THE WALL STREET JOURNAL.
MONEY & INVESTING
THE WALL STREET JOURNAL.
MARKETPLACE
Bargain Bin
Why Certain Stocks Appear to Be Worth More Than Their Price
Cyclicals Like Chrysler Fade As the Economy Softens But Intrigue a Few Buyers
'It Was Screamingly Cheap'
Investors Get More Open-Minded About Quirky Closed-End Funds
HEARD ON THE STREET
By E.S. Browning
Getting Cheaper
How discounts have widened on some closed-end funds in the past three years
Technology IPO Feeding Frenzy Sends Prices of New Issues Soaring
SMALL STOCK FOCUS
By Molly Baker
Technology Stocks Flew High in First Quarter
INDUSTRY FOCUS
Video Games, Computers Find Symbiosis
By Jim Carlton
PC Developers See Pot of Gold in Video Games

Many of the articles and features that appear in *The Wall Street Journal* provide a new and enhanced level of insight into the real world of investments.

Preface

The first edition of *Fundamentals of Investment Management* was published in the early 1980s, and since then many changes have taken place in the financial markets. However, the one constant for this text has been a sincere commitment to present a text that captures the excitement and enthusiasm that we feel for the topic of investment management.

Throughout the book, we attempt to establish the appropriate theoretical base, while at the same time following through with real-world examples. Students ultimately will be able to translate what they have learned in the course to actual participation in the financial markets.

NEW FEATURES AND IMPROVEMENTS TO THE FIFTH EDITION

A number of features have been added to the fifth edition that make using *Fundamentals of Investment Management* an even more exciting and beneficial teaching and learning experience.

The Wall Street Journal Edition

This new option is designed to further integrate *The Wall Street Journal* with *Fundamentals of Investment Management* while still allowing instructors a great deal of flexibility. A special *Wall Street Journal* Edition is available through a unique arrangement with *The Wall Street Journal.* Included in the price of this special edition is a 10-week subscription to *The Wall Street Journal.*

In addition, *The Wall Street Journal* Edition of *Fundamentals of Investment Management* includes a brief introduction explaining how to read and use *The Wall Street Journal* to achieve maximum knowledge and benefits. The introduction guides the reader through *The Wall Street Journal*, explaining how to identify and locate virtually all the important information, tables, and quotes that appear in *The Wall Street Journal.*

Finally, in an effort to make reading *The Wall Street Journal* more interactive for students, *The Wall Street Journal* Projects have been included at the end of every chapter. These projects appear in the standard edition of the text as well, allowing instructors to use them even if students do not subscribe to *The Wall Street Journal* via our special offer. The projects enable the student to use current information from *The Wall Street Journal* in applying material described in the chapter. This includes such exercises as looking up prices of stocks, bonds, commodities; comparing the performance of market indices and then determining which type of stocks have performed best over the past twelve months; and assessing the implications of different asset allocations. Other projects include looking up economic indicators and comparing their movements to changes in the stock and bond market for a given day or time period as well as tracking internal market data such as advances versus declines, volume, and so forth.

Content

Chapter 6 on **industry analysis** has been added. This addition is consistent with the authors' strong emphasis on fundamental analysis. The chapter covers such important topics as industry life cycles, the five competitive forces within industries as developed by Harvard business strategist Michael Porter, the relationship of different industries to the business cycle (rotational investing), and an in-depth comparison of four leading industries.

The emphasis on **international investments** has been expanded. As the framework for portfolio management has become more global, so has *Fundamentals of Investment Management.* The reader will observe that not only is Chapter 18 devoted to "International Securities Markets," but global applications are featured throughout the text. Immediately following the Table of Contents is a List of International Examples covered in various chapters. Emerging markets now receive comparable coverage to that of more developed markets.

Substantial research has challenged the **efficient market hypothesis** in the last decade. Throughout the text, the authors present both sides of the debate. The current edition also includes coverage of the Fama-French study in which the ratio of book value to market value is assigned a large measure of importance by the researchers. Throughout Chapter 10, the reader has the opportunity to study various strategies that appear to provide returns that are superior to those normally associated with traditional risk measures.

The use of **derivatives** has continued to receive increasing attention in the academic and popular press. Options, futures, interest rate swaps, etc. are viewed by some as appropriate tools for portfolio management, while others have categorized them as speculative devices. Firms such as Proctor & Gamble, Bank One Corp., and Gibson Greeting Card Co. have come under substantial criticism for their misuse of derivatives in the mid-1990s. The improper use of derivatives was further dramatized in 1995 by the actions of a trader at the British investment bank, Barings PLC, which caused the collapse of the institution after 233 years of successful operations. The authors have expanded their coverage of derivatives and even included a Critical Thought Case in Chapter 16 on whether derivatives are being properly used by a financial executive.

The topic of **asset allocation** is given greater attention in Chapter 22, which covers risks and returns of portfolio managers. The emphasis is on measuring the effect of allocating investments within the portfolio as compared to simply examining the returns on separate asset categories. *Fundamentals of Investment Management* covers this material in a highly applied fashion in which the reader compares actual returns to benchmark returns. Since it is one of the last topics covered in the book, the material can be used to integrate many previously learned concepts.

The fifth edition also has expanded coverage of **computer databases.** Chapter 4 includes a discussion of on-line services such as America On-Line, Prodigy, Compuserve, and the Dow Jones News Retrieval System. The reader will also find new material on the Internet and how its use can be optimized.

The threat of **inflation** has once again become a reality in the financial markets. The debacle in the bond market in the mid-1990s can be directly traced to fears of rapid price increases. In the fifth edition, the authors have given additional attention to the issue of inflation and its impact on the investment choice between real and financial assets. While

the authors do not know whether inflation has returned to the investment landscape, we do know that it is important that students be prepared to deal with these issues.

From a structural viewpoint, we have moved the chapter on "Time Value of Money and Investment Applications" from the main body of the text to Appendix E. This change was in response to comments from current users that the material was covered previously in financial accounting and financial management courses and should be optional in nature. For those who would like a review of time value of money, the material is retained in Appendix E.

PEDAGOGY

Real World Emphasis

We believe in establishing a very sound base for analysis. For example, in Chapter 7 the student is strongly encouraged to use appropriate valuation techniques to evaluate equities. These include present value techniques under different assumptions of growth rates. Similar approaches are used to evaluate bonds, options, and other forms of investments. At the same time, we consider it essential that real-world material be integrated into the analysis. For example, when valuing equity securities in Chapter 7, the common stock of J. M. Smucker is used rather than a hypothetical firm. Ratio and financial statement analyses in Chapter 8 are focused through the eyes of one reading the Coca-Cola annual report. The discussion of convertible bonds in Chapter 14 is based on securities issued by Telxon. The same principle is followed in virtually every chapter of the book as indicated by the List of Selected Real World Examples immediately following the Table of Contents.

End-of-Chapter Material

In terms of end-of-chapter material, many options are available, thus allowing the instructor to select those end-of-chapter options that best meet his or her objectives.

Key Terms and Concepts At the end of each chapter is a listing of the key terms and concepts with page references. These items are fully defined in the glossary.

Discussion Questions These questions address the important topics covered in each chapter. They can be used for class discussion or completed individually by students.

Problems The problems are carefully annotated in the margin to indicate the topic covered. For each chapter, problems are provided for students to apply the concepts learned in that chapter.

CFA Questions To further reinforce the student's learning process, many of the analytical chapters also have questions and solutions from prior CFA Level I exams. The intent is to illustrate that much of what the students are learning is in line with what professional

financial analysts are expected to know for certification. These questions are denoted by an icon in the margin.

THE *WALL STREET JOURNAL* PROJECTS As previously described, every chapter in the book has a *Wall Street Journal* Project that serves as an extremely effective learning tool. Current information from *The Wall Street Journal* is used to illustrate major points in the chapter. In addition, this feature illustrates the value of *The Wall Street Journal* for both the student and the business finance community.

CRITICAL THOUGHT CASES These cases are presented at the end of Chapters 2, 3, 8, 10, 11, 16 and 19. Designed to stimulate lively class discussion, the cases cover timely topics such as: insider trading, conflicts of interests in broker-customer relationships, and the use and misuse of derivatives.

U.S. EQUITIES ONFLOPPY EXERCISES For those who desire a computer interactive course, U.S. Equities OnFloppy Exercises are included in Chapters 1–8, 10, 18, 21 and 22. These exercises are identified by an icon in the margin. For more information on U.S. Equities OnFloppy, please turn to the section on student supplements.

SELECTED REFERENCES Organized by topic, this list of references provides an up-to-date overview of relevant books and articles.

SUPPLEMENTS

For Instructors

INSTRUCTOR'S MANUAL The Instructor's Manual includes detailed solutions for all text problems (set in large type for convenience in making transparencies), as well as teaching strategies for all 22 chapters.

TEST BANK The Test Bank has well over 1,000 questions, including true-false, multiple-choice, matching quizzes, and many problems for those chapters that lend themselves to problem material.

TRANSPARENCY MASTERS Averaging over a dozen transparency masters per chapter, this supplement allows instructors to visually present important topics in class. The masters include chapter outlines, brief explanations of key concepts, selected examples, and important tables and figures.

INVESTMENTS TEMPLATES These LOTUS 1-2-3 templates are based on the calculations and formulas found in *Fundamentals of Investment Management.* They are designed to test the sensitivity of the investment relationships found in the chapters of the text. The software will allow students to solve many of the end-of-chapter problems. For example, the templates and exercises include the stock valuation models found in Chapter 7, bond valuation, duration calculations, convertible bond analysis, option pricing models, and portfolio analysis models.

Videos Part of the Irwin Finance Video Series, these video segments highlight and reinforce the topics covered in each chapter. Using the videos helps bring finance to life for students.

For Students

Self-Study Software The equivalent of an electronic study guide, this Windows-based software provides students with multiple choice, true/false, matching and fill-in exercises for each chapter of the text. Self-Study Software includes help screens and question hints to aid the student both in using the program and in completing the exercises. Self-Study is sold separately as well as available at a reduced price when packaged with the text.

U.S. Equities OnFloppy A Morningstar product, U.S. Equities OnFloppy is a fundamental database and analysis system of approximately 6,000 companies with common stock trading on the NYSE, AMEX, and NASDAQ national market exchanges. The educational version of U.S. Equities OnFloppy can be packaged with *Fundamentals of Investment Management* at a reduced package price. The software can be used to solve selected end-of-chapter exercises, which are indicated by an icon. The U.S. Equities OnFloppy User's Manual, prepared by William Remaley at Susquehanna University, offers over 60 investment and corporate finance projects to provide your students with even more applications. U.S. Equities OnFloppy data is timely, offered each July for fall orders and updated for the spring semester. Please contact your Irwin representative for further details on how to package U.S. Equities OnFloppy with the fifth edition.

Financial Analysis with an Electronic Calculator Designed to enable students to master the use of financial calculators and develop a working knowledge of financial mathematics and problem-solving, this supplement by Mark A. White, University of Virginia is helpful for the student who needs to enhance skills learned in the introductory financial management course. Complete instructions are included for solving all major problem types on three common models: Hewlett-Packard HP-10B, Sharp Electronics EL-733-A, and Texas Instruments BA II Plus.

ACKNOWLEDGMENTS

The authors wish to express special thanks to Carl Luft for his contribution of the Black-Scholes Option Pricing model material.

We are grateful to the following individuals for their thoughtful reviews and suggestions for the fifth edition: Grace C. Allen, *Western Carolina University;* Laurence E. Blose, *University of North Carolina–Charlotte;* John A. Cole, *Florida A&M University;* Joe B. Copeland, *University of North Alabama;* Don R. Cox, *Appalachian State University;* John Dunkelberg, *Wake Forest University;* Marcus Ingram, *Clark-Atlanta University;* Joe B. Lipscombe, *Texas Christian University;* John Markese, *American Association of Individual Investors;* Mike Miller, *DePaul University;* Carl C. Nielsen, *Wichita State University;* Raj A. Padmaraj, *Bowling Green State University;* Richard Ponarul, *California State University;* and Maneesh Sharma, *Northeast Louisiana University.*

For their prior reviews and helpful comments, we are grateful to Carol J. Billingham, *Central Michigan University;* Gerald A. Blum, *University of Nevada–Reno;* Keith E.

Boles, *University of Colorado–Colorado Springs;* Jerry D. Boswell, *College of Financial Planning;* Paul Bolster, *Northeastern University;* Joe B. Copeland, *University of North Alabama;* Marcia M. Cornett, *Southern Methodist University;* Betty Driver, *Murray State University;* Adrian C. Edwards, *Western Michigan University;* Jane H. Finley, *University of South Alabama;* Adam Gehr, *DePaul University;* Paul Grier, *SUNY–Binghamton;* David Heskel, *Bloomsburg University;* James Khule, *California State University–Sacramento;* Sheri Kole, *Copeland Companies;* Carl Luft, *DePaul University;* John D. Markese, *DePaul University;* Majed R. Muhtaseb, *California State Polytechnic University–Pomona;* Harold Mulherin, *Clemson University;* Roger R. Palmer, *College of St. Thomas;* John W. Peavy III, *Southern Methodist University;* Richard Ponarul, *California State University;* Dave Rand, *Northwest Technical College;* Linda L. Richardson, *University of Southern Maine;* Tom S. Sale, *Louisiana Tech University;* Art Schwartz, *University of South Florida;* Joseph F. Singer, *University of Missouri–Kansas City;* Ira Smolowitz, *Siena College;* Don Taylor, *University of Wisconsin–Platteville;* Frank N. Tiernan, *Drake University;* Allan J. Twark, *Kent State University;* Howard E. Van Auken, *Iowa State University;* and Bismarck Williams, *Roosevelt University.*

Finally we would like to thank Gina Huck, sponsoring editor; Beth Kessler, developmental editor; Jean Lou Hess, project editor; Jim Keefe, senior sponsoring editor; Mike Junior, publisher; and the entire team at Richard D. Irwin for their outstanding help and guidance in developing the fifth edition.

Geoffrey A. Hirt
Stanley B. Block

FUNDAMENTALS OF

INVESTMENT MANAGEMENT

FUNDAMENTALS OF

INVESTMENT MANAGEMENT

GEOFFREY A. HIRT
CHAIRMAN OF THE DEPARTMENT OF FINANCE
DEPAUL UNIVERSITY

STANLEY B. BLOCK, CFA
PROFESSOR OF FINANCE
TEXAS CHRISTIAN UNIVERSITY

Fifth Edition

IRWIN
Chicago • Bogotá • Boston • Buenos Aires • Caracas
London • Madrid • Mexico City • Sydney • Toronto

IRWIN **Concerned About Our Environment**

In recognition of the fact that our company is a large end-user of fragile yet replenishable resources, we at IRWIN can assure you that every effort is made to meet or exceed Environmental Protection Agency (EPA) recommendations and requirements for a "greener" workplace.

To preserve these natural assets, a number of environmental policies, both companywide and department-specific, have been implemented. From the use of 50% recycled paper in our textbooks to the printing of promotional materials with recycled stock and soy inks to our office paper recycling program, we are committed to reducing waste and replacing environmentally unsafe products with safer alternatives.

Irwin Book Team
Sponsoring editor: *Gina M. Huck*
Developmental Editor: *Beth Kessler*
Senior marketing manager: *Ron Bloecher*
Project editor: *Jean Lou Hess*
Production supervisor: *Lara Feinberg*
Designer: *Michael Warrell*
Interior designer: *Deirdre Wroblewski*
Cover designer: *Deirdre Wroblewski*
Cover photographer: *Phyllis Picardi/International Stock*
Interior illustration: *Phyllis Picardi/International Stock*
Art studio: *Carlisle Communications, Ltd.*
Graphics supervisor: *Charlene Breeden*
Compositor: *Carlisle Communications, Ltd.*
Typeface: *10/12 Times Roman*
Printer: *R. R. Donnelley & Sons Company*

▼▼ Times Mirror
◣◢ Higher Education Group

Library of Congress Cataloging-in-Publication Data
Hirt, Geoffrey A.
 Fundamentals of investment management / Geoffrey A. Hirt, Stanley
B. Block. — 5th ed.
 p. cm. — (The Irwin series in finance)
 Includes bibliographical references and index.
 ISBN 0–256–14602–0. —ISBN 0–256–19689–3 (Wall Street Journal
ed.)
 1. Investments. 2. Investments—United States. 3. Investment
analysis. I. Block, Stanley B. II. Title. III. Title: Investment
management. IV. Series.
HG4521.H579 1996
332.6—dc20 95–30454

Printed in the United States of America
2 3 4 5 6 7 8 9 0 DOC 2 1 0 9 8 7 6

To Our Mothers, Lydia and Mary, Who Encouraged Us in Our Education

The Irwin Series in Finance

Stephen A. Ross
Sterling Professor of Economics and Finance
Yale University
Consulting Editor

Financial Management

Block and Hirt
Foundations of Financial Management
Seventh Edition

Brooks
PC Fingame: *The Financial Management Decision Game*
Version 2.0

Bruner
Case Studies in Finance: *Managing for Corporate Value Creation*
Second Edition

Fruhan, Kester, Mason, Piper and Ruback
Case Problems in Finance
Tenth Edition

Harrington
Corporate Financial Analysis: *Decisions in a Global Environment*
Fourth Edition

Helfert
Techniques of Financial Analysis
Eighth Edition

Higgins
Analysis for Financial Management
Fourth Edition

Kallberg and Parkinson
Corporate Liquidity: *Management and Measurement*

Nunnally and Plath
Cases in Finance

Ross, Westerfield and Jaffe
Corporate Finance
Fourth Edition

Ross, Westerfield and Jordan
Essentials of Corporate Finance

Ross, Westerfield and Jordan
Fundamentals of Corporate Finance
Third Edition

Schary
Cases in Financial Management

Stonehill and Eiteman
Finance: *An International Perspective*

White
Financial Analysis with an Electronic Calculator
Second Edition

Investments

Bodie, Kane and Marcus
Essentials of Investments
Second Edition

Bodie, Kane and Marcus
Investments
Third Edition

Cohen, Zinbarg and Zeikel
Investment Analysis and Portfolio Management
Fifth Edition

Hirt and Block
Fundamentals of Investment Management
Fifth Edition

Lorie, Dodd and Kimpton
The Stock Market: *Theories and Evidence*
Second Edition

Morningstar, Inc. and Remaley
U.S. Equities OnFloppy
Annual Edition

Shimko
The Innovative Investor
Version 3.0

Financial Institutions and Markets

Rose
Commercial Bank Management: *Producing and Selling Financial Services*
Third Edition

Rose
Money and Capital Markets: *The Financial System in an Increasingly Global Economy*
Fifth Edition

Rose
Reading on Financial Institutions and Markets
Annual Edition

Rose and Kolari
Financial Institutions: *Understanding and Managing Financial Services*
Fifth Edition

Saunders
Financial Institutions Management: *A Modern Perspective*

Real Estate

Berston
California Real Estate Principles
Seventh Edition

Berston
California Real Estate Practice
Sixth Edition

Brueggeman and Fisher
Real Estate Finance and Investments
Tenth Edition

Smith and Corgel
Real Estate Perspectives: *An Introduction to Real Estate*
Second Edition

Financial Planning and Insurance

Allen, Melone, Rosenbloom and VanDerhei
Pension Planning: *Pensions, Profit-Sharing, and Other Deferred Compensation Plans*
Seventh Edition

Crawford
Law and the Life Insurance Contract
Seventh Edition

Crawford
Life and Health Insurance Law
LOMA Edition

Hirsch
Casualty Claim Practice
Sixth Edition

Kapoor, Dlabay and Hughes
Personal Finance
Fourth Edition

Kellison
Theory of Interest
Second Edition

Rokes
Human Relations in Handling Insurance Claims
Revised Edition

Contents in Brief

Contents

List of Selected Real World Examples

CHAPTER 7

CHAPTER 8

CHAPTER 9

CHAPTER 10

CHAPTER 11

CHAPTER 12

CHAPTER 14

CHAPTER 15

CHAPTER 16

CHAPTER 17

CHAPTER 18

CHAPTER 19

CHAPTER 20

CHAPTER 21

CHAPTER 22

List of Selected International Examples

The Wall Street Journal Preface

We are pleased to able to offer *The Wall Street Journal* edition of *Fundamentals of Investment Management. The Wall Street Journal* is the world's leading business news and finance publication used by professional and individual investors alike to gauge the pulse of companies, industries, economies and markets. It features regular articles on the state of the economy, major issues of concern for corporations and investors, as well as tables for prices of everything from financial assets such as stocks, bond, futures and options, to commodities such as pork bellies, wheat, gold and silver. This preface is designed to introduce you to the many useful features of *The Wall Street Journal*. In addition, it examines each part of *Fundamentals of Investment Management,* indicating ways in which *The Wall Street Journal* can be used in combination with the text. This integration of the text and *The Wall Street Journal* will result in an understanding of investments that is based in the day-to-day activities of the markets. To further enhance the learning experience, *Journal* Projects are included at the end of every chapter, reinforcing the topics covered in each chapter and enabling you to delve into the real world of finance.

THE BASICS OF *THE WALL STREET JOURNAL*

The Wall Street Journal is divided into three major sections (A, B, and C) with an occasional fourth section which covers special topics such as mutual fund performance or technology. At the bottom of page A1 there is a table of contents which includes special topics and articles as well as regular features (Figure 1). Please be aware that *The Wall Street Journal* may add or subtract standard features while this book is in print. While most of the sections will remain as listed in Figure 1, the specific page locations may change. Please note that **Earnings Digest** may appear in any one of the three sections.

FIGURE 1

TODAY'S CONTENTS

THE INDEX TO BUSINESSES APPEARS ON PAGE B2

THREE SECTIONS

HEARD ON THE STREET: Paper-firm shares have their fans, **Page C2.**

COLLECTIBLES: Peace signs and smiley faces hit the art market, **C1.**

YOUR MONEY MATTERS: Industrials do better than pros or luck, **C1.**

ECONOMY: Fed's favorite inflation gauge is supplier delivery, **A2.**

TELEVISION: Murdoch's empire is shaken by one dogged lawyer, **B1.**

FOOD: A primer on the feud over the federal school-lunch program, **B1.**

POLITICS & POLICY: Lamar Alexander's business ties, **A16.**

LAW: More home buyers and sellers do without lawyers, **B1.**

INTERNATIONAL: YPF, with Maxus bid, looks beyond Argentina, **A11.**

REVIEW & OUTLOOK: The Clean Air Act hits the wall, **A14.**

OPINION: If romantic love isn't dead in America, it's ailing, **A14.**

LEISURE & ARTS: New-found old masters in St. Petersburg, **A12.**

FIGURE 2

THE WALL STREET JOURNAL.

© 1995 Dow Jones & Company, Inc. All Rights Reserved.

VOL. LXXVI NO. 127 ★ ★ ★ MIDWEST EDITION FRIDAY, APRIL 14, 1995 NAPERVILLE, ILLINOIS •••• 75 CENTS

Strike Out

Baseball Players' Agent Offers Bargains on Stars In a Buyer's Market

Big Hitters Accept Pay Cuts From Tightfisted Teams; A Steal on Stottlemyre

Finding Tettleton a Position

By JOHN HELYAR
Staff Reporter of THE WALL STREET JOURNAL

SAN DIEGO—Tony Attanasio has made a lot of impassioned pitches on the phone for his ballplayer clients today, but few with a windup quite like this.

"Sandy, you ready for a bomb, you want to become general manager of the

Hardball's Next Circuit

The United Baseball League begins

What's News—

* * *

Business and Finance

THE BANK OF JAPAN CUT its official discount rate by 0.75 percentage point to a postwar low of 1%, and Japan's government unveiled a package of economic measures also meant to cap the yen and stimulate growth. Greater spending would trim Japan's massive $120 billion trade surplus, a key force behind the strong yen.

(Article on Page A8)

* * *

Chrysler faces pressure from large investors to respond to Kirk Kerkorian's $20 billion takeover bid with a major share buyback or other steps, although questions remain about Mr. Kerkorian's ability to finance the deal.

The auto maker posted a 37% drop in first-quar...

* * *

World-Wide

RUBIN PLANNED to press Asian nations to open financial-services markets.

The Treasury chief said he would use a weekend meeting of finance ministers in Bali to urge that Asian markets be opened to U.S. financial-service firms. Rubin termed current proposals "disappointing," saying he would seek better offers. The U.S. effort has targeted Indonesia, Thailand, Malaysia, South Korea and the Philippines. Rubin also will fly to India to hold talks on the issue. (Article on Page A3)

The U.S. is preparing a list of Japanese imports to target for punitive tariffs if an accord isn't reached to open Japan's auto and auto-parts markets.

* * *

Rep. Robert Dornan joined the Republican presidential campaign, saying he wants to force his rivals to put more emphasis on soci... issues. "Winning is not everything,"

Retail Sales

In billions of dollars, seasonally adjusted.

RETAIL SALES rose in March to a seasonally adjusted $191.66 billion from a revised $191.32 billion in February, the Commerce Department reports. (Article on page A2.)

A Corporate Gadfly Takes Boss Seriously —A Serious Mistake

Washington Wire

A Special Weekly Report From The Wall Street Journal's Capital Bureau

SENATE RETIREMENTS stagger Democratic hopes of gaining ground on the GOP.

Illinois Republicans clear the field for their strongest candidate, Lt. Gov. Kustra, to succeed the retiring Simon. Democrats have a shot at keeping Exon's Nebraska seat, but perhaps only if Gov. Nelson runs. Amid GOP gains in the South, even a conservative Democrat faces trouble succeeding Alabama's Heflin; Louisiana Rep. Tauzin probably has the best chance to hold the Johnston seat for Democrats.

Many figure Rhode Island Sen. Pell also will call it quits, though Democrats actually might be stronger with the younger Rep. Reed running. Democrats hope to pick up the seat held by Colorado's Brown, the sole GOP senator to announce retirement so far. But their two strongest candidates, Rep. Skaggs and Gov. Romer, may not run.

One bright spot: The Democratic Senatorial Campaign Committee's fund-rais-

King Kahng

Master of Cheap Clones May Hold Key to Fate Of Apple Computers

He Is Making First Copies Of the Fabled Macintosh, Which Risks Sales Loss

'We Want Him to Succeed'

By JIM CARLTON
Staff Reporter of THE WALL STREET JOURNAL

MILPITAS, Calif.—To understand why some people in Silicon Valley call Stephen Kahng "King," it is essential to understand one of his defining characteristics. He is, by his own admission, cheap.

The millionaire drives an 11-year-old Mercedes with more than 200,000 miles on it. McDonald's value me

1 2 3 4 5 6

Reprinted by permission of *The Wall Street Journal,* ©1995 by Dow Jones & Company. All Rights Reserved Worldwide.

Section A of The Wall Street Journal

As the first section of *The Wall Street Journal*, Section A functions similarly to the first section of any newspaper. It covers the most important news stories and refers you to additional articles and features contained in the paper. While it changes to reflect the latest hot topics, the location of the various features remains the same. Figure 2 is an example of how the first page of *The Wall Street Journal* typically looks. Feature articles appear in the first, fourth, and sixth columns. The second and third columns are always headlined as **What's News,** with one column devoted to Business and Finance and the other to World-Wide stories. Under each of these headings there are one-paragraph summaries of the day's most important news with a page reference given for the full article. Skimming these two columns is a great way for busy people to get the nuts and bolts of important events. The fifth column rotates topics each day. On Mondays, **The Outlook** appears, giving an economic perspective of the domestic economy or focusing on international economic issues. On Tuesdays, **Work Week** appears: a special news report about life on the job and trends taking shape. On Wednesdays, the column contains the **Tax Report** which summarizes and forecasts federal and state tax developments that affect businesses and individuals. Thursday's column is called **Business Bulletin** and presents a special background report on trends in industry and finance. Friday's column ends the five-day cycle with the **Washington Wire,** a special weekly report from *The Wall Street Journal's* capital bureau which can include anything of political interest to businesses and individuals. It should be pointed out that a graph typically appears at the top of the fourth column. This graph provides historical data and current monthly updates of key economic data such as retail sales, housing starts, steel production, unemployment, the leading indicators, etc.

Section B of The Wall Street Journal

This section, entitled **Marketplace,** presents many different stories on marketing and those variables that influence emerging trends. It features regular articles on **Personal Technology, Health, Who's News, Advertising, Corporate**

FIGURE 3

INDEX TO BUSINESSES

This index of businesses mentioned in today's issue of The Wall Street Journal is intended to include all significant references to parent companies. First references to these companies appear in bold type in all articles except those on page one, the editorial pages and the leisure and arts page. The index doesn't cite companies listed solely in the Digest of Earnings, which appears today on page B7, or in the Quarterly Review of Mutual Funds in Section R. Page numbers listed here refer to the pages where the articles begin.

Focus, Industry Trends, Marketing and Media, Enterprise, and more. Especially useful for the investor is the **Index to Businesses,** which lists companies mentioned in that issue of *The Wall Street Journal.* Appearing on page B2, the index makes it easy to follow stories on companies that you may be considering as investments or those in which you are already invested. Figure 3 is an example of what the index looks like.

Section C of The Wall Street Journal

Section C is probably the first section many investors read. This section contains the price data for all the major markets, including the New York and American Stock Exchanges' stock and bond quotes, the Nasdaq's over-the-counter market, government securities, option and futures prices from the Chicago Board of Trade, the Chicago Mercantile Exchange, and many other exchanges from around the world. By examining the data in this section the investor can find out first thing in the morning whether he or she made money during the preceding business day. Regular features such as **World Markets, Credit Markets, Foreign Exchange,** and advertisements for new stock issues appear in this section.

USING *THE WALL STREET JOURNAL* WITH FUNDAMENTALS OF INVESTMENT MANAGEMENT

Since *Fundamentals of Investment Management* is organized into seven parts, it is useful to discuss how *The Wall Street Journal* can be used to enhance the educational value of each group of chapters.

Part 1 Introduction to Investments—Chapters 1-4

Part 1 provides possibilities for daily use of *The Wall Street Journal.* In Chapter 1, real and financial assets are introduced. The prices of most of these assets can be found in Section C of *The Wall Street Journal* under various markets. Chapter 2 provides a description of these security markets. *The Wall Street Journal* can be used to view initial public offerings (IPOs) covered by the Security Act of 1933. Initial public offerings are advertised by investment bankers as part of the distribution process. In the back part of Section C, you will find examples of common stock offerings, corporate bond offerings, and many other securities sold by investment bankers.

FIGURE 4

MARKETS DIARY 4/5/95

STOCKS Dow Jones Industrial Average 4200.57 −1.04

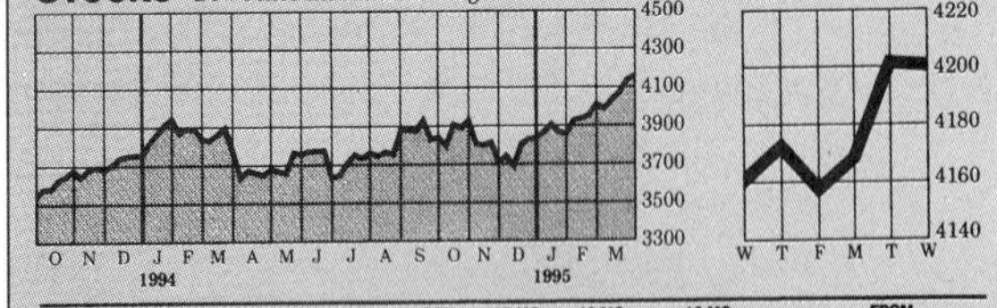

INDEX	CLOSE	NET CHNG	PCT CHNG	12-MO HIGH	12-MO LOW	12-MO CHNG	PCT	FROM 12/31	PCT
DJIA	4200.57	− 1.04	− 0.02	4201.61	3598.71	+ 520.84	+ 14.15	+ 366.13	+ 9.55
DJ Equity	476.36	+ 0.37	+ 0.08	476.36	417.62	+ 51.07	+ 12.01	+ 43.29	+ 10.00
S&P 500	505.57	+ 0.33	+ 0.07	505.57	441.49	+ 57.52	+ 12.84	+ 46.30	+ 10.08
Nasdaq Comp.	816.32	+ 2.60	+ 0.32	826.14	693.79	+ 65.60	+ 8.74	+ 64.36	+ 8.56
DJ World Index	118.08	+ 0.62	+ 0.53	119.86	109.40	+ 6.48	+ 5.81	+ 4.14	+ 3.64
London (FT 100)	3190.2	+ 2.1	+ 0.07	3265.1	2876.6	+ 58.7	+ 1.87	+ 124.7	+ 4.07
Tokyo (Nikkei 225)	15882.49	+ 251.96	+ 1.61	21552.81	15381.29	− 3814.25	− 19.36	− 3840.57	− 19.47

BONDS Lehman Brothers T-Bond Index 5501.62 +9.34

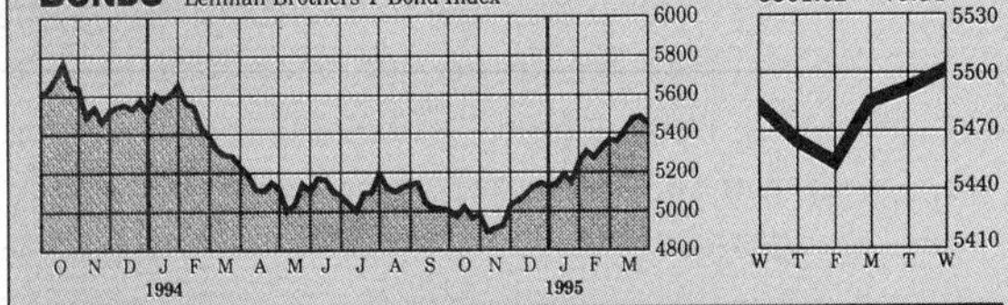

INDEX	WED	WED YIELD	TUES	TUES YIELD	YR AGO	12-MO HIGH	12-MO LOW
Lehman Brothers Long T-Bond	5501.62	7.45%	5492.28	7.46%	5121.60	5507.96	4897.46
DJ 20 Bond (Price Return)	98.61	7.49	98.54	7.49	99.91	99.91	93.56
Salomon mortgage-backed	765.19	7.97	764.37	7.98	731.96	765.82	713.65
Bond Buyer municipal	91-28	6.31	91-20	6.37	89-10	94-9	80-26
Merrill Lynch corporate	716.02	7.96	715.91	7.95	669.23	716.02	656.43

INTEREST Fed Funds (NY Fed, Prebon Yamane) 5.99% −0.10

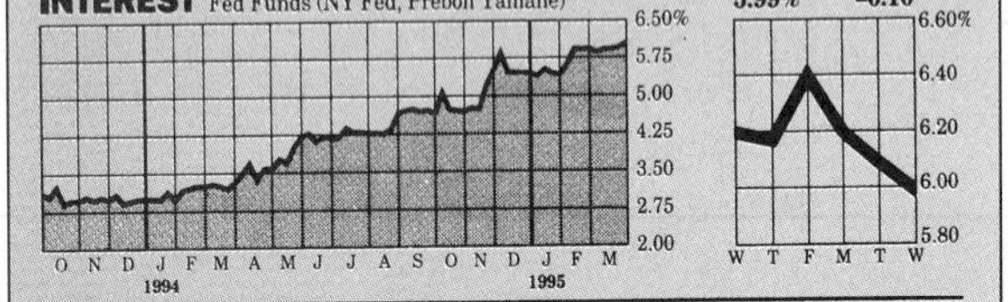

ISSUE	CLOSE	TUES	YEAR AGO	12-MO HIGH	12-MO LOW
3-month T-bill	5.70%	5.73%	3.59%	5.90%	3.53%
3-month CD (new)	5.55	5.57	3.38	5.64	3.37
Dealer Comm. Paper (90 days)	6.14	6.18	3.99	6.32	3.95
3-month Eurodollar deposit	6.25	6.31	4.00	6.50	4.00

U.S. DOLLAR J. P. Morgan Index vs. 19 Currencies 90.4 −0.2

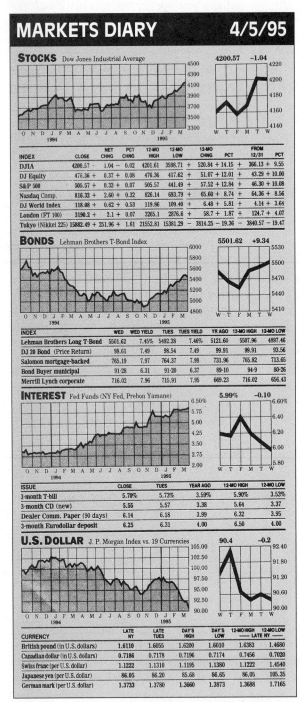

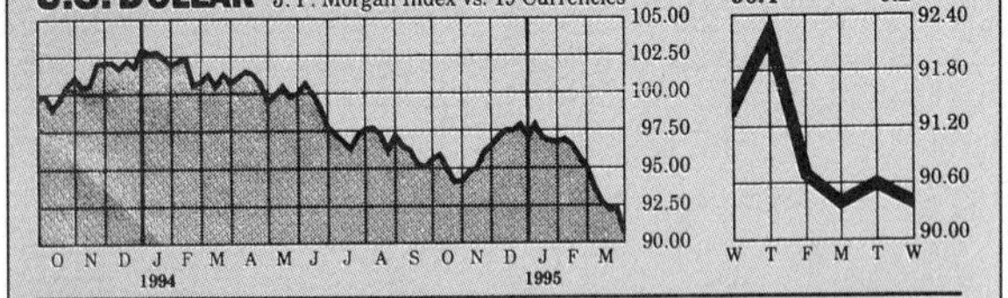

CURRENCY	LATE NY	LATE TUES	DAY'S HIGH	DAY'S LOW	12-MO HIGH — LATE NY —	12-MO LOW — LATE NY —
British pound (in U.S. dollars)	1.6110	1.6055	1.6200	1.6010	1.6383	1.4680
Canadian dollar (in U.S. dollars)	0.7186	0.7178	0.7196	0.7174	0.7456	0.7020
Swiss franc (per U.S. dollar)	1.1222	1.1310	1.1195	1.1380	1.1222	1.4540
Japanese yen (per U.S. dollar)	86.05	86.20	85.68	86.65	86.05	105.35
German mark (per U.S. dollar)	1.3733	1.3780	1.3660	1.3873	1.3688	1.7165

Chapter 3 includes information on many market indexes that are used by professional and individual investors alike. On the first page of Section C, you can find values for everything from indexes of common stocks, like the Dow Jones Industrial Average (DJIA) and the Standard and Poor's 500 Stock Index, to bond indexes and foreign currency prices. Figure 4 is an example of the tables that contain this information and typically appear on page C1. By keeping in touch with this information on a daily basis you will have your finger on the pulse of the markets. Chapter 4 is primarily an informational chapter that highlights the many investments services that are commonly available at university and public libraries. *The Wall Street Journal* can be used to view some of this material.

Part 2 Analysis and Valuation of Equity Securities—Chapters 5–8

Part 2 focuses on fundamental analysis of common stocks. It starts with the economy, moves through industry analysis, and ends up with common stock valuation and analysis of financial statements. *The Wall Street Journal* is necessary reading for anyone keeping up with economic trends on a daily basis. Everyday new information appears on economic indicators such as the consumer price index, industrial production, the series of leading indicators, and others. These strongly influence the performance of individual stocks. For example, improving auto sales would be bullish for General Motors. On Monday of each week there is a table called **Tracking the Economy** that indicates what economic reports will be published during the week and the day they will be published. The table appears on one of the first four pages of Section A, and its location varies from week to week. In terms of specific information, Figure 5 is an example of how the latest data on the leading indicators is presented. This will appear once each month. Depending on what industry is of interest, *The Wall Street Journal* has a daily update of company and industry information. This includes news releases from industry trade groups and individual companies. Additionally, in Section C there is a list of weekly stock

FIGURE 5

LEADING INDICATORS

Here are the net contributions of the components of the Commerce Department's index of leading indicators. After various adjustments, they produced a 0.2% decrease in the index for February and were unchanged for January.

	Feb. 1995	Jan. 1995
Workweek	−.04	.00
Unemployment claims	−.01	−.02
Orders for consumer goods	−.07	.02
Slower deliveries	.00	−.09
Plant and equipment orders	.02	.12
Building permits	−.02	.12
Durable order backlog	.04	.08
Materials prices	−.16	.00
Stock prices	.10	.06
Money supply	−.08	.01
Consumer expectations	−.04	−.01

The seasonally adjusted index numbers (1987=100) for February, and the change from January are:

Index of leading indicators	102.3	−0.2%
Index of coincident indicators	117.0	0.3%
Index of lagging indicators	100.9	0.9%

The ratio of coincident to lagging indicators was 1.16 in February, a decrease from 1.17 in January.

performance by Dow Jones Industry Groups (listed as **DJ Industry Groups** in the table of contents on page A1). Articles on major industries like autos, chemicals, banking and others are highlighted on a rotating basis. On a quarterly basis, a comprehensive summary of industry profitability and company rankings by profits within each industry is typically featured. Earnings reports are issued daily and some financial information on income statements and balance sheet data appears in abbreviated form that can be used to supplement financial analysis.

Part 3 Issues in Efficient Markets—Chapters 9–10

Part 3 looks at the aspects of analysis that include technical analysis, market efficiency, and special situations. Special situations are usually followed in detail by *The Wall Street Journal.* The editors report merger activities and keep you abreast of new and ongoing negotiations between companies. Sometimes *The Wall Street Journal* is used almost as a public forum by both sides involved in the merger, stating their cases for and against the merits of the merger. This activity can go on for days or even weeks as was the case with IBM and Lotus in 1995 and Paramount Communications and Viacom in 1994. Perhaps a merger battle will happen while you are taking this class and you will be able to keep up with the outcome in *The Wall Street Journal.* Other special situations such as earning surprises, dividend increases, and stock splits are announced in *The Wall Street Journal* in regular sections. These can all be found by looking in the index on the front page of *The Wall Street Journal* under **Earnings Digest** and **Dividend News.**

Although technical analysis is not the main focus of the text, it is still important to many investors. Chapter 9 can be augmented by the charts on the Dow Jones Industrial Average found on page C3. Other information relating to technical analysis such as put and call volume, breadth of the market statistics, the advance-decline ratio, and other technical indicators are presented in Section C. **Odd-Lot Trading,** another technical indicator, has its own listing in the table of contents on page A1. Often professional technical analysts will be quoted about their views on the technical strength of the market. This may be discussed in the early part of Section C.

Part 4 Fixed-Income and Leveraged Securities—Chapters 11–14

Part 4 of *Fundamentals of Investment Management* focuses on fixed-income securities, especially bonds. The chapters in this section cover basic bond information, bond valuation, convertible bonds, and the issue of duration, which quantifies the volatility of a bond's price relative to changes in interest rates. While many bonds are traded over the counter, there is a wealth of information available on bond trading, bond interest rates, bond quotes and the tone of the market for U.S. government bonds, mortgage bonds, junk bonds, convertible bonds and more. Since changes in interest rates are the primary determinant of bond prices, *The Wall Street Journal* makes sure to cover interest rates in all bond markets. As an example of the potential changes in bond prices related to interest rate moves, the bonds of AT&T maturing in 2002 were up 10.3 percent in the first half of 1995 as interest rates declined. Additionally, a yield curve showing interest rates on U.S. Government bonds from one to thirty years maturity is shown every day in Section C on **Credit Markets,** which can be located using the table of contents on page A1. Figure 6 shows the

FIGURE 6

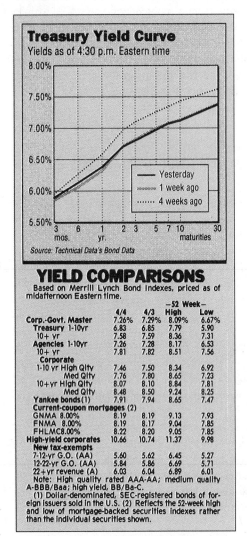

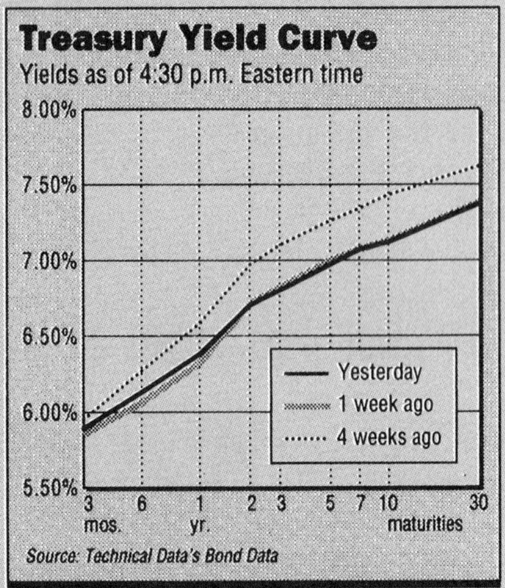

YIELD COMPARISONS

Based on Merrill Lynch Bond Indexes, priced as of midafternoon Eastern time.

	4/4	4/3	–52 Week– High	Low
Corp.-Govt. Master	7.26%	7.29%	8.09%	6.67%
Treasury 1-10yr	6.83	6.85	7.79	5.90
10+ yr	7.58	7.59	8.36	7.31
Agencies 1-10yr	7.26	7.28	8.17	6.53
10+ yr	7.81	7.82	8.51	7.56
Corporate				
1-10 yr High Qlty	7.46	7.50	8.34	6.92
Med Qlty	7.76	7.80	8.65	7.23
10+yr High Qlty	8.07	8.10	8.84	7.81
Med Qlty	8.48	8.50	9.24	8.25
Yankee bonds(1)	7.91	7.94	8.65	7.47
Current-coupon mortgages (2)				
GNMA 8.00%	8.19	8.19	9.13	7.93
FNMA 8.00%	8.19	8.17	9.04	7.85
FHLMC8.00%	8.22	8.20	9.05	7.85
High-yield corporates	10.66	10.74	11.37	9.98
New tax-exempts				
7-12-yr G.O. (AA)	5.60	5.62	6.45	5.27
12-22-yr G.O. (AA)	5.84	5.86	6.69	5.71
22+yr revenue (A)	6.03	6.04	6.89	6.01

Note: High quality rated AAA-AA; medium quality A-BBB/Baa; high yield, BB/Ba-C.

(1) Dollar-denominated, SEC-registered bonds of foreign issuers sold in the U.S. (2) Reflects the 52-week high and low of mortgage-backed securities indexes rather than the individual securities shown.

Reprinted by permission of *The Wall Street Journal*,

graph that appears everyday showing the Treasury Yield Curve and the table of Yield Comparisons that is always given below the graph. When you study this section of the text you should be sure to follow the **Bond Data Bank, Money Rates, Treasury & Government Issues,** and **Credit Markets,** which are listed by title in the table of contents on page A1. A complete examination of these four sections will provide a comprehensive overview of the current character of these markets and the concerns affecting prices and interest rates.

Part 5 Derivative Products—Chapters 15–17

Part 5 of this text presents a wide variety of topics concerning options, futures, options on futures, and index options. *The Wall Street Journal* has a comprehensive listing of prices on options, futures, and other contracts presented in this section of the text. For example, option prices are listed for the Chicago Board Option Exchange, the Pacific Options Exchange and the Philadelphia, Washington and Boston Options Markets. Futures contracts are given for the major markets such as the Chicago Mercantile Exchange, where international currencies (Deutsche Mark, British Pound, Italian Lira, French Franc, Swiss Franc, Canadian Dollar, Mexican Peso, and Japanese Yen) are traded as well as pork bellies and options and futures contracts for the Standard and Poor's 500 Index. The Chicago Board of Trade lists contracts for wheat, corn, soybeans, government bonds and more. The New York Commodities Exchange, where oil futures are traded, is listed as well as other international markets. Examples of these prices are shown in the text chapters as well as in *The Wall Street Journal.* For example, you will find the pages for **Listed Options, CBOE Interest Options, Commodities,** and **Index Options** in the table of contents on page A1.

Part 6 Broadening the Investment Perspective—Chapters 18–20

Part 6 looks at the topics of mutual funds, international investing, and real assets. *The Wall Street Journal* has a comprehensive list of mutual funds, including common stock funds, bond funds, money market funds, and many others. Every day a list is given and in addition to the price and Net Asset Value (NAV) of the fund, new information is given on a rotating basis. Returns for 12 months, 3 years and 5 years are shown as well as some information on fund expenses. Figure 7 is a guide to using mutual fund information and is from a Thursday *Wall Street Journal.* For many individuals, mutual funds are the basic vehicle for investing, making this information quite valuable. **Mutual Funds** is listed in the table of contents on page A1 of *The Wall Street Journal* and found in Section C. International investing has become a very popular form of investing during the 1990s and *The Wall Street*

FIGURE 7

MUTUAL FUND QUOTATIONS

What These Listings Provide...

		NASD DATA			LIPPER ANALYTICAL DATA			
Monday	Inv. Obj.	NAV	Offer Price	NAV Chg.	%Ret YTD	Max Initl Chrg.	Total Exp Ratio	..
Tuesday	Inv. Obj.	NAV	Offer Price	NAV Chg.	—Total Return— YTD	4 wk	1 yr	Rank
Wednesday	Inv. Obj.	NAV	Offer Price	NAV Chg.	—Total Return— YTD	13 wk	3 yr*	Rank
THURSDAY	**Inv. Obj.**	**NAV**	**Offer Price**	**NAV Chg.**	**—Total Return— YTD**	**26 wk**	**4 yr***	**Rank**
Friday	Inv. Obj.	NAV	Offer Price	NAV Chg.	—Total Return— YTD	39 wk	5 yr*	Rank

* Annualized

EXPLANATORY NOTES

Mutual fund data are supplied by two organizations. The daily Net Asset Value (NAV), Offer Price and Net Change calculations are supplied by the National Association of Securities Dealers (NASD) through Nasdaq, its automated quotation system. Performance and cost data are supplied by Lipper Analytical Services Inc.

Daily price data are entered into Nasdaq by the fund, its management company or agent. Performance and cost calculations are percentages provided by Lipper Analytical Services, based on prospectuses filed with the Securities and Exchange Commission, fund reports, financial reporting services and other sources believed to be authoritative, accurate and timely. Though verified, the data cannot be guaranteed by Lipper or its data sources and should be double-checked with the funds before making any investment decisions.

Performance calculations, as percentages, assuming reinvestment of all distributions, and after all asset based charges have been deducted. Asset based charges include advisory fees, other non-advisory fees and distribution expenses (12b-1). Figures are without regard to sales, deferred sales or redemption charges.

INVESTMENT OBJECTIVE (Inv. Obj.) – Based on stated investment goals outlined in the prospectus. The Journal assembled 29 groups based on classifications used by Lipper Analytical in the daily Mutual Fund Scorecard and other calculations. A detailed breakdown of classifications appears [illegible]

TOTAL EXPENSE RATIO (Total Exp Ratio) – Shown as a percentage and based on the fund's annual report, the ratio is total operating expenses for the fiscal year divided by the fund's average net assets. It includes all asset based charges such as advisory fees, other non-[illegible]

Reprinted by permission of *The Wall Street Journal*, ©1995 by Dow Jones & Company. All Rights Reserved Worldwide.

Journal has made sure to include information on this topic. The table of contents lists a section called **International News,** which highlights international issues over several pages. Investors can find much other useful international information, including price quotes on many closed-end mutual funds for individual countries (i.e., Germany Fund) listed on the New York Stock Exchange. The mutual fund section of *The Wall Street Journal* also includes open-end mutual funds specializing in individual countries or regions such as the Asian Fund or Latin American Fund. Many foreign companies now list their shares in the U.S. as ADRs or American Depository Receipts (Honda, Sony, Phillips N.V.), which are denominated in dollars and allow investors to buy shares of individual companies as well as mutual funds. In addition, *The Wall Street Journal* has a separate part in Section C called **World Markets** which is listed in the table of contents on page A1. In Figure 8, stock market indexes from around the world are compared. International investing requires some knowledge of exchange rate movements between countries. Any change in exchange rates between the U.S. dollar and other currencies has an impact on the value of a foreign denominated investment. The currency risk can be evaluated by keeping track of spot exchange rates given in *The Wall Street Journal* as well as the futures contracts on foreign currencies in the Chicago Mercantile Exchange. On a daily basis, *The Wall Street Journal* features a table of Key Currency Cross Rates (Figure 9) which is very useful for keeping track of world currency trends. Chapter 20 discusses investing in real assets such as precious metals, gems, and real estate. **Commodities** lists prices of many of these real assets. Some information on financial instruments pertaining to real estate is included however, there is no special section highlighting real estate investments.

FIGURE 8

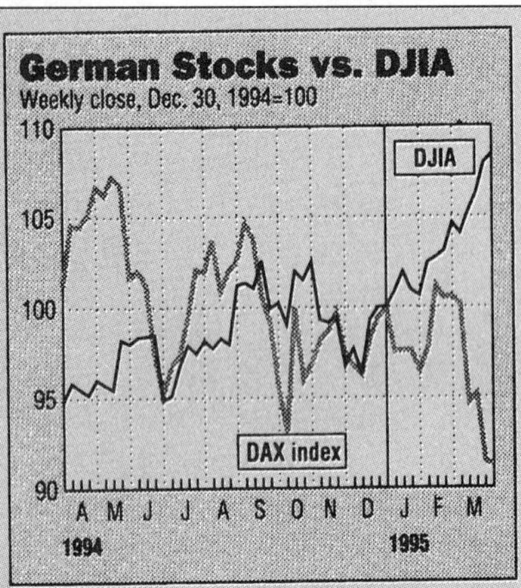

Stock Market Indexes

EXCHANGE	4/5/95 CLOSE	NET CHG	PCT CHG
Tokyo Nikkei 225 Average	15882.49	+ 251.96	+ 1.61
Tokyo Nikkei 300 Index	236.95	+ 1.63	+ 0.69
Tokyo Topix Index	1279.15	+ 8.67	+ 0.68
London FT 30-share	2444	+ 2.2	+ 0.09
London 100-share	3190.2	+ 2.1	+ 0.07
Frankfurt DAX	1969.84	+ 4.83	+ 0.25
Zurich Swiss Market	2536.3	+ 0.1	+ 0.00
Paris CAC 40	1872.92	− 9.85	− 0.52
Milan MIBtel Index	9516	− 52	− 0.54
Amsterdam ANP-CBS General	269.3	+ 0.6	+ 0.22
Stockholm Affarsvarlden	1492.3	− 0.7	− 0.05
Brussels Bel-20 Index	1326.67	+ 0.83	+ 0.06
Australia All Ordinaries	1982.4	+ 46.1	+ 2.38
Hong Kong Hang Seng	closed		
Singapore Straits Times	2101.16	+ 27.11	+ 1.31
Taiwan DJ Equity Mkt	161.47	0	0
Johannesburg J'burg Gold	1572	+ 30	+ 1.95
Madrid General Index	275.01	+ 2.14	+ 0.78
Mexico I.P.C.	1919.09	+ 13.14	+ 0.69
Toronto 300 Composite	4285.1	+ 33.34	+ 0.78
Euro, Aust, Far East MSCI-p	1050.3	+ 11.1	+ 1.07

p-Preliminary
na-Not available

Part 7 Introduction to Portfolio Management—Chapters 21–22

Part 7 develops the basics of portfolio theory and application. While *The Wall Street Journal* does not specifically have a section or special feature on portfolio management, the information in *The Wall Street Journal* is vital to the process of managing a portfolio. Since a portfolio is a collection of assets, a manager must know what is going on in all markets in order to divide up the portfolio into appropriate asset classes. For example, if the manager expects stocks to outperform bonds, he or she may want to have a large percentage of assets invested in common stocks. The manager of an all-equity portfolio needs industry information to make judgments about the weight of each industry in the portfolio. Many managers weigh industries based on their expectations of future industry performance. On the other hand, a bond manager of corporate, convertible, mortgage or government bonds would need to use the information previously mentioned in the discussion of Part 4 of the text. Occasionally *The Wall Street Journal* will run an article comparing the portfolio weightings of competing brokerage firms or money managers. You may also find discussions and interviews with professional money managers concerning their current portfolio strategies.

SUMMARY

Clearly, *The Wall Street Journal* is an invaluable tool for the student of investments. This preface provides an introduction to some of the most commonly used features. As you move through *Fundamentals of Investment Management,* even more uses for *The Wall Street Journal* will become evident. Offering *The Wall Street Journal* Edition provides you with a unique opportunity to experience the real world of investments within the classroom.

FIGURE 9

Key Currency Cross Rates Late New York Trading April 5, 1995

	Dollar	Pound	SFranc	Guilder	Peso	Yen	Lira	D-Mark	FFranc	CdnDlr
Canada	1.3915	2.2417	1.23998	.90640	.21624	.01617	.00081	1.01325	.29035	....
France	4.7925	7.721	4.2706	3.1217	.74476	.05569	.00280	3.4898	....	3.4441
Germany	1.3733	2.2124	1.2238	.89454	.21341	.01596	.00080	....	.28655	.9869
Italy	1711.5	2757.2	1525.13	1114.84	265.97	19.890	....	1246.27	357.12	1230.0
Japan	86.05	138.63	76.680	56.051	13.372	....	.05028	62.659	17.955	61.84
Mexico	6.4350	10.3668	5.7343	4.1916	....	.07478	.00376	4.6858	1.3427	4.6245
Netherlands	1.5352	2.4732	1.3680	....	.23857	.01784	.00090	1.1179	.32033	1.1033
Switzerland	1.1222	1.8079	....	.73098	.17439	.01304	.00066	.81716	.23416	.8065
U K.	.62073	....	.55314	.40433	.09646	.00721	.00036	.45200	.12952	.44609
U.S.	....	1.6110	.89111	.65138	.15540	.01162	.00058	.72817	.20866	.71865

Source: Dow Jones Telerate Inc.

FUNDAMENTALS OF

INVESTMENT MANAGEMENT

PART 1

INTRODUCTION TO INVESTMENTS

OUTLINE

Investing in the securities markets is an exciting process. As you will see throughout the text, the number of potential investments is almost endless. However, the one thing that all investors ask for is a fair, level playing field. That means that all investors should have equal access to information. How intelligently you process that information as an investor is another matter and, in the long run, should determine who the winners and losers are.

You would not want to bet on a football game if other betters knew in advance that the star player for State U. was going to be kicked out of school before the contest for improper behavior. The same principle applies to the stock market. Investors do not like to place their money "at risk" if other investors have access to insider information. But what exactly is insider information, and what separates insider information from other information?

There are a multitude of events that can affect the stock and bond prices of publicly traded companies. For example, mergers, takeovers, corporate restructurings, leveraged buyouts, new products, changes in product sales, a new oil find, or the loss of a major customer can push prices up or down dramatically. If an investor were in a position to have this information and act on it before the general markets, there is no question that a handsome profit might occur. How an investor acquires information is at the heart of the insider trading laws.

Federal law states that you are in violation of the insider trading laws if you trade securities on information that you know or have reason to know is both nonpublic and likely to affect the stock price if the stock were publicly traded. In other words, you cannot trade on confidential stock tips from someone inside the company. Exactly how this law is interpreted by federal enforcement officials and the courts has become clearer in recent years, but many gray areas remain.

When exactly are you in violation of insider trading rules? What if you see a known takeover artist landing in his private jet in a small town where a major company is headquartered and assume he is launching a bid for the company? Anyone could have this knowledge, so no violation occurs. What if you overhear a conversation between two investment bankers at a bar? This becomes touchy because it depends on whether you know who they are or just happen to believe that their conversation is accurate. If you don't know them, acting on their conversation is probably reckless on your part but certainly not a violation of the law. If, however, one of them is your uncle and you act on their conversation, then you are guilty of an insider violation.

In recent years, a reporter for *The Wall Street Journal* was indicted because he acted on information found in *The Wall Street Journal*'s "Heard on the Street" column before it was sold to the public. A truck driver for the publishing house that printed *Business Week* magazine was indicted because he passed on information to a relative before the magazine was put on sale.

Despite these and other recent examples, you don't have to work for a company to be classified as an insider. In many respects, the financial community has received a black eye because of these insider scandals. As a result, the discipline of finance is constantly striving to clean up its house in regard to improper use of insider information. If the financial markets wish to continue to acquire the capital of individual investors, they must demonstrate that the field is, indeed, level. ■

1

The Investment Setting

Between 1982 and 1994 the Dow Jones Industrial Average, the most-watched stock market indicator in the world, gained 380 percent (a gain of approximately 12 percent a year). But not all was smooth sailing. For example, there was the great panic on Monday, October 19, 1987, in which the Dow Jones Industrial Average declined 22.6 percent in *one day.* By contrast, the largest previous single day decline was the fabled stock market crash of 1929 when the market went down slightly over 12 percent on Black Monday of that year.

In the one day crash of 1987, Eastman Kodak declined 26 dollars, Westinghouse Electric 20½ dollars, and Du Pont 18½ dollars. All of these firms eventually recovered.

Perhaps the most interesting example in the last decade is IBM. The stock price of this reknowned computer manufacturer reached a high of 175 ⅞ per share in 1987. At the time, security analysts thought that "Big Blue" could go up forever with its dominance in the traditional mainframe computer market and its emergence as the leader in the rapidly growing personal computer market. Such was not to be. With the conversion of most computer applications from mainframes to microcomputers and the cloning of IBM products by its competitors, IBM rapidly lost market share and began to actually lose money in the early 1990s. This was in stark contrast to the $6 billion per year annual profits it had averaged for the prior decade. By mid-1993, the stock had fallen to 40⅝. Many investors threw up their hands in disgust and bailed out. But by 1995, the firm was once again beginning to show a profit after massive layoffs of employees and restructuring of operations, and the stock price was *up* $40 per share to $80 from its low of 1993. Only time will tell what the remainder of this decade will mean for IBM.

Common stocks are not the only volatile investment. In the past two decades, silver has gone from $5 an ounce to $50 and back again to $5.50. Gold has moved from $35 an ounce to $875 and back to $400 in 1995. The same can be said of investments in oil, real estate, and a number of other items. Commercial real estate lost more than 30 percent of its value in the late 1980s and then began to recover. Other examples are constantly occurring both on the upside and downside as fortunes are made and lost.

How does one develop an investment strategy in such an environment? Suggestions come from all directions. The investor is told how to benefit from the coming monetary disaster as well as how to grow rich in a new era of prosperity. The intent of this text is to help the investor sort out the various investments that are available and to develop analytical skills that suggest what securities and assets might be most appropriate for a given **portfolio.**

We shall define an **investment** as the commitment of current funds in anticipation of receiving a larger future flow of funds. The investor hopes to be compensated for forgoing immediate consumption, for the effects of inflation, and for taking a risk.

Investing may be both exciting and challenging. First-time investors who pore over the financial statements of a firm and then make a dollar commitment to purchase a few shares of stock often have a feeling of euphoria as they charge out in the morning to secure the daily newspaper and read the market quotes. Even professional analysts may take pleasure in leaving their Wall Street offices to evaluate an emerging high-technology firm in Austin or Palo Alto. Likewise, the buyer of a rare painting, late 18th-century U.S. coin, or invaluable baseball card may find a sense of excitement in attempting to outsmart the market. Even the purchaser of a bond or money market instrument must do proper analysis to ensure that anticipated objectives are being met. Let us examine the different types of investments.

FORMS OF INVESTMENT

In the text, we break down investment alternatives between financial and real assets. A **financial asset** represents a financial claim on an asset that is usually documented by some form of legal representation. An example would be a share of stock or a bond. A **real asset** represents an actual tangible asset that may be seen, felt, held, or collected. An example would be real estate or gold. Table 1–1 lists the various forms of financial and real assets.

As indicated in the left column of Table 1–1, financial assets may be broken down into five categories. **Direct equity claims** represent ownership interests and include common stock as well as other instruments that can be used to purchase common stock, such as warrants and options. Warrants and options allow the holder to buy a stipulated number of shares in the future at a given price. Warrants usually convert to one share and are long term, whereas options are generally based on 100 share units and are short term in nature.

Indirect equity can be acquired through placing funds in investment companies (such as a mutual fund). The investment company pools the resources of many investors and reinvests them in common stock (or other investments). The individual enjoys the advantages of diversification and professional management (though not necessarily higher returns).

Financial assets may also take the form of **creditor claims** as represented by debt instruments offered by financial institutions, industrial corporations, or the government. The rate of return is often initially fixed, though the actual return may vary with changing market conditions. Other forms of financial assets are **preferred stock,** which is a hybrid form of security combining some of the elements of equity ownership and creditor

TABLE 1–1 Overview of Investment Alternatives

Financial Assets	Real Assets
1. Equity claims—direct	1. Real estate
Common stock	Office buildings
Warrants	Apartments
Options	Shopping centers
	Personal residences
2. Equity claims—indirect	2. Precious metals
Investment company shares (mutual funds)	Gold
Pension funds	Silver
Whole life insurance	
3. Creditor claims	3. Precious gems
Savings account	Diamonds
Money market funds	Rubies
Commercial paper	Sapphires
Treasury bills, notes, bonds	4. Collectibles
Municipal notes, bonds	Art
Corporate bonds (straight and convertible to common stock)	Antiques
4. Preferred stock (straight and convertible to common stock)	Stamps
5. Commodity futures	Coins
	Rare books
	5. Other
	Cattle
	Oil
	Common metals

claims, and **commodity futures,** which represent a contract to buy or sell a commodity in the future at a given price. Commodities may include wheat, corn, copper, or even such financial instruments as Treasury bonds or foreign exchange.

As shown in the right column of Table 1–1, there are also numerous categories of real assets. The most widely recognized investment in this category is *real estate,* either commercial property or one's own residence. For greater risk, *precious metals* or *precious gems* can be considered, and for those seeking psychic pleasure as well as monetary gain, *collectibles* are an investment outlet. Finally, the *other (all-inclusive)* category includes cattle, oil, and other items that stretch as far as the imagination will go.

Throughout the text, each form of financial and real asset is considered. What assets the investor ultimately selects will depend on investment objectives as well as the economic outlook. For example, the investor who believes inflation will be relatively strong may prefer real assets that have a replacement value reflecting increasing prices. In a more moderate inflationary environment, stocks and bonds may be preferred.

THE SETTING OF INVESTMENT OBJECTIVES

The setting of investment objectives may be as important as the selection of the investment. In actuality, they tend to go together. A number of key areas should be considered.

Risk and Safety of Principal

The first factor investors must consider is the amount of risk they are prepared to assume. In a relatively efficient and informed capital market environment, risk tends to be closely correlated with return. Most of the literature of finance would suggest that those who consistently demonstrate high returns of perhaps 20 percent or more are greater-than-normal risk takers. While some clever investors are able to prosper on their wits alone, most high returns may be perceived as compensation for risk.

And there is not only the risk of losing invested capital directly (a dry hole perhaps) but also the danger of a loss in purchasing power. At 6 percent inflation (compounded annually), a stock that is held for four years without a gain in value would represent a 26 percent loss in purchasing power.

Investors who wish to assume low risks will probably confine a large portion of their portfolio to short-term debt instruments in which the party responsible for payment is the government or a major bank or corporation. Some conservative investors may choose to invest in a money market fund in which the funds of numerous investors are pooled and reinvested in high-yielding, short-term instruments. More aggressive investors may look toward longer-term debt instruments and common stock. Real assets, such as gold, silver, or valued art, might also be included in an aggressive portfolio.

It is not only the inherent risk in an asset that must be considered but also the extent to which that risk is being diversified away in a portfolio. Although an investment in gold might be considered risky, such might not be fully the case if it is combined into a portfolio of common stocks. Gold thrives on bad news, while common stocks generally do well in a positive economic environment. An oil embargo or foreign war may drive down the value of stocks while gold is advancing, and vice versa.

The age and economic circumstances of an investor are important variables in determining an appropriate level of risk. Young, upwardly mobile people are generally in a better position

to absorb risk than are elderly couples on a fixed income. Nevertheless, each of us, regardless of our plight in life, has different risk-taking desires. Because of an unwillingness to assume risk, a surgeon earning $200,000 a year may be more averse to accepting a $2,000 loss on a stock than an aging taxicab driver.

One cruel lesson of investing is that conservative investments do not always end up being what you thought they were when you bought them. This was true of IBM as described at the beginning of the chapter. This has also been true of many other firms. Classic examples can be found in the drug industry where leading firms such as Merek and Pfizer, who have reputations for developing outstanding products for the cure of cardiovascular and other diseases, saw their stock values fall by 30 percent when a strong movement for health care regulation and cost containment began in the 1990s. Even short-term, risk-averse investors in U.S. Treasury bills saw their income stream decline from 12 percent to 4 percent over a decade as interest rates plummeted. This declining cash flow can be a shock to your system if you are living on interest income.

Current Income versus Capital Appreciation

A second consideration in setting investment objectives is a decision on the desire for current income versus capital appreciation. Although this decision is closely tied to an evaluation of risk, it is separate.

In purchasing stocks, the investor with a need for current income may opt for high-yielding, mature firms in such industries as public utilities, machine tools, or apparel. Those searching for price gains may look toward smaller, emerging firms in high technology, energy, or electronics. The latter firms may pay no cash dividend, but the investor hopes for an increase in value to provide the desired return.

The investor needs to understand there is generally a trade-off between growth and income. Finding both in one type of investment is unlikely. If you go for the high-yielding utilities, you can expect slow growth in earnings and stock price. If you opt for high growth such as a biotechnology firm, you can expect no cash flow from the dividend.

Liquidity Considerations

Liquidity is measured by the ability of the investor to convert an investment into cash within a relatively short time at its fair market value or with a minimum capital loss on the transaction.

Most financial assets provide a high degree of liquidity. Stocks and bonds can generally be sold within a matter of minutes at a price reasonably close to the last traded value. Such may not be the case for real estate. Almost everyone has seen a house or piece of commercial real estate sit on the market for weeks, months, or years.

Liquidity can also be measured indirectly by the transaction costs or commissions involved in the transfer of ownership. Financial assets generally trade on a relatively low commission basis (perhaps 1 or 2 percent), whereas many real assets have transaction costs that run from 5 percent to 25 percent or more.

In many cases, the lack of immediate liquidity can be justified if there are unusual opportunities for gain. An investment in real estate or precious gems may provide sufficient return to more than compensate for the added transaction costs. Of course, a bad investment will be all the more difficult to unload.

Investors must carefully assess their own situation to determine the need for liquidity. If you are investing funds to be used for the next house payment or the coming semester's tuition, then immediate liquidity will be essential, and financial assets will be preferred. If funds can be tied up for long periods, bargain-buying opportunities of an unusual nature can also be evaluated.

Short-Term versus Long-Term Orientation

In setting investment objectives, you must decide whether you will assume a short-term or long-term orientation in managing the funds and evaluating performance. You do not always have a choice. People who manage funds for others may be put under tremendous pressure to show a given level of performance in the short run. Those applying pressure may be a concerned relative or a large pension fund that has placed funds with a bank trust department. Even though you are convinced your latest investment will double in the next three years, the fact that it is currently down 15 percent may provide some discomfort to those around you.

Market strategies may also be short term or long term in scope. Those who attempt to engage in short-term market tactics are termed *traders.* They may buy a stock at 15 and hope to liquidate if it goes to 20. To help reach decisions, short-term traders often use technical analysis, which is based on evaluating market indicator series and charting. Those who take a longer-term perspective try to identify fundamentally sound companies for a buy-and-hold approach. A long-term investor does not necessarily anticipate being able to buy right at the bottom or sell at the exact peak.

Research has shown it is difficult to beat the market on a risk-adjusted basis. Given that the short-term trader encounters more commissions than the long-term investor because of more active trading, short-term trading as a rule is not a strategy endorsed by the authors.

Tax Factors

Investors in high tax brackets have different investment objectives than those in lower brackets or tax-exempt charities, foundations, or similar organizations. An investor in a high tax bracket may prefer municipal bonds (interest is not taxable), real estate (with its depreciation and interest write-off), or investments that provide tax credits or limited tax shelters, such as those in oil and gas or railroad cars.

In recent times, many investment advisers have cautioned investors not to be blinded by the beneficial tax aspects of an investment but to look at the economic factors as well. Furthermore, the Tax Reform Act of 1986 greatly diminished the ability to use tax shams and tax shelters to protect income from taxation. One of the best tax-planning features is the individual retirement account (IRA), which is discussed in this and later chapters.

Ease of Management

Another consideration in establishing an investment program is ease of management. The investor must determine the amount of time and effort that can be devoted to an investment portfolio and act accordingly. In the stock market, this may determine whether you want to be a daily trader or to assume a longer-term perspective. In real estate, it may mean the difference between personally owning and managing a handful of rental houses or going

in with 10 other investors to form a limited partnership in which a general partner takes full management responsibility and the limited partners merely put up the capital.

Of course, a minimum amount of time must be committed to any investment program. Even when investment advisers or general partners are in charge, their activities must be monitored and evaluated.

In managing a personal portfolio, the investor should consider opportunity costs. If a lawyer can work for $150 per hour or manage his financial portfolio, a fair question would be, "How much extra return can I get from managing my portfolio, or can I add more value to my portfolio by working and investing more money?" Unless the lawyer is an excellent investor, it is probable that more money can be made by working.

Assume an investor can add a 2 percent extra return to his portfolio but it takes 5 hours per week (260 hours per year) to do so. If his opportunity cost is $40 per hour, he would have to add more than $10,400 ($40 × 260 hours) to his portfolio to make personal management attractive. If we assume a 2 percent excess return can be gained over the professional manager, the investor would need a portfolio of $520,000 before personal management would make sense under these assumptions. This example may explain why many high-income individuals choose to have professionals manage their assets.

Decisions such as these may also depend on your trade-off between work and leisure. An investor may truly find it satisfying and intellectually stimulating to manage a portfolio and may receive psychic income from mastering the nuances of investing. However, if you would rather ski, play tennis, or enjoy some other leisure activity, the choice of professional management may make more sense than a do-it-yourself approach.

Retirement and Estate Planning Considerations

Even the relatively young must begin to consider the effect of their investment decisions on their retirement and the estates they will someday pass along to their "potential families." Those who wish to remain single will still be called on to advise others as to the appropriateness of a given investment strategy for their family needs.

Most good retirement questions should not be asked at "retirement" but 40 or 45 years before because that's the period with the greatest impact. One of the first questions a person is often asked after taking a job on graduation is whether he or she wishes to set up an IRA. An IRA allows a qualifying taxpayer to deduct $2,000 from taxable income and invest the funds at a bank, savings and loan, brokerage house, mutual fund, or other financial institution. The funds are normally placed in interest-bearing instruments, such as a certificate of deposit, or perhaps in other securities, such as common stock. The income earned on the funds is allowed to grow tax-free until withdrawn at retirement. As an example, if a person places $2,000 a year in an IRA for 45 consecutive years and the funds earn 10 percent over that time, $1,437,810 will have been accumulated. Similar retirement and estate-planning issues will be mentioned later.

PROFILE ANALYSIS

Investors often wish to evaluate their own investment situation. In Appendix 1A, a risk profile is presented to see which types of investments are appropriate for investors based on their investment objectives. After you have read the chapter, you may want to try completing it. You can apply the questions to your own or your family's financial goals.

INFLATION—WHY SHOULD I WORRY?

Inflation was very tame from the mid-1980s to the early 1990s, growing at 2 to 3 percent per year. This was a far cry from the double-digit inflation of 11.4 percent in 1979 and 13.4 percent in 1980. Even these rates would have to be considered mild compared with the triple-digit (100+ percent) inflation witnessed during the 1980s in such developing countries as Brazil, Israel, and Mexico.

As you plan your future, you might ask, "What effect could inflation have on my well being?" If inflation is at 3 to 4 percent, the impact is not great. But observe in the table the effect of 6 percent sustained inflation over a 20-year time period. These values indicate why the Federal Reserve remains ever vigilant in trying to hold down the rate of inflation.

Impact of 6 Percent Inflation over 20 Years

	1995 Price	20 Years Later
Average automobile	$12,000	$ 38,484
Mercedes	39,000	125,073
Typical three-bedroom house	90,000	286,630
BBA starting salary	26,000	83,382
MBA starting salary	42,500	136,300
Average private college annual tuition	11,000	35,277
Ivy League annual tuition	21,500	68,950
Poverty level (family of four)	12,500	40,100

MEASURES OF RISK AND RETURN

Now that you have some basic familiarity with the different forms of investments and the setting of investment goals, we are ready to look at concepts of measuring the return from an investment and the associated risk. The return you receive from any investment (stocks, bonds, real estate) has two primary components: capital gains (or increase in value) and current income. The rate of return from an investment can be measured as:

$$\text{Rate of return} = \frac{(\text{Ending value} - \text{Beginning value}) + \text{Income}}{\text{Beginning value}} \qquad (1\text{–}1)$$

Thus, if a share of stock goes from $20 to $22 in one year and also pays a dollar in dividends during the year, the total return is 15 percent. Using Formula 1–1:

$$\frac{(\$22 - \$20) + \$1}{\$20} = \frac{\$2 + \$1}{\$20} = \frac{\$3}{\$20} = 15\%$$

Where the formula is being specifically applied to stocks, it is written as:

$$\text{Rate of return} = \frac{(P_1 - P_0) + D_1}{P_0} \qquad (1\text{–}2)$$

Where:

P_1 = Price at the end of the period.
P_0 = Price at the beginning of the period.
D_1 = Dividend income.

Risk

The risk for an investment is related to the uncertainty associated with the outcomes from an investment. For example, an investment that has an absolutely certain return of 10 percent is said to be riskless. Another investment that has a likely or expected return of 12 percent, but also has the possibility of minus 10 percent in hard economic times and plus 30 percent under optimum circumstances, is said to be risky. An example of three investments with progressively greater risk is presented in Figure 1–1. Based on our definition of risk, investment C is clearly the riskiest because of the large uncertainty (wide dispersion) of possible outcomes.

In the study of investments, you will soon observe that the desired or required rate of return for a given investment is generally related to the risk associated with that

FIGURE 1–1 Examples of Risk

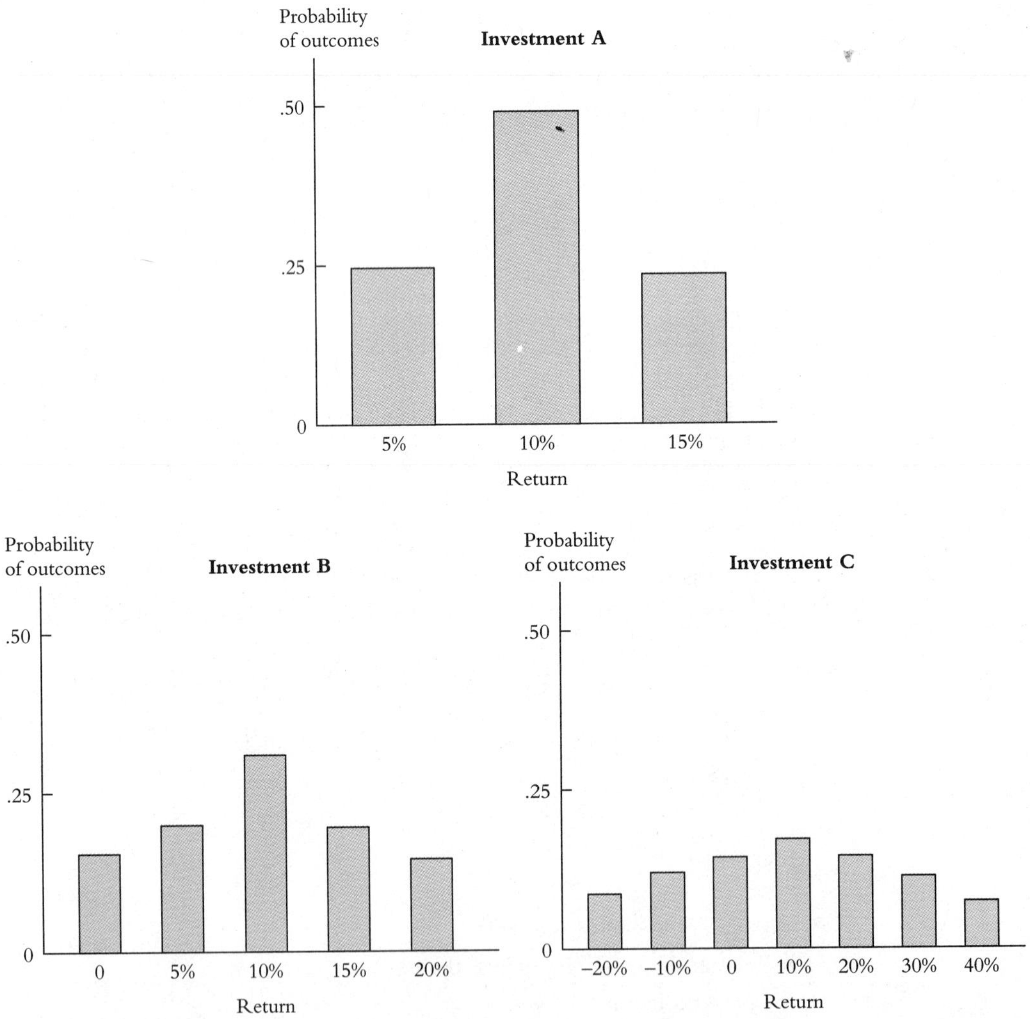

investment. Because most investors do not like risk, they will require a higher rate of return for a more risky investment. That is not to say the investors are unwilling to take risks—they simply wish to be compensated for taking the risk. For this reason, an investment in common stocks (which inevitably carries some amount of risk) may require an anticipated return 6 or 7 percent higher than a certificate of deposit in a commercial bank. This 6 or 7 percent represents a risk premium. You never know whether you will get the returns you anticipate, but at least your initial requirements will be higher to justify the risk you are taking.

ACTUAL CONSIDERATION OF REQUIRED RETURNS

Let's consider how return requirements are determined in the financial markets. Although the following discussion starts out on a theoretical "what if" basis, you will eventually see empirical evidence that different types of investments do provide different types of returns.

Basically, three components make up the required return from an investment:

1. The real rate of return.
2. The anticipated inflation factor.
3. The risk premium.

Real Rate of Return

The **real rate of return** is the return investors require for allowing others to use their money for a given time period. This is the return investors demand for passing up immediate consumption and allowing others to use their savings until the funds are returned. Because the term *real* is employed, this means it is a value determined before inflation is included in the calculation. The real rate of return is also determined before considering any specific risk for the investment.

Historically, the real rate of return in the U.S. economy has been from 2 to 3 percent. During much of the 1980s, it was somewhat higher (4 to 6 percent), but in the early 1990s, interest rates fell more than inflation, and the real rate of return came back to its normal level of 2 to 3 percent, which is probably a reasonable long-term expectation.

Because an investor is concerned with using a real rate of return as a component of a required rate of return, the past is not always a good predictor for any one year's real rate of return. The problem comes from being able to measure the real rate of return only after the fact by subtracting inflation from the nominal interest rate. Unfortunately, expectations and occurrence do not always match. The real rate of return is highly variable (for seven years in the 1970s and early 1980s, it was even negative). One of the problems investors face in determining required rates of return is the forecasting errors involving interest rates and inflation. These forecasting errors are more pronounced in short-run returns than in long-run returns. Let us continue with our example and bring inflation into the discussion.

Anticipated Inflation Factor

The anticipated inflation factor must be added to the real rate of return. For example, if there is a 2 percent real-rate-of-return requirement and the **anticipated rate of inflation** is 3 percent, we combine the two to arrive at an approximate 5 percent required return

factor. Combining the real rate of return and inflationary considerations gives us the required return on an investment before explicitly considering risk. For this reason, it is called the risk-free required rate of return or, simply, **risk-free rate (R_F)**.

We can define the risk-free rate as:

$$\text{Risk-free rate} = (1 + \text{Real rate})\,(1 + \text{Expected rate of inflation}) - 1 \qquad (1\text{–}3)$$

Plugging in numerical values, we would show:

$$\text{Risk-free rate} = (1.02)\,(1.03) - 1 = 1.0506 - 1 = 0.0506 \text{ or } 5.06\%$$

The answer is approximately 5 percent. You can simply add the real rate of return (2 percent) to the anticipated inflation rate (3 percent) to get a 5 percent answer or go through the more theoretically correct process of Formula 1–3 to arrive at 5.06 percent. Either approach is frequently used.

The risk-free rate (R_F) of approximately 5 percent applies to any investment as the minimum required rate of return to provide a 2 percent *real return* after inflation. Of course, if the investor actually receives a lower return, the real rate of return may be quite low or negative. For example, if the investor receives a 2 percent return in a 4 percent inflationary environment, there is a negative real return of 2 percent. The investor will have 2 percent less purchasing power than before he started. He would have been better off to spend the money *now* rather than save at a 2 percent rate in a 4 percent inflationary economy. In effect, he is *paying* the borrower to use his money. Of course, real rates of return and inflationary expectations change from time to time, so the risk-free required rate (R_F) also changes.

We now have examined the two components that make up the minimum risk-free rate of return that apply to investments (stock, bonds, real estate, etc.). We now consider the third component, the risk premium. The relationship is depicted in Figure 1–2.

FIGURE 1–2 The Components of Required Rate of Return

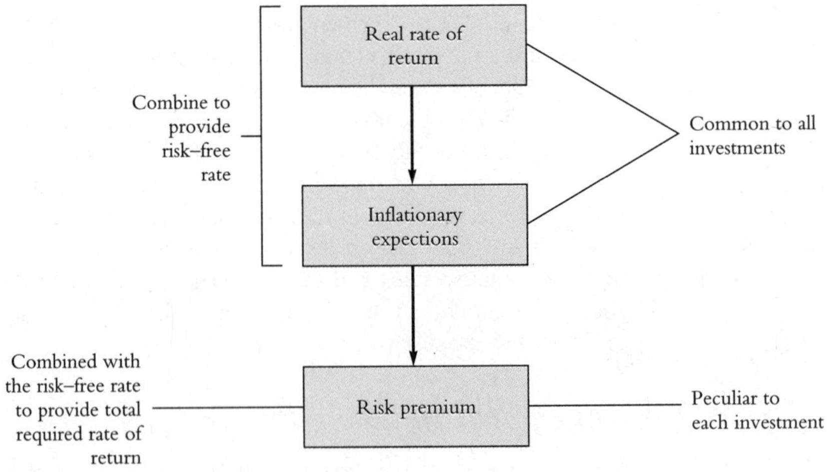

Risk Premium

The **risk premium** will be different for each investment. For example, for a federally insured certificate of deposit at a bank or for a U.S. Treasury bill, the risk premium approaches zero. All the return to the investor will be at the risk-free rate of return (the real rate of return plus inflationary expectations). For common stock, the investor's required return may carry a 6 or 7 percent risk premium in addition to the risk-free rate of return. If the risk-free rate were 5 percent, the investor might have an overall required return of 11 to 12 percent on common stock.

+ Real rate	2%
+ Anticipated inflation	3%
= Risk-free rate	5%
+ Risk premium	6% or 7%
= Required rate of return	11% to 12%

Corporate bonds fall somewhere between short-term government obligations (virtually no risk) and common stock in terms of risk. Thus, the risk premium may be 3 to 4 percent. Like the real rate of return and the inflation rate, the risk premium is not a constant but may change from time to time. If investors are very fearful about the economic outlook, the risk premium may be 8 to 10 percent as it was for junk bonds in 1990 and 1991.

The normal relationship between selected investments and their rates of return is depicted in Figure 1–3 on page 16.

A number of empirical studies tend to support the risk-return relationships shown in Figure 1–3 over a long period. Perhaps the most widely cited is the Ibbotson study presented in Figure 1–4 on page 17, which covers data from 1926 to 1994. Note that the high-to-low return scale is in line with expectations based on risk. Of particular interest is the geometric mean column. This is simply the compound annual rate of return. The arithmetic mean is an average of yearly rates of return and has less meaning. Given that risk is measured by the standard deviation, the distribution of returns, which appears to the right of each security type, indicates which security has the biggest risk. Figure 1–4 shows in practice what we discussed in theory earlier in the chapter.

Because the Ibbotson study in Figure 1–4 covered 68 years (including a decade of depression), the rates of return may be somewhat lower than those currently available. This is particularly true for the bonds and Treasury bills. Table 1–2 on page 17, from the *Stocks, Bonds, Bills and Inflation 1995 Yearbook,* shows returns for eight different decades.

The returns just discussed primarily apply to financial assets (stocks, bonds, and so forth). Salomon Brothers, an investment banking firm, tracks the performance of real assets as well as financial assets. Over long periods of time, common stocks generally tend to perform at approximately the same level as real assets such as real estate, coins, stamps, and so forth, with each tending to show a different type of performance in a

FIGURE 1–3 Risk-Return Characteristics

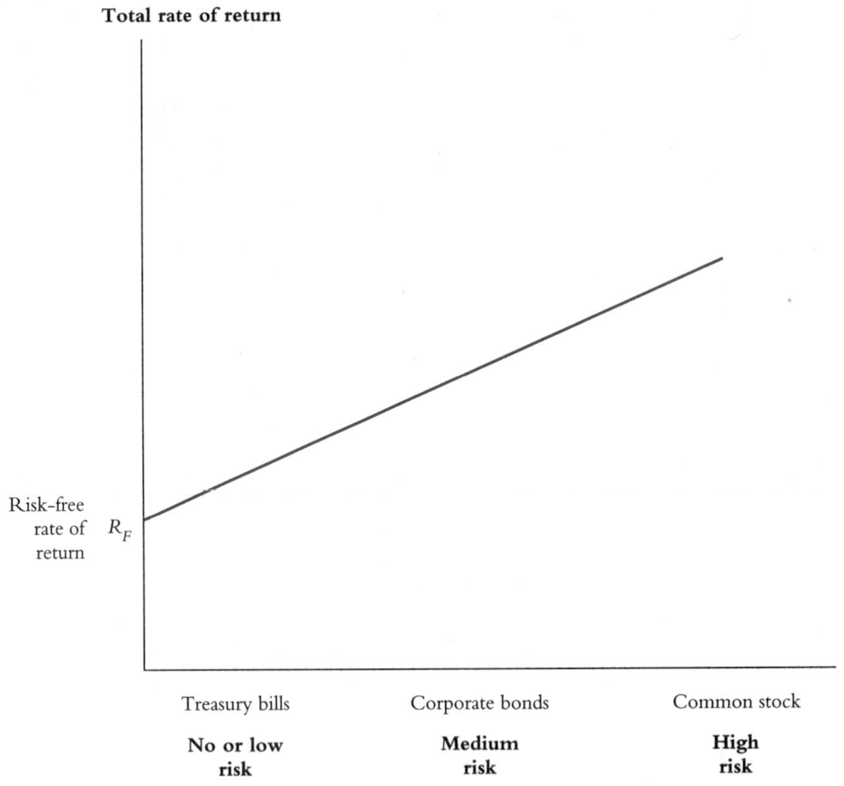

different economic environment.[1] Real assets tend to do best in inflationary environments, while moderate inflation favors financial assets. In 1991, the best long-term performers in the Salomon study were Old Master paintings, Chinese ceramics, gold, diamonds, and stamps. After three years of moderate inflation, stocks and bonds had risen to the top in 1994. No doubt the pattern will shift back and forth many times in the future. More will be said about the impact of inflation and disinflation on investments later in the text.

We have attempted to demonstrate the importance of risk in determining the required rate of return for an investment. As previously discussed, it is the third key component that is added to the risk-free rate (composed of the real rate of return and the inflation premium) to determine the total required rate of return. How does one *actually* determine the risk that is to be rewarded from a given instrument?

---

[1] Examples of other longer-term studies on comparative returns between real and financial assets are: Roger G. Ibbotson and Carol F. Fall, "The United States Wealth Portfolio," *The Journal of Portfolio Management,* Fall 1982, pp. 82–92; Roger G. Ibbotson and Lawrence B. Siegel, "The World Market Wealth Portfolio," *The Journal of Portfolio Management,* Winter 1983, pp. 5–17; and Alexander A. Robichek, Richard A. Cohn, and John J. Pringle, "Returns on Alternative Media and Implications for Portfolio Construction," *Journal of Business,* July 1972, pp. 427–43. (While Ibbotson and Siegel showed superior returns for metals between 1960 and 1980, metals have greatly underperformed other assets in the 1980s.)

FIGURE 1–4 Basic Series: Summary Statistics of Annual Returns (1926–1994)

Series	Geometric Mean	Arithmetic Mean	Standard Deviation
Large Company Stocks	10.2%	12.2%	20.3%
Small Company Stocks	12.2	17.4	34.6
Long-Term Corporate Bonds	5.4	5.7	8.4
Long-Term Government Bonds	4.8	5.2	8.8
Intermediate-Term Government Bonds	5.1	5.2	5.7
U.S. Treasury Bills	3.7	3.7	3.3
Inflation	3.1	3.2	4.6

Distribution

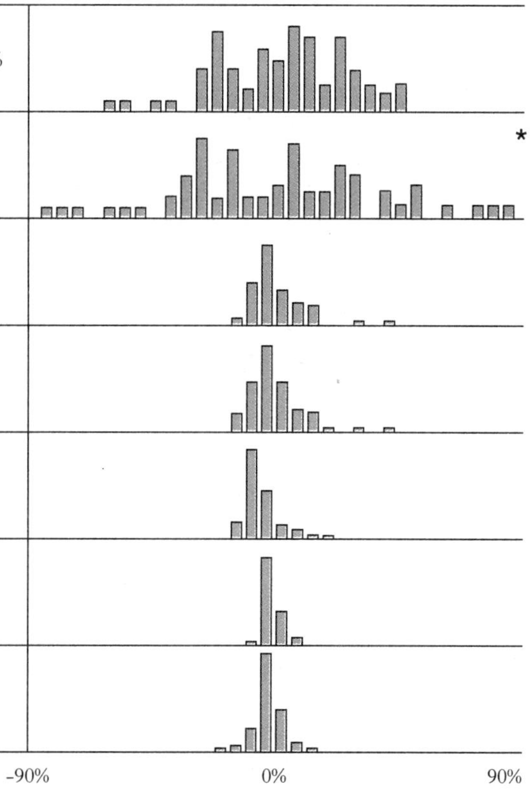

*The 1993 Small Company Stock Total Return was 142.9%.
Source: *Stocks, Bonds, Bills and Inflation 1995 Yearbook* (Chicago: R. G. Ibbotson & Associates, Inc., 1995), p. 33.

TABLE 1–2 Compound Annual Rates of Return by Decade

	1920s*	1930s	1940s	1950s	1960s	1970s	1980s	1990s**	1984–1994
Large company	19.2%	0.1%	9.2%	19.4%	7.8%	5.9%	17.5%	8.7%	14.4%
Small company	−4.5	1.4	20.7	16.9	15.5	11.5	15.8	11.8	11.1
Long-term corporate	5.2	6.9	2.7	1.0	1.7	6.2	13.0	8.4	11.6
Long-term government	5.0	4.9	3.2	−0.1	1.4	5.5	12.6	8.3	11.9
Inter-term government	4.2	4.6	1.8	1.3	3.5	7.0	11.9	7.5	9.4
Treasury bills	3.7	0.6	0.4	1.9	3.9	6.3	8.9	4.7	5.8
Inflation	−1.1	−2.0	5.4	2.2	2.5	7.4	5.1	3.5	3.6

*Based on the period 1926–1929.
**Based on the period 1990–1994.
Source: *SBBI 1995 Yearbook*, p. 18.

Systematic and Unsystematic Risk

You will recall that earlier we defined risk as related to the uncertainty of outcomes for a given investment. But it is not just the risk for an individual security that must be considered. Financial theory also requires that we consider the relationship between two or more investments to determine the combined risk level. Part of the risk of one investment may be **diversified** away with a second investment. For example, an investment in an oil company may be somewhat risky because oil prices may drop, but if you have a second investment in a petrochemical company that will benefit from lower oil prices, then you have diversified away part of the risk. Similarly, investments in foreign stocks often move in the opposite direction of investments in U.S. stocks. If you combine stocks from two or more countries, part of the risk is diversified away. Because diversification can *eliminate* part of the risk in an investment, not all risk is thought to be compensated for by proportionally higher returns.

Financial theory can be used to break down risk that is systematic and unsystematic in nature. **Unsystematic risk** is risk that can be diversified away in a well-constructed portfolio and thus is not assumed to be rewarded with higher returns in the financial markets. It represents the type of risk described in the preceding paragraph. **Systematic risk** is inherent in the investment and cannot be diversified away and is assumed to be rewarded in the marketplace. The relationship is indicated in Figure 1–5.

Systematic risk is measured by the related movement of a stock to the market. Even in a totally diversified portfolio, each stock will be vulnerable to changes in the *overall* market even if individual characteristics of the stocks have been largely diversified away. Based on systematic risk, if the market goes up or down by 10 percent, our stock may go up or down by 10 percent. The joint movement between a security and the market in general is defined as the **beta** coefficient. If a stock has equal volatility to the market (if the market changes by 10 percent, the stock changes by 10 percent), the beta coefficient is 1. If the stock is 50 percent more volatile than the market, the beta coefficient is 1.5 and so on. Systematic risk, as measured by the beta coefficient, is assumed to be compensated for by higher potential returns. That is, stocks that have high systematic risk or betas are assumed to provide higher returns to compensate for the additional risk. This same type of risk analysis can be applied to other types of investments as well.

In a later chapter, we will give a more thorough mathematical definition of how you separate out systematic and unsystematic risk. It is enough for now that you understand that the differences exist and that the two forms of risk are not equally compensated. In the prior discussion of unsystematic risk, we mentioned the importance of diversifying away nonmarket-related risks. We discussed oil versus petrochemicals as presenting potential for diversifying oil price risks. Also foreign stocks versus U.S. stocks were

FIGURE 1–5 Types of Risk

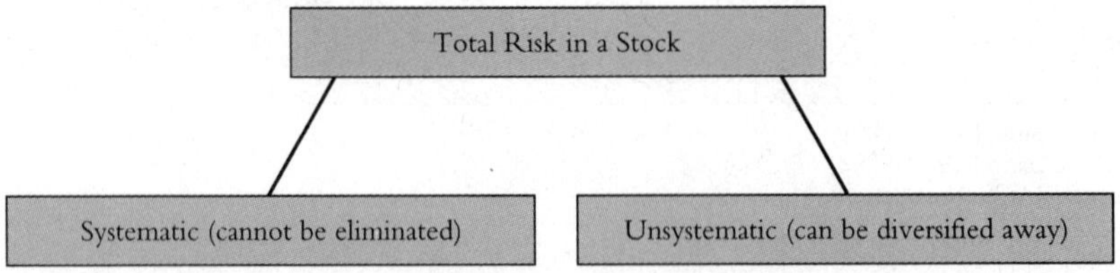

given as an example. The auto parts replacement market may move in the opposite direction of new auto sales; the same can be said for the market for defense systems and public works projects. To establish an efficiently diversified portfolio, the investor must consider how projects correlate with each other. Generally, highly correlated projects provide little diversification benefits, while projects that have low correlations or are negatively correlated provide maximum diversification benefits.

Summary of Return Considerations

Based on our analysis to this point, we can say that each investment requires a total return that comprises a real rate of return, compensation for inflationary expectations, and a risk premium. The risk premium should be related to systematic risk (as opposed to unsystematic risk). In Chapter 7, "Valuation of the Individual Firm," you will become familiar with K_e, which is the total return on common stock. K_e represents a risk-free rate plus a risk premium and this risk premium is directly related to systematic risk.

WHAT YOU WILL LEARN

The first part of the book covers the general framework for investing. You will look at an overview of the security markets (New York Stock Exchange, Chicago Board Options Exchange, and so on). Then you will examine the basics for participating in the market, such as opening an account, executing an order, investing individually or through a mutual fund, and so forth. Also in the first section of the book, you will become familiar with sources of important investment information so you can begin to make your university or public library a valuable asset.

You will then go through the classic process of analyzing and valuing a security. You will start with examining the economy, then move to the industry level, and finally move to the actual company. The authors go through the process of putting a value on a stock. There is also heavy emphasis on financial analysis. One chapter provides an in-depth analysis of the Coca-Cola Company to demonstrate procedures for identifying the strengths and weaknesses of a company. For enthusiasts of charting and other forms of technical analysis, we examine the advantages and disadvantages of such approaches.

You will then move from stocks to bonds. Your level of interest should not diminish because bonds also offer an opportunity for income and, surprisingly, for large gains or losses. Because an emphasis of the book is to present the student with a wide investment horizon from which to choose, we then consider a variety of other investment alternatives. These include convertible securities and warrants, put and call options, commodities and financial futures, stock index futures and options, and real assets such as real estate and precious metals. We realize some of these terms may have little meaning to you now, but they soon will.

You will also study mutual funds and international securities in depth. In the latter part of the book, we also consider the concepts of portfolio theory and how to put together the most desirable package of investments in terms of risk and return. We also consider the consequences of investing in a reasonably efficient stock market environment, one in which information is acted on very quickly. Can superior return be achieved in such a setting?

Many students taking an investments course are not sure of their ultimate career goals. We hope this course can be equally valuable to a future banker, CPA, insurance executive,

marketing manager, or anyone else. However, for those specifically considering a career in investments, the authors present a brief summary of career opportunities in Appendix 1B at the back of this chapter.

KEY WORDS AND CONCEPTS

portfolio, 5
investment, 5
financial asset, 6
real asset, 6
direct and indirect equity claims, 6
creditor claims, 6
preferred stock, 6
commodity futures, 7
liquidity, 8
real rate of return, 13
anticipated rate of inflation, 13
risk-free rate (R_F), 14
risk premium, 15
diversified, 18
unsystematic risk, 18
systematic risk, 18
beta, 18

DISCUSSION QUESTIONS

1. How is an investment defined?
2. What are the differences between financial and real assets?
3. List some key areas relating to investment objectives.
4. Explain the concepts of direct equity and indirect equity.
5. How are equity and creditor claims different?
6. Do those wishing to assume low risks tend to invest long term or short term? Why?
7. How might investing in something generally considered to be risky actually decrease an investor's risk?
8. What are some types of appropriate investments for investors in high tax brackets who wish to diminish their tax obligation? Comment on the effect of the Tax Reform Act of 1986 on tax shams and tax shelters.
9. How is liquidity measured?
10. Explain why conservative investors who tend to buy short-term assets differ from short-term traders.
11. Why is there a minimum amount of time that must be committed to any investment program?
12. In a highly inflationary environment, would an investor tend to favor real or financial assets? Why?
13. What is an individual retirement account (IRA)? What are the tax advantages it offers?
14. What two primary components are used to measure the rate of return achieved from an investment?
15. Many people think of risk as the danger of losing money. Is this the same way that risk is defined in finance?
16. What are the three elements that determine the return an investor should require from an investment?
17. Explain how an investor receiving a 2 or 3 percent quoted return in an inflationary environment may actually experience a negative real rate of return.
18. In Figure 1–4, what has been the highest return investment category over the 68-year period? What has been the lowest? Assuming risk is measured by the standard deviation, what can you say about the relationship of risk to return in Figure 1–4?

19. Why is *all* risk not thought to be compensated by proportionally higher return?
20. If stocks are combined into a portfolio, is it their systematic or unsystematic risk that is being reduced?
21. Explain the concept of a beta coefficient. Should large beta stocks have higher or lower required rates of return?
22. If required returns in the market turn out to be larger than initially anticipated, what is likely to happen to the market value of a previously purchased asset?
23. In considering question 22, suggest some factors that might have caused the required rate of return to rise.

PROBLEMS

Rate of return

1. The stock of Clarkson Corporation went from $50 to $56 last year. The firm also paid $2 in dividends. Compute the rate of return.

Rate of return

2. In the following year, the dividend was raised to $2.25. However, a bear market developed toward the end of the year, and the stock price declined from $56 at the beginning of the year to $48 at the end of the year. Compute the rate of return or (loss) to stockholders.

Risk-free rate

3. Assume the real rate of return in the economy is 2.5 percent, the expected rate of inflation is 5 percent, and the risk premium is 5.8 percent. Compute the risk-free rate (Formula 1–3) and the required rate of return.

Required return

4. Assume the real return in the economy is 4 percent. It is anticipated that the consumer price index will go from 150 to 157.5. Shares in common stock are assumed to have a required return one-third higher than the risk-free rate. Compute the required return on common stock.

THE WALL STREET JOURNAL PROJECT

1. In this chapter, a distinction is made between financial assets and real assets as well as between direct and indirect equity investments. Using *The Wall Street Journal,* bring your knowledge up to date by searching Section C for prices of the following assets (investments).
   a. Financial Assets
      - Minnesota Mining & Manufacturing (MMM) Common Stock. 3M common stock is listed under the M heading on the New York Stock Exchange.
      - Babson Group Growth (OWTH) Mutual Fund (Mutual Fund Quotations).
      - IBM Bond with a 7½ percent coupon and a maturity of 2013 (New York Exchange Bonds). The value you find represents a percentage—multiply the percentage by $1,000 to get your answer.
   b. Real Assets
      - Gold (cash prices)[2]—Engelhard Industrial bullion.
      - Silver (cash prices)—Engelhard Industrial bullion.
      - Copper (cash prices).

---

[2] Cash prices and oil prices are normally found on the page following "Commodities."

- Colombian Coffee (cash prices).
- West Texas Sour Crude Oil (oil prices).

U.S. EQUITIES ONFLOPPY EXERCISES

Please use your U.S. Equities OnFloppy software and manual to complete the following exercise(s).

1. a. Locate IBM, and examine its performance data.
   b. In particular, examine the trend of revenues, earnings, and dividends.
   c. Examine the 60-month and 52-week closing price trends.
2. a. Find the SIC code of IBM, and screen the database to find all companies that have the same first three digits as IBM for their SIC code.
   b. How many companies are there with this SIC code?
3. Investing in the Computer Equipment Manufacturing industry is often thought to involve more risk than investing in the Electric Services industry. Compare the average beta for the companies in these industries. Use SIC 357* and SIC 491*, respectively.

SELECTED REFERENCES

Ibbotson, Roger G., and Carol F. Fall. "The United States Wealth Portfolio." *The Journal of Portfolio Management,* Fall 1982, pp. 82–92.

______, and Lawrence B. Siegel. "The World Market Wealth Portfolio." *The Journal of Portfolio Management,* Winter 1983, pp. 5–17.

Lorie, James H., and Lawrence Fisher. "Rates of Return on Investment in Common Stock." *Journal of Business,* January 1964, pp. 1–17.

"Ranking America's Biggest Brokers." *Institutional Investor,* April 1991, pp. 139–40.

Restoy, Fernando, and G. Michael Rockinger. "On Stock Market Returns and Returns on Investment." *Journal of Finance,* June 1994, pp. 543–56.

Robichek, Alexander A.; Richard A. Cohn; and John J. Pringle. "Returns on Alternative Media and Implications for Portfolio Construction." *Journal of Business,* July 1972, pp. 427–43.

Rozeff, Michael S. "Dividend Yields Are Equity Risk Premiums." *Journal of Portfolio Management,* Fall 1984, pp. 68–75.

Stocks, Bonds, Bills and Inflation, 1995 Yearbook. Chicago: R. G. Ibbotson and Associates, Inc., 1995.

Setting Objectives

Blume, Marshall E., and Irwin Friend. "Risk, Investment Strategy and the Long-Run Rates of Return." *The Review of Economics and Statistics,* August 1974, pp. 259–69.

Editors of *Consumer Guide* with Peter A. Dickinson. *How to Make Money during Inflation Recession.* New York: Harper & Row, 1980.

Lezner, Robert. "The Case for Hard Assets." *Forbes,* June 20, 1994, pp. 146–51.

Paré, Terrence P. "How to Find a Financial Planner." *Fortune,* May 16, 1994, pp. 103–6.

Rosenberg, Barr. "Prediction of Common Stock Investment Risk." *Journal of Portfolio Management,* Fall 1984, pp. 44–53.

Salomon, R. S. "Why I Like Financial Assets." *Forbes,* June 20, 1994, p. 262–63.

Yakov, Amihud, and Haim Mendelson. "Liquidity, Asset Prices and Financial Policy." *Financial Analysts Journal,* November–December 1991, pp. 56–66.

APPENDIX 1A: Investor Risk Profile

Investor Risk Profile

1. Liquidity: the ability to quickly realize cash from the sale at fair market value.
2. Safety of Principal: the principal is safe from bankruptcy or default.
3. Price Stability: the market value of the asset does not change in value.
4. Reinvestment Protection: protection against reinvesting cash flow at lower interest rates as interest rates decline.
5. Growth of Capital: the original investment increases over time to create capital gains.
6. Cash Income: the cash income relative to treasury bills.
7. Growth of Income: the ability of the cash income stream to increase over time.
8. Inflation Hedge: the ability of the total return (cash income plus capital gains) to keep pace with inflation over time.

Circle the appropriate response. If the following risk characteristic is very important to you, circle 7. If the risk is of little concern to you, circle 1. The choice of 4 would indicate that you are moderately concerned about this risk characteristic.

	1 = not too important >>>>>> 7 = very important						
1. Liquidity	1	2	3	4	5	6	7
2. Safety of Principal	1	2	3	4	5	6	7
3. Price Stability	1	2	3	4	5	6	7
4. Reinvestment Protection	1	2	3	4	5	6	7
5. Growth of Capital	1	2	3	4	5	6	7
6. Cash Income	1	2	3	4	5	6	7
7. Growth of Income	1	2	3	4	5	6	7
8. Inflation Hedge	1	2	3	4	5	6	7

A

Total your score: ______

If A totals 48 or more points you want it all. You want to be protected from all risks, which is impossible. You can't have your cake and eat it too.

Your answers would be more consistent if you had high numbers in B and low numbers in C or low numbers in B and high numbers in C. Then you would be stating that you understand that several of these risks go together and several do not blend well.

B

Add Scores for items 1, 2, 3, 4, and 6: ______

If B totals between 30 and 35 you are risk averse and want liquid investments that have stable prices, safety of principal, and generate an above average cash income. You would probably be comfortable buying: Treasury Bills, U.S. Notes, Utility Common Stocks, Certificates of Deposit, Money Market Funds, Income Oriented Mutual Funds, or small % of Blue Chip Stocks.

Your ability to tolerate price instability will determine the length of the maturities you would be willing to buy in the bond market. The more stability you desire, the shorter the maturity you would desire.

C

Add scores for items 5, 7, and 8: ______

If C totals between 18 and 21 you are an aggressive investor seeking growth of income and principal and long-run protection against inflation.

You would probably be comfortable buying Blue Chip Common Stocks, Growth Stocks, small NASDAQ Stocks, High Yield Bonds, Oil Drilling Partnerships, Gold and Silver, or International Stock Funds

If you also have very low numbers in part B between 10 and 12, you are extremely aggressive. If you have moderate numbers in part B between 20 and 25 you would be moderately aggressive.

APPENDIX 1B: Career Opportunities in Investments

Career opportunities in the field of investments include positions as a stockbroker, security analyst or portfolio manager, investment banker, or financial planner.

Stockbroker

A stockbroker (sometimes referred to as an account executive) generally works with the public in advising and executing orders for individual or institutional accounts. Although the broker may have a salary base to cushion against bad times, most of the compensation is in the form of commissions. Successful brokers do quite well financially.

Most brokerage houses look for people who have effective selling skills as well as an interest in finance. In hiring, some (though not all) brokerage houses require prior business experience and a mature appearance. Table 1B–1 lists the 30 largest brokerage houses. Further information on these firms (as well as others not included on the list) can be found in the *Securities Industry Yearbook* published by the Securities Industry Association, 10 Broad Street, New York, N.Y. 10005.

Security Analyst or Portfolio Manager

Security analysts study various industries and companies and provide research reports to their clientele. A security analyst might work for a brokerage house, a bank trust department, or any other type of institutional investor. Security analysts often specialize in certain industries, such as banking or the airlines. They are expected to have an in-depth knowledge of overall financial analysis as well as the variables that influence their industry.

The role of the financial analyst has been upgraded over the years through a certifying program in which you can become a chartered financial analyst (CFA). There are approximately 25,000 CFAs in the United States and Canada. Achieving this designation calls for a three-year minimum appropriate-experience requirement and extensive testing over a three-year period. Each of the annual exams is six hours long and costs approximately $250 (the fee changes from year to year). There is also an initial, one-time registration fee (currently, $250). You can actually begin taking the exams while still in school (you can complete your experience requirement later).

Topics covered in the three years of exams are shown in Table 1B–2 on page 26. An undergraduate or graduate degree in business with a major in finance or accounting or an economics degree is quite beneficial to the exam process (although other degrees are also acceptable). Of course, educational background must be supplemented with additional study prescribed by the Institute of Chartered Financial Analysts. The address for more information is: Association for Investment Management and Research, P.O. Box 3668, Charlottesville, Virginia 22903 (phone 804-980-3668).

While many security analysts are not CFAs, those who carry this designation tend to enjoy higher salaries and prestige. The number of openings for security analysts has shrunk because of the tight research budgets of many brokerage houses. This came about in the mid-1970s when commission charges went from fixed to freely competitive and fewer dollars were allocated to research.

TABLE 1B–1 30 Largest U.S. Brokerage Houses

1993 Rank	Name of Firm	Total Capital ($ millions)
1	Merrill Lynch	$18,954.8
2	Salomon Inc.	17,023.0
3	Goldman, Sachs & Co.	15,249.0
4	Lehman Brothers	11,951.0
5	Morgan Stanley	8,208.8
6	Bear, Stearns & Co.	4,665.3
7	CS First Boston	4,649.0
8	Paine Webber	3,131.0
9	Smith Barney Shearson	2,742.0
10	Prudential Securities	1,842.0
11	Donaldson, Lufkin & Jenrette	1,709.0
12	Dean Witter Reynolds	1,615.0
13	Kidder, Peabody & Co.	1,385.0
14	J. P. Morgan Securities	1,106.0
15	Nomura Securities International	954.0
16	Shelby Cullom Davis & Co.	848.8
17	BT Securities Corp.	814.0
18	UBS Securities	811.5
19	A. G. Edwards, Inc.	752.0
20	Charles Schwab & Co.	459.0
21	Citicorp Securities	453.0
22	Greenwich Capital Markets	424.9
23	D. E. Shaw & Co.	372.0
24	Chemical Securities	363.0
25	Daiwa Securities America	343.5
26	Alex. Brown & Sons	334.0
27	Deutsche Bank Securities Corp.	331.6
28	Oppenheimer & Co.	321.0
29	Fidelity Brokerage Services	311.6
30	Legg Mason	308.0

Source: "The Institutional Investor Ranking," *Institutional Investor,* April 1994, p.156.

Despite this situation, really top analysts are still in strong demand, and six-figure salaries for top analysts are common. The magazine *Institutional Investor* picks an all-American team of security analysts, the best in energy, banking, and so on.

Portfolio managers are responsible for managing large pools of funds, and they are generally employed by insurance companies, mutual funds, bank trust departments, pension funds, and other institutional investors. They often rely on the help of security analysts and brokers in designing their portfolios. They not only must decide which

TABLE 1B–2 Topics Covered in CFA Exams

Ethical and Professional Standards	
Applicable laws and regulations	Ethical conduct and professional obligations
Professional standards of practice	International ethical and professional considerations
Tools and Inputs for Investment Valuation and Management	
Quantitative methods and statistics	Microeconomics
Macroeconomics	Financial standards and accounting
Investment (Asset) Valuation	
Overview of the valuation process	Equity securities
Applying economic analysis in investment valuation	Fixed-income securities
Applying industry analysis in investment valuation	Other investments
Applying company analysis in investment valuation	Derivative securities
Portfolio Management	
Capital market theory	Equity portfolio management
Portfolio policies	Real estate portfolio management
Expectational factors	Specialized asset portfolio management
Asset allocation	Implementing the investment process
Fixed-income portfolio management	Performance management

Source: *The CFA Candidate Study and Examination Program Review,* 1994 (Charlottesville, VA: Association for Investment Management and Research, 1994), pp. 5–13.

stocks to buy or sell, but they also must determine the risk level with the optimum trade-off between the common stock and fixed-income components of a portfolio. Portfolio managers often rise through the ranks of stockbrokers and security analysts.

Investment Banker

Investment bankers are primarily involved in the distribution of securities from the issuing corporation to the public. Investment bankers also advise corporate clients on their financial strategy and may help to arrange mergers and acquisitions.

The investment banker is one of the most prestigious participants in the securities industry. Although the hiring of investment bankers was once closely confined to Ivy League graduates with the right family ties, such is no longer the case. Nevertheless, an MBA and top credentials are usually the first prerequisites.

Financial Planner

A new field of financial planning is emerging to help solve the investment and tax problems of the individual investor. Financial planners may include specially trained representatives of the insurance industry, accountants who have expertise in this area, and certified financial planners (an individual may fall into more than one of these categories).

Certified financial planners (CFPs) are so designated by the College of Financial Planning, a division of the National Endowment for Financial Education. To qualify as a CFP, an applicant must demonstrate proficiency in the five following areas through extensive testing and training.

- Financial planning process and insurance.
- Investment planning.
- Income tax planning.
- Retirement planning and employee benefits.
- Estate planning.

Information on the CFP program can be obtained from the CFP Board, 1660 Lincoln Street, Suite 3050, Denver, Colorado 80264-3001 (phone 303-830-7543).

2

Security Markets: Present and Future

THE MARKET ENVIRONMENT

Changes in the financial markets that began in the 1980s have continued into the 1990s. Deregulation of financial institutions created new competitors for retail brokerage houses and allowed banks and savings and loan associations to offer discount brokerage services and money market deposit accounts. A series of mergers consolidated financial resources into well-capitalized financial-service-oriented companies. Insurance companies entered the financial services arena by offering mutual funds and annuity products to take advantage of retirement planning and the increased emphasis on individual asset management.

After rapid expansion in the 1980s, many financial service firms hit hard times or failed to live up to their promise in the 1990s. Prudential never received the benefits expected from its merger with Bache, and in 1991, Prudential changed management and dropped Bache from the name. Drexel Burnham Lambert went bankrupt, and the "junk bond" market deteriorated with it. The recession of 1990–91 hurt commercial real estate in the Northeast, and real estate prices collapsed in other parts of the country as well.

The early 1990s continued to be a difficult time for financial institutions. Savings and loan associations and banks went out of business at a record pace, and the U.S. government insurance programs (Federal Savings and Loan Insurance Corporation and Federal Deposit Insurance Corporation) had to step in to cover depositors' losses. Unfortunately, these insurance funds did not have enough money to pay off depositors, and the U.S. government had to appropriate funds to make the guarantees good. Also, the U.S. government created the Resolution Trust Corporation to handle sales and liquidations of the assets acquired from the government takeover of failed banks and S&Ls. Insurance companies that had loaded up on risky junk bonds and commercial real estate suffered a serious erosion of capital when these two markets caved in. Several insurance companies, including Mutual Benefit Life and Executive Life of California, were taken over by state insurance commissions.

Despite all these retrenchments in the financial industry, investors probably have more alternative investments (securities) currently available to them than at any other time in history. They can buy traditional stocks and bonds, short-term money market instruments, real estate investments, and international securities as well as other riskier securities. One lesson learned is that it makes a difference what firm you use for your investment transactions.

The markets for stocks, bonds, options, and futures continue to become more international in scope as we approach the year 2000. The increased listing of foreign securities on international stock exchanges has led to around-the-world trading from one time zone to another and virtual 24-hour trading in stocks of large international corporations. Trading starts in Tokyo, is passed to London, then to New York, and back to Tokyo. The three markets encompass enough time zones to make continuous trading almost a reality. With all this trading, international competition is heating up between the equity markets. International markets are covered separately in Chapter 18.

Even the traditional markets for common stocks have changed as the over-the-counter market—through its National Association of Securities Dealers Automated Quotation system (NASDAQ)—has successfully increased its share of equity trades at the expense of the New York and American Stock Exchanges. By the end of 1994, NASDAQ was the second largest equity market in the world based on dollar trading volume. It was second

behind the New York Stock Exchange (NYSE) and ahead of the London and Tokyo markets by more than $500 billion.

Computer and communications technology are not only affecting the way securities are traded in the international market but are also affecting the way individuals and institutional investors trade. Much of the blame for the one day decline of 22.6 percent in the Dow Jones Industrial Average on October 19, 1987, was focused on new trading methods made possible by computerized trading.

The world's futures markets have also increased computerization, and most now have automated trading systems that allow them to trade 24 hours per day. The Chicago Mercantile Exchange (CME), the Chicago Board of Trade, and the Chicago Board Options Exchange are at the center of options and futures trading. The market for stock options and financial futures has become more integrated with the stock and bond markets through stock index options and futures contracts on stock indexes and bonds. Trading volume at the international exchanges such as the London Futures Exchange (LIFE) and the Marche a' Terme International de France (MATIF) has grown tremendously since 1990. Additionally, Asian markets in Japan, Korea, Singapore, Malaysia, and other countries are expected to provide more competition and trading volume during the last half of the decade.

The impact of these changes as well as a complete discussion of securities available for investment will be presented in various chapters throughout the book. In this chapter, we examine how the market system operates, with an eye toward efficiency, liquidity, and allocation of capital. We then look at the role of the secondary or resale markets for stocks, bonds, and other securities. Finally, we examine some key protective legislation for the investor.

MARKET FUNCTIONS

Many times people will call their stockbroker and ask, "How's the market?" What they are referring to is usually the market for common stocks as measured by the Dow Jones Industrial Average, the New York Stock Exchange Index, or some other measure of common stock performance. The stock market is not the only market. There are markets for each different kind of investment that can be made.

A **market** is simply a way of exchanging assets, usually cash, for something of value. It could be a used car, a government bond, gold, or diamonds. There doesn't have to be a central place where this transaction is consummated. As long as there can be communication between buyers and sellers, the exchange can occur. The offering party does not have to own what he sells but can be an agent acting for the owner in the transaction. For example, in the sale of real estate, the owner usually employs a real estate broker/agent who advertises and sells the property for a percentage commission. Not all markets have the same procedures, but certain trading characteristics are desirable for most markets.

Market Efficiency and Liquidity

In general, an **efficient market** occurs when prices respond quickly to new information, when each successive trade is made at a price close to the preceding price, and when the market can absorb large amounts of securities or assets without changing the price significantly. The more efficient the market, the faster prices react to new information; the

closer in price is each successive trade; and the greater the amount of securities that can be sold without changing the price.

For markets to be efficient in this context, they must be liquid. **Liquidity** is a measure of the speed with which an asset can be converted into cash at its fair market value. Liquid markets exist when continuous trading occurs, and as the number of participants in the market becomes larger, price continuity increases along with liquidity. Transaction costs also affect liquidity. The lower the cost of buying and selling, the more likely it is that people will be able to enter the market.

Competition and Allocation of Capital

An investor must realize that all markets compete for funds: stocks against bonds, mutual funds against real estate, government securities against corporate securities, and so on. The competitive comparisons are almost endless. Because markets set prices on assets, investors are able to compare the prices against their perceived risk and expected return and thereby choose assets that enable them to achieve their desired risk-return trade-offs. If the markets are efficient, prices adjust rapidly to new information, and this adjustment changes the expected rate of return and allows the investor to alter investment strategy. Without efficient and liquid markets, the investor would be unable to do this. This allocation of capital occurs on both secondary and primary markets.

Secondary Markets

Secondary markets are markets for existing assets that are currently traded between investors. These markets create prices and allow for liquidity. If secondary markets did not exist, investors would have no place to sell their assets. Without liquidity, many people would not invest at all. Would you like to own $10,000 of Eastman Kodak common stock but be unable to convert it into cash if needed? If there were no secondary markets, investors would expect a higher return to compensate for the increased risk of illiquidity and the inability to adjust their portfolios to new information.

Primary Markets

Primary markets are distinguished by the flow of funds between the market participants. Instead of trading between investors as in the secondary markets, participants in the primary market buy their assets directly from the source of the asset. A common example would be a new issue of corporate bonds sold by AT&T. You would buy the bonds through a brokerage firm acting as an agent for AT&T. Your dollars would flow to AT&T rather than to another investor. The same would be true of buying a piece of art directly from the artist rather than from an art gallery.

Primary markets allow corporations, government units, and others to raise needed funds for expansion of their capital base. Once the assets or securities are sold in the primary market, they begin trading in the secondary market. Price competition in the secondary markets between different risk-return classes enables the primary markets to price new issues at fair prices to reflect existing risk-return relationships. So far, our discussion of markets has been quite general but applicable to most free markets. In the following sections, we will deal with the organization and structure of specific markets.

ORGANIZATION OF THE PRIMARY MARKETS: THE INVESTMENT BANKER

The most active participant in the primary market is the investment banker. Since corporations, states, and local governments do not sell new securities daily, monthly, or even annually, they usually rely on the expertise of the investment banker when selling securities.

Underwriting Function

The **investment banker** acts as a middleman in the process of raising funds and, in most cases, takes a risk by underwriting an issue of securities. **Underwriting** refers to the guarantee the investment banking firm gives the selling firm to purchase its securities at a fixed price, thereby eliminating the risk of not selling the whole issue of securities and having less cash than desired. The investment banker may also sell the issue on a **best-efforts** basis where the issuing firm assumes the risk and simply takes back any securities not sold after a fixed period.

Table 2–1 shows the method of distribution for new corporate securities. Unfortunately, the Securities and Exchange Commission (SEC) stopped collecting and reporting these data, so the table, though dated, is still informative.

TABLE 2–1 Corporate Issues by Method of Distribution and by Type of Security: 1981–1987 (Primary issues registered under the Security Act of 1933) (in millions)

	Underwritten				Best Efforts			
Year	Total	Debt	Preferred	Common	Total	Debt	Preferred	Common
1987	$84,726	$45,871	$6,332	$36,523	$10,053	$2,031	$162	$ 7,860
1986	85,509	45,755	9,319	30,435	10,914	431	11	10,472
1985	54,377	32,288	4,959	17,130	9,833	504	5	9,324
1984	31,168	21,745	3,258	6,165	8,473	224	9	8,240
1983	40,826	16,049	4,918	19,859	8,454	152	16	8,286
1982	36,674	21,570	4,558	10,546	9,935	1,305	10	8,620
1981	46,678	32,499	1,678	12,451	10,139	1,206	4	8,929

	Direct by Issuer			
Year	Total	Debt	Preferred	Common
1987	$4,552	$ 320	$278	$3,954
1986	4,647	1,753	8	2,886
1985	2,683	308	49	2,326
1984	2,940	520	167	2,253
1983	2,543	339	28	2,176
1982	4,138	2,589	6	1,542
1981	6,689	3,091	10	3,589

Source: U.S. Securities and Exchange Commission.

We can see by inspecting Table 2–1 that, on average, the best-efforts offerings in recent years only equal 10 to 15 percent of the total securities sold through public distribution, and the overwhelming majority of these issues were common stock. The more risk the investment banker takes, the higher the selling fee to the corporation. Some stock issues are so risky that the investment banker may charge too much of a fee for underwriting risk and distribution, so the firm chooses the best-efforts method as a cheaper alternative.

With underwriting, once the security is sold, the investment banker will usually make a market in the security, which means active buying and selling to ensure a continuously liquid market and wider distribution. In the case of best efforts and for direct offerings by the issuer, which are even smaller than best efforts, the firm assumes the risk of not raising enough capital and has no guarantees that a continuous market will be made in the company's securities. Table 2–1 shows that most long-term capital-raising efforts by corporations are through investment bankers and not directly by corporations.

Corporations may also choose to raise capital through private placements rather than through a public offering. With a private placement, the company may sell its own securities to a financial institution such as an insurance company, a pension fund, or a mutual fund, or it can engage an investment banker to find an institution willing to buy a large block of stock or bonds. Most private placements involve bonds (debt issues) instead of common stock.

Table 2–2 presents a historical picture of private and public bond offerings. Beginning with 1982, the economic recovery stimulated a huge increase in the volume of bonds issued. Between 1982 and 1984, new debt issues doubled, and between 1984 and 1986, new issues of debt almost tripled as corporations overdosed on their use of debt to finance mergers, acquisitions, leveraged buyouts, and stock repurchases. After 1986, new debt issues increased slightly until 1988 and then turned down as the recession of 1990 decreased the need for new capital.

During the 1991–93 period, interest rates hit their lowest point in decades, and total debt offerings increased by more than 100 percent between 1990 and 1993.[1] As seen in Table 2–2, the basic percentages between publicly offered and privately placed bonds have maintained their historical relationship since 1970, with publicly offered bonds issued through underwriters being by far the most popular method of raising debt capital.

Distribution

In a public offering, the distribution process is extremely important, and on some large issues, an investment banker does not undertake this alone. Investment banking firms will share the risk and the burden of distribution by forming a group called a *syndicate*. The larger the offering in dollar terms, the more participants there generally are in the syndicate. For example, the tombstone advertisement in Figure 2–1 on page 35 for

[1] This pattern once again changed in 1994 when interest rates increased sharply.

TABLE 2–2 Gross Proceeds of Corporate Bonds Publicly Offered and Privately Placed ($ millions)

		Publicly Offered		Privately Placed	
	Total Issues	Amount	% of Total	Amount	% of Total
1950	4,920	2,360	47.97	2,560	52.03
1955	7,420	4,119	55.51	3,301	44.49
1960	8,081	4,806	59.47	3,275	40.53
1965	13,720	5,570	40.60	8,150	59.40
1970	30,315	25,384	83.73	4,931	16.27
1975	42,755	32,583	76.21	10,172	23.79
1976	42,380	26,453	62.42	15,927	37.58
1977	42,015	24,072	57.29	17,943	42.71
1978	36,872	19,815	53.74	17,057	46.26
1979	40,208	25,814	64.20	14,394	35.80
1980	53,206	41,587	78.16	11,619	21.84
1981	44,642	37,653	84.34	6,989	15.66
1982	54,066	44,278	81.90	9,788	18.10
1983	68,495	47,369	69.16	21,126	30.84
1984	109,683	73,357	66.88	36,326	33.12
1985	165,754	119,559	72.13	46,195	27.87
1986	312,697	231,936	74.17	80,761	25.83
1987	301,349	209,279	69.45	92,070	30.55
1988	329,919	202,215	61.29	127,704	38.71
1989	298,813	181,393	60.70	117,420	39.30
1990	276,259	189,271	68.51	86,988	31.49
1991	389,822	286,930	73.61	102,892	26.39
1992	471,502	378,058	80.18	93,444	19.82
1993	642,543	487,924	75.94	154,619	24.06

Source: Selected Issues of the *Federal Reserve Bulletin.*

Duracell International Inc.'s issue of common stock shows two groups of investment bankers. One group sold 9.6 million shares in the United States, and the second group sold 2.4 million shares in foreign countries. This split of the offering demonstrates the globalization of capital flows from country to country.

Merrill Lynch & Co. was the managing underwriter domestically, and Merrill Lynch International Limited was the managing underwriter internationally. Merrill Lynch was joined by Goldman, Sachs and Bear, Stearns as major partners in the underwriting syndicate. It is interesting to note that ABN AMRO, the largest bank in the Netherlands, is part of the international syndicate while no U.S. banks are part of the domestic syndicate. The international syndicate also includes a division of the French bank Credit Lyonnais; a German bank, Deutsche Bank; and a Belgian bank, Banque Bruxelles Lambert S.A. The Glass Stegal Act of the 1930s has prevented U.S. banks from acting as investment bankers, and many major money center banks have complained that they are

FIGURE 2–1

This announcement is under no circumstances to be construed as an offer to sell or as a solicitation of an offer to buy any of these securities.
The offering is made only by the Prospectus.

New Issue **October 21,1991**

12,000,000 Shares

DURACELL INTERNATIONAL INC.

Common Stock

Price $28.75 Per Share

Copies of the prospectus may be obtained in any State or jurisdiction in which this announcement is circulated from only such of the undersigned or other dealers or brokers as may lawfully offer these securities in such State or jurisdiction.

9,600,000 Shares

The above shares were underwriten by the following group of U.S. Underwriters.

Merrill Lynch & Co.

Goldman, Sachs & Co.

Bear, Stearns & Co. Inc.

Alex, Brown & Sons Incorporated — The First Boston Corporation — Dillon. Read & Co. Inc. — Credit Lyonnais Securities (USA) Inc.

Donaldson, Lufkin & Jenrette Securities Corporation — Hambrecht & Quist Incorporated — Kidder, Peabody & Co. Incorporated — Lazard Freres & Co. — Lehman Brothers

Morgan, Stanley & Co. Incorporated — PaineWebber Incorporated — Prudential Securities Incorporated — Robertson, Stephens & Company

Salomon Brothers Inc. — Smith Barney, Harris Upham & Co. Incorporated — S.G. Warburg Securities — Wertheim Schroder & Co. Incorporated — Dean Witter Reynolds Inc.

Allen & Company Incorporated — A.G. Edwards & Sons, Inc. — Kemper Securities Group Inc. — Oppenheimer & Co., Inc.

Advest, Inc. — Robert W. Baird & Co. Incorporated — J.C. Bradford & Co. — Dain Bosworth Incorporated — First Albany Corporation

First of Michigan Corporation — Gruntal & Co., Incorporated — Interstate Johnson Lane Corporation — Janney Montgomery Scott Inc.

C.J. Lawrence Inc. — Legg Mason Wood Walker Incorporated — McDonald & Company Securities, Inc. — Morgan Keegan & Company, Inc. — Neuberger & Berman

Piper, Jaffray & Hopwood Incorporated — Ragen MacKenzie Incorporated — The Robinson-Humphrey Company, Inc. — Stifel, Nicolaus & Company Incorporated

Sutro & Co. Incorporated — Tucker Anthony Incorporated — Wheat First Butcher & Singer Capital Markets

Crowell, Weedon & Co. — Doft & Co., Inc. — Dominick & Dominick Incorporated — Fahnstock & Co. Inc. — First Manhattan Co.

Gabelli & Company, Inc. — J.J.B. Hilliard, W. L. Lyons, Inc. — Johnston, Lemon & Co. Incorporated — Edward D. Jones & Co. — The Ohio Company

Parker/Hunter Incorporated — Pennsylvania Merchant Group Ltd — Branch, Cabell and Company — D.A. Davidson & Co. Incorporated

Gerard Klauer Mattison & Co. — Scott & Stringfellow Investment Corp. — Smith, Moore & Co. — Sturdivant & Co., Inc.

2,400,000 Shares

The above shares were underwriten by the following group of International Underwriters.

Merrill Lynch International Limited

Goldman Sachs International Limited

Bear, Stearns International Limited

Credit Suisse First Boston Limited — S.G. Warburg Securities

ABN AMRO — Banque Bruxelles Lambert S.A. — County NatWest Limited

Credit Lyonnais Securities — Deutsche Bank Aktiengesellschaft — Kleinwort Benson Limited

Nomura International — Paribas Capital Markets Group — ScotiaMcLeod Inc.

at a competitive disadvantage in the international banking arena. The repeal of this act is currently under consideration by the 1995 congress.

Firms are usually listed in the tombstone advertisement based on their clout in the investment banking community. The firms at the top of the advertisement usually have taken the biggest dollar position and the firms at the bottom, a relatively small position. This is true in bond offerings as well as stock offerings. Each participant in the syndicate is responsible for selling the agreed-upon number of bonds or stock.

For most original offerings, the investment banker is extremely important as a link between the original issuer and the security markets. By taking much of the risk, the investment banker enables corporations and others to find needed capital and also allows investors an opportunity to participate in the ownership of securities through purchase in the secondary markets. Notice that the common stock is priced at $28.75 per share in Figure 2–1. This is the price paid by the public. In the case of Duracell International, the investment bankers took a chance that the stock market would not fall much during the offering period. If the price should fall below $28.75 while the shares are still being sold to the public, the investment bankers in the syndicate will not make their original estimated profit on the issue. If the stock price drops too much below $28.75, the investment bankers could lose money on the offering. Actually, investors in Duracell have seen an annualized price increase of more than 12 percent as the stock has increased from its offering price of $28.75 in October 1991, to $43 per share in 1994.

Some significant changes are taking place in the investment banking industry. The number of firms in the syndicate is shrinking, but the size of the individual investment banking firms in the syndicate is increasing as investment bankers expand their capital base to compete in an international market for stocks and bonds. The financial strength of the investment bankers has increased to the point where they are able to assume more risk and thus absorb larger dollar positions in new offerings. Also, the rise of shelf registration under SEC Rule 415 (discussed in Chapter 11) increased the dominance of the large investment bankers. A shelf registration allows issuing firms to register their securities (mostly bonds and notes) with the Securities and Exchange Commission and then sell them at will as funds are needed. This allows investment bankers to buy portions of the shelf issue and immediately resell the securities to institutional clients without forming the normal syndicates or tying up capital for several weeks. Shelf registration is popular with new bond offerings but less so with stock offerings where the traditional syndicated offering tends to exist.

Investment Banking Competition

Table 2–3 shows the top ten lead underwriters of U.S. debt and equity for 1993 compared with 1992. It is interesting to note that the top ten underwriters account for 83.2 percent of total underwriting volume in 1993, leaving the other 17 percent for hundreds of other investment banks.

One of the biggest changes occurring in 1993 was an increased demand for capital from Europe, Latin America, and Asia. Many worried that the large increase in international offerings would have a negative impact on smaller U.S. companies trying to raise capital.

Underwriters are more concerned with the fees from their activities than simply the amount of dollars underwritten. Table 2–4 shows a different picture from Table 2–3 when competition is based on a fee basis. Smith Barney and Dean Witter made the list

TABLE 2–3 Top Underwriters of U.S. Debt and Equity

	Twelve Months 1993		Twelve Months 1992		
Manager	**Amount (In millions)**	**Market Share (%)**	**Amount (In millions)**	**Rank**	**Market Share (%)**
Merrill Lynch	$ 173,783.7	16.4	$140,417.9	1	16.4
Goldman Sachs	127,265.4	12.0	104,329.0	2	12.2
Lehman Brothers	115,996.5	10.9	101,412.4	3	11.8
Kidder Peabody	94,471.0	8.9	77,852.3	5	9.1
Salomon Brothers	91,177.4	8.6	73,935.0	6	8.6
First Boston	90,373.8	8.5	81,533.2	4	9.5
Morgan Stanley	67,717.0	6.4	64,415.8	7	7.5
Bear Stearns	56,236.6	5.3	53,112.1	8	6.2
Donaldson Lufkin	36,911.1	3.5	20,127.3	10	2.4
Paine Webber	29,889.9	2.8	19,846.2	11	2.3
Subtotals	$ 883,822.4	83.2	$736,981.1		86.1
Industry totals	$1,062,871.4	100.0	$856,138.8		100.0

Source: *The Wall Street Journal,* January 3, 1994, p. C1. Reprinted by permission of *The Wall Street Journal,* © 1994 Dow Jones & Company, Inc. All Rights Reserved Worldwide.

TABLE 2–4 Disclosed Fees from New Issue Underwriting

	Twelve Months 1993			Twelve Months 1992			
Manager	**Amount (In millions)**	**% of Market**	**Number of Issues**	**Amount (In millions)**	**Rank**	**% of Market**	**Number of Issues**
Merrill Lynch	$1,786.7	19.6	1,007	$1,420.0	1	20.9	837
Goldman Sachs	1,122.0	12.3	634	915.9	2	13.5	533
Lehman Brothers	744.8	8.2	682	661.0	3	9.7	520
Morgan Stanley	654.6	7.2	413	624.4	4	9.2	359
Salomon Brothers	589.1	6.5	502	328.3	6	4.8	272
First Boston	527.9	5.8	454	484.0	5	7.1	386
Donaldson Lufkin	488.9	5.4	235	238.8	7	3.5	118
Smith Barney	306.3	3.4	171	189.0	11	2.8	101
Dean Witter	286.5	3.1	100	130.0	14	1.9	35
Kidder Peabody	276.4	3.0	307	145.2	13	2.1	285
Subtotals	$6,783.1	74.3%	4,505	$5,136.7		75.7%	3,446
Industry totals	$9,134.8	100.0%	7,211	$6,784.9		100.0%	5,235

Source: *The Wall Street Journal,* January 3, 1994, p. 26. Reprinted by permission of *TheWall Street Journal,* © 1994 Dow Jones & Company, Inc. All Rights Reserved Worldwide.

even though they only sold a small number of issues compared with the other firms. Total industry underwriting fees set a record of $9.13 billion in 1993.

Bringing private companies public for the first time is called an **initial public offering (IPO),** and distribution costs to the selling company are much higher than offerings of additional stock by companies that are already public. Securities Data Co. estimated that the average fee from IPOs was 7.2 percent, while offerings of publicly traded stock averaged about 5.5 percent. Nearly one-third of total underwriting fees came from IPOs issued in 1993: more than 800 companies sold securities in the market for the first time and raised more than $57 billion for a new record, surpassing 1992 by $17 billion. Because companies like Smith Barney and Dean Witter sold mostly IPOs, they managed to make the top ten list in Table 2–4 even though they sold relatively few issues compared with the competition.

Underwriting competition is like a decathlon; there are many events for each contestant. Table 2–5 below presents the total size of each market and the leading investment banker for each market. This table indicates that the dominant player is Merrill Lynch, but it also highlights the market niches and the specialized nature of the investment banking industry.

The worldwide market is becoming more important to all investment bankers, and Table 2–6 looks at the top ten Euromarket underwriters. In 1991 four Japanese investment bankers were in the top ten, but in 1993 only one, Nomura Securities, was still

TABLE 2–5 Who's No. 1 in Each Market

	Full-Year 1993		Full-Year 1992	
Market	**Amount (billions)**	**Top-Ranked Manager**	**Amount (billions)**	**Top-Ranked Manager**
U.S. domestic	$1,062.9	Merrill Lynch	$ 856.1	Merrill Lynch
Straight debt	432.5	Merrill Lynch	313.9	Merrill Lynch
Convertible debt	9.3	Merrill Lynch	7.0	Merrill Lynch
Junk bonds	54.3	Merrill Lynch	38.2	Merrill Lynch
Investments grade debt	378.2	Merrill Lynch	275.7	Merrill Lynch
Mortgage debt	420.6	Kidder Peabody	376.7	Kidder Peabody
Asset-backed debt	59.3	CS First Boston	50.9	CS First Boston
Collateral securities	479.9	Kidder Peabody	427.7	Kidder Peabody
Preferred stock	28.4	Merrill Lynch	29.3	Merrill Lynch
Common stock	101.7	Merrill Lynch	72.8	Merrill Lynch
IPOs	57.4	Merrill Lynch	39.9	Merrill Lynch
Closed-end funds	15.9	Merrill Lynch	16.2	Merrill Lynch
International debt	388.3	Deutsche Bank	268.7	Deutsche Bank
International equity	16.7	S.G. Warburg	13.5	Goldman Sachs
Worldwide issues	1,467.8	Merrill Lynch	1,138.3	Merrill Lynch
U.S. issues	1,048.4	Merrill Lynch	852.0	Merrill Lynch
Municipal new issues	287.4	Merrill Lynch	232.0	Goldman Sachs

Source: *The Wall Street Journal,* January 3, 1994, p. 26. Reprinted by permission of *The Wall Street Journal,* © 1994 Dow Jones & Company, Inc. All Rights Reserved Worldwide.

TABLE 2–6 Top Euromarket Underwriters (Non-U.S. debt and equity)

	Twelve Months 1993		1992
Manager	**Amount (In millions)**	**% of Market**	**% of Market**
Goldman Sachs	$23,874.5	5.9	5.3
Deutsche Bank	23,525.6	5.8	7.9
Morgan Stanley	21,217.2	5.2	2.8
First Boston CS	20,152.3	5.0	6.2
Merrill Lynch	18,999.7	4.7	3.7
Nomura Sec	16,686.7	4.1	6.2
Lehman Brothers	14,115.4	3.5	2.2
Banque Paribas	14,040.3	3.5	4.7
Salomon	13,658.5	3.4	2.0
J.P. Morgan	13,064.0	3.2	4.4
Subtotals	$179,334.3	44.3	45.4
Industry totals	$404,925.5	100.0	100.0

Source: *The Wall Street Journal,* January 3, 1994, p. 26. Reprinted by permission of *The Wall Street Journal,* © 1994 Dow Jones & Company, Inc. All Rights Reserved Worldwide.

there. The list also included one German, one French, one Swiss, and six U.S. underwriters. While these Euromarkets are about 40 percent of the U.S. debt and equity market, they will become increasingly important as the Eastern bloc countries turn to private enterprise and capital markets for economic expansion.

ORGANIZATION OF THE SECONDARY MARKETS

Once the investment banker or the Federal Reserve (for U.S. government securities) has sold a new issue of securities, it begins trading in secondary markets that provide liquidity, efficiency, continuity, and competition. The **organized exchanges** fulfill this need in a central location where trading occurs between buyers and sellers. The **over-the-counter markets** also provide markets for exchange but not in a central location. We will first examine the organized exchanges and then the over-the-counter markets.

Organized Exchanges

Organized exchanges are either national or regional, but both are organized in a similar fashion. Exchanges have a central trading location where securities are bought and sold in an auction market by brokers acting as agents for the buyer and seller. Stocks usually trade at various trading posts on the floor of the exchange. Brokers are registered members of the exchanges, and their number is fixed by each exchange. The national exchanges are the New York Stock Exchange (NYSE) and the American Stock Exchange

TABLE 2–7 Data on Trading Volume (Breakdown of trading in NYSE stocks)

By Market	Monday, October 19, 1987	Tuesday, October 20, 1987	1987 Daily Average
New York	604,330,000	608,120,000	188,937,980
Chicago	21,666,900	24,326,200	12,529,086
Pacific	12,743,900	12,897,600	6,617,917
NASD	4,341,330	4,516,920	4,156,177
Philadelphia	6,602,100	6,294,600	3,072,138
Boston	4,788,100	4,223,900	2,825,407
Cincinnati	1,399,500	1,367,100	928,094
Instinet	261,900	128,100	193,498
Composite	661,874,420	656,133,730	219,260,296

Source: *New York Stock Exchange Fact Book,* 1988, p. 6. *The Wall Street Journal,* October 21, 1987, p. 57. Reprinted by permission of *The Wall Street Journal,* © 1987 by Dow Jones & Company, Inc. All Rights Reserved Worldwide.

(AMEX). Both these exchanges are governed by a board of directors consisting of one-half exchange members and one-half public members.

The regional exchanges began their existence trading securities of local firms. As the firms grew, they became listed on the national exchanges, but they also continued to trade on the regionals. Many cities, such as Chicago, Cincinnati, Philadelphia, and Boston, have regional exchanges. Today, most of the trading on these exchanges is done in nationally known companies. Trading in the same companies is common between the NYSE and such regionals as the Chicago Stock Exchange, the Pacific Coast Exchange in San Francisco and Los Angeles, and the smaller regionals. Over 90 percent of the companies traded on the Chicago and Pacific Coast Exchanges are also listed on the NYSE. This is referred to as dual trading.

October 20, 1987, the day after the crash of '87, was the busiest day in the history of the New York Stock Exchange. On October 19, 1987, the day of the crash, 604 million shares traded, and on the next day, 608 million shares traded. Table 2–7 shows this information as well as data on NYSE listed firms that trade on other markets. The all-time composite trade volume for NYSE firms trading *on all markets* was 661.8 million shares on October 19 (the day of the crash).

Consolidated Tape

Although dual listing and trading have existed for some time, it was not until June 16, 1975, that a consolidated ticker tape was instituted. This allows brokers on the floor of one exchange to see prices of transactions on other exchanges in the dually listed stocks. Any time a transaction is made on a regional exchange or over-the-counter in a security listed on the NYSE, this transaction and any made on the floor of the NYSE are displayed on the composite tape. The composite price data keep markets more efficient and prices more competitive between exchanges at all times.

The NYSE and AMEX are both national exchanges and for years did not allow dual listing of companies traded on their exchanges, but as of August 1976, securities were able to be dually listed between these exchanges. There doesn't seem to be any advantage to this since both are located in New York City, and traditionally, shares that trade on one exchange are not traded on the other.

Table 2–8 on pages 42 and 43 displays the number of trades (not number of shares) on all markets participating in the consolidated tape. Trading volume was rather stable between 1987 and 1990, but it increased dramatically in 1993. While total trades have steadily increased overall, the New York Stock Exchange is getting a smaller piece of trades in its own listed stock. The NYSE has seen its percentage of consolidated tape trades fall from 77.68 percent in 1983 to the 65 to 70 range in the 1990s.[2] The NYSE is seeing tough competition from other exchanges and the over-the-counter NASDAQ system, which has accounted for about 10 percent of total trades for the last three years. While the New York Stock Exchange has suffered from a declining number of trades, each trade is quite large relative to its competitors, and it has managed to maintain at least 81 percent of the total share volume over the last decade.

Listing Requirements for Firms

Securities can be traded on an exchange only if they have met the listing requirements of the exchange and have been approved by the board of governors of that exchange. All exchanges have minimum requirements that must be met before trading can occur in a company's common stock. Since the NYSE is the biggest exchange and generates the most dollar volume in large, well-known companies, its listing requirements are the most restrictive.

Initial Listing Although each case is decided on its own merits, according to the *NYSE Fact Book,* the minimum requirements for a company to be listed on the New York Stock Exchange for the first time are as follows:

1. Demonstrated earning power under competitive conditions of: *either* \$2.5 million before federal income taxes for the most recent year and \$2 million pre-tax for each of the preceding two years *or* an aggregate for the last three fiscal years of \$6.5 million *together with* a minimum in the most recent fiscal year of \$4.5 million. (All three years must be profitable.)
2. Net tangible assets of \$18 million, but greater emphasis is placed on the aggregate market value of the common stock.
3. Market value of publicly held shares currently equal to \$18 million, but subject to adjustment within the following limits:

Maximum	\$18,000,000
Minimum	9,000,000
Present (12/1/94)	18,000,000

[2] While 1993 showed improvement, it is not viewed as a permanent reversal of the trend.

TABLE 2-8 Consolidated Reported Trades (This series includes every transaction in NYSE-listed issues as reported to the Consolidated Tape.)

Consolidated Tape Trades by Market, 1993

	NYSE*	AMEX	PSE	CHX**	PHLX
1993	46,476,295	0	3,806,226	4,050,348	1,851,256
1992	30,557,805	0	3,541,541	3,909,578	1,554,026
1991	27,167,350	0	3,274,499	3,240,894	1,147,522
1990	19,148,610	0	2,355,273	2,810,029	875,100
1989	19,727,062	0	2,378,200	2,970,627	965,448
1988	17,738,727	0	2,051,304	2,366,607	782,674
1987	22,634,989	0	2,863,513	2,749,171	1,074,834
1986	18,971,943	0	2,757,958	2,223,131	953,009
1985	14,648,648	0	1,876,326	1,609,287	752,781
1984	12,953,946	0	1,534,707	1,365,991	705,206
1983	15,050,791	43	1,661,907	1,318,868	751,002

Distribution of Consolidated Tape Trades, 1983–1993

Year	NYSE*	AMEX	PSE	CHX**	PHLX
1993	70.49%	0.00%	5.77%	6.14%	2.81%
1992	65.17	0.00	7.55	8.34	3.31
1991	67.33	0.00	8.13	8.03	2.84
1990	66.17	0.00	8.14	9.71	3.02
1989	69.23	0.00	8.35	10.43	3.39
1988	72.99	0.00	8.44	9.74	3.22
1987	73.60	0.00	9.31	8.94	3.50
1986	72.68	0.00	10.57	8.52	3.65
1985	74.24	0.00	9.51	8.16	3.82
1984	75.40	0.00	8.93	7.95	4.10
1983	77.68	0.00	8.58	6.81	3.88

*Data after 1988 include rights and warrants. **MSE changed its name to CHX on July 8, 1993. ***INST totals included in NASD after March 1, 1993.
Participating markets: NYSE, New York; AMEX, American; PSE, Pacific; CHX, Chicago; PHLX, Philadelphia; BSE, Boston; CSE, Cincinnati; CBOE, Chicago Board Options Exchange; NASD, National Association of Securities Dealers; INST, Instinet.
Source: *New York Stock Exchange Fact Book*, 1994, p. 27.

4. A total of 1.1 million common shares publicly held.
5. *Either* 2,000 holders of 100 shares or more *or* 2,200 total stockholders *together with* average monthly trading volume (for the most recent six months) of 100,000 shares.

The other exchanges have requirements covering the same areas, but the amounts are smaller.

Corporations desiring to be listed on exchanges have decided that public availability of the stock on an exchange will benefit their shareholders by providing liquidity to owners

BSE	CSE	NASD	INST***	Total
1,687,649	1,704,590	6,351,196	2,301	65,929,861
1,485,169	867,926	4,957,152	13,270	46,886,467
1,361,572	298,665	3,847,067	11,542	40,349,111
1,090,871	181,470	2,468,490	9,797	28,939,640
900,529	125,215	1,419,914	7,794	28,494,789
565,878	84,176	706,539	7,678	24,303,583
712,071	81,236	630,559	6,412	30,752,785
588,062	76,833	522,711	8,260	26,101,907
428,112	62,307	334,837	19,163	19,731,461
305,160	58,109	241,424	14,733	17,179,222
241,250	94,171	248,820	7,250	19,374,372

BSE	CSE	NASD	INST***	Total
2.56%	2.59%	9.63%	0.00%	100.00%
3.17	1.85	10.57	0.03	100.00
3.37	0.74	9.53	0.03	100.00
3.77	0.63	8.53	0.03	100.00
3.16	0.44	4.98	0.03	100.00
2.33	0.35	2.91	0.03	100.00
2.32	0.26	2.05	0.02	100.00
2.25	0.29	2.00	0.03	100.00
2.17	0.32	1.70	0.10	100.00
1.78	0.34	1.41	0.09	100.00
1.25	0.49	1.28	0.04	100.00

or by allowing the company a more viable means for raising external capital for growth and expansion. The company must pay annual listing fees to the exchange and some fees based on the number of shares traded each year.

Delisting The New York Stock Exchange also has the authority to remove (delist) a security from trading when the security fails to meet certain criteria. There is much latitude in these decisions, but generally, a company's security may be considered for delisting if there are fewer than 1,200 round-lot (100 shares) owners, 600,000 shares or fewer in public hands, and the total market value of the security is less than $5 million.

A company that easily exceeded these standards on first being listed may fall below them during hard times.

Membership for Market Participants

We've talked about listing requirements for corporations on the exchange, but what about the investment houses or traders that service the listed firms or trade for their own account on the exchanges? These privileges are reserved for a select number of people. The NYSE has 1,366 members who own "seats," which may be leased or sold with the approval of the NYSE. Multiple seats are owned by many member firms such as Merrill Lynch, so the number of member organizations totals 1,192. In recent years, the price of NYSE seats ranged from a low of $35,000 in 1977 to a high of $1,150,000 in 1987. Prices fluctuate with market trends, going up in bull markets and down in bear markets. The members owning these seats can be divided into five distinct categories, each with a specific job.

Commission Brokers The **commission brokers** represent commission houses, such as Merrill Lynch, that execute orders on the floor of the exchange for customers of that firm. Many of the larger retail brokerage houses have more than one commission broker on the floor of the exchange. If you call your account executive (stockbroker) and place an order to buy 100 shares of Exxon, the account executive will teletype your order to the NYSE where it will be transmitted to one of the firm's commission brokers who will go to the appropriate trading post and execute the order.

Floor Brokers You can imagine that commission brokers could get very busy running from post to post on a heavy volume day. In times like these, they will rely on some help from **floor brokers,** who are registered to trade on the exchange but are not employees of a member firm. Instead, floor brokers own their own seat and charge a small fee for services (usually around $4 per 100 shares).

Registered Traders The **registered traders** own their own seats and are not associated with a member firm (such as Merrill Lynch). They are registered to trade for their own accounts and do so with the objective of earning a profit. Because they are members, they don't have to pay commissions on these trades; but in so trading, they help to generate a continuous market and liquidity for the market in general. There is always the possibility that these traders could manipulate the market if they acted in mass, and for that reason, the exchanges have rules governing their behavior and limiting the number of registered traders at one specific trading post.

Odd-Lot Dealers Odd lots (less than 100 shares) are not traded on the main floor of the exchange, so if a customer wants to buy or sell 20 shares of AT&T, the order will end up being processed by an **odd-lot dealer.** Dealers own their own inventory of the particular security and buy and sell for their own accounts. If they accumulate 100 shares, they can sell them in the market, or if they need 20 shares, they can buy 100 in the market and hold the other 80 shares in inventory. A few very large brokerage firms, such as Merrill Lynch, have begun making their own odd-lot market in actively traded securities, and it is expected that this trend will become common at other large commission houses.

Odd-lot trading on other exchanges is usually handled by the specialist in the particular stock.

SPECIALISTS The **specialists** are a very important segment of the exchange and make up about one-fourth of total membership. Each stock traded has a specialist assigned to it, and most specialists are responsible for more than one stock. Specialists have two basic duties with regard to the stocks they supervise. First, they must handle any special orders that commission brokers or floor brokers might give. For example, a special order could limit the price someone is willing to pay for General Telephone (GTE) stock to $30 per share for 100 shares. If the commission broker reaches the General Telephone trading post and GTE is selling at $31 per share, the broker will leave the order with the specialist to execute if and when the stock of GTE falls to $30 or less. The specialist puts these special limit orders in his "book" with the date and time entered so he can execute orders at the same price by the earliest time of receipt. A portion of the broker's commission is then paid to the specialist.

The second major function of specialists is to maintain continuous, liquid, and orderly markets in their assigned stocks. This is not a difficult function in actively traded securities, such as General Motors, Du Pont, and AT&T, but it becomes more difficult in those stocks where there are no large, active markets. For example, suppose you placed an order to buy 100 shares of Ametek at the market price. If the commission broker reaches the Ametek trading post and no seller is present, the broker can't wait for one to appear since he has other orders to execute. Fortunately, the broker can buy the shares from the specialist who acts as a dealer—in this case buying for and selling from his own inventory. To ensure ability to maintain continuous markets, the exchange requires a specialist to have $500,000 or enough capital to own 5,000 shares of the assigned stock, whichever is greater. At times, specialists are under tremendous pressure to make a market for securities. A classic case occurred when President Eisenhower had a heart attack in the 1950s and specialists stabilized the market by absorbing wave after wave of sell orders.

The New York Stock Exchange keeps statistics on specialist performance and their ability to maintain price continuity, quotation spreads, market depth, and price stabilization. These data are given in Table 2–9. Price continuity is measured by the size of the price variation in successive trades. Column 1 is the percentage of transactions with no change in price or a minimum change of ⅛ of a dollar. Column 2 presents the percentage of the quotes where the bid and asked price was equal to or less than ¼ of a point. Market depth (Column 3) is displayed as a percentage of the time that 1,000 to 3,000 shares of volume failed to move the price of the stock more than ⅛ of a point. Finally, the NYSE expects specialists to stabilize the market by buying and selling from their own accounts against the prevailing trend. This is measured in Column 4 as the percentage of shares purchased below the last different price and the percentage of shares sold above the last different price.

While these statistics are not 100 percent, it would be quite unreasonable for us to expect specialists to maintain that kind of a record in all types of markets. However, some critics of the specialist system on the NYSE think these performance measures could be improved by having more than one specialist for each stock. Many market watchers believe competing dealers on the over-the-counter market provide more price stability and fluid markets than the NYSE specialist system.

TABLE 2–9 Market Quality and Specialists' Stabilization: 1984–1993

	(1) Price Continuity	(2) Quotation Spreads	(3) Market Depth*	(4) Stabilization Rate
1993	97.1%	88.9%	88.3%	77.6%
1992	96.4	86.4	87.1	78.3
1991	95.9	84.6	85.5	80.9
1990	95.8	84.5	84.4	83.1
1989	95.9	81.5	87.1	86.0
1988	94.1	78.7	92.1	88.1
1987	89.0	67.5	87.2	90.7
1986	90.2	69.8	89.2	90.2
1985	92.3	70.6	89.8	89.2
1984	91.1	64.7	88.0	88.8

*After 1988 based on 3,000 shares of volume—previous years in 1,000 shares.
Source: *New York Stock Exchange Fact Book,* 1994, p. 21.

Somewhat in response to these criticisms, the New York Stock Exchange created computer systems that help the specialists manage order inflows more efficiently. **Super Dot** (designated order transfer system) allows NYSE member firms to electronically transmit all market and limit orders directly to the specialist at the trading post or the member trading booth. This order routing system takes orders and communicates executions of the orders directly back to the member firm on the same electronic circuit.

As a part of Super Dot, specialists are informed through OARS (Opening Automated Report Service) of market orders received before the opening bell. This preopening knowledge allows specialists to know whether the supply and demand for a stock is in balance because OARS pairs the buy and sell orders. If a sell imbalance exists, the specialist knows before opening that the price will open lower than yesterday's closing price.

The NYSE reports that 98.5 percent of all market orders on Super Dot were received, processed, and reported back to the originator within two minutes. Another feature of Super Dot that greatly aids the specialist is the **Electronic Book.** This data base covers stocks listed on the NYSE and keeps track of limit orders and market orders for the specialist. You can imagine the great improvement in recording, reporting, and error elimination over the old manual entry in the "specialist's book."

OTHER ORGANIZED EXCHANGES

The American Stock Exchange

The American Stock Exchange trades in smaller companies than the NYSE, and except for one dually listed company on the NYSE in 1983, the stocks traded on the AMEX are different from those on any other exchange. Because many of the small companies on the

AMEX do not meet the liquidity needs of large institutional investors, the AMEX has been primarily a market for individual investors.

In an attempt to differentiate itself from the NYSE, the AMEX traded warrants in companies for many years before the NYSE allowed them. Even now, the AMEX has warrants listed for stocks trading on the NYSE. The AMEX also trades put and call options on approximately 200 stocks, with most of the underlying common stocks being listed on the NYSE. This market has been a stabilizing force for the AMEX.

To become more innovative and to attract more business, the American Stock Exchange announced plans in 1991 to trade warrants in foreign stock indexes. As a first step to this plan, the AMEX began providing up-to-the-minute information on:

Euro Top 100: 100 actively traded stocks in nine European countries.

Eurotrack 100: 100 stocks in 10 countries excluding England.

FT-SE 100: 100 large British stocks traded in London.

Eurotrack: Eurotrack 100 and FT-SE 100 combined.

FT-Actuaries: 835 of the largest companies in 14 European countries.

CAC 40: 40 selected foreign stocks traded on the Paris Bourse.

Additionally, in an attempt to compete more directly with the NASDAQ for the market in small stocks, the AMEX created a new market in March 1992 for *emerging companies.*

The Chicago Board Options Exchange

Trading in call options started on the Chicago Board Options Exchange (CBOE) in April 1973 and proved very successful. The number of call options listed grew from 16 in 1973 to over 500 in 1994. A **call option** gives the owner the right to buy 100 shares of the underlying common stock at a set price for a certain period. The CBOE standardized call options into three-month, six-month, and nine-month expiration periods on a rotating monthly series. Other sequences have since been developed. The CBOE and the AMEX currently have many options that are dually listed, and the competition between them is fierce. The two exchanges also trade put options (options to sell). A number of smaller regional exchanges also provide for option trading, and the New York Stock Exchange began trading options in 1985 and ended 1993 with 152 options products.

A new wrinkle in the options game has been options on stock market indexes or industry groupings (called subindexes). The CBOE offers puts and calls on the Standard & Poor's 100 Index; the NYSE has options on the NYSE Index; the AMEX has options on the AMEX Market Value Index, and so on. More about these markets will be presented in Chapter 17.

Futures Markets

Futures markets have traditionally been associated with commodities and, more recently, also with financial instruments. Purchasers of commodity futures own the right to buy a certain amount of the commodity at a set price for a specified period. When the time runs out (expires), the futures contract will be delivered unless sold before expiration. One major futures market is the Chicago Board of Trade, which trades corn, oats, soybeans, wheat, silver, plywood, and Treasury bond futures. There are also other important futures

markets in Chicago, Kansas City, Minneapolis, New York, and other cities. These markets are very important as hedging markets and help set commodity prices. They are also known for their wide price swings and volatile speculative nature.

In recent years, trading volume has increased in foreign exchange futures such as the West German mark, Japanese yen, and British pound as well as in Treasury bill and Treasury bond futures. One recent product having a direct effect in the stock market is the development of futures contracts on stock market indexes. The Chicago Mercantile Exchange, Chicago Board of Trade, New York Futures Exchanges (a division of the NYSE), and the Kansas City Board of Trade have all developed contracts in separate market indexes such as the Standard & Poor's 500 and the Value Line Index. Market indexes will be presented in the following chapter, and we will spend more time discussing futures markets in Chapters 16 and 17.

OVER-THE-COUNTER MARKETS

Unlike the organized exchanges, the over-the-counter markets (OTC) have no central location where securities are traded. Being traded over-the-counter implies the trade takes place by telephone or electronic device and dealers stand ready to buy or sell specific securities for their own accounts. These dealers will buy at a bid price and sell at an asked price that reflects the competitive market conditions. By contrast, brokers on the organized exchanges merely act as agents who process orders. The National Association of Securities Dealers (NASD), a self-policing organization of dealers, requires at least two market makers (dealers) for each security, but often there are 5 or 10 or even 20 for government securities. As previously mentioned, the multiple-dealer function in the over-the-counter market is an attractive feature for many companies in comparison to the single specialist arrangement on the NYSE and other organized exchanges.

OTC markets exist for stocks, corporate bonds, mutual funds, federal government securities, state and local bonds, commercial paper, negotiable certificates of deposits, and various other securities. These securities make the OTC the largest of all markets in the United States in dollar terms.

In the OTC market, the difference between the bid and asked price is the spread; it represents the profit the dealer earns by making a market. For example, if XYZ common stock is bid 10 and asked 10½, this simply means the dealer will buy at least 100 shares at $10 per share or will sell 100 shares at $10.50 per share. If prices are too low, more buyers than sellers will appear, and the dealer will run out of inventory unless he raises prices to attract more sellers and balances the supply and demand. If his price is at equilibrium, he will match an equal number of shares bought and sold, and for his market-making activities, he will earn 50 cents per share traded. Although in the future many OTC stocks will no longer be reported on the basis of bid and asked prices but simply at a closing price, the concept of dealer spreads will remain.

Actually, the over-the-counter stock market has several segments, and the National Association of Securities Dealers divides the more than 6,000 companies into the National Market System, the national list, and regional and local companies. Stocks in the National Market System receive the quickest and best reporting of their trading activity. Requirements for the National Market System are shown in Table 2–10.

Stocks of companies such as Apple Computer, Coors Brewing, Intel, and MCI Communications can be found on the National Market System. These companies all have a diversified geographical shareholder base, while the national list and regional or local companies are usually smaller or closely held by management or the founding family. The small local stocks may not appear in *The Wall Street Journal* but will be found on the financial pages of large city newspapers in Dallas, Cleveland, Chicago, Minneapolis, Los Angeles, and other major cities under the heading "Local Over-the-Counter Markets." Many are also listed on special pink sheets put out by investment houses. OTC markets have always been very popular for smaller bank and insurance stocks because these stocks do not generate enough trading volume or have enough stockholders to merit their listing on the organized exchanges. Another reason is that many have only local interest.

TABLE 2–10 NASDAQ National Market System Quantitative Standards

	Initial NASDAQ National Market Inclusion		
Standard	**Alternative 1**	**Alternative 2**	**Continued NASDAQ National Market Inclusion**
Registration under Section 12(g) of the Securities Exchange Act of 1934 or equivalent	Yes	Yes	Yes
Net tangible assets[a]	$4 million	$12 million	$2 million or $4 million[b]
Net income (in last fiscal year or two of last three fiscal years)	$400,000	—	—
Pretax income (in last fiscal year or two of last three fiscal years)	$750,000	—	—
Public float (shares)[c]	500,000	1 million	200,000
Operating history	—	3 years	—
Market value of float	$3 million	$15 million	$1 million
Minimum bid per share	$5	$3	$1[d]
Shareholders			400[e]
If between 0.5 and 1 million shares publicly held	800	400	—
If more than 1 million shares publicly held	400	400	—
If more than 0.5 million shares publicly held and average daily volume in excess of 2,000 shares	400	400	—
Number of market makers	2	2	2

[a] "Net tangible assets" means total assets (excluding goodwill) minus total liabilities.
[b] Continued NASDAQ National Market inclusion requires net tangible assets of at least $2 million if the issuer has sustained losses from continuing operations and/or net losses in two of its three most recent fiscal years or $4 million if the issuer has sustained losses from the continuing operations and/or losses in three of its four most recent fiscal years. Regardless of the foregoing, the issuer must have at least $1 million in net tangible assets.
[c] Public float is defined as shares that are *not* "held directly or indirectly by any officer or director of the issuer and by any person who is the beneficial owner of more than 10 percent of the total shares outstanding . . ."
[d] Or, in alternative, market value of public float of $3 million and $4 million of net tangible assets.
[e] Or 300 shareholders of round lots.
Source: *NASDAQ Fact Book and Company Directory,* 1994, p. 43.

NASDAQ

NASDAQ stands for the National Association of Securities Dealers Automated Quotations system. This system is linked by a computer network and provides up-to-the-minute quotations on approximately 6,000 of the OTC stocks traded on the NASDAQ system.

Table 2–10 on the previous page presented the qualification standards for initial and continued listing on the NASDAQ National Market System. The big difference between the OTC standards and the NYSE listing requirements is that the OTC requires fewer shareholders of record, smaller assets, and less net income. While these qualifications allow many small companies to be included in the trading system, they do not preclude many large companies such as Apple Computer or MCI from trading. In fact, the National Association of Securities Dealers estimates that more than 600 companies on the National Market System would be eligible for listing on the New York Stock Exchange, and many more would be eligible for the American Stock Exchange.

During the mid-1980s, many articles appeared comparing the New York Stock Exchange and the American Stock Exchange to the over-the-counter market and reporting on the inroads the National Association of Securities Dealers had made in retaining companies on the automated quotation system. Traditionally, companies that would reach listing qualifications for the exchanges would jump to the AMEX and then eventually to the NYSE. This cannot be assumed to happen anymore.

NASDAQ has taken its place in world equity markets. Figure 2–2 shows the relative size of worldwide markets for 1993 based on total dollar trading volume. The NYSE is first followed by NASDAQ, London, and Tokyo. This is a dramatic change for

FIGURE 2–2 1993 Dollar Volume of Equity Trading in Major World Markets

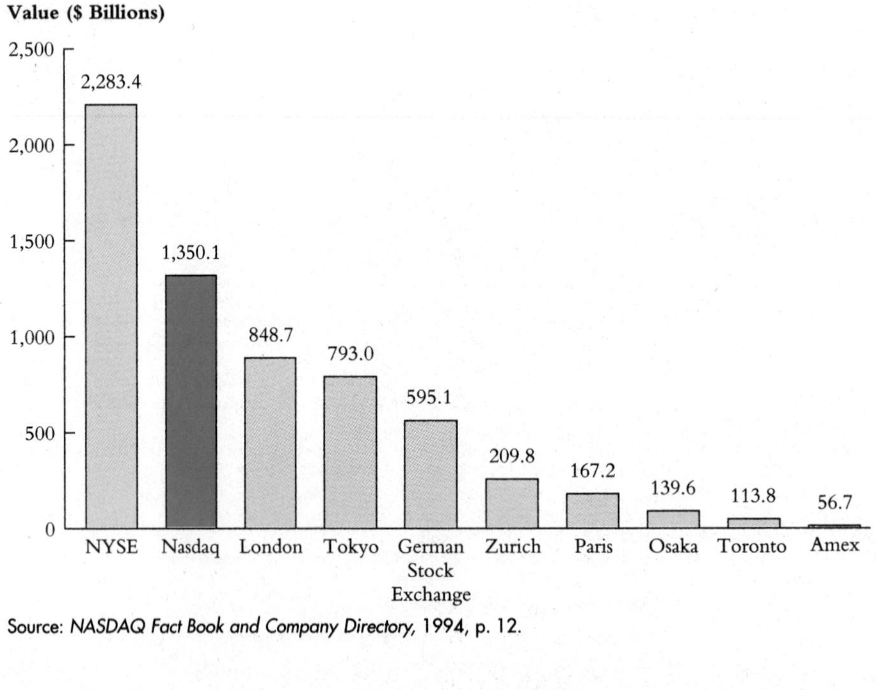

Source: *NASDAQ Fact Book and Company Directory*, 1994, p. 12.

NASDAQ, which was in fifth place in 1990. The U.S. equity market for small growth companies boomed in the 1990s, and this helped to increase NASDAQ's volume. Additionally, its multiple-dealer system, efficient computerized quotation systems, and enhanced reporting capability are other reasons for the increased competitive nature of the OTC markets.

Debt Securities Traded Over-the-Counter

Debt securities also trade over-the-counter. Actually, government securities of the U.S. Treasury provide the largest dollar volume of transactions on the OTC and account for billions of dollars in trades each week. These securities are traded by government securities dealers who are often associated with a division of a large financial institution, such as a New York, Chicago, or West Coast money market bank or a large brokerage house such as Merrill Lynch. These dealers make markets in government securities, such as Treasury bills and Treasury bonds, or federal agency securities such as Federal National Mortgage Association issues.

Municipal bonds of state and local governments are traded by specialized municipal bond dealers who, in most cases, work for large commercial banks. Commercial paper, representing unsecured, short-term corporate debt, is traded directly by *finance* companies, but a large portion of commercial paper sold by *industrial* companies is handled by OTC dealers specializing in this market. Every security has its own set of dealers and its own distribution system. On markets where large dollar trades occur, the spread between the bid and asked price could be as little as $\frac{1}{16}$ or $\frac{1}{32}$ of $1 per $1,000 of securities.

The Third and Fourth Markets: Part of Over-the-Counter Trading

Before the mid-1970s, commissions on the NYSE were fixed. This meant the same commission schedule applied to all transactions of a given size, and one broker could not undercut the other on the New York Stock Exchange. Several OTC dealers, most notably Weeden & Co., decided to make a market in about 200 of the most actively traded NYSE issues and to do this at a much smaller cost than the NYSE commission structure would allow. This trading in NYSE-listed securities in over-the-counter markets became known as the **third market.**

The third market diminished in importance for a while as the NYSE became more price competitive. However, in the 1980s and early 1990s, this market made a comeback. One advantage of the OTC market is that more than one specialist trades a security, making trading flexibility greater. For example, ITT Corporation reported a significant dividend cut and lower earnings after the NYSE was closed, but Jefferies Corporation, an over-the-counter trading firm, traded 3 million shares by the time the NYSE opened the next morning. Another example occurred when the Justice Department announced the breakup of AT&T on a Friday. MCI, a competitor in communications, traded OTC, while AT&T traded on the NYSE. AT&T trading was halted until Monday because the specialist was unable to stabilize the market, whereas the 29 market makers in MCI stock in the OTC market transacted over $75 million of securities before AT&T opened on Monday

morning. At the time of this writing, much discussion is being held at the New York Stock Exchange about trading hours, revising rules, and generally competing more effectively with the third market and the OTC.

The **fourth market** is that market in which institutions trade between themselves, bypassing the middleman broker (replacing the broker with a computer). Much of the trading in this market is done through Instinet, Institutional Networks Inc. Instinet provides a low-cost automated stock trading system, with transactions available on more than 3,500 securities, both listed and over-the-counter. The system allows banks, insurance companies, and mutual and pension funds to enter an order over a computer terminal for up to 1,000 shares. The computer searches a nationwide trading network until it finds the trader with the best price, then the computer holds the order 30 seconds so that another trader may offer a better price. While Instinet is only a small trading system, Merrill Lynch bought 8 percent of the company and has plans to tie the trading system into the quote-terminal desktop computer it is developing with IBM.

THE FUTURE OF THE CAPITAL MARKETS

Financial institutions, such as banks, pension funds, insurance companies, and investment companies (mutual funds), have always invested and traded in securities. However, the growth of these institutions and their participation in the capital markets have increased dramatically in recent years. Part of the increased share activity can be found in the accelerated growth of pension plans during this period. Also, the rapid rise in stock prices during the post–World War II period attracted a lot of individual investors into mutual funds.

Table 2–11, on page 53, on institutional activity shows that significant changes have occurred during the past two decades as institutional trading has accounted for a relatively larger percentage of total trading on the New York Stock Exchange. A block trade is a transaction of 10,000 shares or more and is almost always carried out by institutions rather than individuals. In 1965, block trades accounted for only 3.1 percent of the reported volume on the NYSE, but by 1993, block trades represented 53.7 percent (last column). This increased institutional activity is also evident by an examination of the second column of Table 2–11, which shows that, between 1965 and 1993, the average number of block trades per day increased from 9 to 5,841.

Over this same time period, the individual investor's participation in the market has decreased. This does not mean individuals are getting out of the stock market entirely but that many are investing indirectly in stocks through mutual funds, IRAs, and private pension plans. The market crash of 1987 and the high volatility of stock price movements subsequent to that event have scared off many small investors. However, as markets eventually settle down and new regulations are enacted, the individual investor will continue to have a meaningful role in the market.

The National Market System

A national market system was mandated by Congress in the Securities Amendments Act of 1975. This is envisioned as a coordinated national system of security trading with no barriers between the various exchanges or the OTC market. There is sometimes confusion

TABLE 2–11 Institutional Activity on the New York Stock Exchange

Year	(1) Total Number of Large Block Transactions per Year	(2) Average Number of Large Block Transactions per Day	(3) Block Shares (thousands)	(4) Block Trades as a % of Reported NYSE Volume
1965	2,171	9	49,262	3.1%
1967	6,685	27	N.A.	6.7
1969	15,132	61	N.A.	14.1
1970	17,217	68	450,908	15.4
1971	26,941	106	692,536	17.8
1973	29,223	116	721,356	17.8
1975	34,420	136	778,540	16.6
1977	54,275	215	1,183,924	22.4
1979	97,509	385	2,164,726	26.5
1981	145,564	575	3,771,442	31.8
1982	254,707	1,007	6,742,481	41.0
1983	363,415	1,436	9,842,080	45.6
1984	433,427	1,713	11,492,091	49.8
1985	539,039	2,139	14,222,272	51.7
1986	665,587	2,631	17,811,335	49.9
1987	920,679	3,639	24,497,241	51.2
1988	768,419	3,037	22,270,680	54.5
1989	872,811	3,464	21,316,132	51.1
1990	843,365	3,333	19,681,849	49.6
1991	981,077	3,878	22,474,383	49.6
1992	1,134,832	4,468	26,069,383	50.7
1993	1,477,859	5,841	35,959,117	53.7

Source: *New York Stock Exchange Fact Book,* 1994.

between the concept of a national market system and the National Market System listing segment of the NASDAQ market. The former system is the subject of the present discussion. The latter has already been discussed.

Despite some delay in implementing a national market system due to industry foot-dragging and political changes in Washington, it is still a goal for the future. The system is strongly supported by the SEC. No one knows exactly what form this national market might take, but several things will be required. Some are easily achieved, while others are not. The first is already in place—the composite tape that reflects trades on all exchanges for listed NYSE companies. There will also have to be competition between specialists and market makers. This is already occurring between the regional exchanges and the NYSE in dually listed securities. The prices seem to be more stable and the spreads between the bid and asked prices are closer for securities with competing market makers. A third occurrence is that the NYSE will most likely have to abolish Rule 390,

which prohibits members of the NYSE from trading off the exchange in NYSE-listed securities. This has yet to occur.

Possibly the biggest dilemma in creating a national market system is fully developing a computerized system to execute limit orders. Currently, NYSE specialists execute most limit orders, which specify that a security must be bought or sold at a limited price or better. The national market system will need a computerized system to handle limit orders from all markets. Progress along these lines is being required by the SEC, and by the mid-1990s, the NYSE had created several computer systems to aid in trading.

The national market system mandated by Congress could eventually take the form of NASDAQ, where several competing dealers make markets electronically. Clearly, the National Association of Securities Dealers hopes the national market system will follow its trading practices rather than the auction markets of the exchanges. The exchanges have complained to the SEC that the NASD's use of the term *National Market System* for its largest OTC companies should not be allowed because it gives the appearance that the OTC is *the* national market.

The NYSE will not capitulate easily to an over-the-counter system of trading. The traditional exchange auction markets have been able to absorb block trades without difficulty and serve the needs of institutional customers and individuals. The NYSE does not want to give up its dominant market position, but it had better stop to look at who is catching up.

Any truly national market system will rely on computers more than ever. Some systems in existence today even allow individual investors to use their personal computers to place stock market orders.

Any national market system will also have to interface with international markets whose continuous around-the-clock, around-the-world trading was mentioned earlier in the chapter.

REGULATION OF THE SECURITY MARKETS

Organized securities markets are regulated by the **Securities and Exchange Commission (SEC)** and by the self-regulation of the exchanges. The OTC market is controlled by the National Association of Securities Dealers. Three major laws govern the sale and subsequent trading of securities. The **Securities Act of 1933** pertains to new issues of securities, while the **Securities Exchange Act of 1934** deals with trading in the securities markets. The **Securities Acts Amendments of 1975** is the latest major piece of legislation, and its main emphasis is on a national securities market. The primary purpose of these laws was to protect unwary investors from fraud and manipulation and to make the markets more competitive and efficient.

Securities Act of 1933

The Securities Act of 1933 was enacted after congressional investigations of the abuses present in the securities markets during the 1929 crash and again in 1931. The act's primary purpose was to provide full disclosure of all pertinent investment information whenever a corporation sold a new issue of securities. It is sometimes referred to as the "truth in securities" act. The Securities Act has several important features:

1. All offerings except government bonds and bank stocks that are to be sold in more than one state must be registered with the SEC.[3]
2. The registration statement must be filed 20 days in advance of the date of sale and include detailed corporate information. If the SEC finds the information misleading, incomplete, or inaccurate, it will delay the offering until the registration statement is corrected. The SEC in no way certifies that the security is fairly priced but only that the information seems to be factual and accurate. Under certain circumstances, the previously mentioned shelf registration is being used to modify the 20-day waiting period concept.
3. All new issues of securities must be accompanied by a *prospectus,* a detailed summary of the registration statement. Included in the prospectus is usually a list of directors and officers; their salaries, stock options, and shareholdings; financial reports certified by a certified public accountant (CPA); a list of the underwriters; the purpose and use for the funds to be provided from the sale of securities; and any other reasonable information that investors may need to know before they can wisely invest their money. A preliminary prospectus may be distributed to potential buyers before the offering date, but it will not contain the offering price or underwriting fees. It is called a red herring because stamped on the front in red letters are the words *Preliminary Prospectus.*
4. Officers of the company and other experts preparing the prospectus or registration statement can be sued for penalties and recovery of realized losses if any information presented was fraudulent or factually wrong or if relevant information was omitted.

Securities Exchange Act of 1934

This act created the Securities and Exchange Commission to enforce the securities laws. It was empowered to regulate the securities markets and those companies listed on the exchanges. Specifically, the major points of the 1934 Act are as follows:

1. Guidelines for insider trading were established. Insiders must hold securities for at least six months before they can sell them. This is to prevent them from taking quick advantage of information that could result in a short-term profit. All short-term profits were payable to the corporation. Insiders were generally thought to be officers, directors, major stockholders, employees, or relatives of key employees. In the last two decades, the SEC widened its interpretation to include anyone having information that was not public knowledge. This could include security analysts, loan officers, large institutional holders, and many others who had business dealings with the firm.
2. The Federal Reserve Board of Governors became responsible for setting margin requirements to determine how much credit one had available to buy securities.
3. Manipulation of securities by conspiracies between investors was prohibited.

---

[3] Actually, the SEC did not come into existence until 1934. The Federal Trade Commission had many of these responsibilities before the formation of the SEC.

4. The SEC was given control over the proxy procedures of corporations (a proxy is an absent stockholder vote).
5. In its regulation of companies traded on the markets, it required certain reports to be filed periodically. Corporations must file quarterly financial statements with the SEC, send annual reports to the stockholders, and file 10–K Reports with the SEC annually. The 10–K Report has more financial data than the annual report and can be very useful to an investor or loan officer. Most companies will now send 10–K Reports to stockholders on request. By 1995, the SEC also made company filings available on the Internet under its retrieval system called EDGAR.
6. The act required all securities exchanges to register with the SEC. In this capacity, the SEC supervises and regulates many pertinent organizational aspects of exchanges such as listing and trading mechanics.

The Securities Acts Amendments of 1975

The major focus of the Securities Acts Amendments of 1975 was to direct the SEC to supervise the development of a national securities market. No exact structure was put forth, but the law did assume that any national market would make extensive use of computers and electronic communication devices. Additionally, the law prohibited fixed commissions on public transactions and also prohibited banks, insurance companies, and other financial institutions from buying stock exchange memberships to save commission costs for their own institutional transactions. This is a worthwhile addition to the securities laws since it fosters greater competition and more efficient prices.

Other Legislation

In addition to these three major pieces of legislation, a number of other acts deal directly with investor protection. For example, the Investment Advisor Act of 1940 is set up to protect the public from unethical investment advisers. Any adviser with more than 15 public clients (excluding tax accountants and lawyers) must register with the SEC and file semiannual reports. The Investment Company Act of 1940 provides similar oversight for mutual funds and investment companies dealing with small investors. The act was amended in 1970 and currently gives the NASD authority to supervise and limit commissions and investment advisory fees on certain types of mutual funds.

Another piece of legislation dealing directly with investor protection is the Securities Investor Protection Act of 1970. The **Securities Investor Protection Corporation (SIPC)** was established to oversee liquidation of brokerage firms and to insure investors' accounts to a maximum value of $500,000 in case of bankruptcy of a brokerage firm. It functions much the same as the Federal Deposit Insurance Corporation. SIPC resulted from the problems encountered on Wall Street from 1967 to 1970 when share volume surged to then all-time highs, and many firms were unable to process orders fast enough. A back-office paper crunch caused Wall Street to shorten the hours the exchanges were formally open for new business, but even this didn't help. Investors lost large sums, and for many months, they were unable to use or get possession of securities held in

their names. Even though SIPC insures these accounts, it still does not cover market value losses suffered while waiting to get securities from a bankrupt brokerage firm.

Insider Trading

The Securities Exchange Act of 1934 established the initial restrictions on insider trading. However, over the years, these restrictions have often proved to be inadequate. As previously indicated, the definition of *insider* may go beyond officers, directors, and major stockholders to include anyone with special insider knowledge. Both the Congress and the SEC are attempting to grapple with the issue of making punitive measures severe enough to discourage the illegal use of nonpublic information for profits.[4] Current and future legislation is likely to include tougher civil penalties and stiffer criminal prosecution. Also, the penalties for improper action will expand beyond simple recovery of profits to a penalty three or more times the profits involved.

The 1980s saw a rash of insider trading scandals involving major investment banking houses, traders, analysts, and investors. Ivan Boesky and Dennis Levine were the first of the well-known investors to end up in jail, and in June 1988, Steven Wang, Jr., an analyst at Morgan Stanley, was charged by the SEC of insider trading activities evolving from confidential information passed on to a wealthy Taiwanese businessman, Fred Lee. These insider trading scandals have plagued Wall Street and tarnished its image as a place where investors can get a fair deal.

On balance, all the legislation we have discussed has tended to increase the confidence of the investing public. In an industry where public trust is so critical, some form of supervision, whether public or private, is necessary and generally accepted.

Program Trading and Market Price Limits

Program trading is identified by some market analysts as the primary culprit behind the 508-point market crash on October 19, 1987. **Program trading** simply means computer-based trigger points are established in which large volume trades are initiated by institutional investors. For example, if the Dow Jones Industrial Average (or some other market measure) hits a certain point, a large sale or purchase may automatically occur. When many institutional investors are using program trading simultaneously, this process can have a major cumulative effect on the market. This was thought to be the case not only in the 1987 crash but also for many other highly volatile days in the market.

The New York Stock Exchange reports that program trading has averaged about 11.0 percent of total exchange volume for the five years ending in 1993. However, the percentage has risen every year—from 9.9 percent in 1989 to 11.9 percent in 1993. *The New York Stock Exchange Fact Book* (1994) explains program trading as follows:

> Program trading is defined as a wide range of portfolio trading strategies involving the purchase or sale of a basket of 15 stocks or more and valued at one million dollars or more. Some

[4] Insiders, of course, may make proper long-term investments in a corporation.

examples of program trading strategies are index arbitrage, liquidation of facilitations, liquidation of exchange-for-physicals stock positions, and portfolio management, which includes portfolio realignment and portfolio liquidations. Index arbitrage is the purchase or sale of a basket of stocks in conjunction with the sales or purchase of a derivative product, such as stock index futures, in order to profit from the price difference between the basket and the derivative product.[5]

RULE 80A After the crash of 1987, several studies of the role of program trading in creating market volatility were undertaken. In response to concerns that program trading might create market volatility, the NYSE instituted **Rule 80A.** Under Rule 80A as permanently amended by the SEC, all daily up or down movements in the Dow Jones Industrial Average (DJIA) of 50 points or more cause a tick test to go into effect.[6] In down markets, sell orders can only be executed on an increase in price (a plus tick) and buy orders can only be executed on a decrease in price (a minus tick). The rule stays in effect all day unless the DJIA returns to within 25 points of the previous day's closing price. "Since the implementation of Rule 80A, it has been triggered 23 times in 1990, 20 times in 1991, 16 times in 1992, and 9 times in 1993, and has been widely credited for helping to reduce market volatility."[7]

SUMMARY

A smoothly functioning market is one that is efficient and provides liquidity to the investor. The success of a primary market, in which new issues are generally underwritten by investment bankers, is highly dependent on the presence of an active resale (secondary) market.

Secondary markets may be established in the form of an organized exchange or as an over-the-counter market. The predominant organized market is the New York Stock Exchange, but increasing attention is being directed to various other markets. The possibility of a true national market system looms as a consideration for the future, with the completed first step being the development of a consolidated tape among different markets. NASDAQ (National Association of Securities Dealers Automated Quotations system) has done much to improve the communications network in the over-the-counter market and bring competition to the organized exchanges. The first full year of trading under NASDAQ's National Market System began in 1983, and many companies are choosing to remain on the OTC market rather than be listed on the AMEX or NYSE.

The dominant role of the institutional investor has had an enormous impact on the markets with higher stock turnover and increasing market volatility. An enormous consolidation of market participants has also occurred on Wall Street.

The term *market* is broadening with different types of new investment outlets as witnessed by the expansion of options, futures contracts on stock indexes, options on futures, and many other commodity trading

[5] *New York Stock Exchange Fact Book,* 1994, p. 22.

[6] The rule specifically applies to stocks in the Standard & Poor's 500 Stock Index to protect against index arbitrage, that is, trading in stocks and stock index futures at the same time in order to profit from price differences between the two.

[7] *New York Stock Exchange Fact Book,* 1994, p. 23.

mechanisms. Of equal importance, the term *market* must be viewed from a global viewpoint with securities trading throughout the world on a 24-hour basis.

Finally, problems or imperfections in the marketplace during critical time periods have led to a wide array of securities legislation. The legislation in the 1930s regulated the securities markets and created the SEC. Subsequent laws have dealt with restructuring the market and investor protection. The market crash of 1987 has also called into question the adequacy of our current securities laws. One reaction was the creation of Rule 80A by the New York Stock Exchange, which attempts to control market volatility after the Dow Jones Industrial Average moves up or down by 50 points during a given day.

KEY WORDS AND CONCEPTS

market, 30
efficient market, 30
liquidity, 31
secondary markets, 31
primary markets, 31
investment banker, 32
underwriting, 32
best efforts, 32
syndicate, 33
initial public offering (IPO), 38
organized exchanges, 39
over-the-counter markets, 39
commission brokers, 44
floor brokers, 44
registered traders, 44
odd-lot dealer, 44
specialists, 45
Super Dot, 46
Electronic Book, 46
call option, 47
NASDAQ, 50
third market, 51
fourth market, 52
Securities and Exchange Commission (SEC), 54
Securities Act of 1933, 54
Securities Exchange Act of 1934, 54
Securities Acts Amendments of 1975, 54
Securities Investor Protection Corporation (SIPC), 56
program trading, 57
Rule 80A, 58

DISCUSSION QUESTIONS

1. What is a market?
2. What is an efficient market?
3. What is the difference between primary and secondary markets?
4. What is the difference between an investment banker providing an underwriting function and a "best-efforts" offering?
5. What is a private placement?
6. What generally determines how firms are listed in a tombstone advertisement?
7. Briefly describe the participants on an exchange.
8. How do critics think the specialist system on the NYSE might be improved?
9. How is the over-the-counter market different from the organized exchanges?
10. What is the highest priority segment of the OTC market in terms of reporting trading activity?
11. What is the NASDAQ, and what service does it perform?
12. What are some differences between OTC standards for inclusion and NYSE listing requirements? (Suggest

general categories of differences rather than actual numbers.)

13. Define a block trade. What does the increase in block trades since 1965 tend to indicate about the nature of investors in the market?
14. List some factors that are required for the implementation of a national market system.
15. Indicate the primary purpose of the Securities Act of 1933. Why was it enacted? Does the SEC certify that a security is fairly priced?
16. How has the definition of an insider (inside trader) expanded over the past two decades?
17. Explain the purpose of the Securities Investor Protection Corporation (SIPC).
18. What is program trading? Why does it have the potential to add to market volatility?
19. What is Rule 80A? Should it help to decrease market volatility?
20. The concept of 24-hour market trading is mentioned a number of times in the chapter. What development has led to such a possibility?

THE WALL STREET JOURNAL PROJECTS

1. Generally, a table similar to Table 2–7, called "Data on Trading Volume," appears in *The Wall Street Journal* at the bottom of the Stock Market Data Bank on or near page C2. The table shows the trading volume by market and the total volume on the composite tape. Calculate the percentage market share for each market of the composite market for the most recent day. What is the ranking of each market for volume?
2. When companies decide to raise new capital through a debt or equity offering, their investment banker often places an advertisement announcing the new issue in *The Wall Street Journal.* These advertisements are usually found in the back part of Section C and look similar to Figure 2–1. How many different types of new issues can you find over a three-day time period? What kind of securities are being sold? Is there an international component to the offering?
3. *The Wall Street Journal* has a daily list of New Securities Issues.[8] Identify this list, and see how many new issues are listed and what types of securities are being offered. How do equity offerings compare with other issues?

CRITICAL THOUGHT CASE

The Securities and Exchange Commission is a federal agency created by Congress through the Securities Exchange Acts of 1933 and 1934 to protect investors. The stock market crash of 1929 and the Great Depression led the U.S. Senate to investigate the regulations of the securities industry. The existing laws were found to be inadequate, thus the formation of the securities industry watchdog, the SEC.

[8] To help find this list, look at the page index on the upper left- and right-hand side of page C1.

One of the main provisions of the 1933 act was to ensure full disclosure of facts by companies offering securities for sale to the public. Companies must submit a registration statement to the SEC for approval before securities could be sold. These statements contain financial information essential to a complete analysis of the investment at hand. A company prospectus disclosing this information is made available to the public.

Recently, disclosure of this information has posed many problems. As the world markets become increasingly competitive, foreign companies have access to important financial information about U.S. companies. In many cases, this same financial information on foreign companies is not available to U.S. companies. But, if foreign companies want to sell stock in the United States, the SEC requires them to submit the same financial information as U.S. companies. Many foreign companies are reluctant to do this because they believe it would give away their competitive advantage.

With the globalization of the world's securities markets, the New York Stock Exchange feels very strongly that to remain the leader in the industry, foreign securities must be traded in the United States. The NYSE has been attempting to attract major foreign companies for listing on the exchange, but many of these companies do not want to comply with the stringent financial disclosure requirements. If action is not taken quickly to rectify the situation, the NYSE believes it may lose its competitive position as the world's largest stock exchange.

The NYSE has been trying for some time to persuade the SEC to reduce corporate financial disclosure requirements for foreign companies. Although the SEC agrees in principle that it would be advantageous to investors to have foreign stocks listed on the exchange, it is not willing to lessen the disclosure standards for foreign companies. Investors would be at risk if this were allowed.

Questions

1. Should the SEC, for the sake of maintaining U.S. competitiveness in the world markets, lessen requirements for foreign companies?
2. If so, is this fair to U.S. companies and investors?
3. What are the consequences to the NYSE and New York City if the exchange is no longer the world leader it once was?

U.S. EQUITIES ONFLOPPY EXERCISES

Please use your U.S. Equities OnFloppy software and manual to complete the following exercises.

1. The U.S. Equities OnFloppy database contains companies from the NYSE, the AMEX, and the National Market System (NNM). Determine the respective number of companies in the database that are listed on each of these "exchanges."
2. a. Using the U.S. Equities OnFloppy database determine the average number of shares outstanding and the average market value of the shares outstanding for the firms of the NYSE.
   b. Determine the average number of shares outstanding and the average market value of the shares outstanding for the firms of the AMEX.

c. Determine the average number of shares outstanding and the average market value of the shares outstanding for the firms of the NNM.

3. a. Compare the size of the 25 largest firms from the NYSE, the AMEX, and the NNM, using the average market value of the shares outstanding as the measure.

   b. Compare the size of the 25 smallest firms from the NYSE, the AMEX, and the NNM, using the average market value of the shares outstanding as the measure.

SELECTED REFERENCES

Security Exchanges

Cabanilla, Nathaniel B. "Directly Placed Bonds: A Test of Market Efficiency." *Journal of Portfolio Management,* Winter 1984, pp. 72–74.

Chatterjea, Arkadev; Joseph A. Cherian; and Robert A. Jarrow. "Market Manipulation and Corporate Finance: A New Perspective." *Financial Management,* Summer 1993, pp. 200–09.

Eubank, Arthur E., Jr. "Risk/Return Contrast: NYSE, Amex, and OTC." *Journal of Portfolio Management,* Summer 1977, pp. 25–30.

Kadlec, Gregory B., and John J. McConnell. "The Effect of Market Segmentation on Asset Prices: Evidence from Exchange Listings." *Journal of Finance,* June 1994, pp. 611–36.

Sanger, Gary C., and John J. McConnell. "Stock Exchange Listings, Firm Value, and Security Market Efficiency: The Impact of NASDAQ." *Journal of Financial and Qualitative Analysis,* March 1986, pp. 1–25.

Stoll, Hans R. "The Pricing of Security Dealer Service: An Empirical Study of NASDAQ Stocks." *Journal of Finance,* September 1978, pp. 1153–72.

Trading Patterns by Investors

Hasbrouck, Joel, and George Sofianos. "The Trades of Market Makers: An Empirical Analysis of NYSE Specialists." *Journal of Finance,* December 1993, pp. 1565–93.

Roll, Richard. "A Simple Implicit Measure of the Effective Bid—Ask Spread in an Efficient Market." *Journal of Finance,* September 1984, pp. 1127–39.

Regulation

Gastineau, Gary L., and Robert A. Jarrow. "Larger-Trader Impact and Market Regulation." *Financial Analysts Journal,* July–August 1991, pp. 40–51.

Treynor, Jack. "Securities Law and Public Policy." *Financial Analysts Journal,* May–June 1994, p. 10.

3

Participating in the Market

Many different kinds of investors participate in the market, from the individual to the professional, and each participant needs to know about the structure and mechanics of the market in which he or she might invest. In this chapter, we examine the use of indexes to gauge market performance, the rules and mechanics of opening and trading in an account, and basic tax considerations for the investor.

MEASURES OF PRICE PERFORMANCE: MARKET INDEXES

We first look at tracking market performance for stocks and bonds. Each market has several market indexes published by Dow Jones, Standard & Poor's, Value Line, and other financial services. These indexes allow investors to measure the performance of their portfolios against an index that approximates their portfolio composition; thus, different investors prefer different indexes. While a professional pension fund manager might use the Standard & Poor's 500 Stock Index, a mutual fund specializing in small, over-the-counter stocks might prefer the NASDAQ (National Association of Securities Dealers Automated Quotations) Index, and a small investor might use the Value Line Average as the best approximation of a portfolio's performance.

INDEXES AND AVERAGES

Dow Jones Averages

Since there are many stock market indexes and averages, we will cover the most widely used ones. Dow Jones, publisher of *The Wall Street Journal* and *Barron's,* publishes several market averages of which the **Dow Jones Industrial Average (DJIA)** is the most popular. This average consists of 30 large industrial companies and is considered a "blue-chip" index (stocks of very high quality). Many people criticize the DJIA for being too selective and representing too few stocks. Nevertheless, the Dow Industrials do follow the general trend of the market, and these 30 common stocks comprise more than 25 percent of the market value of the 1,800 firms listed on the New York Stock Exchange. Figure 3–1 shows a listing of the 30 stocks in the Dow Jones Industrial Average as well as the daily price movement for the average over a six-month period.

Dow Jones also publishes an index of 20 transportation stocks and 15 utility stocks. At the top of Table 3–1 on page 66, you see a listing of the daily changes for the three Dow Jones Averages on July 5, 1994. It also shows a Dow Jones 65-stock composite average that summarizes the performance of the Dow Jones industrial, transportation, and utility issues. Many other market averages are presented in the table, which we shall discuss later.

For now, let's return to the Dow Jones Industrial Average of 30 stocks. The Dow Jones Industrial Average used to be a simple average of 30 stocks, but when a company splits its stock price, the average has to be adjusted. For the Dow Jones Industrials, the divisor in the formula has been adjusted downward from the original 30 to below 1. Each time a company splits its shares of stock (or provides a stock dividend), the divisor is reduced to maintain the average at the same level as before the stock split. If this were not done, the lower-priced stock after the split would reduce the average, giving the appearance that investors were worse off.

FIGURE 3–1 Dow Jones Industrial Average

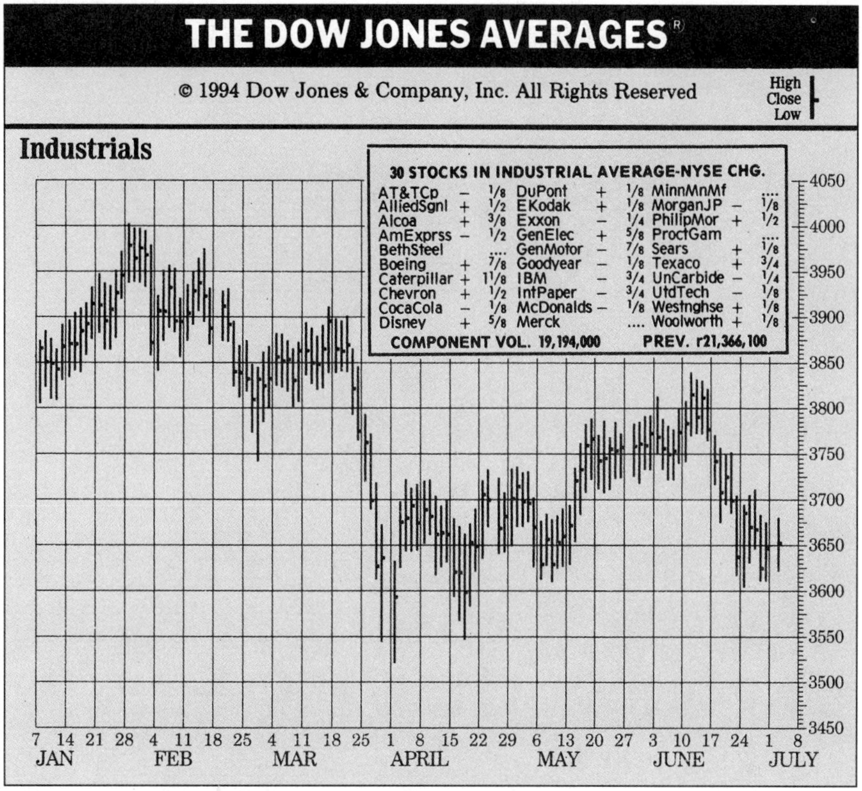

Source: *The Wall Street Journal,* July 6, 1994, p. C3. Reprinted by permission of *The Wall Street Journal,* © 1994 by Dow Jones & Company. All Rights Reserved Worldwide.

The Dow Jones Industrial Average is a **price-weighted average**, which means each stock in the average is weighted by its price. To simplify the meaning of price weighted: if you had three stocks in a price-weighted average that had values of 10, 40, and 100, you would add the prices and divide by three. In this case, you would get an average of 50 (150 divided by 3). A price-weighted average is similar to what you normally use in computing averages. Price-weighted averages tend to give a higher weighting bias to high-price stocks than to low-price stocks. For example, in the above analysis, if the $100 stock goes up by 10 percent, with all else the same, the average will go up over three points from 50 to 53.3. However, if the $10 stock goes up by 10 percent, with all else the same, the average will only go from 50 to 50.3.

In mid-1994, Atlantic Richfield was trading at 103 while Bethlehem Steel was at 18½. Clearly, a 10 percent price movement up or down in Atlantic Richfield would have a greater impact on the Dow Jones Industrial Average than a 10 percent movement in Bethlehem Steel. Thus, we see the bias toward high-priced stocks in the Dow Jones Industrial Average.

Dow Jones also publishes the **Dow Jones Equity Market Index** (the last listing under Dow Jones Averages in Table 3–1). Introduced in October 1988, it includes 700

TABLE 3-1 Indexes and Averages Found in *The Wall Street Journal*

STOCK MARKET DATA BANK 7/5/94

MAJOR INDEXES

HIGH	LOW (†365 DAY)		CLOSE	NET CHG		% CHG		†365 DAY CHG		% CHG		FROM 12/31		% CHG
DOW JONES AVERAGES														
3978.36	3449.93	30 Industrials	x3652.48	+	5.83	+	0.16	+	202.55	+	5.87	−	101.61	− 2.71
1862.29	1495.72	20 Transportation	1604.73	−	5.74	−	0.36	+	76.66	+	5.02	−	157.59	− 8.94
256.46	176.71	15 Utilities	178.09	−	0.07	−	0.04	−	65.85	− 26.99		−	51.21	− 22.33
1447.06	1263.56	65 Composite	x1277.77	−	0.53	−	0.04	+	4.51	+	0.35	−	103.26	− 7.48
456.27	416.31	Equity Mkt. Index	422.21	+	0.05	+	0.01	+	2.33	+	0.55	−	19.98	− 4.52
NEW YORK STOCK EXCHANGE														
267.71	243.14	Composite	246.51	+	0.17	+	0.07	+	1.44	+	0.59	−	12.57	− 4.85
327.93	292.06	Industrials	303.38	+	0.34	+	0.11	+	11.32	+	3.88	−	11.88	− 3.77
246.95	199.04	Utilities	202.64	−	0.47	−	0.23	−	27.81	− 12.07		−	27.28	− 11.86
285.03	231.21	Transportation	243.05	−	0.35	−	0.14	+	8.82	+	3.77	−	27.43	− 10.14
233.33	200.75	Finance	210.29	+	0.29	+	0.14	−	5.84	−	2.70	−	6.53	− 3.01
STANDARD & POOR'S INDEXES														
482.00	438.92	500 Index	446.37	+	0.17	+	0.04	+	4.94	+	1.12	−	20.08	− 4.30
560.59	501.83	Industrials	519.00	+	0.36	+	0.07	+	17.17	+	3.42	−	21.19	− 3.92
453.63	365.22	Transportation	386.29	−	1.08	−	0.28	+	16.06	+	4.34	−	39.31	− 9.24
189.49	148.69	Utilities	153.59	−	0.45	−	0.29	−	20.83	− 11.94		−	18.99	− 11.00
48.40	41.39	Financials	44.60	+	0.07	+	0.16	−	0.14	−	0.31	+	0.33	+ 0.75
184.79	162.44	400 MidCap	165.00	−	0.33	−	0.20	−	2.38	−	1.42	−	14.38	− 8.02
NASDAQ														
803.93	693.79	Composite	703.59	−	3.26	−	0.46	+	1.37	+	0.20	−	73.21	− 9.42
851.80	703.27	Industrials	713.03	−	2.80	−	0.39	−	12.20	−	1.68	−	92.81	− 11.52
956.91	854.85	Insurance	877.55	−	3.39	−	0.38	+	22.70	+	2.66	−	43.04	− 4.68
762.42	612.72	Banks	762.42	+	0.59	+	0.08	+	149.70	+ 24.43		+	72.99	+ 10.59
356.61	307.39	Nat. Mkt. Comp.	312.01	−	1.43	−	0.46	+	1.55	+	0.50	−	31.60	− 9.20
342.72	282.86	Nat. Mkt. Indus.	286.93	−	1.05	−	0.36	−	3.02	−	1.04	−	35.83	− 11.10
OTHERS														
487.89	422.67	Amex	423.70	−	1.02	−	0.24	−	10.07	−	2.32	−	53.45	− 11.20
305.87	273.73	Value-Line(geom.)	276.17	+	0.16	+	0.06	−	0.77	−	0.28	−	19.11	− 6.47
271.08	233.19	Russell 2000	240.73	−	0.39	−	0.16	+	6.81	+	2.91	−	17.86	− 6.91
4804.31	4373.58	Wilshire 5000	4412.17	−	1.22	−	0.03	+	24.11	+	0.55	−	245.65	− 5.27

†-Based on comparable trading day in preceding year.

Source: *The Wall Street Journal*, July 6, 1994, p. C2. Reprinted by permission of *The Wall Street Journal*, © 1994 by Dow Jones & Company. All Rights Reserved Worldwide.

stocks in 82 industry groups. Unlike the Dow Jones Industrial Average, it includes stocks from the New York Stock Exchange, the American Stock Exchange, and the NASDAQ National Market System and is much more broadly based.

Standard & Poor's Indexes

Standard & Poor's Corporation publishes a number of indexes. The best known is the **Standard & Poor's 500 Stock Index**. This index is widely followed by professional money managers and security market researchers as a measure of broad stock market

activity. The S&P 500 Stock Index includes 400 industrial firms, plus 20 transportation firms, 40 utilities, and 40 financial firms. A listing of Standard & Poor's 500 Index and its component parts can be seen in Table 3–1. The stocks in the S&P 500 Stock Index are equivalent to approximately 75 percent of the total value of the 1,800 firms listed on the New York Stock Exchange.[1]

Standard & Poor's also has other special purpose indexes some of which are not shown in Table 3–1. For example, the **Standard & Poor's 100 Index** is composed of 100 blue-chip stocks on which the Chicago Board Options Exchange has individual option contracts. (This terminology will become clearer when we study options later in the text.) The S&P 100 Index closely mirrors the performance of the S&P 500 Stock Index.

In the summer of 1991, Standard & Poor's Corp. introduced its MidCap Index. The **Standard & Poor's MidCap Index** is composed of 400 middle-sized firms that have total market values between $200 million and $5 billion. The index was intended to answer the complaint that the S&P 500 Stock Index shows only the performance of larger firms. For example, Exxon, which is part of the S&P 500 Index, had a total market value of more than $70 billion in mid-1994. By creating an index of middle-sized firms, portfolio managers with comparable-sized holdings could more accurately track their performance against an appropriate measure.

All the S&P measures are true indexes in that they are linked to a base value. For the S&P 500 Stock Index, the base period is 1941–43. The base period price in 1941–43 was 10, so the S&P 500 Stock Index price of 446.37 on July 5, 1994, as previously shown in Table 3–1, represents an increase of 4,363.7 percent over this 50-year-plus period. For the newer indexes, the base period does not go back so far.

Regardless of the base period, the important consideration is how much the index changed over a given time period (such as a day, month, or year) rather than the absolute value. For example, looking back at Table 3–1, you can see that the Dow Jones Industrial Average on July 5, 1994, is down 2.71 percent from December 31 (look at the last column to see the percentage change from the prior year) and that the Standard and Poor's 500 Stock Index is down 4.30 percent over a comparable time period.

The Standard & Poor's Indexes are **value-weighted**, which means each company is weighted in the index by its own total market value as a percentage of the total market value for all firms. For example, in a value-weighted index comprising the following three firms, the weighting would be

Stock	Shares	Price	Total Market Value	Weighting
A	150	$10	$ 1,500	12.0%
B	200	20	4,000	32.0
C	500	14	7,000	56.0
			$12,500	100.0%

[1] Actually, some large, over-the-counter firms are also in the S&P indexes, though the indexes are predominantly made up of New York Stock Exchange firms.

In each case, the weighting is determined by dividing the total market value of the stock by the total market value for all firms. In the case of stock A, that would be $1,500 divided by $12,500, or 12 percent. The same procedure is followed for stocks B and C.

Even though stock C has only the second highest price, it makes up 56 percent of the average because of its high total market value based on 500 shares outstanding. This same basic effect carries through in the Standard & Poor's 500 Index, with large companies such as Exxon, AT&T, and General Motors having a greater impact on the index than smaller companies. Value-weighted indexes do not require special adjustments for stock splits because the increase in the number of shares automatically compensates for the decline in the stock value caused by the split.

Standard & Poor's also compiles value-weighted indexes for more than 100 different industries, and they are reported in the *Outlook,* a weekly Standard & Poor's publication.

Value Line Average

The **Value Line Average** represents 1,700 companies from the New York and American Stock Exchanges and the NASDAQ market. Some individual investors use the Value Line Average because it more closely corresponds to the variety of stocks small investors may have in their portfolios.

Unlike the previously discussed price-weighted average (the Dow Jones Industrial Average) and value-weighted indexes (S&P 500), the Value Line Average is **equal-weighted**. This means each of the 1,700 stocks, regardless of market price or total market value, is weighted equally. It is as if there were $100 to be invested in each and every stock. In this case, IBM or Exxon is weighted no more heavily than Wendy's International or Mattel Inc. This equal-weighting characteristic also more closely conforms to the portfolio of individual investors.

Other Market Indexes

Indexes are also computed and published by the New York Stock Exchange, American Stock Exchange, and the National Association of Securities Dealers. Each index is intended to represent the performance of stocks traded in a particular exchange or market. As is seen in Table 3–1, the NYSE publishes a composite index as well as an industrial, utility, transportation, and financial index. Each index represents the stocks of a broad group or type of company.

The National Association of Securities Dealers, which is the self-governing body of the over-the-counter markets, also constructs several indexes to represent the companies in its market. It publishes the NASDAQ composite, industrial, insurance, and banking indexes. The NASDAQ also publishes subindexes for stocks listed in the National Market System (see Table 3–1).

The American Exchange Market Value Index (AMEX) is composed of all stocks trading on the American Stock Exchange. This index is also shown in Table 3–1.

The indexes of the New York Stock Exchange, NASDAQ, and the American Stock Exchange are all value-weighted indexes.[2]

---

[2] Until October 1973, the American Stock Exchange Index was price-weighted.

A relatively new index is the **Wilshire 5000 Equity Index**. It represents the *total dollar value* of 5,000 stocks, including all New York Stock Exchange and American Stock Exchange issues and the most active over-the-counter issues. By the very fact of including total dollar value, it is *value-weighted.* On July 5, 1994, the Wilshire Index had a value of $4,412.17 billion. The index tells you the total value of virtually all important equities daily.

The Russell indexes have also become popular in recent times. There are three separate but overlapping value-weighted indexes provided by Frank Russell Company, a money management consulting firm in Tacoma, Washington.[3] The **Russell 3000 Index** is comprised of the 3,000 largest U.S. stocks as measured by market capitalization (market value times shares outstanding). The other two indexes allow you to see whether larger or smaller stocks are performing better. For example, the **Russell 1000 Index** includes only the largest 1,000 firms out of the Russell 3000, while the **Russell 2000** specifically includes the smallest 2000 out of the Russell 3000. If the Russell 2000 is outperforming the Russell 1000, you can generally assume that smaller stocks are outperforming larger firms. The reverse would obviously be true if there is a superior performance by the Russell 1000.

International Stock Averages As the internationalization of investments has become progressively more important in the 1990s, so have international market indexes. In January 1993, Dow Jones & Company introduced the **Dow Jones World Stock Index**. As shown in Table 3–2 on page 70, it covers 25 countries in three major sectors of the world (Americas, Europe, and Asia/Pacific). Furthermore, the bottom two rows of the table show the World Index excluding the United States and the overall DJ (Dow Jones) World Stock Index. Note that in the last column, the World (excluding the United States) increased 8.58 percent from year-end while the DJ World Stock Index (which includes the United States) increased only 3.52 percent. Although an in-depth interpretation of the table requires information you will cover in Chapter 18, the strong international performance outside the United States should gain your attention.

Besides the Dow Jones World Stock Market Index, there are other important global indexes such as the Morgan Stanley Capital International Indexes and the Solomon-Russell World Equity Index. The advantage of the Dow Jones World Stock Index is that it is available to the typical investor on a daily basis in *The Wall Street Journal.*

In terms of averages for *specific countries* outside the United States, the **Tokyo Nikkei 225 Average** is probably the most actively watched. Many sophisticated U.S. investors look to the Japanese market immediately after checking local market conditions.

Bond Market Indicators Performance in the bond market is not widely followed by an index or average but is usually gauged by interest-rate movements. Since rising interest rates mean falling bond prices and falling rates signal rising prices, investors can usually judge the bond market performance by yield-curve changes or interest-rate graphs.

[3] Frank Russell Company has other indexes as well.

TABLE 3–2 World Stock Market Average

DOW JONES WORLD STOCK INDEX

Tuesday, July 5, 1994

REGION/ COUNTRY	DJ EQUITY MARKET INDEX, LOCAL CURRENCY	PCT. CHG.	IN U.S. DOLLARS: CLOSING INDEX	CHG.	PCT. CHG.	12-MO HIGH	12-MO LOW	12-MO CHG.	PCT. CHG.	FROM 12/31	PCT. CHG.
Americas			106.41	+ 0.01	+ 0.01	115.99	105.21	− 0.97	− 0.90	− 5.77	− 5.14
Canada	109.20	+ 0.05	90.99	− 0.01	− 0.01	107.30	88.37	− 2.64	− 2.82	− 9.36	− 9.33
Mexico	161.24	+ 0.24	145.68	+ 0.30	+ 0.21	203.25	113.09	+ 31.42	+ 27.50	− 37.20	− 20.34
U.S.	422.21	+ 0.01	422.21	+ 0.05	+ 0.01	456.27	416.31	− 1.60	− 0.38	− 19.98	− 4.52
Europe			112.40	+ 0.46	+ 0.41	122.60	98.02	+ 13.79	+ 13.98	− 3.69	− 3.18
Austria	109.84	− 1.92	105.59	− 1.16	− 1.09	111.50	81.91	+ 23.69	+ 28.92	+ 0.78	+ 0.74
Belgium	121.10	− 1.01	116.35	− 0.29	− 0.25	123.06	98.83	+ 15.82	+ 15.74	+ 4.80	+ 4.30
Denmark	106.17	− 0.18	101.10	+ 0.64	+ 0.64	106.98	80.33	+ 18.02	+ 21.68	+ 5.37	+ 5.61
Finland	209.52	+ 0.56	166.08	+ 1.99	+ 1.21	176.64	107.62	+ 57.03	+ 52.30	+ 27.41	+ 19.77
France	113.07	+ 0.37	108.15	+ 1.44	+ 1.35	124.46	100.32	+ 6.58	+ 6.47	− 9.63	− 8.18
Germany	122.17	− 0.86	117.08	+ 0.22	+ 0.19	125.38	93.21	+ 23.87	+ 25.61	− 1.85	− 1.56
Ireland	132.98	+ 0.66	109.81	+ 1.06	+ 0.98	125.99	93.46	+ 12.03	+ 12.30	− 2.15	− 1.92
Italy	156.02	+ 0.99	123.08	+ 2.35	+ 1.95	143.55	81.75	+ 24.21	+ 24.49	+ 23.97	+ 24.19
Netherlands	133.51	+ 0.31	126.81	+ 1.61	+ 1.29	131.59	105.81	+ 20.66	+ 19.46	+ 1.07	+ 0.85
Norway	125.55	− 0.81	108.53	− 0.03	− 0.03	118.78	87.26	+ 20.99	+ 23.98	+ 5.25	+ 5.09
Spain	122.62	− 2.08	91.26	− 1.17	− 1.27	106.94	78.01	+ 7.97	+ 9.57	− 3.63	− 3.82
Sweden	146.14	− 1.16	103.22	− 2.01	− 1.91	122.77	87.79	+ 14.68	+ 16.58	− 0.84	− 0.81
Switzerland	155.90	− 1.02	159.51	+ 0.19	+ 0.12	172.92	121.91	+ 35.99	+ 29.14	+ 1.24	+ 0.78
United Kingdom	125.03	− 0.07	103.24	+ 0.24	+ 0.23	118.15	94.44	+ 6.46	+ 6.67	− 9.06	− 8.07
Asia/Pacific			127.24	+ 0.76	+ 0.60	127.24	98.67	+ 18.84	+ 17.38	+ 20.47	+ 19.18
Australia	116.62	+ 0.86	111.17	+ 0.25	+ 0.23	128.45	92.11	+ 19.06	+ 20.70	− 2.12	− 1.87
Hong Kong	195.31	− 0.09	196.38	− 0.19	− 0.10	279.65	153.12	+ 32.84	+ 20.08	− 73.98	− 27.36
Indonesia	195.61	− 0.60	181.20	− 1.08	− 0.59	248.28	148.55	+ 24.83	+ 15.88	− 52.73	− 22.54
Japan	99.37	+ 0.63	125.40	+ 0.84	+ 0.67	125.40	91.51	+ 18.80	+ 17.63	+ 29.69	+ 31.02
Malaysia	206.46	+ 0.48	215.75	+ 1.14	+ 0.53	284.09	154.04	+ 56.66	+ 35.62	− 54.24	− 20.09
New Zealand	135.25	− 0.76	148.35	− 1.89	− 1.26	172.58	114.65	+ 33.71	+ 29.40	− 3.17	− 2.09
Singapore	148.25	+ 0.30	157.94	+ 0.52	+ 0.33	184.75	114.99	+ 40.47	+ 34.45	− 21.28	− 11.87
Thailand	208.19	+ 1.57	196.40	+ 3.11	+ 1.61	256.46	120.95	+ 71.20	+ 56.87	− 47.50	− 19.48
Asia/Pacific (ex. Japan)			157.37	+ 0.38	+ 0.24	199.98	124.49	+ 30.41	+ 23.96	− 36.23	− 18.71
World (ex. U.S.)			120.01	+ 0.61	+ 0.51	121.54	102.52	+ 15.59	+ 14.93	+ 9.49	+ 8.58
DJ WORLD STOCK INDEX			114.98	+ 0.38	+ 0.33	119.04	105.33	+ 9.42	+ 8.92	+ 3.90	+ 3.52

Indexes based on 6/30/82=100 for U.S., 12/31/91=100 for World.

Source: *The Wall Street Journal,* July 6, 1994, p. C12. Reprinted by permission of *The Wall Street Journal,*

Nevertheless, there is still a wide menu to choose from in *The Wall Street Journal* when tracking the performance of bond prices as indicated in Table 3–3. The indexes are broken down by different types of bonds: Treasury securities, corporate debt, tax-exempt issues, and mortgage-backed securities. (All of these securities are discussed in Part Four of the text.)

TABLE 3–3 Bond Indexes

BOND MARKET DATA BANK

MAJOR INDEXES

HIGH	LOW	(12 MOS)	CLOSE	NET CHG	% CHG	12-MO CHG	% CHG	FROM 12/31	% CHG
U.S. TREASURY SECURITIES (Lehman Brothers indexes)									
4220.48	3966.84	**Intermediate**	4220.48	+ 3.80	+ 0.09	+ 195.40	+ 4.85	+ 188.05	+ 4.66
5507.96	4897.46	**Long-term**	5501.62	+ 9.34	+ 0.17	+ 380.02	+ 7.42	+ 371.60	+ 7.24
1452.54	1307.21	**Long-term(price)**	1418.57	+ 1.98	+ 0.14	− 13.29	− 0.93	+ 67.76	+ 5.02
4513.29	4199.01	**Composite**	4512.32	+ 4.96	+ 0.11	+ 232.49	+ 5.43	+ 226.92	+ 5.30
U.S. CORPORATE DEBT ISSUES (Merrill Lynch)									
716.02	656.43	**Corporate Master**	716.02	+ 0.11	+ 0.02	+ 46.79	+ 6.99	+ 41.76	+ 6.19
528.76	487.79	**1-10 Yr Maturities**	528.71	+ 0.04	+ 0.01	+ 33.03	+ 6.66	+ 27.76	+ 5.54
544.97	490.84	**10+ Yr Maturities**	544.97	+ 0.13	+ 0.02	+ 39.11	+ 7.73	+ 37.28	+ 7.34
341.94	317.57	**High Yield**	341.94	+ 0.26	+ 0.08	+ 21.89	+ 6.84	+ 20.88	+ 6.50
519.62	477.83	**Yankee Bonds**	519.62	+ 0.11	+ 0.02	+ 32.49	+ 6.67	+ 29.62	+ 6.04
TAX-EXEMPT SECURITIES (Bond Buyer; Merrill Lynch: Dec. 31, 1986 = 100)									
94-9	80-26	**Bond Buyer Municipal**	91-28	+ -8	+ 0.27	+ 2-18	+ 2.87	+ 6-19	+ 7.73
109.20	100.41	**7-12 yr G.O.**	109.20	+ 0.02	+ 0.02	+ 7.86	+ 7.76	+ 5.99	+ 5.80
108.99	97.44	**12-22 yr G.O.**	108.84	+ 0.02	+ 0.02	+ 8.61	+ 8.59	+ 7.56	+ 7.46
106.67	95.67	**22+ yr Revenue**	106.51	− 0.01	− 0.01	+ 9.10	+ 9.34	+ 7.77	+ 7.87
MORTGAGE-BACKED SECURITIES (current coupon; Merrill Lynch: Dec. 31, 1986 = 100)									
217.17	197.64	**Ginnie Mae(GNMA)**	216.34	+ 0.05	+ 0.02	+ 15.50	+ 7.72	+ 12.45	+ 6.11
215.84	197.82	**Fannie Mae(FNMA)**	215.15	+ 0.12	+ 0.06	+ 14.36	+ 7.15	+ 11.36	+ 5.57
131.62	120.58	**Freddie Mac(FHLMC)**	131.19	+ 0.07	+ 0.05	+ 8.76	+ 7.16	+ 6.86	+ 5.52
BROAD MARKET (Merrill Lynch)									
597.75	552.73	**Domestic Master**	597.12	+ 0.25	+ 0.04	+ 35.22	+ 6.27	+ 34.40	+ 6.11
665.78	616.99	**Corporate/Government**	665.56	+ 0.30	+ 0.05	+ 37.12	+ 5.91	+ 34.45	+ 5.46

Source: *The Wall Street Journal,* April 16, 1995, p. C10. Reprinted by permission of *The Wall Street Journal,*

MUTUAL FUND AVERAGES Lipper Analytical Services publishes the Lipper Mutual and Investment Performance Averages shown in Table 3–4. While mutual funds will be considered in depth in Chapter 19, for now it is interesting to observe the various categories that the funds are broken into to compute measures of performance. Also, observe in the next few columns of Table 3–4 that the starting point of the measurement period is very important in relation to the presence or absence of pluses (or minuses) in performance.

DIRECTION OF INDEXES The direction of the indexes are closely related, but they do not necessarily move together. If a pension fund manager is trying to "outperform the market," then the choice of index may be as crucial as to whether the fund manager maintains his or her accounts. The important thing for you, as well as for a professional, when measuring success or failure of performance, is to use an index that represents the risk characteristics of the portfolio being compared with the index.

TABLE 3–4 Lipper Mutual Fund Performance Averages

LIPPER MUTUAL FUND PERFORMANCES AVERAGES

Special Quarterly Summary Report
Friday, April 7, 1995
Cumulative Total Reinvestment Performance

NAV Mil. $	No. Funds		03/31/80- 03/31/95	03/31/85- 03/31/95	03/31/90- 03/31/95	03/31/94- 03/31/95	12/31/94- 03/31/95
General Equity Funds							
41,628.3	156	Capital Appreciation	+ 686.99%	+ 227.61%	+ 70.52%	+ 6.77%	+ 6.45%
197,968.0	588	Growth Funds	+ 695.43%	+ 233.09%	+ 67.74%	+ 8.81%	+ 7.38%
32,141.1	106	Mid Cap	+ 628.50%	+ 251.74%	+ 91.60%	+ 8.62%	+ 7.18%
38,279.8	298	Small Company Growth	+ 641.96%	+ 247.09%	+ 91.26%	+ 7.69%	+ 5.57%
190,061.3	423	Growth and Income	+ 658.20%	+ 224.06%	+ 64.87%	+ 10.35%	+ 7.89%
20,487.7	42	S&P 500 Objective	+ 730.10%	+ 248.28%	+ 68.03%	+ 15.09%	+ 9.59%
68,998.2	135	Equity Income	+ 655.74%	+ 197.87%	+ 68.61%	+ 8.76%	+ 7.39%
589,564.4	1,748	Gen. Equity Funds Avg.	+ 674.86%	+ 229.86%	+ 70.37%	+ 8.96%	+ 7.16%
Other Equity Funds							
4,341.9	18	Health/Biotechnology	N/A	+ 474.32%	+ 124.42%	+ 19.72%	+ 10.26%
3,017.3	38	Natural Resources	+ 496.64%	+ 125.75%	+ 20.88%	+ 4.66%	+ 4.08%
89.4	5	Environmental	N/A	+ 176.81%	+ 7.34%	− 2.33%	+ 5.35%
5,976.7	37	Science & Technol.	+ 566.09%	+ 306.47%	+ 135.27%	+ 17.76%	+ 6.87%
1,960.7	27	Specialty/Misc.	N/A	+ 222.92%	+ 82.88%	+ 7.38%	+ 6.90%
20,827.2	87	Utility Funds	+ 455.63%	+ 167.48%	+ 50.20%	+ 1.91%	+ 4.19%
2,015.6	16	Financial Services	+ 787.22%	+ 255.89%	+ 143.21%	+ 10.46%	+ 7.93%
1,554.5	24	Real Estate	N/A	N/A	+ 40.38%	− 5.46%	− 2.38%
5,558.7	38	Gold Oriented Funds	+ 142.56%	+ 62.26%	+ 7.40%	− 9.62%	− 1:34%
41,914.5	126	Global Funds	+ 827.99%	+ 256.52%	+ 42.85%	− 0.60%	+ 0.04%
6,585.5	23	Global Smal Company	+ 285.00%	+ 155.25%	+ 49.59%	− 2.16%	− 1.18%
66,761.9	237	International Funds	+ 520.87%	+ 305.44%	+ 36.91%	− 1.68%	− 1.84%
2,560.3	11	International Small Co.	N/A	N/A	+ 12.93%	− 10.62%	− 4.66%
6,228.1	48	European Region Fds	N/A	N/A	+ 21.54%	+ 2.45%	+ 2.37%
12,136.8	75	Pacific Region Funds	+ 1,077.75%	+ 320.00%	+ 49.28%	− 4.43%	− 4.25%
8,850.5	48	Emerging Markets	N/A	N/A	+ 53.98%	− 15.23%	− 11.22%
1,707.7	11	Japanese Funds	+ 654.05%	+ 242.16%	− 8.24%	− 8.99%	− 8.83%
3,285.8	20	Latin American Funds	N/A	N/A	N/A	− 37.83%	− 30.38%
356.1	2	Canadian Funds	N/A	N/A	+ 11.82%	− 10.82%	− 0.69%
155,945.9	639	World Equity Fds Avg.	+ 530.22%	+ 224.07%	+ 30.83%	− 3.99%	− 3.10%
785,293.6	2,639	All Equity Funds Avg.	+ 659.65%	+ 230.34%	+ 65.05%	+ 5.89%	+ 4.44%
Other Funds							
28,502.3	158	Flexible Portfolio	+ 422.99%	+ 168.23%	+ 59.38%	+ 6.86%	+ 6.08%
10,679.5	46	Global Flex Port.	N/A	+ 121.36%	+ 40.91%	+ 0.74%	+ 1.94%
52,011.5	220	Balanced Funds	+ 580.98%	+ 197.38%	+ 58.47%	+ 6.84%	+ 6.09%
927.7	13	Balanced Target	N/A	N/A	+ 50.77%	+ 5.03%	+ 5.45%
3,556.3	31	Conv. Securities	+ 636.08%	+ 177.88%	+ 68.54%	+ 3.04%	+ 4.99%
13,752.2	22	Income Funds	+ 541.49%	+ 184.40%	+ 57.70%	+ 6.12%	+ 5.76%
25,018.2	206	World Income Funds	N/A	+ 170.21%	+ 52.09%	+ 1.59%	+ 2.78%
286,548.9	1,419	Fixed Income Funds	+ 399.52%	+ 147.09%	+ 51.07%	+ 2.85%	+ 3.97%
1,206,290.2	4,754	L-T Taxable Fds Aver	+ 599.79%	+ 206.74%	+ 60.05%	+ 4.79%	+ 4.34%
		Medians	+ 582.37%	+ 193.65%	+ 55.91%	+ 4.28%	+ 4.90%
		Funds with % Change	392	665	1,546	3,909	4,688

Securities Market Indexes

Value			03/31/80- 03/31/95	03/31/85- 03/31/95	03/31/90- 03/31/95	03/31/94- 03/31/95	12/31/94- 03/31/95
U.S. Equities							
4,157.69		Dow Jones Ind. Avg. xd	+ 429.14	+ 228.21	+ 53.58	+ 14.35	+ 8.43
500.71		S&P 500 xd	+ 390.46	+ 177.16	+ 47.29	+ 12.33	+ 9.03
596.69		S&P Industrials	+ 417.47	+ 195.87	+ 51.38	+ 14.46	+ 8.96
271.04		NYSE Composite xd	+ 370.16	+ 159.12	+ 45.06	+ 9.71	+ 8.01
464.41		ASE Index	+ 298.57	+ 102.28	+ 28.38	+ 4.81	+ 7.09
260.77		Russell 2000 Index ix p	N/A	N/A	+ 59.36	+ 3.87	+ 4.16
International Equities							
1,922.59		DAX Index	N/A	N/A	− 2.33	− 9.87	− 8.73
3,137.90		FT S-E 100 Index	N/A	+ 145.72	+ 39.59	+ 1.67	+ 2.36
1,614.00		Nikkei 225 Average xd	N/A	+ 28.29	− 46.17	− 15.55	− 18.17

Cumulative Performance With Dividends Reinvested

NAV Mil. $ Current Value	No. Funds		03/31/80- 03/31/95	03/31/85- 03/31/95	03/31/90- 03/31/95	03/31/94- 03/31/95	12/31/94- 03/31/95
500.71		S&P 500 Reinvested[1]	+ 773.39	+ 284.58	+ 71.50	+ 15.54	+ 9.73
4,257.69		Dow Jones Industrials[2]	+ 886.59	+ 364.21	+ 79.28	+ 17.61	+ 9.20

Source: *Barron's*, April 10, 1995, p. MW 76. Reprinted by permission of *Barron's*,

BUYING AND SELLING IN THE MARKET

Once you are generally familiar with the market and perhaps decide to invest directly in common stocks or other assets, you will need to set up an account with a retail brokerage house. Some of the largest and better-known retail brokers are Merrill Lynch, Smith Barney, and Prudential Securities, but there are many other good houses, both regional and national. When you set up your account, the account executive (often called stockbroker) will ask you to fill out a card listing your investment objectives, such as conservative, preservation of capital, income oriented, growth plus income, or growth. The account executive will also ask for your social security number for tax reporting, the level of your income, net worth, employer, and other information. Basically, the account executive needs to know your desire and ability to take risk in order to give good advice and proper management of your assets. Later in this section, we will also talk about discount brokers, that is, brokers who charge very low commissions but give stripped-down service.

Cash or Margin Account

The account executive will need to know if you want a cash account or margin account. Either account allows you three business days to pay for any purchase. A cash account requires full payment, while a **margin account** allows the investor to borrow a percentage of the purchase price from the brokerage firm. The percentage of the total cost the investor must pay is called the margin and is set by the Federal Reserve Board. During the great crash in the 1920s, margin on stock was only 10 percent, but it was as high as 80 percent in 1968. It has been at 50 percent since January 1974. The margin percentage is used to control speculation. When the Board of Governors of the Federal Reserve System thinks markets are being pushed too high by speculative fervor, it raises the margin requirement, which means more cash must be put up. The Fed has been hesitant to take action in this area in recent times.

Margin accounts are used mostly by traders and speculators or by investors who think their long-run return will be greater than the cost of borrowing. Most brokerage houses require a $2,000 minimum in an account before lending money, although many brokerage houses have higher limits. Here is how a margin account works. Assume you purchased 100 shares of Texaco at $60 per share on margin and that margin is 50 percent.

Purchase: 100 shares at $60 per share	$ 6,000
Borrow: Cost × (1 – margin percentage)	–3,000
Margin: Equity contributed (cash or securities)	$ 3,000

You can borrow $3,000 or the total cost times (1 – margin percentage). The percentage cost of borrowing is generally 1 to 2 percent above the prime rate, depending on the size of the account. Rather than putting up $3,000 in cash, a customer could put $3,000 of other approved financial assets into the account to satisfy the margin. Not all stocks may be used for margin purchases. The Securities and Exchange Commission publishes a list of approved securities that may be borrowed against.

One reason people buy on margin is to leverage their returns. Assume that Texaco stock rises to $80 per share. The account would now have $8,000 in stock and an increase in equity from $3,000 to $5,000.

100 shares at $80	$ 8,000
Loan	−3,000
Equity (Margin)	$ 5,000

This $2,000 increase in equity creates a 67 percent return on the initial $3,000 of equity. The 67 percent return was accomplished on the basis of only a 33 percent increase in the price of stock ($60 to $80). With the increased equity in the account, the customer could now purchase additional securities on margin.

Margin is a two-edged sword, however, and what works to your advantage in up markets works to your disadvantage in down markets. If Texaco stock had gone to $40, your equity would decrease to $1,000.

100 shares at $40	$ 4,000
Borrowed	−3,000
Equity (Margin)	$ 1,000

Minimum requirements for equity in a margin account are called *minimum maintenance standards* (usually 25 percent). Your equity would now be at minimum maintenance standards where the equity of $1,000 equals 25 percent of the current market value of $4,000. A fall below $1,000 would bring a margin call for more cash or equity. Many brokerage firms have maintenance requirements above 25 percent, and when margin calls are made, the equity often needs to be increased to 35 percent or more of the portfolio value. Normally, you must maintain a $2,000 minimum in your account, so you would have been called for more equity when the stock was at $50 even though the minimum maintenance requirement had not yet been reached.

One feature of a margin account is that margined securities may not be delivered to the customer. In this case, the Texaco stock would be kept registered in the street name of your retail brokerage house (e.g., Merrill Lynch), and your account would show a claim on 100 shares held as collateral for the loan. It is much like an automobile loan; you don't hold title to the car until you have made the last payment. In the use of margin, however, there is no due date on the loan. The use of margin increases risk and is not recommended for anyone who cannot afford large losses or who has no substantial experience in the market.

Long or Short?—That Is the Question

Once you have opened the account of your choice, you are ready to buy or sell. When investors establish a position in a security, they are said to have a **long position** if they purchase the security for their account. It is assumed the reason they purchased the security was to profit on an increase in price over time and/or to receive dividend income.

Sometimes investors anticipate that the price of a security may drop in value. If they are long in the stock, some may sell out their position. Those who have no position at all

may wish to take a **short position** to profit from the expected decline. When you short a security, you are borrowing the security from the broker and selling it with the obligation to replace the security in the future. How you can sell something you don't own is an obvious question. Your broker will simply lend you the security from the brokerage house inventory. If your brokerage house doesn't have an inventory of the particular stock you want to short, the firm will borrow the stock from another broker.

Once you go short, you begin hoping and praying that the price of the security will go down so that you can buy it back and replace the security at a lower price. In a perverse way, bad news starts to become good news. When you read the morning paper, you look for signs of unemployment, high inflation, and rising interest rates in hopes of a stock market decline.

A short sale can only be made on a trade where the price of the stock advances (an uptick), or if there is no change in price, the prior trade must have been positive. These rules are intended to stop a snowballing decline in stock values caused by short sellers.

A margin requirement is associated with short selling, and it is currently equal to 50 percent of the securities sold short. Thus, if you were to sell 100 shares of Dow Chemical short at $70 per share, you would be required to put up $3,500 in margin (50 percent of $7,000). In a short sale, the margin is considered to be good-faith money and obviously is not a down payment toward purchase. The margin protects the brokerage house in case you start losing money on your account.

You would lose money on a short sales position if the stock you sold short starts going up. Assume Dow Chemical goes from $70 to $80. Since you initially sold 100 shares short at $70 per share, you have suffered a $1,000 paper loss. Your initial margin or equity position has been reduced from $3,500 to $2,500.

Initial margin (Equity)	$ 3,500
Loss	−1,000
Current margin (Equity)	$2,500

We previously specified that there is a minimum 25 percent margin maintenance requirement in buying stock. A similar requirement exists in selling short. The equity position must equal at least 30 percent of the *current* value of the stock that has been sold short. In the present example, the equity position is equal to $2,500, and the current market value of Dow Chemical is $8,000 ($80 × 100). Your margin percentage is 31.25 percent ($2,500 ÷ $8,000) or slightly above the minimum requirement. However, if the stock goes up another point or two and your losses increase, you will be asked to put up more margin to increase your equity position.

Of course, if the value of Dow Chemical stock goes down from its initial base of $70, you would be making profits off the bad news. A 20-point drop in Dow Chemical would mean a $2,000 profit on your 100 shares. Most market observers agree that it requires a "special breed of cat" to be an effective short seller. You often need nerves of steel and a contrarian outlook that cannot be easily shaken by good news.

Aside from risk takers, some investors sell short to establish beneficial tax positions. For example, if you had bought Alcoa at $50 and five months later it was $80, you would have a $30 per share profit on paper. If you want to preserve the profit but wait until next

year to pay the tax, you can **sell short against the box**. This means you can short shares against those you already hold. Since you own the stock and also have a short position, you can neither gain nor lose by price movements in the stock. In the following tax year, you can deliver the shares you hold to cover your short position. At that point, you will incur the tax obligations associated with the transactions. The total net profit will still be $30.

One final point on selling short. In the last 10 or 15 years, some investors have chosen to use other ways to take a negative position in a security. These normally involve put and call options, which are discussed in Chapter 15. Both selling short and option transactions can be effectively utilized for strategic purposes.

TYPES OF ORDERS

When an investor places an order to establish a position, he or she has many different kinds of orders from which to choose. When the order is placed with the account executive on a NYSE-listed stock, it is teletyped to the exchange where it is executed by the company's floor broker in an auction market. Each stock is traded at a specific trading post on the floor of the exchange, so the floor broker knows exactly where to go to find other brokers buying and selling the same company's shares.

Most orders placed will be straightforward market orders to buy or sell. The market order will be carried by the floor broker to the correct trading post and will usually trade close to the last price or within ¼ of a point. For example, if you want to sell 100 shares of AT&T at market, you would probably have no trouble finding a ready buyer since AT&T may be trading a few million shares per day. But if you wanted to sell 100 shares of Bemis, as few as 1,000 shares might be traded in a day, and no other broker would be waiting at the Bemis post to make a transaction with the floor broker. If the broker finds no one else wishing to buy the shares, he will transact the sale with the specialist who is always at the post ready to buy and sell 100-share round lots. If the broker wants to sell, the specialist will either buy the shares for her own account at ⅛ to ¼ less than the last trade or will buy out of her book in which special orders of others are kept.

Two basic special orders are the limit order and the stop order. A **limit order** limits the price at which you are willing to buy or sell and assures you will pay no more than the limit price on a buy or receive no less than the limit price on a sell. Assume you are trying to buy a thinly traded stock that fluctuates in value and you are afraid that with a market order you might risk paying more than you want. So you would place a limit order to buy 100 shares of Bell Industries, as an example, at 16½ or a better price. The order will go to the floor broker who goes to the post to check the price. The broker finds Bell Industries trading at its high for the day of 16⅞, and so he leaves the limit order with the specialist who records it in his book. The entry will record the price, date, time, and brokerage firm. There may be other orders in front of yours at 16½, but once these are cleared, and assuming the stock stays in this range, your order will be executed at 16½ or less. Limit orders are used by investors to buy or sell thinly traded stocks or to buy securities at prices thought to be at the low end of a price range and to sell securities at the high end of the price range. Investors who calculate fundamental values have a basic

idea of what they think a stock is worth and will often set a limit to take advantage of what they view to be discrepancies in values.

Many traders are certain they want their order to be executed if a certain price is reached. A limit order does not guarantee execution if orders are ahead of you on the specialist's book. In cases where you want a guaranteed "fill" of the order, a stop order is placed. A **stop order** is a two-part mechanism. It is placed at a specific price like a limit order, but when the price is reached, the stop turns into a market order that will be executed at close to the stop price but not necessarily at the exact price specified. Often, many short-term traders will view a common stock price with optimism for a certain trading strategy. When the stock hits the price, it may pop up on an abundance of buy orders or decline sharply on a large volume of sell orders, and your "fill" could be several dollars away from the top price. Assume AXE Corporation stock has been trading between $25 and $40 per share over the last six months, reaching both these prices three times. A trader may follow several strategies. One strategy would be to buy at $25 and sell at $40 using a stop buy and a stop sell order. Some traders may put in a stop buy at $41 thinking that if the stock breaks through its peak trading range it will go on to new highs, and finally some may put in a stop sell at $24 to either eliminate a long position or establish a short position with the assumption the stock has broken its support and will trend lower. When used to eliminate a long position, a stop order is often called a *stop-loss order.*

Limit orders and stop orders can be "day orders" that expire at the end of the day if not executed, or they can be GTC (good till canceled) orders. GTC orders will remain on the specialist's books until taken off by the brokerage house or executed. If the order remains unfilled for several months, most brokerage houses will send reminders that the order is still pending so that the client does not get caught buying stock for which he or she is unable to pay. Orders have been known to stay on the specialist's books for years.

COST OF TRADING

Since May 1, 1975, commissions have been negotiated between the broker and customer, with larger orders getting smaller percentage charges. Before "May Day," commissions were fixed, and all brokers charged the same fee out of a published table for a given size order. Now there are individual variations, so check with several brokers. If commissions are of concern, you may want to do business with a "discount" broker who charges a discount of 25 to 75 percent from the old fixed-commission schedule.

Discount brokers are bare-bones operators providing only transactions and no research. They have found a niche with those investors who make up their own minds and do not need advice or personal service. The largest national discount broker is Charles Schwab & Co. To get a quote on the commission for a trade , you can call from anywhere in the country with a toll-free number (listed in your phone book). Many banks in local communities may also have subsidiaries that offer discount brokerage services, so you may wish to check with your local financial institution.

Regular brokerage houses still offer more personal service and more variety of services and are often part of a financial corporation involved in underwriting and investment banking, managing mutual funds and pension funds, economic advising,

TABLE 3–5 Example of Round-Lot Commissions

	Full-Service Brokers Shares/Price				
	200 @ $25	300 @ $20	500 @ $15	500 @ $18	1,000 @ $14
Merrill Lynch	129.50	164.85	205.54	225.23	308.28
Smith Barney	139.61	166.39	212.15	235.26	351.51
Prudential	146.35	173.35	218.35	240.35	359.35
Dean Witter	130.59	155.15	197.15	218.50	341.31
	Discount Brokers				
Charles Schwab	89.00	95.60	101.50	106.60	123.60
Fidelity Brokerage	84.75	90.75	97.25	101.75	116.75
Quick & Reilly	60.50	65.00	77.75	81.50	94.00
Olde Discount	60.00	60.00	80.00	80.00	105.00

government bond dealings, and more. Unfortunately, you pay extra when dealing with a full-service broker. Table 3–5 lists the fees for a sampling of full-service brokers and discount brokers.

TAXES

In making many types of investments, an important consideration will be the tax consequences of your investment (taxes may be more significant than the brokerage commissions just discussed).

This section is intended only as a brief overview of tax consequences. For more information, consult a tax guide. Consultation with a CPA, CFP (Certified Financial Planner), or similar sources may also be advisable.

Before we specifically talk about the tax consequences of investment gains and losses, let's briefly look at the new tax rates under the 1993 Revenue Reconciliation Tax Act. The rates are presented in Table 3–6.

Refer to Table 3–6, and assume you have appropriately computed your taxable income after all deductions as $26,300. Further assume you are single so that you fall into the first category of the table. How much is your tax obligation? The answer is shown below.

	Amount	Rate	Tax
1st	$22,100	15%	$3,315
Next	4,200	28%	1,176
	$26,300		$4,491

TABLE 3–6 Tax Rates under the 1993 Revenue Reconciliation Tax Act*

Single

Taxable Income	Rate (%)
0–$22,100	15
$22,100–$53,500	28
$53,500–$115,000	31
$115,000–$250,000	36
Over $250,000	39.6

Married (Joint return)

Taxable Income	Rate (%)
0–$36,900	15
$36,900–$89,150	28
$89,150–$140,000	31
$140,000–$250,000	36
Over $250,000	39.6

*The tax brackets are adjusted slightly in future years to account for inflation.

The total tax is $4,491. The rates of 15 percent and 28 percent are referred to as marginal tax rates. They apply to income within a given tax bracket. The average tax paid is a slightly different concept. It is simply the amount of taxes paid divided by taxable income, or 17.08 percent in this case.

$$\frac{\text{Taxes paid}}{\text{Taxable income}} = \frac{\$\ 4{,}491}{\$26{,}300} = 17.08\%$$

Capital Gains and Loss Treatment

A **capital gain or loss** occurs when an asset held for investment purposes is sold. Under the 1993 Revenue Reconciliation Tax Act, there is no requirement for how long an asset must be held. Also under the 1993 act, the maximum rate on capital gains is 28 percent (11.6 percent less than the maximum rate applied to other forms of income as described in Table 3–6).[4]

In computing capital gains for the year, the investor subtracts losses from gains. Some timing considerations are significant. The most important is that you can deduct up to $3,000 in security transaction losses in a given year against other forms of income. Thus, if you have a salary of $25,000 and you incur $3,000 in stock trading losses, your taxable income will only be $22,000 for that year.

[4] If you are in a tax bracket under 28 percent, that is the tax rate that is applied to capital gains: 28 percent is the maximum, but not the minimum.

Investors have some incentive to take losses (that is, translate dollar losses on paper to actual losses by selling the security or securities) before year-end. Perhaps an investor has sold $5,000 worth of stock at a profit during the year. When December comes, the investor may attempt to identify up to $8,000 of stocks to sell at a loss to cancel out the profit and create the maximum net loss of $3,000 for the year.

While investors should not let tax considerations override sound investment decisions (don't sell a potential long-term winner just for tax considerations), they have many ways to take losses and still maintain their basic position. For example, an investor might take a loss in one oil stock and buy another similar oil company at the same time (sell Exxon and buy Mobil, or vice versa). Furthermore, even a stock that has been sold for tax purposes can be repurchased after 30 days, and the loss is still deductible. Also, investors have many sophisticated ways to use options, convertibles, and other securities to maintain the potential for an upside move in a security they just sold.

One final point in dealing with the timing of losses. Although the maximum net loss (losses minus gains) deduction is $3,000 per year, a person can carry over larger losses to subsequent years and take up to a maximum of $3,000 in each ensuing year. Table 3–7 below examines loss carryover potential for an investor.

We see the investor had net losses of $8,000 in 1995, of which $3,000 was written off against other income, leaving $5,000 to be carried forward. In 1996, another $3,000 was written off so that $2,000 in losses was carried forward to 1997. In 1997, the investor had net losses of $1,800 during the year so that only $1,200 of the remaining $2,000 was utilized to accumulate the maximum $3,000 deduction. This left $800 to be carried over in subsequent years. Although not explicitly shown in the table, if the investor had net

TABLE 3–7 Tax Loss Carryover Analysis

	1995	
$6,000 Gains	$14,000 Losses	$ 8,000 Net losses −3,000 Tax write-off $ 5,000 Tax loss carryover
	1996	
$7,000 Gains	$7,000 Losses	0 Net loss $3,000 Tax write-off (carried over from 1995) $2,000 Remaining tax loss carryover ($5,000 − $3,000)
	1997	
$4,200 Gains	$6,000 Losses	$1,800 Net loss 1,200 Tax loss carryover $3,000 Tax write-off $ 800 Remaining tax loss carryover ($2,000 − $1,200)

WHO CHEATS ON THEIR INCOME TAXES?

Each year the government loses 17 cents out of every dollar due on income taxes because of cheating by taxpayers. The cheating may take the form of not reporting income or taking nonexistent or unjustified deductions. The total loss to the government is more than $100 billion a year. This represents the unpaid taxes of otherwise honest Americans, not the additional tens of billions hidden by drug czars and other hardened criminals. If all taxes were properly collected, a large portion of our federal deficit could be wiped out.

The most frequent offenders are the self-employed. A 1990 Government Accounting Office (GAO) study revealed that auto dealers, restaurateurs, and clothing store operators underreport their taxable income by nearly 40 percent. Doctors, lawyers, barbers, and *accountants* underpay (cheat?) on 20 percent of their revenues. The most proficient of the nonreporters are in the food-service industry. Collectively, waiters and waitresses fail to report 84 percent of their tips, according to the GAO.

Claiming deductions for dependent children that do not exist is another favorite approach. In 1987, the IRS began requiring taxpayers to report and verify the social security numbers of all dependents over five years of age. The following year 7 million fewer dependents were claimed as deductions. It seems that many people had been listing the same child two or three times and even claiming dogs, cats, and birds as tax-deductible dependents.

Of course, not all feel guilty about not paying their full share of taxes. A shipyard manager who did not report income from yacht repairs on the weekend told *Money* magazine, "The government squanders the money I already pay. Why give more?"

Source: Marguerite T. Smith, "Who Cheats on Their Income Taxes?" *Money,* April 1991, pp. 101–8.

gains of $800 in 1998, the loss carry-forward of $800 would simply mean no taxes would be owed on the gains.

IRAs and Taxes

Another important tax consideration for the investor is the use of individual retirement accounts (IRAs) to reduce current tax burdens and accumulate long-term wealth. The process through which a person may deduct $2,000 a year from current income and invest it tax-free until a future withdrawal is covered in detail in Appendix 3A.

SUMMARY

The investor should have a basic understanding of measures of market performance, the rules and mechanics of opening and trading in an account, and tax considerations.

In gauging the movements in the market, the investor may view the Dow Jones Industrial Average, the Standard & Poor's 500 Stock Index, the Standard & Poor's MidCap Index, the Value Line Average of 1,700 companies, or the NASDAQ Averages (to name a few). To evaluate mutual funds, the investor may turn to the Lipper Mutual Fund Investment Performance Averages. There also are a number of bond indexes, and averages for foreign trading. The investor will try to evaluate performance in light of an index that closely parallels the makeup of the investor's portfolio.

In further considering the advisability of using an index to measure comparative performance, the investor may wish to determine whether it is price-weighted,

value-weighted, or equal-weighted. The weighting measure determines how large an effect the movement of an individual security has on the index.

With some understanding of the various markets and the related means of measurements for those markets (such as the DJIA), the potential investor is now in a position to consider opening an account. The investor may establish either a cash or margin account and use the account to buy securities or to sell short (in which case a margin account is necessary). The investor can also execute a number of different types of orders such as a market order, a limit order, and a stop order. The latter two specify prices where the investor wishes to initiate transactions.

The investor must also consider the tax consequences of his or her actions. Although no one likes to sustain losses from investment activity, when they do occur, they should be properly utilized to shelter other income. The IRS allows a maximum deduction of $3,000 per year, and losses larger than $3,000 can be carried forward. Finally, the investor may wish to route a portion of investments through an individual retirement account (IRA) because the initial contribution is tax deductible and subsequent funds grow tax-free until withdrawn at retirement. This topic is discussed in Appendix 3A.

KEY WORDS AND CONCEPTS

DISCUSSION QUESTIONS

1. Why is the Dow Jones Industrial Average considered a "blue-chip" measure of value?
2. How is the Dow Jones Industrial Average adjusted for stock splits?
3. What are the criticisms and a defense of the Dow Jones Industrial Average?
4. Explain the price-weighted average concept as applied to the Dow Jones Industrial Average.
5. What categories of stocks make up the Standard & Poor's 500 Stock Index?
6. Why was the Standard & Poor's MidCap Index created? What is the size range for firms in the index?
7. What is a value-weighted index? Explain the impact that large firms have on value-weighted indexes such as the S&P 500.

8. What is an equal-weighted average? Which average has this characteristic?
9. Fill in the table at the bottom of the page for the type of weighting system for the various indexes. Put an (x) under the appropriate weighting system.
10. If you did not wish a high-priced or heavily capitalized firm (one with high total market value) to overly influence your index, which of the weighting systems described in this chapter would you be likely to use?
11. Why might one say that the Wilshire 5000 Equity Index is the most comprehensive market measure?
12. If the Russell 2000 Index is outperforming the Russell 1000 Index, what can you generally assume about the relative performance of smaller versus larger stocks?
13. How many countries and sectors of the world are covered in the Dow Jones World Stock Index? Looking at the last column of Table 3–2, what was the percentage change in the Asia/Pacific Index since year-end? If you excluded Japan from the Asia/Pacific Index, what is the percentage change since year-end?
14. Explain the difference between a cash and a margin account.
15. What is meant by the concept of minimum maintenance standards (or requirements) for margin?
16. Why is bad news "good news" to the short seller?
17. Explain how selling short against the box allows one to defer taxes until the following year.
18. Explain what is meant by a limit order. How does a stop order differ from a limit order?
19. What is the difference between day orders and GTC orders?
20. What do you give up and what do you gain when you use a discount broker in preference to a regular broker?
21. What is the difference between the meaning of the marginal tax rate and the average tax rate for a taxpayer?
22. What is the maximum amount of investment losses that can be deducted against other forms of income in any given year? What happens if the losses exceed this amount?

	Price-Weighted	Value-Weighted	Equal-Weighted
NYSE Composite Index	______	______	______
Value Line Average	______	______	______
S&P 500 Index	______	______	______
Dow Jones Industrial Average	______	______	______
NASDAQ Composite	______	______	______

PROBLEMS

Computing an index

1. Assume the following five companies are used in computing an index.

Company	Shares Outstanding	Base Period, January 1, 1972 Market Price	Current Period December 31, 1995 Market Price
A	6,000	$ 6	$12
B	2,000	5	18
C	10,000	8	40
D	1,000	20	10
E	4,000	15	32

a. If the index is price-weighted, what will be the value of the index on December 31, 1995? (Take the average price on December 31, 1995, divide by the average price on January 1, 1972, and multiply by 100.)

b. If the index is value-weighted, what will be the value of the index on December 31, 1995? (Take the total market value on December 31, 1995, divide by the total market value on January 1, 1972, and multiply by 100.)

c. Explain why the answer in part *b* is different from the answer in part *a*.

Changing index values in a value-weighted index

2. Assume the following stocks make up a value-weighted index.

Corporation	Shares Outstanding	Market Price
Reese	4,000	$35
Robinson	16,000	4
Snider	6,000	10
Hodges	40,000	20

a. Compute the total market value and the weights assigned to each stock. (The weights may add up to slightly more than 100 percent due to rounding.)

b. Assume the price of the shares of the Snider Corporation go up by 50 percent, while those of the Hodges Corporation go down by a mere 10 percent. The other two stocks remain constant. What will be the newly established value for the index?

c. Explain why the index followed the pattern it did in part *b*.

Changing values in a value-weighted index

3. In problem 2, if the initial price of the shares of the Snider Corporation double while those of the Hodges Corporation go down by 7.5 percent, would the value of the index change? The other two stocks remain constant. Do the necessary computations.

Margin purchase

4. Assume you buy 100 shares of stock at $40 per share on margin (50 percent). If the price rises to $55 per share, what is your percentage gain on the initial equity?

Margin purchase

5. In problem 4, what would the percentage loss on the initial equity be if the price had decreased to $28?

Minimum margin

6. Assume you have a 25 percent minimum margin standard in problems 4 and 5. With a price decline to $28, will you be called upon to put up more margin to meet the 25 percent rule? Disregard the $2,000 minimum margin balance requirement.

Minimum margin

7. Recompute the answer to problem 6 based on a stock decline to $23.75.

Selling short

8. You sell 100 shares of Norton Corporation short. The price of the stock is $60 per share. The margin requirement is 50 percent.
   a. How much is your initial margin?
   b. If the stock goes down to $42, what is your percentage gain or loss on the initial margin (equity)?
   c. If stock goes up to $67.50, what is your percentage gain or loss on the initial margin (equity)?
   d. In part *c,* if the minimum margin standard is 30 percent, will you be required to put up more margin? (Do the additional necessary calculations to answer this question.)

Margin purchase and selling short

9. You are very optimistic about the personal computer industry, so you buy 200 shares of Microtech Inc. for $45 a share. You are very pessimistic about the machine tool industry, so you sell short 300 shares of King Tools Corporation at $55. Each transaction requires a 50 percent margin balance.
   a. What is the initial equity in your account?
   b. Assume the price of each stock closes as follows for the next three months (month-end). Compute the equity balance in your account for each month.

Month	Microtech Inc.	King Tools Corp.
October	$51	$48
November	39	62
December	37	40

Computing commissions

10. Assume an investor is going to buy 500 shares of stock at $18 per share. Based on the data in Table 3–5:
    a. How much will the commission be if the shares are purchased through Prudential? What is the commission if the shares are purchased through Quick & Reilly?
    b. What percent is the discount broker's commission of the full-service broker's commission?

Computing tax obligation

11. Compute the tax obligation for the following using Table 3–6.
    a. An individual with taxable income of $36,500.
    b. A married couple with taxable income of $116,250.
    c. What is the average tax rate in part *b?*

Tax loss carryover

12. Sam Nelson had the following stock transactions in 1995:

Stock X	$ 6,000	gain
Stock Y	10,000	loss
Stock Z	8,000	loss

a. How much of the loss can he deduct against 1995 income from other sources?
b. How much is his tax loss carryover?

Tax loss carryover

13. Assume that in the next three years Sam Nelson (from problem 12) has the following gains and losses:

	1996	1997	1998
Gains	$5,000	$9,000	$4,500
Losses	7,000	5,000	3,500

How much of the loss carryover computed in problem 12*b* will he use in each of the three years? Recall the maximum net loss write-off in any one year is $3,000. Also, you must take your loss write-offs as quickly as allowed.

Tax loss carryover

14. Alice Tomkins has the following completed security transactions in 1995:

Stock X	$8,000	gain
Stock Y	$4,000	loss
Stock Z	$2,000	gain

She also is holding three stocks in her current portfolio:

Alpha	$5,000	unrealized gain
Beta	2,000	unrealized loss
Gamma	7,000	unrealized loss

An unrealized gain or loss simply means that the gain or loss is on paper, but the stock has not yet been sold.

a. In order for Alice to realize a maximum net $3,000 loss for tax purposes in 1995, what stocks in her portfolio should she sell?
b. Would she always want to follow this course of action?

THE WALL STREET JOURNAL PROJECTS

1. A current picture of Figure 3–1, entitled "The Dow Jones Industrial Average," can be found in *The Wall Street Journal* on page C3. Please find the update, and describe the recent market trend over the last six months.
2. a. A current update of Table 3–1, entitled "Stock Market Data Bank," is also available in *The Wall Street Journal* on page C2. Compare the performance of the various stock indexes over the last 12 months by looking at the 365-day percentage change. Which indexes are performing best? Worst?

b. Are small stocks outperforming or underperforming large stocks? What indexes did you use to reach your conclusions?
c. Are there some economic or market reasons for the difference in these performance measurements?
d. When you compare the performance of the Dow Jones Industrial Average to the Standard & Poor's 500 Stock Index for the 365-day period, what accounts for the fact that these two indexes are not performing at the same percentage rates?

CRITICAL THOUGHT CASE

Elaine and Izzy Polanski have been happily married for the last 10 years. Elaine is a systems engineer for a major West Coast aerospace company, and Izzy is a pilot for a commuter airline flying out of Los Angeles International Airport. Together they anticipate a taxable income of $98,000.

Both Elaine and Izzy are concerned about their potential large tax obligation of $22,909. As the end of the year approached, the Polanskis began to think of ways to reduce their anticipated taxable income. Izzy suggested that they evaluate their stock portfolio to see if they might sell off a stock or two to create a deduction against taxable income. They have six stocks in their portfolio, and only one was trading at a loss from its original purchase price. They hold 500 shares of Atlantic Cellular Company, and the stock has fallen from $58 to $38 a share due to poor third-quarter earnings.

Before they make a decision to sell, the Polanskis completed an intensive investigation of the company and found that the company was still fundamentally sound. It is their view that investors overreacted to the poor third-quarter earnings announcement and that prospects for the fourth quarter looked considerably better. Furthermore, the Polanskis think that Atlantic Cellular Company has an excellent chance of winning a major contract with the U.S. Treasury Department on the installation and use of sophisticated telephone communication equipment. The other bidder on the contract is Atlas Corp., a firm in which the Polanskis currently hold 1,000 shares. Since the Polanskis purchased the stock, it has gone from $10 to $25.

To get a better feel for how the competition on the contract might turn out, Izzy told Elaine he might give Gordon Lewis a call. Mr. Lewis is currently the Vice President of Corporate Development at Atlantic Cellular Company and was Izzy's roommate in college. Elaine isn't sure this is such a good idea. Izzy countered with the argument that it is always best to be as fully informed as possible before making a decision and that Elaine, as a systems engineer, should know this better than anyone.

Questions

1. Do you think Izzy Polanski should call Gordon Lewis, his old college roommate, to get information on the contract bid?
2. Regardless of your answer to question 1, do you think the Polanskis should sell their stock in Atlantic Cellular Company? If they do sell the stock, what's the maximum deduction they can take from their taxable income this year?
3. What strategy do you recommend with their holdings in Atlas Corp.?

U.S. EQUITIES ONFLOPPY EXERCISES

Please use your U.S. Equities OnFloppy software and manual to complete the following exercises.

1. a. The "Portfolios" option of U.S. Equities OnFloppy contains several predefined portfolios including the portfolio containing the Dow Jones Industrial Average (DJI) stocks and the Standard & Poor's (S&P) 500 stocks.
   b. Are any of the DJI stocks not listed on the NYSE?
   c. How many of the S&P 500 stocks are listed on the NYSE? How many are listed on the AMEX?
2. a. Assuming an equal percentage change in the price of all firms included in the DJI average, find the five firms that would have the largest impact on the change in the DJI average.
   b. Assuming an equal percentage change in the price of all firms included in the S&P 500 index, find the five firms that would have the largest impact on the change in the S&P 500 index.
3. a. Use the nine major SIC categories of industry found in the U.S. Equities OnFloppy database, and determine the percentage distribution by industry for the companies of the DJI average.
   b. Construct a similar percentage distribution by industry for the companies of the S&P 500.

SELECTED REFERENCES

Market Indexes

Chakravarty, Subrata, and Dana Wechsler Liden. "Dow Jones: A Belt, Suspenders and Elastic Waistband." *Forbes,* February 3, 1992, pp. 69–74.

Peters, Edgar E. "A Chaotic Attractor: The S&P 500." *Financial Analysts Journal,* March–April 1991, pp. 55–62.

Schultz, John W. "Misleading Averages." *Barron's,* July 7, 1977, p. 5.

Stock Trading

Alexander, Gordon J. "Short Selling and Efficient Sets." *Journal of Finance,* September 1993, pp. 1497–1506.

Chan, K. C. "On the Contrarian Investment Strategy." *Journal of Business,* April 1988, pp. 147–64.

Ippolito, Richard A., and John A. Turner. "Turnover, Fees, and Pension Plan Performance." *Financial Analysts Journal,* November–December 1987, pp. 16–26.

Shepard, Lawrence. "How Good Is Investment Advice for Individuals?" *Journal of Portfolio Management,* Winter 1977, pp. 32–36.

Woolridge, J. Randall, and Amy Dickinson. "Short Selling and Common Stock Prices." *Financial Analysts Journal,* January–February 1994, pp. 20–28.

Brokerage Services

Brennan, Michael J., and Tarun Chordia. "Brokerage Commission Schedules." *Journal of Finance,* September 1993, pp. 1379–1402.

Groth, John C.; Wilbur G. Lewellen; Gary G. Schlarbaum; and Ronald C. Lease. "An Analysis of Brokerage House Securities Recommendations." *Financial Analysts Journal,* January–February 1979, pp. 32–40.

APPENDIX 3A: More Information on IRAs and Taxes

An individual retirement account (IRA) allows some taxpayers to deduct $2,000 from taxable income and invest the funds at a bank, savings and loan, brokerage house, or other financial institution. Not only is the $2,000 allowed to be deducted from earned income to reduce current taxes, but the income is allowed to grow tax-free until withdrawn at retirement. For the young investor who meets Internal Revenue Service restrictions, the use of IRAs may be particularly appropriate as an investment vehicle. Instead of investing $2,000 directly in the market, an investor may wish to set up an IRA with a brokerage house so that he or she can deduct the $2,000 from earned income before it is invested. While an individual may qualify for a $2,000 deduction, a couple filing a joint return may qualify for a $2,250 deduction if there is only one working spouse and $4,000 if there are two working spouses who aren't covered in employer pension plans. The money initially put into an IRA must be earned income and not gifts from others, inheritance funds, and so forth.

In Table 3A–1, we look at the potential accumulation in an IRA account based on annual contributions of $2,000 and various compound rates of growth on the funds. Note that the age at which contributions began and the compounding rate are both significant. For example, a person who begins contributions at age 25 and earns a 10 percent return will accumulate $1,437,810 at age 70. If the same person had waited to age 45, the accumulation at age 70 (based on a 10 percent growth rate) would only be $196,694.

When you begin to withdraw funds from your IRA in later life, you do have to pay your normal tax rate on your annual withdrawals (but you have had the potential for tremendous tax-free accumulation up to that point). It should be pointed out that one can wait to begin withdrawing funds until anywhere from age 59½ up to age 70½ (it's up to you to choose). At that time, you must withdraw a specified minimum amount each year based on your life expectancy and the amount of funds in your IRA. One disadvantage of withdrawing funds before age 59½ is that you pay a 10 percent penalty on the early

TABLE 3A–1 Value of IRA Fund at Age 70 ($2,000 annual contribution)

	Compound Annual Rate of Return			
Age Contributions Begin	8 Percent	10 Percent	12 Percent	14 Percent
20	$1,147,540	$2,327,817	$4,800,036	$9,989,043
25	773,011	1,437,810	2,716,640	5,181,130
30	518,113	885,185	1,534,183	2,684,050
35	344,634	542,049	863,327	1,387,145
40	226,566	329,988	482,665	713,574
45	146,212	196,694	266,668	363,742
50	91,524	114,550	144,105	182,050
55	54,304	63,545	74,559	87,685
60	28,973	31,875	35,097	38,675

withdrawal as well as the normal tax rate on the funds withdrawn (this depends on your marginal tax bracket).

Because IRAs can be such an advantageous way to make stock market investments or draw interest on savings instruments, the IRS restricts the use of IRAs for those who *also* participate in work-related retirement plans. In Table 3A–2, we see the phaseout of allowable annual contributions to an IRA for those who participate in such work-related plans. For example, an individual who makes $30,000 and is in a work-related plan can contribute only $1,100 annually to an IRA as a tax-deductible item. If an individual is not in a work-related retirement plan, he or she can take the full $2,000 taxable deduction regardless of income level. Even those individuals who do not qualify for the $2,000 deduction can still put the funds in an IRA and allow them to grow tax-free until retirement. The taxpayer does not get the initial $2,000 deduction from income, but the subsequent return on the funds grows tax-free until retirement.

In summary, IRAs are generally a desirable way to shelter income from taxation initially (if you qualify) and allow it to grow tax-free until retirement. IRAs, however, are not a desirable investment if you are likely to have a liquidity problem one or two years after you make the contribution and end up having to pay a 10 percent withdrawal penalty[5] as well as your normal taxes on the funds withdrawn. Also, even if you make a contribution to an IRA in one year, you are not required to make a similar contribution in subsequent years (though the accumulations in Table 3A–1 are based on regular annual contributions).

TABLE 3A–2 Phaseout of Allowable IRA Contributions for Taxpayers in a Work-Related Pension Plan

Individual		Joint Filing		
Income Level	**Maximum IRA Deduction**	**Income Level**	**Married, One Spouse Works**	**Married, Two Spouses Work**
$25,000	$2,000	$40,000	$2,250	$4,000
26,000	1,900	41,000	2,138	3,800
27,000	1,700	42,000	1,913	3,400
28,000	1,500	43,000	1,688	3,000
29,000	1,300	44,000	1,463	2,600
30,000	1,100	45,000	1,238	2,200
31,000	900	46,000	1,013	1,800
32,000	700	47,000	788	1,400
33,000	500	48,000	563	1,000
34,000	300	49,000	338	600
35,000	100	50,000	113	200
Over $35,000	0	Over $50,000	0	0

[5] Generally, the break-even point for using an IRA is about five years. That is, it takes about that long for the tax advantages to overcome the withdrawal penalty.

DISCUSSION QUESTIONS

3A–1. Explain why IRAs offer the potential for large wealth accumulation if contributions are made on a regular basis.

3A–2. During what age "time frame" does one normally begin withdrawing funds from an IRA? What are the consequences if funds are withdrawn before this?

3A–3. If a person does not participate in a work-related pension plan, is there any restriction on income level as far as making tax deductible contributions to an IRA?

3A–4. Assuming a taxpayer(s) qualifies for an IRA, what is the maximum deduction for (*a*) an individual, (*b*) a couple filing a joint return if only one spouse works, and (*c*) a couple filing a joint return where both spouses work?

PROBLEMS

3A–1. **a.** Morris Logan, a bachelor, has an income level of $31,000 and participates in a work-related pension plan. What is the maximum contribution (deduction) he can make to an IRA?

b. His sister, Susan, is self-employed as a lawyer and makes $40,000 a year. She also is unmarried. What is the maximum contribution (deduction) she can make to an IRA?

c. Assume Susan makes her maximum contribution from age 30 to age 70 and receives a 12 percent return on her funds. How much will she accumulate at age 70?

4

Sources of Investment Information

We are continually exposed to much information in this world of expanding and rapid communications. As the scope of investments has grown to include more than stocks and bonds, investment information has expanded to cover items such as gold and silver, diamonds, original art, antiques, stamps and coins, real estate, farmland, oil and gas, commodities, mutual funds, and other specialized assets. The problem investors are faced with is not only which investments to choose from the many available, but also where to find relevant information on specific investments.

First, the investor needs a basic knowledge of the economic environment. After determining the economic climate, the investor will proceed to a more detailed analysis of industries and unique variables affecting a specific investment. It is often said that the sign of an educated person is whether he or she knows where to find information to make an intelligent decision. The rest of this chapter will attempt to provide a list and descriptions of the basic information sources for some of the more common forms of investments as well as sources for general economic data.

You may want to refer to this chapter as you go through the chapters that follow. This chapter is not intended to be a guide for analysis—only an overview of what information is available. You may have heard the phrase "a picture is worth a thousand words." You will find that is certainly true of the tables and figures in this chapter. It is virtually impossible to discuss each and every variable found in them. To acquaint yourself more fully with information sources, we suggest you visit your college and local library and browse through their collections of economic and financial services. Appendix 4A at the end of the chapter contains the addresses of a number of the sources mentioned in the chapter.

AGGREGATE ECONOMIC DATA

Economic data are necessary for analyzing the past and predicting trends. The economic environment that exists today and the one expected in the future will bear heavily on the types of investments selected when creating or managing an investment portfolio. Information on inflation, wages, disposable income, interest rates, money supply, demographic trends, and so on are important economic data that will influence investor decisions. This information is available in many publications from the government, commercial banks, and periodicals. What follows is a brief description of some of the major sources of economic data.

Federal Reserve Bulletin

The *Federal Reserve Bulletin* is published monthly by the Board of Governors of the Federal Reserve System, Washington, D.C. It contains an abundance of monetary data such as money supply figures, interest rates, bank reserves, and various statistics on commercial banks. Fiscal variables such as U.S. budget receipts and outlays and federal debt figures are also found in the *Bulletin.* This publication also contains data on international exchange rates and U.S. dealings with foreigners and overseas banks.

A complete description of the *Federal Reserve Bulletin* is outside the scope of this chapter, but a partial listing of the table of contents will provide a better idea of what information it contains. Each heading may be divided into more detailed sections that

provide information for the previous month, the current year on a monthly basis, and several years of historical annual data.

Domestic Financial Statistics
Federal Reserve Banks
Monetary and Credit Aggregates
Commercial Banks
Financial Markets
Federal Finance
Securities Markets and Corporate Finance
Real Estate
Consumer Installment Credit
Domestic Nonfinancial Statistics
International Statistics
Securities Holdings and Transactions
Interest and Exchange Rates

Federal Reserve Banks

The 12 Federal Reserve banks in the Federal Reserve System represent different geographical areas (districts) of the United States. Each bank publishes its own monthly letter or review that includes economic data about its region and sometimes commentary on national issues or monetary policy. The 12 banks by district are as follows: Boston (1), New York (2), Philadelphia (3), Cleveland (4), Richmond (5), Atlanta (6), Chicago (7), St. Louis (8), Minneapolis (9), Kansas City (10), Dallas (11), and San Francisco (12).

Federal Reserve Bank of St. Louis

One district bank, the Federal Reserve Bank of St. Louis, publishes some of the most comprehensive economic statistics on a weekly and monthly basis. *U.S. Financial Data* is published weekly and includes data on the monetary base, bank reserves, money supply, a breakdown of time deposits and demand deposits, borrowing from the Federal Reserve banks, and business loans from the large commercial banks. The publication also includes yields and interest rates on a weekly basis on selected short-term and long-term securities. An example of these published interest rates appears in Figures 4–1 and 4–2 on pages 95 and 96.

Monetary Trends, published monthly, includes charts and tables of monthly data. The information is similar to that found in *U.S. Financial Data* but covers a longer time period. The tables provide compound annual rates of change, while the graphs include the raw data with trend changes over time. Additional data are available on the federal government debt and its composition by type of holder and on the receipts and expenditures of the government for both the National Income Account Budget and the High Employment Budget.

National Economic Trends is also published by the Federal Reserve Bank of St. Louis and presents monthly economic data on employment, unemployment rates, consumer and producer prices, industrial production, personal income, retail sales, productivity, com-

FIGURE 4–1 Federal Reserve Bank of St. Louis: Weekly Yields

YIELDS ON SELECTED SECURITIES

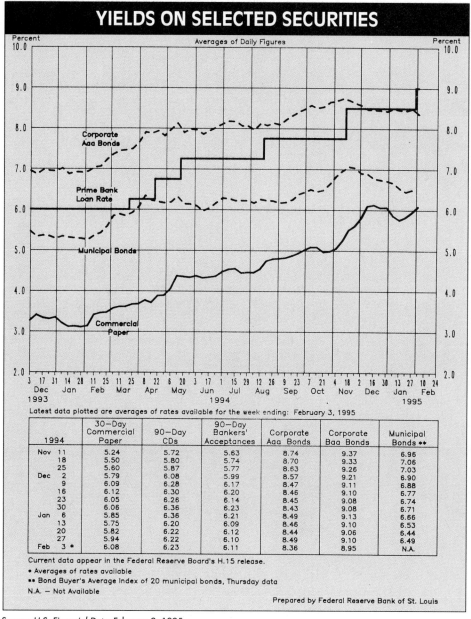

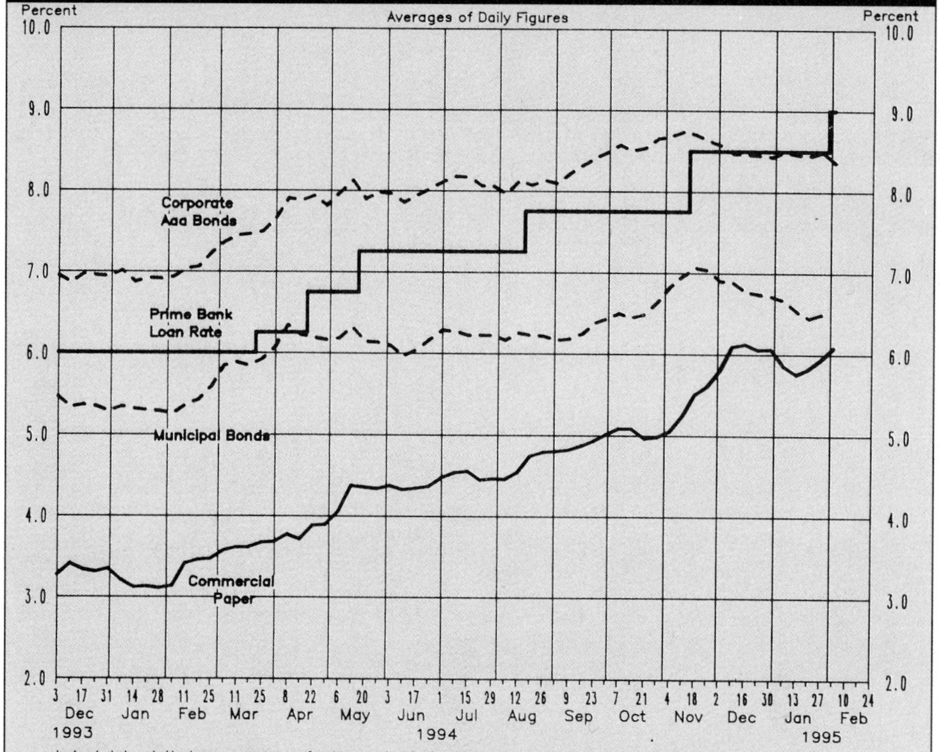

Latest data plotted are averages of rates available for the week ending: February 3, 1995

1994	30-Day Commercial Paper	90-Day CDs	90-Day Bankers' Acceptances	Corporate Aaa Bonds	Corporate Baa Bonds	Municipal Bonds **
Nov 11	5.24	5.72	5.63	8.74	9.37	6.96
18	5.50	5.80	5.74	8.70	9.33	7.06
25	5.60	5.87	5.77	8.63	9.26	7.03
Dec 2	5.79	6.08	5.99	8.57	9.21	6.90
9	6.09	6.28	6.17	8.47	9.11	6.88
16	6.12	6.30	6.20	8.46	9.10	6.77
23	6.05	6.26	6.14	8.45	9.08	6.74
30	6.06	6.36	6.23	8.43	9.08	6.71
Jan 6	5.85	6.36	6.21	8.49	9.13	6.66
13	5.75	6.20	6.09	8.46	9.10	6.53
20	5.82	6.22	6.12	8.44	9.06	6.44
27	5.94	6.22	6.10	8.49	9.10	6.49
Feb 3 *	6.08	6.23	6.11	8.36	8.95	N.A.

Current data appear in the Federal Reserve Board's H.15 release.

* Averages of rates available

** Bond Buyer's Average Index of 20 municipal bonds, Thursday data

N.A. – Not Available

Prepared by Federal Reserve Bank of St. Louis

Source: *U.S. Financial Data,* February 2, 1995.

FIGURE 4–2 Federal Reserve Bank of St. Louis: Weekly Interest Rates

SELECTED INTEREST RATES

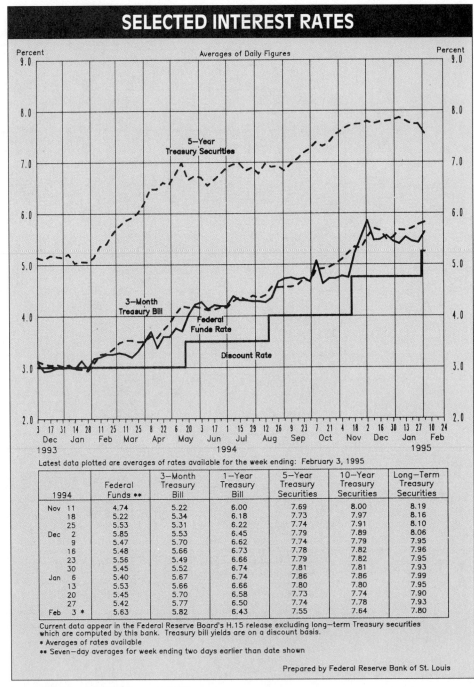

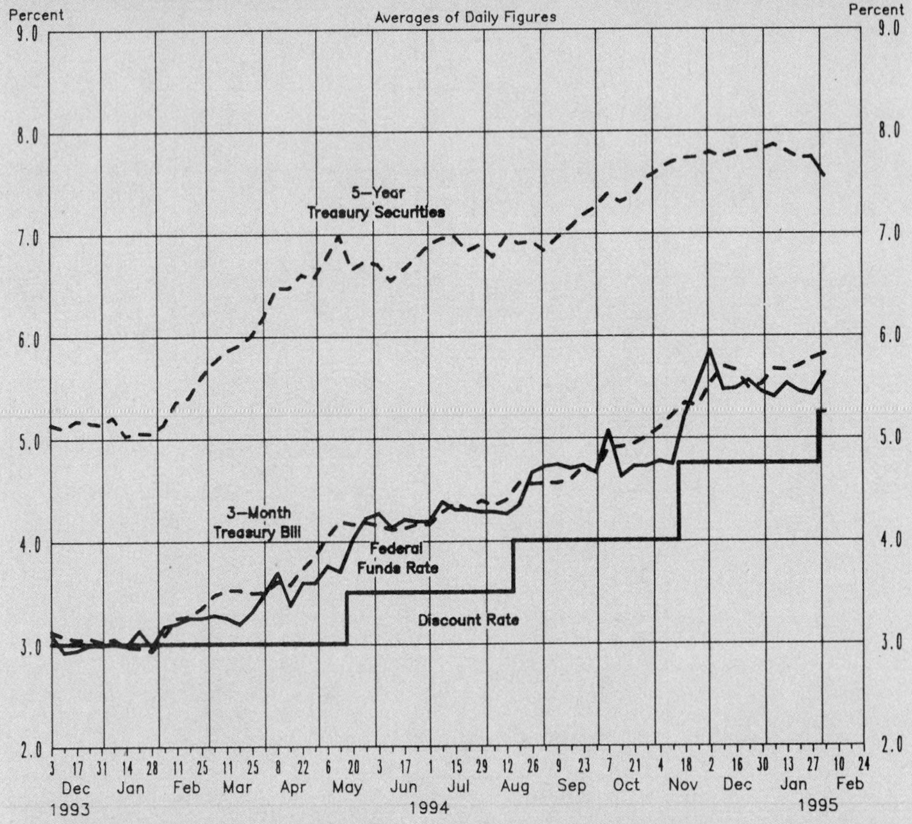

Latest data plotted are averages of rates available for the week ending: February 3, 1995

1994	Federal Funds **	3-Month Treasury Bill	1-Year Treasury Bill	5-Year Treasury Securities	10-Year Treasury Securities	Long-Term Treasury Securities
Nov 11	4.74	5.22	6.00	7.69	8.00	8.19
18	5.22	5.34	6.18	7.73	7.97	8.16
25	5.53	5.31	6.22	7.74	7.91	8.10
Dec 2	5.85	5.53	6.45	7.79	7.89	8.06
9	5.47	5.70	6.62	7.74	7.79	7.95
16	5.48	5.66	6.73	7.78	7.82	7.96
23	5.56	5.49	6.66	7.79	7.82	7.95
30	5.45	5.52	6.74	7.81	7.81	7.93
Jan 6	5.40	5.67	6.74	7.86	7.86	7.99
13	5.53	5.66	6.66	7.80	7.80	7.95
20	5.45	5.70	6.58	7.73	7.74	7.90
27	5.42	5.77	6.50	7.74	7.78	7.93
Feb 3 *	5.63	5.82	6.43	7.55	7.64	7.80

Current data appear in the Federal Reserve Board's H.15 release excluding long-term Treasury securities which are computed by this bank. Treasury bill yields are on a discount basis.
* Averages of rates available
** Seven-day averages for week ending two days earlier than date shown

Prepared by Federal Reserve Bank of St. Louis

Source: *U.S. Financial Data,* February 2, 1995.

pensation and labor costs. It also contains information on gross domestic product (GDP), the implicit price deflator for the GDP, personal consumption expenditures, gross private domestic investment, government purchases of goods and services, disposable personal income, corporate profit after taxes, and inventories. This information is presented in graphic form and in tables showing the compounded annual rate of change on a monthly basis. If raw data are needed, other economic publications are required.

Survey of Current Business

The *Survey of Current Business* is published monthly by the Bureau of Economic Analysis of the U.S. Department of Commerce. During 1991, the Commerce Department stopped publishing the *Business Conditions Digest,* and the *Survey of Current Business* now serves as the major outlet for economic time series data. It also contains a monthly update and evaluation of the business situation, analyzing such data as gross national product (GNP), GDP, business inventories, personal consumption, fixed investment, exports, labor market statistics, financial data, and much more. For example, personal consumption expenditures are broken down into subcategories of durable goods, such as motor vehicles and parts and furniture and equipment; nondurables, such as food, energy, clothing, and shoes; and services.

The survey can be extremely helpful for industry analysis because it breaks data into basic industries. For example, data on inventory, new plant and equipment, production, and more can be found for such specific industries as coal, tobacco, chemicals, leather products, furniture, and paper. Even within industries such as lumber, production statistics can be found on hardwoods and softwoods right down to Douglas fir trees, southern pine, and western pine. To provide a more comprehensive view of what is available in the *Survey of Current Business,* a list of the major series updates follows:

GNP, GDP
National Income
Personal Income
Industrial Production
Housing Starts and Permits
Retail Trade
Labor Force, Employment and Earnings
Manufacturers' Shipments, Inventories and Orders
Consumer Price Index
Producer Price Index
Construction Put in Place
Banking
Consumer Installment Credit
Stock Prices
Value of Exports and Imports
Motor Vehicles

The *Survey of Current Business* includes many graphical presentations of economic time series data including the leading, lagging, and coincident indicators as shown in Figure 4–3 on page 98. Overall, the *Survey* can be very helpful in understanding past economic behavior and in forecasting future economic activity with a higher degree of success.

Other Sources of Economic Data

So far, we have presented the basic sources of economic data. Many more sources are available. What is available to each investor may vary from library to library, so here are some brief notes on other sources of data.

FIGURE 4–3 Cyclical Indicators (Composite indexes and their components)

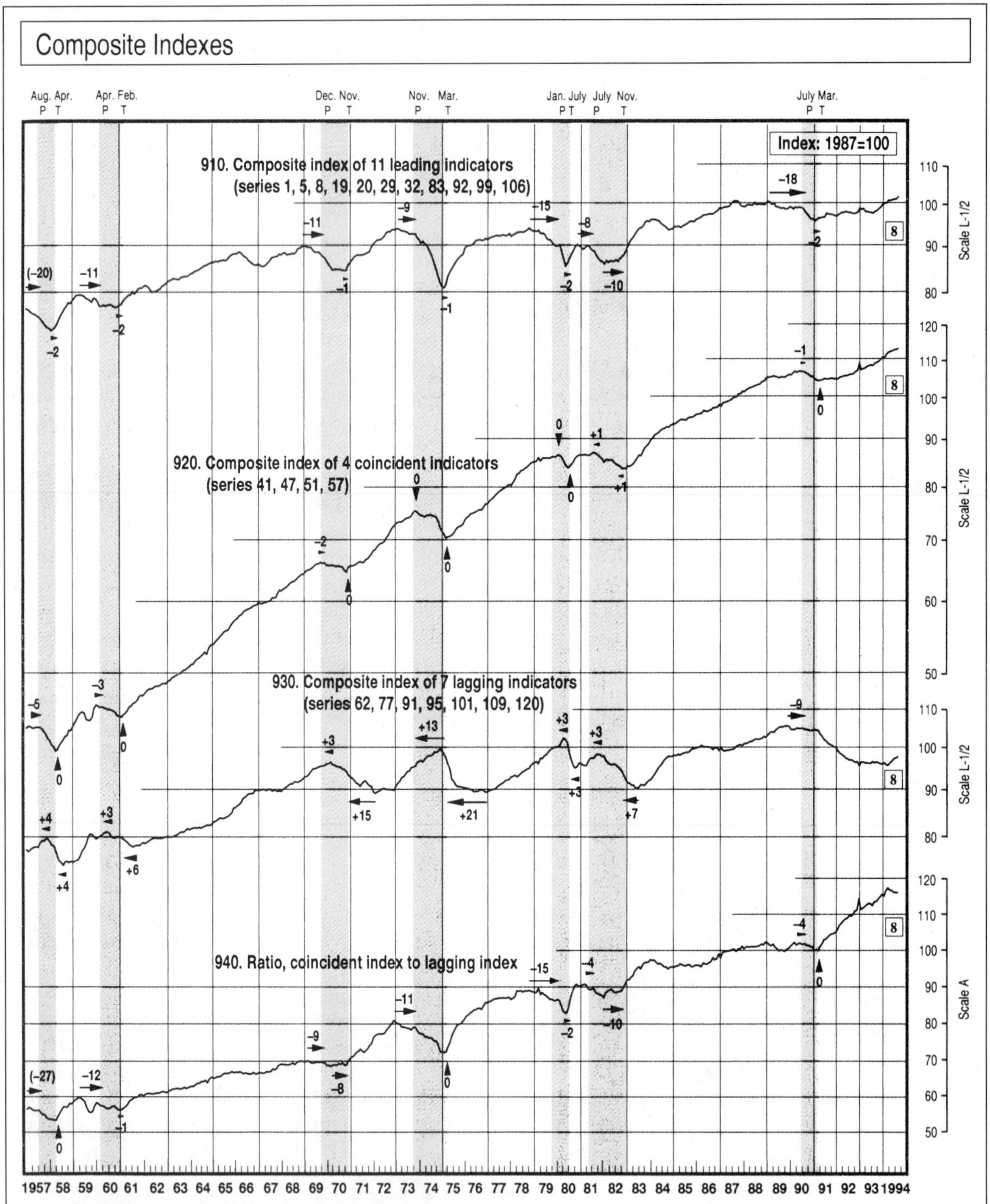

NOTE.—The numbers and arrows indicate length of leads (-) and lags (+) in months from business cycle turning dates. Current data for these series are shown on page C-1.

Source: *Survey of Current Business* (Washington, D.C.: U.S. Department of Commerce Bureau of Economic Analysis, September 1994), p. C-7.

Many universities have bureaus of business research that provide statistical data on a statewide or regional basis. Major banks, such as Citicorp, J. P. Morgan, Harris Trust, and Bank of America, publish monthly or weekly letters or economic reviews, including raw data and analysis. Several other government sources are available, such as *Economic Indicators* prepared by the Council of Economic Advisors and the *Annual Economic Report of the President.* Additionally, many periodicals, such as *Business Week, Fortune,* and *Barron's,* contain raw data as well as economic commentary. Moody's and Standard & Poor's investment services (introduced on the following pages) both publish economic data along with other market-related information.

INVESTMENT ADVISORY SERVICES

Investment information and advice is available from many sources—from large corporate financial services to individuals writing investment letters. A look through such financial magazines as *Barron's, Forbes,* and *Financial World* will turn up hundreds of investment services charging fees large and small for the information they sell. Most public libraries and universities subscribe from several of the major publishers, such as Moody's, Standard & Poor's, or Value Line.

Moody's

Moody's is owned by Dun & Bradstreet and publishes several databases for bonds and stocks. *Moody's Manuals* are widely used and present historical financial data on the companies listed, their officers, and the companies' general corporate condition. The *Manuals* are divided into several categories (Banks and Finance, Industrial, Municipals and Government, OTC Industrial, Public Utility, and Transportation). Each manual has a biweekly news supplement that updates quarterly earnings, dividend announcements, mergers, and other news of interest. *Moody's Manuals* are comprehensive, with each category taking up one or two volumes and several thousand pages.

Moody's Bond Record, a monthly publication, contains data on corporates, convertibles, government and municipal bonds, and ratings on commercial paper and preferred stock. Corporate bond information includes the interest coupon, payment dates, call price, Moody's rating, and yield to maturity. The current price as well as the yearly and historical high-low prices are presented. The total amount of the bond issue outstanding is given with a designation for a sinking fund and the original issue date. Data on convertible bonds also include the conversion price, conversion value, and conversion period. Information on industrial revenue and municipal bonds is usually limited to the Moody's rating. *Moody's Bond Record* also contains historical yield graphs for various types of bonds over at least 30 years.

Moody's also publishes a weekly *Bond Survey* that reviews the week's activity in the bond market, rating changes, new issues, and bonds called for redemption. *Moody's Dividend Record* presents quarterly dividends and the date of declaration, date of record, date payable, and ex-dividend dates. This is an annual publication. *Moody's Handbook of Common Stock* is a quarterly reference guide that summarizes a company's 10-year historical financial data along with a discussion of corporate background, recent developments, and prospects. Approximately 1,000 companies are listed in the *Handbook.*

Only a brief description has been given for each Moody's publication, but enough has been presented for you to know whether a particular one may be worth looking at further.

Standard & Poor's

A second major source of information is the Standard & Poor's Corporation, a subsidiary of McGraw-Hill. Standard & Poor's has very comprehensive coverage of financial data. The following items will not all be discussed, but they provide a good look at what Standard & Poor's makes available to the investor.

Services for Business and Investment Decision Making

Fundamental Company Information
- Corporation Records
- Stock Guide
- Bond Guide
- Stock Reports
- Mutual Fund Profiles
- S&P Compustat

Broad Spectrum Industry Information
- Industry Surveys
- Statistical Service
- Analyst's Handbook
- Industry Reports

Investment Advisory Services
- The Outlook
- Emerging and Special Situations
- Private Label Newsletters
- S&P New Issues Institutional Research

Services Dealing with Indexes, Charting, and Stock Prices
- S&P Index Services
- S&P 100 Information Bulletin
- S&P 500 Information Bulletin
- Daily Stock Price Record
- Trendline Chart Services

Electronically Delivered Services
- S&P MarketScope
- Corporations CD-ROM
- S&P Corporate Descriptions Online
- S&P Daily News Online
- Standard & Poor's Register Online
- S&P ComStock
- Stock Guide/Bond Guide Database
- Index Alert

Law Publications
- Review of Securities and Commodities Regulation
- Review of Banking and Financial Services

Directory Services
- Standard & Poor's Register of Corporations, Directors, and Executives
- Compmark Data Services
- Security Dealers of North America
- Money Market Directory

Standard & Poor's Corporation Records are similar to *Moody's Manuals* except they are organized alphabetically rather than by trade categories. The *Corporation Records* are published monthly, and the six volumes are updated by daily supplements. Information found in the volumes includes historical company background, financial statements, news announcements, earnings updates, and other news of general interest. Companies found in the *Corporation Records* are listed, and their subsidiary companies are cross-listed.

Something that may be overlooked when examining the *Corporation Records* is the statistical section found in the T–Z volume. The statistical section includes a mutual fund summary, an address list of many no-load mutual funds, and foreign bond statistics. Special tables contained in the T–Z volume list new stock and bond offerings on a monthly basis. This volume also presents a classified index of industrial companies listed

by standard industrial classification (SIC) code numbers. For example, if you want to find out about cereal breakfast food companies, you would first find the corresponding SIC number for cereal breakfast foods, which is listed in alphabetical order. The number, 2043, then leads you to the cross-listing of companies. These are the companies one would find listed under *2043 Cereal Breakfast Foods:*

General Mills, Inc.
Gerber Products Co.
Grist Mill Co.
Heinz (H. J.) Co.
Kellogg Company
Nestlé S. A.
The Quaker Oats Co.
RJR Nabisco, Inc.
Ralston Purina Co.

All of these companies make up an industry classification and may be found in the *Corporation Records.* This industry listing can be helpful when trying to compile a list of companies for an industry analysis.

Several other Standard & Poor's publications are quite useful and present concise, thumbnail sketches of companies, common stock variables, and corporate bonds. Table 4–1 on pages 102–103 depicts two pages from the *Stock Guide.* This is a monthly publication that enables investors to take a preliminary look at the common and preferred stock of several thousand companies and hundreds of mutual funds. The introduction to the *Stock Guide* presents name changes, new exchange listings, common stock rating changes, and a graph of Standard & Poor's Stock Price Indexes.

The *Bond Guide* has the same format as the *Stock Guide.* A monthly publication in booklet form, it presents data on corporate and convertible bonds. Table 4–2 on page 104 shows one page on corporate bonds with a long list of Connecticut Light and Power bonds at the top. The Standard & Poor's rating is presented along with other information. Table 4–3 on page 105 shows one page of convertible bonds from the *Bond Guide.* Looking at the table, we see convertible bonds having different coupons, interest payment dates, and maturities. Again, the Standard & Poor's rating is given. All the conversion data are presented with bond prices and common stock prices. Can you find how many shares of common stock an investor will receive for each $1,000 bond of Advest Group?[1]

One of the more popular of Standard & Poor's publications is the *Corporation Reports.* These reports are often mailed from brokerage houses to customers who want basic information on a company. In Table 4–4 on pages 106–107, Hewlett-Packard provides a good example of what one would expect to find in such reports. This information can be compared to the entry in Table 4–1, line 15, for Hewlett-Packard to see the difference in the depth of coverage between the *Corporation Reports* and the *Stock Guide.* The *Corporation Reports* are contained in three separate multiple-volume sets, the New York Stock Exchange Stocks, American Stock Exchange Stocks, and Over-the-Counter and Regional Stocks. Each company is updated quarterly with new earnings, dividends, and recent developments. To develop an appreciation for the other Standard & Poor's services, peruse this material at your library.

---

[1] The answer is 73.69 shares.

TABLE 4–1 Sample Pages, *Standard & Poor's Stock Guide*

96 HEL-HOM

Standard & Poor's

¶ S&P 500 · # MidCap 400 · ✧ SmallCap 600 · • Options

Index	Ticker	Name of Issue (Call Price of Pfd. Stocks)	Market	Com. Rank. & Pfd. Rating	Par Val.	Inst. Hold Cos	Inst. Hold Shs. (000)	Principal Business	Price Range 1971-92 High	1971-92 Low	1993 High	1993 Low	1994 High	1994 Low	Nov. Sales in 100s	November, 1994 Last Sale Or Bid High	Low	Last	%Div Yield	P-E Ratio
1	HHGR	✓Helian Health Group	NNM	NR	1¢	11	1091	Oper out-patient surgery ctrs	10⅜	4½	9	3¾	6¾	4⅛	534	6⅛	5½	5⅝	...	17
2	ZAP	✓Helionetics Inc	AS,Ch,Ph	C	No	13	553	Mfr electronic power prod	29	1¼	7½	1¾	6¼	1⅝	15380	2⅜	1⅝	1⅝B	...	d
3	HELX	✓Helix Technology	NNM	B	1	49	4646	Mfr of cryogenic equipment	9½	3/16	8¾	4¼	19	6¾	18215	19	14	15¼	2.9	18
4	HHH	✓Helm Resources	AS,Ch	C	1¢	7	32	Mkts thermoplastic resins	101¼	7/16	2 5/16	⅞	2	13/16	486	1	13/16	13/16B	...	d
¶5•[1]	HP	✓Helmerich & Payne	NY,B,Ch,Ph	B	10¢	237	16866	Contract driller:o&g prod'n	54⅛	2 5/16	37½	22¼	31⅜	24¾	8501	31⅜	27¾	28	1.8	33
6	HLM	✓Helmstar Group	AS,Ch	C	10¢	1	2	Merchant banking	13⅜	¼	1⅛	9/16	⅞	½	526	¾	½	9/16	...	d
7	HEMA	✓HemaCare Corp	NSC	C	No	8	243	Therapeutic blood services	14¼	¾	8¾	5	7¾	2⅞	2503	4	2⅞	3¼	...	d
8•[2]	HEM	✓Hemlo Gold Mines	AS,Ph	NR	No	84	21257	Gold mining Ontario, Canada	10⅛	5⅞	12⅜	5⅜	11⅞	8½	9959	10¾	9⅛	9¼	◆e1.6	14
9	JKHY	✓Henry(Jack) & Assoc	NNM	B	1¢	27	3080	Data process'g svcs to banks	9¾	⅜	12¾	7¾	11⅞	6½	7633	10¼	8⅜	10⅛	2.0	18
10•[3]	HERB	✓Herbalife Intl	NNM	B–	1¢	66	6075	Weight ctrl/hlth care prod	14½	⅜	18½	8	31	15¼	33381	18⅝	15¼	16	5.5	10
¶11•[3]	HPC	✓Hercules, Inc	NY,B,Ch,P,Ph	B	No	478	32154	Chemical & plastics prod'r	73½	12¼	114⅞	63¼	121½	96⅜	28716	119¾	110⅝	114⅜	2.0	19
12	HERS	✓Heritage Finl Svcs	NNM	A–	0.625	27	1433	Commercial banking,Illinois	14	4⅞	17½	12¾	19¾	15¾	1007	18	16	16¾	2.1	12
13	HTG	✓Heritage Media'A'	AS,Ch,Ph	NR	1¢	78	10054	Broadcasting, in-store adv	23	5⅝	19⅞	8⅜	25¼	15¾	7185	25¼	23⅜	24	...	d
¶14•[4]	HSY	✓Hershey Foods	NY,B,Ch,P,Ph	A+	1	384	22723	Mfr chocolate,candy,pasta	48⅜	1 7/16	55⅞	43½	53½	41⅛	25729	48⅜	45⅞	46¾	2.8	16
¶15•[5]	HWP	✓Hewlett-Packard	NY,B,C,Ch,P,Ph	A	1	994	148848	Electr data:measure/test instr	85	3¾	89¼	64⅜	102½	71⅞	240589	102½	94⅛	97¾	1.2	16
16	HXL	✓Hexcel Corp	NY,Ch,P,Ph	D	1¢	25	2789	Honeycomb cores: plastics	43	1⅞	11¼	2⅛	6⅝	2¾	3665	5⅜	4	4¼	...	d
✧17	HLO	✓Hi-Lo Automotive	NY,Ch,Ph	NR	1¢	58	6520	Retail auto parts/accessories	21½	9⅜	20¾	9½	14⅝	9¼	2445	11¾	10⅛	10¼	...	12
18	HSI	✓Hi-Shear Indus	NY,Ch,Ph	C	10¢	24	3076	Mfr aerospace technology sys	24⅛	2 1/16	6¼	3½	6¾	4¼	568	5⅞	4⅞	4⅞	...	d
19	HSR	✓Hi-Shear Technology	AS,Ch,Ph	NR	.001	1	2	Electr/ordnance prod&sys	....	....	....	....	14¼	3⅜	29069	14¼	3⅞	9⅞	...	d
✧20•[6]	HIB	✓Hibernia Corp Cl'A'	NY,Ch,Ph	C	No	130	35785	Commercial bkg,Louisiana	26	1 9/16	9⅛	5⅞	9⅛	7¼	25333	8½	7⅜	7⅞	3.0	9
21	HICKA	Hickok Elec Instrument'A'	NSC	B	1	2	12	Mfr auto diagnostic equip	24¾	4	24	13½	32½	18	26	32½	27½	29B	1.0	11
22	HIPC	✓High Plains Corp	NNM	B–	10¢	23	1745	Production/mktg of ethenol	8⅛	1/32	9⅜	3⅛	11½	4⅝	22687	11½	8⅞	11⅛	...	d
23	HIW	✓Highwoods Properties	NY,Ch,Ph	NR	1¢	49	4344	Real estate investment trust	....	....	....	....	21⅝	18½	2474	20¾	18½	18⅞	9.0	..
✧24	HRH	✓Hilb,Rogal & Hamilton	NY	B+	No	65	5700	Operates insurance agencies	20⅝	5⅜	16⅞	11⅜	13⅜	11⅛	2349	12⅛	11⅛	11¼	5.0	14
25	HILI	✓Hilite Industries	NNM	NR	1¢	4	197	Mfr automotive components	....	....	....	....	10⅜	6¾	1121	9	7½	8½	...	13
26•[3]	HB	✓Hillenbrand Indus	NY,B,Ch,Ph	A+	No	180	27228	Burial caskets,hosp eq,lugg.	43⅝	11/16	48⅝	36½	43⅝	26⅝	13778	31⅜	29⅜	29⅞	1.9	24
✧27•[4]	HIL	✓Hillhaven Corp(New)	NY,Ch	NR	15¢	126	12111	Operates nursing homes	21⅞	4⅜	21¼	12¾	24	17⅜	10256	22¼	20⅜	21¼	...	10
28	HDS	✓Hills Stores	NY	NR	1¢	57	6068	Regional discount retailer	....	....	21⅝	17½	23	18	5550	21⅛	19½	20⅛	...	9
29	Pr	Sr'A'vtg cm Cv Pfd(20)	NY	NR	No	17	1935		....	....	20½	17¾	22¾	18¼	653	20⅞	19½	20⅛B	...	..
¶30•[7]	HLT	✓Hilton Hotels	NY,B,Ch,P,Ph	B+	2½	314	20103	Own/manage hotels & casinos	115½	1⅛	61	41½	74	49¾	53941	72	57	69½	1.7	28
31	HRSH	✓Hirsch Intl Corp'A'	NNM	NR	1¢	12	519	Distrib embroidery machines	....	....	....	....	9½	6⅞	936	9¼	8	9	s...	10
32•[6]	HIT	✓Hitachi,Ltd ADR[58]	NY,B,Ch,P,Ph	NR	[58]..	79	3544	Elec eq, ind mchy: Japan	145	2⅜	84¾	55½	110⅞	72	1613	103¾	95¾	97½	1.0	50
33	HMG	✓HMG/Courtland Prop	AS	NR	1	4	69	Real estate investment trust	25¼	2⅛	7⅝	4⅜	13¾	6½	13	9¼	8⅞	8⅞	...	4
34	HDT	HMG Digital Tech	AS,Ch	NR	1¢	8	1473	Replication audio/video tapes	6⅜	4⅛	8½	6¼	8¾	5⅛	1455	7¼	6⅜	6⅞	...	46
35	WS.A	'A'wrrt(Pur1com at$6.75)	AS	....	..	..	...		....	....	2	1	2	¾	401	1⅜	1⅛	1⅜	...	..
36	WS.B	'B'wrrt(Pur1com at$7.50)	AS	....	..	..	...		....	....	1⅛	⅞	1⅜	7/16	1331	⅞	⅝	¾B	...	..
37	HMNF	✓HMN Financial	NNM	NR	1¢	8	337	Savings & loan, Minnesota	....	....	....	....	13¾	9⅜	11972	11⅝	9⅜	10⅛	...	..
38	HOEN	Hoenig Group	NNM	NR	1¢	8	332	Global securities broker, svcs	8⅝	4	6¼	3¼	4⅞	3⅜	4140	4	3⅜	3¾	e2.7	11
39	HOGN	✓Hogan Systems	NNM	B	1¢	50	7381	Software prod for bank'g ind	26¼	2	12	5⅝	10⅞	5⅛	12747	6½	5¼	6¼	2.7	17
40	HOL.A	✓Holco Mtge Accept I	AS	NR	1¢	..	...	Invest in GNMA ctfs	7½	2 1/16	2⅞	1½	3⅜	1⅜	95	3	2⅝	2⅝B	...	9
41	HOC	✓Holly Corp	AS,Ph	B	1¢	56	4368	Petroleum refin'g & mktg	41	½	30½	25⅜	33⅜	23¾	485	26½	24¼	25¾	1.6	10
42	HLY	✓Holly Residential Prop[63]	NY	NR	1¢	59	5422	Real estate investment trust	....	....	25¾	19⅞	20¼	13¼	6289	14⅜	13¼	13¾	13.1	19
43	HWCC	✓Hollywood Casino'A'	NNM	NR	.0001	34	5688	Casino gaming operations	....	....	32¾	12	15¼	5	8689	6½	5	5	...	6
44•[8]	HLYW	✓Hollywood Entertainment	NNM	NR	No	59	7464	Oper video rental superstores	....	....	14½	4⅝	35⅛	10	39395	35⅛	28½	33¼	...	65
✧45•[9]	HPRK	✓Hollywood Park	NNM	NR	10¢	74	7824	Horse racing track	17	2¼	35	8⅝	30¾	9¾	16670	13½	9¾	10¼	...	d
46	HLPH	✓Holophane Corp	NNM	NR	1¢	37	2540	Mfr lighting fixtures,systems	....	....	17½	14½	19¼	15¼	3188	18½	15¼	15¾	...	11
47	HBENB	✓Home Beneficial[64]Cl'B'	NNM	A–	.3125	51	5946	Hldg:life,accident,health	29	1 9/16	26½	21½	23	19½	1345	21	19½	20¾	3.9	10
¶48•[10]	HD	✓Home Depot	NY,B,Ch,P,Ph	A–	5¢	882	268803	Bldg mtls,home improv strs	51½	3/16	50⅞	35	48¼	36½	275342	48¼	44½	46¼	0.3	34
49	HHI	✓Home Holdings	NY,Ch	NR	1¢	30	4218	Insur:property & casualty	....	....	17⅜	17	18½	3	15908	7⅜	3	5⅜	...	d

Uniform Footnote Explanations-See Page 1. Other: [1]NY:Cycle 3. [2]ASE,CBOE:Cycle 2. [3]ASE:Cycle 3. [4]ASE:Cycle 2. [5]CBOE:Cycle 2. [6]CBOE:Cycle 1. [7]P:Cycle 1. [8]CBOE,NY:Cycle 1. [9]CBOE:Cycle 3. [10]Ph:Cycle 2. [51]Stk dstr of Tri-Lite Inc,'94. [52]Incl Chapt 11 liabilities. [53]Spl div. [54]Accum on pfd. [55]Incl current amts. [56]4 Mo May'90. [57]®$1.74,'94. [58]ADR's represent'g 10 com par yen 50. [59]Approx. [60]If com exceeds $8.50 - 20 trad days(of30). [61]If com exceeds $8.50 - 20trad.days(of30). [62]To be determined. [63]Vote Dec 14 on Wellsford Redident'l offer,0.75 com. [64]Non-voting.

Source: *Standard and Poor's Stock Guide*, December 1994.

TABLE 4–1 Sample Pages, *Standard & Poor's Stock Guide (concluded)*

Common and Convertible Preferred Stocks

HEL-HOM 97

Splits ◆ Index	Cash Divs. Ea. Yr. Since	Dividends: Latest Payment Period $	Date	Ex. Div.	Total $ So Far 1994	Ind. Rate	Paid 1993	Financial Position Mil-$: Cash& Equiv.	Curr. Assets	Curr. Liab.	Balance Sheet Date
1	....	None Since Public			...	Nil	....	4.40	15.1	3.87	8-31-94
2	....	h[51]....	7-1-94	5-25	h[51]...	Nil	....	5.96	34.5	18.7	6-30-94
3◆	1987	Q0.11	11-15-94	10-26	0.29	0.44	0.20¼	5.35	29.8	9.13	9-30-94
4◆	....	None since 1962			...	Nil	....	0.26	3.99	4.00	6-30-94
5	1959	Q0.12½	12-1-94	11-8	0.49	0.50	0.48	54.0	136	41.8	6-30-94
6	....	None Since Public			...	Nil	....	Equity per shr $1.23			6-30-94
7	....	None Paid			...	Nil	....	1.15	3.25	1.36	9-30-94
8	1987	g†0.20	12-15-94	11-10	g†0.35	0.20	g†0.30	158	179	66.7	j3-31-94
9◆	1990	Q0.05	12-15-94	11-16	0.19½	0.20	0.175	15.2	22.7	12.0	9-30-94
10	1992	Q0.22	11-3-94	10-21	0.76	0.88	0.38	90.0	166	70.3	9-30-94
11	1913	Q0.56	12-21-94	11-28	2.24	2.24	2.24	80.1	1166	810	9-30-94
12◆	1987	Q0.09	11-15-94	10-25	0.36	0.36	0.32	Book Value $8.31			9-30-94
13◆	....	None Since Public			...	Nil	....	5.34	61.5	71.7	9-30-94
14	1930	Q0.32½	12-15-94	11-15	1.25	1.30	1.14	34.7	1067	944	10-02-94
15	1965	Q0.30	1-11-95	12-15	1.10	1.20	0.90	2475	11909	7669	7-31-94
16	....	0.11	11-16-92	10-27	...	Nil	....	File bankruptcy Chapt 11			
17	....	None Since Public			...	Nil	....	1.03	84.5	28.8	6-30-94
18	....	0.05½	8-30-90	8-20	...	Nil	....	0.39	34.6	12.0	8-31-94
19	....	None Since Public			...	Nil	....	3.99	11.6	5.07	8-31-94
20	1993	Q0.06	11-22-94	10-31	0.19	0.24	0.03	Book Value $5.29			6-30-94
21	1989	[53]0.30	1-25-94	12-28	0.30	0.30	0.25	0.35	8.52	2.51	6-30-94
22◆	....	None Paid			...	[54]Nil	....	0.13	4.02	6.26	6-30-94
23	1994	0.50	11-16-94	10-31	0.50	1.70	....	Equity per shr $14.93			6-30-94
24◆	1987	Q0.14	12-30-94	12-9	0.50	0.56	0.45	40.3	86.8	82.9	9-30-94
25	....	None Since Public			...	Nil	....	2.55	15.3	6.59	9-30-94
26◆	1948	Q0.143	11-25-94	10-17	0.57	0.57	0.45	181	566	257	8-27-94
27◆	....	None Since Public			...	Nil	....	56.7	255	207	8-31-94
28	....	None Since Public			...	Nil	....	4.70	452	301	7-30-94
29	....	None Since Public			...	Nil	....	Cv into 1 com, $20			
30	1946	Q0.30	12-23-94	12-5	1.20	1.20	1.20	370	602	305	9-30-94
31	....	5%Stk	8-10-94	7-13	5%Stk	Stk	....	7.80	23.0	11.8	7-31-94
32◆	1951	[59]0.474		9-23	[59]0.947	0.95	0.858	20760	56276	34717	3-31-94
33	....	0.15	9-28-90	9-10	...	Nil	....	Equity per shr $19.09			12-31-93
34	....	None Since Public			...	Nil	....	0.26	12.8	12.3	5-01-94
35	....	Terms&trad. basis should			be checked in detail			Wrrts expire 7-28-97			
36	....	Terms&trad. basis should			be checked in detail			Wrrts expire 7-28-97			
37	....	None Since Public			...	Nil	....	Book Value $14.98			6-30-94
38	1993	Q0.02½	1-6-95	12-19	†0.12½	0.10	0.075	Equity per shr $3.26			6-30-94
39	1991	0.17	6-16-94	5-24	0.17	0.17	0.17	1.64	43.8	28.3	6-30-94
40	1988	0.02	12-1-94	10-26	0.96	[62]...	0.14	Equity per shr $1.54			6-30-94
41◆	1988	Q0.10	10-21-94	10-3	0.37½	0.40	0.30	3.30	152	133	7-31-94
42	1993	Q0.45	10-12-94	9-26	1.80	1.80	0.51	Equity per shr $15.30			9-30-94
43	....	None Since Public			...	Nil	....	48.0	89.2	80.3	6-30-94
44◆	....	None Since Public			...	Nil	....	49.7	59.5	17.3	9-30-94
45◆	....	0.048	3-31-92	3-9	...	Nil	....	64.8	77.0	33.9	6-30-94
46	....	None Since Public			...	Nil	....	13.7	51.5	28.3	9-30-94
47◆	1906	Q0.20	12-9-94	11-14	0.79½	0.80	0.77½	Equity per shr $27.15			9-30-94
48◆	1987	Q0.04	12-21-94	12-1	0.15	0.16	0.11¼	441	2289	1291	7-31-94
49	....	None Since Public			...	Nil	....	Equity per shr $9.05			6-30-94

Index	Capitalization: Lg Trm Debt Mil-$	Shs. 000 Pfd.	Com.	Earnings $ Per Shr. Years End	1990	1991	1992	1993	1994	Last 12 Mos.	Interim Earnings Period	$ per Shr. 1993	1994	Index
1	6.45	...	5438	Nv	0.33	0.26	0.35	d0.55	....	0.33	9 Mo Aug	d0.62	0.26	1
2	1.62	497	25169	Dc	d1.94	d0.06	d0.38	P0.12	....	d0.13	9 Mo Sep	0.16	d0.09	2
3	0.05	...	9666	Dc	0.12	0.33	0.30	Δ0.51	....	0.87	9 Mo Sep	Δ0.37	0.73	3
4	4.55	47	2161	Dc	*0.90	d4.05	Δd3.00	Δ0.11	....	d0.31	9 Mo Sep	Δ0.04	□d0.38	4
5	5.00	...	24702	Sp	1.97	0.88	0.45	1.01	PΔ0.86	0.86				5
6	....	...	6005	Dc	d1.42	d0.48	0.17	d0.23	....	d0.19	6 Mo Jun	d0.09	d0.05	6
7	0.38	...	5366	Dc	d0.33	d0.07	d0.25	d0.55	....	d0.46	9 Mo Sep	d0.42	d0.33	7
8	....	...	96786	Dc	0.27	0.15	0.43	0.47	....	j0.65	9 Mo Sep	0.33	0.51	8
9	....	...	11680	Je	d0.05	0.21	0.36	Δ0.46	0.52	0.55	3 Mo Sep	0.12	0.15	9
10	1.05	...	29921	Dc	d0.13	0.33	0.79	1.47	....	1.68	9 Mo Sep	1.14	1.35	10
11	323	...	39168	Dc	2.04	■2.01	3.69	□4.86	E6.00†	5.93	9 Mo Sep	□3.48	4.55	11
12	....	...	7905	Dc	0.76	0.96	1.18	1.34	....	1.46	9 Mo Sep	0.99	1.11	12
13	340	...	±17512	Dc	Δd3.08	Δd2.40	□d1.51	Δd0.32	....	d0.44	9 Mo Sep	Δd0.52	d0.64	13
14	159	...	±86753	Dc	±▲2.39	±2.43	±2.69	□±3.31	E3.00	2.87	9 Mo Sep	□±2.27	±1.83	14
15	572	...	254229	Oc	3.06	3.02	□3.49	4.65	P6.14	6.14				15
16	[52]181	...	7310	Dc	0.53	0.58	□Δd2.99	Δd12.34	....	d7.77	9 Mo Sep	Δd8.32	d3.75	16
17	33.5	...	10704	Dc	0.77	□0.80	0.89	0.64	E0.84	0.79	9 Mo Sep	0.54	0.69	17
18	9.83	...	5855	My	0.24	d3.01	*0.36	d1.41	d0.96	d0.97	3 Mo Aug	d0.05	d0.06	18
19	0.11	...	6500	My	...	...	...	p0.10	d0.38	d0.24	3 Mo Aug	d0.11	0.03	19
20	....	...	p96883	Dc	d0.40	□d5.12	□d0.27	0.58	E0.90	0.77	9 Mo Sep	□0.44	0.63	20
21	....	10	±598	Sp	±1.33	±0.95	±2.03	±2.54	....	2.59	9 Mo Jun	±1.20	±1.25	21
22	10.2	25	10931	Je	*0.14	*0.16	0.34	Δ0.62	d0.08	d0.07	3 Mo Sep	0.05	0.06	22
23	[55]24.5	...	8986	Dc	...	...	...	p0.80	....	....	9 Mo Sep	n/a	p0.97	23
24	3.49	...	14769	Dc	0.17	0.57	0.71	0.61	....	0.83	9 Mo Sep	0.50	0.72	24
25	2.05	...	4900	Je	0.12	0.19	0.31	0.53	0.66	0.67	3 Mo Sep	0.18	0.19	25
26	215	...	71162	Nv	1.02	1.22	Δ1.47	2.04	E1.25	1.32	9 Mo Aug	1.41	0.69	26
27	580	96	27328	My	p[56]Nil	0.10	d3.85	□1.65	□[57]2.06	2.09	3 Mo Aug	0.31	0.34	27
28	288	5000	9943	Ja	...	...	...	p2.14	....	2.28	9 Mo Oct	p0.35	0.49	28
29	....	5000	...	Ja	...	...	...	....	....	....	Mand red 10-5-2008,$20			29
30	1195	...	48068	Dc	2.34	1.76	2.17	Δ2.14	E2.50	2.40	9 Mo Sep	Δ1.47	1.73	30
31	0.74	...	±4765	Ja	d0.03	0.23	0.54	p0.76	....	0.91	6 Mo Jul	p0.34	0.49	31
32	9954	...	3281724	Mr	4.68	2.78	2.00	1.95	....	1.95				32
33	13.4	...	1167	Dc	d0.51	d0.75	0.47	1.37	....	2.26	3 Mo Mar	d0.10	0.79	33
34	13.1	4	6129	Jl	...	...	...	0.25	P0.15	0.15				34
35	....	...	1354	Jl	...	...	...	....	....	....	Callable at 5¢[60]			35
36	....	...	...	Jl	...	...	...	....	....	....	Callable at 5¢[61]			36
37	36.3	...	6086	Dc	...	...	...	p0.97	....	....	6 Mo Jun	n/a	p0.38	37
38	....	...	10084	Dc	p0.18	p0.25	0.38	0.45	....	0.34	9 Mo Sep	0.36	0.25	38
39	....	...	14383	Mr	0.30	0.14	0.38	Δ0.39	....	0.37	6 Mo Sep	Δ0.12	0.10	39
40	14.4	...	564	Dc	0.60	0.38	0.16	0.20	....	0.29	9 Mo Sep	0.13	0.22	40
41	68.8	...	8254	Jl	2.90	1.42	0.33	□2.42	2.51	2.51				41
42	[55]128	...	7980	Dc	...	...	p0.38	p0.70	....	0.73	9 Mo Sep	p0.49	0.52	42
43	425	...	23748	Dc	*Δd1.63	d0.97	d1.81	□0.02	....	0.79	9 Mo Sep	d0.34	0.43	43
44	4.94	...	14388	Dc	pd0.04	p0.05	p0.18	p0.28	....	0.51	9 Mo Sep	p0.19	0.42	44
45	44.6	28	18314	Dc	d0.38	*0.30	*0.25	0.25	....	d0.05	9 Mo Sep	0.28	d0.02	45
46	32.8	...	7705	Dc	...	...	pΔ0.88	p1.21	....	1.46	9 Mo Sep	p0.94	1.19	46
47	....	...	±17564	Dc	±3.28	±2.51	□±2.50	±2.35	....	2.07	9 Mo Sep	±1.79	±1.51	47
48	841	...	451958	Ja	0.45	0.60	0.82	1.01	E1.35	1.25	9 Mo Oct	0.76	1.00	48
49	[55]755	...	±34814	Dc	...	...	p□1.95	□d14.94	....	d2.21	9 Mo Sep	d16.11	□d3.38	49

◆**Stock Splits & Divs By Line Reference Index** [3]2-for-1,'93,'94. [4]1-for-15 REVERSE,'93. [9]3-for-2,'92,'93:4-for-3,'94. [12]2-for-1,'92. [13]1-for-4 REVERSE,'92. [22]6-for-5,'94(twice):3-for-2,'94. [24]5-for-4,'90. [26]2-for-1,'92. [27]1-for-5 REVERSE,'93. [32]Adj for 5%,'90. [41]No adj for recap,'85:Spl $ dstr,'89. [44]3-for-2,'94. [45]7-for-4,'92:5-for-4,'93. [47]2-for-1,'92. [48]3-for-2,'90,'92:4-for-3,'93.

TABLE 4–2 Page from *Standard & Poor's Bond Guide* (Corporate bonds)

Title-Industry Code & Co. Finances (In Italics) / Individual Issue Statistics / Exchange	Interest Dates (Ind)	S&P Debt Rating (1991)	Date of Last Rating Change (1992)	Prior Rating	Eligible (1993)	Bond Form (Year End)	Regular Price (Cash & Equiv.)	Regular (Begins) Thru (Curr. Assets)	Sinking Fund Price (Curr. Liab.)	Sinking Fund (Begins) Thru (Balance Sheet Date)	Refund/Other Restriction Price (L. Term Debt (Mil $))	Refund/Other Restriction (Begins) Thru	Outst'g (Mil $) (Capital-ization (Mil $))	Underwriting Firm (Total Debt % Capital)	Underwriting Year	Price Range 1994 High	Price Range 1994 Low	Mo. End Price Sale(s) or Bid	Curr. Yield	Yield to Mat.
***Connecticut Lt & Pwr** (Cont.)*																				
1st & Ref SS 9⅜s 2019	mS	BBB+			X	R	106.02	8-31-95	Z100	....	....	....	75.0	S1	'89	106⅝	97½	100	9.38	9.37
1st & Ref UU 7⅝s '97	Ao	BBB+			X	R	103.81	3-31-95	Z100	....	®100	3-31-97	200	S1	'92	105⅞	98⅛	98⅛	7.77	8.55
1st & Ref VV 7¼s '99	jJ	BBB+			X	R	103.72	6-30-95	Z100	....	®100	6-30-97	100	M6	'92	104¾	94⅞	94⅞	7.64	8.65
1st & Ref XX 5¾s 2000	jJ	BBB+			X	R	100	(7-1-98)	Z100	(7-1-98)	....	....	200	M2	'93	99¾	88⅛	88¼	6.52	8.47
1st & Ref YY 7½s 2023	jJ	BBB+			X	R	105.27	(7-1-98)	Z100	....	....	....	100	S1	'93	100¼	82¾	85⅛	8.81	8.95
1st & Ref ZZ 7⅜s 2025	jD	BBB+			X	BE	104.47	(12-1-98)	Z100	(12-1-98)	....	....	125	L3	'93	98½	80⅝	83⅛	8.87	9.00
1st & Ref '94A 5½s '99	Fa	BBB+			X	BE	NC	....	....	....	....	....	140	G1	'94	99¾	90⅛	90⅛	6.10	8.40
1st & Ref '94B 6⅛s 2004	Fa	BBB+			X	BE	101.68	(2-1-99)	Z100	(2-1-99)	....	....	140	S1	'94	98¼	83	84	7.29	8.71
1st & Ref '94C 8½s 2024	Jd	BBB+			X	BE	103.87	(6-1-04)	Z100	(6-1-04)	....	....	115	M6	'94	99¼	92⅜	95⅛	8.94	8.97
Conn.Yankee Atom.Pwr.	*72*	*1.96*	*3.05*		*2.54*	*Dc*	*0.04*	*40.10*	*54.80*	*12-31-93*	*187.0*		*301.0*	*66.9*						
Gen & Ref A[1] 12s 2000	Jd	BBB–	5/90	BB+	X	R	102.40	(6-1-97)	Z100	....	Z104.80	5-31-95	100	S1	'88	121⅝	101⅝	105⅛	11.41	10.72
Conseco Inc.	*35a*	*1.32*	*1.44*		*1.99*	*Dc*				*9-30-94*	*259.0*		*1386*	*18.7*						
• Sr Nts 8⅛s 2003	Fa15	BBB–			X	BE	NC	....	....	....	....	....	200	M2	'93	105⅜	85	91⅞	8.84	9.58
Consolidated Cigar[2]	*69*	*1.38*	*1.88*		*[3]1.36*	*Dc*	*1.34*	*54.50*	*17.60*	*10-1-94*	*132.0*		*171.0*	*77.2*						
Sr Sub Nts[4] 10½s 2003	Ms	B			Y	R	103	(3-1-98)	....	....	[5]Z109	2-28-95	90.0	F1	'93	102	85½	90	11.67	12.48
Consolidated Edison,N.Y.	*75*	*3.84*	*4.08*		*4.36*	*Dc*	*361.0*	*1459*	*1084*	*9-30-94*	*3981*		*10079*	*40.8*						
1st & Ref CC 5s '96	Jj	AA–	2/94	AA	X	R	100	....	▲100	....	....	....	100	M2	'65	100	97⅜	97½	5.13	7.64
1st & Ref DD 5.90s '96	jD15	AA–	2/94	AA	X	R	100.21	12-14-95	▲100	....	....	....	75.0	M6	'66	100¾	96⅛	96¼	6.13	8.00
Deb '90A 9.70s 2025	jD	A+	2/94	AA–	X	R	107.56	(12-1-95)	....	....	....	....	27.4	M2	'90	113⅛	99⅝	108⅛	8.97	8.92
Deb'91A 9⅜s 2026	Jd	A+	2/94	AA–	X	R	106.88	(6-1-96)	....	....	....	....	95.3	G1	'91	125⅜	100½	103⅜	9.07	9.05
Deb '92A 7⅜s 2000	mS15	A+	2/94	AA–	X	R	NC	....	....	....	....	....	150	G1	'92	109½	95⅜	95⅜	7.73	8.41
Deb '92B 7⅝s 2004	Ms	A+	2/94	AA–	X	R	NC	....	....	....	....	....	150	G1	'92	99½	94	94¾	8.05	8.46
Deb '92C 7.60s 2000	Jj15	A+	2/94	AA–	X	R	NC	....	....	....	....	....	125	G1	'92	111	96⅞	96⅞	7.85	8.37
Deb '92D 6½s '99	mS	A+	2/94	AA–	X	R	NC	....	....	....	....	....	75.0	G1	'92	105½	93	93	6.99	8.34
Deb '92E 7⅜s 2005	mS	A+	2/94	AA–	X	R	103.133	(9-1-97)	....	....	....	....	75.0	G1	'92	110	90½	91¾	8.04	8.57
Deb '92F 8.05s 2027	jD15	A+	2/94	AA–	X	R	105.3336	(12-15-97)	....	....	....	....	100	G1	'92	113⅛	88⅛	90¾	8.87	8.92
Deb '93A 6¼s '98	Ao	A+	2/94	AA–	X	R	NC	....	....	....	....	....	100	M2	'93	103⅝	94⅛	94¼	6.63	8.30
Deb '93B 6½s 2001	Fa	A+	2/94	AA–	X	R	NC	....	....	....	....	....	150	L3	'93	105⅝	91	91¼	7.12	8.36
Deb '93C 6⅝s 2002	Fa	A+	2/94	AA–	X	R	NC	....	....	....	....	....	150	L3	'93	106¼	90¼	90½	7.32	8.43
Deb '93D 6⅜s 2003	Ao	A+	2/94	AA–	X	R	NC	....	....	....	....	....	150	L3	'93	102⅝	86¾	87½	7.29	8.51
Deb '93E 5.30s '97	fA	A+	2/94	AA–	X	R	NC	....	....	....	....	....	100	G1	'93	100⅝	93⅜	93⅜	5.68	8.19
Deb '93F 5.70s '98	aO	A+	2/94	AA–	X	R	NC	....	....	....	....	....	100	G1	'93	102	91¾	91¾	6.21	8.30
Deb '93G 7½s 2023	Jd15	A+	2/94	AA–	X	R	103.2725	(6-15-03)	....	....	....	....	380	L3	'93	105	84⅛	86⅜	8.68	8.81
Deb '94A 7⅛s 2029	Fa15	A+			X	R	103.642	(2-15-04)	....	....	....	....	150	G1	'94	98⅞	79⅜	81⅝	8.73	8.84
F/R[6]Deb '94B 5⅝s '99	QJul	A+			X	BE	*100	(7-1-96)	....	....	....	....	150	L3	'94	100	99⅝	99⅝	5.65	....
Consolidated Freightways	*71*	*0.07*	*0.72*		*3.86*	*Dc*	*141.0*	*1043*	*1034*	*9-30-94*	*406.0*		*1104*	*40.5*						
Nts[7] 9⅛s '99	fA15	BB	12/91	BBB–	Y	R	NC	....	....	....	....	....	118	F1	'89	108¾	96⅝	96⅝	9.44	10.05
Consolidated Natural Gas	*73e*	*2.80*	*3.44*		*4.08*	*Dc*	*23.30*	*722.0*	*862.0*	*9-30-94*	*1152*		*3589*	*40.0*						
• SF Deb 8⅝s 2011	jD	AA–	2/90	AA	X	R	105.76	11-30-95	100	(12-1-96)	®105.04	11-30-96	100	M6	'86	106½	106½	95	9.08	9.21
• SF Deb 8¾s 2019	aO	AA–	2/90	AA	X	R	103.80	(10-1-99)	100	(10-1-99)	....	....	150	D7	'89	No Sale		96	9.11	9.16
• Deb 9⅜s '97	Fa	AA–	2/90	AA	X	R	NC	....	....	....	....	....	100	S1	'89	113	103½	101⅜	9.25	8.63
• Deb 5⅞s '98	aO	AA–			X	R	NC	....	....	....	....	....	150	S1	'92	102⅛	91½	92½	6.35	8.23
• Deb 8¾s '99	Jd	AA–	2/90	AA	X	R	NC	....	....	....	....	....	100	S3	'89	109¾	104	100½	8.71	8.61
• Deb 5¾s 2003	fA	AA–			X	R	NC	....	....	....	....	....	150	S1	'93	98⅛	81	81¾	7.03	8.82
• Deb 6⅝s 2013	jD	AA–			X	R	NC	....	....	....	....	....	150	G1	'93	102	98¾	78⅞	8.40	8.96

Uniform Footnote Explanations-See Page 1. Other: [1] Red in whole for plant closure at prices,as def. [2] Subsid of Mafco Hldgs. [3] 10 mos Dec'93. [4] (HRO)On Chge of Ctrl at 101. [5] On Chge of Ctrl or some Pub Eq Off'g(to 3-1-95). [6] Int to 1-1-95,adj qtrly(3 Mo LIBOR&0.1875%). [7] (HRO)At100for Designated Event&Rat'g Decline.

Source: *Standard and Poor's Bond Guide,* December 1994.

TABLE 4–3 Page from *Standard & Poor's Bond Guide* (Convertible bonds)

Convertible Bonds

Exchange ↓ Issue, Rate, Interest Dates and Maturity	S&P Debt Rating	Bond Form	Outstdg. Mil-$	Conv. Ex-pires	Shares per $1,000 Bond	Price per Share	Div. Income per Bond	1994 Price Range High	1994 Price Range Low	Curr Bid Sale(s) Ask(A)	Curr. Yield	Yield to Mat	Stock Value of Bond	Conv Parity	Stock Data Month End	Stock Data P/E Ratio	Earnings Per Share Yr. End	1993	1994	Last 12 Mos
◆Advanced Medical[1]Inc[2]......... 7¼s Jj15 2002	CCC–	R	60.0	2002	55.13	18.14	....	60½	34	s60	12.08	17.28	11⅛	11	◆2	4	Dc	d0.29	....	[9]0.45
•Advest Group 9s Ms15 2008	NR	R	21.0	2008	73.69	13.57	....	103	86	s89¼	10.08	10.52	37⅞	12⅛	•5⅛	15	Sp	Δ0.56	0.34	0.34
AES Corp[3] 6½s Ms15 2002	B+	R	50.0	2002	38.146	26.215	....	110⅝	87⅞	91¼	7.12	8.12	74½	24	19½	19	Dc	0.98	....	[9]1.02
Ag Services of America[1] 7s Mn31 2003	NR	R	13.8	2003	108.10	9.25	....	117	96	97	7.22	7.49	86½	9	8	11	Fb	0.54	....	[11]0.72
Agnico-Eagle Mines (Sr)[45]... 5¾s $Jj27 2004	B+	R	[6]110	2004	55.762	....	5.58	90¼	67½	70¼	8.19	11.02	59¼	12⅝	•10⅝	23	Dc	0.23	....	[9]j0.45
Air & Water Tech[7] 8s Mn15 2015	B–	R	115	2015	[8]33.333	30.00	....	95½	53¼	53¼	15.02	15.68	20	16	◆6	d	Oc	d0.22	....	[7]d8.51
◆Air Express Int'l[9] 6s Jj15 2003	BB–	R	74.8	2003	29.36	34.0625	4.70	100½	84	s100½	5.97	5.92	58¾	34¼	20	17	Dc	0.99	E1.13	[9]1.19
[10]Air Wis Services............... 7¾s Jd15 2010	NR	R	33.0	2010	[11]3.86	259.07	....	115⅞	49½	61½	12.60	13.85	33¾	159⅜	•87⅜	21	Dc	□d5.28	E4.00	[9]d4.42
•Airborne Freight[12] 6¾s fA15 2001	BBB	R	115	2001	28.169	35.50	8.45	116¾	88½	s91½	7.38	8.45	57¾	32½	•20½	10	Dc	Δ1.66	E2.00	[9]2.00
Alaska Air Gr 7¾s Jd15 2010	B	R	14.6	2010	35.40	28.25	....	94¾	85½	94¾	8.18	8.36	53⅛	26⅞	•15	15	Dc	d2.51	E1.00	[9]0.54
•Alaska Air Gr[1] 6⅞s Jd15 2014	B	R	60.2	2014	29.76	33.60	....	88	74	s75¾	9.08	9.66	44¾	25½	•15	15	Dc	d2.51	E1.00	[9]0.54
•Alaska Air Gr[13](Zero)[14] .... [15] 2006	B	R	[6]345	2006	12.396	....	....	42⅛	38	s42⅛	....	7.80	18⅝	34	•15	15	Dc	d2.51	E1.00	[9]0.54
•Albany Int'l[16] 5¼s Ms15 2002	BB–	R	[6]150	2002	38.083	....	13.33	99	83	85½	6.14	7.93	73⅜	22½	•19¼	26	Dc	±0.58	....	[9]0.74
Alexander & Alex Sv............. 11s Ao15 2007	BB–	R	60.2	2007	25.64	39.00	2.56	104½	97⅝	97⅝	11.27	11.36	47½	38⅛	•18½	41	Dc	Δ±0.40	E0.45	[9]d0.74
◆Alexander Haagen Prop('A') 7½s jJ15 2001	NR	R	75.0	2001	55.56	18.00	80.01	100	84	s87	8.62	10.45	88¼	15¾	◆15⅞	..	Dc	p0.06	....	[9]0.06
All Amer Communications[17] ... 6½s aO 2003	NR	R	60.0	2003	86.957	11.50	....	100	71	71	9.15	11.92	54⅜	8¼	6¼	10	Dc	P0.87	....	[9]0.58
•[18]Alleghany Corp................. 6½s Jd15 2014	BBB+	R	59.6	2014	[19]22.88	43.70	20.59	103¾	90½	93	6.99	7.17	67½	40¾	•29½	10	Dc	2.92	E2.75	[9]2.87
•Allegheny Ludlum.............. 5⅞s Ms15 2002	A–	BE	90.0	2002	49.38	20.25	23.70	128	100½	s100½	5.85	5.79	92⅝	20⅜	•18¾	98	Dc	Δ1.06	E0.19	[9]0.24
•Allwaste Inc[1] .... 7¼s Jd 2014	B+	R	30.0	2014	83.75	11.94	....	95	83½	s84¼	8.61	8.98	47⅛	10⅛	•5⅝	15	Au	0.28	0.36	0.36
•ALZA Corp[20](Zero)[21] 2014	BBB–	R	[6]825	2014	12.987	....	....	37¼	33	33	....	5.76	23½	25½	•18	17	Dc	Δ□0.54	E1.05	[9]0.44
[22]Ameribanc,Inc[23] .... 8s Ao 1995	NR	R	13.5	3-17-95	[24]53.45	18.71	59.86	209⅞	160	167⅛	4.79	....	167⅛	31⅜	•31¼	8	Dc	3.32	E3.75	[9]3.69
•Amer Cap Bond Fund[25]........... 8½s Jj 1995	AAA	R	20.1	1-1-95	52.08	19.20	80.20	No Sale		100	8.50	Mat.	87¼	19¼	•16¾	..	Je	....	....	....
[26]Amer Medical Int'l 9½s mN15 2001	B	R	3.19	2001	41.02	24.38	....	109¼	92⅛	99	9.60	9.70	99	24¼	•24⅛	13	Au	□0.87	□1.80	1.80
[26]Amer Medical Int'l .... 8¼s Ao 2008	B	R	7.12	2008	25.00	40.00	....	94½	77⅞	77⅞	10.59	11.55	60⅜	31¼	•24⅛	13	Au	□0.87	□1.80	1.80
•Amer Stores[1] 7¼s mS15 2001	BBB–	R	175	2001	44.444	22.50	21.33	124	107	119½	6.07	3.92	119½	27	•26⅞	11	Ja	□1.85	E2.30	[10]2.23
•[27]Amoco Canada Petroleum 'A' 7⅜s $mS 2013	AA–	R	456	2013	[28]19.05	52.50	41.91	124	112½	s115	6.41	6.02	112¾	60⅜	•59⅛	17	Dc	3.66	E3.35	[9]3.69
•AMR Corp........................ 6⅛s [29]QNov 2024	BB–	R	1000	2004	12.658	79.00	....	80¼	79	80	....	Flat	67½	63¼	•53¼	13	Dc	□d2.05	E4.00	[9]0.50
•AMSCO[30]Int'l[1] 4½s aO15 2002	BB+	R	[6]100	2002	33.22	30.10	....	90¼	75½	s75½	5.96	8.93	30⅜	22¾	•9⅛	16	Dc	0.50	E0.54	[9]d1.66
•Anacomp, Inc[31] 13⅞s Jj15 2002	CCC+	R	[6]23.2	2002	57.14	17.50	....	112	97	98½	....	Flat	11½	17¼	•2	20	Sp	*0.22	Δ0.10	0.10
Andersen Group..................10½s aO15 2002	NR	R	8.04	2002	61.84	16.17	....	93¼	82⅞	85	12.35	13.68	23¼	13¾	3¾	d	Fb	Δd0.86	....	[8]d0.17
[32]Apollo Computer .... 7¼s Fa 2011	AA	R	105	2011	Conv into $729.17			101	88½	90	8.06	8.39	....	....	....	..		....	....	....
Argosy Gaming[17]........................12s Jd 2001	B–	R	100	2001	56.50	17.70	....	110¼	94¼	95	12.63	13.17	67⅛	16⅞	11⅞	44	Dc	p0.38	....	[9]0.27
•Arrow Electronics[1] 5¾s aO15 2002	BB+	R	125	2002	30.188	33.125	....	143	110½	112	5.13	3.95	108⅜	37⅛	•35⅞	12	Dc	2.62	E2.90	[9]2.79

Uniform Footnote Explanations—See Page 224. Other: [1] (HRO)On Chge of Ctrl at 100. [2] Int of 7-15-94 pd 8-17-94. [3] (HRO)For a Redemp Event at 100. [4] Co must offer repurch on Chge of Ctrl. [5] Int of 3.5% pd Jan & Jul 27,bal pd at maturity. [6] Incl disc. [7] (HRO)To 5-15-00 on Chge of Ctrl at 100. [8] Into Cl A com. [9] (HRO)For a Fundamental Chge at declining prices. [10] Mgr into & data of UAL Corp. [11] Conv into UAL Corp com. [12] (HRO)For a Risk Event at 100. [13] (HRO)On 4-18-96('01) at $490.58($700.42). [14] (HRO)To 4-18-96 on Chge of Ctrl. [15] Due 4-18-06. [16] (HRO)On Chge of Ctrl at 87.59 & accr OID. [17] (HRO)On Chge of Ctrl at 101. [18] Conv into & data of Amer Express. [19] Into Amer Express com. [20] (HRO)To 7-14-99,Ctrl Chge, at $354.71&accr OID. [21] (HRO)On 7-14-99(04&09)$459.63($595.58&$771.74). [22] To be exch for com when due. [23] Merged into & data of Mercantile Bancorp. [24] Conv into Mercantile Bancorp. [25] Int thru 12-31-94,adj aft as defined. [26] Now American Medical Hldgs. [27] Subsid & data of Amoco Corp. [28] Into Amoco Corp com. [29] Co may extend the int pyt period(max 20 qtrs). [30] Int to 10-15-95,6.5% aft. [31] Int:1-15-84,pd 3-21-84:7-15-84,pd 8-15-84. [32] Subsid of Hewlett-Packard.

Source: *Standard and Poor's Bond Guide,* December 1994.

TABLE 4–4 Sample Pages, *Standard & Poor's Corporation Reports*

Hewlett-Packard 1137

NYSE Symbol HWP Options on CBOE In S&P 500

Price	Range	P–E Ratio	Dividend	Yield	S&P Ranking	Beta
Dec. 14'94	1994					
95½	102½–71⅞	16	1.20	1.3%	A	1.83

Summary

Hewlett-Packard primarily manufactures a broad array of computer products, including printers, servers, workstations and PCs. The company also features a vast service and support organization. Earnings in fiscal 1994 benefited from significantly higher revenues and controlled operating costs. These trends are expected to fuel further earnings growth in fiscal 1995.

Current Outlook

Earnings for the fiscal year ending October 31, 1995, are estimated at $7.35 a share, up from fiscal 1994's $6.14.

Dividends, increased each year since 1986, were raised 20% in May 1994 to $0.30 quarterly.

HWP is entering fiscal 1995 with strong momentum following an impressive sales and earnings performance in fiscal 1994, particularly in the fourth quarter. Orders in the quarter grew by 25%, signaling continued strong demand for a number of key products. HWP should continue to see strong demand for server and workstation products as customers migrate to open, client-server systems from proprietary systems. The company's dominance in printer products is expected to continue, while targeted assaults on new growth markets, like PCs and uninterruptible power supply (UPS) products, should ensure continue strong revenue growth. Gross margins are likely to continue contracting, due to ongoing competition and product mix shifts, but we expect expense control efforts to offset the margin erosion and lead to favorable earnings comparisons.

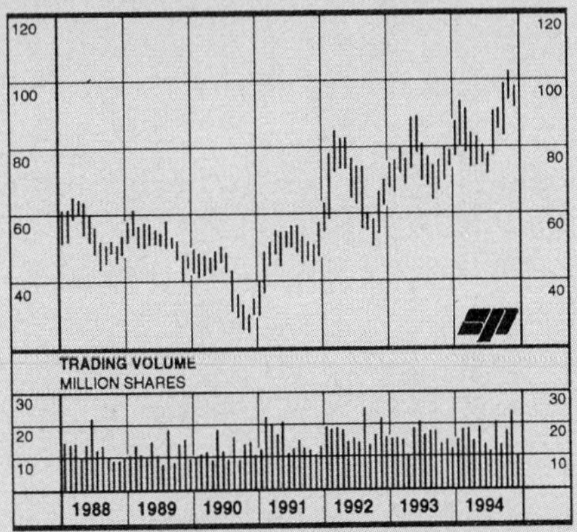

Net Revenues (Billion $)

Quarter:	1994–95	1993–94	1993	1992
Jan.	---	5.68	4.57	3.86
Apr.	---	6.25	5.10	4.18
Jul.	---	6.05	4.96	4.04
Oct.	---	7.00	5.69	4.32
	---	24.99	20.32	16.41

Net revenues for the fiscal year ended October 31, 1994 (preliminary), advanced 23% from the preceding year, led by a 25% gain in computer products, service and support. Gross margins narrowed, hurt by competitive pressures, but SG&A cost rose only 8.1% and net income climbed 36%. Earnings per share, on 2.8% more shares, rose 32% to $6.14 from $4.65.

Common Share Earnings ($)

Quarter:	1994–95	1994	1993	1992
Jan.	E1.75	1.42	1.03	1.19
Apr.	E1.95	1.56	1.38	1.27
Jul.	E1.55	1.33	1.06	0.75
Oct.	E2.10	1.83	1.18	0.28
	E7.35	6.14	4.65	3.49

Important Developments

Oct. '94— HWP announced several new products including the HP OfficeJet personal printer-fax-copier, a new line of uninterruptible power supplies (UPS) and its first color notebook series, the OmniBook 4000 PC. Separately, the company agreed to resell Convex Computer's Exemplar SPP (Scaleable Parallel Processor) through its worldwide sales force.

Next earnings report expected in mid-February.

Per Share Data ($)

Yr. End Oct. 31	1994	1993	1992	1991	1990	[1]1989	1988	1987	1986	1985
Tangible Bk. Val.	**NA**	31.21	27.43	[2]28.90	[2]26.07	21.22	19.35	19.52	17.08	15.50
Cash Flow	**NA**	7.58	6.15	5.24	5.08	5.37	4.81	3.83	3.27	3.07
Earnings[3]	**6.14**	4.65	3.49	3.02	3.06	3.52	3.36	2.50	2.02	1.91
Dividends	**1.100**	0.900	0.725	0.480	0.420	0.360	0.280	0.230	0.220	0.220
Payout Ratio	**18%**	19%	21%	16%	14%	10%	8%	9%	11%	12%
Prices[4]—High	**102½**	89¼	85	57⅜	50⅜	61½	65½	73⅝	49⅝	38⅞
Low	**71⅞**	64⅜	50¼	29⅞	24⅞	40¼	43¾	35¾	35¾	28¾
P/E Ratio—	**17–12**	19–14	24–14	19–10	16–8	17–11	19–13	29–14	25–18	20–15

Data as orig. reptd. **1.** Refl. merger or acq. **2.** Incl. intangibles. **3.** Bef. spec. item of -1.31 in 1992. **4.** Cal. yr. E-Estimated. NA-Not Available.

Standard NYSE Stock Reports
Vol. 61/No. 246/Sec. 23

December 22, 1994

Standard & Poor's
25 Broadway, NY, NY 10004

Source: *Standard and Poor's Corporation Reports*, December 1994.

TABLE 4–4 Sample Pages, *Standard & Poor's Corporation Reports (concluded)*

1137 Hewlett-Packard Company

Income Data (Million $)

Year Ended Oct. 31	Revs.	Oper. Inc.	% Oper. Inc. of Revs.	Cap. Exp.	Depr.	Int. Exp.	[3]Net Bef. Taxes	Eff. Tax Rate	[4]Net Inc.	% Net Inc. of Revs.	Cash Flow
1993	**20,317**	**2,622**	**12.9**	**1,489**	**743**	**121**	**1,783**	**34.0%**	**1,177**	**5.8**	**1,920**
1992	16,410	2,183	13.3	1,032	673	96	1,325	33.5%	881	5.4	1,554
1991	14,494	1,890	13.0	862	555	130	1,127	33.0%	755	5.2	1,310
1990	13,233	1,650	12.5	955	488	172	1,056	30.0%	739	5.6	1,305
[1]1989	11,899	1,630	13.7	915	435	126	1,151	28.0%	829	7.0	1,264
1988	9,831	1,572	16.0	648	353	77	1,142	28.5%	816	8.3	1,169
1987	8,090	1,354	16.7	507	342	50	962	33.1%	[2]644	8.0	986
1986	7,102	1,101	15.5	499	321	NA	780	33.8%	[2]516	7.3	837
1985	6,505	1,057	16.2	632	299	NA	758	35.5%	489	7.5	788
[2]1984	6,044	1,097	18.2	661	237	NA	860	22.7%	665	11.0	902

Balance Sheet Data (Million $)

		Curr.									
Oct. 31	Cash	Assets	Liab.	Ratio	Total Assets	% Ret. on Assets	Long Term Debt	Common Equity	Total Cap.	% LT Debt of Cap.	% Ret. on Equity
1993	**1,644**	**10,236**	**6,868**	**1.5**	**16,736**	**7.7**	**667**	**8,511**	**9,209**	**7.2**	**14.7**
1992	1,035	7,679	5,094	1.5	13,700	6.9	425	7,499	7,973	5.3	11.9
1991	1,120	6,716	4,063	1.7	11,973	6.4	188	7,269	7,700	2.4	10.9
1990	1,106	6,510	4,443	1.5	11,395	6.8	139	6,363	6,763	2.1	12.4
1989	926	5,731	3,743	1.5	10,075	9.4	474	5,446	6,168	7.7	16.5
1988	918	4,420	2,570	1.7	7,497	11.0	61	4,533	4,770	1.3	17.9
1987	2,645	5,490	2,735	2.0	8,133	8.9	88	5,022	5,264	1.7	13.7
1986	1,372	3,814	1,518	2.5	6,287	8.6	110	4,374	4,635	2.4	12.4
1985	1,020	3,342	1,376	2.4	5,680	9.0	102	3,982	4,212	2.4	13.0
1984	938	3,201	1,322	2.4	5,153	14.2	81	3,545	3,738	2.2	20.6

Data as orig. reptd. **1.** Refl. merger or acq. **2.** Refl. acctg. change. **3.** Incl. equity in earns. of nonconsol. subs. **4.** Bef.spec.items. NA-Not Available.

Business Summary

Hewlett-Packard produces a broad range of electronic instruments and systems for measurement, analysis and computation. The company derived 23% of its fiscal 1994 revenues from providing service for its equipment, systems and peripherals. Orders originating outside of the U.S. accounted for 54% of total orders in both fiscal 1994 and fiscal 1993.

Key computer products, services and support (797% of fiscal 1994 revenues) include the HP 3000 series, which runs the proprietary MPE operating systems and is sold for business applications; the 9000 line of UNIX-based technical computers, including workstations; and the HP Vectra series of IBM-compatible personal computers. Both the 3000 and 9000 families are based on the company's Precision Architecture reduced instruction set computing (RISC) design. The company offers software programming services, network services, distributed systems services and data management services. Peripheral products include printers, such as the HP LaserJet and DeskJet families; plotters and page scanners; video display terminals; and disk and tape drives.

Electronic test and measurement instrumentation, systems and services (11%) include voltmeters and multimeters, counters, oscilloscopes and logic analyzers, signal generators and specialized communications test equipment.

Medical electronic equipment and services (4%) include continuous monitoring systems for critical care patients, medical data managment systems and fetal monitors.

Analytical instrumentation and service (3%) includes gas and liquid chromatographs, mass spectrometers and spectrophotometers.

Electronic components (3%) include microwave semiconductor and optoelectronic devices sold primarily to original equipment manufacturers.

Dividend Data

Dividends have been paid since 1965.

Amt. of Divd. $	Date Decl.	Ex-divd. Date	Stock of Record	Payment Date
0.25	Jan. 21	Mar. 17	Mar. 23	Apr. 13'94
0.30	May 20	Jun. 16	Jun. 22	Jul. 13'94
0.30	Jul. 22	Sep. 15	Sep. 21	Oct. 12'94
0.30	Nov. 18	Dec. 15	Dec. 21	Jan. 11'95

Capitalization

Long Term Debt: $547,000,000 (10/94).

Common Stock: 254,229,000 shs. ($1 par). Institutions hold about 59%; the Hewlett & Packard families control 29% (in part held by institutions).

Shareholders of record: 72,598 (11/93).

Office—3000 Hanover St., Palo Alto, CA 94304. **Tel**—(415) 857-1501. **Chrmn, Pres & CEO**—L. E. Platt. **Exec VP-Fin & CFO**—R. P. Wayman. **Secy**—D. C. Nordlund. **Investor Contact**—Steve Beitler. **Dirs**—T. E. Everhart, J. B. Fery, J.-P. G. Gimon, R. A. Hackborn, H. J. Haynes, W. B. Hewlett, S. M. Hufstedler, G. A. Keyworth II, P. F. Miller Jr., S. P. Orr, D. W. Packard, D. E. Petersen, L. E. Platt, R. P. Wayman. **Transfer Agent & Registrar**—Harris Trust & Savings Bank, Chicago. **Incorporated** in California in 1947. **Empl**—98,400.

 John D. Coyle, CFA

Value Line

Value Line Investment Survey, a publication of Arnold Bernhard & Co., is one of the most widely used investment services by individuals, stockbrokers, and small bank trust departments. The *Value Line Investment Survey* follows 1,700 companies, and each common stock is covered in a one-page summary (see the one for Hewlett-Packard in Table 4–5). Value Line is noted for its comprehensive coverage, which can be seen by comparing Table 4–5 with Tables 4–1 and 4–4. Raw financial data are available as well as trendline growth rates, price history patterns in graphic form, quarterly sales, earnings and dividends, and a breakdown of sales and profit margins by line of business. Value Line contains 13 sections divided into several industries each. The first few pages beginning an industry classification are devoted to an overview of the industry, with the company summaries following. Each section is revised on a 13-week cycle.

Value Line has a unique evaluation system that is primarily dependent on historical relationships and regression analysis. From the valuation model, each company is rated 1 through 5, with 1 being the highest positive rating and 5 the lowest. Each company is rated on timeliness and safety. It should be noted that Value Line minimizes human judgment in making its evaluation.

Value Line also publishes two other products: *Value Line Options,* featuring put and call options, and *Value Line Convertibles,* featuring convertible bonds, preferred stocks, and warrants.

Morningstar

Morningstar is a relative newcomer to the data information game but one that has made a name for itself in mutual funds with the following publications: *Morningstar Mutual Funds, Mutual Funds OnDisc, Mutual Fund Sourcebook, Mutual Fund Performance Report, Morningstar Mutual Fund 500, Morningstar Closed-End Funds, Closed End Funds OnFloppy,* and *Closed-End Fund Sourcebook.* These publications provide historical data on fund performance, expense information, asset allocation breakdown, and a ranking system using five stars as the highest ranking and one star as the lowest ranking. Some of these publications will be highlighted in Chapter 19.

After capturing a large share of the market for mutual fund data, Morningstar expanded into other areas such as information on the more than 700 foreign stocks listed as American depository receipts (*Morningstar ADRs*) and information on the Japanese markets (*Morningstar Japan*). Additionally, in late 1994 they bought MarketBase, a firm providing computerized common stock data on disk. This is clearly a new source of information that should prove valuable to an investor and that may provide new products over the coming years.

Other Investment Services

Dun & Bradstreet publishes *Key Business Ratios* in bound form. This publication contains 14 significant ratios on 800 different lines of business listed by SIC code. Examples of ratios included are current assets to current debt, net profits on net sales, and total debt to tangible net worth. This publication has replaced the old Dun & Bradstreet 11-page

TABLE 4–5 The *Value Line Investment Survey*

HEWLETT-PACKARD NYSE-HWP

RECENT PRICE **106** | P/E RATIO **15.1** (Trailing: 17.3 Median: 17.0) | RELATIVE P/E RATIO **1.09** | DIV'D YLD **1.1%** | VALUE LINE **1092**

TIMELINESS (Relative Price Performance Next 12 Mos.) **1** Highest
SAFETY **2** Above Average
(Scale: 1 Highest to 5 Lowest)
BETA 1.40 (1.00 = Market)

1997-99 PROJECTIONS

	Price	Gain	Ann'l Total Return
High	190	(+80%)	17%
Low	140	(+30%)	9%

Insider Decisions

	F	M	A	M	J	J	A	S	O
to Buy	0	0	0	0	0	0	0	0	0
Options	0	4	3	0	0	0	1	5	0
to Sell	0	8	7	0	1	0	2	8	0

Institutional Decisions

	1Q'94	2Q'94	3Q'94
to Buy	183	215	191
to Sell	226	172	182
Hld's(000)	145468	142672	143745

	1983	1984	1985	1986	1987	1988	1989	1990	1991	1992	1993	1994
High:	48.3	45.5	38.9	49.6	73.6	65.5	61.5	50.4	57.4	85.0	89.3	102.5
Low:	34.3	31.1	28.8	35.8	39.3	43.8	40.3	24.9	29.9	50.4	64.4	71.9

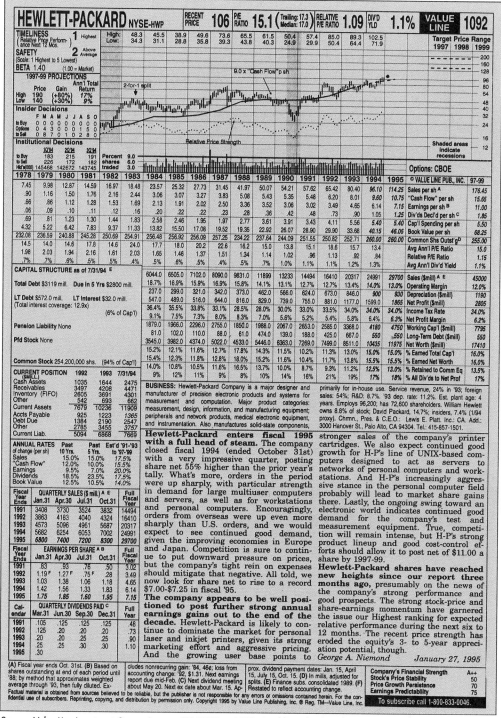

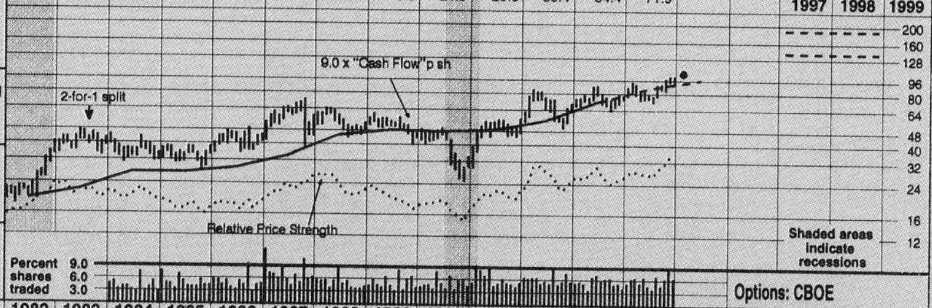

Options: CBOE

1978	1979	1980	1981	1982	1983	1984	1985	1986	1987	1988	1989	1990	1991	1992	1993	1994	1995	© VALUE LINE PUB., INC.	97-99
7.45	9.98	12.87	14.59	16.97	18.48	23.57	25.32	27.73	31.45	41.97	50.07	54.21	57.62	65.42	80.40	*96.10*	*114.25*	Sales per sh [A]	*176.45*
.90	1.16	1.50	1.76	2.16	2.44	3.06	3.07	3.27	3.83	5.08	5.43	5.35	5.48	6.20	8.01	*9.60*	*10.75*	"Cash Flow" per sh	*15.65*
.66	.86	1.12	1.28	1.53	1.69	2.13	1.91	2.02	2.50	3.36	3.52	3.06	3.02	3.49	4.65	6.14	*7.15*	Earnings per sh [B]	*11.00*
.06	.09	.10	.11	.12	.16	.20	.22	.22	.23	.28	.36	.42	.48	.73	.90	1.05	*1.25*	Div'ds Decl'd per sh [C]	*1.85*
.69	.81	1.23	1.30	1.44	1.83	2.58	2.46	1.95	1.97	2.77	3.61	3.91	3.43	4.11	5.56	*5.40*	*5.40*	Cap'l Spending per sh	*5.50*
4.32	5.22	6.42	7.83	9.37	11.33	13.82	15.50	17.08	19.52	19.35	22.92	26.07	28.90	29.90	33.68	*40.15*	*46.05*	Book Value per sh	*68.25*
232.08	236.59	240.88	245.28	250.69	254.91	256.48	256.92	256.09	257.25	234.22	237.64	244.09	251.55	250.82	252.71	*260.00*	*260.00*	Common Shs Outst'g [D]	*255.00*
14.5	14.0	14.6	17.8	14.6	24.0	17.7	18.0	20.2	22.6	16.2	15.0	13.8	15.1	18.6	15.7	13.4		Avg Ann'l P/E Ratio	*15.0*
1.98	2.03	1.94	2.16	1.61	2.03	1.65	1.46	1.37	1.51	1.34	1.14	1.02	.96	1.13	.92	.84		Relative P/E Ratio	*1.15*
.7%	.7%	.6%	.5%	.5%	.4%	.5%	.6%	.5%	.4%	.5%	.7%	1.0%	1.1%	1.1%	1.2%	1.3%		Avg Ann'l Div'd Yield	*1.1%*

1984	1985	1986	1987	1988	1989	1990	1991	1992	1993	1994	1995		97-99
6044.0	6505.0	7102.0	8090.0	9831.0	11899	13233	14494	16410	20317	24991	*29700*	Sales ($mill) [A] [E]	*45000*
18.7%	16.9%	15.9%	16.9%	15.8%	14.1%	13.1%	12.7%	12.7%	13.4%	*14.0%*	*13.0%*	Operating Margin	*12.0%*
237.0	299.0	321.0	342.0	373.0	462.0	566.0	624.0	673.0	846.0	*900*	*930*	Depreciation ($mill)	*1190*
547.0	489.0	516.0	644.0	816.0	829.0	739.0	755.0	881.0	1177.0	1599.0	*1865*	Net Profit ($mill)	*2805*
36.4%	35.5%	33.8%	33.1%	28.5%	28.0%	30.0%	33.0%	33.5%	34.0%	*34.0%*	*34.0%*	Income Tax Rate	*34.0%*
9.1%	7.5%	7.3%	8.0%	8.3%	7.0%	5.6%	5.2%	5.4%	5.8%	6.4%	*6.3%*	Net Profit Margin	*6.2%*
1879.0	1966.0	2296.0	2755.0	1850.0	1988.0	2067.0	2653.0	2585.0	3368.0	*4180*	*4750*	Working Cap'l ($mill)	*7795*
81.0	102.0	110.0	88.0	61.0	474.0	139.0	188.0	425.0	667.0	*550*	*550*	Long-Term Debt ($mill)	*550*
3545.0	3982.0	4374.0	5022.0	4533.0	5446.0	6363.0	7269.0	7499.0	8511.0	*10435*	*11975*	Net Worth ($mill)	*17410*
15.2%	12.1%	11.6%	12.7%	17.8%	14.3%	11.5%	10.2%	11.3%	13.0%	*15.0%*	*15.0%*	% Earned Total Cap'l	*16.0%*
15.4%	12.3%	11.8%	12.8%	18.0%	15.2%	11.6%	10.4%	11.7%	13.8%	*15.5%*	*15.5%*	% Earned Net Worth	*16.0%*
14.0%	10.8%	10.5%	11.6%	16.5%	13.7%	10.0%	8.7%	9.3%	11.2%	*12.5%*	*13.0%*	% Retained to Comm Eq	*13.5%*
9%	12%	11%	9%	8%	10%	14%	16%	21%	19%	*17%*	*18%*	% All Div'ds to Net Prof	*17%*

CAPITAL STRUCTURE as of 7/31/94 [E]

Total Debt $3119 mill. **Due in 5 Yrs** $2800 mill.

LT Debt $572.0 mill. **LT Interest** $32.0 mill.
(Total interest coverage: 12.9x) (6% of Cap'l)

Pension Liability None

Pfd Stock None

Common Stock 254,200,000 shs. (94% of Cap'l)

CURRENT POSITION ($MILL.)	1992	1993	7/31/94
Cash Assets	1035	1644	2475
Receivables	3497	4208	4471
Inventory (FIFO)	2605	3691	4301
Other	542	693	662
Current Assets	7679	10236	11909
Accts Payable	925	1223	*1365*
Debt Due	1384	2190	2547
Other	2785	3455	*3757*
Current Liab.	5094	6868	7669

ANNUAL RATES of change (per sh)	Past 10 Yrs.	Past 5 Yrs.	Est'd '91-'93 to '97-'99
Sales	15.0%	15.0%	*17.5%*
"Cash Flow"	12.0%	10.0%	*15.5%*
Earnings	9.5%	7.0%	*20.0%*
Dividends	18.5%	23.5%	*17.5%*
Book Value	12.5%	10.5%	*14.0%*

Fiscal Year Ends	QUARTERLY SALES ($ mill.) [A] [E] Jan.31	Apr.30	Jul.31	Oct.31	Full Fiscal Year
1991	3408	3730	3524	3832	14494
1992	3863	4183	4040	4324	16410
1993	4573	5096	4961	5687	20317
1994	5682	6254	6053	7002	24991
1995	*6800*	*7400*	*7200*	*8300*	*29700*

Fiscal Year Ends	EARNINGS PER SHARE [A] [B] Jan.31	Apr.30	Jul.31	Oct.31	Full Fiscal Year
1991	.83	.93	.76	.50	3.02
1992	1.19 [F]	1.27 [F]	.75 [F]	.28	3.49
1993	1.03	1.38	1.06	1.18	4.65
1994	1.42	1.56	1.33	1.83	6.14
1995	*1.75*	*1.85*	*1.60*	*1.95*	*7.15*

Cal-endar	QUARTERLY DIVIDENDS PAID [C] Mar.31	Jun.30	Sep.30	Dec.31	Full Year
1991	.105	.125	.125	.125	.48
1992	.125	.20	.20	.20	.73
1993	.20	.20	.25	.25	.90
1994	.25	.25	.30	.30	1.10
1995	.30				

BUSINESS: Hewlett-Packard Company is a major designer and manufacturer of precision electronic products and systems for measurement and computation. Major product categories: measurement, design, information, and manufacturing equipment; peripherals and network products, medical electronic equipment, and instrumentation. Also manufactures solid-state components, primarily for in-house use. Service revenue, 24% in '93; foreign sales: 54%; R&D: 8.7%. '93 dep. rate: 11.2%. Est. plant age: 4 years. Employs 96,200; has 72,600 shareholders. William Hewlett owns 8.8% of stock; David Packard, 14.7%; insiders, 7.4% (1/94 proxy). Chrmn., Pres. & C.E.O.: Lewis E. Platt. Inc.: CA. Add.: 3000 Hanover St., Palo Alto, CA 94304. Tel.: 415-857-1501.

Hewlett-Packard enters fiscal 1995 with a full head of steam. The company closed fiscal 1994 (ended October 31st) with a very impressive quarter, posting share net 55% higher than the prior year's tally. What's more, orders in the period were up sharply, with particular strength in demand for large multiuser computers and servers, as well as for workstations and personal computers. Encouragingly, orders from overseas were up even more sharply than U.S. orders, and we would expect to see continued good demand, given the improving economies in Europe and Japan. Competition is sure to continue to put downward pressure on prices, but the company's tight rein on expenses should mitigate that negative. All told, we now look for share net to rise to a record $7.00-$7.25 in fiscal '95.

The company appears to be well positioned to post further strong annual earnings gains out to the end of the decade. Hewlett-Packard is likely to continue to dominate the market for personal laser and inkjet printers, given its strong marketing effort and aggressive pricing. And the growing user base points to stronger sales of the company's printer cartridges. We also expect continued good growth for H-P's line of UNIX-based computers designed to act as servers to networks of personal computers and workstations. And H-P's increasingly aggressive stance in the personal computer field probably will lead to market share gains there. Lastly, the ongoing swing toward an electronic world indicates continued good demand for the company's test and measurement equipment. True, competition will remain intense, but H-P's strong product lineup and good cost-control efforts should allow it to post net of $11.00 a share by 1997-99.

Hewlett-Packard shares have reached new heights since our report three months ago, presumably on the news of the company's strong performance and good prospects. The strong stock-price and share-earnings momentum have garnered the issue our Highest ranking for expected relative performance during the next six to 12 months. The recent price strength has eroded the equity's 3- to 5-year appreciation potential, though.

George A. Niemond *January 27, 1995*

(A) Fiscal year ends Oct. 31st. (B) Based on shares outstanding at end of each period until '88; by method that approximates weighted average through '93, then fully diluted. Excludes nonrecurring gain: '84, 46¢; loss from accounting change: '92, $1.31. Next earnings report due mid-Feb. (C) Next dividend meeting about May 20. Next ex date about Mar. 15. Approx. dividend payment dates: Jan. 15, April 15, July 15, Oct. 15. (D) In mills, adjusted for splits. (E) Finance subs. consolidated 1989. (F) Restated to reflect accounting change.

Company's Financial Strength	A++
Stock's Price Stability	50
Price Growth Persistence	70
Earnings Predictability	75

Source: *Value Line Investment Survey*, January 27, 1995, p. 1092, Arnold Bernhardt and Company.

pamphlet on key business ratios for 125 lines of business. Another good source of ratios is Robert Morris Associates, which provides ratios on more than 150 industry classifications.

Dun's Marketing Services division of Dun & Bradstreet also publishes the *Million Dollar Directory.* Companies are listed in alphabetical order, by geographical location, and by product classification. The data provide names, addresses, phone numbers, and sales for each company. This could be helpful in identifying companies in the same industry or in writing to request such information as annual reports or product lists.

Another publication is the *Irwin Professional Publishing Business and Investment Almanac.* A section on finance and accounting covers key business ratios, financial statement ratios by industry, and corporate profits and margins. A section on the stock market covers more than 100 pages and includes market averages, mutual funds, dividends, common stock prices and yields, and much more. Information on commodities, banks, financial institutions, economic data, and a great deal more is contained in this 700-page business almanac.

Wiesenberger Services, Inc., publishes one of the best-known sources of information on mutual funds. The annual issue covers a 10-year statistical history (a sample page appears in Chapter 19). Another publication that is like an investment service is the annual issue of *The Individual Investor's Guide to No-Load Mutual Funds* published by the American Association of Individual Investors.

Retail stockbrokers have long provided information to their clients. The more you can afford to pay and the bigger your account, the more research you may receive. Most large brokers, such as Merrill Lynch, Smith Barney, Shearson, Prudential Securities, and Dean Witter, will provide investors information free or perhaps for a fee. You name what you want, and they have it—industry-company analysis, bond market analysis, futures and commodities, options advice, tax shelters in oil and gas and real estate, and so on. The brokerage industry provides much more sophisticated coverage of investments outside of stocks and bonds than they have in the past. This is partly because investors have become more sophisticated and partly because of the increasing numbers and complexity of alternative investments.

INDEXES, SEC FILINGS, PERIODICALS, AND JOURNALS

Indexes

One way to find relevant articles in periodicals and journals is to use indexes. Many will lead an analyst to useful information. The *Business Periodicals Index* references subjects in approximately 170 periodicals in the fields of accounting, advertising, banking, communications, economics, finance, insurance, investments, labor management, marketing, taxation, and other specific topics. The *Funk and Scott Index of Corporations and Industries* covers articles from more than 750 publications in two volumes. Each article covered includes a brief description of its contents. The articles are taken from business, financial, and trade magazines, major newspapers, bank newsletters, and investment advisory services. One very popular index is *The Wall Street Journal Index,* which identifies the date, page, and column of articles appearing in *The Wall Street Journal.* The index is presented in two parts—corporate news and general news. Many libraries have several years of *The Wall Street Journal* on microfiche or microfilm. Among the many

other indexes are *Who's Who in Finance and Industry,* Dun & Bradstreet's *Reference Book of Corporate Management,* and Standard & Poor's *Register of Corporations, Directors, and Executives.* These last three focus on people and can provide important qualitative information about management.

Securities and Exchange Commission Filings

As discussed in Chapter 2, the Securities and Exchange Commission was established by the Securities Exchange Act of 1934 and has the power to regulate trading on the exchanges and to require corporate disclosure of information relevant to the stockholders of publicly traded companies. The SEC even has the power to dictate accounting conventions.

Information available through the SEC consists primarily of corporate income statements, balance sheets, detailed support of accounting information, and internal data not always found in a company's annual report. Companies are required to file specific reports with the SEC. The annual 10-K Report is perhaps the most widely known and can usually be obtained free directly from the company rather than paying the SEC a copying charge. This report should be read in combination with the firm's annual report as it contains the same type of information but in greater detail. The 8-K Report must be filed when the corporation undergoes some important event that stockholders would be interested in knowing about, such as changes in control, bankruptcy, resignation of officers or directors, and other material events. 10-Q statements are filed quarterly no later than 45 days after the end of the quarter. This report includes quarterly financial statements, changes in stockholdings, legal proceedings, and other matters.

There are many other SEC reports. The most common are proxy statements that disclose information relevant to stockholders' votes; a prospectus, which must be issued whenever a new offering of securities is made to the public; and a registration trading statement, which is normally required for new issues by firms trading on an organized exchange or over-the-counter. Figure 4–4 on page 112, from Disclosure Inc., presents a detailed listing of information available from SEC filings, including reports required for tender offers and acquisitions. Investors can also visit the SEC regional office, where the corporation is headquartered, or the SEC's regional New York, Chicago, or Los Angeles offices. A list of SEC addresses is given in Appendix 4B at the end of this chapter. In 1994 the SEC began a service on the internet called EDGAR (Electronic Data Gathering and Retrieval). By 1995 investors were supposed to be able to access on line all SEC year-end December 31, 1994, reports.

Periodicals and Newspapers

After using the *Business Periodical Index,* an investor will most likely be referred to several of the most popular business periodicals such as *Fortune, Business Week, Forbes,* and *Financial World. Fortune* is published biweekly and is known for its coverage of industry problems and specific company analysis. *Fortune* has several regular features that make interesting reading. One, "Business Roundup," usually deals with a major business concern such as the federal budget, inflation, or productivity. Another feature, "Personal Investing," is always a thought-provoking article presenting ideas and analysis for the average investor.

Forbes is also a biweekly publication featuring several company-management interviews. This management-oriented approach points out various management styles and

FIGURE 4–4 Securities and Exchange Commission Filings

REPORT CONTENTS	10-K	19-F 20-F	10-Q	8-K	10-C	6-K	Proxy Statement	Prospects	Registration Statements '34 Act F-10 8-A	Registration Statements '34 Act 8-B	Registration Statements '33 Act "S" Type	ARS	Listing Application	N-1R	N-1Q
Auditor															
Name	A	A						A	A		A	A		A	
Opinion	A	A							A			A		A	
Changes				A											
Compensation Plans															
Equity							F	F	A		F				
Monetary								F	A		F				
Company Information															
Nature of Business	A	A				F		A	A		A				
History	F	A						A			A				
Organization and Change	F	F		A		F		A		F	A				
Debt Structure	A					F		A	A		A	A		A	
Depreciation & Other Schedules	A	A				F		A	A		A				
Dilution Factors	A	A		F		F		A	A		A	A			
Directors, Officers, Insiders															
Identification	F	A				F	A	A	A		A	F			
Background		A				F	F	A			A				
Holdings		A					A	A	A		A				
Compensation		A					A	A	A		A				
Earnings Per Share	A	A	A			F			A			A		A	
Financial Information															
Annual Audited	A	A							A			A		A	
Interim Audited		A													
Interim Unaudited			A			F		F			F	F			
Foreign Operations	A							A	A		A		F		
Labor Contracts									F		F				
Legal Agreements	F								F		F				
Legal Counsel								A			A				
Loan Agreements	F		F						F		F				
Plants and Properties	A	F						F	A		F				
Portfolio Operations															
Content (Listing of Securities)															A
Management														A	
Product-Line Breakout	A							A			A				
Securities Structure	A	A						A	A		A				
Subsidiaries	A	A						A	A		A				
Underwriting								A	A		A				
Unregistered Securities								F			F				
Block Movements				F					A						

TENDER OFFER ACQUISITION REPORTS	13D	13G	14D-1	14D-9	13E-3	13E-4
Name of issuer (Subject Company)	A	A	A	A	A	A
Filing Person (or Company)	A	A	A	A	A	A
Amount of Shares Owned	A	A				
Percent of Class Outstanding	A	A				
Financial Statements of Bidders				F	F	F
Purpose of Tender Offer			A	A	A	A
Source and Amount of Funds	A		A		A	
Identity and Background Information			A	A	A	
Persons Retained, Employed or to be Compensated			A	A	A	A
Exhibits	F		F	F	F	F

Legend A-always included if occurred or significant F-frequently included -special circumstances only

Source: *A Guide to SEC Corporate Filings* (Bethesda, MD: Disclosure, Inc., April 1983), pp. 12–13.

provides a look into the qualitative factors of security analysis. Several regular columnists discuss investment topics from a diversified perspective. *Business Week* is somewhat more general than *Forbes.* It includes a weekly economic update on such economic variables as interest rates, electricity consumption, and market prices while also featuring articles on industries and companies. Many other periodicals, such as *Kiplinger's Personal Finance Magazine* and *Money,* are helpful to the financial manager or personal investor.

Newspapers in most major cities (Chicago, Dallas, and Cleveland, to name a few) have good financial sections. *The New York Times* has an exceptional financial page. However, the most widely circulated financial daily is *The Wall Street Journal,* published by Dow Jones & Company. It is read by millions of investors who want to keep up with the economy and business environment. Feature articles on labor, business, economics, personal investing, technology, and taxes appear regularly. Corporate announcements of all kinds are published. Table 4–6, "Digest of Earnings Reports," is a daily feature that updates quarterly and annual earnings of firms.

TABLE 4–6 *The Wall Street Journal* "Digest of Earnings Reports"

Figures in parentheses are losses.

AMC ENTERTAINMENT INC. (A)

13 wk Sept 29:	1994	1993
Revenues	$164,591,000	$174,750,000
Net income	7,424,000	8,657,000
Shr earns:		
Net income .	.34	.52
26 weeks:		
Revenues	293,072,000	315,369,000
Net income	8,995,000	11,747,000
Shr earns:		
Net income .	.33	.72

ACORDIA INC. (N)

Quar Sep 30:	1994	1993
Revenues	$104,418,000	$54,650,000
Net income	5,851,000	5,850,000
Shr earns:		
Net income .	.42	.45
9 months:		
Revenues	290,534,000	164,930,000
Income	18,560,000	17,670,000
Acctg adj	....	a(776,000)
Net income	18,560,000	16,894,000
Shr earns:		
Income	1.32	1.35
Net income .	1.32	1.29

a-Cumulative effect of an accounting change.

ADVANCED TECHNOL LABS (Nq)

Quar Sep 30:	1994	a1993
Revenues	$67,472,000	$60,966,000
Net income	(4,758,000)	(8,525,000)
Avg shares	13,215,000	13,436,000
Shr earns (com & com equiv):		
Net income .	(.36)	(.63)
9 months:		
Revenues	203,550,000	208,755,000
Net income	(14,403,000)	(7,672,000)
Avg shares	13,151,000	13,690,000
Shr earns (com & com equiv):		
Net income .	(1.10)	(.56)

a-Restated to reflect the acquisition of Interspec Inc., on May 17, 1994 on a pooling-of-interest basis.

AIRTRAN CORP. (Nq)

Quar Sept 30:	1994	1993
Revenues	$36,090,000	$33,046,000
Net income	1,677,000	978,000
Avg shares	9,554,000	8,412,000
Shr earns:		
Net income .	.18	.12
6 months:		
Revenues	69,905,000	65,166,000
Net income	3,014,000	2,136,000
Avg shares	9,625,000	8,455,000
Shr earns:		
Net income .	.31	.25

AMERICAN SENSORS INC. (Nq)

Quar Sept 30:	1994	a1993
Revenues	$10,744,000	....
Net income	2,587,000	....
Shr earns:		
Net income .	.59	....

a-Comparative results not shown; company began operations July 10, 1993.

Corrected from an earlier edition.

ABBREVIATIONS

A partial list of frequently used abbreviations: Acctg adj (Accounting adjustment); Extrd chg (Extraordinary charge); Extrd cred (Extraordinary credit); Inco cnt op (Income from continuing operations); Inco dis op (Income from discontinued operations).

AAMES FINANCIAL CORP. (Nq)

Quar Sept 30:	1994	1993
Revenues	$12,427,000	$8,049,000
Net income	2,172,000	976,000
Avg shares	5,811,000	5,858,000
Shr earns:		
Net income .	.37	.17

AUDIO KING CORP. (Nq)

Quar Sept 30:	1994	1993
Sales	$12,342,446	$9,410,934
Income	104,947	73,404
Acctg adj	....	a(45,000)
Net income	104,947	28,404
Avg shares	2,830,239	2,754,511
Shr earns:		
Income	.04	.03
Net income .	.04	.01

a-Cumulative effect of accounting change

AVID TECHNOLOGY INC. (Nq)

Quar Sept 30:	1994	1993
Revenues	$54,011,000	$30,968,000
Net income	3,883,000	2,088,000
Avg shares	11,869,000	11,420,000
Shr earns:		
Net income .	.33	.18
9 months:		
Revenues	136,678,000	77,074,000
Net income	8,160,000	a655,000
Avg shares	11,747,000	10,166,000
Shr earns:		
Net income .	.69	.06

a-Includes a charge of $3,750,000 from write-off of technology.

BCE MOBILE COMMUNICAT (T)

Quar Sept 30:	1994	1993
Revenues	168,000,000	130,900,000
Net income	12,100,000	4,700,000
Shr earns:		
Net income .	.18	.07
9 months:		
Revenues	460,100,000	370,000,000
Net income	27,600,000	7,400,000
Shr earns:		
Net income .	.40	.11

Amounts in Canadian dollars.

BADGER PAPER MILLS INC. (Nq)

Quar Sept 30:	1994	1993
Sales	$19,751,000	$18,060,000
Net income	(350,000)	261,000
Shr earns:		
Net income .	(.18)	.13
9 months:		
Sales	54,521,000	59,603,000

BANK OF SUFFOLK (Nq)

Quar Sep 30:	1994	1993
Net income	$342,000	$290,000
Shr earns:		
Net income .	.38	.41
9 months:		
Net income	1,039,000	937,000
Shr earns:		
Net income .	1.14	1.33

CAPCO AUTOMOTIVE PRODS (N)

Quar Sept 30:	1994	1993
Sales	$51,997,000	$54,882,000
Net income	5,327,000	6,886,000
Avg shares	11,061,350	10,174,194
Shr earns:		
Net income .	.50	.68
9 months:		
Sales	138,055,000	138,230,000
Net income	8,278,000	9,261,000
Avg shares	10,632,395	10,174,194
Shr earns:		
Net income .	.78	.91

CARENETWORK INC. (Nq)

Quar Sept 30:	1994	1993
Revenues	$35,131,000	$37,592,000
Net income	512,000	a(2,748,000)
Avg shares	4,533,000	4,533,000
Shr earns:		
Net income .	.11	(.61)
9 months:		
Revenues	107,911,000	115,033,000
Net income	860,000	a(9,617,000)
Avg shares	4,533,000	4,533,000
Shr earns:		
Net income .	.19	(2.12)

a-Includes non-recurring charges of $1,500,000 in the quarter and $5,153,000 in the nine months.

CARLISLE PLASTICS INC. (N)

Quar Sept 30:	1994	1993
Sales	$104,258,000	$94,790,000
Net income	122,000	2,665,000
Avg shares	17,704,000	17,686,000
Shr earns (com & com equiv):		
Net income .	.01	.15
9 months:		
Sales	285,352,000	273,388,000
Income	1,292,000	4,400,000
aExtrd chg	(2,462,000)	(234,000)
Acctg adj	....	b1,586,000
Net income	(1,170,000)	5,752,000
Avg shares	17,688,000	17,664,000
Shr earns (com & com equiv):		
Income	.07	.25
Net income .	(.07)	.33

a-From early retirement of debt. b-Cumulative effect of an accounting change.

CASE CORP. (N)

Quar Sept 30:	1994	1993
Revenues	$1,040,000,000	$900,000,000
Net income	29,000,000	28,000,000
Shr earns:		
Net income ..	.39	.37
9 months:		
Revenues ..	3,234,000,000	2,926,000,000
Income	119,000,000	18,000,000

Source: *The Wall Street Journal,* October 27, 1994, p. A6. Reprinted by permission of *The Wall Street Journal,*

TABLE 4–7 New York Stock Exchange Composite Transactions (Common stock prices)

Quotations as of 5 p.m. Eastern Time
Wednesday, October 26, 1994

	52 Weeks Hi	52 Weeks Lo	Stock	Sym	Div	Yld %	PE	Vol 100s	Hi	Lo	Close	Net Chg
			-A-A-A-									
	17⅜	12¼	AAR	AIR	.48	3.9	22	155	12½	12⅜	12⅜	...
	23⅝	16	ABM Indus	ABM	.52	2.6	13	189	20⅛	20	20⅛	...
	12⅝	9¼	ACM Gvt Fd	ACG	1.10a	11.6	...	1083	9½	9¼	9½	+ ⅛
	10¼	6⅞	ACM OppFd	AOF	.80	11.0	...	307	7¼	7	7¼	+ ¼
	12¼	8¼	ACM SecFd	GSF	1.10	13.1	...	1222	8½	8⅜	8⅜	− ⅛
	10⅝	7	ACM SpctmFd	SI	.96	13.2	...	435	7¼	7⅛	7¼	...
	15⅛	10¼	ACM MgmdInc	ADF	1.46	13.6	...	485	10¾	10½	10¾	+ ⅛
	12⅜	7⅜	ACM MgdIncFd	AMF	1.08a	13.1	...	285	8¼	8⅛	8¼	+ ⅛
	9⅜	7⅞	ACM MgdMultFd	MMF	.72	8.9	...	363	8¼	8⅛	8⅛	− ⅛
	14⅜	10	ACM MuniSec	AMU	.90a	8.8	...	270	10¼	10⅛	10¼	+ ⅛
	11⅞	8½	ADT	ADT		...	16	759	11¾	11½	11⅝	...
	36⅛	24¾	♣AFLAC	AFL	.46	1.4	12	924	32¼	32	32¼	...
	52	26½	AGCO Cp	AG	.04	.1	8	224	47¾	47⅜	47⅜	− ½
	68½	39¼	AGCO pf		1.64	2.6	...	2	62⅞	62⅞	62⅞	− ⅛
	17¼	12⅝	AL Pharma	ALO	.18	1.1	52	286	16¾	16½	16¾	+ ⅛
n	23¼	19½	AMLI Resdntl	AML	1.68	8.5	...	16	20	19¾	19⅞	− ⅛
	79⅜	57	♣AMP	AMP	1.68	2.2	25	2261	77¼	76⅜	76¾	− ¼
	72¾	48⅛	AMR	AMR		...	cc	1612	52	50⅝	50⅞	− ¾
	51	40½	ARCO Chm	RCM	2.50	5.1	18	230	49¼	48⅞	49⅛	...
	5	3	♣ARX	ARX		...	7	210	3¾	3½	3⅝	− ⅛
	56⅛	38⅝	ASA	ASA	2.00	4.0	...	652	50¼	49½	49½	− ½
	27⅜	21¼	ATT Cap	TCC	.40f	1.7	11	118	23½	22⅞	22⅞	− ⅝
	58½	49½	AT&T Cp	T	1.32	2.5	18	19692	54⅛	53⅝	53¾	− ⅛
	32	25⅜	AbbotLab	ABT	.76	2.5	17	13298	31	30⅛	30⅛	− ⅜
	8¼	2⅞	Abex	ABE		...	10	7	7⅜	7⅜	7⅜	− ⅛
	15¼	8½	Abitibi g	ABY		...	...	146	13	12⅝	12¾	− ⅛
	18	11⅛	♣AcceptIns	AIF		...	16	296	16⅝	16⅜	16½	− ⅛
	6⅞	2½	AcceptIns wt			...	...	500	5⅜	5⅛	5¼	− ¼
	33½	22¼	ACE Ltd	ACL	.44	2.0	dd	483	23	22¼	22½	− ¼
	15½	8¾	AcmeCleve	AMT	.44	3.3	18	88	13⅝	13⅜	13⅜	− ⅛
	13⅝	**6½**	**AcmeElec**	**ACE**		...	**dd**	**125**	**12⅛**	**11½**	**11½**	**− ⅝**
	28¾	21	♣Acordia	ACO	.60	2.1	14	54	28⅛	28	28	+ ⅛
	13¾	5¾	ActavaGp	ACT	.09j	...	dd	459	9⅛	9	9⅛	+ ¼
	17	**11¼**	**Acuson**	**ACN**		...	**29**	**1455**	**16⅝**	**16**	**16½**	**+1**
	19⅝	16½	AdamsExp	ADX	.48a	2.8	...	152	17⅛	17	17⅛	...
	31¾	16¾	AdvMicro	AMD		...	8	4564	24⅝	24	24½	+ ¼
	64	46½	AdvMicro pf		3.00	5.6	...	13	53½	53	53⅜	+ ⅛
	20	14⅜	Advo	AD	.10	.5	17	107	18¼	17⅞	18¼	+ ¼
n	11⅜	8¼	Advocat	AVC		...	...	1220	10½	10⅛	10¼	− ¼
	63¼	49	AEGON	AEG	2.21e	3.5	11	18	62⅞	62½	62½	− ½
	66¼	44⅝	AetnaLife	AET	2.76	6.1	dd	1355	45⅛	44¾	45⅛	− ⅛
n	19⅝	15⅝	AgreeRlty	ADC	1.80	11.3	...	14	15⅞	15¾	15⅞	...
	22¾	16⅜	Ahmanson	AHM	.88	4.8	11	3918	18⅞	18½	18½	− ½
	27¼	23⅜	Ahmanson pfC		2.10	8.6	...	569	24½	24⅛	24½	+ ⅜
	52	45	Ahmanson pfD		3.00	6.6	...	153	45½	45	45¼	− ¼
	28¼	25⅜	Ahmanson pf		2.40	9.2	...	84	26¼	26⅛	26⅛	...
s	29⅛	22	Ahold	AHO	.61e	2.1	...	24	28⅞	28½	28½	− ¼
	6⅛	1⅜	vjAileen	AEE		...	...	70	1¾	1¾	1¾	...
	50⅜	38¾	AirProduct	APD	.98	2.2	22	946	45	44½	44⅞	+ ¼
▼	39⅞	18¾	AirbornFrght	ABF	.30	1.6	9	7406	19½	18	18½	− ⅝
s	29⅛	17¾	♣Airgas	ARG		...	40	51	28⅝	28⅛	28⅛	− ⅜
	17	14¾	Airlease	FLY	1.84	11.5	12	11	16	15⅞	16	+ ⅛
n	30⅛	19⅞	AirTouch	ATI		...	...	7272	29⅝	29⅛	29⅛	+ ⅛
	26⅞	22¼	AlaPwr pfA		1.90	8.4	...	61	22⅝	22⅜	22½	+ ⅛
n	25½	22	AlaPwr pfD		1.02e	4.5	...	2	22⅞	22⅞	22⅞	+ ¼
	27¼	22	AlaPwr pfH		1.90	8.4	...	7	22⅝	22½	22½	...
n	25½	19½	AlaPwr pfB		1.70	8.4	...	4	20¼	19¾	20¼	+ ¼
	18⅞	13⅝	AlaskaAir	ALK	.05j	...	31	556	16⅞	16⅝	16⅞	...
	21¼	16⅛	♣AlbanyInt	AIN	.35	1.9	25	560	18⅜	18⅜	18⅜	...
	[illegible]	[illegible]	Albemar[illegible]	[illegible]	.15e	1.0		310	15[illegible]	[illegible]	15⅜	+ ⅛
								[illegible]				+ ¼
	27⅛	23	AonCp pfA		2.00	8.5	...	24	23⅝	23⅜	23½	− ⅛
	50¼	45½	AonCp pfB		3.04	6.3	...	11	48¼	48⅛	48⅛	− ⅝
	29¼	**20⅜**	**ApacheCp**	**APA**	**.28**	**1.0**	**39**	**9990**	**27¾**	**25⅝**	**27⅝**	**+2¼**
n	18⅝	16½	ApartmtInv	AIV		...	...	128	17⅞	17¾	17¾	− ⅛
	10¾	8⅜	ApexMunFd	APX	.74e	8.8	...	519	8½	8⅜	8⅜	...
	7½	3½	AppliedMagn	APM		...	dd	417	4	3¾	3⅞	+ ⅛
	25⅛	14½	AppldPwr	APW	.12	.5	19	59	23¾	23½	23½	− ½
	27¾	19¾	♣AptarGp	ATR	.24	.9	18	113	27½	27⅛	27⅜	+ ⅜
	29¼	22¾	Aquarion	WTR	1.62	7.0	13	87	23⅜	22⅞	23¼	...
▼	15¼	7⅞	♣AquilaGasPip	AQP	.04e	.5	...	144	7¾	7¾	7¾	− ⅛
s	**14¾**	**5¾**	**Aracruz**	**ARA**		...	...	**301**	**13**	**12⅜**	**13**	**+ ⅝**
	12⅜	7½	ArborProp	ABR	1.10	11.3	dd	16	9¾	9½	9¾	+ ⅛
	26¼	21¼	ArcadnPtnr	UAN	2.42	9.8	11	263	24⅞	24¼	24⅝	+ ¼
	28¼	20⅝	ArcherDan	ADM	.15f	.5	17	9516	28⅛	27⅜	27⅞	+ ½
	23⅞	18⅞	Argentaria	AGR	.96e	5.1	...	2224	19⅛	19	19	...
	19⅝	12½	ArgntnaFd	AF	.15e	1.0	...	120	14⅝	14⅜	14½	+ ⅛
x	25⅜	20½	ArizPubSvc pfW		1.81	8.7	...	16	21½	20⅞	20⅞	...
	29	25¾	ArkPower pf		2.40	9.2	...	2	26	26	26	− ¼
	6⅞	4½	Armco	AS		...	dd	7633	6⅝	6½	6⅝	...
	29	22⅞	Armco pf		2.10	9.2	...	19	23⅛	22⅞	22⅞	− ⅛
	51⅞	45½	Armco pfA		4.50	9.7	...	7	46¼	46	46¼	...
	58⅞	46	Armco pfB		3.63	7.2	...	620	51	50¾	50¾	+ ⅛
	57½	39⅝	ArmstrngWld	ACK	1.28	3.1	12	4824	41⅛	40⅜	41⅛	+1⅛
	45⅛	33⅝	ArrowElec	ARW		...	13	4586	36⅞	35⅝	36¾	...
	8⅜	4¼	ArtraGp	ATA		...	dd	2	4⅝	4½	4½	...
	33¾	23	♣ArvinInd	ARV	.76	3.2	13	238	24	23⅞	23⅞	− ⅛
	34⅞	17⅜	Asarco	AR	.40	1.3	cc	2130	31¾	31⅛	31⅜	− ⅛
	31¾	22½	AshlandCoal	ACI	.40	1.3	35	1	30⅜	30⅜	30⅜	− ⅛
	44½	31	AshlandOil	ASH	1.00	2.6	13	1474	38½	37¾	38⅜	+ ⅜
	73⅛	56⅜	AshlandOil pf		3.13	5.0	...	271	63	61⅞	63	+1⅛
	25¾	16⅝	AsiaPacFd	APB	2.59e	14.4	...	114	18¼	17⅞	18	+ ⅛
n	16⅞	10¾	AsiaTigers	GRR	.02p	...	...	465	12⅝	12¼	12⅜	...
	3½	1¾	AssetInvest	AIC	.24e	9.6	dd	359	2⅝	2½	2½	− ⅛
n	24⅜	18¾	AssocEstate	AEC	1.60	8.4	...	87	19¼	19	19⅛	...
	38⅛	28¼	AssocNG	NGA	.12	.3	30	1145	37⅝	37½	37½	...
	39	29¾	AtlaGasLt	ATG	2.08	6.4	13	1013	32¾	32⅜	32½	...
	27¼	23½	AtlaGasLt pf		1.93	8.1	...	9	24	23¾	23⅞	...
	22¾	16	AtlanEngy	ATE	1.54	9.6	8	1023	16⅝	16⅛	16⅛	− ¼
	118	92½	AtlanRich	ARC	5.50	5.2	64	5148	106⅜	104⅛	106⅛	+2⅛
	267½	226½	AtlanRich pfC		2.80	1.1	...	2	253	250¼	250¼	+6¼
n	32	24⅞	AtlanRich97	LYX		...	...	842	28	27½	27¾	− ¼
	10	3½	AtlasCp	AZ		...	dd	275	4	3¾	4	...
s	21⅛	16¼	♣ATMOS Eng	ATO	.88	5.2	16	94	16⅞	16⅜	16⅞	...
	12½	8¼	Attwoods	A	.47e	5.2	12	613	9¼	9	9	− ¼
	24⅞	15½	Augat	AUG	.08e	.4	15	1167	18⅞	18¼	18⅞	+ ⅜
	28¼	24⅜	Aus&NZ Bk pf		2.28	9.3	...	57	24⅝	24½	24⅝	− ⅛
	12⅜	8	AustriaFd	OST	.12e	1.5	...	261	8⅛	8	8⅛	...
s	16	10⅞	AuthenticFit	ASM		...	31	120	14⅜	14⅛	14⅜	+ ¼
	4⅜	2⅛	AutoSecHldg	ASI		...	...	2144	2⅝	2½	2⅝	...
	58⅛	47⅝	AutoDataProc	AUD	.60	1.1	23	2193	56⅞	56	56	− ⅝
s	30¾	21⅝	AutoZone	AZO		...	32	4551	25½	24¾	24⅞	− ⅝
n	24¼	19½	AvalonProp	AVN	1.44	7.2	...	75	19⅞	19½	19⅞	+ ¼
	21	13¾	AVEMCO	AVE	.44	3.0	12	25	14½	14½	14½	...
	35⅝	26¼	AveryDensn	AVY	.96	2.9	19	1100	34½	33⅛	33⅜	−1⅛
n	19	7½	Aviall	AVL	.04	.4	...	243	10⅜	10⅛	10⅛	− ¼
	45	30¾	Avnet	AVT	.60	1.7	17	1387	36¼	35½	36¼	+1
	62⅞	47⅝	AvonPdts	AVP	2.00f	3.3	18	5073	60⅜	59¾	60⅜	+ ⅝
	16½	10⅛	Aydin	AYD		...	dd	154	10½	10¼	10½	+ ⅛
	7⅞	5⅜	AztarCp	AZR		...	12	1101	6	5¾	5¾	− ⅛
			-B-B-B-									
	38¾	31¾	BCE Inc g	BCE	2.68	...	...	991	35	34¾	35	+ ¼
	9½	6	BET	BEP	.24e	3.5	...	125	7	6⅞	6⅞	− ⅛
	24⅛	17[illegible]	[illegible]BJ Svc	BJS				[illegible]				
s	1[illegible]											
	26⅝	22⅝	BankBost pfF		1.97	8.6	...	15	23⅛	22⅞	22⅞	...
s	33¼	24⅞	BankNY	BK	1.28f	4.1	8	1584	31	30¼	31	+1
▼	28⅜	24⅞	BankNY pfB		2.15	8.7	...	96	25⅜	24¾	24¾	− ¾
	27¾	24⅞	BkUtdTex pf	BKUA	2.53	10.1	...	27	25⅛	25	25	− ⅛
	50¼	38⅜	BankAmer	BAC	1.60	3.8	8	20224	43	41¾	42⅜	− ⅛
	50⅞	43⅜	BankAmer pfA		3.25	7.4	...	38	44	43⅝	43¾	− ¼
	95½	74	BankAmer pfB		6.00	7.9	...	7	75¾	75½	75¾	−1
	28¼	25½	BankAmer pfF		2.41	9.2	...	83	26½	26¼	26¼	− ⅛
	62¾	51¾	BankAmer pfG		3.25	6.2	...	49	53	52½	52¾	...
	28¼	24⅞	BankAmer pfH		2.25	8.9	...	210	25½	25¼	25⅜	...
	30¼	27½	BankAmer pfI		2.75	9.8	...	19	28	27⅞	28	...
	30½	27⅞	BankAmer pfJ		2.75	9.7	...	39	28⅜	28¼	28¼	− ⅛
	27¼	24	BankAmer pfK		2.09	8.6	...	132	24½	24⅛	24⅜	+ ⅛
	27¼	23⅜	BankAmer pfL		2.04	8.5	...	691	24¼	23¾	24	− ⅛
	26¾	22¾	BankAmer pfM		1.97	8.4	...	211	23⅝	23⅜	23½	...
	27⅝	24⅛	BankAmer pfN		2.13	8.6	...	37	24¾	24½	24¾	+ ⅛
	50⅞	48	BankAm pf1		3.75	7.8	...	21	48¼	48⅛	48⅛	− ⅛
	27⅞	26⅞	BankAm pf2		2.25	8.3	...	156	27⅛	27⅛	27⅛	...
	26½	18	BkrsLife	BLH	.60	3.2	8	2210	19⅞	19	19	− ⅛
	84⅝	62⅞	BankTrst	BT	3.60	5.4	7	2182	66⅞	66⅛	66¾	+ ⅞
n	25⅝	23⅛	BkTrst dep pfQ		1.58	6.7	...	2	23½	23½	23½	− ¼
n	24⅜	23⅛	BkTrst dep pfR			...	...	27	23⅜	23¼	23¼	...
	27¼	23⅝	BankTrst un		2.14	8.7	...	25	24½	24	24½	+ ¼
n	10⅛	6⅛	Banpais	BPS		...	...	106	6⅝	6¼	6⅝	+ ⅛
	1½	⅝	BanyanMtgInv	VMG		...	dd	154	⅝	⅝	⅝	...
	39	30	Barclays	BCS	1.76e	4.7	...	15	37⅞	37¼	37⅝	− ⅛
	27¾	25⅜	Barclays pr		2.78	10.8	...	21	25¾	25½	25¾	+ ¼
	27½	25¼	Barclays prB		2.72	10.7	...	23	25⅝	25⅜	25⅜	− ⅛
	30⅝	26½	Barclays pfD		2.88	10.8	...	3362	26¾	26½	26¾	+ ⅛
	26	21¼	Barclays prE		2.00	9.1	...	173	22⅛	21⅝	21⅞	...
	30⅜	26⅜	Barclays pfC		2.81	10.6	...	64	26¾	26⅜	26⅝	− ⅜
	30½	22¼	Bard CR	BCR	.60	2.5	11	1290	24⅜	24⅛	24⅛	...
	32¼	20	BarnesNoble	BKS		...	58	2032	28¼	27⅝	28	+ ⅝
	39⅞	29½	BarnesGp	B	1.40	3.8	17	12	37⅛	36⅞	37	+ ⅛
	48⅛	37⅜	BarnettBks	BBI	1.64	4.0	9	2175	41	40½	40¾	+ ⅛
	92	80	BarnettBks pfA		4.50	5.6	...	21	81¼	80⅜	80⅜	−1⅛
▼	70½	59½	BarnettBks pfC		4.00	6.7	...	22	59½	58⅞	59½	...
	18½	14⅛	Bass	BAS	.78e	4.4	...	49	17¾	17½	17¾	+ ⅜
	13	8⅞	BattleMtn	BMG	.05	.4	dd	1789	12⅜	12¼	12¼	− ⅛
x	70½	57½	BattleMtn pf		3.25	5.0	...	28	66	65½	65⅝	− ¼
▼	53⅞	31⅞	BauschLomb	BOL	.98	3.2	19	10096	32¼	30⅝	31	−1
	28¾	21⅝	BaxterInt	BAX	1.05f	4.2	dd	12482	25⅜	24¾	24⅞	− ⅛
n	22¾	19¾	BayApartmt	BYA	.82e	4.0	...	298	20⅜	20¼	20¼	− ⅛
	31⅜	23¼	BayStGas	BGC	1.46	5.9	13	34	24⅝	24¼	24⅝	+ ⅛
n	19½	17	BeaconProp	BCN	.16p	...	...	46	18⅝	18½	18⅝	...
	23½	15	BearStearns	BSC	.60b	3.9	7	1931	15½	15¼	15¼	...
	26	21⅞	BearStearns pfB		1.97	8.6	...	102	23⅛	22¾	23	− ⅛
	25⅜	21⅜	BearStearns pfC		1.90	8.7	...	67	21⅞	21½	21¾	− ¼
n	24¾	20¾	BearStnEPICS pfA		2.00	9.4	...	61	21⅜	21	21¼	...
	37½	26⅝	♣BearingsInc	BER	.72f	2.3	18	8	31¾	31¾	31¾	...
n▼	18¾	12⅝	BeazerHm	BZH		...	...	117	12⅝	12½	12½	− ⅛
	32½	23	♣BeckmanInstr	BEC	.40	1.4	dd	81	29⅛	28¾	28¾	− ⅝
	48¼	34	BectonDksn	BDX	.74	1.6	17	769	47⅞	47½	47⅝	+ ⅛
	7¼	4¾	BedfdPrpty	BED	.33e	5.9	11	10	5⅝	5⅝	5⅝	+ ⅛
	21¾	15⅞	♣Belden	BWC	.15e	.8	15	158	19⅜	19	19⅜	...
	64½	49	BellAtlantic	BEL	2.76	5.5	15	3098	50⅝	49⅞	50⅛	+ ⅛
	21⅛	13¾	♣BellIndus	BI		...	13	65	19⅝	19½	19⅝	+ ¼
▼	63⅞	51¼	BellSouth	BLS	2.76	5.4	19	12492	51¾	50¾	50⅞	− ½
	55	**43⅛**	**Belo AH A**	**BLC**	**.60**	**1.1**	**19**	**978**	**54**	**51½**	**53½**	**+2⅞**
	25¾	20⅛	Bemis	BMS	.54	2.3	18	207	24⅜	23⅞	24	− ½
s	44	34½	Beneficial	BNL	1.72f	4.4	10	488	40	38⅝	39⅛	− ⅝
	67¾	56	Beneficial pfA		4.50	8.0	...	z20	56½	56½	56½	−1
	[illegible]	30¼	Beneficial pfV		2.50	7.9	...	1	31½	31½	31½	...
	[illegible]	[illegible]½	B[illegible]tton	BNG	.47p	1[illegible]						

Source: *The Wall Street Journal,* October 27, 1994, p. C3. Reprinted by permission of *The Wall Street Journal,* © 1994 by Dow Jones & Company. All Rights Reserved Worldwide.

New offerings of stocks and bonds are also advertised by investment bankers in the *Journal.* Prices of actively traded securities are presented by the market in which they trade. Common and preferred stock prices are organized by exchange and over-the-counter markets. Table 4–7 is an example of common stock prices on the New York Stock Exchange.

Many other prices are printed in *The Wall Street Journal.* An investor will find prices of government Treasury bills, notes, and bonds, mutual funds, put and call prices from the option exchanges, government agency securities, foreign exchange prices, and commodities futures prices. Table 4–8 is an example of the commodity futures prices from the *Journal.* The prices are listed by category and exchange. Because of the comprehensive price coverage on a daily basis and other features, it is hard to believe that an up-to-date intelligent investor would be able to function without *The Wall*

TABLE 4–8 Commodity Futures Prices

Wednesday, October 26, 1994.

Open Interest Reflects Previous Trading Day.

GRAINS AND OILSEEDS

CORN (CBT) 5,000 bu.; cents per bu.

	Open	High	Low	Settle	Change	Lifetime High	Lifetime Low	Open Interest
Dec	215	216	214¾	215¼	− ¼	277	213¼	121,728
Mr95	226¼	227¼	226	226¾	+ ¼	282½	223¼	59,135
May	234¼	235½	234¼	235	....	285	230½	25,148
July	240	241¼	240	241	+ ¼	285½	235¾	29,520
Sept	245¼	246	245¼	245¾	....	270½	239	2,505
Dec	250	251	250	250¾	....	263	235½	13,138
Mr96	256¾	257¼	256¾	257¼	+ ¼	258	250½	254
July	....	....	....	264	....	266¼	254	418
Dec	250½	251½	250½	251½	+ 1	257	239	286

Est vol 25,000; vol Tues 25,732; open int 252,132, +506.

OATS (CBT) 5,000 bu.; cents per bu.

	Open	High	Low	Settle	Change	Lifetime High	Lifetime Low	Open Interest
Dec	126	127	125¾	126½	+ ½	157¼	116	9,840
Mr95	132	132½	131¾	132¼	+ ½	152¾	121½	3,183
May	135¼	135½	135¼	136	+ ½	151	125	1,489
July	139¼	139¼	139¼	139¼	+ ¼	142½	132	1,331

Est vol 700; vol Tues 828; open int 15,844, −114.

SOYBEANS (CBT) 5,000 bu.; cents per bu.

	Open	High	Low	Settle	Change	Lifetime High	Lifetime Low	Open Interest
Nov	548	549½	545	548	− ¼	699	526¾	39,625
Ja95	559½	561½	557	560	+ ¼	704	537¼	42,648
Mar	569	571½	567¼	570	....	705	547¼	22,365
May	577½	579½	575½	578¼	....	705½	556	10,375
July	583½	585¾	582	584¾	+ ¼	706½	563½	17,646
Aug	587	588½	586	587¼	− ¼	612	566½	1,199
Sept	588½	590	587	588¼	− ¾	616	571	451
Nov	597½	599	596½	598½	− ¼	645	578½	7,473
Ja96	....	....	....	606	− ¾	607	604½	122

Est vol 31,000; vol Tues 42,478; open int 142,017, −481.

SOYBEAN MEAL (CBT) 100 tons; $ per ton.

	Open	High	Low	Settle	Change	Lifetime High	Lifetime Low	Open Interest
Dec	163.30	163.40	162.70	162.90	− .90	209.00	160.30	41,955
Ja95	164.30	164.50	163.90	164.10	− .70	207.50	161.90	17,048
Mar	167.80	167.80	167.20	167.50	− .90	207.50	164.90	14,065
May	171.00	171.00	170.40	170.70	− .70	207.00	167.60	8,262
July	174.80	175.00	174.40	174.70	− .60	206.00	170.70	7,897
Aug	176.20	176.30	176.00	176.00	− .80	182.60	172.00	1,169
Sept	178.30	178.30	177.50	177.50	− 1.00	182.70	173.60	1,202
Oct	179.80	179.80	179.50	179.60	− .70	181.80	175.60	2,420
Dec	182.00	182.00	181.70	181.80	− .70	184.00	176.50	800

Est vol 10,000; vol Tues 10,632; open int 94,819, −1,536.

SOYBEAN OIL (CBT) 60,000 lbs.; cents per lb.

	Open	High	Low	Settle	Change	Lifetime High	Lifetime Low	Open Interest
Dec	25.77	25.98	25.71	25.92	+ .11	28.87	22.00	35,250
Ja95	24.85	25.10	24.85	25.08	+ .17	28.55	22.65	14,257
Mar	24.43	24.65	24.40	24.63	+ .17	28.30	22.91	13,321
May	24.12	24.32	24.12	24.30	+ .16	28.00	22.85	11,239
July	23.93	24.12	23.93	24.08	+ .17	27.85	22.76	7,482
Aug	23.95	24.05	23.95	24.05	+ .15	27.20	22.73	2,146
Sept		....	....	23.92	+ .12	24.75	22.75	1,520
Oct	23.95	23.95	23.88	23.88	+ .13	23.95	22.75	1,578
Dec	23.90	23.90	23.90	23.90	+ .13	23.90	22.80	1,092

Est vol 15,000; vol Tues 20,392; open int 87,886, +2,459.

WHEAT (CBT) 5,000 bu.; cents per bu.

	Open	High	Low	Settle	Change	Lifetime High	Lifetime Low	Open Interest
Dec	398½	404½	397¼	401	+ 1	418¾	309	38,980
Mr95	409	414	407½	411	+ ¾	426¾	327	23,898
May	385	388	383	385½	....	398½	325	4,193
July	352	354½	351¼	352¼	− ½	363¾	311½	9,750
Sept	356½	356½	356½	356½	....	365	351½	232
Dec	364	364	364	365	− ¼	375	362	145

Est vol 14,000; vol Tues 16,095; open int 77,204, +125.

WHEAT (KC) 5,000 bu.; cents per bu.

	Open	High	Low	Settle	Change	Lifetime High	Lifetime Low	Open Interest
Dec	407	411	406	407¼	− ¾	423¼	312½	19,276
Mr95	411	415	410¼	411¾	− ¼	427¼	326½	13,455
May	389	392	389	390	− ¾	403	321½	1,413
July	357½	360	357½	358	− 1	368¼	316½	3,744

Est vol 4,996; vol Tues 4,647; open int 37,975, +473.

WHEAT (MPLS) 5,000 bu.; cents per bu.

	Open	High	Low	Settle	Change	Lifetime High	Lifetime Low	Open Interest
Dec	404	406¾	401¼	404	− ¾	419½	304	11,165
Mr95	413½	417	412¼	414¼	....	431	325¼	6,343
May	409	409.4	06	406¾	....	419¼	332½	647
July	374½	374½	374½	374	+ ½	386	324½	191

Est vol 2,802; vol Tues 2,984; open int 18,442, +16.

RICE--ROUGH (CBT) 2000 cwt; $ per cwt

	Open	High	Low	Settle	Change	Lifetime High	Lifetime Low	Open Interest
Nov	6.350	6.530	6.240	6.240	− .010	6.530	5.970	873
Ja95	6.600	6.730	6.470	6.470	− .10	6.730	6.160	688
Mar	6.800	6.910	6.680	6.680	− .050	6.910	6.340	1,432
May	7.000	7.000	6.950	6.800	− .050	7.000	6.500	183

Est vol 700; vol Tues 752; open int 3,179, −81.

CANOLA (WPG) 20 metric tons; Can. $ per ton

	Open	High	Low	Settle	Change	Lifetime High	Lifetime Low	Open Interest
Nov	388.00	388.00	385.00	385.90	− 3.30	401.00	316.00	8,647
Ja95	392.00	392.00	388.80	389.00	− 3.70	401.50	317.50	16,983
Mar	392.50	393.30	391.30	391.40	− 3.40	403.90	331.00	18,232
June	393.80	396.00	393.80	394.40	− 2.20	409.50	346.50	7,867
Aug	378.00	378.00	377.50	377.50	....	380.00	362.00	218
Nov	373.90	373.90	371.50	372.00	− 1.90	374.90	331.00	707

Est vol 4,015; vol Tues 5,051; open int 52,708, +53.

WHEAT (WPG) 20 metric tons; Can. $ per ton

	Open	High	Low	Settle	Change	Lifetime High	Lifetime Low	Open Interest
Dec	135.80	136.10	135.60	136.10	....	141.70	97.80	6,176
Mr95	138.50	139.00	138.30	139.00	− .10	140.90	100.30	4,033
May		....	....	139.00	....	140.50	100.30	1,420
July		....	....	138.50	+ .40	139.50	101.00	366

Est vol 440; vol Tues 672; open int 12,005, −14.

LIVESTOCK AND MEAT

CATTLE–FEEDER (CME) 50,000 lbs.; cents per lb.

	Open	High	Low	Settle	Change	Lifetime High	Lifetime Low	Open Interest
Oct	72.55	72.60	72.47	72.47	− .10	81.35	70.95	1,169
Nov	74.50	74.55	74.15	74.22	− .30	81.85	71.75	3,628
Ja95	74.40	74.42	74.10	74.12	− .20	80.95	71.40	2,074
Mar	72.45	72.62	72.35	72.47	− .17	80.25	70.35	882
Apr	71.80	71.90	71.55	71.55	− .25	76.90	70.10	497
May	71.50	71.55	71.30	71.30	− .20	76.45	69.80	335
Aug	71.50	71.50	71.30	71.30	....	73.10	69.80	103

Est vol 1,008; vol Tues 2,352; open int 8,701, −347.

CATTLE–LIVE (CME) 40,000 lbs.; cents per lb.

	Open	High	Low	Settle	Change	Lifetime High	Lifetime Low	Open Interest
Dec	69.70	69.85	69.55	69.72	....	74.30	67.20	30,591
Fb95	68.57	68.67	68.37	68.50	− .07	75.25	66.85	20,057
Apr	68.80	68.95	68.77	68.82	....	75.10	67.27	13,003
June	65.35	65.50	65.30	65.47	+ .10	72.50	64.20	4,085
Aug	64.50	64.55	64.40	64.47	+ .05	68.10	63.60	1,381
Oct		....	....	65.30	+ .05	67.55	64.20	256

Est vol 7,661; vol Tues 15,201; open int 69,384, +833.

HOGS (CME) 40,000 lbs.; cents per lb.

	Open	High	Low	Settle	Change	Lifetime High	Lifetime Low	Open Interest
Dec	33.50	33.82	33.25	33.75	+ .35	50.50	32.80	18,052
Fb95	36.60	36.97	36.57	36.90	+ .35	50.80	35.65	7,441
Apr	36.85	37.15	36.85	37.02	+ .30	48.80	36.10	4,356
June	42.12	42.32	41.90	42.27	+ .17	51.55	41.57	1,871
July	42.10	42.27	42.05	42.27	+ .17	49.00	41.60	544
Aug	41.75	41.75	41.60	41.75	+ .05	47.00	41.15	339
Oct	38.65	38.75	38.60	38.75	+ .10	40.50	38.30	283

Est vol 4,087; vol Tues 6,642; open int 32,941, +281.

PORK BELLIES (CME) 40,000 lbs.; cents per lb.

	Open	High	Low	Settle	Change	Lifetime High	Lifetime Low	Open Interest
Feb	39.60	40.17	39.27	39.80	+ .15	60.05	37.40	8,694
Mar	39.57	40.25	39.25	40.02	+ .25	60.20	37.50	998
May	40.95	41.45	40.70	40.97	+ .20	61.15	38.95	318
July	41.35	41.85	41.30	41.70	+ .30	54.00	39.85	301

Est vol 1,411; vol Tues 1,748; open int 10,377, −16.

METALS AND PETROLEUM

COPPER-HIGH (CMX) – 25,000 lbs.; cents per lb.

	Open	High	Low	Settle	Change	Lifetime High	Lifetime Low	Open Interest
Oct	123.30	123.90	122.60	123.55	+ 2.50	123.90	75.20	953
Nov	122.00	123.00	122.00	122.60	+ 2.75	123.00	77.75	1,473
Dec	121.60	122.60	120.85	122.00	+ 2.75	122.60	75.75	39,781
Ja95	121.70	121.70	121.30	121.30	+ 2.65	121.70	76.90	798
Feb	120.00	120.10	120.00	120.60	+ 2.60	120.10	87.85	570
Mar	119.50	120.40	118.95	119.75	+ 2.40	120.40	76.30	8,752
Apr		....	....	118.80	+ 2.25	116.50	90.10	656
May	117.30	117.80	117.30	117.75	+ 2.10	117.80	76.85	2,247
June	117.00	117.00	117.00	117.00	+ 2.10	117.00	106.30	430
July	116.00	116.40	115.75	116.25	+ 1.90	116.40	78.00	1,756
Aug		....	....	115.50	+ 1.90	115.90	111.40	121
Sept	114.70	115.20	114.70	114.75	+ 1.70	115.20	79.10	1,085
Dec	112.50	112.80	112.50	113.10	+ 1.75	113.75	88.00	1,281
Mr96	111.75	111.75	111.75	111.50	+ 1.75	111.80	99.20	256

Est vol 14,000; vol Tues 9,018; open int 60,272, −1,167.

GOLD (CMX) – 100 troy oz.; $ per troy oz.

	Open	High	Low	Settle	Change	Lifetime High	Lifetime Low	Open Interest
Oct	389.50	389.50	389.50	389.30	− .10	417.00	344.00	38
Dec	390.50	391.30	389.20	391.00	− .20	426.50	343.00	83,135
Fb95	394.00	394.90	392.70	394.50	− .20	411.00	363.50	19,529
Apr	398.00	398.00	396.90	398.10	− .20	425.00	385.50	8,139
June	401.30	401.70	400.20	401.70	− .20	430.00	351.00	9,768
Aug		....	....	405.60	− .20	414.50	380.50	6,100
Oct		....	....	409.80	− .20	419.20	401.00	1,514
Dec	413.90	413.90	412.90	414.00	− .20	439.50	358.00	7,848
Fb96		....	....	418.20	− .20	424.50	412.50	1,899
Apr		....	....	422.40	− .20	430.20	418.30	1,965
June		....	....	426.90	− .10	447.00	370.90	5,882
Aug		....	....	431.30	....	....	....	124
Dec	440.40	440.40	440.40	440.50	+ .10	447.50	379.60	3,068
Ju97		....	....	454.60	+ .20	456.00	436.00	1,148
Dec		....	....	469.10	+ .40	477.00	402.00	2,742
Ju98		....	....	484.30	+ .60	489.50	481.70	1,638
Dec		....	....	499.80	+ .80	505.00	468.00	2,023
Ju99		....	....	516.00	1.00	520.00	511.00	994

Est vol 33,000; vol Tues 17,855; open int 157,554, +105.

PLATINUM (NYM) – 50 troy oz.; $ per troy oz.

	Open	High	Low	Settle	Change	Lifetime High	Lifetime Low	Open Interest
Oct	425.90	425.90	425.00	427.00	+ 2.60	435.40	368.00	40
Ja95	425.00	427.40	423.50	427.00	+ 1.60	435.50	374.80	20,367
Apr	429.50	431.00	429.50	431.30	+ 1.60	439.00	390.00	3,648
July		....	....	435.80	+ 1.60	439.00	419.50	1,045
Oct		....	....	440.50	+ 1.60	436.50	422.50	392

Est vol 2,525; vol Tues 1,695; open int 25,494, +196.

PALLADIUM (NYM) 100 troy oz.; $ per troy oz.

	Open	High	Low	Settle	Change	Lifetime High	Lifetime Low	Open Interest
Dec	158.50	158.70	157.50	158.15	+ .35	159.50	122.50	4,322
Mr95	159.30	159.75	159.25	159.35	+ .35	159.75	134.00	1,732
June		....	....	160.35	+ .35	160.50	151.60	376

Est vol 541; vol Tues 490; open int 6,430, −66.

SILVER (CMX) – 5,000 troy oz.; cents per troy oz.

	Open	High	Low	Settle	Change	Lifetime High	Lifetime Low	Open Interest
Oct		....	....	538.6	+ 9.4	561.5	511.5	185
Dec	531.0	542.0	531.0	541.2	+ 9.2	597.0	380.0	75,144
Mr95	540.0	550.0	540.0	549.7	+ 9.2	604.0	416.5	16,835
May	546.5	555.0	546.5	555.8	+ 9.3	606.5	418.0	4,689
July	553.0	560.0	552.0	562.1	+ 9.4	610.0	403.0	3,862
Sept	567.0	567.0	567.0	568.6	+ 9.5	615.0	493.0	2,485
Dec	575.5	576.5	574.5	578.6	+ 9.6	628.0	434.0	2,586
Mr96		....	....	589.7	+ 9.9	622.0	554.0	1,433
July		....	....	604.5	+ 9.9	630.0	524.0	1,303
Dec		....	....	623.8	+ 9.9	670.0	454.0	1,731
Jl97		....	....	652.8	+ 10.4	655.0	588.0	433
Dec		....	....	676.3	+ 10.4	695.0	502.0	307
Dc98		....	....	732.4	+ 10.4	734.0	690.0	109

Est vol 18,000; vol Tues 11,268; open int 111,247, −74.

SILVER (CBT) – 1,000 troy oz.; cents per troy oz.

	Open	High	Low	Settle	Change	Lifetime High	Lifetime Low	Open Interest
Oct		....	....	538.0	+ 10.0	590.0	504.0	2
Dec	531.0	540.0	530.0	539.5	+ 9.0	596.0	414.0	4,759
Ap95	554.0	554.0	552.0	554.0	+ 10.5	605.0	521.0	242
June		....	....	560.0	+ 11.0	605.0	527.0	229

Est vol 200; vol Tues 687; open int 5,377, −4.

CRUDE OIL, Light Sweet (NYM) 1,000 bbls.; $ per bbl.

	Open	High	Low	Settle	Change	Lifetime High	Lifetime Low	Open Interest
Dec	17.60	17.97	17.60	17.95	+ .37	21.25	14.93	108,879
Ja95	na	17.96	17.65	17.92	+ .31	20.12	15.15	61,968
Feb	17.65	17.90	17.65	17.85	+ .27	19.60	15.28	30,376
Mar	na	17.83	17.69	17.81	+ .24	20.66	15.42	23,648
Apr	17.68	17.80	17.68	17.78	+ .22	19.68	15.55	17,516
May	na	17.75	17.70	17.76	+ .19	19.23	15.69	11,707
June	17.58	17.73	17.58	17.74	+ .16	21.21	15.73	21,680
July	17.75	17.76	17.71	17.75	+ .15	18.85	16.28	12,805
Aug	17.78	17.78	17.75	17.77	+ .14	18.85	16.90	6,043
Sept	17.80	17.80	17.75	17.78	+ .13	19.84	16.28	12,083
Oct	17.67	17.77	17.67	17.79	+ .12	18.88	16.42	5,040
Nov	17.78	17.80	17.78	17.79	+ .11	18.87	17.15	5,835
Dec	na	17.85	17.78	17.80	+ .10	20.80	16.50	15,611
Ja96	17.77	17.83	17.77	17.82	+ .09	18.89	17.43	7,422
Feb	17.87	17.87	17.87	17.85	+ .08	18.84	17.68	1,663
Mar	17.91	17.91	17.91	17.88	+ .07	18.80	17.15	6,670
Apr		....	....	17.90	+ .06	18.27	17.81	110
June		....	....	17.94	+ .04	20.40	17.22	15,908
Sept		....	....	18.07	+ .01	18.47	18.38	1,004
Dec		....	....	18.22	....	20.40	17.65	18,258
Ju97		....	....	18.49	− .03	19.60	18.30	6,834

Est vol 108,222; vol Tues 60,800; open int 391,060, −563.

HEATING OIL NO. 2 (NYM) 42,000 gal.; $ per gal.

	Open	High	Low	Settle	Change	Lifetime High	Lifetime Low	Open Interest
Nov	na	.4995	.4940	.4948	+ .0018	.5830	.4600	14,368
Dec	na	.5035	.4975	.4989	+ .0014	.5900	.4680	43,453
Ja95	na	.5090	.5040	.5049	+ .0016	.5850	.4745	32,260
Feb	na	.5125	.5085	.5089	+ .0016	.5875	.4795	18,394
Mar	na	.5100	.5070	.5059	+ .0016	.5750	.4700	11,099
Apr	na	.5030	.5005	.4984	+ .0016	.5500	.4525	6,928
May	na	.4945	.4930	.4924	+ .0021	.5350	.4700	5,482
June	.4920	.4920	.4910	.4899	+ .0026	.5300	.4679	6,570
July	.4940	.4940	.4940	.4919	+ .0026	.5290	.4785	6,291
Aug	.4970	.4970	.4970	.4969	+ .0026	.5390	.4740	1,865
Sept	.5085	.5100	.5085	.5059	+ .0026	.5310	.4845	1,920
Oct		....	....	.5149	+ .0026	.5355	.5110	1,347
Nov		....	....	.5244	+ .0026	.5330	.5200	1,109
Dec		....	....	.5339	+ .0026	.5550	.5270	4,462
Ja96		....	....	.5399	+ .0026	.5525	.5395	526
Feb		....	....	.5399	+ .0026	.5930	.5930	646
Mar		....	....	.5314	+ .0026	.5490	.5470	320

Est vol 29,306; vol Tues 26,900; open int 157,110, −3,694.

GASOLINE-NY Unleaded (NYM) 42,000 gal.; $ per gal.

	Open	High	Low	Settle	Change	Lifetime High	Lifetime Low	Open Interest
Nov	na	.5535	.5250	.5471	+ .0225	.5535	.4275	11,819
Dec	na	.5965	.5840	.5908	+ .0080	.6070	.5080	22,087
Ja95	na	.5685	.5610	.5637	+ .0049	.5860	.5080	14,702
Feb	na	.5535	.5480	.5487	+ .0017	.5825	.5110	6,114
Mar	.5530	.5530	.5450	.5497	+ .0012	.5695	.5340	3,564
Apr	.5850	.5855	.5850	.5839	+ .0004	.6030	.5725	4,468
May		....	....	.5699	....	.5810	.5600	2,023
June		....	....	.5640	....	.5800	.5600	662
July		....	....	.5580	− .0009	.5794	.5530	851
Aug		....	....	.5520	− .0014	.5729	.5490	394
Sept		....	....	.5450	− .0019	.5600	.5350	411
Oct	.5374	.5374	.5374	.5335	− .0019	.5535	.5250	345
Nov		....	....	.5295	− .0019	.5500	.5260	244
Dec		....	....	.5275	− .0019	.5379	.5260	136

Est vol 37,929; vol Tues 27,732; open int 67,820, −2,036.

NATURAL GAS, (NYM) 10,000 MMBtu.; $ per MMBtu's

	Open	High	Low	Settle	Change	Lifetime High	Lifetime Low	Open Interest
Dec	1.950	2.035	1.917	2.031	+ .084	2.740	1.790	31,434
Ja95	na	2.110	2.030	2.103	+ .061	2.720	1.950	18,103

BARLEY (WPG) 20 metric tons; Can. $ per ton

	Vol.	High	Low	Close	Net Change	Lifetime High	Lifetime Low	Open Interest
Nov	706	115.10	114.50	114.50	− 1.00	120.00	88.50	12,611

BRITISH POUND (MCE) 12,500 pounds; $ per pound

	Vol.	High	Low	Close	Net Change	Lifetime High	Lifetime Low	Open Interest
Dec	604	1.6376	1.6296	1.6364	− .0012	1.6386	1.4646	586

CANADIAN GOVT. BONDS (CBT) C$100,000; $ per C$

	Vol.	High	Low	Close	Net Change	Lifetime High	Lifetime Low	Open Interest
Dec	2	98.75	98.20	98.48	+ .15	101.25	97.85	793

CATTLE-LIVE (MCE) 20,000 lb.; ¢ per lb.

	Vol.	High	Low	Close	Net Change	Lifetime High	Lifetime Low	Open Interest
Dec	111	69.75	69.57	69.72	....	74.25	67.50	218

CORN (MCE) 1,000 bu.; cents per bu.

	Vol.	High	Low	Close	Net Change	Lifetime High	Lifetime Low	Open Interest
Dec	467	215¾	214¾	215¼	− ¼	277	213¼	4,823

DEUTSCHEMARK (MCE) 62,500 marks; $ per mark

	Vol.	High	Low	Close	Net Change	Lifetime High	Lifetime Low	Open Interest
Dec	733	.6710	.6674	.6707	+ .0013	.6731	.5045	684

DEUTSCHEMARK FORWARD (CME) 250,000 U.S. $; mark per $

	Vol.	High	Low	Close	Net Change	Lifetime High	Lifetime Low	Open Interest
Dec	110	....	....	149165	− 15.5	154030	154030	8,988

DEUTSCHEMARK–FR. FRANC CROSSRATE (FINEX)
500,000 Dmarks; FFr per DM

	Vol.	High	Low	Close	Net Change	Lifetime High	Lifetime Low	Open Interest
Dec	204	3.4276	3.4252	3.4260	− .0010	3.4511	3.4133	784

DEUTSCHEMARK–JAP. YEN CROSSRATE (FINEX)
125,000 marks; yen per mark

	Vol.	High	Low	Close	Net Change	Lifetime High	Lifetime Low	Open Interest
Dec	1,007	64.68	64.56	64.67	+ .20	64.99	62.66	3,617

DM ROLLING SPOT (CME) $250,000; DM per U.S. $

	Vol.	High	Low	Close	Net Change	Lifetime High	Lifetime Low	Open Interest
Dec	289	1.4989	1.4913	1.4922	− .0015	1.5609	1.4865	6,453

DIAMMONIUM PHOSPHATE (CBT) 100 tons; $ per ton

	Vol.	High	Low	Close	Net Change	Lifetime High	Lifetime Low	Open Interest
Nov	0	....	....	153.00	− .80	160.00	152.00	324

EURODOLLAR (MCE) $500,000; pts. of 100%

	Vol.	High	Low	Close	Net Change	Lifetime High	Lifetime Low	Open Interest
Dec	11	93.98	93.97	93.97	....	95.80	93.67	384

EUROMARK (CME) DM 1,000,000; pts. of 100%

	Vol.	High	Low	Close	Net Change	Lifetime High	Lifetime Low	Open Interest
Dec	0	....	....	94.80	+ .02	95.71	94.05	10

EUROTOP 100 INDEX (CMX) – $100 times index

	Vol.	High	Low	Close	Net Change	Lifetime High	Lifetime Low	Open Interest
Dec	145	1161.0	1152.0	1152.1	+ 3.50	1300.0	1138.0	1,423

The index: High 1157.1; Low 1148.8; Close 1150.0 +4.50

FLAXSEED (WPG) 20 metric tons; Can. $ per ton

	Vol.	High	Low	Close	Net Change	Lifetime High	Lifetime Low	Open Interest
Dec	528	322.50	319.30	319.40	− 3.70	324.00	260.00	2,943

FRENCH FRANC (CME) 500,000 FF; $ per franc

	Vol.	High	Low	Close	Net Change	Lifetime High	Lifetime Low	Open Interest
Dec	84	.19574	.19488	.19570	+ .0036	.19656	.16842	1,269

GOLD-NY (MCE) 33.2 fine troy oz.; cents per troy oz.

	Vol.	High	Low	Close	Net Change	Lifetime High	Lifetime Low	Open Interest
Dec	17	390.60	389.20	391.00	− .20	432.50	357.30	1,247

GOLD-KILO (CBT) 32.15 troy oz.; $ per troy oz.

	Vol.	High	Low	Close	Net Change	Lifetime High	Lifetime Low	Open Interest
Dec	29	391.50	389.30	391.00	− .20	416.40	362.20	585

HOGS (MCE) 20,000 lb.; ¢ per lb.

	Vol.	High	Low	Close	Net Change	Lifetime High	Lifetime Low	Open Interest
Dec	82	33.85	33.32	33.75	+ .35	50.10	32.65	662

JAPANESE YEN (MCE) 6.25 million yen; $ per yen (.00)

	Vol.	High	Low	Close	Net Change	Lifetime High	Lifetime Low	Open Interest
Dec	145	1.0367	1.0343	1.0363	− .0023	1.0490	.9600	393

KC MINI VALUE LINE (KC) – 100 times index

	Vol.	High	Low	Close	Net Change	Lifetime High	Lifetime Low	Open Interest
Dec	209	461.10	457.00	458.75	− .30	476.50	434.90	1,126

KC VALUE LINE INDEX (KC) – 500 times index

	Vol.	High	Low	Close	Net Change	Lifetime High	Lifetime Low	Open Interest
Dec	137	460.90	457.00	458.75	− .25	475.85	441.35	937

The index: High 458.25; Low 456.73; Close 457.54 +.22

LUMBER (CME) 160,000 bd .ft., $ per 1,000 bd.ft.

	Vol.	High	Low	Close	Net Change	Lifetime High	Lifetime Low	Open Interest
Nov	500	319.60	313.50	316.90	− 4.80	453.50	278.00	1,947

OATS (MCE) 1,000 bu.; ¢ per bu.

	Vol.	High	Low	Close	Net Change	Lifetime High	Lifetime Low	Open Interest
Dec	1	....	....	126½	+ ½	148½	116½	161

PLATINUM (MCE) 25 troy oz.; cents per troy oz.

	Vol.	High	Low	Close	Net Change	Lifetime High	Lifetime Low	Open Interest
Jan	1	424.00	424.00	427.00	+ 1.60	431.50	391.20	537

PROPANE (NYM) 42,000 gal.; ¢ per gal.

	Vol.	High	Low	Close	Net Change	Lifetime High	Lifetime Low	Open Interest
Nov	269	32.95	32.65	32.95	+ .40	33.57	28.40	2,107

RUSSELL 2000 INDEX (CME) $500 times index

	Vol.	High	Low	Close	Net Change	Lifetime High	Lifetime Low	Open Interest
Dec	17	251.70	250.40	251.25	+ .25	275.75	241.80	1,808

SILVER (MCE) 1,000 troy oz.; cents per troy oz.

	Vol.	High	Low	Close	Net Change	Lifetime High	Lifetime Low	Open Interest
Dec	97	542.0	532.0	541.2	+ 9.2	596.0	420.0	2,527

SILVER (CBT) 5,000 troy oz.; cents per troy oz.

	Vol.	High	Low	Close	Net Change	Lifetime High	Lifetime Low	Open Interest
Dec	3	539.5	531.0	539.5	+ 9.0	595.0	474.5	2,623

SOYBEANS (MCE) 1,000 bu.; cents per bu.

	Vol.	High	Low	Close	Net Change	Lifetime High	Lifetime Low	Open Interest
Nov	3,850	549¼	545	548	− ¼	699	527	11,136

SOYBEAN MEAL (MCE) 20 tons; cents per ton

	Vol.	High	Low	Close	Net Change	Lifetime High	Lifetime Low	Open Interest
Dec	3	....	....	162.90	− .90	207.50	160.10	173

STERLING-MARK CROSSRATE (FINEX)
125,000 B. Pds; B. Pd per DM

	Vol.	High	Low	Close	Net Change	Lifetime High	Lifetime Low	Open Interest
Dec	1,007	2.4455	2.4425	2.4420	− .0040	2.4530	2.3855	3,617

SWISS FRANC (MCE) 62,500 francs; $ per franc

	Vol.	High	Low	Close	Net Change	Lifetime High	Lifetime Low	Open Interest
Dec	232	.8055	.8002	.8053	+ .0017	.8105	.7014	634

10–YEAR T.NOTES (MCE) 50,000; pts. 32nds of 100%

	Vol.	High	Low	Close	Net Change	Lifetime High	Lifetime Low	Open Interest
Dec	561	100-12	100-00	100-03	− 7	104-19	100-00	1,491

TORONTO 35 INDEX (TFE) $500 x index

	Vol.	High	Low	Close	Net Change	Lifetime High	Lifetime Low	Open Interest
Nov	144	223.40	222.60	223.98	+ 1.48	231.70	221.50	2,970

The index: High 223.53; Low 222.10; Close 223.05 +.92

WHEAT (MCE) 1,000 bu.; cents per bu.

	Vol.	High	Low	Close	Net Change	Lifetime High	Lifetime Low	Open Interest
Dec	605	404½	397½	401	+ 1	419	320½	4,166

WHITE WHEAT (MPLS) 5,000 bu.; cents per bu.

	Vol.	High	Low	Close	Net Change	Lifetime High	Lifetime Low	Open Interest
Dec	156	475	473	473½	− 2½	483	348	1,680

CURRENCY

JAPAN YEN (CME) – 12.5 million yen; $ per yen (.00)

	Open	High	Low	Settle	Change	Lifetime High	Lifetime Low	Open Interest
Dec	1.0387	1.0387	1.0322	1.0366	− .0021	1.0490	.9525	60,841
Mr95	1.0435	1.0451	1.0430	1.0451	− .0021	1.0560	.9680	6,971
June	....	....	....	1.0554	− .0021	1.0670	.9915	441
Sept	....	....	....	1.0653	− .0021	1.0775	1.0200	180

Est vol 15,195; vol Tues 29,782; open int 68,467, +2,108.

DEUTSCHEMARK (CME) – 125,000 marks; $ per mark

	Open	High	Low	Settle	Change	Lifetime High	Lifetime Low	Open Interest
Dec	.6692	.6708	.6670	.6704	+ .0007	.6731	.5590	89,152
Mr95	.6690	.6720	.6690	.6717	+ .0008	.6745	.5798	4,508
June	.6705	.6730	.6705	.6734	+ .0008	.6747	.5980	614
Sept	.6735	.6735	.6735	.6750	+ .0008	.6740	.6290	113

Est vol 28,241; vol Tues 47,272; open int 94,387, −1,327.

CANADIAN DOLLAR (CME) – 100,000 dlrs.; $ per Can $

	Open	High	Low	Settle	Change	Lifetime High	Lifetime Low	Open Interest
Dec	.7413	.7428	.7413	.7416	+ .0002	.7670	.7038	34,910
Mr95	.7416	.7426	.7416	.7416	+ .0002	.7618	.7020	1,719
June	.7420	.7420	.7411	.7409	+ .0002	.7600	.6990	758
Sept	.7402	.7409	.7400	.7397	+ .0002	.7438	.6965	571

Est vol 4,018; vol Tues 8,596; open int 38,021, −509.

BRITISH POUND (CME) – 62,500 pds.; $ per pound

	Open	High	Low	Settle	Change	Lifetime High	Lifetime Low	Open Interest
Dec	1.6354	1.6380	1.6300	1.6364	− .0010	1.6392	1.4400	43,129
Mr95	1.6320	1.6370	1.6280	1.6348	− .0010	1.6370	1.4530	479

Est vol 11,748; vol Tues 13,361; open int 43,616, +278.

SWISS FRANC (CME) – 125,000 francs; $ per franc

	Open	High	Low	Settle	Change	Lifetime High	Lifetime Low	Open Interest
Dec	.8035	.8056	.7992	.8054	+ .0015	.8108	.6885	40,726
Mr95	.8045	.8090	.8040	.8089	+ .0017	.8136	.7287	1,460
June	....	....	....	.8130	+ .0018	.8165	.7193	136

Est vol 17,156; vol Tues 20,105; open int 42,328, −1,104.

AUSTRALIAN DOLLAR (CME) – 100,000 dlrs.; $ per A.$

	Open	High	Low	Settle	Change	Lifetime High	Lifetime Low	Open Interest
Dec	.7370	.7425	.7370	.7413	+ .0068	.7455	.6965	12,560

Est vol 2,776; vol Tues 160; open int 12,615, +14.

U.S. DOLLAR INDEX (FINEX) – 1,000 times USDX

	Open	High	Low	Settle	Change	Lifetime High	Lifetime Low	Open Interest
Dec	85.36	85.62	85.23	83.26	− .03	99.00	85.24	6,704
Mr95	85.46	85.55	85.45	85.42	− .02	96.65	85.28	3,087

Est vol 1,200; vol Tues 2,069; open int 9,925, +281.
The index: High 85.53; Low 85.15; Close 85.17 −.05

INTEREST RATE

TREASURY BONDS (CBT) – $100,000; pts. 32nds of 100%

	Open	High	Low	Settle	Change	Lifetime High	Lifetime Low	Open Interest
Dec	97-10	97-21	96-30	97-08	− 1	118-08	91-19	396,416
Mr95	96-22	97-01	96-10	96-19	− 1	116-20	96-09	27,595
June	96-06	96-08	95-22	96-00	....	113-15	95-26	11,304
Sept	95-21	95-21	95-10	95-14	....	112-15	95-10	256
Dec	....	....	....	94-29	....	111-23	95-00	133

Est vol 380,000; vol Tues 415,844; op int 435,779, +1,790.

TREASURY BONDS (MCE) – $50,000; pts. 32nds of 100%

	Open	High	Low	Settle	Change	Lifetime High	Lifetime Low	Open Interest
Dec	97-14	97-22	96-30	97-04	− 8	114-00	96-30	13,796

Source: *The Wall Street Journal*, October 27, 1994, p. C16. Reprinted by permission of *The Wall Street Journal*,

Street Journal. Each fall, *The Wall Street Journal* publishes an educational edition that explains how to read *The Wall Street Journal* and interpret some of the data presented.

Barron's Business and Financial Weekly, published by Dow Jones every weekend, contains regular features on dividends, put and call options, international stock markets, commodities, a review of the stock market, and many pages of prices and financial statistics. *Barron's* takes a weekly perspective and summarizes the previous week's market behavior. It also has regular analyses of several companies in its section called "Investment News and Views." The common stock section of *Barron's* not only provides weekly high-low-close prices and volume but also informs investors as to the latest earnings per share, dividends declared, and dividend record and payable dates. This can be seen in the bottom portion of Table 4–9.

One unique feature of *Barron's* is the "Market Laboratory" covering seven pages of each issue. Weekly data on major stock and bond markets are presented with the week's market statistics. Tables 4–10 and 4–11 on pages 118 and 119 show some of the tables from *Barron's* "Market Laboratory." Careful reading of this publication will turn up useful data in a compact summary form not found in other publications.

Other major papers are *Investor's Business Daily,* the *Wall Street Transcript* (weekly), and the *Commercial and Financial Chronicle* (weekly). Media General's *Industriscope* is an exceptional source of fundamental and technical indicators for the professional manager. More than 3,400 common stocks are divided into 60 industrial groups and analyzed based on relative strength (whether they are leading or lagging the market), trends, earnings, and other variables that may be useful to the analyst.

Journals

Most journals are academic and, because of this, are more theoretical than investor oriented. However, there are exceptions, such as the *Financial Analysts Journal,* which is a publication of the Association for Investment Management and Research. This journal has both academic and practitioner articles that deal mainly with analytical tools, new laws and regulations, and financial analysis. *The Journal of Portfolio Management* and the *Institutional Investor* are also well read by the profession. The more scholarly, research-oriented academic journals would include the *Journal of Finance,* the *Journal of Financial Economics,* and the *Journal of Financial and Quantitative Analysis.* These journals include information on the development and testing of theories such as the random walk and efficient market hypothesis, the capital asset pricing model, arbitrage pricing theory, and much empirical research on a variety of financial topics. The *Journal of Financial Education* and *Financial Practice and Education* include articles on classroom topics and computer applications.

COMPUTER DATABASES

More computer-accessible databases have become available in the last several years as home computer usage has increased and database storage management has improved. The new craze is the use of compact disks (CD-ROMs) to store information that would take up several hundred floppy disks. Several major sources of data are still available for use in large mainframe computers on magnetic tapes, but this medium is losing its competitive edge as computer networks linking personal computers (PCs) together are replacing mainframes.

TABLE 4–9 Market Transactions from *Barron's*

THE WEEK'S STATISTICS

NEW YORK STOCK EXCHANGE COMPOSITE LIST

ABC

Mkt. Sym	52-Weeks High	52-Weeks Low	Company Name	Tick Sym	Div Amt	Vol 100's	Div Yld	Earn P/E	Week's High	Week's Low	Week's Last	Net Chg.	EARNINGS Interim or Fiscal Year	EARNINGS Year ago	DIVIDENDS Latest divs.	DIVIDENDS Record date	DIVIDENDS Payment date
▼	17⅜	12¼	AAR	AIR	.48	1704	3.7	23	13⅛	12¼	13	+⅛	Aug3m.13	.16	q.12	8-1	9-6
	23⅝	15½	ABM Indus	ABM	.52	363	2.5	13	21¾	20¾	21	−¾	July9m1.12	.98	q.13	10-14	11-3
	12⅝	9½	ACM Gvt Fd	ACG	1.10a	3725	11.3	...	9⅞	9⅝	9¾	... ✚	....	....	M.09⅛	10-7	10-21
	10¼	7	ACM OppFd	AOF	.80	1209	11.2	...	7⅜	7⅛	7⅛	−⅛ ✚	....	....	M.06⅝	10-7	10-21
	12¼	8⅜	ACM SecFd	GSF	1.10	6128	12.6	...	8¾	8½	8¾	+¼ ✚	....	....	M.09⅛	10-7	10-21
	10⅝	7½	ACM SpctmFd	SI	.96	2918	12.8	...	7¾	7½	7½	... ✚	....	....	M.08	10-7	10-21
n	15⅛	10½	ACM MgmdInc	ADF	1.46	2215	13.0	...	11⅜	11	11¼	−⅜ ✚	....	....	M.1219	10-7	10-21
▼	12⅜	8⅛	ACM MgdIncFd	AMF	1.08a	2264	13.1	...	8⅝	8⅛	8¼	−⅜ ✚	....	....	M.09	10-7	10-21
	9⅜	7⅞	ACM MgdMultFd	MMF	.72	1457	8.7	...	8¼	8⅛	8¼	+⅛ ✚	....	....	M.06	10-7	10-21
	14⅜	10¾	ACM MuniSec	AMU	.90a	777	8.2	...	11⅛	10¾	11	+⅛ ✚	....	....	M.07½	10-7	10-21
	11⅝	8⅜	ADT	ADT		11822	...	16	11½	10½	11½	+¾	Jun6m.40	.47	....	....	....
	36⅛	24¾	AFLAC	AFL	.46	9623	1.3	13	34⅛	32¾	34⅛	+1	Jun6m1.34	1.07	q.11½	8-19	9-1 ♣
▲	50⅛	24	AGCO Cp	AG	.04	6867	.1	9	50⅛	44⅜	50⅛	+5¾	Jun6m2.88	1.35	q.01	8-15	9-1
▲	66½	36½	AGCO pf		1.64	440	2.5	...	66½	58⅞	66½	+8	....	....	q.41	8-15	9-1
	18¾	12⅝	AL Labs A	BMD	.18	2052	1.1	53	17¼	15⅜	17	+1⅝	Jun6m.22	.30	q.04½	7-6	7-14
n	23¼	19¾	AMLI Resdntl	AML	1.68	635	7.9	...	21½	20¾	21⅜	+⅜	Jun19w.34	....	.42	8-11	8-22
▲	78¼	57	AMP	AMP	1.68	17314	2.2	25	78¼	75½	77⅜	+⅛	Jun6m1.67	1.41	q.42	8-8	9-1 ♣
▼	72¾	50¾	AMR	AMR		32182	...	dd	53¾	50¾	51½	−1⅝	Jun6m1.48	D.03	Y	...	2-15-80
	51	40½	ARCO Chm	RCM	2.50	1140	5.1	21	50	49⅛	49½	+¼	Jun6m1.18	1.03	q.62½	8-12	9-2 ♣
	5	3	ARX	ARX		1828	...	7	4	3⅝	4	+¼	94June.55	.20	Y	...	5-25-88
	56⅛	38⅜	ASA	ASA	2.00	5706	3.8	...	53¾	51⅞	52¾	−⅛	Jun6m.06	.05	q.50	8-19	8-26
	29¼	21¼	ATT Cap	TCC	.36	977	1.5	14	24⅜	23⅞	24¼	...	Jun6m.74	.71	q.09	8-10	8-31
x	61⅜	49½	AT&T Cp	T	1.32	98128	2.4	17	54⅞	53⅝	54	+⅜	Jun6m1.63	1.44	q.33	9-30	11-1
▲	32	25⅜	AbbotLab	ABT	.76	59058	2.4	18	32	30⅝	31⅜	+¾	Jun6m.91	X.83	q.19	10-14	11-15
	8¼	2⅞	Abex	ABE		844	...	19	8⅛	7¾	8	...	Jun6mX.73	D1.81	....	....	....
	15¼	8¼	Abitibi g	ABY		525	...	...	15⅛	14½	15⅛	+⅜	Jun6mD.76	D.70	Y	...	4-30-93
	15⅝	11⅛	Acceptins	AIF		779	...	14	14⅞	14½	14⅞	+⅛	Jun6m.61	.44	....	....	.... ♣
	5¾	2½	Acceptins wt			857	...	...	4¼	3⅞	4⅛	+⅛	....	....	....	....	....
x	35	22⅜	ACE Ltd	ACL	.44	7036	1.8	dd	24⅝	23⅝	24	−¾	Jun9mD1.86	x4.29	.11	9-30-94	10-19-94
	15½	8¾	AcmeCleve	AMT	.44	1076	3.1	18	14⅜	13¼	14	+⅝	Jun9m.66	.66	q.11	8-8	8-19
	11⅜	6⅜	AcmeElec	ACE		303	...	dd	9⅜	8½	9⅜	+⅝	94JunD1.17	D.14	Y	...	12-3-91
	28¾	21	Acordia	ACO	.60	67	2.2	14	27¼	26¾	27¼	+¼	Jun6m.90	.90	q.15	9-1	9-15 ♣
	13¾	5¾	ActavaGp	ACT	.09j	1498	...	dd	10½	10	10⅛	+⅛	Jun6mD1.02	D.30	Y	...	1-3
▲	16½	11¼	Acuson	ACN		5432	...	29	16½	14¾	16¼	+1⅜	Jun6m.37	D.06	....	....	....
	19⅝	16½	AdamsExp	ADX	1.63e	1266	9.5	...	17¼	17	17⅛	...	....	....	.12	8-22-94	9-1-94
	31¾	16¾	AdvMicro	AMD		30604	...	11	30½	29	29¾	−¼	Jun26w1.78	1.28	....	....	....
	64	46½	AdvMicro pf		3.00	1436	5.0	...	61¼	58¾	59¾	−1	....	....	q.75	9-1	9-15
	8⅛	5	Advest	ADV		265	...	11	5¼	5⅛	5⅛	...	Jun9m.29	.39	Y	...	12-17-91
x	20	14¼	Advo	AD	.10	635	.6	71	17½	16⅜	17	−¼	Jun39w.77	.67	q.02½	10-3	10-14
n	11⅜	8¼	Advocat	AVC		838	...	...	10¾	10	10⅛	−⅜	Jun6m.34	.28	....	....	....
	59½	48	AEGON	AEG	2.21e	1424	3.8	11	58⅝	56⅝	58	−1⅛	ADRJun6m2.82	2.69	.6239	9-6-94	10-7-94
	66¼	44⅝	AetnaLife	AET	2.76	26136	6.0	dd	47½	45½	46⅜	+1	Jun6m1.58	2.62	q.69	7-29	8-15
x	19⅝	16⅛	AgreeRlty	ADC	1.80	338	11.0	...	16⅞	16⅛	16⅜	−⅛	Jun10w.58	....	q.45	9-30	10-14
	31	23⅝	AgriMinl	AMC	2.64	617	9.6	10	27⅞	26⅞	27½	−⅛	Jun6m2.03	1.81	q.66	8-1	8-31
	22¾	16⅜	Ahmanson	AHM	.88	16314	4.2	12	21	20½	20⅞	+⅜	Jun6m.87	D2.33	q.22	8-9	9-1
	27¼	23⅜	Ahmanson pfC		2.10	342	8.5	...	24⅞	24⅜	24⅜	−¼	....	....	q.52½	8-9	9-1
	52	45	Ahmanson pfD		3.00	45	6.1	...	49½	48¾	49¼	...	....	....	.75	8-9	9-1
	28⅜	25⅜	Ahmanson pf		2.40	537	9.3	...	26¼	25¾	25⅞	−⅛	....	....	q.60	8-9	9-1
s	29	22	Ahold	AHO	.61e	172	2.1	...	28⅝	27⅞	28⅜	+¼	....	....	.0014	9-15-94	10-7-94
	22¾	14	Alex&Alex	AAL	.10	3812	.5	dd	19¾	19⅜	19½	+⅛	Jun6mD.05	.48	q.02½	9-1	9-30
	63¼	51½	Alexanders	ALX		121	...	10	54⅞	54⅛	54½	...	Jun28wX.15	X1.60	Y	...	9-9-80
	15⅛	11½	AllAmTerm	AAT	1.20	789	10.2	...	11⅞	11⅝	11¾	+⅛	....	....	M.10	9-16	9-30
	152	133¾	AlleghanyCp	Y	t	74	...	10	146	144	146	+2	Jun6m4.93	6.69	S2%	4-1-94	4-26-94
	24⅞	17	AllegLud	ALS	.48	5350	2.2	61	22⅜	21¼	21½	...	July26wD.15	X.56	q.12	8-31	9-30
s	28	19¾	AllegPwr	AYP	1.64	11683	8.1	10	20⅜	19¾	20⅛	−¼	Jun12m1.93	1.81	q.41	9-16	9-30
s	29⅛	13½	AllenGp	ALN	.16	2669	.8	19	21⅛	20⅛	20⅝	+⅛	Jun6m.46	.57	q.04	9-26	10-10
	28	20	Allergan	AGN	.44f	5227	1.7	15	26⅝	25¼	25⅜	−1	Jun6m.72	.68	q.11	8-26	9-15
▼	4⅜	⅝	Allerion	ALI		2502	...	dd	15/16	⅝	⅞	+⅛	July3mX.17	D.03	....	....	....
	27⅝	17¼	AllncCapMgt	AC	1.63e	906	7.7	13	21⅜	20	21¼	+1¼	Jun6m.83	.09	q.41	8-1	8-8
	7¼	4¾	AllincEntn	CDS		1909	...	...	5½	5⅛	5⅜	+⅛	Jun6m.11	.05	....	....	....
▼	2⅛	⅛	AllincEntn wtA			358	...	...	11/16	⅝	11/16	...	....	....	....	....	....
▼	1 11/16	3/16	AllincEntn wtB			504	...	...	½	7/16	½	−1/16	....	....	....	....	....
	10½	9	AllncGlblEnv	AEF		415	...	...	9⅝	9½	9⅝	...	....	....	Y	...	1-10-92
	16¼	11½	AllianceWrld II	AWF	1.42a	3964	11.7	...	12⅜	12	12⅛	−¼ ✚	....	....	M.1186	10-7	10-21
	22½	12¾	AllianceWrld	AWG	1.68a	1059	12.4	...	13½	13¼	13½	+⅛ ✚	....	....	M.14	10-7	10-21
	33⅝	21¾	AlliantTech	ATK		1194	...	10	31⅝	30⅛	31⅛	+⅞	July3m.68	.83	....	....	....
	27⅝	21½	AlldIrishBk	AIB	1.17e	117	5.1	...	23½	22¾	22¾	+⅛	ADR93Dec.27	.17	.4255	9-2-94	10-11-94
	29¼	25½	AlldIrishBk pf		2.97	280	10.9	...	27½	26⅞	27⅛	−¼	....	....	.57148	7-18-94	8-2-94
	17⅜	10¼	AlliedPdts	ADP		898	...	10	13⅛	12½	12⅝	−⅝	Jun6m1.24	.84	Y	...	11-15-82
s	40⅜	33⅛	AlliedSgnl	ALD	.67	21713	2.0	14	35⅝	34	34⅛	+⅜	Jun6m1.29	1.10	q.16¾	8-19	9-9
s	22⅛	14¼	AllmrPC	APY	.16	5689	1.0	10	17⅛	16⅜	16½	−¼	Jun6m.33	X2.81	q.04	11-1	11-15 ♣
	12	9¼	AllmrST	ALM	.84a	143	9.0	...	9½	9¼	9⅜	+⅛	....	....	q.21	8-31	9-30
	10½	9¼	AllmonTr	GSO	.48e	393	5.0	...	9¾	9½	9⅝	...	....	....	.0066	2-4-94	2-25-94
	34⅛	22⅝	Allstate	ALL	.72	13329	3.0	15	24¾	23¾	23⅞	−¼	Jun6m.28	1.70	q.18	9-8	9-29 ♣
	31¼	24	ALLTEL	AT	.88	4975	3.3	18	27½	26⅝	27	−¼	Jun6m.78	.68	q.22	9-2	10-3
	170	149	ALLTEL pf		2.06	0	1.3	...	162	162	162	...	....	....	q.51½	8-24	9-15
	7	3⅞	Allwaste	ALW		4358	...	21	6½	6	6⅜	+¼	May9m.24	.22	....	....	....
n	35	16¾	Alumax	AMX		11243	...	...	33⅞	30⅝	32⅛	−1⅞	Jun6mD.24	D.52	....	....	....
▲	87¾	64¼	Alcoa	AA	1.60a	27639	1.9	dd	87¾	83¾	84¾	+⅛	Jun6mL.04	.71	q.40	11-4	11-25 ♣
▼	30¾	20⅛	Alza	AZA		20606	...	44	21⅜	20⅛	20⅝	−¼	Jun6m.37	.44	S	5-28-93	6-11-93
	8¼	6	AmaxGold	AU	.06j	13478	...	dd	7⅝	7¼	7⅝	+¼	Jun6mD.12	D.71	Y	...	11-29-93
n▲	55⅝	50	AmaxGold pfB			997	...	...	55⅝	54⅝	55⅝	+1	....	....	....	....	....
	49¾	35¾	Ambac	ABK	.48	2820	1.3	8	37⅝	36¾	37	−¼	Jun6m2.08	2.53	q.12	8-10	9-7 ♣
	25⅞	17⅞	AmcastInd	AIZ	.52f	783	2.2	14	23¼	22⅜	23⅛	+⅝	May9m1.25	1.06	q.13	9-5	9-23 ♣
	2⅝	1½	Amdura	ADU		296	...	23	2⅛	1⅝	1⅞	+¼	Jun6m.04	.07	....	....	....
	54¾	42⅜	AmerHess	AHC	.60	11787	1.3	dd	46¾	45⅛	46½	+¾	Jun6m.72	D1.53	q.15	9-19	9-30
n	25½	20⅞	Amerco pfA		2.13	432	10.0	...	21⅞	21⅛	21⅜	−½	....	....	q.53⅛	8-12	9-1
n	16⅜	12¼	AmWestAir B	AWA		8428	...	...	13⅜	12⅞	13¼	...	....	....	....	....	....
n▼	7⅜	5¼	AmWestAir wt			600	...	...	6⅛	5¼	5⅜	−⅝	....	....	....	....	....
	10	8¾	AmAdjTerm95	ADJ	.34e	477	3.8	...	9	8⅞	8⅞	... ✚	....	....	M.02	10-7	10-26
	9¾	8¼	AmAdjTerm96	BDJ	.43e	1004	5.0	...	8¾	8⅝	8⅝	... ✚	....	....	M.03	10-17	10-26
	9¾	8	AmAdjTerm97	CDJ	.51e	1967	6.0	...	8⅝	8⅜	8½	... ✚	....	....	M.0375	10-17	10-26
	9¾	7⅞	AmAdjTerm98	DDJ	.53e	2292	6.3	...	8½	8⅜	8⅜	... ✚	....	....	M.04	10-17	10-26
	9⅝	7⅞	AmAdjTerm99	EDJ	.55e	1423	6.7	...	8⅜	8¼	8¼	−⅛ ✚	....	....	M.0425	10-17	10-26
	10⅝	8¼	AmAnnuity	AAG	.05e	200	.5	11	9¾	9½	9½	−¼	Jun6m.55	L.27	.05	12-21-93	12-29-93
	31	20⅜	AmBarrick	ABX	.10	93533	.4	32	27⅜	26⅜	26⅝	−⅛	Jun6m.43	.36	sa.05	11-30-94	12-15-94
	37⅛	29⅜	AmBrand	AMB	2.00	22249	5.5	13	36¾	34⅝	36¼	+1⅝	Jun6m1.55	1.97	q.50	8-4	9-1
▲	148	122½	AmBrand pfA		2.67	5	1.8	...	148	138½	148	+9½	....	....	q.66¾	8-4	9-10
	25¾	18¾	AmBusnPdts	ABP	.80	192	3.6	14	22¾	21⅞	22¼	+¼	Jun6m.81	.78	q.20	9-1	9-15
▼	21	16⅝	AmCapBdFd	ACB	1.54	476	9.0	...	17⅜	16⅜	17⅛	+⅛	....	....	.385	9-9	9-30

TABLE 4–10 Market Laboratory—Stocks from *Barron's*

STOCKS

DJ HALF-HOURLY AVERAGES

The Dow Jones Averages current divisors are, respectively: 0.37153418, 0.54354674, 1.8964991 and 2.0087097.

Dow Jones 30 Industrial Average

Daily	Sep 26	27	28	29	30
Open	3833.09	3855.97	3867.75	3879.86	3856.98
10:00	3829.06	3862.70	3879.19	3874.48	3848.57
10:30	3835.78	3868.42	3885.58	3864.38	3866.74
11:00	3836.79	3863.71	3880.87	3855.63	3866.06
11:30	3834.44	3864.72	3882.55	3855.30	3865.05
12:00	3828.72	3859.67	3887.93	3857.32	3867.41
12:30	3829.39	3868.08	3887.60	3858.66	3870.44
1:00	3834.78	3865.73	3886.25	3853.62	3869.09
1:30	3835.45	3858.33	3887.60	3850.59	3872.46
2:00	3835.78	3860.01	3882.89	3854.29	3869.09
2:30	3838.81	3846.21	3880.53	3850.25	3860.68
3:00	3842.51	3854.63	3880.87	3857.32	3856.64
3:30	3839.49	3865.73	3877.84	3856.98	3860.34
Close	**3849.24**	**3863.04**	**3878.18**	**3854.63**	**3843.19**
High (t)	3869.43	3891.63	3904.76	3892.64	3891.30
Low (t)	3804.50	3828.72	3854.29	3834.78	3825.69
High (a)	3849.91	3871.78	3890.96	3878.18	3875.82
Low (a)	3826.36	3844.87	3863.04	3847.90	3838.81
Change	+17.49	+13.80	+15.14	−23.55	−11.44

Theoretical range (t): High 3904.76 Low 3804.50
Actual range (a): High 3890.96 Low 3826.36

Dow Jones 20 Transportation Average

Open	1503.32	1500.10	1495.96	1503.55	1490.44
10.00	1504.01	1501.48	1491.30	1500.79	1480.88
10:30	1504.93	1500.45	1493.89	1494.58	1490.44
11:00	1501.14	1498.26	1497.34	1491.36	1489.41
11:30	1501.25	1496.42	1497.80	1487.68	1490.21
12:00	1498.95	1494.35	1500.33	1486.30	1489.98
12:30	1497.80	1495.27	1502.17	1486.53	1491.59
1:00	1497.34	1495.27	1500.56	1483.77	1491.36
1:30	1496.88	1493.66	1501.48	1482.16	1493.20
2:00	1495.96	1492.97	1499.76	1483.54	1492.05
2:30	1493.20	1492.74	1500.33	1483.08	1489.98
3:00	1492.51	1495.50	1502.17	1487.68	1489.87
3:30	1492.74	1497.80	1502.86	1485.50	1491.94
Close	**1498.03**	**1498.26**	**1502.86**	**1483.54**	**1491.59**
High (t)	1512.98	1514.36	1514.13	1510.68	1502.86
Low (t)	1486.76	1482.39	1481.93	1471.81	1479.86
High (a)	1505.39	1502.40	1503.55	1507.69	1493.20
Low (a)	1491.36	1492.28	1490.21	1481.47	1484.00
Change	−1.38	+ .23	+4.60	−19.32	+8.05

Theoretical range (t): High 1514.36 Low 1471.81
Actual range (a): High 1507.69 Low 1481.47

Dow Jones 15 Utilities Average

Open	176.38	177.17	177.50	178.09	180.27
10:00	176.64	177.17	178.09	178.68	180.07
10:30	176.71	177.56	178.42	178.35	180.40
11:00	176.64	177.56	178.35	178.42	180.46
11:30	176.77	177.56	178.55	178.42	180.73
12:00	176.71	177.56	178.82	178.62	180.79
12:30	176.71	177.76	179.15	178.75	181.32
1:00	176.77	177.89	179.15	178.62	181.58
1:30	176.77	177.70	179.08	178.68	181.72
2:00	176.71	177.70	178.82	179.01	181.65
2:30	176.77	177.63	179.08	178.75	181.65
3:00	176.97	177.83	179.08	178.88	181.58
3:30	176.90	177.89	178.75	179.28	181.39
Close	**177.10**	**177.70**	**178.75**	**180.00**	**181.45**
High (t)	178.03	179.01	179.74	180.20	182.38
Low (t)	175.59	175.92	177.37	177.50	179.21
High (a)	177.37	178.16	179.28	180.00	181.85
Low (a)	176.44	176.64	177.56	178.09	179.87
Change	+ .20	+ .60	+1.05	+1.25	+1.45

Theoretical range (t): High 182.38 Low 175.59
Actual range (a): High 181.85 Low 176.44

Dow Jones 65 Composite Average

Open	1282.29	1286.40	1287.77	1292.62	1286.90
10:00	1281.98	1288.02	1289.26	1291.44	1284.19
10:30	1283.54	1289.17	1291.38	1287.64	1288.82
11:00	1282.63	1287.70	1291.19	1285.15	1288.48
11:30	1282.35	1287.39	1292.00	1284.10	1288.76
12:00	1280.61	1285.90	1293.93	1284.28	1289.14
12:30	1280.42	1287.89	1294.67	1284.78	1290.69
1:00	1281.36	1287.58	1293.99	1282.91	1290.63
1:30	1281.36	1285.53	1294.43	1281.98	1291.87
2:00	1281.11	1285.71	1292.84	1283.35	1290.88
2:30	1280.98	1283.04	1292.87	1282.29	1288.76
3:00	1281.67	1285.53	1293.37	1284.90	1287.86
3:30	1281.11	1288.26	1292.62	1284.62	1288.92
Close	**1284.53**	**1287.70**	**1292.75**	**1284.34**	**1285.78**
High (t)	1293.18	1298.59	1301.64	1298.91	1298.59
Low (t)	1271.77	1275.38	1281.36	1275.13	1277.25
High (a)	1284.72	1289.91	1295.11	1293.31	1292.31
Low (a)	1279.93	1282.54	1286.40	1281.23	1283.38
Change	+3.05	+3.17	+5.05	−8.41	+1.44

Theoretical range (t): High 1301.64 Low 1271.77
Actual range (a): High 1295.11 Low 1279.93

DOW JONES INDUSTRIAL AVERAGE

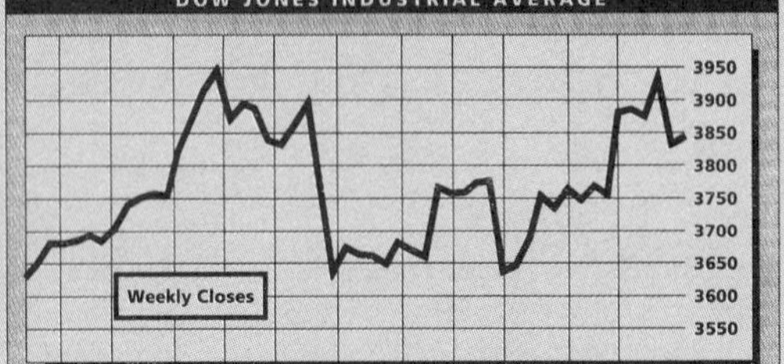

NYSE CUMULATIVE DAILY BREADTH

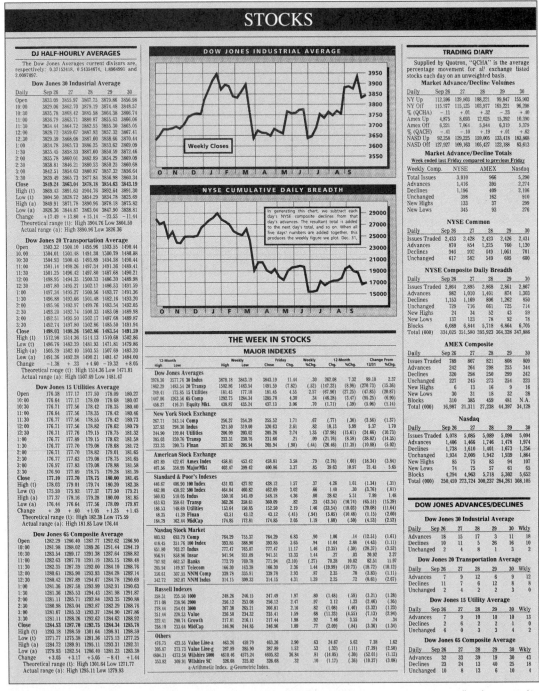

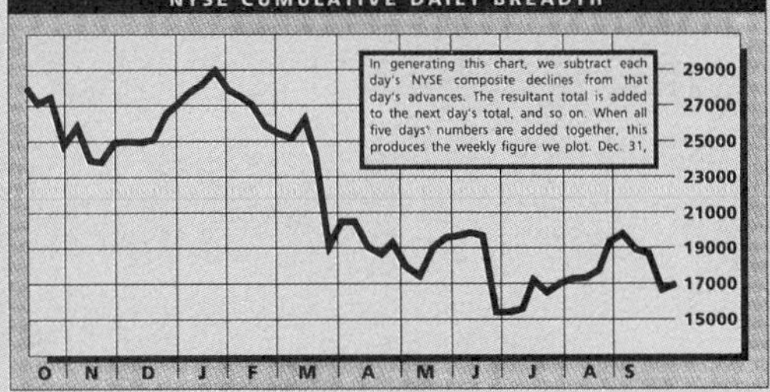

THE WEEK IN STOCKS

MAJOR INDEXES

12-Month High	12-Month Low		Weekly High	Weekly Low	Friday Close	Friday Chg.	Weekly %Chg.	12-Month Chg.	12-Month %Chg.	Change From 12/31	%Chg.
		Dow Jones Averages									
3978.36	3577.76	**30 Indus**	3878.18	3843.19	3843.19	11.44	.30	262.08	7.32	89.10	2.37
1862.29	1483.54	**20 Transp**	1502.86	1483.54	1491.59	(7.82)	(.52)	(147.23)	(8.98)	(270.73)	(15.36)
249.41	175.85	**15 Utilities**	181.45	177.10	181.45	4.55	2.57	(67.96)	(27.25)	(47.85)	(20.87)
1447.06	1263.56	**65 Comp**	1292.75	1284.34	1285.78	4.30	.34	(46.28)	(3.47)	(95.25)	(6.90)
456.27	416.31	**Equity Mkt.**	438.87	435.24	437.13	3.06	.70	(1.71)	(.39)	(5.06)	(1.14)
		New York Stock Exchange									
267.71	243.14	**Comp**	256.37	254.39	255.52	1.71	.67	(.77)	(.30)	(3.56)	(1.37)
327.93	298.30	**Indus**	321.50	319.00	320.63	2.61	.82	18.13	5.99	5.37	1.70
244.90	199.04	**Utilities**	206.09	203.02	205.26	2.74	1.35	(37.98)	(15.61)	(24.66)	(10.73)
285.03	230.76	**Transp**	233.31	230.76	231.66	.21	.09	(21.76)	(8.59)	(38.82)	(14.35)
233.33	200.75	**Finan**	207.02	205.94	205.94	(.90)	(.44)	(26.46)	(11.39)	(10.88)	(5.02)
		American Stock Exchange									
487.89	422.67	**Amex Index**	458.81	453.42	458.81	3.58	.79	(2.78)	(.60)	(18.34)	(3.84)
407.56	358.99	**MajorMkt**	403.47	399.42	400.86	3.37	.85	39.63	10.97	21.45	5.65
		Standard & Poor's Indexes									
446.67	406.90	**100 Index**	431.03	427.92	428.12	1.57	.37	4.26	1.01	(1.34)	(.31)
482.00	438.92	**500 Index**	464.84	460.82	462.69	3.02	.66	1.40	.30	(3.76)	(.81)
560.83	510.05	**Indus**	550.16	545.49	548.18	4.36	.80	28.62	5.51	7.99	1.48
453.63	358.61	**Transp**	362.26	358.61	360.09	.82	.23	(43.34)	(10.74)	(65.51)	(15.39)
186.53	148.69	**Utilities**	153.64	150.85	152.50	2.19	1.46	(33.54)	(18.03)	(20.08)	(11.64)
48.35	41.39	**Finan**	43.51	43.12	43.12	(.41)	(.94)	(5.05)	(10.48)	(1.15)	(2.60)
184.79	162.44	**MidCap**	174.85	172.81	174.85	2.05	1.19	(.88)	(.50)	(4.53)	(2.53)
		Nasdaq Stock Market									
803.93	693.79	**Comp**	764.29	755.37	764.29	6.83	.90	1.06	.14	(12.51)	(1.61)
418.45	351.76	**100 Index**	393.85	388.90	393.85	3.65	.94	11.04	2.88	(4.43)	(1.11)
851.80	703.27	**Indus**	777.47	765.07	777.47	11.17	1.46	(2.35)	(.30)	(28.37)	(3.52)
956.91	858.96	**Insur**	941.94	931.09	941.51	13.33	1.44	.27	.03	20.92	2.27
787.92	662.57	**Banks**	772.79	769.78	771.94	(2.10)	(.27)	70.28	10.02	82.51	11.97
205.94	149.97	**Telecom**	166.30	163.38	166.30	2.36	1.44	(19.99)	(10.73)	(18.72)	(10.12)
356.61	307.55	**NNM Comp**	339.78	335.91	339.78	2.93	.87	2.35	.70	(3.83)	(1.11)
342.72	282.87	**NNM Indus**	314.15	309.33	314.15	4.31	1.39	2.25	.72	(8.61)	(2.67)
		Russell Indexes									
258.31	235.50	**1000**	248.26	246.15	247.49	1.97	.80	(1.48)	(.59)	(3.21)	(1.28)
271.08	238.96	**2000**	256.12	253.08	256.12	2.47	.97	3.12	1.23	(2.46)	(.95)
278.44	254.01	**3000**	267.38	265.21	266.81	2.16	.82	(1.08)	(.40)	(3.32)	(1.23)
251.44	228.53	**Value**	236.50	234.32	235.41	1.59	.68	(11.23)	(4.55)	(7.13)	(2.94)
222.41	200.74	**Growth**	217.81	216.11	217.44	1.98	.92	7.46	3.55	.74	.34
258.10	233.64	**MidCap**	246.96	244.85	246.96	1.89	.77	(2.09)	(.84)	(3.36)	(1.34)
		Others									
476.75	423.55	**Value Line-a**	463.26	459.79	463.26	2.90	.63	24.67	5.62	7.38	1.62
305.87	273.73	**Value Line-g**	287.89	285.90	287.89	1.52	.53	(.32)	(.11)	(7.39)	(2.50)
4804.31	4373.58	**Wilshire 5000**	4610.46	4575.24	4605.82	36.84	.81	(14.05)	(.30)	(52.01)	(1.12)
353.82	309.91	**Wilshire SC**	326.68	325.02	326.68	.32	.10	(1.17)	(.36)	(10.37)	(3.08)

a-Arithmetic Index. g-Geometric Index.

TRADING DIARY

Supplied by Quotron, "QCHA" is the average percentage movement for all exchange listed stocks each day on an unweighted basis.

Market Advance/Decline Volumes

Daily	Sep 26	27	28	29	30
NY Up	112,596	139,803	188,221	99,847	155,903
NY Off	115,377	115,125	103,977	165,221	96,208
% (QCHA)	−.11	+.01	+.32	−.23	+.40
Amex Up	4,875	8,693	12,025	15,392	10,390
Amex Off	6,221	7,064	5,944	6,319	5,379
% (QACH)	−.41	−.10	+.19	+.01	+.62
NASD Up	92,258	129,225	159,005	133,418	183,868
NASD Off	127,927	109,163	105,427	122,188	83,613

Market Advance/Decline Totals

Week ended last Friday compared to previous Friday

Weekly Comp.	NYSE	AMEX	Nasdaq
Total Issues	3,010	966	5,290
Advances	1,416	395	2,274
Declines	1,196	409	2,106
Unchanged	398	162	910
New Highs	133	37	299
New Lows	345	93	276

NYSE Common

Daily	Sep 26	27	28	29	30
Issues Traded	2,433	2,428	2,423	2,426	2,431
Advances	870	854	1,225	760	1,130
Declines	940	992	049	1,061	701
Unchanged	617	582	549	605	600

NYSE Composite Daily Breadth

Daily	Sep 26	27	28	29	30
Issues Traded	2,864	2,895	2,868	2,861	2,867
Advances	982	1,010	1,401	874	1,303
Declines	1,153	1,169	806	1,262	850
Unchanged	729	716	661	725	714
New Highs	24	34	52	43	59
New Lows	137	123	78	92	78
Blocks	6,089	6,844	5,718	6,864	6,705
Total (000)	334,025	351,580	395,923	364,328	347,886

AMEX Composite

Daily	Sep 26	27	28	29	30
Issues Traded	789	807	821	808	809
Advances	242	264	298	255	344
Declines	320	298	250	299	242
Unchanged	227	245	273	254	223
New Highs	6	13	16	9	16
New Lows	30	31	18	32	28
Blocks	310	385	459	481	N.A.
Total (000)	16,987	21,311	27,238	44,397	34,128

Nasdaq

Daily	Sep 26	27	28	29	30
Issues Traded	5,078	5,085	5,089	5,090	5,094
Advances	1,406	1,466	1,746	1,478	1,974
Declines	1,738	1,610	1,401	1,673	1,256
Unchanged	1,934	2,009	1,942	1,939	1,864
New Highs	85	75	83	94	107
New Lows	74	75	57	61	65
Blocks	4,294	4,963	5,718	5,302	5,652
Total (000)	250,459	273,724	300,237	284,261	308,105

DOW JONES ADVANCES/DECLINES

Dow Jones 30 Industrial Average

Daily	Sep 26	27	28	29	30	Wkly
Advances	18	15	17	3	11	18
Declines	10	11	5	26	16	10
Unchanged	2	4	8	1	3	2

Dow Jones 20 Transportation Average

Daily	Sep 26	27	28	29	30	Wkly
Advances	7	9	12	6	9	12
Declines	11	7	6	12	8	8
Unchanged	2	4	2	2	3	0

Dow Jones 15 Utility Average

Daily	Sep 26	27	28	29	30	Wkly
Advances	7	9	10	10	10	13
Declines	2	6	2	2	1	0
Unchanged	6	0	3	3	4	2

Dow Jones 65 Composite Average

Daily	Sep 26	27	28	29	30	Wkly
Advances	32	33	39	19	30	43
Declines	23	24	13	40	25	18
Unchanged	10	8	13	6	10	4

Source: *Barron's*, October 3, 1994, p. 96. Reprinted by permission of *Barron's*,

TABLE 4–11 Market Laboratory—Bonds from *Barron's*

MARKET LABORATORY • BONDS

BOND VOLUME

	Last week	Prev. week	Yr-Ago week
Sales NYSE, th $	116,648	135,282	190,680
Sales AMEX, th $	35,232	24,186	11,441

Daily Bond Volume

Daily	Sept 26	27	28	29	30
NYSE, th $	21,897	24,134	22,869	26,627	21,121
AMEX, th $	11,088	5,759	5,848	7,582	4,955

WEEKLY BOND STATISTICS

	Last Week	Prev. Week	Yr-Ago Week
New Offerings, (mil $) (v)			
Corporate (z)	8,022	r10,203	4,423
Municipal (z)	1,760	1,433	6,296
Best Grade Bonds-y (Barron's index of 10 high-grade corporate bonds.)	8.31	8.31	6.74
Interm-Grade Bonds-y (Barron's index of 10 medium-grade corporate bonds.)	9.01	8.93	7.26
Confidence Index (High-grade index divided by intermediate-grade index; decline in latter vs. former generally indicates rising confidence, pointing to higher stocks.)	92.2	93.1	92.8
Other Confidence Indicators:			
T-Bill/Euro$ Futures (TED) Spread (Difference between nearby contracts; lower spread indicates higher confidence in financial system.)	+0.58	+0.54	+0.40
Lehman Brothers T-Bond Index (Index of prices of long-term government bonds. Dec. 31, 1980=1000.)	1347.11	1351.46	1633.75
Ryan Labs Treasury Index (Index of total return from active Treasury notes and bonds. Dec. 31, 1979=100.)	436.85	437.49	465.70
Bond Buyer 20 Bond Index (Index of yields of 20 general obligation municipal bonds.)	6.43	6.37	5.30
Bond Buyer Municipal Bond Index (Index of 40 actively-traded tax-exempt bonds; component issues are changed regularly to keep the index a current picture of the market. The municipal bond futures contract traded on the Chicago Board of Trade is based on this index.)	6.57	6.53	5.47
Stock/Bond Yield Gap-s (Difference between yield on highest-grade corporate bonds and yield on stocks on the DJIA.)	−5.55	−5.55	−3.89
Yield on Dow Jones Bond Averages:			
20 Bonds, (y)	7.67	7.60	6.26
10 Utils, (y)	8.16	8.15	6.80
10 Inds, (y)	7.19	7.06	5.73

v-Week ended Thursday. y-Yield to maturity, week ended Thursday. (z)-Source: Securities Data Co.

MORTGAGE-RELATED SECURITIES

Quotes for actively traded mortgage-backed securities. Bond-equivalent yields take into account monthly payments vs. semiannual payments for bonds. Bond equivalent yields are calculated based on the latest one month's prepayments. The yield calculations assume that the latest month's prepayments will remain unchanged through the maturity of the issues. Actual yields will depend on future prepayments. As interest rates fall, prepayments tend to rise and vice versa. The Fannie Mae adjustable-rate mortgage (ARM) securities have a rate that floats monthly at 1.25 percentage points above the 11th district cost-of-funds index, which is the key measure of thrift deposit costs in California, Nevada and Arizona. There's no yield on the Fannie Mae ARM issue because the rate on the issue changes monthly. Source: Telerate

(For Trades Totaling $1 Million or More)

(September)	Prices in 32nds			Bond-Equiv.
GNMA	Bid	Ask	Chg.	Yields
7s	90-20	90-24	dn 4	8.79
7 1/2s	93-28	94-00	dn 6	8.76
8s	96-31	91-03	dn 4	8.68
8 1/2s	99-27	99-31	dn 2	8.58
FHLMC (Gold)				
7s	91-30	92-02	dn 6	8.65
7 1/2s	94-27	94-31	dn 6	8.64
8s	97-18	97-22	dn 4	8.60
8 1/2s	100-02	100-06	dn 5	8.51
FNMA				
7s	91-28	92-00	dn 6	8.61
7 1/2	94-25	94-29	dn 6	8.61
8s	97-14	97-18	dn 4	8.58
8 1/2s	100-00	100-04	dn 4	8.47
15 Year 8.0s	99-24	99-28	dn 6	7.98
TREASURY			Yield to Maturity	
10-yr note	97-14	97-18	dn 10	7.60

DOW JONES AVERAGES

Utility Average

Year Ended	Quarter Ended		Close Avg.	12-Mth. Earns	P/E Ratio	Qtrly Divs.
1994	Sept.	30	181.45	N.A.	N.A.	3.23
	June	30	177.17	11.15	15.9	3.28
	Mar.	31	196.28	11.07	17.7	3.27
1993	Dec.	31	229.30	11.17	20.5	3.34
	Sept.	30	249.80	16.64	15.0	3.33
	June	30	244.79	16.95	14.4	3.33

DOW JONES BOND AVERAGES

	9/26	9/27	9/28	9/29	9/30
20 Bonds	97.12	97.09	97.05	96.98	96.68
10 Util	92.46	92.65	92.41	92.63	92.10
10 Ind	101.79	101.54	101.70	101.33	101.26

DOW JONES WEEKLY AVERAGES

	First	High	Low	Last	Chg.
20 Bonds	97.12	97.12	96.68	96.68	− .54
10 Util	92.46	92.65	92.10	92.10	− .36
10 Ind	101.79	101.79	101.26	101.26	− .73

VALUE LINE CONVERTIBLE INDEXES

The Value Line Convertible Price Index is equally weighted, and measures the price performance of 585 convertibles (Bonds, Preferreds and Euro-Converts) followed in Value Line Convertibles. The Value Line Total Return Index includes an income component for issues making timely interest and dividend payments. The Value Line Warrant Index is equally weighted and measures price performance of 72 warrants followed in Value Line Convertibles. 3/1/82=100

Prices as of September 26, 1994

	Index Value	% Chg. 1 Week	% Chg. 12 Mo.	Cur. % Yld
Convertibles	166.35	−1.1	−2.40	6.57
Total Ret.(CVTS)	452.34	−1.0	+3.80	...
Warrants	281.52	+0.6	+6.50	...

J.P. MORGAN EMERGING MARKETS BOND INDEX

This table shows the total return index of bonds issued by the listed nations and denominated in U.S. dollars. The ultimate principal payments on these securities, commonly called "Brady bonds," are backed by U.S. Treasury bonds. The interest payments are the obligations of the individual countries. All data is current through the most recent Friday. In the indexes, 100=the price on the first day of trading, which varies by issue.

Total Return (%)

	Index	Week	YTD	12 Mos.
EMBI	190.00	0.44	−11.24	1.09
Latin only	188.72	0.40	-11.22	1.18
Argentina	123.72	−0.14	−16.16	−2.79
Brazil	236.64	1.43	9.82	21.60
Mexico	183.83	−1.05	−11.11	2.03
Nigeria	143.19	4.58	−23.80	−16.03
Philippines	156.44	−0.23	−9.28	3.19
Venezuela	133.51	1.84	−25.86	−17.39
Fixed-rate	203.81	−0.12	−16.78	−6.64
Floating-rate	175.09	0.86	−6.05	8.66

Source: J.P. Morgan

DOW JONES AVERAGES FOR 1994

	First	High	Low	Last	Chg.	%
20Bds	104.79	105.61	96.43	96.68	− 8.21	− 7.83
10Util	103.31	103.43	92.10	92.10	−11.23	−10.87
10Ind	106.28	107.93	98.76	101.26	− 5.19	− 4.88

NEW YORK EXCHANGE BOND DIARY

	9/26	9/27	9/28	9/29	9/30
Total	326	376	340	375	327
Advances	93	99	154	94	124
Declines	150	182	120	210	122
Unchanged	83	95	66	71	81
NewHighs	2	2	1	4	5
NewLows	29	45	33	54	29
Salesth$	21,897	24,134	22,869	26,627	21,121

GUARANTEED INVESTMENT CONTRACTS

[1]Current Treasury quotes, as reported in the Wall Street Journal. Total issuers quoting: 37. [2]Spreads between GIC/BIC high and Treasury with the same maturity. All rates for non benefit responsive, investment only contracts, net of expenses, no commissions. Source: Fiduciary Capital Management Inc., Woodbury, Conn.

Week Ending: Friday, September 30, 1994

Rates	Three Year Comp.	Three Year Simple	Five Year Comp.	Five Year Simple	Seven Year Comp.	Seven Year Simple
$1 Million						
High	7.25	7.24	7.83	7.75	8.09	7.97
Average	7.00	6.94	7.52	7.43	7.72	7.61
Low	8.53	8.58	6.96	6.99	7.15	7.16
# Issuers	26	30	27	30	24	26
$5 Million						
High	7.31	7.28	7.84	7.75	8.11	7.98
Average	7.09	7.01	7.59	7.49	7.78	7.67
Low	6.53	6.59	6.96	6.99	7.15	7.16
# Issuers	27	31	28	31	24	27
$10 Million						
High	7.36	7.30	7.83	7.77	8.10	7.98
Average	7.15	7.03	7.62	7.49	7.81	7.68
Low	7.00	6.68	7.25	7.15	7.50	7.45
# Issuers	15	17	16	17	12	14
$25 Million						
High	7.36	7.30	7.82	7.76	7.95	7.83
Average	7.19	7.00	7.65	7.46	7.87	7.68
Low	7.05	6.74	7.48	7.15	7.78	7.45
# Issuers	9	10	10	10	7	9
Treasuries[1]						
		6.89		7.29		7.34
Treasuries—GIC/BIC Spreads[2]						
$1 Million	.36	.35	.54	.46	.75	.63
$5 Million	.42	.39	.55	.46	.77	.64
$10 Million	.47	.41	.54	.48	.76	.64
$25 Million	.47	.41	.53	.47	.61	.49
Average	.43	.39	.54	.47	.72	.60

PRICES & YIELDS OF ACTIVE JUNK-BOND ISSUES

Issuer	Cpn.	Maturity	Bid	Ask	Wk. Chg.	%Bid/Yld
American Std.	9⅞	6/1/01	98.750	99.250	+0.000	10.13
Bradlees	9¼	3/1/03	88.500	89.000	−0.250	11.41
Comcast	10¼	10/15/01	101.250	101.750	−0.250	10.00
Inland Steel	12	12/1/98	109.500	110.000	+0.000	9.19
Kroger A	9¾	2/15/04	101.500	102.000	−0.500	9.50
Owens Illinois	10	8/1/02	100.000	100.500	+0.250	9.99
Northwest Stl&W	9½	6/15/01	93.500	94.000	+1.000	10.89
Rogers Cantel	10¾	11/1/01	103.750	104.250	+1.250	9.99
Stone Container	9⅞	2/1/01	93.500	94.000	+0.500	11.34
Unisys	10⅝	10/1/99	100.250	100.750	+0.250	10.56

Source: Lehman Brothers.

J.P. MORGAN OVERSEAS GOVERNMENT BOND INDEX

September 29, 1994

	Local Currency			U.S. Dollar			Yield	
Country	Index	Wkly Chg	YTD Chg	Index	Wkly Chg	YTD Chg	%	YTD Chg
Australia	222.24	−0.27	−8.76	227.90	0.27	−0.48	9.91	3.47
Belgium	172.07	0.64	−4.72	178.47	0.91	8.38	8.21	2.00
Canada	192.64	0.74	−5.13	186.46	0.77	−6.46	8.73	2.20
Denmark	193.93	0.86	−5.98	193.98	1.29	5.27	8.62	2.73
France	189.97	0.66	−6.40	191.45	1.02	4.74	7.82	2.32
Germany	150.68	0.48	−3.85	152.89	0.65	7.99	7.27	1.88
Italy	234.35	1.59	−4.01	174.81	2.42	5.74	11.32	2.68
Japan	145.02	0.02	−4.13	178.21	−0.42	8.62	4.36	1.35
Netherlands	156.27	0.70	−6.06	159.22	0.94	5.34	7.36	1.87
Spain	216.93	0.60	−4.40	181.70	0.77	6.66	10.70	2.95
Sweden	198.88	0.37	−8.24	153.68	0.08	2.24	10.69	4.05
U.K.	192.91	0.60	−9.76	161.71	0.91	−3.57	8.80	2.60
U.S.	173.40	−0.24	−3.21	173.40	−0.24	−3.21	7.43	1.81
Non-U.S.	167.14	0.53	−5.46	162.01	0.65	4.69	7.45	2.05
Global	172.26	0.19	−4.46	171.54	0.26	1.01	7.44	1.94

YTD-Year to date. Yields-Semi-annual. Dec. 31, 1987=100. Source: J.P. Morgan Government Bond Index

BOX SCORE

Adviser Sentiment Polls

Bullish Consensus	Last Week	Two Weeks Ago	Three Weeks Ago
Market Vane			
T-Bonds	32%	33%	33%
Euro$	37	53	50
Consensus Inc.			
T-Bonds	26%	36%	40%
Euro$	15	32	67

Sources: Market Vane, P.O. Box 90490, Pasadena, CA 91109 (818) 395-7436 and Consensus Inc., 1735 McGee Street, Kansas City, MO 64108 (816) 471-3862.

Performance

30-Year T-Bonds	7.81%	7.78%	7.76%
Lehman Index#	1347.11	1351.46	1355.13
Total Return†	436.85	437.49	437.93

#In the Lehman Brothers Index of long Treasury bond prices; Dec. 31, 1980=1000. †Ryan Labs Treasury Index.

BOND RATING CHANGES

Duff & Phelps

DOWNGRADE	FROM	TO
S&A Restaurant Corp.		
sen sec note	B	BB
float rt note	B	BB
sen sub note	B	BB

Moody's

UPGRADE	FROM	TO
The CIT Group Holdings		
note, deb, amort note	A1	Aa3
sub med-term note	A2	A1
DOWNGRADE	FROM	TO
Industrial Bank of Japan		
eurobd, euronote,	Aa3	A1
Vendell Healthcare		
sen note	B1	B2

BARRON'S C.I./YIELD GAP

The figures shown indicate the yield gap between Barron's Best Grade Bonds and the Dow Jones Industrial Stock Average.

Week Ended		Conf. Index	Inrm. Bonds	Best Grade	DJI Yield	Yield Gap
1994						
Sept.	23	93.1	8.93	8.31	2.76	− 5.55
	16	92.8	8.80	8.16	2.68	− 5.48
	9	92.9	8.66	8.05	2.71	− 5.34
	2	92.8	8.62	8.00	2.63	− 5.37
Aug.	26	92.7	8.63	8.00	2.64	− 5.36
	19	92.6	8.61	7.97	2.72	− 5.24
	12	93.0	8.66	8.05	2.70	− 5.35
	5	92.8	8.43	7.82	2.72	− 5.10
July	29	92.6	8.62	7.98	2.72	− 5.26
	22	92.6	8.63	7.99	2.74	− 5.25
	15	92.5	8.63	7.98	2.71	− 5.27
	8	92.1	8.72	8.03	2.74	− 5.29
	1	92.1	8.73	8.04	2.79	− 5.25
June	24	92.1	8.53	7.86	2.75	− 5.11
	17	91.8	8.52	7.82	2.65	− 5.17
	10	92.1	8.41	7.75	2.68	− 5.07
	3	92.3	8.50	7.85	2.68	− 5.17
May	27	92.4	8.52	7.87	2.69	− 5.18
	20	92.5	8.36	7.73	2.69	− 5.04
	13	92.8	8.72	8.09	2.76	− 5.33
	6	92.8	8.46	7.85	2.77	− 5.08
Apr.	29	92.8	8.39	7.79	2.76	− 5.03
	22	92.8	8.36	7.76	2.79	− 4.97
	15	93.2	8.40	7.83	2.77	− 5.06
	8	92.7	8.38	7.77	2.78	− 4.99
Mar.	31	92.6	8.26	7.65	2.81	− 4.84

DOW JONES AVERAGES

65-Stocks Composite Average

Year Ended	Quarter Ended		Clos. Avg.	Qtrly Earns	12-Mth. Earns	P/E Ratio	Qtrly Divs
1994	Sept.	30	1285.78	N.A.	N.A.	N.A.	9.48
	June	30	1269.34	19.39	55.56	22.8	9.11
	Mar.	31	1297.77	12.43	45.98	28.2	9.09
1993	Dec.	31	1381.03	6.43	44.10	31.3	9.01
	Sept.	30	1324.54	17.31	34.83	38.0	8.93
	June	30	1292.59	9.81	27.82	46.5	8.84
	Mar.	31	1279.25	10.55	26.40	48.5	8.75
	Yr. End			44.10			35.53
1992	Dec.	31	1204.55	d2.84	24.89	48.4	9.16
	Sept.	30	1153.46	10.30	14.32	80.5	9.25
	June	30	1165.37	8.39	13.14	88.7	9.02
	Mar.	31	1161.80	9.04	15.94	72.9	8.57
	Yr. End			24.89			36.00

Source: *Barron's,* October 3, 1994, p. 99. Reprinted by permission of *Barron's,*

Internet—A Trip Down the Information Highway

The Internet is part of the "information highway" that has received increasing attention from the national press. Originally, Internet was designed to foster research between government agencies and universities around the world and to allow professors and researchers to communicate through the electronic medium of the telephone cable connecting mainframe computers. For the major part of its existence, the Internet served this purpose—without major cost to the users.

As PCs became more popular (50 million PCs by the end of 1994), commercial providers as well as government agencies tried to devise ways to use Internet to improve information access. As a result, the Internet is becoming more commercial, and some services cost money to use. On the other hand, some government agencies, such as the Securities and Exchange Commission (SEC), have begun to offer free access to data that corporations are required to make public, such as 10-K, 10-Q, 8-K, and other reports. The SEC's on-line database of corporate filings is called *EDGAR* and can be accessed on the Internet through either the *World Wide Web (WWW)* or *Gopher.*

The World Wide Web is a graphical system that is accessed through a program called *MOSAIC* developed and maintained at the University of Illinois at Urbana-Champaign. Another common program found at universities to access the Internet is called *Gopher.* Gopher is a character-based program maintained at the University of Minnesota. WWW and Gopher often lead to the same information.

Students should find out if their university computer labs are connected to the Internet and if their universities provide access to students. If so, the wealth of information will boggle your mind. If you use the WWW, you can go to the subject "finance" and connect to the *FINWeb* at the University of Texas, which then connects you to many other finance file servers all over the world. You can connect to the University of Warsaw and find Polish stock quotes or you can go to New York University and access the EDGAR development project. The Massachusetts Institute of Technology offers the Experimental Stock Market Page with stock-volume graphs on more than 500 companies. A wealth of government data is available from the Department of Commerce, the National Bureau of Economic Research, the Office of Management of the Budget, and even the World Bank. You can find out what the Dow Jones Industrial Average is doing (5-minute delay) by using the FINWeb and looking under Databases: Interactive Stock Market Quotes.

The real power of the Internet for students is that the amount of information at your fingertips is only a keystroke away. This electronic library has more information than can be described in the space of this box. The only way to learn what is available is to explore the WWW and/or Gopher servers as you would wander through library stacks looking for information.

The last several years have seen a great leap forward in commercial on-line services such as America Online, Prodigy, and CompuServe. These services link a user to centralized data that can be accessed through a telephone modem on a time-sharing basis. The fees are reasonable, and the user can access anything from airline travel schedules to stock price information. At the end of 1994, it is estimated that these three providers have more than four million users. For more on-line data, see the box on the Internet.

The Use of Mainframe Computers

The following databases are made to be used on large mainframe computers. Compustat is published by Investors Management Science Company, a subsidiary of Standard & Poor's Corporation. The *Compustat tapes* are very comprehensive, containing 20 years of annual financial data for more than 16,000 companies. Each year's data for the industrial

companies include more than 300 balance sheet, income statement, and market-related items. Compustat has an industrial file that includes company data from the New York and American stock exchanges and the over-the-counter market. Also included is a file on utilities and banks. Besides the annual file, which is updated weekly, users can order tapes with quarterly data, also updated weekly.

A second database created by Compustat is called the Price-Dividend-Earnings tape (PDE), which contains monthly data on per-share performance. These tapes are leased to financial institutions for a fairly large sum or to nonprofit educational institutions at a significant discount. The tapes may be paid for in cash or in soft dollars (commissions funneled through an S&P brokerage subsidiary).

These tapes are useful for analyzing large numbers of companies in a short time. Ratios can be created, analyzed, and compared. Trends and regression analysis can be performed. Searches can be implemented for specific kinds of companies. For example, one could read through the tapes and screen for companies meeting certain parameters, such as:

1. Dividend yield greater than 6 percent.
2. Earnings growth greater than 15 percent per year.
3. Price-earnings ratio less than the Standard & Poor's 500 Stock Index.
4. Market price less than book value.

Interactive Data Corporation also provides the same information as the Compustat tapes on a time-sharing basis.

The *CRSP tapes* are maintained by the University of Chicago in the Center for Research in Security Prices. The information provided is oriented to earnings, dividends, stock prices, and dates of mergers, stock splits, stock dividends, and so on. The tapes are extremely useful (data begin in 1926) for historical research on stock performance. They are widely used in academia for research on the efficient market hypothesis, the capital asset pricing model, and other investment questions.

Value Line also has made computer tapes of its 1,700 companies available. Again, these have market price data as well as financial statement items. The Federal Trade Commission has aggregate industry data, and the Federal Reserve Bank of St. Louis has made tapes of monetary data available for academic researchers.

The Use of Personal Computers

The past few years have brought a proliferation of databases for the personal computer. Most programs have been written for IBM-compatible personal computers operating under DOS. The increased speed of computer chips and larger hard drives allows for large databases and sophisticated programs to analyze the data. As individual investors' computing power increases, they are increasingly using many of these databases.

The owner of a PC with communications ability and a modem (phone hookup) can now dial a family-oriented database such as *Prodigy,* which allows the user to look up information on individual stocks, construct portfolios, and do other personal financial planning involving shopping for consumer goods and travel planning.

If you require more comprehensive data, the Dow Jones News Retrieval System might be better suited to your needs. This database is oriented to the business user and includes financial data, current and historical information on stock quotes, commodity quotes, access to Disclosure's SEC reports mentioned previously, and much more. Other comprehensive information outlets, such as *The Source* and *CompuServe,* also provide financial data, general information, government statistics, and electronic mail. Chase Econometrics and Nite-Line specialize in financial, business, and economic data, while Citishare Corporation offers U.S. economic statistics.

Moody's and Standard & Poor's offer comprehensive databases to the institutional investor, libraries, and corporations. One Moody's service covers news stories on more than 18,000 U.S. companies and 5,000 international companies. It also offers financial company profiles for all NYSE, AMEX, and 1,500 OTC companies. Standard & Poor's offers many on-line services covering data on 55,000 companies from S&P's *Register of Corporations, Directors and Executives.* It provides financial information on stocks, bonds, options, futures, foreign exchange, and more from more than 50 markets and exchanges through an on-line service called S&P ComStock. It also has MarketScope, which includes earnings and dividend forecasts on more than 1,000 companies as well as a reference section and profiles for 5,000 U.S. companies. MarketScope also includes a buy-sell ranking system for 800 companies, technical indicators, economic data, daily commentary, and so on.

Many financial companies such as Value Line and Morningstar are offering their financial data on microcomputer floppy disks with monthly updates. Databases either emphasize fundamental or technical analysis. U.S. Equities OnFloppy and Value Screen II are two of the leading PC databases. They provide mostly fundamental data emphasizing income and balance sheet figures, monthly price, dividend, and earnings data, and calculated financial ratios. These programs allow investors to "screen" (specify characteristics desired and then have the computer look for companies fitting the description). If you subscribe to U.S. Equities OnFloppy, you would be able to search through more than 5,000 companies compared with 1,600 companies for Value Screen II. Additionally, the American Association of Individual Investors produces "Stock Investor" covering 8,000 companies and including Institutional/Brokers/Estimate/Service (I/B/E/S) earnings estimates.

In addition to the databases available for the personal computer, new software to access and analyze the data is being created at an extremely rapid pace. The raw data can either be downloaded (quickly transferred) onto a floppy disk or into your computer memory to save time and be analyzed later, or it can be read directly into a software program designed to perform calculations.

Some programs analyze and create charts of the technical behavior of price movements, and others evaluate the financial data from income statements and balance sheets. Using the Dow Jones Investment Evaluator, you can access the Dow Jones News Retrieval System to obtain information for stocks, bonds, warrants, options, mutual funds, or Treasury issues. Information related to 10-K statements, ratios, earnings growth rates, earnings per share forecasts, and so forth are available on 2,400 companies. The Dow Jones Market Analyzer, the Dow Jones Microscope, and the Dow Jones Investor Workshop all allow access to the Dow Jones information network. Once the correct data

are entered into these software programs, they then create standardized analysis from preprogrammed instructions. Also, new programs are now able to transfer data from a news retrieval service straight into a spreadsheet program such as Lotus 1-2-3 or Excel. This saves time and money and allows the individual the flexibility to create his or her own financial analysis.

Not all these programs are available for every personal computer. Most programs are for the IBM personal computer and compatible systems or for Apple's MacIntosh computer. Before buying a PC, check to make sure which software programs run on your computer. Table 4–12 on page 124 provides information on international databases available for the PC. Most of these are quite expensive and are designed for use by professionals rather than individual investors.

INFORMATION ON NONTRADITIONAL MARKETS

For this section, we define nontraditional as being out of the realm of stocks, bonds, and government securities. A major area that received increased attention during the last decade has been commodities and financial futures. A key source of information on commodities is the *Commodity Yearbook.*

Commodity Yearbook

This is a yearly publication which can be supplemented by the *Commodity Yearbook Statistical Abstract* three times a year. The *Commodity Yearbook* runs several feature articles of educational interest, covering commodities or situations in the forefront of commodity trading.

In addition to the featured articles, the *Yearbook* covers each traded commodity from alcohol to zinc. For example, corn is covered in six pages. The first page is a description of the corn crop and occurrences for the current year. The next five pages cover much data in tabular form for the past 13 years. The tables show world production of corn, acreage, and supply of corn in the United States, corn production estimates, and disposition by value in the United States. Also included are corn supply and disappearance, distribution of corn in the United States, corn price support data, average price received by farmers for corn in the United States, and the weekly high-low-close of the nearest month's futures price. Each commodity has a similarly detailed evaluation and statistical summary.

Other publications about commodities come from mainline brokerage houses and specialty commodity brokers. In addition, the commodities exchanges publish educational booklets and newsletters. The International Monetary Market publishes the *I.M.M. Weekly Report,* which discusses the interest-rate markets, the foreign exchange markets, and gold. It also presents weekly prices for all interest-rate futures, foreign exchange markets, gold, and selected cash market information such as the federal funds rate and the prime rate. The Chicago Board of Trade publishes the *Interest Rate Futures Newsletter.* As investors continue to become active in these markets, an investor (speculator) can be sure to find more available data.

TABLE 4–12 International Data Providers (PC database products) Current Company-Level Data

Name	Non-U.S. Coverage	Scope	Timeliness	Accessibility	History
MSCI PC	2,000 companies 19 markets	Fundamentals Prices	Monthly Daily via modem	Good	20 years available
I/B/E/S	5,400 companies 27 markets	Earnings estimates	Weekly Daily via modem	Depends on delivery platform	3 years
WorldScope via Lotus One-Source	5,000 companies 25 markets	Fundamentals Prices	Weekly	Good CD-ROM	10 years
CIFAR	4,500 companies 40-plus markets	Fundamentals Prices	Monthly	CD-ROM	7 years
Moody's	5,500 companies 100 markets	Background Fundamentals	Quarterly	Text only	3 year balance sheet
IDC (Datasheet)	11,000 prices 1,934 fundamentals 24 markets	Prices Some fundamentals	Daily	Dial up	1982+
Reuters	All companies 110 markets	Prices Some background	Real-time	Dedicated line Excel Link	No
Datastream	12,000 prices 4,200 fundamentals	CAP Prices Fundamentals	Daily Some real-time	Dial up Lotus Link	5–20 years depending on country
EuroEquities	1,200 companies 15 markets	Fundamentals Earnings estimates	Biweekly		8 years
Compustat International Version	3,000 companies 24 markets	Fundamentals		CD-ROM	1982+
IFC Emerging Markets	600 companies 19 markets	Prices Limited fundamentals	Monthly	Lotus spreadsheet	1975+
MSCI Emerging Markets	700 companies 14 markets	Prices	Monthly	Flat file	No

Note: These PC database products are expensive and are primarily used by institutional investors.
Source: Acadian Asset Management, Inc.; Association for Investment Management and Research; and International Society of Financial Analysis, Investing Worldwide II, AIMR, California, 1991, p. 52.

SUMMARY

Information is easy and yet difficult to find. The problem beginners have is knowing where to look and what to look for, and this chapter has attempted to provide some guidance and sample data. The problem advanced investors have is knowing what information is usable. This may also haunt beginners once they find the sources. To become proficient in finding data, spend a day in your library looking through the volumes. Also, determine what software packages are available for your personal computer. This process will increase your awareness of the types of information available. Then do some of the exercises at the end of this chapter to see if you can find specific data. As for knowing what information is useful, the authors hope to shed some light on that as we proceed through the book.

DISCUSSION QUESTIONS

1. What type of information is part of aggregate economic data?
2. The Federal Reserve Bank of St. Louis has a number of comprehensive economic publications. What are they?
3. What is one of the major benefits provided by the *Survey of Current Business* in regard to industry data?
4. What are the three categories of economic time series indicators found in the *Survey of Current Business?*
5. Of the major advisory services for investors, which ones would likely be found in most libraries?
6. What is special about the T–Z volume of Standard & Poor's *Corporation Records?*
7. What is the Standard & Poor's *Stock Guide?*
8. Briefly describe the Value Line evaluation system.
9. Assume one needs information about an industry or company. Suggest three types of indexes for periodicals or journals that can be used.
10. What type of information is contained in the following three filings with the SEC: 10-K, 8-K, 10-Q?
11. Under what category in *Barron's* would weekly data on stock and bond market statistics be found?
12. Who publishes *Compustat?* What type of information is available on *Compustat?*
13. What information is available through the Dow Jones News Retrieval System? Can you access this service with a personal computer?
14. Suggest some sources for information about commodities.

THE WALL STREET JOURNAL PROJECTS

1. *The Wall Street Journal* is an excellent source of current information. It helps keep investors up to date and supplements the historical information found in many of the sources mentioned in Chapter 4.

   For example, Hewlett-Packard is highlighted in Tables 4–1, 4–4, and 4–5. Look up the current common stock price on the New York Stock Exchange and compare it with the price listed in Value Line (Table 4–5). How has the price changed since the Value Line survey was published? Additionally, *The Wall Street Journal* presents an index of companies mentioned in the paper in Section B, page 2. Follow this index, and read and summarize any articles on Hewlett-Packard for one week.
2. Table 4–6, "Digest of Earnings Reports," on page 113, shows a table from *The Wall Street Journal* that appears daily. It shows reported earnings for the latest quarter and also shows earnings for the comparable quarter of the prior year. It further indicates year-to-date information for the current and prior year. For example in Table 4–6, you see Acordia Inc. listed second. Find the quarterly data for the quarter ending September 30 for 1994 and 1993. Right below that, you will see nine-month year-to-date information on Acordia Inc. for 1994 and 1993.

   Find this table in the current issue of *The Wall Street Journal.* Look for it by going to the index on the front page and locating "Earnings Digest." After you have located the Earnings Digest, pick a company that looks interesting to you,

and find a Standard & Poor's report on it in your library. How do current sales and earnings compare with the past trends?

U.S. EQUITIES ONFLOPPY EXERCISES

Please use your U.S. Equities OnFloppy software and manual to complete the following exercises.

1. In Chapter 4, Hewlett-Packard is used as the example to illustrate the information about a company found in the Standard & Poor's Corporate Reports and the Value Line Industry Survey. Locate the data for Hewlett-Packard from the U.S. Equities OnFloppy database, and compare the data with the S&P and Value Line information.

2. **a.** Chapter 4, page 101, lists the companies that are identified by S&P as Cereal Breakfast Companies. According to S&P, these are the companies with an SIC code of 2043. Select the companies from the U.S. Equities OnFloppy database that have an SIC code of 2043, and compare with the prior list.

b. Using the U.S. Equities OnFloppy database, find the SIC code of the nine companies listed on page 101.

3. **a.** According to the U.S. Equities OnFloppy manual, the SIC system groups companies into nine major industries. What are they?

b. Consider all of the companies in the U.S. Equities OnFloppy database, and determine how many companies are in each of the nine major industries. Construct a percentage distribution by industry.

APPENDIX 4A: Names and Addresses of Important Data Sources

Federal Reserve Bank of
Atlanta, GA 30301
Boston, MA 02106
Chicago, IL 60690
Cleveland, OH 44101
Dallas, TX 75222
Kansas City, KS 64198
Minneapolis, MN 55480
New York, NY 10045
Philadelphia, PA 19105
Richmond, VA 23219
San Francisco, CA 94120
St. Louis, MO 63166

Federal Reserve Bulletin
Board of Governors of the
Federal Reserve System
Washington, D.C. 20551

Stock and Commodity Exchanges
American Stock Exchange
86 Trinity Place
New York, NY 10006

Chicago Board of Trade
LaSalle at Jackson
Chicago, IL 60604

Chicago Mercantile Exchange
30 South Wacker Dr.
Chicago, IL 60606

New York Stock Exchange
11 Wall Street
New York, NY 10005

The following U.S. government publications can be requested from the:
Superintendent of Documents
U.S. Government Printing Office
Washington, D.C. 20402

Survey of Current Business
Weekly Business Statistics
Economic Indicators
Economic Report of the President
Statistical Abstract of the United States
Statistical Bulletin

Periodicals

The Wall Street Journal and *Barron's*
Dow Jones & Company
Subscriptions Office
200 Burnett Rd.
Chicopee, MA 01021

Changing Times
The Kiplinger Magazine
1729 H St., N.W.
Washington, D.C. 20006

Disclosure Journal
Disclosure, Inc.
1450 Broadway
New York, NY 10018

Forbes
60 5th Avenue
New York, NY 10011

Financial World
Macro Communications Inc.
150 East 58th Street
New York, NY 10155

Business Week
1221 Avenue of the Americas
New York, NY 10020

Money Magazine
Fortune
Time Inc.
3435 Wilshire Blvd.
Los Angeles, CA 90010

Investor's Daily Financial Services, Inc.
P.O. Box 26991
Richmond, VA 23261

Financial Analysts Journal
1633 Broadway
New York, NY 10019

Investment Services

Moody's Investors Service
99 Church Street
New York, NY 10007

Standard & Poor's Corporation
345 Hudson Street
New York, NY 10014

Value Line Services
Arnold Bernhard & Co.
5 East 44th Street
New York, NY 10017

Dun & Bradstreet
99 Church Street
New York, NY 10007

Dun's Marketing Division
3 Century Drive
Parsippany, NJ 07054

Computer Databases

Compustat
P.O. Box 239
Denver, CO 80201

CRSP Tapes
Center for Research in Security Prices
University of Chicago
Graduate School of Business
Chicago, IL 60637

Interactive Data Corporation
122 East 42nd Street
New York, NY 10017

Morningstar
U.S. Equities OnFloppy
225 West Wacker Drive
Chicago, IL 60606
1-800-876-5005

APPENDIX 4B: Regional and Branch Offices of the SEC

Where You Can Find the Reports: A Directory

Financial and other data included in registration statements, reports, applications, and similar documents filed with the commission are available for study in the public reference room in the main office in Washington, D.C. Copies of these documents may be obtained for 10 cents per page, with a $5 minimum. Cost estimates are available by writing to Public Reference Room, Securities and Exchange Commission, Washington, D.C. 20549.

Current annual reports and other periodic reports filed by companies whose securities are listed on the national exchanges are also available for study in the SEC's New York, Chicago, and Los Angeles regional offices.

Registration statements and subsequent reports filed by those companies whose securities are traded over-the-counter and that register under the Securities Exchange Act are also available at the New York, Chicago, and Los Angeles offices.

SEC filings can also be examined at the regional office serving the area in which the issuer's principal office is located. These regional offices are located in cities shown below and on the following page.

Prospectuses covering recent public offerings of securities registered under the Securities Act may be examined in all regional offices.

Broker-dealer and investment adviser registrations, as well as Regulation A notifications and offering circulars, may be examined in the particular regional office in which they were filed.

Regional and Branch Offices

Region 1
New York Regional Office
26 Federal Plaza
New York, NY 10278
(212) 264-1636
Region: New York and New Jersey.

Region 2
Boston Regional Office
150 Causeway Street
Boston, MA 02114
(617) 223-2721
Region: Maine, New Hampshire, Vermont, Massachusetts, Rhode Island, and Connecticut.

Region 3
Atlanta Regional Office
1375 Peachtree Street, N.E.
Suite 788
Atlanta, GA 30367
(404) 881-4768
Region: Tennessee, Virgin Islands, Puerto Rico, North Carolina, South Carolina, Georgia, Alabama, Mississippi, Florida, and Louisiana east of the Atchafalaya River.

Miami Branch Office
Dupont Plaza Center
300 Biscayne Blvd. Way, Suite 1114
Miami, FL 33131
(305) 350-5765

Region 4
Chicago Regional Office
Northwestern Atrium
500 W. Madison, 14th Floor
Chicago, IL 60601-2511
(312) 353-7390
Region: Michigan, Ohio, Kentucky, Wisconsin, Indiana, Iowa, Minnesota, Missouri, Kansas City, Kansas, and Illinois.

Detroit Branch Office
1044 Federal Bldg.
Detroit, MI 48226
(313) 226-6070

Region 5
Fort Worth Regional Office
411 W. Seventh St.
Fort Worth, TX 76102
(817) 334-3821

Region: Oklahoma, Arkansas, Texas, Louisiana west of the Atchafalaya River, and Kansas (except Kansas City).

Houston Branch Office
Federal Office and Courts Bldg.
515 Rusk Avenue, Room 5615
Houston, TX 77002
(713) 226-4986

Region 6
Denver Regional Office
410 17th Street
Suite 700
Denver, CO 80202
(303) 837-2071
Region: North Dakota, South Dakota, Wyoming, Nebraska, Colorado, New Mexico, and Utah.

Salt Lake Branch Office
Boston Bldg., Suite 810
Nine Exchange Place
Salt Lake City, UT 84111
(801) 524-5796

Region 7
Los Angeles Regional Office
10960 Wilshire Blvd.
Suite 1710
Los Angeles, CA 90024
(213) 473-4511
Region: Nevada, Arizona, California, Hawaii, and Guam.

San Francisco Branch Office
450 Golden Gate Avenue, Box 36042
San Francisco, CA 94102
(415) 556-5264

Region 8
Seattle Regional Office
3040 Federal Building
915 Second Avenue
Seattle, WA 98174
(206) 442-7900
Region: Montana, Idaho, Washington, Oregon, and Alaska.

Region 9
Washington Regional Office
Ballston Center Tower 3
4015 Wilson Blvd.
Arlington, VA 22203
(703) 557-8201
Region: Pennsylvania, Delaware, Maryland, Virginia, West Virginia, and District of Columbia.

Philadelphia Branch Office

William J. Green, Jr., Federal Bldg.
600 Arch Street, Room 2204
Philadelphia, PA 19106
(215) 597-2278

U.S. Securities and Exchange Commission, Washington, D.C. 20549

General Information
Office of Public Affairs
(202) 272-2650

Investor Complaints
Office of Consumer Affairs
(202) 523-5516

Filings by Registered Companies
Public Reference Room
1100 L Street, N.W.
(202) 523-5360

Forms and Publications
(202) 523-3761
For the Official Summary, $70 a year, $6.50 per issue, contact: Superintendent of Documents, Government Printing Office, Washington, D.C. 20402. Phone: (202) 783-3238.

Source: John Markese, "Culling Information from the SEC," *American Association of Individual Investors Journal,* January 1984, pp. 31–34.

PART 2

Analysis and Valuation of Equity Securities

OUTLINE

Historically, the stock market and the economy have been intertwined. Most stock market analysts agree that the stock market usually leads economic activity by six to nine months, but once in gear, the economy drives corporate earnings and dividends, which in turn impact stock values. Occasionally, there are external events that cause shocks to the economy. One recurring economic shock during the last 20 years has been the unpredictability of oil prices.

The Iranian revolution and the Persian Gulf War, started by the Iraqi invasion of Kuwait, are two events that caused wild gyrations in oil prices. Unfortunately, the United States as well as many other industrial economies import a majority of their oil, and any increase in oil prices can have an inflationary impact that ripples through the whole economy. When inflationary expectations rise, so do interest rates, and when that happens bond prices fall and eventually so do stock prices.

Oil has so many uses that a rising oil price affects the price of plastic, fertilizer, automobiles, and many other dependent products. Many industries are severely affected by rapidly increasing oil prices. For example, when gasoline becomes more expensive, many people shift their demand from large cars to smaller, more fuel efficient cars. This has happened many times throughout the last three decades. A steep oil price increase also can reduce the sale of automobiles, gasoline, and products dependent on plastic such as compact disks.

Perhaps one of the most affected industries is the airline industry. Aviation fuel is a major cost of air travel, and even a small increase in the price of oil can affect the earnings of airlines such as Delta, United, or American. In fact, several airlines, including Midway Airlines in Chicago, have been forced to file for bankruptcy as a result of the oil price rise caused by the Persian Gulf War.

If the airline industry raises ticket prices to compensate for the increased cost of operations, passenger traffic can shrink dramatically, sending ripple effects throughout the travel industry. Reduced air travel translates into lost income for hotels, resorts, and car rental firms, as well as other recreational expenditures such as food, golf, and theater. Specific companies such as Hilton, Marriott, Disney, and Hertz can feel the effects of an oil price rise.

A large oil shock, such as the one occurring in 1973–74, can cause a recession if all the negative effects mentioned above occur at the same time. Stock prices in 1973–74 decreased dramatically, and many analysts would say the major blame was on the inflationary impact of the oil price shock. Many times since 1974, oil price increases (or decreases) have played a major role in the fortunes of many industries by influencing profits and consumer demand.

As you go through this section on the economy, industry analysis, and company stock analysis, think about the external shocks that may affect the industry or company being analyzed. Remember that many of these events, both positive and negative, are not controllable by management. On the other hand, management must have a plan for dealing with them. Analysts must be able to quickly factor these economic shocks into their valuation models. ■

5

Economic Activity

To determine the value of the firm, fundamental analysis relies on long-run forecasts of the economy, the industry, and the company's financial prospects. Short-run changes in business conditions are also important in that they influence investors' required rates of return and expectations of corporate earnings and dividends. This chapter presents the basic information for analysis of the economy, while other chapters in this section focus on industry analysis and the individual firm.

Figure 5–1 presents an overview of the valuation process as an inverted triangle. The process starts with a macroanalysis of the economy and then moves into industry variables. Next, common stocks are individually screened according to expected risk-return characteristics, and finally the surviving stocks are combined into portfolios of

FIGURE 5–1 Overview of the Valuation Process

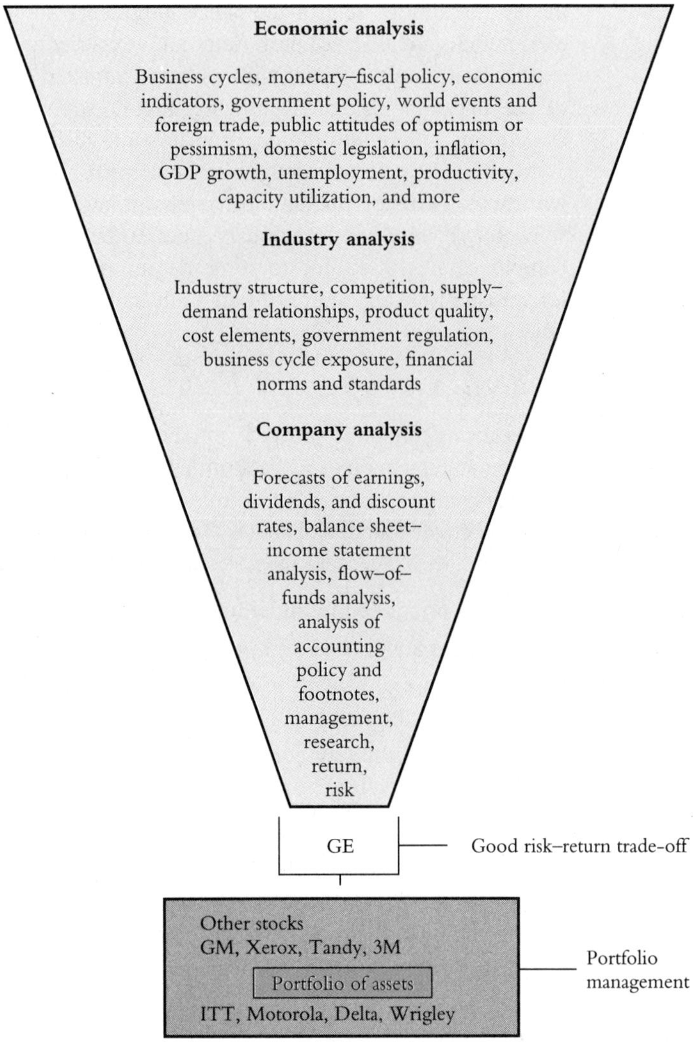

assets. This figure is not inclusive of all variables considered by an analyst, but is intended to indicate representative areas applicable to most industries and companies.

ECONOMIC ACTIVITY AND THE BUSINESS CYCLE

An investor begins the valuation process with an economic analysis. The hope is that an accurate forecast and examination of economic activity will provide the basis for accurate stock market predictions and indicate which industries may prosper. The analyst needs information on present and expected interest rates, monetary and fiscal policy, government and consumer spending patterns, and other economic data. To be successful, investors must understand business cycles and be able to forecast accurately. Unfortunately, these are not easy tasks, but the rewards can be significant if the timing is right.

Whether analysts use statistical methods, such as regression analysis and probability theory, or simply seat-of-the-pants judgment, they are still basing their forecast on expectations related to past data and experiences. Past information usually is not extrapolated into the future without being adjusted to conform with the subjective beliefs of the decision maker. Even when highly sophisticated statistical methods are used, subjectivity enters into the decision in some fashion.

Most likely, past knowledge will be helpful, but modifications for the present effects of worldwide currency fluctuations, international debt obligations, and other factors, which were not so important previously, need to be included in any forecast now. Since most companies are influenced to some degree by the general level of economic activity, a forecast will usually start with an analysis of the government's economic program.

Federal Government Economic Policy

Government economic policy is guided by the Employment Act of 1946 and subsequent position statements by the Federal Reserve Board, the President's Council of Economic Advisors, and other acts of Congress. The goals established by the Employment Act still hold and cover four broad areas. These goals, the focus of monetary and fiscal policy, are as follows with a second interpretation in parentheses:

1. Stable prices (a low inflation rate).
2. Business stability at high levels of production (low levels of unemployment).
3. Sustained real growth in gross domestic product (actual economic growth after deducting inflation).
4. A balance in international payments (primarily a balance of exports and imports but also including cash flows in and out of the United States).

These goals are often conflicting in that they do not all respond favorably to the same economic stimulus. Therefore, goal priorities and economic policies change to reflect current economic conditions. In the 1950s and early 1960s, the United States did not have an international trade problem or spiraling inflation, so economic policy focused on employment and economic growth. The economy grew rapidly between 1961 and 1969, and, because of the Vietnam War, unemployment reached very low levels. The demand for goods and competition for funds were very high during the war, and eventually war expenditures, large budget deficits, full employment, and large increases in the money

supply caused many problems. Inflation accelerated to high levels, interest rates reached record heights, and an imbalance of international payments finally resulted in two devaluations of the U.S. dollar in the early 1970s.

By the time Jimmy Carter took office in January 1977, the primary goals were once again to reduce unemployment, control inflation, and create a moderate level of economic growth that could be sustained without causing more inflation (a very difficult task!). The achievement of these goals was thrown into the hands of the Federal Reserve Board. The Fed's tight money policy caused a rapid increase in interest rates to control inflation, and these high rates depressed common stock prices as the required rate of return by investors reached record levels.

Ronald Reagan inherited most of the problems Carter faced but tried new ways of reaching the goals. As the 1980s began, Reagan instituted a three-year tax cut to increase disposable income and stimulate consumption and thus economic growth, and, at the same time, he negotiated reductions in government spending. These policies were successful in sharply reducing inflation and creating strong growth in the gross domestic product (GDP), but they were accomplished with record government deficits. George Bush followed most of Reagan's domestic policies but focused more on international issues. In the middle of President Bush's term, the record 90-month peacetime expansion came to an end with the start of a recession in July 1990. In looking back, the expansion that began in November 1982 created record employment, reduced unemployment percentages, and lowered interest rates and inflation from the high levels of 1980 and 1981. The stock market began a major bull market in 1982 in response to these improved conditions but also sustained the biggest one day crash ever on October 19, 1987.

Unfortunately, the recession that began in July 1990 was extremely painful. Major companies such as IBM, AT&T, TRW, General Motors, and hundreds of others announced employee reductions totaling more than one-half million employees. In November 1992, President Clinton was elected to office on the promise of more jobs and universal health coverage. The economy was already benefiting from the recovery started in March 1991, and Clinton persuaded Congress to pass an increase in personal and corporate income taxes. Many economists thought the tax increase would create a "fiscal drag" on the economy by reducing spending. By the third quarter of 1992, the economy had slowed down considerably and stagnated at minimal real GDP growth. However, by year end 1993, real GDP growth in the fourth quarter was over 7 percent, and by the end of 1994 had stabilized at between 3.0 and 3.5 percent real growth. The new Republican Congress that came into power in January 1995 was working on a budget overhaul that was expected to have a significant impact on government taxing and spending habits. Whether they will be any more effective than previous Democratic Congresses in reducing the U.S. deficit remains to be seen.

The world has changed dramatically during the last decade. Germany is united, the Union of Soviet Socialist Republics has ceased to exist as a country, and capitalism is springing up all over the former Eastern bloc in countries such as Poland, Hungary, and the Czech Republic. As we enter this new era, we cannot always rely on the past for indications about the future. The changes in Europe will continue as these economies develop and new political alliances arise. The knowledge of economic theory and its applications will increase in importance to investors pursuing international strategies or U.S. companies pursuing foreign opportunities. The ability to interpret these events could have significant financial implications both to the U.S. economy and to those of the other industrial nations.

Fiscal Policy

Fiscal policy can be described as the government's taxing and spending policies. These policies can have a great impact on economic activity. One must realize at the outset that fiscal policy is cumbersome. It has a long implementation lag and is often motivated by political rather than economic considerations since Congress must approve budgets and develop tax laws. Figure 5–2 presents a historical picture of government income and expenditures. When the government spends more than it receives, it runs a **deficit** that must be financed by the Treasury.

A forecaster must pay attention to the size of the deficit and how it is financed to measure its expected impact on the economy. If the deficit is financed by the Treasury selling securities to the Federal Reserve, it is very expansive. The money supply will increase without having any significant short-run effects on interest rates. If the deficit is financed by selling securities to individuals, there is not the same expansion in the money supply, and short-term interest rates will rise unless the Federal Reserve intervenes with open-market trading.

A look at Figure 5–2 shows that **surpluses,** in which revenues exceed expenditures, have been virtually nonexistent from 1961 to 1993, and the annual deficit increased dramatically during the 1980s. Surpluses tend to reduce economic growth as the government slows its demand for goods and services relative to its income. In an analysis of fiscal policy, the important consideration for the investor is the determination of the flow of funds. In a deficit economy, the government usually stimulates GDP by spending on socially productive pro-

FIGURE 5–2 Federal Budget Seasonally Adjusted Annual Rates

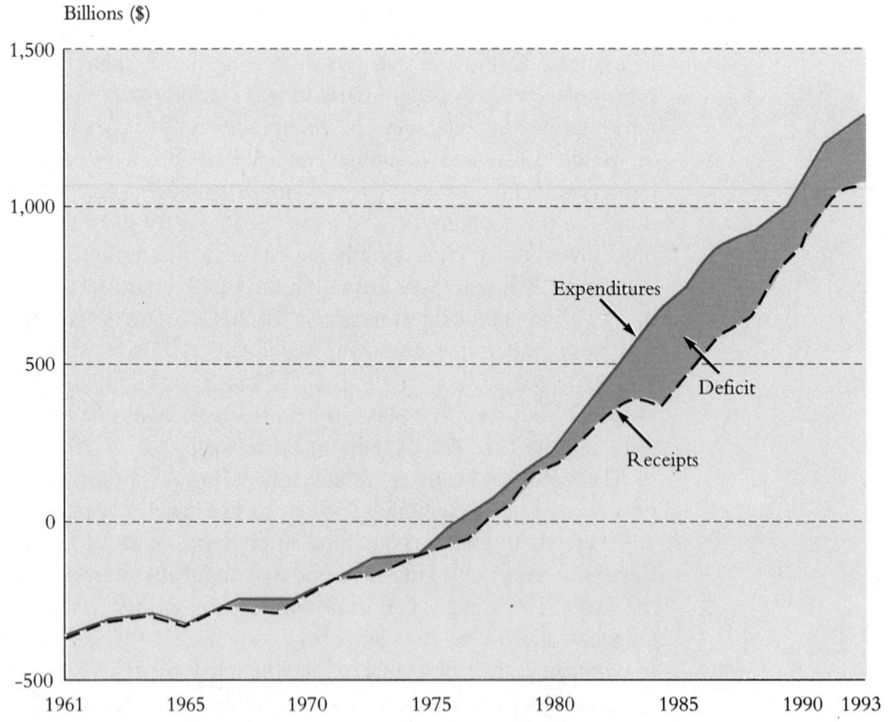

grams or by increasing spending on defense, education, highways, or other government programs. The Reagan administration instituted budget cuts in education and social programs at the same time it reduced tax revenues through tax cuts. This strategy was one that attempted to shift GDP growth from the government sector into the private sector. In the Bush administration, there was inconsistent fiscal policy. Clinton made it clear with his new tax increases that he would use fiscal policy to increase tax revenues to help shrink the fiscal deficit. He instituted a more progressive tax policy by raising rates and reducing deductions for high-income people. His hope was that the wealthy would not slow down their spending and that the increased tax revenues would help decrease the fiscal deficit.

One other area of fiscal policy deals with the government's ability to levy import taxes or tariffs on foreign goods. As a free market economy, we have fought for years with our trading partners to open their countries' markets to U.S. goods. Figure 5–3 depicts the annual trade deficits that started piling up beginning in 1982. This deficit occurred because U.S. consumers purchased more foreign goods than U.S. companies sold to foreigners. As we entered the 1990s, this problem had not gone away. 1992 began with President Bush taking a group of 21 leading executives to Japan to discuss the 1991 $41 billion U.S. trade deficit with Japan. The purpose of this trip was to open Japanese markets to U.S. goods or have the Japanese face the possibility of U.S. trade barriers, such as import tariffs or taxes. These taxes would raise the price of Japanese goods, thus making them less competitive with U.S. goods and eventually reducing this deficit. The conference with Japan produced little in the way of immediate results.

FIGURE 5–3 Imports and Exports in Current Dollars

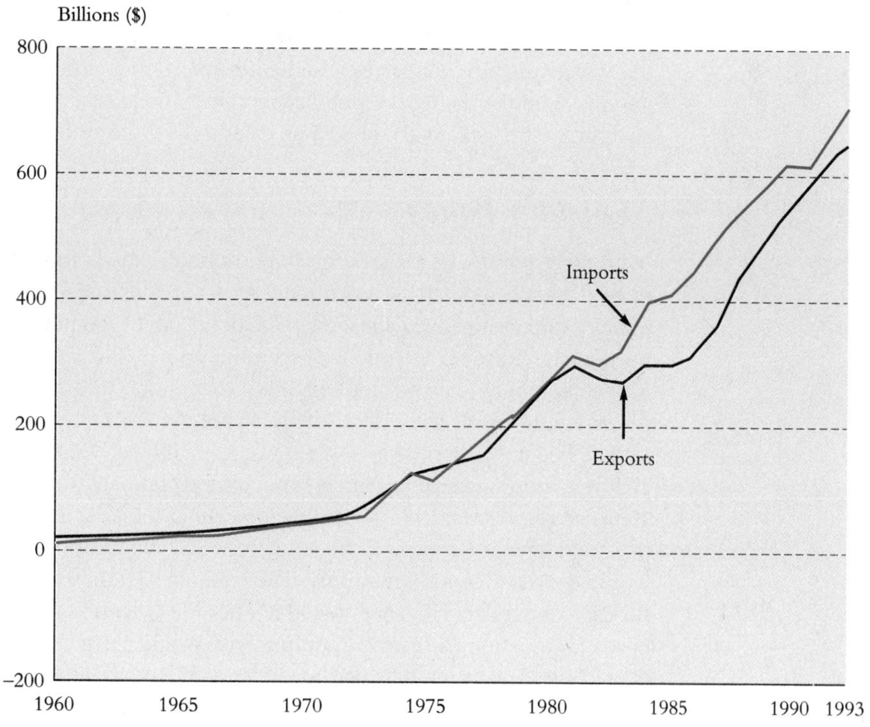

The Clinton administration continued the dialogue with Japan and took what appeared to be a stronger public stance against U.S.–Japanese trading imbalances. In response to years of initiatives, the Japanese have made limited attempts to open their markets to U.S. goods. One example is that when the U.S. automobile manufacturers started selling cars having steering wheels on the right-hand side, demand for U.S. cars increased in Japan. Additionally, Japan has been going through its first serious recession in decades. As the Japanese population looks for ways to get more value for their money, they realize that U.S. goods have become relatively cheap as the yen has increased its value dramatically against the U.S. dollar.

The Japanese example highlights two factors that affect imports and exports. The first is the health of the domestic economy. When a country's economy is healthy with high employment and income, its citizens will spend more in general and will import more goods (especially high-priced luxury goods) from other countries. When a recession is occurring, people spend less, look for less expensive items, and import fewer goods. The second factor is the exchange rate between two currencies. For example, if the U.S. dollar rises against the British pound, U.S. goods become more expensive for British citizens, and British goods become less expensive for U.S. citizens. If the dollar exchange rate stays high or continues to rise, eventually British citizens will change their buying habits and buy fewer U.S. goods, and U.S. citizens will buy more British goods. Also, this effect can be seen in the U.S.–Japanese automobile market. As the Japanese yen rose against the dollar, Americans bought fewer Japanese cars and more U.S. domestic cars. The Japanese consumer did the opposite. Short-term swings in exchange rates will have little effect on imports and exports, but changes in long-term currency relationships will eventually change import-export balances between countries. It usually takes more than a year before the effects of exchange rates on prices show up at the retail level and influence the buying patterns of consumers. As world trade increases, exchange rates and economic trends around the world become more important. While exchange rates and economic activity are influenced by fiscal policy, they are also affected by monetary policy, as discussed in the next section.

Monetary Policy

Monetary policy determines the "appropriate" levels for the money supply and interest rates that accomplish the economic goals of the Employment Act of 1946. Monetary policy is determined by the Federal Open Market Committee (FOMC), which includes the Federal Reserve Board of Governors and the 12 Federal Reserve bank presidents. Monetary policy can be implemented very quickly to reinforce fiscal policy or, when necessary, to offset the effects of fiscal policy.

The Federal Reserve has several ways to influence economic activity. First, it can raise or lower the reserve requirements on commercial bank time deposits or demand deposits. **Reserve requirements** represent the percent of total deposits that a bank must hold as cash in its vault or as deposits in Federal Reserve banks. An increase in reserve requirements would contract the money supply. The banking system would have to hold larger reserves for each dollar deposited and would not be able to lend as much money on the same deposit base. A reduction in reserve requirements would have the opposite effect. The Fed also changes the discount rate periodically to reflect its attitude toward the economy. This **discount rate** is the interest rate the Federal Reserve charges commercial banks on very short-term loans. The Fed does not make a practice of lending funds to a single commercial

bank for more than two or three weeks, and so this charge can influence an individual bank's willingness to borrow money for expansionary loans to industry. The Fed can also influence bank behavior by issuing policy statements, or jawboning.

Beyond these monetary measures, the tool most widely used is **open-market operations** in which the Fed buys and sells U.S. government securities for its own portfolio. When the Fed sells securities in the open market, purchasers write checks to pay for their securities, and demand deposits fall, causing a contraction in the money supply. At the same time, the increase in the supply of Treasury bills sold by the Fed will force prices down and interest rates up to entice buyers to part with their money. The Fed usually accomplishes its adjustments by selling securities to commercial banks, government securities dealers, or individuals.

If the Fed buys securities, the opposite occurs; the money supply increases, and interest rates go down. This tends to encourage economic expansion. As you will see in Chapter 7, the interest rate is extremely important in determining the required rate of return, or discount rate for a stock.

Many economists believe Federal Reserve open-market activity and the resultant changes in the money supply and interest rates are good indicators of the policy position taken by the Fed. If the money supply increases and interest rates fall, the general consensus is that the Fed is encouraging economic expansion. As the money supply decreases or increases slowly and interest rates rise, the expectation is that the Fed is "tightening up" monetary policy to restrict economic growth and inflation. The Federal Reserve cannot totally control the money supply. Money market funds, the resultant monetary expansion created by banks lending money, and changing spending patterns by the population all contribute to the difficulty in controlling the money supply.

In its attempt to stimulate the economy out of the 1990–91 recession, the Federal Reserve Board drove interest rates down to their lowest levels in decades. At the beginning of 1994, the Fed discount rate was 3.0 percent, one-year Treasury bills were in the 4.0 percent range, and the prime rate was 6.0 percent.

After bottoming out in January 1994, rates began to rise as Allen Greenspan, the chairman of the Federal Reserve Board, put pressure on rates to keep inflationary fears in check. By April 1995, the Fed discount rate was up to 5.25 percent, one-year T-bills were 6.5 percent, and the bank prime rate was at 9.00 percent. If the business cycle continues its expansion, rates may keep rising along with inflationary pressures.

Government Policy, Real Growth, and Inflation

In November 1991, the U.S. Commerce Department's Economic Bureau of Analysis shifted from gross national product to gross domestic product as the measure of economic activity for the U.S. economy. The **gross domestic product (GDP)** measurement makes us more compatible with the rest of the world and measures only output from U.S. factories and consumption within the United States. Gross domestic product would not include products made by U.S. companies in foreign countries, but gross national product would. Other U.S. economic measures such as employment, production, and capacity are also measured within the boundaries of the United States, and, with the switch to GDP, we now measure economic output consistently with these other variables.

Figure 5–4 on page 140 depicts 33 years of GDP in current dollars and in inflation-adjusted 1987 dollars. In the bottom of the figure, we see changes in the annual growth rate

FIGURE 5–4 Gross Domestic Product Seasonally Adjusted Annual Rates

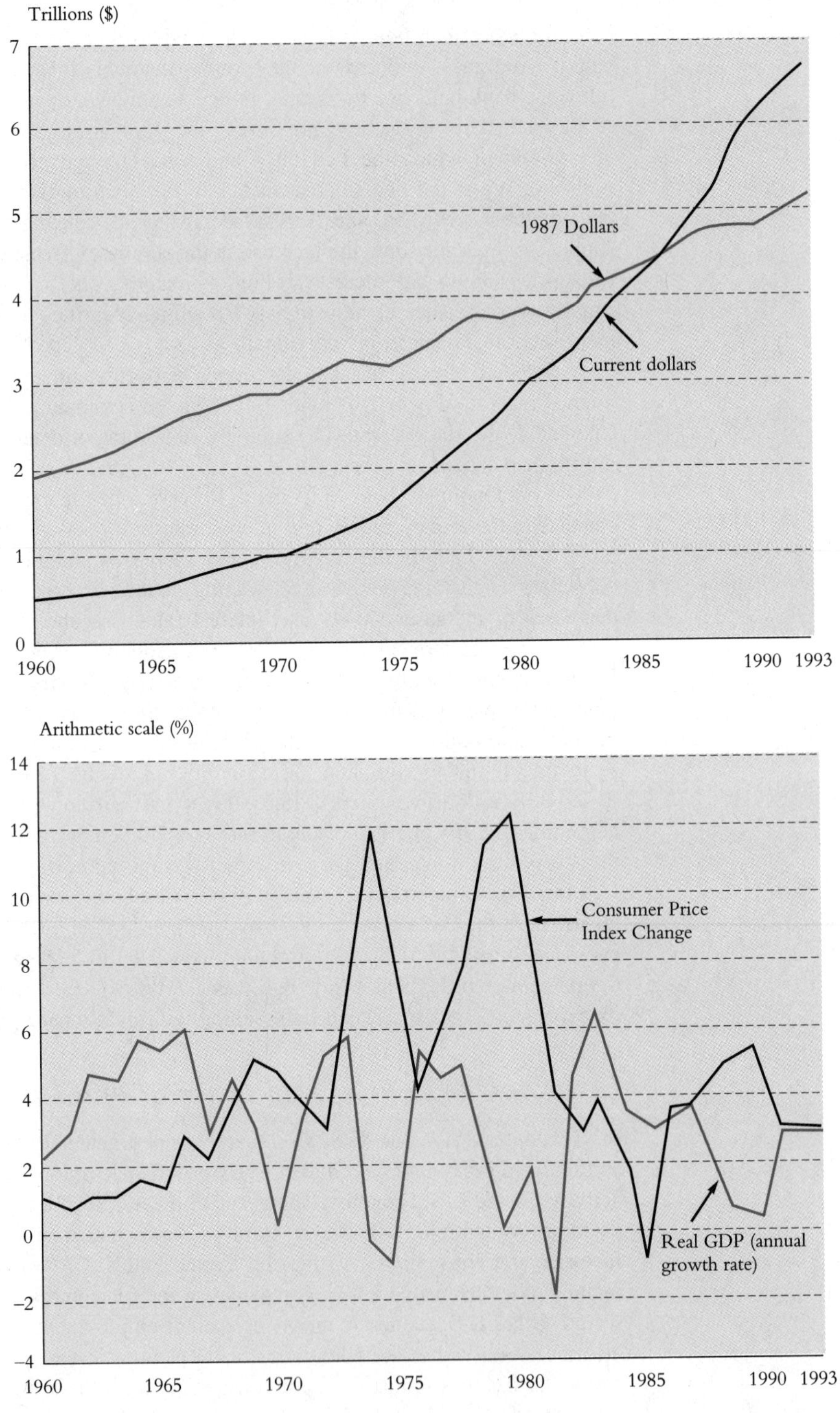

of real GDP. This information in Figure 5–4 needs to be looked at in context with the annual percentage change in the consumer price index (CPI), which is used as a proxy for inflation. Notice the inverse relationship between real GDP and the CPI in the bottom part of Figure 5–4. Since real GDP is the "nominal" GDP adjusted for inflation, the change in real GDP is inversely related to the rate of inflation. As inflation rises, real GDP falls (as indicated in 1970, 1975, 1980–81, and 1989–90), and as inflation subsides, as in 1982–83 and 1985–86, real GDP rises. Since real GDP is the measure of economic output in real physical terms, it does not do any good to stimulate the economy only to have all the gains eroded by inflation.

To understand the major sectors of the economy and the relative influence of each sector, we divide gross domestic product into its four basic areas: personal consumption expenditures, government purchases, gross private investment, and net exports. Figure 5–5 shows the contribution of each one to the total GDP over the past three decades. It becomes clear from Figure 5–5 that personal consumption is growing faster than the other sectors and is the driving force behind economic growth. In the next section we look at the cyclical nature of GDP.

FIGURE 5–5 Breakdown of Gross Domestic Product in Current Dollars

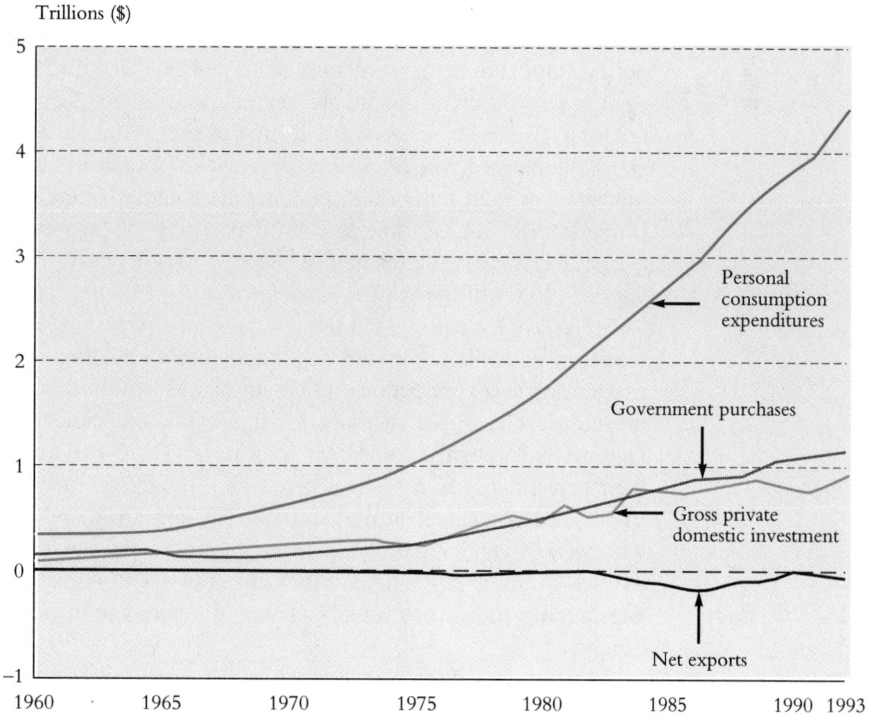

BUSINESS CYCLES AND CYCLICAL INDICATORS

The economy expands and contracts through a **business cycle** process. By measuring GDP and other economic data, we can develop a statistical picture of the economic growth pattern. The National Bureau of Economic Research (NBER) is the final authority in documenting cyclical turning points. The NBER defines recessions as two or more quarters of negative real GDP growth and documents the beginning and end of a recession. Table 5–1 presents a historical picture of business cycle expansions and contractions in the United States. While the modern-day data may be more relevant, it is interesting to see that economic cycles have existed and been defined for more than 130 years.

Table 5–1 measures each contraction and expansion and then presents summary data at the bottom of the table for all business cycles and for cycles in peacetime only. A **trough** represents the end of a recession and the beginning of an expansion, and a **peak** represents the end of an expansion and the beginning of a recession. In general, we see on the last line of Table 5–1 that during peacetime cycles between 1945 and 1991, contractions (recessions) have lasted an average of 11 months, while expansions have averaged 42 months. Thus, one *complete* business cycle during modern *peacetimes* lasts almost four and one-half years whether measured from trough to trough or peak to peak. This has led some to say that the cycle is politically induced by the four-year presidential elections. If business cycles could be so easily influenced by presidential politics, we might assume Presidents Carter and Bush could have exercised enough control over the economy to be elected for a second term. There are many other theories about what causes the economy to cycle.

Predicting business cycles is easier said than done. It is important to realize that each business cycle is unique; no two cycles are alike. Some cycles are related to monetary policy; some are demand related; some are inventory induced. The length and depth of each is also different—some are shallow, and others deep; some are short, while others are long. The last business cycle from November 1982 to July 1990 lasted 92 months and can be compared with those business cycles shown in Table 5–1. Additionally, not all industries or segments of the economy are equally affected by business cycles. However, if investors can make some forecast concerning the beginning and ending of the business cycle, they will be better able to choose which types of investments to hold over the various phases of the cycle.

So far, we have discussed the government's impact on the economy. Fiscal policy and monetary policy both provide important clues to the direction and magnitude of economic expansions and contractions. Other measures are used to evaluate the direction of the business cycle. These measures, called economic indicators, are divided into leading, lagging, and roughly coincident indicators. The NBER classifies indicators relative to their performance at economic peaks and troughs. **Leading indicators** change direction in advance of general business conditions and are of prime importance to the investor who wants to anticipate rising corporate profits and possible price increases in the stock market. Roughly **coincident indicators** move approximately with the general economy, and **lagging indicators** usually change directions after business conditions have turned around.

The National Bureau of Economic Research publishes its indicators in the monthly publication *Survey of Current Business.* This publication includes moving averages, turning dates for recessions and expansions, cyclical indicators, composite indexes and

TABLE 5–1 Business Cycle Expansions and Contractions in the United States

Business Cycle Reference Dates		Duration in Months		Cycle	
Trough	Peak	Contraction (Trough from previous peak)	Expansion (Trough to peak)	Trough from Previous Trough	Peak from Previous Peak
December 1854	June 1857	—	30	—	—
December 1858	October 1860	18	22	48	40
June 1861	April 1865	8	<u>46</u>	30	<u>54</u>
December 1867	June 1989	<u>32</u>	18	<u>78</u>	50
December 1870	October 1873	18	34	36	52
March 1879	March 1882	65	36	99	101
May 1885	March 1887	38	22	74	60
April 1888	June 1890	13	27	35	40
May 1891	January 1893	10	20	37	30
June 1894	December 1895	17	18	37	35
June 1897	June 1899	18	24	36	42
December 1900	September 1902	18	21	42	39
August 1904	May 1907	23	33	44	56
June 1908	January 1910	13	19	46	32
January 1912	January 1913	24	12	43	36
December 1914	August 1918	23	<u>44</u>	35	<u>67</u>
March 1919	January 1920	<u>7</u>	10	<u>51</u>	17
July 1921	May 1923	18	22	28	40
July 1924	October 1926	14	27	36	41
November 1927	August 1929	13	21	40	34
March 1933	May 1937	43	50	64	93
June 1938	February 1945	13	<u>80</u>	63	<u>93</u>
October 1945	November 1948	<u>8</u>	37	<u>88</u>	45
October 1949	July 1953	11	<u>45</u>	48	<u>56</u>
May 1954	August 1957	<u>10</u>	39	<u>55</u>	49
April 1958	April 1960	8	24	47	32
February 1961	December 1969	10	<u>106</u>	34	<u>116</u>
November 1970	November 1973	<u>11</u>	36	<u>117</u>	47
March 1975	January 1980	16	58	52	74
July 1980	July 1981	6	12	64	18
November 1982	July 1990	16	92	28	108
March 1991		8		100	
Average, all cycles:					
1854–1982 (30 cycles)		18	33	51	51*
1854–1919 (16 cycles)		22	27	48	49†
1919–1945 (6 cycles)		18	35	53	53
1945–1991 (9 cycles)		11	50	61	57
Average, peacetime cycles:					
1854–1982 (25 cycles)		19	27	46	46‡
1854–1919 (14 cycles)		22	24	46	47§
1919–1945 (5 cycles)		20	26	46	45
1945–1991 (7 cycles)		11	42	54	53

Note: Underscored figures are the wartime expansions (Civil War, World Wars I and II, Korean War, and Vietnam War), the postwar contractions, and the full cycles that include the wartime expansions.
*29 cycles. †15 cycles. ‡24 cycles. §13 cycles.
Source: *Business Conditions Digest* (U.S. Department of Commerce Bureau of Economic Analysis, July 1988, Nov. 1994).

TABLE 5–2 Cross Classification of Cyclical Indicators by Economic Process and Cyclical Timing

A. Timing at business cycle peaks

Cyclical Timing \ Economic Process	I. Employment and Unemployment (15 series)	II. Production and Income (10 series)	III. Consumption, Trade Orders, and Deliveries (13 series)
Leading (L) Indicators (61 series)	Marginal employment adjustments (3 series) Job vacancies (2 series) Comprehensive employment (1 series) Comprehensive unemployment (3 series)	Capacity utilization (2 series)	Orders and deliveries (6 series) Consumption and trade (2 series)
Roughly Coincident (C) Indicators (24 series)	Comprehensive employment (1 series)	Comprehensive output and income (4 series) Industrial production (4 series)	Consumption and trade (4 series)
Lagging (Lg) Indicators (19 series)	Comprehensive unemployment (2 series)		
Timing Unclassified (U) (8 series)	Comprehensive employment (3 series)		Comsumption and trade (1 series)

B. Timing at business cycle troughs

Cyclical Timing \ Economic Process	I. Employment and Unemployment	II. Production and Income	III. Consumption, Trade Orders, and Deliveries
Leading (L) Indicators (47 series)	Marginal employment adjustments (1 series)	Industrial production (1 series)	Orders and deliveries (5 series) Consumption and trade (4 series)
Roughly Coincident (C) Indicators (23 series)	Marginal employment adjustments (2 series) Comprehensive employment (4 series)	Comprehensive output and income (4 series) Industrial production (3 series) Capacity utilitization (2 series)	Consumption and trade (3 series)
Lagging (Lg) Indicators (41 series)	Job vacancies (2 series) Comprehensive employment (1 series) Comprehensive unemployment (5 series)		Orders and deliveries (1 series)
Timing Unclassified (U) (1 series)			

Source: *Business Conditions Digest* (U.S. Department of Commerce Bureau of Economic Analysis, July 1988).

IV. Fixed Capital Investment (19 series)	V. Inventories and Inventory Investment (9 series)	VI. Price, Costs, and Profits (18 series)	VII. Money and Credit (28 series)
Formation of business enterprises (2 series) Business investment commitments (5 series) Residential construction (3 series)	Inventory investment (4 series) Inventories on hand and on order (1 series)	Stock prices (1 series) Sensitive commodity prices (2 series) Profits and profit margins (7 series) Cash flows (2 series)	Money (5 series) Credit flows (5 series) Credit difficulties (2 series) Bank reserves (2 series) Interest rates (1 series)
Business investment commitments (1 series) Business investment expenditures (6 series)			Velocity of money (2 series) Interest rate (2 series)
Business investment expenditures (1 series)	Inventories on hand and on order (4 series)	Unit labor costs and labor share (4 series)	Interest rate (4 series) Outstanding debt (4 series)
Business investment commitments (1 series)		Sensitive commodity prices (1 series) Profits and profit margins (1 series)	Interest rates (1 series)
Formation of business enterprises (2 series) Business investment commitments (4 series) Residential construction (3 series)	Inventory investment (4 series)	Stock prices (1 series) Sensitive commodity prices (3 series) Profits and profit margins (6 series) Cash flows (2 series)	Money (4 series) Credit flows (5 series) Credit difficulties (2 series)
Business investment commitments (1 series)		Profits and profit margins (2 series)	Money (1 series) Velocity of money (1 series)
Business investment commitments (2 series) Business investment expenditures (7 series)	Inventories on hand and on order (5 series)	Unit labor costs and labor share (4 series)	Velocity of money (1 series) Bank reserves (1 series) Interest rates (8 series) Outstanding debt (4 series)
			Bank reserves (1 series)

their components, diffusion indexes,[1] and information on rates of change. Many of the series are seasonally adjusted and are maintained on a monthly or quarterly basis.

Table 5–2 on pages 144–45 presents a summary of cyclical indicators by economic process and cyclical timing with Part A of the table presenting timing at business cycle peaks and Part B showing timing at business cycle troughs. Thus, in the first part, we see the leading, coincident, and lagging indicators for business cycle peaks, and in the second part, similar indicators for the bottoming out of business cycles (troughs). While we would not expect you to study or learn all the leading or lagging indicators for a cyclical peak or trough, it is important that you know they are heavily relied on by economists and financial analysts. Let's look more specifically at how they are used.

Leading Indicators

Of the 108 leading indicators shown in Parts A and B of Table 5–2, 61 lead at peaks and 47 lead at troughs. Of these, 11 basic indicators have been reasonably consistent in their relationship to the business cycle and are considered most important. These 11 leading indicators have been standardized and used to compute a composite index that is widely followed. It is a much smoother curve than each individual component since erratic changes in one indicator are offset by movements in other indicators. The same can be said for a similar index of four coincident indicators and six lagging indicators.

Figure 5–6 shows the performance of the composite index of leading, lagging, and coincident indicators over several past business cycles. The shaded areas are recessions as defined by the NBER. The minus figures indicate how many months the index preceded the economy. (Lagging indicators have plus signs.)

While the composite index of leading indicators (top of Figure 5–6) has been a better predictor than any single indicator, it has varied widely over time. Table 5–3 on page 148 presents the components for the 11 leading, 4 roughly coincident, and 6 lagging indicators.

Studies have found that the 11 leading indicators do not exhibit the same notice at peaks as they do at troughs. The notice before peaks is quite long, but the warning before troughs is very short, which means it is very easy to miss a turnaround to the upside, but on the downside, you can be more patient waiting for confirmation from other indicators. Indicators occasionally give false signals. Sometimes the indicators give no clear signal, and with the large variability of leads and lags versus the average lead time, an investor is lucky to get close to predicting economic activity within three or four months of peaks and troughs. Despite economic indicators and forecasting methods, investors cannot escape uncertainty in an attempt to manage their portfolios.

One very important fact is that the stock market is the most reliable and accurate of the 11 leading indicators. This presents a very real problem for us because our initial objective is to forecast (as well as we are able) changes in common stock prices. To do this, we are constrained by the fact that the stock market is anticipatory and, in fact, has worked on a lead time of nine months at peaks and five months at troughs.

---

[1] A diffusion index shows the pervasiveness of a given movement in a series. If 100 units are reported in a series, the diffusion index will indicate what percentage followed a given pattern.

FIGURE 5–6 Composite Indexes (Leading, lagging, and coincident indexes)

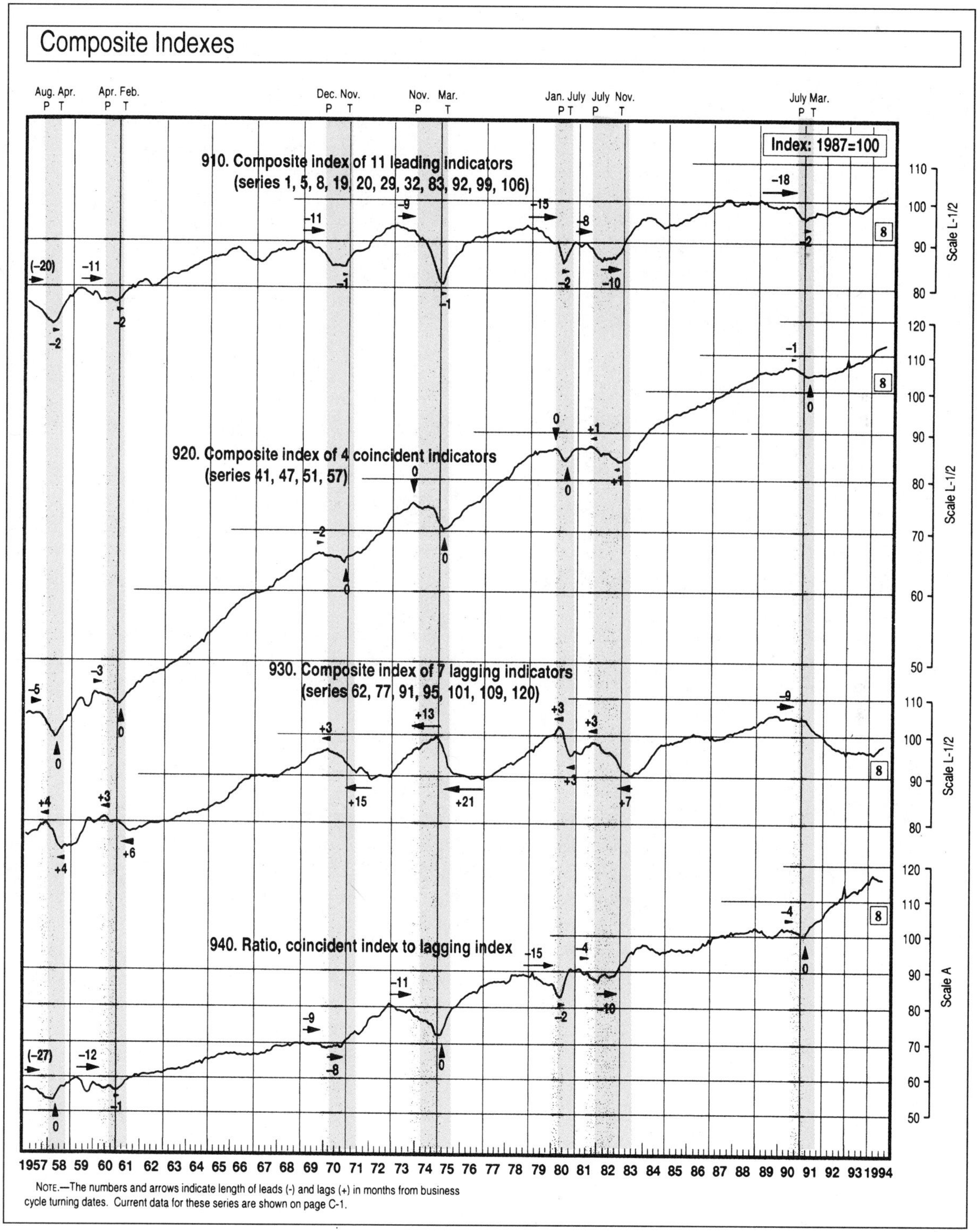

Source: *Survey of Current Business* (U.S. Department of Commerce Bureau of Economic Analysis, September 1994), p. C7.

TABLE 5–3 Components of the Leading, Coincident, and Lagging Indicators (Series title and unit of measure)

Leading indicators

1. Average weekly hours of production or nonsupervisory workers, manufacturing (hours).
5. Average weekly initial claims for unemployment insurance, state programs (thous.).
8. Mfrs. new orders in 1982 dollars, consumer goods and materials industries (bil. dol.).
32. Vendor performance, percent of companies receiving slower deliveries (percent).
20. Contracts and orders for plant and equipment in 1982 dollars (bil. dol.).
29. New private housing units authorized by local building permits (index: 1967 = 100).
36. Change in inventories on hand and on order in 1982 dollars, smoothed (ann. rate, bil. dol.).
99. Change in sensitive materials prices, smoothed (percent).
19. Stock prices, 500 common stocks (index: 1941–43 = 10).
106. Money supply M2 in 1982 dollars (bil. dol.).
111. Change in business and consumer credit outstanding (ann. rate, percent).

Roughly coincident indicators

41. Employees on nonagricultural payrolls (thous.).
51. Personal income less transfer payments in 1982 dollars (ann. rate, bil. dol.).
47. Industrial production (index: 1977 = 100).
57. Manufacturing and trade sales in 1982 dollars (mil. dol.).

Lagging indicators

91. Average duration of unemployment (weeks).
77. Ratio, manufacturing and trade inventories to sales in 1982 dollars (ratio).
62. Labor cost per unit of output, manufacturing-actual data as a percent of trend (percent).
109. Average prime rate charged by banks (percent).
101. Commercial and industrial loans outstanding in 1982 dollars (mil. dol.).
95. Ratio, consumer installment credit outstanding to personal income (percent).

Note: The net contribution of an individual component is that component's share in the composite movement of the group. It is computed by dividing the standardized and weighted change for the component by the sum of the weights for the available components and dividing that result by the index standardization factor. See the February 1983 *Business Conditions Digest* (p. 108) or the 1984 *Handbook of Cyclical Indicators* (pp. 67–88) for the weights and standardization factors.
Source: *Business Conditions Digest* (U.S. Department of Commerce Bureau of Economic Analysis, July 1988).

MONEY SUPPLY AND STOCK PRICES

One variable that has been historically popular as an indicator of the stock market is the money supply. The money supply is supposed to influence stock prices in several ways. Studies of economic growth and the money supply by Milton Friedman and Anna Schwartz found a long-term relationship between these two variables.[2]

Why does money matter? If you are a **monetarist,** money explains much of economic behavior. The quantity theory of money holds that as the supply of money increases relative to the demand for money, people will make adjustments in their portfolios of assets. If they have too much money, they will first buy bonds (a modification of the theory would now include Treasury bills or other short-term monetary assets), stocks, and finally, real assets. This is the direct effect of money on stock prices sometimes referred to as the *liquidity effect.*

[2] Milton J. Friedman and Anna J. Schwartz, "Money and Business Cycles," *Review of Economics and Statistics,* Supplement, February 1963.

FIGURE 5–7 Relationship of Stock Prices to Money Supply

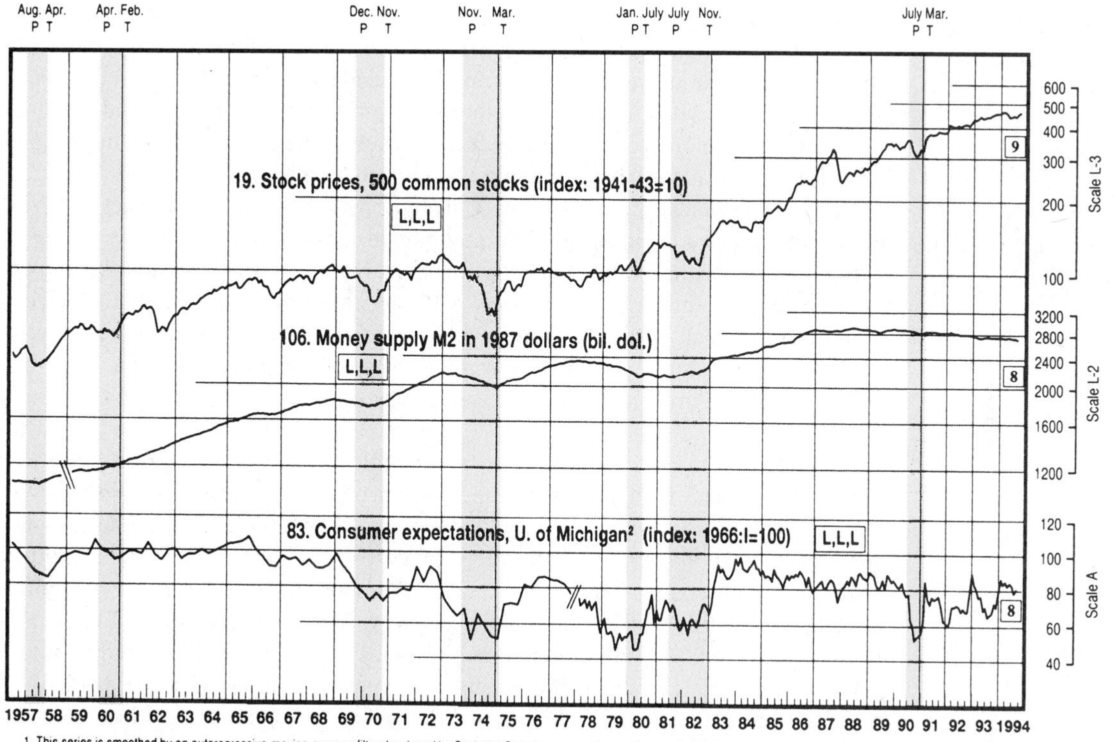

1. This series is smoothed by an autoregressive-moving-average filter developed by Statistics Canada.
2. This is a copyrighted series used by permission; it may not be reproduced without written permission from the University of Michigan, Survey Research Center.

NOTE.—Current data for these series are shown on page C-1.

Source: *Survey of Current Business* (U.S. Department of Commerce Bureau of Economic Analysis, September 1994), p. C10.

The indirect effect of money on stock prices would flow through the GDP's impact on corporate profits. As money influences economic activity, it will eventually influence corporate earnings and dividends and thus returns to the investors. Many studies have found that a significant relationship exists between the money supply variable and stock prices. However, even here, there have been some conflicting patterns in the last decade as shown in Figure 5–7. Note that in the first half of 1982, the money supply (M2) was increasing slightly while stock prices were declining sharply. This goes against the historical norm of comparable movements that can be seen in the same figure. Also note that since 1987, the money supply (M2) has been flat and has not coincided with increasing stock prices.

There are many important predictors of economic patterns and stock market movements, but an investor must be flexible and consider as many variables as possible rather than simply relying on one or two factors. You may wish to acquaint yourself with many of the leading, coincident, and lagging indicators presented previously in Table 5–3 as you become active in the stock market.

BUSINESS CYCLES AND INDUSTRY RELATIONSHIPS

Each industry may be affected by the business cycle differently. Industries where the underlying demand for the product is consumer oriented will quite likely be sensitive to short-term swings in the business cycle. These industries would include durable goods such as washers and dryers, refrigerators, electric and gas ranges, and automobiles. Changes in the automobile industry will also be felt in the tire and rubber industry as well as by auto glass and other automobile component suppliers.

Table 5–4, which appeared in the *Chicago Tribune,* shows the impact of this ripple effect through many industries. The automobile industry purchases 77 percent of the output from the natural rubber industry (tires and bumpers), 67 percent of the output from the lead industry (batteries), and so on to 10 percent of the copper output (electrical and tubing). Additionally, the automobile industry accounts for more than 4 percent of the GDP. The U.S. automobile industry employs 800,000 people, and one in seven workers (12.5 million) in America has a job in an industry somewhat dependent on the automobile industry.

The top of Figure 5–8 shows the automobile industry's sales from 1960 to 1993 relative to the real GDP's growth rate (bottom of figure). Notice the similarity of the pattern. The peaks in economic activity (1965, 1973, 1976–78, 1985) all correspond with peaks in the auto industry. The recessions of 1970, 1974–75, 1981–82, and 1990–91 all correspond with troughs in automobile sales. This close relationship is why it is often said the United States lives in an automobile economy. Also note in the top of Figure 5–8 that in the early 1990s domestic automobile sales increased while foreign auto sales decreased. As the U.S. dollar fell against the Japanese yen and German mark, U.S. cars became better values in U.S. dollars (the dollar had less purchasing power overseas).

Not all industries are so closely related to the business cycle. Necessity-oriented industries, such as food and pharmaceuticals, are consistent performers since people have to eat, and illness is not dependent on the economy. Industries that have products with

TABLE 5–4 Automobile Industry and Its Impact on Other Industries

The automotive industry purchases these percentages of the output of other U.S. industries.*		**What's in a car** A typical American car includes:†
Natural rubber	77%	1,774 pounds of steel
Lead	67	460 pounds of iron
Malleable iron	63	222 pounds of plastic
Synthetic rubber	50	183 pounds of fluids
Platinum	39	146 pounds of aluminum
Zinc	23	135 pounds of rubber
Aluminum	18	86 pounds of glass
Steel	12	25 pounds of copper
Copper	10	24 pounds of lead
		18 pounds of zinc

*Motor Vehicle Manufacturers Association.
†World Book Encyclopedia.

FIGURE 5–8 New Auto Sales and Real GNP, 1961–1993

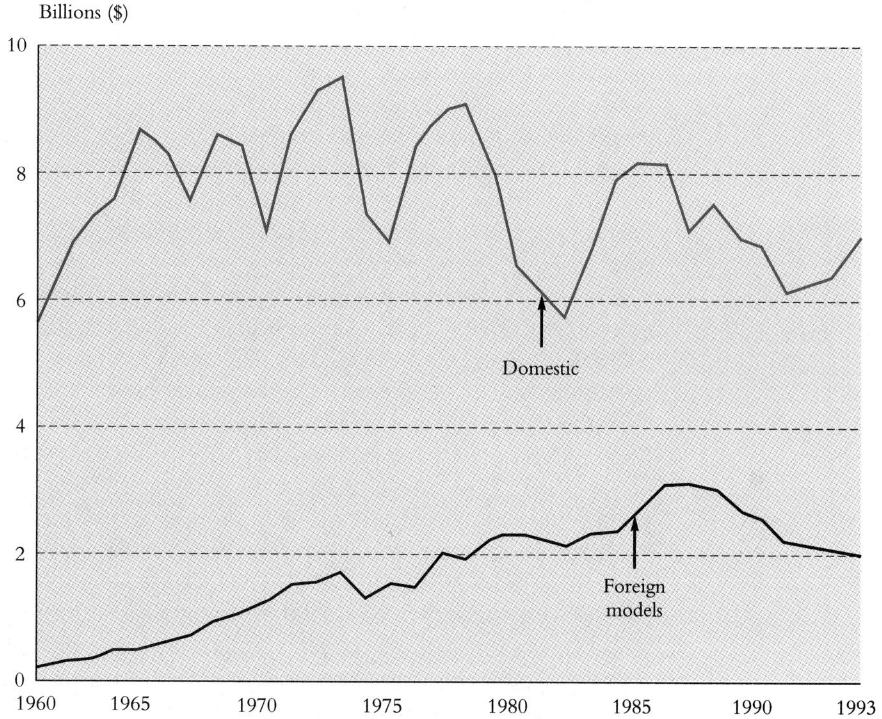

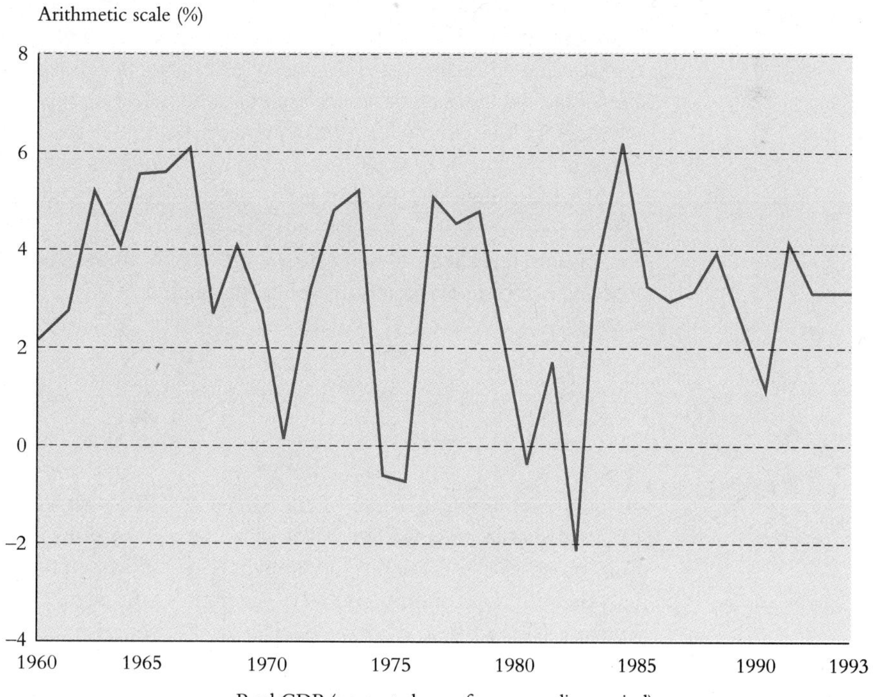

low price elasticities[3] that are habitual in nature, such as cigarettes and alcohol, do not seem to be much affected by business cycles either. In fact, some industries do better during a recession. The movie industry traditionally prospers during a recession as more people substitute low-cost entertainment for more expensive forms. This is one pattern that may not remain the same, however. As cable television and VCRs continue to come into their own, people may find it even more convenient to stay at home than to go to the movies when money is tight. This is one thing that makes investments exciting, the ever-changing environment.

Housing is another example of an industry that historically has done well in recessionary environments. As the economy comes to a standstill, interest rates tend to come down, and prospective home purchasers are once again able to afford mortgage rates on a home. After the period of extremely high mortgage rates in the early 1980s, a precipitous drop in mortgage rates helped to stimulate growth in the housing market. The Federal Reserve followed such a policy again in the early 1990s by pushing interest rates down to their lowest level in decades. Sales of existing housing units picked up, and people refinanced their mortgages at lower rates, giving them more disposable income. As mortgage costs came down, housing became more affordable to more people. For example, if interest rates declined 3 percentage points on a $120,000 loan, the same priced house would now cost $300 per month less in interest expense.

Sensitivity to the business cycle may also be evident in industries that produce *capital* goods for other business firms (rather than consumer goods). Examples would be manufacturers of business plant and equipment, machine tools, or pollution-control equipment. A lag often exists between the recovery from a recession and the increased purchase of capital goods, so recoveries within these industries may be delayed.

Service industries have also become extremely important in our economy. While service-oriented business firms (doctors, lawyers, accountants) are generally less susceptible to the business cycle, there are exceptions. Examples of cyclically oriented service providers include architects, civil engineers, and auto repair shops.

We do not mean to imply that cyclical industries are bad investments or that they should be avoided. We merely point out the cyclical influence of the economy. Often cyclical industries are excellent buys in the stock market because the market does not look far enough ahead to see a recovery and its impact on cyclical profits. We develop these ideas more completely in the next chapter.

SUMMARY

The primary purpose of this chapter is to provide you with a process of valuation and an appreciation of some of the variables that should be considered. The valuation process is based on fundamental analysis of the economy, industry, and company. This method assumes decisions are made based on economic concepts of value over the long-term trend of the stock market. The purpose of the process is to eliminate losers from consideration in your portfolio and to thereby provide you with a good opportunity to build a sound portfolio.

[3] Price elasticity represents the sensitivity of quantity purchased to price.

The first step in the valuation process is an analysis of the economy and long-term economic trends. The difficulties of attaining government policy goals are discussed as a trade-off between conflicting objectives (high growth versus low inflation). Fiscal and monetary policy are discussed as the primary tools used to stimulate economic activity. Interest rates are influenced by inflation, with the end result being a higher required rate of return for the investor.

Business cycles are short-term swings in economic activity; they affect stock prices because they change investor expectations of risk and return. To forecast economic activity, cyclical indicators are presented as leading, lagging, and coincident indexes. The one index potentially most valuable to an investor is the composite index of 11 leading indicators. Unfortunately, stock prices are one of the most accurate leading indicators, and we must try to find another indicator that leads stock prices. The most popular and economically rational leading indicator is the money supply. The money supply influences economic activity by increasing or decreasing interest rates and corporate profits, which, in turn, eventually affect corporate dividends. Money also has a direct effect on stock prices by changing liquidity. An investor cannot escape risk, however, and the money supply is no sure way to forecast stock prices. The leads are too similar, and many factors have clouded the effect of changes in the money supply on the economy and stock prices. The best solution is to use a combination of economic variables that will tend to provide insights into future economic developments and the stock market.

The sensitivity of various types of industries to the business cycle is also examined. Firms in consumer durable goods (automobiles), as well as those in heavy capital goods manufacturing (plant and equipment) are perhaps most vulnerable to the business cycle.

KEY WORDS AND CONCEPTS

fiscal policy, 136
deficit, 136
surpluses, 136
monetary policy, 138
reserve requirements, 138
discount rate, 138
open-market operations, 139
gross domestic product (GDP), 139
business cycle, 141
trough, 142
peak, 142
leading indicators, 142
coincident indicators, 142
lagging indicators, 142
monetarist, 148

DISCUSSION QUESTIONS

1. As depicted in Figure 5–1, what are the three elements in the valuation process?
2. What are the four goals under the Employment Act of 1946?
3. What is fiscal policy? Does it tend to have a long or short implementation period?
4. What is monetary policy?
5. How, specifically, can the Fed influence economic activity? Name three ways.
6. In regard to Federal Reserve open-market activity, if the Fed buys securities, what is the likely impact on the money supply? Is this likely to encourage expansion or contraction of economic activity?

7. What is the historical relationship between real GDP and inflation? What lesson might be learned from observing this relationship?
8. In terms of the business cycle, distinguish between a trough and a peak.
9. What are the four basic areas that make up gross domestic product? Over the past three decades, what area has been growing most rapidly?
10. What is the advantage of using a composite of indicators (such as the 11 leading indicators) over simply using an individual indicator?
11. Do leading indicators tend to give longer warnings before peaks or before troughs? What is the implication for the investor?
12. Explain the quantity theory of money. What is the liquidity effect?
13. Comment on whether each of the following three industries is sensitive to the business cycle. If it is sensitive, does it do better in a boom period or a recession?
    a. Automobiles.
    b. Pharmaceuticals.
    c. Housing.
14. Observe the performance of the 11 leading indicators for the next month. Compare this with changes in stock prices and interest rates.

THE WALL STREET JOURNAL PROJECTS

On a daily basis, *The Wall Street Journal* publishes a graph at the top of the middle column on page 1 that shows the most significant business indicators. Each day a different picture is shown (on a monthly cycle), depicting information such as factory shipments, leading indicators, consumer price index, and housing starts. Cut these out each day, and tape them onto several pages until the cycle restarts (you should end up with about 20 graphs).

1. Discuss the significance of the changes and the implications for economic activity.
2. As this new information becomes public, do you notice any market impact on stock prices? To help you see this relationship, please write down the S&P 500 Index found on page C1 under each graph on the day it appeared. Remember that the data appear the day after the information was reported to the public.
3. How do these graphs and tables help an analyst interpret what is going on in the business cycle? What factor(s) do you see affecting the business cycle?

U.S. EQUITIES ONFLOPPY EXERCISES

Please use your U.S. Equities OnFloppy software and manual to complete the following exercises.

1. Question 13 asked about the sensitivity of three industries (automobiles, pharmaceuticals, and housing) to the business cycle. Determine the average total revenue of GM, Ford, and Chrysler by year for each of the five years for which information is available in the U.S. Securities OnFloppy database, and compare the pattern in these averages to the pattern in real GDP.

2. Use SIC = 283* to identify the companies that represent the pharmaceutical industry. Determine the top 10 by total revenue for the last fiscal year (REV1), and perform the same type of analysis described in exercise 1.
3. Use SIC = 15** to identify the companies that represent the housing industry. Perform the same type of analysis as described in exercise 1.

SELECTED REFERENCES

Business-Cycle Analysis

Darin, Robert, and Robert L. Hetzel. "A Shift Adjusted M2 Indicator for Monetary Policy." *Economic Quarterly,* Federal Reserve Bank of Richmond, Summer 1994, pp. 25–47.

Friedman, Milton J., and Anna J. Schwartz. "Money and Business Cycles." *Review of Economics and Statistics,* Supplement, February 1963.

Hardouvelis, G. A. "Reserve's Announcements and Interest Rates: Does Monetary Policy Matter?" *Journal of Finance,* June 1987, pp. 407–22.

Herbst, Anthony F., and Craig W. Slinkman. "Political-Economic Cycles in the U.S. Stock Market." *Financial Analysts Journal,* March–April 1984, pp. 38–44.

Koretz, Gene. "Inflation Detectives Are Rounding Up the Wrong Suspects." *Business Week,* August 8, 1994, p. 16.

Levin, Jay H. "On the International Transmission of Monetary Policy under Floating Exchange Rates." *Quarterly Review of Economics and Business,* Spring 1984, pp. 78–86.

Rogalski, Richard J., and Joseph D. Vinso. "Stock Returns, Money Supply and the Direction of Causality." *Journal of Finance,* September 1977, pp. 1017–30.

Spindt, P. A., and V. Tarham. "The Federal Reserve's New Operating Procedures: A Postmortem." *Journal of Monetary Economics,* January 1987, pp. 107–23.

Ulan, Michael. "Is the Current Business Cycle Different? Does How We Measure Matter?" *Business Economist,* April 1994, pp. 41–47.

Forecasting

Gray, William. "The Stock Market and the Economy in 1988." *The Journal of Portfolio Management,* September 1984, pp. 73–80.

Heathcotte, Bryan, and Vincent P. Apilado. "The Predictive Content of Some Leading Economic Indicators for Future Stock Prices." *Journal of Financial and Quantitative Analysis,* March 1974, pp. 247–58.

Reichenstein, William. "Touters Trophies: Ranking Economists' Forecasts." *Financial Analysts Journal,* July–August 1991, pp. 20–21.

Renshaw, Edward. "Modeling the Stock Market for Forecasting Purposes." *The Journal of Portfolio Management,* Fall 1993, pp. 76–81.

6

Industry Analysis

We saw in Chapter 5 that *economic analysis* is the first step in the valuation process. Figure 5–1 is funnel shaped and leads from the economy to industry analysis and then to company analysis. This method of choosing common stocks is called the **top-down approach** because it goes from the macroeconomic viewpoint to the individual company. The opposite approach is the **bottom-up approach,** which starts with picking individual companies and then looks at the industry and economy to see if there is any reason an investment in the company should not be made. People who follow the bottom-up approach are sometimes referred to as **stock pickers,** as opposed to industry analysts.

Industry analysis is the second step in the top-down approach used in this text, and it focuses on industry life cycles and industry structure. Industries can be affected by government regulation, foreign and domestic competition, and the economic business cycle. As we shall also see, industry competition is affected by product quality, the cost structures within the industry, and the competitive strategies among companies in the industry. A starting point for industry analysis is determining where an industry's current position is in its industry life cycle.

INDUSTRY LIFE CYCLES

Industry life cycles are created because of economic growth, competition, availability of resources, and the resultant market saturation by the particular goods and services offered. Life-cycle growth influences many variables considered in the valuation process. The particular phase in the life cycle of an industry or company determines the growth of earnings, dividends, capital expenditures, and market demand for products.

An analysis of industry financial data helps place an industry on the life-cycle curve and, in turn, guides the analyst toward decisions on industry growth, the duration of growth, profitability, and potential rates of return. The analyst can determine whether all companies in the industry are in the same stage of the life cycle and translate company differences into various assumptions that will affect their individual valuations.

Figure 6–1 on page 158 shows a five-stage industry life cycle (although it could very well be a company life cycle) and the corresponding dividend policy most likely to be found at each stage. The vertical scale on this graph is logarithmic, which means that a straight line on this scale represents a constant growth rate. The steeper the line, the faster the growth rate, and the flatter the line, the smaller the growth rate. The slope of the line in the life-cycle curve and how it changes over time is very important in the analysis of growth and its duration. We will examine each stage separately and learn why the dividend policy is important in placing an industry or company in a particular stage.

Development—Stage I

The development stage includes companies that are getting started in business with a new idea, product, or production technique that makes them unique. Firms in this stage are usually privately owned and are financed with the owner's money as well as with capital from friends, family, and a bank. If the company has some success, there is a probability that outside money from a venture capital group may increase the financing available to the company. In this case, the company is also the industry or a subset of an existing industry. For example, when Steve Jobs started Apple Computer in the early 1970s, it was

FIGURE 6–1 Industry Life Cycle

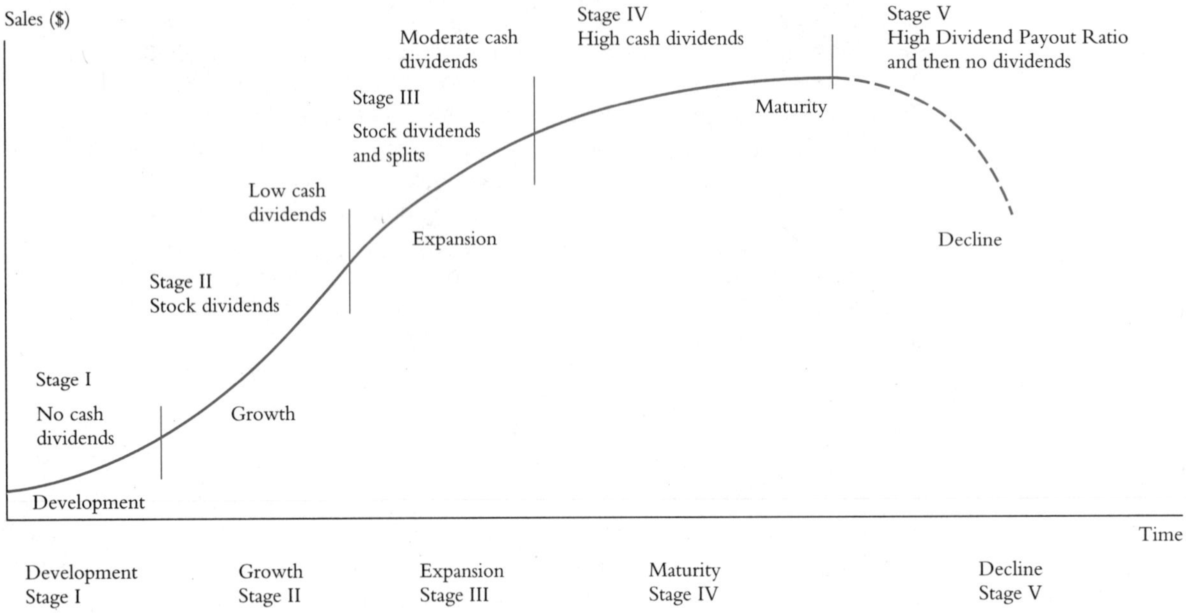

a development startup company that created an entirely new industry. In the beginning, Apple was certainly not taken seriously by IBM, but by the 1990s the personal computer (PC) industry and its related software industry represented a sizable multibillion dollar industry.

The pharmaceutical industry has been around for a long time, but in the 1970s and 1980s many small biotechnology firms were founded that created drugs using different production and research techniques. Hundreds of biotech firms using genetic techniques were created by entrepreneurs in medical research. This focus on medical research created a subset of the pharmaceutical industry, and, eventually, large companies such as Merck and Eli Lilly created joint partnerships with these companies. Some biotech firms such as Genentech eventually produced successful drugs and became large companies themselves.

One thing all these firms have in common is their need for capital. A small firm in the initial stages of development (Stage I) pays no dividends because it needs all of its profits (if there are any) for reinvestment in new productive assets. If the firm is successful in the marketplace, the demand for its products will create growth in sales, earnings, and assets, and the industry or company will move into Stage II.

Growth—Stage II

Stage II growth represents an industry or company that has achieved a degree of market acceptance for its products. At this stage, earnings will be retained for reinvestment, and sales and returns on assets will be growing at an increasing rate. The increasing growth can be seen from the increasing slope of the line in Figure 6–1.

By 1978 Apple Computer's PC was so successful that Apple needed more capital for expansion than could be generated internally, so it made an initial public offering of common stock to finance a major expansion. The success of the personal computer enticed IBM to enter this segment of the market, and, eventually, the IBM PC—with its open architecture—was copied and cloned by companies such as Tandy, Compaq, Gateway, Dell, Zeos, and Micron. All these firms are now publicly traded in U.S. markets.

Companies such as IBM entered the developing PC industry with a small amount of their total assets targeted at this market and were able to fund the move into this market with internal sources of capital. However, the other companies entering this market were "pure plays"; in other words, all they did was make personal computers. These companies were in the early part of Stage II, and they still needed to reinvest their cash flow back into research and development and into new plants and equipment.

In general, companies in Stage II become profitable, and, in their early stage of growth, they want to acknowledge to their shareholders that they have achieved profitability. Since they still need their internal capital, they often pay stock dividends (distributions of additional shares). A stock dividend preserves capital but often signals the market that the firm made a profit. In the latter part of Stage II, low cash dividends may be paid out when the need for new capital declines as new sources of capital appear. A cash dividend policy is sometimes necessary to attract institutional investors to the company stock since some institutions cannot own companies that pay no dividends.

Obviously, industries in Stage I or early Stage II are very risky, and the investor does not really know if growth objectives will be met or if dividends will ever be paid. But if you want to have a chance to make an investment (after careful research) in a high-growth industry with large potential returns, then Stage I or II industries will provide you with opportunities for large gains or losses. Since actual dividends are irrelevant in these stages, an investor will be purchasing shares for capital gains based on expected growth rather than on current income.

Expansion—Stage III

In Stage III, sales expansion and earnings continue but at a decreasing rate. As the industry crosses from the growth stage to the expansion stage, the slope of the line in Figure 6–1 becomes less steep, signaling slower growth. It is this crossover point that is important to the analyst who will also be evaluating declining returns on investment as more competition enters the market and attempts to take away market share from existing firms. The industry has grown to the point where asset expansion slows in line with production needs, and the firms in the industry are more capable of paying cash dividends. Stock dividends and stock splits are still common in Stage III, and the dividend payout ratio usually increases from a low level of 5 to 15 percent of earnings to a moderate level of 25 to 40 percent of earnings by stage IV.

Since industries and companies do not grow in a nice smooth line, it is often difficult to tell when the industry or company has crossed from Stage II growth to Stage III expansion. Determining the crossover point is extremely important to investors who choose to invest in growth companies. Once investors recognize that the past growth rate will not be extrapolated and, instead, is in decline, stock prices can take a sizable tumble

FIGURE 6–2

The Crossover Point

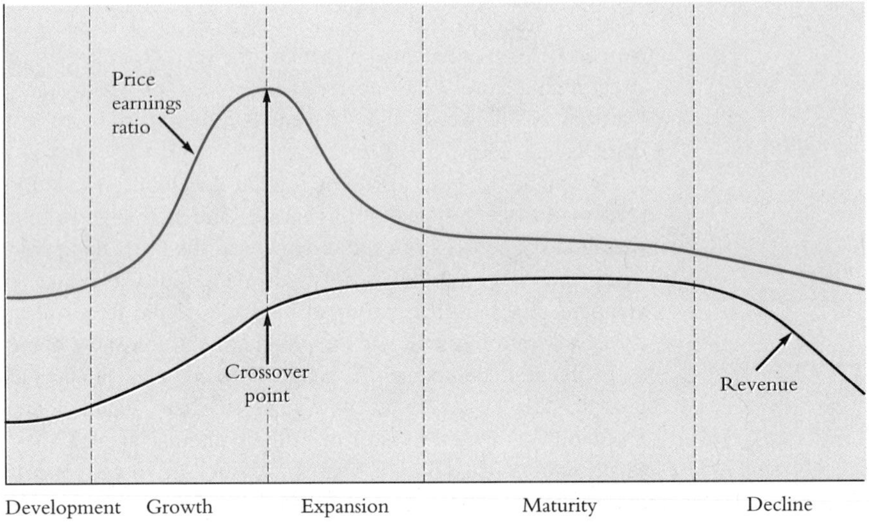

as price-earnings ratios collapse because of slower growth expectations. Figure 6–2 demonstrates this relationship.

Maturity—Stage IV

Maturity occurs when industry sales grow at a rate equal to the economy as measured by the long-term trend in gross domestic product (GDP). Some analysts like to use the growth rate of the Standard & Poor's 500 Index for comparison because the growth rate of these 500 large companies sets the norm for mature companies. Figure 6–3 graphs sales for the S&P 500 and the GDP using a logarithmic graph. The use of a logarithmic graph (sometimes called ratio scale) allows a comparison of growth rates between trend lines since a straight line on a vertical logarithmic scale represents a constant growth rate. The steeper the slope of the line, the faster the growth rate. Notice that on the graph, S&P 500 sales and GDP seem to have similar long-term growth rates (slope).

Automobiles are a good example of a mature industry. You may remember that, in Chapter 5, we looked at the automobile industry as it related to the business cycle. Figure 5–8 showed an industry that was very cyclical and where the number of automobiles sold seemed to be closely related to real GDP. Figure 6–4 shows the relationship between sales of the automobile industry and GDP in current dollars. While automobile sales do not have the relatively smooth line of GDP, the slope of the two lines appears similar. Figure 6–5 on page 162 plots sales for the auto industry against the GDP for the years 1962 through 1994. The scatter diagram again depicts the cyclical nature of automobile sales and a close relationship to that of GDP.

By the time an industry or firm reaches maturity, plant and equipment are in place, financing alternatives are available domestically and internationally, and the cash flow from operations is usually more than enough to meet the growth requirements of the firm.

FIGURE 6–3 S&P Industrials versus GDP

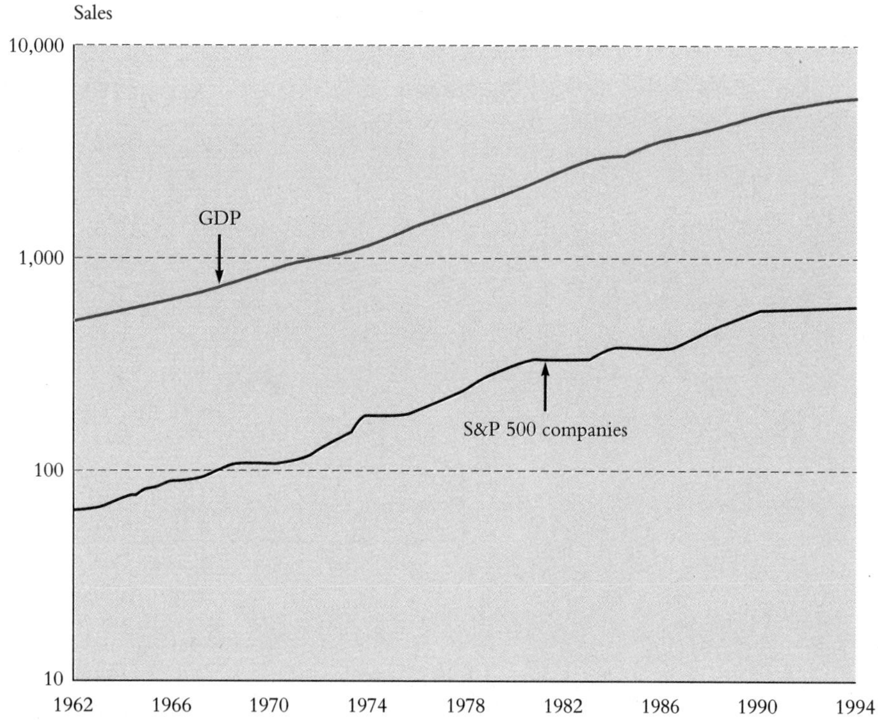

FIGURE 6–4 Automobile Industry versus GDP

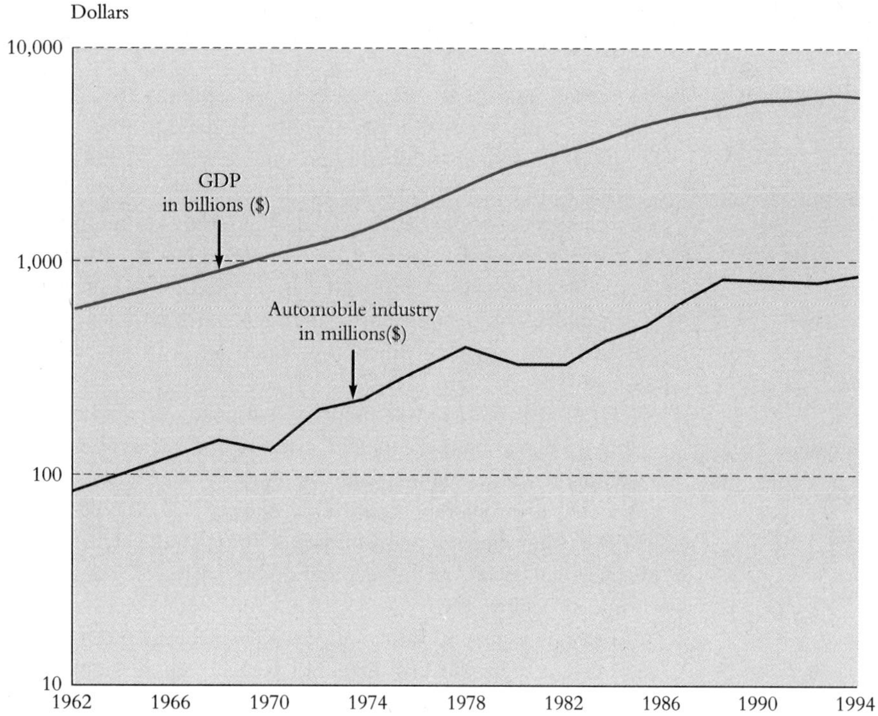

FIGURE 6–5 Automobile Sales versus GDP

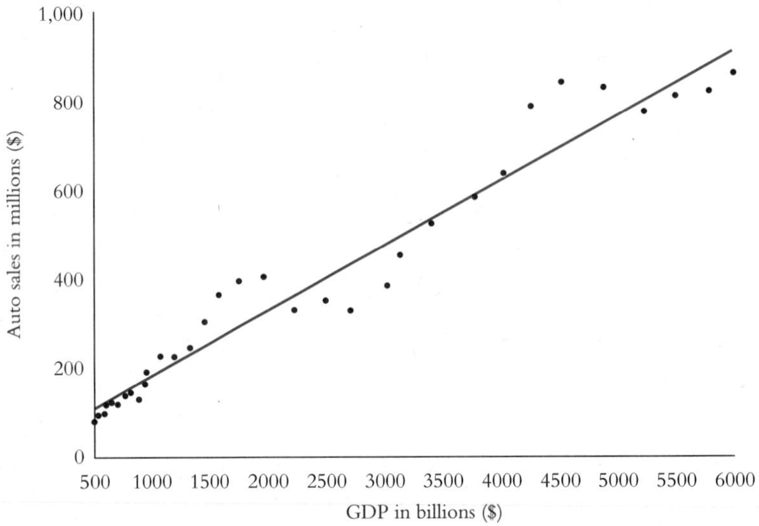

Under these conditions, dividends will usually range from 45 to 60 percent of earnings. These percentages will be different from industry to industry, depending on individual characteristics.

Decline—Stage V

In unfortunate cases, industries suffer declines in sales if product innovation has not increased the product base over the years. Declining industries may be specific to a country; passenger trains are such an example. In Europe, passenger trains are common forms of transportation, while in the United States, passenger trains have been in decline for many decades because competition from automobiles, buses, and airplanes has cut into the market. Besides the famous buggy whip example, black-and-white television, vacuum tubes, and transistor radios are examples of products within an industry that have been in decline. In some cases, the companies producing these products repositioned their resources into growth-oriented products, and, in other cases, the companies went out of business.

Often it is not a whole industry that goes into decline but the weakest company in the industry that cannot compete. Currently, industries such as banks, airlines, and breweries are undergoing consolidation. The number of banks has been declining, and this trend is expected to accelerate as national banking takes hold in the United States. The airline industry has been in consolidation for decades with famous names such as Braniff, Eastern, and Pan Am defunct and others such as TWA and Continental continually on the brink of bankruptcy.

Dividend payout ratios of firms in decline often rise to 100 percent or more of earnings. Often, the firm does not want to signal stockholders that it is in trouble, so it maintains its dividends in the face of falling earnings. This causes the payout ratio to soar

until management realizes that the firm is bleeding to death and needs to conserve cash. Then either drastic dividend cuts follow, or there is an elimination of dividends entirely.

Dividend Policy and the Life-Cycle Curve The dividend payout ratio has an important effect on company growth. As previously pointed out, the more funds a firm retains—and, thus, the lower the dividend payout—the greater the opportunity for growth. This relationship is further demonstrated in Appendix 6A with a discussion of the sustainable growth model.

Growth in Nongrowth Industries

It is also important to realize that growth companies can exist in a mature industry and that not all companies within an industry experience the same growth path in sales, earnings, and dividends. Some companies are simply better managed, have better people, have more efficient assets, and have put more money into productive research and development that has created new products or improved products.

Many U.S. companies, such as Coca-Cola and McDonald's, have found growth by expansion abroad. While their domestic markets are saturated and growing at the rate of GDP or less, the international demand for their products in Asia, Europe, Eastern Europe, Russia, and China has allowed these two companies to maintain double-digit growth rates. This may also be true of other marketing-oriented companies with global trademarks such as Sony, Pepsi, and Heineken.

Electric utilities are generally considered mature, but utilities in states such as Florida, Arizona, and the Carolinas, which have undergone rapid population explosions over the last decade, would still have higher growth rates than the industry in general.

Computer companies such as IBM were fast approaching maturity until technical innovations created new markets. Unfortunately for IBM, demand for its mainframe computers declined worldwide as personal computers and local area networks increased in flexibility and power. To combat this decline in its major product line, IBM restructured in an effort to revive growth from its personal computer, software, and service divisions. Some analysts would place the PC industry in the expansion stage, but IBM as the dominant player in the computer industry is playing catchup to other PC makers who dominate the growth segments.

The warning to the investor is not to become enamored with a company just because it is in a "growth industry." Its time of glory may have passed. Other investors improperly ignore companies that are in the process of revitalization because they no longer carry the growth-stock tag. More will be said about growth stocks in Chapter 7.

INDUSTRY STRUCTURE

The structure of the industry is another area of importance for the analyst. Industry structure determines whether the companies in the industry are profitable, whether there are special considerations such as government regulations that positively or negatively affect the industry, and whether cost advantages and product quality create a dominant company within the industry.

A financial analyst may want to evaluate other significant factors for a given industry. For example, is the industry structure monopolistic like a regulated utility, oligopolistic like the automobile industry, partially competitive like the pharmaceutical industry, or very competitive like the industry for farm commodities? Questions of industry structure are very important in analyzing pricing structures and price elasticities that exist because of competition or the lack of it.

Economic Structure

We often look at the economic structure of an industry to determine how companies compete within the industry. **Monopolies** are generally not common in the United States because of our antitrust laws, but they do exist by government permission in the area of public utilities. Because it would be inefficient to have more than one electric company for a city or state, federal, state, and local governments grant monopolies to electric, gas, water, and local telephone utilities. In return for the monopoly, the government has the right to regulate rates of return on equity and assets and to approve customer fees. This sets the limits of growth and profitability and creates minimums and maximums for the analyst. Monopolies are almost always in mature industries, although the government may occasionally grant a monopoly on emerging technologies and even offer subsidies for the development of new technologies, especially in the defense industry.

Oligopolies have few competitors and are quite common in large mature U.S. industries such as automobiles, steel, oil, airlines, and aluminum to name a few. The competition between companies in an oligopoly can be intense, and profitability can suffer as a result of price wars and battles over market share. Increasingly, oligopolistic industries are facing international competition, which has altered their competitive strategies. Note that many of the industries mentioned earlier have competition from other industrial countries such as Japan, Germany, the Netherlands, Britain, and France.

Pure competition in manufacturing is not widely found in the United States. The food processing industry may be the closest example of this economic form. Generally, companies in pure competition do not have a differentiated product and compete on price such as farmers do with corn, soybeans, and other commodities. Firms will often compete by trying to create perceived differences in product quality or service.

OTHER ECONOMIC FACTORS TO CONSIDER Questions of supply and demand relationships are very important because they affect the price structure of the industry and its ability to produce quality products at a reasonable cost. The cost variable can be affected by many factors. For example, high relative hourly wages in basic industries such as steel, autos, and rubber are somewhat responsible for the inability of the United States to compete in the world markets for these products. Availability of raw material is also an important cost factor. Industries such as aluminum and glass have to have an abundance of low-cost bauxite and silicon to produce their products. Unfortunately, the aluminum industry uses very large amounts of electricity in the production process, so the low cost of bauxite may be offset by the high cost of energy. Energy costs are of concern to all industries, but the availability of reasonably priced energy sources is particularly important to the airline and trucking industries. The list could go on and on, but as analysts become familiar with a specific industry, they learn the crucial variables.

Government Regulation Most industries are also affected by government regulation. This applies to the automobile industry where safety and exhaust emissions are regulated and to all industries where air, water, and noise pollution are of concern. Many industries engaged in interstate commerce—such as utilities, railroads, and telephone companies—are strongly regulated by the government. On the other hand, many other industries—such as airlines, trucking, and natural gas production companies—have been deregulated, and these industries are facing a new climate where the old game plan may no longer prove successful. Most industries are affected by government expenditures; this is especially true for industries involved in defense, education, and transportation.

These are but a few examples to alert you to the importance of having a thorough understanding of your industry. This is why in many large investment firms, trust departments, and insurance companies, analysts are assigned to only one industry or to several related industries so that they may concentrate their attention on a given set of significant factors. Perhaps one of the most important aspects of industry analysis is the competitive structure of the industry.

Competitive Structure

Industries consist of competing firms; some have many firms, others have few. Nevertheless, the existing firms compete with each other and employ different strategies for success. Increasingly, the competition is among large international companies where cultural values and production processes are different. It becomes important for the investment analyst to know the attractiveness of industries for long-term profitability and what factors determine an industry's long-term outlook.

As we discussed previously, just because an industry as a whole is in a certain life-cycle stage, all companies within that industry may not be in the same position. An individual company within the industry may have chosen a poor competitive position or an excellent competitive position. While the industry outlook is important, a company may be able to create a competitive position that shapes the industry environment. There are profitable firms in poor industries and unprofitable firms in good industries.

Perhaps one of the most efficient ways to indicate competitive issues is to consider Michael Porter's elements of industry structure.[1]

Porter divides the competitive structure of an industry into five basic competitive forces: (1) threat of entry by new competitors; (2) threat of substitute goods; (3) bargaining power of buyers; (4) bargaining power of suppliers; and (5) rivalry among existing competitors. All affect price and profitability. The first is the threat of entry by new competitors. If competitors can easily enter the market, firms may have to construct barriers to entry that raise the cost to the firm. This threat places a limit on prices that can be charged and affects profitability. A second force, as we know from economics, is the threat of substitute goods. If we can easily substitute one good for another, this will again affect the price that can be charged and profit margins. An example of this would be in the beverage

[1] Professor Porter is a leading business strategist at Harvard University. See the Selected References at the end of the chapter for a listing of applicable books and articles.

industry. We can drink water (tap or bottled), beer, soft drinks, fruit juice, and so on. If not for the tremendous advertising expenditures from companies trying to get us to drink their beverages, the cost would be considerably lower.

Two other competitive forces are the bargaining power of buyers and the bargaining power of suppliers. A large buyer of goods (Wal-Mart) can influence the price suppliers can charge for their goods. Firms such as McDonald's have stringent requirements for their suppliers, and, because it is a powerful buyer, McDonald's expects and gets costly service and quality control from its suppliers. This behavior restricts the prices that suppliers can charge. On the other hand, there are many powerful suppliers, such as the Middle East oil cartel or DeBeers, the company that controls more than 70 percent of the worldwide diamond market. These suppliers control the cost of raw materials to their customers, and their behavior determines a major part of their customers' profitability.

The last competitive force is the rivalry among existing competitors. The extent of the rivalry affects the costs of competition—from the investment in plant and equipment, to advertising and product development. The automobile industry is a reasonable example of intense rivalry that eventually caused Japanese auto manufacturers, for political reasons, to limit their exports to the United States and instead start producing automobiles in the United States. Because the threat of entry was thought to be small, U.S. automobile companies were complacent for years and did not modernize their production processes with new technology or work flow techniques. Once the Japanese took a large market share, the rivalry intensified and caused a restructuring of the whole U.S. automobile industry. The impact of intense rivalry, therefore, has the same effect as the threat of new entrants.

These five forces vary from industry to industry and directly affect the return on assets and return on equity. The importance of each factor is a function of industry structure or the economic and technical characteristics of an industry. These forces affect prices, costs, and investment in plants, equipment, advertising, and research and development. While each industry has a set of competitive forces that are most important to it in terms of long-run profitability, competitors will devise strategies that may change the industry structure. Strategies that change the environment may improve or destroy the industry structure and profitability. Sometimes it takes several years to see the impact of competitive strategies. The analyst should always look out for firms that will destroy an industry's structure and alter the health of the whole industry.

INDUSTRY TREND ANALYSIS

In this section, we expand the horizon by shifting our attention to four very diverse industries and looking at their comparative trends over time based on their rates of return on equity and their long-term debt-to-equity ratio. The industries chosen for discussion are the airline, brewing, chemical, and pharmaceutical industries. By studying these important industries, the analyst develops a feel for comparative performance in our economy.

The return on equity for the four industries shown in Table 6–1 indicates wide differences in profitability. These data are graphed in Figure 6–6 on page 168, and the trends are more visible. The pharmaceutical industry has the highest returns on equity, with very little variation due to industry or economic effects. A rising profitability trend

TABLE 6–1 Return on Equity (Selected companies—in percent)

	1984	1985	1986	1987	1988	1989	1990	1991	1992	1993
Airline industry	**9.4%**	**4.1%**	**0.4%**	**6.6%**	**14.7%**	**11.7%**	**NMF***	**NMF**	**NMF**	**NMF**
AMR (American)	13.3	15.2	9.3	7.0	14.5	12.1	NMF	NMF	NMF	NMF
Delta	16.7	20.2	3.6	13.6	13.9	17.6	11.6%	NMF	NMF	NMF
Southwest Air	13.7	10.1	9.8	3.4	10.2	12.2	7.8	4.3%	10.7%	15.5%
UAL (United)	13.8	6.8	1.9	0.1	30.6	20.7	5.6	NMF	NMF	NMF
US Air	16.5	12.3	9.3	10.3	8.0	NMF	NMF	NMF	NMF	NMF
Brewing industry	**16.4**	**16.3**	**17.2**	**14.7**	**14.9**	**15.8**	**15.8**	**13.2**	**14.3**	**15.7**
Anheuser-Busch	17.5	18.0	19.9	21.3	23.1	24.7	22.9	21.2	21.5	23.0
Coors (Adolph)	5.0	5.7	6.0	4.7	4.4	3.7	5.3	3.1	5.2	4.0
Labatt Ltd.	15.8	15.0	16.2	16.2	12.2	12.4	7.1	10.9	11.0	13.3
Molson Companies Ltd.	11.3	9.5	9.8	13.3	13.7	14.7	14.8	13.7	9.3	8.9
Chemical industry	**10.9**	**8.1**	**11.9**	**15.1**	**23.6**	**23.1**	**16.0**	**11.2**	**11.7**	**13.1**
Dow	9.6	9.2	14.3	21.6	33.2	31.3	15.9	10.2	7.2	8.0
Du Pont	11.6	9.7	11.5	11.9	13.6	15.7	14.1	10.3	14.4	13.3
Monsanto	12.1	6.3	9.2	10.7	15.6	16.3	12.0	17.0	11.5	16.1
Olin	10.0	5.8	8.9	11.1	14.3	18.6	11.7	10.7	7.4	8.0
Union Carbide	7.4	1.9	12.9	22.9	37.8	26.1	13.2	NMF	9.6	12.5
Pharmaceutical industry	**20.7**	**21.3**	**23.6**	**24.3**	**25.5**	**28.6**	**30.3**	**29.0**	**30.3**	**30.6**
Lilly, Eli	22.1	21.7	20.4	20.6	23.6	25.0	32.5	26.5	28.5	24.1
Merck	19.4	20.5	26.3	42.8	42.3	42.5	46.5	43.2	48.9	29.1
Pfizer	20.4	19.8	19.3	17.8	18.4	16.0	15.7	18.2	23.2	30.3
Upjohn	15.3	15.7	17.2	18.2	19.4	22.3	25.7	26.8	27.9	27.8
Warner-Lambert	15.6	26.6	28.9	33.8	34.1	36.5	34.6	47.8	42.1	44.8

*NMF = not meaningful data (company reported a loss).

is quite visible and has caused some political pressure on the pharmaceutical industry because of exploding health care costs in the United States. The Clinton administration's health care proposals put a damper on pharmaceutical companies' abilities to raise prices, and it is expected that the growth in profitability will slow or even decline over the next several years.

Merck led the group in profitability from 1987 through 1990, and Warner Lambert took the lead in 1991. Even Eli Lilly, with the lowest returns in 1993, is more profitable than all the other companies in the brewing, chemical, and airline industries. This is a very profitable industry.

The brewing industry is next in profitability, but it is perhaps the most stable over the 10-year cycle and remains relatively untouched by business cycle effects. This industry's return on equity is dominated by Anheuser-Busch, which controls more than 40 percent of the market and stands out as a stronger company than Canadian brewers Labatt Ltd. and Molson. While it appears that Coors has been struggling with low returns on equity, it should be noted it used no long-term debt in its capital structure until 1990. Use of debt

FIGURE 6–6 Return on Equity—Airline, Brewing, Chemical, and Pharmaceutical Industries

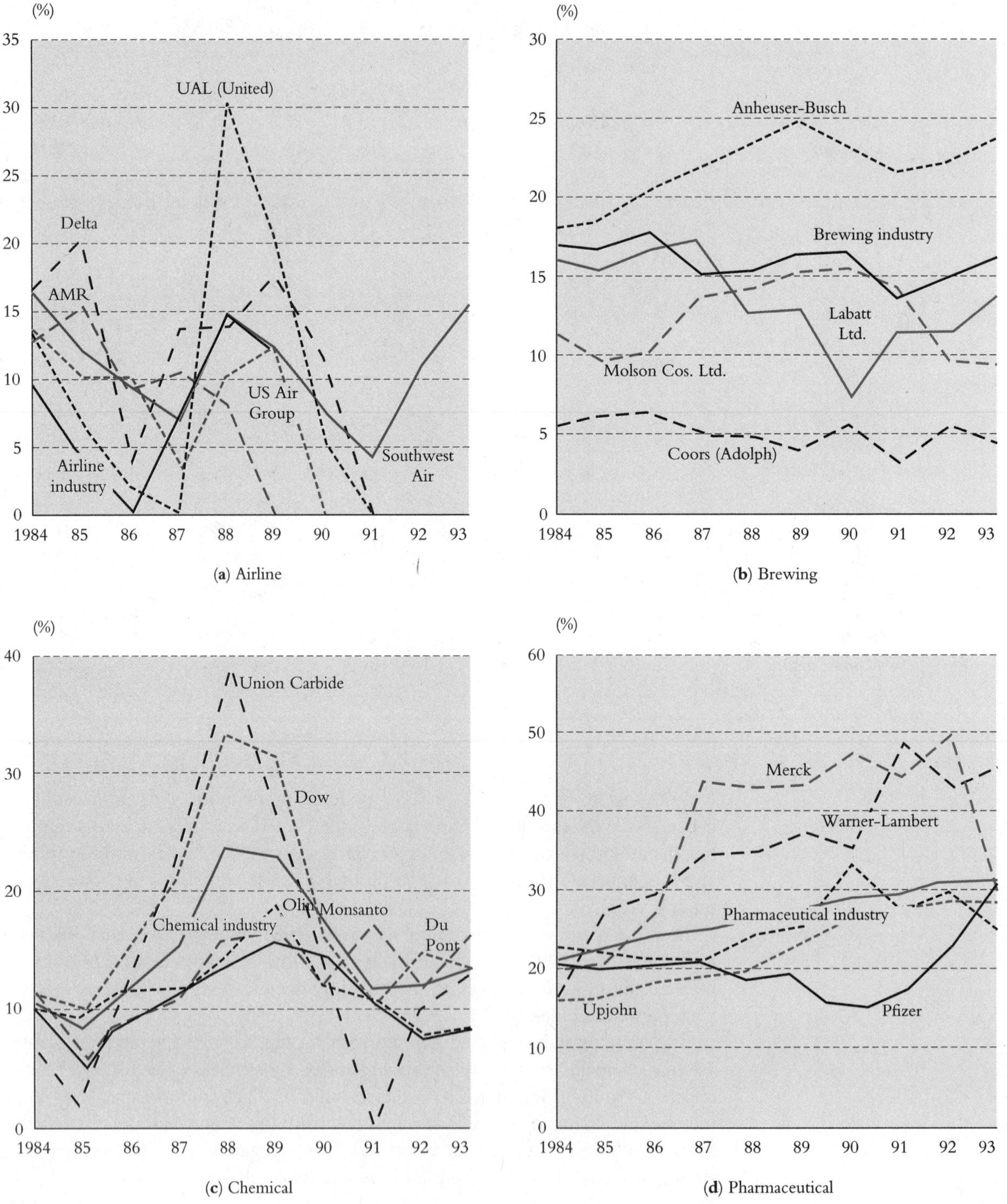

at the same level as Anheuser-Busch would almost double Coors's return on equity but still leave it at the lowest level of the four firms. The comparative returns on this industry do not list Miller Brewing, which is owned by Philip Morris and, therefore, is not broken out separately.

The chemical industry has the third highest returns, but it is more volatile than pharmaceuticals or brewing. This industry shows several distinct periods of high and low profitability because the chemical industry is greatly affected by the business cycle. Figure 6–6 shows the low ROE in the recession of 1991 and the rising returns on equity in the recovery period.

Du Pont and Monsanto exhibit the most consistency, with Dow and Union Carbide showing the most variation of return. Union Carbide's disaster in Bhopal, India, in 1985 killed hundreds of people when a gas leak occurred in one of its chemical plants. As the ROE ratio shows, Union Carbide had barely recovered from a recession when the Bhopal disaster lowered its return to 1.9 percent in 1985. By 1988, the company recovered with the highest return on equity in the industry only to record a loss in 1991. At year-end 1993, the firms were closely bunched in profitability, with Monsanto barely ahead of the others.

The airline industry is by far the most cyclical and least profitable over time. The deregulation of this industry and the rapid expansion that followed hurt profitability. Notice that Table 6–1 shows that only one airline was profitable in 1993 and that three airlines earned no profits for four years in a row with NMF (not meaningful data) indicating losses. In addition to business cycle sensitivity, the airline industry, like the chemical industry, is very sensitive to the price of oil (airline fuel). Southwest Airlines, with its short-haul, low-cost flights, has been the only airline able to keep from losing money during this period. This industry as a whole uses a large percentage of debt to finance its extremely expensive airplanes and terminals.

Although it may be easy to generalize about industries and their relationship to economic cycles, individual companies within each industry seem to stand out. By looking at the industry and companies within the industry together over time, the best and worst become apparent to the trained analyst.

In Table 6–2 and Figure 6–7 on pages 170–171, the same four industries' long-term debt-to-equity ratios are given, which might explain the impact of financial leverage on the return on equity and might possibly explain why some companies and industries are more volatile than others. In general, the airline industry had the most debt, followed by the chemical, brewing, and pharmaceutical industries.

The basic business of airlines requires a large capital commitment in terms of airplanes. A large amount of debt is needed to finance them because profitability is not sufficient to provide internal funds. The airline industry is burdened with debt, and the cyclical nature of the industry compounds earnings swings. The Iraqi invasion of Kuwait in 1991 and the resultant increase in oil prices and reduced passenger traffic spelled the end for several airlines that could not withstand the shock to their fragile financial conditions. Pan American Airlines was sold in parts as various carriers bid for its routes. Midway Airlines declared bankruptcy.

The lack of profitability from 1990 through 1993 has caused a major restructuring of the airline industry and a dramatic increase of long-term debt-to-equity ratios, except for Southwest Air. In 1994, United Airlines employees bought out 55 percent of the

TABLE 6–2 Long-Term Debt-to-Equity Ratios (Selected companies—in percent)

	1984	1985	1986	1987	1988	1989	1990	1991	1992	1993
Airline industry	**123.4%**	**128.3%**	**134.7%**	**72.3%**	**76.8%**	**57.9%**	**81.2%**	**128.4%**	**233.3%**	**199.7%**
AMR (American)	87.3	80.7	96.1	98.3	83.4	61.2	87.8	155.0	234.0	193.3
Delta	64.1	41.6	66.7	52.6	33.0	26.8	50.2	82.1	149.7	186.3
Southwest Air	13.7	81.8	66.2	48.8	65.1	60.3	54.1	98.2	81.8	57.0
UAL (United)	52.1	147.4	90.0	48.8	167.7	85.2	74.7	151.6	512.1	290.4
US Air	56.3	47.2	40.2	94.9	64.4	65.2	126.3	126.2	563.3	504.3
Brewing industry	**29.3**	**32.2**	**42.9**	**35.0**	**44.1**	**53.3**	**49.9**	**48.6**	**50.1**	**15.7**
Anheuser-Busch	37.5	35.0	43.3	48.3	52.1	106.7	85.5	59.6	57.2	72.7
Coors (Adolph)	0.0	0.0	0.0	0.0	0.0	0.0	10.1	20.0	32.1	34.4
Labatt Ltd.	55.2	68.3	87.4	89.0	74.1	60.1	49.0	60.3	61.4	51.7
Molson Companies Ltd.	59.4	58.9	33.1	31.2	25.0	60.1	49.0	52.4	35.3	31.2
Chemical industry	**36.0**	**41.0**	**47.3**	**45.2**	**41.0**	**47.8**	**60.7**	**53.6**	**71.1**	**80.5**
Dow	54.2	66.7	65.9	65.5	46.0	48.4	59.7	64.4	76.7	73.4
Du Pont	28.8	25.9	24.8	21.8	20.7	26.3	34.5	38.6	61.1	78.5
Monsanto	22.7	61.3	43.1	40.1	37.1	37.3	40.4	51.4	47.4	52.5
Olin	42.6	51.6	52.4	56.4	69.4	75.3	65.2	78.1	64.4	90.0
Union Carbide	48.0	43.5	304.2	229.6	125.0	87.3	98.6	45.3	89.9	82.2
Pharmaceutical industry	**11.5**	**11.0**	**19.8**	**13.8**	**11.6**	**18.7**	**17.2**	**15.2**	**14.6**	**11.6**
Lilly, Eli	5.3	10.0	14.4	12.0	12.0	7.2	8.0	8.0	11.9	16.4
Merck	7.0	6.5	6.5	7.9	5.0	3.3	3.2	10.0	9.9	27.0
Pfizer	13.6	11.1	8.4	6.4	5.3	4.2	3.8	7.9	12.1	16.7
Upjohn	33.7	29.1	28.8	26.1	14.1	14.8	30.9	28.5	33.6	34.4
Warner-Lambert	35.6	40.2	37.7	33.6	31.9	26.9	21.8	38.3	36.9	39.9

company; this purchase was in return for worker concessions of $5 billion dollars in wages. Many new airlines are continually being created. These carriers choose to compete on a few select, but profitable, routes and have helped keep profitability low for the whole industry. The ability to start new airlines has been enhanced by an abundance of used planes that can be cheaply bought and financed.

All the other industries are in safe territory in terms of long-term debt. Coors has increased its long-term debt from 1990 through 1993 but still has a small amount, as does Molson Companies Ltd. Until 1992, Du Pont traditionally had the lowest debt ratio in chemicals, but Monsanto now has the lowest long-term debt-to-equity ratio and has been steadily at the low end of the industry. The Bhopal incident forced Union Carbide to increase its debt dramatically in 1986–87 to cover the expenses associated with this disaster, but it has since reduced its long-term debt-to-equity ratio to the industry average. The pharmaceutical industry has traditionally had the lowest long-term debt-to-equity ratio of the four industries, mostly because consistently high returns allow internal generation of funds through retained earnings.

FIGURE 6–7 Long-Term Debt-to-Equity Ratios—Airline, Brewing, Chemical, and Pharmaceutical Industries

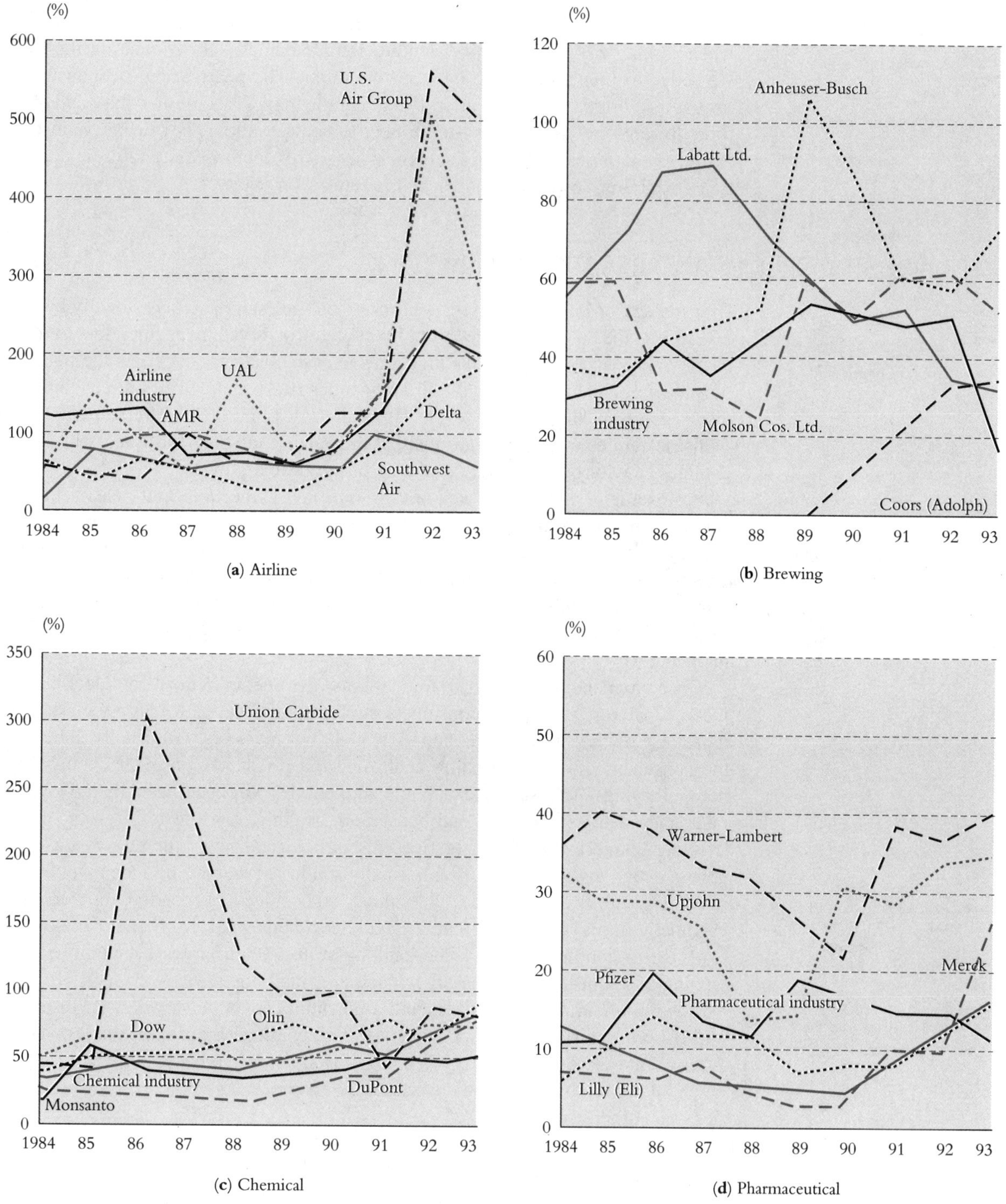

These tables and figures only cover two ratios, but they should show that industry comparisons allow one to pick the quality companies and find the potential losers. These two ratios (return on equity and long-term debt to equity) can be extremely important when making risk-return choices among common stocks. By comparing the two tables, we see a distinct relationship between the ratios. The pharmaceutical industry is in the lowest risk, highest return position by having the highest return on equity and at the same time having the lowest long-term debt-to-equity ratio. The airline industry shows extremely high risk by having the highest long-term debt-to-equity ratios and, at the same time, exhibiting lower and more volatile returns on equity.

INDUSTRY GROUPS AND ROTATIONAL INVESTING

One strategy of investment used by institutional investors and occasionally by individual investors is the concept of **rotational investing.** Rotational investing refers to the practice of moving in and out of various industries over the business cycle. As the business cycle moves from a trough to a peak, different industries benefit from the economic changes that accompany the business cycle. Table 6–3 lists nine Dow Jones Industry Groups; industries are classified into groups that are related in some form and that may exhibit similar behavior during different phases of the business cycle.

For example, as interest rates bottom out, houses become more easily financed and cost less per month to purchase. Because of this, housing stocks, home builders, lumber, and housing-related industries such as household durable goods benefit from the lower interest rates. Earnings of companies in these fields are expected to rise, and investors start buying the common stocks of these companies before any profits are actually visible. The same could be said for the automobile industry because of the effect of low-cost financing.

Once an economic recovery is under way, the unemployment rate declines, personal income starts growing, and consumers start spending more. It may take six quarters or more of growth from the recessionary trough, but investors will usually anticipate when the consumer will start spending again and bid prices of consumer cyclical stocks up before earnings increases appear. While automobiles will be affected by the lower interest rates, they will also get a second boost from healthier consumers.

When interest rates begin to rise, this is not good news for utility stocks. Utilities generate high dividend payouts and usually sell based on their dividend yield. As interest rates rise, utility stock prices fall along with prices of bonds. Another group that eventually loses favor after rates have risen somewhat from their bottom and are expected to continue rising is the banking sector. Rising rates eventually reduce bank lending and squeeze bank margins, which are small anyway.

Investors fearful of rising rates and a potential economic slowdown will often retreat into consumer noncyclical goods such as food, pharmaceuticals, beverages, and tobacco. A move into these industries is often considered defensive because the industries are not much influenced by economic downturns, so their earnings do not suffer nearly as much as cyclical industries.

TABLE 6–3 Dow Jones Industry Groups

Basic Materials
Aluminum
Other nonferrous
Chemicals
Chemicals, commodity
Chemicals, specialty
Forest products
Mining, diversified
Paper products
Precious metals
Steel

Conglomerates

Consumer, Cyclical
Advertising
Airlines
Apparel
Clothing/fabrics
Footwear
Automobile manufacturers
Automobile parts and equipment
Casinos
Home construction
Home furnishings
Lodging
Media
Broadcasting
Publishing
Recreation products
Entertainment
Other recreational products
Toys
Restaurants
Retailers, apparel
Retailers, broadline
Retailers, drug-based
Retailers, specialty

Consumer, Noncyclical
Beverages
Consumer services
Cosmetics/personal care
Food
Foot retailers
Health care providers
Household products
House, durables
House, nondurables
Medical supplies
Pharmaceuticals
Tobacco

Energy
Coal
Oil, drilling
Oil, integrated majors
Oil, secondary
Oilfield equipment and services
Pipelines

Financial
Banks, money center
Banks, regional composite
Banks, central
Banks, east
Banks, south
Banks, west
Financial services, diversified
Insurance composite
Insurance, full line
Insurance, life
Insurance, property and casualty
Real estate investment
Savings and loans
Securities brokers

Industrial
Air freight/couriers
Building materials
Containers and packaging
Electrical components and equipment
Factory equipment
Heavy construction
Industrial and commercial services
Industrial diversified
Marine transportation
Pollution control/waste management
Railroads
Transportation equipment
Trucking

Technology
Aerospace and defense
Communications
Communications (without AT&T)
Computers
Computers (without IBM)
Diversified technology
Industrial technology
Medical and biotechnology
Advanced medical devices
Biotechnology
Office equipment
Semiconductor and related
Software and processing

Utilities
Telephone systems
Electric
Gas
Water

Eventually, as the economy moves through its business cycle, inflation fears return as demand for products pushes up prices of goods. One possible move is into basic materials and energy. The price pressures in the economy will spill over into rising prices for these commodities and rising profits for aluminum, oil, steel, and other companies in these industries. A move into these industry groups usually occurs later in the business cycle.

While we do not necessarily endorse buying and selling common stocks in a rotational manner throughout the business cycle, many investors follow this approach, and you should be well aware of this strategy.

SUMMARY

Chapter 5 presented a three-step model for stock valuation in Figure 5–1. The presentation of industry analysis is the second step in the top-down valuation process we use in the text. One of the most crucial issues in valuing a firm is its potential growth rate in sales, earnings, and cash flow. In order to have some idea of how fast a company can grow, we look at the underlying industry growth characteristics, especially its position on the life-cycle curve.

The industry life-cycle approach includes five stages: development, growth, expansion, maturity, and decline. In the development stage, the firm is usually privately held and makes no profit. The company may make it into the growth stage, which signifies that it has created a market for its product and is becoming profitable. In these first two stages, the firm needs its internal cash flow for reinvestment and, therefore, pays little or no dividends. While the growth stage has sales growing at increasing rates, the expansion stage represents the phase where sales are growing at a decreasing rate. The crossover from the growth to the expansion stage carries the risk that extreme stock price declines may follow the declining growth rate even though dividend payout ratios usually increase during the expansion stage. Stage IV is maturity, and firms in this stage grow at a rate consistent with the Standard & Poor's 500 Stock Index or the gross domestic product. Occasionally firms stumble, lose market share, and go into a decline where sales and earnings decline and eventually dividends evaporate. The life-cycle process is depicted in Figures 6–1 and 6–2.

In addition to life-cycle analysis, the analyst must understand the importance of industry structure. Every industry has an economic structure, for example, monopoly, oligopoly, pure competion, or some other form of competion. The economic structure affects product pricing and returns. Government regulation is another issue that affects many industries. The government regulates profits (utilities), product quality (U.S. Food and Drug Administration), energy consumption (automobile efficiency), and many other areas of commerce such as transportation and education. Other issues that need to be examined are international competition, supply and demand relationships, availability of raw materials, energy costs, and so on.

The competitive structure of industries is crucial to the industry and to companies' profitability. There are five competitive forces that need to be included in an industry analysis: the threat of market entry by new competitors, the threat of substitute goods, the bargaining power of buyers, the bargaining power of suppliers, and the intensity of rivalry among competitors. These five forces vary from industry to industry and directly effect the return on assets and return on equity. Competitive strategies can improve or destroy an industry, and the analyst should know how these forces affect prices, costs, investment in plant and equipment, advertising, and research and development.

The analyst should study general industry trends. We present four industries for comparison: airlines, brewing, chemicals, and pharmaceuticals. Competing firms are compared within each industry, and the industries are compared against each other. The comparisons are presented in Figures 6–6 and 6–7. Finally, the concept of rotational investing is discussed. This concept describes investors who move from one industry to another as business cycle conditions change.

KEY WORDS AND CONCEPTS

top-down approach, 157
bottom-up approach, 157
stock pickers, 157
industry life cycles, 157
monopolies, 164
oligopolies, 164
pure competition, 164
rotational investing, 172

DISCUSSION QUESTIONS

1. Distinguish between a "top-down approach" and a "bottom-up approach" to selecting stocks.
2. List the five stages of the industry life cycle. How does the pattern of cash dividend payments change over the cycle? (A general statement is all that is required.)
3. Why might a firm begin paying stock dividends in the growth stage?
4. If the investor does not correctly identify the crossover point between growth and expansion, what might happen to the price of the stock?
5. Suggest two companies that have continued to grow in nongrowth industries, and explain why.
6. Why are monopolies not common in the United States?
7. How would you describe the nature of competition in oligopolies, and what is the potential effect on profitability? How has international competition affected oligopolies?
8. What are the five competitive forces that affect prices and profitability in an industry?
9. Explain how the automobile industry has responded to intense competition.
10. Why is the airline industry the most cyclical and the least profitable of the four industries discussed under trend analysis?
11. Which of the four industries discussed under trend analysis has the highest return on equity and also the lowest long-term debt-to-equity ratio?
12. What is meant by the concept of rotational investing?
13. Explain why low-interest rates make housing stocks attractive.
14. If an inventor fears higher inflation, what possible industries might he or she choose for investment?

THE WALL STREET JOURNAL PROJECTS

WSJ

1. *The Wall Street Journal* publishes data on world industry groups from 25 countries on a daily basis. This is usually shown in the middle of Section C and is entitled "Dow Jones World Industry Groups." Watch this table for one week, and see if there are industries that are continually leading or lagging. Additionally, look at which countries are represented for each industry, and determine whether the industry performance is a function of a particular country's stock performance for that day.
2. There is another industry table that measures performance on a year-to-date (YTD) basis for the United States, the Americas, Europe, and Asia/Pacific. It is called "Industry Group Performance" and is found right under the table discussed in question 1 above. Compare industry performance across continents to determine if positive and negative trends seem to be dependent on the industry or on the country.

U.S. EQUITIES ONFLOPPY EXERCISES

Please use your U.S. Equities OnFloppy software and manual to complete the following exercises.

1. a. Examine the Electric Services industry (SIC 491*). Compare the growth in revenue of this industry on a year-by-year basis and over the entire five-year period with the growth in revenue of the S&P 500 Index. Does the Elective Services industry appear to be a mature industry?
   b. Identify what appear to be the growth companies in the Electric Services industry. Does there appear to be any difference between the dividend yield of the companies identified as growth companies versus the dividend yield of the other companies in the industry?
2. In Chapter 6 a trend analysis of profitability (as measured by the return on equity) and financial leverage (as measured by the debt-to-equity ratio) was performed on four industries. Perform a similar analysis on the Computer and Office Equipment industry (SIC 357*) and the Grocery Store industry (SIC 541*). Limit your analysis to those firms in each industry with revenues exceeding $5 billion.
3. The Apparel industry (SIC 23**) is generally considered to be a cyclical industry. Compare the year-to-year percentage change in revenue of the companies with total revenues exceeding $200 million in this industry with the year-to-year changes in GDP (Figure 5–8). Can you see any relationship?

SELECTED REFERENCES

Industry Analysis

Cottle, Signey; Roger F. Murray; and Frank E. Block. *Graham and Dodd's Security Analysis,* 5th ed. New York: McGraw-Hill, 1988.

Fama, Eugene F., and Kenneth R. French. "Business Cycles and the Behavior of Metal Prices." *Journal of Finance,* December 1988, pp. 1075–93.

Latane, Henry A., and Donald L. Tuttle. "Profitability in Industry Analysis." *Financial Analysts Journal,* July–August 1968, pp. 51–61.

Livingston, Miles. "Industry Movements of Common Stocks." *Journal of Finance,* June 1977, pp. 861–74.

Porter, Michael E., *Competitive Advantage: Creating and Sustaining Superior Performance.* New York: The Free Press, 1985.

Reilly, Frank K., and Eugene Drzycimski. "Alternative Industry Performance and Risk." *Journal of Financial and Quantitative Analysis,* June 1974, pp. 423–46.

Shriner, Robert D. "The Troubled Airline Industry: Impacts on Plane Makers and the U.S. Economy." *Business Economics,* January 1994, pp. 34–39.

APPENDIX 6A: Sustainable Growth Model

The **sustainable growth model** looks at how much growth a firm can generate by maintaining the same financial relationships as the year before. The process of generating earnings using the sustainable growth model provides many insights into the financial interactions that produce earnings. This method requires an understanding of several ratios—we will examine the return on equity and the retention ratios.

The return on equity can take several forms. First, let's define equity to equal (1) assets – liabilities; (2) net worth; or (3) book value. These are all equal even though we call them by different names. We will use the term *book value* to equal the equity of the firm. The return on equity (ROE) is equal to:

$$\text{ROE} = \frac{\text{Net income or After-tax earnings}}{\text{Book value}} \qquad (6A\text{–}1)$$

We can also express earnings and book value on a per share basis and the formula becomes:

$$\text{ROE} = \frac{\text{Earnings per share (EPS)}}{\text{Book value per share (BVPS)}} \qquad (6A\text{–}2)$$

Because we are using the sustainable growth model, we want to know what the return on equity was, based on the book value at the beginning of the year. This makes sense because it is the book value at the beginning of the year that is in place to generate earnings. Assume the following:

$$\text{ROE} = \frac{\$1.20_{1994}\text{ (full year)}}{\$6.44_{1993}\text{ (year end)*}}$$

$$\text{ROE} = 18.63\%$$

Since we want to forecast earnings per share, we will look at the process of growth on a per share basis. We can rearrange formula 6A–2 by multiplying both sides by the book value per share (BVPS) and we end up with:

$$\text{EPS} = \text{ROE} \times \text{BVPS} \qquad (6A\text{–}3)$$

Using this information, we will examine how earnings per share can grow if the financial relationships stay the same from year to year. Let's say BVPS was $6.44 in 1993 (year end) and return on equity was 18.63 percent, which we already computed. Substituting these numbers into Formula 6A–3 gives us:

$$\text{EPS} = \text{ROE} \times \text{BVPS}$$

$$\$1.20 = 18.63\% \times \$6.44$$

This is the value of earnings per share for 1994. Future growth in earnings comes from the firm reinvesting in new plant and equipment and thus being able to generate more income for next year. In this case, the firm paid out a dividend of $0.38 in 1994 and retained $0.82 ($1.20 – $0.38). The $0.82 gets added to the beginning book value per share to get ending book value of $7.26 ($6.44 + $0.82) for 1994.

---

*We use year end 1993 (beginning of 1994) BVPS to measure return on equity for 1994.

If the firm can continue to earn 18.63 percent on its equity, it will earn \$1.35 per share for 1995. This can be computed as follows:

$$EPS_{1995} = ROE \times BVPS_{\text{year end 1994}}$$
$$EPS_{1995} = 18.63\% \times \$7.26$$
$$EPS_{1995} = \$1.353$$

The growth rate in earnings per share using this model can be calculated by taking the increased earnings of \$0.153 and dividing by beginning earnings of \$1.20. This produces an earnings per share growth rate of 12.7 percent.

One of the conditions of growth is that the firms must retain some earnings. If the firm paid out all its earnings in dividends, it would start 1995 with the same book value and would experience no growth. The more earnings retained, the higher the growth rate would be. In this case, it retained \$0.82 out of \$1.20 in earnings. This is called the **retention ratio,** which is sometimes denoted by B to keep it from being confused with a rate of return symbol.

$$\text{Retention ratio (B)} = \frac{\text{Earnings per share} - \text{Dividends per share}}{\text{Earnings per share}} \qquad (6A\text{–}4)$$
$$\text{Retention ratio (B)} = \frac{\$1.20 - \$.38}{\$1.20}$$
$$\text{Retention ratio (B)} = 0.6833 \text{ or } 68.33\%$$

The outcome of this analysis is that the growth in earnings per share is a function of the return on equity and the retention ratio. We can calculate growth in EPS as follows:

$$\text{Growth } (g) = \text{Return on equity} \times \text{Retention ratio} \qquad (6A\text{–}5)$$
$$g = \text{ROE} \times \text{B}$$

Using our example, we have:

$$g_{eps} = 18.63\% \times 68.33\%$$
$$g_{eps} = 12.7\%$$

The sustainable growth model would predict a 12.7 percent growth rate for 1995 based on dividend policy and return on equity. This rate will continue into the future as long as the firm maintains its return on equity and its retention ratio.

KEY WORDS AND CONCEPTS

sustainable growth model, 177

retention ratio, 178

DISCUSSION QUESTIONS

1. Do you think the sustainable growth model would be appropriate for a highly cyclical firm?
2. Based on the sustainable growth model, if a firm increases the dividend payout ratio (1 – the retention ratio), will this increase or decrease the growth in earnings per share in the future?

PROBLEMS

Sustainable growth model

1. The Bolten Corporation had earnings per share of $2.60 in 1994, and book value per share at the end of 1993 (beginning of 1994) was $13.
   a. What was the firm's return on equity (book value) in 1994?
   b. If the firm pays out $0.78 in dividends per share, what is the retention ratio? How much will book value per share be at the end of 1994? Add retained earnings per share for 1994 to book value per share at the beginning of 1994.
   c. Assume the same rate of return on book value for 1995 as you computed in part *a* for 1994. What will earnings per share be for 1995? Multiply rate of return on book value (part *a*) by book value at the end of 1994 (second portion of part *b*).
   d. What is the growth rate in earnings per share between 1994 and 1995?
   e. If the firm continues to earn the same rate of return on book value and maintains the same earnings retention ratio, what will the sustainable growth rate be for the foreseeable future?

7

Valuation of the Individual Firm

We have been building the foundation for the valuation of the individual firm, which is depicted as the last major step of the valuation process in Figure 5–1 on page 133. **Valuation** is based on economic factors, industry variables, an analysis of the financial statements, and the outlook for the individual firm. Valuation determines the long-run fundamental economic value of a specific company's common stock. In the process, we try to determine whether a common stock is undervalued, overvalued, or fairly valued relative to its market price. Furthermore, the orientation in this chapter is mostly toward long-run concepts of valuation rather than toward determining short-term market pricing factors.

BASIC VALUATION CONCEPTS

The valuation of common stock can be approached in several ways. Some models rely solely on dividends expected to be received during the future, and these are usually referred to as **dividend valuation models.** A variation on the dividend model is the **earnings valuation model,** which substitutes earnings as the main income stream for valuation. Earnings valuation models may also call for the determination of a price-earnings ratio, or multiplier of earnings, to determine value. Some models rely on long-run historical relationships between market price and sales per share, or market price and book value per share. Other methods may include the market value of assets, such as cash and liquid assets, replacement value of plant and equipment, and other hidden assets, such as undervalued timber holdings. For the first part of our discussion, we develop the dividend valuation model and then move to earnings-related approaches. We conclude with a consideration of asset values.

REVIEW OF RISK AND REQUIRED RETURN CONCEPTS

Before moving to the valuation models, it would be helpful to review and consolidate the concepts of risk and required return presented in Chapter 1. Calculation of the required rate of return is extremely important because it is the rate at which future cash flows are discounted to reach a valuation. An investor needs to know the required rate of return on the various risk class of assets to reach intelligent decisions to buy or sell.

Chapter 1 examined rates of returns for various assets and returns based on Ibbotson and Associates data and explained how the risk-free rate is a function of both the real rate of return and an inflation premium. The required return was a function of the risk-free rate plus a risk premium for a specific investment.

In this section, we develop a simple methodology based on the capital asset pricing model for determining a required rate of return when valuing common stocks in a diversified portfolio. First, we determine the risk-free rate. The **risk-free rate** (R_F) is a function of the real rate of return and the expected rate of inflation. Some analysts express the risk-free rate as simply the addition of the real rate of return and the expected rate of inflation, while a more accurate answer is found as follows:

$$R_F \text{ (risk-free rate)} = (1 + \text{Real rate})\,(1 + \text{Expected rate of inflation}) - 1 \qquad (7\text{–}1)$$

We now add a risk component to the risk-free rate to determine K_e, the total **required rate of return.** We show the following relationships.

$$K_e = R_F + b\,(K_M - R_F) \tag{7–2}$$

where:

K_e = Required rate of return
R_F = Risk-free rate
b = Beta coefficient
K_M = Expected return for common stocks in the market
$(K_M - R_F)$ = Equity risk premium (ERP)

The risk-free rate, in practice, is normally assumed to be the return on U.S. Treasury bills. **Beta** measures individual company risk against the market risk (usually the S&P 500 Stock Index). Companies with betas greater than 1.00 have more risk than the market, companies with betas less than 1.00 have less risk than the market, and companies with betas equal to 1.00 have the same risk as the market. It stands to reason then that high beta stocks ($b > 1.00$) would have higher required returns than the market.

The last term $(K_M - R_F)$, the **equity risk premium (ERP),** is very difficult to observe because it represents the extra return or premium the stock market must provide compared with the rate of return an investor can earn on Treasury bills. If we observe the historical relationship between stocks and bills from Figure 1–4 on page 17 in Chapter 1, we see that large stocks have returned an average of 10.2 percent over the 68-year period 1926–94, and Treasury bills have returned an average of 3.7 percent over the same time, or a 6.5 percent equity risk premium. Since K_M is not observable from the market, an analyst calculating K_e usually thinks of $(K_M - R_F)$ as one number, which we express as the equity risk premium (ERP).

The time from 1926 through 1994 is a very long period that included some extreme events such as the depression of the 1930s, World War II, the Vietnam War, and the inflation of the 1970s. Nevertheless, it is a good starting point from which to begin our measurement. For most of the post–World War II period, the normal equity risk premium has been between 5.5 and 6.5 percent, depending on the risk perceived by investors. When investors are more risk averse (pessimistic), the ERP tends to be higher, and when investors are less risk averse (optimistic), the ERP is lower.

Let's compute a required rate of return for a sample company with a beta of 1.17 when the Treasury bill rate is 5 percent. If we assume that a normal equity risk premium (ERP) is 6 percent, we should have a required return as follows:

$$\begin{aligned} K_e &= R_F + b\,(\text{ERP}) \\ &= 5\% + 1.17\,(6\%) \\ &= 5\% + 7.02\% \\ &= 12.02\%\ \text{(We will round to 12\%)} \end{aligned}$$

Now, K_e, the required rate of return, can be used as a discount rate for future cash flows from an investment. This methodology will be helpful as you work through the dividend valuation models for common stock.

DIVIDEND VALUATION MODELS

The value of a share of stock may be interpreted by the shareholder as the present value of an expected stream of future dividends. Although in the short run, stockholders may be influenced by a change in earnings or other variables, the ultimate value of any holding rests with the distribution of earnings in the form of dividend payments. Although the stockholder may benefit from the retention and reinvestment of earnings by the corporation, at some point, the earnings must generally be translated into cash flow for the stockholder.[1] While dividend valuation models are theoretical in nature and subject to many limitations, they are the most frequently used models in the literature of finance. Perhaps this is because they demonstrate so well the relationship between the major variables affecting common stock prices.

General Dividend Model

A generalized stock valuation model based on future expected dividends can be stated as follows:

$$P_0 = \frac{D_1}{(1 + K_e)^1} + \frac{D_2}{(1 + K_e)^2} + \frac{D_3}{(1 + K_e)^3} + \ldots + \frac{D_\infty}{(1 + K_e)^\infty} \qquad (7\text{–}3)$$

where:

P_0 = Present value of the stock price
D_i = Dividend for each year, for example, 1, 2, 3 . . . ∞
K_e = Required rate of return (discount rate)

This model is very general and assumes the investor can determine the right dividend for each and every year as well as the annualized rate of return an investor requires.

Constant Growth Model

Rather than predict the actual dividend each year, a more widely used model includes an estimate of the growth rate in dividends. This model assumes a constant growth rate in dividends to infinity.

If a constant growth rate in dividends is assumed, Formula 7–3 can be rewritten as:

$$P_0 = \frac{D_0(1 + g)^1}{(1 + K_e)^1} + \frac{D_0(1 + g)^2}{(1 + K_e)^2} + \frac{D_0(1 + g)^3}{(1 + K_e)^3} + \ldots + \frac{D_0(1 + g)^\infty}{(1 + K_e)^\infty} \qquad (7\text{–}4)$$

where:

$D_0(1 + g)^1$ = Dividends in the initial year
$D_0(1 + g)^2$ = Dividends in year 2, and so on
g = Constant growth rate in the dividend

[1] Some exceptions to this principle are noted later in the chapter.

The current price of the stock should equal the present value of the expected stream of dividends. If we can correctly predict the growth of future dividends and determine the discount rate, we can ascertain the value of the stock.

For example, assume we wanted to determine the present value of ABC Corporation common stock based on this model. We shall assume ABC anticipates an 8 percent growth rate in dividends per share, and we use a 12 percent discount rate as the required rate of return. The required rate of return is intended to provide the investor with a minimum real rate of return, compensation for expected inflation, and a risk premium. Twelve percent is sufficient to fulfill that function in this example.

Rather than project the dividends for an extremely long period and then discount them back to the present, we can reduce previously presented Formula 7–4 to a more usable form:

$$P_0 = D_1/(K_e - g) \qquad (7\text{–}5)$$

This formula is appropriate as long as two conditions are met. The first is that the growth rate must be constant. For the ABC Corporation, we are assuming that to be the case. It is a constant 8 percent. Second, K_e (the required rate of return) must exceed g (the growth rate). Since K_e is 12 percent and g is 8 percent for the ABC Corporation, this condition is also met. Let's further assume D_1 (the expected dividend at the end of period 1) is \$3.38.

Using Formula 7–5, we determine a stock value of:

$$\begin{aligned} P_0 &= D_1/(K_e - g) \\ &= \$3.38/(0.12 - 0.08) \\ &= \$3.38/0.04 \\ &= \$84.50 \end{aligned}$$

This value, in theory, represents the present value of all future dividends. The meaning is further illustrated in Table 7–1, in which we take the present value of the first 20 years of dividends (\$43.71) and then add in a figure of \$40.79 to arrive at the present value of all future dividends of \$84.50 as previously determined by Formula 7–5. The \$40.79 value represents the present value of dividends occurring between 2016 and infinity (i.e., after the 20th year).[2]

We must be aware that several things could be wrong with our analysis. First, our expectations of dividend growth may be too high for an infinite period. Perhaps 6 percent is a more realistic estimate of expected dividend growth. If we substitute our new estimate into Formula 7–5, we can measure the price effect as dividend growth changes from an 8 percent rate to a 6 percent rate.

$$\begin{aligned} P_0 &= \$3.38/(0.12 - 0.06) \\ &= \$3.38/0.06 \\ &= \$56.33 \end{aligned}$$

A 6 percent growth rate (a 2 percent change) cuts the present value down substantially from the prior value of \$84.50.

We could also misjudge our required rate of return, K_e, which could be higher or lower. A lower K_e would increase the present value of ABC Corporation, whereas a

[2] If you need to brush up on your present value calculations please refer to Appendix E called "Time Value of Money and Investment Applications."

TABLE 7–1 Present Value Analysis of ABC Corporation

Year	Expected Dividends $g = 8\%$	Present Value Factor $K_o = 12\%$*	Present Value of Dividends
1996	$ 3.38	0.893	3.02
1997	3.65	0.797	2.91
1998	3.94	0.712	2.81
1999	4.26	0.636	2.71
2000	4.60	0.567	2.61
2001	4.97	0.507	2.52
2002	5.37	0.452	2.43
2003	5.80	0.404	2.34
2004	6.26	0.361	2.26
2005	6.76	0.322	2.18
2006	7.30	0.287	2.10
2007	7.88	0.257	2.03
2008	8.51	0.229	1.95
2009	9.19	0.205	1.87
2010	9.93	0.183	1.81
2011	10.72	0.163	1.75
2012	11.58	0.146	1.69
2013	12.51	0.130	1.63
2014	13.51	0.116	1.57
2015	14.59	0.104	1.52
PV of dividends for years 1996–2015			43.71
PV of dividends for years 2016 to infinity			40.79
Total present value of ABC Common Stock			$84.50†

*Figures are taken from Appendix C at the end of this book.
†Notice that this value is the same as that found on the previous page using Formula 7–5.

higher K_e would reduce its value. We have made these points to show how sensitive stock prices are to the basic assumptions of the model. Even though you may go through the calculations, the final value is only as accurate as your inputs. This is where a security analyst's judgment and expertise are important—in justifying the growth rate and required rate of return.

A Nonconstant Growth Model

Many analysts do not accept the premise of a constant growth rate in dividends or earnings. As we examined in Chapter 6, industries go through a life cycle in which growth is nonlinear. Growth is usually highest in the infancy and early phases of the life cycle, and as expansion is reached, the growth rate slows until the industry reaches

maturity. At maturity, a constant, long-term growth rate that approximates the long-term growth of the macro economy may be appropriate for a particular industry.

Some companies in an industry may not behave like the industry in general. Companies constantly try to avoid maturity or decline, and so they strive to develop new products and markets to maintain growth.

In situations where the analyst wants to value a company without the constant-growth assumption, a variation of the constant-growth model is possible. Growth is simply divided into several periods with each period having a present value. The present value of each period is summed to attain the total value of the firm's share price. An example of a two-period model may illustrate the concept. Assume that JAYCAR Corporation is expected to have the growth pattern shown in Figure 7–1.

It is assumed that JAYCAR will have a dividend growth rate of 20 percent for the next 10 years and an 8 percent perpetual growth rate after that. JAYCAR's dividend is expected to be $1 next year, and the appropriate required rate of return (discount rate) is 12 percent. Taking the present value for the first 10 years of dividends and then applying the constant dividend growth model for years 11 through infinity, we can arrive at an answer. First, we find the present value of the initial 10 years of dividends.

Year	Dividends (20% growth)	PV Factor (12%)*	Present Value of Dividends First 10 Years
1	$1.00	0.893	$ 0.89
2	1.20	0.797	0.96
3	1.44	0.712	1.03
4	1.73	0.636	1.10
5	2.07	0.567	1.17
6	2.48	0.507	1.26
7	2.98	0.452	1.35
8	3.58	0.404	1.45
9	4.29	0.361	1.55
10	5.15	0.322	1.66
			$12.42

*Figures are taken from Appendix C at the end of this book.

We then determine the present value of dividends after the 10th year. The dividend in year 11 is expected to be $5.56, or $5.15 (for year 10) compounded at the new, lower 8 percent growth rate ($5.15 × 1.08). Since the rest of the dividend stream will be infinite, Formula 7–5 can provide the value of JAYCAR at the end of year 10, based on a discount rate of 12 percent and an expected growth rate of 8 percent.

$$\begin{aligned} P_{10} &= D_{11}/(K_e - g) \\ &= \$5.56/(0.12 - 0.08) \\ &= \$5.56/0.04 \\ &= \$139 \end{aligned}$$

FIGURE 7–1 JAYCAR Growth Pattern

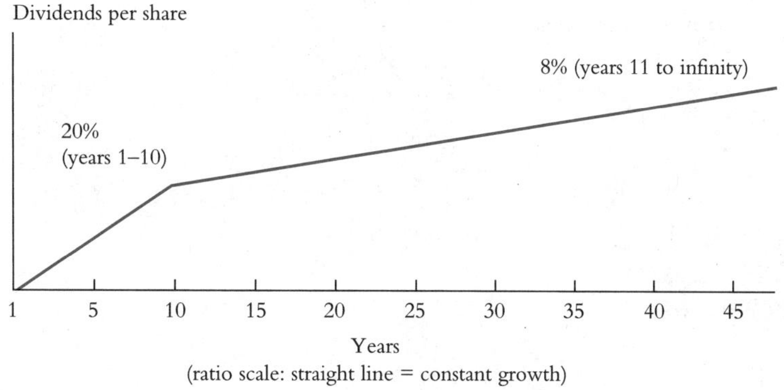

An investor would pay $139 at the end of the 10th year for the future stream of dividends from year 11 to infinity. To get the present value of the 10th year price, the $139 must be discounted back to the present by the 10-year PV factor for 12 percent from Appendix C (0.322). This part of the answer is $139.00 × 0.322, or $44.76. The two parts of this analysis can be combined to get the current valuation per share of $57.18.

Present value of the dividends from years 1 to 10	$12.42
Present value of 10th year price ($139.00 × 0.322)	44.76
Total present value of JAYCAR common stock	$57.18

EARNINGS VALUATION MODELS

Dividend valuation models are best suited for companies in the expansion or maturity life-cycle phase. Dividends of these companies are more predictable and usually make up a larger percentage of the total return than capital gains. Earnings-per-share models are also used for valuation. For example, the investor may take the present value of all future earnings to determine a value. This might be appropriate where the firm pays no cash dividend and has no immediate intention of paying one.

The Combined Earnings and Dividend Model

Another, more comprehensive valuation model relies on earnings per share (EPS) and a price-earnings (P/E) ratio (earnings multiplier) combined with a finite dividend model. The value of common stock can be viewed as a dividend stream plus a market price at the end of the dividend stream. Using J. M. Smucker Co. as an example, we develop a present value for the stock at the beginning of 1995. (The numbers are shown in Table 7–2.)

The total present value (stock price) for Smucker is shown at the bottom of Table 7–2 to be $29.14. Note that Part A of Table 7–2 describes the present value of the future

TABLE 7–2 Smucker Co. Present Value Analysis at Beginning of 1995

Part A: Present Value of Dividends for 5 Years

Year	(1) Estimated Earnings per Share (Growth 13%)	(2) Estimated Payout Ratio	=	(3) Estimated Dividends per Share	×	(4) Present Value Factor (12.00%)	=	(5) Present Value of Dividends
1995	$1.45	40.00%		$0.58		0.893		0.52
1996	$1.64	40.00%		$0.66		0.797		0.53
1997	$1.85	40.00%		$0.74		0.712		0.53
1998	$2.09	40.00%		$0.84		0.636		0.53
1999	$2.36	40.00%		$0.94		0.567		0.53
								$2.64

Part B: Present Value of Common Stock Price at End of 1994

Year	EPS	×	P/E	=	Price	×	PV Factor	=	
1999	$2.36		19.8		$46.73		0.567		26.50
									$29.14

A + B = Total Present Value of Smucker Common Stock at Beginning of 1995

dividends, while Part B is used to determine the present value of the future stock price. These are assumed to be the two variables that determine the current stock price under this model.

In Part A, earnings per share are first projected for the next five years. The earnings are then multiplied by the company's estimated payout ratio of 40 percent to determine anticipated dividends per share for those five years. In this example, we assume the required rate of return to be 12 percent. You need to recognize that this required rate will change continuously with market conditions. The present value of five years of dividends is shown in column (5) of Part A as $2.64.

In Part B, we multiply estimated 1999 earnings per share of $2.36 by the P/E ratio (earnings multiplier) of 19.8 to arrive at an anticipated price five years into the future. This price of $46.73 is then discounted for five years at 12 percent to arrive at a present value of $26.50. This present value of the stock is equal to the present value of the dividend stream for five years ($2.64) plus the present value of the future stock price ($26.50) for a total current value of $29.14 at the beginning of 1995.

This model can be used with your choice of time periods. Five years is not a magic number. As the time period used increases, the estimate of earnings per share becomes more uncertain for cyclical companies, and the future stock price based on an earnings multiplier (P/E ratio) becomes a risky forecast. Some companies in industries such as utilities or food have more predictable earnings streams than those in consumer-sensitive markets such as automobiles and durables, but they still may exhibit fluctuating P/E ratios. The next section develops the concept of the price-earnings ratio, which was used as the earnings multiplier in Table 7–2.

THE PRICE-EARNINGS RATIO

Mathematically, the **price-earnings ratio** (P/E) is simply the price per share divided by earnings per share, and it is ultimately set by investors in the market as they bid the price of a stock up or down in relation to its earnings. Price-earnings ratios are often expressed in the financial press as historical numbers using today's price divided by the latest 12-month earnings.

For companies with cyclical earnings, a P/E using the latest 12-month earnings might be misleading because these earnings could be high. If investors expect earnings to come back to a normal level, they will not bid the price up in relation to this short-term cyclical swing in earnings per share, and the P/E ratio will appear to be low. But if earnings are severely depressed, investors will expect a return to normal higher earnings, and the price will not fall an equal percentage with earnings, and the P/E will appear to be high. This was apparent in the automobile industry during 1991 and 1992. Prices of Ford and General Motors stock went up in early 1992 even as the companies announced losses because investors were anticipating an industry recovery during the summer of 1992.

In the Smucker example in Table 7–2, we used a P/E of 19.8 in 1999. This P/E ratio of 19.8 is determined by historical analysis and by other factors such as expected growth in earnings per share. The P/E of a company is also affected by overall conditions in the stock market. At the time of this writing, Smucker had a P/E of 22, but its five-year average P/E was 23.6, and its 10-year average P/E was 19. The 19.8 used in Table 7–2 is a judgment call.

Even though the current P/E ratio for a stock in the market is known, investors may not agree it is appropriate. Stock analysts and investors probably spend more time examining P/E ratios and assessing their appropriate level than any other variable. Although the use of P/E ratios in valuation approaches lacks the theoretical underpinning of the present value-based valuation models previously discussed in the chapter, P/E ratios are equally important. The well-informed student of investments should have a basic understanding of both the theoretically based present value approach and the more pragmatic, frequently used P/E ratio approach.

What determines whether a stock should have a high or low P/E ratio? Let's first talk about the market for stocks in general, and then we will look at individual securities.

Stocks generally trade at a relatively high P/E ratio (perhaps 15 or greater) when there are strong growth prospects in the economy. However, inflation also plays a key role in determining P/E ratios for the overall market.

To illustrate the latter point, Figure 7–2 on page 190 presents the relationship between the year-end Standard & Poor's 500 composite P/E ratio and the annual rate of inflation measured by the change in the consumer price index (CPI). The graphical relationship between these two variables shows they are inversely related. The price-earnings ratio goes down when the change in the CPI goes up, and the reverse is also true.

The dramatic drop in the P/E ratio in 1973–74 can be attributed in large measure to the rate of inflation increasing from 3.4 percent in 1972 to 12.2 percent in 1974, or a change of more than three times its former level. For a brief period in 1976, inflation decreased to an annual rate of less than 5 percent, only to soar to 13.3 percent by 1979. The average rate of inflation for 1982 was reduced to 3.8 percent, and the market responded by paying higher share prices for one dollar of earnings (that is, higher P/E ratios).

FIGURE 7–2 Inflation and Price-Earnings Ratios

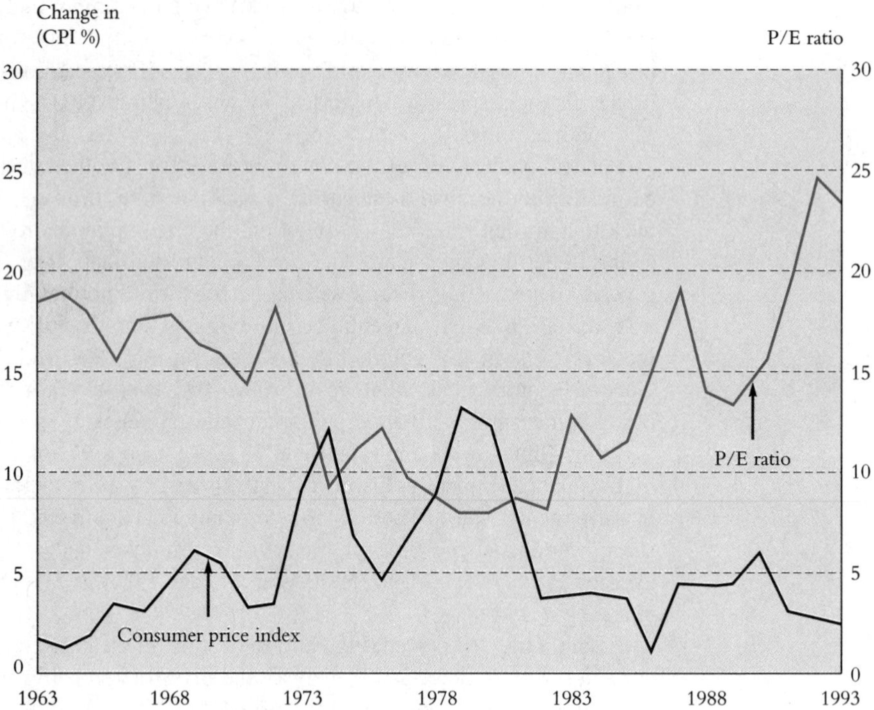

From 1983 through 1985, the consumer price index hovered around 3 to 4 percent, but in 1986, inflation subsided to 1.1 percent, and the S&P price-earnings ratio soared. In 1987, the S&P 500 P/E ratio remained high until the crash of October 1987 brought stock prices down to lower levels. During the sobering and risk-averse period after the crash, market prices were fairly stable.

As fears of higher inflation rose during 1989, the S&P 500 P/E ratio came back to the low-midrange of its 30-year history shown in Figure 7–2. The higher price-earnings ratios in 1991–93 reflect both the impact of falling inflationary expectations and depressed earnings suffered by corporations during the recessionary period of 1990–91, and the slow recovery in 1992 and 1993. As was pointed out in Chapter 1 and earlier in this chapter, required rates of return are directly influenced by the rate of inflation. As inflation changes, the required rate of return on common stock, K_e, changes, and prices go up or down. This is the basic mechanism that causes inflation to influence P/E ratios.

Other factors besides inflationary considerations and growth factors influence the P/E ratio for the market in general. Federal Reserve policy and interest rates, federal deficits, the government's leading indicators, the political climate, the mood and confidence of the population, international considerations, and many other factors affect the P/E ratio for the overall market. The astute analyst is constantly studying a multitude of variables in analyzing the future outlook for P/E ratios.

The P/E Ratio for Individual Stocks

Although the overall market P/E ratio is the collective average of individual P/Es, those factors that influence the market P/E do not necessarily affect P/E ratios of individual companies consistently from one industry to another. An individual firm's P/E ratio is heavily influenced by its growth prospects and the risk associated with its future performance. Table 7–3 shows examples of growth rates and P/E ratios for different industries and firms. Generally, a strong expected future growth rate for 1993–98 (column 4) is associated with a reasonably high P/E for early 1994 (column 5).

In addition to the future growth of the firm and the risk associated with that growth, investors and analysts also consider a number of other factors that influence a firm's P/E ratio. These cannot be easily quantified, but they affect a broad range of stocks. Included in this category are the debt-to-equity ratio and the dividend policy of the firm. All things being equal, the less debt a firm has, the more likely it is to be highly valued in the marketplace.

The dividend policy is more elusive. For firms that show superior internal reinvestment opportunities, low cash dividends may be acceptable. But maturing companies may be expected to pay a high cash dividend. For the latter group, a reduction in cash dividends may be associated with a lower P/E ratio.

Certain industries also traditionally command higher P/E ratios than others. Investors seem to prefer industries that have a high technology and research emphasis. Thus, firms in computers, medical research and health care, and sophisticated telecommunications often have higher P/E ratios than the market in general. This does not mean firms in these industries represent superior investments, but merely that investors value their earnings more highly.[3] Also, fads and other factors can cause a shift in industry popularity. For

TABLE 7–3 P/E and Growth in EPS

(1) Industry	(2) Company	(3) 5-Year EPS Growth, 1989–93	(4) Expected Growth in EPS, 1993–98	(5) Early 1994 P/E
Appliances	Maytag	−12.50%	15.50%	14.0
Newspaper	Dow Jones	−8.50	17.00	23.0
Railroads	CSX	7.50	16.00	11.0
Fast foods	McDonald's	13.50	13.50	14.0
Trucking	Roadway	14.00	11.00	16.0
Tobacco	Philip Morris	23.50	9.00	11.0

Source: Value Line Investment Survey, selected issues (Value Line Inc.).

[3] William Kittrell, Geoffrey A. Hirt, and Roger Potter, "Price-Earnings Multiples, Investors' Expectations, and Rates of Return: Some Analytical and Empirical Findings" (Paper presented at the 1984 Financial Management Association meeting).

example, because Ronald Reagan emphasized military strength, defense-oriented stocks were popular during his administration. Jimmy Carter stressed the need for environmental control, and stocks dealing in air and water pollution control traded at high P/E ratios during his tenure. Bill Clinton's health care proposals lowered P/Es of pharmaceutical stocks dramatically.

The quality of management as perceived by those in the marketplace also influences a firm's P/E ratio. If management is viewed as being highly capable, clever, or innovative, the firm may carry a higher P/E ratio. Investors may look to magazines such as *Forbes* or *Business Week,* which highlight management strategies by various companies, or to management-oriented books. Of course, it is possible that today's trendsetters may represent tomorrow's failures.

Not only is the quality of management important to investors in determining the firm's P/E ratio, but the quality of earnings is also. There are many interpretations of a dollar's worth of earnings. Some companies choose to use very conservative accounting practices so their reported earnings can be interpreted as being very solid by investors (they may even be understated). Other companies use more liberal accounting interpretations to report maximum earnings to their shareholders, and they, at times, overstate their true performance. It is easy to see that a dollar's worth of conservatively reported earnings may be valued at a P/E ratio of 15 to 17 times, whereas a dollar's worth of liberally reported earnings should be valued at a much lower multiple.

All of these factors affect a firm's P/E ratio. Thus, investors will consider growth in sales and earnings, future risk, the debt position, the dividend policy, the quality of management and earnings, and a multitude of other factors in arriving at the P/E ratio. The P/E ratio, like the price of the stock, is set by the interaction of the forces of demand and supply. Those firms that are expected to provide returns greater than the overall economy, with equal or less risk, generally have superior P/E ratios.

The Pure, Short-Term Earnings Model

Often investors/speculators take a very short-term view of the market and ignore using present value analysis with its associated long-term forecasts of dividends and earnings per share. Instead, they only use earnings per share and apply an appropriate multiplier to compute the estimated value.

Applying this approach to Smucker's financial data initially presented in Table 7–2, we can arrive at a value of $29, based on a 1995 earnings estimate of $1.45 and a normal price-earnings ratio of 20.

$$P_0 = \text{EPS}_{1995} \times \text{P/E}_{\text{normal}}$$
$$= \$1.45 \times 20$$
$$P_{1992} = \$29.00^4$$

Every valuation method has its limitations. Although this method is simplified by ignoring dividends and present value calculations, earnings need to be correctly estimated, and the appropriate price-earnings multiplier must be applied. Unfortunately,

[4] This value is not precisely the same as the price in Table 7–2, which was based on discounting future flows.

even if the estimated EPS is correct, you have no assurance that the market will agree with your P/E ratio.

Relating an Individual Stock's P/E Ratio to the Market

Smucker is the leading producer of jams, jellies, and preserves in the United States. The company also makes ice cream toppings, peanut butter, and syrups. While you may have tasted many of Smucker's products, you may not be familiar with the financial data presented in Table 7–4. This table provides a summary of sales per share (SPS), dividends per share (DPS), earnings per share (EPS), cash flow per share (CFPS), book values per share (BVPS), the high and low stock prices, and high and low P/E ratios for the company. Also shown are the high and low P/E ratios for the Standard & Poor's 500 Stock Index over the same period.

In the last two columns, the high and low P/E ratios for Smucker are compared to the high and low P/E ratios for the S&P 500. For example, in 1985, Smucker's high P/E ratio was 23.89, and the S&P 500 high P/E was 14.51. When Smucker's high P/E is divided by the Standard & Poor's 500 high P/E, a relative P/E of 1.65 is calculated in the high relative P/E column. This indicates Smucker's high P/E ratio was at 165 percent of the market, or selling at a 65 percent premium to the market. This relationship did not last.

For each year, a high and low relative P/E ratio was calculated for Smucker with the average of the high and low shown on the last line. Smucker's high relative P/E averages 1.25, and its low relative P/E averages 1.01 percent of the market P/E. When we add the high and low and divide by two, we get an average of 1.13, which indicates Smucker historically sells at 113 percent of the S&P 500 P/E ratio. One could further assume that when the market is high priced, Smucker is priced higher. The low relative P/E shows variability but, on average, is slightly above the market. This indicates that since 1985,

TABLE 7–4 Smucker Stock Valuation Data Table

						Stock Price		P/E Ratio		S&P 500 P/E Ratio		Relative P/E Ratio	
Year	SPS	DPS	EPS	CFPS	BVPS	High	Low	High	Low	High	Low	High	Low
1985	$ 8.95	$0.15	$0.54	$0.74	$3.22	$12.90	$ 6.50	23.89	12.04	14.51	11.20	1.65	1.08
1986	$ 9.80	$0.16	$0.60	$0.83	$3.66	$12.50	$ 9.30	20.83	15.50	17.54	14.05	1.19	1.10
1987	$10.67	$0.19	$0.78	$1.05	$4.26	$15.00	$ 9.80	19.23	12.56	19.24	12.80	1.00	0.98
1988	$12.47	$0.23	$0.94	$1.27	$4.91	$15.70	$11.70	16.70	12.45	11.94	10.22	1.40	1.22
1989	$14.35	$0.28	$1.03	$1.38	$5.68	$19.50	$14.40	18.93	13.98	15.73	12.04	1.20	1.16
1990	$15.40	$0.35	$1.08	$1.47	$6.44	$23.20	$16.10	21.48	14.91	16.98	13.60	1.27	1.10
1991	$16.37	$0.37	$1.16	$1.59	$7.18	$38.90	$20.00	35.53	17.24	25.60	19.12	1.39	0.90
1992	$16.83	$0.41	$1.27	$1.73	$7.55	$39.00	$24.50	30.71	19.29	23.12	20.67	1.33	0.93
1993	$17.57	$0.47	$1.13	$1.66	$8.05	$32.40	$20.30	25.92	16.24	21.51	19.60	1.21	0.83
1994	$23.10	$0.53	$1.35	$1.95	$9.10	$26.00	$20.50	19.26	15.19	21.22	19.37	0.91	0.78
Average	**$14.55**	**$0.31**	**$0.99**	**$1.37**	**$6.01**	**$23.51**	**$15.31**	**23.25**	**14.94**	**18.74**	**15.27**	**1.25**	**1.01**

TABLE 7–5 Projected Earnings and Relative P/E Valuation Model

Part A: Smucker's Estimated 1995 Earnings per Share = $1.45

Part B: Relative P/E Model

	Relative P/E		S&P 500 Current P/E		Smucker's Expected P/E		Smucker's Estimated 1995 EPS		Smucker's Estimated Value Based on Relative P/E
Average high P/E	1.25	×	17	=	21.25	×	1.45	=	$30.81
Average low P/E	1.01	×	17	=	17.17	×	1.45	=	$24.90
Average P/E	1.13	×	17	=	19.21	×	1.45	=	$27.85

investors have been willing to pay a premium for Smucker's common stock at the peaks and troughs of the market.

To apply this knowledge to a model, we must indicate earnings per share, and we also have to know the current S&P P/E ratio at the time we calculate the value. Part A of Table 7–5 indicates earnings per share are expected to be $1.45 for 1995.

At the time of the analysis, the S&P 500 Stock Index was selling at a P/E ratio of 17.0 times earnings. The relative P/E model shown in Part B of Table 7–5 uses the high, low, and average P/E relative times the S&P 500 P/E to find the appropriate price-earnings ratio for Smucker based on its relationship to the current market level. When applied to the $1.45 EPS estimate, we find that Smucker should be selling between $30.81 per share at its high price and $24.90 at its low price. This would indicate that at a market price of less than $25, Smucker would probably be a good buy. Since Smucker was selling at $23 per share at the time of this analysis, the relative P/E model indicates it is a buy.

OTHER VALUATION MODELS USING AVERAGE PRICE RATIOS AND 10-YEAR AVERAGES

Table 7–4 also included data for other variables such as sales per share (SPS), dividends per share (DPS), book value per share (BVPS), and cash flow per share (CFPS) for Smucker. Some people like to look at the relationship of these price variables when deciding to buy or sell a stock. These models use the average price to average per share data (bottom line of Table 7–4) to determine whether a stock is selling for a price that is above or below its historical relationship.

Using the data in Table 7–4, we develop these four models in Table 7–6. In each case in Table 7–6, we multiply the historical ratio times the estimated 1995 amount to compute the estimated value. For example, in Part A of Table 7–6, Smucker exhibits a price-to-sales ratio of 1.33, or 133 percent, which indicates that over the 10 years covered, Smucker stock has sold at 133 percent of its sales per share. Multiplying this ratio times estimated sales per share for 1995 of $24.65 produces a value of $32.78. The dividend-to-price ratio (in Part B) indicates Smucker has sold at more than 62 times its annual dividend, which is not unusual for a growth stock. This dividend model indicates a value of $37.57 per share.

TABLE 7–6 Other Valuation Models Using Average Price Ratios and 10-Year Averages

A. Price-to-Sales Model

$$\frac{\text{Average price*}}{\text{Average sales per share}} = \frac{\$19.41}{14.55} = 1.33 \text{ Price-to-sales ratio}$$

$$\begin{aligned}\text{Value} &= \text{Price-to-sales ratio} \times \text{Estimated 1995 SPS} \\ &= 1.33 \times 24.65 = \$32.78\end{aligned}$$

B. Price-to-Dividend Model

$$\frac{\text{Average price*}}{\text{Average dividends per share}} = \frac{\$19.41}{0.31} = 62.61 \text{ Price-to-dividend ratio}$$

$$\begin{aligned}\text{Value} &= \text{Price-to-dividend ratio} \times \text{Estimated 1995 DPS} \\ &= 62.61 \times \$0.60 = \$37.57\end{aligned}$$

C. Price-to-Book Value Model

$$\frac{\text{Average price*}}{\text{Average book value per share}} = \frac{\$19.41}{6.01} = 3.23 \text{ Price-to-book value ratio}$$

$$\begin{aligned}\text{Value} &= \text{Price-to-book value ratio} \times \text{Estimated 1995 BVPS} \\ &= 3.23 \times \$10.10 = \$32.62\end{aligned}$$

D. Price-to-Cash Flow Model

$$\frac{\text{Average price*}}{\text{Average cash flow per share}} = \frac{\$19.41}{1.37} = 14.17 \text{ Cash flow per share ratio}$$

$$\begin{aligned}\text{Value} &= \text{Price-to-cash flow ratio} \times \text{Estimated 1995 CFPS} \\ &= 14.17 \times \$2.15 = \$30.47\end{aligned}$$

*This represents the average of the 10-year high and low stock prices in Table 7–4, that is, $23.51 plus $15.31 divided by 2.

The book value model in Part C shows Smucker has sold at 3.23 times its book value per share and indicates a price of $32.62 per share. The cash flow model in Part D became popular during the leverage buyout days of the 1980s and produces a value of $30.47. These values are all higher than the market price of $23 per share at the time these calculations were done, which implies that Smucker is selling lower than its fair value relative to these models. These models are sometimes used because these variables are more stable than earnings per share, and, thus, the models present more "normal" values.

FORECASTING EARNINGS PER SHARE

The other side of choosing an appropriate P/E ratio is forecasting the earnings per share of a company with the proper growth rate. Investors can get earnings forecasts in several ways. They can rely on professional brokerage house research, investment advisory firms such as Value Line or Standard & Poor's, or financial magazines such as *Forbes* or *Business Week,* or they can do it themselves.

Least Squares Trendline

One of the most common ways of forecasting earnings per share is to use regression or **least squares trend analysis.** The technique involves a statistical method whereby a trendline is fitted to a time series of historical earnings. This trendline, by definition, is a straight line that minimizes the distance of the individual observations from the line. Figure 7–3 depicts a scattergram for the earnings per share of XYZ Corporation. The earnings of this company have been fairly consistent, and so we get a good trendline with a minimum of variation. The compounded growth rate for the whole 10-year period was 16.5 percent, with 9.8 percent for the first 5 years and 20.4 for the last 5 years. This shows up in Figure 7–3 as two distinct five-year trendlines. There are many statistical programs on PCs and mainframes that run regression analysis, and even handheld calculators have the ability to compute a growth rate from raw data.

Whenever a mechanical forecast is made, subjectivity still enters the decision in choosing the data that will be considered in the regression plot.

Using CSX, a fairly stable railroad company, and Potlatch Corporation, a cyclical forest products paper company, we compare earnings-per-share trends in Table 7–7. Potlatch has been much more subject to the ups and downs in the economy.

The values are plotted in Figure 7–4. From that figure, it is clear that CSX would provide the more reliable forecast based on past data. Its trendline is fairly consistent with a few minor ups and downs. To forecast Potlatch, you would not want to start in 1989 and end in 1993 (peak to trough). Clearly, a Potlatch forecast based on 10 or 12 years of data is more reliable than a three- or five-year forecast. With companies that follow economic cycles, the best forecasting period encompasses at least two peaks and two troughs, or several business cycles.

FIGURE 7–3

Least Squares Trendline for EPS of XYZ Corporation

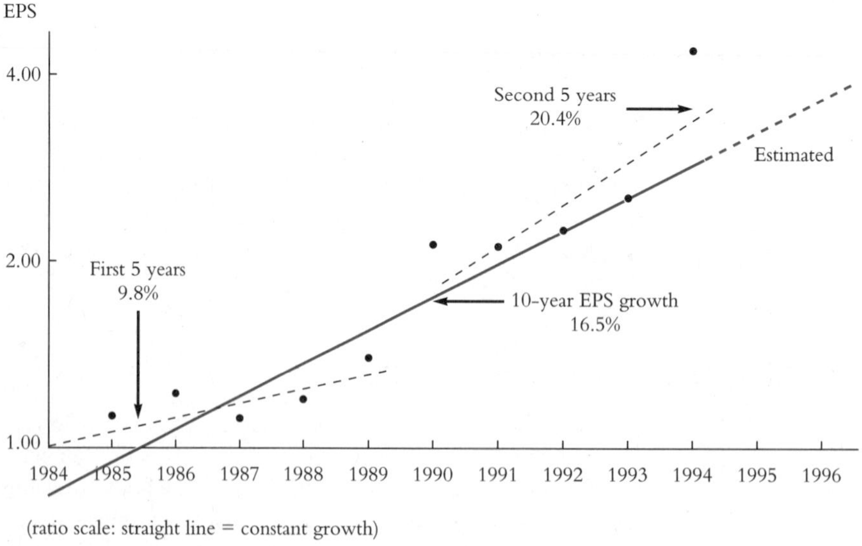

TABLE 7–7 Growth in Earnings per Share

Year	Earnings per Share CSX Corporation (Past 10-year EPS)	Earnings per Share Potlatch Corporation (Past 10-year EPS)
1985	2.92	1.30
1986	2.73	2.49
1987	2.78	2.98
1988	2.86	3.78
1989	3.45	4.56
1990	3.63	3.41
1991	3.81	1.92
1992	4.57	2.20
1993	4.53	1.22
1994	6.00	1.50

FIGURE 7–4 CSX Corporation and Potlatch Corporation Trendlines

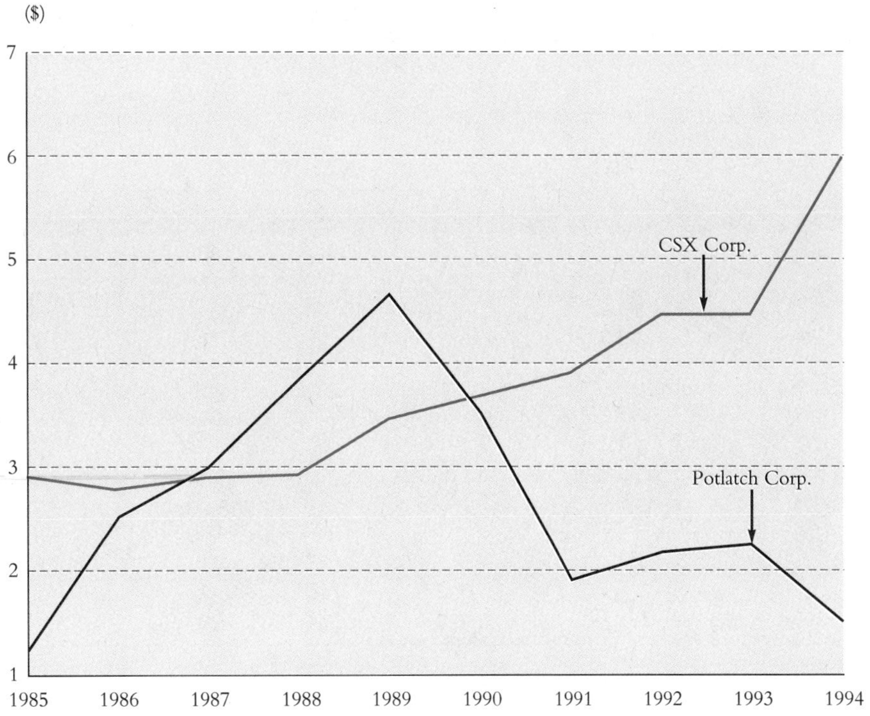

The Income Statement Method

A more process-oriented method of forecasting earnings per share is to start with a sales forecast and create a standardized set of financial statements based on historical relationships. The sales forecast must be accurate if the earnings estimates are to have any significance. This method can be involved and provides a student with a very integrated understanding of the relationships that go into the creation of earnings.

Several important factors are included in this method of forecasting. The analyst is forced to examine profitability and the resultant fluctuations in profit margins before and after taxes. The impact of short-term interest expense and any new bond financing can be factored into the analysis as well as any increase in shares of common stock from new equity financing.

Most analysts use an abbreviated method of forecasting earnings per share. They use a sales forecast combined with after-tax profit margins. For example, let us assume the Hutchins Corporation has a sales and profit margin history as set forth in Table 7–8. The sales have been growing at a 10 percent growth rate, so the forecast is a simple extrapolation. However, the profit margin has fluctuated between 6.7 and 9.1 percent, with 8.2 percent being the average. Common stock outstanding has also grown by an average of 1.4 million shares per year. Given the cyclical nature of the profit margin, 8.2 percent was used for 1995, which is expected to be an average year. Nine percent was used for 1996, a year expected to be economically more robust. Multiplying the profit margin times the estimated sales produced an estimate of earnings that was divided by the number of shares outstanding to find the earnings per share. Once the EPS is found, it still must be plugged into a valuation model to determine an appropriate value.

TABLE 7–8 Abbreviated Income Statement Method—Hutchins Corporation

Year	Sales ($000s)	×	After-Tax Profit Margin	=	Earnings ($000s)	÷	Shares (000s)	=	Earnings per Share
1989	$1,250,000		7.9%		$ 98,750		30,000		$3.29
1990	1,375,000		9.1		125,125		31,500		3.97
1991	1,512,500		8.5		128,562		33,200		3.87
1992	1,663,750		6.7		111,471		35,000		3.18
1993	1,830,125		8.3		151,900		35,200		4.31
1994	2,013,137		8.5		171,117		37,000		4.62
1995e	2,214,452		8.2		181,585		38,400		4.73
1996e	2,435,896		9.0		219,230		39,800		5.50

e = Estimated.

GROWTH STOCKS AND GROWTH COMPANIES

In assessing the worth of an investment, stockholders, analysts, and investors often make reference to such terms as growth stock and growth companies. As part of the process of improving your overall valuation skills, you should have some familiarity with these terms.

A **growth stock** may be defined as the common stock of a company generally growing faster than the economy or market norm. These companies are usually predictable in their earnings growth. Many of the more popular growth stocks, such as 3M, Coca-Cola, and McDonald's, are really in the middle-to-late stages of the expansion phase. They tend to be fully valued and recognized in the marketplace.

Growth companies, on the other hand, are those companies that exhibit rising returns on assets each year and sales that are growing at an increasing rate (growth phase of the life cycle curve). Growth companies may not be as well-known or recognized as growth stocks. Companies that may be considered to be growth companies might be in such industries as cable television, cellular telephones, biotechnology, medical electronics, and so on. These companies are growing very rapidly, and extrapolations of growth trends can be very dangerous if you guess incorrectly. Growth companies have many things in common. Usually, they have developed a proprietary product that is patented and protected from competition like the original Xerox process (now other companies can use the dry process). This market protection allows a high rate of return and generates cash for new-product development.

There are also other indicators of growth potential. Companies should have sales growth greater than the economy by a reasonable margin. Increasing sales should be translated into similar earnings growth, which means consistently stable and high profit margins. Additionally, the earnings growth should show up in earnings per share growth (no dilution of earnings through unproductive stock offers). The firm should have a low labor cost as a percentage of total cost since wages are prone to be inflexible on the downside but difficult to control on the upside.

The biggest error made in searching for growth-oriented companies is that the price may already be too high. By the time you identify the company, so has everyone else, and the price is probably inflated. If the company has one quarter where earnings do not keep up with expectations, the stock price could tumble. The trick is to find growth companies before they are generally recognized in the market, and this requires taking more risk in small companies trading over-the-counter.

ASSETS AS A SOURCE OF STOCK VALUE

Until now, our emphasis has been primarily on earnings and dividends as the source of value. However, in certain industries, asset values may have considerable importance. These assets may take many forms—cash and marketable securities, buildings, land, timber, old movies, oil, and other natural resources. At times, any one of these assets may dominate a firm's value. Furthermore, companies with heavy cash positions are attractive merger and acquisition candidates because of the possibility that a firm with highly liquid assets could be taken over and its own cash used to pay back debt incurred in the takeover.

In the last two decades, natural resources also had an important influence on value. Let's briefly examine this topic.

Natural Resources

Natural resources such as timber, copper, gold, and oil often give a company value even if the assets are not producing an income stream. This is because of the present value of the future income stream that is expected as these resources are used up. Companies such as International Paper, Weyerhaeuser, and other forest product companies have timberlands with market values far in excess of their book values and, in some cases, in excess of their common stock prices.

Oil companies with large supplies of oil in the ground may have to wait 20 years before some of it is pumped, but there may be substantial value there. In the case of natural gas pipeline companies, increasing reserves have changed the way these companies are viewed by the market. They were considered similar to utilities because of their natural gas transmission system, but now they are also being valued based on their hidden assets (energy reserves). The term **hidden assets** refers to assets that are not readily apparent to investors in a traditional sense but that add substantial value to the firm.

Investors should not overlook hidden assets because of naive extrapolation of past data or failure to understand an industry or company. Furthermore, assets do not always show up on the books of a company. They may be fully depreciated, like the movies *Sound of Music, Jaws,* or *Star Wars,* but still have substantial value in the television or VCR market.

SUMMARY

This chapter presents several common stock valuation models that rely on dividends and earnings per share. For the valuation to be accurate, the forecast of earnings and dividends needs to be correct.

Firms can be valued in many ways, and an analyst may use several methods to substantiate estimates. Valuation models based primarily on dividends look at future projections of dividends and the associated present values of the dividends. Assumptions must be made as to whether the dividend growth pattern is constant, accelerating, or decreasing.

Valuation using the earnings method requires that a price-earnings ratio be used as a multiplier of EPS. Price-earnings ratios are influenced by many variables, such as growth, risk, capital structure, dividend policy, level of the market in general, industry factors, and more. A careful study of each situation must be concluded before choosing the appropriate P/E. The price-earnings ratio is a function of two fluctuating variables—earnings and price. The two variables combine to form a ratio that is primarily future oriented. High price-earnings ratios usually indicate positive expectations of the future, whereas low price-earnings ratios connote negative expectations.

To choose a P/E that is reasonable, the analyst must have some idea about the expected growth rate in earnings per share. Investors may find earnings estimates in investment advisory services, in statistical forecasts by brokerage houses, through their own time series statistical regression analysis, or by using the income statement method. Growth stocks were discussed more with the view of alerting the student to what to look for

when trying to identify a growth stock or company than with the concept of valuation. The previously developed methods of valuation can be used on growth stocks as long as care is taken to evaluate the duration and level of growth.

We also presented some basic ideas about the value of companies based not on their earnings or dividend stream but on their assets such as cash or natural resources. Throughout the chapter, it was pointed out that every industry and company is unique. Management, products, organization structure, accounting systems, and philosophy are different for each. The role of an analyst is to understand the intricacies of several related industries and companies so as to enlighten the investing public.

KEY WORDS AND CONCEPTS

DISCUSSION QUESTIONS

1. To determine the required rate of return, K_e, what factor is added to the risk-free rate? (Use Formula 7–2.)
2. What does beta represent?
3. What does the equity risk premium (ERP) represent?
4. How is value interpreted under the dividend valuation model?
5. What two conditions are necessary to use Formula 7–5?
6. How can companies with nonconstant growth be analyzed?
7. In considering P/E ratios for the overall market, what has been the relationship between price-earnings ratios and inflation?
8. What factors besides inflationary considerations and growth factors influence P/E ratios for the general market?
9. For cyclical companies, why might the current P/E ratio be misleading?
10. What two factors are probably most important in influencing the P/E ratio for an *individual stock?* Suggest a number of other factors as well.
11. What type of industries tends to carry the highest P/E ratios?
12. What is the essential characteristic of a least squares trendline?
13. What two elements go into an abbreviated income statement method of forecasting?
14. What is the difference between a growth company and a growth stock?
15. What are some industries in which there are growth companies?
16. How should a firm with natural resources be valued?
17. What is an example of a valuable asset that might not show any "value" on a balance sheet?

PROBLEMS

Equity risk premium

1. If R_F = 6 percent, b = 1.3, and the equity risk premium (ERP) equals 6.5 percent, compute K_e (the required rate of return).

Constant growth dividend model

2. Assume D_1 = \$1.60, K_e = 13 percent, and g = 8 percent. Using Formula 7–5 for the constant growth dividend valuation model, compute P_0.

Constant growth dividend model

3. Using the data from problem 2:
   a. If D_1 and K_e remain the same but g goes up to 9 percent, what will the new stock price be? Briefly explain the reason for the change.
   b. If D_1 and g retain their original value (\$1.60 and 8 percent) but K_e goes up to 15 percent, what will the new stock price be? Briefly explain the reason for the change.

Proof of constant growth dividend model

4. Using the original data from problem 2, find P_0 by following the steps described.
   a. Project dividends for years 1 through 3 (the first year is already given). Round all values that you compute to two places to the right of the decimal point throughout this problem.
   b. Find the present value of the dividends in part *a* with a 13 percent discount rate.
   c. Project the dividend for the fourth year (D_4).
   d. Use Formula 7–5 to find the present value of all future dividends, beginning with the fourth year's dividend. The present value you find will be at the end of the third year (the equivalent of the beginning of the fourth year).
   e. Discount back the value found in part *d* for three years at 13 percent.
   f. Observe that in part *b* you determined the present value of dividends for the first three years and, in part *e,* the present value of an infinite stream after the first three years. Now add these together to get the total present value of the stock.
   g. Compare your answers in part *f* to your answer to problem 2. There may be a slight 5 to 10 cent difference due to rounding. Comment on the relationship between following the procedures in problem 2 and problem 4.

Appropriate use of constant dividend growth model

5. If D_1 = \$3.00, K_e = 10 percent, and g = 12 percent, can Formula 7–5 be used to find P_0? Explain the reasoning behind your answer.

Nonconstant growth dividend model

6. The Fleming Corporation anticipates a nonconstant growth pattern for dividends. Dividends at the end of year 1 are \$2 per share and are expected to grow by 16 percent per year until the end of year 5 (that's four years of growth). After year 5, dividends are expected to grow at 6 percent as far as the company can see into the future. All dividends are to be discounted back to the present at a 10 percent rate (K_e = 10 percent).
   a. Project dividends for years 1 through 5 (the first year is already given as \$2). Round all values that you compute to two places to the right of the decimal point throughout this problem.
   b. Find the present value of the dividends in part *a.*
   c. Project the dividend for the sixth year (D_6).
   d. Use Formula 7–5 to find the present value of all future dividends, beginning with the sixth year's dividend. The present value you find will be at the end of the fifth year. Use Formula 7–5 as follows: $P_5 = D_6/(K_e - g)$.

e. Discount back the value found in part *d* for five years at 10 percent.
f. Add together the values from parts *b* and *e* to determine the present value of the stock.
g. Explain how the two elements in part *f* go together to provide the present value of the stock.

Nonconstant growth dividend model

7. Rework problem 6 with a new assumption—that dividends at the end of the first year are $1.60 and that they will grow at 18 percent per year until the end of the fifth year, at which point they will grow at 6 percent per year for the foreseeable future. Use a discount rate of 12 percent throughout your analysis. Round all values that you compute to two places to the right of the decimal point.

Combined earnings and dividend model

8. J. Jones investment bankers will use a combined earnings and dividend model to determine the value of the Aikman Corporation. The approach they take is basically the same as that in Table 7–2 in the chapter. Estimated earnings per share for the next five years are:

1995	$3.20
1996	3.60
1997	4.10
1998	4.62
1999	5.20

a. If 40% of earnings are paid out in dividends and the discount rate is 11 percent, determine the present value of dividends. Round all values you compute to two places to the right of the decimal point throughout this problem.
b. If it is anticipated that the stock will trade at a P/E of 15 times 1999 earnings, determine the stock's price at that time, and discount back the stock price for five years at 11 percent.
c. Add together parts *a* and *b* to determine the stock price under this combined earnings and dividend model.

P/E ratio analysis

9. Mr. Phillips of Southwest Investment Bankers is evaluating the P/E ratio of Madison Electronic Conveyors (MEC). The firm's P/E is currently 17. With earning per share of $2, the stock price is $34.

The average P/E ratio in the electronic conveyor industry is presently 16. However, MEC has an anticipated growth rate of 18 percent versus an industry average of 12 percent, so 2 will be added to the industry P/E by Mr. Phillips. Also, the operating risk associated with MEC is less than that for the industry because of its long-term contract with American Airlines. For this reason, Mr. Phillips will add a factor of 1.5 to the industry P/E ratio.

The debt-to-total asset ratio is not as encouraging. It is 50 percent, while the industry ratio is 40 percent. In doing his evaluation, Mr. Phillips decides to subtract a factor of 0.5 from the industry P/E ratio. Other ratios, including dividend payout, appear to be in line with the industry, so Mr. Phillips will make no further adjustments along these lines.

However, he is somewhat distressed by the fact that the firm only spent 3 percent of sales on research and development last year; the industry norm is 7 percent. For this reason, he will subtract a factor of 1.5 from the industry P/E ratio.

Despite the relatively low research budget, Mr. Phillips observes that the firm has just hired two of the top executives from a competitor in the industry. He decides to add a factor of 1 to the industry P/E ratio because of this.

a. Determine the P/E ratio for MEC based on Mr. Phillips's analysis.

b. Multiply this by earnings per share, and comment on whether you think the stock might possibly be under- or overvalued in the marketplace at its current P/E and price.

P/E ratio analysis

10. Refer to Table 7–4. Assume that because of unusually bright long-term prospects, analysts determine that Smucker's P/E ratio in 1995 should be 60 percent above the average high S&P 500 P/E ratio for the last 10 years. (Carry your calculation of the P/E ratio two places to the right of the decimal point in this problem.) What would the stock price be based on previously projected earnings per share of $1.45 (for 1995)?

P/E ratio analysis

11. Refer to problem 10, and assume new circumstances cause the analysts to reduce the anticipated P/E in 1995 to 10 percent below the average low S&P 500 P/E for the last 10 years. Furthermore, projected earnings per share are reduced to $1.16. What would the stock price be?

Income statement method of forecasting

12. Security analysts following Health Sciences, Inc., use a simplified income statement method of forecasting. Assume that 1995 sales are $30 million and are expected to grow by 11 percent in 1996 and 1997. The after-tax profit margin is projected at 6.1 percent in 1996 and 5.9 percent in 1997. The number of shares outstanding are projected to be 700,000 in 1996 and 710,000 in 1997. Project earnings per share for 1996 and 1997. Round to two places to the right of the decimal point throughout the problem.

P/E ratio and price

13. The average P/E ratio for the industry that Health Science, Inc., is in is 14. If the company has a P/E ratio 20 percent higher than the industry average of 14 in 1996 and 25 percent higher than the industry ratio (also of 14) in 1997:

a. Indicate the appropriate P/E ratios for the firm in 1996 and 1997.

b. Combine this with the earnings per share data in problem 12 to determine the anticipated stock price for 1996 and 1997. Round to two places throughout the problem.

P/E ratio and price

14. Relating to problems 12 and 13, assume you wish to determine the probable price range in 1997 if the P/E ratio is between 16 and 20. What is the price range?

CFA MATERIAL

The following material contains sample questions and solutions from a prior Level I CFA exam. While the terminology is slightly different from that in this text, you can still view the skills necessary for the CFA exam.

CFA Exam Question

3. As a firm operating in a mature industry, Arbot Industries is expected to maintain a constant dividend payout ratio and constant growth rate of earnings for the foreseeable future. Earnings were $4.50 per share in the recently completed fiscal year. The dividend payout ratio has been a constant 55 percent in recent years and is expected to remain so. Arbot's return on equity (ROE) is expected to remain at 10 percent in the future, and you require an 11 percent return on the stock.

a. Using the constant growth dividend discount model, *calculate* the current value of Arbot common stock. *Show* your calculations.

After an aggressive acquisition and marketing program, it now appears that Arbot's earnings per share and ROE will grow rapidly over the next two years. You are aware that the dividend discount model can be useful in estimating the value of common stock even when the assumption of constant growth does not apply.

b. *Calculate* the current value of Arbot's common stock using the dividend discount model assuming Arbot's dividend will grow at a 15 percent rate for the next two years, returning in the third year to the historical growth rate and continuing to grow at the historical rate for the foreseeable future. *Show* your calculations.

Solution: Question 3—Morning Session (I–91) (15 points)

a. Constant growth (single-stage) dividend discount model:

$$\text{Value}_0 = \frac{D_1}{K - g}$$

where:

D_1 = Next year's dividend

K = Required rate of return

g = Constant growth rate

$D_1 = (\text{EPS}_0)(1 + g)(\text{P/O}) = (4.50)(1.045)(0.55) = \$2.59$

K = given at 11% or 0.11

$g = (\text{ROE})(1 - \text{P/O}) = (0.10)(1 - 0.55) = 0.045$

$$\text{Value}_0 = \frac{\$2.59}{11 - 0.045} = \frac{\$2.59}{0.065} = \$39.85$$

b. Multistage dividend discount model (where $g_1 = 0.15$ and g_2 is 0.045):

$$\text{Value}_0 = \frac{D_1}{(1 + K)} + \frac{D_2}{(1 + K)^2} + \frac{\text{D}_3/(\text{K} - g_2)}{(1 + K)^2}$$

$$D_1 = (\text{EPS}_0)(1 + g_1)(\text{P/O}) = (4.50)(1.15)(0.55) = \$2.85$$

$$D_2 = (D_1)(1 + g_1) = (\$2.85/(1.15) = \$3.27$$

$$K = \text{given at } 11\% \text{ or } 0.11$$

$$g_2 = 0.045$$

$$D_3 = (D_2)(1 + g_2) = (\$3.27)(1.045) = \$3.42$$

$$\text{Value}_0 = \frac{\$2.85}{(1.11)} + \frac{\$3.27}{(1.11)^2} + \frac{\$3.42/(0.11 - 0.045)}{(1.11)^2}$$

$$= \frac{\$2.85}{(1.11)} + \frac{\$3.27}{(1.11)^2} + \frac{\$52.62}{(1.11)^2}$$

$$= \$2.56 + \$2.65 + \$42.71$$

$$= \$47.92$$

CFA Exam Question

7. The constant growth dividend discount model can be used both for the valuation of companies and for the estimation of the long-term total return of a stock.

Assume: $20 = Price of a stock today
8% = Expected growth rate of dividends
$0.60 = Annual dividend one year forward

a. Using *only* the above data, *compute* the expected long-term total return on the stock using the constant growth dividend discount model. *Show* calculations.
b. *Briefly discuss three* disadvantages of the constant growth dividend discount model in its application to investment analysis.
c. *Identify three* alternative methods to the dividend discount model for the valuation of companies.

Solution: Question 7—Morning Session (I–90)(10 points)

(Reading reference: Cohen, Zinbarg, & Ziekel, Chapter 10)

a. The dividend discount model is: $P = \dfrac{d}{k-g}$

where:

P = Value of the stock today
d = Annual dividend one year forward
k = Discount rate
g = Constant dividend growth rate

$$\text{Solving for k: } (k - g) = \frac{d}{p}; \text{ then } k = \frac{d}{p} + g$$

So k becomes the estimate for the long-term return of the stock.

$$k = \frac{\$0.60}{\$20.00} + 8\% = 3\% + 8\% = 11\%$$

b. Many professional investors shy away from the dividend discount framework analysis due to its many inherent complexities.
   (1) The model cannot be used where companies pay very small or no dividends and speculation on the level of future dividends could be futile. (Dividend policy may be arbitrary.)
   (2) The model presumes one can accurately forecast long-term growth of earnings (dividends) of a company. Such forecasts become quite tenuous beyond two years out. (A short-term valuation may be more pertinent.)
   (3) For the variable growth models, small differences in g for the first several years produce large differences in the valuations.
   (4) The correct k or the discount rate is difficult to estimate for a specific company as an infinite number of factors affect it that are themselves difficult to forecast, e.g., inflation, riskless rate of return, risk premium on stocks, and other uncertainties.
   (5) The model is not definable when $g > k$ as with growth companies, so it is not applicable to a large number of companies.
   (6) Where a company has low or negative earnings per share or has a poor balance sheet, the ability to continue the dividend is questionable.
   (7) The components of income can differ substantially, reducing comparability.

c. Three alternative methods of valuation would include: (1) price-earnings ratios; (2) price-asset value ratios (including market and book asset values); (3) price-sales ratios; (4) liquidation or breakup value; and (5) price-cash flow ratios.

THE WALL STREET JOURNAL PROJECT

Chapter 7 presents the required rate of return K_e for an individual common stock as follows:

$$K_e = R_F + b\,(K_M - R_F)$$
$$= R_F + b\,(\text{ERP})$$

1. a. What would be the required return for J. M. Smucker using the one-year yield on a Treasury bill for R_F, the beta for J. M. Smucker as found in the *Value Line Survey,** and an equity risk premium of 6 percent. Find R_F in *The Wall Street Journal* in Section C under "Treasury Bonds, Notes & Bills." Use the Ask Yield (last column) for the last Treasury bill listed.

   b. Plug your numbers for Smucker into the dividend discount model, and determine the market value of J. M. Smucker. Use the expected annual dividend shown in *Value Line* for the next year and a growth rate of 10 percent:

$$P_0 = D_1/(K_e - g)$$

---

*Beta is found in the upper left corner of the *Value Line* data sheet for Smucker.

c. Look up the common stock price of Smucker in *The Wall Street Journal,* and determine whether Smucker common stock is undervalued or overvalued based on your analysis. Would you buy or sell?

U.S. EQUITIES ONFLOPPY EXERCISES

Please use your U.S. Equities OnFloppy software and manual to complete the following exercises.

1. a. Determine K_e, the required rate of return, for Teco Energy Inc. Use the User Fields option of U.S. Equities OnFloppy to calculate the required rate of return using Formula 7–2 from Chapter 7. Use 5 percent for R_F, and assume $(K_M - R_F)$; i.e., the equity risk premium is 6 percent. The equation thus becomes $K_e = 0.05 + \text{beta}\ (0.06)$.

   b. Use the User Fields option to enter the constant growth model, $P_o = D_o\ (1 + g)/(K_e - g)$. Use the dividend for the last full year, Div 1, for D_o. Use the compound growth rate of total earnings over the past five years for *g,* EA%C15, and K_e from part *a* to estimate a price for Teco Energy Inc. Compare this estimate with the actual price of Teco Energy Inc.

2. The constant growth model is appropriate only when two conditions are met. The two conditions are (*a*) the growth rate must be constant and (*b*) K_e, the required rate of return, must be greater than *g,* the growth rate. Use the Display option of U.S. Equities OnFloppy to analyze the degree to which these two conditions are met for the companies in the Grocery Stores industry, SIC = 541*. Specifically, (1) analyze the percentage change in total revenue by year for the five years for which data are available, and (2) compare K_e, using the formula specified in part *a,* to *g* as measured by the compound annual percentage change in total revenue from five years ago to the last full year for which data is available, EA%C15.

3. a. Select the firms in the Computer and Office Equipment industry (SIC 357*) that have (1) positive EPS for the last 12 months and the last fiscal year; (2) EPS the last full year greater than the prior year; (3) EPS two years ago greater than three years ago, that is, EPS2 > EPS3; and (4) a greater percentage annual increase in EPS to the last full year than the previous percentage annual increase, that is, EPS%12 > EPS%23.

   b. Determine the high P/E ratio and the low P/E ratio over the previous 12 months. That is, use the User Fields option to define HIPE = HPR/EPS and LOPE = LPR/EPS.

   c. Use the User Fields option to enter a formula to project the trailing 12-month EPS figure ahead at the compound annual growth in EPS over the previous two full years (EPS%C13).

   d. Multiple the high P/E ratio and the low P/E ratio by the projected EPS to get an estimated high and low price.

   e. Prepare a report using the Display option that shows the estimated high and low prices versus the actual price for all of the firms selected in part *a.*

SELECTED REFERENCES

Considerations in Valuing Securities

Bierman, Harold, Jr. "Accounting for Valuation and Evaluation." *The Journal of Portfolio Management,* Spring 1994, pp. 64–67.

Fergeson, Robert. "How to Find Next Year's Best Performing Stock." *Financial Analysts Journal,* March–April 1994, p. 10.

Loderer, Claudio F.; Dennis P. Sheehan; and Gregory P. Kadlec. "The Pricing of Equity Offerings." *Journal of Financial Economics,* March 1991, pp. 35–57.

Miller, Merton, and Franco Modigliani. "Dividend Policy, Growth, and the Valuation of Shares." *Journal of Business,* October 1961, pp. 411–33.

Muller, Frederick. "Equity Securities Analysis in the U.S." *Financial Analysts Journal,* January–February 1994, pp. 6–9.

Tobin, James. "A Mean-Variance Approach to Fundamental Valuations." *Journal of Portfolio Management,* Fall 1984, pp. 26–33.

Price-Earnings Ratio Considerations

Basu, S. "Investment Performance of Common Stocks in Relation to Their Price-Earnings Ratios: A Test of the Efficient Market Hypothesis." *Journal of Finance,* June 1977, pp. 663–82.

Beaver, William, and Dale Morse. "What Determines Price-Earnings Ratios?" *Financial Analysts Journal,* July–August 1978, pp. 65–76.

Good, Walter R. "When Are Price/Earnings Ratios Too High—or Too Low?" *Financial Analysts Journal,* July–August 1991, pp. 9–12.

Leibowitz, Martin L., and Stanley Kogelman. "The Growth Illusion: The P/E Cost of Earnings Growth." *Financial Analysts Journal,* March–April 1994, pp. 36–48.

Earnings Forecast

Klemkosky, Robert C., and William P. Miller. "When Forecasting Earnings, It Pays to Be Right!" *Journal of Portfolio Management,* Summer 1984, pp. 13–18.

Moses, O. Douglas. "Cash Flow Signals and Analysts' Earnings Forecast Revisions." *Journal of Business, Finance and Accounting,* November 1991, pp. 807–32.

Growth Stocks

Mao, James C. T. "The Valuation of Growth Stocks: The Investment Opportunities Approach." *Journal of Finance,* March 1966, pp. 95–102.

Statman, Meir. "Growth Opportunities vs. Growth Stocks." *Journal of Portfolio Management,* Spring 1984, pp. 70–74.

8

Financial Statement Analysis

Financial statements present a numerical picture of a company's financial and operating health. Since each company is different, an analyst needs to examine the financial statements for industry characteristics as well as for differences in accounting methods. The major financial statements are the balance sheet, the income statement, and the statement of cash flows. A very helpful long-term financial overview also is provided by a 5- or 10-year summary statement found in the corporate annual report. One must further remember that the footnotes to these statements are an integral part of the statements and provide a wealth of in-depth explanatory information. More depth can often be found in additional reports such as the 10-K filed with the Securities and Exchange Commission and obtainable on request (free) from most companies.

Fundamental analysis depends on variables internal to the company, and the corporate financial statements are one way of measuring fundamental value and risk. Financial statement analysis should be combined with economic and industry analysis before a final judgment is made to purchase or sell a specific security. Chapter 7 presented methods of valuation that used forecasts of dividends and earnings per share. Earnings per share combined with an estimated price-earnings ratio was also used to get a future price. Careful study of financial statements provides the analyst with much of the necessary information to forecast earnings and dividends, to judge the quality of earnings, and to determine financial and operating risk.

THE MAJOR FINANCIAL STATEMENTS

In the first part of this chapter, we examine the three basic types of financial statements—the income statement, the balance sheet, and the statement of cash flows—with particular attention paid to the interrelationships among these three measurement devices. In the rest of the chapter, ratio analysis is presented in detail, and deficiencies of financial statements are discussed along with the role of the security analyst in interpreting financial statements.

Income Statement

The **income statement** is the major device for measuring the profitability of a firm over a period of time. An example of the income statement is presented in Table 8–1 for the Coca-Cola Company. Note that the income statement is for a defined period, whether it be one month, three months, or a year. The statement is presented in a stair-step fashion so that we may examine the profit or loss after each type of expense item is deducted.

For 1993, the Coca-Cola Company had net operating revenues (sales) of approximately $14 billion. After subtracting the cost of goods sold, and selling, administrative, and general expenses, the firm's operating income was $3.1 billion. Because of a high level of cash, cash equivalents, and marketable securities during 1993, Coca-Cola had interest income that was 85.7 percent of its interest expense. This is an uncommonly high ratio of interest income to interest expense, but this pattern occurred in all three years shown in the consolidated income statements. An analyst might conclude that Coca-Cola has a policy of keeping a high level of cash as a current asset. Coca-Cola also had income of $91 million from equity interests in other publicly held companies.

TABLE 8–1 Coca-Cola Income Statement

THE COCA-COLA COMPANY AND SUBSIDIARIES
Consolidated Statements of Income
for the Years Ended December 31, 1991, 1992, 1993
(Dollars in thousands except per share data)

Year Ended December 31,	1993	1992	1991
—Net operating revenues	$13,957,000	$13,074,000	$11,572,000
Cost of goods	5,160,000	5,055,000	4,649,000
Gross profit	8,797,000	8,019,000	6,923,000
Selling, administrative, and general expenses	5,695,000	5,249,000	4,604,000
—Operating income	3,102,000	2,770,000	2,319,000
—Interest income	144,000	164,000	175,000
—Interest expense	168,000	171,000	192,000
—Equity income	91,000	65,000	40,000
Other income (deductions)—net	4,000	(82000)	41,000
Gain on issuance of stock by subsidiaries	12,000	—	—
—Income before income taxes and changes in accounting principles	3,185,000	2,746,000	2,383,000
Income taxes	997,000	863,000	765,000
—Income before changes in accounting principles	2,188,000	1,883,000	1,618,000
Transition effects in accounting principles			
Postemployment benefits	(12,000)	—	—
Postretirement benefits other than pensions			
Consolidated operations	—	(146,000)	—
Equity investments	—	(73,000)	—
Net income	2,176,000	1,664,000	1,618,000
Preferred stock dividends	—	—	1
Net income available to common shareholders	2,176,000	1,664,000	1,617,000
—Income (loss) per common share			
—Before changes in accounting principles	$1.68	$1.43	$1.21
Transition effects on changes in accounting principles			
Postemployment benefits	(0.01)	—	—
Postretirement benefits other than pensions			
Consolidated operations	—	(0.11)	—
Equity investments	—	(0.06)	—
—Net income per common share	$1.67	$1.26	$1.21
—Average common shares outstanding (in thousands)	1,302,000	1,317,000	1,333,000

Source: *The Coca-Cola Company Annual Report*, 1993, p. 56.

Altogether, Coca-Cola reported income from continuing operations before taxes and changes in accounting principles of approximately $3.2 billion. After paying taxes of almost $1 billion, net income available to common stockholders was approximately $2.2 billion.

In 1992, the total net income per share was $1.43, before $0.17 in charges from postretirement benefits. In comparing 1993 earnings per share, it would look as though Coca-Cola had a much better year than it really did because EPS rose from $1.26 to $1.67 instead of from $1.43 to $1.68. Since the analyst is primarily concerned with income from

continuing operations as an indicator of future earnings, it would make more sense to compare the $1.43 in 1992 to the $1.68 from continuing operations in 1993. If we compare the year 1991 to 1992, it also makes more sense to compare the $1.21 EPS to $1.43. Since the postretirement benefits are one-time nonrecurring charges, we minimize their importance in comparisons.

Coca-Cola has been repurchasing shares of common stock. Notice how shares outstanding in computing earnings per share (last row) have fallen from 1.333 billion in 1991 to 1.302 billion in 1993. Generally, shares outstanding can be calculated by taking issued shares on the balance sheet and subtracting treasury stock. Since shares outstanding for annual purposes are usually computed on an averaging basis, it is likely that fewer shares were outstanding at 1993 year-end. In forecasting earnings, the analyst also needs to know how long the company's strategy of repurchasing shares will continue.

Are these good income figures or bad? As we shall see later, the analyst's interpretation of the numbers will depend on historical figures, on industry data, and on the relationship of income to balance sheet items such as assets and net worth.

Balance Sheet

The **balance sheet** indicates what the firm owns and how these assets are financed in the form of liabilities or ownership interest. While the income statement purports to show the profitability of the firm, the balance sheet delineates the firm's holdings and obligations. Together, these statements are intended to answer two questions: How much did the firm make or lose, and what is a measure of its worth? A balance sheet for the Coca-Cola Company is presented in Table 8–2.

Note that the balance sheet is given at one point in time, in this case December 31, 1993. It does not represent the result of transactions for a specific month, quarter, or year but rather is a cumulative chronicle of all transactions that have affected the corporation since its inception. This is in contrast to the income statement, which measures results only over a short, quantifiable period. Generally, balance sheet items are stated on an original cost basis rather than at market value.

The Coca-Cola Company was chosen for analysis because of its product diversification, its international scope, and its well-known soft drinks such as Coca-Cola, Tab, Sprite, and Diet Coke. Its food division's major product is Minute Maid orange juice. This division accounted for 12.7 percent of revenues but only 4.1 percent of operating income in 1993. Coca-Cola began a major restructuring in 1985 by spinning off wholly owned subsidiaries but retaining minority interests in several of the newly owned public firms. In a major sale in 1989, Coca-Cola sold Columbia Pictures to Sony, the Japanese entertainment giant. This sale provided several billion dollars in cash, which Coca-Cola used for stock repurchases over the following years.

Companies where Coca-Cola still holds minority interests show up in the balance sheet under the section "Investments and other assets." These companies are Coca-Cola Enterprises, Inc., Coca-Cola Amatil Limited, and other assets that are principally bottling companies. The Coca-Cola Company reports the earnings of these companies using the equity method of reporting. In 1993, Coca-Cola reported $91 million in equity income, which represented their percentage of earnings from their minority owned investments.

TABLE 8–2 Coca-Cola Balance Sheet

COCA-COLA COMPANY AND SUBSIDIARIES
Consolidated Balance Sheets
for the Years Ended December 31, 1992 and 1993
(Dollars in thousands except per share data)

Assets	1993	1992
Current		
Cash and cash equivalents	$ 998,000	$ 956,000
Marketable securities, at cost (approximates market)	80,000	107,000
Trade accounts receivable, less allowances of	1,078,000	1,063,000
$39,000 in 1993 and $33,000 in 1992	1,210,000	1,055,000
Finance subsidiary—receivables	33,000	31,000
Inventories	1,049,000	1,019,000
Prepaid expenses and other assets	1,064,000	1,080,000
Total current assets	4,434,000	4,248,000
—Investments and other assets		
Investments		
Coca-Cola Enterprises, Inc.	498,000	518,000
Coca-Cola Amatil Limited	592,000	548,000
Other, principally bottling companies	1,125,000	1,097,000
Finance subsidiary—receivables	226,000	95,000
Long-term receivables and other assets	868,000	637,000
	3,309,000	2,895,000
Property, plant, and equipment		
Land	197,000	203,000
Buildings and improvements	1,616,000	1,529,000
Machinery and equipment	3,380,000	3,137,000
Containers	403,000	374,000
	5,596,000	5,243,000
Less allowance for depreciation	1,867,000	1,717,000
Fixed assets	3,729,000	3,526,000
Goodwill and other intangible assets	549,000	383,000
Total assets	12,021,000	11,052,000

Source: *The Coca-Cola Annual Report*, 1993, pp. 54–55.

Statement of Cash Flows

In November 1987, the accounting profession designated the **statement of cash flows** as the third required financial statement, along with the balance sheet and income statement. Referred to as Financial Accounting Standards Board (FASB) *Statement No. 95,* it replaced the old statement of changes in financial position (and the sources and uses of funds statement).

TABLE 8–2 Coca-Cola Balance Sheet *(concluded)*

	1993	1992
Liabilities and shareholders' equity		
Current liabilities		
Accounts payable and accrued expenses	$ 2,217,000	$ 2,253,000
Loans and notes payable	1,409,000	1,967,000
Finance subsidiary	244,000	105,000
Current maturities of long-term debt	19,000	15,000
Accrued taxes	1,282,000	963,000
Total current liabilities	5,171,000	5,303,000
Long-term debt	1,428,000	1,120,000
Other liabilities	725,000	659,000
Deferred income taxes	113,000	82,000
Total liabilities	$ 7,437,000	$ 7,164,000
Shareholders' equity		
Common stock $.25 par value—		
Authorized: 2,800,000,000 shares; Issued: 1,703,526,299 shares in 1993; 1,696,202,840 shares in 1992	$ 426,000	$ 424,000
Capital surplus	1,086,000	871,000
Reinvested earnings	9,458,000	8,165,000
Unearned compensation related to outstanding restricted stock	(85,000)	(100,000)
Foreign currency translation adjustment	(420,000)	(271,000)
	10,465,000	9,089,000
Less treasury stock, at cost (406,072,817 common shares in 1993; 389,431,622 common shares in 1992)	5,881,000	5,201,000
Stockholders' equity	4,584,000	3,888,000
Total liabilities and shareholders' equity	$12,021,000	$11,052,000

The purpose of the statement of cash flows is to emphasize the critical nature of cash flow to the operations of the firm. Cash flow generally represents cash or cash-equivalent items that can easily be converted into cash within 90 days (such as a money market fund).

The income statement and balance sheet are normally based on the accrual method of accounting, in which revenues and expenses are recognized as they occur, rather than when cash actually changes hands. For example, a $100,000 credit sale may be made in December 1995 and shown as revenue for that year—despite the fact the cash payment would not be received until March 1996. When the actual payment is finally received under accrual accounting, no revenue is recognized (it has already been accounted for previously). The primary advantage of accrual accounting is that it allows us to match revenues and expenses in the period in which they occur to appropriately measure profit; but a disadvantage is that adequate attention is not directed to the actual cash flow position of the firm.

One can think of situations in which a firm made a \$1 million profit on a transaction but will not receive the actual cash payment for two years. Or perhaps the \$1 million profit is in cash, but the firm increased its asset purchases by \$3 million (a new building). If you merely read the income statement, you might assume the firm is in a strong \$1 million cash position; but if you go beyond the income statement to cash flow considerations, you would observe the firm is \$2 million short of funds for the period.

As a last example, a firm might show a \$100,000 loss on the income statement; but if it had a depreciation expense write-off of \$150,000, the firm would actually have \$50,000 in cash. Since depreciation is a noncash deduction, the \$150,000 deduction in the income statement for depreciation can be added back to net income to determine cash flow.

The statement of cash flows addresses these issues by translating income statement and balance sheet data into cash flow information. A corporation that has \$1 million in accrual-based accounting profits can determine whether it can actually afford to pay a cash dividend to stockholders, buy new equipment, or undertake new projects. In the cash-tight era of today, cash flow analysis has taken on a very special meaning.

The three primary sections of the statement of cash flows are:

1. Cash flows from operating activities.
2. Cash flows from investing activities.
3. Cash flows from financing activities.

After each of these sections is completed, the results are added to compute the net increase or decrease in cash flow for the corporation. An example of this process is shown in Figure 8–1. This statement informs us about how the cash was created (operations, investing, financing), where it was spent, and the net increase or decrease of cash for the entire year.

Let's look at Coca-Cola's statement of cash flows in Table 8–3 on page 218. Cash provided from operating activities (top one-third of the statement) was \$2.5 billion in 1993. The major items were net income, and depreciation and amortization. Second, investing activities used \$885 million of cash.

In 1993, financing activities used \$1.54 billion of cash. Coca-Cola issued new debt to raise \$445 million but then paid off \$567 million of debt, retired common stock valued at \$680 million, sold new common stock for \$145 million (mostly for corporate stock options), and paid dividends of \$883 million.

An analysis of this statement can pinpoint many strengths or weaknesses in a company's cash flow. We can see that Coca-Cola has made some major moves within the last three years. The company has a strong positive cash flow even after repurchasing large amounts of its common stock.

If we add together cash flow from operating, investing, and financing activities, we arrive at the following (in millions):

Net cash provided by operating activities	\$ 2,508
Net cash provided by (used in) investing activities	(885)
Net cash used in financing activities	(1,540)
	\$ 83

FIGURE 8–1 Illustration of Concepts behind Statement of Cash Flows

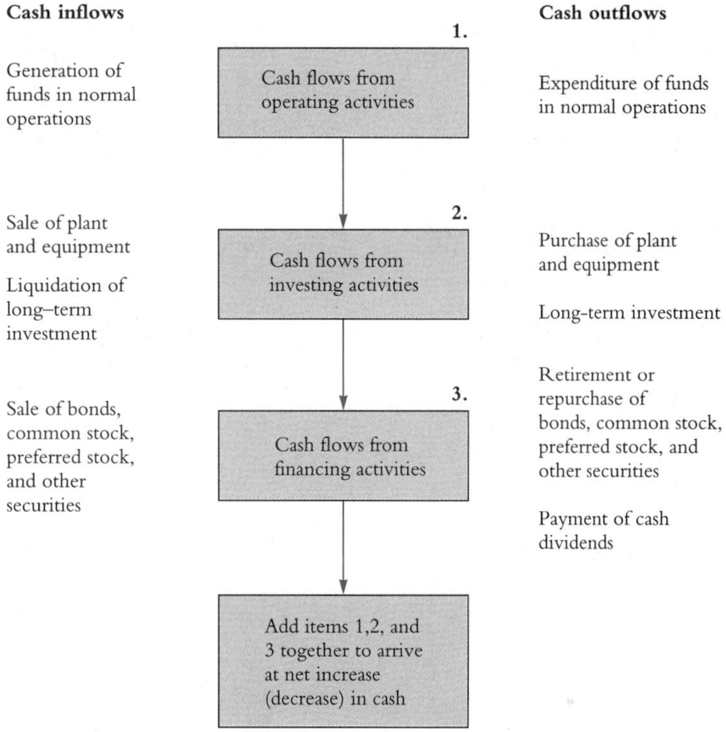

From this $83 million figure, we subtract $41 million to indicate the effect of exchange rate changes on cash and cash equivalents. This leaves Coca-Cola with a net increase in cash and cash equivalents of $42 million in 1993, as shown on the third line from the bottom of Table 8–3 on page 218. This figure can be added to the $956 million balance at the beginning of the year (1993) to arrive at a balance at the end of the year of $998 million. This number is also the same as the cash balance shown on the first line of the balance sheet for 1993 as previously presented in Table 8–2.

Many companies are not as fortunate as Coca-Cola in generating cash. For example, a number of hard-pressed firms in the energy industry in the 1980s and early 1990s had insufficient earnings to pay dividends or to maintain or expand long-term asset commitments. In such cases, short-term borrowing is required to meet long-term needs. This can lead to a reduction of short-term working capital and a dangerous operating position.

TABLE 8–3 Coca-Cola Statement of Cash Flows

THE COCA-COLA COMPANY AND SUBSIDIARIES
Consolidated Statements of Changes in Financial Position (Dollars in thousands)

Year Ended December 31,	1993	1992	1991
Operating activities:			
Net income	$2,176,000	$1,664,000	$1,618,000
Transition effects of changes in accounting principles	12,000	219,000	0
Depreciation and amortization	360,000	322,000	261,000
Deferred income taxes	(62,000)	(27,000)	(94,000)
Equity income, net of dividends	(35,000)	(30,000)	(16,000)
Foreign currency adjustments	9,000	24,000	66,000
Gain on sale of businesses and investments before income taxes	(84,000)	0	(35,000)
Other noncash items	78,000	103,000	33,000
Net change in operating assets and liabilities	54,000	(43,000)	251,000
Net cash provided by operating activities	2,508,000	2,232,000	2,084,000
Investing activities:			
Decrease (increase) in marketable securities	29,000	(52,000)	3,000
Additions to finance subsidiary receivables	(177,000)	(54,000)	(210,000)
Collections of finance subsidiary receivables	44,000	254,000	52,000
Purchases of investments and other assets	(816,000)	(717,000)	(399,000)
Proceeds from disposals of investments and other assets	621,000	247,000	180,000
Purchase of property, plant, and equipment	(800,000)	(1,083,000)	(792,000)
Proceeds from disposals of property, plant, and equipment	312,000	47,000	44,000
All other investment activities	(98,000)	(1,000)	(2,000)
Net cash provided by (used in) investing activities	(885,000)	(1,359,000)	(1,124,000)
Net cash provided by operations after reinvestment	1,623,000	873,000	960,000
Financing activities:			
Issuances of debt	445,000	1,381,000	990,000
Payment of debt	(567,000)	(432,000)	(1,246,000)
Preferred stock redeemed	0	0	(75,000)
Common stock issued	145,000	131,000	39,000
Purchases of common stock for treasury	(680,000)	(1,259,000)	(399,000)
Dividends (common and preferred)	(883,000)	(738,000)	(640,000)
Net cash used in financing activities	(1,540,000)	(917,000)	(1,331,000)
Effect of exchange rate changes on cash and cash equivalents	(41,000)	(58,000)	—
Cash and cash equivalents:			
Net increase (decrease) during the year	42,000	(102,000)	(371,000)
Balance at beginning of year	956,000	1,058,000	1,429,000
Balance at end of year	$998,000	$956,000	$1,058,000

Source: *The Coca-Cola Company Annual Report*, 1993, p. 57.

KEY FINANCIAL RATIOS FOR THE SECURITY ANALYST

We have just summarized the three major financial statements that will be the basis of your analysis in this section emphasizing financial ratios. Ratio analysis brings together balance sheet and income statement data to permit a better understanding of the firm's past and current health, which will aid you in forecasting the future outlook.

Ratio Analysis

Ratios are used in much of our daily life. We buy cars based on miles per gallon, we evaluate baseball players by their earned run averages and batting averages and basketball players by field goal and foul shooting percentages, and so on. These are all ratios constructed to judge comparative performance. Financial ratios serve a similar purpose, but you must know what is being measured to construct a ratio and to understand the significance of the resultant number.

Financial ratios are used to weigh and evaluate the operating performance and capital structure of the firm. While an absolute value such as earnings of $50,000 or accounts receivable of $100,000 may appear satisfactory, its acceptability can be measured only in relation to other values.

For example, are earnings of $50,000 actually good? If a company earned $50,000 on $500,000 of sales (10 percent profit-margin ratio), that might be quite satisfactory, whereas earnings of $50,000 on $5 million could be disappointing (a meager 1 percent return). After we have computed the appropriate ratio, we must compare our firm's results to the achievement of similar firms in the industry as well as to our own firm's past performance. Even then, this "number-crunching" process is not always adequate because we are forced to supplement our financial findings with an evaluation of company management, physical facilities, and numerous other factors.

Ratio analysis will not uncover "gold mines" for the analyst. It is more like a physical exam at the doctor's office. You hope you are all right, but if not, you may be content to know what is wrong and what to do about it. Just as with medical illness where some diseases are easier to cure than others, the same is true of financial illness. The analyst is the doctor. He or she determines the illness and keeps track of management to see if they can administer the cure. Sometimes ailing companies can be very good values. Penn-Central went into bankruptcy, and its common stock could have been purchased at $2 per share for several years. In the 1990s, Penn-Central traded in the $17 to $27 range after a three-for-two stock split in 1982 and a two-for-one stock split in 1988. Chrysler and Lockheed were both on the brink of bankruptcy in the 1970s until the government made guaranteed loans available. Both Chrysler and Lockheed could have been bought at less than $3 per share. After recovering and generating higher stock prices, they both split their common stock. These were all sick companies that returned to health, and any investor willing to take such great risk would have been well rewarded.

Bankruptcy Studies

In a sense, ratio analysis protects an investor from picking continual losers more than it guarantees picking winners. Several studies have used ratios as predictors of financial failure. The most notable studies are by William Beaver and Edward Altman. Beaver

found that ratios of failing firms signal failure as much as five years ahead of bankruptcy, and as bankruptcy approaches, the ratios deteriorate more rapidly, with the greatest deterioration in the last year. The Beaver studies also found (*a*) "Investors recognize and adjust to the new solvency positions of failing firms," and (*b*) "The price changes of the common stocks act as if investors rely upon ratios as a basis for their assessments, and impound the ratio information in the market prices."[1]

The first Altman research study indicated that five ratios combined were 95 percent accurate in predicting failure one year ahead of bankruptcy and were 72 percent accurate two years ahead of failure, with the average lead time for the ratio signal being 20 months.[2] Altman developed a Z score that was an index developed through multiple discriminate analysis that could predict failure. Altman modified and improved his model's accuracy even further by increasing the number of ratios to seven.[3] This service is currently sold to institutional investors by Zeta Services Inc. The Z (zeta) score relies on the following variables:

1. Retained earnings/total assets (cumulative profitability).
2. Standard deviation of operating income/total assets (measure of earnings stability during the last 10 years).
3. Earnings before interest and taxes/total assets (productivity of operating assets).
4. Earnings before interest and taxes/interest (leverage ratio, interest coverage).
5. Current assets/current liabilities (liquidity ratio).
6. Market value of common stock/book value of equity (a leverage ratio).
7. Total assets (proxy for size of the firm).

The greater the firm's bankruptcy potential, the lower its Z score. The ratios were not equally significant, but together they separated the companies into a correct bankruptcy group and nonbankruptcy group a high percentage of the time. Retained earnings/total assets has the heaviest weight in the analysis, and leverage is also very important. In the next section, we present six classifications of ratios that are helpful to the analyst. Many more would be used, but these represent the most widely used measures.

Classification System

We divide 20 significant ratios into six primary groupings:

A. Profitability ratios:
   1. Operating margin.
   2. After-tax profit margin.

---

[1] William H. Beaver, "Market Prices, Financial Ratios, and the Prediction of Failure," *Journal of Accounting Research,* Autumn 1968, p. 192.

[2] Edward I. Altman, "Financial Ratios, Discriminant Analysis, and the Prediction of Corporate Bankruptcy," *Journal of Finance,* September 1968, pp. 589–609.

[3] Edward I. Altman, *Corporate Financial Distress* (New York: John Wiley & Sons, 1983).

3. Return on assets.
4. Return on equity.

B. Asset-utilization ratios:
5. Receivables turnover.
6. Inventory turnover.
7. Fixed-asset turnover.
8. Total asset turnover.

C. Liquidity ratios:
9. Current ratio.
10. Quick ratio.
11. Net working capital to total assets.

D. Debt-utilization ratios:
12. Long-term debt to equity.
13. Total debt to total assets.
14. Times interest earned.
15. Fixed charge coverage.

E. Price ratios:
16. Price to earnings.
17. Price to book value.
18. Dividends to price (dividend yield).

F. Other ratios:
19. Average tax rate.
20. Dividend payout.

The users of financial statements will attach different degrees of importance to the six categories of ratios. To the potential investor, the critical consideration is profitability and debt utilization. For the banker or trade creditor, the emphasis shifts to the firm's current ability to meet debt obligations. The bondholder, in turn, may be primarily influenced by debt to total assets—while also eyeing the profitability of the firm in terms of its ability to cover interest payments in the short term and principal payments in the long term. Of course, the shrewd analyst looks at all the ratios, with different degrees of attention.

A. Profitability Ratios The **profitability ratios** allow the analyst to measure the ability of the firm to earn an adequate return on sales, total assets, and invested capital. The profit-margin ratios (1, 2) relate to income statement items, while the two return ratios (3, 4) relate the income statement (numerator) to the balance sheet (denominator). Many of the problems related to profitability can be explained, in whole or in part, by the firm's ability to effectively employ its resources. We shall apply these ratios to Coca-Cola's income statement and balance sheet for 1993, which were previously presented in Tables 8–1 and 8–2. The values are rounded for ease of computation (dollars in millions).

Profitability ratios (Coca-Cola, 1993—in millions):

1. Operating margin $= \frac{\text{Operating income}}{\text{Sales (revenue)}} = \frac{\$3,102}{\$13,957} = 22.23\%$

2. After-tax profit margin $= \frac{\text{Net income}}{\text{Sales}} = \frac{\$2,176}{\$13,957} = 15.59\%$

3. Return on assets

(*a*) $\frac{\text{Net income}}{\text{Total assets}} = \frac{\$2,176}{\$12,021} = 18.10\%$

(*b*) $\frac{\text{Net income}}{\text{Sales}} \times \frac{\text{Sales}}{\text{Total assets}} = 15.59\% \times 1.161 = 18.10\%$

4. Return on equity

(*a*) $\frac{\text{Net income}}{\text{Stockholders' equity}^{4}} = \frac{\$2,176}{\$4,584} = 47.47\%$

(*b*) $\frac{\text{Return on assets}}{(1\text{-Debt/Assets})^{5}} = \frac{18.10\%}{1-.6187} = 47.47\%$

The profitability ratios indicate that Coca-Cola is quite profitable, but the analysis of its return on equity using 4(*b*) indicates that its high return on stockholders' equity is largely a result of heavy total debt to assets. The disparity between return on assets and return on equity is solely the result of financing 61.87 percent of assets with debt.

Du Pont Analysis Notice that the return on assets and return on equity have parts (*a*) and (*b*), or two ways to determine the ratio. The methods employed in (*b*), which arise from the Du Pont Company's financial system, help the analyst see the relationship between the income statement and the balance sheet. The return on assets is generated by multiplying the after-tax profit margin (income statement) by the asset-turnover ratio (combination income statement–balance sheet ratio).

The Du Pont Company was a forerunner in stressing that satisfactory return on assets may be achieved through high profit margins or rapid turnover of assets, or a combination of both. The Du Pont system causes the analyst to examine the sources of a company's profitability. Since the profit margin is an income statement ratio, a high profit margin indicates good cost control, whereas a high asset turnover ratio demonstrates efficient use of the assets on the balance sheet. Different industries have different operating and

[4] A working definition of stockholders' equity is the preferred and common stock accounts plus retained earnings. Coca-Cola also has a few other adjustments. The total can be found on the second line from the bottom at the end of Table 8–2 on page 215.

[5] Debt/assets = $7,437/$12,021 = 0.6187

financial structures. For example, in the heavy capital goods industry (machinery and equipment), the emphasis is on a high profit margin with a low asset turnover, while in food processing, the profit margin is low, and the key to satisfactory returns on total assets is a rapid turnover of assets.

Du Pont analysis further stresses that the return on equity stems from the return on assets adjusted for the amount of financial leverage by using the total debt-to-asset ratio. About 62 percent of the Coca-Cola Company's assets are financed by debt, and the return on equity reflects a high level of debt financing because the return on equity of 47.47 percent is 2.6 times as large as return on assets of 18.1 percent. As a detective, the financial analyst can judge how much debt a company employs by comparing these two measures of return. Of course, you will want to check this clue with the debt-utilization ratios. The total relationship between return on assets and return on equity under the Du Pont system is depicted in Figure 8–2.

In computing return on assets and equity, the analyst must also be sensitive to the age of the assets. Plant and equipment purchased 15 years ago may be carried on the books far below its replacement value in an inflationary economy. A 20 percent return on assets that were purchased in the late 1960s or early 1970s may be inferior to a 15 percent return on newly purchased assets.

B. Asset-Utilization Ratio With **asset-utilization ratios**, we measure the speed at which the firm is turning over accounts receivable, inventory, and longer-term assets. In other words, asset-utilization ratios measure how many times per year a company sells its inventory or collects its accounts receivable. For long-term assets, the utilization ratio tells us how productive the fixed assets are in terms of sales generation.

FIGURE 8–2 Du Pont Analysis

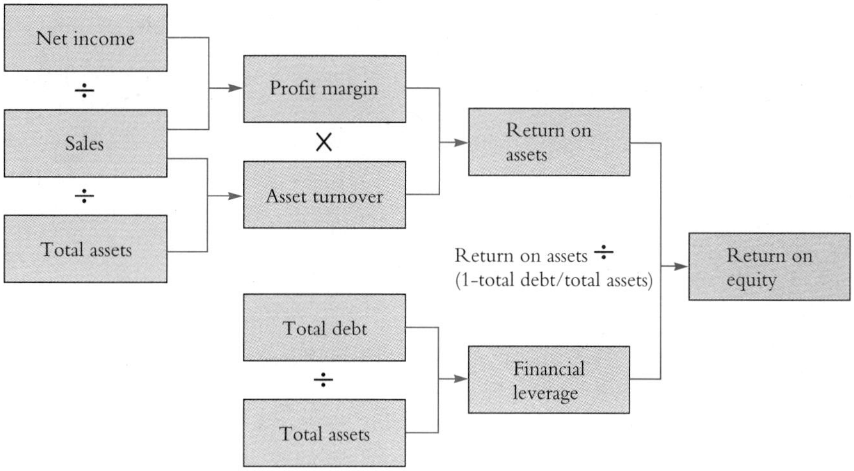

Asset-utilization ratios (Coca-Cola, 1993—in millions):

$$5.\ \text{Receivables turnover} = \frac{\text{Sales}}{\text{Receivables}} = \frac{\$13{,}957}{\$1{,}210} = 11.53\times$$

$$6.\ \text{Inventory turnover} = \frac{\text{Sales}}{\text{Inventory}} = \frac{\$13{,}957}{\$1{,}049} = 13.31\times$$

$$7.\ \text{Fixed-assets turnover} = \frac{\text{Sales}}{\text{Fixed assets}} = \frac{\$13{,}957}{\$3{,}729} = 3.74\times$$

$$8.\ \text{Total asset turnover} = \frac{\text{Sales}}{\text{Total assets}} = \frac{\$13{,}957}{\$12{,}021} = 1.16\times$$

The asset-utilization ratios relate the income statement (numerator) to the various assets on the balance sheet. Given that Coca-Cola's primary products are soft drinks and food, the receivables-turnover and inventory-turnover ratios reflect high turnover. Since most of the company's consumable products are not perishable, these ratios seem satisfactory. However, the large amount of cash and marketable securities, as seen on the balance sheet, reduces the total asset turnover.

C. Liquidity Ratios The primary emphasis of the **liquidity ratios** is a determination of the firm's ability to pay off short-term obligations as they come due. These ratios can be related to receivables and inventory turnover in that a faster turnover creates a more rapid movement of cash through the company and improves liquidity. Again remember that each industry will be different. A jewelry store chain will have much different ratios from a grocery store chain.

Liquidity ratios (Coca-Cola, 1993—in millions):

9. Current ratio

$$\frac{\text{Current assets}}{\text{Current liabilities}} = \frac{\$4{,}434}{\$5{,}171} = 0.857$$

10. Quick ratio

$$\frac{\text{Current assets} - \text{Inventory}}{\text{Current liabilities}} = \frac{\$4434 - 1049}{\$5{,}171} = 0.655$$

11. Net working capital to total assets

$$\frac{\text{Current assets} - \text{Current liabilities}}{\text{Total assets}} = \frac{\$4434 - \$5171}{\$12{,}021} = -0.061$$

The first two ratios (current and quick) indicate whether the firm can pay off its short-term debt in an emergency by liquidating its current assets. The quick ratio looks only at the most-liquid assets, which include cash, marketable securities, and receivables. Cash and securities are already liquid, but receivables usually will be turned into cash during the collection period. If there is concern about the firm's

liquidity, the analyst will want to cross-check the liquidity ratios with receivable and inventory turnover to determine how fast the current assets are turned into cash during an ordinary cycle.

The last liquidity ratio is a measure of the percentage of current assets (after short-term debt has been paid) to total assets. This indicates the liquidity of the assets of the firm. The higher the ratio, the greater the short-term assets relative to fixed assets, and the safer a creditor is. Net working capital to total assets is negative but small for Coca-Cola. In some firms, this would indicate serious trouble, but for Coca-Cola it is probably not a problem. The total borrowing power of the firm remains strong, but this ratio, along with the low current ratio, indicates a high reliance on short-term borrowing, which could be a disadvantage to the firm if interest rates increase. The quick ratio probably indicates most correctly in Coca-Cola's case that liquidity is not a problem. Since the company holds more than $1.0 billion in cash and marketable securities, the quick ratio is adequate. Also consider that the firm generated net cash flow of $42 million in 1993 after the repurchase of $680 million of common stock. Remember, ratios are pieces of the puzzle, and you cannot tell by looking at one piece whether the firm is healthy.

D. Debt-Utilization Ratios The **debt-utilization ratios** provide an indication of the way the firm is financed between debt (lenders) and equity (owners) and therefore helps the analyst determine the amount of financial risk present in the firm. Too much debt can not only impair liquidity with heavy interest payments but can also damage profitability and the health of the firm during an economic recession or industry slowdown.

Debt-utilization ratios (Coca-Cola, 1993—in millions):

$$12.\ \text{Long-term debt to equity} = \frac{\text{Long-term debt}}{\text{Stockholder's equity}} = \frac{\$1{,}428}{\$4{,}584} = 31.15\%$$

$$13.\ \text{Total debt to total assets} = \frac{\text{Total debt}}{\text{Total assets}} = \frac{\$7{,}437}{\$12{,}021} = 61.87\%$$

$$14.\ \text{Times interest earned} = \frac{\text{Income before interest and taxes}^{6}}{\text{Interest}} = \frac{\$3{,}102}{\$168} = 18.46\times$$

$$15.\ \text{Fixed-charge coverage} = \frac{\text{Income before fixed charges and taxes}^{7}}{\text{Fixed charges}^{8}} = \frac{\$3{,}102}{\$168} = 18.46\times$$

We have already discussed the impact of financial leverage on return on equity, and the first two ratios in this category indicate to the analyst how much financial leverage is

[6] Income before interest and taxes is the same as operating income as shown in Table 8–1.

[7] Since there are no other fixed charges besides interest, the numerators are the same in Formulas 14 and 15.

[8] The denominators are also the same in Formulas 14 and 15.

being used by the firm. The more debt, the greater the interest payments and the more volatile the impact on the firm's earnings. Companies with stable sales and earnings such as utilities can afford to employ more debt than those in cyclical industries such as automobiles or airlines. Ratio 12, long-term debt to equity, provides information concerning the long-term capital structure of the firm. In the case of Coca-Cola, long-term liabilities represent 31.15 percent of the stockholders' equity base provided by the owners of the firm. Ratio 13, total debt to total assets, looks at the total assets and the use of borrowed capital. Each firm must consider its optimum capital structure, and the analyst should be aware of industry fluctuations in assessing the firm's proper use of leverage. Coca-Cola seems safe, given that its business is not subject to large swings in sales.

The last two debt-utilization ratios indicate the firm's ability to meet its cash payments due on fixed obligations such as interest, leases, licensing fees, or sinking-fund charges. The higher these ratios, the more protected the creditor's position. Use of the fixed-charge coverage is more conservative than interest earned since it includes all fixed charges. Now that most leases are capitalized and show up on the balance sheet, it is easier to understand that lease payments are similar in importance to interest expense. Charges after taxes such as sinking-fund payments must be adjusted to before-tax income. For example, if a firm is in the 40 percent tax bracket and must make a $60,000 sinking-fund payment, the firm would have had to generate $100,000 in before-tax income to meet that obligation. The adjustment would be as follows:

$$\text{Before-tax income required} = \frac{\text{After-tax payment}}{1 - \text{Tax rate}}$$

$$= \frac{\$60{,}000}{1 - 0.40} = \$100{,}000$$

Coca Cola's fixed-charge coverage is the same as its interest-earned ratio because it has no fixed charges other than interest expense.

E. Price Ratios The **price ratios** relate the internal performance of the firm to the external judgment of the marketplace in terms of value. What is the firm's end result in market value? The price ratios indicate the expectations of the market relative to other companies. For example, a firm with a high price-to-earnings ratio has a higher market price relative to $1 of earnings than a company with a lower ratio.

Price ratios (Coca-Cola, December 31, 1993—in millions):

$$\text{16. Price to earnings} = \frac{\text{Common stock price}}{\text{Earnings per share}} = \frac{\$44.63}{\$1.67} = 26.72\times$$

$$\text{17. Price to book value} = \frac{\text{Common stock price}}{\text{Book value per share}^{9}} = \frac{\$44.63}{\$3.52} = 12.68\times$$

[9] $\text{Book value per share} = \frac{\text{Stockholders' equity}}{\text{Number of shares}} = \frac{\$4{,}584}{1302} = \$3.52$

18. Dividends to price (Dividend yield) $= \frac{\text{Dividends per share}}{\text{Common stock price}} = \frac{\$0.68}{\$44.63} = 1.52\%$

Coca-Cola's price-earnings ratio indicates that the firm's stock price represents $26.72 for every $1 of earnings. This number can be compared with that of other companies in the soft drink industry and/or related industries. As indicated in Chapter 7, the price-earnings ratio (or P/E ratio) is influenced by the earnings and the sales growth of the firm and also by the risk (or volatility in performance), the debt-equity structure of the firm, the dividend-payment policy, the quality of management, and a number of other factors. The P/E ratio indicates expectations about the future of a company. Firms that are expected to provide greater returns than those for the market in general, with equal or less risk, often have P/E ratios higher than the overall market P/E ratio.

Expectations of returns and P/E ratios do change over time, as Table 8–4 illustrates. Price-earnings ratios for a selected list of U.S. firms in 1981, 1988, and 1994 show that during this 13-year period, price-earnings ratios rose between 1981 (the year before the bull market began) and 1988. By 1994, the economy had recovered from a recession, corporate earnings were rising, and stock prices were high due to lower interest rates and expectations of growing earnings. It was no surprise, given this scenario, that the market P/E ratio in 1994, measured by the Standard and Poor's 500 Stock Index (bottom line) was higher than in 1988.

The P/E ratios are more complicated than they may appear at first glance. The level of the market was higher in 1994, but not all companies exhibited higher P/E ratios. A high

TABLE 8–4 Price-Earnings Ratios for Selected U.S. Corporations

			P/E Ratio*	
Corporation	**Industry**	**December 31, 1981**	**October 24, 1988**	**September 29, 1994**
Exxon	International oil	5	12	15
Texas Utilities	Public utility	6	7	26
Union Carbide	Chemical	5	10	26
Bank America	Banking	7	9	10
CBS	Broadcasting	7	16	17
Halliburton	Oil service	11	26	dd**
Winn-Dixie	Retail	8	15	18
IBM	Computers	9	14	31
Upjohn	Ethical drugs	10	18	17
McDonald's	Restaurant franchise	10	15	18
Texas Instruments	Semiconductors	15	13	12
S&P 500	Market index	8	13	18

* P/E is calculated by taking the market price and dividing by the previous 12 months' earnings per share.
**dd—indicates loss in the most recent four quarters.
Source: *Barrons,* September 29, 1994.

P/E ratio can result from many sets of assumptions. P/E ratios can be high because of high expected growth in earnings per share. For a company in a cyclical industry, the P/E ratio can be high because of low earnings. For example, both IBM and Texas Utilities suffered from very low earnings per share. Because their prices did not fall as much as EPS, the P/E ratios were very high. According to Table 8–4, the "dd" symbol on the P/E ratio on September 29, 1994, indicates that Halliburton had a loss in the most recent four quarters.

The price-to-book-value ratio relates the market value of the company to the historical accounting value of the firm. In a company that has old assets, this ratio may be quite high, but in one with new, undepreciated fixed assets, the ratio might be lower. This information needs to be combined with a knowledge of the company's assets and of industry norms.

The **dividend yield** is part of the total return that an investor receives along with capital gains or losses. It is usually calculated by annualizing the current quarterly dividend since that is the cash value a current investor is likely to receive over the next year.

The price-to-earnings and price-to-book-value ratios are often used in computing stock values. The simple view of these ratios is that when they are relatively low compared with a market index or company history, the stock is a good buy. In the case of the dividend yield, the opposite is true. When dividend yields are relatively high compared with the company's historical data, the stock may be undervalued. Of course, the application of these simple models is much more complicated. The analyst has to determine if the company is performing the same as it was when the ratios were at what the analyst considers a normal level.

F. Other Ratios The other ratios presented in category F are to help the analyst spot special tax situations that affect the profitability of an industry or company and to determine what percentage of earnings are being paid to the stockholder and what is being reinvested for internal growth.

Other ratios (Coca-Cola, 1993—in millions):

$$\text{19. Average rax rate} = \frac{\text{Income tax}}{\text{Taxable income}} = \frac{\$997}{\$3{,}185} = 31.30\%$$

$$\text{20. Dividend payout} = \frac{\text{Dividends per share}}{\text{Earnings per share}} = \frac{\$0.68}{\$1.67} = 40.72\%$$

These other ratios are calculated to provide the analyst with information that may indicate unusual tax treatment or reinvestment policies. For example, the tax ratio for forest products companies will be low because of the special tax treatment given timber cuttings. A company's tax rate may also decline in a given year as a result of special tax credits. Thus, earnings per share may rise, but we need to know if it is from operations or favorable tax treatment. If it is from operations, we will be more sure of next year's forecast, but if it is from tax benefits, we cannot normally count on the benefits being continued into the future.

The **dividend-payout ratio** provides data concerning the firm's reinvestment strategies. It represents dividends per share divided by earnings per share. A high payout ratio tells the analyst that the stockholder is receiving a large part of the earnings and that the company is not retaining much income for investment in new plant and equipment. High payouts are usually found in industries that do not have great growth potential, while low payout ratios are associated with firms in growth industries.

USES OF RATIOS

The previous section presented 20 ratios that may be helpful to the analyst in evaluating a firm. How can we further use the data we have gathered to check the health of companies we are interested in analyzing?

One way is to compare the company to the industry. This is becoming more difficult as companies diversify into several industries. Twenty years ago, firms competed in one industry, and ratio comparisons were more reliable. Now companies have a wide range of products and markets.

Table 8–5 shows that while the food division dominates the asset-turnover (revenue/assets) ratio with a 2.32 turnover, its low operating profit margin of 7.19 percent drags down operating return on total assets. The biggest contributor to Coca-Cola's bottom line is the international soft drinks division. The company has more invested internationally than domestically and this seems to be prudent policy based on profitability. While the food division is not a major contributor to the Coca-Cola Company currently, improvements in its operating performance and profitability could enhance the stock price. Coca-Cola evidently thinks the food division is worth the investment since it continues to put capital expenditures into this area.

Table 8–6 on page 230 presents further information on the business segments in which Coca-Cola operates. Soft drinks and foods comprise the business segments with soft drinks divided into United States and International. The soft drink segment is by far the largest segment, accounting for 87 percent of the operating revenues and virtually all of the operating income in 1993. The interesting fact is that the international soft drink division accounts for 66 percent of consolidated operating revenues and 89 percent of consolidated operating income. The foods division is not

TABLE 8–5 Selected Ratios by Segment for the Coca-Cola Company, 1993

	USA Soft Drinks	International Soft Drinks	Food
Revenue/assets	1.52×	1.58×	2.32×
Operating income/assets	31.60%	47.39%	16.69%
Operating income/sales	20.84%	29.91%	7.19%

TABLE 8–6 Coca-Cola's Lines of Business

The company operates in two major lines of business: soft drinks and foods (principally, juice-based beverages). Information concerning operations in these businesses at December 31, 1993, 1992, and 1991, and for the years then ended, is presented below (in millions):

	Soft Drinks				
	United States	**International**	**Foods**	**Corporate**	**Consolidated**
1993					
Net operating revenues	$2,966.0	$9,205.0	$1,766.0	$20.0	$13,957.0
Operating income	618.0	2,753.0	127.0	(396.0)	3,102.0
Identifiable operating assets	1,956.0	5,809.0	761.0	1,280.0**	9,806.0
Equity income				91.0	91.0
Investments (principally bottling companies)				2,215.0	2,215.0
Capital expenditures	136.0	557.0	30.0	77.0	800.0
Depreciation and amortization	91.0	172.0	38.0	59.0	360.0
1992					
Net operating revenues	$2,813.0	$8,551.0	$1,675.0	$35.0	$8,622.3
Operating income	510.0	2521.0	112.0	(373.0)	1,725.8
Identifiable operating assets	1812.0	5251.0	791.0	1,035.0**	6,352.1
Equity income				65.0	65.0
Investments (principally bottling companies)				2,163.0	2,163.0
Capital expenditures	169.0	736.0	38.0	140.0	1,083.0
Depreciation and amortization	87.0	157.0	35.0	43.0	322.0
1991					
Net operating revenues	$2,645.0	$7,245.0	$1,636.0	$46.0	$11,572.0
Operating income	496.0	2141.0	104.0	(395.0)	2,319.0
Identifiable operating assets	1447.0	4742.0	755.0	1,124.0**	8,068.0
Equity income				40.0*	40.0
Investments (principally bottling companies)				2,121.0	2,121.0
Capital expenditures	131.0	547.0	57.0	57.0	792.0
Depreciation and amortization	82.0	112.0	30.0	37.0	261.0

* Reduced by $44 million related to restructuring charges recorded by Coca-Cola Enterprise.
**General corporate identifiable operating assets are composed principally of marketable securities and fixed assets.
Source: *The Coca-Cola Company Annual Report*, 1993, p. 69.

nearly as profitable as soft drinks. The corporate category is misleading since it holds the identifiable assets associated with the equity interest in other investments. It also includes overhead and staff but generates no income.

Companies in oligopolies such as Coca-Cola in the soft drink industry are hard to evaluate on a ratio basis because one or two firms (Pepsi and Coke) dominate the industry, and so industry ratios are not a helpful measure of performance. In the case of the food division of Coca-Cola, this would not be the case since this industry consists of many firms, and industry comparison would be helpful. Table 8–7 looks at Coca-Cola compared with the food industry, and since Coca-Cola dominates the soft drink industry, we must compare its performance to another competitive industry, the beverage industry (beer).

Given the set of ratios in Table 8–7, Coca-Cola compares favorably with the ratios for both the food and beverage industries. The beverage industry is dominated by Budweiser, while the food industry is not dominated by any one company. Because Coca-Cola has low long-term debt, its interest expense may be lower than that of the food and beverage industries, allowing it to bring more of its operating profit down to the after-tax profit margin.

Coca-Cola's return on equity is higher than those of the comparative industries and reflects a better level of profitability. The fact that the profitability ratios favor Coca-Cola has been translated into the market in terms of a higher P/E ratio for Coca-Cola. Additionally, the market may think Coca-Cola will grow faster than the two industries.

In general, after reviewing all the financial statements and ratios, Coca-Cola looks to be in good financial shape. The food division needs to improve profitability, and Coca-Cola needs to use more long-term debt in its capital structure to replace short-term borrowings that have more volatile interest rates and therefore may carry more risk as a financing vehicle.

TABLE 8–7 Selected Ratio Comparisons for the Coca-Cola Company, 1993

		Industries	
	Coca-Cola	**Food**	**Beverage**
Operating margin	22.7%	12.2%	19.0%
After-tax profit margin	15.6%	5.2%	9.9%
Return on equity	47.5%	20.0%	25.4%
Long-term debt to equity	31.1%	36.2%	41.3%
Price-to-earnings ratio	26.7×	14.5×	19.0×
Dividend yield	1.5%	2.3%	1.7%
Average tax rate	31.3%	38.0%	34.0%
Payout ratio	40.72%	34.0%	33.0%

It is important to realize that Coca-Cola is an international company that may be affected by political and economic events abroad. Foreign revolts and a rising dollar can hurt Coca-Cola's earnings. Unfortunately, its earnings during 1992–93 suffered from a rising dollar. This made the translation of foreign profits less valuable in dollars and reduced Coca-Cola's earnings per share. In 1995, however, the falling dollar increased earnings per share.

Table 8–8 shows the breakdown of the company's worldwide sales and profitability by region. Using the 1993 data for computations, all U.S. products account for about 33 percent of net operating revenues, but they account for only 23 percent of operating income. The European Community is the second largest market with 27 percent of revenues, and the Pacific and Canadian market is third with 21 percent of revenues, but it provides the highest amount of operating income ($1,010 million) of all regions. The international markets all provide operating profit margins (operating income/net operating revenues) of 11 to 31 percent; the United States is low with a 16 percent profit margin.

When international sales growth is analyzed, it becomes clear that Coca-Cola's revenue growth is occurring in its most profitable markets. An economist might credit this phenomenon to a lack of competition from alternative beverages in these regions compared with the competition from many alternatives in the United States. One concern has to be future competition in Europe, Latin America, the Pacific Rim, and Africa. If competitors such as Pepsi and Budweiser become more aggressive and successful, Coca-Cola's profit margins and resulting earnings could grow more slowly, and the P/E and stock price could suffer declines.

COMPARING LONG-TERM TRENDS

Over the course of the business cycle, sales and profitability may expand and contract, and ratio analysis for any one year may not present an accurate picture of the firm. Therefore, we look at **trend analysis** of performance over a number of years to examine long-term performance.

Table 8–9 on pages 234 and 235 presents the 10-year summary of selected financial data for Coca-Cola. One can see the strong growth in net operating revenues since 1983. Net income has also grown rapidly. Furthermore, note the large accumulation in cash and marketable securities by Coca-Cola over the last decade. This 10-year summary statement provides other in-depth perspectives on the company and its relative performance.

For example, Table 8–9 provides 5- and 10-year compound growth rates so that comparisons can be made over time. An analyst can see that there is a high rate of consistency between the long-term, 10-year period and the shorter term, 5-year period. Although the growth rates seem to be higher in the last five-year period, there is very little disparity. This could indicate to the analyst that a high level of predictability exists. One long-term trend that is apparent is the decline in shares of common stock outstanding. The number of shares has declined from 1.635 billion in 1983 to 1.302 billion in 1993. This 20 percent decline in shares has caused net income per share (EPS) to grow faster than net income.

TABLE 8–8 Coca-Cola's Operations in Geographic Areas

Operations in geographic areas. Information about the company's operations in different geographic areas at December 31, 1993, 1992, and 1991, and for the years then ended, as presented below (in millions):

	United States	Africa	European Community	Latin America	Northeast Europe/ Middle East	Pacific and Canada	Corporate	Consolidated
1993								
Net operating revenues	$4,586	$255	$3,834	$1,683	$677	$2,902	$20	$13,957
Operating income	730	152	872	582	152	1,010	(396)	3,102
Identifiable operating assets	2,682	153	2,777	1,220	604	1,090	1,280	9,806
Equity income							91	91
Investments							2,215	2,215
Capital expenditures	165	6	239	141	129	43	77	800
Depreciation and amortization	127	3	99	33	22	17	59	360
1992								
Net operating revenues	$4,339	$242	$3,984	$1,383	$546	$2,545	$35	$1,320,474
Operating income	608	129	889	502	108	907	(373)	2,770
Identifiable operating assets	2,563	139	2,587	1,185	435	945	1,035	8,889
Equity income							65	65
Investments							2,163	2,163
Capital expenditures	204	12	386	188	120	33	140	1,083
Depreciation and amortization	121	3	99	27	14	15	43	322
1991								
Net operating revenues	$4,125	$206	$3,338	$1,103	$408	$2,346	$46	$532,312
Operating income	560	105	768	405	99	777	(395)	2,319
Identifiable operating assets	2,161	126	2,558	815	297	987	1,124	8,068
Equity income							40	40
Investments							2,121	2,121
Capital expenditures	185	6	331	106	55	52	57	792
Depreciation and amortization	111	2	66	23	7	15	37	261

Source: *The Coca-Cola Company Annual Report*, 1993, p. 70.

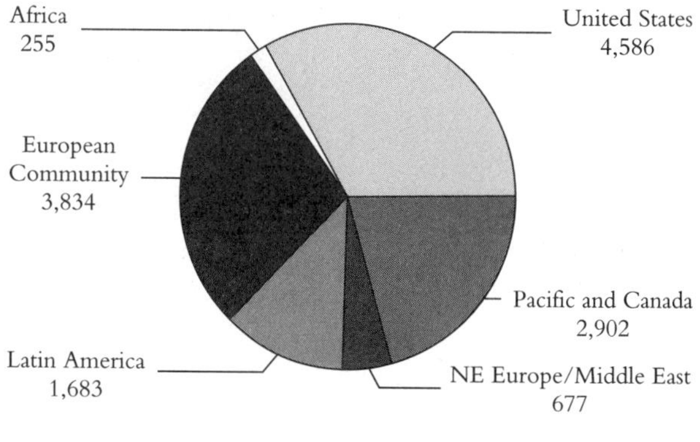

(a) Net operating revenues (in millions)

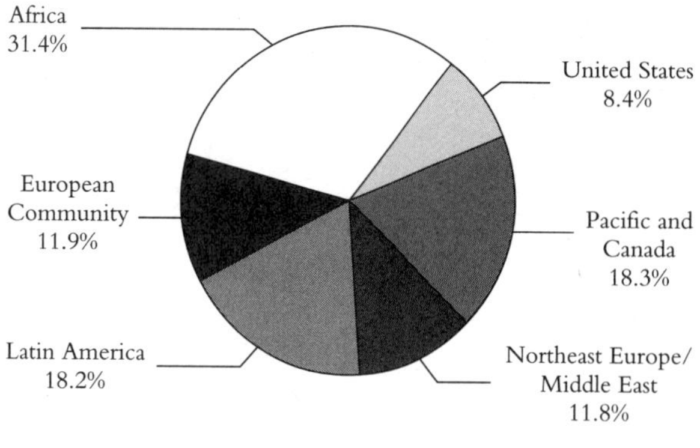

(b) Operating margin

TABLE 8–9 Selected Financial Data for the Coca-Cola Company

(In millions except per share data, ratios, and growth rates)	Compound Growth Rates 5 Years	10 Years	Year Ended December 31 1993[1]	1992[2,3]
Summary of Operations				
Net operating revenues	11.6%	10.7%	$13,957	$13,074
Cost of goods sold	8.5%	7.2%	5,160	5,055
Gross profit	13.7%	13.5%	8,797	8,019
Selling, administrative, and general expenses	13.4%	13.2%	5,695	5,249
Operating income	14.2%	14.1%	3,102	2,770
Interest income			144	164
Interest expense			168	171
Equity income			91	65
Other income (deductions)—net			4	(82)
Gain on issuance of stock by subsidiaries			12	—
Income from continuing operations before income taxes and changes in accounting principles	14.4%	13.8%	3,185	2,746
Income taxes	13.2%	10.3%	997	863
Income from continuing operations before changes in accounting principles	15.0%	15.8%	$ 2,188	$ 1,883
Net income	15.8%	14.6%	$ 2,176	$ 1,664
Preferred stock dividends			—	—
Net income available to common share owners	16.0%	14.6%	$ 2,176	$ 1,664
–Average common shares outstanding			1,302	1,317
PER COMMON SHARE DATA				
Income from continuing operations before changes in accounting principles	17.8%	18.4%	$1.68	$ 1.43
Net income	18.7%	17.3%	1.67	1.26
Cash dividends	17.8%	11.9%	0.68	0.56
Market price at December 31	31.9%	25.9%	44.63	41.88
Balance Sheet Data				
Cash, cash equivalents, and current marketable securities			$ 1,078	$ 1,063
Property, plant, and equipment—net			3,729	3,526
Depreciation			333	310
Capital expenditures			800	1,083
Total assets			12,021	11,052
Long-term debt			1,428	1,120
Total-debt			3,100	3,207
Share-owners' equity			4,584	3,888
Total capital			7,684	7,095
Other Key Financial Measures				
Total-debt-to-total-capital			40.3%	45.2%
Net-debt-to-net-capital			26.2%	31.9%
Return on common equity			51.7%	46.4%
Return on capital			31.2%	29.4%
Dividend payout ratio			40.6%	44.3%
Economic profit			$1,495	$1,293

[1] In 1993, the Company adopted SFAS No. 112, "Employers' Accounting for Postemployment Benefits."
[2] In 1992, the Company adopted SFAS No. 106, "Employers' Accounting for Postretirement Benefits Other Than Pensions."
[3] The company adopted SFAS No. 109, "Accounting for Income Taxes," in 1992 by restating financial statements beginning in 1989.
[4] Net income available to common share owners in 1989 includes after-tax gains of $604 million ($0.44 per common share) from the sales of the company's equity interest in Columbia Pictures Entertainment, Inc., and the company's bottled water business and the transition effect of $265 million related to the change in accounting for income taxes. Excluding these nonrecurring items, the dividend payout ratio in 1989 was 39.9 percent.

TABLE 8–9 Selected Financial Data for the Coca-Cola Company, *(concluded)*

	1991[3]	1990[3]	1989[3]	1988	1987	1986	1985	1984	1983
	$11,572	$10,236	$ 8,622	$8,065	$7,658	$6,977	$5,879	$5,442	$5,056
	4,649	4,208	3,548	3,429	3,633	3,454	2,909	2,738	2,580
	6,923	6,028	5,074	4,636	4,025	3,523	2,970	2,704	2,476
	4,604	4,076	3,348	3,038	2,701	2,626	2,163	1,855	1,648
	2,319	1,952	1,726	1,598	1,324	897	807	849	828
	175	170	205	199	232	154	151	133	90
	192	231	308	230	297	208	196	128	77
	40	110	75	92	64	45	52	42	35
	41	13	66	(33)	—	35	69	13	2
	—	—	—	—	40	375	—	—	—
	2,383	2,014	1,764	1,626	1,363	1,298	883	909	878
	765	632	553	537	496	471	314	360	374
	$ 1,618	$ 1,382	$ 1,211	$1,089	$ 867	$ 827	$ 569	$ 549	$ 504
	$ 1,618	$ 1,382	$ 1,537	$1,045	$ 916	$ 934	$ 722	$ 629	$ 559
	1	18	21	7	—	—	—	—	—
	$ 1,617	$ 1,364	$ 1,516[4]	$1,038	$ 916	$ 934	$ 722	$ 629	$ 559
	1,333	1,337	1,384	1,458	1,509	1,547	1,573	1,587	1,635
	$ 1.21	$ 1.02	$ .86	$ 0.74	$ 0.57	$ 0.53	$ 0.36	$ 0.35	$ 0.31
	1.21	1.02	1.10[4]	0.71	0.61	0.60	0.46	0.40	0.34
	0.48	0.40	0.34	0.30	0.28	0.26	0.25	0.23	0.22
	40.13	23.25	19.31	11.16	9.53	9.44	7.04	5.20	4.46
	$ 1,117	$ 1,492	$ 1,182	$1,231	$1,489	$ 895	$ 843	$ 768	$ 559
	2,890	2,386	2,021	1,759	1,602	1,538	1,483	1,284	1,247
	254	236	181	167	152	151	130	119	111
	792	593	462	387	304	346	412	300	324
	10,189	9,245	8,249	7,451	8,606	7,675	6,341	5,241	4,540
	985	536	549	761	909	996	801	631	428
	2,288	2,537	1,980	2,124	2,995	1,848	1,280	1,310	520
	4,239	3,662	3,299	3,345	3,187	3,479	2,948	2,751	2,912
	6,527	6,199	5,279	5,469	6,182	5,327	4,228	4,061	3,432
	35.1%	40.9%	37.5%	38.8%	48.4%	34.7%	30.3%	32.3%	15.2%
	19.2%	23.7%	14.7%	18.9%	15.4%	10.9%	15.6%	19.7%	5.6%
	41.3%	41.4%	39.4%	34.7%	26.0%	25.7%	20.0%	19.4%	17.7%
	27.5%	26.8%	26.5%	21.3%	18.3%	20.1%	16.8%	16.7%	16.4%
	39.5%	39.2%	31.0%[4]	42.1%	46.0%	43.1%	53.8%	57.9%	65.3%
	$1,029	$ 878	$ 821	$ 748	$ 417	$ 311	$ 269	$268	$138

The Stock Market and the Spin Doctor

In a stock market environment, all new information is thought to be quickly reflected in the value of a stock. Of course, the quality of the information can always be questioned. For example, stock brokerage firms are much more likely to paint a rosy picture than a negative one. In a study by researchers of 6,000 brokerage house recommendations, 87 percent of the time the brokers suggested a buy, while a sell was advised only 13 percent of the time.* Keep in mind that brokerage houses are often investment bankers for the firms they are researching and may have a vested interest in seeing the firm's stock do well. Furthermore, a buy recommendation has the potential to generate two commissions—a sell generates only one.

Companies themselves are not averse to painting a positive picture. Items that feature good news about improved earnings or the signing of a new contract may be prominently featured in the middle of the day, while dismal announcements may be deferred to the weekend.

There is the old story about a chief executive officer (CEO) who was interviewing two candidates for the position of chief financial officer. One had a CPA, an MBA from Harvard, and five years of experience with Arthur Andersen. The other had taken two bookkeeping courses on weekends. When the CEO asked the two candidates how much 2 + 2 added up to, the first candidate couldn't believe the simplicity of the question but quickly answered, "Four." The second candidate thought a bit longer and responded, "Anything you want it to." Guess who got the job?

While this example is meant to represent the extreme case, there is enough flexibility in financial reporting that the prudent analyst must always look behind the numbers. One such firm, David Tice and Associates of Dallas, Texas, does that exclusively. These independent analysts specialize in reporting overly aggressive procedures firms have used in reporting earnings. They have taken on small and large firms alike, including General Electric. Their phone call to corporate headquarters is not always met with excitement. Not all firms want a second opinion after the spin doctor has put his out.

* J. C. Groth, W. Lewellen, G. Schlarbaum, and R. Lease, "An Analysis of Brokerage House Security Recommendations," *Financial Analysts Journal,* January/February 1979, pp. 32–40.

DEFICIENCIES OF FINANCIAL STATEMENTS

Several differences occur between companies and industries, and, at times, inflation has additionally clouded the clarity of accounting statements. Some of the more important difficulties occur in the area of inflation-adjusted accounting statements, inventory valuation, depreciation methods, pension fund liabilities, research and development, deferred taxes, and foreign exchange accounting. We do not have space to cover all of them, but we will touch on the most important ones.

Inflation Effects

Inflation causes phantom sources of profit that may mislead even the most alert analyst. Revenue is almost always stated in current dollars, whereas plant and equipment or inventory may have been purchased at lower price levels. Thus, profit may be more a function of increasing prices than of satisfactory performance.

Distortion of inflation also shows up on the balance sheet since most of the values on the balance sheet are stated on a historical or original-cost basis. This may be particularly troublesome in the case of plant and equipment and inventory, which may now be worth

two or three times the original cost or—from a negative viewpoint—may require many times the original cost for replacement.

The accounting profession has been groping with this problem for decades, and the discussion becomes particularly intense each time inflation rears its ugly head. In October 1979, the Financial Accounting Standards Board (FASB) issued a ruling that required about 1,300 large companies to disclose **inflation-adjusted accounting** data in their annual reports. This information shows the effects of inflation on the financial statements of the firm. The ruling on inflation adjustment was extended for five more years in 1984 but was later made optional. As inflation temporarily slowed, many companies chose not to disclose inflation-adjusted statements in addition to the historical cost statements.

From a study of 10 chemical firms and 8 drug companies using current-cost (replacement-cost) data found in the financial 10-K statements these companies filed with the SEC, it was found that the changes shown in Table 8–10 occurred in their assets, income, and other selected ratios. The impact of these changes is important as an example of the changes that take place on ratio analysis during periods of high inflation.

The comparison of replacement-cost and historical-cost accounting methods in Table 8–10 shows that replacement cost increases assets but at the same time reduces income. This increase in assets lowers the debt-to-assets ratio since debt is a monetary asset that is not revalued because it is paid back in current dollars.

The decreased debt-to-assets ratio would indicate that the financial leverage of the firm decreased, but a look at the interest-coverage ratio tells a different story. Because the interest-coverage ratio measures the operating income available to cover interest expense, the declining income penalizes the ratio, and the firm shows a decreased ability to cover its interest cost.

As long as prices continue to rise in an inflationary environment, profits appear to feed on themselves. The main objection is that when prices do level off, management and unsuspecting stockholders have a rude awakening as expensive inventory is charged

TABLE 8–10 Comparison of Replacement-Cost Accounting to Historical-Cost Accounting

	10 Chemical Companies		8 Drug Companies	
	Replacement Cost	**Historical Cost**	**Replacement Cost**	**Historical Cost**
Increase in assets	28.4%	—	15.4%	—
Decrease in net income before taxes	(45.8)	—	(19.3)	—
Return on assets	2.8	6.2%	8.3	11.4%
Return on equity	4.9	13.5	12.8	19.6
Debt-to-assets ratio	34.3	43.8	30.3	35.2
Interest-coverage ratio (times interest earned)	7.1×	8.4×	15.4×	16.7×

Note: Replacement cost is but one form of current cost. Nevertheless, it is widely used as a measure of current cost.
Source: Jeff Garnett and Geoffrey A. Hirt, "Replacement Cost Data: A study of the Chemical and Drug Industry for Years 1976 through 1978" (Working paper).

against softening retail prices. A 15 to 20 percent growth rate in earnings may be little more than an "inflationary illusion." Industries most sensitive to inflation-induced profits are those with cyclical products, such as lumber, copper, rubber, and food products, as well as those in which inventory is a significant percentage of sales and profits. Reported profits for the lumber industry have been influenced as much as 50 percent by inventory pricing, and profits of a number of other industries have been influenced by 15 to 20 percent.

Inventory Valuation

The income statement can show considerable differences in earnings, depending on the method of inventory valuation. The two basic methods are FIFO (first-in, first-out) and LIFO (last-in, first-out). In an inflationary economy, a firm could be reporting increased profits even though no actual increase in physical output occurred. The example of the Rhoades Company will illustrate this point. We first observe its income statement for 1995 in Table 8–11. It sold 1,000 units for $20,000 and shows earnings after taxes of $4,200 and an operating margin and after-tax margin of 35 percent and 21 percent, respectively.

Assume that in 1996 the number of units sold remains constant at 1,000 units. However, inflation causes a 10 percent increase in price, from $20 to $22 per unit as shown in Table 8–12. Total sales will go up to $22,000, but with no actual increase in physical volume. Further assume the firm uses FIFO inventory pricing so that inventory first purchased will be written off against current sales. We will assume that 1,000 units of 1995 inventory at a cost of $10 per unit are written off against 1996 sales revenue. If Rhoades used LIFO inventory and if the cost of goods sold went up 10 percent also, to $11 per unit, income will be less than under FIFO. Table 8–12 shows the 1996 income statement of Rhoades under both inventory methods.

The table demonstrates the difference between FIFO and LIFO. Under FIFO, Rhoades Corporation shows higher profit margins and more income even though no

TABLE 8–11 Rhoades Corporation Income Statement

RHOADES CORPORATION
First-Year Income Statement
Net Income for 1995

Sales	$20,000	(1,000 units at $20)
Cost of goods sold	10,000	(1,000 units at $10)
Gross profit	10,000	
Selling and administrative expense	2,000	
Depreciation	1,000	
Operating profit	7,000	
Taxes (40 percent)	2,800	
Earnings after taxes	$ 4,200	
Operating margin	$ 7,000/$20,000 = 35%	
After-tax margin	$ 4,200/$20,000 = 21%	

TABLE 8–12 Rhoades Corporation Income Statement

RHOADES CORPORATION
Second-Year Income Statement Using FIFO and LIFO
Net income for 1996

	FIFO	LIFO
Sales	$22,000 (1,000 at $22)	$22,000 (1,000 at $22)
Cost of goods sold	10,000 (1,000 at $10)	11,000 (1,000 at $11)
Gross profit	12,000	11,000
Selling and administrative expense	2,200 (10% of sales)	2,200 (10% of sales)
Depreciation	1,000	1,000
Operating profit	8,800	7,800
Taxes (40 percent)	3,520	3,120
Earnings after taxes	$ 5,280	$ 4,680
Operating margin	$ 8,800/$22,000 = 40%	$ 7,800/$22,000 = 35.4%
After-tax margin	$ 5,280/$22,000 = 24%	$ 4,680/$22,000 = 21.2%

physical increase in sales occurs. This is because FIFO costing lags behind current prices, and the company generates "phantom profits" due to capital gains on inventory. Unfortunately, this inventory will need to be replaced next period at higher costs. When and if prices turn lower in a recessionary environment, FIFO will have the opposite effect and drag down earnings. LIFO inventory costing, on the other hand, relates current costs to current prices, and although profits rise in dollar terms from 1995, the margins stay basically the same. The only problem with LIFO inventory accounting is that low-cost layers of inventory build up on the balance sheet of the company and understate inventory. This will cause inventory turnover to appear higher than under FIFO.

While many companies shifted to LIFO accounting in the past, FIFO inventory valuation still exists in some industries, and the analyst must be alert to the consequences of both methods.

Extraordinary Gains and Losses

Extraordinary gains and losses may occur from the sale of corporate fixed assets, lawsuits, or similar events that would not be expected to occur often, if ever, again. Some analysts argue that such extraordinary events should be included in computing the current income of the firm, while others would leave them off when assessing operating performance. The choice can have a big impact on ratios that rely on earnings or earnings per share. Extraordinary gains can inflate returns and lower payout ratios if they are included in earnings. The analyst concerned about forecasting should include only those earnings from continuing operations; otherwise, the forecast will be seriously off its mark. Unfortunately, there is some inconsistency in the manner in which nonrecurring losses are treated despite determined attempts by the accounting profession to ensure uniformity.

Pension Fund Liabilities

One area of increasing concern among financial analysts is the unfunded liabilities of corporate pension funds. These funds eventually will have to pay workers their retirement income from the pension fund earnings and assets. If the money is not available from the pension fund, the company is liable to make the payments. These unfunded pensions may have to come out of earnings in future years, which would penalize shareholders and limit the corporation's ability to reinvest in new assets.

Foreign Exchange Transactions

Foreign currency fluctuations have a major impact on the earnings of those companies heavily involved in international trade. The drug industry is significantly affected. Coca-Cola, with more than 75 percent of operating income coming from foreign operations in 1993, is a prime example of a company greatly affected by swings in the currency markets. For example, when the dollar declines relative to foreign currencies, earnings from foreign subsidiaries get translated into more U.S. dollars and help the earnings of U.S. companies such as Coca-Cola. The opposite is true when the dollar increases in value. Coca-Cola's foreign exchange currency transactions had a negative effect of $41 million in 1993. Since Coca-Cola is available in 155 countries, the firm has a diversification effect with some currencies rising and others falling. However, a major change in a given part of the world could cause this diversification effect to lose its impact, as was the case in 1993.

Other Distortions

Other problems exist in accounting statements and methods of reporting earnings. A mention of some of them might provide you with areas that require further investigation. Additional areas for detective work are in accounting methods for the following: research and development expenditures, deferred taxes, tax credits, merger accounting, intangible drilling and development costs, and percentage depletion allowances. As you can see, many issues cause analysts to dig further and to be cautious about accepting bottom-line earnings per share.

SUMMARY

Chapter 8 presents the basics of accounting statements and ratio analysis. After going through an income statement, a balance sheet, and the statement of cash flows, ratios are presented that help tie together these statements.

Ratio analysis is used to evaluate the operating performance and capital structure of a firm. Ratios will not help to find a gold mine, but they can help to avoid buying sick companies. Using ratio analysis, a brief description of two bankruptcy studies was given that emphasized the ability of ratios to spot troubled firms with a potential for failure.

Twenty ratios were classified into six categories that measured profitability, asset utilization, liquidity, debt utilization, relative prices, and taxes and dividend policy. The Coca-Cola Company was

used as an example as we computed each ratio. The Du Pont method was presented to demonstrate the relationship between assets, sales, income, and debt for creating returns on assets and equity.

Ratios are best used when compared with industry norms, company trends, and economic and industry cycles. It is becoming more difficult to use ratio analysis on an industry basis as firms become more integrated and diversified into several industries.

Finally, the deficiencies of financial statements were discussed. The effect on ratios was examined for replacement cost versus historical cost data. Other distortions were discussed such as extraordinary gains and losses and pension fund liabilities.

Financial analysis is a science as well as an art, and experience certainly sharpens the skills. It would be unrealistic for someone to pick up all the complex relationships involved in ratio analysis immediately. This is why analysts are assigned industries they learn inside and out. After much practice, the analytical work is easier, and the true picture of financial performance becomes focused.

KEY WORDS AND CONCEPTS

income statement, 211
balance sheet, 213
statement of cash flows, 214
profitability ratios, 221
asset-utilization ratios, 223
liquidity ratios, 224
debt-utilization ratios, 225
price ratios, 226
dividend yield, 228
dividend-payout ratio, 229
trend analysis, 232
inflation-adjusted accounting, 237
extraordinary gains and losses, 239

DISCUSSION QUESTIONS

1. Does a balance sheet that is dated year-end 1995 reflect only transactions for that year?
2. Explain why the statement of cash flows is particularly relevant in light of the fact that the accrual method of accounting is used in the income statement and balance sheet.
3. Can we automatically assume that a firm that has an operating loss on the income statement has reduced the cash flows for the firm during the period?
4. What ratios are likely to be of greatest interest to the banker or trade creditor? To the bondholder?
5. If a firm's operating margin and after-tax margin are almost the same (an unusual case), what can we say about the firm?
6. Comment on the heavy capital goods industry and the food-processing industry in terms of performance under the Du Pont system of analysis.
7. In computing return on assets and return on equity, how does the age of the assets influence the interpretation of the values?
8. If a firm's return on equity is substantially higher than the firm's return on assets, what can the analyst infer about the firm?
9. How do the asset-utilization ratios relate to the liquidity ratios?

10. Can public utility firms better justify the use of high debt than firms in the automobile or airline industry? Comment.
11. Why will the fixed-charge-coverage ratio always be equal to or *less* than times interest earned?
12. What might a high dividend-payout ratio suggest to an analyst about a company's growth prospects?
13. Comment on the relative profitability of Coca-Cola's international soft drinks and food divisions using data from Table 8–5. Is the difference due to a better turnover of assets?
14. Using data from Table 8–7, comment on Coca-Cola's profitability ratios in comparison to those of the beverage and food industries. Do the price-earnings ratios in the table reflect relative profitability?
15. Explain the probable impact of replacement-cost accounting on the ratios of return on assets, debt to total assets, and times interest earned for a firm that has substantial old fixed assets.
16. In examining Table 8–11 and the first column of Table 8–12, explain why earnings after taxes and the ratios have improved despite a constant unit sales volume.

PROBLEMS

Du Pont analysis

1. Given the following financial data: net income/sales = 4 percent; sales/total assets = 3.5 percent; debt/total assets = 60 percent; compute:
   a. Return on assets.
   b. Return on equity.

Du Pont analysis

2. Explain why in problem 1 return on equity was so much higher than return on assets.

Du Pont analysis

3. A firm has a return on assets of 12 percent and a return on equity of 18 percent. What is the debt-to-total assets ratio?

General ratio analysis

4. A firm has the following financial data:

Current assets	$600,000
Fixed assets	400,000
Current liabilities	300,000
Inventory	200,000

If inventory increases by $100,000, what will be the impact on the current ratio, the quick ratio, and the net-working-capital-to-total-assets ratio. Show the ratios before and after the changes.

General ratio analysis

5. Given the financial data starting on the next page, compute:
   a. Return on equity.
   b. Quick ratio.
   c. Long-term debt to equity.
   d. Fixed-charge coverage.

Assets:	
Cash	$ 2,500
Accounts receivable	3,000
Inventory	6,500
Fixed assets	8,000
Total assets	$20,000
Liabilities and stockholders' equity:	
Short-term debt	$ 3,000
Long-term debt	2,000
Stockholders' equity	15,000
Total liabilities and stockholders' equity	$20,000
Income before fixed charges and taxes	$ 4,400
Interest payments	800
Lease payments	400
Taxes (35 percent tax rate)	1,120
Net income (after taxes)	$ 2,080

Coverage of sinking fund

6. Assume in part *d* of problem 5 that the firm had a sinking-fund payment obligation of $200. How much before-tax income is required to cover the sinking-fund obligation? Would lower tax rates increase or decrease the before-tax income required to cover the sinking fund?

Return on equity

7. In problem 5, if total debt were increased to 50 percent of assets, and interest payments went up by $300, what would be the new value for return on equity?

Stock price ratios

8. Assume the following financial data:

Short-term assets	$300,000
Long-term assets	500,000
Total assets	$800,000
Short-term debt	$200,000
Long-term debt	168,000
Total liabilities	368,000
Common stock	200,000
Retained earnings	232,000
Total stockholders' equity	432,000
Total liabilities and stockholders' equity	$800,000
Total earnings (after-tax)	$72,000
Dividends per share	$1.44
Stock price	$45
Shares outstanding	24,000

a. Compute the P/E ratio (stock price to earnings per share).
b. Compute book value per share (note that book value equals stockholders' equity).
c. Compute the ratio of stock price to book value per share.
d. Compute the dividend yield.
e. Compute the payout ratio.

Tax considerations and financial analysis

9. Referring to problem 8:
   a. Compute after-tax return on equity.
   b. If the tax rate were 40 percent, what could you infer the value of before-tax income was?
   c. Now assume the same before-tax income computed in part *b,* but a tax rate of 25 percent; recompute after-tax return on equity (using the simplifying assumption that equity remains constant).
   d. Assume the taxes in part *c* were reduced largely as a result of one-time nonrecurring tax credits. Would you expect the stock value to go up substantially as a result of the higher return on equity?

Divisional analysis

10. The Multi-Corporation has three different operating divisions. Financial information for each is as follows:

	Clothing	Appliances	Sporting Goods
Sales	$3,000,000	$15,000,000	$25,000,000
Operating income	330,000	1,250,000	3,200,000
Net income (A/T)	135,000	870,000	1,400,000
Assets	1,200,000	10,000,000	8,000,000

   a. Which division provides the highest operating margin?
   b. Which division provides the lowest after-tax profit margin?
   c. Which division has the lowest after-tax return on assets?
   d. Compute net income (after-tax) to sales for the entire corporation.
   e. Compute net income (after-tax) to assets for the entire corporation.
   f. The vice president of finance suggests the assets in the Appliances division be sold off for $10 million and redeployed in Sporting Goods. The new $10 million in Sporting Goods will produce the same after-tax return on assets as the current $8 million in that division. Recompute net income to total assets for the entire corporation assuming the above suggested change.
   g. Explain why Sporting Goods, which has a lower return on sales than Appliances, has such a positive effect on return on assets.

Approaches to security evaluation

11. Security Analyst A thinks that the Collins Corporation is worth 14 times current earnings. Security Analyst B has a different approach. He assumes that 45 percent of earnings (per share) will be paid out in dividends and the stock should provide a 4 percent current dividend yield. Assume total earnings are $12 million and that 5 million shares are outstanding.
   a. Compute the value of the stock based on Security Analyst A's approach.
   b. Compute the value of the stock based on Security Analyst B's approach.

c. Security Analyst C uses the constant dividend valuation model approach presented in Chapter 7 as Formula 7–5. She uses Security Analyst B's assumption about dividends (per share) and assigns a growth rate, g, of 9 percent and a required rate of return, K_e, of 12 percent. Is her value higher or lower than that of the other security analysts?

CFA MATERIAL

The following material contains sample questions and solutions from a prior Level I CFA exam. While the terminology is slightly different from that in this text, you can still view the skills necessary for the CFA exam.

CFA Exam Question

Question 1 is composed of two parts, for a total of 15 minutes.

1. As shown in Table 1, Tennant's operating results have been less favorable during the 1980s than the 1970s based on three representative years, 1975, 1981, and 1987. To develop an explanation, you decide to examine Tennant's operating history employing the industrial life cycle model, which recognizes four stages as follows:

   I. Early development.

   II. Rapid expansion.

TABLE 1 Tennant Company

Selected Historic Operating and Balance Sheet Data
As of December 31, 1975, 1981, and 1987
(in thousands)

	1975	1981	1987
Net sales	$47,909	$109,333	$166,924
Cost of goods sold	27,395	62,373	95,015
Gross profits	20,514	46,960	71,909
Selling, general, and administrative expenses	11,895	29,649	54,151
Earnings before interest and taxes	8,619	17,311	17,758
Interest on long-term debt	0	53	248
Pretax income	8,619	17,258	17,510
Income taxes	4,190	7,655	7,692
After-tax income	$ 4,429	$ 9,603	$ 9,818
Total assets	$33,848	$ 63,555	$106,098
Total common stockholders' equity	25,722	46,593	69,516
Long-term debt	6	532	2,480
Total common shares outstanding	5,654	5,402	5,320
Earnings per share	$ 0.78	$ 1.78	$ 1.85
Dividends per share	0.28	0.72	0.96
Book value per share	4.55	8.63	13.07

III. Mature growth.
IV. Stabilization or decline.

a. Describe the behavior of revenues, profit margins, and total profits as a company passes through *each* of the *four* stages of the industrial life cycle.
b. Using 1975, 1981, and 1987 results as representative, discuss Tennant's operating record from 1975 through 1987 in terms of the industrial life-cycle record.

(*15 minutes*)

Solution: Question 1—Morning Section (I–88) (15 points)

a. During the early development stage, revenue growth is rapid. However, profit margins are negative until revenues reach a critical mass. From that point forward, rapidly improving margins combine with continued strong revenue growth to create extremely rapid earnings progress.

Profit margins continue to expand during the rapid expansion phase but level out during the mature growth phase. Despite gradual tapering of profit margins, earnings continue to rise during the mature growth phase due to continuing revenue growth. However, earnings progress is significantly slower than during the rapid expansion phase.

The final stage of earnings stabilization or decline is characterized by a continuing moderation in the rate of sales growth and deteriorating profit margins. In the extreme, declining revenues in combination with decreasing profit margins lead to significant earnings declines.

b. Tennant appeared to be in the rapid expansion to the mature growth stage between 1975 and 1981. Although pretax margins weakened, the company was able to double pretax earnings, while sales revenues increased even more rapidly. However, a sharp change occurred after 1981. Sales growth moderated, and profit margins declined sharply. On this basis, Tennant clearly entered the mature growth stage between 1981 and 1987. Based on profit trends, it could be argued that the company had progressed to Stage IV, stabilization and decline. However, a continuation of reasonably strong revenue growth suggests this is not the case.

(Good answers to this question will recognize that the life cycle of a corporation is identified primarily by trends in revenue growth and profit margins. An ideal answer might include simple calculations along the line shown below.)

	1975	1981	1987
Sales	$47,909	$109,333	$166,924
Percent change during prior 6 years	N.A.	128.2%	52.7%
Pretax earnings	$ 8,619	$ 17,311	$ 17,758
Percent change during prior 6 years	N.A.	100.8%	2.6%
Pretax margins	18.0%	15.8%	10.6%

Question 2 is composed of two parts, for a total of 25 minutes.

2. The director of research suggests that you use the Du Pont model to analyze the components of Tennant's return on equity during 1981 and 1987 to explain the change that has occurred in the company's return on equity. She asks you to work with the five factors listed below.

I. EBIT margin.
II. Asset turnover.
III. Interest burden.
IV. Financial leverage.
V. Tax retention rate.

a. Compute 1981 and 1987 values of *each* of these *five* factors.
(*15 minutes*)

b. Identify the individual component that had the greatest influence on the change in return on equity from 1981 and 1987, and briefly explain the possible reasons for the changes in the value of this component between the two years.
(*10 minutes*)

Solution: Question 2—Morning Section (I–88) (25 points)

a.

	Value	
Tennant Equity Return Components	**1981**	**1987**
I. EBIT margins	15.8%	10.6%
II. Asset turnover	1.72x	1.57x
III. Interest burden	0.1%	0.2%
IV. Financial leverage	1.36x	1.53x
V. Tax retention rate	55.6%	56.1%

b. Increases in financial leverage and the tax retention rate acted to increase return on equity between 1981 and 1987. Declining EBIT margins, a decline in asset turnover, and an increase in interest burden tended to reduce profitability.

The dominant factor was the 33 percent decline in EBIT margins. This was due to the increase in SG&A and Tennant's entering mature growth. Interest burden was a relatively trivial factor, and the tax-retention rate changed only nominally. The decrease in asset turnover and increase in financial leverage were more meaningful but tended to cancel each other.

THE WALL STREET JOURNAL PROJECTS

1. Chapter 8 features Coca-Cola as the sample company under analysis. Follow *The Wall Street Journal* (page B2) for any stories affecting Coca-Cola.

a. Locate the stock price, price-earnings ratio (P/E), and dividends from *The Wall Street Journal* in section C. Use *The Value Line Investment Survey* to find the book value.

(1) Calculate the dividends-to-price (dividend yield).

(2) Calculate the price-to-book value.

b. Calculate Coca-Cola's P/E ratio using today's price and estimated year-end earnings per share as found in the *Value Line Survey.* Is there a difference between the P/E calculated this way versus the one in part *a?* If there is, can you explain why?

2. Examine the companies listed in Table 8–4, and compare their current price-earnings (P/E) ratios from section C in *The Wall Street Journal* to those in the table. Do stock prices on a relative P/E basis seem to be higher or lower than they were in late 1994? What do you think is the reason for this relationship?

CRITICAL THOUGHT CASE

Barry Minkow founded ZZZZ Best Co., a carpet-cleaning firm, when he was 15 years old. He ran the business from his family's garage in Reseda, California. The company became one of the biggest carpet-cleaning firms in California, and Minkow was a millionaire by age 18. Minkow took his company public by selling its stock when he was 21, and his personal worth was estimated at close to $10 million. At that time, ZZZZ Best ("Zee Best") had 1,300 employees and 1986 sales of $4.8 million. Minkow boldly predicted that 1987 revenues would exceed $50 million.

In July 1990, ZZZZ Best management filed for bankruptcy protection and sued Minkow for misappropriating $21 million in company funds. In addition, several customers accused ZZZZ Best of overcharging them in a credit-card scam. Minkow publicly admitted the overcharges but blamed them on subcontractors and employees. He also said he had fired those responsible and had personally repaid the charges.

The Securities and Exchange Commission and other law enforcement agencies began investigating Minkow and his company. It became apparent that ZZZZ Best was built on a foundation of lies, dishonesty, and inconsistent accounting practices. The company had submitted phoney credit-card charges and had issued press releases claiming millions of dollars in bogus contracts, sending the price of the company's stock even higher. The SEC investigated other charges, including the possibility of phoney receivables, bogus financial accounting statements, organized crime connections, and securities law violations by Minkow and other executives. The SEC placed an independent trustee in charge of the company until its accounting records could be sorted out.

The Los Angeles Police Department investigated charges that ZZZZ Best was a money-laundering operation for organized crime. The investigation linked Minkow and ZZZZ Best with drug dealings and organized crime members.

These allegations ultimately led Minkow to resign from ZZZZ Best for "health reasons." But his resignation was not the end of his troubles. ZZZZ Best's new management sued Minkow for embezzling $3 million of the company's funds for his personal use and misappropriating $18 million to perform fictitious insurance restoration

work. The suit charged that Minkow actually diverted this money to an associate's refurbishing business, which was part of an elaborate scheme designed to allow Minkow to take corporate funds for his own and others' personal use. According to the suit, these discrepancies in the company's accounting practices were the reasons behind the bankruptcy filing. As a result, ZZZZ Best's accounting firm quit.

Questions

1. Given the extent of fraud in this case, should ZZZZ Best's accounting firm be held responsible for not discovering the fraudulent activities?
2. What is the responsibility of the broker and financial analyst in recommending the company to investors? To what extent are they responsible for their investment recommendations?

U.S. EQUITIES ONFLOPPY EXERCISES

Please use your U.S. Equities OnFloppy software and manual to complete the following exercises.

1. **a.** Use the User Fields option to define the following ratios referred to in Chapter 8:
   (1) After-tax profit margin
   (2) Return on assets
   (3) Return on equity
   (4) Inventory turnover
   (5) Total asset turnover
   (6) Current ratio
   (7) Quick ratio
   (8) Net working capital to total assets
   (9) Total debt to total assets
   (10) Price to earnings
   (11) Price to book value
   (12) Dividends to price
   (13) Dividend payout
   Define these ratios to calculate the values for the last full year of data. For example, after-tax profit margin, ROR1 = EA1/REV1, return on assets, ROA1 = EA1/ (CL1 + LTD1 + PFD1 + EQ1).

   b. Use the ratios defined in part *a* to analyze Pepsico and Coca-Cola.
2. The Du Pont system of analysis expresses (*a*) return on assets (EA/TA) as the product of the profit margin (EA/REV) and total asset turnover (REV/TA) and (*b*) return on equity (EA/EQ) as the product of return on assets (EA/TA) and the equity multiplier (TA/EQ). Analyze the values of these five variables for a portion of the Heavy Capital Goods industry (SIC 351* and SIC 352*) versus the Food Stores industry (SIC 54**). Use the data from the last full year, EA1, REV1, and

so forth. Consider only those firms that have a positive return on assets and return on equity. Further limit your analysis to the largest (market capitalization) 10 firms.

3. **a.** Select the companies that have an ROE of at least 20 percent. How many are there?
   b. From those companies selected in part *a,* select the companies that have a dividend yield of at least 5 percent. How many companies remain?
   c. From the analysis of parts *a* and *b,* what conclusion would you draw?
   d. Suggest some reasons to explain your conclusion.

SELECTED REFERENCES

Financial Reporting

Bierman, Harold, Jr. "Accounting for Valuation and Evaluation." *The Journal of Portfolio Management,* Spring 1994, pp. 64–67.

Briloff, Abraham J. "Cannibalizing the Transcendent Margin: Reflections on Conglomeration, LBOs, Recapitalizations and Other Manifestations of Corporate Mania." *Financial Analysts Journal,* May–June 1988, pp. 74–82.

Chaney, Paul K., and Debra C. Jeter. "The Effect of Deferred Taxes on Security Prices." *Journal of Accounting, Auditing and Finance,* Winter 1994, pp. 91–116.

Frankel, Micah, and Robert Trezevant. "The Year-End LIFO Inventory Purchasing Decision: An Empirical Test." *The Accounting Review,* April 1994, pp. 382–98.

Joy, O. Maurice; Robert H. Litzenberger; and Richard W. McEnally. "The Adjustment of Stock Prices to Announcements of Unanticipated Changes in Quarterly Earnings." *Journal of Accounting Research,* Autumn 1977, pp. 207–25.

Safian, Kenneth. "Corporate Profits and Valuation: A Different Approach." *Financial Analysts Journal,* January–February 1988, pp. 8–13.

Swales, George S., Jr. "Another Look at the President's Letter to Stockholders." *Financial Analysts Journal,* March–April 1988, pp. 71–72.

Warshawsky, Mark J.; H. Fred Mittelstaedt; and Carrie Cristea. "Recognizing Retiree Health Benefits: The Effect of SFA 106." *Financial Management,* Summer 1993, pp. 188–99.

The Use of Ratios

Backer, Morton, and Martin L. Gosman. "The Use of Financial Ratios in Credit Downgrade Decisions." *Financial Management,* Spring 1980, pp. 53–56.

Chen, Kung H., and Thomas A. Shimerda. "An Empirical Analysis of Useful Financial Ratios." *Financial Management,* Spring 1981, pp. 51–60.

Distortions in Reported Data

Choi, Frederick D. S., and Richard M. Levich. "International Accounting Diversity: Does It Affect Market Participants?" *Financial Analysts Journal,* July–August 1991, pp. 73–82.

Fabozzi, Frank J., and Robert Fonfeder. "Have You Seen Any Good Quarterly Statements Lately?" *Journal of Portfolio Management,* Winter 1983, pp. 71–74.

"Pension Liabilities: Improvement Is Illusory." *Business Week,* September 14, 1981, pp. 114–18.

PART 3

Issues in Efficient Markets

OUTLINE

A few thousand highly paid portfolio managers have basically replaced individual investors as the key players in the marketplace. Has the age of sophisticated stock analysis replaced the "hot tip" days of yesteryear?

The Great Market Crash of 1929 was caused, in part, by a *herd* instinct. The market was dominated by individual investors rather than professional money managers, and the mood of the day went from blind optimism to panic as the market crashed. Investors followed each other like sheep to slaughter.

In the following decades, the nature of market participants changed. Although 60 percent of the stocks in the United States are still owned by individuals, professional money managers do most of the daily trading. These money managers are supposedly brilliant and dispassionate professionals armed with their MBA degrees and computers. One would assume they could pick stocks scientifically. Hire them, and the return on your investment would likely be much greater than if you invested on your own.

Not so, says Bob Glauber, a Harvard Business School professor. Glauber headed the Brady Commission that investigated and reported on the market crash of October 1987. He says it is easy to forget that professional investors are also human beings subject to the same emotions as the rest of us. They tend to look at what everybody else is doing and follow the herd. Thus, seven decades after the crash of the 1920s, there is still a herd instinct on Wall Street, only carried out by a more sophisticated, trained group of analysts and money managers.

Of course, there are exceptions to the "follow the leader" mentality. Some would suggest that unusually insightful analysis can produce high returns that set one apart from the pack. This may well be true, but for how long? A new insight or technique that produces superior returns is likely to be quickly copied in the great electronic markets in the United States, London, or Japan.

The herd instinct may eventually turn a good idea into a disaster. For example, one may use short-selling or options to protect against a fall in stock values in a portfolio. This is basically a conservative strategy, but it turns into an ill-fated one if everyone does it at the same time.

The creative individual investor may have a better chance to outperform the market than a hard-driven, computer-inspired MBA who is constantly watching the market tape. ■

9

A Basic View of Technical Analysis and Market Efficiency

In the preceding four chapters, we followed a fundamental approach to security analysis. That is, we examined the fundamental factors that influence the business cycle, the performance of various industries, and the operations of the individual firms. We have further examined the financial statements and tools of measurement that are available to the security analyst. In following a fundamental approach, one attempts to evaluate the appropriate worth of a security and perhaps ascertain whether it is under- or overpriced.

In this chapter, we shall examine a technical approach to investment timing. In this approach, analysts and market technicians examine prior price and volume data, as well as other market-related indicators, to determine past trends in the belief that they will help forecast future ones. Technical analysts place much more emphasis on charts and graphs of *internal market data* than on such fundamental factors as earnings reports, management capabilities, or new-product development. They believe that even when important fundamental information is uncovered, it may not lead to profitable trading because of timing considerations and market imperfections.

We shall also devote much time and attention in this chapter to the concept of market efficiency; that is, the ability of the market to adjust very rapidly to the supply of new information in valuing a security. This area of study has led to the efficient market hypothesis, which states that all securities are correctly priced at any point.

At the outset, be aware there are many disagreements and contradictions in the various areas we will examine. As previously implied, advocates of technical analysis do not place much emphasis on fundamental analysis, and vice versa. Even more significant, proponents of the efficient market hypothesis would suggest that neither technical nor fundamental analysis is of any great value in producing superior returns.

In light of the various disagreements that exist, we believe it is important that the student be exposed to many schools of thought. For example, we devote the first part of the chapter to technical analysis and then later offer research findings that relate to the value of the technical approach as well as the fundamental approach. Our philosophy throughout the chapter is to recognize that there sometimes is a gap between practices utilized by brokerage houses (and on Wall Street) and beliefs held in the academic community, yet the student should be exposed to both.

TECHNICAL ANALYSIS

Technical analysis is based on a number of basic assumptions:

1. Market value is determined solely by the interaction of demand and supply.
2. It is assumed that though there are minor fluctuations in the market, stock prices tend to move in trends that persist for long periods.
3. Reversals of trends are caused by shifts in demand and supply.
4. Shifts in demand and supply can be detected sooner or later in charts.
5. Many chart patterns tend to repeat themselves.[1]

For our purposes, the most significant items to note are the assumptions that stock prices tend to move in trends that persist for long periods, and these trends can be

---

[1] R. D. Edwards and John Magee, Jr., *Technical Analysis of Stock Trends* (Springfield, MA: John Magee, 1958).

detected in charts. The basic premise is that past trends in market movements can be used to forecast or understand the future. The market technician generally assumes there is a lag between the time he perceives a change in the value of a security and when the investing public ultimately assesses this change.

In developing the tools of technical analysis, we shall divide our discussion between (*a*) the use of charting and (*b*) the key indicator series to project future market movements.

THE USE OF CHARTING

Charting is often linked to the development of the Dow theory in the late 1890s by Charles Dow.[2] Mr. Dow was the founder of the Dow Jones Company and editor of *The Wall Street Journal.* Many of his early precepts were further refined by other market technicians, and it is generally believed the Dow theory was successful in signaling the market crash of 1929.

Essential Elements of the Dow Theory

The **Dow theory** maintains that there are three major movements in the market: daily fluctuations, secondary movements, and primary trends. According to the theory, daily fluctuations and secondary movements (covering two weeks to a month) are only important to the extent they reflect on the long-term primary trend in the market. Primary trends may be characterized as either bullish or bearish in nature.

In Figure 9–1, we look at the use of the Dow theory to analyze a market trend. Note that the primary movement in the market is positive despite two secondary movements that are downward. The important facet of the secondary movements is that each low is

FIGURE 9–1 Presentation of the Dow Theory

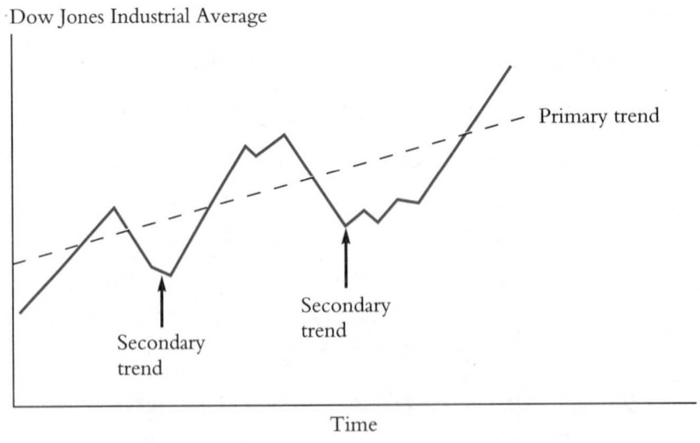

[2] *The Wall Street Journal,* December 19, 1900.

FIGURE 9–2

Market Reversal and Confirmation

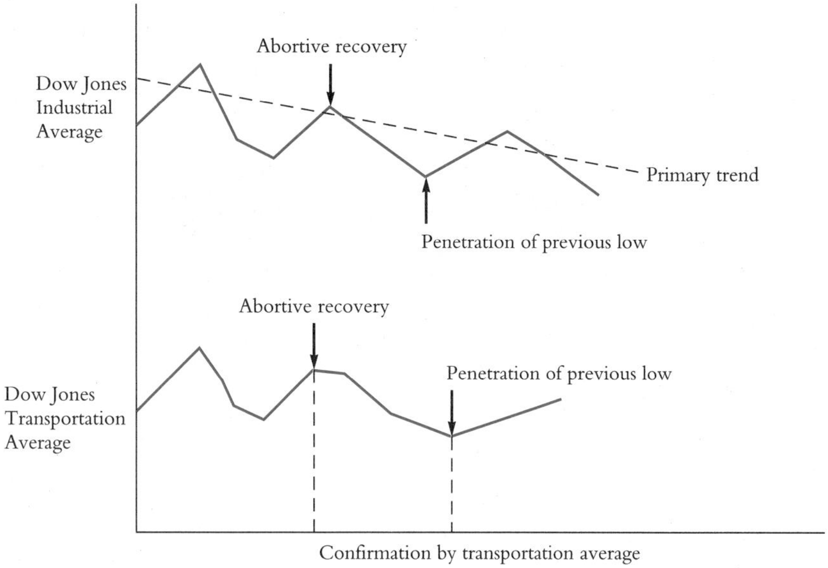

higher than the previous low and each high is higher than the previous high. This tends to confirm the primary trend, which is bullish.

Under the Dow theory, it is assumed that this pattern will continue for a long period, and the analyst should not be confused by secondary movements. However, the upward pattern must ultimately end. This is indicated by a new pattern in which a recovery fails to exceed the previous high (abortive recovery) and a new low penetrates a previous low as indicated in the top part of Figure 9–2. For a true turn in the market to occur, the new pattern of movement in the Dow Jones Industrial Average must also be confirmed by a subsequent movement in the Dow Jones Transportation Average as indicated on the bottom part of Figure 9–2.

A change from a bear to a bull market would require similar patterns of confirmation. While the Dow theory has proved helpful to market technicians, there is always the problem of false signals. For example, not every abortive recovery is certain to signal the end of a bull market. Furthermore, the investor may have to wait a long time to get full confirmation of a change in a primary trend. By the time the transportation average confirms the pattern in the industrial average, important market movements may have already occurred.

Support and Resistance Levels

Chartists attempt to define trading levels for individual securities (or the market) where there is a likelihood that price movements will be challenged. Thus, in the daily financial press or on television, the statement is often made that the next barrier to the current market move is at 4000 (or some other level). This assumes the existence of support and

FIGURE 9–3 Support and Resistance

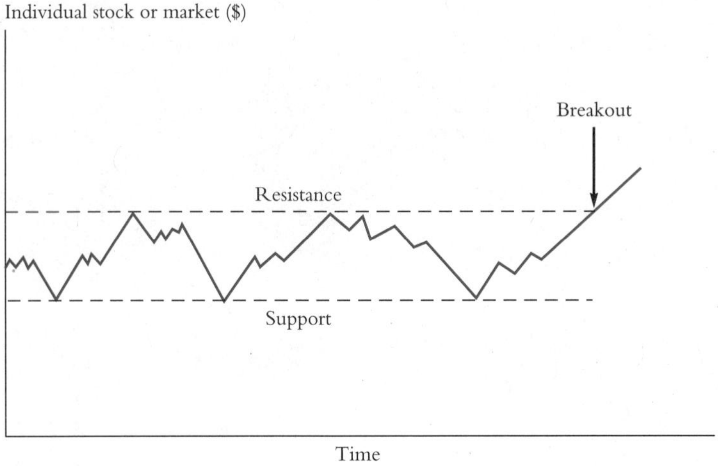

resistance levels. As indicated in Figure 9–3, a support level is associated with the lower end of a trading range and a resistance level with the upper end.

Support may develop each time a stock goes down to a lower level of trading because investors who previously passed up a purchase opportunity may now choose to act. It is a signal that new demand is coming into the market. When a stock reaches the high side of the normal trading range, **resistance** may develop because some investors who bought in on a previous wave of enthusiasm (on an earlier high) may now view this as a chance to get even. Others may simply see this as an opportunity to take a profit.

A breakout above a resistance point (as indicated in Figure 9–3) or below a support level is considered significant. The stock is assumed to be trading in a new range, and higher (lower) trading values may now be expected.

Volume

The amount of volume supporting a given market movement is also considered significant. For example, if a stock (or the market in general) makes a new high on heavy trading volume, this is considered to be bullish. Conversely, a new high on light volume may indicate a temporary move that is likely to be reversed.

A new low on light volume is considered somewhat positive because of the lack of investor participation. When a new low is established on the basis of heavy trading volume, this is considered to be quite bearish.

In the mid-1990s, the New York Stock Exchange averaged a volume of 250 to 275 million shares daily. When the volume jumped to 350 to 400 million shares, analysts took a very strong interest in the trading pattern of the market.

Types of Charts

Until now, we have been using typical line charts to indicate market patterns. Technicians also use bar charts and point and figure charts. We shall examine each.

Bar Chart A bar chart shows the high and low price for a stock with a horizontal dash along the line to indicate the closing price. An example is shown in Figure 9–4.

We see on November 12 the stock traded between a high of 41 and a low of 38 and closed at 40. Daily information on the Dow Jones Industrial Average is usually presented in the form of a bar chart, with daily volume shown at the bottom as indicated in Figure 9–5 on page 260.

Trendline, published through a division of Standard & Poor's, provides excellent charting information on a variety of securities traded on the major exchanges and is available at many libraries and brokerage houses. Market technicians carefully evaluate the charts, looking for what they perceive to be significant patterns of movement. For example, the pattern in Figure 9–4 might be interpreted as a head-and-shoulder pattern (note the head in the middle) with a lower penetration of the neckline to the right indicating a sell signal. In Figure 9–6 on page 261, we show a series of the price-movement patterns presumably indicating market bottoms and tops.

Though it is beyond the scope of this book to go into interpretation of chart formations in great detail, special books on the subject are suggested at the end of our discussion of charting.

FIGURE 9–4 Bar Chart

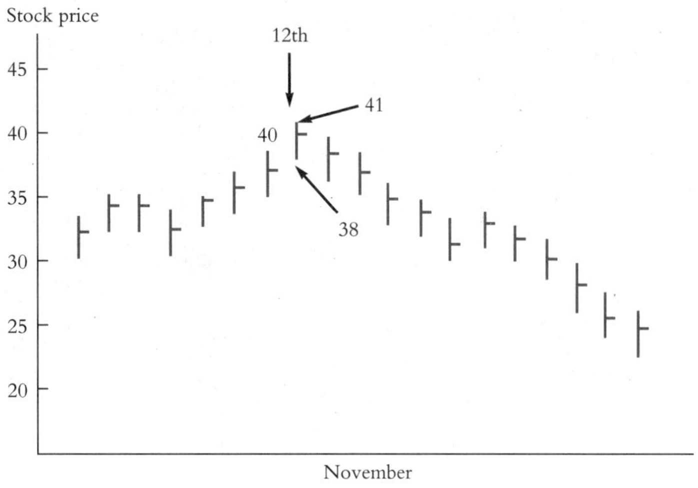

FIGURE 9–5 Bar Chart of Market Average

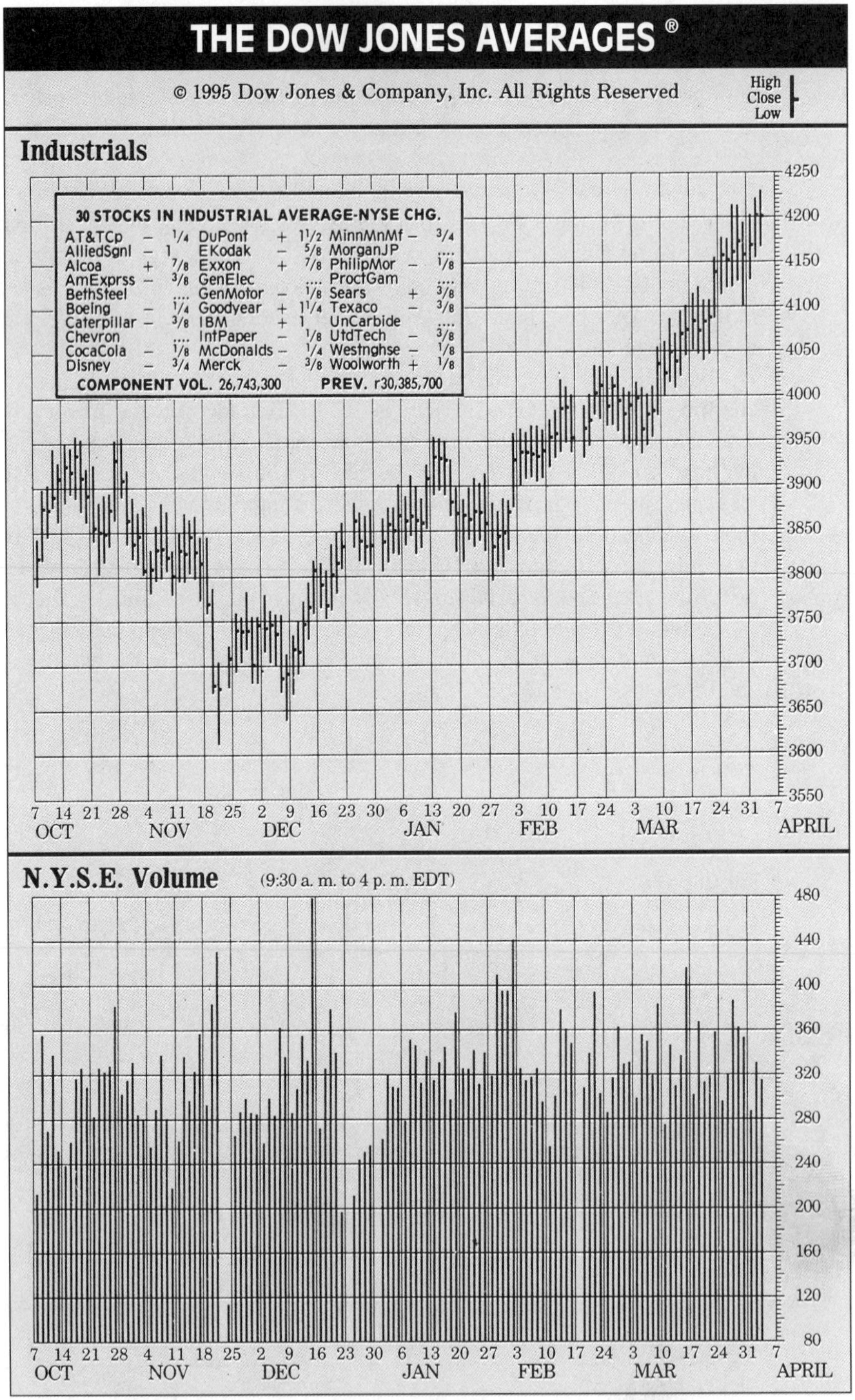

Source: *The Wall Street Journal*, April 6, 1995, p. C3. Reprinted by permission of *The Wall Street Journal*, © 1994 by Dow Jones & Company, Inc. All Rights Reserved Worldwide.

FIGURE 9–6 Chart Representation of Market Bottoms and Tops

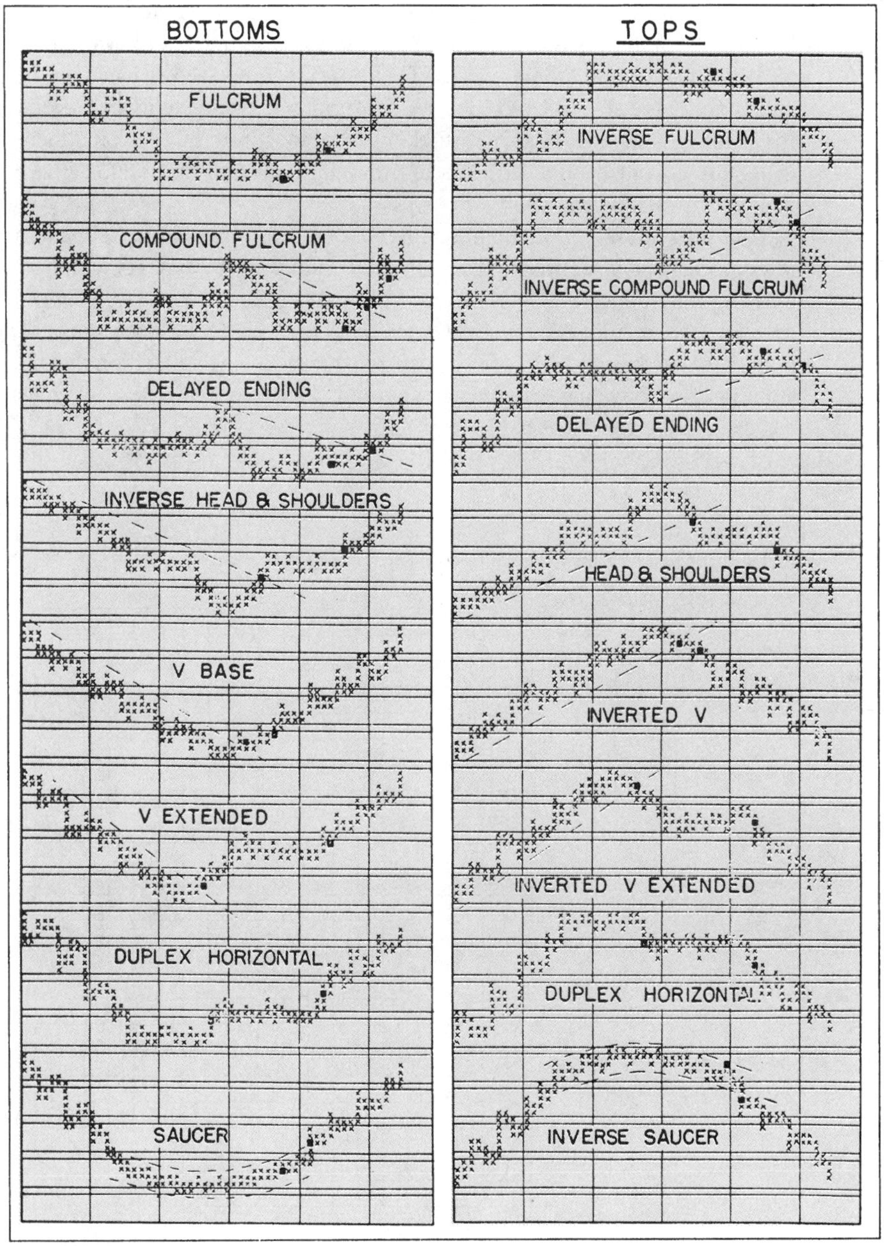

Source: Irwin Shishko, "Techniques of Forecasting Commodity Prices," *Commodity Yearbook* (New York: Commodity Research Bureau, 1965), p. 4.

Point and Figure Chart A point and figure chart (PFC) emphasizes significant price changes and the reversal of significant price changes. Unlike a line or bar chart, it has no time dimension. An example of a point and figure chart is presented in Figure 9–7.

The assumption is that the stock starts at 30. Only moves of two points or greater are plotted on the graph (some may prefer to use one point). Advances are indicated by Xs, and declines are shown by Os. A reversal from an advance to a decline or vice versa calls for a shift in columns. Thus, the stock initially goes from 30 to 42 and then shifts columns in its subsequent decline to 36 before moving up again in column 3. A similar pattern persists throughout the chart.

Chartists carefully read point and figure charts to observe market patterns (where there is support, resistance, breakouts, congestion, and so on). Students with a strong interest in charting may consult such books as Colby and Meyers, *The Encyclopedia of Technical Market Indicators,*[3] and Zweig, *Understanding Technical Forecasting.*[4] The problem in reading charts has always been to analyze patterns in such a fashion that they truly predict stock market movements before they unfold. To justify the effort, one must assume there are discernible trends over the long term.

FIGURE 9–7

Point and Figure Chart

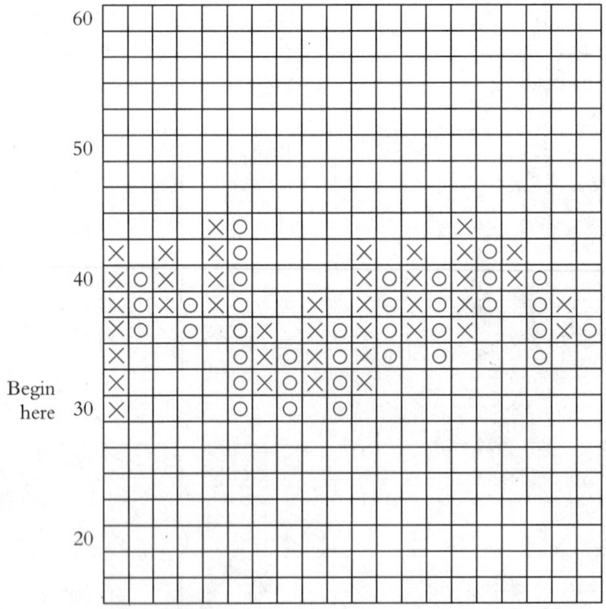

[3] Robert W. Colby and Thomas A. Meyers, *The Encyclopedia of Technical Market Indicators* (Homewood, IL: Business One Irwin, 1988).

[4] Martin E. Zweig, *Understanding Technical Forecasting* (Princeton, NJ: Dow Jones, 1978).

KEY INDICATOR SERIES

In the television series "Wall Street Week," host Louis Rukeyser watches a number of indicators on a weekly basis and compares the bullish and bearish indicators to determine what the next direction of the market might be.

In this section, we will examine bullish and bearish technical indicator series. We will first look at contrary opinion rules, then smart money rules, and finally, overall market indicators.

Contrary Opinion Rules

The essence of a **contrary opinion rule** is that it is easier to figure out who is wrong than who is right. If you know your neighbor has a terrible sense of direction and you spot him taking a left at the intersection, you automatically take a right. In the stock market there are similar guidelines.

Odd-Lot Theory An odd-lot trade is one of less than 100 shares, and only small investors tend to engage in odd-lot transactions. The odd-lot theory suggests you watch very closely what the small investor is doing and then do the opposite. *The Wall Street Journal* reports odd-lot trading on a daily basis, and *Barron's* reports similar information on a weekly basis. It is a simple matter to construct a ratio of odd-lot purchases to odd-lot sales. For example, on May 19, 1994, 949,800 odd-lot shares were purchased, and 1,317,500 shares were sold, indicating a ratio of 0.721. The ratio has historically fluctuated between 0.50 and 1.35.

The odd-lot theory actually suggests that the small trader does all right most of the time but badly misses on key market turns. As indicated in Figure 9–8, the odd-lot trader is on the correct path as the market is going up; that is, selling off part of the portfolio in an up market (the name of the game is to buy low and sell high). This net selling posture is reflected by a declining odd-lot index (purchase-to-sales ratio). However, as the market

FIGURE 9–8 Comparing Standard & Poor's 500 Index and the Odd-Lot Index

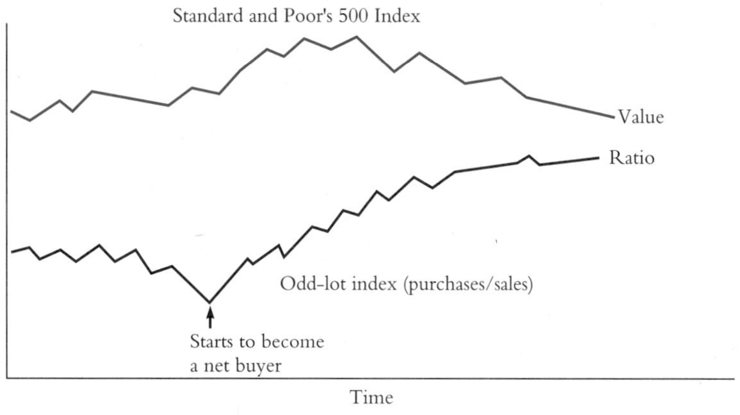

continues upward, the odd-lot trader suddenly thinks he or she sees an opportunity for a killing in the market and becomes a very strong net buyer. This precedes a fall in the market.

The odd-lot trader is also assumed to be a strong seller right before the bottom of a bear market. Presumably, when the small trader finally gets grandfather's 50 shares of AT&T out of the lockbox and sells them in disgust, it is time for the market to turn upward.

As if to add injury to insult, a corollary to the odd-lot theory says one should be particularly sensitive to what odd-lot traders do on Monday because odd-lotters tend to visit each other over the weekend, confirm each other's opinions or exchange hot tips, and then call their brokers on Monday morning. The assumption is that their chatter over the barbeque pit or in the bowling alley is even more suspect than their own individual opinions.

While the odd-lot theory appeared to have some validity in the 1950s and 1960s, it was not a particularly valuable tool in the last two decades. For one thing, the odd-lotters outguessed many of the professional money managers in selling off before the stock market debacle of the mid-1970s and late 1980s, and they began buying in advance of a recovery.

Short Sales Position A second contrary opinion rule is based on the volume of short sales in the market. As you recall from Chapter 3, a short sale represents the selling of a security you do not own with the anticipation of purchasing the security in the future to cover your short position. Investors would only engage in a short sale transaction if they believed the security would, in fact, be going down in price in the near future so they could buy back the security at a lower price to cover the short sale. When the aggregate number of short sellers is large (that is, they are bearish), this is thought to be a bullish signal.

The contrary opinion stems from two sources: first, short sellers are sometimes emotional and may overreact to the market; second and more important, there now is a built-in demand for stocks that have been sold short by investors who will have to repurchase the shares to cover their short positions.

Daily short sale totals for the New York Stock Exchange are recorded in *The Wall Street Journal.* Also once a month (around the 20th), *The Wall Street Journal* reports on total short sale figures for the two major exchanges as well as securities traded on those exchanges (based on midmonth data). This feature usually contains comments about current trends in the market.

Technical analysts compute a ratio of the total short sales positions on an exchange to average daily exchange volume for the month. The normal ratio is between 2.5 and 5.0. A ratio of 3.0 would indicate that the current short sales position is equal to three times the day's average trading volume.

As the short sales ratio (frequently called the short interest ratio) approaches the higher end of the normal trading range, this would be considered bullish (remember this is a contrary opinion trading rule). As is true with many other technical trading rules, its use in predicting future performance has produced mixed results.[5]

---

[5] Randall Smith, "Short Interest and Stock Market Prices," *Financial Analysts Journal,* November–December 1968, pp. 151–54; and Barton M. Briggs, "The Short Interest—A False Proverb," *Financial Analysts Journal,* July–August 1966, pp. 111–16.

Investment Advisory Recommendations A further contrary opinion rule states that you should watch the predictions of the investment advisory services and do the opposite. This has been formalized by Investors Intelligence (an investment advisory service itself) into the Index of Bearish Sentiment. When 60 percent or more of the advisory services are bearish, you should expect a market upturn. Conversely, when only 15 percent or fewer are bearish, you should expect a decline.[6]

Figure 9–9 gives a summary of bullish and bearish sentiments as published in the "Market Laboratory—Economic Indicators" section of *Barron's*. Investors Intelligence as well as three other sources of sentiments are presented. Let's concentrate our attention on Investors Intelligence. Since the bears were closing in on 60 percent in the survey (in column 1 at 52.1 percent versus 29.1 percent for the bulls), this indicates a possible buy under contrary opinion rules.

FIGURE 9–9 Investor Sentiment Readings

INVESTOR SENTIMENT READINGS

In Investors Intelligence's poll, the correction figure represents advisers who are basically bullish, but are looking for some sort of short-term weakness. High bullish readings in that poll, in Consensus Inc., or in Market Vane's usually are signs of market tops; low ones, market bottoms.

Investors Intelligence

	Last Week	Two Weeks Ago	Three Weeks Ago
Bulls	29.1%	29.1%	30.2%
Bears	52.1	50.4	50.8
Correction	18.8	20.5	19.0

Source: Investors Intelligence, 30 Church Street, New Rochelle, N.Y. 10801 (914) 632-0422.

Consensus Index

Bullish Opinion	24%	34%	27%

Source: Consensus Inc., 1735 McGee Street, Kansas City, Mo. 64108 (816) 471-3862.

AAII Index

Bullish	22%	38%	32%
Bearish	42	30	36
Neutral	36	32	32

Source: American Association of Individual Investors, 625 N. Michigan Ave., Chicago, Ill 60611 (312) 280-0170.

Market Vane

Bullish Consensus	32%	34%	42%

Source: Market Vane, P.O. Box 90490, Pasadena, CA 91109 (818) 395-7436.

Source: *Barron's*, May 23, 1994, p. MW101. Reprinted by permission of *Barron's*, © 1994 by Dow Jones & Company. All Rights Reserved Worldwide.

[6] John R. Dortman, "The Stock Market Sign Often Points the Wrong Way," *The Wall Street Journal*, January 26, 1989, p. C1.

Lest one take investment advisory services too lightly, however, observe the market impact of a recommendation by Joseph Granville, publisher of the *Granville Market Letter.* On Tuesday, January 6, 1981, Mr. Granville issued a late-evening warning to his subscribers to "sell everything." He helped cause a $40 billion decline in market values the next day. Although subsequent events proved Mr. Granville wrong in his prediction of an impending bear market, the fact that one man could trigger such a reaction is an indication of the number of people who are influenced by the suggestions of advisory services. Mr. Granville has been followed by many other so-called gurus in the 1980s and early 1990s, most of whom have their day in the sun and then eventually fall into disrepute as they fail to call a major turn in the market or begin reversing their positions so often that investors lose confidence. No doubt a new series of such stars will appear in the mid-1990s.

Put-Call Ratio A final contrary opinion rule applies to the put-call ratio. Puts and calls represent options to sell or buy stock over a specified time period at a given price. A put is an option to sell, and a call is an option to buy. Options have become very popular since they began trading actively on organized exchanges in 1973. As you will see in Chapter 15, there are many sophisticated uses for options to implement portfolio strategies (particularly to protect against losses). However, there is also a great deal of speculation by individual investors in the options market. Because some of this speculation is ill conceived, ratios based on options may tell you to do the opposite of what option traders are doing.

The ratio of put (sell) options to call (buy) options is normally about 0.60. There are generally fewer traders of put options than call options. However, when the ratio gets up to 0.70 or higher, this indicates increasing pessimism by option traders. Under a contrary opinion rule, this indicates a buy signal (he turned left so you turn right). If the put-call ratio goes down to 0.40, the decreasing pessimism (increasing optimism) of the option trader may indicate that it is time to sell if you are a contrarian. The put-call ratio has a better than average record for calling market turns. Put-call ratio data can be found in the "Market Week-Options" section of *Barron's.*

Smart Money Rules

Market technicians have long attempted to track the pattern of sophisticated traders in the hope that they might provide unusual insight into the future. We shall briefly observe theories related to bond market traders and stock exchange specialists.

Barron's Confidence Index The *Barron's* **Confidence Index** is used to observe the trading pattern of investors in the bond market. The theory is based on the premise that bond traders are more sophisticated than stock traders and will pick up trends more quickly. The theory would suggest that a person who can figure out what bond traders are doing today may be able to determine what stock market investors will be doing in the near future.

Barron's Confidence Index is actually computed by taking the yield on 10 top-grade corporate bonds, dividing by the yield on 40 intermediate-grade bonds,[7] and multiplying by 100.

[7] The 40 bonds compose the Dow Jones 40 bond averages.

$$\textit{Barron's} \text{ Confidence Index} = \frac{\text{Yield on 10 top-grade corporate bonds}}{\text{Yield on 40 intermediate-grade bonds}} \times 100 \qquad (9\text{–}1)$$

The index is published weekly in the "Market Laboratory—Bonds" section of *Barron's.* What does it actually tell us? First, we can assume that the top-grade bonds in the numerator will always have a smaller yield than the intermediate-grade bonds in the denominator. The reason is that the higher quality issues can satisfy investors with smaller returns. The bond market is very representative of a risk-return trade-off environment in which less risk requires less return and higher risk necessitates a higher return.

With top-grade bonds providing smaller yields than intermediate-grade bonds, the Confidence Index will always be less than 100 (percent). The normal trading range is between 80 and 95, and it is within this range that technicians look for signals on the economy. If bond investors are bullish about future economic prosperity, they will be rather indifferent between holding top-grade bonds and holding intermediate-grade bonds, and the yield differences between these two categories will be relatively small. This would indicate the Confidence Index may be close to 95. An example is presented below in which top-grade bonds are providing 8.4 percent and intermediate-grade bonds are yielding 9.1 percent.

$$\textit{Barron's} \text{ Confidence Index} = \frac{\text{Yield on 10 top-grade corporate bonds}}{\text{Yield on 40 intermediate-grade bonds}} \times 100$$

$$= \frac{8.4\%}{9.1\%} \times 100 = 92(\%)$$

Now let us assume that investors become quite concerned about the outlook for the future health of the economy. If events go poorly, some weaker corporations may not be able to make their interest payments, and thus, bond market investors will have a strong preference for top-quality issues. Some investors will continue to invest in intermediate- or lower-quality issues but only at a sufficiently high yield differential to justify the risk. We might assume that the *Barron's* Confidence Index will drop to 83 because of the increasing spread between the two yields in the formula.

$$\textit{Barron's} \text{ Confidence Index} = \frac{\text{Yield on 10 top-grade corporate bonds}}{\text{Yield on 40 intermediate-grade bonds}} \times 100$$

$$= \frac{8.9\%}{10.7\%} \times 100 = 83(\%)$$

The yield on the intermediate-grade bonds is now 1.8 percentage points higher than that on the 10 top-grade bonds, and this is reflected in the lower Confidence Index reading. As confidence in the economy is once again regained, the yield spread differential will narrow, and the Confidence Index will go up.

Market technicians assume there are a few months of lead time between what happens to the Confidence Index and what happens to the economy and stock market. As is true with other such indicators, it has a mixed record of predicting future events. One problem is that the Confidence Index is only assumed to consider the impact of investors' attitudes

on yields (their demand pattern). We have seen in the 1980s and early 1990s that the supply of new bond issues can also influence yields. Thus, a very large bond issue by AT&T or Exxon may drive up high-grade bond yields even though investor attitudes indicate they should be going down.

Short Sales by Specialists Another smart money index is based on the short sales positions of specialists. Recall from Chapter 2 that specialists make markets in various securities listed on the organized exchanges. Because of the uniquely close position of specialists to the action on Wall Street, market technicians ascribe unusual importance to their decisions. One measure of their activity that is frequently monitored is the ratio of specialists' short sales to the total amount of short sales on an exchange.

When we previously mentioned short sales in this chapter, we suggested that a high incidence of short selling might be considered bullish because short sellers often overreact to the market and provide future demand potential to cover their short position. In the case of market specialists, this is not necessarily true. These sophisticated traders keep a book of limit orders on their securities so that they have a close feel for market activity at any given time, and their decisions are considered important.

The normal ratio of specialist short sales to short sales on an exchange is about 45 percent. When the ratio goes up to 50 percent or more, market technicians interpret this as a bearish signal. A ratio under 40 percent is considered bullish.

Overall Market Rules

Our discussion of key indicator series has centered on both contrary opinion rules and smart money rules. We now briefly examine two overall market indicators: the breadth of the market indicator series and the cash position of mutual funds.

Breadth of the Market A breadth of the market indicator attempts to measure what a broad range of securities is doing as opposed to merely examining a market average. The theory is that market averages, such as the Dow Jones Industrial Average of 30 stocks or the Standard & Poor's 500 Stock Average, are weighted toward large firms and may not be representative of the entire market. To get a broader perspective of the market, an analyst may examine all stocks on an exchange.

The technician often compares the advance-declines with the movement of a popular market average to determine if there is a divergence between the two. Advances and declines usually move in concert with the popular market averages but may move in the opposite direction at a market peak or bottom. One of the possible signals for the end of a bull market is when the Dow Jones Industrial Average is moving up but the number of daily declines consistently exceeds the number of daily advances on the New York Stock Exchange. This indicates that conservative investors are investing in blue-chip stocks but that there is a lack of broad-based confidence in the market. In Table 9–1, we look at an example of divergence between the advance-decline indicators on the New York Stock Exchange and the Dow Jones Industrial Average (DJIA).

In column 4, we see the daily differences in advances and declines. In column 5, we look at the cumulative pattern by adding or subtracting each new day's value from the

TABLE 9–1 Comparing Advance-Decline Data and the Dow Jones Industrial Average (DJIA)

Day	(1) Advances	(2) Declines	(3) Unchanged	(4) Net Advances or Declines	(5) Cumulative Advances or Declines	(6) DJIA
1	1150	1050	650	+100	+100	+13.38
2	1100	1110	640	− 10	+ 90	+10.51
3	1092	1121	637	− 29	+ 61	+ 3.08
4	1080	1128	642	− 48	+ 13	+15.21
5	1019	1190	641	−171	−158	− 2.02
6	1102	1112	636	− 10	−168	+ 5.43
7	1033	1174	643	−141	−309	+ 3.01
8	892	1312	640	−420	−729	+ .52

previous total. We then compare the information in column 4 and column 5 to the Dow Jones Industrial Average (DJIA) in column 6. Clearly, the strength in the Dow Jones Industrial Average is not reflected in the advance-decline data, and this may be interpreted as signaling future weakness in the market.

Breadth of the market data can also be used to analyze upturns in the market. When the Dow Jones Industrial Average is going down but advances consistently lead declines, the market may be positioned for a recovery. Some market technicians develop sophisticated weighted averages of the daily advance-declines to go along with the data in Table 9–1. Daily data on the Dow Jones Industrial Average and advancing and declining issues can be found in the "Stock Market Data Bank" section of *The Wall Street Journal.*

While a comparison of advance-decline data to market averages can provide important insights, there is also the danger of false signals. Not every divergence between the two signals a turn in the market, so analysts must be careful in their interpretation. The technical analyst generally looks at a wide range of variables.

Mutual Fund Cash Position Another overall market indicator is the cash position of mutual funds. This measure indicates the buying potential of mutual funds and is generally representative of the purchasing potential of other large institutional investors. The cash position of mutual funds, as a percentage of their total assets, generally varies between 5 and 20 percent.[8]

At the lower end of the boundary, it would appear that mutual funds are fully invested and can provide little in the way of additional purchasing power. As their cash position goes to 15 percent or higher, market technicians assess this as representing significant purchasing power that may help to trigger a market upturn. While the overall premise is valid, there are problems in identifying just what is a significant cash position for mutual funds in a given market cycle. It may change in extreme market environments.

[8] The cash dollars are usually placed in short-term credit instruments as opposed to stocks and bonds.

Put Your Book Away and Turn on the Tube—"The Super Bowl Effect"

Twenty-eight Super Bowl games were played between 1967 and 1994. Stock market analysts found an amazing pattern in evaluating the results of those games. In years in which the game was won by a team from the National Football Conference (or teams that were once part of the National Football League such as Baltimore or Pittsburgh), the stock market went up 19 out of 21 years. In years in which the game was won by a team from the American Football Conference, the stock market went down six out of seven years.

This means that an investor could have used the results of the Super Bowl, which is played in January, to correctly predict the performance of the stock market for the year in 25 out of the 28 years. A market technician that could come up with a better predictive device than the Super Bowl would no doubt be considered one of the great market gurus of all time. The so-called Super Bowl Effect was even analyzed in an article in the highly prestigious *Journal of Finance* by Professors Krueger and Kennedy. They found the predictive power of the Super Bowl to be significant at almost any conceivable level of testing.* Even though there is a high correlation, there is obviously no cause and effect between football and stock prices.

*Thomas M. Krueger and William F. Kennedy, "An Examination of the Super Bowl Stock Market Predictor," *Journal of Finance,* June 1990, pp. 691–97.

EFFICIENT MARKET HYPOTHESIS

We shift our attention from technical analysis to that of examining market efficiency. As indicated at the beginning of the chapter, we shall now view any contradictions between the assumptions of fundamental or technical analysis and findings of the **efficient market hypothesis (EMH).**

Earlier in the text, we said that an efficient market is one in which new information is very rapidly processed so that securities are properly priced at any given time.[9] An important premise of an efficient market is that a large number of profit-maximizing participants are concerned with the analysis and valuation of securities. This would seem to describe the security market environment in the United States. Any news on IBM, AT&T, an oil embargo, or tax legislation is likely to be absorbed and acted on very rapidly by profit-maximizing individuals. For this reason, the efficient market hypothesis assumes that no stock price can be in disequilibrium or improperly priced for long. There is almost instantaneous adjustment to new information. The EMH applies most directly to large firms trading on the major security exchanges.

The efficient market hypothesis further assumes that information travels in a random, independent fashion and that prices are an unbiased reflection of all currently available information.

More generally, the efficient market hypothesis is stated and tested in three different forms: the weak form, the semistrong form, and the strong form. We shall examine each of these and the related implications for technical and fundamental analysis.

---

[9] A slightly more precise definition is that securities are priced in an unbiased fashion at any given time. Because information is assumed to travel in a random, independent fashion, there is no consistent upside or downside pricing bias mechanism. Although the price adjustment is not always perfect, it is unbiased and cannot be anticipated in advance.

WEAK FORM OF THE EFFICIENT MARKET HYPOTHESIS

The **weak form of the efficient market hypothesis** suggests there is no relationship between past and future prices of securities. They are presumed to be independent over time. Because the efficient market hypothesis maintains that current prices reflect all available information and information travels in a random fashion, it is assumed that there is little or nothing to be gained from studying past stock prices.

The weak form of the efficient market hypothesis has been tested in two different ways—tests of independence and trading rule tests.

Tests of Independence

Tests of independence have examined the degree of correlation between stock prices over time and have found the correlation to be consistently small (between +0.10 and –0.10) and not statistically significant. This would indicate that stock price changes are independent.[10] A further test is based on the frequency and extent of runs in stock price data. A run occurs when there is no difference in direction between two or more price changes. An example of a series of data and some runs is presented below.

$$(\underbrace{+\ +\ +\ +}_{\uparrow\ \text{run}}\ -\ +\ -\ +\ -\ +\ \underbrace{-\ -\ -}_{\uparrow\ \text{run}}\ +\ -\ +)$$

Runs can be expected in any series of data through chance factors, but an independent data series should not produce an unusual amount of runs. Statistical tests have indicated that security prices generally do not produce any more runs than would be expected through the process of random number generation.[11] This would also tend to indicate that stock price movements are independent over time.[12]

Trading Rule Tests

A second method of testing the weak form of the efficient market hypothesis (that past trends in stock prices are not helpful in predicting the future) is through trading rule tests. Because practicing market technicians maintain that tests of independence (correlation studies and runs) are too rigid to test the assumptions of the weak form of the efficient market hypothesis, additional tests by academic researchers have been developed. These are known as trading rule or filter tests. These tests determine whether a given trading rule based on past price data, volume figures, and so forth can be used to beat a naive buy-and-hold approach. The intent is to simulate the conditions under which a given trading rule is used and then determine if superior returns were produced after considering transaction costs and the risks involved.

---

[10] Sidney S. Alexander, "Price Movements in Speculative Markets: Trends or Random Walks," *Industrial Management Review,* May 1961, pp. 7–26; and Eugene F. Fama, "The Behavior of Stock Market Prices," *Journal of Business,* January 1965, pp. 34–105.

[11] Ibid.

[12] A possible exception to this rule was found in small stocks. A sample study is Jennifer Conrad and Gantam Kaul, "Time Variation and Expected Returns," *Journal of Business,* October 1988, pp. 409–25.

As an example of a trading rule, if a stock moves up 5 percent or more, the rule might be to purchase it. The assumption is that this represents a breakout and should be considered bullish. Similarly, a 5 percent downward movement would be considered bearish and call for a sell strategy (rather than a buy-low/sell-high strategy, this is a follow-the-market-trend strategy). Other trading rule tests might be based on advance-decline patterns, short sales figures, and similar technical patterns. Research results have indicated that in a limited number of cases, trading rules may produce slightly positive returns, but after commission costs are considered, the results are neutral and sometimes negative in comparison to a naive buy-and-hold approach.[13]

Implications for Technical Analysis

The results of the *tests of independence* and *trading rules* would seem to uphold the weak form of the efficient market hypothesis. Security prices do appear to be independent over time or, more specifically, move in the pattern of a random walk.

Some challenge the research on the basis that academic research in this area does not capture the personal judgment an experienced technician brings forward in reading charts. There is also the fact that there are an infinite number of trading rules, and not all of them can or have been tested. Nevertheless, research on the weak form of the EMH still seems to suggest that prices move independently over time, that past trends cannot be used to easily predict the future, and that charting and technical analysis may have limited value.

SEMISTRONG FORM OF THE EFFICIENT MARKET HYPOTHESIS

The **semistrong form of the efficient market hypothesis** maintains that all public information is already impounded into the value of a security, and therefore, one cannot use fundamental analysis to determine whether a stock is undervalued or overvalued.

Basically, the semistrong form of the efficient market hypothesis would support the notion that there is no learning lag in the distribution of public information. When a company makes an announcement, investors across the country assess the information with equal speed. Also, a major firm listed on the New York Stock Exchange could hardly hope to utilize some questionable accounting practice that deceptively leads to higher reported profits and not expect sophisticated analysts to pick it up. (This may not be equally true for a lesser known firm that trades over-the-counter and enjoys little investor attention.)

Researchers have tested the semistrong form of EMH by determining whether investors who have acted on the basis of newly released public information have been able to enjoy superior returns. If the market is efficient in a semistrong sense, this information is almost immediately impounded in the value of the security, and little or no trading profits would be available. The implications would be that one could not garner superior returns by trading on public information about stock splits, earnings reports, or other similar items.

---

[13] Eugene F. Fama and Marshall Blume, "Filter Rules and Stock Market Trading Profits," *Journal of Business,* supplement, January 1966, pp. 226–41; and George Pinches, "The Random Walk Hypothesis and Technical Analysis," *Financial Analysts Journal,* March–April 1970, pp. 104–10.

Tests on the semistrong form of the efficient market hypothesis have generally been on the basis of risk-adjusted returns. Thus, the return from a given investment strategy must be compared with the performance of popular market indicators with appropriate risk adjustments. As will be described in Chapter 21, the risk measurement variable is usually the beta. After such adjustments are made, the question becomes: Are there abnormal returns that go beyond explanations associated with risk? If the answer is yes and can be shown to be statistically significant, then the investment strategy may be thought to refute the semistrong form of the efficient market hypothesis. The investor must also cover transaction costs in determining that a given strategy is superior.

For example, assume a stock goes up 15 percent. The security is 20 percent riskier than the market. Further assume the overall market goes up by 10 percent. On a risk-adjusted basis, the security would need to go up in excess of 12 percent (the 10 percent market return × 1.2 risk factor) to beat the market.

The risk adjustment measure may be viewed as:

$$K_i = a_i + b_i K_M + e_i$$

Actual return (K_i) — *Intercept* (a_i) — *Risk variable* (b_i) — *Market return* (K_M) — *Random error term* (e_i)

Each of these items will receive further attention in Chapter 21. For now, our concern is whether an investment strategy can produce consistently superior, abnormal returns.

Tests examining the impact of such events as stock splits and stock dividends, corporate announcements, and changes in accounting policy have indicated that the market is generally efficient in a semistrong sense. For example, a study by Fama, Fisher, Jensen, and Roll indicated that almost all of the market impact of a stock split occurs before a public announcement.[14] There is little to be gained from acting on the announcement.

According to the semistrong form of the efficient market hypothesis, investors not only digest information very quickly, but they also are able to see through mere changes in accounting information that do not have economic consequences. For example, the switching from accelerated depreciation to straight-line depreciation for financial reporting purposes (but not tax purposes) would tend to make earnings per share look higher but would provide no economic benefit for the firm. Research studies indicate this would have no positive impact on valuation.[15]

Similarly, investors are not deceived by mere accounting changes related to inventory policy, reserve accounts, exchange translations, or other items that appear to have no economic benefits. The corporate treasurer who switches from LIFO to FIFO accounting to make earnings look better in an inflationary economy will probably not see the firm's stock price rise as investors look at the economic consequences of higher taxes associated with the action and disregard the mere financial accounting consequences of higher

---

[14] Eugene F. Fama, Lawrence Fisher, Michael G. Jensen, and Richard Roll, "The Adjustment of Stock Prices to New Information," *International Economic Review,* February 1969, pp. 2–21.

[15] T. Ross Archibald, "Stock Market Reaction to Depreciation Switch-Back," *Accounting Review,* January 1972, pp. 22–30; and Robert S. Kaplan and Richard Roll, "Investor Evaluation of Accounting Information: Some Empirical Evidence," *Journal of Business,* April 1972, pp. 225–57.

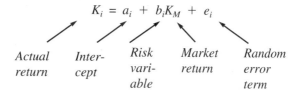

reported profits.[16] Under this circumstance, the effect on stock may be neutral or negative.

Implications for Fundamental Analysis

If stock values are already based on the analysis of all available public information, it may be assumed that little is to be gained from additional fundamental analysis. Under the semistrong form of the efficient market hypothesis, if General Motors is trading at $45, the assumption is that every shred of public information about GM has been collected and evaluated by thousands of investors, and they have determined an equilibrium price of $45. The assumption is that anything you read in *The Wall Street Journal* or Standard & Poor's publications has already been considered many times over by others and is currently impounded in the value of the stock. If you were to say you think GM is really worth $47 because of some great new product, proponents of the semistrong form of the efficient market hypothesis would suggest that your judgment cannot be better than the collective wisdom of the marketplace in which everyone is trying desperately to come out ahead.

Ironically, although many would suggest that fundamental analysis may not lead to superior profits in an efficient market environment, it is fundamental analysis itself that makes the market efficient. Because everyone is doing fundamental analysis, there is little in the way of unabsorbed or undigested information. Therefore, one extra person doing fundamental analysis is unlikely to achieve superior insight.

Although the semistrong form of the efficient market hypothesis has research support, there are exceptions. These are referred to as **anomalies** or deviations from the basic proposition that the market is efficient. For example, Basu has found that stocks with low P/E ratios consistently provide better returns than stocks with high P/E ratios on both a non-risk-adjusted and risk-adjusted basis.[17] Since a P/E ratio is publicly available information that may be used to generate superior returns, this flies in the face of the more common conclusions on the semistrong form of the efficient market hypothesis. Banz[18] and Reinganum's[19] research indicates that small firms tend to provide higher returns than larger firms even after considering risk. Perhaps fewer institutional investors in smaller firms make for a less-efficient market and superior potential opportunities. Oppenheimer and Schlarbaum have also shown that investors can generate superior risk-adjusted returns by following widely disseminated rules by Graham and Dodd on such factors as dividends, capitalization, firm size, and P/E ratios and by using only public information.[20]

---

[16] Shyam Sunder, "Stock Price and Risk Related to Accounting Changes in Inventory Valuation," *Accounting Review,* April 1975, pp. 305–15.

[17] S. Basu, "Investment Performance of Common Stocks in Relation to Their Price-Earnings Ratios: A Test of the Efficient Market Hypothesis," *Journal of Finance,* June 1977, pp. 663–82. Also, S. Basu, "The Information Content of Price-Earnings Ratios," *Financial Management,* Summer 1975, pp. 53–64.

[18] Rolf W. Banz, "The Relationship between Returns and Market Value of Common Stocks," *Journal of Financial Economics,* March 1981, pp. 3–18.

[19] Marc R. Reinganum, "Misspecification of Capital Asset Pricing—Empirical Anomalies Based on Earnings Yield and Market Values," *Journal of Financial Economics,* March 1981, pp. 19–46.

[20] Henry R. Oppenheimer and Gary R. Schlarbaum, "Investing with Ben Graham: An Ex Ante Test of the Efficient Market Hypothesis," *Journal of Financial and Quantitative Analysis,* September 1981, pp. 341–60.

Additional evidence of this nature continues to accumulate, and in Chapter 10, covering special situations, we present an extended discussion of some of the above items and other possible contradictions to the acceptance of the semistrong version of the efficient market hypothesis. We also comment on measurement problems in that chapter.

Thus, even if the semistrong form of the efficient market hypothesis appears to be generally valid, exceptions can be noted. Also, it is possible that while most analysts may not be able to add additional insight through fundamental analysis, there are exceptions to every rule. It can be assumed that some analysts have such *extraordinary* insight and capability in analyzing publicly available information that they can perceive what others cannot. Also, if you take a very long-term perspective, the fact that a stock's value is in short-term equilibrium may not discourage you from taking a long-term position or attempting to find long-term value.

Before we move on, it is also appropriate to point out that there is not only debate about whether the market is efficient in a semistrong sense but also over whether market researchers are appropriately testing for efficiency. For example, if risk is not properly measured, then conclusions to research studies can be questioned. This is an issue that cannot be easily settled and will be discussed again at the end of Chapter 10.

STRONG FORM OF THE EFFICIENT MARKET HYPOTHESIS

The **strong form of the efficient market hypothesis** goes beyond the semistrong form to state that stock prices reflect not only all public information but *all* information. Thus, it is hypothesized that insider information is also immediately impounded into the value of a security. In a sense, we go beyond the concept of a market that is highly efficient to one that is perfect.

The assumption is that no group of market participants or investors has monopolistic access to information. If this is the case, then no group of investors can be expected to show superior risk-adjusted returns under any circumstances.

Unlike the weak and semistrong forms of the efficient market hypothesis, major test results are not supportive of the strong form of the hypothesis. For example, specialists on security exchanges have been able to earn superior rates of return on invested capital.[21] The book they keep on unfilled limit orders would appear to provide monopolistic access to information. An SEC study actually found that specialists typically sell above their latest purchase 83 percent of the time and buy below their latest sell 81 percent of the time.[22] This implies wisdom that greatly exceeds that available in a perfect capital market environment. Likewise, an institutional investor study, also sponsored by the SEC, indicated that specialists' average return on capital was more than 100 percent.[23] While these returns have decreased somewhat recently in a more competitive environment, specialists still appear to outperform the market.

---

[21] Victor Niederhoffer and M. F. M. Osborne, "Market-Making and Reversal on the Stock Exchange," *Journal of the American Statistical Association,* December 1966, pp. 897–916.

[22] Securities and Exchange Commission, *Report of the Special Study of the Security Markets,* part 2 (Washington, D.C.: U.S. Government Printing Office, 1965).

[23] Securities and Exchange Commission, *Institutional Investor Study Report* (Washington, D.C.: U.S. Government Printing Office, 1971).

Another group that appears to use nonpublic information to garner superior returns is corporate insiders. As previously described, an insider is considered to be a corporate officer, member of the board of directors, or substantial stockholder. The SEC requires that insiders report their transactions to that regulatory body. A few weeks after reporting to the SEC, the information becomes public. Researchers can then go back and determine whether investment decisions made by investors appeared, on balance, to be wise. Did heavy purchases by insiders precede strong upward price movements, and did sell-offs precede poor market performance? The answer appears to be yes. Research studies indicate insiders consistently achieve higher returns than would be expected in a perfect capital market.[24] Although insiders are not allowed to engage in short-term trades (of six months or less) or illegal transactions to generate trading profits, they are allowed to take longer-term positions, which may prove to be profitable. It has even been demonstrated that investors who follow the direction of inside traders after information on their activity becomes public may enjoy superior returns.[25] (This, of course, represents contrary evidence to the semistrong form of the efficient market hypothesis as well.)

Even though there is evidence on the activity of specialists and insiders that would cause one to reject the strong form of the efficient market hypothesis (or at least not to accept it), the range of participants with access to superior information is not large. For example, tests on the performance of mutual fund managers have consistently indicated they are not able to beat the market averages over the long term.[26] Although mutual fund managers may get the first call when news is breaking, that is not fast enough to generate superior returns.

While the strong form of the efficient market hypothesis suggests more opportunity for superior returns than the weak or semistrong forms, the premium is related to monopolistic access to information rather than other factors.

It should also be pointed out that those who act *illegally* with insider information may initially achieve superior returns from their special access to information, but the price of their actions may be high. For example, Ivan Boesky and Michael Milken, convicted users of illegal insider information in the late 1980s, were forced to give up their gains, pay heavy fines, and serve jail sentences. In their particular cases, they traded on insider information about mergers well before the public was informed. Although they were not officers of the companies or on the boards, they had special fiduciary responsibilities as money managers that they violated.

---

24 James H. Lorie and Victor Niederhoffer, "Predictive Statistical Properties of Insider Trading," *Journal of Law and Economics,* April 1966, pp. 35–53; Joseph E. Finnerty, "Insiders and Market Efficiency," *Journal of Finance,* September 1976, pp. 1141–48; Jeffrey Jaffe, "Special Information and Insider Trading," *Journal of Business,* July 1974, pp. 410–28; and Shannon P. Pratt and Charles W. DeVere, "Relationship between Insider Trading and Rates of Return for NYSE Common Stocks, 1960–1966," in *Modern Developments in Investment Management,* ed. James H. Lorie and Richard Beasley (New York: Praeger, 1972), pp. 268–79.

25 Pratt and DeVere, "Relationship," pp. 268–79.

26 Michael Jensen, "The Performance of Mutual Funds in the Period 1945–1964," *Journal of Finance,* May 1968, pp. 389–416.

SUMMARY

Following the discussion of fundamental analysis in Chapters 5 through 8, we examined technical analysis in this chapter and, more significantly, the impact of the efficient market hypothesis (EMH) on both fundamental and technical analysis.

While fundamental analysis deals with financial analysis and determinants of valuation, technical analysis is based on the study of past price and volume data as well as associated market trends to predict future price movements. Technical analysis relies heavily on charting and the use of key market indicators to make forecasts.

Charting came into prominence with the development of the Dow theory in the late 1800s by Charles Dow. The theory stresses the importance of primary trends that may be temporarily obscured by daily and secondary movements. For a long-term, bullish trend to be reversed, there must be an abortive recovery followed by penetrations of previous lows, and patterns in the Dow Jones Industrial Average must be ultimately confirmed by the Dow Jones Transportation Average. Similar patterns of movement in the opposite direction would signal the end of a bear market.

Technical analysts also observe support and resistance levels in the market as well as data on volume. Line, bar, and point and figure charts are used to determine turns in the market.

Market technicians also follow a number of key indicator series to predict the stock market—contrary opinion indicators, smart money indicators, and general market indicators.

Although there have been traditional arguments about whether fundamental or technical analysis is more important, a great deal of current attention is directed to the efficient market hypothesis and its implications for all types of analysis.

The efficient market hypothesis maintains that the market adjusts very rapidly to the supply of new information, and because of this, securities tend to be correctly priced at any given time (or very rapidly approaching this equilibrium value). The EMH further assumes information travels in a random, independent fashion and prices are an unbiased reflection of all currently available information. Furthermore, past trends in prices mean little or nothing.

The efficient market hypothesis has been stated and tested in three different forms.

1. The weak form states there is no relationship between past and future prices (they are independent over time).
2. The semistrong form suggests all public information is currently impounded in the price of a stock and there is no concept of under- or overvaluation based on publicly available information.
3. The strong form suggests *all* information, public or otherwise, is included in the value of a security. The implication of the strong form is that security prices are not only highly efficient, they are perfect.

Research tends to support the weak form of the efficient market hypothesis, which causes many researchers to seriously question the overall value of technical analysis. However, many on Wall Street would vigorously debate this position. The semistrong form of the efficient market hypothesis is also reasonably supported by research, and this fact would

tend to question the value of fundamental analysis by the individual investor. (It is, however, the collective wisdom of all fundamental analysis that leads to the efficient market hypothesis in the first place.) There are some contradictions to the semistrong form of the efficient market hypothesis, and much research is aimed at supplying additional contradictory data. The semistrong form probably does not apply with equal emphasis to smaller firms that are not in the institutional investor's limelight.

The strong form of the efficient market hypothesis is not generally accepted. Thus, the market does not perfectly adjust to all information (insider as well as public). Evidence suggests stock exchange specialists and corporate insiders may be able to achieve superior returns based on the monopolistic use of nonpublic data. However, very few groups demonstrate successful access or use of nonpublic information.

KEY WORDS AND CONCEPTS

technical analysis, 255
Dow theory, 256
support, 258
resistance, 258
contrary opinion rule, 263
Barron's Confidence Index, 266
efficient market hypothesis (EMH), 270
weak form of the efficient market hypothesis, 271
semistrong form of the efficient market hypothesis, 272
anomalies, 274
strong form of the efficient market hypothesis, 275

DISCUSSION QUESTIONS

1. What is technical analysis?
2. What are the views of technical analysts toward fundamental analysis?
3. Outline the basic assumptions of technical analysis.
4. Under the Dow theory, if a recovery fails to exceed the previous high and a new low penetrates a previous low, what does this tell us about the market?
5. Also under the Dow theory, what other average is used to confirm movements in the Dow Jones Industrial Average?
6. What is meant by a support level for a stock or a market average? When might a support level exist?
7. In examining Figure 9–7, if the next price movement is to 34, will a shift to a new column be indicated? (Assume the current price is 36.)
8. What is the logic behind the odd-lot theory? If the odd-lot index starts to move higher in an up market, what does the odd-lot theory indicate the next movement in the market will be?
9. If the Investors Intelligence Service has a bearish sentiment of 70 percent, would you generally want to be a buyer or seller?
10. What is the logic behind *Barron's* Confidence Index?
11. If the advance-decline movement in the market is weak (more declines

than advances) while the DJIA is going up, what might this indicate to a technician about the market?

12. Categorize the following as either contrary opinion or smart money indicators (as viewed by technicians):
    a. Short sales by specialists.
    b. Odd-lot positions.
    c. Short sales positions.
    d. *Barron's* Confidence Index.
    e. Investment advisory recommendations.
    f. Put-call ratio.
13. Under the efficient market hypothesis, what is the assumption about the processing of new information, and what effect does this have on security pricing?
14. What does the weak form of the efficient market hypothesis suggest? What are the two major ways in which it has been tested?
15. Would low correlation coefficients over time between stock prices tend to prove or disprove the weak form of the efficient market hypothesis?
16. Under the semistrong form of the efficient market hypothesis, is there anything to be gained from a corporate treasurer changing accounting methods to increase earnings per share when there is no associated economic benefit or gain?
17. Why does fundamental analysis tend to make the market efficient?
18. Suggest some studies that would indicate the market is not completely efficient in the semistrong form.
19. What does the strong form of the efficient market hypothesis suggest? Are major test results generally supportive of the strong form?
20. How do specialists, insiders, and mutual fund managers fare in terms of having access to superior information to generate large returns? (Comment on each separately.)

THE WALL STREET JOURNAL PROJECTS

WSJ

1. In Section C, page 2, *The Wall Street Journal* carries a table called "DIARIES." This table gives data on advances and declines for NYSE, NASDAQ, and AMEX stocks. It also includes data for these markets on new highs—new lows, advancing volume—declining volume, and block trades. The closing tick is given for the NYSE as the net difference between stocks closing higher than their previous trade and those closing lower than their previous trade. For example, if the tick is negative, more stocks closed lower than higher than their previous trade.

   Use this data to create a table similar to Table 9–1 on page 269. For this assignment, use the advances and declines on the New York Stock Exchange (NYSE) and also use the Dow Jones Industrial Average (DJIA). Track the pattern for 10 market days. Do you see any pattern evolving?
2. Find the graph usually found on page C3 in *The Wall Street Journal* similar to Figure 9–5. Make a determination about the support and resistance level you see in the market, and indicate how volume supports your judgment.

3. Another technical indicator (contrary opinion) is the put-call ratio. Find the total put and call volume* from *The Wall Street Journal,* and calculate the ratio. Using the presentation in Chapter 9, determine whether the put-call ratio indicates a bullish or bearish market or gives no clear signal. Explain your answer.

SELECTED REFERENCES

Technical Analysis

Blume, Lawrence; David Easley; and Maureen O'Hara. "Market Statistics and Technical Analysis: The Role of Volume." *Journal of Finance,* March 1994, pp. 153–81.

Conrad, Jennifer, and Gantam Kaul. "Time Variation and Expected Returns." *Journal of Business,* October 1988, pp. 409–25.

Edwards, R. D., and John Magee, Jr. *Technical Analysis of Stock Trends,* 5th ed. Springfield, MA: Stock Trends Service, 1966.

Krueger, Thomas M., and William F. Kennedy. "An Examination of the Super Bowl Stock Market Predictor." *Journal of Finance,* June 1990, pp. 691–97.

Murphy, J. Austin. "Futures Fund Performance: A Test of the Effectiveness of Technical Analysis." *Journal of Futures Markets,* Summer 1986, pp. 175–86.

Sweeney, Richard J. "Some New Filter Rule Tests: Methods and Results." *Journal of Financial and Quantitative Analysis,* September 1988, pp. 285–300.

Fundamental Analysis

Basu, S. "Investment Performance of Common Stocks in Relation to Their Price-Earnings Ratios: A Test of the Efficient Market Hypothesis." *Journal of Finance,* June 1977, pp. 663–82.

______. "The Information Content of Price-Earnings Ratios." *Financial Management,* Summer 1975, pp. 53–64.

Bernstein, Barbara, and Peter L. Bernstein. "Where the Postcrash Studies Went Wrong." *Institutional Investor,* April 1988, pp. 173–77.

Brennan, Michael J., and Patricia J. Hughes. "Stock Prices and the Supply of Information." *Journal of Finance,* December 1991, pp. 1665–91.

Fama, Eugene F.; Lawrence Fisher; Michael G. Jensen; and Richard Roll. "The Adjustment of Stock Prices to New Information." *International Economic Review,* February 1969, pp. 1–21.

Mott, Claudia E., and Daniel P. Coker. "Earnings Surprise in the Small-Cap World." *Journal of Portfolio Management,* Fall 1993, pp. 64–93.

Reinganum, Marc R. "Misspecification of Capital Asset Pricing—Empirical Anomalies Based on Earnings Yield and Market Values." *Journal of Financial Economics,* March 1981, pp. 19–46.

Efficient Markets

Fama, Eugene F. "Efficient Capital Markets: II." *Journal of Finance,* December 1991, pp. 1575–1617.

Oppenheimer, Henry R., and Gary G. Schlarbaum. "Investing with Ben Graham: An Ex Ante Test of the Efficient Market Hypothesis." *Journal of Financial and Quantitative Analysis,* September 1981, pp. 341–60.

Saunders, Edward M. "Testing the Efficient Market Hypothesis without Assumptions." *Journal of Portfolio Management,* Summer 1994, pp. 28–30.

---

*The total put and call volume is found as the last item in the lower right corner of the "Listed Options Quotations" page in Section C of *The Wall Street Journal.*

10

Investments in Special Situations

In a previous discussion of market efficiency in Chapter 9, we suggested that while the security markets were generally efficient in the valuing of securities, there were still opportunities for special returns in a number of circumstances. Just what these circumstances are is subject to debate.

In most instances, special or **abnormal returns** refer to gains beyond what the market would normally provide after adjustment for risk. Transactions costs must also be covered. In this chapter, we will explore such topics as market movements associated with mergers and acquisitions, the underpricing of new stock issues, the impact of an exchange listing on a stock's valuation, the stock market impact of a firm repurchasing its own shares, and the small-firm and low-P/E effects.

MERGERS AND ACQUISITIONS

Many stocks that were leaders in daily volume and price movement in the last decade represented firms that were merger candidates—that is, companies that were being acquired or anticipated being acquired by other firms. The stocks of these acquisition candidates often increased by 60 percent or more over a relatively short period. The list of acquired companies includes such well-known names as Conoco, Gulf Oil, Kraft, EDS, General Foods, and Hospital Corporation of America.

Premiums for Acquired Company

The primary reason for the upward market movement in the value of the acquisition candidate is the high premium that is offered over current market value in a merger or acquisition. The **merger price premium** represents the difference between the offering price per share and the market price per share for the candidate (before the impact of the offer). For example, a firm that is selling for $25 per share may attract a purchase price of $40 per share. Quite naturally, the stock will go up in response to the offer and the anticipated consummation of the merger.

As expected, researchers have consistently found that there are abnormal returns for acquisition candidates.[1] A study has indicated the average premium paid in a recent time period was approximately 60 percent, and there was an associated upward price movement of a similar magnitude.[2] This is a much larger average premium than in prior time periods and may be attributed to the recognition of high replacement value in relationship to current market value. The premium was based on the difference between the price paid and the value of the acquisition candidate's stock *three months* before announcement of the merger. Some examples of premiums paid during the last decade are presented in Table 10–1.

---

[1] Gershon Mandelker, "Risk and Return: The Case of Merging Firms," *Journal of Financial Economics,* December 1974, pp. 303–35; Donald R. Kummer and J. Ronald Hoffmeister, "Valuation Consequences of Cash Tender Offers," *Journal of Finance,* May 1978, pp. 505–6; Peter Dodd, "Merger Proposals, Management Discretion and Stockholder Wealth," *Journal of Financial Economics,* December 1980, pp. 105–38; and Steven Kaplan, "The Effect of Management Buyouts on Operating Performance and Value," *Journal of Financial Economics,* October 1989, pp. 217–54.

[2] Henry Oppenheimer and Stanley Block, "An Examination of Premiums and Exchange Ratios Associated with Merger Activity during the 1975–78 Period" (Financial Management Association Meeting, 1980).

TABLE 10–1 Premiums Paid in Mergers and Acquisitions

Acquiring Firm	Acquired Firm	Price Paid in Cash for Acquired Company's Stock	Value of Acquired Firm Three Months before Announcement	Premium Paid (percent)
Roche	Syntex	$24.00	$15.25	57.38%
Beatrice Food Co.	Harmon International Inc.	35.25	20.00	76.25
Parker Pen Co.	Manpower, Inc.	15.20	11.50	32.18
Colt Industries	Menaso Manufacturing	26.60	15.00	77.33
Pepsico, Inc.	Pizza Hut, Inc.	38.00	22.375	69.83
Walter Kidde & Co.	Victor Comptometer	11.75	7.375	59.32
Dana Corporation	Weatherford Co.	14.00	9.375	49.33
Allis Chalmers Corporation	American Air Filter	34.00	19.50	74.36
Time, Inc.	Inland Containers	35.00	20.75	68.67
Chemical Bank	Texas Commerce Bank	32.75	20.25	61.73

The only problem from an investment viewpoint is that approximately two-thirds of the price gain related to large premiums occurs before public announcement. It is clear that people close to the situation are trading on information leaks. In the early 1980s, the highly prestigious investment banking house of Morgan Stanley was embarrassed by charges brought by the U.S. Attorney's Office that two of its former merger and acquisition specialists were conspiring to use privileged information on takeovers to make profits on secret trading accounts.[3] Later in the 1980s, notorious insider traders Ivan Boesky, Michael Milken, and Dennis Levine served jail sentences for their misuse of information related to unannounced mergers.

Those who attempt to legitimately profit by investing in mergers and acquisitions can follow a number of routes. First, some investors try to identify merger candidates before public announcement to capture maximum profits. This is difficult. While researchers have attempted to identify financial and operating characteristics of acquisition candidates, the information is often contradictory and may even change over time.[4] In prior time periods, acquisition candidates were often firms with sluggish records of performance, whereas many of the recent acquirees are high-quality companies that have unusually good records of performance (Cellular Communications, Pillsbury, and Steak and Ale).

Some alert analysts keep a close eye on such sources as *Industriscope's* "Stocks in the Spotlight," which pinpoints securities undergoing unusual volume or pricing patterns (this could be for any number of reasons). Other investors identify industries where

---

[3] "Two Former Morgan Stanley Executives Accused of Plot Involving Takeover Data," *The Wall Street Journal,* February 4, 1981, p. 2.

[4] Robert J. Monroe and Michael A. Simkowitz, "Investment Characteristics of Conglomerate Targets: A Discriminant Analysis," *Southern Journal of Business,* November 1971, pp. 1–15; and Donald J. Stevens, "Financial Characteristics of Merger Firms: A Multivariate Analysis," *Journal of Financial and Quantitative Analysis,* March 1973, pp. 149–58.

companies are being quickly absorbed and attempt to guess which firm will be the next to be acquired. Prime examples of such industries in recent times were natural resource firms being acquired by multinational oil companies and food companies being absorbed by tobacco companies or other firms in the food or consumer product industry.

While trying to guess an acquisition candidate before public announcement can be potentially profitable, it requires that an investor tie up large blocks of capital in betting on an event that may never come to pass. Others prefer to invest at the time of announcement of a merger or acquisition. A gain of the magnitude of 20 percent or more may still be available (over a few months' time period). Perhaps a stock that was $25 before any consideration of merger is up to $34 on announcement. If the acquisition price is $40, there may still be a nice profit to be made. The only danger is that the announced merger may be called off, in which case the stock may sharply retreat in value. This happened to Kemper in 1994 when General Electric made a bid for its shares only to be outbid by Conseco Insurance at $62 per share. When Conseco could not arrange financing, the bid fell through and the stock plunged into the low $40s until Zurich Insurance offered $49 per share in 1995. Examples of other price drops associated with merger cancellations are shown in Table 10–2.

The wise investor must carefully assess the likelihood of cancellation. Special attention must be given to such factors as the possibility of antitrust action, the attitude of the target company's management toward the merger, the possibility of unhappy stockholder suits, and the likelihood of poor earnings reports or other negative events. In a reasonably efficient market environment, the potential price gain that exists at announcement may be well correlated with the likelihood of the merger being successfully consummated. That is to say, if it appears the merger is almost certain to go through, the stock may be up to $37.50 at announcement based on an anticipated purchase price of $40. If a serious question remains, the stock may only be at $33. When a merger becomes reasonably certain, arbitrageurs come in and attempt to lock in profits by buying the acquisition candidate at a small spread from the purchase price.

One of the most interesting features of the latest merger movement was the heavy incidence of **unfriendly takeovers,** that is, the bidding of one company for another against its will. Such events often lead to the appearance of a third company on the scene, referred to as a **"white knight,"** whose function is to save the target company by buying it out, thus thwarting the undesired suitor. The new suitor is generally deemed to be friendly to the interests of the target company and may be invited by it to partake in the

TABLE 10–2 Stock Movement of Potential Acquirees in Canceled Mergers

Acquirer–Potential Acquiree	Preannouncement	One Day after Announcement	One Day after Cancellation
Mead Corporation—Occidental Petroleum	20 ⅜	33 ¼	23 ¼
Olin Corp.—Celanese	16	23 ¾	16 ¾
Chicago Rivet—MITE	20 ¾	28 ⅛	20 ¾

process. Examples of white knights occurred when Gulf Oil thwarted an offer from Mesa Petroleum and went with Standard Oil of California (renamed Chevron). Similarly, Marathon Oil rejected an offer from Mobil to merge with U.S. Steel.

As one might guess, these multiple-suitor bidding wars often lead to unusually attractive offers. A 40 to 60 percent premium may ultimately parlay into an 80 to 100 percent gain or more. For example, the bidding for Gulf Oil sent the stock from 38 to 80.

Acquiring Company Performance

What about the acquiring company's stock in the merger and acquisition process? Is this a special situation; that is, does this stock also show abnormal market gains associated with the event? A study by Mandelker indicated that it did not.[5] Long-term economic studies have indicated that many of the anticipated results from mergers may be difficult to achieve.[6] There is often an initial feeling of optimism that is not borne out in reality. The **synergy,** or "2 + 2 = 5," effect associated with broadening product lines or eliminating overlapping functions may be offset by the inability of management to mesh divergent philosophies. However, companies do appear to be more adept at the process than in prior periods; conservatively managed firms, such as General Motors, Du Pont, and AT&T, have replaced the funny-money conglomerate gunslingers of another decade. Nevertheless, most investors would prefer to position themselves with the acquired firm, which is certain to receive a high premium, rather than with the acquiring firm, which has to pay it.

Form of Payment

Another consideration in a merger is the form of payment. Cash offers usually carry a slightly higher premium than stock offers because of the immediate tax consequences to the acquired firm's shareholders. When stock is offered, the tax obligation usually may be deferred by the acquired company's stockholders until the stock of the acquiring firm is actually sold. This may occur relatively soon or many years in the future.

The recent merger movement has seen a much heavier utilization of cash as a medium of payment than in prior time periods (in the 50 percent range as opposed to 25 percent earlier). Many of the old accounting advantages associated with stock or residual stock items (convertibles, warrants) in mergers have been diminished by accounting rule changes.

Leveraged Buyouts

Some corporations are also taken over through **leveraged buyouts** (LBOs). Here, either the management of the company or some other investor group borrows the needed cash to repurchase all the shares of the company. The balance sheet of the company serves as

---

[5] Mandelker, "Risk and Return," pp. 303–35. Also see Anup Agrawal, Jeffrey F. Jaffe, and Gershon Mandelker, "The Post-Merger Performance of Acquiring Firms," *Journal of Finance,* September 22, 1992, pp. 1605–21.

[6] T. Hogarty, "The Profitability of Corporate Managers," *Journal of Business,* July 1970, pp. 317–27. For a contrary opinion, see Paul M. Healy, Krisha G. Paleps, and Richard S. Ruback, "Does Corporate Performance Improve after Mergers?" *Journal of Financial Economics,* April 1992, pp. 132–65.

the collateral base to make the borrowing possible. After the leveraged buyout, the company may be taken private for a period, in which unprofitable assets are sold and debts reduced. The intent is then to bring the company to the public market once again (or resell it to another company) at a large profit over the initial purchase price. Successful leveraged buyouts, in which profits of 50 percent or more were made, include those of Blue Bell, Leslie Fay, Metromedia, SFN, and Uniroyal. The largest leveraged buyout (or financial transaction of any kind) involved RJR Nabisco in 1988. The price tag was in excess of $25 billion.

Not all leveraged buyouts are successful. Sometimes the debt burden associated with the transaction is so large that a company has difficulty recovering after an LBO. A classic case is the Southland Corporation (owners of 7-Eleven convenience stores), which found itself in bankruptcy court after putting an unmanageable amount of debt on its books.

NEW STOCK ISSUES

Another form of a special situation is the initial issuance of stock by a corporation. There is a belief in the investment community that securities may be underpriced when they are issued to the public for the first time. That is to say, when a company **goes public** by selling formerly privately held shares to new investors in an initial public offering, the price may not fully reflect the value of the security.

Why does this so-called underpricing occur, and what is the significance to the investor? The underpricing may be the result of the investment banker's firm commitment to buy the shares when distributing the issue. That is, the investment banker normally agrees to buy the stock from Company A at a set price and then resells it to the public (along with other investment bankers, dealers, and brokers). The investment banker must be certain the issue will be fully subscribed to at the initial public market price or the banker (and others) will absorb losses or build up unwanted inventory. To protect his position, the investment banker may underprice the issue by 5 to 10 percent to ensure adequate demand.

Studies by Miller and Reilly;[7] Ibbotson, Sindelar, and Ritter;[8] and Muscarella and Vetsuypens,[9] and others have indicated positive excess returns are related to the issue of the stock. Miller and Reilly, for example, observed positive excess returns of 9.9 percent one week after issue. However, the efficiency of the market comes into play after the stock is actively trading on a regular basis, and any excess returns begin to quickly disappear. The lesson to be learned is that, on average, the best time to buy a new, unseasoned issue is on initial distribution from the underwriting syndicate (investment bankers, dealers, brokers), and the best time to sell is shortly after.

---

7 Robert E. Miller and Frank K. Reilly, "An Examination of Mispricing Returns, and Uncertainty for Initial Public Offerings," *Financial Management*, Winter 1987, pp. 33–38.

8 Roger G. Ibbotson, J. Sindelar, and Jay R. Ritter, "Initial Public Offerings," *Journal of Applied Corporate Finance*, Fall 1988, pp. 37–45.

9 Chris Muscarella and Mike Vetsuypens, "A Simple Test of Barron's Model of IPO Underpricing," *Journal of Financial Economics*, September 1989, pp. 125–35.

The point has been strongly made by recent research by Barry and Jennings.[10] They calculated positive excess returns of 8.69 percent on the first date of trading for new issues, but discovered that 90 percent of that gain occurred on the opening transaction.

Participating in the distribution of a new issue is not always as easy as it sounds. A really hot new issue may be initially oversubscribed, and only good customers of a brokerage house may be allocated shares. Such was the case in the feverish atmosphere that surrounded the initial public trading of NexGen, Microsoft, Apple Computer, and Genentech. Genentech actually went from $35 to $89 in the first 20 minutes of trading (only to quickly come back down). For the most part, customers with a regular brokerage account and a desire to participate in the new-issues market can find adequate opportunities for investment, though perhaps in less spectacular opportunities than those described above.

Performance of Investment Bankers

Research studies indicate that large, prestigious investment banking houses do not generally provide the highest initial returns to investors in the new issues they underwrite.[11] The reason for this is that the upper-tier investment bankers tend to underwrite the issues of the strongest firms coming into the market. Less risk is associated with these strong firms.[12] These firms generally shop around among the many investment bankers interested in their business and eventually negotiate terms that would allow for very little underpricing when they reach the market. (They want most of the benefits to go to the corporation, not to the initial stockholders.)

Factors to Consider in a New Issue

Although the best strategy in a new public offering is often to sell the stock soon after it becomes public, some investors may choose to take a longer-term position. In this case, the investor should consider the management of the firm and its performance record. In most cases, a firm that is going public will have past sales and profit figures that can be compared to others in the industry. In one study, the average sales volume for a firm approaching the new issues market was $22.9 million with $1.8 million in after-tax profits and $14.6 million in assets.[13]

The investor also should take a close look at the intended use of funds from the public distribution. There are many legitimate purposes, such as the construction of new plant

---

[10] Christopher B. Barry and Robert H. Jennings, "The Opening Performance of Initial Offerings of Common Stock," *Financial Management* (forthcoming).

[11] Brian M. Neuberger and Carl T. Hammond, "A Study of Underwriters' Experience with Unseasoned New Issues," *Journal of Financial and Quantitative Analysis,* March 1974, pp. 165–74. Also, see Dennis E. Logue, "On the Pricing of Unseasoned New Issues, 1965–1969," *Journal of Financial and Quantitative Analysis,* January 1973, pp. 91–103; and Brian M. Neuberger and Chris A. La Chapelle, "Unseasoned New Issue Price Performance on Three Tiers: 1976–1980," *Financial Management,* Autumn 1983, pp. 23–28.

[12] Richard Carter and Steven Manaster, "Initial Public Offerings and Underwriter Reputation," *Journal of Finance,* September 1990, pp. 1045–67.

[13] Stanley Block and Marjorie Stanley, "The Financial Characteristics and Price Movement Patterns of Companies Approaching the Unseasoned Securities Market in the Late 1970's," *Financial Management,* Winter 1980, pp. 30–36.

and equipment, the expansion of product lines, or the reduction of debt. The investor should be less enthusiastic about circumstances in which funds are being used to buy out old stockholders or to acquire property from existing shareholders.

EXCHANGE LISTINGS

A special situation of some interest to investors is an **exchange listing,** in which a firm trading over-the-counter now lists its shares on an exchange (such as the American or New York Stock Exchange). Another version of a listing is for a firm to step up from an American Stock Exchange listing to a New York Stock Exchange listing.

An exchange listing may generate interest in a security (particularly when a company moves from the over-the-counter market to an organized exchange). The issue will now be assigned a specialist who has responsibility for maintaining a continuous and orderly market.[14] Furthermore, there may be greater marketability for the issue as well as more readily available price quotes. An exchange listing may also make the issue more acceptable for margin trading and short selling. Large institutional investors and foreign investors may also consider a listed security more appropriate for inclusion in their portfolios.

Listed firms must meet certain size and performance criteria provided in Table 10–3 (and previously mentioned in Chapter 2 for the NYSE). Although the criteria are not highly restrictive, meeting these standards may still signal a favorable message to investors.

A number of research studies have examined the stock market impact of exchange listings. As might be expected, a strong upward movement is associated with securities

TABLE 10–3 Minimum Requirements for NYSE Exchange Listing

1. Demonstrated earning power under competitive conditions of: *either* $2.5 million before federal income taxes for the most recent year and $2 million pretax for each of the preceding two years, *or* an aggregate for the last three fiscal years of $6.5 million *together with* a minimum in the most recent fiscal year of $4.5 million. (All three years must be profitable.)
2. Net tangible assets of $18 million, but greater emphasis is placed on the aggregate market value of the common stock.
3. Market value of publicly held shares, at least equal to $18 million.
4. A total of 1,100,000 common shares publicly held.
5. *Either* 2,000 holders of 100 shares or more, *or* 2,200 total stockholders *together with* average monthly trading volume (for the most recent six months) of 100,000 shares.

---

14 This is not always a superior arrangement to having multiple market makers in the over-the-counter market. It depends on how dedicated the specialist is to maintaining the market. Some banks and smaller industrial firms may choose the competitive dealer system in the over-the-counter market in preference to the assigned specialist. For a truly extensive overview of research on stock listings, see H. Kent Baker and Sue E. Meeks, "Research on Exchange Listings and Delistings: A Review and Synthesis," *Financial Practice and Education,* Spring 1991, pp. 57–71.

that are to be listed, but there is also a strong sell-off after the event has occurred. Research by Van Horne,[15] Fabozzi,[16] and others[17] indicates that the total effect may be neutral. Research by Ying, Lewellen, Schlarbaum, and Lease (YLSL) would tend to indicate an overall gain.[18]

The really significant factor is that regardless of whether a stock has a higher net value a few months after listing as opposed to a few months before listing, there still may be profits to be made. This would be true if the investor simply bought the stock four to six weeks before listing and sold it on listing. Because an application approval for listing is published in the weekly bulletin of the American Stock Exchange or the New York Stock Exchange well before the actual date of listing, a profit is often possible. The study by YLSL, cited above, indicates there may be an opportunity for abnormal returns on a risk-adjusted basis in the many weeks between announcement of listing and actual listing (between 4.40 percent and 16.26 percent over normal market returns, depending on the time period). In this case, YLSL actually reject the semistrong form of the efficient market hypothesis by suggesting there are substantial profits to be made even after announcement of a new listing. The wise investor may wish to sell on the eventual date of listing because sometimes a loss in value may occur at that point.

The reader should also be aware of the potential impact of delisting on a security, that is, the formal removal from a New York Stock Exchange or American Stock Exchange listing, and a resumption of trading over-the-counter. This may occur because the firm has fallen substantially below the requirements of the exchange. As you would expect, this has a large negative effect on the security. Merjos found that 48 of the 50 firms in her study declined between the last day of trading on an exchange and the resumption of trading over-the-counter.[19] The average decline was 17 percent. While the value was not risk adjusted, it is large enough to indicate the clear significance of the event. Other studies have found similar results.[20]

STOCK REPURCHASE

The **repurchase** by a firm of its own shares provides for an interesting special situation. The purchase price is generally over current market value and tends to increase the demand for the shares while decreasing the effective supply. Before we examine the

---

[15] James C. Van Horne, "New Listings and Their Price Behavior," *Journal of Finance,* September 1970, pp. 783–94.

[16] Frank J. Fabozzi, "Does Listing on the AMEX Increase the Value of Equity?" *Financial Management,* Spring 1981, pp. 43–50.

[17] Richard W. Furst, "Does Listing Increase the Market Value of Common Stock?" *Journal of Business,* April 1970, pp. 174–80; and Waldemar M. Goulet, "Price Changes, Managerial Accounting and Insider Trading at the Time of Listing," *Financial Management,* Spring 1974, pp. 303–6.

[18] Louis K. W. Ying, Wilbur G. Lewellen, Gary G. Schlarbaum, and Ronald C. Lease, "Stock Exchange Listing and Securities Returns," *Journal of Financial and Quantitative Analysis,* September 1977, pp. 415–32.

[19] Anna Merjos, "Stricken Securities," *Barron's,* March 4, 1963, p. 9.

[20] Gary C. Sanger and James D. Paterson, "An Empirical Analysis of Common Stock Delistings," *Journal of Financial and Quantitative Analysis,* June 1990, pp. 261–72.

stock market effects of a repurchase, we will briefly examine the reasons behind the corporate decision.

Reasons for Repurchase

In some cases, management believes the stock is undervalued in the market. Prior research studies have indicated that repurchased securities have generally underperformed the popular market averages before announcement of repurchase.[21] Thus, management or the board of directors may perceive this to be an excellent opportunity because of depressed prices. Others, however, might see the repurchase as a sign that management is not creative or that it lacks investment opportunities for the normal redeployment of capital.[22] Empirical study indicates that firms that engage in repurchase transactions often have lower sales and earnings growth and lower return on net worth than other, comparable firms.[23] There also tends to be a concentration of these firms in the lower growth areas, such as apparel, steel, food products, tobacco, and aerospace.

Another reason for the repurchase of shares is the acquisition of treasury stock to be used in future mergers and acquisitions or to fulfill obligations under an employee stock option plan. Shares may also be acquired to reduce the number of voting shares outstanding and thus diminish the vulnerability of the corporation to an unwanted or unsolicited takeover attempt by another corporation. Finally, the repurchase decision may be closely associated with a desire to reduce stockholder servicing cost, that is, to eliminate small stockholder accounts that are particularly unprofitable for the corporation to maintain.

Actual Market Effect

From the viewpoint of a special situation, the key question is, What is the stock market impact of the repurchase? Is there money to be made here or not? Much of the earlier research said no.[24] However, more recent research would tend to indicate there might be positive returns to investors in a repurchase situation.[25] Most of the higher returns are

---

[21] Richard Norgaard and Connie Norgaard, "A Critical Evaluation of Share Repurchase," *Financial Management,* Spring 1974, pp. 44–50; and Larry Y. Dann, "Common Stock Repurchases: An Analysis of Returns to Bondholders and Stockholders," *Journal of Financial Economics,* June 1981, pp. 113–38.

[22] Charles D. Ellis and Allen E. Young, *The Repurchase of Common Stock* (New York: The Ronald Press, 1971), p. 61.

[23] Norgaard and Norgaard, "A Critical Evaluation."

[24] A good example is Ellis and Young, *The Repurchase of Common Stock,* p. 156.

[25] Terry E. Dielman, Timothy J. Nantell, and Roger L. Wright, "Price Effects of Stock Repurchasing: A Random Coefficient Regression Approach," *Journal of Financial and Quantitative Analysis,* March 1980, pp. 175–89; Larry Y. Dann, "Common Stock Repurchases: An Analysis of Returns to Bondholders and Stockholders," *Journal of Financial Economics,* June 1981, pp. 113–38; Theo Vermaelen, "Common Stock Repurchases and Market Signaling: An Empirical Study," *Journal of Financial Economics,* June 1981, pp. 139–83; R. W. Masulis, "Stock Repurchase by Tender Offer: An Analysis of the Causes of Common Stock Price Changes," *Journal of Finance,* May 1980, pp. 305–19; and Josef Lakonishok and Theo Vermaelen, "Anomalous Price Behavior around Repurchase Tender Offers," *Journal of Finance,* June 1990, pp. 455–77.

confined to formal tender offers to repurchase shares (perhaps 10 to 20 percent of the shares outstanding) rather than the use of informal, unannounced, open-market purchases. Under a formal tender offer, the corporation will specify the purchase price, the date of purchase, and the number of shares it wishes to acquire.

Of particular interest is the fact that most of the positive market movement comes *on* and *after* the announcement rather than before it. The implications are that there may be trading profits to be made here.

Dann determined that the average premium paid over the stock price (the day prior to announcement) was 22.46 percent as indicated on the top line of Table 10–4.

This high premium helps to generate a return of 8.946 percent on the day of announcement and 6.832 percent one day after announcement as indicated in Table 10–5. This represents a two-day return of approximately 15.8 percent.[26]

The predominant argument for the beneficial effects of the repurchase is that management knows what it is doing when it purchases its *own* shares. In effect, management is acting as an insider for the benefit of the corporation, and we previously observed in Chapter 9 that insiders tend to be correct in their investment decisions. This factor, combined with the high premium, may provide positive investment results. Of course, these are merely average results over many transactions, and not all tender offers will prove to be beneficial events. The investor must carefully examine the premium offered, the number of shares to be repurchased, the reasons for repurchase, and the future impact on earnings and dividends per share.

TABLE 10–4 Summary Statistics for the Tender Offer Sample, 1962–1976 (143 observations)

Characteristic of Offers	Mean (percent)	Median (percent)
Tender offer premium relative to closing market price one *day* prior to announcement	22.46%	19.40%
Tender offer premium relative to closing market price one *month* prior to announcement	20.85	18.83
Percentage of outstanding shares sought	15.29	12.57
Percentage of outstanding shares acquired	14.64	11.93
Percentage of outstanding shares tendered	18.04	14.27
Number of shares tendered ÷ number of shares sought	142.30	115.63
Number of shares acquired ÷ number of shares sought	111.35	100.00
Value of proposed repurchase relative to preoffer market value of equity	19.29	15.28
Value of actual repurchase relative to preoffer market value of equity	18.63	13.90
Duration of offer	22 days	20 days

Source: Larry Y. Dann, "Common Stock Repurchases: An Analysis of Returns to Bondholders and Stockholders," *Journal of Financial Economics*, June 1981, p. 122.

[26] Professor Dann's observations are based on raw data rather than normalized returns. However, they are of sufficient magnitude to be important.

TABLE 10–5 Common Stock Rates of Return over a 121-Day Period around Announcement of Common Stock Repurchase Tender Offer

Trading Day	Mean Rate of Return (percent)	Trading Day	Mean Rate of Return (percent)
−60	0.217%	0	8.946%
−50	−0.034	1	6.832
−40	0.058	2	0.908
−30	−0.562	3	−0.041
−25	−0.125	4	0.133
−20	−0.071	5	0.158
−19	0.026	6	0.230
−18	−0.346	7	0.129
−17	−0.317	8	0.051
−16	−0.413	9	−0.211
−15	0.377	10	0.213
−14	−0.228	11	0.172
−13	−0.738	12	−0.024
−12	0.051	13	0.181
−11	−0.424	14	−0.143
−10	−0.578	15	0.497
− 9	0.188	16	−0.105
− 8	−0.391	17	−0.236
− 7	0.107	18	0.148
− 6	0.417	19	0.141
− 5	−0.169	20	−0.057
− 4	0.943	25	−0.003
− 3	0.239	30	−0.025
− 2	0.490	40	0.133
− 1	0.959	50	−0.069
		60	0.161

Source: Larry Y. Dann, "Common Stock Repurchases: An Analysis of Returns to Bondholders and Stockholders," *Journal of Financial Economics,* June 1981, p. 124.

One of the major developments of 1987 (the year of the crash) was the unusually large number of stock repurchases. More than 1,400 companies announced plans to buy back over $80 billion in stock. Many of these buybacks came after the Dow Jones Industrial Average declined 508 points on Black Monday, October 19, 1987. As one example, Citicorp sold $1.2 billion in new stock in September 1987 at $58.25 a share only to buy back almost $200 million on October 20 at a mere $37.50 a share. The largest announced stock buybacks for the historic year of 1987 are shown in Table 10–6.

TABLE 10-6 Biggest Announced Stock Buybacks of 1987

Company	Common Shares (in millions)	Value	Company	Common Shares (in millions)	Value
General Motors	64.0	$ 4.72 billion	Procter & Gamble	10.0	$810.0 million
Sante Fe Southern Pacific	60.0	3.38 billion	Salomon	21.3	808.7 million
			Hewlett-Packard	15.3	750.0 million
Ford	27.9	2.00 billion	Nynex	10.0	736.3 million
Coca-Cola	40.0	1.80 billion	Chrysler	27.0	729.0 million
Henley Group	64.5	1.76 billion	Burlington Industries	8.0	640.0 million
Gencorp	12.5	1.63 billion	Monsanto	8.0	627.0 million
IBM	12.9	1.57 billion	ITT	10.0	625.0 million
American Express	40.0	1.35 billion	Hospital Corporation of America	12.0	612.0 million
Allied-Signal	25.0	1.11 billion			
Owens-Illinois	20.0	1.11 billion	Atlantic Richfield	8.3	600.0 million
J. C. Penny	20.0	1.04 billion	Schlumberger	20.0	595.0 million
Hercules	15.0	1.02 billion	Tektronix	15.6	593.2 million
IC Industries	30.8	1.00 billion	Boeing	15.0	592.5 million
Merck	5.4	1.00 billion	Kimberly-Clark	9.0	547.5 million
Philip Morris	10.0	933.5 million	Kraft	10.0	547.5 million
Bristol-Myers	25.0	925.0 million	Eaton	8.5	500.0 million
NCR	14.0	825.3 million	Kmart	17.9	500.0 million

Note: Figures represent announcements, not actual purchases, and may include more than one announcement. Values are actual dollar amounts when available or estimates based on closing prices before announcements.
Sources: Merrill Lynch & Co.; *The Wall Street Journal,* January 4, 1988, p. 8B. Reprinted by permission of *The Wall Street Journal,* © 1988 by Dow Jones & Company, Inc. All Rights Reserved Worldwide.

THE SMALL-FIRM AND LOW-P/E-RATIO EFFECT

Two University of Chicago doctoral studies in the early 1980s contended that the true key to superior risk-adjusted rates of return rests with investing in firms with small **market capitalizations.** (Market capitalization refers to shares outstanding times stock price.) In a study of New York Stock Exchange firms, covering from 1936 to 1975, Banz indicates that the lowest quintile (bottom 20 percent) firms in terms of market capitalization provide the highest returns even after adjusting for risk. Banz suggests, "On average, small NYSE firms have had significantly larger risk-adjusted returns than larger NYSE firms over a 40-year period."[27]

Some criticized Banz for using only NYSE firms in his analysis and for using a time period that included the effects of both a depression and a major war. Small firms had

---

[27] Rolf W. Banz, "The Relationship between Returns and Market Value of Common Stocks," *Journal of Financial Economics,* March 1981, pp. 3–18.

incredibly high returns following the Depression. A similar type study, produced by Reinganum[28] at about the same time, overcame these criticisms. Reinganum examined 2,000 firms that were traded on the New York Stock Exchange or the American Stock Exchange between 1963 and 1980. He annually divided the 2,000 firms into 10 groupings based on size, with the smallest category representing less than $5 million in market capitalization and the largest grouping representing a billion dollars or more.

A synopsis of the results from the Reinganum study is presented in Table 10–7.

Column (2) indicates the median value of the market capitalization for the firms in each group. Column (3) is the median stock price for firms in each group, while column (4) indicates average annual return associated with that category.

As observed in column (4), the smallest capitalization group (MV 1) outperformed the largest capitalization group (MV 10) by more than 23 percentage points per year. Although not included in the table, in 14 out of the 18 years under study, the MV 1 group showed superior returns to the MV 10 group. In another similar analysis, Reinganum found that $1 invested in the smallest capitalization group would have grown to $46 between 1963 and 1980, while the same dollar invested in the largest capitalization group would have only grown to $4. As did Banz, Reinganum adjusted his returns for risk and continued to show superior risk-adjusted returns.

TABLE 10–7 Synopsis of Results—Reinganum Study

(1) Grouping	(2) Median Market Value (Capitalization, in millions)	(3) Median Share Price	(4) Average Annual Return
MV 1	$ 4.6	$ 5.24	32.77%
MV 2	10.8	9.52	23.51
MV 3	19.3	12.89	22.98
MV 4	30.7	16.19	20.24
MV 5	47.2	19.22	19.08
MV 6	74.2	22.59	18.30
MV 7	119.1	26.44	15.64
MV 8	209.1	30.83	14.24
MV 9	434.6	34.43	13.00
MV 10	1,102.6	44.94	9.47

* MV = Market value.
Source: Marc R. Reinganum, "Portfolio Strategies Based on Market Capitalization," *Journal of Portfolio Management,* Winter 1983, pp. 29–36.

28 Marc R. Reinganum, "Misspecification of Capital Asset Pricing—Empirical Anomalies Based on Earnings Yield and Market Values," *Journal of Financial Economics,* March 1981, pp. 19–46. Also, "A Direct Test of Roll's Conjecture on the Firm Size Effect," *Journal of Finance,* March 1982, pp. 27–35; and "Portfolio Strategies Based on Market Capitalization," *Journal of Portfolio Management,* Winter 1983, pp. 29–36.

Such superior return evidence drew criticisms from different quarters. Roll suggested that small-capitalization studies underestimate the risk measure (beta) by failing to account for the infrequent and irregular trading patterns of stocks of smaller firms.[29] Stoll and Whaley maintained that transaction costs associated with dealing in smaller capitalization firms might severely cut into profit potential.[30] They indicated the average buy-sell spread on small-capitalized, low-priced stocks might be four or five times that of large-capitalization firms. Reinganum has maintained that even after accounting for these criticisms, small-capitalization firms continue to demonstrate superior risk-adjusted returns.[31]

Given that there might be advantages to investing in smaller firms, why haven't professional money managers picked up on the strategy? This, in part, is a catch-22. Part of the reason for the inefficiency in this segment of the market that allows for superior returns is the absence of institutional traders. This absence means less information is generated on the smaller firms, and the information that is generated is reacted to in a less immediate fashion. Studies suggest an important linkage between the absence of organized information and superior return potential.[32]

Advocates of the small-firm effect argue that it is this phenomenon alone, rather than others, such as the low-P/E-ratio effect, that leads to superior risk-adjusted returns. Peavy and Goodman would argue that the low-P/E-ratio effect is also important.[33] In following up on the earlier work of Basu[34] on the importance of P/E ratios, they compensated for other factors that may have resulted in superior returns, such as the small size of the firm, the infrequent trading of stock, and the overall performance of an industry. They did this by using firms that had a market capitalization of at least $100 million, that had an active monthly trading volume of at least 250,000 shares, and that were in the same industry. Thus, none of these factors was allowed to be an intervening variable in the relationship between returns and the level of P/E ratios.

After following these parameters, Peavy and Goodman showed a significant relationship between the firm's P/E ratios and risk-adjusted returns. Firms were broken down into quintiles based on the size of their P/E ratios. Quintile 1 contained firms with the lowest P/E ratios, quintile 2 had the next lowest P/E ratios, and so on up the scale. A portion of their results is presented in Table 10–8 on page 296.

Note that lower P/E stocks have higher risk-adjusted returns. While Table 10–8 shows data only for the electronics industry, a similar pattern was found for other industries.

In summarizing this section, some researchers such as Banz and Reinganum argue that small size is the primary variable leading to superior returns, while others argue that it is the low-P/E-ratio effect.

---

29 Richard Roll, "A Possible Explanation of the Small Firm Effect," *Journal of Finance,* September 1981, pp. 879–88.

30 H. A. Stoll and R. E. Whaley, "Transaction Costs and the Small Firm Effect," *Journal of Financial Economics,* March 1985, pp. 121–43.

31 Reinganum, "Misspecification of Capital Asset Pricing," pp. 19–46.

32 Avner Arbel and Paul Strebel, "Pay Attention to Neglected Firms," *Journal of Portfolio Management,* Winter 1983, pp. 37–42.

33 John W. Peavy III and David A. Goodman, "The Significance of P/Es for Portfolio Returns," *Journal of Portfolio Management,* Winter 1983, pp. 43–47.

34 S. Basu, "Investment Performance of Common Stocks in Relation to Their Price-Earnings Ratios: A Test of the Efficient Market Hypothesis," *Journal of Finance,* June 1977, pp. 663–82.

TABLE 10–8 P/E Ratios and Performance: The Electronics Industry (1970–1980)

Quintile	Average P/E	Average Quarterly Return (Risk-adjusted)	Average Beta
1	7.1	8.53	1.15
2	10.3	4.71	1.12
3	13.4	4.34	1.13
4	17.4	2.53	1.19
5	25.5	1.86	1.29

Source: John W. Peavy III and David A. Goodman, "The Significance of P/Es for Portfolio Returns," *Journal of Portfolio Management,* Winter 1983, pp. 43–47.

THE LATEST THEORY—THE BOOK VALUE TO MARKET VALUE EFFECT

Just to make sure that finance professors and their students do not sleep too soundly at night, we have yet another theory to explain why certain stocks outperform the market. Professors Fama and French maintain that the ratio of book value to market value is more important than either the size or P/E ratio in explaining superior stock performance. Their study says that the higher the ratio of book value to market value (lower the ratio of market value to book value) the higher the potential return on the stock.[35]

This conclusion is somewhat surprising to students who have been taught that book value, which is based on historical cost rather than current replacement value, is not an important predictor. The newer logic is that stocks that have a book value that approaches market value are more likely to be undervalued than stocks that have book values that are perhaps only 20 percent of market value. The latter figure would imply that the stock is trading at five times its book value (or net worth) as shown on the corporate books.

$$\frac{\text{Book value}}{\text{Market value}} = \frac{\text{Market value}}{\text{Book value}}$$
$$0.20 \qquad\qquad 5\times$$

The high ratio of 5× means the company may be due for a correction as opposed to a stock that is trading at very close to book value.

With this third theory in mind, the investor may wish to keep his or her eye on stocks that meet some or all of the attributes previously discussed, that is, small size, low P/E ratios, and a high book-to-market value ratio.

---

35 Eugene F. Fama and Kenneth R. French, "The Cross Section of Stock Returns," *Journal of Finance,* June 1992, pp. 427–65.

IT'S THE "JANUARY EFFECT," BUT WILL IT OCCUR IN JANUARY?

Something mysterious happens every January in stock and bond markets around the world.

Small-company stocks rise sharply—overwhelming increases in large-company stocks for that month. High-yield, high-risk "junk" bonds also get a large hunk of their yearly appreciation in January.

Why it happens still isn't understood. One thing is known, however: A growing number of traders and speculators believe it is possible to make a short-term profit by playing the January effect.

The strategy is simple. Around mid-December, investors buy small-company stocks selling for depressed prices or a mutual fund that invests in small-company stocks. After prices surge in early January, these investors lock in their gains by selling the stocks or switching out of their mutual fund and into a money market fund. Some investors take a similar approach with mutual funds that invest in junk bonds.

Still, it is possible to lose money trying to play the January effect. In bear markets like the Januaries of 1978 and 1982, small stocks lost money. "Even though they outperform large stocks, they can't fight the tape," says one trader.

One problem for investors trying to capitalize on the January effect is transaction costs. Brokers' commissions, poor prices from wide bid-and-asked spreads on thinly traded over-the-counter stocks, and taxes can all erode returns, points out Robert Haugen, coauthor of *The Incredible January Effect.* "Still, historically, the force is with you," he says.

Since the effect first got wide notice in 1981, Goldman, Sachs & Co. says the performance difference between small stocks and large stocks in January has been narrowing. Since 1982, small stocks rose an average of 4.2 percent in January, compared with 3.8 percent for large stocks. That's not nearly as significant as the 7.4 percent versus 1.4 percent comparison for 1926 to 1981.

Earl C. Gottschalk, Jr., *The Wall Street Journal,* December 14, 1988, pp. C1, C16. Reprinted by permission of *The Wall Street Journal,* ©1988 by Dow Jones & Co., Inc. All Rights Reserved Worldwide.

OTHER STOCK-RELATED SPECIAL SITUATIONS

Although the authors have attempted to highlight the major special situations related to stocks in the preceding pages, there are other opportunities as well. While only brief mention will be made in this section, the student may choose to follow up the footnoted references for additional information.

THE JANUARY EFFECT Because stockholders may sell off their losers in late December to establish tax losses, these stocks are often depressed in value in early January and may represent bargains and an opportunity for high returns.[36] In fact, the January effect and the potential for high returns has attracted so much attention that it often is used as a variable to explain other phenomena as well as itself. For example, Keim has found that

[36] Ben Branch and J. Ryan, "Tax-Loss Trading: An Inefficiency Too Large to Ignore," *Financial Review,* Winter 1980, pp. 20–29.

roughly half the small-firm effect for the year occurs in January. In other words, if you want to play the small-firm effect game, start early in the year.[37]

The Weekend Effect Research evidence indicates that stocks tend to peak in value on Friday and generally decline in value on Monday. Thus, the theory is that the time to buy is on late Monday and the time to sell is on late Friday. While over many decades this observation is valid,[38] generally the price movement is too small to profitably cover transaction costs. However, if you *know* you are going to sell a stock that you have held for a long time, you may prefer to do so later in the week rather than early in the week.

The Value Line Ranking Effect *The Value Line Investment Survey* contains information on approximately 1,700 stocks. Using a valuation model, each company is rated from 1 through 5 for profitable market performance over the next 12 months. One is the highest possible rating, and 5 is the lowest. One hundred stocks are always in category 1. Researchers have generally indicated that category 1 stocks provide superior risk-adjusted returns over the other four categories and the market in general.[39] Of course, frequent trading may rapidly cut into these profits. Figure 10–1 graphs the strong performance of the Value Line group 1 category compared with the other four categories.

The Surprise-Earnings Effect As indicated in Chapter 9 in the discussion of efficient markets, accounting information tends to be quickly impounded in the value of a stock, and there appears to be little opportunity to garner superior returns from this data. Even if a firm reports a 20 percent increase in earnings, there is likely to be little market reaction to the announcement if the gain was generally anticipated. However, an exception to this rule may relate to truly *unexpected* earnings announcements.[40] If they are very positive, the stock may go up for a number of days after the announcement and thus provide a superior investment opportunity. The opposite would be true of a totally unexpected negative announcement.

---

37 Donald B. Keim, "Size-Related Anomalies and Stock Return Seasonality," *Journal of Financial Economics,* March 1983, pp. 13–32. Also see Richard Roll, "Vas ist das? The Turn of the Year Effect and the Return Premium of Small Firms," *Journal of Portfolio Management,* Winter 1983, pp. 18–28.

38 Frank Cross, "The Behavior of Stock Prices on Fridays and Mondays," *Financial Analysts Journal,* November–December 1973, pp. 67–69; Kenneth R. French, "Stock Returns and the Weekend Effect," *Journal of Financial Economics,* March 1980, pp. 55–69; and Lawrence Harris, "A Transaction Data Study of Weekly and Interdaily Patterns in Stock Returns," *Journal of Financial Economics,* May 1986, pp. 99–117.

39 Fisher Black, "*Yes,* Virginia, There Is Hope: Test of the Value Line Ranking System," *Financial Analysts Journal,* September–October 1973, pp. 10–14; Clark Holloway, "A Note on Testing an Aggressive Strategy Using Value Line Ranks," *Journal of Finance,* June 1981, pp. 711–19; and Scott E. Stickel, "The Effect of *Value Line Investment Survey* Rank Changes on Common Stock Prices," *Journal of Financial Economics,* March 1985, pp. 121–43.

40 Richard Rendleman, Charles Jones, and Henry A. Latane, "Empirical Anomalies Based on Unexpected Earnings and the Importance of Risk Adjustments," *Journal of Financial Economics,* November 1982, pp. 269–87.

FIGURE 10–1 Performance of Value Line Groups

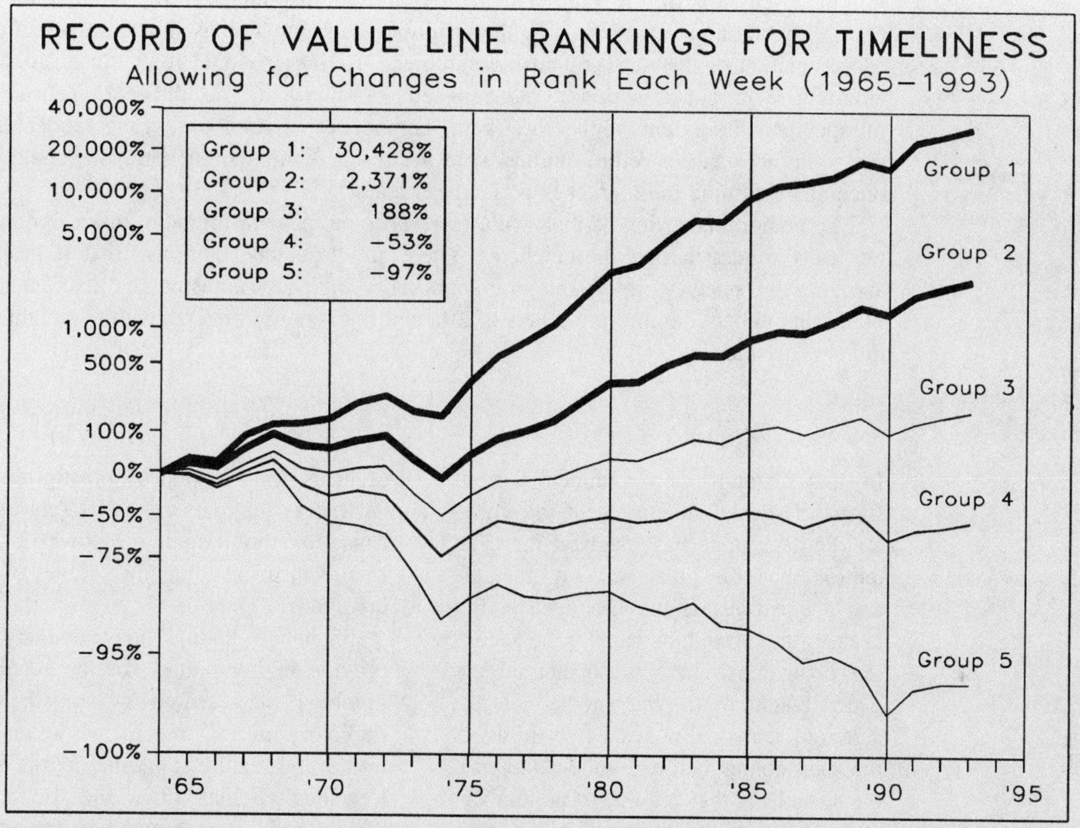

Record of Value Line Rankings for Timeliness (Allowing for Changes in Rank Each Week)
April 16, 1965 to December 31, 1993

Group	'65*	'66	'67	'68	'69	'70	'71	'72	'73	'74	'75	'76	'77	'78	'79
1	28.8%	– 5.5%	53.4%	37.1%	–10.4%	7.3%	30.6%	12.6%	–19.1%	–11.1%	75.6%	54.0%	26.6%	32.6%	54.7%
2	18.5	– 6.2	36.1	26.9	–17.5	– 3.2	13.7	7.4	–28.9	–29.5	47.4	31.2	13.4	18.3	38.0
3	6.7	–13.9	27.1	24.0	–23.8	– 8.0	9.3	3.5	–33.6	–34.1	40.7	29.0	1.3	3.0	20.7
4	– 0.4	–15.7	23.8	20.9	–33.3	–16.3	8.4	– 7.1	–37.9	–40.6	39.3	28.8	– 6.9	– 3.8	12.8
5	– 3.2	–18.2	21.5	11.8	–44.9	–23.3	– 5.5	–13.4	–43.8	–55.7	40.9	26.7	–17.6	– 3.2	10.4

Group	'80	'81	'82	'83	'84	'85	'86	'87	'88	'89	'90	'91	'92	'93	'65* To '93
1	52.6%	13.6%	50.6%	40.9%	– 2.1%	47.0%	22.9%	5.4%	9.5%	27.9%	–10.4%	55.4%	10.0%	13.4%	30,428%
2	35.7	1.8	31.0	19.1	– 0.8	30.7	14.4	– 2.4	20.4	26.5	–10.2	34.1	14.3	12.4	2,371
3	15.4	– 3.3	17.9	20.2	– 5.6	22.8	7.7	–12.6	16.1	13.7	–24.4	18.9	11.0	9.8	188
4	7.4	– 8.7	5.1	25.0	–17.4	11.4	– 6.8	–15.8	17.6	2.6	–33.7	16.7	6.2	8.5	–53
5	2.9	–21.4	–10.9	19.0	–31.0	– 5.6	–19.6	–28.0	11.4	–19.2	–45.5	25.5	15.4	0.3	–97

***April through December**

Source: *Value Line Selection and Opinion,* January 21, 1994.

TRULY SUPERIOR RETURNS OR MISMEASUREMENT?

In our discussion in the previous chapter and in this chapter, we pointed out the possibility that high returns may be the result of a superior strategy in a less than efficient capital market or the result of mismeasurement. The latter would refer, for example, to assuming you got a superior risk-adjusted return when you did not. You simply misspecified the extent of the risk (beta) component or used the wrong model. If all risk-adjusted superior return studies were the result of misspecification, we could then once again assume the market is perfectly efficient.

The predominant view is that while there is some mismeasurement, many opportunities truly reflect market inefficiencies. There are "special situations" that if properly analyzed provide an opportunity for abnormally high risk-adjusted returns. The most literal and unbending interpretations of efficient markets no longer carry the weight they did two decades ago.[41]

SUMMARY

In this chapter, we examined various forms of special situations for the investor. Perhaps none has received more attention than the great wave of mergers and acquisitions of the last decade. Because of the premiums paid by the acquiring companies, there is substantial upward potential in the stocks of the acquired firms. However, two-thirds of the gain comes before public announcement, and for that reason, some analysts attempt to identify potential target companies before announcements are made. One of the problems of investing in mergers and acquisitions is that announced plans may be called off, and there may be substantial retractions in value for the stock of the target company.

Next, we observe the price patterns of firms going public (selling their stock to the general public for the first time). There appear to be abnormal returns after issue, and then the efficiency of the market comes strongly into play. The reason for the initial excess returns is the underpricing by investment bankers to ensure a good reception for the new issue. Stocks of firms underwritten by prestigious underwriters may show smaller returns because of the bargaining power of the issuing firm and the lower level of risk involved.

Exchange listings may or may not provide higher values for the securities involved; the research is somewhat contradictory in this regard. However, the interesting feature suggested by the Ying, Lewellen, Schlarbaum, and Lease research is that there may be excess returns between the point of announcement and listing (regardless of whether there is a sell-off after listing). This is at variance with the semistrong form of the efficient market hypothesis.

There is also conflicting evidence on the impact of a firm's repurchase of its own shares in the marketplace. Recent research, however, indicates the high premiums paid (22.46 percent) on cash tender offers may provide upward market movement at and immediately after the point of announcement.

Studies of the small-firm effect indicate there may be superior return poten-

[41] Eugene F. Fama, "Efficient Capital Markets: II," *Journal of Finance,* December 1991, pp. 1575–1617.

tial in investing in smaller capitalization firms. Others suggest it is the low P/E ratios or high book value to market value of many of these firms that leads to superior returns.

Finally, researchers have indicated some special opportunities for profits related to seasonality, unexpected earnings reports, and the Value Line ranking system.

KEY WORDS AND CONCEPTS

abnormal returns, 282
merger price premium, 282
unfriendly takeovers, 284
white knight, 284
synergy, 285
leveraged buyouts, 285
going public (initial public offering), 286
exchange listing, 288
repurchase, 289
market capitalizations, 293

DISCUSSION QUESTIONS

1. Define special or abnormal returns.
2. What is the basis for upward movement in the stock of an acquisition candidate?
3. What is an unfriendly takeover?
4. What is the primary danger in investing in merger and acquisition candidates?
5. What factor(s) will determine the extent of upward price potential for an acquisition candidate at the time of a merger announcement?
6. Do the stocks of acquiring companies tend to show strong upward market movement as a result of the merger process? Comment on the reasoning behind your answer.
7. Why do cash tender offers frequently carry a higher premium than stock offers?
8. Why does abnormal return potential sometimes exist in the new-issues market?
9. What are some factors to consider before buying a new issue?
10. Why might firms that are underwritten by large, prestigious investment banking houses not necessarily provide the highest initial returns to investors in the new-issue market?
11. What are some reasons a firm may wish to have its security listed on an exchange?
12. What was the major finding of the Ying, Lewellen, Schlarbaum, and Lease study? How does this relate to the semistrong form of the efficient market hypothesis?
13. What are some reasons a firm may repurchase its own stock?
14. What are some negative connotations associated with a firm repurchasing its own shares?
15. Relate the existence of positive returns on stock repurchases to the type of offer (formal versus informal).
16. According to researchers such as Banz and Reinganum, what is the general performance of small firms relative to larger firms?
17. What does the term *market capitalization* mean?
18. What criticisms of the small-firm effect were offered by Roll and Stoll and Whaley? Were these considered valid by Reinganum?

19. What explanation might be offered for the possible market inefficiency in the small-firm segment of the market?
20. What problem does an institutional investor have when he or she tries to purchase shares of a small firm?
21. Advocates of the small-firm effect argue that it is this factor *alone* that leads to superior risk-adjusted returns. Does the Peavy and Goodman study support this position?
22. What does Table 10–8 indicate about the relationship between a firm's P/E ratio and its average quarterly return?
23. What does the research by Fama and French indicate about the importance of the ratio of book value to market value? If a stock has a book value that is 20 percent of market value, is it thought to possibly be undervalued or overvalued (due for a correction)?
24. Why might the first week in January be a good time to purchase stocks that were losers in the prior year?
25. If a corporation has an anticipated large positive earnings report, is that a good time to buy? What if the positive report were unexpected?
26. What is meant by the statement that "mismeasurement or misspecification of risk could give the false appearance of superior returns"?

THE WALL STREET JOURNAL PROJECT

When *The Wall Street Journal* reports corporate earnings in the "Digest of Earnings Reports,"* it usually includes a section on earnings surprises. Find the box on earnings surprises, and identify the company having the biggest positive earnings surprise and the biggest negative earnings surprise. Compare the price of the common stock from the day before the surprise announcement with the day after the surprise announcement, and explain any relationships between performance and earnings per share changes.

CRITICAL THOUGHT CASE

Jane Hailey, the vice president of finance for Global Retail Stores, Inc., was excited about the way preliminary negotiations had gone for Modern Woman Corp., a retail chain of 45 stores that specialized in professional wear for the working female. The Modern Woman Corp. traded on the NASDAQ at a price of 18 bid, 18½ ask. Jane's own analyses indicated a buyout price as high as $30 could be justified based on the firm's futures prospects. The initial secret discussions had touched on a price in the $26 to $28 range, but Jane thought the officers of the Modern Woman Corp. were probably eyeing at least 10 percent more for their stock. Otherwise, the negotiations were very amicable.

*This information can be located by going to the index on the front page of *The Wall Street Journal* and locating "Earnings Digest." It should be noted that the earnings surprise information is not always available. It is most likely to be found during periods of high quarterly earnings announcements.

Jane's annual salary exceeded $200,000 a year, but like many successful people she would have liked even more. However, she knew it was illegal for her to trade on such privileged inside information. Fortunately, she thought, she had a younger brother who was a senior in medical school and could benefit from the potential upward movement in Modern Woman's stock once the news became public. Although she would tell him of the impending merger, she would be very careful not to lend or advance him any funds for fear of reprisal by the Securities and Exchange Commission. If he made any investment, it would be purely on his own.

Question

1. Comment on Jane Hailey's intended action.

U.S. EQUITIES ONFLOPPY EXERCISES

Please use your U.S. Equities OnFloppy software and manual to complete the following exercises.

1. This Chapter identifies and discusses a number of market anomalies including the small-firm, P/E-ratio, and P/B-ratio effects. In an attempt to capture these effects, select firms with the following characteristics:
   a. Market value between $10 and $100 million.
   b. Price-to-book (P/B) value greater than 1.
   c. Price-earnings ratio greater than the growth rate in total earnings, that is, EA%12.
   d. Consider only those firms that have had positive earnings for the last three years and increasing earnings for the past two years, that is, EA3 > 0, EA2 > EA3, and EA1 > EA2.
   e. Eliminate all firms that have an SIC between 6000 and 6999, that is, the financial firms.
2. Pick the five firms you prefer (justify selection), and check on their future performance.

SELECTED REFERENCES

Market Inefficiency

Beebower, G. L., and A. P. Varikooty. "Measuring Market Timing Strategies." *Financial Analysts Journal,* November–December 1991, pp. 78–84.

Fama, Eugene F. "Efficient Capital Markets: II." *Journal of Finance,* December 1991, pp. 1575–1617.

Rosenberg, Barr; Kenneth Reid; and Ronald Lanstein. "Persuasive Evidence of Market Inefficiency." *Journal of Portfolio Management,* Spring 1985, pp. 9–16.

Mergers and Acquisitions

Agrawal, Anup; Jeffrey F. Jaffe; and Gershon Mandelker. "The Post-Merger Performance of Acquiring Firms." *Journal of Finance,* September 22, 1992, pp. 1605–21.

Healy, Paul M.; Krisha G. Paleps; and Richard S. Ruback. "Does Corporate Performance Improve after Mergers?" *Journal of Financial Economics,* April 1992, pp. 132–65.

Kaplan, Steven. "The Effect of Management Buyouts on Operating Performance." *Journal of Financial Economics,* October 1989, pp. 217–54.

Mandelker, Gershon. "Risk and Return: The Case of Merging Firms." *Journal of Financial Economics,* December 1974, pp. 303–35.

New Stock Issues (Initial Public Offerings)

Baron, D. P. "A Model for the Demand for Investment Bank Advising and Distribution Services for New Issues." *Journal of Finance,* September 1982, pp. 955–76.

Barry, Christopher B., and Robert H. Jennings. "The Opening Performance of Initial Offerings of Common Stock." *Financial Management,* Spring 1993, pp. 54–63.

Barry, Christopher B.; Chris J. Muscarella; and Michael R. Vetsuypens. "Underwriter Warrants, Underwriter Compensation and Cost of Going Public." *Journal of Financial Economics,* March 1991, pp. 113–35.

Block, Stanley, and Marjorie Stanley. "The Financial Characteristics and Price Movement Patterns of Companies Approaching the Unseasoned Securities Market in the Late 1970s." *Financial Management,* Winter 1980, pp. 30–36.

Carter, Richard, and Steven Manaster. "Initial Public Offering and Underwriter Reputation." *Journal of Finance,* September 1990, pp. 1045–67.

Ibbotson, Roger G. "Price Performance of Common Stock New Issues." *Journal of Financial Economics,* September 1975, pp. 235–72.

______; J. Sindelar; and Jay R. Ritter. "Initial Public Offerings." *Journal of Applied Corporate Finance,* Fall 1988, pp. 37–43.

Miller, Robert E., and Frank K. Reilly. "An Examination of Mispricing Returns, and Uncertainty for Initial Public Offerings." *Financial Management,* Winter 1987, pp. 33–38.

Muscarella, Chris, and Mike Vetsuypens. "A Simple Test of Barron's Model of IPO Underwriting." *Journal of Financial Economics,* September 1989, pp. 123–35.

Neuberger, Brian M., and Chris A. La Chapelle. "Unseasoned New Issues' Price Performance on Three Tiers: 1975–1980." *Financial Management,* Autumn 1983, pp. 23–28.

Ritter, Jay. "The Long-Term Performance of Initial Public Offerings." *Journal of Finance,* March 1991, pp. 3–27.

Rock, K. "Why New Issues Are Underpriced." *Journal of Financial Economics,* January–February 1986, pp. 187–212.

Exchange Listings Effect

Fabozzi, Frank J., and Richard W. Furst. "Does Listing Increase the Market Value of Common Stock?" *Journal of Business,* April 1970, pp. 174–80.

Goulet, Waldemar. "Price Changes, Managerial Accounting and Insider Trading at the Time of Listing." *Financial Management,* Spring 1974, pp. 303–6.

Sanger, Gary C., and James D. Peterson. "An Empirical Analysis of Common Stock Delistings." *Journal of Financial and Quantitative Analysis,* June 1990, pp. 261–72.

Ying, Louis K. W.; Wilbur G. Lewellen; Gary G. Schlarbaum; and Ronald C. Lease. "Stock Exchange Listing and Securities Returns." *Journal of Financial and Quantitative Analysis,* September 1977, pp. 415–32.

Stock Repurchases

Dann, Larry Y. "Common Stock Repurchases: An Analysis of Returns to Bondholders and Stockholders." *Journal of Financial Economics,* June 1981, pp. 113–38.

Dielman, Terry E.; Timothy J. Nantell; and Roger L. Wright. "Price Effects of Stock Repurchasing: A Random Coefficient Regression Approach." *Journal of Financial and Quantitative Analysis,* March 1980, pp. 175–89.

Lakonishok, Josef, and Theo Vermaelen. "Anomalous Price Behavior around Repurchase Tender Offers." *Journal of Finance,* June 1990, pp. 455–77.

Masulis, R. W. "Stock Repurchase by Tender Offer: An Analysis of the Causes of Common Stock Price Changes." *Journal of Finance,* May 1980, pp. 305–19.

Norgaard, Richard, and Connie Norgaard. "A Critical Evaluation of Share Repurchase." *Financial Management,* Spring 1974, pp. 44–50.

Vermaelen, Theo. "Common Stock Repurchases and Market Signaling: An Empirical Study." *Journal of Financial Economics,* June 1981, pp. 139–83.

The Small-Firm Effect

Arbel, Avner, and Paul Strebel. "Pay Attention to Neglected Firms." *Journal of Portfolio Management,* Winter 1983, pp. 37–42.

Banz, Rolf W. "The Relationship between Returns and Market Value of Common Stocks." *Journal of Financial Economics,* March 1981, pp. 3–18.

Barry, Christopher B., and Stephen J. Brown. "Differential Information and the Small-Firm Effect." *Journal of Financial Economics,* June 1984, pp. 283–94.

Reinganum, Marc R. "Misspecification of Capital Asset Pricing—Empirical Anomalies Based on Earnings Yield and Market Values." *Journal of Financial Economics,* March 1981, pp. 19–46.

______. "A Direct Test of Roll's Conjecture on the Firm Size Effect." *Journal of Finance,* March 1982, pp. 27–35.

______. "Portfolio Strategies Based on Market Capitalization." *Journal of Portfolio Management,* Winter 1983, pp. 29–36.

Roll, Richard. "A Possible Explanation of the Small-Firm Effect." *Journal of Finance,* September 1981, pp. 879–88.

______. "Vas ist das? The Turn of the Year Effect and the Return Premium of Small Firms." *Journal of Portfolio Management,* Winter 1988, pp. 18–28.

Stoll, H. R., and R. E. Whaley. "Transaction Costs and the Small-Firm Effect." *Journal of Financial Economics,* June 1983, pp. 57–80.

Low-P/E Effect

Basu, S. "Investment Performance of Common Stocks in Relation to Their Price-Earnings Ratios: A Test of the Efficient Market Hypothesis."*Journal of Finance,* June 1977, pp. 663–82.

Goodman, David A., and John W. Peavy III. "The Risk Universal Nature of the P/E Effect." *Journal of Portfolio Management,* Summer 1985, pp. 14–17.

Peavy, John W., III, and David A. Goodman. "The Significance of P/Es for Portfolio Returns." *Journal of Portfolio Management,* Winter 1983, pp. 43–47.

Book Value to Market Value Effect

Fama, Eugene F., and Kenneth R. French. "The Cross Section of Stock Returns." *Journal of Finance,* June 1992, pp. 427–65.

The January Effect

Branch, Ben, and J. Ryan. "Tax-Loss Trading: An Inefficiency Too Large to Ignore." *Financial Review,* Winter 1980, pp. 20–29.

Keim, Donald B. "Dividend Yields, Size, and the January Effect." *Journal of Portfolio Management,* Winter 1986, pp. 54–61.

The Daily and Weekend Effect

Cross, Frank. "The Behavior of Stock Prices on Fridays and Mondays." *Financial Analysts Journal,* November–December 1973, pp. 67–69.

French, Kenneth R. "Stock Returns and the Weekend Effect." *Journal of Financial Economics,* March 1980, pp. 55–69.

Harris, Lawrence. "A Transaction Data Study of Weekly and Interdaily Patterns in Stock Returns." *Journal of Financial Economics,* May 1986, pp. 99–117.

The Value Line Effect

Black, Fisher. "*Yes,* Virginia, There Is Hope: Test of the Value Line Ranking System." *Financial Analysts Journal,* September–October 1973, pp. 10–14.

Holloway, Clark. "A Note on Testing an Aggressive Strategy Using Value Line Ranks." *Journal of Finance,* June 1981, pp. 711–19.

Stickel, Scott E. "The Effect of *Value Line Investment Survey* Rank Changes on Common Stock Prices." *Journal of Financial Economics,* March 1985, pp. 121–43.

The Earnings Effect

Kormendi, Roger, and Robert Lipe. "Earnings Innovations, Earnings Persistence, and Stock Returns." *Journal of Business,* July 1987, pp. 323–46.

Rendleman, Richard; Charles Jones; and Henry A. Latane. "Empirical Anomalies Based on Unexpected Earnings and the Importance of Risk Adjustments." *Journal of Financial Economics,* November 1982, pp. 269–87.

PART 4

Fixed-Income and Leveraged Securities

OUTLINE

The fixed income markets include many different types of securities from municipal bonds to convertible corporate bonds, but the dominant group of securities are the U.S. government's bills, notes, and bonds. U.S. government securities markets are the prime markets around the world. In time of political trouble, U.S. government securities provide a safe haven for investors from Japan to Germany. Billions of dollars trade every day in these markets where it is not unusual for the U.S. Treasury Department to offer $10 to $15 billion of new securities in one day.

However, one mistake that investors sometimes make in dealing with U.S. government securities is failing to differentiate between credit risk and interest rate risk. While there is virtually no risk that the U.S. government will default on the payments related to its obligations (that is, no credit risk), there is still a second risk that can be all too real for investors: Once the securities are issued, interest rates in the market may change, and this can cause the prices of outstanding bonds to change. Take, for example, a 30-year, $1,000 U.S. government bond that is issued at 8 percent. If interest rates rise to 10 percent shortly after issue, the bond will fall in price to $811. This price adjustment takes place because investors are now demanding a 10 percent return on their money, so the previously issued 8 percent bond must be valued downward to meet their demands. (The mechanics of this price adjustment process will be explained in Chapter 12; for now it is enough that you understand that it can take place.)

Many unsophisticated investors are duped into thinking that there is no risk associated with government securities. Furthermore, some mutual fund salespeople and aggressive stockbrokers, at times, talk about the extra measure of safety associated with government securities, but they fail to differentiate between credit risk and interest rate risk. Actually, there is more interest rate risk associated with U.S. government bonds than any other type of bonds (for example, those issued by corporations or by cities and states). The reason is that the price of U.S. government bonds is influenced *only* by changes in interest rates, while corporate or municipal bonds may also trade up or down as the issuer's creditworthiness improves or declines.

Of course, one can argue that the bonds will return to their original $1,000 price when they mature (in 30 years in our example). However, this is small consolation to the investor who may need his or her funds a couple of years after the investment and is forced to sell the bonds at a large loss.

The impact of interest rate changes can also work in the other direction. If interest rates go down after the original purchase, the value of the newly purchased bond will go up. Because U.S. government securities are the most price sensitive to interest rate changes, the price appreciation will be greater than for any other type of bond.

The point to be made is that even though there is no credit risk associated with U.S. government securities, there is still interest rate uncertainty, which can make you substantially richer or poorer. ■

11

BOND AND FIXED-INCOME FUNDAMENTALS

As the reader will observe in various sections of this chapter, bonds actually represent a more substantial portion of new offerings in the capital markets than common stock. Some of the most financially rewarding jobs on Wall Street go to sophisticated analysts and dealers in the bond market.

In this chapter, we will examine the fundamentals of the bond instrument for both corporate and government issuers, with an emphasis on the debt contract and security provisions. We will also look at the overall structure of the bond market and the ways in which bonds are rated. The question of bond market efficiency is also considered. While most of the chapter deals with corporate and government bonds, other forms of fixed-income securities also receive attention. Thus, there is a brief discussion of short-term, fixed-income investments (such as certificates of deposit and commercial paper) as well as preferred stock.

In Chapter 12, we will shift the emphasis to actually evaluating fixed-income investments and devising strategies that attempt to capture profitable opportunities in the market. In Chapter 13, we will look at the interesting concept of *duration.* We begin our discussion by considering the key elements that go into a bond contract.

THE BOND CONTRACT

A bond normally represents a long-term contractual obligation of the firm to pay interest to the bondholder as well as the face value of the bond at maturity. The major provisions in a bond agreement are spelled out in the **bond indenture,** a complicated legal document often more than 100 pages long, administered by an independent trustee (usually a commercial bank). We shall examine some important terms and concepts associated with a bond issue.

The **par value** represents the face value of a bond. Most corporate bonds are traded in $1,000 units, while many federal, state, and local issues trade in units of $5,000 or $10,000.

Coupon rate refers to the actual interest rate on the bond, usually payable in semiannual installments. To the extent that interest rates in the market go above or below the coupon rate after the bond is issued, the market price of the bond will change from the par value. A bond initially issued at a rate of 8 percent will sell at a substantial discount from par value when 12 percent is the currently demanded rate of return. We will eventually examine how the investor makes and loses substantial amounts of money in the bond market with the swings in interest rates. A few corporate bonds are termed **variable-rate notes** or **floating-rate notes,** meaning the coupon rate is fixed for only a short period and then varies with a stipulated short-term rate such as the rate on U.S. Treasury bills. In this instance, the interest payment rather than the price of the bond varies up and down. In recent times, zero-coupon bonds have also been issued at values substantially below maturity value. With **zero-coupon bonds,** the investor receives return in the form of capital appreciation over the life of the bond since no semiannual cash interest payments are received.

The **maturity date** is the date on which final payment is due at the stipulated par value.

Methods of bond repayment can occur under many different arrangements. Some bonds are never paid off, such as selected **perpetual bonds** issued by the Canadian and

British governments, and have no maturity dates. A more normal procedure would simply call for a single-sum lump payment at the end of the obligation. Thus, the issuer may make 40 semiannual interest payments over the next 20 years plus one lump-sum payment of the par value of the bond at maturity. There are also other significant means of repayment.

The first is the **serial payment** in which bonds are paid off in installments over the life of the issue. Each serial bond has its own predetermined date of maturity and receives interest only to that point. Although the total bond issue may span more than 20 years, 15 to 20 maturity dates are assigned. Municipal bonds are often issued on this basis. Second, there may be a **sinking-fund provision** in which semiannual or annual contributions are made by a corporation into a fund administered by a trustee for purposes of debt retirement. The trustee takes the proceeds and goes into the market to purchase bonds from willing sellers. If no sellers are available, a lottery system may be used to repurchase the required number of bonds from among outstanding bondholders.

Third, debt may also be retired under a call provision. A **call provision** allows the corporation to call or force in all of the debt issue prior to maturity. The corporation usually pays a 5 percent to 10 percent premium over par value as part of the call provision arrangement. The ability to call is often *deferred* for the first five years of an issue (it can only occur after this time period).

The opposite side of the coin for a bond investor is a put provision. The **put provision** enables the bondholder to have an option to sell a long-term bond back to the corporation at par value after a relatively short period (such as three to five years). This privilege can be particularly valuable if interest rates have gone up since the initial issuance and if the bond is currently trading at 75 to 80 percent of par. A put bond generally carries a lower interest rate than conventional bonds (perhaps 1 to 2 percent lower) because of this protective put privilege. If one buys a put bond and interest rates go down and bond prices up (perhaps to $1,200), the privilege is unnecessary and is merely ignored.

SECURED AND UNSECURED BONDS

We have discussed some of the important features related to interest payments and retirement of outstanding issues. At least of equal importance is the nature of the security provision for the issue. Bond market participants have a long-standing practice of describing certain issues by the nature of asset claims in liquidation. In actuality, pledged assets are sold and the proceeds distributed to bondholders only infrequently. Typically, the defaulting corporation is reorganized, and existing claims are partially satisfied by issuing new securities to the participating parties. Of course, the stronger and *better secured* the initial claim, the higher the quality of the security to be received in a reorganization.

A number of terms are used to denote **secured debt,** that is, debt backed by collateral. Under a **mortgage** agreement, real property (plant and equipment) is pledged as security for a loan. A mortgage may be senior or junior in nature, with the former requiring satisfaction of claims before payment is given to the latter. Bondholders may also attach an **after-acquired property clause** requiring that any new property be placed under the original mortgage.

A very special form of a mortgage or collaterialized debt instrument is the **equipment trust certificate** used by firms in the transportation industry (railroads, airlines, etc.). Proceeds from the sale of the certificate are used to purchase new equipment, and this new equipment serves as collateral for the trust certificate.

Not all bond issues are secured or collateralized by assets. Most federal, state, and local government issues are unsecured. A wide range of corporate issues also are unsecured. There is a set of terminology referring to these unsecured issues. A corporate debt issue that is unsecured is referred to as a **debenture.** Even though the debenture is not secured by a specific pledge of assets, there may be priorities of claims among debenture holders. Thus, there are senior debentures and junior or subordinated debentures.

If liquidation becomes necessary because all other avenues for survival have failed, secured creditors are paid off first out of the disposition of the secured assets. The proceeds from the sale of the balance of the assets are then distributed among unsecured creditors, with those holding a senior ranking being satisfied before those holding a subordinate position (subordinated debenture holders).[1]

Unsecured corporate debt may provide slightly higher yields because of the greater suggested risk. However, this is partially offset by the fact that many unsecured debt issuers have such strong financial statements that security pledges may not be necessary.

Companies with less favorable prospects may issue income bonds. **Income bonds** specify that interest is to be paid only to the extent that it is earned as current income. There is no legally binding requirement to pay interest on a regular basis, and failure to make interest payments cannot trigger bankruptcy proceedings. These issues appear to offer the corporation the unusual advantage of paying interest as a tax-deductible expense (as opposed to dividends) combined with freedom from the binding contractual obligation of most debt issues. But any initial enthusiasm for these issues is quickly reduced by recognizing that they have very limited appeal to investors. The issuance of income bonds is usually restricted to circumstances where new corporate debt is issued to old bondholders or preferred stockholders to avoid bankruptcy or where a troubled corporation is being reorganized.

THE COMPOSITION OF THE BOND MARKET

Having established some of the basic terminology relating to the bond instrument, we are now in a position to take a more comprehensive look at the bond market. Corporate issues must vie with offerings from the U.S. Treasury, federally sponsored credit agencies, and state and local governments (municipal offerings). The relative importance of the four types of issues is indicated in Figure 11–1.

Over the 20-year period presented in Figure 11–1, the two fastest growing users of funds (borrowers) were the U.S. government and corporations. The former's needs can be attributed to persistent federal deficits that must be financed by increased borrowing. In the case of corporations, low profitability, combined with internal expansions and

---

[1] Those secured creditors who are not fully satisfied by the disposition of secured assets may also participate with the unsecured creditors in the remaining assets.

FIGURE 11–1 Long-Term Funds Raised by Business and Government

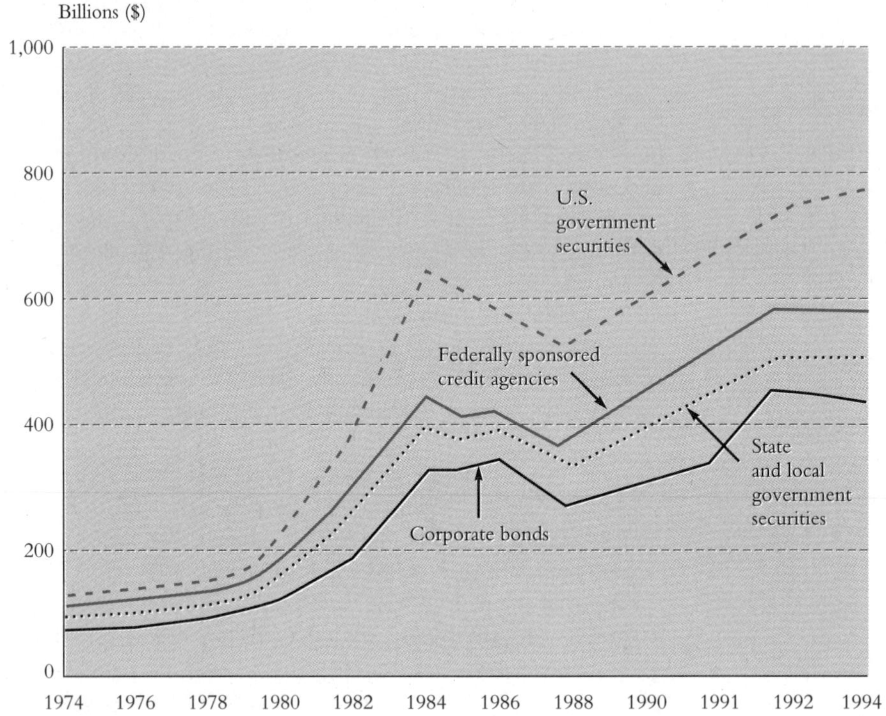

mergers, has led to tremendous borrowing needs. State and local governments have been active participants with municipal bond issues used to finance local growth and cover local deficits. Finally, federally sponsored credit agencies must call on the long-term funds market. Please observe the explosive growth in long-term borrowing by all sectors of the economy since 1980.

U.S. Government Securities

U.S. government securities take the form of Treasury bills, Treasury notes, and Treasury bonds (only the latter two are considered in Figure 11–1). The distinction among the three categories relates to the life of the obligation.

Treasury bills (T-bills) have a maximum maturity of one year and common maturities of 91 and 182 days. Treasury bills trade on a discount basis, meaning the yield the investor receives occurs as a result of the difference between the price paid and the maturity value (and no actual interest is paid). A further discussion of this is presented later in the chapter.

Treasury bills trade in minimum units of $10,000, and there is an extremely active secondary, or resale, market for these securities. Thus, an investor buying a Treasury bill

from the government with an initial life of approximately six months would have no difficulty selling it to another investor after two or three weeks. Since the T-bill now has a shorter time to run, its market value would be a bit closer to par.

A second type of U.S. government security is the **Treasury note,** which is considered to be of intermediate term and generally has a maturity of 1 to 10 years. Finally, **Treasury bonds** are long term in nature and mature in 10 to 30 years. Unlike Treasury bills, Treasury notes and bonds provide direct interest and trade in units of $1,000 and higher. Because there is no risk of default (unless the government stops printing money or the ultimate bomb explodes), U.S. government securities provide lower returns than other forms of credit obligations. Interest on U.S. government issues is fully taxable for IRS purposes but is exempt from state and local taxes.

Some Treasury notes and bonds have been repackaged into zero-coupon bonds by major brokerage firms and investment bankers such as Merrill Lynch and Goldman Sachs. These firms buy U.S. "governments" and put these securities in trust (usually a commercial bank acts as trustee). A security is divided into two parts—one generating a cash flow from the interest payments and the other providing principal at maturity. These two parts are then sold separately to investors with specific needs. The principal payment part is generically called a zero-coupon Treasury bond, but each investment bank labels its own product with names such as TIGRs (for Merrill Lynch's Treasury Investment Growth Receipts) and RATs, CATs, and GATORs for other firms. For example, Merrill Lynch's TIGRs are called Principal TIGRs (the zero-coupon part) and Serial TIGRs (which pay interest at six-month intervals for up to 40 payments). In the mid-1980s, the U.S. Treasury also began trading zero-coupon bonds on its own.

Since zero-coupon bonds pay no interest, all returns to the investor come in the form of increases in the value of the investment. For example, 15-year zero-coupon bonds might initially sell for 18 percent of par value. You might buy a $1,000 instrument for $180.[2]

The Internal Revenue Service taxes zero-coupon bonds as if interest were paid annually even though no cash flow is received until maturity. The tax is based on amortizing the built-in gain over the life of the instrument. For tax reasons, zero-coupons are usually only appropriate for nontaxable accounts such as individual retirement accounts, Keogh plans, or other nontaxable pension funds.

Federally Sponsored Credit Agency Issues

Referring back to Figure 11–1, the second category represents securities issued by federal agencies. The issues represent obligations of various agencies of the government such as the Federal National Mortgage Association and the Federal Home Loan Bank.

---

[2] On zero-coupon bonds, the yield to maturity is a true rate over the life of the security since the price paid includes the assumption of continuous compounding at the yield to maturity. Zero-coupon securities are the most price sensitive to a change in interest rates of any bond having the same maturity. This is fine when interest rates decline but can be disastrous when rates rise. More will be said about zero-coupon bonds in Chapter 13.

Although these issues are authorized by an act of Congress and are used to finance federal projects, they are not direct obligations of the Treasury but rather of the agency itself.

Although the issues are essentially free of risk (there is always the implicit standby power of the government behind the issues), they carry a slightly higher yield than U.S. government securities simply because they are not directly issued by the Treasury. Agency issues have been particularly active as a support mechanism for the housing industry. The issues generally trade in denominations of $5,000 and up and have varying maturities of from 1 to 40 years, with an average life of approximately 15 years. Examples of some agency issues are presented below.

	Minimum Denomination	Life of Issue
Federal Home Loan Bank	$10,000	12–25 years
Federal Intermediate Credit Banks	5,000	Up to 4 years
Federal Farm Credit Bank	50,000	1–10 years
Export-Import Bank	5,000	Up to 7 years
Resolution Funding Corporation	10,000	40 years

Interest on agency issues is fully taxable for IRS purposes and is generally taxable for state and local purposes although there are exceptions. (For example, interest on obligations issued by the Federal Housing Administration are subject to state and local taxes, but those of the Federal Home Loan Bank are not.)

One agency issue that is of particular interest to the investor because of its unique features is the **GNMA (Ginnie Mae) pass-through certificate.** These certificates represent an undivided interest in a pool of federally insured mortgages. Actually, GNMA, the Government National Mortgage Association, buys a pool of mortgages from various lenders at a discount and then issues securities to the public against these mortgages. Security holders in GNMA certificates receive monthly payments that essentially represent a pass through of interest and principal payments on the mortgages. These securities come in minimum denominations of $25,000, are long term, and are fully taxable for federal, state, and local income tax purposes. A major consideration in this investment is that the investor has fully consumed his or her capital at the end of the investment. (Not only has interest been received monthly but also all principal has been returned over the life of the certificate, and therefore, there is no lump-sum payment at maturity.)

Because mortgages that are part of GNMA pass-through certificates are often paid off early as a result of the sale of a home or refinancing at lower interest rates, the true life of a GNMA certificate tends to be much less than the quoted life. For example, a 25-year GNMA certificate may actually be paid off in 12 years. This feature can be a negative consideration because GNMA certificates are particularly likely to be paid off early when interest rates are going down and homeowners are refinancing. The investor in the GNMA certificate is then forced to reinvest the proceeds in a low interest rate environment.

State and Local Government Securities

Debt securities issued by state and local governments are referred to as **municipal bonds.** Examples of issuing agencies include states, cities, school districts, toll roads, or any other type of political subdivision. The most important feature of a municipal bond is the tax-exempt nature of the interest payment. Dating back to the U.S. Supreme Court opinion of 1819 in *McCullough v. Maryland,* it was ruled that the federal government and state and local governments do not possess the power to tax each other. An eventual by-product of the judicial ruling was that income from municipal bonds cannot be taxed by the IRS. Furthermore, income from municipal bonds is also exempt from state and local taxes if bought within the locality in which one resides. Thus, a Californian buying municipal bonds in that state would pay no state income tax on the issue. However, the same Californian would have to pay state or local income taxes if the originating agency were in Texas or New York.

We cannot overemphasize the importance of the federal tax exemption that municipal bonds enjoy. The consequences are twofold. First, individuals in high tax brackets may find highly attractive investment opportunities in municipal bonds.[3] The formula used to equate interest on municipal bonds to other taxable investments is:

$$Y = \frac{i}{(1 - T)} \tag{11–1}$$

where:

Y = Equivalent before-tax yield on a taxable investment
i = Yield on the municipal obligation
T = Marginal tax rate of the investor

If an investor has a marginal tax rate of 36 percent and is evaluating a municipal bond paying 6 percent interest, the equivalent before-tax yield on a taxable investment would be:

$$\frac{6\%}{(1 - 0.36)} = \frac{6\%}{0.64} = 9.38\%$$

Thus, the investor could choose between a *non*-tax-exempt investment paying 9.38 percent and a tax-exempt municipal bond paying 6 percent and be indifferent between the two. Table 11–1 on page 318 presents examples of trade-offs between tax-exempt and non-tax-exempt (taxable) investments at various interest rates and marginal tax rates. Clearly, the higher the marginal tax rate, the greater the advantage of tax-exempt municipal bonds.

A second significant feature of municipal bonds is that the yield the issuing agency pays on municipal bonds is lower than the yield on taxable instruments. Of course, a municipal bond paying 6 percent may be quite competitive with taxable instruments paying more. Average differentials are presented in Table 11–2 on page 318. You should notice in Table 11–2 that the yield differences between municipal bonds and corporate bonds was normally 2 to 4 percentage points. A major distinction that is also important to the bond issuer and investor is whether the bond is of a general obligation or revenue nature.

[3] It should be noted that any capital gain on a municipal bond is taxable as would be the case with any investment.

TABLE 11–1 Marginal Tax Rates and Return Equivalents

Yield on Municipal (percent)	28 Percent Bracket	36 Percent Bracket	39.6 Percent Bracket
5%	6.94%	7.81%	8.28%
6	8.33	9.38	9.93
7	9.72	10.94	11.59
8	11.11	12.50	13.25
9	12.50	14.06	14.90
10	13.89	15.63	16.56

TABLE 11–2 Comparable Yields on Long-Term Municipals and Taxable Corporates (Yearly Averages)

Year	Municipals Aa	Corporates Aa	Yield Difference
1994	6.40%	8.60%	2.20
1993	5.51	7.40	1.89
1992	6.30	8.46	2.16
1991	6.80	9.09	2.29
1990	7.15	9.56	2.41
1989	7.51	9.46	1.95
1988	8.38	9.66	1.28
1987	8.50	9.68	1.18
1986	7.35	9.47	2.12
1985	8.81	11.82	3.01
1984	9.95	12.25	2.30
1983	9.20	12.42	3.22
1982	11.39	14.41	3.02
1981	10.89	14.75	3.86
1980	8.06	12.50	4.44
1979	6.12	9.94	3.82
1978	5.68	8.92	3.24
1977	5.39	8.24	2.85
1976	6.12	8.75	2.63
1975	6.77	9.17	2.40
1974	6.04	8.84	2.80

Source: *Moody's Municipal & Government Manual, Moody's Industrial Manual,* and *Moody's Bond Record* (published by Moody's Investors Service, Inc., New York, NY), selected issues.

The Bond Rating Game: Who Really Runs the Corporation?

When Shell Canada, an integrated oil company with many U.S. investors, decided to sell its coal business, it called Moody's and Standard & Poor's first. Although its own financial analysis indicated the move was appropriate, it would not have made the decision without the blessings of the two major U.S. bond-rating agencies as well as similar rating agencies in Canada. The sell-off provided a $120 million write-off that could have caused a downgrading of Shell Canada's double-A rating, and the firm was not about to take a chance.

The firm's concern was well justified. Its action was taken in June 1991 (a recession year). During the first six months of 1991, 422 corporations suffered a downgrading in ratings while only 88 had an increase. In the prior decade, the big causes for downgradings were the aftereffects of acquisitions or attempts by corporations to defend themselves against takeovers. In the 1990s, these factors were less important, and the major concern was poor earnings performance in a debt-laden economy.

Three good rules for firms to follow in dealing with bond-rating agencies is never surprise the agencies, tell all, and show good intent. A number of years ago, Manville Corporation was severely downgraded not for poor performance, but because it took Chapter 11 bankruptcy protection because it faced asbestos damage litigation. The decision may have been right at the time, but the firm did not have the blessings of the bond-rating agencies.

General Obligation versus Revenue Bonds A **general obligation issue** is backed by the full faith, credit, and "taxing power" of the governmental unit. For a **revenue bond,** on the other hand, the repayment of the issue is fully dependent on the revenue-generating capability of a specific project or venture, such as a toll road, bridge, or municipal colosseum.

Because of the taxing power behind most general obligation (GO) issues, they tend to be of extremely high quality. Approximately three-fourths of all municipal bond issues are of the general obligation variety, and very few failures have occurred in the post–World War II era. Revenue bonds tend to be of more uneven quality, and the economic soundness of the underlying revenue-generating project must be carefully examined (though most projects are quite worthwhile).

Municipal Bond Guarantee A growing factor in the municipal bond market is the third-party guarantee. Whether dealing with a general obligation or revenue bond, a fee may be paid by the originating governmental body to a third-party insurer to guarantee that all interest and principal payments will be made. There are four private insurance firms that guarantee municipal bonds, the largest of which are the Municipal Bond Investors Assurance (MBIA) and the American Municipal Bond Assurance Corporation (AMBAC). Municipal bonds that are guaranteed carry the highest rating possible (AAA) because all the guaranteeing insurance companies are rated AAA. Approximately 30 percent of municipal bond issues are guaranteed.

A municipal bond that is guaranteed will carry a lower yield and have a better secondary or resale market. This may be important because municipal bonds, in general, do not provide as strong a secondary market as U.S. government issues. The market for

a given municipal issue is often small and fragmented, and high indirect costs are associated with reselling the issue.

Corporate Securities

While corporate bonds represent approximately half of the total bond market (which also includes U.S. government securities, federally sponsored credit agencies, and municipal bonds as shown in Figure 11–1), they are the dominant source of new financing for the U.S. corporation. The importance of corporate bonds as a significant form of new financing for U.S. corporations is shown in Figure 11–2.

FIGURE 11–2 Long-Term Corporate Financing

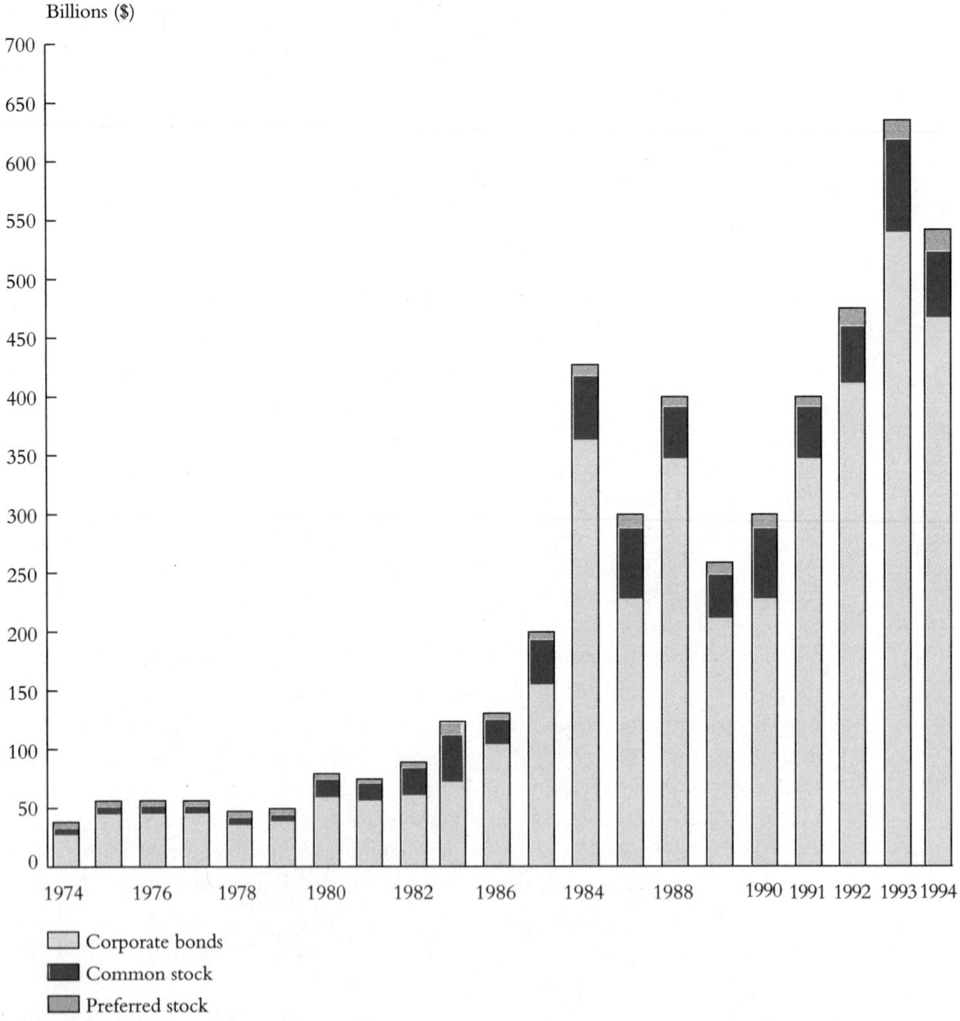

Bonds normally supply 80 to 85 percent of firms' external financial needs. Even during the great bull stock market of 1982 to 1986, corporations looked as heavily as ever to the debt markets to provide financing (this was justified by the decreasing interest rates during this period).

The corporate market may be divided into a number of subunits, including *industrials, public utilities, rails* and *transportation,* and *financial issues* (banks, finance companies, etc.). The industrials are a catchall category that includes everything from high-technology companies to discount chain stores. Public utilities represent the largest segment of the market and have issues that run up to 40 years in maturity. Because public utilities are in constant need of funds to meet ever-expanding requirements for power generation, telephone services, and other essentials, they are always in the bond market to raise new funds. The needs associated with rails and transportation as well as financial issues tend to be less than those associated with public utilities or industrials. Table 11–3 shows comparative yields for the two main categories.[4]

TABLE 11–3 Comparative Yields on Aa Bonds among Corporate Issuers

	Industrial	Public Utility
1994	8.41%	8.74%
1993	7.05	7.19
1992	8.24	8.65
1991	9.01	9.25
1990	9.41	9.65
1989	9.35	9.55
1988	9.41	10.20
1987	9.73	9.83
1986	9.49	9.44
1985	11.57	12.02
1984	12.39	13.02
1983	11.94	12.74
1982	15.01	16.48
1981	13.01	14.03
1980	11.16	11.95
1979	9.24	9.70
1978	8.42	8.76
1977	7.90	8.41
1976	8.87	9.39
1975	8.81	9.45
1974	7.85	8.15

Source: *Moody's Bond Record* (published by Moody's Investors Service, Inc., New York, NY), selected issues.

[4] Financial and transportation issues are generally not broken out of the published data.

The higher yields on public utility issues represent a supply-demand phenomenon more than anything else. A constant stream of new issues to the market can only be absorbed by a higher yield pattern. In other cases, the higher required return may also be associated with quality deterioration as measured by profitability and interest coverage. During 1983–84, the default of the Washington State Power Authority on bonds issued to construct power-generating facilities sent waves through the bond market. Again in 1984, when Public Service of Indiana canceled construction of a partially complete nuclear power plant, nuclear utility issues (both stocks and bonds) suffered severe price erosion, and the bond market demanded high risk premiums on bonds of almost all nuclear utilities.

Corporate bonds of all types generally trade in units of $1,000, and this is a particularly attractive feature to the smaller investor who does not wish to purchase in units of $5,000 to $10,000 (which is necessary for many Treasury and federally sponsored credit agency issues). Because of higher risk relative to government issues, the investor will generally receive higher yields on corporates as well. All income from corporates is taxable for federal, state, and local purposes. Finally, corporate issues have the disadvantage of being subject to calls. When buying a bond during a period of high interest rates, the call provision must be considered a negative feature because the high-yielding bonds may be called in for early retirement as interest rates go down.

The list of innovative products in the corporate debt market is ever growing. Appendix 11A provides an example of developments as presented by John D. Finnerty.

BOND MARKET INVESTORS

Having considered the issuer or supply side of the market, we now comment on the investor or demand side. The bond market is dominated by large institutional investors (insurance companies, banks, pension funds, mutual funds) even more than the stock market. Institutional investors account for 80 to 85 percent of the trading in key segments of the bond market. However, the presence of the individual investor is partially felt in the corporate and municipal bond market where the incentives of low denomination ($1,000) corporate bonds or tax-free municipal bonds have some attraction. Furthermore, in the 1990s individual investors have made their presence felt in the bond market through buying mutual funds that specialize in bond portfolios. The activities of individuals in mutual funds will be covered in detail in Chapter 19, so for now we will concentrate on institutional investors.

Institutional investors' preferences for various sectors of the bond market are influenced by their tax status as well as by the nature of their obligations or liabilities to depositors, investors, or clients. For example, banks traditionally have been strong participants in the municipal bond market because of their substantial tax obligations. Their investments tend to be in short- to intermediate-term assets because of the short-term nature of their deposit obligations (the funds supplied to the banks). One problem that banks find in their bond portfolios is that such investments are often preferred over loans to customers when the economy is weak and loan demand is sluggish. Not so coincidentally, this happens to be the time period when interest rates are low. When the economy improves, interest rates go up, and so does loan demand. To meet

the loan demand of valued customers, banks liquidate portions of their bond portfolios. The problem with this recurring process is that banks are buying bonds when interest rates are *low* and selling them when interest rates are *high.* This can cause losses in the value of the bank portfolio.

The bond investor must be prepared to deal in a relatively strong primary market (new issues market) and a relatively weak secondary market (resale market). While the secondary market is active for many types of Treasury and agency issues, such is not the case for corporate and municipal issues. Thus, the investor must look well beyond the yield, maturity, and rating to determine if a purchase is acceptable. The question that must be considered is: How close to the going market price can I dispose of the issue if that should be necessary? If a 5 or 10 percent discount is involved, that might be unacceptable. Unlike the stock market, the secondary market in bonds tends to be dominated by over-the-counter transactions (although listed bonds are traded as well).

A significant development in the 1990s has been the heavy participation of foreign investors in U.S. bond markets. Foreign investors now bankroll between 10 to 15 percent of the U.S. government's debt. While these investors have helped to finance the U.S. government's deficits, they can be a disruptive factor in the market when they decide to partially withdraw their funds. This happened in the mid-1990s when the declining value of the dollar and fear of inflation in the United States caused many foreign investors to temporarily cash in their investments. Because the U.S. government fears the flight of funds provided by foreign investors, it is sensitive to their needs and desires.

DISTRIBUTION PROCEDURES

In February 1982, the Securities and Exchange Commission began allowing a process called shelf registration under SEC Rule 415. **Shelf registration** permits large companies to file one comprehensive registration statement that outlines the firm's plans for future long-term financing. Then, when market conditions seem appropriate, the firm can issue the securities through an investment banker without further SEC approval. Future issues are said to be sitting on the shelf, waiting for the most advantageous time to appear. An issue may be on the shelf for up to two years.

Approximately half of the new public bond issues are distributed through the shelf registration process. The rest are issued under more traditional procedures in which the bonds are issued shortly after registration by a large syndicate of investment bankers in a highly structured process.

Private Placement

A number of bond offerings are sold to investors as a **private placement;** that is, they are sold privately to investors rather than through the public markets. Private placements are most popular with investors such as insurance companies and pension funds, and they are primarily offered in the corporate sector by industrial firms rather than public utilities. The lender can generally expect to receive a slightly higher yield than on public issues to compensate for the extremely limited or nonexistent secondary market and the generally smaller size of the borrowing firm in a private placement.

BOND RATINGS

Bond investors tend to place much more emphasis on independent analysis of quality than do common stock investors. For this reason, both corporate financial management and institutional portfolio managers keep a close eye on bond rating procedures. The difference between an AA and an A rating may mean the corporation will have to pay ¼ point more interest on the bond issue (perhaps 9½ percent rather than 9¼ percent). On a $100 million, 20-year issue, this represents $250,000 per year (before tax), or a total of $5 million over the life of the bond.

The two major bond-rating agencies are Moody's Investors Service (a subsidiary of Dun & Bradstreet, Inc.) and Standard & Poor's (a subsidiary of McGraw-Hill, Inc.). They rank thousands of corporate and municipal issues as well as a limited number of private placements, commercial paper, preferred stock issues, and offerings of foreign companies and governments. U.S. government issues tend to be free of risk and therefore are given no attention by the bond-rating agencies. Moody's, founded in 1909, is the older of the two bond-rating agencies and covers twice as many securities as Standard & Poor's (particularly in the municipal bond area). Other less well-known bond-rating agencies include Duff & Phelp, Inc., and Fitch Investors Service, Inc. (an old-line rating agency that specializes in bank securities).

The bond ratings, generally ranging from an AAA to a D category, are decided on a committee basis at both Moody's and Standard & Poor's. There are no fast and firm quantitative measures that specify the rating a new issue will receive. Nevertheless, measures pertaining to cash flow and earnings generation in relationship to debt obligations are given strong consideration. Of particular interest are coverage ratios that show the number of times interest payments, as well as all annual contractual obligations, are covered by earnings. A coverage of 2 or 3 may contribute to a low rating, while a ratio of 5 to 10 may indicate the possibility of a strong rating. Operating margins, return on invested capital, and returns on total assets are also evaluated along with debt-to-equity ratios.[5] Financial-ratio analysis makes up perhaps 50 percent of the evaluation. Other factors of importance are the nature of the industry in which the firm operates, the relative position of the firm within the industry, the pricing clout the firm has, and the quality of management. Decisions are not made in a sterile, isolated environment. Thus, it is not unusual for corporate management or the mayor to make a presentation to the rating agency, and on-sight visitations to plants or cities may occur.

The overall quality of the work done by the bond-rating agencies may be judged by the agencies' acceptance in the business and academic community. Their work is very well received. Although Paine Webber and some other investment houses have established their own analysts to shadow the activities of the bond-rating agencies and look for imprecisions in their classifications (and thus potential profits), the opportunities are not great. Academic researchers have generally found that accounting and financial data were well considered in the bond ratings and that rational evaluation appeared to exist.[6]

---

[5] Similar appropriate measures can be applied to municipal bonds, such as debt per capita or income per capita within a governmental jurisdiction.

[6] James O. Horrigan, "The Determination of Long-Term Credit Standing with Financial Ratios," *Empirical Research in Accounting: Selected Studies,* supplement to *Journal of Accounting Research* 4 (1966), pp. 44–62; Thomas F. Pogue and Robert M. Soldofsky, "What's in a Bond Rating?" *Journal of Financial and Quantitative Analysis,* June 1969, pp. 201–8;

One item lending credibility to the bond-rating process is the frequency with which the two major rating agencies arrive at the same grade for a given issue (this occurs well over 50 percent of the time). When "split ratings" do occur (different ratings by different agencies), they are invariably of a small magnitude. A typical case might be AAA versus AA rather than AAA versus BBB. While one can question whether one agency is looking over the other's shoulder or "copying its homework," this is probably not the case in this skilled industry.

Nevertheless, there is room for criticism. While initial evaluations are quite thorough and rational, the monitoring process may not be wholly satisfactory. Subsequent changes in corporate or municipal government events may not trigger a rating change quickly enough. One sure way a corporation or municipal government will get a reevaluation is for them to come out with a new issue. This tends to generate a review of all existing issues.

Actual Rating System

Table 11–4 shows an actual listing of the designations used by Moody's and Standard & Poor's. Note that Moody's combines capital letters and small *a*'s, and Standard & Poor's uses all capital letters.

The first four categories are assumed to represent investment-grade quality. Large institutional investors (insurance companies, banks, pension funds) generally confine their activities to these four categories. Moody's also modifies its basic ratings with numerical values for categories Aa through B. The highest in a category is 1, 2 is the midrange, and 3 is the lowest. An Aa2 rating means the bond is in the midrange of Aa. Standard & Poor's has a similar modification process with pluses and minuses applied. Thus, AA+ would be on the high end of an AA rating, AA would be in the middle, and AA− would be on the low end.

It is also possible for a corporation to have issues outstanding in more than one category. For example, highly secured mortgage bonds of a corporation may be rated AA, while unsecured issues carry an A rating.

The level of interest payment on a bond is inverse to the quality rating. If a bond rated AAA by Standard & Poor's pays 8.5 percent, an A quality bond might pay 9.5 percent; a BB, 11.5 percent; and so on. The spread between these yields changes from time to time and is watched closely by the financial community as a barometer of future movements in the financial markets. A relatively small spread between two rating categories would indicate that investors generally have confidence in the economy. As the yield spread widens between higher and lower rating categories, this may indicate loss of confidence. Investors are demanding increasingly higher yields for lower rated bonds. Their loss of confidence indicates they will demand progressively higher returns for taking risks. This logic was previously covered in Chapter 9 as part of the discussion of the *Barron's* Confidence Index.

and George E. Pinches and Kent A. Mingo, "A Multivariate Analysis of Industrial Bond Ratings," *Journal of Finance,* March 1973, pp. 1–18.

TABLE 11–4 Description of Bond Ratings

Quality	Moody's	Standard & Poor's	Description
High grade	Aaa	AAA	Bonds that are judged to be of the best quality. They carry the smallest degree of investment risk and are generally referred to as "gilt edge." Interest payments are protected by a large or exceptionally stable margin, and principal is secure.
	Aa	AA	Bonds that are judged to be of high quality by all standards. Together with the first group, they comprise what are generally known as high-grade bonds. They are rated lower than the best bonds because margins of protection may not be as large.
Medium grade	A	A	Bonds that possess many favorable investment attributes and are to be considered as upper-medium-grade obligations. Factors giving security to principal and interest are considered adequate.
	Baa	BBB	Bonds that are considered as medium-grade obligations—they are neither highly protected nor poorly secured.
Speculative	Ba	BB	Bonds that are judged to have speculative elements; their future cannot be considered as well assured. Often the protection of interest and principal payments may be very moderate.
	B	B	Bonds that generally lack characteristics of the desirable investment. Assurance of interest and principal payments or of maintenance of other terms of the contract over any long period may be small.
Default	Caa	CCC	Bonds that are of poor standing. Such issues may be in default, or there may be elements of danger present with respect to principal or interest.
	Ca	CC	Bonds that represent obligations that are speculative to a high degree. Such issues are often in default or have other marked shortcomings.
	C		The lowest-rated class in Moody's designation. These bonds can be regarded as having extremely poor prospects of attaining any real investment standing.
		C	Rating given to income bonds on which interest is not currently being paid.
		D	Issues in default with arrears in interest and/or principal payments.

Sources: *Moody's Bond Record* (published by Moody's Investors Service, Inc., New York, NY) and *Bond Guide* (Standard & Poor's).

JUNK BONDS

Lower quality bonds are sometimes referred to as **junk bonds.** Any bond that is not considered to be of investment quality by Wall Street analysts is put in the junk bond category. As previously indicated, investment quality means the bond falls into one of the four top investment grade categories established by Moody's and Standard & Poor's. This indicates investment grade bonds extend down to Baa in Moody's and BBB in Standard & Poor's (Table 11–4). A wide range of quality is associated with junk bonds. Some are very close to investment quality (such as the Ba and BB bonds), while others carry ratings in the C and D category.

Bonds tend to fall into the junk bond category for a number of reasons. First are the so-called fallen angel bonds issued by companies that once had high credit rankings but now face hard times. Second are emerging growth companies or small firms that have not yet established an adequate record to justify an investment-quality rating. Finally, the largest part of the junk bond market is made of companies undergoing a restructuring either as a result of a leveraged buyout or as part of fending off an unfriendly takeover offer. In both these cases, equity capital tends to be replaced with debt and a lower rating is assigned.

Many junk bonds behave more like common stock than bonds and rally on good news, actual interest payments, or improving business conditions. Several institutions such as Merrill Lynch and Fidelity Investments manage mutual funds with a junk bond emphasis.

The main appeal of junk bonds historically is that they provided yields 300 to 800 basis points higher than that for AAA corporate bonds or U.S. Treasury securities. Also, until the recession of 1990–91, there were relatively few defaults by junk bond issuers. Thus, the investor got a substantially higher yield with only a small increase in risk.

However, in the 1990–91 recession, junk bond prices tumbled by 20 to 30 percent, while other bond values stayed firm. Examples of junk bond issues that dropped sharply in value included those issued by Rapid-American Corporation, Revco, Campeau Corporation, and Resorts International. Many of these declines were due to poor business conditions. However, the fall of Drexel Burnham Lambert, the leading underwriter of junk bond issues, also contributed to the difficulties in the market. That problem was further compounded when Michael Milken, the guru of junk bond dealers, was sentenced to 10 years in prison for illegal insider trading.

As the economy came out of the recession of 1990–91, junk bonds once again gained in popularity and value. Many of these issues had their prices battered down so low that they appeared to be bargains. It was not unusual to see yields of 15 to 18 percent. As a result, junk bonds enjoyed a two-year rally. These securities appear to have a place in the portfolio of investors with a reasonable risk tolerance. This is particularly true for bonds that are in the middle to lower B categories.

BOND QUOTES

The Wall Street Journal and a number of other sources publish bond values on a daily basis. Table 11–5 on page 328 provides an excerpt from the daily quote sheet for corporate bonds.

In the first column, the company name is followed by the annual coupon rate and the maturity date. For example, the table shows Best Buy (BST Buy) bonds with a coupon rate of 8⅝ percent maturing in 00 (the year 2000). The current yield (Cur Yld) represents the annual interest or coupon payment divided by the price and is 8.8 percent. The volume (Vol) is 187 bonds traded, and the closing price is 98⅜. The bond quote does not represent actual dollars but percent of par value. Since bonds trade in units of \$1,000, 98⅜ represents \$983.75 (\$1,000 × 98.375%).

A student interested in further information on a bond could proceed to *Moody's Bond Record,* published by Moody's Investors Service, or the *Bond Guide,* published by

TABLE 11–5 Daily Quotes on Corporate Bonds

CORPORATION BONDS
Volume, $25,397,000

Bonds	Cur Yld	Vol	Close	Net Chg
AMR 9s16	9.4	39	96	– 1½
ATT 7½06	7.6	40	99¼	– ⅝
ATT 6s00	6.3	161	94¾	– ¼
ATT 5⅛01	5.7	5	90	...
ATT 8⅝31	8.4	128	103¼	– ½
ATT 7⅛02	7.2	306	99½	– ⅛
ATT 8⅛22	8.1	752	100⅜	+ ⅜
ATT 8⅛24	8.0	5	101	+ ¼
ATT 4½96	4.6	14	97⅞	+ ⅜
ATT 6¾04	7.1	225	95⅝	– ⅞
Actava 9⅞97	10.0	27	99	...
Actava 9½98	10.0	6	95	– 1
Advst 9s08	cv	5	97	...
AlskAr 6⅞14	cv	13	80¾	– 1¼
AlskAr zr06	...	5	40⅜	– ¼
AlbnyInt 5s02	cv	2	89	– ½
AlldC zr98	...	19	74½	– 1¼
AlldC zr96	...	1	90⅛	– ⅛
AlldC zr2000	...	48	64½	– ⅞
AlldC zr03	...	5	50¾	+ ¼
AlldC zr05	...	15	42⅛	– 1⅞
AlegCp 6½14	cv	15	98	+ 1½
Allwst 7¼14	cv	10	94	– 1
AmBrnd 8½03	8.2	5	104	+ 3
AmBrnd 7½99	7.4	50	101⅝	...
Amsco 2002	cv	8	82	+ 1½
AnnTaylr 8¾00	9.0	11	97⅝	– ⅜
ArmI 9.2s00	9.5	8	96½	+ ½
ArmI 8½01	8.9	32	95⅜	+ ⅜
Arrow 5¾02	cv	2	120	– 4
AshO 6¾14	cv	50	100	+ 1
ARch 10⅜95	9.9	15	104⅞	– ¼
AubrnHI 12⅜20f	...	7	135¼	– 1⅞
AutDt zr12	...	1	41	...
Avnet 6s12	cv	39	99¼	+ 1¼
Bally 10s06f	cv	22	89½	+ ¼
BncFla 9s03	cv	5	128	+ 1
BkNY 7½01	cv	7	156¼	– 5¾
Barnt 8½99	8.1	5	105	+ ⅜
BellPa 7⅛12	7.7	37	93	...
BellPa 8⅛17	8.1	90	100½	...
BellsoT 8¼32	8.2	78	100⅞	+ ¼
BellsoT 7⅞32	8.1	10	97	– ⅞
BellsoT 6½00	6.6	55	97¾	– ⅛
BellsoT 7s05	7.2	98	97⅞	– ⅜
Bellso 6¼03	6.7	40	93	– ⅛
BellsoT 7½33	8.1	37	92⅞	– ⅝
Bellso 5⅞09	6.9	115	85¾	+ ¼
Bellso 6¾33	8.0	51	84⅜	– ⅛
BstBuy 8⅝00	8.8	187	98⅜	+ ¼
BethSt 8⅜01	8.6	21	97	...
Bevrly 7⅝03	cv	23	99½	...
Boeing 8⅜96	8.1	54	103¾	– ⅜
Bordn 8⅜16	8.7	25	96⅛	+ ⅝
BorgWS 9⅛03	9.4	30	97	...
BwnFer 6¼12	cv	35	98¾	...
BurNo 9¼06	8.3	3	111	...
BurN 6.55s20 O	8.1	20	81⅛	+ ⅛
BurNo 3.20s45	7.4	20	43¼	+ 5⅛
BurNo 9s16	8.7	211	103½	...
CIGNA 8.2s10	cv	52	107½	+ 1
CarnCp 4½97	cv	1	140	– ⅛
CaroFrt 6¼11	cv	57	77¼	...

Bonds	Cur Yld	Vol	Close	Net Chg
vjColuG 10¼11f	...	311	121	+ 1
vjColuG 10½12f	...	20	120⅝	+ ⅝
CmwE 8s03	8.3	75	96¾	– ½
CmwE 8⅛07J	8.4	5	96¾	...
CmwE 8¼07	8.5	25	97⅝	...
CompUSA 9½00	10.7	859	88½	+ ½
ConrPer 6¾01	cv	59	81	+ ½
ConrPer 6½02	cv	73	83¼	...
CnNG 5⅞98	6.0	40	97⅞	+ 1⅝
ConNG 7¼15	cv	6	103	+ ¼
CnPw 6⅞98	6.9	5	99	+ 1
CnPw 7½01	7.7	10	97½	+ 1⅝
vjCtlInf 9s06f	cv	105	9	– ½
Coopr 10⅝05f	...	1	70	...
CrayRs 6⅛11	cv	25	84	+ ⅞
CrossTmb 5¼03	cv	5	90	+ 4
DatGen 8⅜02	9.2	15	90¾	– 1⅛
DataGn 01	cv	33	80	+ 1
Datpnt 8⅞06	cv	90	60½	– 2
DiaSTel 7s08	7.5	18	93½	– ½
Dole 7s03	7.6	125	92⅝	– ⅜
Dole 6¾00	7.1	20	95¼	– ¼
duPnt dc6s01	6.5	162	92½	+ ½
EMC 4¼01	cv	26	93	...
Eckerd 9¼04	9.6	681	96½	– ⅝
EBP 6¾06	cv	9	75	– ⅛
F&M 11½03	15.5	332	74	+ ½
FairCp 12s01	12.5	15	96	...
FairCp 13s07	13.3	27	98	...
Fldcst 6s12	cv	30	79	+ ½
Frpt dc6.55s01	cv	39	90⅞	– ⅛
FremntGn zr13	...	5	33½	+ ¼
GMA dc6s11	7.5	97	79½	...
GMA zr12	...	5	220	– 1¼
GMA zr15	...	22	183¼	+ 4¼
GMA 8¼16	8.5	182	96¾	+ ½
GMA 8⅜97	8.0	50	104½	+ ⅛
GPA Del 8¾98	10.5	60	83	+ ½
GnCorp 8s02	7.8	1	102	+ 1½
GEICap 7⅞06	7.6	1	104	+ 2
GHost 11½02	11.6	90	98⅞	...
GHost 8s02	cv	68	84½	+ ½
GnSgnl 5¾02	cv	1	103½	...
Gene 10⅜03	12.4	173	84	– 2
Genrad 7¼11	cv	10	77	+ ½
GaGlf 15s00	13.9	5	107⅞	+ 1½
GrnTrFn 10¼02	9.1	15	112¼	– ¼
Gulfrd 6s12	cv	2	89½	– 1
Hallb zr06	...	5	49½	+ ½
Hallwd 7s00	10.9	50	64½	– 1½
HlthsoR 9½01	9.6	52	99¼	– ¾
Hlttrst 10¾02	10.2	205	105⅝	– ⅜
Hlttrst 8¾05	9.4	124	93	+ ¼
Hilhvn 7¾02	6.2	5	126	– 1
HomeDp 4½97	cv	26	119⅝	– ⅜
HostM 10⅝00	10.5	3	101	+ ⅝
HostM 9⅞01	9.8	4	100½	+ ½
HostM 10½06	10.5	49	100	– ⅜
HostM 11s07	11.0	25	100⅛	...
HostM 10⅜11	10.3	80	100½	+ ½
ICN 12⅞98	12.6	27	102	...
IMC Fer 6¼01	cv	15	91	...
IllBel 7⅝06	7.7	33	99⅝	...
IBM 9s98	8.7	248	103⅛	...
IBM 8⅜19	8.3	229	101	...

Source: *The Wall Street Journal,* June 17, 1994, p. C16. Reprinted by permission of *The Wall Street Journal,*

Standard & Poor's. For example, using *Moody's Bond Record,* as shown in Table 11–6, the reader could determine information about a firm. Let's look at Burlington Northern, Inc., 9.00s of 2016. The designation in the left margin indicates the industry classification of the firm. The firm has a Moody's bond rating of Baa1 and a call price of 105.40 percent of par or $1,054 ($1,000 × 105.40%). *Moody's Bond Record* further indicates that interest is payable on April and October 1 of each year (Interest Dates column). The current price of the bond is $1,035 ($1,000 × 103.5%).

TABLE 11–6 Background Data on Bond Issues

20 BROW—Card **MOODY'S BOND RECORD** June 1994

CUSIP	ISSUE	MOODY'S RATING	INTEREST DATES	CURRENT CALL PRICE	CALL DATE	SINK FUND PROV	CURRENT PRICE		YIELD TO MAT.	1994 HIGH	1994 LOW	AMT. OUTST. MIL. $	ISSUED	PRICE	YLD.
115885AE	**BROWNING-FERRIS IND. INC.** deb. 9.25 2021	A2 r	M&N 1	N.C.	----	No	107 3/8	bid	8.54	122 1/2	106 5/8	100	5-7-91	100.00	
117043AE	Brunswick Corp. deb. 7.375 2023	Baa2	M&S 1	N.C.	----		87	bid	8.58	99 3/4	86 3/8	125	8-25-93	99.28	7.44
117043AD	nts. 8.125 1997	Baa2 r	A&O 1	N.C.	----	No	101 3/4	bid	7.42	107 1/4	101 1/2	99.7	3-26-87	99.50	8.20
11815HAA	Buckeye Cellulose Corp. sr.nts. 10.25 2001	B2	M&N 15		----		----	bid	----	----	----	70.0	5-20-93	100.00	10.25
----	Burlington Holdings Inc. sr.deb. 0.00 2002	B1	A&O 1	N.C.	----	No	----		----	----	----	283.4	8-5-91	00.00	
121867AA	Burlington Motor Holdings sr.sub.nts. 11.50 2003	B3	M&N 1	105.75 fr	11-1-98		98	bid	11.86	104 1/4	93 1/2	100	11-22-93	100.00	11.50
121897WT	Burlington Northern Inc. nts. 7.40 1999	Baa1	M&N 15		----		100	bid	7.38	100 5/8	100	150	5-17-94		
121897WR	nts. 7.00 2002	Baa1	F&A 1	N.C.	----	No	95 1/4	bid	7.79	106 3/8	94 1/4	150	7-29-92	98.27	
121897WS	nts. 7.50 2023	Baa1	J&J 15		----		89 5/8	bid	8.46	102 1/2	89	150	7-7-93	98.53	7.63
121897WP •	deb. 9.00 2016	Baa1 r	A&O1	§105.40 to	3-31-95	Yes	103 1/2	bid	8.64	106	101 1/4	200	Ref. fr. 4-1-96 @ 104.50		
121897WQ	nts. 8.75 2022	Baa1 r	F&A 25	N.C.	----	No	104 3/8	bid	8.33	119 3/8	103 5/8	200	2-19-92	98.64	8.88
121899BY	•Burlington Northern R.R. cons.mtg. J 10.00 1997	A3 r	M&N 1	100.00 fr	11-1-94	No	102	sale	9.30	105 1/2	100 1/2	150	10-28-87	99.66	10.10
121899BX •	cons.mtg. H 9.25 2006	A3 r	A&O 1	N.C.	----	No	108	bid	8.20	122	116	275	9-26-86	99.88	9.26
121899DF	certificates 7.25 2012	Aa3 r	J&D 28	N.C.	----	No	----		----	----	----	72.04	9-22-92	100.00	7.25
121899CD •	cons.mtg. K 6.55 2020	A3 r	J&J 1	N.C.	----	No	80 5/8	bid	8.40	96 5/8	84 1/4	3.987	11-19-90	100.00	6.55
121899CC •	cons.mtg. L 3.80 2020	A3 r	J&J 1	N.C.	----	No	53 3/4	bid	8.11	61	53	6.195	11-19-90	100.00	3.80
121899CF •	cons.mtg. N 8.15 2020	A3 r	JAJ&O1	N.C.	----	No	98 1/2	bid	8.29	103	98	2.506	11-19-90	100.00	8.15
121899CE •	cons.mtg. O 6.55 2020	A3 r	J&J 1	N.C.	----	No	79 1/2	bid	8.53	97 1/2	81	15.38	11-19-90	100.00	6.55
121899CG •	cons.mtg. P 8.15 2020	A3 r	J&J 1	N.C.	----	No	102	bid	7.96	104	102	5.566	11-19-90	100.00	8.15
121899CH •	cons.mtg. M 3.20 2045	A3 r	JAJ&O1	N.C.	----	No	40	bid	8.21	49	38 1/8	13.09	11-19-90	100.00	3.20
122014AF	Burlington Resources, Inc nts. 6.875 1999	A3	F&A 1	N.C.	----		97 3/8	bid	7.48	105 1/2	96 3/4	150	8-4-92	99.74	
122014AG	nts. 7.15 1999	A3	M&N 1	N.C.	----		99 1/8	bid	7.33	99 7/8	98 3/4	300	5-2-94	99.73	7.21
122014AB	nts. 9.625 2000	A3 r	J&D 15	N.C.	----	No	110	bid	7.53	120 5/8	109 1/8	150	6-21-90	99.77	9.66
122014AD	nts. 8.50 2001	A3 r	A&O 1	N.C.	----	No	103 3/8	bid	7.87	115 3/8	102 1/2	150	10-10-91	99.72	8.54
122014AC	deb. 9.875 2010	A3 r	J&D 15	N.C.	----	No	114 1/2	bid	8.22	130 1/4	113 1/8	150	6-21-90	99.77	9.90

Source *Moody's Bond Record* (published by Moody's Investor's Service, Inc. New York, NY), June 1994, p. 20.

Table 11–7 on page 330 features quotes on U.S. government securities. Treasury notes and bonds are traded as a percentage of par value, similar to corporate bonds. Historically, price changes in the market have been rather small, and bonds are quoted in $\frac{1}{32}$ of a percentage point. For example, the price for the $6\frac{3}{8}$ Treasury note due July 1999 is quoted at 99.08 bid and 99.10 asked.[7] These prices translate into $99\frac{8}{32}$ and $99\frac{10}{32}$ percent of $1,000. The bid price on a $1,000 bond would be 99.25% × $1,000 or $992.50:

$$\begin{array}{r} 99.25\% \text{ (same as } 99\tfrac{8}{32}) \\ \times \$1{,}000 \\ \hline \$992.50 \end{array}$$

The asked price is 99.3125% × $1,000 or $993.125:

$$\begin{array}{r} 99.3125\% \text{ (same as } 99\tfrac{10}{32}) \\ \times \$1{,}000 \\ \hline \$993.125 \end{array}$$

The total spread between the bid and asked price is $0.625:

Bid price	$993.125
Asked price	992.500
Spread	$0.625

While Treasury notes and bonds are quoted on the basis of price, Treasury bills are quoted on the basis of yield. Look at the Treasury bills on the right side of Table 11–7. These yields represent the discount from the par value of $10,000. As a general example,

[7] The bid price is the value at which the bond can be sold, and the asked price is the value at which it can be bought.

TABLE 11–7 Daily Quotes on Government Issues—Treasury Bonds, Notes, and Bills

TREASURY BONDS, NOTES & BILLS

GOVT. BONDS & NOTES

Rate	Maturity Mo/Yr	Bid	Asked	Chg.	Ask Yld.
$5\frac{1}{8}$	May 94n	100:01	100:03	....	0.84
5	Jun 94n	100:03	100:05	....	3.44
$8\frac{1}{2}$	Jun 94n	100:15	100:17	− 1	3.31
8	Jul 94n	100:21	100:23	+ 1	2.98
$4\frac{1}{4}$	Jul 94n	100:00	100:02	+ 1	3.87
$6\frac{7}{8}$	Aug 94n	100:19	100:21	....	3.95
$8\frac{5}{8}$	Aug 94n	101:00	101:02	....	3.91
$8\frac{3}{4}$	Aug 94	101:01	101:03	....	3.90
$12\frac{5}{8}$	Aug 94n	101:30	102:00	− 1	3.80
$4\frac{1}{4}$	Aug 94n	99:30	100:00	....	4.21
4	Sep 94n	99:26	99:28	+ 1	4.33
$8\frac{1}{2}$	Sep 94n	101:13	101:15	+ 1	4.25
$9\frac{1}{2}$	Oct 94n	101:29	101:31	....	4.40
$4\frac{1}{4}$	Oct 94n	99:27	99:29	+ 2	4.46
6	Nov 94n	100:19	100:21	+ 1	4.59
$8\frac{1}{4}$	Nov 94n	101:21	101:23	+ 1	4.57
$10\frac{1}{8}$	Nov 94	102:18	102:20	+ 1	4.51
$11\frac{5}{8}$	Nov 94n	103:08	103:10	....	4.54
$4\frac{5}{8}$	Nov 94n	99:30	100:00	+ 1	4.63
$4\frac{5}{8}$	Dec 94n	99:27	99:29	+ 2	4.78
9	May 98n	109:06	109:08	+ 10	6.33
$5\frac{3}{8}$	May 98n	96:16	96:18	+ 10	6.36
$5\frac{1}{8}$	Jun 98n	95:15	95:17	+ 10	6.38
$8\frac{1}{4}$	Jul 98n	106:22	106:24	+ 13	6.37
$5\frac{1}{4}$	Jul 98n	95:26	95:28	+ 11	6.39
$9\frac{1}{4}$	Aug 98n	110:12	110:14	+ 13	6.40
$4\frac{3}{4}$	Aug 98n	93:27	93:29	+ 11	6.40
$4\frac{3}{4}$	Sep 98n	93:23	93:25	+ 11	6.41
$7\frac{1}{8}$	Oct 98n	102:18	102:20	+ 12	6.43
$4\frac{3}{4}$	Oct 98n	93:17	93:19	+ 11	6.43
$3\frac{1}{2}$	Nov 98	92:31	93:31	+ 11	5.02
$8\frac{7}{8}$	Nov 98n	109:09	109:11	+ 12	6.44
$5\frac{1}{8}$	Nov 98n	94:27	94:29	+ 12	6.44
$5\frac{1}{8}$	Dec 98n	94:22	94:24	+ 11	6.46
$6\frac{3}{8}$	Jan 99n	99:21	99:23	+ 12	6.45
5	Jan 99n	94:04	94:06	+ 13	6.46
$8\frac{7}{8}$	Feb 99n	109:19	109:21	+ 14	6.47
$5\frac{1}{2}$	Feb 99n	96:00	96:02	+ 12	6.47
$5\frac{7}{8}$	Mar 99n	97:12	97:14	+ 12	6.50
7	Apr 99n	102:00	102:02	+ 13	6.50
$6\frac{1}{2}$	Apr 99n	99:30	100:00	+ 12	6.50
$9\frac{1}{8}$	May 99n	111:00	111:02	+ 15	6.49
$6\frac{3}{8}$	Jul 99n	99:08	99:10	+ 13	6.53
8	Aug 99n	106:10	106:12	+ 12	6.54
6	Oct 99n	97:11	97:13	+ 12	6.58
$7\frac{7}{8}$	Nov 99n	105:27	105:29	+ 14	6.57
$6\frac{3}{8}$	Jan 00n	98:28	98:30	+ 13	6.60

TREASURY BILLS

Maturity	Days to Mat.	Bid	Asked	Chg.	Ask Yld.
May 26 '94	3	3.02	2.92	−0.51	2.96
Jun 02 '94	10	3.65	3.55	−0.17	3.60
Jun 09 '94	17	3.67	3.57	−0.11	3.63
Jun 16 '94	24	3.66	3.56	−0.05	3.62
Jun 23 '94	31	3.72	3.68	−0.07	3.74
Jun 30 '94	38	3.72	3.68	−0.09	3.75
Jul 07 '94	45	3.76	3.72	−0.10	3.79
Jul 14 '94	52	3.78	3.74	−0.13	3.81
Jul 21 '94	59	3.87	3.85	−0.10	3.93
Jul 28 '94	66	3.94	3.92	−0.09	4.00
Aug 04 '94	73	4.05	4.03	−0.05	4.12
Aug 11 '94	80	4.07	4.05	−0.08	4.14
Aug 18 '94	**87**	**4.13**	**4.11**	**−0.06**	**4.21**
Aug 25 '94	94	4.19	4.17	−0.04	4.27
Sep 01 '94	101	4.20	4.18	−0.06	4.29
Sep 08 '94	108	4.23	4.21	−0.06	4.32
Sep 15 '94	115	4.24	4.22	−0.06	4.34
Sep 22 '94	122	4.26	4.24	−0.07	4.36
Sep 29 '94	129	4.30	4.28	−0.05	4.41
Oct 06 '94	136	4.35	4.33	−0.05	4.46
Oct 13 '94	143	4.39	4.37	−0.05	4.51
Oct 20 '94	150	4.40	4.38	−0.06	4.52
Oct 27 '94	157	4.42	4.40	−0.06	4.55
Nov 03 '94	164	4.47	4.45	−0.05	4.61
Nov 10 '94	171	4.45	4.43	−0.08	4.59
Nov 17 '94	**178**	**4.48**	**4.46**	**−0.07**	**4.62**
Dec 15 '94	206	4.53	4.51	−0.07	4.68
Jan 12 '95	234	4.61	4.59	−0.07	4.77
Feb 09 '95	262	4.70	4.68	−0.08	4.88
Mar 09 '95	290	4.74	4.72	−0.10	4.93
Apr 06 '95	318	4.81	4.79	−0.09	5.02
May 04 '95	346	4.84	4.82	−0.09	5.06

Source: *The Wall Street Journal*, May 22, 1994, p. C16. Reprinted by permission of *The Wall Street Journal*, ©1994 by Dow Jones & Company. All Rights Reserved Worldwide.

a $10,000 Treasury bill quoted at 5 percent, with one year to maturity, would provide $500 in interest and would sell on a discount basis for $9,500. The effective yield would be 5.26 percent ($500/$9,500). The same 5 percent Treasury bill with six months to maturity would provide $250 in interest ($500/2) and sell for $9,750. The effective yield would be 5.12 percent ($250/$9,750 × 2).

BOND MARKETS, CAPITAL MARKET THEORY, AND EFFICIENCY

In many respects, the bond market appears to demonstrate a high degree of rationality in recognition of risk and return. Corporate issues promise a higher yield than government issues to compensate for risk, and furthermore, federally sponsored credit agencies pay a higher return than Treasury issues for the same reason. Also, lower rated bonds consistently trade at larger yields than higher quality bonds to provide a risk premium.

Taking this logic one step further, bonds should generally pay a lower return than equity investments since the equity holder is in a riskier position because of the absence of a contractual obligation to receive payment. As was pointed out in Chapter 1, researchers have attributed superior returns to equity investments relative to debt over the long term.

A number of studies have also investigated the efficiency of the bond market. A primary item under investigation was the extent of a price change that was associated with a change in a bond rating. If the bond market is efficient, much of the information that led to the rating change was already known to the public and should have been impounded into the value of the bond before the rating change. Thus, the rating change should not have led to major price movements. Major research has generally been supportive of this hypothesis.[8] Nevertheless, there is evidence that the bond market may still be less efficient than the stock market (as viewed in terms of short-term trading profits.)[9] The reason behind this belief is that the stock market is heavily weighted toward being a secondary market in which *existing* issues are constantly traded between investors. The bond market is more of a primary market, with the emphasis on new issues. Thus, bond investors are not constantly changing their portfolios with each new action of the corporation. Many institutional investors, such as insurance companies, are not active bond traders in existing issues but, instead, buy and hold bonds to maturity.

OTHER FORMS OF FIXED-INCOME SECURITIES

Our interest so far in this chapter has been on fixed-income securities, primarily in the form of bonds issued by corporations and various sectors of the government. There are other significant forms of debt instruments from which the investor may choose, and they are primarily short term in nature.

CERTIFICATES OF DEPOSIT (CDs) The **certificates of deposit (CDs)** are provided by commercial banks and savings and loans (or other thrift institutions) and have traditionally been issued in small amounts such as $1,000 or $10,000, or large amounts such as $100,000. The investor provides the funds and receives an interest-bearing certificate in return. The smaller CDs usually have a maturity of anywhere from six months to eight years, and the large $100,000 CDs, 30 to 90 days.

The large CDs are usually sold to corporate investors, money market funds, pension funds, and so on, while the small CDs are sold to individual investors. One main difference between the two CDs, besides the dollar amount, is that there may be a secondary market for the large CDs, which allows these investors to maintain their liquidity without suffering an interest penalty. Investors in the small CDs have no such liquidity. Their only option when needing the money before maturity is to redeem the certificate to the borrowing institution and suffer an interest loss penalty.

---

8 Steven Katz, "The Price Adjustment Process of Bonds to Rating Classifications: A Test of Bond Market Efficiency," *Journal of Finance,* May 1974, pp. 551–59; and George W. Hettenhouse and William S. Sartoris, "An Analysis of the Informational Content of Bond Rating Changes," *Quarterly Review of Economics and Business,* Summer 1976, pp. 65–78.

9 George E. Pinches and Clay Singleton, "The Adjustment of Stock Prices to Bond Rating Changes," *Journal of Finance,* March 1978, pp. 29–44.

Small CDs have been traditionally regulated by the government, with federal regulatory agencies specifying the maximum interest rate that can be paid and the life of the CD. In 1986, all such interest-rate regulations and ceilings were phased out, and the free market now determines return. Any financial institution is able to offer whatever it desires. Almost all CDs are federally insured for up to $100,000 in the event of the collapse of the financial institution offering the instrument. This feature became particularly important in the late 1980s and early 1990s as a result of the problems in the savings and loan and banking industries.

Commercial Paper Another form of a short-term credit instrument is **commercial paper,** which is issued by large business corporations to the public. Commercial paper usually comes in minimum denominations of $25,000 and represents an unsecured promissory note. Commercial paper will carry a higher yield than small CDs or government Treasury bills and will be in line with the yield on large CDs. The maturity is usually 30, 60, or 90 days (though up to six months is possible).

Bankers' Acceptance This instrument often arises from foreign trade. A **bankers' acceptance** is a draft drawn on a bank for approval for future payment and is subsequently presented to the bank for payment. The investor buys the bankers' acceptance from an exporter (or other third party) at a discount with the intention of presenting it to the bank at face value at a future date. Bankers' acceptances provide yields comparable to commercial paper and large CDs and have an active secondary or resale market.

Money Market Funds The **money market funds** represent a vehicle to buy short-term fixed-income securities through a mutual fund arrangement.[10] An individual with a small amount to invest may pool funds with others to buy higher-yielding large CDs and other similar instruments indirectly through the fund. There is a great deal of flexibility in withdrawing funds through check-writing privileges.

Money Market Accounts The **money market accounts** are similar to money market funds but are offered by financial institutions rather than mutual funds. Financial institutions introduced money market accounts in the 1980s to compete with money market funds. These accounts pay rates generally competitive with money market funds and normally allow up to three withdrawals a month without penalty. One advantage of a money market account over a money market fund is that it is normally insured by the federal government for up to $100,000. However, due to the high quality of investments of money market funds, this advantage is not particularly important in most cases.

---

[10] Most brokerage houses also offer money market fund options.

Both money market funds and money market accounts normally have minimum balance requirements of $500 to $1,000. Minimum withdrawal provisions may also exist. Each fund or account must be examined for its rules. In any event, both provide much more flexibility than a certificate of deposit in terms of access to funds with only a slightly lower yield.

PREFERRED STOCK AS AN ALTERNATIVE TO DEBT

Finally, we look at preferred stock as an alternative to debt because some investors may elect to purchase preferred stock to satisfy their fixed-income needs. **Preferred stock** pays a stipulated annual dividend but does not include an ownership interest in the corporation. A $50 par value preferred stock issue paying $4.40 in annual dividends would provide an annual yield of 8.8 percent.

Preferred stock as an investment falls somewhere between bonds and common stock as far as protective provisions for the investor. In the case of debt, the bondholders have a contractual claim against the corporation and may force bankruptcy proceedings if interest payments are not forthcoming. Common stockholders have no such claim, but are the ultimate owners of the firm and may receive dividends and other distributions after all prior claims have been satisfied. Preferred stockholders, on the other hand, are entitled to receive a stipulated dividend and must receive the dividend before any payment to common stockholders. However, the payment of preferred stock dividends is not compelling to the corporation as is true in the case of debt. In bad times, preferred stock dividends may be omitted by the corporation.

While preferred stock dividends are not tax deductible to the corporation, as would be true with interest on bonds, they do offer certain investors unique tax advantages. The tax law provides that any corporation that receives preferred or common stock dividends from another corporation must add only 30 percent of such dividends to its taxable income. Thus, if a $5 dividend is received, only 30 percent of the $5, or $1.50, would be taxable to the corporate recipient.[11]

Because of this tax feature, preferred stock may carry a slightly lower yield than corporate bond issues of similar quality as indicated in Table 11–8 on page 334.

Features of Preferred Stock

Preferred stock may carry a number of features that are similar to a debt issue. For example, a preferred stock issue may be *convertible* into common stock. Also, preferred stock may be *callable* by the corporation at a stipulated price, generally slightly above par. The call feature of a preferred stock issue may be of particular interest in that preferred stock has no maturity date as such. If the corporation wishes to take preferred stock off the books, it must call in the issue or purchase the shares in the open market at the going market price.

[11] An individual investor does not enjoy the same tax benefit.

TABLE 11–8 Yields on Corporate Bonds and High-Grade Preferred Stock

Year	(1) High-Grade Bonds (percent)	(2) High-Grade Preferred Stock (percent)	(2) – (1) Spread
1994	8.50%	7.75%	−0.75
1993	7.40	6.89	−0.51
1992	8.46	7.46	−1.00
1991	8.97	8.55	−0.42
1990	9.40	9.14	−0.26
1989	9.33	9.08	−0.25
1988	9.75	9.05	−0.70
1987	9.68	8.37	−1.31
1986	9.47	8.76	−0.71
1985	11.82	10.49	−1.33
1984	13.31	11.59	−1.72
1983	12.42	10.55	−1.87
1982	14.41	11.68	−2.73
1981	14.75	11.64	−3.11
1980	12.50	10.11	−2.39
1979	9.94	8.54	−1.40
1978	8.92	7.76	−1.16
1977	8.24	7.12	−1.12
1972	7.49	6.56	−0.93
1967	5.66	5.13	−0.53
1962	4.47	4.21	−0.26

Source: *Moody's Industrial Manual* and *Moody's Bond Record* (published by Moody's Investor Service, Inc., New York, NY), selected issues.

An important feature of preferred stock is that the dividend payments are usually *cumulative* in nature. That is, if preferred stock dividends are not paid in any one year, they accumulate and must be paid before common stockholders can receive any cash dividends. If preferred stock carries an $8 dividend and dividends are not paid for three years, the full $24 must be paid before any dividends go to common stockholders. This provides a strong incentive for the corporation to meet preferred stock dividend obligations on an annual basis even though preferred stock does not have a fixed, contractual obligation as do bonds. If the corporation gets behind in preferred stock dividends, it may create a situation that is difficult to get out of in the future. Being behind or in arrears on preferred stock dividends can make it almost impossible to sell new common stock because of the preclusion of common stock dividends until the preferred stockholders are satisfied.

Examples of existing preferred stock issues are presented in Table 11–9. The issues are listed in *Moody's Bond Record,* and the daily price quotes may be found in the NYSE Composite Stock Transactions section of *The Wall Street Journal* or other newspapers.

TABLE 11–9 Examples of Outstanding Preferred Stock Issues, June 1994

Issuer	Moody's Rating*	Par Value	Call Price	Market Price	Yield (percent)
Duke Power Company 7.72% cumulative preferred	aa2	$100	103.93	103.25	7.48%
Ohio Edison Company 8.20% cumulative preferred	baa2	100	102.07	90.91	9.02
Interstate Power 6.40% cumulative preferred	a1	50	53.20	40.00	8.01

* Lowercase letters are used by Moody's to rate preferred stock.
Source: *Moody's Bond Record* (published by Moody's Investor Service, Inc., New York, NY).

SUMMARY

Debt continues to play an important role in our economy from both the issuer's and investor's viewpoints. The primary fundraisers in the bond market are the U.S. Treasury, federally sponsored credit agencies, state and local governments, and corporations. The corporate sector is made up of industrials, public utilities, rails and transportation, as well as financial issues. The amount of new, long-term debt financing in the United States greatly exceeds the volume of equity financing.

Bond instruments are evaluated on the basis of a number of factors, including yield, maturity, method of repayment, security provisions, and tax treatment. The greater the protection and privileges accorded the bondholder, the lower the yield. Thus, U.S. Treasury securities generally provide a lower yield than federally sponsored credit agency issues, and corporate securities provide a higher yield than governmental offerings. Because interest received on municipal bonds is tax-exempt to the recipient, they provide the lowest promised yield. However, when one converts this figure to an equivalent before-tax return on a taxable instrument, the return may be attractive. Preferred stock also offers some unique tax advantages in the form of a 70 percent tax exemption on dividends paid to corporate purchasers.

A significant feature for a bond issue is the rating received by Moody's Investors Service or Standard & Poor's. The ratings generally range from AAA to D and determine the required yield to sell a security in the marketplace. Although there are no firm and fast rules to determine a rating, strong attention is given to such factors as cash flow and earnings generation in relation to interest and other obligations (coverage ratios) as well as to operating margins and return on invested capital and total assets. Financial-ratio analysis makes up perhaps 50 percent of the evaluation, with other factors of importance including the nature of the industry, the relative position of the firm within the industry, the pricing ability of the firm, and the overall quality of management (similar criteria have also been developed for municipal bonds).

The bond market appears to be reasonably efficient in terms of absorbing new information into the price of existing issues. Some researchers have suggested that the bond market may be slightly less efficient than the stock market in pricing

outstanding issues because of the lack of a highly active secondary, or resale, market for certain issues. Insurance companies, pension funds, and bank trust departments are not normally active traders in their bond portfolios.

Short-term investors with a need for fixed income may look to certificates of deposit, commercial paper, bankers' acceptances, money market funds, money market accounts, and the previously discussed government securities as sources of investment. Such factors as maturity, yield, and minimum amount must be considered.

Finally, preferred stock may also be thought of as an alternative form of a fixed-income security. Although dividends on preferred stock do not represent a contractual obligation to the firm as would be true of interest on debt, they must be paid before common stockholders can receive any payment. The preferred stock alternative may be important to the issuing firm because it provides some balance to the corporate capital structure.

KEY WORDS AND CONCEPTS

bond indenture, 311
par value, 311
coupon rate, 311
variable-rate notes, 311
floating-rate notes, 311
zero-coupon bonds, 311
maturity date, 311
perpetual bonds, 311
serial payment, 312
sinking-fund provision, 312
call provision, 312
put provision, 312
secured debt, 312
mortgage, 312
after-acquired property clause, 312
equipment trust certificate, 313
debenture, 313
income bonds, 313
Treasury bills, 314
Treasury note, 315
Treasury bonds, 315
GNMA (Ginnie Mae) pass-through certificate, 316
municipal bonds, 317
general obligation issue, 319
revenue bond, 319
shelf registration, 323
private placement, 323
junk bonds, 326
certificates of deposit (CDs), 331
commercial paper, 332
bankers' acceptance, 332
money market funds, 332
money market accounts, 332
preferred stock, 333

DISCUSSION QUESTIONS

1. What are some of the major provisions found in the bond indenture?
2. Does a serial bond normally have only one maturity date? What types of bonds are normally issued on this basis?
3. Explain how a sinking fund works.
4. Why do you think the right to call a bond is often deferred for a time?
5. What is the nature of a mortgage agreement?
6. What is a senior security?
7. Discuss the statement, "A debenture may not be more risky than a secured bond."

8. How do zero-coupon bonds provide returns to investors? How is the return taxed?
9. Explain the concept of a pass-through certificate.
10. What is an agency issue? Are they direct obligations of the U.S. Treasury?
11. What tax advantages are associated with municipal bonds?
12. Distinguish between general obligation and revenue bonds.
13. How might an investor reduce the credit risk in buying a municipal bond issue?
14. What is an industrial bond?
15. What is shelf registration?
16. What is meant by the private placement of a bond issue?
17. What is a split bond rating?
18. What is meant by the term *junk bond?* What quality rating does it fail to meet?
19. What does a bond quote of 72¼ represent in dollar terms?
20. Why might the bond market be considered less efficient than the stock market?
21. What is the advantage of a money market fund? How does it differ from a money market account?
22. Why would a corporate investor consider preferred stock over a bond? What is meant by the cumulative feature of preferred stock issues?

PROBLEMS

Municipal bond

1. If an investor is in a 39.6 percent marginal tax bracket and can purchase a municipal bond paying 7.25 percent, what would the equivalent before-tax return from a nonmunicipal bond have to be to equate the two?

Bond quotes

2. Using the data in Table 11–5, indicate the closing *dollar* value of the American Brands (shown as AmBrnd in the table) bonds that pay 7½ interest and mature in 1999 (the year is shown as 99). State your answer in terms of dollars based on a $1,000 par value bond.

Treasury bill

3. Assume a $10,000 Treasury bill is quoted to pay 8 percent interest over a six-month period.
   a. How much interest would the investor receive?
   b. What will be the price of the Treasury bill?
   c. What will be the effective yield?

Treasury bill

4. In problem 3, if the Treasury bill had only three months to maturity:
   a. How much interest would the investor receive?
   b. What will be the price of the Treasury bill?
   c. What will be the effective yield?

Treasury note quotes

5. Using the data in Table 11–7, indicate the bid price for the 5⅞ March 1999 Treasury notes. The bid price is the sales price for the bonds. State your answer based on a $1,000 bond value.

Comparative after-tax returns

6. A corporation buys $100 par value preferred stock of another corporation. The dividend payment is 7.8 percent of par. The corporation is in a 35 percent tax bracket.

a. What will be the after-tax return on the dividend payment? Fill in the following table.

Par value	________
Dividend payment (%)	________
Actual dividend	________
Taxable income (30% of dividend)	________
Taxes (35% of taxable income)	________
After-tax return (Actual dividend − Taxes)	________
Percent return = $\frac{\text{After-tax return}}{\text{Par value}}$	________

b. Assume a second investment in a $1,000 par value corporate bond pays 8.6 percent interest. What will be the after-tax return on the interest payment? Fill in the following table.

Par value	________
Interest payment (percent)	________
Actual interest	________
Taxes (35 percent of interest)	________
After-tax return (Actual interest − Taxes)	________
Percent return = $\frac{\text{After-tax return}}{\text{Par value}}$	________

c. Should the corporation choose the corporate bond over the preferred stock because it has a higher quoted yield (8.6 percent versus 7.8 percent)?

CFA MATERIAL

The following material contains sample questions and solutions from a prior Level I CFA exam. While the terminology is slightly different from that in this text, you can still view the skills that are necessary for the CFA exam.

CFA Exam Question

The investment manager of a corporate pension fund has purchased a U.S. Treasury bill with 180 days to maturity at a price of $9,600 per $10,000 face value. He has computed the discount yield at 8 percent.

a. *Calculate* the bond equivalent yield for the Treasury bill. *Show* calculations. (*3 minutes*)

b. *Briefly state two* reasons why a Treasury bill's bond equivalent yield is always different from the discount yield. (*2 minutes*)

Solution: Morning Section (I–86) (5 points)

a.

$$\text{BEY} = \frac{(\text{F} - \text{P})}{\text{P}} \times \frac{365}{\text{N}}$$

where:

BEY = Bond equivalent yield
F = Face value
P = Price
N = Days to maturity

$$\text{BEY} = \frac{(\$100 - \$96)}{\$96} \times \frac{365}{180} = 8.45\%$$

b. (1) The bond equivalent yield is computed using the actual purchase price of the instrument in the denominator, while the discount yield is calculated using the face value.

(2) The bond equivalent yield is based on a 365-day year, whereas the discount yield is computed using a 360-day year.

THE WALL STREET JOURNAL PROJECT

Look for "Government Agency & Similar Issues" in Section C of *The Wall Street Journal;* there you will find prices for federally sponsored credit agencies. Look up the current price and yield for the following securities:

a. Federal National Mortgage Association (FNMA)—coupon of 6.90 percent and maturity of March 2004.
b. Federal Home Loan Bank—coupon of 9.5 percent and maturity of February 2004.
c. Federal Farm Credit Bank—coupon of 7.95 percent and maturity of April 2002.
d. Student loan marketing—coupon of 7.00 percent and maturity of December 2002.
e. Compare the yields to a U.S. government bond due in February 2000 carrying a coupon of 8.5 percent. This bond is found on the same page or a page close by under "Treasury Bonds, Notes & Bills." Explain the differences in yields between the agency issues and the U.S. government bond.
f. What can you say about the relative risk between these bonds?

CRITICAL THOUGHT CASE

Gail Rosenberg still had her head in the clouds when she joined Salomon Brothers, Inc., in June 1990. While she was proud of her newly awarded MBA from the Wharton School of Business at the University of Pennsylvania, she was even prouder of joining the most prestigious investment banking house on Wall Street, the famous Salomon Brothers. She had received five job offers, but this was the one she wanted. Not only would she train with the best and brightest on Wall Street, but she also would be working for a firm in

which 90 employees made over $1 million a year. How many Fortune 500 companies, law firms, or other employers could claim such a record? She was pleased with her own starting salary of $70,000 a year and could see matters only getting better in the future.

After some general training and apprenticeship-type work, she was assigned to the government bond trading unit in February 1991. Here she would help in the bidding and distributing of U.S. Treasury bills and notes. Salomon Brothers was the largest participant among investment banking houses in this field, so she knew she would quickly learn the ropes.

Her first major participation would be in the Treasury bill auction for May 1991. Salomon Brothers would bid on behalf of many of its clients and probably have some influence on the ultimate price and yield at which the Treasury bills were sold. As Gail got on her PC to help process orders, she noticed Salomon Brothers submitted bids for clients that did not exist. It was no surprise to Gail that Salomon Brothers captured 85 percent of the bidding and virtually controlled the pricing of the securities.

In a state of shock, Gail went to her immediate supervisor and reported what she had observed on her computer screen. She was told to calm down, that she was no longer in school, and she was witnessing a common practice on "The Street." She was further informed that John Gutfreund, chairman of the board of Salomon Brothers, and President Thomas Strauss implicitly approved of such practices. She felt a little like Oliver North in the Iran-Contra affair coverup. She had worked very hard to get to this tender point in her career and was now disillusioned.

Question

1. What strategy or advice can you offer to Gail Rosenberg?

SELECTED REFERENCES

General Bond Information

Altman, Edward I. "Defaults and Returns on High-Yield Bonds through the First Half of 1991." *Financial Analysts Journal,* November–December 1991, pp. 67–77.

Nunn, Kenneth P., Jr.; Joanne Hill; and Thomas Schneeweis. "Corporate Bond Price Data Sources and Return/Risk Management." *Journal of Financial and Quantitative Analysis,* June 1986, pp. 197–208.

Municipal and U.S. Government Bonds

Van Hore, James C. "Call Risk and Municipal Bonds." *Journal of Portfolio Management,* Winter 1984, pp. 53–57.

Yawitz, Jess B.; George H. Hempel; and William J. Marshall. "A Risk-Return Approach to the Selection of Optimal Government Bond Portfolios." *Financial Management,* Autumn 1976, pp. 36–45.

Bond Management Strategies

Chance, Don M.; Wayne Marr; and G. Rodney Thompson. "Hedging Shelf Registrations." *Journal of Futures Markets,* Spring 1986, pp. 11–27.

Johnson, James M. "When Are Zero-Coupon Bonds the Better Buy?" *Journal of Portfolio Management,* Spring 1984, pp. 36–41.

Trainer, Francis H., Jr.; David A. Levine; and Jonathan A. Reiss. "A Systematic Approach to Bond Management in Pension Funds." *Journal of Portfolio Management,* Spring 1984, pp. 30–35.

Research on Bond Ratings

Crabbe, Leland, and Mitchell A. Post. "The Effect of a Rating Downgrade on Outstanding Commercial Paper." *Journal of Finance,* March 1994, pp. 39–56.

Gentry, James A.; David T. Whitfold; and Paul Newbold. "Predicting Industrial Bond Ratings with a Probit Model and Funds Flow Components." *Financial Review,* August 1988, pp. 269–86.

Hettenhouse, George W., and William S. Sartoris. "An Analysis of the Informational Content of Bond Rating Changes." *Quarterly Review of Economics and Business,* Summer 1976, pp. 65–78.

Pinches, George E., and Kent A. Mingo. "A Multivariate Analysis of Industrial Bond Ratings." *Journal of Finance,* March 1973, pp. 1–18.

APPENDIX 11A: Evaluation of Debt Innovations

Security	Distinguishing Characteristics	Yield Reduction or Risk Reallocation	Enhanced Liquidity	Reduction in Transaction Costs	Other Benefits
Zero-coupon bonds	Non-interest-bearing. Payment in one lump sum at maturity.	Issuer assumes reinvestment risk. Issues sold in Japan carried below-market yields reflecting their tax advantage over conventional debt issues.			Straight-line amortization of original issue discount pre-TEFRA. Japanese investors realize significant tax savings.
Stripped Treasury securities	Coupons separated from corpus to create a series of zero-coupon bonds that can be sold separately.	Yield curve arbitrage; sum of the parts can exceed the whole.			
Adjustable-rate notes and floating-rate notes	Coupon rate floats with some index, such as the 91-day Treasury bill rate.	Issuer exposed to floating interest-rate risk, but initial rate is lower than for fixed-rate issue.	Price remains closer to par than the price of a fixed-rate note.		

Source: John D. Finnerty, *Financial Management Collection,* Financial Management Association, Winter 1988, p. 4.

Security	Distinguishing Characteristics	Yield Reduction or Risk Reallocation	Enhanced Liquidity	Reduction in Transaction Costs	Other Benefits
Extendible notes	Interest rate adjusts every 2 to 3 years, at which time note holder has the option to put the notes back to the issuer if the new rate is unacceptable.	Coupon based on 2- to 3-year put-date, not on final maturity.		Lower transaction costs than issuing 2- or 3-year notes and rolling them over.	
Putable bonds and adjustable tender securities	Issuer can periodically reset the terms, in effect rolling over debt without having to redeem it for cash until the final maturity.	Coupon based on the type of interest-rate period selected, not on final maturity.		Lower transaction costs than having to perform a series of refundings.	
Medium-term notes	Notes are sold in varying amounts and in varying maturities on an agency basis.			Agents' commissions are lower than underwriting spreads.	
Negotiable certificates of deposit	Certificates of deposit are registered and sold to the public on an agency basis.		More liquid than nonnegotiable CDs.	Agents' commissions are lower than underwriting spreads.	
Mortgage pass-through certificates	Investor buys an undivided interest in a pool of mortgages.	Reduced yield due to the benefit to the investor of diversification and greater liquidity.	More liquid than individual mortgages.		
Collateralized mortgage obligations (CMOs)	Mortgage payment stream is divided into 3 to 5 classes, which are prioritized in terms of their right to receive principal payments.	Reduction in prepayment risk to classes with prepayment priority. Designed to appeal to different classes of investors; sum of the parts can exceed the whole.	More liquid than individual mortgages.		

Security	Distinguishing Characteristics	Yield Reduction or Risk Reallocation	Enhanced Liquidity	Reduction in Transaction Costs	Other Benefits
Receivable backed securities	Investor buys an undivided interest in a pool of receivables.	Reduced yield due to the benefit to the investor of diversification and greater liquidity. Significantly cheaper than pledging receivables to a bank.	More liquid than individual receivables.		
Euro-notes and Euro-commercial paper	Euro-commercial paper is similar to U.S. commercial paper.	Elimination of intermediary brings savings that lender and borrower can share.		Corporations invest in each other's paper directly rather than through an intermediary.	
Interest-rate swaps	Two entities agree to swap interest-rate-payment obligations, typically fixed rate for floating rate.	Weaker credits can borrow from banks and swap for fixed rate so as to achieve a lower fixed rate than they could by borrowing directly from traditional fixed-rate lenders.			
Credit-enhanced debt securities	Issuer's obligation to pay is backed by an irrevocable letter of credit or surety bond.	Stronger credit rating of the letter of credit or surety bond issuer leads to lower yield, which can more than offset letter of credit/surety bond fees.			Enables a privately held company to borrow publicly while preserving confidentiality.

12

Principles of Bond Valuation and Investment

The old notion that a bond represents an inherently conservative investment can be quickly dispelled. A $1,000, 10 percent coupon rate bond with 25 years to maturity could rise $214.80 or fall $157.60 in response to a 2 percent change in interest rates in the marketplace. Investors enjoyed a total return of 43.79 percent on long-term high-grade corporate bonds in 1982 and 25.37 percent in 1985. However, the same bond investors would have had a negative total return in 9 out of the 27 years between 1968 and 1994. Losses were as high as 10 percent.

In this chapter, we will examine the valuation process for bonds, the relationship of interest-rate changes to the business cycle, and various investment and speculative strategies related to bond maturity, quality, and pricing.

FUNDAMENTALS OF THE BOND VALUATION PROCESS

The price of a bond at any given time represents the present value of future interest payments plus the present value of the par value of the bond at maturity. We say that:

$$V = \sum_{t=1}^{n} \frac{C_t}{(1+i)^t} + \frac{P_n}{(1+i)^n} \tag{12–1}$$

where:

V = Market value or price of the bond
n = Number of periods
t = Each period
C_t = Coupon or interest payment for each period, t
P_n = Par or maturity value
i = Interest rate in the market

We can use logarithms and various mathematical calculations to find the value of a bond or simply use Tables 12–1 and 12–2 on page 346 to determine the present value of C_t and P_n and add the two. (Expanded versions of these two tables are presented in appendixes at the end of the text.)

Assume a bond pays 10 percent interest or $100 ($C_t$) for 20 years ($n$) and has a par ($P_n$) or maturity value of $1,000. The interest rate (i) in the marketplace is assumed to be 12 percent. The present value of the bond, using annual compounding, is shown to be $850.90 as follows:

Present Value of Coupon Payments (C_t) (from Table 12–1 or Appendix D)	**Present Value of Maturity Value (P_n) (from Table 12–2 or Appendix C)**
n = 20, i = 12%	n = 20, i = 12%
$100 × 7.469 = $746.90	$1,000 × 0.104 = $104.00
Present value of coupon payments	= $746.90
Present value of maturity value	= 104.00
Value of bond	= $850.90

TABLE 12–1 Present Value of an Annuity of $1 (Coupon payments, C_t)

Number of periods (n)	Interest Rate (i): 4 Percent	5 Percent	6 Percent	8 Percent	9 Percent	10 Percent	12 Percent
1	0.962	0.952	0.943	0.926	0.917	0.909	0.893
2	1.886	1.859	1.833	1.783	1.759	1.736	1.690
3	2.775	2.723	2.673	2.577	2.531	2.487	2.402
4	3.630	3.546	3.465	3.312	3.240	3.170	3.037
5	4.452	4.329	4.212	3.993	3.890	3.791	3.605
10	8.111	7.722	7.360	6.710	6.418	6.145	5.650
15	11.118	10.380	9.712	8.559	8.061	7.606	6.811
20	13.590	12.462	11.470	9.818	9.129	8.514	7.469
30	17.292	15.372	13.765	11.258	10.274	9.427	8.055
40	19.793	17.160	15.046	11.925	10.757	9.779	8.244

TABLE 12–2 Present Value of a Single Amount of $1 (Par or maturity value, P_n)

Number of Periods (n)	Interest Rate (i): 4 Percent	5 Percent	6 Percent	8 Percent	9 Percent	10 Percent	12 Percent
1	0.962	0.952	0.943	0.926	0.917	0.909	0.893
2	0.925	0.907	0.890	0.857	0.842	0.826	0.797
3	0.889	0.864	0.840	0.794	0.772	0.751	0.712
4	0.855	0.823	0.792	0.735	0.708	0.683	0.636
5	0.822	0.784	0.747	0.681	0.650	0.621	0.567
10	0.676	0.614	0.558	0.463	0.422	0.386	0.322
15	0.555	0.481	0.417	0.315	0.275	0.239	0.183
20	0.456	0.377	0.312	0.215	0.178	0.149	0.104
30	0.308	0.231	0.174	0.099	0.075	0.057	0.033
40	0.208	0.142	0.097	0.046	0.032	0.022	0.011

Because the bond pays 10 percent of the par value when the competitive market rate of interest is 12 percent, investors will pay only $850.90 for the issue. This bond is said to be selling at a discount of $149.10 from the $1,000 par value. The discount is determined by several factors, such as the years to maturity, spread between the coupon and market rates, and the level of the coupon payment. While the $850.90 price was calculated using annual compounding, coupon payments on most bonds are paid

semiannually. To adjust for this, we *divide* the annual coupon payment and required interest rate in the market by two and *multiply* the number of periods by two. Using the same example as before but with the appropriate adjustments for semiannual compounding, we show a slightly lower price of $849.30 as follows:

Present Value of Coupon Payments (C_t) (from Table 12–1 or Appendix D)	**Present Value of Maturity Value (P_n) (from Table 12–2 or Appendix C)**
$n = 40$, $i = 6\%$	$n = 40$, $i = 6\%$
$50 × 15.046 = $752.30	$1,000 × 0.097 = $97.00
Present value of coupon payments	= $752.30
Present value of maturity value	= 97.00
Value of bond	= $849.30

We see a minor adjustment in price as a result of using the more exacting process. To check our answer, Table 12–3 presents an excerpt from a bond table indicating prices for 10 percent and 12 percent annual coupon rate bonds at various market rates of interest (yields to maturity) and time periods. Though the values are quoted on an annual basis, the assumption is that semiannual discounting, such as that shown in our second example, was utilized. Note that for a bond with a 10 percent coupon rate, a 12 percent market rate (yield to maturity), and 20 years to run, the value in the table is 84.93. This is assumed to represent 84.93 percent of par value. Since the par value of the bond in our example was $1,000, the answer would be $849.30 ($1,000 × 84.93%). This is the answer we got in our second example. A typical modern bond table may be 1,000 pages long and cover time periods up to 30 years and interest rates from ¼ to 30 percent. For professionals working with bonds on a continual basis, financial calculators and computers are quite common and have a quicker response time.

TABLE 12–3 Excerpts from Bond Value Table

	Coupon Rate (10 percent)				Coupon Rate (12 percent)				
Yield to Maturity (percent)	**1 Year**	**5 Years**	**10 Years**	**20 Years**	**1 Year**	**5 Years**	**10 Years**	**20 Years**	**Yield to Maturity (percent)**
8%	101.89%	108.11%	113.50%	119.79%	103.77%	116.22%	127.18%	139.59%	8%
9	100.94	103.96	106.50	109.20	102.81	111.87	119.51	127.60	9
10	100.00	100.00	100.00	100.00	101.86	107.72	112.46	117.16	10
11	99.08	96.23	94.02	91.98	100.92	103.77	105.98	108.02	11
12	98.17	92.64	88.53	84.93	100.00	100.00	100.00	100.00	12
13	97.27	89.22	83.47	78.78	99.09	96.41	94.49	92.93	13
14	96.38	85.95	78.81	73.34	98.19	92.98	89.41	86.67	14

Source: Reprinted by permission from the *Thorndike Encyclopedia of Banking and Financial Tables*, 1981.

RATES OF RETURN

Bonds are evaluated on a number of different types of returns, including current yield, yield to maturity, yield to call, and anticipated realized yield.

Current Yield

The **current yield,** which is shown in *The Wall Street Journal* and many daily newspapers, is the annual interest payment divided by the price of the bond. An example might be a 10 percent coupon rate $1,000 par value bond selling for $950. The current yield would be:

$$\frac{\$100}{\$950} = 10.53\%$$

The 10.53 percent indicates the annual cash rate of return an investor would receive in interest payments on the $950 investment but does not include any adjustments for capital gains or losses as bond prices change in response to new market interest rates. Another problem with current yield is that it does not take into consideration the maturity date of a debt instrument. A bond with 1 year to run and another with 20 years to run would have the same current yield quote if interest payments were $100 and the price were $950. Clearly, the one-year bond would be preferable under this circumstance because the investor would not only get $100 in interest but also a $50 gain in value ($1,000 – $950) within a *one-year* period, as the price goes to its $1,000 maturity value.

Yield to Maturity

Yield to maturity is a measure of return that considers annual interest received, the difference between the current bond price and its maturity value, and the number of years to maturity. More importantly, **yield to maturity** is the same concept as the internal rate of return or true yield on an investment. That is, it is the interest rate (i) at which you can discount the future coupon payments (C_t) and maturity value (P_n) to arrive at a known current value (V) of the bond. Now, we are assuming that you know the current value (price) of the bond (perhaps from *The Wall Street Journal*), the coupon payments, the maturity value, and the number of periods to maturity and that you want to know what the true yield to maturity is on the bond.

Restating Formula 12–1 below, the unknown is now assumed to be *i,* the interest rate in the market. The interest rate in the market is always going to be the same as the yield to maturity (the bond will yield what the market dictates):

$$V = \sum_{t=1}^{n} \frac{C_t}{(1 + \textcircled{i})^t} + \frac{P_n}{(1 + \textcircled{i})^n}$$

$$\nwarrow \quad \nearrow$$

Unknown

Let us compute the value of i. We will use annual analysis to facilitate the calculations. First, we will do an easy problem to demonstrate the process, and then we will extend the analysis to a more involved calculation.

Assume V (market value or price of the bond) is \$850.90, C_t (coupon or interest payment for each period) is \$100, P_n (par or maturity value) is \$1,000, and n (number of periods) is 20. What i will force the future inflows to equal \$850.90? Let's use 12 percent, and prove that it works.

Present Value of Coupon Payments (C_t) (from Table 12–1 or Appendix D)	Present Value of Maturity Value (P_n) (from Table 12–2 or Appendix C)
n = 20, i = 12%	n = 20, i = 12%
\$100 × 7.469 = \$746.90	\$1,000 × 0.104 = \$104.000
Present value of coupon payments	= \$746.90
Present value of maturity value	= 104.00
Value of bond	= \$850.90

An i of 12 percent gave us the \$850.90 we desired because we used the same *12 percent* we employed earlier in the chapter to get \$850.90. (We turned the problem around.) Thus, 12 percent is the yield to maturity.

Let us now go to a situation where we presumably do not know the answer in advance. It should be mentioned at this point that if you have a financial calculator, you may wish to follow the recommended steps for the calculator (such as those shown in Appendix F for the Texas Instruments BA-35 or the Hewlett-Packard 12C) to find yield to maturity. Since the authors cannot assume this is the case, we will introduce you to a trial-and-error method of solution. Please feel free to use the approach that is best for you.

Assume a bond is paying a 7 percent coupon rate (C_t), has 15 periods to maturity (n), is selling for \$839.27 (V), and has a par maturity value (P_n) of \$1,000. What is the value of i? Using a trial-and-error process, we will need to make a first guess at the value of i and try it out. Since the bond is selling for less than par value (\$1,000), we can assume that the interest rate is greater than 7 percent. Why? Anytime a bond is trading at an interest rate (i) greater than the coupon rate, it will sell for less than par value, and that is the case in this example. Of course, if the coupon rate were greater than the interest rate (i), the bond would sell for more than par value. It would be paying more than the market is demanding and would sell at a premium rather than a discount.

Remember that our first trial-and-error calculation in this example must be at an interest rate (i) greater than 7 percent. Let's try 8 percent for the 15 periods to maturity:

Present Value of Coupon Payments (C_t) (from Table 12–1 or Appendix D)	Present Value of Maturity Value (P_n) (from Table 12–2 or Appendix C)
n = 15, i = 8%	n = 15, i = 8%
\$70 × 8.559 = \$599.13	\$1,000 × 0.315 = \$315
Present value of coupon payments	= \$599.13
Present value of maturity value	= 315.00
Value of bond	= \$914.13

The answer of $914.13 is higher than our desired answer of $839.27. To bring the answer down, we will use a higher interest rate. The next try will be at 9 percent:

Present Value of Coupon Payments (C_t) (from Table 12–1 or Appendix D)	**Present Value of Maturity Value (P_n) (from Table 12–2 or Appendix C)**
$n = 15$, $i = 9\%$	$n = 15$, $i = 9\%$
$70 × 8.061 = $564.27	$1,000 × 0.275 = $275
Present value of coupon payments	= $564.27
Present value of maturity value	= 275.00
Value of bond	= $839.27

Obviously, 9 percent is the interest rate that equates the future coupon payments (C_t) *and maturity value* (P_n) to the bond value of $839.27. Thus, we say that 9 percent is the yield to maturity.

Interpolation We cannot always assume that the value we derive from the interest rates in the tables will allow us to arrive at exactly the current value for the bond. Therefore, we may wish to interpolate between two values derived from the table.

Actually, interpolation represents a lot of tedious work and does not convey enough new knowledge to warrant extensive discussion. However, an example of the use of interpolation is presented in Appendix 12A for those who wish to pursue the calculation.

The Formula for Approximate Yield to Maturity Most textbooks present a formula for *approximate* yield to maturity, and we shall also. Although the formula gives a less precise answer than that determined by financial calculators, computers, or the trial-and-error method, it is an appropriate tool for getting an approximation for the yield on a bond.

The formula is:[1]

$$Y' = \frac{C_t + \dfrac{P_n - V}{n}}{(0.6)\,V + (0.4)\,P_n} \qquad (12\text{–}2)$$

Plugging values into the formula on an annual basis, we find:

Y' = Approximate yield to maturity

C_t = Coupon payment = $100

P_n = Par or maturity value = $1,000

V = Market value = $850.90

n = Number of periods = 20

[1] This formula is recommended by Gabriel A. Hawawini and Ashok Vora, "Yield Approximations: A Historical Perspective," *Journal of Finance,* March 1982, pp. 145–56. It tends to provide the best approximation.

$$Y' = \frac{\$100 + \dfrac{\$1{,}000 - \$850.90}{20}}{(0.6)\$850.90 + (0.4)\$1{,}000}$$

$$= \frac{\$100 + \dfrac{\$149.10}{20}}{\$510.54 + \$400}$$

$$= \frac{\$100 + 7.45}{910.54}$$

$$= \frac{\$107.45}{\$910.54} = 11.80\%$$

Actually, the true yield to maturity is 12.00 percent, so the approximate yield to maturity of 11.80 percent is 0.20 percent below the actual price. In the jargon of bond trading, each 1/100 of 1 percent is referred to as a **basis point,** so the difference is 20 basis points. The approximate yield to maturity method tends to understate exact yield to maturity for issues trading at a discount (in this case, the bond is priced at $850.90). The opposite effect occurs for bonds trading at a premium (above par value).[2]

In the interest of simplicity, we will use approximation formulas in the next two sections related to yield to call and anticipated realized yield, but keep in mind these are only estimates of the exact answer.

Yield to Call

As discussed in the preceding chapter on bond fundamentals, not all fixed-income securities are held to maturity. To the extent a debt instrument may be called in before maturity, a separate calculation is necessary to determine yield to the call date. The answer is termed the **yield to call.** Assume a 20-year bond was initially issued at 11.5 percent interest rate, and after two years, rates have dropped. Let us assume the bond is currently selling for $1,180, and the yield to maturity on the bond is 9.48 percent. However, the investor who purchases the bond for $1,180 may not be able to hold the bond for the remaining 18 years because the issue can be called. Under these circumstances, yield to maturity may not be the appropriate measure of return over the expected holding period.

In the present case, we shall assume the bond can be called at $1,090 five years after issue. Thus, the investor who buys the bond two years after issue can have his bond called back after three more years at $1,090. To compute yield to call, we determine the approximate interest rate that will equate a $1,180 investment today with $115 (11.5 percent) per year for the next three years plus a payoff or call price value of $1,090 at the end of three years. We can adjust Formula 12–2 (approximate yield to maturity) to Formula 12–3 (approximate yield to call).

---

[2] In all our bond problems, we assume we buy the bond at the beginning of an interest payment period. To the extent there is accrued interest, we would have to modify our calculations slightly.

$$Y'_c = \frac{C_t + \dfrac{P_c - V}{n_c}}{(0.6)\,V + (0.4)\,P_c} \qquad (12\text{–}3)$$

On an annual basis, we show:

Y'_c = Approximate yield to call
C_t = Coupon payment = \$115
P_c = Call price = \$1,090
V = Market value = \$1,180
n_c = Number of periods to call = 3

$$Y'_c = \frac{\$115 + \dfrac{\$1{,}090 - \$1{,}180}{3}}{(0.6)\$1{,}180 + (0.4)\$1{,}090}$$

$$= \frac{\$115 + \dfrac{-\$90}{3}}{\$708 + \$436}$$

$$= \frac{\$115 - \$30}{\$1{,}144}$$

$$= \frac{\$85}{\$1{,}144}$$

$$= 7.43\%$$

The yield to call figure of 7.43 percent is 205 basis points less than the previously cited yield to maturity figure of 9.48 percent. Clearly, the investor needs to be aware of the differential, which represents the decrease in yield the investor would receive if the bond is called. Generally, any time the market price of a bond is equal to or greater than the call price, the investor should do a separate calculation for yield to call.[3]

In the case where market interest rates are much lower than the coupon, there is always the chance the company will call the bond. Because of this possibility, the call price often serves as an upper price limit, and further reductions in market interest rates will not cause this callable bond to increase in price. In other words, investors' capital gain potentials may be quite limited with bonds subject to a call.

[3] Bond tables may also be used to find the exact value for yield to call. A source is *Thorndike Encyclopedia of Banking and Financial Tables* (Boston: Warren, Gorham & Lamont, 1981).

Anticipated Realized Yield

Finally, we have the case where the investor purchases the bond with the intention of holding the bond for a period that is different from either the call date or the maturity date. Under this circumstance, we examine the **anticipated realized yield.** This represents the return over the holding period.

Assume an investor buys a 12.5 percent coupon bond for $900. Based on her forecasts of lower interest rates, she anticipates the bond will go to $1,050 in three years. The formula for the approximate realized yield is:

$$Y'_r = \frac{C_t + \dfrac{P_r - V}{n_r}}{(0.6)V + (0.4)P_r} \tag{12–4}$$

The terms are:

Y'_r = Anticipated realized yield

C_t = Coupon payment = $125

P_r = Realized price = $1,050

V = Market price = $900

n_r = Number of periods to realization = 3

$$Y'_r = \frac{\$125 + \dfrac{\$1{,}050 - \$900}{3}}{(0.6)\$900 + (0.40)\$1{,}050}$$

$$= \frac{\$125 + \dfrac{\$150}{3}}{\$540 + \$420}$$

$$= \frac{\$175}{\$960}$$

$$= 18.23\%$$

The anticipated return of 18.23 percent would not be unusual in periods of falling interest rates.

Reinvestment Assumption

Throughout our analysis, when we have talked about yield to maturity, yield to call, and anticipated realized yield, we have assumed that the determined rate also represents an appropriate rate for reinvestment of funds. If yield to maturity is 11 or 12 percent, then it is assumed that coupon payments, as they come in, can also be reinvested at that rate. To the extent that this is an unrealistic assumption, investors will wish to temper their

So You Want a Long Maturity—How About 1,000 Years?

That's right—bonds of Canadian Pacific Limited have a 1,000-year maturity. By then the cost of a postage stamp should be a few billion dollars.

On a more serious note, in 1993 five major corporations began offering 50-year bonds, the longest maturities in U.S. history. The following firms participated:

TVA	$1 billion
Boeing	$275 million
Conrail	$250 million
Ford Motor	$200 million

All were issued at about ¼ percent above comparable 30-year issues of the same firm. Because long-term interest rates were considered low at the time for highly rated corporate bonds (approximately 8 percent), one can clearly see the motivation to the issuing firm.

What about the investor? Half a century is a long time to be tied in to an investment. Look back 50 years ago; we didn't know about computers, space shots to the moon, or artifical heart transplants. What new events will transpire during the next 50 years?

Nevertheless, approximately $2 billion of these 50-year issues were absorbed in the marketplace. Some investors were motivated by the fact that the maturity of the issues matched their liabilities. An example would be insurance companies with long-term policy commitments. Others recognized that the price sensitivity of a 50-year bond is not much greater than a 30-year bond. Although bond price sensitivity increases with maturity, it increases at a greatly decreasing rate with long maturity obligations. For example, an interest rate increase of 2 percent on a 30-year, 8 percent, $1,000 par value bond will cause a price decline to $811.16. On a 50-year bond, the same 2 percent increase will cause a price decline to $802.20—only about a $9 difference. The extra ¼ percent interest on the 50-year bonds apparently justified accepting the small price sensitivity exposure.

Also keep in mind that if interest rates fall below the initial issue rate any time over the next 50 years, the investor may have the opportunity for capital appreciation. Fifty years is a long opportunity to wait for a depression, a stock market crash, or other type event that might drive down interest rates.

An added feature was that the issuers were all in the A to AAA category so that the threat of bankruptcy was thought to be relatively small. However, keep in mind that a lot can happen over a 50-year period. By the year 2043, there may not even be conventional airplanes, automobiles, or gasoline, the primary products of many of the issuers.

thinking. For example, if it is anticipated that returns can be reinvested at a higher rate in the future, this increases true yield, and the opposite effect would be present for a decline in interest rates. The reinvestment topic is more fully developed in Chapter 13.

THE MOVEMENT OF INTEREST RATES

In developing our discussion of bond valuation and investments, we have observed that lower interest rates bring higher bond prices and profits. A glance back at Table 12–3 (right-hand portion) indicates a 12 percent coupon rate, 20-year bond will sell for $1,171.60 if yields to maturity on competitive bonds decline to 10 percent and for $1,276.00 when yields decline to 9 percent. The maturity of the bond is also important, with the impact on price being greater for longer-term obligations.

The investor who wishes to make a substantial profit in the bond market must try to anticipate the turns and directions of interest rates. While much of the literature on

efficient markets would indicate that this is extremely difficult,[4] Wall Street economists, bank economists, and many others rely on interest-rate forecasts to formulate financial strategies. The fact that short-term and long-term rates do not necessarily move in the same direction or move with the same magnitude makes the task even more formidable. Nevertheless, some historical analysis and knowledge of interest-rate patterns over the business cycle are useful in making investment decisions.

Interest rates have long been viewed as a coincident indicator in our economy; that is to say, they are thought to move in concert with industrial production, gross domestic product, and similar measures of general economic health. This is generally true, although in the last five recessions, the change in interest rates has actually lagged behind the decline in industrial production.

While inflationary expectations have the greatest influence on long-term rates, a number of other factors also influence overall interest rates. The demand for funds by individuals, businesses, and the government represents one side of the equation, with the desire for savings and Federal Reserve policy influencing the supply side. A classic study by Feldstein and Eckstein found that bond yields were inversely related to the money supply (the slower the growth, the higher the interest rates) and directly related to economic activity, the demand for loanable funds by the government, the level of inflation, and changes in short-term interest rate *expectations.*[5]

Term Structure of Interest Rates

Of general importance to understanding the level of interest rates is the development of an appreciation for the relationship between the level of interest rates and the maturity of the debt obligation. There is no one single interest rate but, rather, a whole series of interest rates associated with the given maturity of bonds.

The **term structure of interest rates** depicts the relationship between maturity and interest rates. It is sometimes called a yield curve because yields on existing securities having maturities from three months to 30 years are plotted on a graph to develop the curve. To eliminate any business risk consideration, the securities analyzed are usually U.S. Treasury issues. Examples of four different types of term structures are presented in Figure 12–1 on page 356.

In panel *a,* we see an ascending term structure pattern in which interest rates increase with the lengthening of the maturity dates. When the term structure is in this posture, it is a general signal that interest rates will rise in the future. In panel *b,* we see a descending pattern of interest rates, with this pattern generally predictive of lower interest rates. Panel *c* is a variation of panel *b,* with the hump representing intermediate-term interest rates. This particular configuration is an even stronger indicator that interest rates may be

[4] Michael J. Prell, "How Well Do the Experts Forecast Interest Rates?" Federal Reserve Bank of Kansas City, *Monthly Review,* September–October 1973, pp. 3–13; Oswald D. Bowlin and John D. Martin, "Extrapolations of Yields over the Short Run: Forecast or Folly?" *Journal of Monetary Economics,* 1975, pp. 275–88; and Richard Roll, *The Behavior of Interest Rates* (New York: Basic Books, 1970).

[5] Martin Feldstein and Otto Eckstein, "The Fundamental Determinants of the Interest Rate," *The Review of Economics and Statistics,* November 1970, pp. 363–75.

FIGURE 12–1 Term Structure of Interest Rates

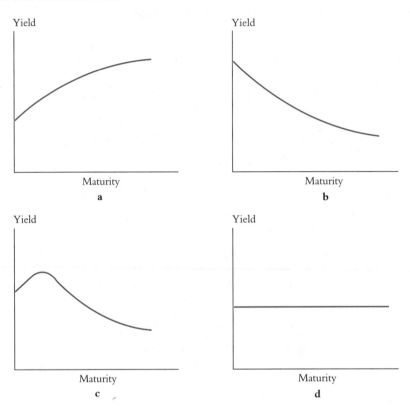

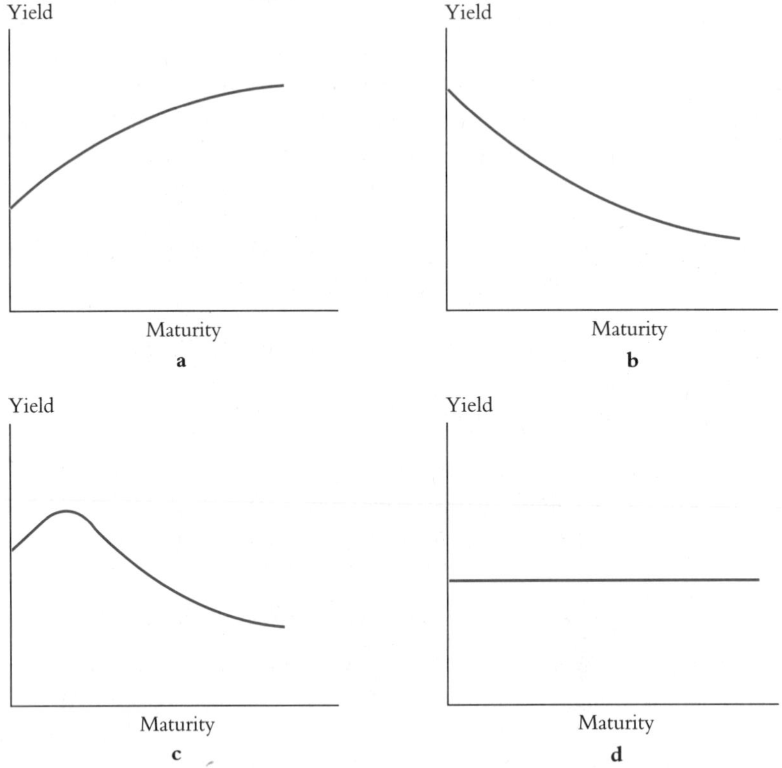

declining in the future. Finally, in panel *d,* we see a flat-term structure indicating investor indifference between debt instrument maturity. This generally indicates that there is no discernible pattern for the future of interest rates. Several theories of interest rates are used to explain the particular shape of the yield curve. We shall review three of these theories.

Expectations Hypothesis The dominant rationale for the shape of the term structure of interest rates rests on a phenomenon called the **expectations hypothesis.** The hypothesis is that any long-term rate is an average of the expectations of future short-term rates over the applicable time horizon. Thus, if lenders expect short-term rates to be continually increasing, they will demand higher long-term rates. Conversely, if they anticipate short-term rates to be declining, they will accept lower long-term rates. An example may be helpful. Suppose the interest rate on a one-year Treasury bill is 6 percent, and that after one year, it is assumed that a new one-year Treasury bill may be bought to yield 8 percent. At the end of year 2, it is assumed that a third one-year Treasury bill may be

bought to yield 10 percent. In other words, the investor can buy (this is sometimes called roll over) three one-year Treasury bills in yearly succession, each with an expected one-year return.

But what about investors who buy one-, two-, or three-year securities today? The yield they will require will be based on expectations about the future. For the one-year security, there is no problem. The 6 percent return will be acceptable. But investors who buy a two-year security now will want the average of the 6 percent they could expect in the first year and the 8 percent expected in the second year, or 7 percent.[6] An investor who buys a three-year security will demand an average of 6, 8, and 10 percent, or an 8 percent return. Higher expected interest rates in the future will mean that longer maturities will carry higher yields than will shorter maturities. The reverse would be true if interest rates were expected to go down.

The expectations hypothesis tends to be reinforced by lender/borrower strategies. If investors (lenders) expect interest rates to increase in the future, they will attempt to lend short-term and avoid long-term obligations so as to diminish losses on long maturity obligations when interest rates go up. Borrowers have exactly the opposite incentive. When interest rates are expected to go up, they will attempt to borrow long term now to lock in the lower rates. Thus, the desire of lenders to lend short term (and avoid long term) and the desire of borrowers to borrow long term (and avoid short term) accentuates the expected pattern of rising interest rates. The opposite motivations are in effect when interest rates are expected to decline.

Liquidity Preference Theory The second theory used to explain the term structure of interest rates is called the **liquidity preference theory,** which states that the shape of the term structure curve tends to be upward sloping more than any other pattern. This reflects a recognition of the fact that long maturity obligations are subject to greater price-change movements when interest rates change. Because of the increased risk of holding longer-term maturities, investors demand a higher return to hold long-term securities relative to short-term securities. This is called the liquidity preference theory of interest rates. Since short-term securities are more easily turned into cash without the risk of large price changes, investors will pay a higher price for short-term securities and thus receive a lower yield.

Market Segmentation Theory The third theory related to the term structure of interest rates is called the **market segmentation theory** and focuses on the demand side of the market. The theory is that there are several large institutional participants in the bond market, each with its own maturity preference. Banks tend to prefer short-term liquid securities to match the nature of their deposits, whereas life insurance companies prefer long-term bonds to match their long-run obligations. The behavior of these two institutions, as well as that of savings and loans, often creates pressure on short-term or

---

[6] The expectations hypothesis actually uses the geometric mean (compound growth rate) rather than the arithmetic mean (simple average) used in the example. For a short number of years, the two means would be quite similar.

long-term rates but very little in the intermediate market of five- to seven-year maturities. This theory helps to focus on the accumulation or liquidation of securities by institutions during the different phases of the business cycle and the resultant impact on the yield curve.

As stated earlier, the expectations hypothesis is probably the most dominant theory, but all three theories have some part in the creation of the term structure of interest rates. Also, as we discussed, the curve takes on many different shapes over time. For example, as viewed in Figure 12–2, in May 1981, the yield curve had reached new high levels and was steeply downsloping in anticipation of lower interest rates. Lower rates came, and by May 1983, the curve had shifted down significantly for all maturities and was now presenting a more normal upsloping yield curve. Over the two-year period from May 1981 to May 1983, three-month Treasury bills dropped from 16.99 to 8.48 percent, for a total decline of 851 basis points. Long-term Treasuries went from 13.26 to 10.75 percent over the same two-year period for a decline of only 251 basis points. One year later, by May 1984, interest rates had started to rise on fears that large government deficits would rekindle rampant inflation. Between May 1983 and May 1984, long-term rates rose to 14.21 percent, or a change of 346 basis points, more than wiping out the previous decrease.

Moving forward to January 1988, interest rates were down considerably from their former level. Part of this decline can be attributed to the stock market crash a few months earlier, which caused the Federal Reserve to sharply lower interest rates to avoid a financial panic. By October 1993, interest rates on all maturities were at their lowest level in more than 30 years. This was due to a recession-riddled, no-growth economy in which the Federal Reserve drove down interest rates in hopes of stimulating business activity. Also, the lack of a desire by businesses to borrow and expand contributed to lower interest rates. By September 1994, the Federal Reserve had changed its policy through a number of increases in short-term interest rates in an attempt to slow down a rapidly improving economy in order to head off the threat of inflation.

The question being asked during 1995 was, What would be the next major movement in the term structure of interest rates? Would a strong economic recovery raise inflationary expectations and cause interest rates to go even higher or would moderation set in and cause interest rates to level off or decline.

In studying Figure 12–2, you cannot hope to remember all the shifts in interest rates that have taken place. The important factor to appreciate is that the interest-rate environment often changes radically, and these changes are very important to bond investors. Students of today may have trouble believing the yield curve of May 22, 1981, in which interest rates were between 13 and 17 percent.

Before concluding our discussion of the term structure of interest rates and proceeding to the development of investment strategies, one final observation is significant. Short-term rates, which are most influenced by Federal Reserve policy in attempting to regulate the money supply and economy, are much more volatile than long-term rates. An examination of Figure 12–3 on page 360 indicates that *short-term* prime commercial paper rates move much more widely than *long-term,* high-grade corporate bond rates.

FIGURE 12–2 Yield Curve Patterns

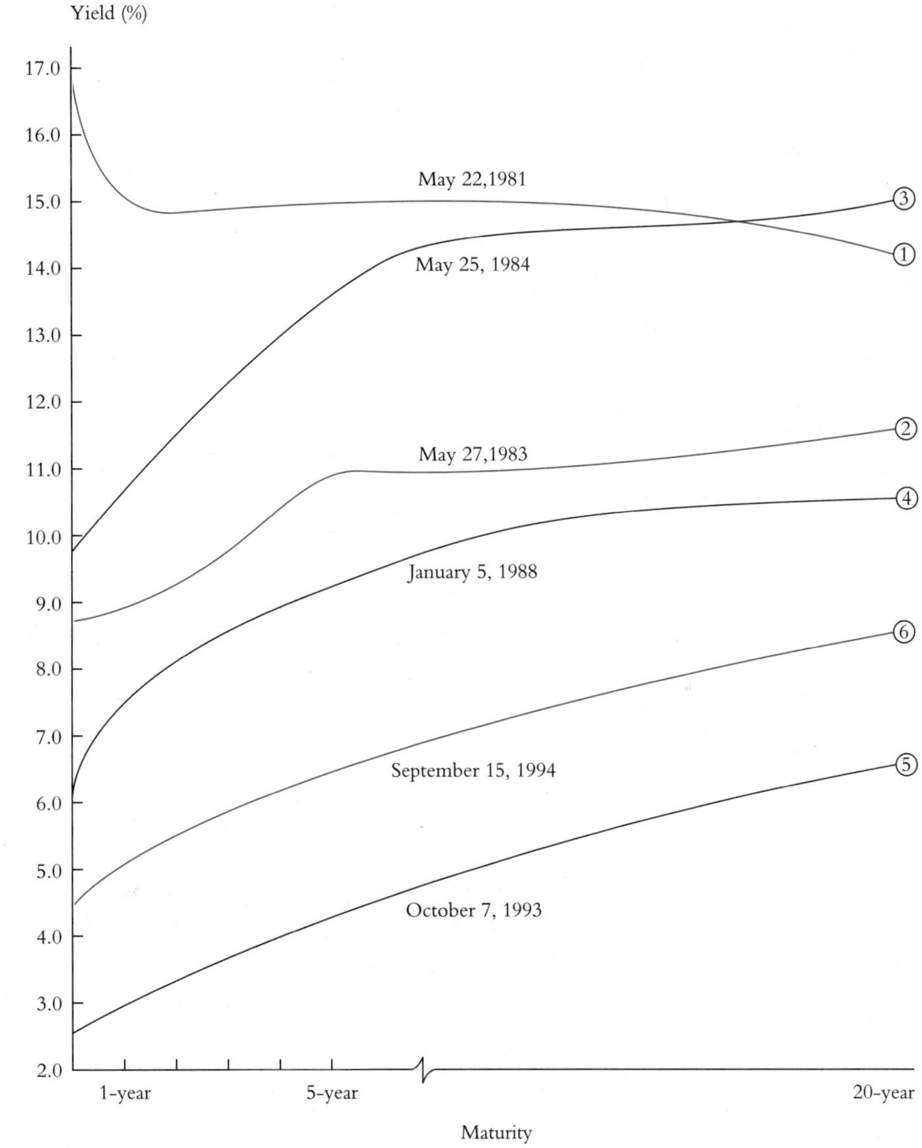

FIGURE 12–3 Relative Volatility of Short-Term and Long-Term Interest Rates

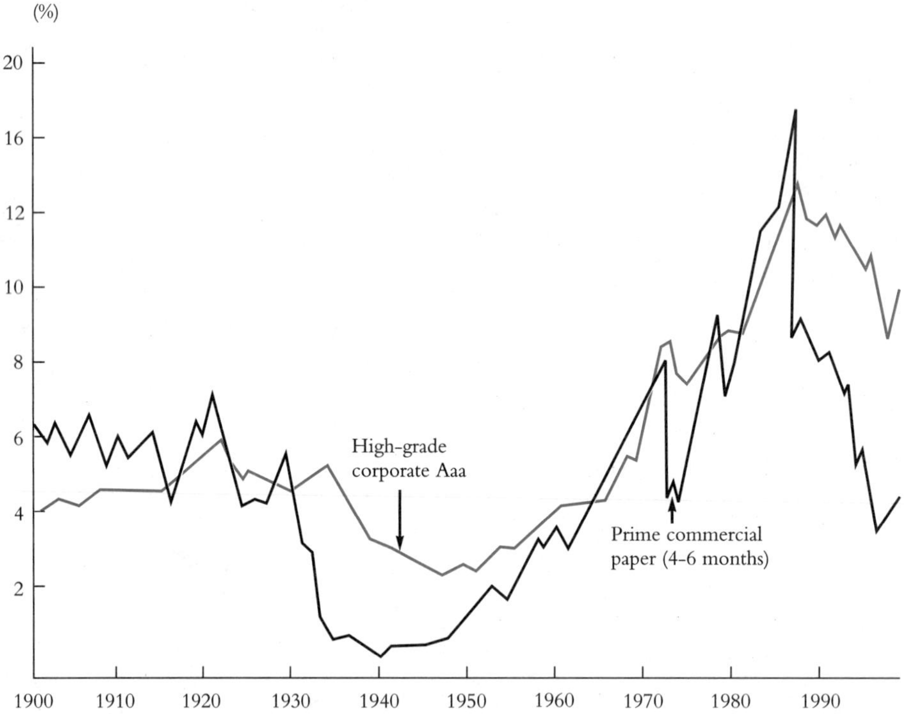

Source: *Federal Reserve Bulletin* (Washington, D.C.: Federal Reserve Board of Governors).

INVESTMENT STRATEGY: INTEREST-RATE CONSIDERATIONS

Thus far in this chapter, we have examined the different valuation procedures for determining the price or yield on a bond and the methods for evaluating the future course of interest rates. We now bring this knowledge together in the form of various investment strategies.

When the bond investor believes interest rates are going to fall, he will take a bullish position in the market by buying long-term bonds and try to maximize the price movement pattern associated with a change in interest rates. The investor can do this by considering the *maturity, coupon rate,* and *quality* of the issue.

Because the impact of an interest-rate change is much greater on long-term securities, the investor will generally look for extended maturities. The impact of various changes in yields on bond prices for a 12 and a 6 percent coupon rate bond can be examined in Table 12–4. For example, looking at the –2% line for the 12 percent coupon bond, we see a 2 percent drop in competitive yields would cause a 1.86 percent increase in value for a bond with 1 year to maturity but an 18.93 percent increase in value for a bond with 30 years to maturity. For the same 2 percent drop in rates, the 6 percent coupon bond would increase 1.92 percent (1 year to maturity) and 34.59 percent (30 years to maturity). The

TABLE 12–4 Change in Market Prices of Bonds for Shifts in Yields to Maturity

12 Percent Coupon Rate

	Maturity (Years)				
Yield Change (percent)	1	5	10	20	30
+3%	−2.69%	−10.30%	−15.29%	−18.89%	−19.74%
+2	−1.81	−7.02	−10.59	−13.33	−14.04
+1	−0.91	−3.57	−5.01	−7.08	−7.52
−1	+0.92	+3.77	+5.98	+8.02	+8.72
−2	+1.86	+7.72	+12.46	+17.16	+18.93
−3	+2.81	+11.87	+19.51	+27.60	+30.96

6 Percent Coupon Rate

	Maturity (Years)				
Yield Change (percent)	1	5	10	20	30
+3%	−2.75%	−11.67%	−19.25%	−27.39%	−30.82%
+2	−1.85	−7.99	−13.42	−19.64	−22.52
+1	−0.94	−4.10	−7.02	−10.60	−12.41
−1	+0.95	+4.33	+7.72	+12.46	+15.37
−2	+1.92	+8.90	+16.22	+27.18	+34.59
−3	+2.91	+13.74	+25.59	+44.63	+58.80

relationship between these two bonds further shows that the lower 6 percent coupon bond is more price sensitive than the higher 12 percent coupon bond.

We can also observe that the effect of interest-rate changes is not symmetrical. Drops in interest rates will cause proportionally greater gains than increases in interest rates will cause losses, particularly as we lengthen the maturity. An evaluation of the 30-year column in Table 12–4 confirms that both bonds are more price sensitive to a decline in yields than to a rise in yields.[7]

Although we have emphasized the need for long maturities in maximizing price movement, the alert student will recall that short-term interest rates generally move up and down more than long-term interest rates as was indicated in Figure 12–3. What if short-term rates are more volatile—even though long-term rates have a greater price

[7] A sophisticated investor would also consider the concept of *duration.* Duration is defined as the weighted average time to recover interest and principal. For a bond that pays interest (which includes most cases except zero-coupon bonds), duration will be shorter than maturity in that interest payments start almost immediately. Portfolio strategy may call for maximizing duration rather than maturity in order to achieve maximum movement. A complete discussion of this topic is presented in Chapter 13.

impact—which then do we choose? The answer is fairly direct. The mathematical impact of long maturities on price changes far outweighs the more volatile feature of short-term interest rates. A 1-year, 12 percent debt instrument would need to have an interest-rate *change* of almost 9 *percent* to have the equivalent impact of a 1 percent change in a 30-year debt obligation.

Bond-Pricing Rules

The relationships we have presented in this section can be summarized in a set of bond-pricing rules. Prices of existing bonds have a relationship to maturities, coupons, and market yields for bonds of equal risk. These relationships are evident from an examination of previously presented Table 12–4. If you look at the change in bond prices in Table 12–4, you may be able to describe many of the relationships presented in the following list.

1. Bond prices and interest rates are inversely related.
2. Prices of long-term bonds are more sensitive to a change in yields to maturity than short-term bonds.
3. Bond price sensitivity increases at a decreasing rate as maturity increases.
4. Bond prices are more sensitive to a decline in market yields to maturity than to a rise in market yields to maturity.
5. Prices of low-coupon bonds are more sensitive to a change in yields to maturity than high-coupon bonds.
6. Bond prices are more sensitive when yields to maturity are low than when yields to maturity are high.

Understanding these six bond-pricing relationships is at the heart of creating bond trading and investment strategies. The next chapter on duration provides a more comprehensive analysis of price sensitivity, coupon rates, maturity, market rates, and their combined impact on bond prices.

Example of Interest-Rate Change

Assume we buy 20-year, $1,000 Aaa bonds at par providing a 12 percent coupon rate. Further assume interest rates on these bonds in the market fall to 10 percent. Based on Table 12–5, the new price on the bonds would be $1,171.60 ($1,000 × 117.16).

Although we could assume the gain in price from $1,000 to $1,171.60 occurred very quickly, even if the time horizon were one year, the gain is still 17.16 percent. This is only part of the picture. An integral part of many bond-interest-rate strategies is the use of margin or borrowed funds. For government securities, it is possible to use margin as low as 5 percent, and on high-quality utility or corporate bonds, the requirement is generally 30 percent. In the preceding case, if we had put down 30 percent cash and borrowed the balance, the rate of return on invested capital would have been 57.2 percent:

TABLE 12–5 Bond Value Table (Coupon rate 12 percent)

Yield to Maturity (percent)	Number of Years 10	20	30
8%	127.18%	139.59%	145.25%
10	112.46	117.16	118.93
12	100.00	100.00	100.00
14	89.41	86.55	85.96

Source: Reprinted by permission from the *Thorndike Encyclopedia of Banking and Financial Tables,* 1981.

$$\frac{\text{Return}}{\text{Investment}} = \frac{\$171.60}{\$300.00} = 57.2\%$$

Although we would have had to pay interest on the $700 we borrowed, the interest on the bonds (which belongs to the borrower/investor) would have partially or fully covered this expense. Also, if interest rates drop further to 8 percent, our leveraged return could be over 100 percent on our original investment.

Lest the overanxious student sell all his or her worldly possessions to participate in this impressive gain, there are many admonitions. Even though we think interest rates are going down, they may do the opposite. A 2 percent *increase* in interest rates would cause a $133.30 loss or a negative return on a leveraged investment of $300 or a 44.4 percent loss. At the very time it appears that interest rates should be falling due to an anticipated or actual recession, the Federal Reserve may generate the opposite effect by tightening the money supply as an anti-inflation weapon as it did in 1970, 1974, 1979, and 1981.

Deep Discount versus Par Bonds

Another feature in analyzing a bond is the current pricing of the bond in regard to its par value. Bonds that were previously issued at interest rates significantly lower than current market levels may trade at deep discounts from par. These are referred to as **deep discount bonds.** As an example, the Missouri Pacific 4¾ percent bonds due to mature in 2020 were selling at $605 in the fall of 1994. Their bond rating was A, and the yield to maturity was 8.25 percent.

Deep discount bonds generally trade at a lower yield to maturity than bonds selling at close to par. There are two reasons for this. First, a deep discount bond has almost no chance to be called away. Even if prices go up because of falling interest rates, the price is still likely to be below par value. Because of this protection against a call, the investor in deep discount bonds accepts a lower yield. Second, investors in deep discount bonds have the potential for higher percentage price increases (because of the low price base at which the investment is made).

Yield Spread Considerations

As discussed in the previous chapter, different types or grades of bonds provide different yields. For example, the yield on Baa corporate bonds is always above that of corporate Aaa obligations to compensate for risk. Similarly, Aaa corporates pay a higher yield than long-term government obligations. In Figure 12–4, we observe the actual yield spread between Moody's corporate Baa's, Moody's corporate Aaa's, and long-term government securities.

Let's direct our attention to total spread between corporate Baa bonds and government securities (corporate Aaa's fall somewhere in between). Over the long term, the spread appears to be between 75 and 100 basis points.[8] Nevertheless, at certain phases of the

FIGURE 12–4 Yield Spread Differentials on Long-Term Bonds

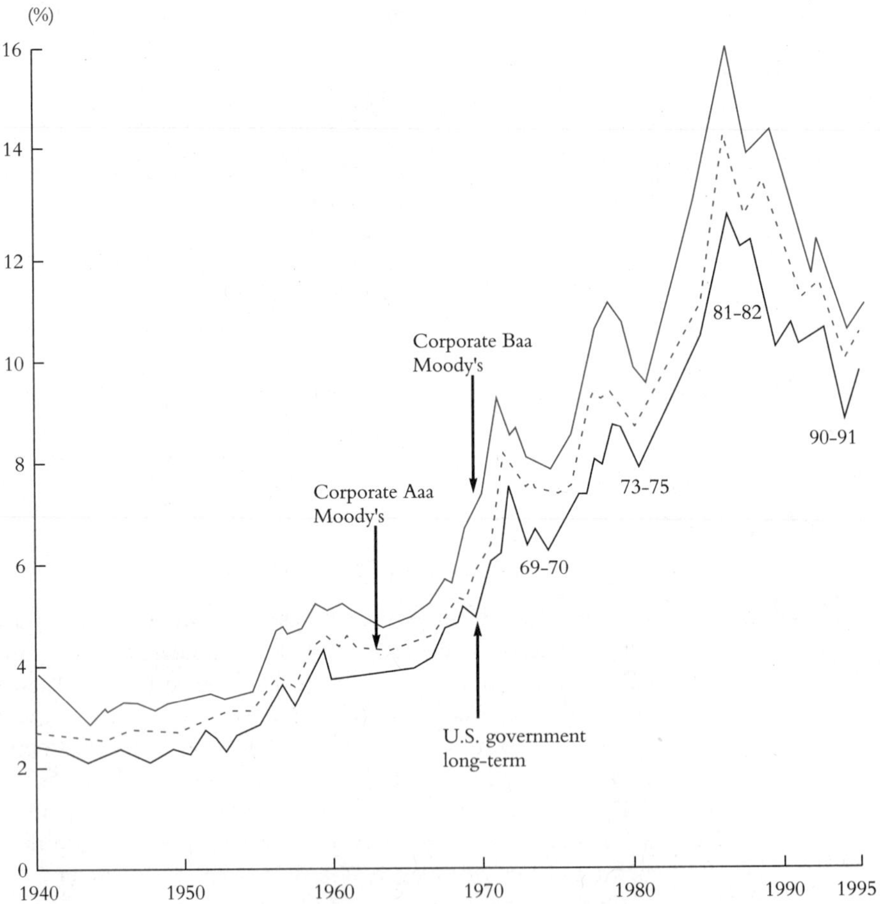

Source: *Federal Reserve Bulletins* (Washington, D.C.: Federal Reserve Board of Governors).

[8] The concept of higher yields on Baa bonds should not be confused with that of junk bonds. In the latter case, the yield is substantially higher, but so is the risk of default.

business cycle, the yield spread changes. For example, in the early phases of a recession, confidence tends to be at a low ebb, and as a consequence, investors will attempt to shift out of lower grade securities into stronger instruments. The impact on the yield spreads can be observed in the recessions of 1969–70, 1973–75, 1981–82, and 1990–91. In all cases, the yield spread between corporate Baa's and government securities went over 150 basis points, only to narrow again during the recovery. Remember that in Chapter 9, on technical analysis, one of the market indicators was the *Barron's* Confidence Index, which measured the ratio of high-grade bonds to medium-grade bonds. The closer the confidence index is to 1.00, the smaller the spread between rates and the more optimistic investors are about the economy. The further the index is below 1.00, the greater the spread in yields and the less the confidence.

Investors must determine how the yield spread affects their strategy. If they do not need to increase the quality of the portfolio during the low-confidence periods of a recession, they can enjoy unusually high returns on lower-grade instruments relative to higher grades.

BOND SWAPS

The term **bond swap** refers to selling out of a given bond position and immediately buying into another one with similar attributes in an attempt to improve overall portfolio return or performance.[9]

Often there are bonds that appear to be comparable in every respect with the exception of one characteristic. For example, *newly issued bonds* that are the equivalent in every sense to outstanding issues generally trade at a slightly higher yield.

Swaps may also be utilized for tax-adjustment purposes and are very popular at the end of the year. Assume you own an AAA rated AT&T bond that you bought five months ago, and you are currently sitting on a 20 percent capital loss because of rising interest rates. You can sell the bond and claim the loss (up to $3,000) against other income.[10] This will save you taxes equal to the loss times your marginal tax rate. You can then take the proceeds from the sale and reinvest in a bond of equal risk, and you will have increased your total cash returns because of tax benefits.

Another common swap is the **pure pickup yield swap** in which a bond owner thinks he can increase the yield to maturity by selling a bond and buying a different bond of equal risk. The key to this swap is that the bond price of one or both bonds has to be in disequilibrium. This assumes that the market is less than totally efficient. By selling the bond that is overpriced and purchasing the bond that is underpriced, the investor is increasing the yield on the investment. If by chance the true quality and risk of the two bonds are different, the bond trader may have swapped for nothing or may even end up losing on the trade. Other types of swaps exist for arbitrages associated with interest-payment dates, call transactions, conversion privileges, or any quickly changing factor in the market.

---

[9] Interest rate swaps are a somewhat different concept and will be discussed in Chapter 16.

[10] Losses greater than $3,000 can be carried forward to future years.

SUMMARY

The price of a bond is based on the concept of the present value of future interest payments plus the present value of a single-sum payment at maturity. The true return on a bond investment may be measured by yield to maturity, yield to call, or anticipated realized yield. A study of interest rates in the business cycle indicates that while interest rates were at one time a coincident indicator, their movement has tended to lag behind the drop in business activity during recent recessions.

The term structure of interest rates depicts the relationship between maturity and interest rates over a long time horizon. The slope of the curve gives some indication as to future movements, with an ascending pattern generally followed by higher interest rates and a descending pattern associated with a possible decline in the future. While these movements hold true in the long run, it is somewhat difficult to project interest movements in the short run.

An investor who wishes to capture maximum gains from an anticipated interest-rate decline should maximize the length of the portfolio while investing in low-coupon, interest-sensitive securities. Deep discount bonds also offer some protection from call provisions.

A complete analysis of a bond portfolio will also include a consideration of the yield spreads between low- and high-quality issues. The spread between long-term U.S. government bonds and corporate Baa's has been as high as 150 basis points or more during certain periods in the 1970s, 1980s, and early 1990s. This factor can have a strong influence on bond portfolio construction.

KEY WORDS AND CONCEPTS

current yield, 348
yield to maturity, 348
basis point, 351
yield to call, 351
anticipated realized yield, 353
term structure of interest rates, 355
expectations hypothesis, 356
liquidity preference theory, 357
market segmentation theory, 357
deep discount bonds, 363
bond swap, 365
pure pickup yield swap, 365

DISCUSSION QUESTIONS

1. Why are bonds not necessarily a conservative investment?
2. How can the market price of a bond be described in terms of present value?
3. Why does a bond price change when interest rates change?
4. Why is current yield not a good indicator of bond returns? (Relate your answer to maturity considerations.)
5. Describe how yield to maturity is the same concept as the internal rate of return (or true yield) on an investment.

6. What is the significance of the yield-to-call calculation?
7. What is the bond reinvestment assumption? Is this necessarily correct?
8. What is the meaning of term structure of interest rates?
9. What does an ascending term structure pattern tend to indicate?
10. Explain the general meaning of the expectations hypothesis as it relates to the term structure of interest rates.
11. Explain the liquidity preference theory as it relates to the term structure of interest rates.
12. How might the market segmentation theory help to explain why short-term rates on government securities increase when bank loan demand becomes high?
13. Under what circumstances would the yield spread on different classes of debt obligations tend to be largest?
14. List the six principles associated with bond-pricing relationships.
15. How do margin requirements affect investor strategy for bonds?
16. Explain the benefits derived from investing in deep discount bonds.
17. What is a bond swap investment strategy? Explain how it might relate to tax planning.

PROBLEMS

Bond price

1. Given a 15-year bond that sold for $1,000 with a 9 percent coupon rate, what would be the price of the bond if interest rates in the marketplace on similar bonds are now 12 percent? Interest is paid semiannually. Assume a 15-year time period.

Bond price

2. Given the facts in problem 1, what would be the price if interest rates go down to 8 percent? (Once again, do a semiannual analysis.)

Current yield

3. What is the current yield of an 8 percent coupon-rate bond priced at $877.60?

Yield to maturity

4. What is the yield to maturity for the data in problem 3? Assume there are 10 years left to maturity. It is a $1,000 par value bond. Use the trial-and-error approach with annual analysis. [**Hint:** Since the bond is trading for less than par value, you can assume the interest rate (*i*) for which you are solving is greater than the coupon rate of 8 percent.]

Yield to maturity

5. What is the yield to maturity for a 10 percent coupon rate bond priced at $1,090.90? Assume there are 20 years left to maturity. It is a $1,000 par value bond. Use the trial-and-error approach with annual analysis. (**Hint:** Since the bond is trading at a price above par value, first decide whether your initial calculation should be at an interest rate above or below the coupon rate.)

Approximate yield to maturity

6. What is the approximate yield to maturity of a 14 percent coupon-rate, $1,000 par value bond priced at $1,160 if it has 16 years to maturity? Use Formula 12–2.

Yield to call

7. **a.** Using the facts given in problem 6, what would be the yield to call if the call can be made in four years at a price of $1,080? Use Formula 12–3.

b. Explain why the answer is lower in part *a* than in problem 6.
c. Given a call value of $1,080 in four years, is it likely that the bond price would actually get to $1,160?

Anticipated realized yield

8. a. Using the facts given in problem 6, what would be the anticipated realized yield if the forecast is that the bond can be sold in three years for $1,280? Use Formula 12–4. Continue to assume the bond has a 14 percent coupon rate ($140) and a current price of $1,160.
b. Now break down the anticipated realized yield between current yield and capital appreciation. (**Hint:** Compute current yield and subtract this from anticipated realized yield to determine capital appreciation.)

Use of bond table

9. An investor places $800,000 in 30-year bonds (12 percent coupon rate), and interest rates decline by 3 percent. Use Table 12–4 to determine the current value of the portfolio.

Expectations hypothesis

10. The following pattern for one-year Treasury bills is expected over the next four years:

Year 1:	5%
Year 2:	7%
Year 3:	10%
Year 4:	11%

a. What return would be necessary to induce an investor to buy a two-year security?
b. What return would be necessary to induce an investor to buy a three-year security?
c. What return would be necessary to induce an investor to buy a four-year security?
d. Diagram the term structure of interest rates for years 1 through 4.

Margin purchase

11. a. Assume an investor purchases a 10-year, $1,000 bond with a coupon rate of 12 percent. The market rate almost immediately falls to 9 percent. What would be the percentage return on the investment if the buyer borrowed part of the funds with a 25 percent margin requirement? Assume the interest payments on the bond cover the interest expense on the borrowed funds. (You can use Table 12–3 in this problem to determine the new value of the bond.)
b. Assume the same bond in part *a* is purchased with 25 percent margin, but market rates go up to 14 percent from 12 percent instead of going down to 9 percent. You can once again use Table 12–3 to determine the price of the bond. What is the percentage loss on the cash investment?

Deep discount bond

12. Assume an investor is trying to choose between purchasing a deep discount bond or a par value bond. The deep discount bond pays 6 percent interest, has 20 years to maturity, and is currently trading at $656.80 with a 10 percent yield to maturity. It is callable at $1,050.

The second bond is selling at its par value of $1,000. It pays 12 percent interest and has 20 years to maturity. Its yield to maturity is also 12 percent. The bond is callable at $1,080.

a. If the yield to maturity on the deep discount bond goes down by 2 percent to 8 percent, what will the new price of the bond be? Do semiannual analysis.
b. If the yield to maturity on the par value bond goes down by 2 percent to 10 percent, what will the new price of the bond be? Do semiannual analysis.
c. Based on the facts in the problem and your answers to parts *a* and *b,* which bond appears to be the better purchase? (Consider the call feature as well as capital appreciation.)

Tax swap

13. Mr. Conrad bought $10,000 of bonds six months ago. The 10-year bonds were purchased at par with a 10 percent coupon rate. Now interest rates in the market are 13 percent for similar obligations with 10 years to maturity. The rapid rise in interest rates was caused by an unexpected increase in inflation.
a. Determine the current value of Mr. Conrad's portfolio. Use Table 12–3 to help accomplish this.
b. How large a deduction from other income can Mr. Conrad take if he sells the bonds?
c. If he is in a 36 percent tax bracket, what is the tax write-off worth to him?
d. Assume he will replace the old 10 percent bonds with 11.9 percent bonds selling at $927. Based on your answer in part *a,* how many new bonds can be purchased? Round to the nearest whole number.

CFA MATERIAL

The following material contains sample questions and solutions from a prior Level I CFA Exam. While the terminology is slightly different from that in this text, you can still view the skills that are necessary for the CFA exam.

CFA Exam Question

4. a. *Briefly explain* why bonds of different maturities have different yields in terms of the (1) expectations, (2) liquidity, and (3) segmentation hypotheses. *(5 minutes)*
b. Briefly describe the implications of each of the three hypotheses when the yield curve is (1) upward sloping, and (2) downward sloping. *(5 minutes)*

Solution: Question 4—Morning Section (I–86) (10 points)

a. (1) The expectations hypothesis maintains that the current long-term rate should equal the average of current and expected future short-term rates. Unless the current and expected future rates are all equal, the averages will be different for different maturities.
(2) The liquidity hypothesis maintains that since longer securities have greater risk, interest rates should increase with maturity as a compensation to investors.
(3) The segmentation hypothesis maintains that individual borrowers are constrained to particular segments of the maturity spectrum. The interest rate for a given maturity will thus depend on the supply and demand for funds in each segment.

b. *Upward sloping yield curve:*

(1) Expectations—short-term interest rates are expected to be higher in the future.
(2) Liquidity—as predicted, longer-term securities have higher return to compensate for risk.
(3) Segmentation—signifies relatively less demand for long-term bonds than short-term bonds.

Downward sloping yield curve:

(1) Expectations—short-term interest rates are expected to be lower in the future.
(2) Liquidity—this is inconsistent with the liquidity hypothesis. When liquidity plus expectations is considered, a decrease in future short-term rates that is larger than the liquidity premium is indicated.
(3) Segmentation—signifies relatively higher demand for long-term bonds than for short-term bonds.

CFA Exam Question

5. You are considering the purchase of a 10 percent, 10-year bond with a par value of $1,000.

a. Using Tables I and II, *compute* the price you should pay for this bond assuming semiannual interest payments and 8 percent yield to maturity. *(2 minutes)*

b. A year from now, you expect that the yield to maturity for this bond will be 6 percent. Using Tables I and II, *compute* the realized compound yield during the year, assuming a reinvestment rate of 5 percent and semiannual interest payments. *Identify* and *comment* on the significance of each of the components of the calculated realized compound yield. *(7 minutes)*

Solution: Question 5—Morning Section (I–87) (10 points)

a.	$50 × 13.5903 (4% – 20 periods)	$679.52
	$1,000 × 0.4564	456.40
	Value	$1,135.92
b.	$50 × 13.7535 (3% – 18 periods)	$687.68
	$1,000 × 0.5874	587.40
	Value of bond 1 year from now	$1,275.08

Realized compound yield:

Ending wealth value:

$1,275.08	—ending price of bond
50.00	—interest at end of year
50.00	—mid-year interest payment
1.25	— 5% interest on interest for ½ year
$1,276.33	

$$\text{Realized compound yield} = \frac{\$1,376.33}{\$1,135.92} - 1 = 1.2116 - 1$$
$$= 21.16\%$$

TABLE I Present Value of $1

Periods	3 Percent	4 Percent	5 Percent	6 Percent	7 Percent	8 Percent
4	0.8885	0.8548	0.8227	0.7921	0.7629	0.7350
6	0.8375	0.7903	0.7462	0.7050	0.6663	0.6302
8	0.7874	0.7307	0.6768	0.6274	0.5820	0.5403
10	0.7441	0.6756	0.6139	0.5584	0.5083	0.4632
12	0.7014	0.6246	0.5568	0.4970	0.4440	0.3971
14	0.6611	0.5775	0.5051	0.4423	0.3878	0.3405
16	0.6232	0.5339	0.4581	0.3936	0.3387	0.2919
18	0.5874	0.4936	0.4155	0.3503	0.2959	0.2502
19	0.5703	0.4746	0.3957	0.3305	0.2765	0.2317
20	0.5537	0.4564	0.3769	0.3118	0.2584	0.2145

TABLE II Present Value of $1 Annuity

Periods	3 Percent	4 Percent	5 Percent	6 Percent	7 Percent	8 Percent
4	3.7171	3.6299	3.5460	3.4651	3.3872	3.3121
5	5.4172	5.2421	5.0757	4.9173	4.7665	4.6229
8	7.0197	6.7327	6.4632	6.2098	5.9713	5.7466
10	8.5302	8.1109	7.7217	7.3601	7.0236	6.7101
12	9.9540	9.3851	8.8633	8.3838	7.9427	7.5361
14	11.2961	10.5631	9.8986	9.2950	8.7455	8.2442
16	12.5611	11.6523	10.8378	10.1059	9.4466	8.8514
18	13.7535	12.6593	11.6896	10.8276	10.0591	9.3719
19	14.3238	13.1339	12.0853	11.1581	10.3356	9.6036
20	14.8775	13.5903	12.4622	11.4699	10.5940	9.8181

There are three components of the realized compound yield calculated above: price appreciation due to decline in rates from 8 percent to 6 percent, coupon interest, and interest on interest.

The total return in dollars for the year was $240.41. Of that total return, $139.16, or about 58 percent, was due to price appreciation; $100, or about 42 percent, was due to coupon interest; and about 0.5 percent was due to interest on interest.

Because the realized compound yield is calculated over only one year in which rates have fallen, the interest-on-interest component will be very small, and the appreciation component is the largest. Had the coupon been smaller than 10 percent, the appreciation component would have been even larger.

THE WALL STREET JOURNAL PROJECTS

1. Look up "Treasury Bonds, Notes & Bills" in Section C of *The Wall Street Journal.* Use this information to plot the term structure of interest rates as illustrated in Figure 12–1 on page 356. Follow these steps:
   a. Find the Ask Yld. (yield) on a Treasury bill that matures approximately 6 months in the future.
   b. Find the Ask Yld. under the "Government Bonds & Notes" subheading on a security that matures approximately five years into the future. Follow this same procedure for a security maturing approximately 10, 20, and 30 years in the future. Exact dates are not critical.
   c. Plot the dates on the horizontal axis.
   d. Plot the yields on the vertical axis.
   e. Which of the four patterns in Figure 12–1 does your term structure most resemble?
2. Every day *The Wall Street Journal* publishes a term structure of interest rates called the Treasury Yield Curve. You can find the yield curve under "Credit Markets" in Section C. Use the index on page C1 to locate this section.
   a. Compare the change in the yield curve over the four-week time period.
   b. Are there any economic conditions you can link to the stability or change in yield curves?
   c. How would the three theories of interest rates as related to the term structure be applied to describe the shape of the yield curve?

SELECTED REFERENCES

Investment Strategies with Bonds

Brick, Ivan E., and S. Abraham Ravid. "Interest Rate Uncertainty and the Optimal Debt Maturity Structure." *Journal of Financial and Quantitative Analysis,* March 1991, pp. 63–81.

Fong, H. Gifford, and Frank J. Fabozzi. "How to Enhance Bond Returns with Naive Strategies." *Journal of Portfolio Management,* Summer 1985, pp. 57–60.

Leibowitz, Martin L. "Goal Oriented Bond Portfolio Management." *Journal of Portfolio Management,* Summer 1979, pp. 13–18.

McAdams, Lloyd, and Evangelos Karagiannis. "Using Yield Curve Shapes to Manage Bond Portfolios." *Financial Analysts Journal,* May–June 1994, pp. 57–59.

Mulvey, John M., and Stavros A. Zenios. "Dynamic Diversification of Fixed Income Portfolios." *Financial Analysts Journal,* January–February 1994, pp. 30–38.

Rosenberg, Hilary. "The New Lure of Foreign Bonds." *Institutional Investor,* March 1988, pp. 143–47.

Bond Yields

Ferri, Michael G. "How Do Call Provisions Influence Bond Yields?" *Journal of Portfolio Management,* Winter 1979, pp. 55–57.

Heynen, Ronald; Angelien Kemna; and Tom Vorst. "Analysis of the Term Structure of Implied Volatilities." *Journal of Financial and Quantitative Analysis,* March 1994, pp. 31–56.

Homer, S., and M. L. Leibowitz. *Inside the Yield Book: New Tools for Bond Market Strategy.* Englewood Cliffs, NJ: Prentice Hall, 1972.

Empirical Studies

Dann, Larry Y., and Wayne H. Mikkelson. "Convertible Debt Issuance, Capital Structure Change and Financing—Related Information: Some New Evidence." *Journal of Financial Economics,* June 1984, pp. 155–86.

Yawitz, Jess B.; Kevin J. Maloney; and Louis H. Ederington. "Taxes, Default Risk, and Yield Spreads." *Journal of Finance,* September 1985, pp. 1127–40.

APPENDIX 12A: Interpolating to Find Yield to Maturity

Interpolation allows you to find a more exact answer to a bond yield problem.

Assume a bond has a coupon rate of 7 percent ($70), has 15 years to maturity (*n*), and is selling at $875.00.

We will assume that at an interest rate of 8 percent, you got a bond price of $914.13, and at 9 percent, the value was $839.27. Thus, the interest rate associated with $875.00 must fall between 8 and 9 percent. Using interpolation, we find the yield y* as follows:

Interest rate	Bond price		
8%	$914.13	$39.13 ↑ Difference between upper and middle value (8% to y*)	$74.86 ↑ Difference between upper and lower value (8% to 9%)
y^*	875.00		
9%	839.27		

$$8\% + \frac{\$39.13}{74.86}(1\%) = 8\% + 0.52\% = 8.52\%$$

The interpolated answer between 8 and 9 percent is 8.52 percent.

13

Duration and Reinvestment Concepts

REVIEW OF BASIC BOND VALUATION CONCEPTS

In Chapter 12, we discussed the principles of bond valuation. The value of a bond was established in Formula 12–1 as follows:

$$V = \sum_{t=1}^{n} \frac{C_t}{(1+i)^t} + \frac{P_n}{(1+i)^n}$$

where:

V = Market value or price of the bond
n = Number of periods
t = Each period
C_t = Coupon or interest payment for each period, t
P_n = Par or maturity value
i = Interest rate in the market

Based on this equation, as interest rates in the market rise, the price of the bond will decline because the present value of the cash flows is worth less at a higher discount rate. The opposite is true if interest rates decline. We also demonstrated in Table 12–4 that bonds with long-term maturities were generally more sensitive to changes in interest rates than were short-term bonds. Reproduction of part of Table 12–4 below shows that a 30-year bond exhibits larger price changes in response to a change in yield than do shorter-term obligations. For example, a 2 percent drop in interest rates would cause a 1.86 percent increase in value for a bond with one year to maturity, but an 18.93 percent increase in value for a bond with 30 years to maturity. Given the relationship between the life of a bond and the price sensitivity just described, it is particularly important that we have an appropriate definition of the life or term of a bond.

(Reproduction of Table 12–4) Change in Market Prices of Bonds for Shifts in Yields to Maturity (12 Percent Coupon Rate)

Yield Change (Percent)	**Maturity (Years)**				
	1	**5**	**10**	**20**	**30**
+3%	−2.69%	−10.30%	−15.29%	−18.89%	−19.74%
+2	−1.81	−7.02	−10.59	−13.33	−14.04
+1	−0.91	−3.57	−5.01	−7.08	−7.52
−1	+0.92	+3.77	+5.98	+8.02	+8.72
−2	+1.86	+7.72	+12.46	+17.16	+18.93
−3	+2.81	+11.87	+19.51	+27.60	+30.96

The first inclination is to say that the term of a bond is an easily determined matter. One supposedly merely needs to look up the maturity date (such as 2000 or 2004) in a bond book, and the matter is settled. However, the notion of effective life of a bond is more complicated than this. The situation is somewhat analogous to the quoted coupon rate on the bond, not really conveying the true yield on the obligation. Similarly, the maturity date on a bond may not convey all important information about the life of a bond.

In studying the true characteristics about the life of a bond, not only must the final date and amount of the maturity payment be considered but also the pattern of coupon payments that occurs in the interim. If you were to receive $1,000 after 20 years and no interest payments during the term of the obligation, clearly the effective life is 20 years. But suppose in addition to the $1,000, you were also to receive $100 per year for the next 20 years. Part of the payment is coming early and part of the payment is coming late, and the weighted average term of the payout is certainly less than 20 years. The higher the coupon payments relative to the maturity payment, the shorter the weighted average life of the payout. The **weighted average life** refers to the time period over which the coupon payments and maturity payment on a bond are recovered. In the next section, we shall go through the simple mathematics of computing the weighted average life of the payout; for now it is enough to know that such a concept exists.

The important consideration is that *bond price sensitivity* can be more appropriately related to *weighted average life* than to just the maturity date. While many bond analysts simply relate price sensitivity to maturity (and we did that also in Chapter 12), there is a more sophisticated approach related to weighted average life.

Before we move on to calculate weighted average life, there is an investment decision we wish you to consider. Assume you have to decide whether to invest in an 8 percent coupon rate bond with a 20-year maturity or a 12 percent coupon rate bond with a 25-year maturity. Which bond will have the larger increase in price if interest rates decline? You may choose the 25-year, 12 percent coupon rate bond because it has the longer maturity, but don't answer too quickly on this. Let's consider weighted average life and then come back to this question of price sensitivity.

DURATION

The concept of weighted average life of a bond falls under the general topic of duration. We shall first of all do a simple example of weighted average life and then more formally look at duration. Assume we have a five-year bond that provides $80 per year for the next five years plus $1,000 at the end of five years. For ease of calculation, we are using annual coupon payments in our analysis. Semiannual analysis would change the answer only slightly. An approach to computing weighted average life is presented in Table 13–1.

First, we see that the weighted average life of the bond, based on the annual cash flows, is 4.4290 years. Let's see how this is calculated. In column (1) is the year in which each cash flow falls, and in column (2) is the size of the cash flow for each year plus the total cash flow. Column (3) calls for dividing the annual cash flow in column (2) by the total cash flow at the bottom of column (2) to determine what percentage of the total it represents. For example, the annual cash flow of $80 on the first line of column (2) represents 0.0571 of the total cash flow of $1,400. ($80 ÷ $1,400 = 0.0571.) The same basic procedure is followed for all subsequent years. In column (4), each year is multiplied by the weights (percentages) developed in column (3). For example, year 1 is multiplied by 0.0571 to arrive at 0.0571 in column (4). Year 2 is multiplied by 0.0571 to arrive at 0.1142 in column (4). This procedure is followed for each year and each weight. The final answer is 4.4290 for the weighted average life of the bond.

If you can understand the approach presented in Table 13–1, you should have no difficulty following a more formal and appropriate definition of weighted average life

TABLE 13–1 Simple Weighted Average Life

(1) Year *t*	(2) Cash Flow	(3) Annual Cash Flow (2) ÷ by Total Cash Flow	(4) Year × Weight (1) × (3)
1	$ 80	0.0571	0.0571
2	80	0.0571	0.1142
3	80	0.0571	0.1713
4	80	0.0671	0.2284
5	80	0.0571	0.2855
5	1,000	0.7145	3.5725
Total cash flow →	$1,400	1.0000	4.4290

called duration. **Duration** represents the weighted average life of a bond where the weights are based on the *present value* of the individual cash flows relative to the *present value* of the total cash flows. An example of duration is presented in Table 13–2. Present value calculations are based on the market rate of interest (yield to maturity) for the bond, which in this case, we shall assume to be 12 percent.

The only difference between Table 13–1 and Table 13–2 is that in Table 13–2, the cash flows are present valued before the weights are determined. Thus, the cash flows (2) are multiplied by the present value factors at 12 percent (3) to arrive at the present value of cash flows (4). The total present value of cash flows at the bottom of column (4) is also the same as the price of the bond. In column (5), weights for each year are

TABLE 13–2 Duration Concept of Weighted Average Life

(1) Year, t	(2) Cash Flow *(CF)*	(3) *PV* Factor at 12 percent	(4) *PV* of Cash Flow *(CF)*	(5) *PV* of Annual Cash flow (4) ÷ by Total *PV* of Cash Flows	(6) Year × Weight (1) × (5)
1	$ 80	0.893	$ 71.44	0.0835	0.0835
2	80	0.797	63.76	0.0745	0.1490
3	80	0.712	56.96	0.0666	0.1998
4	80	0.636	50.88	0.0595	0.2380
5	80	0.567	45.36	0.0530	0.2650
5	$1,000	0.567	567.00	0.6629	3.3145
		Total *PV* of cash flows (*V*) →	$855.40	1.0000	4.2498 ↑ Duration

determined by dividing the present value of each annual cash flow (4) by the total present value of cash flows (bottom of column 4). For example in year 1, the present value of the cash flow is $71.44, and this is divided by the total present value of cash flows of $855.40 to arrive at 0.0835 in column (5). Similarly, the weight in year 2, as shown in column (5), is determined by dividing $63.76 by $855.40 to arrive at 0.0745. In column (6), each year is multiplied by the weights developed in column (5). For example, year 1 is multiplied by 0.0835 to arrive at 0.0835 in column (6). Year 2 is multiplied by 0.0745 to arrive at 0.1490. This procedure is followed for each year, and the values are then summed. The final answer for duration (the weighted average life based on present value) is 4.2498. Duration, once determined, is the most representative value for effective bond life and the measure against which bond price sensitivity should be evaluated.

The formula for duration can be formally stated as:

$$\text{Duration} = \underbrace{\frac{CF\ PV}{V}}_{\text{Weight}}\underbrace{(1)}_{\text{Year}} + \underbrace{\frac{CF\ PV}{V}}_{\text{Weight}}\underbrace{(2)}_{\text{Year}} + \underbrace{\frac{CF\ PV}{V}}_{\text{Weight}}\underbrace{(3)}_{\text{Year}} + \ldots + \underbrace{\frac{CF\ PV}{V}}_{\text{Weight}}\underbrace{(n)}_{\text{Year}} \qquad (13\text{–}1)$$

where:

CF = Yearly cash flow for each time period

PV = Present value factor for each time period (from Appendix C at the end of the book)

V = Total present value or market price of the bond

n = Number of periods to maturity[1]

In Table 13–3, we observe durations for an 8 percent coupon rate bond with maturities of 1, 5, and 10 years. The discount rate is 12 percent. The procedure used to compute duration in Table 13–3 is the same as that employed in Table 13–2. Although many calculations are involved, you should primarily direct your attention to the last value presented in column (6) for each of the three bonds. This value represents the duration of the issue.

---

[1] Using the symbols from Formula 12–1, duration can also be stated as:

$$\text{Duration} = \sum_{t=1}^{n} \frac{C_t \dfrac{1}{(1+i)^t}}{V}(t) + \frac{P_n \dfrac{1}{(1+i)^n}}{V}(n)$$

If semiannual analysis is used throughout the calculation, the answer should be divided by two to convert the figure to annual terms.

TABLE 13–3 Duration for an 8 Percent Coupon Rate Bond with Maturities of 1, 5, and 10 Years Discounted at 12 Percent

1-Year Bond

(1) Year, t	(2) Cash Flow (CF)	(3) PV Factor at 12 Percent	(4) PV of Cash Flow (CF)	(5) PV of Annual Cash Flow (4) ÷ by Total PV of Cash Flows	(6) Year × Weight (1) × (5)
1	$ 80	0.893	$ 71.44	0.0741	0.0741
1	1,000	0.893	893.00	0.9259	0.9259
		Total PV of cash flows →	$964.44	1.0000	1.0000 ↑ Duration

5-Year Bond

1	$ 80	0.893	$ 71.44	0.0835	0.0835
2	80	0.797	63.76	0.0745	0.1490
3	80	0.712	56.96	0.0666	0.1998
4	80	0.636	50.88	0.0595	0.2380
5	80	0.567	45.36	0.0530	0.2650
5	1,000	0.567	567.00	0.6629	3.3145
		Total PV of cash flows →	$855.40	1.0000	4.2498 ↑ Duration

10-Year Bond

1	$ 80	0.893	$ 71.44	0.0923	0.0923
2	80	0.797	63.76	0.0824	0.1648
3	80	0.712	56.96	0.0736	0.2208
4	80	0.636	50.88	0.0657	0.2628
5	80	0.567	45.36	0.0586	0.2930
6	80	0.507	40.56	0.0524	0.3144
7	80	0.452	36.16	0.0467	0.3269
8	80	0.404	32.32	0.0418	0.3344
9	80	0.361	28.88	0.0373	0.3357
10	80	0.322	25.76	0.0330	0.3330
10	1,000	0.322	322.00	0.4160	4.1600
		Total PV of cash flows →	$774.08	1.0000	6.8381 ↑ Duration

We see in Table 13–3 that the duration for a one-year bond is 1.0. Since all cash flows are paid at the end of year 1, duration equals the maturity.[2] As maturity increases (to 5 and 10 years), duration increases but less than the maturity of the bond. With a 5-year bond, duration is 4.2498, and with a 10-year bond, duration is 6.8381. Duration is increasing at a decreasing rate because the principal repayment in the last year becomes a smaller percentage of the total present value of cash flow, and the annual coupon payments become more important.[3]

DURATION AND PRICE SENSITIVITY

Once duration is computed, its most important use is in determining the price sensitivity of a bond. In Table 13–4, we consider the maturity, duration, and percentage price change for an 8 percent coupon rate bond based on a 2 percent decrease and on a 2 percent increase in interest rates. The *market* rate of interest for computing duration in Table 13–4 is 8 percent. Duration is related not only to maturity but also to coupon rate and market rate of interest. For example, in Table 13–3, the coupon rate of interest was 8 percent, and the market rate of interest was 12 percent. In the calculations in Table 13–4, the coupon rate is 8 percent, and the initial market rate of interest is assumed to be 8 percent. Because of the different market rates of interest in Tables 13–3 and 13–4, the duration for a given maturity (such as 5 or 10 years) will be different. The point just discussed will be further clarified later in the chapter, so even if you do not fully understand it, you should still continue to read on.

We see in Table 13–4 that the longer the maturity or duration, the greater the impact of a 2 percent change in interest rates on price. However, we shall also observe how much

TABLE 13–4 Duration and Price Sensitivity (8 Percent Coupon Rate Bond)

(1) Maturity	(2) Duration	(3) Impact of a 2 Percent Decline in Interest Rates on Price	(4) Impact of a 2 Percent Increase in Interest Rates on Price
1	1.0000	+ 1.89%	− 1.81%
5	4.3121	+ 8.42	− 7.58
10	7.2470	+14.72	−12.29
20	10.6038	+22.93	−17.03
25	11.5290	+25.57	−18.50
30	12.1585	+27.53	−18.85
40	12.8787	+30.09	−19.55
50	13.2123	+31.15	−19.83

[2] If semiannual analysis were used, the duration would be slightly less than the maturity in the first year.

[3] A sinking-fund provision can also have an effect on duration, causing the weighted average life of the bond to be shorter.

more closely the percentage change in price parallels the change in duration as compared with maturity. For example, between 25 and 50 years, duration increases very slowly (column 2), and the same can be said for the increase in the percentage impact that a 2 percent decline in interest rates has on price (column 3). This is true despite the fact that the maturity period has increased by 100 percent, from 25 to 50 years.

As a rough measure of price sensitivity, one can multiply duration times the change in interest rates to determine the percentage change in the value of a bond.

$$\text{Percentage change in the value of a bond approximately equals} \rightarrow \text{Duration} \times \text{Change in interest rates}$$

The sign in the final answer is reversed because interest-rate changes and bond prices move in opposite directions. For example, if a bond has a duration of 7.2470 years, and interest rates go down by 2 percent, a rough measure of bond value appreciation is +14.494 percent (7.2470 × 2). Columns (2) and (3) in Table 13–4, across from 10 years maturity, indicate this is a good approximation. That is, when duration was 7.2470, a 2 percent drop in interest rates produced a 14.72 percent increase in bond prices (not too many basis points away from our formula value of +14.494 percent). The approximation gets progressively less accurate as the term of the bond is extended.[4] It is also a less valid measure for interest-rate increases (and the associated price decline). Even with these qualifications, one can observe a more useful relationship between price changes and duration than between price changes and maturity.

It is for this reason that the analyst must have a reasonable feel for the factors that influence duration. The length of the bond affects duration, but as previously mentioned, it is not the only variable. Duration is also influenced by market rate of interest and the coupon rate on the bond. It is theoretically possible for these two factors to outweigh maturity in determining duration. That is to say, it is possible that a bond with a shorter maturity than another bond may actually have a longer duration and be more price sensitive to interest rate changes.

Duration and Market Rates

Market rates of interest (yield to maturity) and duration are inversely related. The higher the market rate of interest, the lower the duration. This is because of the present-value effect that is part of duration. Higher market rates of interest mean lower present values. For example, in Table 13–2 on page 377, if the market rate of interest in column (3) had been 16 percent instead of 12 percent, the final answer for duration would have been 4.1859. The new value is computed in Table 13–5 on page 382. Clearly, it is less than the 4.2498 duration value in Table 13–2.

To expand our analysis, in Table 13–6 on page 382 we see the duration values for an 8 percent coupon rate bond at different market rates of interest. As market rates of interest

[4] The approximation can be slightly improved by using modified duration instead of actual duration. Modified duration is defined as: Duration ÷ (1 + Market rate of interest/Number of coupon payments per period). For more information, see Michael H. Hopewell and George C. Kaufman, "Bond Price Volatility and Term to Maturity: A Generalized Respecification," *American Economic Review,* September 1973, pp. 749–53.

TABLE 13–5 Duration of an 8 Percent Coupon Rate Bond with a 16 Percent Market Rate of Interest

(1) Year, *t*	(2) Cash Flow (*CF*)	(3) *PV* Factor at 16 Percent	(4) PV of Cash Flow (*CF*)	(5) PV of Annual Cash Flow (4) ÷ by Total *PV* of Cash Flows	(6) Year × Weight (1) × (5)
1	$ 80	0.862	$ 68.96	0.0935	0.0935
2	80	0.743	59.44	0.0806	0.1612
3	80	0.641	51.28	0.0695	0.2085
4	80	0.552	44.16	0.0598	0.2392
5	80	0.476	38.08	0.0516	0.2580
5	1,000	0.476	476.00	0.6451	3.2255
		Total *PV* of cash flows →	$737.92	1.0000	4.1859 ↑ Duration

increase, duration decreases. This can be easily seen in the 20-year row (reading across). At a 4 percent market rate of interest, duration for the 8 percent coupon rate bond is 12.3995. At 8 percent, it is 10.6038, and at 12 percent, 8.9390.

Also note in Table 13–6 that an equal change in market rates of interest will have a bigger impact on duration when rates move down than when they move up. For example, in the 50-year row, a 4 percentage point decrease in market rates of interest (say, from 8 percent to 4 percent) causes duration to increase by 7.0358 years, from 13.2123 to 20.2481 years. A similar increase from 8 percent to 12 percent would cause duration to decrease by only 3.8407 years, from 13.2123 to 9.3716 years.

TABLE 13–6 Duration Values at Varying Market Rates of Interest (Based on 8 Percent Coupon Rate Bond)

	Market Rates of Interest				
Maturity (Years)	4 Percent	6 Percent	8 Percent	10 Percent	12 Percent
1	1.0000	1.0000	1.0000	1.0000	1.0000
5	4.3717	4.3423	4.3121	4.2814	4.2498
10	7.6372	7.4450	7.2470	7.0439	6.8381
→ 20	12.3995	11.4950	10.6038	9.7460	8.9390
25	14.2265	12.8425	11.5290	10.3229	9.2475
30	15.7935	13.8893	12.1585	10.6472	9.3662
40	18.3274	15.3498	12.8787	10.9176	9.3972
50	20.2481	16.2494	13.2123	10.9896	9.3716

Duration and Coupon Rates

In the previous section, we learned that duration is inversely related to the market rate of interest. We now look at the relationship between duration and the coupon rate on a bond. As the coupon rate rises, duration decreases. Why? The answer is that high coupon rate bonds tend to produce higher annual cash flows before maturity and thus tend to weight duration toward the earlier to middle years. On the other hand, low coupon rate bonds produce less annual cash flows before maturity and have less influence on duration. Duration is weighted more heavily toward the final payment at maturity, and duration tends to be somewhat closer to the actual maturity on the bond. At the extreme, a zero-coupon bond has the same maturity and duration.

The relationship between duration and coupon rates can be seen in Table 13–7. Here three different coupon rate bonds are presented. Each bond is assumed to have a maturity of 25 years. The best way to read the table is to pick a market rate of interest in the first column and then read across the table to determine the duration at various coupon rates. For example, at an 8 percent market rate of interest, duration is 13.2459 at a 4 percent coupon rate, 11.5290 at an 8 percent coupon rate, and 10.8396 at a 12 percent coupon rate. Clearly, the higher the coupon rate, the lower the duration (and vice versa).

The impact of coupon rates on duration is also demonstrated in Figure 13–1 on page 384. Note that with a zero-coupon bond, the line is at a 45-degree angle; that is, duration and years to maturity are always the same value. There is only one payment, and it is at maturity.

You can also observe in Figure 13–1 that progressively higher coupon rates lead to a lower duration. As an example, go to point N on the horizontal axis and observe duration for 4 percent, 8 percent, and 12 percent interest. Clearly the higher the coupon rate, the lower the duration value.

Because the higher the duration, the greater the price sensitivity, it follows that an investor desiring maximum price movements will look toward lower coupon rate bonds. As previously demonstrated, low coupon rate and high duration go together, and high duration leads to maximum price sensitivity. The relationship of low coupon rates to price sensitivity was briefly discussed in Chapter 12 under investment strategy. We now see that the unnamed explanatory variable at that point was duration.

TABLE 13–7 Duration and Coupon Rates (25-Year Bonds)

	Coupon Rates		
Market Rate of Interest	**4 Percent**	**8 Percent**	**12 Percent**
4%	16.2470	14.2265	13.3278
6	14.7455	12.8425	12.0407
8	13.2459	11.5290	10.8396
10	11.8112	10.3229	9.7501
12	10.4912	9.2475	8.7844

FIGURE 13–1 The Effect of Coupon Rates on Duration

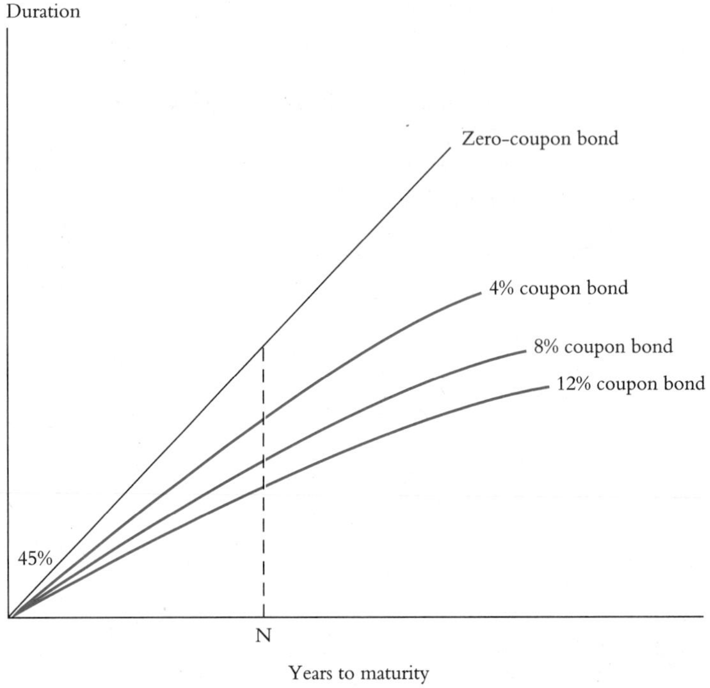

BRINGING TOGETHER THE INFLUENCES ON DURATION

The three factors that determine the value of duration are the maturity of the bond, the market rate of interest, and the coupon rate. Duration is positively correlated with maturity but moves in the opposite direction of market rates of interest and coupon rates; that is, the higher the market rate of interest or the coupon rate, the lower the duration. Earlier in this chapter, you were asked to consider whether you should invest in an 8 percent coupon rate, 20-year bond or a 12 percent coupon rate, 25-year bond. Since we were assuming interest rates were going to go down, you were looking for maximum price volatility. Had you not studied duration, you probably would have selected the bond with the longer maturity. This would generally be a valid assumption as indicated in Chapter 12. However, the primary emphasis to the sophisticated bond investor when assessing price volatility, or sensitivity, is duration.

Note that the bond with the longer maturity (25 years versus 20 years) also has a higher coupon rate (12 percent versus 8 percent). The first factor (longer maturity) would indicate higher duration, but the second factor (higher coupon rate) would indicate a lower duration. What is the net effect? The answer can be found in earlier tables in this chapter. Let's assume that the *market rate* of interest is 12 percent for both bonds. Table 13–6 presented information on 8 percent coupon rate bonds for varying maturities and market rates of interest. To determine the duration on the 8 percent coupon rate, 20-year bond, assuming a 12 percent market rate of interest, we read across the 20-year

row to the last column in the table and see the answer is 8.9390. (Note that all bonds in Table 13–6 have an 8 percent coupon rate, so we must identify the value associated with 20 years and a 12 percent market rate of interest.)

To determine the duration for the 12 percent coupon rate, 25-year bond with a 12 percent market rate of interest, we must go to Table 13–7 on page 383. Note that all bonds in this table have a 25-year maturity, so read down to a market rate of interest of 12 percent and across to a coupon rate of 12 percent. The value for duration on this bond is 8.7844.

Based on this analysis, the answer to the question posed earlier in the chapter is that the bond with the shorter maturity (8 percent coupon rate for 20 years) has a higher duration than the bond with the greater maturity (12 percent for 25 years) and thus is the most price sensitive.[5]

Bond	Duration
8%, 20 years	8.9390 ← greater price sensitivity
12%, 25 years	8.7844

In actuality, if interest rates went down by 2 percent, the 8 percent, 20-year bond would go up by 18.5 percent, while the 12 percent, 25-year bond would only increase by 17.9 percent.

DURATION AND ZERO-COUPON BONDS

Characteristics of zero-coupon bonds were briefly described in Chapter 11. As previously mentioned, Figure 13–1 depicts the duration of zero-coupon bonds as a 45-degree line relative to years to maturity. This graphically indicates that the duration of a zero-coupon bond equals the number of years it has to maturity. For all bonds of equal risk and maturity, the zero-coupon bond has the greatest duration and therefore the greatest price sensitivity. This price risk is one that is often lost in the image of safety that zero-coupons have when backed by U.S. government securities.

A headline in *The Wall Street Journal* on June 1, 1984, appeared as follows: "Zero-Coupon Bonds' Price Swings Jolt Investors Looking for Security."[6] It was reported that between March 31, 1983, and March 31, 1984, Salomon Brothers' 30-year CATs declined 25 percent in price, while returns on conventional 30-year government bonds declined only a few percentage points. The article cited one client buying $100,000 of zero coupons, thinking they were similar to short-term Treasury bill investments, only to find out four weeks later that his zero-coupon bonds had declined in value by $24,000.

To put the volatility of a zero-coupon bond into better perspective, we compare the duration of a zero-coupon bond to that of an 8 percent coupon bond for several maturities in Table 13–8 on page 386.

---

[5] As previously indicated, if we vary the market rate of interest, we can also influence the outcome to our question.

[6] Randall Smith, "Zero-Coupon Bonds' Price Swings Jolt Investors Looking for Security," *The Wall Street Journal,* June 1, 1984, p. 19.

TABLE 13–8 Duration of Zero-Coupon versus 8 Percent Coupon Bonds (Market Rate of Interest is 12 Percent)

(1) Years to Maturity	(2) Duration of Zero-Coupon Bond	(3) Duration of 8 Percent Coupon Bond	(4) Relative Duration of Zero-Coupon to 8 Percent Coupon Bonds (2) ÷ (3)
10	10	6.8374	1.4625
20	20	8.9390	2.2374
30	30	9.3662	3.2030
40	40	9.3972	4.2566
50	50	9.3716	5.3353

The far right column in Table 13–8 indicates the ratio of duration between zero-coupon and 8 percent coupon rate bonds. As stressed throughout the chapter, duration represents a measure of price sensitivity. Thus, for a 10-year maturity period, a zero-coupon bond is almost 1½ times as price sensitive as an 8 percent coupon rate bond (the ratio in the last column is 1.4625). For a 20-year maturity period, it is over two times more price sensitive (2.2374), and for 50 years the price sensitivity ratio is over five times greater (5.3353). This might explain why zero-coupons were much more sensitive to rising interest rates during 1983–84 as described in the story in *The Wall Street Journal.* Of course, tremendous profits can be made in zero-coupon bonds when there is a sharp drop in interest rates as in early 1985 and again in 1991–92.

THE USES OF DURATION

Duration is primarily used as a measure to judge bond price sensitivity to interest-rate changes. Since duration includes information on several variables (maturity, coupon rate, and market rate of interest), it captures more information than any one of them. It therefore allows more accurate decisions for complex bond strategies. One such strategy involves the timing of investment inflows to provide a needed cash outlay at a known future date. Perhaps $1 million is needed after five years. Everything is tailored to this five-year time horizon. If interest rates go up, there will be a decline in the value of the portfolio but a higher reinvestment rate opportunity for inflows. Similarly, if interest rates go down, there will be capital appreciation for the portfolio but a lower reinvestment rate opportunity. By tying all the investment decisions to a duration period, the portfolio manager can take advantage of these counter forces to ensure a necessary outcome. This strategy is called **immunization** and is used by insurance companies, pension funds, and other institutional money managers to protect their portfolios against swings in interest rates. For a more comprehensive discussion of immunization strategies, an article by Fisher and Weil is an appropriate source.[7] For an excellent criticism of duration and

[7] Lawrence Fisher and Roman L. Weil, "Coping with Risk of Interest Rate Fluctuations: Returns to Bondholders from Naive and Optimal Strategies," *Journal of Business,* October 1971, pp. 408–31.

immunization strategy, see Yawitz and Marshall.[8] One of the problems with duration analysis is that it often assumes a parallel shift in yield curves. Although long-duration bonds are clearly more price sensitive than shorter-duration bonds, there is no assurance that long- and short-term interest rates will move by equal amounts.

BOND REINVESTMENT ASSUMPTIONS AND TERMINAL WEALTH ANALYSIS

Reinvestment Assumptions

As indicated in the previous section, one concern an investor may have when purchasing bonds is that the interest income will not be reinvested to earn the same return the coupon payment represents. This may not be a problem for an individual consuming the interest payments, but it could be a serious concern for individuals building a retirement portfolio or a pension fund manager accumulating funds for future payout to retirees. The crucial issue is the amount of money accumulated at the time the retirement fund will be used to cover living expenses. One major determinant of the ending value of a retirement fund is the rate of return on coupon payments as they are reinvested.

Since the late 1960s, interest rates have generally been higher and more volatile than during previous periods. This has caused more emphasis on the management of fixed-income securities, not only in the selection of maturity but also in the switching from short- to long-term securities. These volatile high rates have caused more emphasis on concepts such as duration to measure bond price sensitivity and on total return as a measure of bond management success. Given that interest rates change daily and by large amounts over a year, what impact would a lower or higher **reinvestment assumption** have on the outcome of your retirement nest egg?

First, let us look at a partial reproduction of Appendix A at the back of the text (reproduced in Table 13–9). The material covers the compound sum of $1. Appendix A assumes all interest is reinvested at the stated rate in order to find the ending value of $1 invested to maturity. For our current analysis, we are assuming annual interest (though the answer changes only slightly if we use semiannual interest).

The table values are given in $1 amounts, so for a $1,000 bond we would just move the decimal three places to the right. A $1,000 bond having a 12 percent coupon rate with

TABLE 13–9 Compound Sum of $1.00 (From Appendix A)

Period	7 Percent	8 Percent	9 Percent	10 Percent	11 Percent	12 Percent
10	$ 1.967	$ 2.159	$ 2.367	$ 2.594	$ 2.839	$ 3.106
20	3.870	4.661	5.604	6.727	8.062	9.646
30	7.612	10.063	13.268	17.449	22.892	29.960
40	14.974	21.725	31.409	45.259	65.001	93.051

[8] Jess B. Yawitz and William J. Marshall, "The Shortcomings of Duration as a Risk Measure for Bonds," *Journal of Financial Research,* Summer 1981, pp. 91–101.

interest being reinvested at 12 percent would compound to $93,051 over 40 years, while a 7 percent coupon bond reinvested at 7 percent would compound to only $14,974 over a similar period. A difference of 5 points in the rates creates a total difference of $78,077. This is quite a large difference. Notice that the longer the compounding period, the larger the amount. From further inspection of Table 13–9, other comparisons can be made between years and total ending values.

The importance of the reinvestment assumption can also be viewed from the perspective of its contribution to total wealth. For example, an investor owning a 40-year bond with a 12 percent coupon rate and an assumed reinvestment rate of 12 percent will have an accumulated value of $93,051. In terms of payout, $4,800 (40 × $120) comes directly from 40 years of 12 percent interest payments, $1,000 comes from principal, and the balance of $87,251 comes from interest that is earned on the annual interest payments. In this case, interest on interest represents 93.8 percent of the overall return ($87,251/ $93,051).

Terminal Wealth Analysis

Now, we will assume a reinvestment assumption different from the coupon rate. Take the two extreme values from Table 13–9 of 12 percent and 7 percent. Assume you buy a bond having a 12 percent coupon rate, but the interest can only be reinvested at 7 percent. To find the ending value of this investment, we will need to use a **terminal wealth table.**

Table 13–10 is called a terminal wealth table because it generates the ending value of the investment at the end of each year, assuming the bond has a *maturity* date corresponding to that year. Let's use 10 years as an example in examining Table 13–10. If the bond matures in 10 years, the $1,000 principal in column (2) will be recovered. Also the investor will receive $120 in annual interest (12 percent of $1,000) in year 10 as indicated in column (3). In column (4), the accumulated interest up to the *beginning* of year 10 is shown. The reinvestment rate on this previously accumulated interest is a mere 7 percent as indicated in column (5). The interest on the previously accumulated interest is $100.62 (0.07 × $1,437.38). Finally, the total interest for year 10 is shown in column (7). This consists of the coupon interest of $120 and the interest on interest of $100.62 and totals to $220.62. The total ending value of the portfolio is shown in column (8). The ending value consists of the recovered principal of $1,000 plus the accumulated interest of $1,437.38 up to the beginning of year 10 plus the total interest paid in year 10 of $220.62. The ending wealth value (portfolio sum) thus shown in column (8) is $2,658.00. The value is summarized below.

Recovered principal	$1,000.00	Column (2)
Accumulated interest (beginning of year 10)	1,437.38	Column (4)
Total annual interest (during year 10)	220.62	Column (7)
Ending wealth value (portfolio sum)	$2,658.00	Column (8)

A $1,000 investment that grows to $2,658.00 after 10 years is the equivalent of a $1 investment that grows to 2.65800 as indicated in column (9). The annual percentage

TABLE 13–10 Terminal Wealth Table (12 Percent Coupon with 7 Percent Reinvestment Rate on Interest)

(1) Years to Maturity	(2) Principal	(3) Annual Coupon Interest	(4) Accumulated Interest*	(5) Reinvestment Rate on Interest	(6) Interest on Interest	(7) Total Annual Interest	(8) Portfolio Sum	(9) Compound Sum Factor	(10) Annual Percentage Return
0.0	$1,000.00								
1.0	1,000.00	$120.00	$ 0.00			$ 120.00	$ 1,120.00	1.12000	12.00%
2.0	1,000.00	120.00	120.00	0.07	$ 8.40	128.40	1,248.40	1.24840	11.73
3.0	1,000.00	120.00	248.40	0.07	17.39	137.39	1,385.79	1.38579	11.48
4.0	1,000.00	120.00	385.79	0.07	27.01	147.01	1,532.80	1.53280	11.26
5.0	1,000.00	120.00	532.80	0.07	37.30	157.30	1,690.10	1.69010	11.06
6.0	1,000.00	120.00	690.10	0.07	48.31	168.31	1,858.41	1.85841	10.86
7.0	1,000.00	120.00	858.41	0.07	60.90	180.09	2,038.50	2.03850	10.71
8.0	1,000.00	120.00	1,038.50	0.07	72.70	192.70	2,231.20	2.23120	10.55
9.0	1,000.00	120.00	1,231.20	0.07	86.18	206.18	2,437.38	2.43738	10.40
10.0	1,000.00	120.00	1,437.38	0.07	100.62	220.62	2,658.00	2.65800	10.26
11.0	1,000.00	120.00	1,658.00	0.07	116.06	236.06	2,894.06	2.89406	10.14
12.0	1,000.00	120.00	1,894.06	0.07	132.58	252.58	3,146.64	3.14664	10.02
13.0	1,000.00	120.00	2,146.64	0.07	150.26	270.26	3,416.90	3.41690	9.91
14.0	1,000.00	120.00	2,416.90	0.07	169.18	289.18	3,706.08	3.70608	9.80
15.0	1,000.00	120.00	2,706.08	0.07	189.43	309.43	4,015.51	4.01551	9.71
16.0	1,000.00	120.00	3,015.51	0.07	211.09	331.09	4,346.60	4.34660	9.61
17.0	1,000.00	120.00	3,346.60	0.07	234.26	354.26	4,700.86	4.70086	9.54
18.0	1,000.00	120.00	3,700.86	0.07	259.06	379.06	5,079.92	5.07992	9.44
19.0	1,000.00	120.00	4,079.92	0.07	285.59	405.59	5,485.51	5.48551	9.37
20.0	1,000.00	120.00	4,485.51	0.07	313.99	433.99	5,919.50	5.91950	9.29
21.0	1,000.00	120.00	4,919.50	0.07	344.37	464.37	6,383.87	6.38387	9.22
22.0	1,000.00	120.00	5,383.87	0.07	376.87	496.87	6,880.74	6.88074	9.16
23.0	1,000.00	120.00	5,880.74	0.07	411.65	531.65	7,412.39	7.41239	9.09
24.0	1,000.00	120.00	6,412.39	0.07	448.87	568.87	7,981.26	7.98126	9.04
25.0	1,000.00	120.00	6,981.26	0.07	488.69	608.69	8,589.95	8.58995	8.98
26.0	1,000.00	120.00	7,589.95	0.07	531.30	651.30	9,241.25	9.24125	8.92
27.0	1,000.00	120.00	8,241.25	0.07	576.89	696.89	9,938.14	9.93814	8.87
28.0	1,000.00	120.00	8,938.14	0.07	625.67	745.67	10,683.81	10.68381	8.82
29.0	1,000.00	120.00	9,683.81	0.07	677.87	797.87	11,481.68	11.48168	8.78
30.0	1,000.00	120.00	10,481.68	0.07	733.72	853.72	12,335.40	12.33540	8.73
31.0	1,000.00	120.00	11,335.40	0.07	793.48	913.48	13,248.88	13.24888	8.69
32.0	1,000.00	120.00	12,248.88	0.07	857.42	977.42	14,226.30	14.22630	8.65
33.0	1,000.00	120.00	13,226.30	0.07	925.84	1,045.84	15,272.14	15.27214	8.61
34.0	1,000.00	120.00	14,272.14	0.07	999.05	1,119.05	16,391.19	16.39119	8.57
35.0	1,000.00	120.00	15,391.19	0.07	1,077.38	1,197.38	17,588.57	17.58857	8.53
36.0	1,000.00	120.00	16,588.57	0.07	1,161.20	1,281.20	18,869.77	18.86977	8.50
37.0	1,000.00	120.00	17,869.77	0.07	1,250.88	1,370.88	20,240.65	20.24065	8.46
38.0	1,000.00	120.00	19,240.65	0.07	1,346.85	1,466.85	21,707.50	21.70750	8.43
39.0	1,000.00	120.00	20,707.50	0.07	1,449.53	1,569.53	23,277.03	23.27703	8.40
40.0	1,000.00	120.00	22,277.03	0.07	1,559.39	1,679.39	24,956.42	24.95642	8.37

*At beginning of year.

return for a $1 investment that grows to 2.65800 after 10 years is 10.26 percent as indicated in column (10).

A similar analysis can be done for all other maturity periods running from 1 to 40 years. One thing to notice from Table 13–10 is that the longer the maturity period of the bond, the greater the effect the low 7 percent reinvestment rate has on the bond. For 5 years, the annual percentage return (column 10) is 11.06 percent; for 15 years, 9.71 percent; and for 40 years, 8.37 percent.

What is the actual difference between the ending value for a 40-year, 12 percent coupon rate bond assuming a *12 percent* reinvestment rate and the 40-year, *7 percent* reinvestment rate just presented in Table 13–10? Earlier in this section Table 13–9 demonstrated that a 12 percent coupon rate bond with an assumed 12 percent reinvestment rate for 40 years would grow to $93,051. In Table 13–10, we see that a 12 percent coupon rate bond with a 7 percent reinvestment rate will grow to only $24,956.42 after 40 years. It should be evident that it is not only the coupon rate that matters but the reinvestment rate as well.

If the bond were not held to maturity in our analysis, then we would have to rely on the realized rate of return analysis developed in Chapter 12. The realized rate of return approach would assume that the bond is not held to maturity and that it is sold at either a gain or a loss. In the case of the bond analyzed in the terminal wealth table (Table 13–10), we know that since interest rates are assumed to decline, any sale of the bond before maturity should result in a capital gain. How large that capital gain would be will be dependent on its duration. Terminal wealth analysis is a way of analyzing the reinvestment assumption when bonds are held to maturity, while the realized yield approach assumes bonds are actively traded to take advantage of interest-rate swings.

Zero-Coupon Bonds and Terminal Wealth

One of the benefits of zero-coupon bonds is that they lock in a compound rate of return (or reinvestment rate) for the life of the bond *if held to maturity.* There are no coupon payments during the life of the bond to be reinvested, so the originally quoted rate holds throughout if held to maturity. If a $1,000 par value, 15-year zero-coupon bond is quoted at a price of $183 to yield 12 percent, you truly have locked in a 12 percent reinvestment rate. Some would say you have not only locked in 12 percent but have thrown away the key. In any event, zero-coupon bonds allow you to predetermine your reinvestment rate.

Of course, if a zero-coupon bond is sold before maturity, there could be large swings in the sales price of the bond because of its high duration characteristics. Under this circumstance, the locked-in reinvestment concept for the zero-coupon bond loses much of its meaning. It is valid only when the zero-coupon bond is held to maturity.

SUMMARY

In Chapter 13, we have taken the concepts developed in Chapter 12 and expanded on the principles of bond price volatility and total return. We developed the concept of duration so that the student has a basic understanding of its meaning and some of its applications. In general, we have shown that duration is the number of years, on a present-value basis, that it takes to recover an initial investment in

a bond. More specifically, each year is weighted by the present value of the cash flow as a proportion of the present value of the bond, and is then summed. The higher the duration, the more sensitive the bond price is to a change in interest rates. Duration as one number captures the three variables—maturity, coupon rate, and market rate of interest—to indicate the price sensitivities of bonds with unequal characteristics. Generally, bond duration increases with the increase in number of years to maturity. Duration also increases as coupon rates decline to zero, and finally, duration declines as market interest rates increase.

Zero-coupon bonds are highlighted as the most price sensitive of bonds to a change in market interest rates, and comparisons are made between zero-coupon bonds and coupon bonds. Duration's primary use is in explaining price volatility, but it also has applications in the insurance industry and other areas of investments where interest-rate risk can be reduced by matching duration with predictable cash outflows in a process called immunization.

An important concept has to do with the reinvestment of interest at rates other than the coupon rate. The method used to explain the effect on the total return is terminal wealth analysis, which assumes that the investment is held to maturity and that all proceeds over the life of the bond are reinvested at the reinvestment rate. In general, the longer the maturity, the more total annualized return approaches the reinvestment rate. If the reinvestment rate is significantly different from the coupon rate, the annualized return can differ greatly from the coupon rate in as little as five years.

KEY WORDS AND CONCEPTS

weighted average life, 376
duration, 377
immunization, 386
reinvestment assumption, 387
terminal wealth table, 388

DISCUSSION QUESTIONS

1. Why is the weighted average life of a bond less than the maturity date?
2. Define duration.
3. How can duration be used to determine a rough measure of the percentage change in the price of a bond as a result of interest-rate changes?
4. Comment on the statement, "It is possible that a bond with a shorter maturity than another bond may actually have a longer duration and be more price sensitive to interest-rate changes." Explain why a bond with a shorter maturity than another bond could have a longer duration.
5. As market rates of interest become higher, what impact does this have on duration?
6. What happens to duration as the coupon rate on a bond issue declines from 12 percent to 0 percent with the maturity date remaining constant?
7. Why are the maturity date and duration the same for a zero-coupon bond?
8. Should an investor who thinks interest rates are going down seek low or high coupon rate bonds? Relate your answer to duration and price sensitivity.

9. Why are zero-coupon bonds the most price sensitive of any type of bond issue?
10. Why is the reinvestment rate assumption critical to bond portfolio management?
11. What is a terminal wealth table? How is terminal wealth analysis different from the realized yield approach in Chapter 12?
12. Why is it said that zero-coupon bonds lock in the reinvestment rate?
13. Is the locked-in reinvestment assumption valid for zero-coupon bonds if they are sold before maturity? Explain.

PROBLEMS

Weighted average life

1. Compute the simple weighted average life for the following data. Use an approach similar to that in Table 13–1.

Year	Cash Flow
1	$ 105
2	105
3	105
4	105
5	105
5	1,000

Duration

2. Compute the duration for the data in problem 1. Use an approach similar to that in Table 13–2. A discount rate of 13 percent should be applied.

Price sensitivity

3. As part of the your answer to problem 2, you computed the price of the bond (column 4). This is the same as the PV of cash flows in column 4.
   a. Recompute the price of a bond based on an 11 percent discount rate (market rate of interest).
   b. What is the percentage change in the price of the bond as interest rates decline by 2 percent from 13 percent to 11 percent?
   c. Approximate this same value by multiplying the duration computed in problem 2 times the change in interest rates (2 percent). The answer in part *c* should come reasonably close to the answer in part *b*. However, they will not be exactly the same.

Comparative duration

4. **a.** Compute the duration for the following data. Use a discount rate of 13 percent.

Year	Cash Flow
1	$50
2	50
3	50
4	50
5	50
5	1,000

b. Explain why the answer to part *a* is higher than the answer to problem 2.

c. If in part *a* the discount rate were 10 percent rather than 13 percent, would duration be longer or shorter? You do not need to actually compute a value; merely indicate an answer based on the discussion material in the text.

Comparative duration

5. You are considering the purchase of two $1,000 bonds. Your expectation is that interest rates will drop, and you want to buy the bond that provides the maximum capital gains potential. The first bond has a coupon rate of 6 percent with four years to maturity, while the second has a coupon rate of 14 percent and comes due six years from now. The market rate of interest (discount rate) is 8 percent. Which bond has the best price movement potential? Use duration to answer the question.

Comparative duration

6. Ted Bear thinks that recent Federal Reserve policy is going to push interest rates up. He is considering keeping only one of the three bonds in his portfolio. He knows that bond A has a duration of 5.3128, bond B has a duration of 3.2056, and bond C has the following characteristics:

Par Value	$1,000
Life	4 years
Coupon rate	5 percent
Discount rate	10 percent

Which one of the three bonds should he keep?

Comparative duration

7. Assume you desire maximum duration to take advantage of anticipated interest-rate declines. Answer the following questions based on information taken from Tables 13–6 and 13–7.

a. Would you prefer an 8 percent coupon rate bond with a 20-year maturity or a 4 percent coupon rate bond with a 25-year maturity? The market rate of interest is 12 percent.

b. Would you prefer an 8 percent coupon rate bond with a 20-year maturity or a 12 percent coupon rate bond with a 25-year maturity? The market rate of interest is 12 percent.

c. Would you prefer an 8 percent coupon rate bond with a 20-year maturity or a 12 percent coupon rate bond with a 25-year maturity? The market rate of interest is 8 percent.

Zero-coupon bond and duration

8. A 30-year, $1,000 par value zero-coupon bond provides a yield of 11 percent.

a. Compute the current price of the zero-coupon bond. (**Hint:** Simply take the present value of the ending $1,000 payment.)

b. What is the duration of the bond?

c. Does the bond have a longer or shorter duration than a 50-year, 8 percent coupon rate bond, where the duration on the latter bond is based on a 12 percent market rate of interest (consult Table 13–6).

d. Assume you were going to put the zero-coupon bond(s) from part *a* in a nontaxable individual retirement account. If you wish to have $30,000 after 30 years, how much would you need to invest today?

e. If a $1,000 par value zero-coupon rate bond had a 40-year maturity and provided a yield of 13 percent, what would be the current price of the zero-coupon bond?

Return on zero-coupon bond

9. Assume you buy a 20-year, $1,000 par value zero-coupon rate bond that provides a 10 percent yield. Almost immediately after you buy the bond, yields go down to 8 percent.

a. What will be your dollar gain on the investment?

b. What will be your percentage gain?

Reinvestment assumption

10. You have invested $1,000 in a 13 percent coupon bond that matures in five years. This bond is held in your individual retirement account, and you are not concerned about tax consequences. You are investing the interest income in a money market fund earning 8 percent. At the end of five years, what will be your portfolio sum? Follow the procedure in Table 13–10 (first eight columns).

Annual return with reinvestment assumption

11. In problem 10, what is the annual percentage return? Use Appendix A near the end of the book to help you find the answer. An approximation will be sufficient.

CFA MATERIAL

The following material contains sample questions and solutions from a prior Level I CFA exam. While the terminology is slightly different from that in this text, you can still view the skills that are necessary for the CFA exam.

CFA Exam Question

Question 7 is composed of two parts, for a total of 10 minutes.

7. You are asked to consider the following bond for possible inclusion in your company's fixed-income portfolio:

Issuer	Coupon	Yield to Maturity	Maturity	Duration
Wiser Company	8%	8%	10 Years	7.25 years

a. **I.** Explain why the Wiser bond's duration is less than its maturity.

II. Explain whether a bond's duration or its maturity is a better measure of the bond's sensitivity to changes in interest rates.
(4 minutes)

b. Briefly explain the impact on the duration of the Wiser Company bond under *each* of the following conditions:

I. The coupon is 4 percent rather than 8 percent.

II. The yield to maturity is 4 percent rather than 8 percent.

III. The maturity is 7 years rather than 10 years.
(6 minutes)

Solution: Question 7—Morning Section (10 points)

a. **I.** The Wiser bond's duration is less than its maturity because some of the bond's cash flow payments (i.e., the coupons) occur before maturity. Since duration measures the weighted average time until cash flow payment, its duration is less than its maturity. Bond duration is defined as

$$D = \frac{\sum_{t=1}^{N} PVCF_t \times t}{\sum_{t=1}^{N} PVCF_t}$$

II. For coupon bonds, duration is a better measure of the bond's sensitivity to changes in interest rates. Using the bond's maturity is deficient as a benchmark because it measures only when the final cash flow is paid and ignores all of the interim flows. Duration is a better measure because it measures the weighted average time until cash flow and thus is a more representative measure of the bond's overall cash flow sensitivity to interest-rate changes. Duration takes into account coupon (inverse relationship) and yield to maturity (inverse relationship) as well as time to maturity.

b. **I.** Duration will increase. As the coupon decreases, a proportionately higher weight is given to the redemption payment, and therefore, the duration increases.

II. Duration will increase. As rates decline, all of the cash flows increase in value, but the longest ones increase at the greatest rate. Therefore, the redemption payment has much greater effect, causing the duration to increase.

III. Duration will decrease. The elapsing of time is accompanied by the reduction of total coupon payments and the shortening of time until the redemption payment. Therefore, because the redemption payment comes sooner, the duration decreases.

THE WALL STREET JOURNAL PROJECT

Go to "Treasury Bonds, Notes and Bills" in Section C of *The Wall Street Journal.* Take a Treasury note (toward the bottom of the first column) with a maturity of five years from the current month, and calculate its duration. The annual cash flow can be found by taking the coupon rate in the left column and multiplying it by $1,000. Assume the final payment is $1,000. The discount rate is the "Ask Yield" in the right column (round it to the nearest whole number).

After you have found the duration, assume interest rates will go down 2 percent in the near future. Approximate how much the price of the Treasury note will rise.

SELECTED REFERENCES

Duration and Price Volatility

Babcock, Guilford C. "Duration as a Link between Yield and Value." *Journal of Portfolio Management,* Summer 1984, pp. 58–65.

Hopewell, Michael H., and George G. Kaufman. "Bond Price Volatility and Term to Maturity: A Generalized Respecification." *American Economic Review,* September 1973, pp. 749–53.

Applications of Duration

Arak, Marcelle; Laurie S. Goodman; and Joseph Snailer. "Duration Equivalent Bond Swaps: A New Tool." *Journal of Portfolio Management,* Summer 1986, pp. 26–32.

Bierwag, G. O., and George G. Kaufmann. "Durations of Non-Default-Free Securities." *Financial Analysts Journal,* July–August 1988, pp. 39–46.

Dunetz, Mark L., and James M. Mahoney. "Using Duration and Convexity in the Analysis of Callable Bonds." *Financial Analysts Journal,* May–June 1988, pp. 53–72.

Nawalkha, Sanjoy K. "Convexity of Bonds with Special Cash Flow Streams." *Financial Analysts Journal,* January–February 1991, pp. 80–87.

Reilly, Frank K., and Rupindner S. Sidha. "The Many Uses of Bond Duration." *Financial Analysts Journal,* July–August 1980, pp. 58–72.

Yawitz, Jess B., and William J. Marshall. "The Use of Futures in Immunized Portfolios." *Journal of Portfolio Management,* Winter 1985, pp. 51–58.

Shortcomings in the Use of Duration Analysis

Yawitz, Jess B., and William J. Marshall, "The Shortcomings of Duration as a Risk Measure for Bonds." *Journal of Financial Research,* Summer 1981, pp. 91–101.

The Reinvestment Assumption

Bernstein, Peter L. "How to Take Reinvestment Risk without Really Trying." *Journal of Portfolio Management,* Spring 1984, p. 4.

14

Convertible Securities and Warrants

An investment in convertible securities or warrants offers the market participant special opportunities to meet investment objectives. For conservative investors, convertible securities can offer regular income and potential downside protection against falling stock prices. Convertibles also offer capital gains opportunities for an investor desiring the appreciation potential of an equity investment. Warrants are more speculative securities than convertibles and also offer the chance for leveraged returns.

These securities have been used as financing alternatives by corporations in periods of high interest rates or tight money. Also, convertibles have been utilized as a medium of exchange for acquiring other companies' stock in mergers and acquisitions. Convertibles and warrants have advantages to the corporation and to the owner of the security. It is important to realize as we go through this chapter that what is an advantage to the corporation is often a disadvantage to the investor, and vice versa. These securities involve trade-offs between the buyer and the corporation that are considered in the pricing of each security.

CONVERTIBLE SECURITIES

A **convertible security** is a bond or share of preferred stock that can be converted into common stock at the option of the holder. Thus, the owner has a fixed-income security that can be transferred to common stock if and when the performance of the firm indicates such a conversion is desirable.

For this discussion, we will use a Telxon 7.5 percent convertible bond. (Note that the firm's name is pronounced "Telzon.") Telxon makes hand-held computers that are used to take inventory based on bar codes. You have probably seen them used by employees in grocery stores. The company has had an extremely volatile existence in sales, profits, and stock prices with a high stock price of $28.50 and a low stock price of $4.75. The Telxon convertible security was originally a 25-year long-term bond, and it demonstrates the benefits and perils of owning any convertible security. During the first 30 months of its existence (June 1, 1987, through December 15, 1989) the price of the convertible bond ranged between $1,000 and $555.

In general, the best time to buy convertible bonds is when interest rates are high (bond prices are depressed) and when stock prices are relatively low. A purchase at times like these increases the probability of a successful investment because rising stock prices and falling interest rates both exert upward pressure on the price of a convertible security. This will become more apparent as we proceed through the chapter.

CONVERSION PRICE AND CONVERSION RATIO

The Telxon annual report states that this 7.5 percent convertible bond is a subordinated bond with a sinking fund and is due June 1, 2012. One bond is convertible into shares of common stock of the company at a conversion price of $26.75 per share. The bonds are redeemable by the company at a premium over par of 2.5 percent in 1995, 1.5 percent in 1996, 0.75 percent in 1997, and at par value of $1,000 thereafter.

While there is standard information about the coupon being 7.5 percent and the maturity date being June 1, 2012, one piece of information is not answered directly. How many shares of common stock are you entitled to receive on conversion? The annual

report states that the bonds are convertible at $26.75 per share. This is called the **conversion price.**

The face value ($1,000) or par value never changes (the market price does), so by dividing the face value by the conversion price, we get the number of shares received on conversion of one $1,000 bond. This is called the **conversion ratio:**

$$\frac{\text{Face value}}{\text{Conversion price}} = \text{Conversion ratio} \qquad (14\text{–}1)$$

For the Telxon convertible bond, an investor would receive 37.38 shares for each bond:

$$\frac{1{,}000 \text{ (Face value)}}{\$26.75 \text{ per share (Conversion price)}} = 37.38 \text{ shares}$$

Value of the Convertible Bond

The Telxon bond was originally sold at $1,000, and the common stock price on the New York Stock Exchange on the day of this offering closed at $22. If the bondholder converted the bond into 37.38 shares of common stock, what would be the market value of the common stock received? We can find this by multiplying the conversion ratio by the market price per share of the common stock, and we get a value of $822.36, which we round to $822:

$$\text{Conversion ratio} \times \text{Common stock price} = \text{Conversion value} \qquad (14\text{–}2)$$

$$37.38 \text{ shares} \times \$22 = \$822.36$$

This value is called the **conversion value** and indicates the value of the underlying shares of common stock each bond represents.

The convertible bond also has what is called a **pure bond value.** This represents its value as a straight bond (nonconvertible). In the case of Telxon, straight bonds of similar risk (B2 rating) had a yield to maturity of about 13 percent at the time of issue. A rating of B2 is considered a high-yield bond (junk bond), and considerable risk is associated with the 13 percent yield to maturity. If the Telxon 7.5 percent convertible bond were valued at 13 percent yield to maturity, the pure bond value would be $596.[1] This pure bond value is considered the **floor value,** or minimum value, of the bond. The conversion value and the pure bond value can be seen in Figure 14–1 on page 400, which depicts the Telxon convertible bond. You should be aware that it is possible for the pure bond value to change if interest rates change. In other words, the pure bond value will be inversely related to changes in interest rates just like any other fixed-income security. This point is not reflected in Figure 14–1.

In examining Figure 14–1, you can see that the market price of the bond will not go below the pure bond value regardless of what happens to the price of the common stock. If the stock price went down to $10 and the conversion value fell to $373.80 ($10 × 37.38 shares), the market value of the bond would at least equal its pure bond value of $596.

[1] Using present value procedures or a calculator, the pure bond value comes out to be $596 for a bond with 25 years to maturity and a yield to maturity of 12.98 percent. We rounded to 13 percent in the text.

FIGURE 14–1

Telxon 7.5 Percent Convertible Bond on Day of Issue (June 1, 1987)

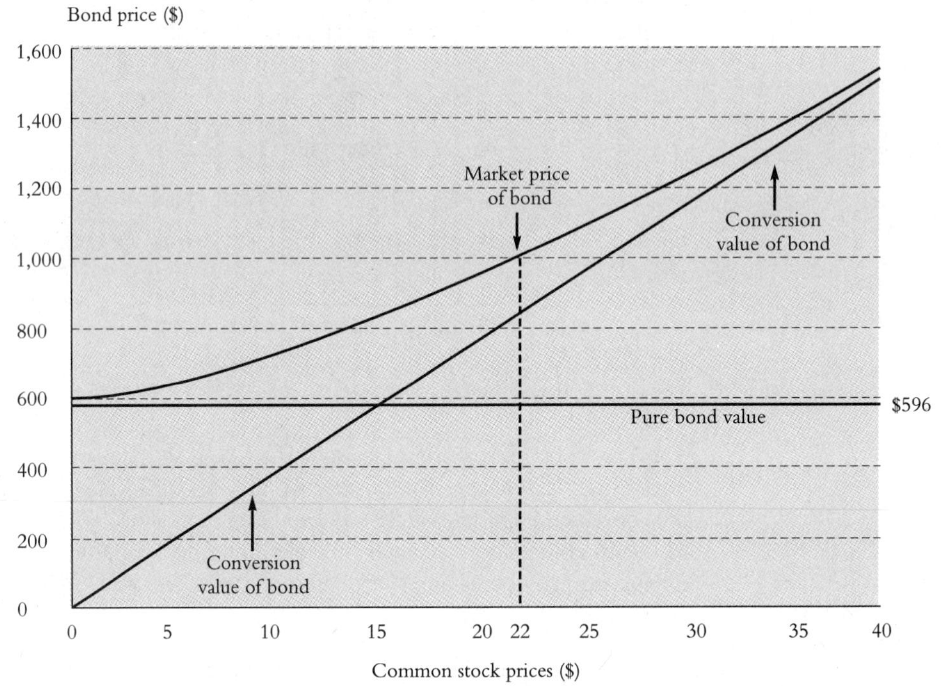

The convertibility of the bond loses much of its meaning at low stock prices, and the pure bond value is the controlling factor on price. Of course, if the common stock goes up to $35 or $40 per share, the market price of the bond will approach $1,500 because of the conversion feature. At a high bond price, the pure bond value of $596 loses much of its meaning. When a bond is selling at $1,500, it is little comfort to know the bond has a pure bond value or floor price of $596. You would lose $904 before the bond got down to the floor price.

In summary, you can see in Figure 14–1 that if the stock price is low or declining, pure bond value is very important in determining the bond price. When stock prices are booming, the conversion value is the controlling factor. The bond's minimum price will always be the pure bond value or the conversion value, whichever has the highest price.

Bond Price and Premiums

You may wonder how a company can originally sell a bond for $1,000 with both a conversion value of $822 (rounded) and a pure bond value of $596. Let's examine these values. The difference between the bond's market price ($1,000) and the conversion value ($822) is a premium of $178; it is usually expressed as a percentage of the conversion value and thus is called the **conversion premium.** In this case, the conversion premium at issue was 21.65 percent:

$$\text{Conversion premium} = \frac{\text{Market price of bond} - \text{Conversion value}}{\text{Conversion value}} \tag{14–3}$$

$$= \frac{\$1{,}000 - 822}{\$822} = \frac{\$178}{\$822}$$

$$= 21.65\%$$

The $178 premium indicates the extra amount paid for the 37.38 shares of stock. Remember, in essence, you paid $26.75 per share for 37.38 shares by purchasing the bond at $1,000; you could have had the same number of shares purchased on the NYSE for $22 and had $178 in cash left. Instead, the investor buying the convertible security paid a premium for the benefits offered by this type of security.

People pay the conversion premium for several reasons. In the case of Telxon's convertible bond, the premium is about the usual 20 percent. First, at the time, Telxon common stock paid $0.01 per share in dividends ($0.01 × 37.38) or approximately $0.37 per year for 37.38 shares. The bond paid $75 per year. If the bondholder owns the bond for approximately 2.5 years, he recovers the premium through the differential between interest and dividend income. This analysis of interest income versus dividend income is always important in comparing a stock purchase with a convertible bond purchase.

Additionally, the bond price will rise as the stock price rises because of the convertible feature, but there is a downside limit if the stock should decline in price. This **downside limit** is established by the pure bond value, which in this case is $596. This downside protection is further justification for the conversion premium. One way to compute this downside protection is to calculate the difference between the market price of the bond and pure bond value as a percentage of the market price. We call this measure **downside risk.**

$$\text{Downside risk} = \frac{\text{Market price of bond} - \text{Pure bond value}}{\text{Market price of bond}} \tag{14–4}$$

$$= \frac{\$1{,}000 - 596}{\$1{,}000} = \frac{\$404}{\$1{,}000}$$

$$= 40.4\%$$

Telxon has a downside risk of 40.4 percent, which is the maximum percentage the bond will decline in value if the stock price falls. One important warning is necessary—the pure bond value is sensitive to market interest rates. As competitively rated B2 bond interest rates rise, the pure bond value will decline. Therefore, downside risk can vary with changing interest rates.

The conversion premium is also affected by several other variables. The more volatile the stock price as measured by beta or standard deviation of returns, the higher the conversion premium. This occurs because the potential for capital gains is larger than on less volatile stocks. The longer the term to maturity, the higher the premium—because there is a greater chance the stock price could rise, making the bond more valuable.

Figure 14–2 on page 402 presents two graphs of the Telxon convertible bond and depicts the conversion premium in panel (*a*) and the downside risk in panel (*b*). Note in panel (*a*)

FIGURE 14–2 Telxon Convertible Bond—7.5 Percent, 2012 Maturity (Convertible into 37.38 shares of common stock)

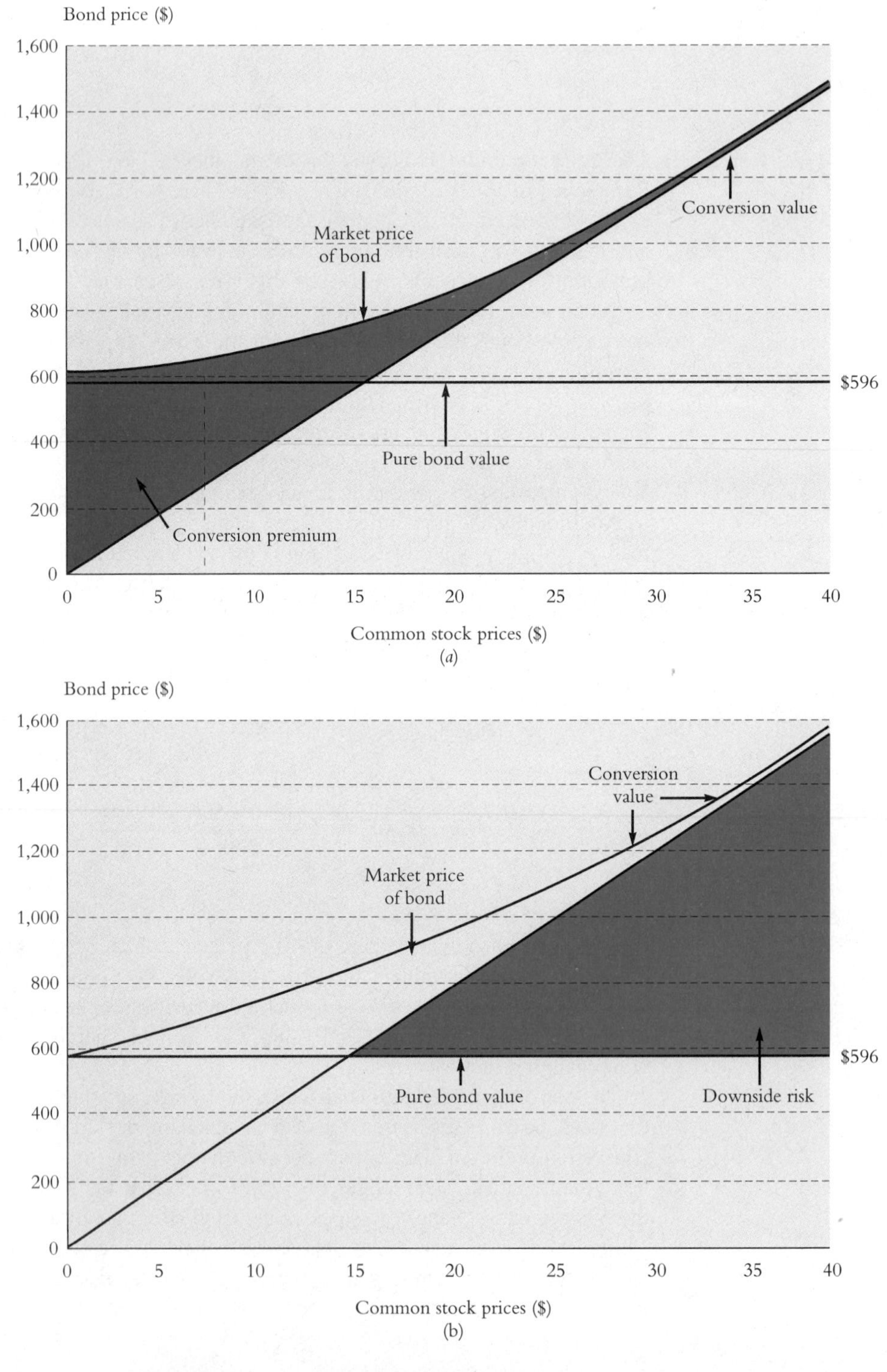

TABLE 14–1 Telxon Convertible Bond Price Performance—7.5 Percent, 2012 Maturity

	June 1, 1987	December 15, 1989	October 17, 1994
Market price of bonds	$1,000.00	$555.00	$865.00
Common stock price	$ 22.00	$ 7.50	$13.00
Conversion ratio	37.38	37.38	37.38
Conversion value	$ 822.36	$280.35	$485.94
Conversion premium	21.65%	96.18%	78.01%
Pure bond value	$ 596.00	$555.00	$770.00
Downside risk	40.4%	0%	11%

that as the stock price gets higher, the conversion premium the investor is willing to pay becomes lower. This is because the investor is getting almost no downside protection. This is confirmed by the presence of large downside risk at high stock prices in panel (*b*).

You can track the actual performance of the Telxon bond in Table 14–1. The analysis is over a seven-year period.

Note that between June 1, 1987, and December 15, 1989, the common stock price fell sharply from $22 to $7.50 per share—a decline of $14.50 or 65.9 percent. Because the conversion ratio remained constant at 37.38 shares, the conversion value fell by an equal percentage amount. However, the actual bonds only fell 44.5 percent from $1,000 to $555 because they had the security of a pure bond value on December 15, 1989, of $555 to back them up. The pure bond level had declined slightly from its previous level of $596 due to increasing interest rates.

By October 17, 1994, the stock had demonstrated an improved performance, increasing from $7.50 on December 15, 1989, to $13 on October 17, 1994, five years later. This increase in stock value helped trigger an increase in the convertible bond value to $865. Additionally, interest rates declined during this period, and the pure bond value increased to $770.

Telxon's common stock was not callable until 1995. Assume that Telxon common stock reached $30 during 1996, which is not such a farfetched possibility since Telxon had a high stock price of $28.125 in 1992 and $28.25 in 1993. If Telxon calls the bond at 101.5 ($1,015), what action would an owner take? You have the choice of receiving 37.38 shares worth $1,121.40 ($30 × 37.38 shares) or receiving $1,015 in cash. It should be obvious that the 37.38 shares are the best choice. If the company would call the bonds, all convertible bondholders would be "forced" to take the shares of common stock to maximize their value. This is called a **forced conversion** when the company calls the convertible security knowing that the owners will take stock and thus convert debt to equity. The advantage to the company's balance sheet is an obvious reduction in the debt-to-equity ratio and less financial risk. However, on the initial announcement of the call, the common stock will usually decline somewhat because of the increased number of shares on the market and the potential for many bondholders to liquidate their shares for other fixed-income investments. This is why companies generally wait until the conversion price is well above the call price before forcing the call. If the price drops enough so

that the conversion value falls below the call price, the company could get stuck having to come up with cash instead of shares of stock.

Comparison with Common Stock

Would you have been better off putting $1,000 in Telxon common stock on June 1, 1987, or $1,000 in the convertible bond? At $22, $1,000 in Telxon stock would have purchased 45.45 shares, while $1,000 invested in the bond got the investor the right to convert into 37.38 shares. As shown in Table 14–2, in October 1994, a stock investment would have been worth $590.85 plus $2.59 in dividends for a total of $593.44, and the convertible bond would be worth $865 plus approximately $525 in interest payments over the seven years for a total of $1,390. This amount would be even higher if we assume the interest payments were reinvested at market rates over the seven years. The convertible bond investor would definitely have been better off under this situation, but if the 45.45 shares of stock had gone over $30.58,[2] then the stock would have been a better investment than the $1,390 value from the bond. Given that Telxon is considered a technology stock, one or two good quarters of higher than expected earnings could double the stock price very quickly.

TABLE 14–2 Comparative Telxon Investments—Convertible Bond versus Common Stock

	Amount Invested June 1987	Shares	Stock Price October 1994	Ending Stock or Bond Value	Total Income	Total Value
Stock	$1,000	45.45	$13	$590.85	$2.59	$593.44
Bond	$1,000	37.38	$13	$865	$525	$1,390

The trade-off the investor makes in the stock versus the convertible security decision is whether to buy stock, receiving more shares and a lower cash flow from dividends, or to buy the convertible security with its option of fewer shares but higher cash flow from interest payments. In this case, the cash flow difference between dividends ($2.59) and interest ($525) was very high, and since the stock price declined, the differential was impossible to make up.

Table 14–3 presents a selection of convertible bonds and preferred stock and helps to illustrate several basic points. First, notice that no bonds are rated Aa or Aaa. While an occasional convertible bond such as the Avnet 6%, 2012 carries an A3 rating, in general, convertible bonds are usually lower-quality bonds. Notice that the Anacomp bond has a conversion premium of 676.9 percent. This indicates that the stock price has fallen since the original issue and that the bond price is trading based on its pure bond value (investment value) or interest-paying ability rather than the stock price. The conversion value is extremely low relative to the bond price, and the common stock price would have to go up sharply before an investor would begin to benefit from an increased bond price.

---

[2] At a price of $30.58, the stock is worth $1,390 (45.45 × $30.58).

TABLE 14–3 Selected Convertible Bonds and Preferred Stock

Selected Convertible Bonds—December 5, 1994

Issue	Coupon	Maturity	Moody's Performance Rank	Bond Price	Conversion Price	Conversion Ratio	Common Stock Price	Conversion Value	Conversion Premium	Pure Bond Value	Stock Dividend Yield	Current Yield	Call Price
American Stores Co.	7.25%	2001	Ba1	$1,167.50	$22.50	44.44	$25.88	$1,150.11	1.5%	$ 870.00	1.9%	6.2%	$1,045.30
Anacomp	13.88%	2002	Ba3	$ 998.80	$17.50	57.14	$ 2.25	$ 128.57	676.9%	$1,000.00	Nil	13.9%	$1,000.00
Avnet	6.00%	2012	A3	$1,020.00	$43.00	23.26	$36.38	$ 846.20	20.5%	$ 770.00	1.6%	5.9%	$1,018.00
Bank of New York	7.50%	2001	Baa1 r	$1,445.00	$39.10	51.15	$28.50	$1,457.78	-0.9%	$ 940.00	4.5%	5.2%	NCB
Bolt, Bemack, and Newman	6.00%	2012	B3 r	$ 770.00	$30.00	33.33	$19.50	$ 649.94	18.5%	$ 550.00	0.3%	7.8%	$1,018.00
Champion International Group	6.50%	2011	Baa2 r	$1,035.00	$34.75	28.78	$33.88	$ 975.07	6.1%	$ 810.00	0.6%	6.3%	$1,013.00
Delta Air Lines	3.23%	2003	Ba3	$ 702.50	$78.86	12.68	$49.75	$ 630.83	11.4%	$ 580.00	4.0%	4.6%	NCB
Masco Corporation	5.25%	2012	Baa2 r	$ 795.00	$42.28	23.65	$23.00	$ 543.95	46.2%	$ 690.00	3.1%	6.6%	$1,015.80
Mead Corporation	6.75%	2012	Baa1 r	$ 970.00	$52.85	18.92	$45.38	$ 858.59	13.0%	$ 820.00	2.2%	7.0%	$1,020.30
Unisys Corporation	8.25%	2000	B2	$1,052.50	$10.23	97.75	$ 9.00	$ 879.75	19.6%	$ 890.00	Nil	7.8%	NCB
Wendy's International, Inc.	7.00%	2006	Baa3 r	$1,240.00	$12.30	81.30	$13.88	$1,128.44	9.9%	$ 880.00	1.7%	5.6%	NCB

Selected Convertibles Preferred Stock—December 5, 1994

Issue	Dividend	Call Date	Preferred Stock Price	Common Stock Price	Coversion Ratio	Conversion Value	Conversion Premium	Pure Value*	Common Stock Dividend Yield	Preferred Stock Dividend Yield
Diamond Shamrock	$2.50	6/15/00	$53.25	$25.75	1.89	$48.59	9.6%	$25.00	2.2%	4.7%
Ford	$4.20	12/7/97	$88.00	$26.88	3.27	$87.85	0.2%	$48.00	3.3%	4.8%
Mobile Telecom Tech	$2.25	10/24/96	$27.13	$17.56	1.10	$19.51	39.1%	$20.00	Nil	8.3%
Property Trust of America	$1.75	11/30/03	$21.63	$16.25	1.22	$19.75	9.5%	$16.00	6.2%	8.1%
Transco Energy	$3.50	10/31/99	$40.50	$12.75	2.50	$31.88	27.0%	$35.00	4.7%	8.6%

* Value based strictly on dividend-paying level of the preferred stock.
r — denotes fully registered bond.
NCB — denotes noncallable bond.
Sources: Value Line Convertible Index and Moody's Bond Record.

The American Stores bond and the Ford preferred stock (bottom of table) both have very low conversion premiums of less than 2 percent, which indicates that these securities are selling close to their conversion value. In the case of the Bank of New York bond, the conversion premium is actually negative (–0.9%) because the conversion value is slightly greater than the bond value by $12.78. This indicates a market disequilibrium most likely because the prices of the stock and bond were not determined or traded at the same time.

Disadvantages of Convertibles

It has been said that everything has a price, and purchasing convertible securities at the wrong price can eliminate one of their main advantages. For example, once convertible bonds begin going up in value, or the pure bond value declines substantially, the downside protection becomes meaningless. In the case of the Bank of New York in Table 14–3, the market price of the bond is $1,445, while the pure bond value is $940. If the investor buys the bond at $1,445 and the common stock declines significantly, the investor is exposed to a potential decline of slightly over $500 (hardly adequate protection for a true risk averter). Also, don't forget that if market yields rise, the floor price or pure bond value could decline from $940, thus creating even greater downside risk.

Another drawback with convertible bonds is that the purchaser is invariably asked to accept below-market yields on the debt instrument. The interest rate on convertibles is generally one-third below that for instruments in a similar risk class (perhaps 6 percent instead of 9 percent).

From the institutional investor's standpoint, many convertible securities lack liquidity because of small trading volume or even the small amount of convertibles issued by one company. The institutions prefer to own convertible issues where the size of the total bond issue is $100 million or more.

When to Convert into Common Stock

Convertible securities generally have a call provision, such as the Telxon bond had (in the earlier description), which gives the corporation the option of redeeming the bond at a specified price before maturity. The call price is usually at a premium over par value ($1,000) in the early years of callability, and it generally declines over time to par value. We know that as the price of the common stock goes up, the convertible security will rise along with the stock so the investor has no incentive to convert bonds into stock. However, the corporation may use the call privilege to force conversion before maturity. Companies usually force conversion when the conversion value is well above the call price. Investors will take the shares rather than the call price since the shares are worth more. This enables the company to turn debt into equity on its balance sheet and makes new debt issues a better risk for future lenders because of higher interest coverage and a lower debt-to-equity ratio.

Corporations may also encourage voluntary conversion by using a step-up in the conversion price over time. When the bond is issued, the contract may specify the following conversion provisions.

	Conversion Price	Conversion Ratio
First five years	$40	25.0 shares
Next three years	45	22.2 shares
Next two years	50	20.0 shares
Next five years	55	18.2 shares

At the end of each time period, there is a strong inducement to convert rather than accept an adjustment to a higher conversion price and a lower conversion ratio. This is especially true if the bond's conversion value is the dominating influence on the market price of the bond. In the case where the conversion value is below the pure bond value and where the interest income is greater than the dividend income, an investor will most likely not be induced to convert through the step-up feature.

About the only other reason for voluntary converting is if the dividend income received on the common stock is greater than the interest income on the bond. Even in this case, risk-averse investors may want to hold the bond because interest payments are legally required whereas dividends may be reduced. As with most investment decisions, investors must consider their expectations of future corporate and market conditions. Hard-and-fast rules are difficult to find, and different investors may react according to their own risk aversion and objectives.

ADVANTAGES AND DISADVANTAGES TO THE ISSUING CORPORATION

Having established the fundamental characteristics of the convertible security from the investor's viewpoint, let us now examine the factors a corporate financial officer must consider in weighing the advisability of a convertible offer for the firm.

It has been established that the interest rate paid on convertible issues is lower than that paid on a straight debt instrument. Also, the convertible feature may be the only device for allowing smaller corporations access to the bond market.

Convertible bonds are also attractive to a corporation that believes its stock is undervalued. For example, assume a corporation's $1,000 bonds are convertible into 20 shares of common stock at a conversion price of $50. Also assume the company's common stock has a current price of $45, and new shares of stock might be sold at only $44.[3] Thus, the corporation will effectively receive $6 over current market price, assuming future conversion. Of course, one can also argue that if the firm had delayed the issuance of common stock or convertibles for a year or two, the stock might have gone up from $45 to $60 or $65, and new common stock might have been sold at this lofty price.

To translate this to overall numbers for the firm, if a corporation needs $10 million in funds and offers straight stock now at a new price of $44, it must issue 227,272 shares

[3] There is always a bit of underpricing to ensure the success of a new offering.

($10 million/$44 per share). With convertibles, the number of shares potentially issued is only 200,000 shares ($10 million/$50 per share). Finally, if no stock or convertible bonds are issued now and the stock goes up to a level at which new shares can be offered at a price of $60, only 166,667 will be required ($10 million/$60).

Another matter of concern to the corporation is the accounting treatment accorded to convertibles. In the funny-money days of the 1960s' conglomerate merger movement, corporate management often chose convertible securities over common stock because the convertibles had a nondilutive effect on earnings per share. As indicated in the following section on reporting earnings for convertibles, the rules were changed.

ACCOUNTING CONSIDERATIONS WITH CONVERTIBLES

Before 1969, the full impact of the conversion privilege as it applied to convertible securities, warrants (long-term options to buy stock), and other dilutive securities was not adequately reflected in reported earnings per share. Since all of these securities may generate additional common stock in the future, the potential effect of this **dilution** should be considered. Let us examine the unadjusted (for conversion) financial statements of the XYZ Corporation in Table 14–4.

An analyst would hardly be satisfied in accepting the unadjusted earnings per share figure of $1.50 for the XYZ Corporation. In computing earnings per share, we have not accounted for the 400,000 additional shares of common stock that could be created by converting the bonds. How then do we make this full disclosure? According to *APB Opinion No. 15,* issued by the American Institute of Certified Public Accountants, we need to compute earnings per share using two different methods when there is potential dilution: **primary earnings per share** and **fully diluted earnings per share.**

TABLE 14–4 XYZ Corporation

1. Capital section of balance sheet:	
Common stock (1 million shares at $10 par)	$10,000,000
4.5% convertible debentures (10,000 debentures of $1,000; convertible into 40 shares per bond, or a total of 400,000 shares)	10,000,000
Retained earnings	20,000,000
Net worth	$40,000,000
2. Condensed income statement:	
Earnings before interest and taxes	$ 2,950,000
Interest (4.5% of $10 million of convertibles)	450,000
Earnings before taxes	$ 2,500,000
Taxes (40%)	1,000,000
Earnings after taxes	$ 1,500,000
3. Earnings per share (unadjusted):	

$$\frac{\text{Earnings after taxes}}{\text{Shares of common stock}} = \frac{\$1{,}500{,}000}{1{,}000{,}000} = \$1.50$$

1. Primary earnings per share

$$= \frac{\text{Adjusted earnings after taxes}}{\text{Shares outstanding} + \text{Common stock equivalents}} \quad (14\text{–}5)$$

Common stock equivalents include warrants, other options, and any convertible securities that paid less than two-thirds of the going interest rate at time of issue.[4]

2. Fully diluted earnings per share

$$= \frac{\text{Adjusted earnings after taxes}}{\text{Shares outstanding} + \text{Common stock equivalents} + \text{All convertibles regardless of the interest rate}} \quad (14\text{–}6)$$

The intent in computing both primary and fully diluted earnings per share is to consider the effect of potential dilution. Common stock equivalents represent those securities that are capable of generating new shares of common stock in the future. Note that convertible securities may or may not be required in computing primary earnings per share depending on rates, but they must be included in computing fully diluted earnings per share.

In the case of the XYZ Corporation in Table 14–4, the convertibles pay 4.5 percent interest. We assume the going interest rate was 9 percent at the time they were issued, so they are considered as common stock equivalents and are included in both primary and fully diluted earnings per share.

We get new earnings per share for the XYZ Corporation by assuming that 400,000 new shares will be created from potential conversion, while at the same time, allowing for the reduction in interest payments that would occur as a result of the conversion of the debt to common stock. Since before-tax interest payments on the convertibles are \$450,000, the after-tax interest cost (\$270,000) will be saved and can be added back to income. After-tax interest cost is determined by multiplying interest payments by one minus the tax rate or \$450,000 (1 – 0.4) = \$270,000. Making the appropriate adjustments to the numerator and denominator, we show adjusted earnings per share:

$$\text{Primary earnings per share}^{5} = \frac{\text{Adjusted earnings after taxes}}{\text{Shares outstanding} + \text{Common stock equivalents}}$$

$$= \frac{\underset{\text{earnings}}{\text{Reported}}\ \$1{,}500{,}000 + \underset{\text{savings}}{\text{Interest}}\ \$270{,}000}{1{,}000{,}000 + 400{,}000} = \frac{\$1{,}770{,}000}{1{,}400{,}000} = \$1.26$$

We see a \$0.24 reduction from the earnings per share figure of \$1.50 in Table 14–4. The new figure is the value that a sophisticated security analyst would utilize.

---

[4] The going interest rate was initially defined as the prime interest rate in *APB Opinion No. 15* (1969). In 1982, the Financial Accounting Standards Board defined the going interest rate as the average Aa bond yield at the time of issue.

[5] Same as fully diluted in this instance.

INNOVATIONS IN CONVERTIBLE SECURITIES

Not all convertible securities are convertible into the common stock of the company issuing the convertible. Some convertibles are convertible into bonds, preferred stock, stock of another company, or another type of asset.

Another type of new convertible security bears mentioning. For many companies recovering from years of losses and having tax-loss carryforwards, "convertible exchangeable preferred stock" is a security that can improve the firm's balance sheet and provide high returns to investors. A firm with losses does not need tax-deductible interest expenses but does need balanced financing. Since no taxes are due, preferred dividends are no different from interest expenses to the issuing company. When the issuing firm becomes taxable again, it can exchange the preferred stock for debt with the same conversion ratio and can then utilize the tax savings from the deductible interest expense. The exchange occurs without the cost of new underwriting fees.

SPECULATING THROUGH WARRANTS

A **warrant** is an option to buy a stated number of shares of stock at a specified price over a given time period. The nine warrants listed in Table 14–5 demonstrate the relationships discussed in the following sections. For example, Viacom (last line) was once a very hot stock and involved in several potential mergers with telecommunications companies and movie studios. The stock hit a high of $78 in 1994, but when its attempt to take over Paramount failed, its stock price fell dramatically ($36.38 in the table). The table lists a warrant currently available for the firm that allows the holder to buy the stock for $70 [column (4)] until June 6, 1999. The common stock price would have to rise considerably for the warrant to have any value. If Viacom gets back into the merger game or becomes a takeover target itself, the stock may rise again, but it would have to go to over $70 for the warrant to have any intrinsic value. Some investors are willing to pay $4.13 [column (2)] for the right to buy Viacom shares for $70 per share. Since they have almost five years before the warrant expires, they must think there is a possibility that the stock could rise to more than $74.13 ($70 Option price + $4.13 Warrant price) so that they would make a profit.

Warrants are usually issued as a sweetener to a bond offering, and they may enable the firm to issue debt when this would not be feasible otherwise. The warrants allow the bond issue to carry a lower coupon rate and are usually detachable from the bond after the issue date. After being separated from the bond, warrants have their own market price and may trade on a different market from the common stock. After the warrants are exercised, the initial debt with which they were sold remains in existence.

The Bache Group, a financial company (now Prudential Securities), had a bond offering October 30, 1980. It offered 35,000 units of $1,000 debentures due in the year 2000 with a coupon interest rate of 14 percent. To each bond, 30 warrants were attached. Each warrant allowed the holder to buy one share of stock at $18.50 until November 1, 1985. At the time of issue, the warrant had no true value since the common stock was selling below $18.50. During 1981, however, the stock went up as several merger offers were made for retail brokerage companies. On May 29, 1981, Bache common stock was

TABLE 14–5 Selected Warrants as of October 12, 1994

(1) Name of Firm, Place of Warrant Listing, and Stock Listing*	(2) Warrant Price	(3) Per Share Stock Price	(4) Per Share Option Price	(5) Intrinsic Value** [(3)-(4)]	(6) Speculative Premium [(2)-(5)]	(7) Percentage Stock Must Rise to Break Even	(8) Number of Shares per Warrant	(9) Due Date
1. Anacomp Inc. ASE	$ 1.63	$ 2.88	$ 1.87	$ 1.01	$ 0.62	21.5%	1	11/11/00
2. BankAmerica, NYSE, OTC	$28.50	$45.88	$17.50	$28.38	$ 0.12	0.3%	1	10/22/97
3. Bank of New York, NYSE, OTC	$11.13	$30.75	$62.00	0	$11.13	137.8%	1	11/29/98
4. Carter Hawley Hale, OTC	$ 2.25	$ 9.38	$17.00	0	$ 2.25	105.2%	1	9/8/99
5. Lone Star Ind., NYSE	$ 7.38	$17.75	$18.75	0	$ 7.38	47.2%	1	12/30/00
6. Metropolitan Financial, NYSE	$23.78	$23.75	$ 5.21	$18.54	$ 5.24	21.9%	1	11/19/00
7. Quidel, OTC	$ 1.38	$ 3.31	$ 7.50	0	$ 1.38	168.3%	1	4/30/02
8. Scios Nova, OTC	$ 1.88	$ 5.88	$26.75	0	$ 1.88	386.9%	1	6/30/98
9. Viacom B, ASE	$ 4.13	$36.38	$70.00	0	$ 4.13	103.8%	1	6/6/99

* OTC = Over-the-counter market, NYSE = New York Stock Exchange, ASE = American Stock Exchange.

** When column (4) is larger than column (3), the intrinsic value will calculate as a negative number. Since the intrinsic value of a warrant cannot be less than worthless, we put a zero in column (5) in these cases.

selling at 31½, and each warrant traded at 13⅝. The 30 warrants received with each bond were now worth $408.75 and provided the sweetener every bondholder had hoped for.

Because a warrant is dependent on the market movement of the underlying common stock and has no "security value" as such, it is highly speculative. If the common stock of the firm is volatile, the value of the warrants may change dramatically.

Valuation of Warrants

Because the value of a warrant is closely tied to the underlying stock price, we can develop a formula for the minimum or intrinsic value of a warrant:

$$I = (M - OP) \times N \tag{14–7}$$

where:

I = The intrinsic or minimum value of the warrant
M = The market value of the common stock
OP = The option or exercise price of the warrant
N = The number of shares each warrant entitles the holder to purchase

Assume that the common stock of the Graham Corporation is $25 per share and that each warrant carries an option to purchase one share at $20 over the next 10 years. The purchase price stipulated in the warrant is the **option** or **exercise price.** Using Formula 14–7, the intrinsic value is $5 [($25 – 20) × 1]. The **intrinsic value** in this case is equal to the market price of the common stock minus the option price of the warrant. Since the warrant has 10 more years to run and is an effective vehicle for speculative trading, it may well trade for over $5. If the warrant were selling for $9, we would say it had an intrinsic value of $5 and a speculative premium of $4. The **speculative premium** is equal to the price of the warrant minus the intrinsic value.

Even if the stock were trading at less than $20 (the option price on the warrant), the warrant might still have some value in the market. Speculators might purchase the warrant in the hope that the common stock value would increase sufficiently to make the option provision valuable. If the common stock were selling for $15 per share, thus giving the warrant a negative intrinsic value of $5, the warrant might still command a value of $1 or $2 in anticipation of increased common stock value.

In many cases, firms would have negative intrinsic values because the stock price is below the warrant's option price, but a warrant cannot be less than worthless, so a zero value is denoted for the intrinsic value, as shown in Table 14–5 on page 411. In some cases, firms with zero intrinsic values still have large speculative premiums. This is true even when the stock price has to more than double in price by expiration before the warrant breaks even on the original investment. This **warrant break-even** value can be calculated by adding the speculative premium to the option price (exercise price).

As an example of an extreme case, the Bank of New York's common stock was trading $31.25 below the exercise price of $62.00 on the warrant, and yet the warrant still traded for $11.13. Bank of New York common stock would have to rise $42.38 ($31.25 + 11.13) before the warrant holder would break even. This would be a 137.8 percent increase on the $30.75 stock price. The Bank of New York warrant is due to expire November 29, 1998, so a warrant holder has four years to wait for a profit. As the economy recovers and banks return to profitability, a doubling in price could take much less than four years and could handsomely reward the warrant holder for the $11.13 investment.

The typical relationship between the market price and the intrinsic value of a warrant is depicted in Figure 14–3. We assume the warrant entitles the holder to purchase one new share of common stock at $20.

Although the intrinsic value of the warrant is theoretically negative at a common stock price between 0 and $20, the warrant still carries some value in the market. Also, observe that the difference between the market price of the warrant and its intrinsic value is diminished at the upper ranges of value. Two reasons may be offered for this declining premium.

First, the speculator loses the ability to use leverage to generate high returns as the price of the stock goes up. When the price of the stock is relatively low, say, $25, and the warrant is in the $5 to $10 range, a 10-point movement in the stock could mean a 200 percent gain in the value of the warrant, as indicated in part A of Table 14–6. At the upper levels of stock value, much of this leverage is lost, as indicated in part B of the table. At a stock value of $50 and a warrant value of approximately $30, a 10-point movement in the stock would produce only a 33 percent gain in the warrant.

FIGURE 14–3 Market Price Relationships for a Warrant

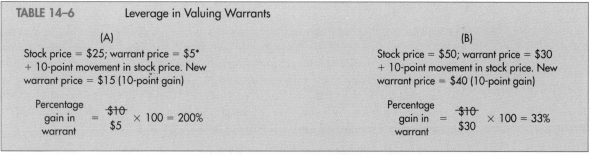

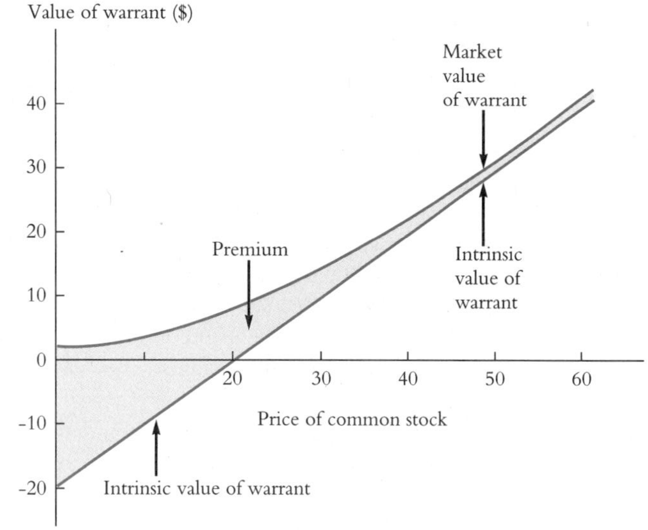

TABLE 14–6 Leverage in Valuing Warrants

(A)

Stock price = \$25; warrant price = \$5*
+ 10-point movement in stock price. New warrant price = \$15 (10-point gain)

$$\text{Percentage gain in warrant} = \frac{\$10}{\$5} \times 100 = 200\%$$

(B)

Stock price = \$50; warrant price = \$30
+ 10-point movement in stock price. New warrant price = \$40 (10-point gain)

$$\text{Percentage gain in warrant} = \frac{\$10}{\$30} \times 100 = 33\%$$

* The warrant price would, of course, be greater than \$5 because of a premium. Nevertheless, we use \$5 for ease of computation.

Another reason speculators pay a very low premium at higher stock prices is that there is less downside protection. A warrant selling at \$30 when the stock price is \$50 is more vulnerable to downside movement than is a \$5 to \$10 warrant when the stock is in the 20s.

Warrant premiums are also influenced by the same factors that affect convertible bond premiums. More volatile common stocks will have greater potential to create short-run profits for warrant speculators, so the higher the price volatility, the greater the premium. Also, the longer the option has before expiration, the higher the premium will be. This "time premium" is worth more the longer the common stock has to reach and surpass the option price of the warrant.

Use of Warrants by Corporations

As previously indicated, warrants may allow for the issuance of debt under difficult circumstances. While a straight debt issue may not be acceptable or may be accepted only at extremely high rates, the same security may be well received because detachable warrants are included. Warrants may also be included as an add-on in a merger or acquisition agreement. A firm might offer $20 million in cash plus 10,000 warrants in exchange for all the outstanding shares of the acquisition candidate.

The use of warrants has traditionally been associated with such aggressive, "high-flying" firms as biotechs, airlines, and conglomerates.

As a financing device for creating new common stock, warrants may not be as desirable as convertible securities. A corporation with convertible bonds outstanding may force the conversion of debt to common stock through a call, while no similar device is available to the firm with warrants. The only possible inducement might be a step-up in the option price—whereby the warrant holder must pay a progressively higher option price if he does not exercise by a given date.

The capital structure of the firm after the exercise of a warrant also is somewhat different from that created after the conversion of a debenture. In the case of a warrant, the original debt outstanding remains in existence after the detachable warrant is exercised, whereas the conversion of a debenture extinguishes the former debt obligation.[6]

ACCOUNTING CONSIDERATIONS WITH WARRANTS

As with convertible securities, the potential dilutive effect of warrants must be considered. Warrants are generally included in computing both primary and fully diluted earnings per share.[7] The accountant must compute the number of new shares that could be created by the exercise of all warrants, with the provision that the total can be reduced by the assumed use of the cash proceeds to purchase a partially offsetting amount of shares at the market price. Assume that warrants to purchase 10,000 shares at $20 are outstanding and the current price of the stock is $50. We show the following:

1.	New shares created	10,000
2.	Reduction of shares from cash proceeds (computed below)	4,000
	Cash proceeds— 10,000 shares at $20 = $200,000	
	Current price of stock—$50	
	Assumed reduction in shares outstanding from cash proceeds = $200,000/$50 = 4,000	
3.	Assumed net increase in shares from exercise of warrants (10,000 – 4,000)	6,000

[6] A number of later financing devices can blur this distinction. See Jerry Miller, "Accounting for Warrants and Convertible Bonds," *Management Accounting,* January 1973, pp. 36–38.

[7] Under some circumstances, where the market price is below the option price, dilution need not be considered (*APB Opinion No. 15*).

In computing earnings per share, we will add 6,000 shares to the denominator with no adjustment to the numerator, which will lower earnings per share. If earnings per share had previously been $1 based on $100,000 in earnings and 100,000 shares outstanding, EPS would now be reduced to $0.943:

$$\frac{\text{Earnings}}{\text{Shares}} = \frac{\$100{,}000}{106{,}000} = \$0.943$$

With warrants included in computing both primary and fully diluted earnings per share, their impact on reported earnings is important from both the investor and corporate viewpoints.

SUMMARY

Convertible securities and warrants offer the investor an opportunity for participating in increased common stock values without owning common stock directly. Convertible securities may be in the form of debt or preferred stock, though most of our examples refer to debt.

Convertible securities provide a guaranteed income stream and a floor value based on required yield on the investment. At the same time, they have an established conversion ratio to common stock (par value/conversion price). The conversion value of an issue is equal to the conversion ratio times the current value of a share of common stock. The conversion value is generally less than the current market price of the convertible issue. Actually, the difference between the market price of the convertible issue and the conversion value is referred to as the conversion premium. The conversion premium is influenced by the volatility of the underlying common stock, the time to maturity, the dividend payment on common stock relative to the interest rate on the convertibles, and other lesser factors. Generally, when the common stock price has risen well above the conversion price (and the convertible is trading well above par), the conversion premium will be quite small, as indicated in panel (*a*) of Figure 14–2. The small premium is attributed to the fact that the investor no longer enjoys significant downside protection.

A convertible issue is considered to be potentially dilutive to the reported earnings of the corporation, and since 1969, primary and/or fully diluted earnings per share must consider the impact of potential conversion. Actually, the corporation may ultimately have the opportunity to force conversion through calling the issue at slightly over par value when, in fact, it is selling at a substantially higher price. In the absence of a call, there is generally little incentive to convert since the convertible security will move up and down with the common stock issue.

A warrant is an option to buy a stated number of shares of stock (usually one) at a specified price over a given time period. Warrants are often issued as a sweetener to a bond issue and may allow the firm to issue debt where it would not normally be feasible. The warrants are generally detachable from the bond issue. Thus, if the warrants are exercised, the bond issue still remains in existence (this is clearly different from a convertible security). The difference between the market price of a warrant and its minimum or intrinsic value represents a premium that the investor is willing to pay. This premium represents

the speculative potential in the warrant. Warrants are dilutive to earnings and must generally be considered in computing primary and fully diluted earnings per share.

KEY WORDS AND CONCEPTS

convertible security, 398
conversion price, 399
conversion ratio, 399
conversion value, 399
pure bond value, 399
floor value, 399
conversion premium, 400
downside limit, 401
downside risk, 401
forced conversion, 403
dilution, 408
primary earnings per share, 408
fully diluted earnings per share, 408
warrant, 410
option price (of warrant), 412
exercise price (of warrant), 412
intrinsic value (of warrant), 412
speculative premium, 412
warrant break-even, 412

DISCUSSION QUESTIONS

1. Why would an investor be interested in convertible securities? (What do they offer to the investor?)
2. What are the disadvantages of investing in convertible securities?
3. When is the best time to buy convertible bonds?
4. How can you determine the conversion ratio from the conversion price?
5. How do you determine the conversion value?
6. What is meant by the pure bond value?
7. For bonds that have conversion premiums in excess of 100 percent, what can you generally infer about the stock price?
8. How does the volatility of a stock influence the conversion premium?
9. How might a step-up in the conversion price force conversion?
10. Why do corporations use convertible bonds?
11. What is meant by the dilutive effect of convertible securities?
12. What is a warrant?
13. For what reasons do firms issue warrants?
14. Why are warrants highly speculative?
15. Why do investors tend to pay a smaller premium for a warrant as the price of the stock goes up?
16. If warrants were initially a detachable part of a bond issue, will the amount of debt be reduced if the warrants are eventually exercised? Contrast this with a convertible security.
17. What type of firm generally issues warrants?

PROBLEMS

Conversion terms

1. A convertible bond has a face value of $1,000, and the conversion price is $50 per share. The stock is selling at $42 per share. The bond pays $60 per year interest and is selling in the market for $930. It matures in 15 years. Market rates are 10 percent per year.

a. What is the conversion ratio?
b. What is the conversion value?
c. What is the conversion premium (in dollars and in percent)?
d. What is the floor value or pure bond value? (You may wish to review material in Chapter 12 for computing bond values.)

Downside risk

2. Compute the downside risk as a percentage in problem 1. What does this mean?

Downside risk

3. Under what circumstances might the downside risk increase? Relate your answer to interest rates in the market.

Conversion premium

4. Lowrey Metals Company has a $1,000 convertible bond outstanding that has a market value of $1,100. It has a coupon rate of 7 percent and matures in 10 years. The conversion price is $40. The common stock currently is selling for $37.
   a. What is the conversion premium (in percentage terms)?
   b. At what price does the common stock need to sell for the conversion value to be equal to the current bond price?

Pure bond value

5. In problem 4, market rates of interest for comparable bonds are 10 percent, and the pure bond value is $813.17. What will happen to the pure bond value if market rates of interest go to 12 percent? (Once again, you may wish to consult Chapter 12 for computing bond values.)

Comparative analysis of stock and convertible bonds

6. Assume you bought a convertible bond two years ago for $900. The bond has a conversion ratio of 32. At the time the bond was purchased, the stock was selling for $25 per share. The bond pays $75 in annual interest. The stock pays no cash dividend. Assume the stock price rises to $35 after two years, and the firm forces investors to convert to common stock by calling the bond (there is no conversion premium at this time).

   Would you have been better off if you (*a*) had bought the stock directly or (*b*) had bought the convertible bond and eventually converted it to common stock? Assume you would have invested $900 in either case. Disregard taxes, commissions, and so forth. (**Hint:** Consider appreciation in value plus any annual income received. See Table 14–2 for an example.)

EPS and convertibles

7. Given the following data, compute unadjusted earnings per share and fully diluted earnings per share. There are no other potentially dilutive securities outstanding, and the 7 percent interest is greater than two-thirds of the going interest rate at time of issue.

Common stock (500,000 shares at $4.00 per)	$2,000,000
Convertible debentures at 7 percent (6,000 bonds at $1,000 each; convertible into 20 shares per bond)	6,000,000
Retained earnings	8,000,000
Earnings before interest and taxes	3,420,000
Interest	420,000
Earnings before taxes	3,000,000
Taxes (34%)	1,020,000
Earnings after taxes	$1,980,000

Valuing warrants

8. Assume a firm has warrants outstanding that permit the holder to buy one new share of stock at $25 per share. The market price of the stock is now $34.
   a. What is the intrinsic value of the warrant?
   b. Why might the warrant sell for $2 on the market even if the stock price is $22.

Valuing warrants

9. Northern Airlines has warrants outstanding that allow the holder to purchase 1.45 shares per warrant at $15 per share (option price). The common stock is currently selling for $19.
   a. What is the intrinsic value of the warrant?
   b. If the stock sold for $12.50, how large would the negative intrinsic value be?

Valuing warrants

10. Assume in Table 14–5 that Anacomp had a warrant price of $2.50 instead of $1.63 in column (2). The per share stock price in column (3) remains $2.88, and the per share option price is still $1.87 in column (4). Based on the new information, compute:
   a. Intrinsic value. (Does it change?)
   b. Premium (warrant price minus intrinsic value).
   c. Percent the stock must rise to break even. (First determine what price the stock must go to for the warrant to equal $2.50; then determine how large an increase that is from the current stock value.) This assumes no premium.

Comparative analysis of stock and warrants

11. A firm has warrants outstanding that allow the holder to buy one share of stock at $25 per share. Also, assume the stock is selling for $30 per share, and the warrants are now selling for $7 per warrant (this, of course, is above intrinsic value). You can invest $1,000 in the stock or the warrants (for purposes of the computation, round to two places to the right of the decimal point). Assume the stock goes to $40, and the warrants trade at their intrinsic value when the stock goes to $40. Would you have a larger total dollar profit by initially investing in the stock or in the warrants?

EPS and warrants

12. Assume a corporation has $400,000 in earnings and 200,000 shares outstanding ($2 in earnings per share). Also assume there are warrants outstanding to purchase 40,000 shares at $25 per share. The stock is currently selling at $40 per share. In considering the effect of the warrants outstanding, what would revised earnings per share be?

CFA MATERIAL

The following material contains a sample question and solution from a prior Level I CFA exam. While the terminology is slightly different from that in this text, you can still view the skills that are necessary for the CFA exam.

CFA Exam Question

6. In examining a company's straight debentures and subordinated convertible debentures, both issued at the same time with the same maturity and at par, you note that the coupon and yield for the subordinated convertible debenture are lower than for the straight debenture. *Discuss* the return potential for the

convertible bond in an environment of stable interest rates and rising stock prices that would explain its lower coupon and yield.
(*5 minutes*)

Solution: Question 6—Morning Section (5 points)
The reason for the lower coupon and yield is that convertible bonds and preferred stock have the ability to act like common stock on the upside and be valued as a straight bond on the downside. This is demonstrated by the graph in Figure 14–4.

As shown, it has the upside potential of common stock and the downside protection of a bond. Thus, it could have a rate of return approaching common stock with substantially lower risk because it is protected on the downside. Also, the convertible bond has an income advantage relative to common stock until the point at which parity value drives the current yield below the dividend yield.

FIGURE 14–4 Return Distributions—Stocks, Bonds, Convertible Securities

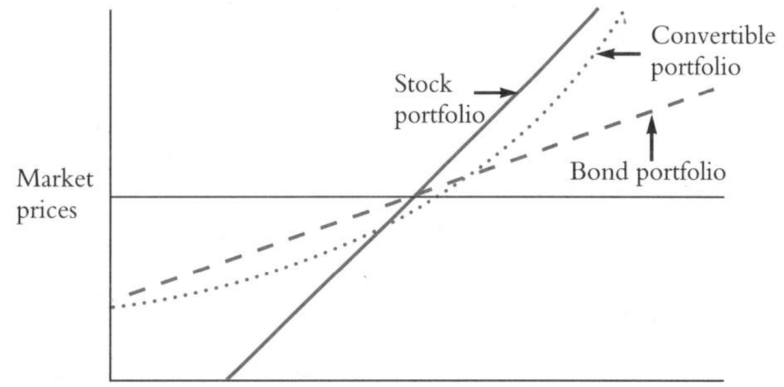

THE WALL STREET JOURNAL PROJECTS

This assignment uses part of the data in Table 14–3. You will work with the convertible bonds of Masco Corporation, Mead Corporation, and Wendy's International, Inc.

1. For each company, using the conversion ratio in Table 14–3, compute the current conversion value. You need to multiply the conversion ratio from the table by the price of the common stock for each company as currently shown in the "New York Stock Exchange Composite Transactions" in Section C of *The Wall Street Journal.*
2. Compute the conversion premium for each of the three companies. The appropriate equation to use is Formula 14–3, which is restated below. The answer should be shown as a percentage:

$$\text{Conversion premium} = \frac{\text{Market price of bond} - \text{Conversion value}}{\text{Conversion value}}$$

You have already determined the conversion value for each of the three bonds in part 1 of this assignment. You will need to look up the market price of the bonds to complete the equation. To accomplish that task, look up the current bond price for each company in the table labeled "New York Exchange Bonds" in Section C of *The Wall Street Journal.* To correctly show the bond price, keep in mind that

the value you found in the table represents the percentage of par value of $1,000. Thus, as an example, 98¾ would represent 98.75 percent × $1,000, or $987.50. Similarly, 102½ would represent 102.5% × $1,000, or $1,025. Also if you cannot find a bond quote on a given day, merely go back a day or two in the *Journal* until you find it.

Note: Remember that the conversion premium is the percent convertible bond holders are willing to pay over the conversion value of the bond and is influenced by the comparative yield between the bond and stock, the amount of downside protection the convertible bond has, the volatility of the stock, the amount of time left to maturity, and a number of other factors. Although you do not have enough information to check out the factors at play in this example, undoubtedly most or all of them are having some effect.

SELECTED REFERENCES

Innovations in Convertible-Type Securities

Cowan, Arnold R.; Nandkumar Nayar; and Ajai K. Singh. "Calls of Out-of-the-Money Convertible Bonds." *Financial Management,* Winter 1993, pp. 106–16.

Heston, C. "How to Get Stocks and Bonds in One Package." *Futures,* September 1986, pp. 50–51.

Pershing, A. C. "Rupert Murdoch's New Convertible." *Institutional Investor,* August 1986, p. 27.

Valuing Convertibles

Brennan, M. J., and E. S. Schwartz. "Convertible Bonds: Valuation and Optimal Strategies for Call and Conversion." *Journal of Finance,* December 1977, pp. 1699–1715.

Hoffmeister, J. R. "Conditions Affecting the Timing of Convertible Bond Sales." *Journal of Business Research,* February 1987, pp. 101–6.

Call Features with Convertibles

Calamos, John P. "Convertible Securities as an Asset Class for the 1990s." *The Journal of Investing,* Spring 1994, pp. 63–65.

Emery, Douglas R.; Mai E. Iskandar; and Johg-Chul Rhim. "Capital Structure Management as a Motivation for Calling Convertible Debt." *The Journal of Financial Research,* Spring 1994, pp. 91–116.

Ingersoll, Jonathan. "An Examination of Corporate Call Policies on Convertible Securities." *Journal of Finance,* May 1977, pp. 463–78.

Singh, Ajai; Arnold R. Cowan; and Nandkumer Nayar. "Underwritten Calls of Convertible Bonds." *Journal of Financial Economics,* March 1991, pp. 173–96.

Accounting Issues and Convertibles

Hagler, J. L., and P. B. Thomas. "Should FASB 84–Induced Conversions of Convertible Debt Apply to Convertible Preferred Stock?" *CPA Journal,* May 1986, pp. 86–88.

King, T. E., and A. K. Ortegren. "Accounting for Hybrid Securities: The Case of Adjustable-Rate Convertible Notes." *The Accounting Review,* July 1988, pp. 522–35.

Investing in Warrants

Miller, Jerry D. "Effects of Longevity on Values of Stock Purchase Warrants." *Financial Analysts Journal,* November–December 1971, pp. 78–85.

Stone, Bernell K. "Warrant Financing." *Journal of Financial and Quantitative Analysis,* March 1976, pp. 143–53.

PART 5

DERIVATIVE PRODUCTS

OUTLINE

Derivatives are securities whose value is derived from the value of some underlying asset, such as stocks, bonds, commodities, and foreign currencies. The derivative allows the investor to gain or lose money based on the performance of the underlying asset. Options, futures contracts, swaps, and other instruments are termed derivatives.

To understand how a derivative works, suppose you purchase an option to buy a stock or bond in the future at a price that is specified now (it may be different from the current price). If the stock or bond goes way up in value, your option will also increase in value since it derives its value from the underlying security. Of course, if the stock or bond goes down, your option may end up being worthless.

In order for you to buy the option or any other derivative, a second party must be willing to sell it to you. For example, if you purchase an option to buy 100 shares of General Motors at $50 dollars a share over the next six months for an option price of $500, another party must be willing to sell you that contract. (You may not deal directly with him or her but rather through an intermediate third party.) The party who is on the other side of the contract is essentially betting that General Motors will not go up enough in value to make your purchase of the option valuable. He or she hopes to pocket part or all of the $500 you put up, without any further obligation.

The financial press has painted a picture of derivatives as being highly speculative instruments. However, this is not necessarily the case. As you will see throughout the next four chapters, as you read about put and call options, commodity and financial futures, swaps, and so forth, derivatives may actually be used to reduce risk rather than to speculate. Derivatives themselves are *neutral;* it is only how they are used that makes them either speculative or defensive.

For example, the person purchasing the option to buy General Motors stock may be offsetting another type of risk. He may have a concurrent short sales position in General Motors and needs protection against the stock going up in value. He is using a derivative to help accomplish this objective. Similarly, a person who is fearful that interest rates on a loan will go up can purchase a derivatives contract in the futures market that will only be profitable if interest rates go up. You will begin to understand the mechanics of these transactions as you read through the following chapters. ■

15

PUT AND CALL OPTIONS

The word **option** has many different meanings, but most of them include the ability or right to choose a certain alternative. One definition provided by *Webster's* is "the right, acquired for a consideration, to buy or sell something at a fixed price within a specified period of time." This definition is very general and applies to puts, calls, warrants, real estate options, or any other contract entered into between two parties where a choice of action or decision can be put off for a limited time at a cost. The person acquiring the option pays an agreed-upon sum to the person providing the option. For example, someone may want to buy your house for its sale price of $75,000. The buyer does not have the money but will give you $2,000 in cash if you give him the right to buy the house at $75,000 for the next 60 days. If you accept, you have given the buyer an option and have agreed not to sell the house to anyone else for the next 60 days. If the buyer raises $75,000 within the 60-day limit, he may buy the house, giving you the $75,000. Perhaps he finds the $75,000 but also finds another house he likes better for $72,000. He will not buy your house, but you have $2,000 and must now find someone else to buy your house. By selling the option, you tied up the sale of your house for 60 days, and if the option is not exercised, you have forgone an opportunity to sell the house to someone else.

The most widely known options are puts and calls on common stock. A **put** is an option to sell 100 shares of common stock at a specified price for a given period. **Calls** are the opposite of puts and allow the owner the right to buy 100 shares of common stock from the option seller (writer). Contracts on listed puts and calls have been standardized and can be bought on several different exchanges.

OPTIONS MARKETS

Before the days of options trading on exchanges, puts and calls were traded over-the-counter by the Put and Call Dealers Association. These dealers would buy and sell puts and calls for their own accounts for stocks traded on the New York Stock Exchange and then try to find an investor, hedger, or speculator to take the other side of the option. For example, if you owned 1,000 shares of Chevron and you wanted to write a call option giving the buyer the right to buy 1,000 shares of Chevron at $40 per share for six months, the dealer might buy the calls and look for someone who would be willing to buy them from him.

This system had several disadvantages. Dealers had to have contact with the buyers and sellers, and the financial stability of the option writer had to be endorsed (guaranteed) by a brokerage house. The option writer either had to keep the shares on deposit with the brokerage firm or put up a cash margin. Options in the same stock could exist in the market at various strike prices (price at which the option could be exercised) and scattered expiration dates. This meant that when an option buyer wanted to exercise or terminate the contract before expiration, he or she would have to deal directly with the option writer. This does not make for an efficient, liquid market. Unlisted options also reduced the striking price of a call by any dividends paid during the option period, which did not benefit the writer of the call.

Listed Options Exchanges

The Chicago Board Options Exchange was established in 1973 as the first exchange for call options. The market response was overwhelming, and within three years, the American, Pacific, and Philadelphia exchanges were also trading call options. By 1994,

the list of stocks with available option contracts increased dramatically from the original list of 16 companies to 1,600 companies, and puts as well as calls were traded for many companies. On many days, the number of underlying shares of stock represented by options traded on the option exchanges is greater than the number of actual shares traded on the NYSE in those same issues.

Table 15–1, from the *Chicago Board Options Exchange's Market Statistics,* shows the growth in options trading since 1973. Besides the Chicago Board Options Exchange (CBOE), the American Exchange (AMEX), the Philadelphia Exchange (PHLX), the Pacific Coast Exchange (PSE), and the New York Stock Exchange (NYSE) currently trade options.

One can now also buy a put or call option on *stock indexes.* For example, the Standard & Poor's 500 Stock Index or the S&P 100 Stock Index are traded on the CBOE, and options on the New York Stock Exchange Index are traded on the NYSE. Options on stock indexes are covered in detail in Chapter 17, while this chapter concentrates on options for individual common stocks.

There are several reasons the listed options markets are so desirable compared with the previous method of over-the-counter trading for options. The contract period was standardized with three-, six-, and nine-month expiration dates on three calendar cycles.

TABLE 15–1 Total Options Contract Volume by Exchange (for Individual Stocks)

	CBOE*	AMEX	PHLX	PSE	NYSE	Total
1993	140,348,955	47,883,957	25,699,888	16,364,744	2,052,965	232,350,509
1992	121,467,604	42,314,942	22,947,867	13,066,618	2,177,041	201,974,072
1991	121,689,918	38,805,589	22,365,110	13,852,604	2,059,969	198,773,190
1990	129,500,018	40,914,962	22,808,688	13,881,269	2,817,811	209,922,748
1989	126,765,253	49,873,264	27,970,765	18,091,434	4,315,944	227,016,660
1988	111,784,045	45,022,497	23,165,112	13,349,148	2,627,789	195,948,591
1987	182,112,636	70,988,990	29,155,308	19,410,875	3,499,095	305,166,904
1986	180,357,774	65,440,500	24,467,468	14,075,872	4,823,782	289,165,396
1985	148,889,091	48,559,122	18,134,575	12,793,451	4,426,855	232,803,094
1984	123,273,736	40,104,605	16,109,050	11,366,056	4,093,816	194,947,263
1983	82,468,750	38,967,725	16,808,125	11,155,906	656,480	150,056,986
1982	75,735,739	38,790,852	13,466,652	9,309,563	—	137,302,806
1981	57,584,175	34,859,475	10,009,565	6,952,567	—	109,405,782
1980	52,916,921	29,048,323	7,758,101	5,486,590	—	95,209,935
1979	35,379,600	17,467,018	4,952,737	3,856,344	—	61,655,699
1978	34,277,350	14,380,959	3,270,378	3,289,968	—	55,218,655
1977	24,838,632	10,077,578	2,195,307	1,925,031	—	39,036,548
1976	21,498,027	9,035,767	1,274,702	550,194	—	32,358,690
1975	14,431,023	3,530,564	140,982	—	—	18,102,569
1974	5,682,907	—	—	—	—	5,682,907
1973	1,119,177	—	—	—	—	1,119,177

* The Midwest Stock Exchange Options Program was consolidated with the CBOE on June 2, 1980.
Source: *The Chicago Board Options Exchange's Market Statistics,* 1994.

Cycle 1: January/April/July/October.

Cycle 2: February/May/August/November.

Cycle 3: March/June/September/December.

The use of three cycles spread out the expiration dates for the options so that not all contracts came due on the same day.[1] Each contract expires at 11:59 P.M. Eastern time on the Saturday immediately following the third Friday of the expiration month. For all practical purposes, any closing out of positions must be done on that last Friday while the markets are open.

In an attempt to satisfy demand for longer-term options, **long-term equity anticipation securities (LEAPS)** were added and provided options with up to two years of expiration. LEAPS have generally been limited to blue-chip stocks such as Coca-Cola, Dow Chemical, General Electric, IBM, and others. LEAPS have the same characteristics as the short-term options, but because of their length, they have higher premiums.

Another important feature of option trading is the standardized **exercise price** (strike price). This is the price the contract specifies for a buy or sell. For all stocks over $25 per share, the striking price normally changes by $5 intervals, and for stocks selling under $25 per share, the strike price usually changes by $2.50 a share. As the underlying stocks change prices in the market, options with new striking prices are added. For example, a stock selling at $30 per share when the January option is added will have a striking price of 30, but if the stock gets to 32½ (halfway to the next striking price), the exchange may add another option (to the class of options) with a 35 strike price.

This standardization of expiration dates and strike prices creates more certainty when buying and selling options in a changing market and allows more efficient trading strategies because of better coordination between stock prices, strike prices, and expiration dates. Dividends no longer affect the option contract as they did in the unlisted market. Transactions occur at arm's length between the buyer and seller without any direct matchmaking needed on the part of the broker. The ultimate result of these changes in the option market is a highly liquid, efficient market where speculators, hedgers, and arbitrageurs all operate together.

Telephonos DeMexico put and call options are presented in Table 15–2 as an example of different strike prices (35, 40, 45, 50) and expiration months. Telmex stock closed at

TABLE 15–2 Telephonos DeMexico, January 6, 1995

		Calls—Last			Puts—Last		
Stock Price Close	**Strike Price**	**January**	**February**	**May**	**January**	**February**	**May**
Telmex							
36⅞	35	2⅞	3¾	—	13/16	1 11/16	2⅜
36⅞	40	11/16	1 7/16	2 13/16	3⅝	4¼	5
36⅞	45	⅛	5/16	1⅜	8½	8½	r
36⅞	50	1/16	¼	1 1/16	13¼	r*	r

* r = not traded.

[1] Additional cycles have also been added.

36⅞ on January 6, 1995. The values within Table 15–2, such as 2⅞ or 3¾, reflect the price of the various options contracts. This information will take on greater meaning as we go through the chapter.

THE OPTIONS CLEARING CORPORATION

Much of the liquidity and ease of operation of the option exchanges is due to the role of the **Options Clearing Corporation,** which functions as the issuer of all options listed on the five exchanges—the CBOE, the AMEX, the Philadelphia Exchange, the Pacific Coast Exchange, and the NYSE. Investors who want to trade puts and calls need to have an approved account with a member brokerage firm; on opening an account, they receive a prospectus from the Options Clearing Corporation detailing all aspects of option trading.

Options are bought and sold through a member broker the same as other securities. The exchanges allow special orders, such as limit, market, and stop orders, as well as orders used specifically in options trading, such as spread orders and straddle orders. The order process originates with the broker and is transacted on the floor of the exchange. Remember that for every order there must be a buyer and seller (writer) so that the orders can be "matched." Once the orders are matched, they are filed with the Options Clearing Corporation, which then issues the necessary options or closes the position. Four basic transactions are handled:

Opening purchase transaction—A transaction in which an investor intends to become the holder of an option.

Opening sale transaction—A transaction in which an investor intends to become the writer (seller) of an option.

Closing purchase transaction—A transaction in which an investor who is obligated as a writer of an option intends to terminate his obligation as a writer. This is accomplished by "purchasing" an option in the same series as the option previously written. Such a transaction has the effect, upon acceptance by the Options Clearing Corporation, of canceling the investor's preexisting position as a writer.

Closing sale transaction—A transaction in which an investor who is the holder of an outstanding option intends to liquidate his position as a holder. This is accomplished by "selling" an option in the same series as the option previously purchased. Such a transaction has the effect, upon acceptance by the Options Clearing Corporation, of liquidating the investor's preexisting position as a holder of the option.

In a transaction, holders and writers of options are not contractually linked but are committed to the Options Clearing Corporation. Since no certificates are issued for options, a customer must maintain a brokerage account as long as he or she holds an option position and must liquidate the option through the broker originating the transaction unless a brokerage transfer is completed before an ensuing transaction. If an option is traded on more than one exchange, it may be bought, sold, or closed on any exchange and cleared through the Options Clearing Corporation. Basically, the aggregate obligation of the option holders is backed up by the aggregate obligation of the option

writers. If holders choose to exercise their options, they must do so through the Clearing Corporation, which randomly selects a writer from all Clearing member accounts in the same option series.[2] This would be true whether the holder chooses to exercise early or at expiration. Upon notice from the Options Clearing Corporation, a call writer must sell 100 shares of the underlying common stock at the exercise price, while the put writer must buy 100 shares from the holder exercising the put.

All option contracts are adjusted for stock splits, stock dividends, or other stock distributions. For example, a two-for-one stock split for a stock selling at 60, with options available at 70, 60, and 50 strike prices, would cause the stock to trade at 30 and the strike prices to be 35, 30, and 25.

OPTION PREMIUMS

Before investors or speculators can understand various option strategies, they must be able to comprehend what creates option premiums (prices). In Table 15–3 on page 430, using Intel as an example, we can see that the common stock closed at $57 13/16 per share on the NYSE and that calls and puts are available for the following strike prices—50, 55, 60, 65, and 70. The January 50 call closed at 8 1/4 ($825 for one call on 100 shares), while the January 55 call closed at 4 1/4. The 50 and 55 call options are said to be **in the money** because the market price (57 13/16) is above the strike (or purchase) price of 50 or 55. The 60 call is **out of the money** since the strike price is above the market price. If Intel common were trading at 60, the 60 call and put would be at the money. Let's once again assume the stock is selling for 57 13/16. Since a put allows you to sell the stock at the strike price, in the money *puts* would be at the 60, 65, and 70 strike price, and out of the money puts would be at 50 and 55.

Intrinsic Value

In the money *call* options have an **intrinsic value** equal to the market price minus the strike price. In the case of the Intel April 50 call, the intrinsic value is 7 13/16 as indicated by Formula 15–1.

$$\text{Intrinsic value (call)} = \text{Market price} - \text{Strike price} \qquad (15\text{–}1)$$

$$\text{Intrinsic value} = 57\tfrac{13}{16} - 50$$

$$= 7\tfrac{13}{16} \text{ (Intel April call)}$$

Options that are out of the money have no positive intrinsic value. If we use Formula 15–1 for the Intel 60 April call, we calculate a negative 2 3/16 intrinsic value. When the market price minus the strike price is negative, the negative value represents the amount the stock price must increase to have the option at the money where the strike price and market price are equal.

---

2 Few option holders choose to exercise their options and take possession of securities. During the 1980s approximately 15 percent of all call options were exercised, while only 7 percent of put options were exercised. Assuming the option holder does not want to exercise the option, he may close out the position on the open market through a closing sale transaction.

TABLE 15–3

LISTED OPTIONS QUOTATIONS

Option/Strike		Exp.	Call Vol.	Call Last	Put Vol.	Put Last
21 5/8	22 1/2	Jul	33	3 1/4	10	3 1/8
21 5/8	25	Jan	123	3/16	15	3 3/8
21 5/8	25	Apr	173	1 1/8	...	...
21 5/8	25	Jul	36	1 7/8	...	...
E Sys	40	Jan	...	...	55	1 1/4
EastCh	50	Jun	25	3 3/4	60	2 5/16
EKodak	45	Jan	325	1 3/4	9	1/2
EchoB	10	Jan	524	3/4	5	1/4
10 5/8	10	Apr	50	1 3/8	4	7/8
10 5/8	10	Jul	37	1 1/2	33	3/4
10 5/8	12 1/2	Jan	181	1/16	110	2 1/4
Egghed	7 1/2	Jun	...	...	26	1/4
11 1/4	12 1/2	Mar	50	1/2	...	...
Elan	35	Apr	40	1 7/8	30	3 1/8
EleArt	20	Jan	79	3/4	10	2 3/8
18 5/8	20	Feb	13	1 1/8	110	2 7/8
18 5/8	20	Mar	96	1 1/2	...	...
18 5/8	22 1/2	Jan	31	3/8	...	...
18 5/8	25	Jun	81	13/16	...	...
EmrsEl	55	Jan	250	6 3/8	...	...
61 5/8	65	Jan	250	5/16	255	3 3/4
61 5/8	65	Mar	208	7/8	...	...
EBP	12 1/2	Jun	272	3/16	...	...
Emplca	22 1/2	Jan	100	4	20	3/16
25 7/8	25	Jan	...	...	150	7/8
25 7/8	25	Apr	...	...	50	1 3/4
25 7/8	25	Jul	...	...	100	2
25 7/8	30	Jan	150	5/16	103	4 1/8
25 7/8	30	Apr	804	1 5/16	240	4 7/8
ELaMd	25	Jan	60	1	...	...
ENSCO	10	Jan	100	2 1/2	...	...
Enron	25	Jan	100	5 1/8	...	...
Entrgy	22 1/2	Jun	5	13/16	34	1 1/16
EnzoBl	10	Jan	200	1	...	...
10 3/8	12 1/2	Jan	120	1/4	20	2 3/8
Epitpe	17 1/2	Jan	17	3 1/8	60	5/16
20 5/8	20	Jan	309	1 3/4	85	15/16
20 5/8	22 1/2	Jan	149	5/8	40	2 5/8
20 5/8	22 1/2	Apr	58	2 1/8	...	...
20 5/8	25	Jan	422	3/8	...	...
20 5/8	25	Apr	60	1 1/2	...	...
Exbyte	20	Jan	25	1 1/8	...	...
19 5/8	20	May	25	2 1/2	...	...
19 5/8	25	May	100	1	...	...
Exxon	50	Jan	55	11 1/2	...	...
61 1/2	60	Jan	137	2 1/4	...	...
61 1/2	60	Apr	350	3 1/4	500	1 1/4
61 1/2	65	Jan	378	3/16	30	3 5/8
61 1/2	65	Apr	30	13/16	...	...
61 1/2	65	Jul	328	1 5/8	50	4 3/4
FamDlr	12 1/2	Jan	40	7/16	...	...
Fastenl	40	Jan	...	...	32	1 11/16
39 3/4	40	Aug	...	...	30	4 3/8
FedExp	60	Jan	156	1 1/8	2	3 1/8
FHLB	55	Feb	100	11/16	...	...
F N M	60	Jan	70	14	...	...
74	70	Jan	69	4 3/4	113	7/16
74	70	Mar	42	5 3/8	25	1 1/2
74	75	Jan	404	1 1/8	134	2 1/8
74	80	Mar	205	1	9	7 3/8
FedPap	30	Jan	26	5/8	...	...
FedDSt	15	Jan	800	3 3/4	...	...
18 3/4	20	Feb	50	5/8	...	...
Fldcrs	25	Jun	27	2 1/4	...	...
23 7/8	30	Mar	35	3/8	...	...
Finght	12 1/2	Feb	50	2 7/16	...	...
14 3/4	15	Apr	107	1 5/8	...	...
FstAlrt	15	Jan	20	3 7/8	35	1/4
18 3/4	17 1/2	Jan	6	1 11/16	25	15/16
18 3/4	20	Jan	129	9/16	...	...
FstChl	50	Jan	53	11/16	...	...
47 7/8	50	Feb	69	1 1/4	...	...
47 7/8	50	Apr	336	2 1/4	...	...
47 7/8	50	Jul	25	3 3/8	...	...
47 7/8	55	Jan	102	1/4	...	...
47 7/8	55	Apr	110	1 1/8	...	...
47 7/8	55	Jul	30	1 3/4	...	...
FtData	45	Feb	...	...	200	1
47	50	Feb	215	7/8	...	...
FFB	45	Jan	60	1 1/2	11	5/8
45 7/8	50	Mar	25	1/2	...	...
FtMiss	22 1/2	Apr	58	2	20	2 1/8
FtPcNt	5	Jan	21	3/16	50	1 3/8

Option/Strike		Exp.	Call Vol.	Call Last	Put Vol.	Put Last
68	60	Apr	...	...	45	2 9/16
68	65	Jan	173	5	66	1 5/16
68	70	Jan	699	2 3/16	35	3 5/8
68	70	Jul	50	7 3/8	...	...
68	75	Jan	75	13/16	...	...
68	75	Apr	28	3 1/2	...	...
68	80	Jan	206	9/16	...	...
HlywdE	30	Jul	...	...	37	3 1/2
31 1/4	35	Jan	30	7/16	...	...
HmeDp	40	Feb	...	...	155	3/8
46 1/8	45	Jan	84	2	165	3/4
46 1/8	45	May	270	4 1/8	...	...
46 1/8	45	Aug	270	5 1/8	...	...
46 1/8	50	Jan	35	3/16	...	...
46 1/8	50	Feb	62	1/2	...	...
46 1/8	50	May	100	1 1/2	100	4 3/4
46 1/8	50	Aug	62	2 1/2	100	5 1/8
Homstk	17 1/2	Jan	255	1/2	19	3/4
17	17 1/2	Jul	25	2	...	...
17	20	Jan	364	1/8	64	3 1/4
17	20	Apr	56	5/8	350	3 3/8
17	20	Jul	...	...	414	3 5/8
Honwll	30	Jan	30	1 1/2	10	11/16
30	35	Feb	36	5/8	...	...
30	35	May	134	1 1/8	...	...
30	35	Aug	80	1 5/8	...	...
Horshm	10	Apr	57	2 1/2	...	...
12 1/8	12 1/2	Apr	270	7/8	10	7/8
HospFS	20	Jan	50	4	...	...
Humana	20	Jan	34	2 1/2	5	5/16
22 3/8	20	Feb	115	2 3/4	...	...
22 3/8	22 1/2	Jan	79	1	...	...
22 3/8	22 1/2	Feb	70	1 3/8	...	...
22 3/8	22 1/2	May	...	...	55	2 1/8
22 3/8	25	Feb	46	7/16	...	...
IBP	35	Jan	106	5/8	...	...
ICN o	22	Jan	125	3/16	...	...
IDB Cm	10	Mar	42	1/4	...	...
IMC Gl	40	Apr	26	4	4	2 1/2
ITT	75	Jan	100	6 1/8	...	...
81 1/2	80	Jan	2	2 7/16	50	2
81 1/2	85	Mar	39	2 1/8	...	...
Imungn	5	Mar	...	...	35	2 1/4
ImunRs	7 1/2	Feb	26	3/8	15	1 11/16
5 3/4	10	Feb	...	...	35	4 1/4
5 3/4	10	May	66	1/4	...	...
Imunex	12 1/2	Jan	30	2 15/16	...	...
Inco	30	Jan	40	7/8	...	...
InfoRs	12 1/2	Feb	25	2 5/16	...	...
13 1/4	15	Jan	53	1/2	...	...
Infrmx	25	Jan	2	2 3/8	42	1 1/16
25 7/8	30	Jan	61	1/2	...	...
25 7/8	30	Feb	52	1 1/16	4	4 1/8
25 7/8	30	May	25	2 1/4	...	...
IngRnd	30	Jan	...	...	33	3/4
IntgDv	22 1/2	Jan	47	4 1/8	...	...
25 3/4	22 1/2	Feb	29	4 3/8	33	13/16
25 3/4	25	Jan	...	...	96	1 1/8
25 3/4	25	Feb	30	3	...	...
25 3/4	30	Jan	50	3/8	...	...
Intel	50	Jan	60	8 1/4	239	1/4
57 13/16	50	Apr	90	10	128	15/16
57 13/16	55	Jan	264	4 1/4	3916	1 1/16
57 13/16	55	Feb	18	5	3462	1 5/8
57 13/16	55	Apr	52	6 1/2	1470	2 1/4
57 13/16	55	Jul	4	7 1/2	55	3
57 13/16	60	Jan	3558	1 7/16	1946	3 1/8
57 13/16	60	Feb	428	2 1/8	89	3 7/8
57 13/16	60	Apr	1925	3 1/2	349	4 1/2
57 13/16	65	Jan	2397	1/4	677	7 1/4
57 13/16	65	Feb	171	11/16	1	7 5/8
57 13/16	65	Apr	250	1 3/4	36	7 3/4
57 13/16	65	Jul	106	3 1/8	39	8
57 13/16	70	Jan	93	1/8	...	...
57 13/16	70	Apr	324	7/8	53	12 1/4
57 13/16	70	Jul	40	1 13/16	...	...
Intelcm	12 1/2	Jan	200	1 1/4	10	3/4
12 3/4	12 1/2	Mar	30	1 13/16	6	1 3/8
12 3/4	15	Jan	90	3/8	...	...
12 3/4	15	Mar	27	13/16	75	2 13/16
12 3/4	17 1/2	Mar	47	3/8	...	...
IntelEl	7 1/2	Jan	30	11/16	18	1/2
7 3/4	10	Jun	135	13/16	...	...

Option/Strike		Exp.	Call Vol.	Call Last	Put Vol.	Put Last
Melvil	35	May	40	1/2	...	...
MercSt	35	Jan	12	5 1/8	66	5/8
39 7/8	35	Mar	33	7	...	...
39 7/8	40	Jan	136	2 3/16	4	2 1/4
39 7/8	40	Jun	100	5 5/8	...	...
39 7/8	45	Jan	48	7/8	...	...
39 7/8	55	Jun	29	1 9/16	...	...
39 7/8	60	Jun	40	1	...	...
Merck	30	Jan	60	8 3/8	76	1/16
38 1/8	35	Jan	869	3 1/2	15	1/4
38 1/8	35	Apr	39	4 1/8	26	5/8
38 1/8	35	Jul	68	4 3/4	...	...
38 1/8	40	Jan	2461	3/8	15	2 1/4
38 1/8	40	Apr	229	1 1/4	10	2 7/8
38 1/8	40	Jul	162	2 1/8	12	3 1/2
Merril	30	Jan	11	5 1/2	400	3/16
35 3/8	30	Apr	...	...	60	13/16
35 3/8	32 1/2	Jan	4	2 7/8	229	9/16
35 3/8	35	Jan	431	1 9/16	1348	1 3/16
35 3/8	40	Jan	134	1/8	38	4 3/4
35 3/8	45	Jul	30	13/16	...	...
Methnx	10	Jan	50	4	...	...
13 3/4	12 1/2	Jan	5	1 3/4	50	3/8
13 3/4	15	Jan	431	1/2	19	1 5/8
13 3/4	15	Feb	25	1	...	...
13 3/4	17 1/2	Jan	50	1/8	5	3 3/4
MichNt	70	Jan	...	...	30	1/2
Micrchp	25	Jan	45	1 7/8	103	1 1/2
Mcrchp o	26 5/8	Apr	95	3 7/8	10	3 3/8
Micrchp	30	Jan	265	5/8	20	5 1/8
Microcm	12 1/2	Jan	120	5/16	...	...
10 7/8	12 1/2	Feb	30	11/16	...	...
10 7/8	12 1/2	Jul	200	1 1/4	...	...
MicrTc	30	Jan	27	10 1/2	...	...
40 3/8	35	Jan	478	6	786	7/16
MicrTc o	36	Jan	...	...	37	5/8
MicrTc	40	Jan	585	2 1/4	669	1 7/8
40 3/8	40	Feb	94	3 3/8	457	2 5/8
40 3/8	40	Apr	172	4 3/4	...	...
40 3/8	45	Jan	1752	11/16	129	5
40 3/8	45	Feb	30	1 3/8	...	...
40 3/8	45	Apr	33	2 3/4	...	...
40 3/8	50	Jan	60	3/16	10	9 1/2
Microp	10	Jan	70	5/16	...	...
Micsft	52 1/2	Jan	...	...	186	1/16
62 5/8	55	Jan	323	8 1/2	1015	3/16
62 5/8	55	Apr	...	...	92	1
62 5/8	55	Jul	80	11	...	...
62 5/8	57 1/2	Jan	...	...	520	1/4
62 5/8	60	Jan	1217	3 7/8	1269	7/8
62 5/8	60	Feb	...	...	36	1 1/2
62 5/8	60	Apr	29	6	427	2 3/8
62 5/8	65	Jan	338	1	441	3 1/8
62 5/8	65	Feb	25	1 7/8	...	...
62 5/8	70	Feb	54	1/2	...	...
62 5/8	70	Apr	33	1 3/4	1	8
MAWste	7 1/2	Jan	80	5/8	...	...
MidAtl	22 1/2	Jan	29	1 3/8	20	1 1/8
22 5/8	25	Jan	219	1/2	...	...
Midlan	25	Jan	32	1 3/4	15	5/8
MirRst	25	Feb	48	1/4	...	...
MblTel	20	Jan	84	3/8	...	...
18 1/16	20	Feb	31	11/16	...	...
18 1/16	20	Mar	44	1	...	...
18 1/16	20	Jun	104	1 3/4	...	...
Mohawk	12 1/2	Jan	210	3/8	...	...
12	12 1/2	Feb	30	3/4	10	1
MolBio	7 1/2	Apr	30	3 7/8	...	...
11 3/8	10	Jan	25	1 1/2	...	...
11 3/8	12 1/2	Jan	34	1/4	...	...
11 3/8	12 1/2	Feb	35	11/16	...	...
11 3/8	15	Apr	...	...	30	4 1/8
Monsan	75	Jan	40	1 1/8	...	...
Moore	20	Apr	20	5/8	30	2 3/8
MorgSt	60	Jan	5	2 1/4	40	2
59 3/4	65	May	...	...	40	6 3/8
Morgan	55	Jan	10	2 1/4	46	3/4
57 1/4	55	Feb	50	2 3/4	...	...
57 1/4	60	Mar	25	7/8	40	4
57 1/4	65	Jan	318	1/8	33	8 7/8
MorrKn	12 1/2	Feb	38	1 1/16	...	...
12 7/8	12 1/2	Apr	...	...	206	1
12 7/8	15	Jan	36	1/4	10	2

Source: *The Wall Street Journal*, December 20, 1994, p. C13. Reprinted by permission of *The Wall Street Journal*,

The intrinsic value for the in the money *put* options equals the strike price minus the market price. In the case of the Intel 60 April put, the intrinsic value is $2\frac{3}{16}$ as indicated by Formula 15–2.

$$\text{Intrinsic value put} = \text{Strike price} - \text{Market price} \qquad (15\text{–}2)$$

$$\text{Intrinsic value} = 60 - 57\tfrac{13}{16}$$

$$= 2\tfrac{3}{16} \text{ (Intel 60 April put)}$$

Since puts allow the owner to sell stock at the strike price, in the money put options exist where the strike price is above the market price of the stock. Out of the money puts have market prices for common stock above the strike price.

Speculative Premium

Returning to the Intel 50 April call, we see in Table 15–3 that the total premium is 10, while the previously computed intrinsic value is $7\frac{13}{16}$. This call option has an additional speculative premium of $2\frac{3}{16}$ due to other factors. The total premium (option price) is a combination of the intrinsic value plus a **speculative premium.** This relationship is indicated in Formula 15–3 and shown in Figure 15–1.

$$\text{Total premium} = \text{Intrinsic Value} + \text{Speculative premium} \qquad (15\text{–}3)$$

$$10 = 7\tfrac{13}{16} + 2\tfrac{3}{16}$$

Generally, the higher the volatility of the common stock—as measured by its stock price's standard deviation or by its beta—and the lower the dividend yield, the greater the speculative premium.[3] The longer the exercise period, the higher the speculative premium, especially if market expectations over the duration of the option are positive. Finally, the deeper the option is in the money, the smaller the leverage potential and therefore the smaller the speculative premium. Most often, we examine the speculative premium separately to see if it is a reasonable premium to pay for the possible benefits.

The speculative premium can be expressed in dollars or as a percentage of the common stock price. A speculative premium expressed in percent indicates the increase in

FIGURE 15–1 Components of the Total Premium on a Call Option

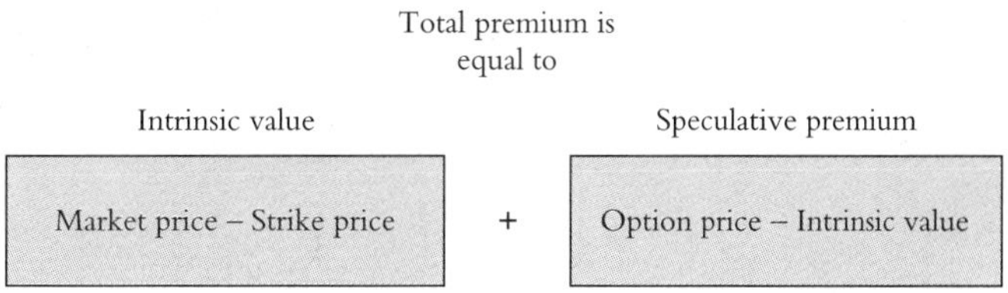

[3] Some people refer to the speculative premium as the time premium because time may be the overriding factor affecting the speculative premium.

the stock price needed for the purchaser of a call option to break even on the expiration date. Table 15–4 shows this point.[4] Notice that the Intel April 50 call option, which is deep in the money, has the lowest speculative premium, while the 70 call option has the highest. Realize that the 70 call option has a cash value of only ⅞ (the total premium), and the other 12³⁄₁₆ represents the required increase in the stock price for the market price and the strike price to be equal. The 22.59 percent speculative premium for the April 70 call option represents the percentage movement in stock price by the expiration date for a break-even position. At expiration, there will be no speculative premium. The option will reflect only the intrinsic value and possibly even a discount because of commission expenses incurred on exercise.

Speculative Premiums and the Time Factor Table 15–5 provides a look at premiums for the in the money and out of the money call options with varying times to expiration. Since the quotes are as of January, the January options will expire first, then the February options, and finally the April options. The option premiums increase with more time to expiration.

Intel's speculative premiums in Table 15–5 demonstrate that percentage speculative premiums increase with time across all series of strike prices. The speculative premiums are lowest with the in the money 50 and 55 calls because of the low leverage potential and the downside risk if the stock declines. The 70 call option has a high speculative premium, but an option writer (seller) would *not reap much cash inflow.* Generally, out of the money call options have high speculative premiums, but little of the premium may be in the form of cash. For example, the January 70 call has a total premium of ⅛. The fact that the cash premium is only 12.5 cents is an important consideration for an option writer.

Speculative Premiums, Betas, and Dividend Yields Table 15–6 demonstrates the relationship of betas and dividend yields to the speculative premium. The four options listed are all January calls from Table 15–3. In general, the speculative premiums (in percent) are

TABLE 15–4 Speculative Premiums on December 19, 1994, for Intel Options

Market Price	Intel Strike Price	Total Premium (Price)	–	Intrinsic Value	=	Speculative Premium	Speculative Premium as a Percent of Stock Price
57¹³⁄₁₆	50 April call	10		7¹³⁄₁₆		2³⁄₁₆	3.78%
57¹³⁄₁₆	55 April call	6½		2¹³⁄₁₆		3¹¹⁄₁₆	6.38
57¹³⁄₁₆	60 April call	3½		(2³⁄₁₆)		5¹¹⁄₁₆	9.84
57¹³⁄₁₆	65 April call	1¾		(7³⁄₁₆)		8¹⁵⁄₁₆	15.46
57¹³⁄₁₆	70 April call	⅞		(12³⁄₁₆)		13¹⁄₁₆	22.59

[4] As applied to put options, the speculative premium indicates the decrease in stock price needed for the purchaser of a put option to break even on the expiration date.

TABLE 15–5 Speculative Premiums over Time (Intel Option Calls, December 19, 1994)

Market Price	Strike Price	January Total Premium* (Price)	Speculative Premium Dollars	Speculative Premium Percent	February Total Premium** (Price)	Speculative Premium Dollars	Speculative Premium Percent	April Total Premium*** (Price)	Speculative Premium Dollar	Speculative Premium Percent
57 13/16	50	8 1/4	7/16	0.76%	r†	—	—	10	2 3/16	3.78%
57 13/16	55	4 1/4	1 7/16	2.49	5	2 3/16	3.78%	6 1/2	3 11/16	6.38
57 13/16	60	1 7/16	1 5/8	6.27	2 1/8	4 5/16	7.46	3 1/2	5 11/16	9.84
57 13/16	65	1/4	7 7/16	12.86	11/16	7 7/8	13.62	1 3/4	8 15/16	15.46
57 13/16	70	1/8	12 5/16	21.30	r	—	—	7/8	13 1/16	22.59

* January—32 days to expiration.
** February—60 days to expiration.
*** April—123 days to expiration.
†r = not traded.

TABLE 15–6 Speculative Premiums Related to Betas and Dividend Yields

	January Strike	Market Price	Total Premium	Speculative Premium Dollars	Speculative Premium Percent	Beta	Expected Dividend Yield
Exxon	60	61 1/2	2 1/4	3/4	1.22%	0.60	4.88%
Home Depot	45	46 1/8	2	7/8	1.90	1.60	0.35
Merck	35	38 1/8	3 1/2	3/8	0.98	1.20	3.14
Morgan (J.P.)	55	57 1/4	2 1/4	0	0.00	1.10	5.24

higher for the high-beta, low-dividend yield stocks, and lower for the low-beta, high-dividend stocks. A classic example in the table is Home Depot.

High-beta stocks have a greater probability of participating in a market upturn, and so speculators will pay a higher speculative premium on a call for the chance to participate in an up market. High-dividend-yield stocks are the ones favored by call writers, and therefore, the speculative premiums are lower because there is a larger number of call writers for these stocks. Other factors, such as market attitudes or individual company conditions, can also have a strong bearing on the speculative premium.

Speculative Premiums per Day Speculative premiums can be deceiving. The novice may attempt to write the options with the highest total premium or speculative premium, while the buyer may think the smallest dollar investment provides the greatest advantage. These are not usually true if we look at speculative premiums on a per day basis. For example,

the Intel calls in Table 15–5 have the following speculative premiums per day. The information is based on a strike price of 55 and expiration months of January, February, and April. Note that the speculative premium is divided by the number of days to expiration to arrive at the speculative premium per day.

Month	Strike	Speculative Premium	Days to Expiration	Speculative Premium per Day
January	55	2.49%	32	0.078
February	55	3.78	60	0.063
April	55	6.38	123	0.052

An examination of daily premiums would suggest that call writers should write short-lived calls on a continuous basis to get a maximum return. In this case, the January calls give the maximum premium per day. On the other hand, call buyers get more time for less premium per day by purchasing the April calls.

Understanding option premiums is important to make sense out of option strategies. Various strategies involving calls and puts are covered in the next section. Appendix 15A presents the Black-Scholes option pricing model, a much more sophisticated way of analyzing option prices and their time premiums and speculative premiums. This appendix is primarily designed for those who wish to achieve a more advanced understanding of the theoretical basis for option pricing; it is not essential for the standard reading of the text.

BASIC OPTION STRATEGIES

Option strategies can be very aggressive and risky, or they can be quite conservative and used as a means of reducing risk. Option buyers and writers both attempt to take advantage of the option premiums discussed in the preceding section. In theory, many option strategies can be created, but in practice, the market must be liquid to execute these strategies. After a decade of explosive growth, option volume on individual common stocks has not expanded as much in the late 1980s and early 1990s as in the first years of the Chicago Board Options Exchange. Although volume on the underlying common stock has continued to increase, much of the option activity has been absorbed by options on the Standard & Poor's 100 and 500 Stock Indexes, where large institutional investors can transact portfolio strategies on the market rather than on individual stocks.

A reduction of individual option trading reduces the ability to create workable strategies for specific companies. For example, the lack of a liquid market can keep institutional investors from executing hedging strategies involving several hundred thousand shares. Even with these limitations in mind, the average investor can still find many opportunities for option strategies. In this section, we discuss the possible uses of calls and puts to achieve different investment goals. Table 15–7 provides option quotes at three time periods for our examples. We have ignored commissions in most examples, but commissions can be a significant hidden cost in some types of option strategies.

TABLE 15–7 Option Quotes over Three Months

		November 4, 1994 74 days to Expiration		December 2, 1994 46 Days to Expiration		January 6, 1995 11 Days to Expiration	
Name	Strike Price	Option Premium	Common Stock Price	Option Premium	Common Stock Price	Option Premium	Common Stock Price
Apple	Jan. 40	3⅜	40⅜	1¼	36 9/16	2⅞	42
GM	Jan. 40	2	39¼	1 1/16	38½	3⅜	43¼
Intel	Jan. 60	3¾	60⅜	4½	62⅞	5¼	65
Intel	Jan. 65	1 11/16	60⅜	1⅞	62⅞	1 5/16	65
Lilly	Jan. 60	4¾	62½	4½	61¾	5½	65⅛
Lilly	Jan. 65	1 11/16	62½	2⅛	61¾	1⅜	65⅛
Merck	Jan. 35	1 9/16	35⅛	3¾	37¾	2¾	37½
Motorola	Jan. 50	9½	58½	8	57¼	8⅛	57⅞
Motorola	Jan. 55	6½	58½	4	57¼	3¾	57⅞
Motorola	Jan. 55 P*	1½	58½	1¾	57¼	11/16	57⅞
Motorola	Jan. 60	2 11/16	58½	1⅝	57¼	15/16	57⅞
Motorola	Jan. 60 P*	3⅜	58½	3⅞	57¼	3	57⅞
Newbridge Networks	Jan. 30	2⅜	27⅞	—	32⅝	6⅝	36⅜
Newbridge Networks	Jan. 35	—	27⅞	1½	32⅝	1⅞	36⅜
Novell	Jan. 15	3⅝	18⅛	4⅜	19½	2⅝	17½
Novell	Jan. 17 ½	2	18⅛	2 13/16	19½	⅜	17½
Novell	Jan. 17 ½ P*	1⅛	18⅛	½	19½	⅜	17½
TelMex	Jan. 50	7¼	56⅜	4	52½	1/16	36⅞
TelMex	Jan. 55	4	56⅜	1 9/16	52½	1/16	36⅞

* P = Put Contract.

Buying Call Options

The Leverage Strategy Leverage is a very common reason for buying call options when the market is expected to rise during the exercise period. The use of calls in this way is similar to warrants discussed in Chapter 14, but calls have shorter lives. The call option is priced much lower than common stock, and the leverage is derived from a small percentage change in the price of the common stock that can cause a large percentage change in the price of the call option. For example, on November 4, 1994, General Motors (GM) common stock closed at $39.25 per share, and the call closed at $2.00 (see Table 15–7).

Two months later, on January 6, 1995, the stock closed at $43.25 for a $4.00 point gain of 10.2 percent ($4.00/$39.25). The January 40 call closed at $3.375 for a $1.375 gain of

68.8 percent ($1.375/$2.00). The call option increased by more than six times the percentage move in the common stock. The relationship is indicated below.

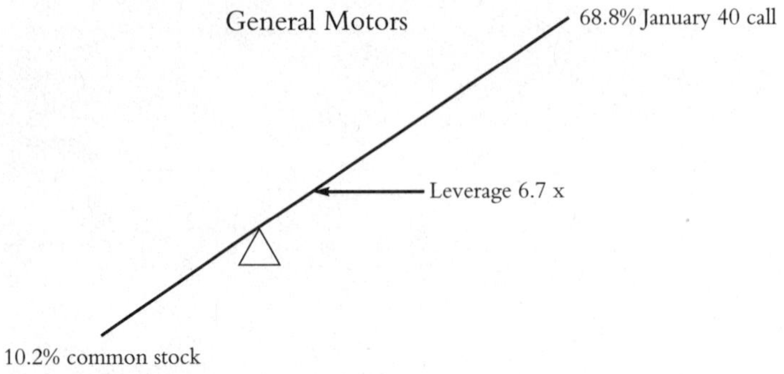

Figure 15–2 depicts the relationship between profit and loss opportunities for the General Motors January 40 call option, assuming the option is held until the day of expiration (no speculative premium exists at expiration).

As long as the common stock closes under $40, the call buyer loses the whole premium of $2 (100 shares × $2 = $200). At a price of $42, the call buyer breaks even as the option is worth an intrinsic value of $2. As the stock increases past $42, the profit starts accumulating. At a price of $46, the profit equals $400 at expiration. If the option is sold before expiration, a speculative premium may increase the profit potential.

FIGURE 15–2 General Motors January 40 Call Option (Excludes commissions)

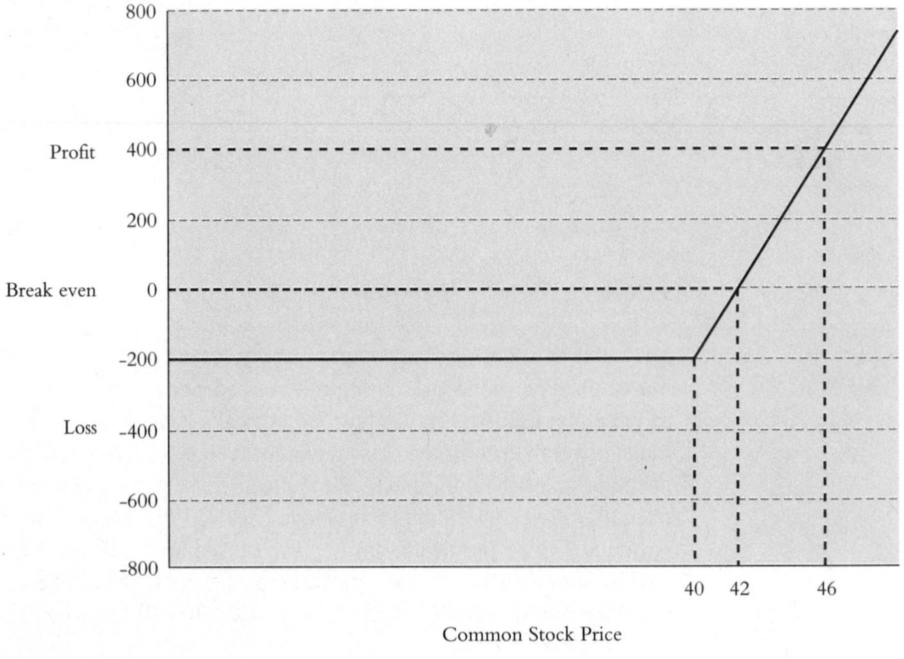

An investor striving for maximum leverage will generally buy options that are out of the money or slightly in the money. Buying high-priced options for $10 or $15 that are well in the money limits the potential for leverage. You may have to invest almost as much in the options as you would in the stock.

Playing the leverage game does not always work. Let's once again look at Table 15–7. If on December 2, 1994, a speculator assumed Telephonos deMexico (TelMex) would go up and bought the January 50 call for $4, approximately one month later on January 6, 1995, the TelMex 50 call option would have been worth $0.0625. A $3.9375 point loss occurred. The decline in TelMex common stock from $52.50 to $36.875 would have caused a $393.75 loss (100 shares × $3.9375) for the option buyer. Although the stock declined $15.625, or 29.8 percent, the call declined $3.9375 points, or 98.4 percent. If the stock price stays below $50 until expiration, the owner of the January 50 call can expect to lose the current call premium of $0.0625 because the intrinsic value at a market price of $50 is zero. It is not hard to lose all your money under these circumstances—leverage works in reverse, too.

Call Options Instead of Stock Many people do not like to risk losing large amounts of money and view call options as a way of controlling 100 shares of stock without a large dollar commitment. For example, using Table 15–7 for the November 4, 1994, prices, Motorola common stock could have been purchased at $58.50 or $5,850 for 100 shares. A January 55 call purchased on November 4, 1994, could also be bought for $6.50 ($650), which would leave $5,200 ($5,850 – $650) for an investment elsewhere while still controlling 100 shares of Motorola at 55 through the option.

Assume the call is purchased for $650, and the $5,200 is left to be invested in a money market fund at 5 percent until January 6, 1995. The interest income would be about $44.87 for the 63 days.[5] During this time, the stock declined from $58.50 to $57.875 for a loss of $0.625, or $62.50 on 100 shares. As would be expected, the call option also went down from $6.50 to $3.75. That's a loss of $275 ($2.75 × 100) that was partially offset by the $44.87 of interest income from the investment of leftover cash in a money market fund. The net loss associated with the call option is $230.13 ($275 – $44.87). In this case, the net loss on the call option of $230.13 is more than the net loss of $62.50 on the stock purchased because so much time premium evaporated as expiration approached. For this strategy to work a little better, the investor should buy a call option that is in the money or slightly out of the money.

Nevertheless, had Motorola stock really declined in value, say, to $40, the advantage of the limited dollar loss exposure of the option would be quite apparent. The purchaser of 100 shares of stock would have lost $1,850 as the stock declined from $58.50 to $40. The purchaser of the option cannot lose more than the initial purchase price of $650 ($6.50 × 100). Even this loss is slightly offset by the $44.87 of interest from the investment of leftover cash in a money market account.[6] Of course, if the stock rises to $80 or $90, both the stock purchaser and option buyer will show substantial profits.

---

[5] The approximate calculation is $5,200 × 5% × (63/365) = $44.87.

[6] It should be pointed out we are talking about *absolute* dollar losses. On a percentage basis, the options would be the bigger losers.

Protecting a Short Position Calls are often used to cover a short sale against the risk of rising stock prices. This is called hedging your position: By purchasing a call, the short seller guarantees a loss of no more than a fixed amount while at the same time reducing any potential profit by the total premium paid for the call. Again refer to Table 15–7, and assume you sold 100 shares of Intel short at $60.375 on November 4, 1994, and bought a January 60 call for $3.75 as protection against a rise in the price of the stock. By January 6, 1995, the stock has risen to $65 for a $4.625 ($60.375 – $65) loss per share on the short position. This loss has been partially offset by an increase in the January 60 call option price from $3.75 to $5.25, or a $1.50 gain. Instead of losing $4.625 per share, the short position is only out $3.125 so far ($4.625 – $1.50). Based on 100 shares, the loss has been cut from $462.50 to $312.50, or reduced by $150.

Reconsider the initial $3.75 call premium. If the stock goes up, the call limits your loss, but if the stock goes down as expected, your profit on the short position may be reduced by the call premium. In the case of Intel, the stock would have to decline to $56.625 ($60.375 – $3.75) before the short seller with call protection would break even. After that point, the combined short sell/call option position would begin to make money. As is true of most option plays, there are advantages and disadvantages to most strategies.

Guaranteed Price Often, an investor thinks a stock will rise over the long term but does not have cash currently available to purchase the stock. The important point for this strategy is that the investor wants to own this stock eventually but does not want to miss out on a good buying opportunity now (based on expectations). Perhaps the oil stocks are depressed, or semiconductors have hit bottom. A call option can be utilized. The investor could be anticipating a cash inflow in the future when he or she plans to exercise the call option with a tax refund, a book royalty, or even the annual Christmas bonus.

For example, on November 4, 1994, Michelle Trudeau buys a Newbridge Networks January 30 call option for $2.375, which is all speculative premium since Newbridge is selling for $27.875 per share on that date (as shown in Table 15–7). By January 6, 1995, she has received her $3,000 royalty check and exercises the option to buy the stock at 30 when the stock is selling at $36.375. For tax purposes, the cost or basis of these 100 shares of Newbridge is the strike price ($30) plus the option premium ($2.375), or $32.375 per share. Since most investors will not pursue this strategy if they expect prices to fall, they will usually seek out the deepest in the money option they can afford because it is likely to have the lowest speculative premium.

Writing Call Options

Writers of call options take the opposite side of the market from buyers. The writer is similar to a short seller in that he or she expects the stock to decline or stay the same. For short sellers to profit, prices may decline, but since writers of call options receive a premium, they can make a profit if prices stay the same or even rise less than the speculative premium. Option writers can write **covered options,** meaning they own the underlying common stock, or they can write **naked options,** meaning they do not own the underlying stock.

Writing covered call options is often considered a hedged position because if the stock price declines, the writer's loss on the stock is partially offset by the option premium. A

potential writer of a covered call must decide if he is willing to sell the underlying stock if it closes above the strike price and if the option is exercised.

Returning to Table 15–7 for another set of option quotes, find the TelMex options on November 4, 1994. The market price of the common stock is 56.375, and the writer for a January call option chooses the 50 strike price.

Remember, the writer agrees to sell 100 shares at the strike price as the consideration for the premium. The 50 strike price is deeper in the money than the 55 strike and would be a good write if the stock closed at less than 50 because the call would not get exercised, and the writer would profit by the amount of the $7.25 premium. If the stock closed at 50 or higher, then the call could get exercised, and the writer would have to deliver 100 shares at 50. More likely, the option writer would buy back the option for its price in the market to avoid having the option exercised. If the ending value of the stock were 55, the option writer could buy back the 50 call option for 5 and still have a profit of $2.25 ($225 on 100 shares) before commissions. If the stock closed at more than $57.25 (the strike price plus the option premium of $7.25), the call writer would buy back the option at a loss. Figure 15–3 shows this relationship between profit and loss and the common stock price in writing the option.

By January 6, 1995, TelMex stock closed at 36.875, and at that point, the covered call writer would lose money, and a naked option writer would make a profit. The covered option writer is assumed to have bought 100 shares at 56.375 at the time he or she wrote the option for $7.25 on November 4. The naked option writer merely sold the option for $7.25. It is further assumed the covered option writer would receive a $76 dividend

FIGURE 15–3 TelMex January 50 Call (Excludes commissions)

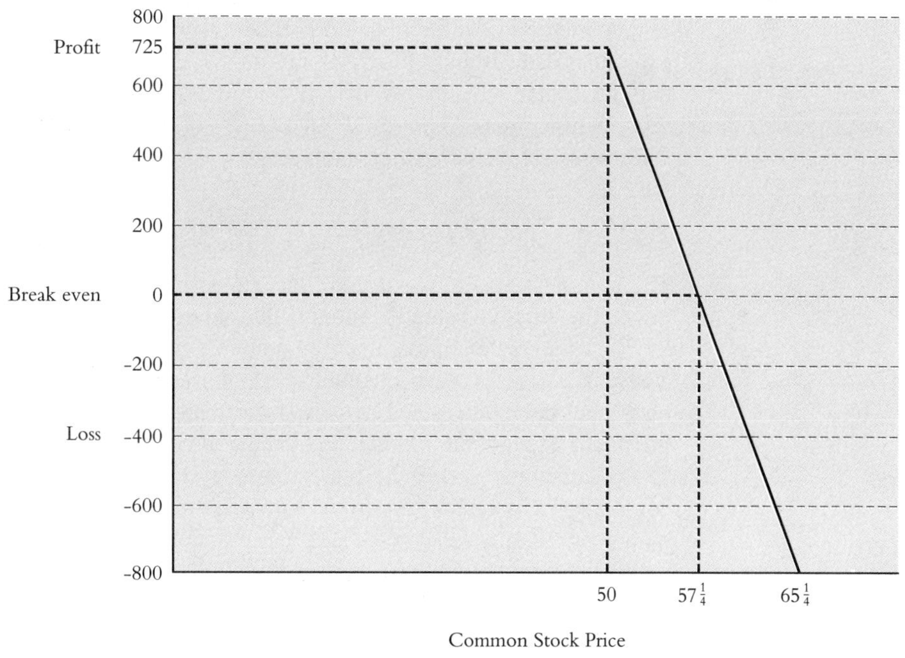

during December. Also note that the option is only worth 1/16 or $0.0625. The analysis is presented below.

Covered Writer		Naked Writer	
– Initial investment (100 × 56.375)	($5,637.50)	– Margin (30% of stock price)	($1,691.50)
+ Option premium (100 × 7.25)	725.00	+ Option premium (100 × 725.00)	725.00
+ Dividend	76.00	(no dividends received)	—
+ Ending value stock (100 × 36.875)	3,687.50	+ Ending value margin	1,691.50
– Repurchase of option (100 × 0.0625)	(6.25)	– Repurchase of option	(6.25)
Loss	$1,155.25	Profit	$ 718.75
Percent return (loss) on initial investment	–20.49%	Percent return on initial investment	42.5%

The covered writer hedged the loss on his stock ($1,950) as it fell from 56.375 to 36.875 to a loss of $1,155.25 through profits from the option and a dividend. The naked option writer made money and a high percentage return on his initial margin (42.5 percent) for a two-month investment, or close to a 255 percent annualized return. The naked writer was required to put up margin on 30 percent of the value of the stock to ensure his ability to close out the option write if the stock should rise significantly. The capital was returned to him when it was no longer needed as collateral. If the stock price had risen, the naked writer was exposed to unlimited risk as he or she either had to close out the position at a loss or purchase the stock above the strike price and deliver it at a loss. The covered writer had limited risk because he or she owned the stock and could deliver it or close out the position before it is called. If the owner of the stock had not written a call, she would have lost $1,950 (34.6%) instead of $1,555.25 (20.5%).

Another critical decision for a call writer is the choice of months. In the section on option premiums, we examined percentage premiums per day and found that the shortest expiration dates usually provided the highest daily speculative premium. In most cases, the call writer will choose the short-term options and, as they expire, write another short-term option. *Annualized* returns of 12 to 15 percent are not uncommon for continuously covered writing strategies.

Buying Put Options

The owner (buyer) of a put may sell 100 shares of stock to the put writer at the strike price. The strategy behind a put is similar to selling short or writing a call except losses are limited to the total investment (premium), and no more risk exposure is possible if the stock rises. Buying a put in anticipation of a price decline is one method of speculating on market price changes. The same factors influencing call premiums also apply to put premiums except that expectations for the direction for the market are the opposite.

On December 2, 1994, Novell common stock was 19.50, and a 17.50 January put could be purchased for 1/2 or $0.50 (see Table 15–7 and look for put prices as designated by a P rather than call prices). The put was out of the money by $2.00. A period of 1.5 months (46 days) remained until expiration. The buyer of the put would expect a price decline with the idea that the intrinsic value of the put would increase. By January 6, 1995, Novell declined to 17.50 (its strike price) with the January 17.50 put trading at 3/8.

TABLE 15–8 Loss on Put and Gain on Stock

Loss on Put		Gain on Stock	
Purchase price (December 2, 1994)	$ 1.75	Value (December 2, 1994)	$ 57.25
Latest price (January 6, 1995)	0.6875	Latest price (January 6, 1995)	57.875
Loss	1.0625	Gain	$ 0.625
× 100	100	× 100	100
Total loss	$106.25	Total gain	$ 62.50

The intrinsic value was zero, and the speculative premium was ⅜. At this time, the owner of the put had a ⅛ loss on the original $0.50 investment. Assume that Novell closed at $16 on the day of expiration. The intrinsic value of the $17.50 put would be $1.50, and the owner of the put would have a $1.00 profit on a $0.50 investment or a 200 percent return in one and one-half months. On the other hand, if Novell closes at $17.50 or above, the put option expires worthless, and the put owner is out $50 ($0.50 × 100 shares).

Puts can make money in a down market and also possibly help offset a loss in the value of the common stock. As an example of the latter case, an owner of 100 shares of Novell at an ending price of 16 would drop $3.50 (19.50 – 16.00), and the gain of $1.00 on the put would offset some of the loss suffered on the common stock.

Hedges do not always work as expected. For example, assume on December 2, 1994, that an owner of 100 shares of Motorola stock thought the stock was going to decline because of expectations of rising interest rates, but he or she did not want to sell the stock and pay a capital gains tax on these shares that were profitably held for many years. Instead, the owner bought a January 55 put for $1.75 when the stock was trading at $57.25 (see Table 15–7). One month later on January 6, 1995, Motorola was up to $57.875 (the decline never materialized), and the January 55 put had no intrinsic value and was trading at 11/16 ($.6875), providing a loss of $106.25 on the put. This $106.25 loss more than offset the $62.50 (⅝ per share or $62.50 total) gain on the stock and eliminated the profit on the stock as shown in Table 15–8. Of course, one can think of the $106.25 loss as insurance against a price decline that never happened. Much like auto insurance, we pay a premium for something we hope never happens.

USING OPTIONS IN COMBINATIONS

Spreads

Now that you have studied puts and calls from both the buyer's and writer's perspectives, we proceed with a discussion of spreads. Most combinations of options are called **spreads** and consist of buying one option (going long) and writing an option (going short) on the same underlying stock. Spreads are for the sophisticated investor and involve many variations on a theme. Vertical spreads involve buying and writing two contracts at different striking prices with the same month of expiration. Horizontal spreads consist of buying and writing two options with the same strike price but different months, and a

TABLE 15–9 Spreads (Call options)

Vertical Spread

			Option Prices		
	Market Price	**Strike Price**	**October**	**January**	**April**
XYZ	36⅜	35	4	6	6½
	36⅜	40	2	3⅜	4
	36⅜	45	11/16	1½	6

Horizontal Spread

	Market Price	Strike Price	October	January	April
XYZ	36⅜	35	4	6	6½
	36 /8	40	2	3⅜	4
	36⅜	45	11/16	1½	6

Diagonal Spread

	Market Price	Strike Price	October	January	April
XYZ	36⅜	35	4	6	6½
	36⅜	40	2	3⅜	4
	36⅜	45	11/16	1½	6

diagonal spread is a combination of the vertical and horizontal spread. Table 15–9 presents an example of XYZ Corporation demonstrating the options, months, and strike prices involved in each type of spread. There are more complicated spreads than these, such as the butterfly spread, variable spread, and domino spread. We cannot attempt to explain all of these spreads in the space available, so we will concentrate on vertical bull spreads and vertical bear spreads.

Since spreads require the purchase of one option and the sale of another option, a speculator's account will have either a debit or credit balance. If the cost of the long option position is greater than the revenue from the short option position, the speculator has a net cash outflow and a debit in his account. When your spread is put on with a debit, it is said you have "bought the spread." You have "sold the spread" if the receipt from writing the short option position is greater than the cost of buying the long option position and you have a credit balance. For example, the difference between the option prices for a vertical spread on XYZ Corporation in Table 15–9 with October strike prices of 35 and 40 is \$2 (\$4 – \$2). The \$2 difference between these two option prices could be either a debit or credit, depending on whether a bull or bear spread is used. In either case, the profit or loss from a spread position results in the change between the two option prices over time as the price of the underlying stock goes up or down.

VERTICAL BULL SPREAD In a bull spread, the expectation is that the common stock price will rise. The speculator can buy the common stock outright, or if he wants to profit from an expected price increase but reduce his risk of loss, he can enter into a bull spread. Vertical bull spreads limit both the maximum gain and maximum loss available. They are usually debit positions because the spreader buys the higher-priced, in the money option and

TABLE 15–10 Profit on Vertical Bull Spread

XYZ October 35		XYZ October 40		Price Spread
Bought at	4	Sold at	2	2
Sold at	7½	Bought at	4½	3
Gain	3½	(Loss)	(2½)	1
		Net gain	$100	
		Investment	$200	
		Return	50%	

shorts (writes) an inexpensive, out of the money option. Using Table 15–9 for an XYZ October vertical bull spread, we would buy the October 35 at 4 and sell the October 40 at 2 for a debit of 2 (price spread). This represents a $200 investment. Assume that three weeks later, XYZ stock rises from 36⅜ to 42 with the October 35 selling at 7½ (previously purchased at 4) and the October 40 at 4½ (previously sold at 2). Table 15–10 shows the result of closing out the spread.

Because the investment was only $200, the total return of $100 provided a 50 percent return. However, returns on spreads can be greatly altered by commissions. If the following spread incurred commissions of $25 in and $25 out, the percentage return could be cut in half to 25 percent.

The maximum profit at expiration is equal to the difference in strike prices ($5 in this case) minus the initial price spread ($2 in this case). For the XYZ vertical bull spread, the maximum profit is $300, and the maximum loss is the original debit of $200. At expiration, all speculative premiums are gone, and each option sells at its intrinsic value. Table 15–11 shows maximum profit and loss at various closing market prices at expiration. Remember, our initial investment is $200.

As Table 15–11 indicates, profit does not increase after the stock moves through the 40 price range. Every dollar of increased profit on the long position is offset by $1 of loss

TABLE 15–11 XYZ Vertical Bull Spread

XYZ Stock Price at Expiration 35				XYZ Stock Price at Expiration 40				XYZ Stock Price at Expiration 45			
October 35		**October 40**		**October 35**		**October 40**		**October 35**		**October 40**	
Bought at	4	Sold at	2	Bought at	4	Sold at	2	Bought at	4	Sold at	2
Expired at*	0	Expired at*	0	Sold at*	5	Expired at*	0	Sold at*	10	Bought at*	5
(Loss)	(4)	Gain	2	Gain	1	Gain	2	Gain	6	Loss	(3)
(Net loss) (2)				Net gain 3				Net gain 3			
($200) = 100 percent loss				$300 = 150 percent gain				$300 = 150 percent gain			

*All call options on date of expiration equal their intrinsic value.

FIGURE 15–4 Profit and Loss Relationships on Spreads and Calls

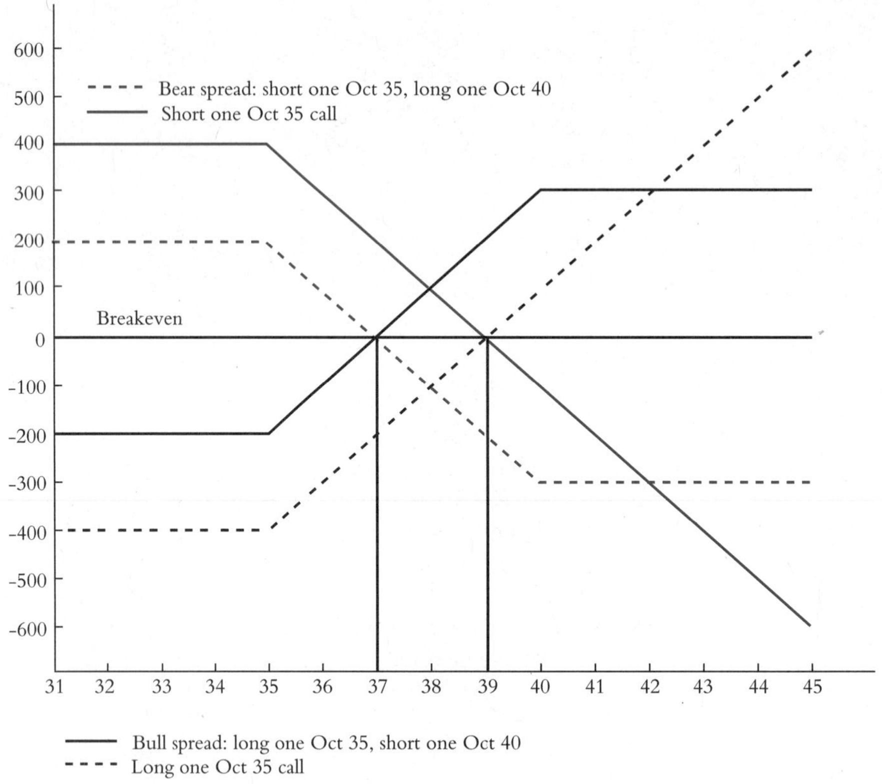

on the short position after the stock passes a price of 40. One of the important but difficult aspects of spreading is forecasting a range of prices rather than just the direction prices will move. If a speculator is bullish, he or she may buy a call instead of spreading. The potential loss is higher with the call but still limited, while the possible gain is unlimited. The relationship between long calls and bull spreads starts in the *bottom* of Figure 15–4. Note the maximum loss with the bull spread is $200 and $400 with a long call. The break-even point is also $2 less for the bull spread ($37 versus $39). However, the long call has unlimited profit potential, and the bull spread is locked in at $300 at a stock price of $40 or higher. The spread position lowers the break-even point by $2 per share but also limits potential returns—a classic case of risk-return trade-off.

Vertical Bear Spread The speculator enters a bear spread anticipating a decline in stock prices. Instead of selling short or writing a call with both having unlimited risk, he spreads by selling short the call with the lower strike price (highest premium) and covers the upside risk with the purchase of a call having a higher strike price. This creates a credit balance. In a sense, the bear spread does the opposite of the vertical bull spread as seen in Table 15–12 in which we show profits and losses from the strategy if XYZ ends up at 35 or at 40. With a bear spread, the price spread of 2 is the maximum gain if the

TABLE 15–12 XYZ Vertical Bear Spread

XYZ Stock Price at Expiration 35				XYZ Stock Price at Expiration 40			
October 35		**October 40**		**October 35**		**October 40**	
Sold at	4	Bought at	2	Sold at	4	Bought at	2
Expired at	0	Expired at	0	Bought at	5	Expired at	0
Gain	4	(Loss)	(2)	(Loss)	1	(Loss)	2
	Net gain 2				Net loss (3)		
	$200				$(300)		

stock closes at 35 or less at expiration, while the maximum loss equals 3, the difference between the exercise prices minus the price spread. The relationship between bear spreads and writing a call option is also demonstrated in Figure 15–4 (the comparison starts at the *top* of the figure).

Straddles

A **straddle** is a combination of a put and call on the same stock with the same strike price and expiration date. It is used to play wide fluctuations in stock prices and is usually applied to individual stocks with high betas and a history of large, short-term fluctuations in price. The speculator using a straddle may be unsure of the direction of the price movement but may be able to make a large enough profit on one side of the straddle to cover the cost of both options even if one option expires worthless.

For example, assume a put and a call can be bought for $5 apiece on an ABC October 50 when ABC Corporation is selling at 50 with six months to expiration. The total investment is 10 ($1,000). If the stock should rise from 50 to 65 at expiration, the call would provide a profit of 10 (15 value – 5 cost), and the put would be left to expire worthless for a loss of 5. This would provide a net gain of 5, or $500. The same type of example can be drawn if the price goes way down. Some who engage in spreads or straddles might attempt to close out one position before the other. This expands the profit potential but also increases the risk.

OTHER OPTION CONSIDERATIONS

Many factors have not been covered in detail because of their changing nature over time. Tax laws relating to options are constantly changing, and some items, such as capital gains, have been revised several times in the last few years. We do know that the tax laws have a significant impact on spread positions and also on the tax treatment where put options are involved. The recognition of the year in which a gain or loss is declared can still be affected by option strategies in combination with stock positions. The best advice we can give is to check the tax consequences of any option strategy with your accountant or stockbroker.

Commissions vary among brokerage houses and are not easy to pinpoint for option transactions since quantity discounts exist. Because many option positions involve small dollar investment outlays, commissions of $25 to $50 for buying and selling can significantly alter your returns and even create losses. Commissions on acquiring common stock through options are higher than the transaction costs of options, and this is a motivating force in closing out option transactions before expiration. Overall, commissions on options tend to be more significant than commissions on commodities or other highly leveraged investments.

SUMMARY

Put and call options are an exciting area of investment and speculation. We have discussed the past history of over-the-counter options trading and more recent trading of options on the listed options exchanges, such as the CBOE. The markets are more efficient, and the standardized practices of the listed exchanges have made options more usable for many investors and widened the number of option strategies that can be employed.

Option premiums (option prices) are affected by many variables such as time, market expectations, stock price volatility, dividend yields, and in the money/out of the money relationships. The total premium consists of an intrinsic value plus a speculative premium that declines to zero by the expiration date. Calls are options to buy 100 shares of stock, while puts are options to sell 100 shares of stock.

Understanding the benefits and risks of trading options is complicated. Options can be risky or used to reduce risk. Calls can be bought for leverage, to cover a short position, or as an alternative to investing in the underlying common stock while buying time to purchase the stock (waiting for the financial resources to exercise the call). Calls are written either as a hedge on a long position in the underlying stock or to speculate on a price decline. Puts are bought to hedge a long position against a price decline or as an alternative to selling short. A writer of a put may speculate on a price increase or use the write as a hedge against a short position (if the price goes up, he will come out ahead on the writing of the put to partially offset the loss on the short sale).

Spreads are combinations of buying and writing the same options for an underlying common stock. In general, spreads reduce the risk of loss while limiting the gain. Spreads can be created to profit from rising prices, falling prices, or no price change. The important part is having the correct expectations. Straddles are a combination of a put and a call option in a stock at the same exercise date and strike price. They are used to profit from stocks showing large, short-term price fluctuations.

Other factors affect option profitability, such as taxes and commissions, and in general, each investor or speculator should check out his or her own situation and factor in the appropriate information with regard to taxes and commissions.

KEY WORDS AND CONCEPTS

option, 425
put, 425
calls, 425
long-term equity anticipation securities (LEAPS), 427
exercise price, 427
Options Clearing Corporation, 428

opening purchase transaction, 428
opening sale transaction, 428
closing purchase transaction, 428
closing sale transaction, 428
in the money, 429
out of the money, 429
intrinsic value, 429
speculative premium, 431
covered options, 438
naked options, 438
spreads, 441
straddle, 445

DISCUSSION QUESTIONS

1. What exchanges trade stock options?
2. How has the option market been expanded to go beyond individual stocks?
3. What is meant by the exercise or strike price on an option?
4. Explain how the Options Clearing Corporation operates.
5. What factors influence a speculative premium on an option?
6. Why might an option price reflect a discount at expiration?
7. Why does an option that is deep in the money often have a low speculative premium?
8. Why would a high-beta stock often have a greater speculative premium than a low-beta stock?
9. Comment on the statement, "The novice may attempt to write the options with the highest total premium or speculative premium, while the buyer may think the smallest investment provides the greatest leverage."
10. What does the speculative premium as a percent of stock price indicate for a call option?
11. Comment on how leverage works in purchasing a call option.
12. Assume you wish to control the price movement of 100 shares of stock. You may buy 100 shares of stock directly or purchase a call option on the 100 shares. Which strategy is likely to expose you to the larger potential dollar amount of loss? Which strategy is likely to expose you to the larger potential percentage loss on your investment?
13. Explain how options can be used to protect a short position.
14. What are two option strategies to take advantage of an anticipated decline in stock prices? (Relate one to call options and the other to put options.)
15. What is the difference between writing a covered and a naked call option?
16. In general, if the price of the underlying stock is going up, what will happen to the price of a put option? Briefly explain.
17. What is a vertical spread? A horizontal spread? A diagonal spread?
18. Is a vertical bear spread likely to be more or less risky than selling short or writing a naked call option?
19. What is a straddle? Why is it used?
20. Why might small commissions of $25 to $50 be important in option trades?

PROBLEMS

Option trading prices

1. Look at the option quotes in Table 15–3.
   a. What is the closing price of the common stock of Merck?
   b. What is the highest strike price listed?
   c. What is the price of an April 35 call option?
   d. What is the price of an April 35 put option?
   e. Explain the reason for the difference between the prices of the put and the call.

Option trading terms

2. Assume that a stock is selling for $66.75 with options available at 60, 65, and 70 strike prices. The 65 call option price is at $4.50.
   a. What is the intrinsic value of the 65 call?
   b. Is the 65 call in the money?
   c. What is the speculative premium on the 65 call option?
   d. What percent does the speculative premium represent of common stock price?
   e. Are the 60 and 70 call options in the money?

Option trading terms

3. In the case of Humana in Table 15–3:
   a. What is the intrinsic value of the February 20 call?
   b. What is the total premium?
   c. How much is the speculative premium?

Option trading terms

4. In the case of Microsoft (Micsft) in Table 15–3:
   a. What is the intrinsic value of the February 70 call?
   b. How much is the speculative premium?
   c. By what percent does the stock need to go up by expiration to break even on the call option?

Speculative premium per day

5. Assume that on May 1 you are considering a stock with three different expiration dates for the 60 call options. The percentage speculative premium for each date is as follows:

May	2.8%
August	6.7
November	10.9

   Each contract expires at 11:59 P.M. Eastern time on the Saturday immediately following the third Friday of the expiration month. For purposes of this problem, assume the May option has 21 days to run, the August option has 112 days, and the November option has 203 days.
   a. Compute the percentage speculative premium per day for each of the three dates.
   b. From the viewpoint of a call option purchaser, which expiration date appears most attractive (all else being equal)?
   c. From the viewpoint of a call option writer, which expiration date appears most attractive (all else being equal)?

Leverage strategy

6. In Table 15–7, calculate the leverage from holding a Newbridge Networks option (January 30 call) from November 4, 1994, until January 6, 1995. (The best approach for doing this is to compute the percentage gain from holding the option, then compute the percentage gain from holding the stock, and, finally, divide the first value by the second value.)

Naked call options

7. Assume that an investor writes a call option for 100 shares at a strike price of 30 for a premium of $5\frac{3}{4}$. This is a naked option.
   a. What would his gain or loss be if the stock closed at 26?
   b. What would the break-even point be in terms of the closing price of the stock?

Covered call options

8. Assume you purchase 100 shares of stock at $44 per share and wish to hedge your position by writing a 100-share call option on your holdings. The option has a 40 strike price and a premium of 8.50. If the stock is selling at 38 at the time of expiration, what will be the overall dollar gain or loss on this covered option play? (Consider the change in stock value as well as the gain or loss on the option.) Note that the stock does not pay a cash dividend.

Covered call options

9. In problem 8, what would be the overall dollar gain or loss if the stock ended up at (*a*) $41, (*b*) $25, (*c*) $57, (*d*) $70. [Disregard the stock being called away in (*a*), (*c*), and (*d*). Assume you will repurchase the option.]

Commission considerations

10. Though commissions are not explicitly considered in problems 7 through 9, might they be significant?

Put options

11. Assume a 40 July put option is purchased for $6\frac{1}{2}$ on a stock selling at $35 per share. If the stock ends up on expiration at $38\frac{3}{4}$, what will be the value of the put option?

Put options

12. In problem 11, at what ending stock price would the investor break even?

Vertical bull spread

13. A stock is selling for $47. You buy a July 45 call option for $3\frac{1}{4}$, and short (write) a July 50 call option for 1. If the stock is $53 at expiration, what will your profit or loss be on the spread? (Note: You do not own any stock directly.)

Protecting a short position with options

14. Assume you sell 100 shares of Bowie Corporation short at $72. You also buy a 70 call option for $5\frac{1}{4}$ to protect against the stock price going up.
    a. If the stock ends up at $90, what will be your overall gain or loss?
    b. If the stock ends up at $50, what will be your overall gain or loss?
    c. If you have an unprotected short sale position (no call option), what is the most you could lose?

THE WALL STREET JOURNAL PROJECTS

Find the options for General Electric in the "Listed Options Quotations" section of *The Wall Street Journal.*

1. Assume you buy a General Electric call option that is in the money by the smallest amount. You will buy the nearest month possible. If the price of General

Electric common stock goes up by 10 percent at the expiration of the option, what will be your dollar profit or loss? Assume you close out your option position.

2. Assume you buy a General Electric put option that is in the money by the smallest amount. You will buy the nearest month possible. If the price of General Electric common stock goes down by 5 percent at the expiration of the option, what will be your dollar profit or loss? Assume you close out your position.

SELECTED REFERENCES

Option Trading Strategy

Black, Fischer. "Fact and Fantasy in the Use of Options." *Financial Analysts Journal,* July–August 1975, pp. 36–41.

Degler, William. "Option for Professionals: Tools of the Trade." *Futures,* April 1987, pp. 52–55.

Finucane, Thomas J. "Put-Call Parity and Expected Returns." *Journal of Financial and Quantitative Analysis,* December 1991, pp. 445–57.

French, Dan W., and Glenn V. Henderson. "Substitute Hedged Option Portfolios: Theory and Evidence." *Journal of Financial Research,* Spring 1981, pp. 21–31.

Gambola, Michael J.; Rodney L. Roenfeldt; and Philip L. Cooley. "Spreading Strategies in CBOE Options: Evidence on Market Performance." *Journal of Financial Research,* Winter 1978, pp. 35–44.

Hauser, R. J., and J. S. Eales. "On Marketing Strategies with Options: A Technique to Measure Risk and Return." *Journal of Futures Markets,* Summer 1986, pp. 273–78.

Labuszewski, John. "Setting Up Your Options Trading Battle Plan." *Futures,* November 1988, pp. 44–45.

Merton, Robert C.; Myron S. Scholes; and Mathew L. Gladstein. "The Returns and Risk of Alternative Call Option Investment Strategies." *Journal of Business,* April 1978, pp. 183–242.

Naik, Vasanttilak. "Option Valuation and Hedging Strategies with Jumps in the Volatility of Asset Returns." *Journal of Finance,* December 1993, pp. 1969–84.

Rendleman, Richard J., Jr. "Optional Long-Run Option Investment Strategies." *Financial Management,* Spring 1981, pp. 61–76.

Valuing Options

Black, Fischer, and Myron Scholes. "The Valuation of Option Contracts and a Test of Market Efficiency." *Journal of Finance,* May 1972, pp. 399–417.

______. "The Pricing of Options and Corporate Liabilities." *Journal of Political Economy,* May–June 1973, pp. 637–54.

Fleming, Jeff, and Robert E. Whaley. "The Value of Wildcard Options." *Journal of Finance,* March 1994, pp. 215–36.

Geske, Robert, and Kuldeep Shastri. "Valuation by Approximation: A Comparison of Alternative Option Valuation Techniques." *Journal of Financial and Quantitative Analysis,* March 1985, pp. 45–71.

Woodward, R. S. "The Effect of Monetary Surprises on Financial Futures Prices." *Journal of Futures Markets,* Fall 1986, pp. 375–84.

APPENDIX 15A: The Black-Scholes Option Pricing Model*

Theory

In 1973, Fischer Black and Myron Scholes published their derivation of a theoretical option pricing model. They started with three securities: riskless bonds, shares of common stock, and call options. The shares of common stock and call options were combined to form a riskless hedge that, by definition, had to duplicate the return of a discount bond with the same maturity length as the option. Using the riskless-hedge concept as a basis, Black and Scholes then proceeded with their model derivation.

Black and Scholes made the following assumptions:

1. Markets are frictionless. This means there are no taxes or transactions costs; all securities are infinitely divisible; all market participants may borrow and lend at the known and constant riskless rate of interest; there are no penalties for short selling.
2. Stock prices are lognormally distributed, with a constant variance for the underlying returns.
3. The stock neither pays dividends nor makes any other distributions.
4. The option may be exercised only at maturity.

Given the above assumptions and the riskless hedging strategy, Black and Scholes derived a call option pricing model that may be expressed as:

$$c = (S)(N(d_1)) - (X)(e^{-rt})(N(d_2)) \qquad (15A\text{–}1)$$

where:

$$d_1 = \frac{\ln(S/X) + (r + (\sigma^2/2))(T)}{(\sigma)(\sqrt{T})} \qquad (15A\text{–}2)$$

$$d_2 = d_1 - (\sigma)(\sqrt{T}) \qquad (15A\text{–}3)$$

The terms are defined as follows:

c = Price of the call option

S = Prevailing market price of a share of common stock on the date the call option is written

X = Call option's striking price (exercise price)

r = Annualized prevailing short-term riskless rate of interest

T = Length of the option's life expressed in annual terms

σ^2 = Annualized variance associated with the underlying security's price changes

$N(\cdot)$ = Cumulative normal density function

---

* This appendix was developed by Professor Carl Luft of DePaul University in consultation with the authors.

At maturity ($T = 0$), the call option must sell for either its intrinsic value or zero, whichever is greater. This boundary condition may be expressed mathematically as:

$$c = \text{Max}\ (0, S - X) \tag{15A–4}$$

It can be shown that given a put option and a call option, with the same striking price, and one share of the underlying stock, one can form a portfolio that will earn an amount equal to the option's striking price no matter what value the stock takes at expiration. From this relationship, the value of a put option can be determined mathematically as:

$$p = (X)(e^{-rt}) - S + c \tag{15A–5}$$

with the boundary condition,

$$p = \text{Max}(O, X - S) \tag{15A–6}$$

Formula 15A–5 is known as the put-call parity relationship, and Formula 15A–6 shows that at maturity the put must sell for either its intrinsic value or zero.

Inspection of Formulas 15A–1 through 15A–6 reveals that both the call and put option prices are a function of only five variables: S, the underlying stock's market price; X, the striking price; T, the length of the option's life; σ^2, the volatility of the stock price changes; and r, the riskless rate of interest. All of these variables are easily observed or estimated. Previously developed option pricing models relied on variables that were based on individual investor risk preferences or on expected values of the stock price. Since the Black-Scholes model does not rely on such variables, it is superior to prior models.

To understand the behavior of options, it is necessary to examine the relationship of the option price to each of the five inputs. For call options, the price is positively related to the stock's price, the riskless rate of interest, the volatility, and the time to maturity; whereas an inverse relationship exists between the call option price and the striking price. Put options exhibit positive relationships with the striking price and volatility, negative relationships with the underlying stock price and riskless rate, and either a positive or negative relationship with time.

These relationships are easy to grasp if one realizes that options will not be exercised unless they have an intrinsic value. Consider first the price of the underlying stock. As it increases, calls go in the money and gain intrinsic value while puts fall out of the money and lose intrinsic value. If the stock price declines, then the reverse is true. This explains the positive relationship between the call price and the stock price and the inverse relationship between the put price and the stock price. Higher striking prices cause lower intrinsic values for call options but result in greater intrinsic values for put options. In this case, the loss of intrinsic value causes the inverse relationship between the call option and striking price, while the gain in intrinsic value causes the positive relationship between the put price and the striking price. The positive relationship of both put and call prices to the volatility can be explained by the fact that options written on higher volatility stocks have a relatively better chance of being in the money at expiration than do options written on lower volatility stocks. The positive relationship of the call price to the risk-free rate reflects the fact that the intrinsic value increases because the present value of the exercise price decreases as the risk-free rate rises. For put options, such rate increases and declining present values of exercise prices cause a loss of intrinsic value

and account for the inverse relationship between the put option price and risk-free rate. Finally, the positive relationship of the call price to time is caused by an increasing intrinsic value due to lower present values of the exercise price for longer time periods. A more complex relationship exists for put options.

Intuitively, one might expect a strictly positive relationship between the put option price and time. Such a relationship will occur if the put is at the money or out of the money, while a negative relationship can exist for deep in the money puts. The reason for this inverse relationship lies embedded in the stock's price behavior. Since stock prices cannot be less than zero, the put option has a maximum value that equals the strike price. Investors who own deep in the money put options that are close to their maximum value because of extremely low stock prices are prohibited from exercising these options by assumption 4. Thus, time is working against these investors since they run the risk of losing intrinsic value if the stock price rises before expiration.

After deriving the model, Black and Scholes subjected it to empirical testing. They implemented the riskless-hedging strategy by combining options and stock in proportions dictated by the model and comparing these hedged returns to observed Treasury bill returns. They hypothesized that if the model provided equilibrium, or fair option prices, then the hedged returns should equal the returns generated by the investment in riskless securities. In effect, they attempted to create a synthetic Treasury bill by combining options and stock. If the returns from the option-stock hedge were not equal to the Treasury bill return, it meant the model was unable to provide equilibrium option prices. On the other hand, if there was no significant difference between the hedge and Treasury bill returns, then it could be concluded that the model provided equilibrium prices. The results of the Black-Scholes empirical test showed no significant difference between the option-stock hedged returns and the Treasury bill returns. Thus, Black and Scholes concluded the model did provide equilibrium prices.

The theoretical derivation and empirical justification of an option pricing model by Black and Scholes was an extremely important accomplishment with far-reaching implications. Basically, it meant that model-generated prices could be considered as the equilibrium, or correct, prices. Thus, an investor could use the model to determine whether the market had mispriced an option. Mispriced options spawn arbitrage opportunities. Given such an opportunity, the most obvious way to benefit is to form a riskless hedge by combining options and stock and then maintaining the hedge until the option's market price adjusts to the equilibrium model price. This strategy will provide arbitrage profits since the level of risk that is being assumed equals that of a Treasury bill, but the profits earned when the mispriced option adjusts to the equilibrium, or model price, will exceed the profits earned from investing in a Treasury bill.

Application

The data in Table 15A–1 illustrate the mechanics of the Black-Scholes option pricing model.

Column (1) simply denotes the stock's ticker symbol, while columns (2) through (7) provide the required inputs for the model. Notice that the option maturity is expressed in calendar days and the volatility is given as the standard deviation of returns. The call and put option prices (for both stocks) implied by the data will not be computed.

TABLE 15A–1 Illustrative Data for Black-Scholes Option Model

(1) Stock Symbol	(2) (*S*) Stock Price	(3) (*X*) Strike Price	(4) (*T*) Days to Maturity Divided by Days in Year	(5) (*r*) Risk-Free Rate	(6) (σ) Standard Deviation of Returns	(7) (σ^2) Variance of Stock Returns
CFL	33	35	180/365	0.09	0.20	0.04
GAH	42	40	50/365	0.10	0.23	0.0529

When the values from Table 15A–1 for CFL stock are used in Formulas 15A–2 and 15A–3, we obtain the following answers for d_1 and d_2:

$$d_1 = \frac{1n(33/35) + (0.09 + (0.04/2))(0.4932)}{(0.2)(\sqrt{0.4932})}$$

$$= \frac{-0.0588 + 0.0543}{0.1405}$$

$$= -0.032$$

$$d_2 = -0.032 - 0.1405$$

$$= -0.1725$$

To obtain values for $N(d_1)$ and $N(d_2)$, the Standard Normal Distribution Function Table (Table 15A–2) must be used. The $N(d_1)$ and $N(d_2)$ values are found by first locating the row and column entries in the table that correspond to the computed d_1 and d_2 values. For CFL stock, the row entry is –0.0, and the column entry is 3. This value of –0.03 approximates the computed d_1 value of –0.032. For d_2, the row entry is –0.1, and the column entry is 7, yielding a value of –0.17, approximating the computed value of –0.1725 for d_2.

Locating the d_1 and d_2 values yield the table entries that define the values of $N(d_1)$ and $N(d_2)$. For CFL stock, the $N(d_1)$ value is 0.4880, while the $N(d_2)$ value is 0.4325. In this example, these values are only approximations, since –0.03 and –0.17 are approximations. If one desires more precise $N(d_1)$ and $N(d_2)$ values, they can be obtained through interpolation. For these examples, the approximations are sufficient.

At this point, all the necessary values for computing the option price have been found. Determining the options' prices via Formulas 15A–1 and 15A–5 is all that remains to be done. Thus, the CFL call option price is:

$$c = (33)(0.4880) - (35)(e^{-(0.09)(0.4932)})(0.4325)$$

$$= 16.1040 - (35)(0.9566)(0.4325)$$

$$= 16.1040 - 14.4805$$

$$= 1.6235$$

TABLE 15A–2 Standard Normal Distribution Function

t	0	1	2	3	4	5	6	7	8	9
−3	.0013									
−2.9	.0019	.0018	.0017	.0017	.0016	.0016	.0015	.0015	.0014	.0014
−2.8	.0026	.0025	.0024	.0023	.0023	.0022	.0021	.0021	.0020	.0019
−2.7	.0035	.0034	.0033	.0032	.0031	.0030	.0029	.0028	.0027	.0026
−2.6	.0047	.0045	.0044	.0043	.0041	.0040	.0039	.0038	.0037	.0036
−2.5	.0062	.0060	.0059	.0057	.0055	.0054	.0052	.0051	.0049	.0048
−2.4	.0082	.0080	.0078	.0075	.0073	.0071	.0069	.0068	.0066	.0064
−2.3	.0107	.0104	.0102	.0099	.0096	.0094	.0091	.0089	.0087	.0084
−2.2	.0139	.0136	.0132	.0129	.0125	.0122	.0119	.0116	.0113	.0110
−2.1	.0179	.0174	.0170	.0166	.0162	.0158	.0154	.0150	.0146	.0143
−2.0	.0227	.0222	.0217	.0212	.0207	.0202	.0197	.0192	.0188	.0183
−1.9	.0287	.0281	.0274	.0268	.0262	0.256	.0250	.0244	.0239	.0233
−1.8	.0359	.0351	.0344	.0336	.0329	.0322	.0314	.0307	.0300	.0294
−1.7	.0446	.0436	.0427	.0418	.0409	.0401	.0392	.0384	.0375	.0367
−1.6	.0548	.0537	.0526	.0516	.0505	.0495	.0485	.0475	.0465	.0455
−1.5	.0668	.0655	.0643	.0630	.0618	.0606	.0594	.0582	.0571	.0559
−1.4	.0808	.0793	.0778	.0764	.0749	.0735	.0721	.0708	.0694	.0681
−1.3	.0968	.0951	.0934	.0918	.0901	.0885	.0869	.0853	.0838	.0823
−1.2	.1151	.1131	.1112	.1093	.1075	.1056	.1038	.1020	.1003	.0985
−1.1	.1357	.1335	.1314	.1292	.1271	.1251	.1230	.1210	.1190	.1170
−1.0	.1587	.1562	.1539	.1515	.1492	.1469	.1446	.1423	.1401	.1379
−.9	.1841	.1814	.1788	.1762	.1736	.1711	.1685	.1660	.1635	.1611
−.8	.2119	.2090	.2061	.2033	.2005	.1977	.1949	.1921	.1894	.1867
−.7	.2420	.2389	.2358	.2326	.2297	.2266	.2236	.2206	.2177	.2148
−.6	.2743	.2709	.2676	.2643	.2611	.2578	.2546	.2514	.2483	.2451
−.5	.3085	.3050	.3015	.2981	.2946	.2912	.2877	.2843	.2810	.2776
−.4	.3446	.3409	.3372	.3336	.3300	.3264	.3228	.3192	.3156	.3121
−.3	.3821	.3783	.3745	.3707	.3669	.3632	.3594	.3557	.3520	.3483
−.2	.4207	.4168	.4129	.4090	.4052	.4013	.3974	.3936	.3897	.3859
−.1	.4602	.4562	.4522	.4483	.4443	.4404	.4364	.4325	.4286	.4247
−.0	.5000	.4960	.4920	.4880	.4840	.4801	.4761	.4721	.4681	.4641

t	0	1	2	3	4	5	6	7	8	9
.0	.5000	.5040	.5080	.5120	.5160	.5199	.5239	.5279	.5319	.5359
.1	.5398	.5438	.5478	.5517	.5557	.5596	.5636	.5675	.5714	.5753
.2	.5793	.5832	.5871	.5910	.5948	.5987	.6026	.6064	.6103	.6141
.3	.6179	.6217	.6255	.6293	.6331	.6368	.6406	.6443	.6480	.6517
.4	.6554	.6591	.6628	.6664	.6700	.6736	.6772	.6808	.6844	.6879
.5	.6915	.6950	.6985	.7019	.7054	.7088	.7123	.7157	.7190	.7224
.6	.7257	.7291	.7324	.7357	.7389	.7422	.7454	.7486	.7517	.7549
.7	.7580	.7611	.7642	.7673	.7704	.7734	.7764	.7794	.7823	.7852
.8	.7881	.7910	.7939	.7967	.7995	.8023	.8051	.8079	.8106	.8133
.9	.8159	.8186	.8212	.8238	.8264	.8289	.8315	.8340	.8365	.8189
1.0	.8413	.8438	.8461	.8485	.8508	.8531	.8554	.8577	.8599	.8621
1.1	.8643	.8665	.8686	.8708	.8729	.8749	.8770	.8790	.8810	.8830
1.2	.8849	.8869	.8888	.8907	.8925	.8944	.8962	.8980	.8997	.9015
1.3	.9032	.9049	.9066	.9082	.9099	.9115	.9131	.9147	.9162	.9177
1.4	.9192	.9207	.9222	.9236	.9251	.9265	.9279	.9292	.9306	.9319
1.5	.9332	.9345	.9357	.9370	.9382	.9394	.9406	.9418	.9429	.9441
1.6	.9452	.9463	.9474	.9484	.9495	.9505	.9515	.9525	.9535	.9545
1.7	.9554	.9564	.9573	.9582	.9591	.9599	.9608	.9616	.9625	.9633
1.8	.9641	.9649	.9656	.9664	.9671	.9678	.9686	.9693	.9700	.9706
1.9	.9713	.9719	.9726	.9732	.9738	.9744	.9750	.9756	.9761	.9767
2.0	.9773	.9778	.9783	.9788	.9793	.9798	.9803	.9808	.9812	.9817
2.1	.9821	.9826	.9830	.9834	.9838	.9842	.9846	.9850	.9854	.9857
2.2	.9861	.9864	.9868	.9871	.9875	.9878	.9881	.9884	.9887	.9890
2.3	.9893	.9896	.9898	.9901	.9904	.9906	.9909	.9911	.9913	.9916
2.4	.9918	.9920	.9922	.9925	.9927	.9929	.9931	.9932	.9934	.9936
2.5	.9938	.9940	.9941	.9943	.9945	.9946	.9948	.9949	.9951	.9952
2.6	.9953	.9955	.9956	.9957	.9959	.9960	.9961	.9962	.9963	.9964
2.7	.9965	.9966	.9967	.9968	.9969	.9970	.9971	.9972	.9973	.9974
2.8	.9974	.9975	.9976	.9977	.9977	.9978	.9979	.9979	.9980	.9981
2.9	.9981	.9982	.9982	.9983	.9984	.9984	.9985	.9985	.9986	.9986
3.	.9987									

and the CFL put option price is:

$$\begin{aligned} p &= (35)(e^{-(0.09)(0.4932)}) - 33 + 1.6235 \\ &= (35)(0.9566) - 33 + 1.6235 \\ &= 2.1045 \end{aligned}$$

Since each option controls 100 shares of stock, the theoretical call price is \$162.35, while the put's theoretical price is \$210.45.

A second example (using GAH stock) again uses the variables from Table 15A–1 and substitutes them into Formulas 15A–2 and 15A–3 to derive d_1 and d_2 as follows:

$$\begin{aligned} d_1 &= \frac{\ln(42/40) + (0.10 + (0.0529/2))(0.1370)}{(0.23)(\sqrt{0.1370})} \\ &= \frac{0.0488 + 0.0173}{0.0851} \\ &= 0.7767 \\ d_2 &= 0.7767 - 0.0851 \\ &= 0.6916 \end{aligned}$$

The $N(d_1)$ and $N(d_2)$ values from the standard normal distribution table (Table 15A–2) are 0.7823 and 0.7549, respectively. As mentioned in the previous example, greater precision is possible through interpolation.

Given the above values, the GAH call and put prices are computed as:

$$\begin{aligned} c &= (42)(0.7823) - (40)(e^{-(0.10)(0.1370)})(0.7549) \\ &= 32.8566 - (40)(0.9864)(0.7549) \\ &= 32.8566 - 29.7853 \\ &= 3.0713 \\ p &= (40)(e^{-(0.10)(0.1370)}) - 42 + 3.0713 \\ &= (40)(0.9864) - 42 + 3.0713 \\ &= 0.5273 \end{aligned}$$

These calculations indicate the theoretically correct price (for 100 shares) for the call is \$307.13 and that \$52.73 is the theoretically correct price for the put.

Suppose the market had priced the GAH call at \$262.50. How would you be able to earn arbitrage profits? According to Black and Scholes, you would buy the undervalued calls at \$262.50 and sell shares of GAH stock at \$42 per share to form a riskless hedge and thus obtain arbitrage profits when equilibrium is established. However, to implement such a strategy, an investor must know how many shares to combine with each option to form the riskless hedge. This information is provided by $N(d_1)$ and is known as the hedge ratio or delta.

Since each option controls 100 shares of stock, the appropriate arbitrage activity in this example is to sell 0.7823 shares of GAH stock for every option purchased. Practically speaking, one cannot buy and sell fractional shares. Thus, 78 shares should be sold for each option that is purchased. If the market had overpriced the option, then the arbitrageur would sell options and purchase 78 shares for each option sold. In either case, the hedge's risk level will equal that of a Treasury bill, but the hedge's returns will exceed the Treasury bill's return, thus generating arbitrage profits.

16

COMMODITIES AND FINANCIAL FUTURES

What do pork bellies, soybeans, Japanese yen, and Treasury bills have in common? They are all items on which contracts may be traded in the commodities and financial futures markets.

A **futures contract** is an agreement that provides for the delivery of a specific amount of a commodity at a designated time in the future at a given price. An example might be a contract to deliver 5,000 bushels of corn next September at $2.15 per bushel. The person who sells the contract does not need to have actual possession of the corn, nor does the purchaser of the contract need to plan on taking possession of the corn. Almost all commodities futures contracts are closed out or reversed before the actual transaction is to occur. Thus, the seller of a futures contract for the delivery of 5,000 bushels of corn may simply later buy back a similar contract for the purchase of 5,000 bushels and close out his position. The initial buyer also reverses his position. More than 97 percent of all contracts are closed out in this fashion rather than through actual delivery. The commodities futures market is similar to the options market in that there is a tremendous volume of activity, but very few actual items ever change hands.

The futures markets were originally set up to allow grain and livestock producers and processors to **hedge** (protect) their positions in a given commodity. For example, a wheat producer might have a five-month lead time between the planting of his crop and the actual harvesting and delivery to the market. While the current price of wheat might be $4 a bushel, there is a tremendous risk that the price might change before delivery to the market. The wheat farmer can hedge his position by offering to sell futures contracts for the delivery of wheat. Even though he will probably close out or reverse these futures contracts before the call for actual delivery, he will still have effectively hedged his position. Let's see how this works. If the price of wheat goes down, he will have to sell his crop for less than he anticipated when he planted the wheat, but he will make up the difference on the wheat futures contracts. That is, he will be able to buy back the contracts for less than he sold them. Of course, if the price of the wheat goes up, the extra profit he makes on the crop will be lost on the futures contracts as he now has to buy back the contracts at a higher price.[1]

A miller who uses wheat as part of his processing faces the opposite dilemma in terms of pricing. The miller is afraid the price of wheat might go up and ultimately cut into his profit margin when he takes actual delivery of his product. He can hedge his position by buying futures contracts in wheat. If the actual price of wheat does go up, the extra cost of producing his product will be offset by the profits he makes on his futures contracts.

The commodities market allows the many parties in need of hedging opportunities to acquire contracts. Although some of this could be accomplished on a private basis (one party in Kansas City calls another party in Chicago on the advice of his banker), this would be virtually impossible to handle on a large-scale basis. Liquid, fluid markets such as those provided by the commodity exchanges are necessary to accomplish this function.

While the hedgers are the backbone and basic reason for the existence of commodity exchanges, they are not the only significant participants. We also have the speculators who take purely long or short positions without any intent to hedge actual ownership. Thus, there is the speculator in wheat or silver who believes that the next major price move can be predicted to such an extent that a substantial profit can be made. Because

[1] The hedger not only reduces risk of loss but also eliminates additional profit opportunities. This may be appropriate for farmers since they are not in the risk-taking business but rather in agriculture.

commodities are purchased on the basis of a small investment in the form of margin (usually running 2 to 10 percent of the value of the contract), there is substantial leverage on the investment, and percentage returns and losses are greatly magnified. The typical commodities trader often suffers many losses with the anticipation of a few very substantial gains. Commodities speculation, as opposed to hedging, represents somewhat of a gamble, and stories have been told of reformed commodities speculators who gave up the chase to spend the rest of their days merely playing the slot machines. Nevertheless, commodity speculators are quite important to the liquidity of the market.

TYPES OF COMMODITIES AND EXCHANGES

Commodities and financial futures can be broken down into a number of categories based on their essential characteristics. As indicated in Table 16–1, there are six primary categories. In each case, we show representative items that fall under the category.

The first five categories represent traditional commodities, but category six came into prominence in the 1970s and 1980s—with foreign exchange futures originating in 1972, interest rate futures beginning in 1975, and stock index futures in 1982. Because many financial futures have tremendous implications for financial managers, we will give them special attention later in this chapter. We will defer discussion of stock index futures to Chapter 17 so that they can be given *complete coverage* as a separate topic.

TABLE 16–1 Categories of Commodities and Financial Futures

(1)	(2)	(3)
Grains and oilseeds:	Livestock and meat:	Food and fiber:
Corn	Cattle—feeder	Cocoa
Oats	Cattle—live	Coffee
Soybeans	Hogs—live	Cotton
Wheat	Pork bellies	Orange juice
Barley	Turkeys	Potatoes
Rye	Broilers	Sugar
		Rice
		Butter
(4)	**(5)**	**(6)**
Metals and petroleum:	Wood:	Financial futures:
Copper	Lumber	*a.* Foreign exchange:
Gold	Plywood	Pound, yen, franc, etc.
Platinum		*b.* Interest rate futures:
Silver		Treasury bonds
Mercury		Treasury bills
Heating oil no. 2		Municipal bonds
		Eurodollars
		c. Stock index futures:
		S&P 500
		Value Line

TABLE 16–2 **Major United States and Canadian Commodity Exchanges**

American Commodities Exchange (ACE)
Chicago Board of Trade (CBT)
Chicago Mercantile Exchange (CME)
Also controls International Monetary market (IMM)
Commodity Exchange (CMX)
Kansas City Board of Trade (KC)
Minneapolis Grain Exchange (MPLS)
New Orleans Commodity Exchange
New York Coffee, Sugar, and Cocoa Exchange (CSCE)
New York Cotton Exchange (CTN)
New York Futures Exchange (NYFE)
Subsidiary of the New York Stock Exchange
New York Mercantile Exchange (NYM)
Pacific Commodities Exchange (PCE)
Winnipeg Grain Exchange (WPG)

The commodities listed in Table 16–1 trade on various commodity exchanges in the United States and Canada (see Table 16–2). While the exchanges are well organized and efficient in their operation, they are still run by an open auction complete with outcries of bids and various hand-signal displays.

The largest commodity exchange is the Chicago Board of Trade (CBT) with the Chicago Mercantile Exchange (CME) in second place. While some exchanges are highly specialized, such as the New York Cotton Exchange, most exchanges trade in a number of securities. For example, the Chicago Board of Trade deals in such diverse products as corn, oats, soybeans, wheat, silver, and Treasury bonds.

The activities of the commodity exchanges are primarily regulated by the Commodity Futures Trading Commission (CFTC), a federal regulatory agency established by Congress in 1975. The CFTC has had a number of jurisdictional disputes with the SEC over the regulation of financial futures.

Types of Commodities Contracts

The commodity contract lists the type of commodity and the denomination in which it is traded (bushels, pounds, troy ounces, metric tons, percentage points, etc.). The contract will also specify the standardized unit for trade (5,000 bushels, 30,000 pounds, etc.). A further designation will indicate the month in which the contract ends, with most commodities having a whole range of months from which to choose. Typically, contracts run as far as a year into the future, but some interest rate futures contracts extend as far as three years.

Examples of the sizes of futures contracts are presented in Table 16–3 on page 462. Be aware that there may be many different forms of the same commodity (such as spring wheat or amber/durum wheat).

TABLE 16–3 Size of Commodity Contracts

Contract	Trading Units	Size of Contract Based on Mid-1994 Prices (in dollars)
Corn	5,000 bushels	$ 10,750
Oats	5,000 bushels	7,500
Wheat	5,000 bushels	20,000
Pork bellies	38,000 pounds	15,200
Coffee	37,500 pounds	70,500
Cotton	50,000 pounds	34,485
Sugar	112,000 pounds	14,414
Copper	25,000 pounds	31,250
Gold	100 troy ounces	40,000
Silver	5,000 troy ounces	26,625
Treasury bonds	$100,000	97,110
Treasury bills	$1,000,000	945,300

ACTUAL COMMODITIES CONTRACT

To examine the potential gain or loss in a commodities contract, let's go through a hypothetical investment. Assume we are considering the purchase of a December wheat contract (it is now May 1). The price on the futures contract is $4 per bushel. Since wheat trades in units of 5,000 bushels, the total price is $20,000. As we go through our example, we will examine many important features associated with commodity trading—beginning with margin requirements.

Margin Requirements

Commodity trading is based on the use of margin rather than on actual cash dollars. Margin requirements are typically 2 to 10 percent of the value of the contract and may vary over time or even among exchanges for a given commodity. For our example, we will assume a $600 margin requirement on the $20,000 wheat contract.[2] That was the specified margin in 1995. The $600 would represent 3 percent of the value of the contract ($20,000).

Margin requirements on commodities contracts are much lower than those on common stock transactions, where 50 percent of the purchase price has been the requirement since 1974. Furthermore, in the commodities market, the margin payment is merely considered to be a good-faith payment against losses. There is no actual borrowing or interest to be paid.[3]

[2] The amount of margin required also differs between speculative and hedging activities. For example, $600 represents the margin for speculation. The margin for hedging is $400 in this case.

[3] It should also be pointed out that a customer may need a minimum account balance of $5,000 or greater to open a commodity account.

In addition to the initial margin requirements, **margin maintenance requirements** (minimum maintenance standards) run 60 to 80 percent of the value of the initial margin. In the case of the wheat contract, the margin maintenance requirement might be \$400 (67% × \$600). If our initial margin of \$600 is reduced by \$200 due to losses on our contract, we will be required to replace the \$200 to cover our margin position. If we do not do so, our position will be closed out, and we will take our losses.

The margin requirement, relative to size, is even less for financial futures. For example, on a \$1 million Treasury bill contract, the investor must post only an initial margin of \$675. Similar requirements exist for other types of financial futures.

Note that the high risk inherent in a commodities contract is not so much a function of volatile price movements as it is the impact of high leverage made possible by the low initial margin requirements. A 5 percent price move may equal or exceed the size of our initial investment in the form of the margin deposit. This is similar to the type of leverage utilized in the options market as described in Chapter 15. However, the action in the commodities market is much quicker. You can be asked to put up additional margin within hours after you establish your initial position.

Market Conditions

Because the price of every commodity moves in response to market conditions, each investor must determine the key market variables that influence the value of his or her contract. In the case of wheat, the investor may be particularly concerned about such factors as weather and crop conditions in the Midwest, the price of corn as a substitute product, the carryover of wheat supply from the previous year, and potential wheat sales to other countries.

Gains and Losses

In the present example, assume we guessed right in our analysis of the wheat market; we purchased a December futures contract for \$4 per bushel, and the price goes to \$4.12 per bushel (recall that the contract was for 5,000 bushels). With a \$0.12 increase per bushel, we have established a dollar gain of \$600 (5,000 bushels × \$0.12 per bushel profit). With an initial margin requirement of \$600, we have made a percentage profit of 100 percent as indicated in the following formula:[4]

$$\frac{\text{Dollar gain}}{\text{Amount of margin deposit}} = \frac{\$600}{\$600} \times 100 = 100\%$$

If this transaction occurred over one month, the annualized gain would be 1,200 percent (100% × 12 = 1,200%). Note that this was all accomplished by a \$0.12 movement in the price of a December wheat contract from \$4 to \$4.12.

Actually, we may choose to close out the contract or attempt to let the profits run. We also may use the profits to establish the basis for margin on additional futures

[4] This does not include commissions, which are generally less than \$100 for a complete transaction (buy and sell).

contracts. A paper gain of $600 is enough to provide the $600 margin on a second wheat contract.

We are now in a position to use an inverse pyramid to expand our position. With two contracts outstanding, a mere $0.06 price change will provide $600 in profits.

$ .06	Price change
× 10,000	Bushels (two contracts)
$600	Profits (can be applied to third contract)

The new $600 in profits can be used to purchase a third contract, and now with 15,000 bushels under control, a $0.04 price change will generate enough profits for a fourth contract.

$ 0.04	Price change
× 15,000	Bushels (three contracts)
$600	Profits (can be applied to fourth contract)

Inverse pyramiding begins to sound astounding since eventually a 1¢ or ½¢ change in the price of wheat will trigger enough profits for a new contract. Of course, great risks are associated with such a process. It is like building a house with playing cards. If one tumbles, the whole house comes down. The investor can become so highly leveraged that any slight reversal in price can trigger off margin calls. While it is often wise to let profits run and perhaps do some amount of pyramiding, prudence must be exercised.

Our primary attention up to this point has been on contracts that are making money. What are the implications if there is an immediate price reversal after we have purchased our December wheat contract? You will recall there was a margin maintenance requirement of $400 based on our initial margin of $600. In this case, a $200 loss would call for an additional deposit to bring our margin position up to $600. How much would the price of wheat have to decline for us to get this margin call to increase our deposit? With a 5,000-bushel contract, we are talking about a mere decline of $0.04 per bushel.

$$\frac{\$200 \text{ loss}}{5{,}000 \text{ bushels}} = \$0.04 \text{ per bushel}$$

This could happen in a matter of minutes or hours after our initial purchase. When we get the margin call, we can either elect to put up the additional $200 and continue with the contract or tell our commodities broker to close out our contract and take our losses. If we put up the $200, our broker could still be on the phone a few minutes later asking for more margin because the price has shown further deterioration. Because investors often buy multiple contracts, such as 10 December wheat contracts, the process can be all the more intense. In the commodities market, the old adage of "cut your losses short and let your profits run" probably has its greatest significance. Even a seasoned commodities trader might determine that he is willing to lose 80 percent of the time and win only 20 percent of the time, but those victories will represent home runs and the losses mere outs.

TABLE 16–4 Maximum Daily Price Changes

Commodity	Exchange*	Normal Price Range	Maximum Daily Price Change (from Previous Close)**
Corn	CBT	$2.00–$3.00	$0.10 per bushel
Oats	CBT	$1.00–$1.75	$0.10 per bushel
Wheat	CBT	$2.50–$4.50	$0.20 per bushel
Pork bellies	CBT	$0.40–$0.75	$0.02 per pound
Copper	CMX	$0.90–$1.40	$0.03 per pound
Silver	CBT	$3.50–$6.50	$1.00 per ounce
Treasury bills	IMM of CME	85% of par and up	No limit

*CBT (Chicago Board of Trade), CMX (Commodity Exchange), IMM (International Monetary Market), CME (Chicago Mercantile Exchange).
**These values may change slightly from exchange to exchange and are often temporarily altered in response to rampant speculation.

Price Movement Limitations

Because of the enormous opportunities for gains and losses in the commodities markets, the commodity exchanges do limit maximum daily price movements in a commodity. Some examples are shown in Table 16–4.

These daily trading limits obviously must affect the efficiency of the market somewhat. If market conditions indicate that the price of wheat should decline by $0.30 and the daily limit is $0.20, then obviously the price of wheat is not in equilibrium as it opens the following morning. However, the desire to stop market panics tends to override the desire for total market efficiency in the commodity markets. Nevertheless, the potential intraday trading range is still large. Recall, for example, that a $0.20 change in the price of wheat, which is the daily limit, is more than enough to place tremendous pressure on the investor to repeatedly increase his margin position. On the typical 5,000-bushel contract, this would represent a daily loss of $1,000.

READING MARKET QUOTES

We turn our attention to interpreting market quotes in the daily newspaper. Table 16–5 on page 466 shows an excerpt from the October 26, 1994, edition of *The Wall Street Journal* covering 21 different types of contracts (this represents about 40 percent of the contracts reported for that day).

In each case, we see a wide choice of months for which a contract may be purchased. For example, corn, which trades on the Chicago Board of Trade (CBT), has futures contracts for March, May, July, September, and December. Some commodities offer a contract for virtually every month. To directly examine some of the terms in the table, we produce a part of the corn contract (CBT) in Table 16–6 on page 467.

The second line in the table indicates that we are dealing in corn traded on the CBT. We then note that corn is traded in 5,000-bushel units and quoted in cents per bushel.

TABLE 16–5 Examples of Price Quotes on Commodity Futures

Tuesday, October 25, 1994.

Open Interest Reflects Previous Trading Day.

GRAINS AND OILSEEDS

CORN (CBT) 5,000 bu.; cents per bu.

	Open	High	Low	Settle	Change	Lifetime High	Lifetime Low	Open Interest
Dec	216¾	217½	215	215½	− 1¾	277	213¼	122,839
Mr95	228	228½	226¼	226½	− 1¾	282½	223¼	58,288
May	236½	236¾	234¾	235	− 1¾	285	230½	25,131
July	242	242¼	240¼	240¾	− 1½	285½	235¾	29,092
Sept	247½	247½	245¼	245¾	− 1½	270½	239	2,463
Dec	251½	251¾	250¼	250¾	− 1	263	235½	12,865
Mr96	257¾	257¾	256½	257	− 1	258	250½	245
July	....	....	....	264	− 1	266¼	254	418
Dec	....	....	....	250½	− 1	257	239	285

Est vol 36,000; vol Mon 44,775; open int 251,626, +3,278.

OATS (CBT) 5,000 bu.; cents per bu.

	Open	High	Low	Settle	Change	Lifetime High	Lifetime Low	Open Interest
Dec	127½	127½	125	126	− 1½	157¼	116	9,998
Mr95	133½	133½	131	131¾	− 2	152¾	121½	3,146
May	137	137	135½	135½	− 1¾	151	125	1,489
July	139¾	139¾	139	139	− 1½	142½	132	1,324

Est vol 800; vol Mon 632; open int 15,958, −85.

SOYBEANS (CBT) 5,000 bu.; cents per bu.

	Open	High	Low	Settle	Change	Lifetime High	Lifetime Low	Open Interest
Nov	553	554½	546¾	548¼	− 4¾	699	526¾	43,741
Ja95	564	566	558½	559¾	− 4½	704	537¼	39,888
Mar	575	576¼	568½	570	− 4¾	705	547¼	22,210
May	582	583	576¼	578¼	− 4¼	705½	556	10,187
July	588½	590½	583¼	584½	− 4½	706½	563½	17,232
Aug	591½	592	587	587½	− 4½	612	566½	1,153
Sept	592	594	588½	589	− 2½	616	571	420
Nov	601½	602½	597	598¾	− 3	645	578½	7,455
Ja96	607	607	607	606¾	− ¾	607	604½	105

Est vol 44,000; vol Mon 52,077; open int 142,498, −5,715.

SOYBEAN MEAL (CBT) 100 tons; $ per ton.

	Open	High	Low	Settle	Change	Lifetime High	Lifetime Low	Open Interest
Dec	164.80	165.20	163.60	163.80	− .90	209.00	160.30	43,501
Ja95	166.00	166.20	164.70	164.80	− 1.00	207.50	161.90	16,938
Mar	169.40	169.70	168.10	168.40	− .90	207.50	164.90	14,041
May	172.30	173.00	171.30	171.40	− .90	207.00	167.60	8,105
July	176.30	177.20	175.30	175.30	− 1.20	206.00	170.70	8,203
Aug	178.60	178.20	177.00	176.80	− 1.20	182.60	172.00	1,172
Sept	179.50	180.50	178.60	178.50	− 1.20	182.70	173.60	1,161
Oct	181.50	181.70	180.30	180.30	− 1.50	181.80	175.60	2,419
Dec	182.50	182.50	182.50	182.50	− 1.50	184.00	176.50	814

Est vol 15,000; vol Mon 13,672; open int 96,355, +181.

SOYBEAN OIL (CBT) 60,000 lbs.; cents per lb.

	Open	High	Low	Settle	Change	Lifetime High	Lifetime Low	Open Interest
Dec	26.18	26.24	25.78	25.81	− .32	28.87	22.00	33,743
Ja95	25.22	25.27	24.89	24.91	− .26	28.55	22.65	13,804
Mar	24.65	24.73	24.45	24.46	− .16	28.30	22.91	13,043
May	24.25	24.34	24.12	24.14	− .09	28.00	22.85	11,121
July	24.12	24.12	23.90	23.91	− .06	27.85	22.76	7,415
Aug	23.95	23.95	23.90	23.90	− .05	27.20	22.73	2,146
Sept	24.00	24.00	23.80	23.80	− .07	24.75	22.75	1,475
Oct	23.82	23.82	23.75	23.75	− .02	23.88	22.75	1,578
Dec	23.75	23.75	23.75	23.77	....	23.85	22.80	1,092

Est vol 18,000; vol Mon 19,381; open int 85,427, +10.

WHEAT CBT) 5,000 bu.; cents per bu.

	Open	High	Low	Settle	Change	Lifetime High	Lifetime Low	Open Interest
Dec	404	405½	398	400	− 4	418¾	309	39,430
Mr95	415	415¾	408½	410¼	− 4¾	426¾	327	23,575
May	391	391	384½	385½	− 5¾	398½	325	4,097
July	355	356	351½	352¾	− 3¼	363¾	311½	9,601
Sept	356	356	356	356½	− 1½	365	351½	232
Dec	366½	367	365¼	365¼	− 2¼	375	362	138

Est vol 15,000; vol Mon 16,065; open int 77,079, +1,348.

WHEAT (KC) 5,000 bu.; cents per bu.

	Open	High	Low	Settle	Change	Lifetime High	Lifetime Low	Open Interest
Dec	412	413¼	407	408	− 4¼	423¼	312½	19,324
Mr95	416½	418	411½	412	− 5¼	427¼	326½	13,097
May	393	393	388¾	390¾	− 4¼	403	321½	1,400
July	360	361	357¼	359	− 1	368¼	316½	3,598

Est vol 4,647; vol Mon 4,077; open int 37,502, +385.

WHEAT (MPLS) 5,000 bu.; cents per bu.

	Open	High	Low	Settle	Change	Lifetime High	Lifetime Low	Open Interest
Dec	407½	409½	403¼	404¾	− 3	419½	304	11,337
Mr95	419	420½	414	414¼	− 5½	431	325¼	6,281
May	413	414	406	406¾	− 5¼	419¼	332½	521
July	375	375	375	373½	− 1½	386	324½	191

Est vol 2,999; vol Mon 2,327; open int 18,426, +153.

METALS AND PETROLEUM

COPPER-HIGH (CMX)—25,000 lbs.; cents per lb.

	Open	High	Low	Settle	Change	Lifetime High	Lifetime Low	Open Interest
Oct	119.55	121.10	119.55	121.05	+ 1.70	122.10	75.20	1,113
Nov	119.00	119.00	119.00	119.85	+ 1.60	119.80	77.75	1,486
Dec	118.20	119.70	117.90	119.25	+ 1.35	120.50	75.75	41,106
Ja95		....	....	118.65	+ 1.30	119.40	76.90	813
Feb		....	....	118.00	+ 1.25	117.70	87.85	570
Mar	116.70	117.60	116.15	117.35	+ 1.20	118.40	76.30	8,522
Apr		....	....	116.55	+ 1.00	116.50	90.10	656
May	115.10	115.20	114.70	115.55	+ .80	116.10	76.85	2,183
June		....	....	114.90	+ .60	115.65	106.30	430
July	113.80	113.80	113.40	114.35	+ .60	116.10	78.00	1,749
Aug		....	....	113.60	+ .30	115.90	111.40	121
Sept	112.90	112.90	112.90	113.05	+ .20	113.30	79.10	1,106
Dec	111.00	111.20	111.00	111.35	+ .10	113.75	88.00	1,215
Mr96		....	....	109.75	....	111.80	99.20	256

Est vol 8,000; vol Mon 6,659; open int 61,439, −194.

GOLD (CMX)—100 troy oz.; $ per troy oz.

	Open	High	Low	Settle	Change	Lifetime High	Lifetime Low	Open Interest
Oct	390.10	390.30	390.00	389.40	− .20	417.00	344.00	39
Dec	391.60	392.10	390.70	391.20	− .20	426.50	343.00	82,901
Fb95	395.10	395.60	394.30	394.70	− .20	411.00	363.50	19,588
Apr	398.50	398.50	398.30	398.30	− .20	425.00	385.50	8,198
June	402.30	402.80	401.90	401.90	− .20	430.00	351.00	9,882
Aug		....	....	405.80	− .20	414.50	380.50	6,100
Oct		....	....	410.00	− .10	419.20	401.00	1,414
Dec		....	....	414.20	− .10	439.50	358.00	7,849
Fb96		....	....	418.40	− .10	424.50	412.50	1,899
Apr		....	....	422.60	− .10	430.20	418.30	1,965
June		....	....	427.00	....	447.00	370.90	5,882
Aug		....	....	431.30	....	....	....	124
Dec	441.00	441.00	441.00	440.40	....	447.50	379.60	3,063
Ju97		....	....	454.40	+ .10	456.00	436.00	1,148
Dec		....	....	468.70	+ .10	477.00	402.00	2,742
Ju98		....	....	483.70	+ .10	489.50	481.70	1,638
Dec		....	....	499.00	+ .10	505.00	468.00	2,023
Ju99		....	....	515.00	+ .10	520.00	511.00	994

Est vol 18,000; vol Mon 16,699; open int 157,449, +157.

PLATINUM (NYM)—50 troy oz.; $ per troy oz.

	Open	High	Low	Settle	Change	Lifetime High	Lifetime Low	Open Interest
Oct	426.00	426.00	424.90	424.40	− .30	435.40	368.00	86
Ja95	427.00	428.00	424.10	425.40	− .30	435.50	374.80	20,352
Apr	431.50	431.50	429.00	429.70	− .30	439.00	390.00	3,553
July		....	....	434.20	....	439.00	419.50	947
Oct		....	....	438.90	+ .70	436.50	422.50	358

Est vol 1,697; vol Mon 1,532; open int 25,298, +1,255.

PALLADIUM (NYM) 100 troy oz.; $ per troy oz.

	Open	High	Low	Settle	Change	Lifetime High	Lifetime Low	Open Interest
Dec	156.50	158.90	156.50	157.80	+ 1.35	159.50	122.50	4,502
Mr95	158.00	158.00	158.00	159.00	+ 1.45	159.75	134.00	1,626
June	159.00	160.50	159.00	160.00	+ 1.45	160.50	151.60	368

Est vol 492; vol Mon 403; open int 6,496, +54.

SILVER (CMX)—5,000 troy oz.; cents per troy oz.

	Open	High	Low	Settle	Change	Lifetime High	Lifetime Low	Open Interest
Oct		....	....	529.2	− 2.1	561.5	511.5	108
Dec	536.0	537.0	531.5	532.0	− 2.2	597.0	380.0	75,593
Mr95	544.0	546.0	540.0	540.5	− 2.2	604.0	416.5	16,563
May	548.0	548.0	547.0	546.5	− 2.2	606.5	418.0	4,684
July	554.5	555.0	553.0	552.7	− 2.2	610.0	403.0	3,860
Sept		....	....	559.1	− 2.2	615.0	493.0	2,485
Dec	575.0	575.0	569.0	569.0	− 2.2	628.0	434.0	2,573
Mr96		....	....	579.8	− 2.2	622.0	554.0	1,433
July		....	....	594.6	− 2.2	630.0	524.0	1,303
Dec	613.0	613.0	613.0	613.9	− 2.2	670.0	454.0	1,732
Jl97		....	....	642.4	− 2.2	655.0	588.0	433
Dec		....	....	665.9	− 2.2	695.0	502.0	307
Dc98		....	....	722.0	− 2.2	734.0	690.0	109

Est vol 12,000; vol Mon 11,509; open int 111,321, +43.

SILVER (CBT)—1,000 troy oz.; cents per troy oz.

	Open	High	Low	Settle	Change	Lifetime High	Lifetime Low	Open Interest
Oct	527.0	528.0	527.0	528.0	− 4.0	590.0	504.0	4
Dec	536.0	536.0	529.0	530.5	− 2.5	596.0	414.0	4,771
Ap95	548.0	548.0	543.5	543.5	− 2.5	605.0	521.0	242
June	554.0	554.0	549.0	549.0	− 3.5	605.0	527.0	225

Est vol 200; vol Mon 170; open int 5,381, −16.

CRUDE OIL, Light Sweet (NYM) 1,000 bbls.; $ per bbl.

	Open	High	Low	Settle	Change	Lifetime High	Lifetime Low	Open Interest
Dec	17.47	17.60	17.35	17.58	+ .13	21.25	14.93	111,120
Ja95	na	17.62	17.44	17.61	+ .09	20.12	15.15	61,380
Feb	na	17.59	17.46	17.58	+ .07	19.60	15.28	28,966
Mar	na	17.56	17.45	17.57	+ .07	20.66	15.42	23,908
Apr	na	17.53	17.46	17.56	+ .06	19.68	15.55	17,882

Source: *The Wall Street Journal*, October 26, 1994, p. C18. Reprinted by permission of *The Wall Street Journal*,

TABLE 16–6 Price Quotes for Corn Contracts

(1)	Open	High	Low	Settle	Change	Lifetime High	Lifetime Low	Open Interest
(2) Corn (CBT)-5,000 bu.; cents per bu.								
Dec	216¾	217½	215	215½	−1¾	277	213¼	122,839
Mr 95	228	228½	226¼	226½	−1¾	282½	223¼	58,288
May	236½	236¾	234¾	235	−1¾	285	230½	25,131
July	242	242¼	240¼	240¾	−1½	285½	235¾	29,092

Source: *The Wall Street Journal,* October 26, 1994, p. C18. Reprinted by permission of *The Wall Street Journal,*

Quotations in cents per bushel require some mental adjustment. For example, 200 cents per bushel would actually represent $2 per bushel. We generally move the decimal point two places to the left and read the quote in terms of dollars. For example, the December 1994 opening price was 216¾, or $2.1675 per bushel.

Across the top of the table we observe that we are given information on the open, high, low, settle (close), and change from the previous day's close as well as the lifetime high and low for that particular contract. The last column represents the open interest, or the number of actual contracts presently outstanding for that delivery month.

THE CASH MARKET AND THE FUTURES MARKET

Many commodity futures exchanges provide areas where buyers and sellers can negotiate **cash** (or **spot**) **prices.** The cash price is the actual dollar value paid for the immediate transfer of a commodity. Unlike a futures contract, there must be a transfer of the physical possession of the goods. Prices in the cash market are somewhat dependent on prices in the futures market. Thus, it is said that the futures markets provide an important service as a price discovery mechanism. By cataloging price trends in everything from corn to cattle, the producers, processors, and handlers of more than 50 commodities are able to observe price trends in categories of interest.

THE FUTURES MARKET FOR FINANCIAL INSTRUMENTS

The major event in the commodities markets for the last two decades has been the development of financial futures contracts. With the great volatility in the foreign exchange markets and in interest rates, corporate treasurers, investors, and others have felt a great need to hedge their positions. Financial futures also appeal to speculators because of their low margin requirements and wide swings in value.

Financial futures may be broken down into three major categories: currency futures, interest-rate futures, and stock index futures (the latter is covered in depth in Chapter 17). Trading in currency futures began in May 1972 on the International Monetary Market (part of the Chicago Mercantile Exchange). Interest-rate futures started trading on the Chicago Board of Trade in October 1975 with the GNMA certificate. Trading in financial

futures, regardless of whether they are currency or interest-rate futures, is very similar to trading in traditional commodities such as corn, wheat, copper, or pork bellies. There is a stipulated contract size, month of delivery, margin requirement, and so on. We will first look at currency futures and then shift our attention to interest-rate futures.

CURRENCY FUTURES

Futures are currently available in the currencies listed below.

British pound	Swiss franc
Australian dollar	German mark
Canadian dollar	French franc
Japanese yen	Mexican peso

The futures market in currencies provides many of the same functions as the older and less formalized market in foreign exchange operated by banks and specialized brokers, who maintain communication networks throughout the world. In either case, one can speculate or hedge. The currency futures market, however, is different in that it provides standardized contracts and a strong secondary market.

Let's examine how the currency futures market works. Assume you wish to purchase a currency futures contract in Japanese yen. The standardized contract is 12.5 million yen. The value of the contract is quoted in cents per yen. Assume you purchase a December futures contract in May, and the price on the contract is \$0.010387 per yen. The total value of the contract is \$129,837.50 (12.5 million yen × \$0.010387). The typical margin on a yen contract is \$2,300.

We will assume the yen strengthens relative to the dollar. This might happen because of decreasing U.S. interest rates, declining inflation in Japan, or any number of other reasons. Under these circumstances, the currency might rise to \$0.010485 per yen (the yen is now worth more cents than it was previously). The value of the contract has now risen to \$131,062.50 (12.5 million × \$0.010485). This represents an increase in value of \$1,225:

Current value	\$131,062.50
Original value	129,837.50
Gain	\$ 1,225.00

With an original margin requirement of \$2,300, this represents a return of 53.3 percent:

$$\frac{\$1,225}{\$2,300} \times 100 = 53.3\%$$

On an annualized basis, it could even be higher. Of course, the contract could produce a loss if the yen weakens against the dollar as a result of higher interest rates in the United States or increasing inflation in Japan. With a normal margin maintenance requirement of \$1,700, a \$600 loss on the contract will call for additional margin.

Corporate treasurers often try to hedge an exposed position in their foreign exchange dealings through the currency futures market. Assume a treasurer closes a deal today to receive payment in two months in Japanese yen. If the yen goes down relative to the

TABLE 16–7 Contracts in Currency Futures

Currency	Trading Units	Size of Contract Based on Mid-1994 Prices
British pound	62,500	$102,300
Canadian dollar	100,000	74,140
Swiss franc	62,500	50,240
German mark	125,000	83,710

dollar, he will have less value than he anticipated. One solution would be to sell a yen futures contract (go short). If the value of the yen goes down, he will make money on his futures contract that will offset the loss on the receipt of the Japanese yen in two months.

Table 16–7 lists the typical size of contracts for four other foreign currencies that trade on the International Monetary Market.

INTEREST-RATE FUTURES

Since the inception of the interest-rate futures contract with GNMA certificates in October 1975, the market has been greatly expanded to include Treasury notes, Treasury bills, municipal bonds, federal funds, and Eurodollars. There is almost unlimited potential for futures contracts on interest-related items.

Interest-rate futures trade on a number of major exchanges, including the Chicago Board of Trade, the International Monetary Market of the Chicago Mercantile Exchange, and the New York Futures Exchange. There is strong competition between Chicago and New York City for dominance in this business, with Chicago being not only the historical leader but also the current leader.

Table 16–8 on page 470 shows examples of quotes on interest-rate futures. Direct your attention to the first category, Treasury bonds (CBT), trading on the Chicago Board of Trade.

The bonds trade in units of $100,000, and the quotes are in percent of par value taken to 32nds of a percentage point. Although it is not shown in these data, the bonds on which the futures are based are assumed to be new, 15-year Treasury instruments paying 8 percent interest. In the first column for the December contract for Treasury bonds, we see a price of 97-06. This indicates a value of 97$\frac{6}{32}$ percent of stated (par) value. We thus have a contract value of $97,187.50 (96$\frac{6}{32}$ × $100,000). This represents the opening value. The entire line in Table 16–8 reads as follows:

						Lifetime		
	Open	High	Low	Settle	Change	High	Low	Open Interest
Dec	97-06	97-17	97-03	97-12	+4	118-08	91-19	390,012

The **settle,** or closing, **price** is 97-12, which represents a positive change of $\frac{4}{32}$ from the close of the previous day. The close for the previous day is not always the same as the

TABLE 16–8 Examples of Price Quotes on Interest-Rate Futures

TREASURY BONDS (CBT)–$100,000; pts. 32nds of 100%

	Open	High	Low	Settle	Change	Lifetime High	Lifetime Low	Open Interest
Dec	97-06	97-17	97-03	97-12	+ 4	118-08	91-19	390,012
Mr95	96-15	96-27	96-14	96-23	+ 4	116-20	96-09	27,492
June	96-03	96-05	95-31	96-03	+ 3	113-15	95-22	11,313
Sept	....	....	....	95-17	+ 3	112-15	95-10	256
Dec	....	....	....	95-00	+ 3	111-23	95-00	133

Est vol 295,000; vol Wed 349,849; op int 429.281, −6,498.

TREASURY BONDS (MCE)–$50,000; pts. 32nds of 100%

	Open	High	Low	Settle	Change	Lifetime High	Lifetime Low	Open Interest
Dec	97-09	97-17	97-04	97-11	+ 7	114-00	96-30	13,932

Est vol 4,200; vol Wed 4,822; open int 13,957, +133.

TREASURY NOTES (CBT)–$100,000; pts. 32nds of 100%

	Open	High	Low	Settle	Change	Lifetime High	Lifetime Low	Open Interest
Dec	100-04	100-10	100-01	100-05	....	114-21	99-31	275,127
Mr95	99-15	99-17	99-11	99-14	+ 1	111-07	99-09	9,393
June	98-27	98-28	98-25	98-26	+ 1	105-22	98-23	105

Est vol 53,555; vol Wed 70,133; open int 284,630, +2,042.

5 YR TREAS NOTES (CBT)–$100,000; pts. 32nds of 100%

	Open	High	Low	Settle	Change	Lifetime High	Lifetime Low	Open Interest
Dec	101-11	01-155	101-10	01-115	− 1.0	104-20	101-05	173,061
Mr95	100-27	100-27	00-235	00-245	− 0.5	103-09	00-215	7,923

Est vol 40,300; vol Wed 40,816; open int 180,985, −3,914.

2 YR TREAS NOTES (CBT)–$200,000, pts. 32nds of 100%

	Open	High	Low	Settle	Change	Lifetime High	Lifetime Low	Open Interest
Dec	101-18	01-195	101-18	101-18	....	102-25	101-16	31,657

Est vol 1,000; vol Wed 1,024; open int 31,657, +43.

30-DAY FEDERAL FUNDS (CBT)-$5 million; pts. of 100%

	Open	High	Low	Settle	Change	Lifetime High	Lifetime Low	Open Interest
Oct	95.24	95.24	95.23	95.24	....	95.63	94.63	2,688
Nov	94.94	94.96	94.94	94.95	+ .02	95.52	94.50	5,896
Dec	94.48	94.49	94.47	94.49	+ .02	96.00	94.38	2,515
Ja95	94.30	94.31	94.30	94.31	+ .02	94.66	94.24	1,332
Feb	94.16	94.16	94.15	94.15	+ .01	94.56	94.14	458
Mar	....	....	....	93.95	+ .01	94.44	93.92	235

Est vol 2,222; vol Wed 1,379; open int 13,124, +339.

TREASURY BILLS (CME)–$1 mil.; pts. of 100%

	Open	High	Low	Settle	Chg	Discount Settle	Discount Chg	Open Interest
Dec	94.57	94.60	94.57	94.59	+ .02	5.41	− .02	17,940
Mr95	94.07	94.10	94.07	94.09	+ .02	5.91	− .02	10,605
June	93.60	93.64	93.60	93.64	+ .02	6.36	− .02	5,839

Est vol 1,227; vol Wed 2,344; open int 34,389, +1,326.

Source: *The Wall Street Journal,* October 28, 1994, p. C14. Reprinted by permission of *The Wall Street Journal,* © 1994 by Dow Jones & Company, Inc. All Rights Reserved Worldwide.

open for the current day.[5] Since the value of the futures contract went up, we can assume interest rates declined. We can also observe the lifetime high and low for this contract. Finally, we see an open interest of 390,012, indicating the number of contracts previously outstanding for December.

Assume we buy a December futures contract for $97\frac{12}{32}$ or \$97,375 ($97\frac{12}{32} \times$ \$100,000). The margin requirement on the Chicago Board of Trade is \$2,400 with a \$1,750 margin maintenance requirement. In this case, it may be that we bought the futures contract because we anticipate easier monetary policy by the Federal Reserve, which will trigger a decline in interest rates and an increase in bond prices. If interest rates decline by 0.6 percent (60 basis points), Treasury bond prices will increase by approximately $1\frac{17}{32}$.[6] On a \$100,000 par value futures contract, this would represent a gain of \$1,531.25 as indicated below:

$$\begin{array}{r} \$100{,}000 \\ \times \quad 1\frac{17}{32}\% \ (1.53125\%) \\ \hline \$1{,}531.25 \end{array}$$

[5] A number of overnight events can cause the difference. In this case, we can assume the close for the previous day was 97-08.

[6] This is derived from a standard bond table and not explicitly calculated in the example.

With a \$2,400 initial margin, the \$1,531.25 profit represents an attractive return on our original \$2,400 investment of 63.8 percent:

$$\frac{\$1{,}531.25}{\$2{,}400.00} = 63.8\%$$

Note, however, that if interest rates go up by even a small amount, our Treasury bond futures contract value will fall, and there may be a margin call.

As is true of other commodities, when we trade in interest rate futures, we do not take actual title or possession of the commodity unless we fail to reverse our initial position. The contract merely represents a bet or hedge on the direction of future interest rates and bond prices.

Hedging with Interest-Rate Futures

Interest-rate futures have opened up opportunities for hedging that can only be compared with the development of the agricultural commodities market more than a century ago. Consider the following potential hedges against interest-rate risks.

1. A corporate treasurer is awaiting a new debt issue that will occur in 60 days. The underwriters are still putting the final details together. The great fear is that interest rates will rise between now and then. The treasurer could hedge his or her position in the futures market by selling a Treasury bond or other similar security short. If interest rates go up, the price to buy back the interest-rate futures will be lower, and a profit will be made on the short position. This will partially or fully offset the higher interest costs on the new debt issue.
2. A corporate treasurer is continually reissuing commercial paper at new interest rates or borrowing under a floating prime agreement at the bank. He or she fears that interest rates will go up and make a big dent in projected profits. By selling (going short) interest-rate futures, the corporate treasurer can make enough profit on interest-rate futures if interest rates go up to compensate for the higher costs of money.
3. A mortgage banker has made a forward commitment to provide a loan at a set interest rate one month in the future. If interest rates go up, the resale value of the mortgage in the secondary market will go down. He or she can hedge the position by selling or going short on an interest rate futures contract.
4. A pension fund manager has been receiving a steady return of 8 percent on his short-term portfolio in 90-day Treasury bills. He is afraid interest rates will go down and he will have to adjust to receiving lower returns on the managed funds. His strategy might be to buy (go long on) a Treasury bill futures contract. If interest rates go down, he will make a profit on his futures contract that will partially or fully offset his decline in interest income for one period. Of course, if he is heavily invested in long-term securities and fearful of an interest-rate rise, a sell or short position that would provide profits on an interest-rate rise would be advisable. This would offset part of the loss in the portfolio value due to increasing interest rates.

5. A commercial banker has most of her loans on a floating prime basis, meaning the rate she charges will change with the cost of funds. However, some of the loans have a fixed rate associated with them. If the cost of funds goes up, the fixed-rate loans will become unprofitable. By selling or going short on interest-rate futures, the danger of higher interest rates can be hedged away by the profits she will make on the interest-rate futures. Similarly, a banker may make a commitment to pay a set amount of interest on certificates of deposit for the next six months. If interest rates go down, the banker may have to lend the funds at a lower rate than she is currently paying. If she buys a futures contract, then lower interest rates will increase the value of the contract and provide a profit. This will offset the possible negative profitability spread described earlier.

An Actual Example

Assume an industrial corporation has a $10 million, 15-year bond to be issued in 60 days. Long-term rates for such an issue are currently 10.75 percent, and there is concern that interest rates will go up to 11 percent by the time of the issue. The corporate treasurer has figured out that the extra ¼ point would have a present value cost of $179,775 over the life of the issue (on a before-tax basis):

	$10,000,000	
×	¼%	
$	25,000	
×	7.191	Present value factor for 15 years at 11 percent (Appendix D)
$	179,775	Present value of futures costs

To establish a hedge position, he sells 109 Treasury bond futures short. We assume they are currently selling at 92 (92 percent of $100,000), equaling $92,000 each. The total value of the hedge would be $10,028,000. This is roughly equivalent to the $10 million size of the corporate bond issue. If interest rates go up by ¼ point, the profit on the Treasury bond futures contract (due to falling prices with a short position) will probably offset the present value of the increased cost of the corporate bond issue.

Of course, we do not suggest that both rates (on Treasury bonds and corporate bonds) would move exactly together. However, the general thrust of the example should be apparent. We are actually establishing a **cross-hedging** pattern by using one form of security (Treasury bonds) to hedge another form of security (corporate bonds). This is often necessary. Even when the same security is used, there may be differences in maturity dates so that a perfect hedge is difficult to establish.

Many financial managers prefer **partial hedges** to complete hedges. They are willing to take away part of the risk but not all of it. Others prefer no hedge at all because it locks in their position. While a hedge ensures them against loss, it precludes the possibility of an abnormal gain.

Nevertheless, in a risk-averse financial market environment, most financial managers can gain by hedging their position as described in the many examples in this section. Companies such as Burlington Northern, Eastman Kodak, and McDonald's have estab-

lished reputations for just such actions. Others have not yet joined the movement because of a lack of appreciation or understanding of the highly innovative financial futures market. Much of this will change with the passage of time.

OPTIONS AS WELL AS FUTURES

In late 1982, many exchanges began offering options on financial instruments and commodities. For example, the Chicago Board Options Exchange began listing put and call options on Treasury bonds. Also, the American Stock Exchange started trading options on Treasury bills and Treasury notes, and the Philadelphia Exchange offered foreign currency options. The Chicago Board of Trade, the Chicago Mercantile Exchange, and other exchanges have also attached options to futures contracts. The relationship, similarities, and dissimilarities between option contracts and futures contracts are given much greater attention in the following chapter. For now it will suffice to say that the futures contract requires an initial margin, which can be parlayed into large profits or immediately wiped out, whereas an option requires the payment of an option premium, which represents the full extent of an option purchaser's liability. In Chapter 17, we will also see there are options to purchase futures, which combine the elements of both types of contracts.

INTEREST-RATE SWAPS

No chapter relating to hedging interest-rate risk would be complete without a discussion of the latest instrument, the **interest-rate swap.**

The basic premise of interest-rate swaps is that one party is able to trade one type of risk exposure to another party, and both parties are able to rebalance their portfolios with less risk. For example, bank A may be obligated to pay a fixed rate on a $100,000 certificate of deposit (CD) for the next five years. The bank is fearful that rates may go down and that it will be paying more on the CD than it will be receiving on loans. Under these circumstances, bank A may try to find a "counterparty" who has the opposite type of problem. Perhaps company B is borrowing money from a finance company at a variable rate and is fearful that rates will go up. Assume it has a $100,000 loan that is also due over the next five years.

Under these circumstances, bank A will agree to pay company B a variable rate on a hypothetical $100,000 of principal (referred to as notational principal).[7] In return, company B will agree to pay bank A a fixed rate on the same hypothetical principal. Both parties have used this swap agreement to eliminate their risk. Let's see how.

Because bank A is paying a variable rate and receiving a fixed rate, if rates go down (its original fear), it will come out ahead on the swap agreement. Let's say rates start out at 8 percent (fixed and variable), but variable rates go down to 5 percent. Bank A will receive a net payment of $3,000 from company B on the hypothetical principal:

---

[7] There is no principal actually put up. The $100,000 is merely used to keep score on who owes whom and is referred to as "notational principal."

Can Derivatives Be Dangerous?

Derivatives such as futures, options, swaps, caps, floors, and collars keep making headlines. While derivatives are basically neutral instruments, their misuse or overindulgence by investors may not be. Not only are derivatives growing into a multitrillion dollar market, but they are spreading worldwide. Congressional committees and governmental organizations such as the Federal Reserve and U.S. Treasury Department are calling for increased regulation.

Why? The answer may be that many derivatives intended for use in a neutral or defensive way are being utilized in a speculative, highly risky fashion. One can compare the misuse of a derivative with driving an automobile in an irresponsible manner. Although the automobile is basically sound, if it is driven at 95 miles per hour in a rainstorm down a steep hill, it can indeed be a danger to society.

Corporate treasurers at such firms as Procter & Gamble and Banc One Corporation found themselves behind the "eight ball" when they went from using derivatives to protect against interest-rate exposure to attempting to generate huge profits from guessing the next move in interest rates. They had unprotected, exposed positions that became very costly when they guessed wrong. (Both firms have since corrected the situation.)

Because derivatives can be used in a highly sophisticated fashion, derivatives trading is not easily understood by many corporate auditors. The derivatives trader may take positions that move in five directions on financial markets throughout the world, which the auditor may not have the expertise to follow and analyze. For that reason, it is particularly important that the board of directors and top management of a corporation have clearly stated policies and boundaries on the trading of derivatives. They also must implement adequate monitoring policies to ensure that their directions are being followed.

$100,000 Hypothetical Principal	
Bank A pays variable (5%)	$5,000
Company B pays fixed (8%)	8,000
Net payment of B to A	$3,000

The swap agreement has effectively protected bank A against lower interest-rate exposure that it has with the customer who owns the $100,000 CD. It has achieved this through an entirely unrelated interest-rate swap agreement with company B.

At the same time, company B has protected itself against its original fear that interest rates will go up. For example, if interest rates go from 8 percent to 11 percent, it will make $3,000 on the interest rate swap with bank A:

$100,000 Hypothetical Principal	
Bank A pays variable (11%)	$11,000
Company B pays fixed (8%)	8,000
Net payment of A to B	$ 3,000

This $3,000 profit will offset the exposure that company B has on its loan with the finance company. It has also achieved its goal through a completely unrelated interest-rate swap agreement with bank A.

We have presented the most basic type of swap agreement (although you may not think so!). The point is that interest-rate swap agreements are not, initially, as structured as are futures and options contracts (contract months, strike prices, etc.). The counterparties can start out with a blank piece of paper and put together any kind of deal they desire. Major financial institutions such as Goldman Sachs, Chase Manhattan, and Credit Swiss/CS often serve as facilitators or dealers in bringing parties together for a transaction.

SUMMARY

In this chapter, we broke down the commodities futures market into traditional commodities (such as grains, livestock, and meat) and financial futures primarily in currencies and interest rates.

A commodities futures contract is an agreement that provides for the delivery of a specific amount of a commodity at a designated time in the future. It is not intended that the purchaser of a contract take actual possession of the goods but, rather, that he or she reverse or close out the contract before delivery is due. The same is true for the seller.

Primary participants in the commodities market include both speculators and hedgers. We first examine speculators. A speculator buys a commodities contract (goes long) or sells a commodities contract (goes short) because he believes he can anticipate the direction in which the market is going to move. Because of low margin (initial deposit) requirements of 2 to 10 percent, large profits or losses are possible with small price movements. If the market moves against someone who has a commodity contract, that person may be asked to put up additional margin.

A hedger buys or sells a commodities futures contract to protect an underlying position he or she might have in the actual commodity. For example, a wheat farmer may sell (go short on) a futures contract in wheat to protect against a price decline. If prices go down, he can buy back his contract at a lower price than he sold it and record a profit on the transaction. This may offset any losses he incurs as a result of selling wheat at a lower price to its intended user. Of course, if the price goes up, he will lose on his futures contract but make up the difference on the actual sale of wheat. Millers or bakers who know they will have to purchase wheat in the future may buy (go long) a futures contract. If the price goes up, they will make money on the contract, and this will offset the added production costs.

Many commodity futures exchanges provide areas where buyers and sellers can negotiate cash (or spot) prices. The cash price is the actual dollar paid for the immediate delivery of the goods. Near-term futures prices and cash prices tend to approximate each other.

Currency and interest rate futures represent important financial futures. Although these markets only came into existence in the 1970s, they have seen explosive growth. The contract on financial futures is very similar to that on

basic, traditional commodities; only the items traded and units of measurement are different.

Currency futures relate to many different currencies and enable financial managers to hedge their position in foreign markets. There is also active participation by speculators.

Interest-rate futures cover Treasury bonds, Treasury bills, Treasury notes, certificates of deposit, and similar items. Many other items are on the drawing board. Interest-rate futures generally trade in units of $100,000 or $1 million with extremely low margin requirements. There is a battle between the traditional commodity exchanges in Chicago and the New York Futures Exchange (part of the New York Stock Exchange) and the Amex Commodity Exchange (part of the American Stock Exchange) to see which will ultimately have a dominant position in the financial futures markets.

In the current environment of volatile interest rates, interest-rate futures offer an excellent opportunity to hedge dangerous interest-rate risks. Possible hedgers include corporate financial officers, pension fund managers, mortgage bankers, and commercial bankers. As sophistication and understanding in the use of these hedging techniques increase, the market in financial futures will continue to grow. An additional tool, interest-rate swaps, is also discussed in this chapter. Swaps can be tailored to the needs of the participating parties.

KEY WORDS AND CONCEPTS

DISCUSSION QUESTIONS

1. What is a futures contract?
2. Do you have to take delivery or deliver the commodity if you are a party to a futures contract?
3. Explain what hedging is.
4. Why is there substantial leverage in commodity investments?
5. What are the basic categories of items traded on the commodity exchanges?
6. What group has primary regulatory responsibility for the activities of the commodity exchanges?
7. How does the concept of margin on a commodities contract differ from that of margin on a stock purchase?
8. Indicate some factors that might influence the price of wheat in the commodities market.
9. What is meant by a daily trading limit on a commodities contract?
10. Refer to Table 16–5, and explain the quotation for March (Mr) 1995 corn on the Chicago Board of Trade (CBT).

11. How does the cash market differ from the futures market for commodities?
12. What are the three main categories of financial futures? Which two are discussed in this chapter?
13. How does the currency futures market differ from the foreign exchange market?
14. Describe the Treasury bonds that are part of the futures contract that trades on the Chicago Board of Trade (size of units, maturity, assumed initial interest rate).
15. How can using the financial futures markets for interest rates and foreign exchange help financial managers through hedging? Briefly explain, and give one example.
16. Explain how interest-rate swaps can reduce risks for the counterparties.

PROBLEMS

Gain on commodities contract

1. You purchase a 5,000-bushel contract for corn at $2.20 per bushel ($11,000 total). The initial margin requirement is 7 percent. The price goes up to $2.28 in one month. What is your percentage profit and the annualized gain?

Hedging

2. Farmer Tom Hedges anticipates taking 100,000 bushels of oats to the market in three months. The current cash price for oats is $1.25. He can sell a three-month futures contract for oats at $1.30. He decides to sell ten 5,000-bushel futures contracts at that price. Assume that in three months, when Farmer Hedges takes the oats to market and also closes out the futures contracts (buys them back), the price of oats has tumbled to $1.13.
   a. What is his total loss in value over the three months on the actual oats he produced and took to market?
   b. How much did his hedge in the futures market generate in gains?
   c. What is his overall net loss considering the answer in part *a* and the partial hedge in part *b?*

Hedging

3. The Health Food Corporation anticipates the need to purchase 80,000 bushels of soybeans in six months to use in their products. The current cash price for soybeans is $5.50 a bushel. A six-month futures contract for soybeans can be purchased at $5.53.
   a. Explain why Health Food Corporation might need to purchase futures contracts to hedge their position.
   b. To completely hedge their exposure, how many contracts will they need to purchase? Soybeans trade in 5,000-bushel contracts.
   c. If the cash price of soybeans ends up at $5.75 per bushel after six months, by how much will the cost of 80,000 bushels of soybeans have gone up?
   d. After the futures contracts are closed out (sold at $5.75 also), what will be the gain on the futures contracts?
   e. Considering the answers to parts *c* and *d,* what is their net position?

Margin maintenance

4. With a 5,000-bushel contract for $25,000, assume the margin requirement is $2,000, and the maintenance margin is 80 percent of the margin requirement. How much would the price per bushel have to fall before additional margin is required?

Generating margin

5. If contracts are written on a 5,000-bushel basis requiring $3,000 of margin and you control 12 contracts, how much would the price per bushel have to change to generate enough profit to purchase an additional contract?

Pyramiding

6. Referring to problem 5, how many contracts would need to be controlled to generate enough profit for a new margin contract if the price changed by only 1 cent per bushel?

Currency futures

7. You purchase a futures contract in German marks for $85,000. The trading unit is 125,000 marks.
   a. What is the ratio of cents to marks in this contract? (Divide the dollar contract size by the size of the trading unit.)
   b. Assume you are required to put up $2,100 in margin and the mark increases by 3 cents (per mark). What will be your return as a percentage of margin?

Treasury bond futures

8. Maxwell Securities buys a $100,000 par value, March 1995 Treasury bond contract at the quoted settle price in Table 16–8 (near the top).
   a. What is the dollar value of the contract? Use the settle price in your calculation.
   b. There is an initial margin requirement of $2,400 and a margin maintenance requirement of $1,750. If an interest rate increase causes the bond to go down by 0.8 percent of par value, will Maxwell be called upon to put up more margin?
   c. Assume Maxwell's investment is for six months. To have a 100 percent annualized return on the initial $2,400 margin, by what percent of par value must the bond increase?

Hedging by corporate treasurer

9. The treasurer of the Barton Corporation is going to bring an $8 million issue to the market in 45 days. It will be a 25-year issue. The interest-rate environment is highly volatile, and even though interest rates are currently 10¼ percent, there is a fear that interest rates will be up to 11 percent by the time the bonds get to the market.
   a. If interest rates go up by ¾ percent, what is the present value of the extra interest this increase will cost the corporation? Use an 11 percent discount rate, and disregard tax considerations.
   b. Assume the corporation is going to short June 1995 Treasury bonds as quoted near the top of Table 16–8 for the CBT (Chicago Board of Trade). Based on the settle price, how many contracts must they sell to equal the $8 million exposed position? Round to the nearest whole number of contracts.
   c. Based on your answer in part *b,* if Treasury bond prices increase by 2.8 percent of par value in each contract in response to a ½ percent decline in interest rates over the next 45 days, what will be the total loss on the futures contracts?

Hedging by corporate treasurer

10. Should the treasurer of the Barton Corporation feel he has failed in his tasks if the circumstance in part *c* of problem 9 takes place?

THE WALL STREET JOURNAL PROJECT

Using *The Wall Street Journal,* find the settle (closing) price for the nearest term contract (the one listed first) for the following commodities and financial futures. To find the placement of the quotes, go to the index on the first page of Section C and look up

"Commodities." When you are writing down the prices of the commodities in group A, move the decimal price two places to the left; that is, 132 ½ would translate to $1.3250.

Group A*

1. Wheat (CBT)
2. Pork bellies (CME)
3. Coffee (CSCE)
4. Gold (CMX)
5. Silver (CMX)

After you have written down the quote for the nearest term contract, indicate whether contracts in the future have a higher or lower value for each commodity. What might this tell you about investor expectations concerning the future price of the commodity?

Group B

Once again write down the settle (closing) price for the nearest term contract. For the financial futures in this group, you do *not* need to move the decimal point two places to the left. However, for the Treasury bonds, use the procedures in the chapter shown under "Interest-Rate Futures" to properly state the quote.

1. Deutschemark (CME)
2. British pound (CME)
3. Treasury bonds (CBT)

After you have written down the quote for the nearest term contract, indicate whether contracts in the future have a higher or lower value. Indicate what this might tell you about investor expectations for each contract.

CRITICAL THOUGHT CASE

Milt Samuals joined Garrett Construction Company in 1989 in the budgeting section of the corporate treasurer's office. He worked with a team of two accountants and a senior vice president of finance to provide pro forma budgets and financial statements. Although his undergraduate degree was in finance with an emphasis on investments, he still felt he was acquiring experience with his budgeting work. Nevertheless, he was quite excited when he learned that he was being shifted to a new department in the treasurer's office in which he would share responsibility for managing the excess funds of the corporation as well as participate in the hedging function that the corporation undertook to offset interest-rate exposure.

By 1993, he had moved to the top position in the hedging area. Samuals had the major responsibility for hedging against interest-rate increases that might take place from the

*The item in parentheses is the exchange the commodity trades on. The full name of the exchange can be found at the bottom of the "Commodities" page in the "Exchange Abbreviation" box.

time Garrett Construction Company agreed to undertake a project until the time it was completed. The period often ran from 6 to 12 months. Samuals used financial derivatives such as interest-rate futures and swaps to accomplish his purpose. Most often, he employed Treasury bond futures. He would sell (short) them to protect against interest-rate increases. If interest rates went up, the market value of the bonds covered under the contract would go down, and he could close out or cover his position at a profit. As he explained it, he would establish the sales price at approximately $100,000, and if interest rates went up, he could buy them back at perhaps $95,000. The $5,000 profit he made on the derivatives would help cover the added interest expense that Garrett Construction Company experienced on its loan at the bank as a result of increasing interest rates. Of course, if interest rates went down, he would lose money on the futures contract, but that would be offset by the lower interest the company would pay. Basically, he was neutralizing the company's position regardless of what happened to interest rates. If the company had a large amount of interest rate exposure, Samuals might engage in 10 or 20 contracts at one time.

Although Samuals was acquiring expertise in his hedging function, he eventually found himself becoming somewhat bored with his normal hedging activities. While he continued to hedge the company's interest-rate exposure, he also began speculating on interest-rate movements for the company. These contracts had nothing to do with the company's interest-rate exposure. For example, if he thought interest rates were going down, he would buy Treasury bond futures contracts. If rates did go down, the value of the bonds covered under the contract would go up, and he would sell (cover) his position at a nice profit. Since only a small amount of margin (cash) was involved, he could really use leverage to establish spectacular gains (though sometimes there were losses).

For the most part, Samuals was doing well, and he could not wait to tell Roger Garrett, the president of the company, about the new activity he had decided to undertake and how well he was doing for the company. He felt certain an added bonus was coming.

Question

1. If you were Roger Garrett, would you be inclined to reward Milt Samuals with an added bonus?

SELECTED REFERENCES

General Source

Extensive bibliography presented regularly by Robert T. Diagler in the *Journal of Futures Markets.*

Trading Strategy and Hedging

Block, Stanley B., and Timothy J. Gallagher. "How Much Do Bank Trust Departments Use Derivatives?" *Journal of Portfolio Management,* Fall 1988, pp. 12–16.

Miller, Merton. "Financial Innovation: The Last Twenty Years and the Next." *Journal of Financial and Quantitative Analysis,* December 1986, pp. 459–71.

Shefrin, Hersh, and Meir Statman. "Behavioral Aspects of the Design of Financial Products." *Financial Management,* Summer 1993, pp. 123–34.

Usmen, Nilufer. "Currency Swaps, Financial Arbitrage, and Default Risk." *Financial Management,* Summer 1994, pp. 43–56.

Returns on Futures

Cox, John; Jonathan Ingersoll, Jr.; and Stephen Ross. "The Relation between Forward and Futures Prices." *Journal of Financial Economics,* December 1981, p. 346.

Fabozzi, Frank J.; Christopher K. Ma; and James E. Briley. "Holiday Trading in Futures Markets." *Journal of Finance,* March 1994, pp. 307–24.

Nelson, Ray, and Robert Collins. "A Measure of Hedging Performance." *Journal of Futures Markets,* Spring 1985, pp. 45–56.

Treasury Futures

Hegde, Shantaram P., and Bill McDonald. "On the Information Role of Treasury Bill Futures." *Journal of Futures Markets,* Winter 1986, pp. 629–45.

Simpson, W. Gary, and Timothy C. Ireland. "The Impact of Financial Futures on the Cash Market for Treasury Bills." *Journal of Financial and Quantitative Analysis,* September 1985, pp. 371–79.

Foreign Currency Futures

Nesbitt, Stephen L. "Currency Hedging Plans for Plan Sponsors." *Financial Analysts Journal,* March–April 1991, pp. 73–81.

Shastri, Kuldeep, and Kishore Tandon. "Valuation of Foreign Currency Options: Some Empirical Tests." *Journal of Financial and Quantitative Analysis,* June 1986, pp. 145–60.

Interest-Rate Swaps

Filler, R. "Credit Risks and Costs in Interest-Rate Swaps." *Journal of Cash Management,* January–February 1993, pp. 38–41.

Kim, S. H., and G. D. Koppenhaver. "An Empirical Analysis of Bank Interest-Rate Swaps." *Journal of Financial Services Research,* February 1993, pp. 57–72.

17

Stock Index Futures and Options

In February 1982, the Kansas City Board of Trade began trading futures on a stock index, the Value Line Index. This event ushered in a new era of futures and options trading.

A future or option on an index allows the investor to participate in the movement of an entire index rather than an individual security. Currently, futures and options relate to such indexes as the Standard & Poor's 500 Stock Index, the Standard & Poor's 100 Stock Index, the New York Stock Exchange Composite Index, and many other old and new market measures.[1]

If an investor purchases a **futures contract on a stock market index,** he puts down the required margin and gains or loses on the transaction based on the movement of the index. For example, an investor may purchase a futures contract on the Standard & Poor's 500 Stock Index with $11,250 in margin. The actual contract value is based on the index value times 500. If the S&P 500 Futures Index were at 470, the initial contract value would be $235,000 (500 × 470). If the index went up or down by two points, the investor would gain or lose $1,000 (500 × ± 2). Because the initial investment is $11,250 in margin, we see a gain or loss of 8.9 percent (8.9 percent = $1,000/$11,250). Since this might happen over a one- or two-day period, the annualized return or loss could be high.

If the investor is trading in **stock index options** instead of futures, he may choose to participate in the Standard & Poor's 100 Stock Index. The S&P 100 Index is a smaller version of the S&P 500 Index and is composed of 100 blue-chip stocks on which the Chicago Board Options Exchange currently has individual option contracts. Included in the S&P 100 Index are such firms as IBM, General Motors, AT&T, and so on. The value of the S&P 100 Index tends to be about 35 points lower than the S&P 500 Index. If the S&P 100 Index were at 435 at a given time, an option to purchase the index at a strike price of 435 in two months might carry a premium (option price) of $5. The option price is multiplied by 100 to get a total value for the option of $500 (100 × $5). If the S&P 100 Index closed out at 445 on expiration, the option price will be $10, and a profit of $500 will be achieved over the two months:

Final value (100 × $10)	$ 1,000
Purchase price (100 × $5)	−500
Profit	$ 500

As we go further into the chapter, you will see there are not only futures and options on stock market indexes, but also **options to purchase futures** on stock market indexes. This represents a combination of a futures and option contract.

Stock index futures have grown faster than any new futures trading outlet in history. In their first six months of trading, the average daily volume was 4.5 times as great as the volume on Treasury bond futures during a comparable period of infancy. The same sort of pattern has occurred in index option trading.

THE CONCEPT OF DERIVATIVE PRODUCTS

Trading in stock index futures and options has had a tremendous impact on the financial markets in the United States. Stock index futures and options are sometimes referred to as **derivative products** because they derive their existence from actual market indexes but

[1] To date, there is no contract on the Dow Jones Industrial Average because Dow Jones & Company has resisted having its venerable index used for this purpose.

have no intrinsic characteristics of their own.[2] These derivative products are thought to make market movements more volatile. The primary reason is that enormous amounts of securities can be controlled by relatively small amounts of margin payments or option premiums. Also, these derivative products are often used as part of program trading. As discussed in Chapter 2, **program trading** means that computer-based trigger points are established in which large volume trades are initiated by institutional investors. Stock index futures and options facilitate program trading because a large volume of securities can be controlled. The presence of program trading, as supported by the use of stock index futures and options, was blamed by many for the market crash of 508 points in the Dow Jones Industrial Average on October 19, 1987. It was thought that too many institutional investors were moving in the same direction (to sell) at one time. Increased stock price volatility since the market crash has also been blamed on program trading and the use of stock index futures and options.

Actually, these are somewhat controversial topics. A study by the Chicago Mercantile Exchange suggests program trading and the use of derivative products has no negative effect on the market volatility per se. These trading tools merely help the market reach a new equilibrium level (in terms of value) more quickly.[3]

It is the contention of the authors that stock index futures and options have many useful purposes, which we will cover throughout the chapter. We will also try to point out potential negatives where they exist.

Before going into further discussion of futures and options on stock market indexes, the student should have read Chapter 15, Put and Call Options, and Chapter 16, Commodities and Financial Futures.

TRADING STOCK INDEX FUTURES

There are major stock index futures contracts on the S&P 500 Index (Chicago Mercantile Exchange), the S&P MidCap 400 (Chicago Mercantile Exchange), the Nikkei 225 Stock Average (Chicago Mercantile Exchange), the Major Market Index (Chicago Mercantile Exchange), and the New York Composite Index (New York Financial Exchange).[4] An example of these stock index futures contracts is shown in Table 17–1.[5]

We mentioned some of these indexes in Chapter 3 with the exception of the Major Market Index. The Major Market Index (MMI) is a price-weighted index composed of 20 of the largest firms in the United States. It is a convenient way to imitate movements in the Dow Jones Industrial Average and has a 97 percent correlation with that average (although its price movements are from a different base). Since Dow Jones & Company has prohibited the use of the Dow Jones Industrial Average for futures and options trading, this is an alternative way to play the game. Seventeen of the firms in the Major Market Index are part of the Dow Jones Industrial Average.

You will note in Table 17–1 that the title line for each contract (such as the S&P 500 Index) indicates the appropriate multiple times the value in the table. For the S&P 500

[2] Interest-rate futures and options are also considered to be derivative products.

[3] *Report of the Committee of Inquiry Appointed by the Chicago Mercantile Exchange to Examine the Events Surrounding October 19, 1987* (Chicago: The Chicago Mercantile Exchange, December 17, 1987).

[4] The NYFE (New York Financial Exchange) is a division of the New York Stock Exchange.

[5] There are also a number of other contracts. The Kansas City Board of Trade continues to trade contracts on the Value Line Index (though the volume is relatively low).

TABLE 17–1 Stock Index Futures (October 13, 1994)

INDEX

	Open	High	Low	Settle	Chg	High	Low	Open Interest
S&P 500 INDEX (CME) $500 times index								
Dec	467.50	473.75	467.10	469.15	+ 1.50	487.10	438.85	215,350
Mr95	475.10	476.85	471.90	472.25	+ 1.45	484.00	441.45	8,707
June		....	....	475.95	+ 1.40	487.40	449.50	2,574
Sept	482.50	485.00	480.30	480.30	+ 1.25	486.00	462.00	278
Est vol 94,875; vol Wed 60,686; open int 226,909, +1,475.								
Indx prelim High 471.30; Low 465.56; Close 467.79 +2.32								
S&P MIDCAP 400 (CME) $500 times index								
Dec	178.20	178.70	176.10	176.15	– .05	187.05	163.50	13,682
Est vol 965; vol Wed 393; open int 13,696, +63.								
The index: High 176.78; Low 175.03; Close 175.17 +.19								
NIKKEI 225 STOCK AVERAGE (CME)–$5 times index								
Dec	20175.	20280.	20165.	20180.	– 5.0	21800.	17030.	25,842
Est vol 1,5000; vol Wed 1,361; open int 25,844, +73.								
The index: High 20176.64; Low 20042.81; Close 20148.83 +59.11								
MAJOR MARKET INDEX (CME)–$500 times index								
Oct	407.00	408.75	404.70	405.00	+ 1.30	409.30	378.45	2,576
Dec	408.00	409.00	405.40	405.40	+ 1.30	408.20	361.75	198
Est vol 795; vol Wed 163; open int 2,871, +29.								
The index: High 408.00; Low 402.94; Close 404.86 +1.92								
NYSE COMPOSITE INDEX (NYFE)–500 times index								
Dec	260.40	260.80	257.85	258.05	+ .65	264.50	244.15	4,452
Mr95	261.60	261.60	259.45	259.45	+ .65	264.60	248.50	192
Est vol 2,731; vol Wed 1,690; open int 4,719, +6.								
The index: High 259.07; Low 256.35; Close 257.43 +1.08								

Source: *The Wall Street Journal,* October 14, 1994, p. C14.

Index, the multiplier is 500. This is also the value for the S&P MidCap 400 Index, the Major Market Index, and the NYSE Composite Index. For the Nikkei 225 Stock Average, the multiplier is 5. Looking at the December settle price in each of the five indexes, we see the value of the contracts in Table 17–2.

If the investor thinks the market is going up, he will purchase a futures contract. If he thinks the market is going down, he will sell a futures contract and hope the market will decline so that the contract can be closed out (repurchased) at a lower value than the sales price. Selling futures contracts can also be used to hedge a large stock portfolio. If the market goes down, what you lose on your portfolio you recoup in your futures contract.

In the example in Table 17–2, the investor has five indexes from which to choose.

We shall direct our attention for now to the S&P 500 Index futures contract (though the same basic principles would apply to other indexes). Part of the material from Table 17–1

TABLE 17–2 Value of Contracts

	December 1994 Settle Price	Multiplier	Contract Value
S&P 500 Index	469.15	500	$234,575
S&P MidCap 400	176.15	500	88,075
Nikkei Stock Average	20,180	5	100,900
Major Market Index	405.00	500	202,500
NYSE Composite Index	258.05	500	129,025

TABLE 17–3 S&P Index Futures Contract (CME), 500 Multiplier (October 13, 1994)

Contract Month	Open	High	Low	Settle	Change
December 1994	467.50	473.75	467.10	469.15	+ 1.50
March 1995	475.10	476.85	471.90	472.25	+ 1.45
June	—	—	—	475.95	+ 1.40
September	482.50	485.00	480.30	483.30	+ 1.25
Value of S&P 500 Stock Index (October 13, 1994) 467.79					

that pertains to the S&P 500 Index futures contract is reproduced in Table 17–3 so we can examine a number of key features related to the contract.

Trading Cycle

The trading cycle in the table is made up of the four months of March, June, September, and December. The last day of trading for a contract is the third Thursday of the ending month. The contracts in Table 17–3 extend 11 months into the future.

Margin Requirement

As previously mentioned, the basic margin requirement for buying or selling an S&P 500 futures contract on the Chicago Mercantile Exchange was $11,250 in 1994. Based on the December 1994 contract value of $234,575 (found on the top line in Table 17–2), this represents a margin requirement of 4.80 percent ($11,250/$234,575). There is also a margin maintenance requirement of $10,000. Thus, if the initial margin or equity in the account falls to this level, the investor will be required to supply sufficient cash or securities to bring the account back up to $11,250. Since the contract trades at 500 times the index, a decline of 2½ points in the S&P contract value would cause a loss of $1,250. In this instance, the margin position would be reduced from $11,250 to $10,000, and the investor would be asked to supply $1,250 in funds.

If the investor can prove he is hedging a long position, the margin requirement will be less. For example, if an investor owns a portfolio of stocks that roughly equals the value of the index futures contract ($234,575 in this case), the initial margin requirement is only $10,000. Since a hedged position is not as risky as a speculative position, less initial margin is required.[6]

Minimum Price Change

The minimum price change per trade for the S&P 500 Futures Index contract is 0.05. Thus, if the December futures contract is at 469.15, the smallest possible price move would be down to 469.10 or up to 469.20. Since the contract is multiplied by 500 to

[6] It should be mentioned that on a hedged position, the margin maintenance requirement is the same as the original margin—$10,000 in this case.

determine value, an index movement of 0.05 represents \$25 (500 × 0.05 = \$25). Therefore, the smallest possible price change is \$25.

Cash Settlement

In traditional commodity futures markets, the potential for physical delivery exists. One who is trading in wheat could actually decide to deliver the commodity to close out the contract. As discussed in Chapter 16, this happens only a very small percentage of the time, but it is possible. The stock index futures market, on the other hand, is purely a **cash-settlement** market. There is never the implied potential for future delivery of the Standard & Poor's 500 Stock Index. An investor simply closes out (or reverses) his position before the settlement date. If he does not, his account is automatically credited with his gains or debited with his losses, and the transaction is completed.[7]

One of the advantages of a cash-settlement arrangement is that it makes it impossible for a "short squeeze" to develop. A short squeeze occurs when an investor attempts to corner a market in a commodity, such as silver, so that it is not possible for those who have short positions to make physical delivery. Clearly, with a cash-settlement position, this can never happen.

Basis

The term **basis** represents the difference between the stock index futures price and the value of the actual underlying index.[8] We can now turn back to Table 17–3 to see a numerical example of basis. On the date of the table, the S&P 500 futures contract for December was quoted at a settle (closing) price of 469.15 (second item from the right in the first row). The actual S&P 500 Stock Index, as shown at the bottom of Table 17–3, closed at 467.79. The basis, or difference, between the futures price and the actual underlying index was 1.36:

Stock index futures price	469.15
Actual underlying index	–467.79
Basis	1.36

Moving to the March 1995 contract in Table 17–3, the basis is the difference between the March contract settle value of 472.25 and the value of the underlying index, which, of course, is still 467.79. The difference is 4.46. For the data in Table 17–3, the basis indicates that a premium is being paid over the actual underlying index value, and furthermore, the premium expands with the passage of time. This is generally thought to be a positive sign. If the index futures price is below the actual underlying index, there is a negative basis.

An excellent discussion of the ability of stock index futures to forecast the actual underlying index is presented in an article by Zeckhauser and Niederhoffer in the *Financial Analysts Journal.*[9] A part of their thesis is that futures contracts move

[7] Actually, the account is adjusted daily to reflect the gains and losses. This is known as marking the customer's position to market.

[8] The same concept can be applied to other types of futures contracts.

[9] Richard Zeckhauser and Victor Niederhoffer, "The Performance of Market Index Futures Contracts," *Financial Analysts Journal,* January–February 1983, pp. 59–65.

instantaneously to reflect market conditions, whereas the actual underlying index moves more slowly. If the market makes an important move, some of the stocks that are part of the actual underlying index will not yet have reacted. Thus, initial, significant, and potentially predictive information may be found in the futures market quotes.

Also, at times, futures or options markets stay open later or begin trading earlier than the actual underlying stock markets. This can be very beneficial not only in providing lead time information on market movements, but also in giving the trader an opportunity to take a position before the opening or after the closing of the stock market.

Overall Features

Many of the important features related to stock index futures on the various exchanges are presented in Table 17–4. This table can serve as a ready reference guide to trading commodities in various markets.

TABLE 17–4 Specifications for Stock Index Futures Contracts

Index and Exchange	Index	Contract Size and Value (in dollars)	Contract Months
S&P 500 Index Index and Options Market (IOM) of Chicago Mercantile Exchange (CME)	Value of 500 selected stocks on NYSE, AMEX, and OTC, weighted to reflect market value of issues	500 × S&P 500 Index	March June September December
S&P MidCap 400 Index and Options Market (IOM) of Chicago Mercantile Exchange (CME)	Index of 400 medium-sized stocks with values from $200 million to $5 billion, weighted to reflect market value of issues	500 × S&P MidCap 400	March June September December
Nikkei 225 Stock Average Index and Options Market (IOM) of Chicago Mercantile Exchange (CME)	Index of 225 Japanese stocks, weighted to reflect market value of issues	5 × Nikkei Stock Average	March June September December
Major Market Index Index and Options Market (IOM) of Chicago Mercantile Exchange (CME)	Index of 20 major stocks, weighted to reflect market value of issues	500 × Major Market Index (MMI)	March June September December
NYSE Composite Index New York Futures Exchange (NYFE) of the New York Stock Exchange	Index of 1,550 NYSE stocks, weighted to reflect market value of issues	500 × NYSE Composite Average	March June September December

USE OF STOCK INDEX FUTURES

There are a number of actual and potential users of stock index futures. As is true of most commodity futures contracts, the motivation may be either speculation or the opportunity to hedge.

Speculation

The speculator may use stock index futures in an attempt to profit from major movements in the market. He or she may have developed a conviction about the next move in the market through fundamental or technical analysis. For example, those who utilize fundamental analysis may determine that P/E ratios are at a 10-year low or that earnings performance should be extremely good in the next two quarters, so they wish to bet on the market moving upward. Market technicians might observe that a resistance or support position in the market is being penetrated and that it is time to take a position based on the anticipated consequences of that penetration.

While the market participant could put his or her money in individual stocks, it might be more efficient and less time consuming to simply invest in stock index futures. In buying futures on the S&P 500 Index, the investor is capturing the performance of 500 securities; with the S&P MidCap, 400 securities; with the New York Stock Exchange Index, 1,550 securities; and with the Nikkei Average, 225 Japanese stocks.

As discussed in Chapter 1, two types of risks are associated with investments: systematic or market-related risks, and unsystematic or firm-related risks. Since only systematic risk is assumed to be rewarded in an efficient capital market environment (unsystematic risk can be diversified away), the investor may wish to be exposed only to systematic risk. Stock index futures represent an efficient approach to only taking systematic, market-related risk.

Another advantage of stock index futures is that there is less manipulative action and insider trading than with individual securities. While it is possible (though not legal) for "informed" insider trading to cause an individual stock to move dramatically in the short term, such activity is not as likely for an entire index. This advantage, however, should not be overstated. Unusual trading activity of stock index futures comes under the scrutiny of federal regulators from time to time.

Stock index futures also offer leverage potential. A $230,000 to $240,000 S&P futures contract can be established for $11,250 in margin and with no interest on the balance.[10] If you were investing $240,000 in actual stocks through margin, you would have to put up a minimum of $120,000 (50 percent) in margin and pay interest on the balance. The margin requirement is still considerably lower than that on an outright stock purchase. Also, the commissions on a stock index futures contract are minuscule in comparison with commissions on securities of comparable value.

Volatility and Profits or Losses Before the market crash of 1987, the average daily move on the S&P 500 Index was approximately 0.50 (one-half of a point per day). Since the crash, the average daily movement has been in the 0.75 to 1.00 range. A 0.90 upward move in an S&P 500 futures contract (say, from 470 to 470.90) means a daily gain of

[10] As mentioned in Chapter 16, margin on futures contracts merely represents good-faith money, and there is never any interest on the balance.

$450 (recall the contract has a multiplier of 500). With a margin requirement of $11,250, that is a 4 percent, one-day return on your money:

Gain in futures contract	$ .90
Multiplier	× 500
Dollar gain	$ 450
Margin	$11,250
Percentage gain	4%

This translates into a 1,440 percent annualized return (4 percent × 360). By contrast, if the $11,250 were invested in a 6 percent certificate of deposit, only $1.87 in interest would accrue on a daily basis. The difference here, of course, is that the $450 average daily movement related to the index may be up or down, whereas the $1.87 is only up.

When a stock index futures contract starts to run against an investor, he or she can bail out and cut losses. If the contract value is going down rapidly, the investor will be continually called on to put up more margin as the margin position is being depleted. That puts tremendous pressure on the investor. He or she must decide whether to put up more margin and hold the position in hopes of a comeback or close out the position and take a loss.

Not all speculation in stock index futures must necessarily be based on the market going up. You can also speculate that the market will go down. You simply sell a contract with the anticipation of repurchasing it at a lower price later. Margin requirements are similar, and gains come from a declining market and losses from an increasing market. If the index goes up rapidly, the investor will be called on to put up more margin.[11]

Hedging

Up to now our discussion of stock index futures has mainly related to speculating (or anticipating the next major move in the market). Perhaps the most important use of stock index futures is for hedging purposes. One who has a large diversified portfolio may think the market is about to decline. A portfolio manager who suffers a 20 percent decline in his or her portfolio actually requires a 25 percent gain from the new lower base to break even.

A portfolio manager faced with the belief that a declining market is imminent may be inclined to sell part or all of the portfolio. The question becomes, is this realistic? First, large transaction costs are associated with selling part or all of a portfolio and then repurchasing it later. Second, it may be difficult to liquidate a position in certain securities that are thinly traded. For example, a mutual fund or pension fund that tries to sell 10,000 shares of a small over-the-counter stock may initially find a price quote of $25 but only be able to close out its relatively large position at $23.50. A $15,000 loss would be suffered. Furthermore, the fund might find the same type of problem in reacquiring the stock after the overall market decline is over. This problem could be multiplied by 25 or 50 times, depending on the number of securities in the portfolio. Although larger, more liquid holdings would be easier to trade, significant transactions costs are still involved.

[11] The margin maintenance requirements are similar to those on a long position.

A more easily executed defensive strategy would be to sell one or more stock index futures as a hedge against the portfolio. If the stock market does go down, the loss on the portfolio will be partially or fully offset by the profit on the stock index futures contract(s) because they are bought back at a lower price than the initial sales price.

As an example, assume a corporate pension fund has $20 million in stock holdings. The investment committee for the fund is very bearish in its outlook, fearing that the overall market could go down by 20 percent in the next few months and a $4 million loss would be suffered. The pension fund decides to fully hedge its position.

The fund is going to use S&P 500 Index futures for the hedge. We shall assume the futures can be sold for 470, with a settlement date in three months. Before the number of contracts for execution is determined, the portfolio manager must consider the relative volatility of his portfolio. If the portfolio is more volatile than the market, this must be factored into the decision-making process. As discussed in Chapter 1, the beta coefficient indicates how volatile a stock is relative to the market. If a stock has a beta of 1.20, it is 20 percent more volatile than the market (or market index). We shall assume the $20 million portfolio discussed above has a weighted average beta of 1.15 (that is, the portfolio is 15 percent more volatile than the market).

To determine the number of contracts necessary to hedge the position, we use the following formula:

$$\frac{\$\text{ Value of portfolio}}{\$\text{ Value of contract}} \times \begin{matrix}\text{Weighted beta} \\ \text{of portfolio}\end{matrix} = \begin{matrix}\text{Number of} \\ \text{contracts}\end{matrix} \qquad (17\text{–}1)$$

In the example under discussion, we would show:

$$\frac{\$20{,}000{,}000}{470 \times \$500} \times 1.15 = \text{Number of contracts}$$

In the first term of the formula, the numerator is the size of the portfolio being hedged. The denominator is the size of each contract and, in this example, is found by multiplying the S&P futures contract value of 470 by 500. The first term is then multiplied by the weighted beta value of 1.15. The answer works out as:

$$\frac{\$20{,}000{,}000}{\$235{,}000} \times 1.15 = 85.11 \times 1.15 = 98 \text{ contracts (rounded)}$$

The portfolio can be effectively hedged with 98 contracts.

Assume the market does go down but only by 10 percent instead of the 20 percent originally anticipated. Let's demonstrate that the hedge has worked. Since the portfolio has a beta of 1.15, its decline would be 11.5 percent (10 percent × 1.15). With a $20 million portfolio, the loss would be $2.3 million. To offset this loss, we will have a gain on 98 contracts. The gain is shown as follows:

S&P Index futures contract (sales price)	470.0
Decline in price on the futures contract (10% × 470)	– 47.0
Ending value (purchase price)	423.0

The 47-point decline on the index futures contract indicates the profit made on each contract.[12] They were sold for 470.0 and repurchased for 423.0. With 98 contracts, the profit on the stock index futures contracts comes out as $2,303,000:

Profit per contract (47.0 × $500)	$ 23,500
Number of contracts	× 98
Total profit	$2,303,000

The gain of $2,303,000 on the stock index futures contracts offsets the loss of $2.3 million on the portfolio. The small difference between the two values represents the fact that we rounded up our position from 97.87 contracts to 98 contracts. Actually, executing a perfect hedge may be further complicated by a number of other factors such as the lack of an appropriate index to match against the portfolio and the change in basis over time. Also, the portfolio may not move exactly in accordance with the beta. No doubt, many real-world factors can complicate any hedge.

While a stock index futures hedge offers the advantage of protecting against losses, it takes away the upside potential. If the market goes up by 10 percent instead of down, the gain on the portfolio may be wiped out by the loss on the stock index futures contracts. The investor could be forced to buy back the futures contract for 10 percent more than the selling price. Because some portfolio managers are afraid of losing all their upside potential in a hedged position, they may wish to hedge less than 100 percent of their portfolio.

While the hedging procedure just described can be potentially beneficial to portfolio managers, it can be potentially detrimental to the market in general if overused. Actually, protecting a large portfolio against declines is sometimes referred to as **portfolio insurance.** It is potentially a good strategy, but what if many investors initiate their portfolio-insurance strategies at the same time? Perhaps they are worried because there has been an increase in the prime rate or a bad report on inflation. An overload of stock index futures sales hitting the market at the same time drives down not only stock index futures prices but the stocks in the indexes as well (such as those in the S&P 500 Stock Index). An overall panic can result. The chain reaction is that a whole new round of portfolio-insurance-induced sales is triggered.

Partially to protect against a recurrence of the events that were part of the market crash of 1987, the Chicago Mercantile Exchange and New York Stock Exchange introduced so-called circuit breakers in 1990. **Circuit breakers** call for the temporary halt in trading of futures contracts when the market is tumbling. For example, the Chicago Mercantile Exchange has a rule that prevents market participants from trading Standard & Poor's 500 Stock Index futures at lower prices for 30 minutes after the S&P 500 Index has fallen 12 points. The New York Stock Exchange temporarily bars most program-trading-related activities any time the Dow Jones Industrial Average changes by 50 points.[13] While these circuit breakers have worked effectively since their introduction in the summer of 1990,

[12] Note that the futures contract is assumed to move on a one-to-one basis with the market. The actual relationship may not be this precise.

[13] Under Rule 80A, the New York Stock Exchange mandates that stock index arbitrage, in which computer-assisted traders rapidly buy or sell stocks in New York with offsetting trades in stock futures in Chicago, must be conducted in a technically stabilizing way once the Dow Jones Industrial Average swings 50 points.

they have not been fully tested. In a true panic, the circuit breakers themselves could add to fear as traders and hedgers are not able to execute their transactions.

Other Uses of Hedging Hedging with stock index futures has a number of other uses besides attempting to protect the position of a long-term investment portfolio. These include the following.

Underwriter Hedge As described in Chapter 10, the investment banker (underwriter) has a risk exposure from buying stock from the issuing corporation with the intention of reselling it in the public markets. If there is weakness during the distribution period, the potential resale price could fall below the purchase price, and the underwriter's profit would be wiped out. To protect against this market risk, the underwriter could sell stock index futures contracts. If the market goes down, presumably, the loss on the stock will be compensated for by the gain on the stock index futures contract as a result of being able to repurchase it at a lower price. This, of course, is not a perfect hedge. It is possible that the individual stock could go down while the market is going up, and losses on both the stock and stock index futures contract would occur (writing options directly against the stock might be more efficient, but in many cases such options are not available).

Specialist or Dealer Hedge As indicated in Chapter 2, a specialist on an exchange or a dealer in the over-the-counter market buys and sells stocks for his own inventory for temporary holding. He may, at times, assume a larger temporary holding than desired, with all the risks associated with that exposure. Stock index futures can reduce the market (or systematic) risk, although the futures cannot reduce the specific risk associated with a security.

Retirement or Estate Hedge As we move into the next two or three decades, large retirement funds will be accumulated from voluntary retirement plans. A retirement plan participant who has accumulated a large sum in an equity fund may feel a need to hedge his or her position in certain time periods in the economy (where liquidation is neither legal nor possible). A futures contract may provide that hedge. Also, a person with responsibility for an estate may be locked into a portfolio during the period of probate (validation of the will process) and wish to hedge his or her position with a stock index futures contract.

Tax Hedge An investor may have accumulated a large return on a diversified portfolio in a given year. To maintain the profitable position but defer the taxable gains until the next year, futures contracts may be employed.

Arbitraging

While stock index futures started out as a major tool for speculating and hedging, they are now also widely used for arbitraging. Basically, an **arbitrage** is set up when a simultaneous trade (a buy and a sell) occurs in two different markets and a profit is locked in. Assume the S&P 500 Stock Index has a value of 468 based on the market value of all the stocks in the index. Also, assume the S&P 500 Stock Index futures contract, due to

expire in two months, is selling for 469. There is a one-point positive basis between the futures contract and the underlying index. A sophisticated institutional investor may decide to arbitrage based on this difference. He or she will simultaneously sell a futures contract for 469 and buy a basket of stocks that matches the S&P 500 Stock Index for 468.[14] Because at expiration, the futures contract and underlying index will have the same value, a one-point profit is locked in at the time of arbitraging. For example, if at expiration, the S&P 500 Stock Index has a value of 466, a gain of three will occur on the sale, and a loss of two will be associated with the purchase for a net profit of one. If thousands of such contracts are involved, the profits can be substantial, and the potential for losses in a true arbitrage is nonexistent.

As you might assume, index arbitraging is in the exclusive providence of wealthy, sophisticated investors. For this reason, many smaller investors are somewhat resentful of the process and claim it tends to disrupt the normal operations of the marketplace. While there is nothing inherently wrong with arbitraging and it may even make the markets more efficient, it is sometimes a target for criticism by regulators. This is because it involves the process of program trading, discussed earlier in the chapter.

TRADING STOCK INDEX OPTIONS

Stock index options also allow the market participant to speculate or hedge against major market movements, although there is no opportunity for arbitraging. Stock index options are similar in many respects to the standard put and call options on individual stocks discussed in Chapter 15. The purchaser of an option pays an initial premium and then closes out the option at a given price in the future. One essential difference between stock index options and options on individual securities is that in the former case, there is only a cash settlement of the position, whereas in the latter case (individual securities), you can force the option writer to deliver the securities.

Examples of stock index options are presented in Table 17–5. They are:

Standard and Poor's 100 Index (Chicago Board Options Exchange)
Russell 2000 (Chicago Board Options Exchange)
Major Market Index (American Stock Exchange)
Wilshire Index (Pacific Coast Exchange)
New York Stock Exchange Index (New York Stock Exchange)

There are many other indexes on which options can be written such as the Standard and Poor's 500 Stock Index (Chicago Board Options Exchange) and the Standard and Poor's MidCap Index (American Stock Exchange).

We have discussed many of these indexes either in Chapter 3 or in this chapter. One item to observe is that the stock index option contract often trades on a different exchange than the previously discussed stock index futures contract. For example, the Major Market Index futures contract trades on the Chicago Mercantile Exchange, while the

[14] Actually, arbitraging has become sufficiently sophisticated through mathematics and computer analysis that all 500 stocks do not actually have to be purchased. Perhaps 10 or 15 key stocks bought in large quantities will be sufficient to adequately represent the S&P 500 Index. Commissions on such transactions tend to be extremely small.

TABLE 17–5 Stock Index Options (October 13, 1994)

INDEX OPTIONS TRADING

CHICAGO

S & P 100 INDEX(OEX)

Index Value 433.34

Oct	415 c	2,040	19	+ 1 1/8	10,035
Oct	415 p	10,721	1/2	− 1/16	43,690
Nov	415 c	630	21 1/4	+ 2 3/8	4,425
Nov	415 p	4,469	2 7/16	− 3/16	17,843
Dec	415 c	20	28	+ 6 5/8	1,240
Dec	415 p	1,690	4 1/8	− 5/8	3,779
Jan	420 p	167	7	− 1	2,698
Oct	420 c	19,347	14 1/2	+ 1 1/2	38,022
Oct	420 p	27,219	7/8	− 1/16	68,927
Nov	420 c	1,663	16 1/2	+ 1 3/8	9,319
Nov	420 p	7,499	3 1/4	− 1/4	43,737
Dec	420 c	11	20 1/2	+ 2 1/2	1,497
Dec	420 p	8,623	5 1/2	− 1/2	22,542
Oct	425 c	20,368	10	+ 1 1/8	40,299
Oct	425 p	35,951	1 5/16	− 3/16	62,347
Nov	425 c	11,188	13	+ 1 1/8	10,854
Nov	425 p	8,587	4 1/8	− 1/2	19,249
Dec	425 c	1,114	16 1/2	+ 2	4,573
Dec	425 p	1,851	6 3/4	− 1/4	6,494
Jan	430 c	24	15	+ 5/8	2,636
Jan	430 p	108	9 1/2	− 1 3/8	3,928
Oct	430 c	44,370	5 3/4	+ 3/4	55,140
Oct	430 p	52,517	2 5/16	− 5/16	57,976
Nov	430 c	8,597	9 1/8	+ 5/8	19,784
Nov	430 p	12,903	5 5/8	− 5/8	21,550
Dec	430 c	590	13 1/8	+ 1 7/8	9,325
Dec	430 p	1,513	8 1/4	− 1/4	9,968
Oct	435 c	60,079	2 3/4	+ 1/2	60,839
Oct	435 p	39,714	4 1/8	− 1	23,272
Nov	435 c	6,777	6	+ 5/8	22,292
Nov	435 p	7,715	7 3/4	− 1/2	12,125
Dec	435 c	536	9 1/8	+ 5/8	4,328
Dec	435 p	257	9 3/8	− 1 3/8	2,622
Jan	440 c	328	9 7/8	+ 1 1/2	2,777
Jan	440 p	31	13 1/2	− 1 3/4	2,076
Oct	440 c	50,008	7/8	+ 3/16	60,775
Oct	440 p	12,688	7 1/2	− 1 1/2	6,821
Nov	440 c	9,693	3 5/8	+ 11/16	28,147
Nov	440 p	1,168	10 3/4	− 5/8	4,829
Dec	440 c	1,325	6 1/4	+ 3/4	14,525
Dec	440 p	173	12 1/4	− 1	4,167
Oct	445 c	20,831	5/16	+ 1/16	55,370
Oct	445 p	773	12 1/4	− 1 1/4	1,292
Nov	445 c	5,491	1 15/16	+ 1/2	24,132
Nov	445 p	90	14	− 1 1/4	610
Dec	445 c	881	4	+ 1/2	4,462
Dec	445 p	7	14 1/4	− 2 1/4	163
Jan	450 c	338	5 1/2	+ 1 3/8	3,110
Jan	450 p	2	18	− 3 1/4	97
Oct	450 c	12,643	1/8	...	36,339
Oct	450 p	15	15 3/4	− 3	352
Nov	450 c	6,394	15/16	+ 1/4	26,584
Nov	450 p	23	15 1/8	− 5 1/4	206
Dec	450 c	1,301	2 7/8	+ 7/8	13,684
Dec	450 p	26	17 3/4	− 2 1/4	367
Oct	455 c	3,335	1/16	...	24,207
Nov	455 c	6,123	7/16	+ 3/16	22,594
Dec	455 c	1,254	1 3/8	+ 5/16	9,532
Dec	455 p	2	21 1/2	− 3 1/8	25

RUSSELL 2000(RUT)

Index Value 255.12

Dec	235 p	50	1 1/2	− 3/8	5,232
Oct	250 c	100	7 3/8	+ 1 5/8	449
Oct	250 p	90	5/16	− 3/4	236
Nov	250 p	23	2 1/8	− 1/2	644
Oct	255 c	15	3	+ 1 1/2	373
Dec	255 c	50	7 3/4	+ 1 1/4	1,537
Dec	255 p	510	5	− 5 1/4	1,537
Oct	260 p	10	4 5/8	− 5/8	358
Nov	260 c	50	3 1/8	+ 5/16	80
Nov	260 p	100	6 5/8	+ 3/8	471
Oct	265 c	50	5/16	...	...
Nov	265 p	50	9 3/8	...	...

Call vol. .... 265 Open Int........ 38,606
Put vol. .... 850 Open Int........ 48,975

AMERICAN

MAJOR MARKET(XMI)

Index Value 404.86

Nov	325 p	10	1/4	+ 1/16	329
Dec	350 p	8	13/16	− 7/16	894
Oct	370 p	10	1/16	...	1,312
Oct	380 c	10	28 1/2	+ 5 1/2	78
Oct	380 p	10	1/8	− 1/16	2,347
Nov	380 p	30	1 1/4	− 1/4	114
Oct	385 c	8	19 5/8	+ 2 1/4	105
Oct	385 p	755	1/4	− 1/16	2,493
Nov	385 p	10	1 1/2	− 5/8	360
Dec	385 p	3	3 3/4	− 1 3/4	4
Oct	390 c	5	17 3/4	+ 3 7/8	461
Oct	390 p	81	7/16	− 1/4	795
Nov	390 p	116	2 1/4	− 3/4	1,125
Oct	395 c	21	11 1/2	+ 2	915
Oct	395 p	483	1	− 1/4	1,929
Nov	395 p	665	3 3/4	+ 1/8	4,629
Oct	400 c	91	7 5/8	+ 2 1/4	1,274
Oct	400 p	377	1 7/8	− 3/8	1,310
Nov	400 c	5	11 1/2	+ 3 3/8	207
Nov	400 p	48	4 3/8	− 5/8	2,711
Dec	400 c	2	14 1/4	+ 3 3/4	100
Dec	400 p	35	7	− 5 5/8	150
Oct	405 c	988	3 1/4	+ 1	1,341
Oct	405 p	151	3 1/2	− 1	3,185
Nov	405 c	76	6 1/4	+ 5/8	116
Nov	405 p	20	5 3/8	− 1 7/8	10
Dec	405 c	5	9 3/4	+ 3 1/4	31
Oct	410 c	447	1 5/16	+ 3/8	789
Oct	410 p	241	6 1/8	− 1 3/4	341
Nov	410 c	42	5 1/8	+ 2 1/4	132
Nov	410 p	4	7 1/2	− 2 5/8	48
Dec	410 c	1	7 5/8	+ 2 1/8	250
Oct	415 c	159	1/4	+ 1/16	458
Oct	415 p	10	8 1/4	− 4 1/8	336
Nov	415 c	1	2 5/8	+ 1 15/16	38
Nov	415 p	10	11 1/2	...	...
Dec	415 c	1	4 3/4	...	...
Oct	420 c	5	1/16	...	155
Nov	420 c	825	1 5/8	+ 1 3/8	99
Nov	425 c	50	5/8	...	...
Dec	425 c	500	1 3/4	+ 1	2,450
Dec	425 p	2	18	− 14 3/4	2,000

Call vol. ....3,240 Open Int........31,118
Put vol. ....3,069 Open Int........41,403

PACIFIC

WILSHIRE INDEX(WSX)

Index Value 329.38

Oct	320 c	10	8 5/8	+ 1	101
Oct	325 c	10	4 3/4	+ 1 5/8	329
Oct	325 p	9	1 9/16	− 9/16	138
Oct	330 c	5	1 7/16	+ 5/16	17
Oct	330 p	7	2 15/16	− 2 7/16	10
Oct	335 c	12	3/8	− 5/8	35
Nov	335 c	5	2 9/16	+ 1/8	132
Nov	340 c	5	1	− 1 1/16	...

Call vol. ....47 Open Int..........1,329
Put vol. ....16 Open Int............709

NEW YORK

NYSE INDEX new(NYA)

Index Value 259.07

Oct	245 p	3	1/16	− 1/4	33
Oct	250 p	3	1/4	− 1/16	58
Nov	250 c	3	11	+ 2 1/2	3
Oct	255 c	15	3 1/8	+ 1 3/4	186
Oct	255 p	3	7/8	− 11/16	12
Nov	255 c	2	6 7/8	+ 2 1/8	2
Nov	255 p	25	2 3/8	− 7/8	195
Oct	260 c	15	7/8	− 9/16	152
Oct	260 p	7	1 3/4	− 5 3/4	11
Nov	260 p	170	3 7/8	− 1 7/8	21
Oct	265 c	4	3/16	− 1	...
Oct	265 p	3	6 5/8	− 1 3/4	...
Nov	265 c	2	1 1/8	− 1 3/8	125

Call vol. ....41 Open Int..........1,513
Put vol. ....214 Open Int............596

Source: *The Wall Street Journal,* October 14, 1994, p. C15. Reprinted by permission of *The Wall Street Journal,*

Major Market Index option contract trades on the American Stock Exchange. Also, the Standard & Poor's 500 Stock Index futures contract trades on the Chicago Mercantile Exchange, while the Standard & Poor's 500 Stock Index option contract trades on the Chicago Board Options Exchange. The point is that some exchanges have greater expertise in options (such as the Chicago Board Options Exchange and the American Stock Exchange), while others specialize in futures (the Chicago Mercantile Exchange and the Chicago Board of Trade). There is tremendous competition among exchanges to find the appropriate niche in stock index futures and options.

Actual Trade in the S&P 100 Index

Let's take a closer look at the most popular of the stock index options, the Standard & Poor's 100 Index options trading on the Chicago Board Options Exchange. We reproduce a part of Table 17–5 covering this index in Table 17–6. For ease of presentation, we will reconstruct the data in columns for calls and columns for puts.

You may recall from an earlier discussion that the S&P 100 Index is composed of 100 blue-chip stocks on which the Chicago Board Options Exchange currently has individual option contracts. It is a smaller version of the S&P 500 Index and generally has a value of about 35 points less (though it closely parallels the overall movements of the S&P 500). Both indexes are value weighted.

Note at the bottom of Table 17–6 that the S&P 100 Index closed on October 13, 1994, at 433.34. With this value in mind, we can examine the strike prices and premiums for the various contracts. The premium in each case is multiplied by 100 to determine the total cash value involved. Let's read down to the 435 strike price and across to the November call option (second monthly column). The premium is 6.

TABLE 17–6 S&P 100 Index Stock Options (October 13, 1994)

	Calls			Puts		
Strike Price	October	November	December	October	November	December
415	19	21¼	28	½	2 7/16	4⅛
420	14½	16½	20½	⅞	3¼	5½
425	10	13	16½	1 9/16	4⅛	6¾
430	5¾	9⅛	13⅛	2 9/16	5⅝	8¼
435	2¾	6	9⅛	4⅛	7¾	9⅜
440	⅞	3⅜	6¼	7½	10¾	12¼
445	5/16	1 15/16	4	12¼	14	14¼
450	⅛	15/16	2⅞	15	15⅛	17¾
455	1/16	7/16	1⅜	—	—	21½

The multiplier times the premium is 100.
Value of the S&P 100 Index (October 13, 1994) = 433.34.

Assume an investor bought a November 435 contract for a premium of 6 on October 13, 1994, and that when the November contract expired, the S&P 100 Index was 452 under an optimistic assumption and 418 under a pessimistic assumption. At an index value of 452, the option value is 17 (452 – 435). The ending or expiration price is 17 points higher than the strike price. Keep in mind that the option cost is 6. The profit is shown below to be $1,100.

At an ending value of 418 (pessimistic assumption), the option is worthless, and there is a loss of $600. Remember these are 435 call options.

	452 Optimistic Assumption	418 Pessimistic Assumption
Final value (100 × 17)	$1,700	$ 0.00
Purchase price (100 × 6)	– 600	–600.00
Profit or loss	$1,100	$–600.00

We have been working with call options. Now let's shift our attention to put options. If a 435 put option (the option to sell at 435 rather than buy at 435) had been acquired on October 13, 1994, we can see in Table 17–6 (November put column, fifth row from the bottom) that the initial price of our put option would be 7¾ ($775.00). Let's assume that when the November put contract expired, the S&P 100 Index was 452 under what is now the pessimistic assumption and 418 under what is now the optimistic assumption.

At an index value of 452, no value is associated with a put option. That allows you to sell at 435. No one would want to use the option to sell at 435 if the index value is 452. Since the put option costs 7¾, there is a $775.00 loss. At a final value of 418, the put option to sell at 435 has a value of 17. With a cost of 7¾, a profit of $925.00 occurs. The profit and losses are indicated below:

	452 Pessimistic Assumption	418 Optimistic Assumption	
Final value	$ 0.00	(100 × 17)	$1,700.00
Purchase price (100 × 7.75)	775.00	(100 × 7.75)	775.00
Profit or loss	$–775.00		$ 925.00

HEDGING WITH STOCK INDEX OPTIONS

The discussion of stock index options thus far has pertained to speculation about market moves. Stock index options can also be used for hedging. Like stock index futures, stock index options can be used to protect a portfolio or for special purposes by underwriters, specialists, dealers, tax planners, and others.

At times, options may offer a hedging advantage over futures to investors who are limited by law from purchasing futures contracts.[15] On the other hand, futures generally

[15] It should be pointed out that there are stock index options that apply to specific industries such as banking stocks, pharmaceutical stocks, and utility stocks. Stock index futures do not offer these opportunities.

allow for a more efficient hedge than options. If the market goes down by 20 or 25 percent, chances are good that a completely hedged short futures position (selling futures contracts) will compensate for losses in a portfolio. An option write, used to hedge a portfolio, may be inadequate. Perhaps the option premium income represents 10 percent of the portfolio, but the market goes down by 25 percent. Fifteen percent of the loss will be unprotected. Buying a put option may overcome this problem, but the cash outflow to purchase the put option could involve substantial funds. Clearly, both futures and options have their advantages and disadvantages.

OPTIONS ON STOCK INDEX FUTURES

We have discussed *stock index futures* and *stock index options,* so a natural extension of our discussion is to consider the third form of stock index trading, *options on stock index futures.* The three forms of index trading are listed below for reference. The contrast between them is shown in Figure 17–1.

1. Stock index futures.
2. Stock index options.
3. Options on stock index futures.

An option on stock index futures (item 3 above) gives the holder the right to purchase the stock index *futures contract* at a specified price over a given period. This is slightly

FIGURE 17–1 Comparison of Option Contracts

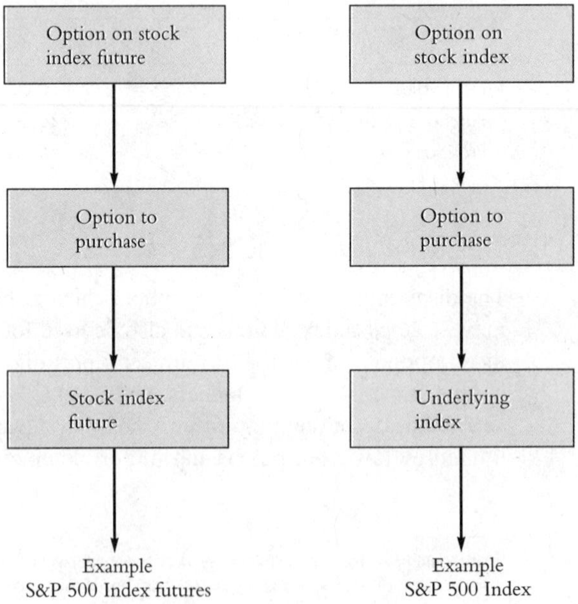

different from the stock index option (item 2) that gives the holder the right to purchase the *underlying index* at a specified price over a given time period.[16]

The primary topic for discussion in this section is represented by the lefthand column in Figure 17–1, an option on a stock index futures contract. The value of an option to purchase a stock index futures contract will depend on the outlook for the futures contract. Quotes on options to purchase stock index futures are shown in Table 17–7.

As indicated in Table 17–7, options on stock index futures are available for the S&P 500 Stock Index. A call option to buy a December S&P 500 Stock Index futures contract at a price of 470 has a premium of 9.65. On these option contracts, the premium is multiplied by 500 to get the value of the contract. Thus, the cost of the contract is $4,825 (500 × 9.65).

In examining Table 17–7, note that the premiums on the call options increase substantially with the passage of time from October to December. This gain in value is not only a function of the extended time period associated with the option but is also due to the fact that the S&P futures contract has a higher value with the passage of time.[17] For example, on October 13, 1994, the S&P 500 October contract traded at 467.85, while the December contract traded at 469.15. Thus, options on stock index futures not only have a time premium (all options do) but may also have an additional premium (or discount) depending on the relationship of the far-term futures market to the near-term futures market.

Options on stock index futures may be settled on a cash basis, or the holder of a call option may exercise the option and force the option writer to produce a specified futures contract. There are also puts for options on stock index futures.

TABLE 17–7 Options on Stock Index Futures (October 13, 1994)

INDEX

S&P 500 STOCK INDEX (CME)
$500 times premium

Strike	Calls –Settle			Puts –Settle		
Price	Oct	Nov	Dec	Oct	Nov	Dec
460	10.30	13.35	16.20	1.15	4.25	7.15
465	6.35	9.75	12.75	2.20	5.60	8.65
470	3.15	6.65	9.65	4.00	7.50	10.50
475	1.15	4.10	7.00	7.00	9.90	12.80
480	0.35	2.45	4.80	11.20	13.25	15.55
485	0.10	1.30	3.00	15.95	17.05	18.70

Est vol 21,578 Wed 9,914 calls 21,-
158 puts
Op int Wed 81,263 calls 149,111 puts

Source: *The Wall Street Journal,* October 14, 1994, p. C15. Reprinted by permission of *The Wall Street Journal,* © 1994 by Dow Jones & Company, Inc. All Rights Reserved Worldwide.

[16] Because of cash-settlement procedures, the actual index will never actually be purchased, and the gain or loss will be settled for cash.

[17] Of course, if the market outlook were highly pessimistic, there would be a decline in the S&P futures contract with the passage of time.

Commodity Trading: Make Room for the Newest Players

No job in the commodities market is tougher than being a trader. You are constantly buying and selling futures contracts in the trading pits with some of the pushiest people in the world. But according to a September 13, 1991, *Wall Street Journal* article, women are making their presence known in this rock-em, sock-em world of finance. The article stated, "Many women traders are earning far more than they did in their previous careers: It's not unusual for traders to earn $100,000 or more a year, and the sky's the limit for very good or very lucky traders."* Now a number of years later, women continue to increase in importance as commodity traders as more and more women graduate with MBAs from the top business schools in the country. How do traders actually operate?

The traders stand toe to toe using hand signals to indicate their buy or sell intentions for stock index futures, pork bellies, soybeans, and other items. Although sexist jokes float around and locker room talk is often the mode of communication, women are holding their own. Why? When all is said and done, all that counts is performance. It is very easy to measure success, the bottom line, and it shows up every day of trading. Often, the article pointed out, women are better suited to trading because they do not let egos get in their way. They simply use straight logic to get the job done.

*Elyse Tanouye, "Women Traders Make Headway on the Futures Floor," *The Wall Street Journal,* September 3, 1991, p. C1.

SUMMARY

For the investor who wishes to trade in stock indexes, there are three basic types of securities: stock index futures, stock index options, and options on stock index futures.

Stock index futures and options offer the potential for speculation as well as for hedging. With stock index futures, the margin is relatively low, which allows for a strong leverage potential. In hedging a portfolio position, the investor should consider the beta of his or her portfolio and adjust the number of contracts accordingly. Basis in the futures market represents the difference between the stock index futures price and the value of the actual underlying index. Basis may present the investor with a potential clue about the future direction of the market. The stock index futures market and the stock index option market trade on a cash-settlement basis. No securities ever change hands as the settlement is always in cash.

Investors in stock index futures may also engage in arbitraging procedures in which a simultaneous trade (a buy and a sell) occurs in the stock index futures contract and in the underlying securities in the index. This allows the investor to lock in a profit. The use of arbitraging, portfolio insurance, and program trading has been blamed by some for the market crash in October 1987 and the subsequent volatility in the market after the crash. This is subject to debate. Nevertheless, the Chicago Mercantile Exchange and the New York Stock Exchange have established circuit breakers that call for the temporary halt in trading of futures contracts when the market is tumbling.

The stock index option contract is generally similar to the option contract on individual securities. The investor has an opportunity to buy puts and calls, and the premium is related to the future prospects for the index.

The third form of stock index contracts, an option on stock index futures, combines the option concept with the futures market. Instead of an option on an actual index, you have an option on a stock index futures contract. The contract may be settled either with cash or with securities.

The two forms of option contracts offer an investment outlet to some investors who are constrained by law from investing in commodity contracts and thus cannot participate in stock index futures. On the other hand, stock index futures do provide a more efficient hedging device in that the gain on the futures contract may offset the loss on the portfolio. With an option, this may be more difficult or expensive to establish.

KEY WORDS AND CONCEPTS

futures contract on a stock market index (stock index futures), 483
stock index options, 483
options to purchase futures, 483
derivative products, 483
program trading, 484
cash settlement, 487
basis, 487
portfolio insurance, 492
circuit breakers, 492
arbitrage, 493

DISCUSSION QUESTIONS

1. Why are stock index futures and options sometimes referred to as derivative products? Why do some investors believe derivative products make the markets more volatile?
2. How many stocks are in the Major Market Index? With what other market average does it closely correlate?
3. Why does a hedging position require less initial margin than a speculative position?
4. What is meant by the concept of cash settlement?
5. What does the term *basis* mean in the futures market? If there is a premium and it expands with the passage of time, what is the general implication?
6. Why does a down market put tremendous pressure on a speculator if he or she is the purchaser of a contract in anticipation of a market increase? Relate this answer directly to margin.
7. Why is it unrealistic for a portfolio manager to sell a large portion of his portfolio if he thinks the market is about to decline?
8. How does the beta of a portfolio influence the number of contracts that must be used in the hedging process?
9. What are some complicating factors in attempting to hedge a portfolio?
10. Why might the overuse of portfolio insurance be dangerous to the market?
11. What is an arbitrage position?
12. What is an essential difference between stock index options and options on individual securities in terms of settlement procedures?

13. Under what circumstance might a portfolio manager be more likely to use index option contracts instead of futures contracts to hedge a portfolio? What is the counter argument for futures contracts over index options?

14. Explain the difference between a stock index option and an option on stock index futures.

15. Suggest two reasons why an option on a stock index futures contract that has a distant expiration date might have a high premium.

PROBLEMS

Stock index futures

1. Based on the information in Table 17–1, what is the total value of an S&P 500 Index futures contract for March 1995? Use the settle price and the appropriate multiplier. Also, if the required margin is $11,250, what percent of the contract value does margin represent?

Gain on S&P futures

2. In problem 1, if the S&P Index futures contract goes up to 480.50, what will be the total dollar profit on the contract? What is the percent return on the initial margin? If this price change occurred over four months, what is the annualized return?

Loss on S&P futures and margin

3. Return to problem 1, and assume that margin must be maintained at a minimum level of $10,000. If the S&P Index futures contract goes from its initial value down to 468.70, will there be a call for more margin?

Computing settle price

4. Based on the information in Table 17–1, assume you buy a Major Market Index December contract at the settle price. You hold the contract for one month and enjoy a gain in value of $10,000. What was the settle price after one month?

Computing basis

5. Examine Table 17–3. Using settle prices, what is the value of the basis for the June 1995 and September 1995 contracts?

Hedging and basis

6. Eastern States Life Insurance Company has a $14 million stock portfolio. The company is very aggressive, and the portfolio has a weighted beta of 1.25.
   a. Assume they use S&P 500 Index futures contracts to hedge the portfolio for the next 90 days and the contracts can be sold at 472. The contracts have a multiplier of 500. With the appropriate beta adjustment factor, how many contracts should be sold? Round your final answer to the nearest whole number.
   b. If NYSE Composite Index contracts selling at 262 were used instead, how many contracts should be sold? These contracts also have a multiplier of 500. Once again, consider the appropriate beta adjustment factor and round your final answer to the nearest whole number.

Hedging and betas

7. The New Century Pension Fund decides to hedge its $40 million stock portfolio on October 1. The portfolio has a beta of 1.10. It will use Major Market Index futures contracts selling at 406 to hedge. These contracts have a multiplier of 500. The fund intends to hedge the portfolio for the next 60 days.
   a. With the appropriate beta adjustment factor and rounding the final answer to the nearest whole number, how many contracts should be sold?
   b. Assuming that by December 1, the market has gone down by 20 percent and the stock portfolio moves in accordance with its beta, what will be the total dollar decline in the portfolio?

c. Assume the Major Market Index futures contracts decline by 20 percent from 406. What will be the total dollar gain on the futures contracts? In the process, compare the sales price of 406 with the current value, multiply by 500, and then multiply this value by the number of contracts. How does the total dollar gain on the futures contracts compare with the portfolio loss in part *b*?

d. Now assume that because of changing basis, the stock index futures contract does not move parallel to the market. Although the market goes down by 20 percent, the stock index futures decline by only 15 percent. What will be the gain on the futures contracts? How does this compare with the loss in portfolio value in part *b*?

S&P 100 call options

8. This problem relates to data in Table 17–6. Assume you purchase a December 435 (strike price) S&P 100 call option. Compute your total dollar profit or loss if the index has the following values at expiration.
   a. 460
   b. 440
   c. 380

S&P 100 call options

9. Using data from Table 17–6, assume you purchase a December 430 (strike price) S&P 100 put option. Compute your total dollar profit or loss if the index has the following values at expiration.
   a. 465
   b. 425
   c. 390

Hedging with the Major Market Index

10. The Bowman Company has a $1 million funded pension plan for its employees. The portfolio beta is equal to 1.12. Assume the company sells (writes) 30 December 400 (strike price) call (c) option contracts on the American Stock Exchange Major Market Index as shown in Table 17–5. Each contract trades in units of 100. At the time the options were written, the index had a value of 404.86.
    a. What are the proceeds from the sale of the call options?
    b. Assume the market goes down by 14 percent. Considering the portfolio beta, what will be the total dollar decline in the portfolio?
    c. Assume the American Stock Exchange Major Market Index also goes down by 14 percent at expiration. What will be the value of the index at that time?
    d. Based on your answer to part *c*, what will be your profit on the option writes?
    e. Considering your answers to parts *b* and *d*, what is your net gain or loss?

Using puts to hedge

11. Assume that in problem 10 the firm had purchased 30 December 400 put (p) option contracts on the American Stock Exchange Major Market Index listed in Table 17–5 instead of selling the call options. If the American Stock Exchange Major Market Index goes down by 14 percent at expiration,
    a. What will be your profit on the puts? Comparing that to your loss on the stock portfolio in problem 10*b*, what is your net overall gain or loss?
    b. Compare the protection afforded by the call-writing hedge in problem 10 with the protection afforded by the put purchase in this problem.
    c. Suggest any modifications to the call writing or put purchase strategy that would allow you to increase your protection even more. A general statement is all that is required.

Using calls and puts to hedge

12. Sterling Money Management Incorporated is in charge of a $50 million portfolio. Its beta is equal to the market. To hedge its position, it sells (writes) 700 December 445 call (c) option contracts on the S&P 100 Stock Index as shown in Table 17–5. It also buys 800 December 450 put (p) option contracts on the same index shown in Table 17–5. Instead of going down, the market goes up by 10 percent (as does the portfolio), and the S&P 100 Stock Index ends at 485.

    Consider the change in the portfolio value and the gains or losses on the call and put options. Each option contract trades in units of 100. What is the overall net gain or loss of Sterling Money Management as a result of the changes in the market?

Option on stock index futures

13. The State Teachers Retirement Fund purchases a call on a stock option futures contract. The quote can be found in Table 17–7. The option is on the S&P 500 Stock Index. It has a strike price of 465 for December (1994).
    - **a.** What is the quoted option premium (price)?
    - **b.** Referring to Table 17–1, what is the quote for the December 1994 (futures) contract for the S&P 500 Stock Index? (Use the settle price.)
    - **c.** Also referring to Table 17–1, what was the actual quote (value) for the S&P 500 Stock Index? (Use the closing price at the bottom of the S&P 500 Stock Index data. It can be found on the line above the S&P MidCap 400.)
    - **d.** By how much does the futures quote (part *b*) exceed the actual index quote (part *c*)? That is, how much is the basis?
    - **e.** By how much does the quoted option premium calculated in part *a* exceed the basis calculated in part *d*?
    - **f.** If the basis were to suddenly go to zero and the option declined by a similar amount, what would the new option premium be?

THE WALL STREET JOURNAL PROJECT

Assume you are working for a bank trust department that wishes to hedge to protect a $5 million portfolio for one of its clients. The portfolio has a beta of 1.25 and is made up primarily of MidCap stocks (stocks that each have a total market value of between $200 million and $5 billion).

You are asked to determine how many futures contracts the bank trust department customer needs to protect her position.

Use Formula 17–1 from the chapter plus information from *The Wall Street Journal* to determine your answer. Go to the "Commodities" portion of Section C of the *Journal,* and find the S&P MIDCAP 400. It is located under the "Index" subheading of the "Future Prices" section. Use the nearest term settle (closing) price. (On many days there is only one S&P MidCap 400 contract listed, so use that one—it is obviously the nearest term.)

Apply Formula 17–1 by dividing the dollar value of the portfolio by the dollar value of the contract and multiplying by the weighted beta of the portfolio of 1.25. The dollar value of the contract is equal to 500 times the settle price of the S&P MidCap 400 futures contract. Round your answer to a whole number.

SELECTED REFERENCES

Use of Stock Index Futures and Options

Castelino, Mark G.; Jack C. Francis; and Avner Wolf. "Cross Hedging: Basis Risk and Choice of the Optimal Hedging Vehicle." *Financial Review,* May 1991, pp. 179–210.

Fung, Hung-Gay Fung; Wai-Chung Lo; and John E. Peterson. "Examining the Dependency in Intra-day Stock Index Futures." *The Journal of Futures Markets,* June 1994, pp. 405–19.

Holden, Craig W. "Index Arbitrage and the Media." *Financial Analysts Journal,* September–October 1991, pp. 8–9.

Junkus, Joan C., and Cheng F. Lee. "Use of Three Stock Index Futures in Hedging Decisions." *Journal of Futures Markets,* Summer 1985, pp. 201–22.

Moster, James T. "A Note on the Crash and Participation in Stock Index Futures." *The Journal of Futures Markets,* February 1994, pp. 117–19.

Nordhauser, Fred. "Using Stock Index Futures to Reduce Market Risk." *Journal of Portfolio Management,* Spring 1984, pp. 56–69.

Valuation of Stock Index Futures and Options

Cornell, Bradford. "Taxes and the Pricing of Stock Index Futures: Empirical Results." *Journal of Futures Markets,* Spring 1985, pp. 89–102.

Marchard, Patrick H.; James T. Lindley; and Richard A. Followill. "Further Evidence on Parity Relationships in Options on S&P 500 Index Futures." *The Journal of Futures Markets,* September 1994, pp. 757–71.

Modest, David M. "On the Pricing of Stock Index Futures." *Journal of Portfolio Management,* Summer 1984, pp. 51–57.

Shastri, Kuldeep, and Kishore Tandon. "Options on Futures Contracts: A Comparison of European and American Pricing Models." *Journal of Futures Markets,* Winter 1986, pp. 593–618.

Program Trading

Kritzman, Mark. "What's Wrong with Portfolio Insurance." *Journal of Portfolio Management,* Fall 1986, pp. 13–16.

Stoll, Hans, and Robert Whaley. "Program Trading and Expiration-Day Effects." *Financial Analysts Journal,* March–April 1987, pp. 16–28.

PART 6

BROADENING THE INVESTMENT PERSPECTIVE

OUTLINE

Nomura Securities is the most profitable brokerage house in the world. If you want to work there, plan to get to work early and stay late. The Japanese are among the best savers in the world, and in recent times, much of their funds have gone into equities. The rest of the world better hope they do not lose their appetite for investments.

Wall Street is the main place for securities trading in the United States. Kibudatu is the financial district of Tokyo. It is where you will find the Tokyo Stock Exchange.

The most profitable stock brokerage house in the world is Nomura Securities. If you were to work there, you would need to set your alarm for 6 A.M. and hit the ground running the moment it goes off. "Work harder" is the battle cry of Nomura. Brokers are held to rigorous sales quotas and are publicly humiliated if they fail to meet them. The company isn't afraid to trumpet the pressure it puts on its people. A new employee is expected to meet at least a thousand clients during the first three months with the company.

Many relationships with customers are long-standing. For example, Fumie Mitobe is part of the female sales force at Nomura. She has been selling Nomura's products door to door since the end of World War II. In the 1950s, she would visit the families in her neighborhood and give them a savings box, and she would keep the key. A month later, she would return, remove whatever money had been saved and invest for the family, usually in securities. She and others like her helped build a huge client base.

Among working-age people in Japan, 8 out of 10 own stock. This is not surprising, as the Japanese people are the world's greatest savers, putting away one-fourth of their income. In the United States, the individual savings rate is closer to 5 percent.

Over the decades, Japanese savers have transferred much of their savings from low-yielding bank accounts to stocks and bonds. This was a great strategy as long as the market climbed to even higher levels. But in the early 1990s, the Tokyo Nikkei Average fell by 50 percent. The decline was caused by the unusually high valuation assigned in the marketplace to Japanese securities. At one time, price-earnings ratios of 70-80 were the norm.

Still, the rest of the world (and particularly the United States) continues to closely watch the developments in the Tokyo markets. We have all become dependent on the Japanese saver to provide part of our capital. If these funds are withdrawn, who will help finance the U.S. deficit of hundreds of billions of dollars a year? ■

18

INTERNATIONAL SECURITIES MARKETS

In Chapter 1, we discussed the advantage of diversification in terms of risk reduction. To reduce risk exposure, the investor may desire a broad spectrum of securities from which to choose. An investor who lives in California would hardly be expected to limit all his investments to that geographic boundary. The same might be said for an investor living in the United States or Germany or Japan. The advantages of crossing international boundaries may be substantial in terms of diversification benefits.

Companies operating in different countries will be affected differently by international events such as crop failures, energy prices, wars, tariffs, trade between countries, and the value of local currencies relative to other currencies, especially the U.S. dollar. Furthermore, despite the up and down markets in the United States, there is almost certain to be a bull market somewhere in the world for the investor who likes to keep his chips on the table at all times.

Of course, there are some disadvantages to investing in international securities. The main drawback would appear to be the more complicated nature of the investment. Currently, one cannot simply pick up the phone and ask a broker to buy 100 shares of any stock listed on a foreign exchange. Some foreign markets have very low liquidity or require citizenship for ownership, or U.S. brokers may be restricted from dealing in these securities.

The primary focus of this chapter is international equities, although investments may certainly include fixed-income securities and real assets. We shall examine the composition of world equity markets, the diversification and return benefits that can be derived from foreign investments, the obstacles that are present, and finally, the methods of participating in foreign investments directly and indirectly.

THE WORLD EQUITY MARKET

The world equity markets have grown dramatically. At the beginning of 1994, the United States accounted for 42 percent of the world's securities markets in terms of total market valuation, followed by Japan with 24 percent. Table 18–1 on page 510 lists the major developed markets at year-end 1990 and 1993 by their market capitalization. The U.S. share of the world market increased significantly from 35 percent to 42 percent, while Japan decreased from 33 percent to 24 percent due to its first significant recession in the last 20 years.

Figure 18–1 at the bottom of page 510 depicts the geographical breakdown of major developed markets showing Europe, North America, and the Pacific region.

While the developed world securities markets continue to expand, major growth in securities markets has occurred in the "emerging" markets such as Argentina, Brazil, Chile, Nigeria, Taiwan, Turkey, and Zimbabwe. Additionally, the Eastern European countries of Poland, the Czech Republic, and Hungary have instituted capitalistic economic reforms including fledgling equity markets. East Germany and West Germany united to create a new German state that already had the benefits of a developed capital market. Table 18–2 on page 511 lists the market capitalizations of the emerging markets. The total value in 1993 of $1.6 trillion ranks the emerging markets (as a whole) in third place among developed countries. Some of these emerging markets, such as Korea and Taiwan, China, are bigger than markets in developed countries, but because these countries have a low per-capita gross domestic product, they are listed with the emerging economies.

TABLE 18–1 Market Capitalization of Developed Countries (in millions of U.S. dollars)

Country	Year-End 1990	Percent of Total (1990)	Year-End 1993	Percent of Total (1993)
Kuwait	—	0.00%	10,103	0.08%
Luxembourg	10,456	0.12	19,337	0.16
Finland	22,721	0.26	23,562	0.19
New Zealand	8,836	0.10	25,597	0.21
Norway	26,130	0.30	27,380	0.22
Austria	11,476	0.13	28,437	0.23
Denmark	39,063	0.44	41,785	0.34
Israel	3,324	0.04	50,773	0.41
Belgium	65,449	0.74	78,067	0.63
Sweden	92,102	1.05	107,376	0.86
Spain	111,404	1.26	119,264	0.96
Singapore	34,308	0.39	132,742	1.06
Italy	148,766	1.69	136,153	1.09
Netherlands	119,825	1.36	181,876	1.46
Australia	107,611	1.22	203,964	1.64
Switzerland	160,044	1.82	271,713	2.18
Canada	241,920	2.75	326,524	2.62
Hong Kong	83,397	0.95	385,247	3.09
France	314,384	3.57	456,111	3.66
Germany	355,073	4.03	463,476	3.72
United Kingdom	848,866	9.63	1,151,646	9.24
Japan	2,917,679	33.11	2,999,756	24.07
United States	3,089,651	35.06	5,223,768	41.91

Source: *Emerging Stock Markets Factbook, 1994* (Washington, D.C.: International Finance Corporation, 1994), p. 15.

FIGURE 18–1 Developed Markets by Geographical Region (Market capitalization in 1993, U.S. dollars in trillions)

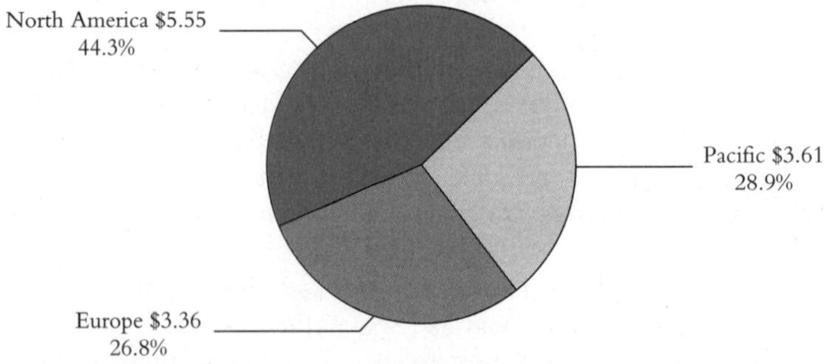

Source: Data from *Emerging Stock Markets Factbook, 1994* (Washington, D.C.: International Finance Corporation, 1994), p. 14.

TABLE 18–2 Market Capitalization of Emerging Markets (in millions of U.S. dollars)

Country	Year-End 1990	Percent of Total (1990)	Year-End 1993	Percent of Total (1993)
Argentina	$3,268	0.53%	$43,967	2.69%
Bangladesh	321	0.05	454	0.03
Barbados	280	0.05	326	0.02
Botswana	—	0.00	261	0.02
Brazil	16,354	2.67	99,430	6.08
Chile	13,645	2.23	44,622	2.73
China	—	0.00	40,567	2.48
Colombia	1,416	0.23	9,237	0.56
Costa Rica	—	0.00	433	0.03
Cote d'Ivoire	549	0.09	415	0.03
Cyprus	—	0.00	981	0.06
Ecuador	—	0.00	1,566	0.10
Egypt	1,835	0.30	3,800	0.23
Ghana	—	0.00	118	0.01
Greece	15,228	2.49	12,319	0.75
Hungary	—	0.00	812	0.05
India	38,567	6.31	97,976	5.99
Indonesia	8,081	1.32	32,953	2.01
Iran	—	0.00	1,297	0.08
Jamaica	911	0.15	1,469	0.09
Jordan	2,001	0.33	4,891	0.30
Kenya	453	0.07	1,421	0.09
Korea	110,594	18.08	139,420	8.52
Malaysia	48,611	7.95	220,328	13.47
Mauritius	265	0.04	799	0.05
Mexico	32,725	5.35	200,671	12.27
Morocco	966	0.16	2,662	0.16
Namibia	—	0.00	3,443	0.21
Nigeria	1,372	0.22	1,029	0.06
Oman	1,274	0.21	1,605	0.10
Pakistan	2,850	0.47	11,602	0.71
Panama	—	0.00	421	0.03
Peru	812	0.13	5,113	0.31
Philippines	5,927	0.97	40,327	2.46
Poland	—	0.00	2,706	0.17
Portugal	9,201	1.50	12,417	0.76
South Africa	137,540	22.49	217,110	13.27
Sri Lanka	917	0.15	2,498	0.15
Swaziland	17	0.00	297	0.02
Taiwan, China	100,710	16.46	195,198	11.93
Thailand	23,896	3.91	130,510	7.98
Trinidad and Tobago	696	0.11	490	0.03
Tunisia	533	0.09	955	0.06
Turkey	19,065	3.12	37,496	2.29
Uruguay	38	0.01	251	0.02
Venezuela	8,361	1.37	8,010	0.49
Zimbabwe	2,395	0.39	1,433	0.09
IFC Global Index Markets*	465,996	76.18	1,354,965	82.82
All Emerging Markets	$611,674	100.00%	$1,636,106	100.00%

*International Finance Corporation.
Source: *Emerging Stock Markets Factbook, 1994* (Washington, D.C.: International Finance Corporation, 1994), pp. 14–15.

FIGURE 18–2 Regional Weights of Emerging Markets (Based on market capitalization in U.S. dollars)

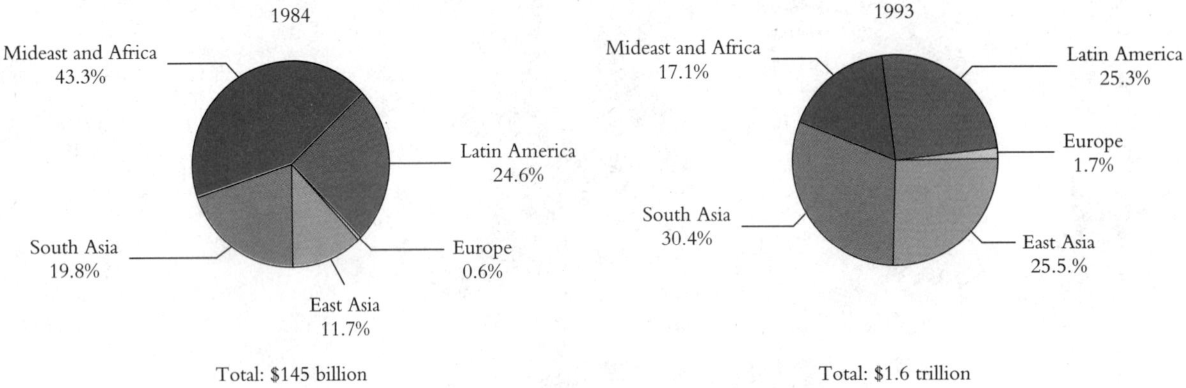

Source: *Emerging Stock Market Factbook, 1994* (Washington, D.C.: International Finance Corporation, 1994), pp. 14–15.

A geographical breakdown of the emerging markets is depicted in Figure 18–2 for 1984 and 1993. The relationships among the emerging countries have changed dramatically. The Mideast and Africa fell from 43.3 to 17.1 percent of the total emerging market capitalization as the economies of this region suffered from high inflation, too much debt, slow real economic growth, and war. A rising share of market value in the emerging markets goes to the high-growth countries of East Asia (from 11.7 to 25.5 percent) and to South Asia (from 19.8 to 30.4 percent). The total value of all emerging markets increased from $145 billion to $1.6 trillion over this 10-year period, an increase of more than 27 percent annually. As emerging markets have grown, there are more opportunities to own equity positions. It is useful to look at the different market structures and institutional characteristics of these and other markets.

In 1988, Richard Roll published an article in the *Financial Analysts Journal* that analyzed the different institutional distinctions in many of the world's capital markets after the market crash in October 1987.[1] Table 18–3 shows the institutional arrangements in world markets. Continuous auction markets (second column) are the standard in markets such as the United States, Japan, United Kingdom, Germany, Canada, Hong Kong, and others. Table 18–3 also summarizes the use of specialists, the use of forward contracts, automated quotations, and many other factors.

While the next section points out the benefits of diversification using foreign securities, the crash of 1987 was an international phenomenon where 19 out of 23 markets declined more than 20 percent. This is unusual given the low degree of correlation between the historical returns of different countries. Richard Roll's article points out that the most significant factor relating to the size of the market decline in each country was the beta of that market to the world market index.

---

[1] Richard Roll, "The International Crash of 1987," *Financial Analysts Journal,* September–October 1988, pp. 19–35.

TABLE 18–3 Institutional Arrangements in World Markets

Country	Auction	Official Special-ists	Forward Trading on Exchange	Automated Quota-tions	Computer-Directed Trading	Options/ Futures Trading	Price Limits	Transac-tion Tax (Round Trip)	Margin Require-ments	Trading Off Exchange
Australia	Continuous	No	No	Yes	No	Yes	None	0.6%	None	Infrequent
Austria	Single	Yes	No	No	No	No	5%	0.3%	100%	Frequent
Belgium	Mixed	No	Yes	No	No	No[a]	10%	0.375%	100%/	Occasional
							None[b]	0.195%	25%[b]	
Canada	Continuous	Yes	No	Yes	Yes	Yes	None[c]	0	50%[d]	Prohibited
Denmark	Mixed	No	No	No	No	No	None	1%	None	Frequent
France	Mixed	Yes	Yes	Yes	Yes	Yes	4%/	0.3%	100%/	Prohibited
							7%[e]		20%[f]	
Germany	Continuous	Yes	No	No	No	Options	None	0.5%	None	Frequent
Hong Kong	Continuous	No	No	Yes	No	Futures	None[g]	0.6%+	None	Infrequent
Ireland	Continuous	No	No	Yes	No	No	None	1%	100%	Frequent
Italy	Mixed	No	Yes	No	No	No	10-20%[h]	0.3%	100%	Frequent
Japan	Continuous	Yes	No	Yes	Yes	No[i]	−10%	0.55%	70%[j]	Prohibited
Malaysia	Continuous	No	No	Yes	No	No	None	0.03%	None	Occasional
Mexico	Continuous	No	Yes	No	No	No	10%[k]	0	None	Occasional
Netherlands	Continuous	Yes	No	No	No	Options	Variable[l]	2.4%[m]	None	Prohibited
New Zealand	Continuous	No	No	No	No	Futures	None	0	None	Occasional
Norway	Single	No	No	No	No	No	None	1%	100%	Frequent
Singapore	Continuous	No	No	Yes	No	No[n]	None	0.5%	71%	Occasional
South Africa	Continuous	No	No	Yes	No	Options	None	1.5%	100%	Prohibited
Spain	Mixed[o]	No	No	No	No	No	10%[p]	0.11%	50%[p]	Frequent
Sweden	Mixed	No	No	Yes	No	Yes	None	2%	40%	Frequent
Switzerland	Mixed	No	Yes	Yes	No	Yes	5%[q]	0.9%	None	Infrequent
United Kingdom	Continuous	No	No	Yes	Yes	Yes	None	0.5%	None	Occasional
United States	Continuous	Yes	No	Yes	Yes	Yes	None	0	Yes	Occasional

[a] Calls only on just five stocks.
[b] Cash/forward.
[c] None on stocks; 3–5% on index futures.
[d] 10% (5%) for uncovered (covered) futures.
[e] Cash/forward, but not always enforced.
[f] Cash/forward; 40% if forward collateral is stock rather than cash.
[g] "Four Spread Rule": offers not permitted more than four ticks from current bids and asks.
[h] Hitting limit suspends auction; auction then tried a second time at end of day.
[i] Futures on the Nikkei Index are traded in Singapore.
[j] Decreased to 50% on October 21, 1987, "to encourage buyers."
[k] Trading suspended for successive periods, 15 and then 30 minutes; effective limit: 30–40%.
[l] Authorities have discretion. In October, 2% limits every 15 minutes used frequently.
[m] For nondealer transactions only.
[n] Only for Nikkei Index (Japan).
[o] Groups of stocks are traded continuously for 10 minutes each.
[p] Limits raised to 20% and margin to 50% on October 27.
[q] Hitting limit causes 15-minute trading suspension. Limits raised to 10–15% in October.

Source: Richard Roll, "The International Crash of 1987," *Financial Analysts Journal,* September–October 1988, p. 29.

DIVERSIFICATION BENEFITS

Not all foreign markets move in the same direction at any point in time. In Table 18–4, we see the stock market movements for a number of key countries over 18 years. Each year there is a wide range of performance numbers among these nine countries; the highest and lowest yearly returns are highlighted in boldface type. There are several issues worth noting. First, no country continually outperforms the others on an annual basis. Hong Kong has the highest returns 7 out of 18 years, while Canada never has had the highest return. Second, in all but five years (1978, 1988, 1989, 1991, 1993), one of these countries in the table had a loss.

Let us look at a U.S. investor based on the data in Table 18–4. In 1976, a 23.8 percent return could be earned in the United States, while a 12.7 percent loss occurred in the United Kingdom. In 1977, this situation was reversed with a 7.2 percent loss in the United States and a 58 percent return in the United Kingdom. If an investor had held equal positions in both countries, returns would have been less volatile (risky), and a U.S. investor would have had a greater total return. Diversification reduces portfolio volatility and at the same time offers opportunities for higher returns than a single country portfolio.

Another way to consider **diversification benefits** is to measure the extent of correlation of stock movements. The correlation coefficient measures the movement of

TABLE 18–4 The Best Performing Equity Markets, 1976–1993

	Germany	Switzerland	United Kingdom	Australia	Hong Kong	Japan	Singapore/ Malaysia	Canada	United States
1976	6.6	10.5	**(12.70)**	(10.2)	**40.7**	25.6	13.9	9.7	23.8
1977	25.8	28.7	**58.0**	11.9	**(11.20)**	15.9	5.9	(2.1)	(7.2)
1978	26.9	21.9	14.6	21.8	18.5	**53.3**	45.1	20.4	**6.5**
1979	(2.2)	12.1	22.1	43.6	**83.5**	**(11.9)**	28.5	51.8	18.5
1980	**(9.1)**	(7.3)	41.1	55.3	**72.7**	30.3	62.8	22.6	32.4
1981	(8.2)	(9.5)	(10.6)	**(23.9)**	(15.8)	15.8	**18.3**	(10.7)	(4.9)
1982	12.3	3.4	9.2	(22.6)	**(44.5)**	(0.5)	(16.7)	2.4	**21.5**
1983	25.9	19.3	17.2	**56.0**	**(3.0)**	24.9	31.7	33.4	22.2
1984	(3.8)	(11.1)	5.4	(12.6)	**46.8**	17.1	**(25.9)**	(7.6)	6.2
1985	**139.2**	107.4	52.8	20.9	51.6	43.4	**(22.2)**	15.9	31.6
1986	37.2	34.3	27.1	43.8	56.0	**99.7**	45.2	**(10.7)**	18.2
1987	**(23.4)**	(8.8)	36.5	10.3	(4.1)	**43.2**	2.3	14.6	5.2
1988	23.1	**7.1**	**7.1**	**38.0**	28.0	35.5	33.3	18.0	16.5
1989	**48.8**	27.1	23.1	10.8	8.3	**1.8**	42.2	25.2	31.4
1990	(10.8)	(7.8)	**6.0**	(21.0)	3.7	**(36.4)**	(13.1)	(15.3)	(5.6)
1991	8.7	13.6	12.0	n.a.	**43.4**	**6.5**	20.9	8.7	30.3
1992	(13.2)	13.3	(6.2)	(16.2)	**28.3**	**(23.1)**	6.3	(15.7)	2.8
1993	33.7	47.5	**3.2**	36.3	**107.7**	25.3	63.4	17.0	9.0

n.a. Not sufficient information.

Note: Numbers represent total return, assuming reinvestment of dividends in U.S. dollars of the Morgan Stanley Capital International Index for each country. (Bold color numbers represent lowest returns and bold black numbers represent highest returns for one year.)

Source: Templeton International; Morgan Stanley Capital International Perspective, Geneva.

one series of data over time to another series of data, in this case stock market returns. The correlation coefficient can be between −1 and +1. A coefficient of +1 indicates a perfect positive relationship as the two variables move together up and down. A coefficient of −1 indicates a perfect negative relationship as the two variables move opposite of each other. A zero coefficient describes a series that has no relationship. Any time you can diversify into assets that have a correlation coefficient of less than +1, you reduce the amount of risk assumed. Such a measure is presented in Table 18–5, in which stock movements for a number of developed countries are compared with those of the United States. Two sets of correlation coefficients are presented, one long-term set from 1960 through 1980 and a short-term set of data from June 1981 through September 1987. The countries are listed from the highest correlation to the lowest based on 1960–80 data. By comparing the two sets of correlations, we can see there is not a great amount of stability between the two time periods, with some countries such as Hong Kong going from the top of the list to the bottom. However, correlations of returns with the U.S. market are still quite low on average, with the median correlation being 0.389 in the first period and 0.328 in the second period.

The best risk-reduction benefits can be found by combining U.S. securities with those from countries having low correlations such as Spain and Austria in both periods. Countries with high correlations provide the least benefit from diversification. Even though countries like Germany and Italy have fairly stable correlations between the two periods, France and Norway display a significant switching of rankings between the two periods. According to

TABLE 18–5 Correlation of Foreign Stock Movements with U.S. Stock Movements

Country	Correlation 1960–1980	Correlation June 1981–September 1987
United States	1.000	1.000
Hong Kong	0.814 (1)	0.114 (17)
Netherlands	0.730 (2)	.473 (4)
Canada	0.710 (3)	0.720 (1)
Australia	0.699 (4)	0.328 (9) median
United Kingdom	0.617 (5)	0.513 (2)
Singapore	0.579 (6)	0.377 (6)
Switzerland	0.454 (7)	0.500 (3)
Sweden	0.398 (8)	0.279 (11)
Belgium	0.389 (9) median	0.250 (12)
Denmark	0.243 (10)	0.351 (8)
Japan	0.216 (11)	0.326 (10)
France	0.214 (12)	0.390 (5)
Germany	0.210 (13)	0.209 (15)
Italy	0.208 (14)	0.224 (13)
Norway	0.009 (15)	0.356 (7)
Austria	−0.076 (16)	0.138 (16)
Spain	−0.115 (17)	0.214 (14)

Source: Roger G. Ibbotson, Richard C. Carr, and Anthony W. Robinson, "International Equity and Bond Returns," *Financial Analysts Journal*, July–August 1982, p. 71; and Richard Roll, "The International Crash of 1987," *Financial Analysts Journal*, September–October 1988, pp. 20–21.

TABLE 18–6 Statistics of the IFC* Global Total Return Indexes (In U.S. dollars; December 1988–December 1993)

Market	Number of Months	Mean of Percent Change	Standard Deviation	Annualized Mean	Annualized Standard Deviation	Correlation with S&P 500
Latin America						
Argentina	60	8.26	33.63	99.12	116.50	0.06
Brazil	60	4.05	21.92	48.60	75.93	0.20
Chile	60	3.45	7.46	41.40	25.84	0.16
Colombia	60	4.12	10.76	49.44	37.27	0.09
Mexico	60	3.91	7.76	46.92	26.88	0.33
Peru	12	3.42	12.76	41.04	44.20	0.53
Venezuela	60	3.17	14.68	38.04	50.85	−0.08
East Asia						
China	12	1.15	19.81	13.80	68.62	−0.69
Korea	60	0.06	8.52	0.72	29.51	0.19
Philippines	60	2.52	10.53	30.24	36.48	0.34
Taiwan, China	60	1.57	15.03	18.84	52.07	0.15
South Asia						
India	60	1.86	11.09	22.32	38.42	−0.17
Indonesia	48	0.91	9.34	10.92	32.35	0.17
Malaysia	60	2.43	6.68	29.16	23.14	0.42
Pakistan	60	2.74	9.00	32.88	31.18	0.06
Sri Lanka	12	4.56	7.95	54.72	27.54	−0.12
Thailand	60	3.27	9.31	39.24	32.25	0.31
Europe/Mideast/Africa						
Greece	60	2.46	14.01	29.52	48.53	0.03
Hungary	12	2.08	7.25	24.96	25.11	0.41
Jordan	60	1.18	5.72	14.16	19.81	0.22
Nigeria	60	1.21	11.89	14.52	41.19	−0.11
Poland	12	22.31	30.26	267.72	104.82	0.21
Portugal	60	0.42	7.19	5.04	24.91	0.36
Turkey	60	4.67	20.50	56.04	71.01	−0.19
Zimbabwe	60	0.84	9.28	10.08	32.15	0.03
Regions						
Composite	60	1.48	6.40	17.76	22.17	0.25
Latin America	60	3.24	8.90	38.88	30.83	0.25
Asia	60	1.19	7.61	14.28	26.36	0.18
Developed						
U.S., S&P 500	60	1.20	3.76	14.40	13.03	1.00
MSCI, EAFE	60	0.36	5.91	4.32	20.47	0.43
FT EuroPac	60	0.33	6.10	3.96	21.13	0.41

* International Finance Corporation.

one researcher, Bruno Solnik, a well-diversified international portfolio can achieve the same risk-reduction benefits as a pure U.S. portfolio that is twice the size in terms of securities.[2]

In Table 18–5, we examined developed countries. Using Table 18–6 for emerging markets and several regional indexes, we see correlations using data for five years ending in 1993. Looking down the last column of numbers gives each country's correlation coefficient against the U.S. market as measured by the Standard & Poor's 500 Index. Six countries (Venezuela, China, India, Sri Lanka, Nigeria, and Turkey) have negative correlations with the United States. Three of these countries have only been in the index for 12 months, so their negative correlations do not cover the 60-month period used in the calculations for the other countries. The highest positive correlation for 60 months with the United States is 0.42 for Malaysia. It is interesting to note in the last two lines that the Morgan Stanley Capital International (MSCI) EAFE Index (Europe, Australia, and Far East) and the Financial Times (FT) EuroPacific Index both have correlation coefficients slightly above 0.40 against the U.S. market. These two indexes compared with the U.S. market indicate the scope of diversification available to today's investors.

RETURN POTENTIAL IN INTERNATIONAL MARKETS

Actually, risk reduction through effective international diversification is only part of the story. Not only does the investor have less risk exposure, but there is also the potential for higher returns in many foreign markets. Why? A number of countries have had growth rates superior to that of the United States in terms of real GDP. These would include Japan, Norway, Singapore, and Hong Kong. Second, many countries have become highly competitive in traditional U.S. products such as automobiles, steel, and consumer electronics. Third, many nations (Germany, Japan, France, Canada) enjoy higher individual savings rates than the United States, and this leads to capital formation and potential investment opportunity. This is not to imply that the United States does not have the strongest and best regulated securities markets in the world. It clearly does. However, it is a more mature market than many others, and there may be abundant opportunities for superior returns in a number of foreign markets.

We have already presented the annual returns for nine developed countries in Table 18–4. However, we present five different international indexes of investment performance in Figure 18–3 on page 518, showing the wealth that would have accumulated by the end of 1993 from an investment of $1 in each index at the beginning of 1969. The Pacific region has performed much better than the others, while the North American index (Canada and the United States) was at the bottom. The annualized rates of return for each index over this 24 year period are as follows:

---

[2] Bruno H. Solnik, "Why Not Diversify Internationally Rather than Domestically?" *Financial Analysts Journal,* July–August 1974, pp. 48–54.

Region	Annualized Rates of Return
Pacific	15.81%
EAFE*	13.43
Europe	12.51
World Index	11.64
North America	11.09

*Europe, Australia, and Far East.

Figure 18–3 represents a long-term perspective. There are, of course, time periods when the United States outperforms foreign markets. The performance figures represent the rapid growth experienced in the Pacific region between 1985 and 1988 and the subsequent 34 percent decline in 1990. The U.S. markets suffered greatly in 1973 (17.6 percent decline) and 1974 (29.86 percent decline). By 1978, the $1 invested in the North American market was worth only $1.03. If we measure returns from 1978 to 1993, the North American annualized return increases to 15.37 percent versus 15.06 percent over this same time for the Pacific region.

FIGURE 18–3 U.S. Dollar-Adjusted Cumulative Wealth Indexes of World Equities: 1969–1993

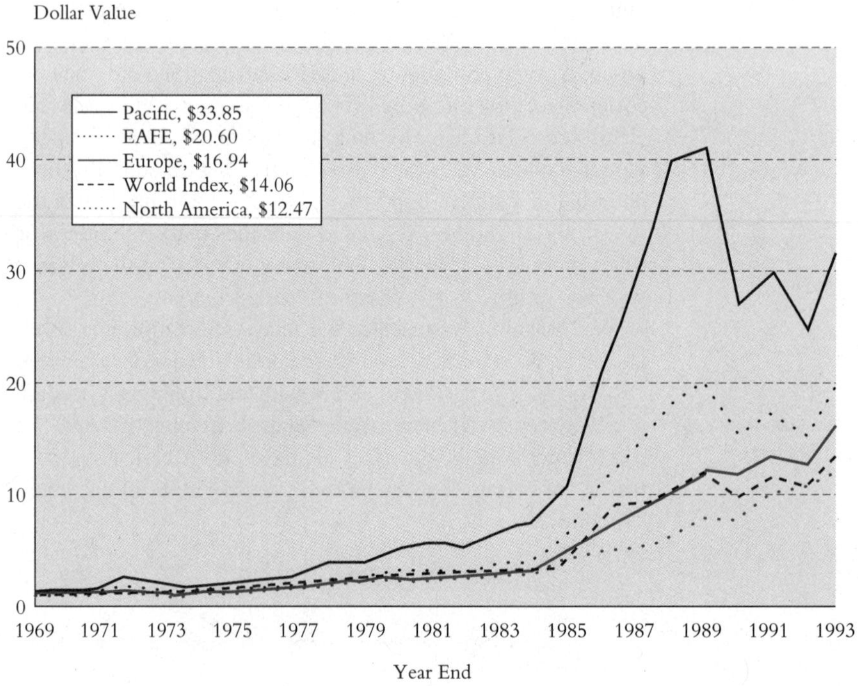

Current Quotations on Foreign Market Performance

To track the current performance of selected world markets, *The Wall Street Journal* provides daily quotes of price movements, while *Barron's* presents a weekly summary of the major global markets. The closing quotes of September 29, 1994, for *Barron's* are presented in Table 18–7.

The quotes are shown in local currencies as well as in U.S. dollars. For a U.S. investor, the returns in U.S. dollars are the best comparative measure against an investment in U.S. stocks. Under the U.S. dollars columns, you can first observe the percentage change from

TABLE 18–7 Global Stock Markets

	In Local Currencies				In U.S. Dollars*			
Index	Percent Change	9/29/94	52-Week Range High	52-Week Range Low	Percent Change	9/29/94	52-Week Range High	52-Week Range Low
The World	−0.2	461.1	442.4	495.7	−0.3	627.2	567.7	644.0
EAFE**	−0.6	572.5	536.8	628.5	−0.6	1056.8	901.5	1094.4
Australia	0.2	425.5	407.9	483.5	0.8	281.3	237.2	308.9
Austria	−1.5	406.0	405.6	491.4	−1.4	969.8	908.5	1052.9
Belgium	−0.3	462.4	445.2	526.2	0	727.4	632.4	775.3
Canada	0	458.5	404.9	481.3	0	369.2	319.6	394.6
Denmark	−0.5	773.5	736.1	929.8	−0.1	956.0	867.1	1043.8
Finland	2.4	147.3	106.6	153.6	3.4	119.2	72.2	121.1
France	−1.1	579.6	576.6	716.2	−0.8	609.0	580.9	674.4
Germany	−1.4	296.4	281.8	330.9	−1.2	701.3	631.6	749.7
Hong Kong	0.5	6791.0	5345.3	8460.7	0.6	4880.6	3837.6	6083.2
Ireland	−1.2	194.5	169.7	211.2	−0.9	182.5	147.8	192.2
Italy	2.7	591.9	431.0	681.8	3.6	238.1	158.7	267.3
Japan	−0.6	930.8	802.8	1008.2	−1.1	3407.5	264.5	3612.5
Malaysia	−4	398.5	312.8	465.7	−4.3	386.9	305.8	440.6
Netherlands	0.9	446.1	415.1	496.3	1.1	932.6	820.1	969.6
New Zealand	1	110.0	96.2	121.0	1.5	100.8	79.9	105.0
Norway	0.5	836.8	722.9	966.5	0.8	883.2	724.2	950.2
Singapore	3.3	1271.8	1003.1	1336.2	2.6	2632.9	1948.9	2632.9
Spain	1.7	252.5	245.9	313.6	1.8	138.0	129.0	156.0
Sweden	−0.5	1887.5	1690.1	2086.6	−0.8	1305.1	1032.5	1362.0
Switzerland	−1.6	330.2	310.9	401.1	−1.3	1105.7	936.5	1185.9
United Kingdom	−0.9	917.5	881.6	1082.5	−0.6	604.5	566.6	674.4
United States	0.4	432.6	410.2	450.5	0.4	432.6	410.2	450.5

Base: January 1, 1970 = 100.

* Adjusted for foreign exchange fluctuations relative to the U.S. dollar.

** Europe, Australia, and the Far East Index.

Source: Morgan Stanley Capital International Perspective, Geneva.

TABLE 18–8 Comparative Valuations of Emerging Countries*

	Price-Earnings Ratio			Price-to-Book-Value Ratio			Dividend Yield		
Market	Year-End 1993	Relative to World*	Year-End 1992	Year-End 1993	Relative to World*	Year-End 1992	Year-End 1993	Relative to World*	Year-End 1992
Latin America									
Argentina	41.90	1.46	37.99	1.94	0.85	1.20	2.28	0.99	1.93
Brazil	12.59	0.44	−24.43	0.55	0.24	0.37	0.40	0.17	0.68
Chile	20.04	0.70	12.99	2.11	0.92	1.71	2.74	1.19	3.82
Colombia	25.54	0.89	27.95	1.80	0.79	1.73	1.88	0.82	1.89
Mexico	19.45	0.68	12.28	2.59	1.13	1.99	1.65	0.72	0.99
Peru	44.01	1.53	25.91	3.62	1.58	2.66	0.79	0.34	—
Venezuela	17.44	0.61	15.63	1.85	0.81	1.61	2.35	1.02	0.98
East Asia									
China	—	—	—	—	—	—	—	—	—
Korea	25.12	0.88	21.43	1.38	0.60	1.06	0.63	0.27	1.81
Philippines	38.77	1.35	14.13	5.23	2.28	2.45	0.35	0.15	1.02
Taiwan, China	34.73	1.21	16.57	3.93	1.72	2.15	0.83	0.36	1.77
South Asia									
India	39.68	1.38	33.74	4.90	2.14	4.74	1.00	0.43	0.73
Indonesia	28.93	1.01	12.19	3.09	1.35	1.60	1.25	0.54	2.06
Malaysia	43.49	1.52	21.84	5.39	2.35	2.53	1.05	0.46	2.36
Pakistan	27.64	0.96	21.86	4.20	1.83	2.55	1.55	0.67	2.55
Sri Lanka	27.81	0.97	—	4.22	1.84	—	1.65	0.72	—
Thailand	27.54	0.96	13.93	4.71	2.06	2.52	1.51	0.66	2.62
Europe/ Mideast/Africa									
Greece	10.18	0.35	6.89	1.94	0.85	1.67	4.85	2.11	11.02
Hungary	52.42	1.83	—	1.65	0.72	—	2.73	1.19	—
Jordan	17.95	0.63	14.49	1.96	0.86	1.61	2.71	1.18	2.51
Nigeria	8.36	0.29	8.98	1.76	0.77	1.74	6.87	2.99	5.10
Poland	31.47	1.10	—	5.69	2.48	—	0.43	0.19	—
Portugal	17.97	0.63	9.05	1.69	0.74	1.02	2.95	1.28	4.68
Turkey	36.34	1.27	6.95	7.18	3.14	1.29	2.39	1.04	8.14
Zimbabwe**	8.84	0.31	2.03	0.91	0.40	0.31	3.62	1.57	6.13

* Relative to the MSCI World Index.

** The composite P/E and P/BV are averages of the companies in the IFC indexes weighted by market capitalization; the dividend yield represents a 12-month moving yield for the indexes.

Source: *Emerging Stock Markets Factbook, 1994* (Washington, D.C.: International Finance Corporation, 1994), p. 36.

the last weekly quote. Next observe the index values shown under the 9/29/94 column (third column from the right) for U.S. dollar values. The base period for the index is 1970. Over the 24-year period, the indexes of Japan (3407.5) and Hong Kong (4880.6) have substantially outperformed the United States (432.6). The wide disparity in index values over time indicates the differing movements in foreign markets.

At the top of Table 18–7 on page 519 is the **World Index,** which is a value-weighted index of the performance in 19 major countries as compiled by Morgan Stanley Capital International Perspective, Geneva, Switzerland.

Other Market Differences

There are large differences among cultures, including willingness to take risk, desire for dividend income versus growth in share value, the number and type of companies available to stockholders, and bureaucratic differences such as accounting conventions and government regulation of markets. In a book of this type, we do not intend to cover each issue but simply bring them to your attention. Table 18–8 presents differences in price-earnings ratios, price-to-book value ratios, and dividend yields from the *Emerging Stock Market Factbook, 1994,* published by International Finance Corporation of Washington, D.C.

Many developing countries have higher price-earnings ratios in their stock markets than the rest of the World. For example, Argentina has an average P/E of 41.9 for 1993. However, the P/E ratios in Latin America vary widely from country to country ranging from 41.9 in Argentina to 12.5 in Brazil. Clearly, individual country differences account for these disparities, but in all cases, those countries with high expected growth in "real" earnings and dividends will have higher price-earnings ratios than those with lower expected growth. This is the same impact found in the U.S. market as discussed in Chapter 7.

To some extent, the price-to-book-value ratio in each country corresponds to each country's P/E ratio. Countries with high P/Es have high P/BV ratios and vice versa. The dividend yields show a wide difference with Nigeria having a yield of 6.87 percent and the Philippines having a 0.35 percent dividend yield. This wide difference is mostly attributable to country differences, inflation rates, different accounting methods, and risk-return preferences of the stockholders.

CURRENCY FLUCTUATIONS AND RATES OF RETURN

We must explicitly consider the effect of **currency fluctuations** (changes in currency values) as well as rates of return in different countries. For example, assume an investment in France produces a 10 percent return. But suppose at the same time the French franc declines in value by 5 percent against the U.S. dollar. The French franc profits are thus worth less in dollars. In the present case, the gain on the investment would be shown as follows:

110%	(Investment with 10% profit)
	(Adjusted value of French franc relative to U.S. dollar)
× 0.95	(1.00 – .05 decline in currency)
104.5%	Percent of original investment

The actual return in U.S. dollars would be 4.5 instead of 10 percent. Of course, if the French franc appreciated by 5 percent against the dollar, the French franc profits

converted to dollars would be worth considerably more than 10 percent. The values are indicated below:

110%	(Investment with 10% profit)
	(Adjusted value of French franc relative to U.S. dollar)
× 1.05	(1.00 + .05 increase in currency)
115.5%	Percent of original investment

The 10 percent gain in the French franc investment has produced a 15.5 percent gain in U.S. dollars. A U.S. investor in foreign securities must consider not only the potential trend of security prices but also the trend of foreign currencies against the dollar. This point will become more apparent as we look at Table 18–9.

Let's examine currency effects in London. In this instance, the one-year return in the local currency was 15.2 percent (second column), but the currency (British pound) declined 16.9 percent (fifth column) against the U.S. dollar for the one-year period, causing an overall *loss* on the investment of 4.3 percent (second column from the right for London). The values are computed as follows:

115.2%	(Investment with 15.2% profit)
	(Adjusted value of British pound to the U.S. dollar)
× 0.831	(1.000 − 0.169 decline in currency)
95.7%	Percent of original investment

The ending value of 95.7 percent indicates a loss of 4.3 percent from the initial value of 100 percent.[3] If one were merely to subtract the foreign currency loss of 16.9 percent from the 15.2 percent profit, the answer would be a loss of 1.7 percent, but this is not the

TABLE 18–9 Return on World Stock Markets

	Return in Each Currency (Percent)			Currency Valuation (Percent)			Return in U.S. Dollars (Percent)		
	3 Months	1 Year	5 Years	3 Months	1 Year	5 Years	3 Months	1 Year	5 Years
New York	8.8%	36.6%	11.4%	0.0%	0.0%	0.0%	8.8%	36.6%	11.4%
Tokyo	4.0	15.7	8.7	− 2.0	3.5	− 1.7	1.9	19.8	6.8
London	9.8	15.2	7.2	− 8.3	−16.9	− 4.5	0.6	− 4.3	2.4
Toronto	10.1	36.6	15.2	− 0.7	− 0.8	− 1.7	9.3	35.5	13.2
Frankfurt	19.1	26.5	2.7	− 2.2	− 0.7	− 3.9	16.5	25.6	− 1.3
Sydney	5.6	11.0	10.8	−11.9	−17.7	− 5.4	− 6.9	− 8.7	4.8
Paris	20.5	10.8	8.6	− 7.4	−13.9	− 9.1	11.6	− 4.5	− 1.3
Zurich	9.0	22.4	1.3	− 3.7	− 7.2	− 2.6	5.0	13.7	− 1.3
Hong Kong	27.1	14.6	17.3	− 3.7	−13.0	− 7.2	22.4	−25.7	8.8
Milan	28.5	4.8	28.5	− 5.3	− 8.4	−10.1	21.7	− 4.0	15.6
Amsterdam	29.4	49.9	7.1	4.0	− 2.0	− 4.6	24.1	47.0	2.2
Singapore	18.5	19.3	24.9	1.1	2.3	2.1	19.8	22.0	27.5

[3] Due to rounding and other statistical adjustments, not all values adjusted to U.S. dollars come out as precisely as this.

correct procedure. The gain of 15.2 percent was on an initial base of 100 percent, but the foreign currency loss of 16.9 percent was on an ending value of 115.2 percent (which comes out to an actual loss in currency value of 19.5 percent).

Those who track the performance in foreign markets usually make adjustments so that the reported returns are in U.S. dollars that have already been adjusted for **foreign currency effects.** For example, most of the returns in prior tables of this chapter have already been adjusted for the foreign currency effect.

One might justifiably ask, how important is the foreign currency effect in relation to the overall return performance in the foreign currency? Do events in foreign exchange markets tend to overpower actual returns achieved in specific investments in foreign countries? Normally, the foreign currency effect is only about 10 to 20 percent as significant as the actual return performance in the foreign currency.[4] However, when the dollar is rising or falling rapidly over a short period, the impact can be much greater. For example, the returns to U.S. investors in Japanese securities between 1985 and 1988 were increased by 50 percent from the gain in the yen against the dollar.

In a well-diversified international portfolio, the changes in foreign currency values in one part of the world normally tend to cancel changes in other parts of the world. Also, those who do not wish to have foreign currency exposure of any sort may use forward exchange contracts, futures market contracts, or put options on foreign currency to hedge away the risk. Finally, there are those who believe in parity theories that suggest one should get additional compensation in local returns to make up for potential losses in foreign currency values. This latter point is a purely theoretical matter that provides little comfort in the short run.

The authors would suggest that those considering international investments be sensitive to the foreign currency effect, but not be overly discouraged by it. The superior return potentials from foreign investments previously shown in Figure 18–3 (and most other places in this chapter) are constructed *after* considering the foreign exchange effect on U.S. dollar returns. While foreign currency swings have been *wider* in recent times, they are still not a major deterrent to an internationally diversified portfolio.

OTHER OBSTACLES TO INTERNATIONAL INVESTMENTS

Other problems are peculiar to international investments. Let us consider some of them.

Political Risks

Many firms operate in foreign political climates that are more volatile than that of the United States. There is the danger of nationalization of foreign firms or the blockage of capital flows to investors. There also may be the danger of a violent overthrow of the political party in power. Furthermore, many countries have been unable to meet their foreign debt obligations, and this has important political implications.

The informed investor must have some feel for the political/economic climate of the foreign country in which he or she invests. Of course, problems sometimes create opportunities. Local investors may overreact to political changes occurring in their

---

[4] Bertrand Jacquillat and Bruno Solnik, "Multinationals Are Poor Tools for Diversification," *Journal of Portfolio Management,* Winter 1978, pp. 8–12.

environment. Because all their eggs are in one basket, they may engage in an oversell in regard to political changes. A less impassioned outside investor may identify an opportunity for profit.

Nevertheless, political risk represents a potential deterrent to foreign investment. The best solution for the investor is to be sufficiently diversified around the world so that a political or economic development in one foreign country does not have a major impact on his or her portfolio (this can be accomplished through a mutual fund or through other means discussed later in the chapter).

Tax Problems

Many major foreign countries may impose a 15 to 30 percent withholding tax against the dividends or interest paid to nonresident holders of equity or debt securities. However, it is often possible for *tax-exempt* U.S. investors to secure an exemption or rebate on part or all of the withholding tax. Also, taxable U.S. investors can normally claim a U.S. tax credit for taxes paid in foreign countries. The problem is more likely to be one of inconvenience and paper shuffling rather than loss of funds.

Lack of Market Efficiency

U.S. capital markets tend to be the most liquid and efficient in the world. Therefore, an investor who is accustomed to trading on the New York Stock Exchange may have some difficulties adjusting to foreign markets. A larger spread between the bid (sell) and asked (buy) price in foreign countries is likely. Also, an investor may have more difficulty handling a large transaction (the seller may have to absorb a larger discount in executing the trade). Furthermore, as a general rule, commission rates are higher in foreign markets than in the United States.

Administrative Problems

There can also be administrative problems in dealing in foreign markets in terms of adjusting to the various local systems. For example, in the Hong Kong, Swiss, and Mexican stock markets, you must settle your account one day after the transaction; in London, there is a two-week settlement procedure; and in France, there are different settlement dates for cash and forward markets. The different administrative procedures of foreign countries simply add up to an extra dimension of difficulty in executing trades. (As implied throughout this chapter, there are ways to avoid most of these difficulties by going through mutual funds and other investment outlets.)

Information Difficulties

The U.S. securities markets are the best in the world at providing investment information. The Securities and Exchange Commission, with its rigorous requirements for full disclosure, is the toughest national regulator of investment information. Also, the United States has the Financial Accounting Standards Board (FASB) continually providing pronouncements on generally accepted accounting principles for financial reporting.

Publicly traded companies are required to provide stockholders with fully audited annual reports. In the United States, we are further spoiled by the excellent evaluative reports and ratings generated by Moody's, Standard & Poor's, Value Line, and other firms. We also have extensive economic data provided by governmental sources such as the Department of Commerce and the Federal Reserve System.

Many international firms, trading in less sophisticated foreign markets, simply do not provide the same quantity or quality of data. This would be particularly true of firms trading in some of the smaller foreign markets. Even when the information is available, there may be language problems for the analyst who does not speak German, French, Portuguese, and so on.

Also, the analyst must be prepared to analyze the firm in light of the standards that are generally accepted in the foreign market in which the company operates. For example, Japanese companies often have much higher debt ratios than U.S. firms. A debt-to-equity ratio of three times is not unusual in Japan, whereas in the United States, the standard is closer to 1:1. The analyst may be inclined to "mark down" the Japanese firm for high debt unless he or she realizes the different features at play in the Japanese economy. For example, in Japan there are normally very close relationships between the lending bank and the borrower, with the lender perhaps having an equity position in the borrower and with interlocking boards between the two. This diminishes the likelihood of the lender calling in the loan in difficult economic periods. Also, the Japanese make extensive use of reserve accounts that tend to give the appearance of a smaller asset or equity base than actually exists. This pattern of understatement is further aided by a strict adherence to historical cost valuation even though Japanese land values have increased more rapidly than almost anywhere else in the world since the end of World War II. When appropriate adjustments are made for these effects on financial reporting, a Japanese debt-to-equity ratio of 3:1 may not be a matter of any greater concern than a U.S. debt-to-equity ratio of 1:1.

METHODS OF PARTICIPATING IN FOREIGN INVESTMENTS

The avenues to international investment include investing in firms in their own foreign markets, purchasing the shares of foreign firms trading in the United States (shown in Table 18–10 on pages 526–27), investing in mutual funds and closed-end funds with a global orientation, buying the shares of multinational corporations, and entrusting funds to private money managers who specialize in international equities. We shall examine each of these alternatives.

Direct Investments

The most obvious but least likely alternative would be to directly purchase the shares of a firm in its own foreign market through a foreign broker or an overseas branch of a U.S. broker. The investor might consider such firms as Toshiba or Fanuc on the Tokyo Stock Exchange, Consolidated Rutile on the Sydney Stock Exchange, or Hoechst on the Frankfurt Stock Exchange. This approach is hampered by all the difficulties and administrative problems associated with international investments. There could be information-gathering problems, tax problems, stock-delivery problems, capital-transfer problems, and communication difficulties in executing orders. Only the most sophisti-

TABLE 18–10 Foreign Firms Trading on the New York Stock Exchange (December 31, 1993)

Country	Company
Argentina	Banco Frances del Rio de la Plata*
	BAESA—Buenos Aires Embotelladora, S.A.*
	YPF Sociedad Anonima*
Australia	Australia and New Zealand Banking Group Ltd. (PFD)
	Broken Hill Proprietary Company Limited*
	Coles Myer Ltd.*
	FAI Insurances Limited*
	National Australia Bank Limited*
	News Corporation Ltd.*
	Orbital Engine Corporation Limited*
	Western Mining Corp. Holdings Ltd.*
	Westpac Banking Corporation*
	Westpac Banking Corporation* (PFD)
Bermuda	ACE Limited
	Sphere Drake Holdings Limited
Brazil	Aracruz Celulose, S.A.*
British West Indies	Club Med, Inc.
Canada	Abitibi-Price Inc.
	Alcan Aluminum Ltd.
	American Barrick Resources Corporation
	BCE Inc.
	Campbell Resources Inc.
	Canadian Pacific Limited
	Cineplex Odeon Corporation
	Domtar Inc.
	Glamis Gold Ltd.
	Horsham Corporation
	Inco Limited
	InterTAN Inc.
	LAC Minerals Ltd.
	Laidlaw Inc. (Class A)
	Laidlaw Inc. (Class B)
	Magna International Inc.
	Mitel Corporation
	Moore Corporation Limited
	Northern Telecom Limited
	Northgate Exploration Limited
	NOVA Corporation of Alberta
	Placer Dome Inc.
	Potash Corporation of Saskatchewan Inc.
	Premdor Inc.
	Ranger Oil Limited
	Seagram Company Ltd.
	TransCanada Pipelines Limited
	United Dominion Industries Limited
	Westcoast Energy Inc.
Cayman Islands	Elf Overseas Ltd. Ser. A (PFD)
	Elf Overseas Ltd. Ser. B (PFD)
	Espirito Santo Overseas (PFD)
	Extecapital Ltd. (PFD)
	NewsCorp. Cayman Islands Ltd.* (PFD)
	NewsCorp. Overseas Ltd., Ser. A (PFD)
	Santander Finance Ltd. (PFD)
Chile	Compania de Telefonos de Chile, S.A.*
	Enersis, S.A.*
	Madeco, S.A.*
	MASISA—Maderas y Sinteticos Sociedad Anonima*
	Sociedad Quimica y Minera de Chile, S.A.*
Denmark	Novo-Nordisk A/S*
France	Alcatel Alsthom Compagnie Générale d'Electricité*
	Rhone-Poulenc, S.A.* Ord. A
	Rhone-Poulenc Overseas (PFD)
	Rhone-Poulenc, S.A.* 1/4A (PFD)
	Societe National Elf Aquitaine*
	TOTAL*
Germany	Daimler–Benz AG*
Hong Kong	Amway Asia Pacific Ltd.
	Brilliance China Automotive Holdings Limited
	China Tire Holdings Limited
	Ek Chor China Motorcycle Company, Ltd.
	Hong Kong Telecommunications Ltd.*
	Tommy Hilfiger Corporation
Ireland	Allied Irish Banks PLC*
	Allied Irish Banks PLC* (PFD)
Israel	Elscint Limited
	Tadiran Limited
Italy	Benetton Group, S.p.A.*
	Fiat, S.p.A.* 5 Ord.
	Fiat, S.p.A.* 5 (PFD)
	Fiat, S.p.A.* 5 Svg. (PFD)
	Fila Holdings, S.p.A.*
	Industrie Natuzzi, S.p.A.*

TABLE 18–10 *(continued)*

Country	Company
Italy	Luxottica Group, S.p.A.*
	Montedison, S.p.A.*
	Montedison, S.p.A.* (PFD)
Japan	Hitachi, Ltd.*
	Honda Motor Company, Ltd.*
	Kubota Corporation*
	Kyocera Corporation*
	Matsushita Electric Industrial Company, Ltd.*
	Mitsubishi Bank Ltd.*
	Pioneer Electronic Corporation*
	Sony Corporation*
	TDK Corporation*
Liberia	Royal Caribbean Cruises Ltd.
Luxembourg	Espirito Santo Financial Holdings, S.A.*
Mexico	Bufete Industrial, S.A.*
	Coca-Cola Femsa, S.A. de C.V.*
	Consorcio G Grupo Dina, S.A. de C.V.*
	Empresas ICA Sociedad Controladora, S.A. de C.V.*
	Grupo Casa Autrey, S.A. de C.V.*
	Grupo Financiero Serfin, S.A. de C.V.*
	Grupo Mexicano de Desarrollo, S.A. de C.V.* (Ser. B)
	Grupo Mexicano de Desarrollo, S.A. de C.V.* (Ser. L)
	Grupo Radio Central, S.A. de C.V.*
	Grupo Televisa, S.A.***
	Grupo Tribasa, S.A. de C.V.*
	Telefonos de Mexico, S.A. de C.V.*
	Transportacion Maritima Mexicana, S.A. de C.V.* (Ser. L)
	Transportacion Maritima Mexicana, S.A. de C.V.* Ord.
	Vitro, S.A.*
Netherlands	AEGON N.V.**
	Elsag Bailey Process Automation N.V.
	KLM Royal Dutch Airlines**
	Koninklijke Ahold N.V.*
	Philips N.V.**
	Polygram N.V.**
	Royal Dutch Petroleum Company**
	Unilever N.V.**
Netherlands	Schlumberger Limited
Antilles	Singer Company N.V.
New Zealand	Fletcher Challenge Ltd.*
	Fletcher Challenge Ltd. Forest Division Shares*
	Telecom Corporation of New Zealand Ltd.*
Norway	A/S Eksportfinans (PFD)
	Hafslund Nycomed AS*
	Norsk Hydro a.s.*
Panama	Banco Latinoamericano de Exportaciones, S.A.
	Panamerican Beverages, Inc.
People's Republic of China	Shanghai Petrochemical Company, Ltd.*
Philippines	Benguet Corporation
Portugal	Banco Comercial Portugues, S.A.*
South Africa	ASA Limited
Spain	ARGENTARIA-Corporacion Bancaria de Espana, S.A.*
	Banco Bilbao Vizcaya, S.A.*
	Banco Bilbao Vizcaya Int. (Gibraltar)* (PFD)
	Banco Bilbao Vizcaya Int. (Gibraltar)* (PFD)
	Banco Bilbao Vizcaya Int. (Gibraltar)* (PFD)
	Banco Central, S.A.*
	Banco de Santander, S.A.*
	Empresa Nacional de Electricidad, S.A.*
	Repsol, S.A.*
	Telefonica de Espana, S.A.*
Sweden	Aktiebolaget Svensk Exportkredit (PFD)
United Kingdom	Attwoods PLC*
	Automated Security (Holdings) PLC*
	Barclays Bank PLC* (PFD)
	Barclays Bank PLC* (PFD)
	Barclays Bank PLC* (PFD)
	Barclays Bank PLC* (PFD)
	Barclays Bank PLC* (PFD)
	Barclays Bank PLC*
	Bass PLC*
	BET Public Limited Company*
	British Airways PLC*
	British Gas PLC*
	British Petroleum Co. PLC*
	British Steel PLC*
	British Telecommunications PLC*
	Cable and Wireless Public Limited Company*
	Carlton Communications PLC (PFD)
	English China Clays PLC*
	Enterprise Oil PLC*

(continued)

TABLE 18–10 (concluded)

Country	Company	Country	Company
United Kingdom	Enterprise Oil PLC Ser. A* (PFD)		Royal Bank of Scotland Group PLC* (PFD)
	Enterprise Oil PLC Ser. B* (PFD)		Royal Bank of Scotland Group PLC* (PFD)
	Glaxo Holdings PLC*		RTZ Corporation PLC*
	Grand Metropolitan PLC*		Saatchi & Saatchi Company PLC*
	Hanson PLC*		Shell Transport & Trading Company, PLC*
	Huntingdon International Holdings PLC*		SmithKline Beecham PLC* (Class A)
	Imperial Chemical Industries PLC*		SmithKline Beecham PLC* (Class B)
	Lasmo PLC*		Tiphook PLC*
	Lasmo PLC Ser. A*		Unilever PLC*
	Midland Bank PLC* (PFD)		Vodafone Group PLC*
	National Westminster Bank PLC*		Willis Corroon PLC*
	National Westminster Bank PLC* (PFD)		Wellcome PLC*
	National Westminster Bank PLC* (PFD)		Waste Management International PLC*
	National Westminster Bank PLC (PFD)		Zeneca Group PLC*
	Royal Bank of Scotland Group PLC*		
		Venezuela	Corimon C.A.*

* American depositary receipts/shares
** NY shares and/or guilder shares
*** Global depositary shares

cated money manager would probably follow this approach (though this may change somewhat in the future as foreign markets become better coordinated).

A more likely route to direct investment would be to purchase the shares of foreign firms that actually trade in U.S. securities markets. Hundreds of foreign firms actively trade their securities in the United States as shown in Table 18–10.

Firms such as Alcan Aluminium Ltd., Campbell Resources, Inc., and Ranger Oil Limited trade their stocks *directly* on the New York Stock Exchange. Most of the other firms in the table (as well as other large foreign firms) trade their shares in the United States through **American depository receipts (ADRs).** The ADRs represent the ownership interest in a foreign company's common stock. In Table 18–10, such firms have an asterisk after their names. The process is as follows: The shares of the foreign company are purchased and put in trust in a foreign branch of a New York bank. The bank receives and can issue depository receipts to the American shareholders of the foreign firm. These ADRs (that is, depository receipts) allow foreign shares to be traded in the United States.

When you call your broker and ask to purchase Sony Corporation or Honda Motor Company, Ltd. (which are represented by ADRs), you will notice virtually no difference between this transaction and buying shares of General Motors or Eastman Kodak. You can receive a certificate that looks very much like a U.S. stock certificate. You will receive your dividends in dollars and get your reports about the company in English. Generally, you will pay your normal commission rates.

Table 18–11 shows a page from *Standard & Poor's Stock Guide* that includes Sony Corporation's ADRs. Note that the financial information is basically the same as that for

TABLE 18–11 Sample Page from *Standard & Poor's Stock Guide*

178 **SNY-SOU** Standard & Poor's

¶ S&P 500
# MidCap 400
✣ SmallCap 600
• Options

Index	Ticker	Name of Issue (Call Price of Pfd. Stocks)	Market	Com. Rank. & Pfd. Rating	Par Val.	Inst. Hold Cos	Inst. Hold Shs. (000)	Principal Business	Price Range 1971-92 High	1971-92 Low	1993 High	1993 Low	1994 High	1994 Low	Nov. Sales in 100s	November, 1994 Last Sale Or Bid High	Low	Last	%Div Yield	P-E Ratio
✣1•[1]	SNY	✓Snyder Oil Corp	NY	NR	1¢	140	15020	Oil&gas explor,dev,prod'n	10½	4¾	23	10	21⅜	15⅛	17740	17½	15⅛	15½	1.7	27
2	Pr	$4.00 cm Cv[51]Ex Pfd([52]52.50)	NY	B+	1¢	19	650		65¾	46	126¼	64	118	85¼	383	90	85¼	85½B	4.7	. .
3	Pr A	Dep [54]cm Cv Ex[55]Pfd([56]26.05)	NY,Ch	B+	1¢	54	2958		. . . .	. . . .	31¾	25	29⅝	20½	3090	23½	20½	21¼	7.1	. .
4	SQM	✓Sociedad Quimica Y Minera ADS[57]	[2]	NR	[57]. .	45	3593	Produce natural nitrates	. . . .	. . . .	30¾	23¼	38	25⅜	5103	33¾	26¾	28	1.3	25
5	SODK	✓Sodak Gaming	NNM	NR	.001	48	1855	Mfr electr slot/video mach	. . . .	. . . .	39½	16	30¼	10	13932	18	13¼	14	. . .	18
6•[3]	SDG	✓Sofamor/Danek Group	NY,Ph	NR	No	99	6036	Mfr spinal implant devices	44¾	7½	45	25½	37⅛	10⅜	10162	17⅛	15¼	16⅛	. . .	16
7	SDSK	✓Softdesk Inc	NNM	NR	1¢	35	1818	Dvlp architecture softwr prd	. . . .	. . . .	. . . .	. . . .	23¾	10¾	10228	23¾	19	23¼	. . .	51
8	SOFT	✓SofTech Inc	NNM	B–	10¢	17	556	Devel software svcs & prod	25⅛	1	7¼	2⅜	9⅞	5¼	3084	7⅝	6⅜	6⅜	. . .	11
9	SOF	✓Softnet Systems	AS	C	1¢	7	98	Hlth care cost mgmt svcs	14⅞	¾	7⅛	2⅝	9	5⅛	778	8	6⅝	7¼	. . .	d
10•[4]	SPCO	✓Software Publishing	NNM,Ph	C	No	48	4610	Mkts pkgd applicat'n software	35¼	3⅛	14½	5½	8½	3	19109	6	4¾	5⅜	. . .	d
11	SOI	✓S.O.I. Industries	AS,Ph	B–	.000025	5	162	Mfr cabinets/lamps&tape duplicat'n	3⅝	5/16	4	⅜	3⅞	1⅝	5839	3¼	2¾	2⅞	. . .	15
12•[5]	SLR	✓Solectron Corp	NY,Ph	B	No	191	37913	Mfr computer prod/subsys	18¾	1½	29¾	16⅝	34	23⅜	27364	28¼	25⅝	27⅛	. . .	21
13	SGT.EC	✓Soligen Technologies	ECM	NR	No	1	15	Dvlp stg: metal fabricat'g sys	. . . .	. . . .	. . . .	. . . .	2	½	1268	⅞	⅝	¾	. . .	d
14	SOMA	✓Somatix Therapy	NNM	C	1¢	38	7019	Cellular medical technology	79	1½	9⅝	5⅛	9	3¼	9129	5⅛	3¼	3⅝	. . .	d
15•[5]	SMTG	✓Somatogen Inc	NNM	NR	0.001	51	4940	Dvlp stge:human blood subst	50½	13	22¾	6¾	10½	6¼	15606	8	7⅛	7¼	. . .	d
16	SOMR	✓Somerset Group	NNM	B–	No	13	333	Construction prd/sv,banking	18	5	11½	6¾	14¼	9¾	650	13½	12½	13½	1.5	9
¶17•[6]	SNT	✓Sonat, Inc	NY,B,C,Ch,P,Ph	B	1	517	58880	Nat'l gas P.L.: drill'g o&g	28	3⅜	36½	21⅝	34⅞	26	49417	32½	27⅝	28⅛	3.8	15
✣18•[7]	RIG	✓Sonat Offshore Drilling	NY	NR	1¢	92	15560	Offshore oil&gas drilling svcs	. . . .	. . . .	23½	15¼	21½	15⅝	7564	20	18½	19½	1.2	32
✣19	SONC	✓Sonic Corp	NNM	NR	1¢	58	5269	Oper fast food drive-in restr	33	12¼	30¾	19	26½	16¾	9811	23¾	19¼	22	. . .	23
#20	SONO	✓Sonoco Products	NNM	A–	No	226	28816	Mfr paper packaging products	25¼	⅝	24⅞	19¾	25¾	19¾	30241	22¾	20¾	21⅛	2.7	16
21•[3]	SNE	✓Sony Corp[60]ADR	[8]NY,B,C,Ch,P,Ph,Mo	NR	[60]. .	125	11845	Color TV sets,tape rec,radio	59¾	2⅝	50⅝	32	63¼	49⅜	14083	60⅞	50⅜	53⅛	0.8	. .
#22•[9]	BID	✓Sotheby's Hldgs Cl'A'	NY,Ch	NR	10¢	158	30991	Worlds largest art auctioneer	37	7¾	17¼	10¾	19¾	11⅜	18250	12¾	11⅜	11¾	2.0	29
23	SJI	✓South Jersey Indus	NY,B,Ch,Ph	B+	1.25	48	1553	Hldg co: gas, fuel oil, sand	23⅛	4½	27½	21⅞	24	16⅝	1612	17½	16⅝	16⅞	s8.5	12
24	SWP	✓South West Prop Tr	NY,Ch	NR	1¢	86	11882	Real estate investment trust	77½	2½	15⅜	10½	14	11	8826	12½	11	11¼	8.2	18
#25	SDW	✓Southdown, Inc	NY,Ch,Ph	C	1¼	121	15812	Cement:concrete:environ'l svc	31½	1⅜	25⅞	9⅝	30¼	15¼	14314	18	15¼	17⅛	. . .	43
26	PrD	$2.875cm Cv Sr'D'Pfd([64]50)	NY	B	5¢	39	1737		. . . .	. . . .	. . . .	. . . .	56¾	33¼	2431	37¼	33¼	34¾	8.3	. .
27	SMGS	✓Southeastern Mich Gas Ent	NNM	A	1	31	663	Integrated natural gas sys	18⅝	2 5/16	24½	16½	21⅝	17	636	19	17¾	17¾	s4.5	16
✣28	SCW	✓Southern Cal Water	NY	A–	2.5	51	1617	Water supply, some elec	20⅝	4¼	24⅜	19⅝	22	15¼	1503	15⅞	15¼	15⅞	7.6	11
¶29•[10]	SO	✓Southern Co	NY,B,C,Ch,P,Ph	A–	5	577	188066	Elec util hldg:Southeast	19⅝	4	23⅝	18½	22⅛	17	223660	21	18⅞	20¾	5.7	14
30	SECX	✓Southern Electronics	NNM	NR	1¢	37	2150	Dstr computers/eqp so'estn US	14½	⅞	18½	9¾	12½	4¾	4874	6⅝	5¼	6⅛	. . .	8
✣31	SEHI	✓Southern Energy Homes	NNM	NR	.0001	52	4339	Producer of manufactured homes	. . . .	. . . .	21¼	13	19⅛	11¾	3041	14¼	11¾	12⅝	. . .	11
32	SIG	✓Southern Indiana G&E	NY,Ch,Ph	A	No	92	3752	Utility:elec/gas,Evansville	34⅛	4⅛	35½	31⅞	33⅞	24	2392	26¾	24	25⅝	6.4	11
33	SNB	✓Southern National	NY,Ph	A	5	76	6302	Comm'l bkg,North&So.Carolina	19¾	2¾	23½	18½	22	17¾	11104	21	17¾	18⅜	4.4	7
34	Pr A	6.75% cm Cv[70]Dep Pfd([71]26.0125)	NY	BB+	5	21	1513		32	25	37⅜	29⅝	33¼	27⅜	1834	31½	27⅜	28	6.0	. .
#35•[11]	SNG	✓Southern New Eng Telecom	[12]NY,B,Ch	A–	1	232	21929	Supplies telecommunic svcs	46½	6⅜	38⅜	33⅝	36¼	28¼	9884	35⅝	32⅛	33	5.3	13
36•[10]	RSP	✓Southern Pacific Rail	NY,Ch	NR	.001	208	82569	Railroad freight transport'n	. . . .	. . . .	21⅜	13½	24⅜	16⅝	71371	19⅞	17⅛	18¼	. . .	18
37	SUG	✓Southern Union	AS,B,Ch	NR	1	39	2450	Natural gas dstr: oil & gas	12⅞	7⅝	20⅛	9	23⅜	16⅜	1061	18¼	16¾	17⅞	s. . .	56
38	SLCMC	✓Southland Corp	NNM	NR	.0001	42	26640	Oper 7-Eleven convenience strs	4¼	½	7⅝	3	6¾	3¾	24019	5¼	4⅜	4⅝	. . .	66
#39•[4]	SOTR	✓SouthTrust Corp	NNM	A	2½	190	32550	Commercial bkg,Alabama	18⅛	⅞	22⅛	16⅝	22⅛	17	36063	19¼	17	18⅛	3.8	9
40	SWTX	✓Southwall Technologies	NNM	C	.001	17	1811	Produces thin film coatings	12	2⅞	6⅛	2¼	5⅝	2⅛	2017	3¼	2½	2¾	. . .	d
¶41•[3]	LUV	✓Southwest Airlines	NY,B,Ch,P,Ph	B+	1	404	77720	Airline svc mid-so'west U.S.	19⅞	1/32	37⅝	18⅛	39	20⅛	138824	23⅝	20⅛	21⅛	0.2	15
42	OKSB	✓Southwest Bancorp	NNM	NR	1	4	605	Commercial banking,Oklahoma	. . . .	. . . .	12½	11¾	15	11	501	14⅝	13¾	14½	1.4	11
✣43	SWX	✓Southwest Gas	NY,B,Ch,P,Ph	B	1	95	7337	Natural gas,banking,R.E. dvlp	26¾	6⅛	18½	13⅜	19⅜	14⅝	6916	17⅛	14⅝	15¼	5.4	15
44	SWST	✓Southwest Securities Grp	NNM	NR	10¢	24	1280	Securities/brokerage svcs	9⅞	5⅝	14¼	8	12¾	5⅞	4292	7¼	6⅜	6⅞	2.0	10
45	SWWC	✓Southwest Water Co	NNM	B	1	22	326	Water utility:serves CA,NM,TX	24	2½	18	8½	12¼	8	481	9¾	9	9⅛	4.4	d
¶46•[13]	SBC	✓Southwestern Bell Corp[73].	[12]NY,B,Ch,P	A	1	950	222003	Tel svc:Ark,Kan,Mo,Okl,Tex	37⅜	9⅛	47	34¼	44⅜	36¾	164548	43⅛	40	41⅜	3.8	15
✣47	SWN	✓Southwestern Energy	NY,Ch,Ph	A–	10¢	141	15353	Hldg gas utility,Ark: o & g	14	⅝	21⅞	12⅛	18⅞	15⅛	9063	17¾	15½	15¾	1.5	13
48	SLC	✓Southwestern Life	AS,Ch,P	B–	1	61	16584	Ins hldg:life,accident,health	32⅝	⅜	7⅜	3¾	7⅝	2 1/16	40374	4⅜	2 1/16	2⅜	. . .	d
49	Pr A	$1.75cmCv Ex'86 Pfd([75]25.350)	AS,Ch	CCC+	No	17	542		25¾	7½	18⅝	13⅛	19⅞	9¼	11826	15¼	9¼	9⅝	18.2	. .

Uniform Footnote Explanations-See Page 1. Other: [1]ASE:Cycle 3. [2]NY,Ch [3]CBOE:Cycle 3. [4]P:Cycle 3. [5]CBOE:Cycle 1. [6]ASE:Cycle 1. [7]Ph:Cycle 2. [8]To [9]ASE,CBOE,P:Cycle 1. [10]CBOE:Cycle 2. [11]NY:Cycle 1. [12]Ph [13]P:Cycle 1. [51]Co opt fr 12-31-92 exch for $50 amt 8% Cv 2006. [52]Fr 12-31-94 scale to $50 in 2000. [53]If conv price equal/exceed150%com-20trad'g days. [54]Dep for 0.25 shrs $6.00 Cv Exch Pfd. [55]Fr 3-31-96,scale to $25 in 2003. [56]Co opt fr 3-31-94 exch for $100 amt 6% Cv 2008. [57]Ea ADS rep 10 Sr'B',no-par. [58]Stk dstr of Newcare Health Corp. [59]®$1.18,'94. [60]ADR equal 1 ord shr, 50y. [61]Approx. [62]Subsid Pfd. [63]Incl $0.19375 non-taxable,'93. [64]Fr 1-27-2001. [65]If com exceeds 130% Cv price-20 trad.days. [66]Excl $3.1M subsid pfd. [67]Excl $1333 subsid Pfd. [68]12 Mo Dec'92. [69]®$2.13,'93. [70]Dep for 0.25 shr 6.75% cm Cv Series'A'Pfd. [71]Fr 3-1-96,scale to $25 in 2002. [72]Incl curr amts. [73]Plan Apr'95 vote on name chge:SBC Communications. [74]®$3.53,'93. [75]Co opt exch for $25amt 7%Cv 2011.

Source: Reprinted by permission of Standard and Poor's, one of the McGraw-Hill Companies.

other U.S. corporations trading on a major exchange or over-the-counter. The Sony ADRs also receive coverage from Value Line, Morningstar, and other reporting services. *The Wall Street Journal* has daily quotes just as it would have for any company. Since these ADRs trade on the New York Stock Exchange, the quote would be found in that section of the paper.

Indirect Investments

The forms of indirect investments in the international securities include (*a*) purchasing shares of multinational corporations, (*b*) purchasing mutual funds or closed-end investment funds specializing in worldwide investments, and (*c*) engaging the services of a private firm specializing in foreign investment portfolio management.

Purchasing Shares of Multinational Corporations **Multinational corporations,** that is, firms with operations in a number of countries, represent an opportunity for international diversification. For example, the major oil companies have investments and operations throughout the world. The same can be said for large banking firms and mainframe computer manufacturers. When one buys Exxon, to some extent one is buying exposure to the world economy (77.3 percent of sales are foreign for this firm). A list of the 20 largest U.S. multinational firms is presented in Table 18–12 on page 530. Of particular interest is the third column from the left, which represents foreign revenue as a percentage of total revenue, and the fourth column from the right, which represents foreign profit as a percentage of total profit.

Although buying shares in a U.S. multinational firm is an easy route to take to experience worldwide economic effects, some researchers maintain that multinationals do not provide the major *investment* benefits that are desired. Jacquillat and Solnik found that multinationals provide very little risk reduction over and above purely domestic firms (perhaps only 10 percent).[5] The prices of multinational shares tend to move very closely with U.S. financial markets despite their worldwide investments. Thus, U.S. multinationals may not do well in a U.S. bear market even if they have investments in strong markets in other countries. This leaves us to turn to mutual funds and closed-end investment companies as potential international investments.

Mutual Funds and Closed-End Investment Companies As will be described in Chapter 19, mutual funds offer the investor an opportunity for diversification as well as professional management. Nowhere is the mutual fund concept more important than in the area of international investments. Those who organize the funds usually have extensive experience in investing overseas and are prepared to deal with the administrative problems. This, of course, does not necessarily lead to superior returns, but the likelihood for inexperienced blunders is reduced.

One may also invest in closed-end investment companies specializing in international equity investments. As later described in Chapter 19, a closed-end investment company has a fixed supply of shares outstanding and trades on a national exchange or

[5] Ibid.

TABLE 18–12 Largest U.S. Multinational Corporations (in millions of U.S. dollars)

		Revenue			Net Profit[a]			Assets		
1993 Rank	Company	Foreign	Total	Foreign as Percent of Total	Foreign	Total	Foreign as Percent of Total	Foreign	Total	Foreign as Percent of Total
1	Exxon	75,639	97,825	77.3	4,066	5,280	77.0	47,445	84,145	56.4
2	General Motors	38,646	138,220	28.0	2,244	2,466	91.0	40,145	188,034	21.3
3	Mobil	38,535[b]	57,077[b]	67.5[c]	1,917[c]	2,401	79.8	25,420	40,585	62.6
4	IBM	37,013	62,716	59.0	−2,389	−7,987	D-D[d]	44,703	81,113	55.1
5	Ford Motor	32,860	108,521	30.3	−293	2,529	D-P[e]	51,669	198,938	26.0
6	Texaco	24,292	45,395	53.5	760	1,468[c]	51.8	11,895	30,410	39.1
7	Citicorp	20,762	32,196	64.5	1,560[c]	1,919	81.3	117,123[f]	228,240[f]	51.3
8	El du Pont de Nemours	16,756	32,621	51.4	565	566	99.8	13,807	37,053	37.3
9	Chevron	16,601	40,352	41.1	848	1,265	67.0	20,541	37,223	55.2
10	Procter & Gamble	15,856	30,433	52.1	175	269	65.1	10,157	24,932	40.7
11	Philip Morris	15,315	50,621	30.3	1,278	3,568	35.8	15,619	51,205	30.5
12	Hewlett-Packard	10,971	20,317	54.0	675	1,177	57.3	7,508	16,736	44.9
13	American International Group	10,148[g]	20,135	50.4	1,034[g]	1,918	53.9	36,532[g]	101,015	36.2
14	General Electric	10,036	60,562	16.6	323	4,424	7.3	31,791	251,506	12.6
15	Coca-Cola	9,351	13,957	67.0	1,484	2,188	67.8	5,844	12,021	48.6
16	Xerox[h]	9,242	19,434	47.6	141	−189	P-D[i]	10,119	39,677	25.5
17	Digital Equipment	9,152	14,371	63.7	114	−251	P-D[i]	6,641	10,950	60.6
18	Dow Chemical	8,775	18,060	48.6	279	919[j]	30.4	10,602	25,505	41.6
19	United Technologies	8,148[b]	21,081[b]	38.7	356	573[j]	63.7	4,403	15,618	28.2
20	Eastman Kodak	7,980	16,364	48.8	197	475	41.5	6,588	20,325	32.4

[a] From continuing operations.
[b] Includes other income.
[c] Net income before corporate expense.
[d] D-D: Deficit to deficit.
[e] D-P: Deficit to profit.
Source: Reprinted by permission of *Forbes* Magazine© Forbes Inc. 1994.

[f] Average assets.
[g] Excludes Canadian operations.
[h] Includes proportionate interest in unconsolidated subsidiaries or affiliates.
[i] P-D: Profit to deficit.
[j] Net income before minority interest.

The Growth of American Depository Receipts

After almost 70 years of going unnoticed, the benefits that American depositary receipts (ADRs) offer American investors are better understood. To avoid investor difficulties in collecting dividends, receipts were created that provided proof of ownership of the shares held abroad. This made it is less expensive and less troublesome for shareholders to collect dividends on their own.

ADRs are widely traded in America's markets. In 1994 alone, $266 billion worth of ADRs were exchanged on the various stock exchanges in America. Wall Street has become increasingly more global, and worldwide companies are being sold side by side with large American companies.

Many companies from around the world are scrambling to get their stocks traded on American exchanges. This move to Wall Street allows foreign companies to expand their capital while filling the growing demand for ADRs by American investors. Although ADRs are considered to be more liquid, less expensive, and easier to trade than buying foreign companies' stock directly on that country's exchange, there are some drawbacks.

ADRs are treated like domestic stock on the American front and are traded in dollars, but they are still traded in their local currencies on their home market. The gains or losses an investor can receive from changes in the currency exchange rate can also be offset by capital gains or losses on the investment itself. For those with short time horizons, this can be a serious problem, but for those with long-run interests, many experts argue that the dollar will usually even itself out, and high returns will win out.

There is still a lack of communication between companies and their shareholders abroad. It is difficult for individual investors to keep daily tabs on a foreign company without the aid of a broker.

Even though the SEC requires companies trading ADRs on American exchanges to use the U.S. standard of accounting, many "pink-sheet" ADRs not traded on an exchange are free from such restrictions. Pink sheets are price quotes for smaller or thinly traded over-the-counter companies. These companies are trying, however, to improve their accounting methods to catch the interests of foreign investors.

Politics can also be a disadvantage in ADRs. If a country is going through political turmoil, such unrest can send the stock price soaring or cause it to crash. The hefty taxes the foreign government takes out of the dividends can also be burdensome. To be reimbursed for the amount deducted, a U.S. investor has to request a credit by the Internal Revenue Service.

A final warning is to beware of management. History shows that in emerging economies, unexperienced companies often have tried to expand their business into markets in which they have little knowledge.

over-the-counter, much as an individual company does. It may trade at a premium or discount from its net asset value. An example is the Japan Fund.

A listing of internationally oriented funds is presented in Table 19–8 of the next chapter. The addresses of these funds can be found in *Forbes* magazine or the Wiesenberger Investment Companies Service (also discussed in the next chapter).

Specialists in International Securities The large investor may consider the option of engaging the services of selected banks and investment counselors with specialized expertise in foreign equities. Major firms include Morgan Guaranty Trust Company, State Street Bank and Trust Company, Batterymarch Financial Management, and Fidelity Trust Company of New York. These firms provide a total range of advisory and management services. However, they often require a minimum investment well in excess of $100,000 and are tailored to the needs of the large institutional investor.

SUMMARY

Investments in international securities allow the investor to diversify a portfolio beyond the normal alternatives. Because different foreign markets are influenced by varying and often contradictory factors, effective risk reduction can be provided. An example might be a sharp and unexpected increase in energy prices. The negative impact on oil importers will likely be offset by the positive impact on oil exporters.

Investments in selected foreign equity markets may also provide excellent return opportunities. A number of countries have had superior real GDP growth performance in comparison with the United States. They may also have greater savings rates and higher capital formation. Furthermore, a number of countries are becoming more competitive in traditional U.S. products such as automobiles, steel, and consumer electronics. Emerging countries may offer even greater return and risk-reduction benefits than investments in better established markets. However, many of the problems of international investments can surface in these less developed countries.

The impact of currency fluctuations on returns is an added dimension to international investments. Not only must the investor determine whether the security will provide a positive return, but he or she must also evaluate the possibility of the return being enhanced or diminished by changes in currency relationships with the U.S. dollar.

Other obstacles to foreign investment include political risks associated with foreign nations, tax problems, market efficiency and liquidity concerns, administrative problems, and gaps in information transference. The latter issue draws attention because of the comprehensive reporting system in the United States compared with the rest of the world. Also, the analyst must evaluate a security within the norms of the country in which the firm resides. This can be a problem for the uninitiated investor.

Fortunately, most of these obstacles can be overcome by appropriate investment routes into foreign markets. ADRs (American depository receipts) represent the ownership interest in a foreign company's common stock. The shares of the foreign company are put in trust in the foreign branch of a New York bank. The bank receives and can issue depository receipts to the American shareholders of the foreign firm.

Indirect means of participation include the purchase of shares in multinational firms or, more importantly, investing in mutual funds or closed-end investment companies specializing in foreign securities. An international fund offers the advantages of partial or comprehensive worldwide diversification and the removal of administrative and information-gathering problems.

The reader can readily observe that one who wishes to participate in foreign equities has many feasible alternatives.

KEY WORDS AND CONCEPTS

DISCUSSION QUESTIONS

1. Does an investor who achieves international diversification through foreign investments necessarily have to accept lower returns?
2. Why does Canada represent a relatively poor outlet for achieving risk reduction for U.S. investors? (Merely use your own judgment in answering this question.)
3. In discussing return potential in foreign markets, indicate why a number of foreign countries may have higher return possibilities than the United States.
4. According to researcher Bruno Solnik, how much larger would a pure U.S. portfolio have to be in relation to a well-diversified international portfolio to achieve the same risk-reduction benefits?
5. Examine Table 18–8 and indicate which South Asian country has firms with the highest price-to-book-value ratio and the second lowest dividend yield for 1993.
6. Explain how currency fluctuations affect the return on foreign investments.
7. Suggest two types of strategies to reduce or neutralize the impact of currency fluctuations on portfolio returns.
8. Suggest how foreign political risk may create a potential investment opportunity.
9. Are foreign markets likely to be more or less efficient than U.S. markets? What effect does this have on bid-ask spreads and the ability to absorb large transactions?
10. Explain why high debt ratios in Japan may not be as great a problem as one might first assume.
11. What are some of the key problems in investing directly in foreign securities?
12. Explain the concept of an ADR.
13. Why did Jacquillat and Solnik indicate that multinational firms may provide very little risk-reduction benefits in comparison with domestic firms?
14. Why might mutual funds be particularly beneficial in the international area?

PROBLEMS

Foreign currency effects

1. Assume you invest in the German equity market and have a 20 percent return (quoted in German marks).
   a. If during this period the mark appreciated by 10 percent against the dollar, what would be your actual return translated into U.S. dollars?
   b. If the mark declined by 15 percent against the dollar, what would your actual return be translated into dollars?
   c. Recompute the answer based on a 25 percent decline in the mark against the dollar.

Foreign currency effects

2. Assume you invest in the French equity market and have a 20 percent return (quoted in francs). However, during the course of your investment, the franc declines versus the dollar. By what percent could the franc decline relative to the dollar before all your gain is eliminated?

CFA MATERIAL

The following material contains a sample question and solution from a prior Level I CFA exam. While the terminology is slightly different from that in this text, you can still view the skills that are necessary for the CFA Exam.

CFA Exam Question

2. Unique risks are associated with international investing. Briefly describe *four* such risks. *(5 minutes)*

Solution: Question 2—Morning Section (5 points)

Four primary risks are:

1. *Currency fluctuations.* If the value of the investors' domestic currency strengthens after the purchase of foreign securities, the value of the investment declines.
2. *Availability of information.* Quality information about foreign companies may be less readily available to analysts than information about domestic companies. This results because of varying requirements for corporate disclosure, less exhaustive analysis conducted by the foreign financial community, and the use of accounting conventions that differ from those in the country of the investor.
3. *Liquidity.* Foreign equity issues may tend to be smaller (or larger) than those in the investor's country making the accumulation of substantial positions more (or less) difficult.
4. *Sovereign risks.* These risks include the potential for disruptive political, sociological, or psychological developments. Examples of political risk are the possibility of nationalization of local companies, expropriation of assets owned by foreign investors, punitive taxation, and restrictions on the withdrawal of capital.

Other unique risks that might be addressed are:

5. High transaction costs, including taxes.
6. Administrative cost/settlement problems.
7. Difficulty in assessing manager skill and high fee structure.

THE WALL STREET JOURNAL PROJECTS

1. There are many ADRs listed on the New York Stock Exchange in Section C of *The Wall Street Journal* under "New York Stock Exchange Composite Transactions." Find the closing price and dividend yield (%) for the ADRs representing six different countries:

Novo Nordisk (NVO)	Danish
Banco Santander (STD)	Spanish
Telephones de Mexico (TMX)	Mexican
Sony Corporation (SNE)	Japanese
Daimler–Benz (DIA)	German
Hanson PLC (HAN)	British

2. Section C of *The Wall Street Journal* carries a page on world markets.
   a. Using the Dow Jones World Stock Index listed under "World Markets," compare the 12-month percentage change of the American, European, and Asia/Pacific regions.
   b. Further compare the returns within the European sector. Which two countries have the highest returns, and which two countries have the lowest returns? How does this comparison contribute to the concept of diversification through international investing?

U.S. EQUITIES ONFLOPPY EXERCISES

Please use your U.S. Equities OnFloppy software and manual to complete the following exercises.

1. a. Using the list of foreign firms from Table 18–10, create a portfolio of 10 firms for each of the following countries: Australia, Canada, Japan, Mexico, Netherlands, and the United Kingdom. (If 10 firms are not listed for a particular country, use all that are listed.) Perhaps the best way of achieving this is to (1) find each firm using the Display a Stock option, (2) make a note of each firm's ticker symbol, (3) use the Portfolios option to enter the ticker symbols for the firms from each country, and (4) save each portfolio.
   b. Prepare a report on each portfolio that will show for each firm in the portfolio its price/earnings ratio, dividend yield, price/sales ratio, price/book ratio, institutional holding percentage, and closely held percentage. Analyze the report, and comment on any patterns you observe.
   c. Prepare a second report on each portfolio containing the dividend payout ratio, current ratio, long-term debt as a percentage of capital, ROR, ROA, and ROE for each firm. Analyze the report, and comment on any patterns you observe.
2. a. Use the Portfolio option to retrieve the portfolio of the stocks that make up the Dow Jones Industrial Index, and then prepare the same reports as described in problems 1*b* and 1*c* for this portfolio.
   b. Using the reports prepared earlier, compare the characteristics of the U.S. firms with those of the firms of the six countries specified earlier. Comment on your findings.

SELECTED REFERENCES

Risk and Return Considerations

Alexander, Gordon J.; Cheol S. Eun; and S. Janakiramanan. "International Listings and Stock Returns: Some Empirical Evidence." *Journal of Financial and Quantitative Analysis,* June 1988, pp. 135–52.

Bergstrom, Gary L. "A New Route to Higher Returns and Lower Risks." *Journal of Portfolio Management,* Fall 1975, pp. 30–38.

Bergstrom, Gary L.; John K. Koeneman; and Martin J. Siegel. "International Security Market." In *Readings in Financial Management,* ed. Frank J. Fabozzi. Homewood, IL: Richard D. Irwin, 1983.

Bostock, Paul, and Paul Woolley. "A New Way to Analyze International Equity Performance." *Financial Analysts Journal,* January–February 1991, pp. 32–38.

Ibbotson, Roger G.; Richard C. Carr; and Anthony W. Robinson. "International Equity and Bond Returns." *Financial Analysts Journal,* July–August 1982, pp. 61–83.

Ibbotson, Roger G., and Laurence B. Siegel. "The World Market Wealth Portfolio." *Journal of Portfolio Management,* Winter 1983, pp. 5–17.

Lessard, Donald R. "World, Country, and Industry Relationships in Equity Returns." *Financial Analysts Journal,* January–February 1976, pp. 32–38.

Logue, Dennis E. "An Experiment in International Diversification." *Journal of Portfolio Management,* Fall 1982, pp. 22–27.

Solnik, Bruno. "Why Not Diversify Internationally Rather than Domestically?" *Financial Analysts Journal,* July–August 1974, pp. 48–54.

Speidell, Lawrence S., and Ross Seppenfield. "Global Diversification in a Shrinking World." *Journal of Portfolio Management,* Fall 1992, pp. 57–67.

Emerging Markets

Barry, Christopher B., and John W. Peavy, III. "A Bibliography of Research on Emerging Capital Markets." Working Paper, Texas Christian University, 1994.

Divecha, Arjun; Jaime Drach; and Dan Stefek. "Emerging Markets: A Quantitative Perspective." *Journal of Portfolio Management,* Fall 1992, pp. 41–56.

Errunza, Vihang R., and Etienne Losq. "How Risky Are Emerging Markets? Myths and Perceptions versus Theory and Evidence." *Journal of Portfolio Management,* Fall 1987, pp. 62–67.

Mullin, John. "Emerging Equity Markets in the Global Economy." *FRBNY Quarterly Review,* Summer 1993, pp. 54–83.

Stone, Douglas. "The Emerging Markets and Strategic Asset Allocation." *Journal of Investing,* Summer 1992, pp. 40–45.

Currency Considerations

Chang, Jack, and Latha Shanker. "Hedging Effectiveness of Currency Options and Currency Futures." *Journal of Futures Markets,* Summer 1986, pp. 289–306.

Glen, Jack, and Philippe Jorion. "Currency Hedging for International Portfolios." *Journal of Finance,* December 1993, pp. 1865–86.

International Market Crash of 1987

Roll, Richard. "The International Crash of 1987." *Financial Analysts Journal,* September–October 1988, pp. 19–35.

19

Mutual Funds

Mutual funds have become a very important part of investing. Between 1983 and 1994, mutual fund shareholder accounts grew from 25 million to more than 90 million accounts. During this time, the total assets of this industry grew from slightly more than $290 billion in 1983 to more than $2.1 trillion by the beginning of 1994.

The concept of a mutual fund is best understood by an example. Suppose you and your friends are too busy to develop the expertise needed to manage your own assets. One of your neighbors, however, has studied investments and security markets extensively. He has also had years of hands-on experience as a trustee of his company's pension fund. You and your friends decide to pool your money and have this experienced investor act as your investment advisor. He will be compensated by receiving a small percentage of the average amount of assets under his management during the forthcoming year.

By common agreement, the pooled money is to be invested in the common stock of large, stable companies with the objective of capital appreciation and moderate dividend income; funds not so invested are to be placed in short-term T-bills to earn interest. Group members collectively contribute $100,000 and decide to issue shares in the fund at a rate of one share for each $10 contributed—a total of 10,000 shares. Since you put in $10,000, you receive 1,000 shares of the fund—or 10 percent of the fund's shares. Over the next few weeks, your investment advisor uses $90,000 to purchase common stock in a number of companies representing several different industries and puts $10,000 in T-bills. The portfolio looks like this:

Common stocks grouped by industry:

Computers:
- Hewlett-Packard
- IBM
- Digital Equipment

Financial services:
- American Express
- Chemical Bank
- Merrill Lynch
- Northwestern National Life Insurance Company

Consumer retail:
- Kmart
- Toys "Я" Us
- Dayton Hudson

Treasury bills:
- $10,000

Since you own 10 percent of this portfolio, you are entitled to 10 percent of all income paid out to shareholders and 10 percent of all realized capital gains or losses.

The initial value of the portfolio is $100,000, or $10 per share. Assume your investment manager picked some winning stocks, and the portfolio rises to $115,000. Now each share is worth $11.50.

Your group of investors has many characteristics of a mutual fund: ownership interest represented by shares, professional management, stated investment objectives, and a diversified portfolio of assets. A billion dollar mutual fund would operate with many of the same concepts and principles—only the magnitude of the operation would be thousands of times larger.

ADVANTAGES AND DISADVANTAGES OF MUTUAL FUNDS

Mutual funds offer an efficient way to diversify your investments. For many small investors, diversification may be difficult to achieve. The normal trading unit for listed stocks—the "round lot"—is 100 shares. If proper diversification required a portfolio of at least 10 different stocks, the investor should purchase 100 shares of each of them. If each stock had a market value of $30, cost would be (excluding commission) $30,000 ($30 × 100 × 10). That's a big bite for most individuals just to get started.

With a mutual fund, you are also buying the expertise of the fund management. In many cases, fund managers have a long history of investment experience and may be specialists in certain areas such as international securities, gold stocks, or municipal bonds. By entrusting your funds to capable hands, you are freeing your time for other pursuits. This may be particularly important to people such as doctors or lawyers who may be capable of earning $150 to $200 an hour in their normal practice but are novices in the market.

As will be demonstrated throughout the chapter, you have a multitude of funds from which to choose to satisfy your investment objectives. Thus, another advantage of mutual funds is that they can be used to buy not only stocks but also U.S. government bonds, corporate bonds, municipal securities, and so on. Also, they represent an efficient way to invest in foreign securities. With many of these advantages in mind, it is not surprising that mutual funds have enjoyed enormous growth in the last decade.

Having stated some of the advantages of mutual funds, let's look at the disadvantages. First, mutual funds, on average, do not outperform the market. That is to say, over long periods, they do no better than the Standard & Poor's 500 Stock Index, the Dow Jones Industrial Average, and so on. Nevertheless, they provide an efficient means for diversifying your portfolio. Also, a minority of funds have had exceptional returns over time (many of these have had exposure to international investments).

Some mutual funds can be expensive to purchase. However, this factor should not overly concern you because a high commission can often be avoided. As you read further into the chapter, you will become very proficient at identifying the absence or presence of a commission and whether it is justified.

An investor in mutual funds must also be sensitive to the excessive claims sometimes made by mutual fund salespeople. Often, potential returns to the investor are emphasized without detailing the offsetting risks. The fact that a fund made 20 to 25 percent last year in no way ensures such a return in the future. Although the Securities and Exchange Commission has begun clamping down on false or overly enthusiastic advertising practices by members of the industry, the buyer still needs to be cautious. We will also help develop your skills in measuring actual performance as we progress through the chapter.

A final potential drawback to mutual funds is actually a reverse view of an advantage. With more than 5,000 mutual funds from which to choose, an investor has as much of a problem in selecting a mutual fund as a stock. For example, there are approximately 1,500 stocks on the New York Stock Exchange, considerably less than the number of mutual funds in existence. Nevertheless, if you sharpen your goals and objectives, you will be able to focus on a handful of funds that truly meet your needs.

Having discussed the general nature of mutual funds and some of the potential advantages and disadvantages, we now examine the actual mechanics. In the remainder of

this chapter, we shall discuss closed-end versus open-end funds, load versus no-load funds, fund objectives, considerations in selecting a fund, and measuring the return on a fund. There is also a brief description of unit investment trusts (UITs) in Appendix 19A. UITs have some attributes similar to mutual funds.

CLOSED-END VERSUS OPEN-END FUNDS

There are basically two types of investment funds, the closed-end fund and the open-end fund. We shall briefly discuss the closed-end fund and then move on to the much more important type of arrangement, the open-end fund.

Actually, these terms refer to the manner in which shares are distributed and redeemed. A **closed-end fund** has a fixed number of shares, and purchasers and sellers of shares must trade with each other. You cannot buy the shares directly from the fund (except at the inception of the fund) because of the limitation on shares outstanding. Furthermore, the fund does not stand ready to buy the shares back from you.

As we shall eventually see, an open-end fund represents exactly the opposite concept. The **open-end fund** stands ready at all times to sell you new shares or buy back your old shares. Having made this distinction, let's stay with the closed-end fund for now. The shares of closed-end funds trade on security exchanges or over-the-counter just as any other stock might. Instead of the firm being involved in the manufacturing of automobiles or the discovery of new drugs, it is involved in the investment and management of a security portfolio. An example of a closed-end fund that trades on a security exchange is shown in Table 19–1 on page 542. Note the Royce Value Trust Fund, a closed-end fund specializing in equities, is presented the same as any other common stock, such as Royal Dutch Petroleum shown directly above it. If you wish to buy or sell shares in the Royce Value Trust Fund, you call your broker and place your order.

One of the most important considerations in purchasing a closed-end fund is whether it is trading at a discount or premium from net asset value. First, let's look at the formula for net asset value.

$$\text{Net asset value (NAV)} = \frac{\text{Total value of securities} - \text{Liabilities}}{\text{Shares outstanding}} \qquad (19\text{–}1)$$

The **net asset value (NAV)** is equal to the current value of the securities owned by the fund minus any liabilities divided by the number of shares outstanding. For example, assume a fund has securities worth \$140 million, liabilities of \$5 million, and 10 million shares outstanding. The NAV is \$13.50:

$$\text{NAV} = \frac{\$140 \text{ million} - \$5 \text{ million}}{10 \text{ million shares}} = \frac{\$135 \text{ million}}{10 \text{ million}} = \$13.50$$

The NAV is computed at the end of each day for a fund.

Intuitively, one would expect a closed-end fund to sell at its net asset value, but that is not the case. Many funds trade at a discount from NAV because they have a poor record of prior performance, are heavily invested in an unpopular industry, or are thinly traded (illiquid). A few trade at a premium because of the known quality of their management, the nature of their investments, or the fact they have holdings in nonpublicly traded

TABLE 19–1 A Closed-End Fund Quote on the New York Stock Exchange

	52 Weeks Hi	Lo	Stock	Sym	Div	Yld %	PE	Vol 100s	Hi	Lo	Close	Net Chg
	35	26	Repsol	REP	.92e	3.4	...	92643	27¼	27	27¼	...
	15⅜	7¼	♣RepGypsum	RGC	.24f	2.3	12	106	10⅜	10	10¼	...
	52¼	41⅞	RepNY	RNB	1.32	2.9	8	507	46⅛	45¼	45¾	+ ½
	62¼	48¾	RepNY pf		3.38	6.7	...	3	50⅝	50¼	50⅝	+ ⅛
	26⅞	22¼	RepNY pfC		1.94	8.5	...	10	22¾	22¾	22¾	...
n	25	20½	RepNY pfD		.92e	4.4	...	164	21⅛	21	21⅛	– ⅛
	30	9½	ResouMtg	RMR	1.92	17.9	4	460	10⅞	10⅝	10¾	+ ⅛
	24½	13⅞	Revco	RXR		...	28	843	23¾	23	23	– ⅝
	23¼	14⅜	RexStores	RSC		...	13	10	16⅜	16¼	16⅜	+ ⅛
	18	2⅞	♣Rexene	RXN		...	cc	590	12¼	11¾	12¼	+ ⅜
s	26⅝	19¾	Reyn&Reyn	REY	.40f	1.7	16	1338	25⅛	23⅞	24	–1
	59⅜	40⅜	ReynMetl	RLM	1.00	2.0	dd	2247	49⅜	48¾	49⅛	+ ⅛
n	55½	44⅝	Reyn pf prides		3.31	6.8	...	52	48½	48⅜	48½	+ ⅛
	20¼	**8¼**	**Rhodes**	**RHD**		...	**10**	**314**	**12**	**11⅜**	**11⅜**	**–1⅛**
	25	20	RhonPLnc prA		2.03	9.9	...	165	20½	20⅛	20½	– ¼
	42⅝	30½	RhonPlRorer	RPR	1.12	3.1	17	213	36¾	36¼	36½	...
	27⅝	20⅞	RhonePoulnc	RP		...	...	318	23⅛	22⅞	22⅞	– ¼
	21½	13⅜	RhonPoulnc A		1.45e	10.2	...	4	14¼	14¼	14¼	+ ½
n	15¾	10	RightChoice A	RIT		...	...	246	14½	14	14¼	+ ¼
	24	15¾	♣RiteAid	RAD	.60	2.6	cc	2892	23⅜	23	23¼	– ⅛
	4 11/16	2 13/16	♣Roadmstr	RDM		...	13	646	3⅝	3½	3½	– ⅛
s	26¾	12⅝	RobtHalfInt	RHI		...	29	429	24	23⅛	23¼	– ¾
	4	2⅜	RobrtsonCeco	RHH		...	dd	2	3¼	3¼	3¼	...
	26½	19¾	RochG&E	RGS	1.80f	8.6	12	730	21	20⅞	21	+ ⅛
	8⅜	3¾	RockeCtr	RCP	.60	12.0	8	709	5⅛	5	5	...
	44⅛	33½	Rockwell	ROK	1.08	3.0	12	1413	35⅝	35	35½	– ¼
	7⅞	3⅝	RodmanRen	RR		...	12	62	3⅞	3¾	3⅞	...
	68½	53¼	RohmHaas	ROH	1.48	2.6	16	870	57	56⅜	56½	– ⅝
	12⅛	8	Rohr	RHR		...	74	658	10⅜	10¼	10⅜	...
	6⅜	4	RollinsEnvr	REN		...	dd	760	4⅞	4⅝	4⅞	– ⅛
	30¾	22⅛	RollinsInc	ROL	.50	2.2	17	311	23	22½	23	– ⅛
s	14⅜	10⅞	RollinsLeas	RLC	.16	1.4	13	440	11⅝	11⅜	11½	– ⅜
n	34¼	19¾	RougeSteel A	ROU	.06e	.2	...	645	29	28⅝	28⅝	– ¼
	9¼	5¾	RowanCos	RDC		...	dd	1238	6⅜	6⅛	6¼	...
s	12¾	4⅝	RoweFurn	ROW	.08	1.6	11	71	5⅛	5	5⅛	+ ⅛
	6¼	3¼	RoylAppl	RAM		...	23	349	3⅝	3½	3⅝	+ ⅛
	27⅝	24⅞	RoylBkScot A		2.81	10.9	...	31	25⅞	25⅝	25¾	– ¼
	29¼	24¾	RoylBkScot B	RBSB	2.80	10.7	...	44	26½	26¼	26¼	...
	27⅛	21¾	RoylBkScot C		2.38	10.6	...	286	22⅞	22½	22 35/64	– ⅛
n	24¾	21¾	RoylBkScot cap A		2.13	9.4	...	18	23	22¾	22¾	– ⅛
	30½	23⅝	♣RoylCaribn	RCL	.44	1.6	13	407	28½	27⅝	27⅝	– ⅞
	116¾	96⅞	RoylDutchP	RD	4.83e	4.5	19	3048	108⅛	107½	108⅛	+ ⅜
	13⅜	10⅞	RoyceValTr	RVT	1.05e	9.2	...	292	11⅜	11⅛	11⅜	+ ⅜
	35¾	23⅝	Rubbermaid	RBD	.50f	1.7	21	2837	28¾	28⅜	28¾	...
	23⅛	15⅝	Ruddick	RDK	.28a	1.5	14	49	19⅛	18¾	18⅞	– ¼
	15⅝	12¾	RussBerr	RUS	.60	4.4	dd	144	13⅞	13½	13¾	...
	32⅝	24	Russell	RML	.48f	1.5	17	308	31¼	30⅞	31⅛	– ¼
	24½	10¾	RustIntl	RST		...	14	122	11¼	11	11¼	+ ⅛
	28	19⅞	♣RyderSys	R	.60	2.7	12	1351	22½	21¾	22½	+ ½
	22½	17⅝	Rykoff	RYK	.04e	.2	7	88	20⅜	20⅜	20⅜	...
	25⅝	12⅞	♣RylandGp	RYL	.60	4.0	9	58	15	14¾	15	...
	4½	**1⅝**	**Rymer**	**RYR**		...	**5**	**64**	**3¼**	**3**	**3**	**– ¼**

Source: *The Wall Street Journal,* January 4, 1995, p. C6. Reprinted by permission of *The Wall Street Journal,* © 1995 by Dow Jones & Company, Inc. All Rights Reserved Worldwide.

securities that are believed to be undervalued on their books. Note in Table 19–2 the predominance of common stock funds trading at discounts from NAV in December 1994 (last column). This has normally been the case over the last decade. Some researchers even use the fact that closed-end funds do not sell for what they are worth (in terms of their holdings) as evidence that the market is something less than truly efficient in valuing securities (see the accompanying box on naive investors).

How Naive Can Investors Be?

It is assumed that the stock market is reasonably efficient; that is, information is quickly absorbed by investors and impounded into the value of securities. An associated feature of market efficiency is that stocks tend to be correctly priced at any point in time. Forget it! While IBM and General Motors might be correctly priced, such is not the case with closed-end investment companies. Clearly, the true value per share of a closed-end investment company is the total current value of the stock holdings (less any liabilities) divided by the number of shares outstanding. If a fund has a net asset value of $10, but is selling at a 15 percent discount for $8.50, all the fund management has to do is liquidate the assets of the fund and give each stockholder $10 per share. Forget about whether the fund is popular or not; its assets still have an immediate liquidation value of $10.

It is indeed surprising that 75 to 80 percent of closed-end funds sell at a discount from actual value (normally 10 to 20 percent below). The discount tends to be well in excess of the relatively small costs to liquidate the fund or simply convert it into an open-end fund (where it immediately trades at full net asset value).

Even more surprising is the fact that closed-end funds are almost always initially issued at a premium above net asset value. Then, within the first couple of weeks of trading, they slip to a discount. Why would anyone buy a fund with such a high probability of a loss? To directly quote *Forbes* magazine, "How Dumb Can Investors Be?"* If an investor wants to invest in a closed-end fund, why not buy an existing one at a discount and hope for a liquidation? Why pay the initial premium and then wait to take a beating?

The most plausible answer, according to *Forbes* and other sources, is that this is the least sophisticated part of the investment community. Naive investors engage in a mass misunderstanding about their own self-interest when they buy into an initial distribution of a closed-end fund. Rest assured there are very few institutional investors or enlightened finance majors playing this game.

*Mark Fadiman, "Muni Mystery," *Forbes,* September 3, 1990, p. 174.

TABLE 19–2 Premiums or Discounts from Net Asset Value

Fund Name	Stock Exch	NAV	Market Price	Prem /Disc	52 week Market Return
Friday, December 30, 1994					
General Equity Funds					
Adams Express	N	17.97	15 5/8	−13.0	−3.6
Alliance All-Mkt	N	18.90	16 1/8	−14.7	N/A
Baker Fentress	N	17.50	13 3/4	−21.4	−7.1
Bergstrom Cap -ag	A	94.51	84 7/8	−10.2	−4.0
Blue Chip Value	N	6.99	6 1/8	−12.4	−12.7
Central Secs	A	16.82	15 3/4	−6.4	12.0
Charles Allmon	N	9.95	8 1/2	−14.6	−11.4
Engex	A	9.15	6 7/8	−24.9	−35.3
Equus II	A	19.24	12 7/8	−33.1	−9.5
Gabelli Equity	N	9.46	9 5/8	+1.7	−5.5
General American	N	22.27	19	−14.7	−7.6
Inefficient Mkt	A	11.78	9 1/2	−19.4	−8.2
Jundt Growth	N	14.95	13 5/8	−8.9	4.3
Liberty All-Star	N	9.27	8 3/8	−9.7	−15.3
Morgan FunShares -c	O	7.36	7	−4.9	N/A
Morgan Gr Sm Cap	N	10.21	8 7/8	−13.1	−7.1
NAIC Growth -ac	C	11.52	9 3/8	−18.6	−0.4
Royce Value	N	12.40	11	−11.3	−6.4
Salomon SBF	N	12.87	10 5/8	−17.4	−3.8
Source Capital	N	38.52	37	−3.9	−6.1
Spectra	O	13.61	11	−19.2	4.0
Tri-Continental	N	23.70	19 7/8	−16.1	−5.0
Z-Seven	O	16.68	16 1/2	−1.1	−9.6
Zweig	N	10.33	10 3/8	+0.4	−16.3

Source: *Barron's,* January 2, 1995, p. 75. Reprinted by permission of *Barron's.* © 1995 by Dow Jones & Company, Inc. All Rights Reserved Worldwide.

INVESTING IN OPEN-END FUNDS

As previously indicated, an open-end fund stands ready at all times to sell new shares or buy back old shares from investors at net asset value. Over 95 percent of the investment funds in the United States are open-ended. Actually, the term *mutual fund* applies specifically to *open-end* investment companies, although closed-end funds are sometimes loosely labeled as mutual funds as well. We shall be careful to make the distinction where appropriate.

Transactions with open-end funds are made at the net asset value as described in Formula 19–1 (though there may be an added commission). If the fund has 100 million shares outstanding at an NAV of $10 per share ($1 billion) and sells 20 million more shares at $10 per share, the new funds ($200 million) are redeployed in investments worth $200 million, and the NAV remains unchanged. The only factor that changes the NAV is the up and down movement of the securities in the fund's portfolio. The primary distinctions between closed-end and open-end funds are presented in Table 19–3. All of our subsequent discussion will be about open-end (mutual) funds. These include such established names as Fidelity, Dreyfus, Vanguard, IDS, T. Rowe Price, and Templeton.

Load versus No-Load Funds

Some funds have established selling agreements with stockbrokers, financial planners, insurance agents, and others licensed to sell securities. These selling agents receive a commission for selling the funds. The funds are termed **load funds** because there is a commission associated with the purchase of the fund shares. The commission may run as high as 7.25 percent.

Several stock funds are referred to as **low-load funds** because their sales charges are 2 to 3 percent instead of 7.25 percent. In recent years, a number of funds have also introduced a back-end load provision. While there may or may not be a front-end load in buying such a fund, there is an exit fee in selling a fund with a **back-end load** provision. The fee may be 3 to 5 percent of the selling price, but typically declines with the passage of time.

No-Load Funds

No-load funds do not charge commissions and are sold directly by the investment company through advertisements, prospectuses, and 800-number telephone orders. As of 1994, no-load funds made up about 32 percent of all mutual fund assets and accounted for

TABLE 19–3 Distinction between Closed-End and Open-End Funds

	Method of Purchase	Number of Shares Outstanding	Shares Traded at Net Asset Value
Closed-end fund	Stock exchange or over-the-counter	Fixed	No—there may be a discount or premium from NAV; there will be a commission
Open-end fund	Direct from fund or fund salesperson	Fluctuates	Yes—but there may be a commission

36 percent of new sales. Some wonder how no-load funds justify their existence since they charge no commission to purchase their shares. The answer is because of the fee they charge to manage the assets in the fund. This management fee plus expenses normally average .75 to 1.25 percent. On a billion dollar fund, this represents approximately $10 million a year and can be more than adequate to compensate the fund managers. It should also be pointed out that load funds also have similar management fees.

The question then becomes, why pay the load (commission)? Studies indicate there is no significant statistical difference in the investment performance of load and no-load funds. Consequently, most astute investors shop around for a no-load fund to fit their needs rather than pay a commission. This statement is not intended to dismiss the possibility that apprehensive or uncomfortable investors may benefit from the consultation and advice of a competent mutual fund salesman or financial advisor, and thus receive a commensurate service from paying the commission. Also, some specialized funds may exist only in the form of load funds. However, whenever possible, investors are better off using the commission toward the purchase of new shares rather than the payment of a sales fee.

If you invest $1,000 in a mutual fund and pay a 7.25 percent commission, only 92.75 percent will go toward purchasing your shares. A $1,000 investment will immediately translate into a holding of $927.50. This means the fund must go up by $72.50 or 7.82 percent, just for you to break even:

$$\frac{\$72.50}{\$927.50} = 7.82 \text{ percent}$$

With these thoughts in mind, you should become proficient in recognizing funds that are charging a load and those that are not. To accomplish this goal, observe Table 19–4 on page 546, which is an excerpt on mutual fund quotations from *The Wall Street Journal.*

The bold letters in the table represent the name of the mutual fund sponsor. For example, AARP (the second listed group) has six different mutual funds dedicated to serving diverse needs ranging from Capital Growth (CaGr) to Tax-Free Bonds (TXFBd). The table has three primary columns that allow us to determine whether a fund is a load or a no-load. As examples of load funds, observe the AAL Mutual Funds at the top of the table or the ABT group below the AARP group. In each case, the NAV (net asset value) is different from the offer price. This means a commission must be paid. For example, for the first ABT group (Emrg), the NAV is $13.32, and the offer price is $13.98. This means the fund has a net asset value of $13.32 per share but is offered to the public for $13.98. The difference between $13.32 and $13.98 of $.66 represents the commission:

Offer price	$13.98
NAV (net asset value)	13.32
Commission	$ 0.66

In this case, the commission represents 4.72 percent of the offer price ($0.66/$13.98 = 4.72%).[1] You will buy a fund valued at $13.32 for $13.98 because of the sales charge.

Contrast this with no-load funds where you buy and sell at the same price. You can identify no-load funds by the symbol NL under the offer price column in Table 19–4.

[1] It also represents 4.95 percent of the net asset value ($0.66/$13.32).

MUTUAL FUND QUOTATIONS

Wednesday, December 28, 1994

Ranges for investment companies, with daily price data supplied by the National Association of Securities Dealers and performance and cost calculations by Lipper Analytical Services Inc. The NASD requires a mutual fund to have at least 1,000 shareholders or net assets of $25 million before being listed. Detailed explanatory notes appear elsewhere on this page.

	Inv. Obj.	NAV	Offer Price	NAV Chg.	– Total Return – YTD	26 wks	4 yrs	R
AAL Mutual:								
Bond p	BIN	9.29	9.75	−0.01	−4.7	−0.8	+6.4	D
CaGr p	GRO	14.80	15.54	−0.05	−1.0	+4.0	+9.8	D
MuBd p	GLM	10.18	10.69	+0.01	−5.7	−1.9	+6.1	D
SmCoStk p	MID	10.22	10.73	−0.01	−5.9	+15.3	NS	..
Util p	SEC	9.20	9.66	+0.02	NS	−1.7	NS	..
AARP Invst:								
BalS&B	S&B	14.31v	NL	−0.22	NS	+1.2	NS	..
CaGr	GRO	30.09v	NL	−0.82	−10.2	+2.4	+11.5	C
GiniM	MTG	14.57	NL	−0.01	−1.7	+0.6	+6.4	C
GthInc	G&I	31.68v	NL	−1.59	+2.9	+2.0	+13.4	B
HQ Bd	BND	14.98	NL	−0.02	−4.2	−0.1	+7.1	D
TxFBd	ISM	16.54	NL	+0.01	−6.3	−2.4	+6.5	B
ABT Funds:								
Emrg p	CAP	13.32	13.98	−0.09	−10.1	+5.0	+21.2	A
FL HI	MFL	9.60	10.08	...	−4.5k	−2.6k	NS	..
FL TF	MFL	10.37	10.89	+0.01	−4.7	−1.5	+7.0	B
GthIn p	G&I	10.28	10.79	−0.03	−4.2	+0.6	+7.7	E
UtilIn p	SEC	10.65	11.18	+0.02	−11.9	−1.2	+5.7	E
AHA Funds:								
Balan	S&B	11.20	NL	−0.03	−1.5	+1.2	+10.8	C
Full	BND	9.28	NL	−0.01	−3.2	+0.2	+7.6	C
Lim	BST	9.90	NL	−0.01	+0.7	+0.7	+5.9	C
AIM Funds:								
Agrsv p	SML	28.16	29.80	−0.11	+15.2	+20.0	+32.3	A
BalB t	S&B	14.61	14.61	−0.05	−6.3	−0.5	NS	..
Chart p	G&I	8.12	8.59	−0.04	−4.5	−0.7	+10.0	D
Const p	MID	17.04	18.03	−0.08	+0.4	+10.2	+23.7	A
BalA p	S&B	14.61	15.34	−0.04	−5.5	−0.1	+14.6	A
GlAgGrA	WOR	9.99	10.49	+0.04	NS	NS	NS	..
GlAgGrB	WOR	9.98	9.98	+0.04	NS	NS	NS	..
GoScA p	MTG	9.01	9.46	...	−3.3k	−0.2k	+5.7k	D
GovSecB	MTG	9.00	9.00	...	−4.1k	−0.8k	NS	..
GrthA p	GRO	10.27	10.87	−0.04	−5.5	+7.6	+7.8	E
GrthB t	GRO	10.15	10.15	−0.05	−6.4	+6.9	NS	..
HYldA p	BHI	8.94	9.39	+0.01	−1.8k	−2.2k	+18.4k	B
HYldB t	BHI	8.93	8.93	...	−2.6k	−2.7k	NS	..
IncoA p	BND	7.23	7.59	+0.01	−7.3k	+0.5k	+7.9k	C
IntlE p	ITL	12.16	12.87	+0.10	−3.0	+0.9	NS	..
LimM p	BST	9.77	9.87	−0.01	+0.7	+0.6	+5.3	D
MuniA p	GLM	7.78	8.17	...	−3.8k	−1.3k	+7.4k	A
Sumit	GRO	8.88	NA	−0.05	−3.4	+5.4	+12.2	C
TeCt p	SSM	10.33	10.85	...	−3.5k	−0.9k	+7.1k	A
TF Int	IDM	10.38	10.48	+0.01	−1.4k	−0.5k	+6.3k	B
UtilA p	SEC	11.89	12.58	...	−11.3k	+0.4k	+7.4k	D
UtilB t	SEC	11.89	11.89	...	−12.0k	0.0k	NS	..
ValuA p	GRO	21.05	22.28	−0.06	+2.8	+6.0	+19.7	A
ValuB t	GRO	21.04	21.04	−0.06	+2.0	+5.6	NS	..
Weing p	GRO	15.17	16.05	−0.05	−0.6	+6.3	+10.2	D
AMCORE Vintage Fds:								

	Inv. Obj.	NAV	Offer Price	NAV Chg.	– Total Return – YTD	26 wks	4 yrs	R
GvTIA p	BIN	8.00	8.40	−0.01	−4.0	−0.3	NS	..
GvTIB t	BIN	8.00	8.00	−0.01	−4.8	−0.8	NS	..
GvTIC t	BIN	8.00	8.00	−0.01	−4.8	−0.8	NS	..
GvT97 p	BND	13.12	13.53	...	−2.8	−0.2	+7.2	D
HarbA p	S&B	13.20	14.01	−0.02	−6.6	−0.8	+9.4	D
HarbB t	S&B	13.15	13.15	−0.03	−7.5	−1.3	NS	..
HiYldA p	BHI	5.87	6.16	...	−3.7	−3.0	+17.4	C
HiYldB t	BHI	5.88	5.88	...	−4.4	−3.4	NS	..
MunBA p	GLM	9.62	10.10	...	−3.5	−1.3	+6.9	B
MunBB t	GLM	9.62	9.62	...	−4.2	−1.7	NS	..
PaceA p	GRO	9.77	10.37	−0.04	−3.9	+0.8	+10.2	D
PaceB t	GRO	9.73	9.73	−0.05	−4.7	+0.3	NS	..
ReEstA p	SEC	9.26	9.72	...	NS	−0.9	NS	..
ReEstB t	SEC	9.25	9.25	...	NS	−1.2	NS	..
ReEstC t	SEC	9.26	9.26	...	NS	−1.1	NS	..
TxE IA p	ISM	10.70	11.23	+0.01	−3.4	−1.2	+5.6	D
TxE IB t	ISM	10.69	10.69	...	−4.1	−1.6	NS	..
TXMSA p	SSM	9.45	9.92	...	−3.7	−1.2	NS	..
TEHYA p	HYM	10.56	11.09	+0.01	+0.1	+0.7	+7.4	B
TEHYB t	HYM	10.55	10.55	+0.01	−0.7	+0.3	NS	..
UtilA p	SEC	8.36	8.78	−0.01	−6.8	+0.6	NS	..
UtilB t	SEC	8.36	8.36	−0.01	−7.4	+0.3	NS	..
American Funds:								
A Bal p	S&B	12.02	12.75	−0.01	+0.5	+2.4	+11.3	B
Amcp p	GRO	11.67	12.38	−0.04	−0.6	+3.8	+12.9	B
AMutl p	G&I	20.15	21.38	−0.06	+0.5	+1.4	+10.9	D
Bond p	BND	12.69	13.32	...	−5.0	−1.1	+10.0	A
CapIB p	EQI	31.78	33.72	+0.10	−2.1	+3.2	+12.2	C
CapW p	WBD	15.18	15.94	+0.10	−1.0	+4.2	+7.9	A
CapWGr p	WOR	17.48	18.55	+0.09	+1.3	+4.8	NS	..
Eupac p	ITL	21.09	22.38	+0.18	+0.9	+2.7	+13.8	A
FdInv p	G&I	17.45	18.51	−0.07	+1.0	+2.4	+14.4	A
Govt p	MTG	12.69	13.32	−0.01	−4.7	−0.5	+6.7	B
Gwth p	GRO	25.40	26.95	−0.09	−0.5	+4.8	+13.6	B
HiInMuni	HYM	14.05	14.75	...	NS	NS	NS	..
HI Tr p	BHI	13.08v	13.73	−0.17	−6.1	−4.2	+13.6	E
Inco p	EQI	13.15	13.95	−0.31	NE	NE	NE	..
IntBd p	BIN	12.93	13.57	−0.01	−2.9	−0.3	+6.8	C
ICA p	G&I	17.68	18.76	−0.04	+0.2	+1.9	+11.1	C
LtdTEBd p	IDM	13.58	14.26	...	−2.9	−1.1	NS	..
NEco p	GRO	13.67	14.50	+0.02	−8.6	+1.3	+16.0	A
N Per p	WOR	14.37	15.25	+0.08	+3.0	+5.0	+13.8	B
SmCp p	WOR	21.16	22.45	+0.05	−4.0	+2.9	+15.7	A
TxEx p	GLM	11.11	11.66	...	−4.9	−1.7	+6.5	C
TECA p	MCA	14.60	15.33	+0.01	−5.1	−2.2	+6.3	B
TEMd p	SSM	14.33	15.04	+0.01	−4.9	−1.6	+5.7	E
TEVA p	SSM	14.79	15.53	...	−4.9	−1.7	+6.1	D
Wsh p	G&I	16.91	17.94	−0.06	+0.9	+2.2	+11.5	C
A GthFd	GRO	7.33	7.78	...	−3.7	−2.9	+13.8	B
A Heritg	CAP	0.83	NL	−0.01	−36.9	−13.0	+20.8	A
A HeritgGr	GRO	3.41	NL	−0.01	NS	+14.4	NS	..
Amer Natl Funds:								
Grth	GRO	3.82	4.05	−0.03	+4.7	+5.2	+11.2	C
Inco	EQI	18.88	20.03	−0.05	−0.7	+1.1	+10.1	D
Triflex	S&B	14.31	15.18	−0.06	+1.4	+1.7	+8.6	D
API Gr fp	CAP	12.32	12.32	+0.07	−4.0	+4.4	+14.4	C
Am Perform:								
AggGro	SML	12.17	12.68	...	−6.5	+9.8	NS	..
Bond	BND	8.81	9.18	−0.01	−3.6	−0.6	+6.9	E
Equity	GRO	10.10	10.52	−0.01	−1.2	+3.4	+7.6	E

	Inv. Obj.	NAV	Offer Price	NAV Chg.	– Total Return – YTD	26 wks	4 yrs	R
GroInc	G&I	12.52	13.11	−0.03	−0.7	+0.6	+11.2	C
IntlEqInv	ITL	9.89	10.36	...	NS	−1.0	NS	..
MoTF	SSM	10.61	11.11	...	−5.7	−2.2	+6.3	C
US Gov	MTG	10.09	10.57	−0.03	−2.6	+0.3	+6.5	B
ArielApp p	MID	20.69	NL	−0.10	−9.6	−4.7	+10.2	E
ArielGro p	SML	28.35	NL	+0.06	−6.1	+1.0	+11.3	E
Amstng	GRO	8.50	NL	−0.01	+5.1	+10.9	+11.4	C
Arrow Funds:								
Equity	GRO	9.64	9.99	−0.04	−2.0	+1.9	NS	..
FxdIncm	BND	9.23	9.56	−0.03	−6.4	−0.9	NS	..
Muni	GLM	9.63	9.98	+0.01	−4.4	−1.6	NS	..
AtlantaGr p	SEC	10.38	10.78	−0.03	−5.0	+0.3	NS	..
Atlas Funds:								
CaInsA	IDM	9.65	9.95	+0.01	−4.0	−1.4	NS	..
CaMuniA	MCA	10.31	10.63	...	−5.9	−2.4	+6.7	A
GvtScA	MTG	9.56	9.86	−0.01	−3.3	−0.2	+6.7	B
GroIncA	G&I	13.57	13.99	−0.08	−2.3	+3.0	+11.0	D
NaMuniA	GLM	10.40	10.72	...	−5.6	−1.9	+7.2	A
AVESTA Trust:								
Balanced	S&B	17.18	17.18	−0.03	−2.2	+2.0	+8.0	E
EqGro	GRO	18.44	18.44	−0.04	−0.9	+3.4	+9.4	E
EqIncm	EQI	17.95	17.95	−0.05	−3.1	+0.6	+8.9	D
Income	BND	15.42	15.42	−0.03	−4.3	−0.1	+6.0	E
BB&T:								
BalT	S&B	9.62	NL	−0.02	−1.6	+0.5	NS	..
GroIncT	G&I	10.97	NL	−0.05	−0.5	+1.4	NS	..
IntGovT	BIN	9.18	NL	−0.01	−4.0	−0.6	NS	..
NCIntT	IDM	9.63	NL	...	−2.8	−0.7	NS	..
SIGovT	BST	9.46	NL	−0.01	−2.0	−0.1	NS	..
BEA Funds:								
EmgMktEq	ITL	20.01	20.01	+0.40	−21.3	−3.9	NS	..
IntlEq	ITL	18.31	18.31	+0.14	−9.3	−4.8	NS	..
MuniBd	GLM	14.42	14.42	...	NS	NA	NS	..
ShDurClt	BST	4.89	4.89	...	+2.7	+2.2	NS	..
ShDurInv	BST	4.89	4.89	...	+2.8	+2.1	NS	..
StgcFxIn	BHI	15.16	15.16	−0.05	−8.2	−1.7	NS	..
USCFxIn	BND	14.34	14.34	−0.01	NS	−0.9	NS	..
BFMShDu	BST	9.59	9.59	...	+1.5	+1.3	NS	..
BJB GIncA p	WBD	10.88	11.33	−0.03	−7.3	−1.0	NS	..
BJB IEqA p	ITL	10.28	10.71	+0.02	−33.8	−6.1	NS	..
BT:								
CapApp	GRO	11.99	NL	−0.05	+2.3	+12.6	NS	..
InstAstMg	S&B	9.42	NL	−0.03	−3.1	+1.0	NS	..
InstEqIx	G&I	10.59	NL	−0.04	+1.7	+4.1	NS	..
InvEqApp	MID	10.06	NL	−0.03	+2.7	+12.8	NS	..
InvEqIx	G&I	10.57	NL	−0.04	+1.4	+3.9	NS	..
InvIntlEq	ITL	13.37v	NL	−0.24	+4.1	+2.9	NS	..
InvIntTxf	IDM	9.72	NL	...	−3.9	−1.4	NS	..
InvLaAmEq	ITL	10.51	NL	+0.13	−14.3	−3.6	NS	..
InvLGvt	...	9.61	NL	...	NA	NA	NA	..
InvUtil	SEC	9.07x	NL	−0.14	−12.0	−1.5	NS	..
LcyMRg	S&B	9.18	NL	−0.01	−3.3	+0.6	NS	..
PacBasEq	ITL	10.23	NL	−0.02	−16.6	−2.3	NS	..
SmCap	SML	12.22	NL	−0.01	+16.8	+23.3	NS	..
Babson Group:								
Bond L	BND	1.47	NL	...	−3.4	−0.4	+7.5	D
Bond S	BST	9.43	NL	...	−2.1	+0.2	+6.9	A
Enterp2	SML	15.90	NL	+0.10	−9.0	−3.6	NS	..
Enterp	SML	15.00	NL	−0.02	+1.4	+2.2	+20.7	B
Gwth	GRO	11.96	NL	−0.07	−0.6	+1.1	+10.9	D
Intl	ITL	15.31	NL	+0.03	+0.4	−2.3	+11.2	B

Source: *The Wall Street Journal*, December 29, 1994, p. C17. Reprinted by permission of *The Wall Street Journal*,

TABLE 19–5

MUTUAL FUND QUOTATIONS

What These Listings Provide...

		NASD DATA			LIPPER ANALYTICAL DATA			
Monday	Inv. Obj.	NAV	Offer Price	NAV Chg.	%Ret YTD	Max Initl Chrg.	Total Exp Ratio	..
Tuesday	Inv. Obj.	NAV	Offer Price	NAV Chg.	Total Return YTD	4 wk	1 yr	Rank
WEDNESDAY	**Inv. Obj.**	**NAV**	**Offer Price**	**NAV Chg.**	**Total Return YTD**	**13 wk**	**3 yr***	**Rank**
Thursday	Inv. Obj.	NAV	Offer Price	NAV Chg.	Total Return YTD	26 wk	4 yr*	Rank
Friday	Inv. Obj.	NAV	Offer Price	NAV Chg.	Total Return YTD	39 wk	5 yr*	Rank

* Annualized

EXPLANATORY NOTES

Mutual fund data are supplied by two organizations. The daily Net Asset Value (NAV), Offer Price and Net Change calculations are supplied by the National Association of Securities Dealers (NASD) through Nasdaq, its automated quotation system. Performance and cost data are supplied by Lipper Analytical Services Inc.

Daily price data are entered into Nasdaq by the fund, its management company or agent. Performance and cost calculations are percentages provided by Lipper Analytical Services, based on prospectuses filed with the Securities and Exchange Commission, fund reports, financial reporting services and other sources believed to be authoritative, accurate and timely. Though verified, the data cannot be guaranteed by Lipper or its data sources and should be double-checked with the funds before making any investment decisions.

Performance calculations, as percentages, assuming reinvestment of all distributions, and after all asset based charges have been deducted. Asset based charges include advisory fees, other non-advisory fees and distribution expenses (12b-1). Figures are without regard to sales, deferred sales or redemption charges.

INVESTMENT OBJECTIVE (Inv. Obj.) – Based on stated investment goals outlined in the prospectus. The Journal assembled 27 groups based on classifications used by Lipper Analytical in the daily Mutual Fund Scorecard and other calculations. A detailed breakdown of classifications appears at the bottom of this page.

NET ASSET VALUE (NAV) – Per share value prepared by the fund, based on closing quotes unless noted, and supplied to the NASD by 5:30 p.m. Eastern time.

OFFER PRICE – Net asset value plus sales commission, if any.

NAV CHG. – Gain or loss, based on the previous NAV quotation.

TOTAL RETURN – Performance calculations, as percentages, assuming reinvestment of all distributions. Sales charges aren't reflected. Percentages are annualized for periods greater than one year. For funds declaring dividends daily, calculations are based on the most current data supplied by the fund within publication deadlines. A YEAR TO DATE (YTD) change is listed daily, with results ranging from 4 weeks to 5 years offered throughout the week. See chart on this page for specific schedule.

MAXIMUM INITIAL SALES COMMISSION (Max Initl Chrg) – Based on prospectus; the sales charge may be modified or suspended temporarily by the fund, but any percentage change requires formal notification to the shareholders.

TOTAL EXPENSE RATIO (Total Exp Ratio) – Shown as a percentage and based on the fund's annual report, the ratio is total operating expenses for the fiscal year divided by the fund's average net assets. It includes all asset based charges such as advisory fees, other non-advisory fees and distribution expenses (12b-1).

RANKING (R) – Funds are grouped by investment objectives defined by The Wall Street Journal and ranked on longest time period listed each day. Performance measurement begins at either the closest Thursday or month-end for periods of more than one year. Gains of 100% or more are shown as a whole number, not carried out one decimal place. A=top 20%; B=next 20%; C=middle 20%; D=next 20%; E=bottom 20%.

QUOTATIONS FOOTNOTES

e-Ex-distribution. **f**-Previous day's quotation. **s**-Stock split or dividend. **x**-Ex–dividend.

p-Distribution costs apply, 12b-1 plan. **r**-Redemption charge may apply.

g-Footnotes x and s apply. **j**-Footnotes e and s apply. **t**-Footnotes p and r apply. **v**-Footnotes x and e apply. **z**-Footnotes x, e and s apply.

NA-Not available due to incomplete price, performance or cost data. **NE**-Deleted by Lipper editor; data in question. **NL**-No Load (sales commission). **NN**-Fund doesn't wish to be tracked. **NS**-Fund didn't exist at start of period.

k-Recalculated by Lipper, using updated data. **i**-No valid comparison with other funds because of expense structure.

Source: *The Wall Street Journal,* January 4, 1995, p. C18. Reprinted by permission of *The Wall Street Journal,*

For example, the AARP group (second listed funds) are no-loads, and you will see NL (no-load) under the offer price column. Looking at the Capital Growth (CaGr) fund under the AARP group, the NAV is $30.09. Because there is no commission, the offer price shows NL for no-load, and the investor knows the offer price equals the net asset value. (Incidentally, the fourth column in the table indicates whether the NAV changed for the day.)

During 1994, *The Wall Street Journal* began providing Lipper Analytical Data on a daily basis with its mutual fund quotes. Every day the Lipper Analytical Data covers returns for a different period. On Monday it provides expense ratios; on Tuesday, a 4-week and 1-year return; on Wednesday, a 13-week and 3-year return; on Thursday a 26-week and 4-year return; and on Friday a 39-week and 5-year return. Table 19–5 on page 547 shows the daily variation in data and explains the mutual fund table that appears in *The Wall Street Journal.*

Another way to determine whether a fund is load or no-load is by examining the *Forbes* annual mutual fund survey published each August. An excerpt from approximately 50 pages of data is presented in Table 19–6. Observe that the maximum sales charge is shown in the second column from the right. Clearly, the term *none* indicates a no-load.

As you can see, you will get a great deal of other information from Table 19–6 as well. This can be important if you are trying to pick an appropriate no-load fund because you will have to select the fund and initiate the action on your own. Remember, there is no salesperson to call on you with a no-load fund or even some low-load funds such as Fidelity. (But opening a no-load fund is an easy, routine process.)

Some of the information from *Forbes* in Table 19–6 will be discussed later in the chapter, but note for now that you get a rating on performance in up and down markets (left margin), average annual return data for a decade (June 1983 to June 1994), returns for the latest 12 months and 5 years, size of total assets, weighted average P/E, median market capitalization, maximum sales charges, and annual expenses per $100. Although not specifically listed, most of these funds have an initial minimum investment of $500 to $1,000, but the amount may vary from fund to fund (later additional contributions may be smaller).

Assume you select a number of funds that interest you from the funds listed in *Forbes* or some other source. The next step is to contact the fund by mail or telephone (most have toll-free numbers). You can then ask any questions, and you will receive a detailed prospectus describing the fund.

The same August *Forbes* issue that provided financial information on funds in Table 19–6 also supplies information about mailing addresses and telephone numbers for all major funds. An excerpt is presented in Table 19–7 on page 550. Other sources of similar mutual fund information include *Consumer Reports, Business Week, Kiplinger,* and *Money* magazine. For more comprehensive information to use in screening a fund, *Morningstar Mutual Funds* is an excellent source. You may also wish to consult the *Wiesenberger Investment Companies Service* publication (produced annually by Warren, Gorham, and Lamont, Boston). This hardback, oversized book has a complete page of information on all mutual funds and can be found in most libraries. An excerpt is presented in Figure 19–1 on page 551, which presents data on the T. Rowe Price New Era Fund, Inc. Finally, you may wish to contact the Investment Company Institute to get its annual directory of mutual funds.[2]

---

[2] The price is approximately $5. The address is the Investment Company Institute, P.O. Box 66140, Washington, D.C. 20035-6140. The phone number is (202) 293-7700.

TABLE 19–6 Stock Funds (Fund Survey)

Performance UP —markets—	DOWN	Fund/distributor	—Annualized total return— 6/83 to 6/94	last 12 months	5-year	Assets 6/30/94 ($mil)	Weighted average P/E	Median market cap ($bil)	Maximum sales charge	Annual expenses per $100
		Standard & Poor's 500 stock average	13.1%	1.5%	10.3%		18.3	$26.5		
		Forbes stock fund composite	10.5%	2.0%	10.6%		26.7	$13.0		$1.23
A+	F	**AIM Equity–Constellation**/AIM	12.6%	1.5%	18.6%	$3,079	24.2	$4.8	5.50%	$1.20
B	D	**AIM Equity–Weingarten**/AIM	11.7	–1.4	11.1	3,838	16.6	12.0	5.50	1.13a
D	C	**AIM Growth Fund-A**/AIM	8.2	–7.0	6.1	142	25.3	7.8	5.50	1.17
B	D	**AIM Summit Fund**/AIM	9.3	–3.1	11.1	679	20.0	3.3	**	0.79
		AIM Utilities Fund-A/AIM	—*	–12.0	8.3	201	13.7	5.8	5.50	1.16
A	■C	**AIM Value Fund-A**/AIM	—*	4.9	16.9	1,372	16.6	7.2	5.50	1.09
■B	■C	**Alger Fund–Growth**/Alger	—*	4.1	15.3	63	24.5	8.9	5.00b	2.34
		Alger Fund–Small Capitalization/Alger	—*	–3.4	13.3	256	29.2	0.9	5.00b	2.17
■D	■B	**Alliance Counterpoint Fund-A**/Alliance	—*	–0.2	6.8	45	15.7	22.4	4.25	1.87
B	D	**Alliance Fund-A**/Alliance	10.7	1.2	11.6	782	15.2	13.2	4.25	1.01
C	B	**Alliance Growth & Income-A**/Alliance	11.9	–0.4	8.1	516	16.1	27.5	4.25	1.07
		Alliance Growth Fund-A/Alliance	—*	7.3	—*	686	NA	NA	4.25	1.40a
		Alliance Premier Growth-A/Alliance	—*	–0.1	—*	187	18.0	9.1	4.25	2.18
B	D	**Alliance Quasar Fund-A**/Alliance	8.5	–1.7	2.2	174	17.1	0.6	4.25	1.65
A+	F	**Alliance Technology Fund-A**/Alliance	8.9	6.1	15.7	175	21.8	5.7	4.25	1.73
B	C	**Amcap Fund**/American Funds	11.1	3.5	9.8	2,814	16.8	12.5	5.75	0.72
		Amcore Vintage Equity/Winsbury	—*	1.3	—*	131	20.0	7.3	4.25	0.54a
D	B	**American Capital Comstock-A**/American Cap	10.2	–0.4	9.3	910	18.6	22.2	5.75	0.96
B	D	**American Capital Emerging Growth-A**/American Cap	9.6	–4.2	16.6	622	28.0	1.0	5.75	1.14
B	D	**American Capital Enterprise-A**/American Cap	10.0	0.0	10.8	790	22.0	14.3	5.75	0.99
C	B	**American Capital Growth & Income**/American Cap	10.0	5.3	9.6	216	19.0	17.1	5.75	1.16
D	B	**American Capital Pace-A**/American Cap	9.7	–0.9	8.2	2,190	19.7	18.4	5.75	1.01
		American Gas Index/Rushmore	—*	–10.7	5.4	201	15.5	3.0	none	0.84
D	A	**American Growth Fund**/American Growth	9.3	8.9	13.2	67	15.2	22.6	5.75	1.42
		American Heritage Fund/Amer Heritage	—*	–22.7	8.3	91	8.4	8.2	none	2.41
C	A	**American Leaders Fund-A**/Federated	12.7	2.4	10.3	265	15.6	20.4	4.50	1.18
D	A	**American Mutual Fund**/American Funds	12.4	2.1	9.6	5,116	19.4	19.0	5.75	0.59
D	D	**American National Growth**/Securities Mgmt	7.8	6.9	8.5	109	20.6	32.4	5.75	1.00
D	A	**American National Income**/Securities Mgmt	10.4	4.5	10.3	115	18.7	20.7	5.75	1.17
		American Performance Equity/Winsbury	—*	0.5	—*	79	18.0	15.8	4.00	1.13a
		AmSouth Equity Fund[1]/Winsbury	—*	5.3	9.7	200	17.3	10.1	4.50	0.95a
		AmSouth Regional Equity[2]/Winsbury	—*	4.4	13.1	53	26.5	3.7	4.50	0.80a
C	C	**Amway Mutual Fund**/Amway	10.1	–3.2	10.7	60	NA	NA	3.00	1.10
F	A+	**Analytic Optioned Equity**/Analytic	9.3	1.6	6.9	65	16.4	25.9	none	1.07a
■B	■D	**API Trust–Growth**/Yorktown	—*	4.4	8.5	46	23.0	2.4	none	2.24a
		Atlas Growth & Income-A/Atlas	—*	–2.0	—*	66	19.1	14.2	3.00	1.07a
A	■D	**Babson Enterprise Fund**/Jones & Babson	—*	6.4	12.2	185	18.2	0.2	†	1.09
		Babson Enterprise Fund II/Jones & Babson	—*	8.1	—*	35	15.5	0.7	none	1.60

■Fund rated for two periods only; maximum allowable grade A. *Fund not in operation or did not meet asset minimum for full period. †Closed to new investors. ** Available only through monthly contractual plan. a: Net of absorption of expenses by fund sponsor. b: Includes back-end load that reverts to distributor. NA: Not applicable or not available. [1]Formerly ASO Outlook Group Equity. [2]Formerly ASO Outlook Group Regional Equity.

Source: Reprinted by permission of *Forbes,* August 29, 1994, p. 176.

TABLE 19–7 Addresses of Mutual Funds (Fund Distributors)

Fund/minimum initial investment ($)	Type
AAL Capital Management 222 West College Avenue Appleton, WI 54919-0007 **(800) 553-6319**	
AAL Bond Fund/1,000	BD
AAL Capital Growth/1,000	ST
AAL Municipal Bond/1,000	MU
AAL Smaller Company Stock/1,000	ST
ABT Financial Services 340 Royal Palm Way Palm Beach, FL 33480 **(800) 553-7838**	
ABT Growth & Income Trust/1,000	ST
ABT Invest–Emerging Growth/1,000	ST
ABT Southern Master–Fla T-F/1,000	MU
ABT Utility Income/1,000	ST
Acorn Investment Trust 227 West Monroe Street Chicago, IL 60606-5016 **(312) 634-9200 (local); (800) 922-6769**	
Acorn Fund†	ST
Acorn International Fund†	FS
Addison Capital Fund/1,000 1608 Walnut Street Philadelphia, PA 19103 **(800) 526-6397**	ST
Advest Group 280 Trumbull Street Hartford, CT 06103 **(203) 525-1421 (local); (800) 243-8115**	
Advantage Government Securities/500	BD
Advantage Growth Fund/500	ST
Advantage High Yield Bond/500	JU
Advantage Income Fund/500	BA
Advantage Special Fund/500	ST
Scottish Widows International/1,000	FS
AIM Distributors Eleven Greenway Plaza Houston, TX 77046 **(713) 626-1919 (local); (800) 347-1919**	
AIM Aggressive Growth†	ST
AIM Balanced Fund-A/500	BA
AIM Equity–Charter/500	ST
AIM Equity–Constellation/500	ST
AIM Equity–Weingarten/500	ST
AIM Government Securities-A/500	BD
AIM Growth Fund-A/500	ST
AIM High Yield-A/500	JU
AIM Income Fund-A/500	BD
AIM International–Equity/500	FS
AIM Limited Maturity Treas Shares/500	BD
AIM Municipal Bond-A/500	MU
AIM Summit Fund**	ST
AIM Utilities Fund-A/500	ST
AIM Value Fund A/500	ST
Fred Alger & Co 30 Montgomery Street Jersey City, NJ 07302 **(800) 992-3863**	
Alger Fund–Growth‡	ST
Alger Fund–Small Capitalization‡	ST
Alliance Fund Services 500 Plaza Drive Secaucus, NJ 07094 **(800) 247-4154**	
Alliance Balanced Shares-A/250	BA
Alliance Bond–Corporate Bond-A/250	BD
Alliance Bond–US Government-A/250	BD
Alliance Conservative Investors-A/250	BA
Alliance Counterpoint Fund-A/250	ST
Alliance Fund-A/250	ST
Alliance Funds–Balanced-A/250	BA
Alliance Global Small Cap-A/250	GS
Alliance Growth & Income-A/250	ST
Alliance Growth Fund-A/250	ST
Alliance Growth Investors-A/250	BA
Alliance Income Builder-A/250	GB
Alliance International Fund-A/250	FS
Alliance Mortgage Secs Income-A/250	BD
Alliance Mortgage Strategy Trust-A/250	BD
Alliance Multi-Market Strategy-A/250	GB
Alliance Muni Income–Calif-A/250	MU
Alliance Muni Income–Ins Calif-A/250	MU
Alliance Muni Income–Ins Natl-A/250	MU
Alliance Muni Income–National-A/250	MU
Alliance Muni Income–New York-A/250	MU
Alliance New Europe-A/250	FS
Alliance North American Govt Inc-A/250	GB
Alliance Premier Growth-A/250	ST
Alliance Quasar Fund-A/250	ST
Alliance Short-Term Multi-Market-A/250	GB
Alliance Technology Fund-A/250	ST
Alliance World Income Trust/10,000	GB

Fund	Symbol
Balanced	BA
Foreign stock	FS
Global bond	GB
Global stock	GS
Junk bond	JU
Money market	MM
Municipal bond	MU
Stock	ST
Taxable bond	BD

Source: Reprinted by permission of *Forbes*, August 29, 1994, p. 246–47.

Price (T. Rowe) New Era

Energy/Natural Resources (ENR)

12/31/93 CDA Rating (1 = lowest, 10 = highest) **6**

Overview

The investment objective of the T. Rowe Price New Era Fund is long-term growth of capital. It may seek this in any industry, but its current portfolio consists largely of securities of companies in the energy sources area, precious metals and other metals and minerals, other basic commodities, and companies which own or develop land. Investments in companies which provide consumer products and services are included, as well as companies operating in technological areas, such as the manufacture of labor-saving machinery and instruments.

Portfolio Characteristics as of 12/93

Largest Holdings	Pct.	Sector Breakdown	Pct.
WAL MART STORES INC	7.7	Basic Industries	40.6
MOBIL CORP	5.2	Cap. Goods & Tech.	7.4
ATLANTIC RICHFIELD CO	4.8	Consumer Cyclicals	13.6
NEWMONT MNG CORP	4.7	Consumer Staples	3.3
DU PONT E I DE NEMOURS & CO	4.7	Energy	26.8
AMERICAN BARRICK RES CORP	4.2	Finance	0.6
UNION PAC CORP	4.0	Transportation	5.9
TVX GOLD INC	3.0	Utilities	0.0
ROYAL DUTCH PETE CO	2.6	Miscellaneous	1.9
ROUSE CO	2.5		
Avg. P/E	37.5	**Market Cap. (mil$)**	17055.6

Administration

Directors: George J. Collins; Anthony W. Deering; Karl J. Ladner; F. Pierce Linaweaver; Lawrence P. Naylor, III; Govenor Emmett J. Rice; James S. Riepe; John Sagan; John G. Schriber; Peter Van Dyke; Marna C. Whittington; Henry H. Hopkins; Veena A. Kutler; Heather R. Landon; James M. McDonald; Edmund Notzon; Charles P. Smith; Lenora V. Hornung; Carmen F. Deyesu; David S. Middleton
Portfolio Manager(s): George Roche since 1979
Investment Advisor: Price (T. Rowe) Associates
Max / Actual '93 Management Fee (%): 0.600 / 0.600
Distributor: Price (T. Rowe) Inv Services
Fiscal Year End / Ticker Symbol: December / PRNEX

Shareholder Information

Minimum initial investment: $2,500
Minimum subsequent investment: $100
Sales Charge: None
Transfer Agent: T. Rowe Price Services
Qualified for Sale: In all states, DC and PR
Address: P.O. Box 89000; Baltimore, MD 21289
Telephone: (800) 638-5660; (410) 547-2308

Statistical History

	At Year-End							Annual Data				
					% of Assets in							
Year	Net Assets (mil$)	# of Accounts (000s)	NAV ($)	Yield (%)	Csh Eqv	Bds Pfds	Com Stks	Inc. Divs ($)	Cap. Gains ($)	Exp. Ratio (%)	Total Return	+/-% S&P 500
1993	752.5	36.2	20.35	1.8	8	0	92	0.38	1.03	0.80	15.3	5.3
1992	699.6	40.6	18.88	2.3	0	29	71	0.45	0.94	0.81	2.1	-5.5
1991	756.8	47.0	19.86	2.7	8	0	92	0.55	0.73	0.85	14.7	-15.7
1990	707.5	51.8	18.48	3.2	18	0	82	0.62	0.71	0.83	-8.8	-5.6
1989	826.6	55.4	21.73	2.5	11	0	89	0.56	1.05	0.83	24.3	-7.3
1988	726.5	61.8	18.79	2.7	8	1	91	0.53	0.61	0.89	10.3	-6.2
1987	756.5	66.5	18.08	4.9	15	0	85	0.98	1.77	0.82	17.8	12.6
1986	496.2	39.2	17.76	2.4	15	0	85	0.50	3.25	0.73	16.0	-2.6
1985	529.0	42.1	18.67	3.4	8	0	92	0.68	1.41	0.69	23.4	-8.3
1984	472.0	45.8	17.13	3.3	10	0	90	0.61	1.29	0.68	3.3	-2.8
1983	485.1	47.2	18.44	4.4	12	6	82	0.81	0.07	0.68	25.5	3.0
1982	411.5	46.4	15.53	4.7	11	0	89	0.86	3.04	0.71	2.5	-19.1

Commenced Operations: 01/20/69

Performance as of 12/31/93

Ann'lzd Total Return	Fund	Avg. ENR	S&P 500
1 Yr.	15.3	21.2	10.1
3 Yr.	10.5	8.3	15.6
5 Yr.	8.9	8.7	14.5
10 Yr.	11.4	7.7	14.9
Bull*	43.4	29.0	68.8
Bear*	-14.1	-8.2	-14.5

MPT Stats.	Fund	Avg. ENR	S&P 500
Alpha	-1.68	-2.58	-
Beta	0.74	0.65	-
Std Dev	2.69	4.11	3.01

Risk-to-Reward

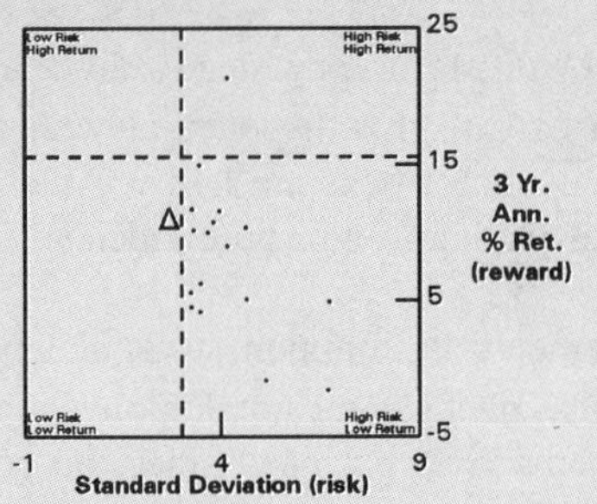

Fd (Δ) vs. all ENR; Intersect: S&P 500

Performance on $10,000 Investment

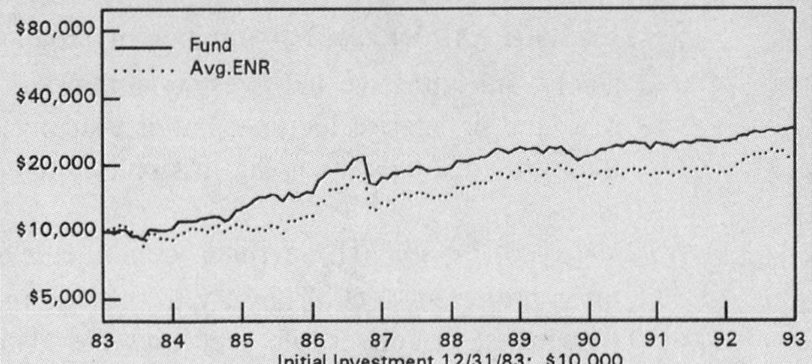

Initial Investment 12/31/83: $10,000
Value at 12/31/93: $29,460

* Returns for most recent market cycle dates are not annualized Bull: 10/31/90 - 12/31/93 Bear: 05/31/90 -10/31/90

Source: Reprinted by permission from *Wiesenberger Investment Companies Service,* 1994, © Warren, Gorham and Lamont, 210 South Street, Boston, MA. All rights reserved.

DIFFERING OBJECTIVES AND THE DIVERSITY OF MUTUAL FUNDS

Recognizing that different investors have different objectives and sensitivities to risk, the mutual fund industry offers a large group of funds from which to choose. In 1994, there were more than 5,000 mutual funds, each unique in terms of stated objectives, investment policies, and current portfolio. To make some sense out of this much variety, funds can be classified in terms of their stated objectives.

MONEY MARKET FUNDS Money market funds have been the phenomenon of the last two decades. (*Forbes* Mutual Fund Survey provides a helpful list of funds.) Money market mutual funds invest in short-term securities, such as U.S. Treasury bills and Eurodollar deposits, commercial paper, jumbo bank certificates of deposit (CDs), and repurchase agreements.

Money market funds are no-load, and most require minimum deposits of $500 to $1,000. Most have check-writing privileges, but usually the checks must be written for at least $250 to $500.

Because the maturities of assets held in money market portfolios generally range from 20 to 50 days, the yields of these funds closely track short-term market interest rates. Money market funds give small investors an opportunity to invest in securities that were once out of reach.

GROWTH FUNDS The pursuit of capital appreciation is the emphasis here. This class of funds includes those called aggressive growth funds and those concentrating on more stable and predictable growth. Both types invest primarily in common stock. Aggressive funds concentrate on speculative issues, emerging small companies, and "hot" sectors of the economy and frequently use financial leverage to magnify returns. Regular growth funds generally invest in common stocks of more stable firms. They are less inclined to stay fully invested in stocks during periods of market decline, seldom use aggressive techniques such as leverage, and tend to be long term in orientation.

The best way to determine the type of growth fund is to carefully examine the fund's prospectus and current portfolio.

GROWTH WITH INCOME A number of large, growing firms pay steady dividends. Their stocks are attractive to investors interested in capital growth potential with a base of dividend or interest income. Funds that invest in such stocks are less volatile and risky than growth funds investing in small companies paying low or no dividends.

BALANCED FUNDS These funds combine investments in common stock and bonds and often preferred stock. They try to provide income plus some capital appreciation. Funds that invest in convertible securities are also considered balanced since the convertible security is a hybrid fixed-income security with the opportunity for appreciation if the underlying common stock rises.

BOND FUNDS Income-oriented investors have always been attracted to bonds. Because bonds represent a contractual obligation on the part of the issuer to the bondholder, they normally offer a certain return. But as pointed out in Chapter 12, rising interest rates can

undercut the market value of all classes of fixed-income securities. During the early 1980s and mid-1990s, a time of intense interest-rate fluctuations, many bondholders watched the principal value of even their "safe" government bonds drop to 75 percent of face value. Bonds held in mutual funds were affected by the same market forces. Returns from bonds are historically lower than those from stocks, and bond funds are no exception.

Bond mutual funds can be roughly subdivided into corporate, government, and municipal funds.

Some corporate bond funds are particularly targeted to low-rated, high-yielding bonds. These funds are termed *junk bond funds.* They may have a yield of 4 or 5 percent over the typical corporate bond fund but also possess greater risk in terms of potential default by the securities in the bond portfolio. Just how much greater that risk is was discovered in the fall of 1989 when a number of low-rated bonds in these funds defaulted on their interest payments and prices for all junk bonds fell.

Because municipal bond funds buy only tax-exempt securities, interest income to shareholders is free of federal tax. Special tax-exempt funds also have been established for the benefit of investors in states with high state and local income taxes. For example, fund managers of New York municipal bond funds establish portfolios of tax-exempt securities issued within the boundaries of that state. Under current tax law, interest income from these funds is exempt from federal, state, and local taxes for New York residents—a very appealing feature to high-bracket taxpayers.

Sector Funds Special funds have been created to invest in specific sectors of the economy. Sector funds exist for such areas as energy, medical technology, computer technology, leisure, and defense.

Because stock performance of companies within a particular industry, or sector, tend to be positively correlated, these funds offer investors less diversification and higher loss/reward potential.

Investors should be cautious with regard to the initial offering of new sector funds. An initial offering usually occurs after the sector has already been the subject of intense interest based on recent spectacular performance. As a result, stocks in that sector are often fully priced or overpriced.

Foreign Funds As noted in Chapter 18, investors seeking participation in foreign markets and foreign securities confront a number of obstacles, but the rewards can be remarkable. The mutual fund industry has made overseas investing convenient by establishing funds whose policies mandate investing on a global basis (Templeton World Fund), within the markets of a particular locale (Canadian Fund, Inc.), or within a region (Merrill Lynch Pacific). Some funds even specialize in Third World countries.

Foreign funds as a group outperformed all other kinds of mutual funds in the last decade. A listing of some important international funds is presented in Table 19–8 on page 554. The mutual fund industry distinguishes between global and international funds. Global funds have foreign stocks plus U.S. stocks, while international have only foreign stocks.

Specialty Funds Some mutual funds have specialized approaches that do not fit neatly into any of the preceding categories. Their names are often indicative of their investment

TABLE 19–8 Internationally Oriented Funds

Name of Fund	Open- or Closed-End	Load (L) No-Load (NL)	Where Invested
Canadian Fund, Inc.	Open	L	Canada
International Investors Incorporated	Open	L	Gold mines
G. T. Pacific Fund, Inc.	Open	NL	Asia (Japan, Hong Kong, etc.)
Fidelity Overseas Fund	Open	L	Worldwide
Kemper International Fund, Inc.	Open	L	Worldwide
Merrill Lynch Pacific	Open	L	Far East
Merrill Lynch International Holdings	Open	L	Worldwide
Putnam International Equities Fund	Open	L	Worldwide
Research Capital Fund, Inc.	Open	L	Foreign mining
T. Rowe Price International Fund, Inc.	Open	NL	Worldwide
Scudder International Fund, Inc.	Open	NL	Worldwide
Strategic Investments Fund, Inc.	Open	L	South African gold mines
Templeton World Fund, Inc.	Open	L	Worldwide
Transatlantic Fund, Inc.	Open	NL	Worldwide
United International Growth Fund	Open	L	Worldwide
ASA Limited	Closed	Commission	South African gold mines
Mexican Fund	Closed	Commission	Mexico
U.S. and Foreign Securities	Closed	Commission	Worldwide

objectives or policies: the Phoenix Fund (rising from the ashes?), the Calvert Social Investment Fund, and United Services Gold Shares, to name just a few.

There is even a "fund of funds" (FundTrust) that manages a portfolio of different mutual fund shares.

Owing to some fund managers' poor records in attempting to outperform the market, a number of funds have taken up the maxim that "if you can't beat 'em, join 'em!" Calling themselves index funds, these mutual funds establish portfolios that replicate some major market index, such as the S&P 500. Fund performance is almost exactly correlated with performance of "the market."

Matching Investment Objectives with Fund Types

Investors must consider how much volatility of return they can tolerate. Investors who require safety of principal with very little deviation of returns should choose money market funds first and intermediate-term bond funds second. They should also expect to receive lower returns based on historical evidence. While aggressive growth stock funds provide the highest return, they also have the biggest risk.

Liquidity objectives are met by all mutual funds since redemption can occur any time. If investors need income, bond funds provide the highest annual current yield, while aggressive growth funds provide the least. Growth-income and balanced funds are most appropriate for investors who want growth of principal with moderate current income.

Many investors diversify by fund type. For example, at one stage in the business cycle, an investor may want to have 50 percent of assets in common stocks, 35 percent in bonds, 10 percent in money market funds, and 5 percent in an international stock fund. These percentages could change as market conditions change. If interest rates are expected to decline, it would be better to have a higher percentage of bonds and fewer money market securities since bond prices will rise as rates decline. Investing with a "family of funds" allows the investor a choice of many different types of funds and the privilege of switching between funds at no or low cost. Some of the larger families of funds are managed by American Capital, Dreyfus Group, Federated Funds, Fidelity Investments, T. Rowe Price Funds, and the Vanguard Group. In addition, most major retail brokerage firms, such as Merrill Lynch, Dean Witter, and Prudential, have families of mutual funds.

Each mutual fund has a unique history and management team. There is no guarantee that past performance will be repeated. Investors should check on a fund's longevity of management, historical returns, trading history, and management expenses. A very key instrument in providing information in this regard is the fund prospectus.

THE PROSPECTUS

The Investment Companies Act of 1940, which established the standard of practice for all investment companies, requires that the purchaser of fund shares be provided with a current prospectus. The **prospectus** contains information deemed essential by the SEC in providing "full disclosure" to potential investors regarding the fund's investment objectives and policies, risks, management, and expenses. The prospectus also provides information on how shares can be purchased and redeemed, sales and redemption charges (if any), and shareholders' services. Other fund documents are available to the public on request including the Statement of Additional Information and the fund's annual and quarterly reports.

While it is beyond the scope of this chapter to provide a complete discourse on interpreting a prospectus, investors need to understand the following essentials.

INVESTMENT OBJECTIVES AND POLICIES This section is always found in the beginning of the prospectus. It usually describes the fund's basic objectives such as:

> The Fund will invest only in securities backed by the full faith and credit of the U.S. Government. At least 70% of the Fund's assets will be invested in certificates issued by the Government National Mortgage Association (GNMA). It may also purchase other securities issued by the U.S. Government, its agencies, or instrumentalities as long as these securities are backed by the full faith and credit of the U.S. Government.

The prospectus normally goes on to detail investment management policies under which it intends to operate—typically with regard to the use of borrowed money, lending of securities, or something like the following:

> The Fund may, under certain circumstances, sell covered call options against securities it is holding for the purpose of generating additional income.

PORTFOLIO (OR "INVESTMENT HOLDINGS") This section lists the securities held by the fund as of the date indicated. Since investment companies are only required to publish their

prospectuses every 14 months, the information is probably dated. Still, the portfolio should be compared with the stated objectives of the fund to see if they are consistent.

MANAGEMENT FEES AND EXPENSES Besides sales and redemption charges, the prospectus also provides information and figures on fund managers' reimbursement and the fund's housekeeping expenses. Annual fees for the investment advisor are expressed as a percentage of the average daily net assets during the year (usually 0.50 percent). Other expenses include legal and auditing fees, the cost of preparing and distributing annual reports and proxy statements, directors' fees, and transaction expenses. When lumped together with investment advisory fees, a fund's total yearly expenses typically range from 0.75 to 1.25 percent of fund assets. Experienced mutual fund investors cast a jaundiced eye on funds with expense ratios that exceed this figure. It is required that all expenses appear on one page in a table format.

A controversial SEC ruling—Rule 12b-l—allows mutual funds to use fund assets for marketing expenses, which are included in the expense ratio. Since marketing expenses have nothing to do with advancing shareholders' interests and everything to do with increasing the managers' fees, investors should be alert to this in the prospectus.

TURNOVER RATE A number of mutual funds trade aggressively in pursuit of profits; others do just the opposite. In one year, the Fidelity Contrafund had a 243 percent turnover rate; the rate for the Oppenheimer Special Fund was 9 percent.

In reality, transaction costs amount to more than just commissions, and they are not accounted for in the expense ratio. When fund assets are traded over-the-counter, the dealer's spread between the bid and asked price is not considered. Nor is the fact that large block trades—the kind mutual funds usually deal in—are made at less favorable prices than are smaller volume transactions.

The prospectus also contains audited data on the turnover rate, the expense ratio, and other important data in the section on per-share income and capital changes.

DISTRIBUTION AND TAXATION

The selling of securities by a mutual fund's portfolio results in capital losses or gains for the fund. After netting losses against gains, mutual funds distribute net capital gains to shareholders annually.

Funds with securities that pay dividends or interest also have a source of investment income. The fund, in turn, distributes such income to shareholders either quarterly or annually.

A fund that distributes at least 90 percent of its net investment income and capital gains is not subject, as an entity, to federal income tax. It is simply acting as a "conduit" in channeling taxable sources of income from securities held in the portfolio to the fund's shareholders. Most funds operate this way. But while the mutual fund may not be subject to taxation, its shareholders are.

At the end of every calendar year, each fund shareholder receives a Form 1099-DIV. This document notifies the shareholder of the amount and tax status of his or her distributions.

When the investor actually sells (redeems) shares in a mutual fund, another form of taxable event occurs. It is precisely the same as if stocks, bonds, or other securities were

sold. The investor must consider the cost basis, the selling price, and any gain or loss and appropriately report the tax consequences on his or her tax form.

SHAREHOLDER SERVICES

Most mutual funds offer a number of services to their shareholders. Some can be used in the investor's strategy. Common services include:

Automatic reinvestment. The fund reinvests all distributions (usually without sales charge). Shares and fractional shares are purchased at the net asset value. Purchases are noted on annual and periodic account statements.

Safekeeping. While shareholders are entitled to receive certificates for all whole shares, it is often convenient to let the fund's transfer agent hold the shares.

Exchange privilege. Many large management companies sponsor a family of funds. They may have five or more funds, each dedicated to a different investment objective. Within certain limits, shareholders are free to move their money between the different funds in the family on a net asset value basis. Transfers can often be done by telephone; a minimal charge is common to cover paperwork. These exchanges are taxable events.

Preauthorized check plan. Many people lack the discipline to save or invest regularly. Those who recognize this trait in themselves can authorize a management company to charge their bank account for predetermined amounts on a regular basis. The amounts withdrawn are used to purchase new shares.

Systematic withdrawal plan. Every shareholder plans to convert shares into cash at some time. The investor who wants to receive a regular amount of cash each month or quarter can do so by arranging for such a plan. The fund sells enough shares on a periodic basis to meet the shareholder's cash requirement.

Checking privileges. Most money market mutual funds furnish shareholders with checks that can be drawn against the account, provided that the account balance is above a minimum amount (usually $1,000). A per-check minimum of $250 to $500 is common.

INVESTMENT FUNDS, LONG-TERM PLANNING, AND DOLLAR-COST AVERAGING

Perhaps more than anything else, the liquidity and conveniences inherent in mutual funds lend themselves best to financial planning activities. The most important of these is the gradual accumulation of capital assets.

Using the preauthorized check plan, investors can have fixed amounts regularly withdrawn from their checking accounts to purchase fund shares. Just as savers can have their banks channel a specific amount from their paychecks into savings accounts, so too can investors make regular, lump-sum fund share purchases on an "out of sight, out of mind" basis. Reinvestment of distributions enhances this strategy.

What distinguishes the mutual fund from the bank savings strategy is the fact that fund shares are purchased at different prices. The investor can even use a passive strategy known as dollar-cost averaging. Under **dollar-cost averaging,** the investor buys a fixed dollar's worth of a given security at regular intervals regardless of the security's price or

TABLE 19–9 Dollar-Cost Averaging

(1) Month	(2) Investment	(3) Share Price	(4) Shares Purchased
January	$200	$12	16.66
February	200	14	14.28
March	200	16	12.50
April	200	19	10.52
May	200	15	13.33
June	200	12	16.66
Totals	$1,200	$88	83.95 total shares
		Average price $14.67	Average cost $14.29

the current market outlook. By using such a strategy, investors concede they cannot outsmart the market. The intent of dollar-cost averaging is to avoid the common practice of buying high and selling low. In fact, investors are forced to do the opposite. Why? They commit a fixed-dollar amount each month (or year) and buy shares at the current market price. When the price is high, they are buying relatively fewer shares; when the price is low, they are accumulating more shares. An example is presented in Table 19–9. Suppose we use the preauthorized check plan to channel $200 per month into a mutual fund. The price ranges from a low of $12 to a high of $19.

Note that when the share price is relatively low, such as in January, we purchased a larger number of shares than when the share prices were high, as in April. In this case, the share price ended in June at the same price it was in January ($12).

What would happen if the price merely ended up at the average price over the six-month period? The values in column 3 total $88, so the average price over six months is $14.67 ($88/6). Actually, we would still make money under this assumption because the average *cost* is less than this amount. Consider that we invested $1,200 and purchased 83.95 shares. This translates to an average cost of only $14.29:

$$\frac{\text{Investment}}{\text{Shares purchased}} = \frac{\$1{,}200}{83.95} = \$14.29$$

The average cost ($14.29) is less than the average price ($14.67) because we bought relatively more shares at the lower price levels, and they weighed more heavily in our calculations. Thus, under dollar-cost averaging, investors can come out ahead over a period of investing fixed amounts, even if the share price ends up less than the average price paid on each transaction.[3]

The only time investors lose money is if the eventual price falls below the average cost ($14.29) and they sell at that point. While dollar-cost averaging has its advantages, it is not without criticism. Clearly, if the share price continues to go down over a long period, it is hard to make a case for continued purchases. However, the long-term performance

[3] This does not consider any sales charges or commissions, which could be important but can generally be avoided.

Some Funds Don't Like Quick-Change Artists

A few mutual funds are starting to discourage the troublesome clients that most people in the industry regard as Fund Enemy No. 1.

These pesky customers are the market timers—money managers who dash in and out of mutual funds with the aim of catching broad market swings.

The chief complaint about timers is that their frenzied switching forces funds to buy and sell huge blocks of securities, penalizing other, often smaller, shareholders. Many fund groups have accelerated their antitimer campaigns in recent months by imposing limits and fees on switches.

Timers are drawn most often to no-load fund groups—which don't levy an upfront sales charge—because they offer the fastest and cheapest way to switch in and out of stocks.

Fund operators over the years have abruptly kicked out a number of timers who have failed to heed pleas to curb switching. Fidelity Investments has responded with a series of ever-tighter restrictions on switches. They now are limited to four a year for most funds and five a month for its select funds, which usually invest in one industry and are intended to handle much faster turnover.

The timers' strategy continues to pose a basic dilemma. Says the president of one investment management firm: "If we trade too often, we get kicked out by the funds. And if we don't perform, we get kicked out by our clients."

Source: *The Wall Street Journal,* November 22, 1988, p. C1. Reprinted by permission of *The Wall Street Journal,* © 1988 by Dow Jones & Company, Inc. All Rights Reserved Worldwide.

of most diversified mutual funds has been positive, and long-term investors may find this strategy useful in accumulating capital assets for retirement, children's education funds, or other purposes.

EVALUATING FUND PERFORMANCE

Throughout this chapter, we referred to mutual fund performance. We will now consider the issue more directly by actually comparing mutual fund performance with the market in general. This topic will also be considered more fully in Chapter 22.

A good place to start the current discussion is to return to Table 19–6, page 549, which covers *Forbes* mutual fund information. Direct your attention to total returns in the middle three columns of the table. The first column shows the average annual total return over an 11-year period (1983–94).[4] This total return figure is composed of capital appreciation plus dividend income. Notice toward the top of the table that the Standard & Poor's 500 Stock Average (a measure of the total market) had an average annual return of 13.1 percent, while the Forbes Stock Fund Composite (a measure of mutual funds) had a return of 10.5 percent.

The next column shows return data for the most recently reported 12 months. The Standard & Poor's 500 Stock Average was up 1.5 percent, while the Forbes Stock Fund Composite showed a gain of 2.0 percent. Over the 11-year time period shown in Table 19–6, the Standard & Poor's 500 Stock Average outperformed the Forbes Stock Fund Composite. However, this is not always the case. If we were to look at the one-year

[4] The period covers June 1983 to June 1994.

and five-year periods, the Forbes Stock Fund Composite outperformed the Standard & Poor's 500 Stock Average. In some periods, mutual funds as a group beat the popular market averages, while in other periods they do not.

You can also identify the performance of individual funds in Table 19–6. An example of a strong performer is AIM Equity-Constellation with a 12.6 percent 11-year return and an 18.6 percent 5-year return. An obvious underperformer is American National Growth with a 7.8 percent 11-year return and an 8.5 percent 5-year return.

Grades are assigned to fund performance in the first two columns on the far left side of Table 19–6. The grades are based on how the funds performed in up and down markets over the past 10 years. The grades theoretically range from A+ to F. Most investors like funds that do reasonably well in both types of markets. Notice that there are no funds getting an A in both up and down markets. Of course, if you feel strongly that the market is about to move in one direction rather than another, you will adjust your emphasis accordingly.

One warning: Past performance in no way guarantees future performance. A fund that did well in the past may do poorly in the future and vice versa.[5] Nevertheless, all things being equal, investors generally prefer funds that have a prior record of good performance. Investors do not know whether the funds can reproduce the performance, but at least the funds have indicated the capacity for good returns in the past. The same cannot be said for underperformers.

Lipper Mutual Fund Performance Averages

As you can see in Table 19–10, mutual fund performance can also be broken down by type of fund. This information was previously presented in Chapter 3 under the discussion of stock market indexes and averages but now takes on greater meaning in the current context of mutual fund evaluation. You can observe that certain types of funds did better or worse and how their performance changed with differing periods for measurement. The Lipper Mutual Fund Performance Averages shown in Table 19–10 are published weekly in *Barron's.*

Computing Total Return on Your Investment

Assume you own a fund for a year and want to determine the total return on your investment. There are three potential sources of return:

Change in net asset value (NAV).
Dividends distributed.
Capital gains distributed.[6]

[5] The factor is covered more fully in Chapter 22.

[6] This represents net capital gains that the fund actually had as a result of selling securities. They are distributed to shareholders.

TABLE 19–10 Lipper Mutual Fund Performance Reports

Weekly Summary Report: Thursday, December 29, 1994
Cumulative Performances With Dividends Reinvested

NAV Mil. $	No. Funds		10/11/90-12/29/94	07/12/90-12/29/94	12/30/93-12/29/94	12/31/93-12/29/94	12/22/94-12/29/94
General Equity Funds:							
40,991.8	155	Capital Appreciation	+ 89.38%	+ 45.88%	− 3.26%	− 3.58%	+ 1.05%
196,181.4	684	Growth Funds	+ 81.18%	+ 41.65%	− 2.06%	− 2.15%	+ 0.80%
32,005.4	99	Mid Cap Funds	+ 118.86%	+ 62.33%	− 1.69%	− 2.35%	+ 1.64%
38,824.5	283	Small Company Growth	+ 127.03%	+ 63.51%	− 0.45%	− 1.35%	+ 1.72%
190,435.7	412	Growth and Income	+ 73.41%	+ 43.25%	− 1.00%	− 0.88%	+ 0.45%
19,639.8	40	S&P 500 Objective	+ 73.81%	+ 41.95%	+ 0.84%	+ 1.32%	+ 0.41%
69,164.2	121	Equity Income	+ 69.07%	+ 42.83%	− 2.53%	− 2.48%	+ 0.22%
585,242.8	1,674	Gen. Equity Funds Avg.	+ 86.13%	+ 46.15%	− 1.60%	− 1.79%	+ 0.89%
Other Equity Funds:							
4,283.5	18	Health/Biotechnology	+ 95.30%	+ 66.05%	+ 4.56%	+ 4.12%	+ 1.13%
3,065.0	36	Natural Resources	+ 19.97%	+ 11.77%	− 4.26%	− 4.77%	+ 0.13%
120.6	6	Environmental	+ 12.64%	− 14.28%	− 10.12%	− 11.32%	+ 0.81%
5,186.4	37	Science & Technol.	+ 188.81%	+ 94.94%	+ 11.30%	+ 10.81%	+ 2.67%
2,236.9	27	Specialty/Misc.	+ 110.55%	+ 59.84%	− 2.37%	− 2.59%	+ 0.70%
22,172.1	86	Utility Funds	+ 47.95%	+ 41.18%	− 9.24%	− 8.95%	− 0.13%
2,321.1	16	Financial Services	+ 183.42%	+ 111.69%	− 2.71%	− 2.90%	+ 0.21%
1,445.4	21	Real Estate	+ 76.38%	+ 42.16%	− 3.65%	− 3.28%	+ 0.20%
6,772.5	38	Gold Oriented Funds	+ 28.39%	+ 22.06%	− 11.95%	− 12.39%	+ 3.16%
42,221.0	123	Global Funds	+ 52.18%	+ 29.00%	− 3.01%	− 3.15%	+ 0.59%
6,612.9	23	Global Small Co. Funds	+ 75.16%	+ 40.34%	− 2.61%	− 3.37%	+ 1.17%
87,470.6	223	International Funds	+ 45.01%	+ 23.98%	− 1.03%	− 1.16%	+ 0.53%
2,728.4	11	International Small Co.	+ 34.57%	+ 5.40%	− 5.48%	− 5.75%	+ 0.72%
6,535.0	47	European Region Fds	+ 23.47%	+ 4.97%	+ 0.50%	+ 0.53%	+ 0.67%
13,158.4	69	Pacific Region Funds	+ 65.36%	+ 36.16%	− 11.66%	− 12.06%	− 0.47%
10,308.4	47	Emerging Markets Funds	+ 93.99%	+ 52.57%	− 10.77%	− 11.08%	− 0.19%
1,886.6	12	Japanese Funds	+ 6.39%	− 14.30%	+ 15.13%	+ 16.06%	+ 1.70%
4,373.1	19	Latin American Funds	N/A	N/A	− 13.86%	− 13.99%	+ 0.49%
410.0	2	Canadian Funds	+ 21.11%	+ 11.22%	− 13.30%	− 13.92%	+ 0.81%
162,474.9	614	World Equity Funds Avg.	+ 43.44%	+ 23.15%	− 3.96%	− 4.17%	+ 0.81%
788,548.7	2,535	All Equity Funds Avg.	+ 79.80%	+ 43.30%	− 2.22%	− 2.40%	+ 0.79%
Other Funds:							
29,588.2	149	Flexible Portfolio	+ 60.03%	+ 42.36%	− 2.65%	− 2.65%	+ 0.35%
11,005.7	45	Global Flex Port.	+ 43.54%	+ 31.55%	− 4.86%	− 4.81%	+ 0.41%
51,441.9	196	Balanced Funds	+ 60.87%	+ 41.95%	− 2.45%	− 2.47%	+ 0.43%
962.6	13	Balanced Target	+ 56.69%	+ 42.98%	− 5.39%	− 5.46%	+ 0.51%
3,809.8	31	Conv. Securities	+ 77.61%	+ 51.97%	− 3.71%	− 3.97%	+ 0.23%
14,317.1	22	Income Funds	+ 55.84%	+ 44.52%	− 3.00%	− 2.97%	+ 0.07%
28,450.8	198	World Income Funds	+ 26.62%	+ 35.80%	− 5.49%	− 5.50%	+ 0.03%
304,518.7	1,375	Fixed Income Funds	+ 42.22%	+ 39.66%	− 3.24%	− 3.25%	+ 0.16%
1,232,643.5	4,564	Long-Term Average	+ 66.04%	+ 42.05%	− 2.72%	− 2.84%	+ 0.53%
		Long-Term Median	+ 58.80%	+ 38.91%	− 2.68%	− 2.65%	+ 0.31%
		Funds with % Change	1,597	1,552	3,545	3,674	4,451
		Securities Market Indexes					
Value		**U.S. Equities:**					
3,833.43		Dow Jones Ind. Avg. xd	+ 62.08	+ 29.06	+ 1.52	+ 2.11	+ 0.46
481.16		S&P 500 xd	+ 58.08	+ 26.19	− 1.60	− 1.13	+ 0.32
549.91		S&P 400 xd	+ 58.54	+ 26.89	+ 1.41	+ 1.78	+ 0.45
251.44		NYSE Composite xd	+ 55.02	+ 26.15	− 3.21	− 2.95	+ 0.29
431.36		ASE Index	+ 48.87	+ 19.08	− 8.72	− 9.80	+ 0.90
246.89		Russell 2000 Index xd	+ 105.71	+ 45.72	− 3.83	− 4.62	+ 1.36
Value		**International Equities:**					
2,077.03		DAX Index	+ 48.41	+ 8.39	− 8.37	− 8.37	− 1.12
3,065.60		FT S-E 100 Index	+ 45.83	+ 29.32	− 10.59	− 10.32	− 0.84
1,975.30		Nikkei 225 Average xd	− 12.54	− 39.36	+ 13.41	+ 13.41	+ 0.61
		Fund Management Companies					
Value:							
1,318.46		Stock-price Index	N/A	N/A	− 0.64	− 2.07	+ 0.21

xd-Price only index. Calculated without reinvestment of dividends. The Nikkei index value is divided by 10 due to space limitation. Source: Lipper Analytical Services Inc., Summit, New Jersey 07901

Source: *Barron's,* January 2, 1995, p. 57. Reprinted by permission of *Barron's,*

Assume the following:

Beginning NAV	$14.05	
Ending NAV	15.10	
Change in NAV (+)	1.05	
Dividends distributed	0.40	} 0.72
Capital gains distributed	0.32	
Total return	$ 1.77	

In this instance, there is a total return of $1.77. Based on a beginning NAV of $14.05, the return is 12.60 percent:

$$\frac{\text{Total return}}{\text{Beginning NAV}} = \frac{\$1.77}{\$14.05} = 12.60 \text{ percent}$$

As a further consideration, assume that instead of taking dividends and capital gains income in cash, you decide to automatically reinvest the proceeds to purchase new mutual fund shares. To compute the percentage return in this instance, you must compare the total value of your ending shares to the total value of your beginning shares. Assume you owned 100 shares to start, and you received $0.72 in dividends plus capital gains per share (see prior example). This would allow you to reinvest $72 (100 shares × $0.72 per share). Further assume you bought new shares at an average price of $14.40 per share. This would provide you with five new shares.[7]

$$\frac{\text{Dividends and capital gains allocated to the account}}{\text{Average purchase price of new shares}} =$$

$$\frac{\$72}{\$14.40} = 5 \text{ new shares}$$

In comparing the ending and beginning value of the investment based on the example in this section, we show the following:

$$\text{Total return} = \frac{\begin{pmatrix}\text{Number of}\\ \text{ending shares}\\ \times \text{ Ending price}\end{pmatrix} - \begin{pmatrix}\text{Number of}\\ \text{beginning shares}\\ \times \text{ Beginning price}\end{pmatrix}}{\text{Number of beginning shares} \times \text{Beginning price}} \tag{19–2}$$

$$= \frac{(105 \times \$15.10) - (100 \times \$14.05)}{(100 \times \$14.05)}$$

$$= \frac{\$1{,}585.50 - \$1{,}405}{\$1{,}405}$$

$$= \frac{\$180.50}{\$1{,}405} = 12.85\%$$

[7] In this case, the number of new shares came out to be a whole number. It is also possible to buy fractional shares in a mutual fund.

In determining whether the returns computed in this section are adequate, you must compare your returns with the popular market averages and with the returns on other mutual funds. While the returns might be considered quite good for a conservative fund, such might not be the case for an aggressive, growth-oriented fund. You must also consider the amount of risk you are taking in the form of volatility of returns. These factors of risk and return are more fully developed in the chapters on portfolio management.

SUMMARY

Investment funds allow investors to pool their resources under the guidance of professional managers. Some funds are closed-end, which means there is a *fixed* number of shares, and purchasers and sellers of shares must deal with each other. They normally cannot buy new shares from the fund. Much more important is the open-end fund, which stands ready at all times to sell new shares or buy back old shares. Actually, it is the open-end investment fund that technically represents the term *mutual fund.*

An important consideration with an open-end fund is whether it is a load fund or a no-load fund. The former requires a commission that may run as high as 7.25 percent, while the latter has no such charge. Because there is no proof that load funds deliver better performance than no-load funds, the investor should think long and hard before paying such a commission. Important sources of information on mutual funds include the *Forbes* annual August issue and the *Wiesenberger Investment Companies Service* guide. *Consumer Reports, Business Week, Financial World,* and *Money* also provide good mutual fund information.

Mutual funds may take many different forms such as those emphasizing money market management, growth in common stocks, bond portfolio management, special sectors of the economy (such as energy or computers), or foreign investments. The funds with an international orientation have enjoyed strong popularity in the last decade.

Through examining a fund's prospectus, the investor can become familiar with the fund's investment objectives and policies, its portfolio holdings, its turnover rate, and the fund's management fees. The investor can also become aware of whether the fund offers such special services as automatic reinvestment of distributions (when desired), exchange privileges among different funds, systematic withdrawal plans, and check-writing privileges.

Some investors use mutual funds as part of a strategy for long-term investment planning and may purchase the fund on a dollar-cost averaging basis, in which fixed amounts are placed in the fund on a regular basis regardless of present net asset value or the short-term economic outlook.

Return to fund holders may come in the form of capital appreciation or yield. Over the long term, mutual funds have not outperformed the popular market averages. However, they do offer an opportunity for low-cost, efficient diversification, and they normally have experienced management. Also, a minority of funds have turned in above-average performances.

KEY WORDS AND CONCEPTS

closed-end fund, 541	load funds, 544	no-load funds, 544
open-end fund, 541	low-load funds, 544	prospectus, 555
net asset value (NAV), 541	back-end load, 544	dollar-cost averaging, 557

DISCUSSION QUESTIONS

1. Do mutual funds, on average, outperform the market?
2. Do mutual funds generally provide efficient diversification?
3. Explain why the vast array of mutual funds available to the investor may be a partial drawback and not always an advantage.
4. What is the basic difference between a closed-end fund and an open-end fund?
5. Define net asset value. Do closed-end funds normally trade at their net asset value? What about open-end funds?
6. Is it mandatory that you pay a load fee when purchasing an open-end mutual fund? What is a low-load fund?
7. Should you get better performance from a load fund in comparison to a no-load fund?
8. If there is a difference between the net asset value (NAV) and the offer price for a mutual fund, what does that tell us about the fund?
9. How can you distinguish between regular growth funds and aggressive growth funds?
10. What type of fund is likely to invest in convertible securities?
11. Why might there be some potential danger in investing in sector funds?
12. What does Rule 12b-1 enable mutual funds to do? Is this normally beneficial to current mutual fund shareholders?
13. Are earnings of mutual funds normally taxed at the fund level or the shareholder level?
14. What is the advantage of investing in a mutual fund that offers an exchange privilege?
15. What is dollar-cost averaging? If you were a particularly astute investor at timing moves in the market, would you want to use dollar-cost averaging?
16. How does *Forbes* magazine rate fund performance in up and down markets?

PROBLEMS

Net asset value

1. The Twenty-First Century closed-end fund has \$350 million in securities, \$8 million in liabilities, and 20 million shares outstanding. It trades at a 10 percent discount from net asset value (NAV).
   a. What is the net asset value of the fund?
   b. What is the current price of the fund?
   c. Suggest two reasons why the fund may be trading at a discount from net asset value.

Load funds

2. An open-end fund is set up to charge a load. Its net asset value is $8.72, and its offer price is $9.40.
   a. What is the dollar value of the load (commission)?
   b. What percent of the offer price does the load represent?
   c. What percent of the net asset value does the load represent?
   d. Do load funds necessarily outperform no-load funds?
   e. How do no-load funds earn a return if they do not charge a commission?

Load funds

3. In problem 2, assume the fund increased in value by $0.32 the first month after you purchased 300 shares.
   a. What is your total dollar gain or loss? (Compare the total current value with the total purchase amount.)
   b. By what percent would the net asset value of the shares have to increase for you to break even?

Loads versus no-loads

4. Examine Table 19–4 and fill in the table below.

	Load or No-Load	If Load, Percent of Offer Price Load Represents
American Funds		
A Bal		
Babson Group		
INTL		
AIM Funds		
GRTHA		

Comparative fund performance and loads

5. Use Table 19–10 for this problem.
   a. What was the strongest performing group of funds between December 31, 1993, and December 29, 1994 (second column from the right)?
   b. If you purchased a low-load fund in this group at $10.30 and it had a net asset value of $10.00, what is the percent load?
   c. If the fund's performance percentagewise equaled that of the rest of the group, what would its new net asset value be? (Refer back to parts *a* and *b* and round to the nearest cent.)
   d. What is your dollar profit or loss per share based on your purchase price?
   e. What is your percentage return on your purchase price?

Total returns on a fund

6. An investor buys the Go-Go Mutual fund on January 1 at a net asset value of $21.20. At the end of the year, the price is $25.40. Also, the investor receives $0.50 in dividends and $0.35 in capital gains distributions. What is the total percentage return on the beginning net asset value? (Round to two places to the right of the decimal point.)

Total returns on a fund

7. Dan Herman purchases the Ivy Tower New Horizon Fund at a net asset value of $11.25. During the course of the year, he receives $0.50 in dividends and $0.14 in capital gains distributions. At the end of the year, the fund's price is $10.90. What

is the total percentage return or loss on the beginning net asset value? (Round to two places to the right of the decimal point.)

Total returns with reinvestment

8. Alice Oliva had 200 shares of the Quest Fund on January 1. The shares had a value of $17.60. During the year she received $90 in dividends and $270 in capital gains distributions. She used the funds to purchase new shares at an average price of $18 per share. By the end of the year, the shares were up to $18.50. What is her percentage total return? Use Equation 19–2, and round to two places to the right of the decimal point. Recall you first must determine the number of new shares.

Dollar-cost averaging

9. Under dollar-cost averaging, an investor will purchase $6,000 worth of stock each year for three years. The stock price is $40 in year 1, $30 in year 2, and $48 in year 3.
   - **a.** Compute the average price per share.
   - **b.** Compute the average cost per share.
   - **c.** Explain why the average cost is less than the average price.

THE WALL STREET JOURNAL PROJECTS

1. Take a Monday *Wall Street Journal* and compare the expense ratios of several mutual fund families. Mutual fund data can be found in Section C of the *Journal.* Specifically compare the expense ratios in general between the load funds sold by Merrill Lynch Group A Funds and the no-load funds sold by Price Funds (T. Rowe Price). Which group on average has higher expense ratios? Can you offer an opinion on how this might affect your investment return?
2. Use a Friday *Wall Street Journal* and compare the five-year rates of return between the Merrill Lynch Euro A international fund and the Price Europe international fund. Which one has the higher return? Is there any relationship between the higher fees charged (Monday's *Journal* part 1) and the return earned?

CRITICAL THOUGHT CASE

Al Harris was particularly glad to have an opportunity to visit with Mildred Frazier. Al had been selling mutual funds for the last five years, and he believed he was about to make his best sale of the year.

Mildred, age 70, had inherited $500,000 on the death of her husband four months ago. Her husband had been a successful businessman and had managed their financial affairs up to the time of his death. Although their home mortgage had been paid, Mildred had $500,000 in CDs, money market funds, and widely diversified stocks and bonds to manage. Her first inclination had been to turn over the assets to the trust department of the largest bank in town and let it manage the funds for a 1½ percent fee.

When she mentioned this plan to Al at a church gathering, he responded that bank trust departments were so conservative in their management policies that she probably would not get a return high enough to keep up with inflation.

He suggested she put her $500,000 in the New Era Science and Technology fund. He emphasized that the fund had enjoyed an increase in net asset value of 20 percent per year over the past five years for a total compounded gain of 148.8 percent. He suggested a

$500,000 investment could easily be worth $1,244,000 five years from now as the same pattern was likely to persist.

When Mildred asked if there were any expenses involved in buying the fund, Al said there was a courtesy commission of 7¼ percent at the time of purchase. Also, there was a back-end fee of 5 percent if she decided to sell the fund. He stressed that the 7¼ percent commission was insignificant when one considered the enormous return potential. Furthermore, he said, the 5 percent back-end sales commission would be reduced by 1 percent each year and would be eliminated after five years.

Mildred was excited about the information Al had given her and promised to consider it very carefully.

Question

1. Comment on the practices used by Al Harris.

SELECTED REFERENCES

Investment Strategy

Brealey, Richard A. "How to Combine Active Management with Index Funds." *Journal of Portfolio Management,* Winter 1986, pp. 4–10.

Fisher, David. "Lessons from the Third World." *Institutional Investor,* October 1988, pp. 243–45.

Gordon, Marion, and Janice Horowitz. "Inside Moves: Market Timing with Mutual Funds." *Personal Investor,* July 1985, pp. 32–39.

Healy, Thomas J., and Donald J. Hardy. "Alternative Investments Grow Rapidly at Tax Exempt Funds." *Journal of Investing,* Spring 1994, pp. 12–18.

Ruth, Simon. "Why Good Brokers Sell Bad Funds." *Money,* July 1991, pp. 94–99.

Simonds, Richard R. "Mutual Fund Strategies for IRA Investors." *Journal of Portfolio Management,* Winter 1986, pp. 40–43.

Mutual Fund Performance

Gallagher, Timothy J. "Mutual Fund Size and Risk-Adjusted Performance." *Illinois Business Review,* August 1988, pp. 11–13.

Goetzmann, William N., and Roger G. Ibbotson. "Do Winners Repeat?" *Journal of Portfolio Management,* Winter 1994, pp. 9–18.

Ippolito, Richard A. "On Studies of Mutual Fund Performance, 1962–1991." *Financial Analysts Journal,* January–February 1993, pp. 42–50.

Jensen, Michael C. "Risk, Capital Assets and Evaluation of Portfolios." *Journal of Business,* April 1969, pp. 167–247.

Kon, Stanley J., and Frank C. Jen. "The Investment Performance of Mutual Funds: An Empirical Investigation of Timing, Selectivity, and Market Efficiency." *Journal of Business,* April 1979, pp. 263–89.

Mutual Fund Guides and Surveys

"A Guide to Mutual Funds." *Consumer Reports* (published annually).

"Individual Investor's Guide to Low-Load Mutual Funds." *American Association of Individual Investors* (published annually).

"Morningstar Mutual Funds." *Morningstar Inc.* (published every other week).

"Tallying the Totals: Mutual Fund Scorecard." *Financial World* (published annually).

"The Money Ranking of Mutual Funds." *Money* (published annually).

"The Mutual Fund Survey." *Forbes* (published annually).

Wiesenberger Investment Companies Service. Boston: Warren, Gorham and Lamont (published annually).

Closed-End Funds

Anderson, Seth Copeland. "Closed-End Funds vs. Market Efficiency." *Journal of Portfolio Management,* Fall 1986, pp. 63–65.

APPENDIX 19A: Unit Investment Trusts (UITs)

Unit investment trusts (UITs) are investment companies organized for the purpose of purchasing a pool of securities—usually tax-exempt municipal bonds. UITs issue units to investors, representing a proportionate interest in the assets of the trust. Investors also receive a proportionate share in the interest or dividends received by the trust.

Unit investment trusts are passive investments. They normally purchase assets and hold them for the benefit of owners for a specified period.

To understand UITs better, consider the following hypothetical example. Nuveen, Inc.—a prominent firm in this field—announces the formation of the next in its series of tax-exempt unit trusts: Nuveen Series 200. Through advertising and selling agents, Nuveen will raise $4 million; investors will pay approximately $1,000 per unit. After deducting 2 to 3 percent for sales commissions, Nuveen will use the remaining cash to purchase large blocks of municipal securities from 10 to 20 different issuers. Once this diversified pool of bonds is acquired, Nuveen will play a passive role. It will collect and pass on to unit holders all interest payments received and all principal repayments resulting from maturing or recalled bonds. While UITs usually hold bonds until maturity, the trust custodian may sell off bonds whose future ability to pay interest and principal is altered by events.

The majority of UITs formed in the past decade have invested in tax-exempt securities. Often, trusts are formed to purchase tax-exempt securities from issuers in specific, high-tax states, such as New York, Massachusetts, and Minnesota. Unit holders residing in these states expect to receive a stream of income exempt from federal, state, and local taxation.

Even unit investment trusts dedicated to tax-exempt bonds have different investment objectives. Some deal strictly in long-term, high-rated issues. Others seek higher yields by purchasing issues with low ratings.

Units of a trust are redeemable under terms set forth in the prospectus. In most cases, this means a unit holder can sell units back to the trust at their net asset value, which is the current market value of each trust unit.

A secondary market for unit trusts is evolving among broker-dealers. Investors seeking to acquire or sell units can sometimes find a better deal in this market. However, most investors in UITs do not intend to redeem early.

Investors in UITs benefit by professional selection of securities, by diversification, and by avoiding the housekeeping chores of collecting coupon payments. As a large buyer, a UIT can usually purchase securities at a better price than the individual who buys in small lots.

Essential Difference between a Unit Investment Trust and a Mutual Fund

There is an important difference between UITs and mutual funds. UITs are formed with the intention of keeping all the initially purchased assets until maturity. The investment strategy, as described above, is strictly passive. A UIT of $4 million with a 10-year life will draw interest over that time period, while only cashing in bonds as they mature and returning the funds to the investors. The UIT will cease to exist after 10 years. Because of the features just described, there is very little interest-rate risk associated with UITs. Since all bonds are intended to be held until maturity, the investor can be reasonably well assured of recovering his initial investment (plus interest). The fact that interest rates and bond prices are changing at any point in time during the life of the UIT makes little difference.[1]

A bond-oriented mutual fund has no such assurance of recovering the initial investment. First, mutual funds have no stipulated life. Second, the bonds in the portfolio are actively managed and frequently sold off before their maturity dates at large profits or losses. Thus, the purchaser of a bond-oriented mutual fund may experience large capital gains or losses as well as receiving interest income.

The message is that if preservation of capital is of paramount importance to the investor, the UIT may be a better investment than a mutual fund. Of course, if one thinks interest rates are going down and bond prices up, the bond-oriented mutual fund would be a better investment.

[1] Of course, if the investor needs to redeem shares before the end of the life of the trust, there will be fluctuations in value.

20

INVESTMENTS IN REAL ASSETS

In this chapter, we turn our attention to **real assets;** that is, tangible assets that may be seen, felt, held, or collected. Examples of such assets are real estate, gold, silver, diamonds, coins, stamps, and antiques. This is no small area from which to consider investments. For example, the total market value of all real estate holdings in the United States in the mid-1990s was in excess of $6 trillion.

As further evidence of value, in the late 1980s, a Van Gogh painting sold for $40 million, and a 132-carat diamond earring set sold for $6.6 million. Coins and stamps also sell for values well into the hundreds of thousands.

A number of the traditional stock brokerage houses have moved into the area of real estate. Also, 25 million people in the United States are stamp collectors, and 8 million collect and invest in coins.

As was pointed out in Chapter 1, in inflationary environments, real assets have at times outperformed financial assets (such as stocks and bonds). With this in mind, the reader is well advised to become familiar with these investment outlets—not only to take advantage of the investment opportunities but also to be well aware of the pitfalls. A money manager who is challenged by clients to include real assets in a portfolio (such as real estate or precious metals) must be conversant not only with the opportunities but also with the drawbacks.

ADVANTAGES AND DISADVANTAGES OF REAL ASSETS

As previously mentioned, real assets may offer an opportunity as an inflation hedge because inflation means higher replacement costs for real estate, precious metals, and other physical items. Real assets also serve as an investment hedge against the unknown and feared. When people become concerned about world events, gold and other precious metals may be perceived as the last safe haven for investments.

Real assets also may serve as an effective vehicle for portfolio diversification. Since financial and real assets at times move in opposite directions, some efficient diversification may occur. A study by Robichek, Cohn, and Pringle in the *Journal of Business* actually indicates that movements among various types of real and monetary assets are less positively correlated than are those for monetary assets alone.[1] The general findings indicate that enlarging the universe of investment alternatives would benefit the overall portfolio construction in terms of risk-return alternatives.

A final advantage of an investment in real assets is the psychic pleasure that may be provided. One can easily relate to a beautiful painting in the living room, a mint gold coin in a bank lockbox, or an attractive real estate development.

There are many disadvantages to consider as well. Perhaps the largest drawback is the absence of large, liquid, and relatively efficient markets. Whereas stocks or bonds can generally be sold in a few minutes at a value close to the latest quoted trade, such is not likely to be the case for real estate, diamonds, art, and other forms of real assets. It may take many months to get the desired price for a real asset, and even then, there is an air of uncertainty about the impending transaction until it is consummated.

Furthermore, there is the problem of dealer spread or middleman commission. Whereas in the trading of stocks and bonds where spreads or commissions are very small

---

[1] Alexander A. Robichek, Richard A. Cohn, and John J. Pringle, "Return on Alternative Media and Implications for Portfolio Construction," *Journal of Business,* July 1972, pp. 427–43.

(usually 1 or 2 percent), dealer spreads for real assets can be as large as 20 to 25 percent or more. This is particularly true for small items that do not have great value. On more valuable items, such as rare paintings, valuable jewels, or mint gold coins, the dealer spread tends to be smaller (perhaps 5 to 10 percent) but still more than that on securities.

The investor in real assets generally receives no current income (with the possible exception of real estate) and may incur storage and insurance costs. Furthermore, there may be the problem of high unit cost for investments. You cannot easily acquire multiple art masterpieces.

A final drawback or caveat in real assets is the hysteria or overreaction that tends to come into the marketplace from time to time. Gold, silver, diamonds, and coins may be temporarily bid all out of proportion to previously anticipated value. The last buyer, who arrives too late, may end up owning a very unprofitable investment. The trick is to get into the recurring cycle early enough to take advantage of the large capital gains opportunities that regularly occur for real assets. Also, you should buy items of high enough quality so that you can ride out the setbacks if your timing is incorrect.

In the remainder of this chapter, we will examine real estate, gold, silver, diamonds, and other collectibles as investment outlets. Because real estate lends itself more directly to analytical techniques familiar to students of finance, it will receive a proportionately larger share of our attention.

REAL ESTATE AS AN INVESTMENT

Approximately half the households in the United States own real estate as a home or investment. Also, many firms in the brokerage and investment community have also moved into real estate. As an example, Merrill Lynch has acquired real estate affiliates to broker property, conduct mortgage banking activities, and package real estate syndications. Pension fund managers are also increasing the real estate component in their portfolio, going from virtually no representation two decades ago to almost 10 percent in the 1990s.

Some insight into changing real estate values may be gained from Figure 20–1. We see the gain for a dollar invested in real estate in 1946 as compared with fixed-income investments and common stock.

Real estate investments may include such outlets as your own home, duplexes and apartment buildings, office buildings, shopping centers, industrial buildings, hotels and motels, as well as undeveloped land. The investor may participate as an individual, as part of a limited partnership real estate syndicate, or through a real estate investment trust.

Throughout the rest of the section, we will discuss real estate in the last decade and relate it to the future outlook. We will also evaluate a typical real estate investment, consider new methods of real estate financing, and examine limited partner syndicates and real estate investment trusts.

Real Estate in the Last Decade and the Future Outlook

The mid-1980s started out as a bad time for real estate with the passage of the Tax Reform Act of 1986. As part of this legislation, the life over which a real estate investor could write off depreciation for tax purposes was extended from 19 years to 27½ years

FIGURE 20–1 Growth in Value: 1946–1994 ($1 of investment)

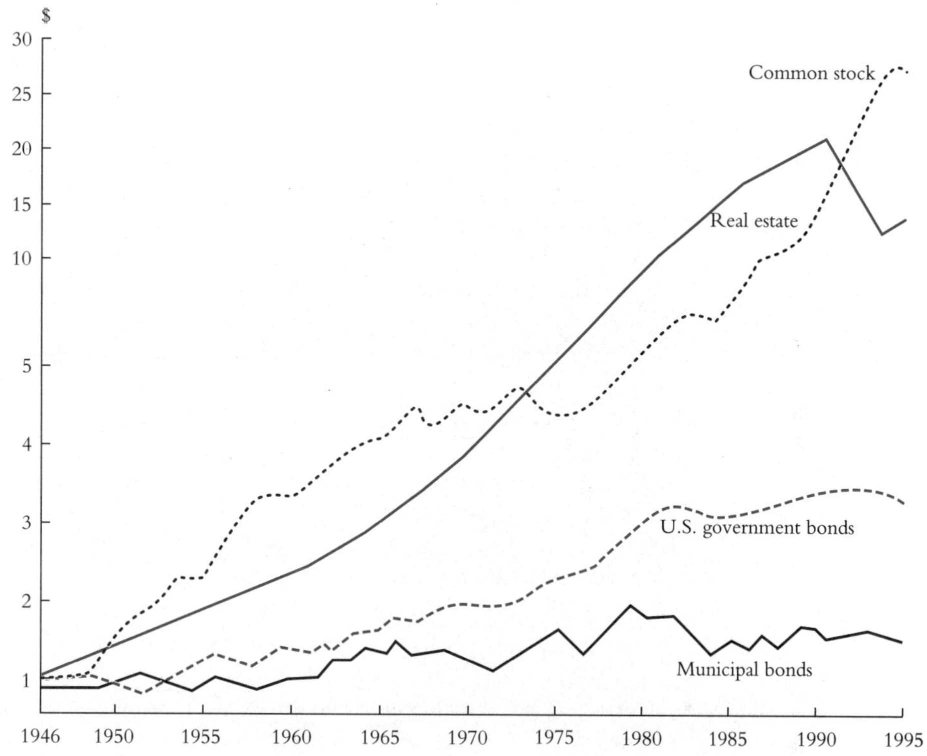

for residential rental property and to 31½ years for commercial property.[2] This meant that an investor had to wait longer to take full advantage of tax deductions related to real estate. Also, real estate investors not actively involved in the management of property were severely restricted in writing off paper losses from real estate against other forms of income.[3]

The effect of tax reform was to make real estate a less attractive investment. Because of the loss of many traditional tax benefits for real estate, some existing properties had less value, and new construction proceeded at a slower pace.

The initial negative impact of tax reform on real estate was also associated with declining economic conditions in various sections of the country during the late 1980s and early 1990s. First, the Southwest (and Texas in particular) was hit with a 70 percent plunge in oil prices in 1986. This meant office buildings, shopping centers, and homes built on an assumption of increasing energy prices to stimulate economic growth went begging for buyers. It was not unusual for a home that was purchased in Dallas,

---

[2] The time period for depreciating commercial property was extended to 39 years under the Revenue Reconciliation Tax Act of 1993.

[3] A paper loss is a taxable loss associated with positive cash flow. It may take place because of large noncash tax deductions.

Oklahoma City, or Denver for $300,000 in 1986 to be sold at 50 to 60 percent of that amount five years later. Even as the Southwestern economy began to slowly recover in the early 1990s, real estate–related problems moved into the Northeast, with Massachusetts being hit particularly hard. The next area to suffer was the supposedly immune West Coast in the mid-1990s. Few thought it possible that the ever-growing state of California would see the real estate bubble burst in such dynamic areas as Los Angeles and the San Francisco Bay area.

Real estate investors and home buyers were not the only ones hurt; so were the financial institutions that loaned money to them. In 1989, the Resolution Trust Corporation (RTC) was formed by Congress in an attempt to help savings and loans liquidate their bad real estate loans. The eventual cost to the government (and taxpayers) of the S&L bailout is likely to be over $200 billion.

Over the long term, however, real estate may still be a good investment. Why? With fewer new properties being developed as a result of tax reform and economic conditions, the glut in office space and apartments in certain sections of the country will eventually disappear. Furthermore, with fewer new properties brought to the market, rents will eventually go up on existing properties. The eventual effect of higher rents should be higher valuation. Evidence of "smart" money starting to flow into depressed real estate markets can be seen in the Dallas–Fort Worth area where Texas billionaire H. Ross Perot is buying everything he can get his hands on.

An Actual Example

Let's look at an actual real estate investment example. Assume we are considering investing $170,000 in a new fourplex (four-unit apartment housing project). The land costs will be $30,000, and the actual physical structure will cost $140,000. This latter amount will be the value to be depreciated. We assume that we borrow 75 percent of the total property value of $170,000, which represents a loan of $127,500. Although we are dealing with relatively small numbers for ease of computation, the same types of considerations would apply to a multimillion dollar shopping center or office building. Before we actually evaluate our cash inflows and outflows, we consider tax and accounting factors related to depreciation in real estate.

Depreciation Effects

In the present case, we can write off depreciation on residential real estate property over 27½ years. Furthermore, under the Tax Reform Act of 1986, only **straight-line depreciation** (equal annual depreciation) can be applied to any form of real estate investment. There is no potential for accelerated depreciation as there was before the passage of this act.

Returning to our example, the $140,000 physical structure would be depreciated over 27½ years using straight-line depreciation. The annual depreciation charge would be $5,091:

$$\frac{\$140,000}{27.5} = \$5,091 \text{ annual depreciation}$$

Cash Flow Considerations

The only aspect of our investment we have considered so far is depreciation. We have established the fact that on a $170,000 investment with $30,000 in land and $140,000 in the building, we could take annual depreciation of $5,091. Depreciation is a noncash tax-deductible expense that is used to lower tax obligations. We now must consider various cash flow items, such as the receipt of the rent, the payment of interest, property taxes, insurance, maintenance expenses, and so on. An overall example of cash flow analysis is presented in Table 20–1. This is assumed to represent the first year of the investment.

We see in Table 20–1 that we have a loss of $1,797 before federal income tax, and this provides a tax-shelter benefit of $557 against other income.[4] We also add depreciation of $5,091 back in to get cash flow because, although it was subtracted out, it is really a noncash item. The negative and two positive values at the bottom of the table provide a positive cash flow of $3,851.

In terms of investor return in the first year, we first consider that the initial cash investment is $42,500. This is based on the total value of the property of $170,000 minus the initial loan of $127,500, requiring the investor to put up $42,500 in cash. With a cash inflow of $3,851 in the first year, the cash-on-cash return in the first year is 9.06 percent ($3,851/$42,500).

TABLE 20–1 Cash Flow Analysis for an Apartment (Fourplex) Investment

Gross annual rental (4 units at $490 per month or $5,880 per year for each unit		$23,520
Less 5 percent vacancy		1,176
Net rental income		$22,344
Interest expense on a loan of 75 percent of property value at 12 percent interest:		
75% x $170,000 = $127,500		
12% x $127,500 = $15,300	$15,300	
Property taxes	2,000	
Insurance	750	
Maintenance	1,000	
Depreciation	5,091	
Total expenses		24,141
Before-tax income or (loss)		$ (1,797)
Tax benefit (assumes 31 percent tax rate)		557
Depreciation		5,091
Cash flow		$ 3,851

[4] The assumption in this case is that we have an active participation in the property and are allowed to deduct the tax loss. This is a tricky matter in real estate because some real estate losses are considered to be passive and nondeductible. However, there are exceptions.

TABLE 20–2 Interest Payments for a 20-Year Loan (Principal amount equals $127,500)

	8 Percent	10 Percent	12 Percent	14 Percent	16 Percent
Annual payment	$ 12,986	$ 14,975	$ 17,070	$ 19,251	$ 21,504
First year interest expense	10,200	12,750	15,300	17,850	20,400
Total interest over the life of the loan	132,220	172,000	213,900	257,520	302,580

However, we should point out that in considering the cost of the loan in Table 20–1, we have evaluated only interest payments. We might wish to consider repayment of principal as well. In the present case, we are assuming that in the first year we are paying 12 percent on a loan balance of $127,500, or $15,300 in interest (as shown in the second line of Table 20–2). Assuming a 20-year loan, the total first-year payment for interest and principal is $17,070 (also shown in Table 20–2). These figures indicate that $1,770 is applied toward the repayment of principal:

Payment − Interest = Repayment of principal
$17,070 − $15,300 = $1,770

On this basis, our net cash flow figure will be reduced to $2,081:

Cash flow	−	Repayment of principal	=	Net cash flow[5]
$3,851	−	$1,770	=	$2,081

With a net cash flow of $2,081 (after repayment of principal), the cash-on-cash return in the first year is 4.90 percent ($2,081/$42,500). This value will be different from year to year as rental income, expenses, and repayment of principal change.

While the return appears to be low, it should be pointed out that the investor will build up equity or ownership interest by the amount of repayment toward principal each year as well as any increase in property value resulting from inflation. If the property increases by 5 percent in the first year, this represents an added benefit of $8,500 (5 percent times the $170,000 value of the property). Actually, return benefits associated with price appreciation may exceed all other considerations. An investor may be willing to accept relatively low cash flow if he or she can enjoy inflation-related gains. Note in the present case, the $8,500 gain from price appreciation alone would represent a first-year return on cash investment of 20 percent ($8,500/$42,500).

This gain is particularly relevant because most of the tax advantages of real estate have been largely reduced, so there is a dependence on cash generation and *inflation.*

[5] One could argue that we are building up equity or ownership interest through the repayment of principal. However, our focus for now is simply on the amount of cash flow going in and out. We will consider buildup in equity very shortly.

You can readily see the twin factors that make real estate potentially attractive are depreciation write-offs and appreciation in value due to price appreciation. Apartments, office buildings, warehouses, and shopping centers have served particularly well as good performers in inflationary environments. However, the clear downside is that in a weak economic environment there may not be enough cash inflow to cover the financial obligations associated with the investment. As previously mentioned, this happened all too often in various sections of the country during the late 1980s and early 1990s.

FINANCING OF REAL ESTATE

One of the essential considerations in any real estate investment analysis is the cost of financing. In the prior example, we said a loan for $127,500 over 20 years at 12 percent interest would have yearly payments of $17,070. Note in Table 20–2 the effects of various interest rates on annual payments.

We see that the difference in annual payments ranges from $12,986 at 8 percent up to $21,504 at 16 percent. Even more dramatic is the increase in total interest paid over the life of the loan; it goes from $132,220 at 8 percent to $302,580 at 16 percent. (Keep in mind that the total loan was only $127,500.)

An investor who has the unlikely opportunity to shift out of the loan at 16 percent into one at 8 percent might be willing to pay as much as $83,692.72 for the privilege (tax effects are not specifically considered here):

$$\text{16 percent interest} - \text{8 percent interest} = \text{Dollar difference in annual payments}$$
$$\$21{,}504 - \$12{,}986 = \$8{,}518$$

The present value of $8,518 over 20 years assuming an 8 percent discount rate (see Appendix D on page 656) is:

$$\$8{,}518 \times 9.818 = \$83{,}629.72$$

Thus, it is easy to appreciate the role of interest rates in a real estate investment decision. No industry is more susceptible to the impact of changing interest rates than real estate. Each time the economy overheats and interest rates skyrocket, the real estate industry comes to a standstill. With the eventual easing of interest-rate pressures, the industry once again enjoys a recovery.

New Types of Mortgages

In actuality, a whole new set of mortgage arrangements has appeared as alternatives to the fixed-interest-rate mortgage (particularly for home mortgages). The borrower must now be prepared to consider such alternative lending arrangements as the **adjustable rate mortgage,** the **graduated payment mortgage,** and the **shared appreciation mortgage.**

Adjustable Rate Mortgage (ARM) Under this mortgage arrangement, the interest rate is adjusted regularly. If interest rates go up, borrowers may either increase their normal payments or extend the maturity date of the loan at the same fixed-payment level to fully compensate the lender. Similar downside adjustments can also be made if interest rates fall. Generally, adjustable rate mortgages are initially made at rates 1 to 2 percent below

fixed-interest-rate mortgages because the lender enjoys the flexibility of changing interest rates and is willing to share the benefits with the borrower. Adjustable rate mortgages currently account for more than half of the residential mortgage market. Although adjustable rate mortgages usually have an upper boundary (such as 15 or 18 percent), there is a real possibility of default for many borrowers if interest rates reach high levels.

Graduated Payment Mortgage (GPM) Under this type of financial arrangement, the payments start out on a relatively low basis and increase over the life of the loan. This type of mortgage may be well suited to the young borrower who has an increasing repayment capability over the life of the loan. An example would be a 30-year, $60,000 loan at 9 percent that would normally require monthly payments of $583.99 under a standard fixed-payment mortgage. With a graduated payment mortgage, monthly payments might start out as $350 or $400 and eventually progress to more than $700. The GPM plan has been referred to by a few of its critics as the "gyp 'em" plan, in that early payments may not be large enough to cover interest, and therefore, later payments must cover not only the amortization of the loan but also interest on the accumulated, unpaid, early interest. This is not an altogether fair criticism but merely an interpretation of what the graduated payment stream represents.

Shared Appreciation Mortgage (SAM) Perhaps the newest and most innovative of the mortgage payment plans is the shared appreciation mortgage. This provides the lender with a hedge against inflation because he directly participates in any increase in value associated with the property being mortgaged. The lender may enjoy as much as 30 to 40 percent of the appreciation in value over a specified time period, such as 10 years. The lender may take his return from the selling of the property or from the refinancing of the appreciated property value with a new lender. In return for this appreciation-potential privilege, the lender may advance funds at well below current market rates (perhaps at three-fourths of current rates). The shared appreciation mortgage is not yet legal in all states.

Other Forms of Mortgages Somewhat similar to the shared appreciation mortgage is the concept of equity participation that is popular in commercial real estate. Under an **equity participation** arrangement, the lender not only provides the borrowed capital but part of the equity or ownership funds as well. A major insurance company or savings and loan thus may acquire an equity interest of 10 to 25 percent (or more). This financing arrangement becomes popular each time inflation rears its head. Some lenders are simply unwilling to commit capital for long periods without a participation feature.

Borrowers may also look toward a *second mortgage* for financing. Here, a second lender provides additional financing beyond the first mortgage in return for a secondary claim or lien. The second mortgage is generally for a shorter period of time than the initial mortgage. Primary suppliers of second mortgages in recent times have been sellers of property. Often, to consummate a sale, it is necessary for the seller to supplement the financing provided by a financial institution. Sellers providing second mortgages generally advance the funds at rates below the first mortgage rate to facilitate the sale, whereas other second mortgage lenders (nonsellers) will ask for a few percentage points

above the first mortgage rate to compensate for the extra risk of being in a secondary claim position.

In some cases, sellers may actually provide all the financing to the buyer. Usually the terms of the mortgage are for 20 to 30 years, but the seller has the right to call in the loan after three to five years if so desired. The assumption is that the buyer may have an easier time finding his own financing at that point in time. This may or may not be true.

FORMS OF REAL ESTATE OWNERSHIP

Ownership of real estate may take many forms. The investor may participate as an individual, in a regular partnership, through a real estate syndicate (generally a limited partnership), or through a real estate investment trust (REIT).

Individual or Regular Partnership

Investing as an individual or with two or three others in a regular partnership offers the simplest way of getting into real estate from a legal viewpoint. The investors pretty much control their own destinies and can take advantage of personal knowledge of local markets and changing conditions to enhance their returns.

As is true with most smaller and less complicated business arrangements, there is a well-defined center of responsibility that often leads to quick corrective action. However, there may be a related problem of inability to pool adequate capital to engage in large-scale investments as well as the absence of expertise to develop a wide range of investments. Furthermore, there is unlimited liability to the investor(s).

Syndicate or Limited Partnership

To expand the potential for investor participation, a syndicate or limited partnership has traditionally been formed.[6] The **limited partnership** works as follows: A general partner forms the limited partnership and has unlimited liability for the partnership liabilities. The general partner then sells participation units to the limited partners whose liability is limited to the extent of their initial investment (such as $5,000 or $10,000). Limited liability is particularly important in real estate because mortgage debt obligations may exceed the net worth of the participants. The general partner is normally responsible for managing the property, while the limited partners are merely investors.

Although the restricted liability feature of the limited partnership remains attractive, the Tax Reform Act of 1986 generally restricted the use of limited partnerships as tax shelters. Historically, real estate limited partnerships generated large paper losses through accelerated depreciation (though not cash losses), and these paper losses were used to shelter other forms of income (such as a doctor's salary) from taxation. Under the Tax Reform Act of 1986, a taxpayer is no longer allowed to freely use passive losses to offset other sources of income such as salary or portfolio income. Such losses can only be used to offset income from other passive investments.

---

[6] A syndicate may take the form of a corporation, but this is not common. The term *real estate syndicate* has become virtually synonymous with the limited partnership form of operation.

It is easy to see why the Tax Reform Act of 1986 had a damaging effect on real estate values. Investors who had bought into real estate limited partnerships a number of years before the act was passed had their tax write-off privileges rapidly phased out after the passage of the act. All of a sudden, investors in existing real estate limited partnerships were bailing out. They were refusing to make required annual payments into the partnership, and as a result, many of the limited partnerships (as well as their investors) were disposing of property at fire-sale prices.

As previously mentioned, the initial impact of the act has already occurred, so real estate has the potential to be a bargain in the future. Real estate limited partnerships still exist but more for limited liability than for tax reasons. The successful partnerships stress strong cash flow generation and capital appreciation potential. In the analysis in Table 20–1, a limited partnership was not involved, and the investor actively participated in managing the property. Some small tax write-offs were allowed, but note that the success of the project was much more dependent on cash flow and potential capital appreciation.

If you decide to invest in a limited partnership, you should follow certain guidelines. You must be particularly sensitive to the front-end fees and commissions the general partner might charge. These can vary anywhere from 5 to 10 percent to as large as 20 to 25 percent. The investor must also be sensitive to any double-dealing the general partner might be doing. An example would be selling property between different partnerships the general partner has formed and taking a commission each time. The inflated paper profits may prove quite deceptive and costly to the uninformed limited partner.

In assessing a general partner and his associated real estate deal, the investor should look at a number of items. First, he should review the prior record of performance of the general partner. Is this the 1st or 10th deal that the general partner has put together? The investor will also wish to be sensitive to any lawsuits against the general partner that might exist. The investor might also wish to ascertain whether he or she is investing in a **blind pool** arrangement where funds are provided to the general partner to ultimately select properties for investment or if specific projects have already been identified and analyzed.

Finally, the investor may have to decide whether to invest in a limited partnership/syndication that is either *public* or *private* in nature. A public offering generally involves much larger total amounts and has gone through the complex and rigorous process of SEC registration. Of course, SEC registration only attempts to ensure that full disclosure has occurred—it does not judge the prudence of the venture. A private offering of a limited partnership syndication is usually local in scope and restricted to a maximum of 35 investors.

Secondary (resale) markets for both public and private limited partnerships exist, but the dealer spreads and commissions tend to be very high. The spreads on desirable property are perhaps 10 to 15 percent; on less desirable property, 20 to 30 percent or more. Really bad property may approach total illiquidity. As you might anticipate, a public limited partnership has much more resale potential than a private one.

Real Estate Investment Trust

Another form of real estate investment is the **real estate investment trust (REIT).** REITs are similar to mutual funds or investment companies and trade on organized exchanges or over-the-counter. They pool investor funds, along with borrowed funds, and invest them directly in real estate or use them to make construction or mortgage loans to investors.

The advantage to the investor of a REIT is that he or she can participate in the real estate market for as little as $10 to $20 per share. Furthermore, this is the most liquid type of real estate investment because of the large secondary market for the shares.

REITs were initiated under the Real Estate Investment Trust Act of 1960. Like other investment companies, they enjoy the privilege of single taxation of income (only the stockholder pays and not the trust). To qualify for the tax privilege of a REIT, a firm must receive at least 75 percent of its income from real estate (i.e., rents and interest on mortgage loans) and distribute at least 95 percent of its income as cash dividends.

REITs may take any of three different forms or combinations thereof. **Equity trusts** buy, operate, and sell real estate as an investment; **mortgage trusts** make long-term loans to real estate investors; and **hybrid trusts** engage in the activities of both equity and mortgage trusts. REITs are generally formed and advised by affiliates of commercial banks, insurance companies, mortgage bankers, and other financial institutions. Representative issues include Bank American Realty, and Connecticut General Mortgage.

Although REITs were enormously popular investments during the 1960s and early 1970s, the bottom fell out of the REIT market in the mid-1970s. Many had made questionable loans that came to the surface in the tight money, recessionary period of 1973–75. Nevertheless, REITs have now regained some of their earlier popularity. The investor in REITs normally hopes to receive a reasonably high yield because 95 percent of income must be paid out in the form of dividends plus a modest capital appreciation in stock value. In some cases, outside investors have taken over REITs with the intention of liquidating assets at higher than current stock market values.

There are more than 200 REITs from which the investor may choose. Further information on REITs may be acquired from the National Association of Real Estate Investment Trusts, 1101 17th St., N.W., Washington, D.C. 20036. In Figure 20–2 on page 582, a Value Line data sheet is presented for HRE Properties, a typical REIT.

GOLD AND SILVER

We now examine a number of other forms of real asset investments. Precious metals represent the most volatile of the investment alternatives. Gold and silver tend to move up in troubled times and show a decline in value during stable, predictable periods. Observe the movement in the price of gold between 1976 and 1994 in Figure 20–3 on page 583.

Gold

Major factors that tend to drive up gold prices are fear of war, political instability, and inflation (these were particularly evident in Figure 20–3 for 1979 with the takeover of U.S. embassies in Iran and double-digit inflation). Conversely, moderation in worldwide tensions and lower inflation cause a decline in gold prices. This pattern has generally been in place since 1987 but could easily change if there is a substantial increase in inflation or an extended period of world tensions.

Gold may be owned in many different forms, and a survey by *Changing Times* indicated 30 percent of the U.S. population with incomes of more than $30,000 per year

FIGURE 20–2 Data Sheet for a REIT

HRE PROPERTIES NYSE-HRE

RECENT PRICE	P/E RATIO	(Trailing: NMF / Median: NMF)	RELATIVE P/E RATIO	DIV'D YLD	VALUE LINE
15	44.1	Trailing: NMF, Median: NMF	2.64	7.7%	1175

TIMELINESS 3 Average
(Relative Price Performance Next 12 Mos.)
SAFETY 3 Average
(Scale: 1 Highest to 5 Lowest)
BETA .75 (1.00 = Market)

	1982	1983	1984	1985	1986	1987	1988	1989	1990	1991	1992	1993
High:	19.9	26.0	26.0	27.4	27.5	27.8	26.4	26.4	23.3	16.3	14.9	16.4
Low:	14.5	17.6	20.5	23.1	23.1	17.3	21.1	21.5	10.5	10.4	11.0	11.8

1996-98 PROJECTIONS

	Price	Gain	Ann'l Total Return
High	20	(+35%)	*14%*
Low	14	(-5%)	*7%*

Insider Decisions

	A	M	J	J	A	S	O	N	D
to Buy	0	0	0	0	0	0	0	1	0
Options	0	0	0	0	0	0	0	0	0
to Sell	0	0	0	0	0	0	0	0	0

Institutional Decisions

	1Q'93	2Q'93	3Q'93
to Buy	5	1	2
to Sell	5	1	0
Hld's(000)	264	199	225

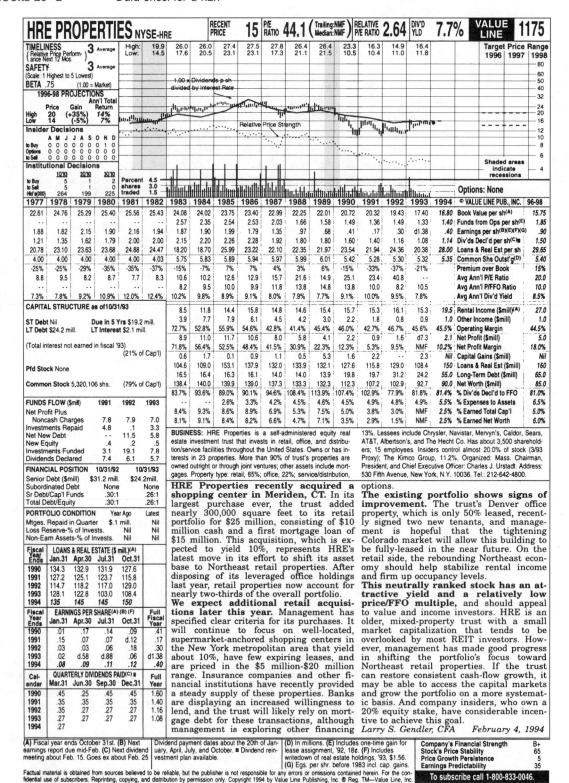

Options: None

1977	1978	1979	1980	1981	1982	1983	1984	1985	1986	1987	1988	1989	1990	1991	1992	1993	1994	© VALUE LINE PUB., INC.	96-98
22.61	24.76	25.29	25.40	25.56	25.43	24.08	24.02	23.75	23.40	22.99	22.25	22.01	20.72	20.32	19.43	17.40	*16.80*	Book Value per sh(A)	*15.75*
--	--	--	--	--	--	2.57	2.35	2.54	2.53	2.03	1.66	1.58	1.49	1.36	1.49	1.33	*1.40*	Funds from Ops per sh(E)	*1.85*
1.88	1.82	2.15	1.90	2.16	1.94	1.87	1.90	1.99	1.79	1.35	.97	.68	.41	.17	.30	d1.38	*.40*	Earnings per sh(B)(E)(F)(G)	*.90*
1.21	1.35	1.62	1.79	2.00	2.00	2.15	2.20	2.26	2.28	1.92	1.80	1.80	1.60	1.40	1.16	1.08	*1.14*	Div'ds Decl'd per sh(C)■	*1.50*
20.78	23.10	23.63	23.68	24.88	24.47	18.20	18.70	25.99	23.22	22.10	22.35	21.97	23.54	21.94	24.36	20.38	*28.00*	Loans & Real Est per sh	*29.65*
4.00	4.00	4.00	4.00	4.00	4.03	5.75	5.83	5.89	5.94	5.97	5.99	6.01	5.42	5.28	5.30	5.32	*5.35*	Common Shs Outst'g(D)	*5.40*
-25%	-25%	-29%	-35%	-35%	-37%	-15%	-7%	7%	7%	4%	3%	6%	-15%	-33%	-37%	-21%		Premium over Book	*15%*
8.8	9.5	8.2	8.7	7.7	8.3	10.6	10.2	12.6	12.9	15.7	21.6	14.9	25.1	23.4	40.8	--		Avg Ann'l P/E Ratio	*20.0*
--	--	--	--	--	--	8.2	9.5	10.0	9.9	11.8	13.8	14.8	13.8	10.0	8.2	10.5		Avg Ann'l P/FFO Ratio	*10.0*
7.3%	7.8%	9.2%	10.9%	12.0%	12.4%	10.2%	9.8%	8.9%	9.1%	8.0%	7.9%	7.7%	9.1%	10.0%	9.5%	7.8%		Avg Ann'l Div'd Yield	*8.5%*
						8.5	11.8	14.4	15.8	14.8	14.6	15.4	15.7	15.3	16.1	15.3	*19.5*	Rental Income ($mill)(A)	*27.0*
						3.9	7.7	7.9	6.1	4.5	4.2	3.0	2.2	1.8	0.8	0.9	*1.0*	Other Income ($mill)	*1.0*
						72.7%	52.8%	55.9%	54.6%	42.8%	41.4%	45.4%	46.0%	42.7%	46.7%	45.6%	*45.5%*	Operating Margin	*44.5%*
						8.9	11.0	11.7	10.6	8.0	5.8	4.1	2.2	0.9	1.6	d7.3	*2.1*	Net Profit ($mill)	*5.0*
						71.8%	56.4%	52.5%	48.4%	41.5%	30.9%	22.3%	12.3%	5.3%	9.5%	NMF	*10.2%*	Net Profit Margin	*18.0%*
						0.6	1.7	0.1	0.9	1.1	0.5	5.3	1.6	2.2	--	2.3	*Nil*	Capital Gains ($mill)	*Nil*
						104.6	109.0	153.1	137.9	132.0	133.9	132.1	127.6	115.8	129.0	108.4	*150*	Loans & Real Est ($mill)	*160*
						16.5	16.4	16.3	16.1	14.0	14.0	13.9	19.8	19.7	31.2	24.2	*55.0*	Long-Term Debt ($mill)	*65.0*
						138.4	140.0	139.9	139.0	137.3	133.3	132.3	112.3	107.2	102.9	92.7	*90.0*	Net Worth ($mill)	*85.0*
						83.7%	93.6%	89.0%	90.1%	94.6%	108.4%	113.9%	107.4%	102.9%	77.9%	81.8%	*81.4%*	% Div'ds Decl'd to FFO	*81.0%*
						--	--	2.6%	3.3%	4.2%	4.5%	4.6%	4.5%	4.9%	4.8%	4.9%	*5.5%*	% Expenses to Assets	*6.5%*
						8.4%	9.3%	8.6%	8.9%	6.9%	5.3%	7.5%	5.0%	3.8%	3.0%	NMF	*2.5%*	% Earned Total Cap'l	*5.0%*
						8.1%	9.1%	8.4%	8.2%	6.6%	4.7%	7.1%	3.5%	2.9%	1.5%	NMF	*2.5%*	% Earned Net Worth	*6.0%*

CAPITAL STRUCTURE as of 10/31/93

ST Debt Nil **Due in 5 Yrs** $19.2 mill.
LT Debt $24.2 mill. **LT Interest** $2.1 mill.

(Total interest not earned in fiscal '93)
(21% of Cap'l)

Pfd Stock None

Common Stock 5,320,106 shs. (79% of Cap'l)

FUNDS FLOW ($mill)	1991	1992	1993
Net Profit Plus Noncash Charges	7.8	7.9	7.0
Investments Repaid	4.8	.1	3.3
Net New Debt	--	11.5	5.8
New Equity	.4	.2	.5
Investments Funded	3.1	19.1	7.8
Dividends Declared	7.4	6.1	5.7

FINANCIAL POSITION	10/31/92	10/31/93
Senior Debt ($mill)	$31.2 mill.	$24.2mill.
Subordinated Debt	None	None
Sr Debt/Cap'l Funds	.30:1	.26:1
Total Debt/Equity	.30:1	.26:1

PORTFOLIO CONDITION	Year Ago	Latest
Mtges. Repaid in Quarter	$.1 mill.	Nil
Loss Reserve-% of Invests.	Nil	Nil
Non-Earn Assets-% of Invests.	Nil	Nil

Fiscal Year Ends	LOANS & REAL ESTATE ($ mill.)(A) Jan.31	Apr.30	Jul.31	Oct.31
1990	134.3	132.9	131.9	127.6
1991	127.2	125.1	123.7	115.8
1992	114.7	118.2	117.0	129.0
1993	128.1	122.8	103.0	108.4
1994	*135*	*145*	*145*	*150*

Fiscal Year Ends	EARNINGS PER SHARE(A)(B)(F) Jan.31	Apr.30	Jul.31	Oct.31	Full Fiscal Year
1990	.01	.17	.14	.09	.41
1991	.15	.07	.07	d.12	.17
1992	.03	.03	.06	.18	.30
1993	.02	d.58	d.88	.06	d1.38
1994	*.08*	*.09*	*.11*	*.12*	*.40*

Cal-endar	QUARTERLY DIVIDENDS PAID(C)■ Mar.31	Jun.30	Sep.30	Dec.31	Full Year
1990	.45	.25	.45	.45	1.60
1991	.35	.35	.35	.35	1.40
1992	.35	.27	.27	.27	1.16
1993	.27	.27	.27	.27	1.08
1994	.27				

BUSINESS: HRE Properties is a self-administered equity real estate investment trust that invests in retail, office, and distribution/service facilities throughout the United States. Owns or has interests in 23 properties. More than 90% of trust's properties are owned outright or through joint ventures; other assets include mortgages. Property type: retail, 65%; office, 22%; service/distribution, 13%. Lessees include Chrysler, Navistar, Mervyn's, Caldor, Sears, AT&T, Albertson's, and The Hecht Co. Has about 3,500 shareholders; 15 employees. Insiders control almost 20.0% of stock (3/93 Proxy); The Kimco Group, 11.2%. Organized: Mass. Chairman, President, and Chief Executive Officer: Charles J. Urstadt. Address: 530 Fifth Avenue, New York, N.Y. 10036. Tel.: 212-642-4800.

HRE Properties recently acquired a shopping center in Meriden, CT. In its largest purchase ever, the trust added nearly 300,000 square feet to its retail portfolio for $25 million, consisting of $10 million cash and a first mortgage loan of $15 million. This acquisition, which is expected to yield 10%, represents HRE's latest move in its effort to shift its asset base to Northeast retail properties. After disposing of its leveraged office holdings last year, retail properties now account for nearly two-thirds of the overall portfolio.

We expect additional retail acquisitions later this year. Management has specified clear criteria for its purchases. It will continue to focus on well-located, supermarket-anchored shopping centers in the New York metropolitan area that yield about 10%, have few expiring leases, and are priced in the $5 million-$20 million range. Insurance companies and other financial institutions have recently provided a steady supply of these properties. Banks are displaying an increased willingness to lend, and the trust will likely rely on mortgage debt for these transactions, although management is exploring other financing options.

The existing portfolio shows signs of improvement. The trust's Denver office property, which is only 50% leased, recently signed two new tenants, and management is hopeful that the tightening Colorado market will allow this building to be fully-leased in the near future. On the retail side, the rebounding Northeast economy should help stabilize rental income and firm up occupancy levels.

This neutrally ranked stock has an attractive yield and a relatively low price/FFO multiple, and should appeal to value and income investors. HRE is an older, mixed-property trust with a small market capitalization that tends to be overlooked by most REIT investors. However, management has made good progress in shifting the portfolio's focus toward Northeast retail properties. If the trust can restore consistent cash-flow growth, it may be able to access the capital markets and grow the portfolio on a more systematic basis. And company insiders, who own a 20% equity stake, have considerable incentive to achieve this goal.

Larry S. Gendler, CFA *February 4, 1994*

(A) Fiscal year ends October 31st. (B) Next earnings report due mid-Feb. (C) Next dividend meeting about Feb. 15. Goes ex about Feb. 25 Dividend payment dates about the 20th of January, April, July, and October. ■ Dividend reinvestment plan available. (D) In millions. (E) Includes one-time gain for lease assignment, '92, 18¢. (F) Includes writedown of real estate holdings, '93, $1.56. (G) Egs. per shr. before 1983 incl. cap. gains.

Company's Financial Strength	B+
Stock's Price Stability	65
Price Growth Persistence	5
Earnings Predictability	35

FIGURE 20–3 Dollar per Troy Ounce

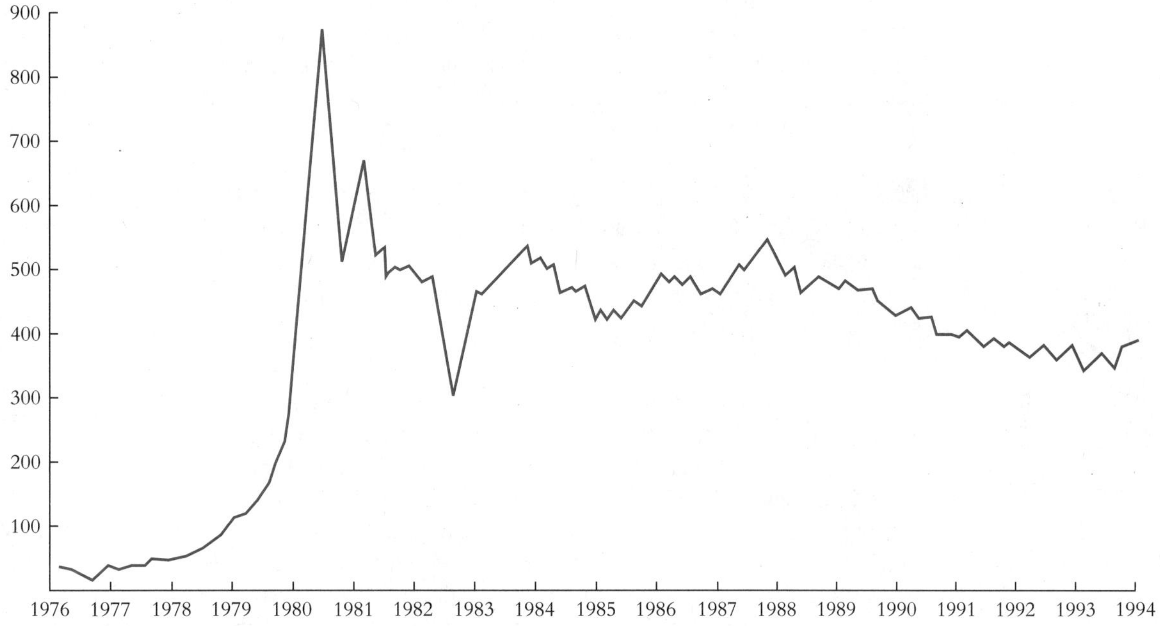

owned gold (directly or indirectly) or other forms of precious metals. Let's examine the different forms of gold ownership.

Gold Bullion Gold bullion includes gold bars or wafers. The investor may own anywhere from 1 troy ounce to 10,000 troy ounces (valued at approximately $4 million in 1994). Smaller bars generally trade at a 6 to 8 percent premium over pure gold bullion value, with larger bars trading at a 1 to 2 percent premium. Gold bullion may provide storage problems, and unless the gold bars remain in the custody of the bank or dealer who initially sells them, they must be reassayed before being sold.

Gold Coins Many of the storing and assaying costs associated with gold bullion can be avoided by investing directly in gold coins. There are three basic outlets for investing in gold coins. First, there are *gold bullion coins,* such as the South African Krugerrand, the Mexican 50 peso, and the Canadian Maple Leaf. These coins trade at a small premium of 2 to 3 percent over pure bullion value and afford the investor an excellent outlet for taking a position in the market. A second form is represented by *common date gold coins* that are no longer minted, such as the U.S. double eagle, the British sovereign, or the French Napoleon. These coins may trade at as much as 50 to 100 times their pure gold bullion value because of their value as collectibles. Finally, there are gold coins that are *old* and *rare* and that may trade at a numismatic value into the thousands or hundreds of thousands of dollars.

Gold Stocks In addition to gold bullion and gold coins, the investor may take a position in gold by simply buying common stocks that have heavy gold-mining positions. Examples of companies listed on U.S. exchanges include Battle Mountain (U.S. based), Placer Dome Inc. (Canadian based), and Homestake Mining (U.S. based). Because these securities often move in the opposite direction of the stock market as a whole, they may provide excellent portfolio diversification.

Gold Futures Contracts Finally, the gold investor may consider trading in futures contracts. Gold futures are traded on five different U.S. exchanges and on many foreign exchanges.[7]

Silver

Silver has many of the same investment characteristics as gold in terms of being a hedge against inflation and a safe haven for investment during troubled times. Silver moved from $4 a troy ounce in 1976 to over $50 an ounce in early 1980 and then back to $4 an ounce in the early 1990s. In 1995, silver was still trading in the $5 to $6 range.

More so than gold, silver has heavy industrial and commercial applications. Areas of utilization include photography, electronic and electrical manufacturing, electroplating, dentistry, and silverware and jewelry. It is estimated that industrial uses of silver exceed annual production by 150 million ounces per year. Furthermore, the supply of silver does not necessarily increase with price because silver is a by-product of copper, lead, zinc, and gold. Because of the undersupply factor, many consider silver to be appropriate for long-term holding.

Investment in silver can also take many different forms. Some may choose to buy *silver bullion* in the form of silver bars. Because the price of silver generally is 1/25 to 1/75 the price of gold and larger bulk is involved for an equivalent dollar size investment, the storage and carrying costs can be quite high. Second, *silver coins* may be bought in large bags or as rare coins for their numismatic value. Keep in mind that dimes, quarters, and half-dollars minted during and before 1965 were 90 percent pure silver. As a third outlet, the investor may wish to consider *silver futures contracts.* Finally, the investor may purchase *stocks* of firms that have interests in silver mining, such as Sunshine Mining or Hecla Mining.

PRECIOUS GEMS

Precious gems include diamonds, rubies, sapphires, and emeralds. Diamonds and other precious gems have appeal to investors because of their small size, easy concealment, and great durability. They are particularly popular in Europe because of a long-standing distrust of paper currencies as a store of value.

---

[7] There are also options on gold futures on the Comex.

The reason diamonds are so valuable can be best understood by considering the production process. It is estimated that 50 to 200 *tons* of rock or sand is required to uncover one carat (1/142 of an ounce) of quality diamonds.

The distribution of diamonds is under virtual monopolistic control by De Beers Consolidated Mines of South Africa, Ltd. It controls the distribution of approximately 80 percent of the world's supply and has a stated policy of maintaining price control. Diamonds have generally enjoyed a steady, somewhat spectacular movement in price. For example, the price of a "D" color, one-carat, flawless, polished diamond increased more than tenfold between 1974 and 1980.

Of course, not all diamonds have done so well. Furthermore, there have been substantial breaks in the market, such as in 1974 and 1980–82 when diamond prices declined by one-fourth and more. Even with large increases in value, the diamond investor does not automatically come out ahead. Dealer markups may be anywhere from 10 to 100 percent so three to five years of steady gain may be necessary to show a substantial profit.

In no area of investment is product and market knowledge more important. Either you must be an expert yourself or know that you are dealing with an "honest" expert. Diamonds are judged on the basis of the four *c*'s (color, clarity, carat weight, and cut), and the assessment of any stone should be certified by a member of the Gemological Institute of America. As is true of most valuable items, the investor is well advised to purchase the highest quality possible. You are considerably better off using the same amount of money to buy a higher quality, smaller carat diamond than a lesser quality, high-carat diamond.

OTHER COLLECTIBLES

A listing of other collectibles for investment might include art, antiques, stamps, Chinese ceramics, rare books, and other items that appeal to various sectors of our society. Each offers psychic pleasure to the investor as well as the opportunity for profit.

Anyone investing in a collectible should have some understanding of current market conditions and of the factors that determine the inherent worth of the item. Otherwise, you may be buying someone else's undesirable holding at a premium price. It is important not to get swept away in a buying euphoria. The best time to buy art, antiques, or stamps is when the bloom is off the market and dealers are overburdened with inventory, not when there is a weekly story in *The Wall Street Journal* or *Business Week* about overnight fortunes being made. There seems to be a pattern or cycle in the collectibles market the same as in other markets (arts, antiques, and stamps actually do move together).

As is true of other markets, the wise investor in the collectibles market must be sensitive to dealer spreads. A price guide that indicates a doubling in value every two or three years may be meaningless if the person with whom you are dealing sells for $100 and buys back for $50. The wise investor/collector can best maintain profits by dealing with other collectors or investors and eliminating the dealer or middleman from the transaction where possible.

Such periodicals as *Money* magazine and the *Collector/Investor* provide excellent articles on the collectibles market. Specialized periodicals, such as *American Arts and Antiques, Coin World, Linn's Stamp News, The Sports Collectors Digest,* and *Antique Monthly,* also are helpful. The interested reader can find books on almost any type of collectible in a public library or large bookstore.

Baseball Cards as Collectibles

Although we most often associate baseball cards with the 10-year-old child who coaxes $1.00 from his parents to buy a pack of cards in the drugstore, there is actually a half-billion dollar a year industry out there. There are 100,000 serious baseball card collectors and millions of child arbitragers doing business on a daily basis.

And why not? In a Sotheby's Holdings Inc.'s New York auction in March 1991, a Honus Wagner 1910 tobacco baseball card sold for $451,000. Only six years ago in the 3rd edition of this book, the card had reportedly been sold for the then seemingly unbelievable sum of $110,000. Why is this card so valuable? Wagner did not approve of smoking and when his card appeared in a tobacco-related set around 1910, he forced the American Tobacco Company to pull all but 100 off the market. Now, only 40 known Wagner cards exist, and the one sold at the Sotheby's auction was in exceptional condition. The law of demand and supply has clearly set in over the decades.

Among other items, a Mickey Mantle Topps card that could be purchased for 1¢ in 1952 as part of a gum pack went for $49,500 at the same auction.

If you are a Nolan Ryan fan, be prepared to pay $2,000 for his rookie card in mint condition. For the modern collector, such stars as Ken Griffey Jr. and Barry Bonds promise appreciation in value.

Other forms of sports memorabilia have value as well. A baseball clearly autographed by Babe Ruth is worth about $2,500. An authentic Lou Gehrig game-worn uniform carries a $125,000 price tag. A truly enterprising collector went so far as to pay $500 for the dental records of Eddie Cicotte, a long-deceased pitcher for the infamous Chicago Black Sox of 1919.

SUMMARY

Investments in real assets must be considered in a total portfolio concept. They offer a measure of inflation protection, an opportunity for efficient diversification, and psychic pleasure to the investor.

A disadvantage is the absence of a large, liquid market such as that provided by the securities markets. There also may be a large dealer or middleman spread, and the investor may have to forgo current income.

The hysteria that grips these markets from time to time not only creates substantial opportunities for profit but also dictates that the investor must be particularly cautious about market timing. It can be quite expensive to be the last buyer in a gold or silver boom.

Investors in real estate should be aware of the impact the Tax Reform Act of 1986 had on real estate values. The combined effect of lengthening the depreciation write-off, lowering the marginal tax rate, and disallowing passive losses to be written off against other forms of income drove down commercial real estate values across the country. However, all markets tend to adjust over time, and some bargain opportunities may exist in real estate in the 1990s. Because of the disallowance of many tax advantages in real estate, the emphasis now is on cash flow generation and the potential for capital appreciation.

The financing of real estate is becoming increasingly complicated as lenders seek alternatives to fixed-rate mortgages. Thus, we have seen the creation of the adjustable rate mortgage (ARM) and other floating-rate plans, the graduated payment mortgage (GPM), and the shared appreciation mortgage (SAM).

Gold and silver represent two highly volatile forms of real assets in which price movements often run counter to events in the economy and the world. Bad news is good news (and vice versa) for precious-metal investors. Gold and silver may generally be purchased in bullion or bulk form, as coins, in the commodities futures market, or indirectly through securities of firms specializing in gold or silver mining.

Precious gems and other collectibles, such as art, antiques, stamps, Chinese ceramics, and rare books, have caught the attention of investors in recent times. Although there are many warning signs, the wise and patient investor can do well over the long run. The investor should understand the factors that determine value before taking a serious investment position.

KEY WORDS AND CONCEPTS

real assets, 571
straight-line depreciation, 574
adjustable rate mortgage, 577
graduated payment mortgage, 577
shared appreciation mortgage, 577
equity participation, 578
limited partnership, 579
blind pool, 580
real estate investment trust (REIT), 580
equity trusts, 581
mortgage trusts, 581
hybrid trusts, 581

DISCUSSION QUESTIONS

1. Why might real assets offer an opportunity as an inflation hedge?
2. Explain why real assets might add to effective portfolio diversification.
3. What are some disadvantages of investing in real estate?
4. What two factors hurt real estate in the last decade? Why might the future outlook be more positive?
5. In what way does real estate provide for a high degree of leverage?
6. What is an adjustable rate mortgage?
7. For what type of borrower is the graduated payment mortgage best suited?
8. Explain a shared appreciation mortgage.
9. What is meant by a seller loan with a call privilege?
10. How is liability handled in a limited partnership?
11. What are REITs? What are the various types of REITs?
12. What are some factors that drive up the price of gold? What are factors that drive it down?
13. What are three different ways to invest in gold coins?
14. Suggest some commercial and industrial uses of silver. What forms can silver investments take?
15. Explain how the dealer spread can affect the rate of return on a collectible item.

PROBLEM

Real estate investment analysis

1. An investor owns a rental duplex with land valued at $25,000 and the building valued at $125,000. Straight-line depreciation over 27½ years will be taken. The investor will be actively involved in the management of the property. He is in a 36 percent tax bracket.
   a. What is the annual depreciation deduction? (Round to the nearest dollar throughout this problem.)
   b. Assume revenue minus all other expenses besides depreciation provides $3,000 of net income in the first year. Now, considering the depreciation computed in part *a,* how much will cash flow be in the first year? Add together lines (3), (4), and (5) below to get your answer.

(1) Net income before depreciation	$3,000
(2) – Depreciation	______
(3) Before-tax income (or loss)	______
(4) + Tax benefit (36% rate)	______
(5) + Depreciation	______
(6) Cash flow	______

   c. Assume a 25-year loan equal to 70 percent of the total value of the property at 10 percent interest. Annual payments will be $11,568. How much of the annual payment will go toward interest and how much will go toward the repayment of principal in the first year?
   d. Based on the information in parts *b* and *c,* compute net cash flow.

Cash flow (line (6) of part *b*)	______
– Repayment of principal	______
Net cash flow	______

   e. What is the ratio of net cash flow to initial cash investment? Initial investment equals total investment minus the loan.
   f. If there is 3.5 percent inflation related to total property value in the first year, what will be the ratio of inflationary gains to initial cash investment?
   g. Comment on the comparative importance of your answers to parts *e* and *f.*

THE WALL STREET JOURNAL PROJECT

Income-oriented investors often put their money in real estate investment trusts (REITs). To compare the yield on a REIT to current money market yields, go to the "Credit Markets/Money Rates" table in section C of *The Wall Street Journal* found under "Money Rates." Write down the yields on Treasury bills for 13 and 26 weeks. Also record the yield on the Merrill Lynch Ready Asset Trust.

Now compare these yields to the dividend yield that can be earned on the following REITs:

Federal Realty (FedRlty)

New Plant Realty Trust (NewPlnRlty)

The dividend yields for the REITs can be found after the company's name in "The New York Stock Exchange Composite Transactions" part of section C. The yield is located in the third column after the company's name. The column is labeled Div Yld %.

Are these two REITs providing a current yield higher or lower than the money market rates you recorded? You also may want to keep in mind that the stock prices of REITs may go up or down.

SELECTED REFERENCES

Portfolio Considerations with Real Assets

Lenzner, Robert. "The Case for Hard Assets." *Forbes,* June 20, 1994, pp. 146–51.

Robichek, Alexander A.; Richard A. Cohn; and John J. Pringle. "Return on Alternative Media and Implications for Portfolio Construction." *Journal of Business,* July 1972, pp. 427–43.

Investments in Real Estate

Alpert, Mark. "Office Buildings for the 1990s." *Fortune,* November 18, 1991, pp. 140–42.

Folger, H. Russell. "20% in Real Estate: Can Theory Justify It?" *Journal of Portfolio Management,* Winter 1984, pp. 6–13.

Grissom, Terry V.; James L. Kuhle; and Carl H. Walther. "Diversification Works in Real Estate, Too." *Journal of Portfolio Management,* Winter 1987, pp. 66–71.

Hartzell, David J.; Robert H. Pittman; and David H. Downs. "An Updated Look at the Size of the U.S. Real Estate Market Portfolio." *The Journal of Real Estate Research,* Spring 1994, pp. 197–212.

Kaplan, Howard M. "Farmland as a Portfolio Investment." *Journal of Portfolio Management,* Winter 1985, pp. 73–79.

Lipscomb, Joseph. "Discount Rates for Cash Equivalent Analysis." *Appraisal Journal,* January 1981, pp. 23–33.

Meyers, William. "Real Estate: A High Water Mark?" *Institutional Investor,* January 1988, pp. 129–36.

O'Brien, Thomas J.; Lawrence J. Graubling; and Mauricio Rodriguez. "An Introduction to the Collectible Sportscard Market." (Forthcoming, *Managerial Finance*).

Saderion, Zahra; Burton Smith; and Charles Smith. "An Integrated Approach to the Evaluation of Commercial Real Estate." *Journal of Real Estate Research,* Spring 1994, pp. 151–67.

Precious Metals and Precious Gems

Regular articles featured in: *Money, Personal Investor, Consumer Reports,* and *Changing Times.*

Collectibles

Periodicals: *American Arts and Antiques, Antique Monthly, Coin World, Collector/Investor, Linn's Stamp News,* and *Sports Collectors Digest.*

PART 7

Introduction to Portfolio Management

OUTLINE

Modern portfolio managers are being held accountable not only for the return they make, but also for the risk of their portfolio. One way to reduce this risk is through portfolio insurance (insuring a portfolio against decline), but does this technique work?

Suppose you bought a beautiful new BMW or Mercedes (no, this is not a fairy tale). One of your first concerns, besides being sure that everyone on campus saw you behind the wheel of your treasured automobile, would be that you had adequate insurance to protect against an unexpected event. This might include a crash with another car, a burglary, a fire, and so on.

The same need for insurance applies to those who manage large pools of money. Although professional money managers normally hope the market will go up, they need financial protection against a sharp drop in the market. Although the protection involves some expense, the cost is justified just as the auto insurance premium you pay can normally be justified as a prudent business expense.

Actually, specialized computer programs that assist the money manager represent a form of portfolio insurance. These programs keep an eye out for a downturn in the market; when the market drops, the program automatically presells baskets of stocks in the futures market. That selling action protects the money manager against a crash.

A money manager who has $100 million in a diversified stock portfolio would normally absorb a loss of $20 million if the market went down by 20 percent. But with portfolio insurance, the manager is simultaneously selling futures contracts that can be bought back at a lower price as the market falls. Thus, the manager is insured (hedged) against the consequences of a falling market.

The popularity of portfolio insurance can be linked to the development of modern portfolio theory in which money managers are held accountable not only for the return they generate, but also for the risks they take in generating that return. Portfolios that have widely changing values from quarter to quarter are thought to be much less desirable than steadily performing portfolios even though their total return might be equal over 5 or 10 years.

Portfolio insurance may be a good approach for lessening risk if only a handful of portfolio managers are using it, but what happens if a large number of portfolio managers are committed to a similar plan?

Event number one: The stock market falls sharply due to bad economic news for a variety of reasons.

Event number two: The money managers' computer programs see the drop and automatically presell a number of baskets of stocks in the futures market as insurance against the crash.

Event number three: The stock market continues to plummet, partially as a result of the activation of the portfolio insurance sell programs.

Event number four: The computer programs kick in again and presell more baskets of stocks. And on and on!

Where does this all end? Does the initial protection provided by portfolio insurance actually create a new round of larger losses by the actual presence of the insurance? Market researchers are very concerned about this. ■

21

A Basic Look at Portfolio Management and Capital Market Theory

In this chapter, we develop a more complete understanding of how the investor perceives risk and demands compensation for it. We eventually build toward a theory of portfolio management that incorporates these concepts. While the use of mathematical terms is an essential ingredient to a basic understanding of portfolio theory, more involved or complicated concepts are treated in appendixes at the end of the chapter.

As indicated in Chapter 1, risk is generally associated with uncertainty about future outcomes. The greater the dispersion of possible outcomes, the greater the risk. We also observed in Chapter 1 that most investors tend to be risk-averse; that is, all things being equal, investors prefer less risk to more risk and will increase their risk-taking position only if a premium for risk is involved. Each investor has a different attitude toward risk. The inducement necessary to cause a given investor to withdraw funds from a savings account to drill an oil well may be quite different from yours. For some, only a very small premium for risk is necessary, while others may not wish to participate unless there are exceptionally high rewards. We begin the chapter with a formal development of risk measures.

FORMAL MEASUREMENT OF RISK

Having defined risk as uncertainty about future outcomes, how do we actually measure risk? The first task is to design a probability distribution of anticipated future outcomes. This is no small task. The possible outcomes and associated probabilities are likely to be based on economic projections, past experience, subjective judgments, and many other variables. For the most part, we are forcing ourselves to write down what already exists in our head. Having established the probability distribution, we then determine the expected value and the dispersion around that expected value. The greater the dispersion, the greater the risk.

Expected Value

To determine the **expected value**, we multiply each possible outcome by its probability of occurrence. Assume we are considering two investment proposals where *K* represents a possible outcome and *P* represents the probability of that outcome based on the state of the economy. If we were dealing with stocks, *K* would represent the price appreciation potential plus the dividend yield (total return). Table 21–1 presents the data for two investments, *i* and *j*.

TABLE 21–1 Return and Probabilities for Investments i and j

Investment $_i$			Investment $_j$	
K_i	P_i (Probability of K_i Occurring)	Possible State of the Economy	K_j	P_j (Probability of K_j Occurring)
5%	0.20	Recession	20%	0.20
7	0.30	Slow growth	8	0.30
13	0.30	Moderate growth	8	0.30
15	0.20	Strong economy	6	0.20

We will say that $\overline{K}_i$ (the expected value of investment i) equals $\Sigma K_i P_i$. In this case, the answer would be 10.0 percent, as shown under Formula 21–1:

$$\overline{K}_i = \Sigma K_i P_i \tag{21–1}$$

K_i	P_i	$K_i P_i$
5%	0.20	1.0%
7	0.30	2.1
13	0.30	3.9
15	0.20	3.0
		10.0% = $\Sigma K_i P_i$

Standard Deviation

The commonly used measure of dispersion is the **standard deviation**, which is a measure of the spread of the outcomes around the expected value. The formula for the standard deviation is:

$$\sigma_i = \sqrt{\Sigma (K_i - \overline{K}_i)^2 P_i} \tag{21–2}$$

Let's determine the standard deviation for investment i around the expected value ($\overline{K}_i$) of 10 percent.

K_i	$\overline{K}_i$	P_i	$(K_i - \overline{K}_i)$	$(K_i - \overline{K}_i)^2$	$(K_i - \overline{K}_i)^2 P_i$
5%	10%	0.20	−5%	25%	5.0%
7	10	0.30	−3	9	2.7
13	10	0.30	+3	9	2.7
15	10	0.20	+5	25	5.0
					15.4% = $\Sigma (K_i - \overline{K}_i)^2 P_i$

$$\sigma_i = \sqrt{\Sigma (K_i - \overline{K}_i)^2 P_i} = \sqrt{15.4\%} = 3.9\%$$

The standard deviation of investment i is 3.9 percent (rounded). To have some feel for the relative risk characteristics of this investment, we compare it with a second proposal, investment j.

We assume investment j is a countercyclical investment. It does well during a recession and poorly in a strong economy. Perhaps it represents a firm in the housing industry that is most profitable when the economy is sluggish and interest rates are low. Under these circumstances, people will avail themselves of low-cost financing to purchase a new home, and the stock of the firm will do well. In a booming economy, interest rates will advance rapidly, and the financing of housing will become expensive. Thus, we have a countercyclical investment. The outcomes and probabilities of outcomes for investment j are as follows:

The expected value for investment j is:

$$\bar{K}_j = \Sigma K_j P_j$$

K_j	P_j	$K_j P_j$
20%	0.20	4.0%
8	0.30	2.4
8	0.30	2.4
6	0.20	1.2
		$\bar{K}_j$ = 10.0%

The standard deviation for investment j is:

$$\sigma_j = \sqrt{\Sigma (K_j - \bar{K}_j)^2 P_j}$$

K_j	$\bar{K}_j$	P_j	$(K_j - \bar{K}_j)$	$(K_j - \bar{K}_j)^2$	$(K_j - \bar{K}_j)^2 P_j$
20%	10%	0.20	+10%	100%	20.0%
8	10	0.30	−2	4	1.2
8	10	0.30	−2	4	1.2
6	10	0.20	−4	16	3.2
					25.6% = $\Sigma(K_j - \bar{K}_j)^2 P_j$

$$\sigma_j = \sqrt{\Sigma (K_j - \bar{K}_j)^2 P_j} = \sqrt{25.6\%} = 5.1\% \text{ (rounded)}$$

We now see we have two investments, each with an expected value of 10 percent but with varying performances in different types of economies and different standard deviations (3.9 percent versus 5.1 percent).[1]

PORTFOLIO EFFECT

An investor who is holding only investment i may wish to consider bringing investment j into the portfolio. If the stocks are weighted evenly, the new portfolio's expected value will be 10 percent. We define K_p as the expected value of the portfolio:

$$K_p = X_i \bar{K}_i + X_j \bar{K}_j \qquad (21\text{–}3)$$

The X values represent the weights assigned by the investor to each component in the portfolio and are 50 percent for both investments in this example. The $\bar{K}_i$ and $\bar{K}_j$ values were previously determined to be 10 percent. Thus we have:

$$K_p = 0.5(10\%) + 0.5(10\%) = 5\% + 5\% = 10\%$$

[1] Actually, rather than use the standard deviation, we can also use its squared value, termed the *variance*, to describe risk. That is, we may use σ^2 (the standard deviation squared) to describe the risk in an individual security.

What about the standard deviation for the combined portfolio (σ_p)? If a weighted average were taken of the two investments, the new standard deviation would be 4.5 percent:

$$X_i\sigma_i + X_j\sigma_j$$
$$0.5(3.9\%) + 0.5(5.1\%) = 1.95\% + 2.55\% = 4.5\%$$

The interesting element is that the investor in investment i would appear to be losing from the combined investment. His expected value remains at 10 percent, but his standard deviation has increased from 3.9 to 4.5 percent. Given that he is risk-averse, he appears to be getting more risk rather than less risk by expanding his portfolio.

There is one fallacy in the analysis. The standard deviation of a portfolio is not based on the simple weighted average of the individual standard deviations (as the expected value is). Rather, it considers significant interaction between the investments. If one investment does well during a given economic condition while the other does poorly and vice versa, there may be significant risk reduction from combining the two, and the standard deviation for the portfolio may be less than the standard deviation for either investment (this is the reason we do not simply take the weighted average of the two).

Note in Figure 21–1 the risk-reduction potential from combining the two investments under study. Investment i alone may produce outcomes anywhere from 5 to 15 percent, and investment j, from 6 to 20 percent. By combining the two, we narrow the range for investment (i, j) to from 7.5 to 12.5 percent. Thus, we have reduced the risk while keeping the expected value constant at 10 percent. We now examine the appropriate standard deviation formula for the two investments.

FIGURE 21–1 Investment Outcomes under Different Conditions

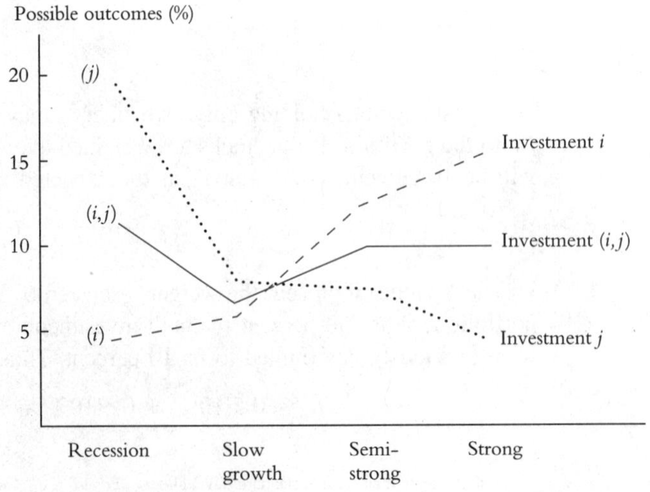

Standard Deviation for a Two-Asset Portfolio

The standard deviation for a two-asset portfolio is presented in Formula 21–4[2]:

$$\sigma_p = \sqrt{X_i^2\sigma_i^2 + X_j^2\sigma_j^2 + 2X_iX_jr_{ij}\sigma_i\sigma_j} \qquad (21\text{–}4)$$

The only new term in the expression is r_{ij}, the **correlation coefficient** or measurement of joint movement between the two variables. The value for r_{ij} can be from −1 to +1, although for most variables, the correlation coefficient falls somewhere in between these two values. Figure 21–2 demonstrates the concept of correlation. In panel A, assets *i* and *j* are perfectly correlated, with r_{ij} equal to +1. As *i* increases in value, so does *j* in exact proportion to *i*. In panel B, assets *i* and *j* exhibit a perfect negative correlation, with r_{ij} equal to −1. As *i* increases, *j* decreases in exact proportion to *i*. Panel C demonstrates assets *i* and *j* having no correlation at all, with r_{ij} equal to 0.

The actual computation of the correlation coefficient for investments *i* and *j* is covered in Appendix 21A. It is not necessary to go through Appendix 21A before proceeding with our discussion, though some readers may wish to do so. As indicated in Appendix 21A,

FIGURE 21-2 Correlation Analysis

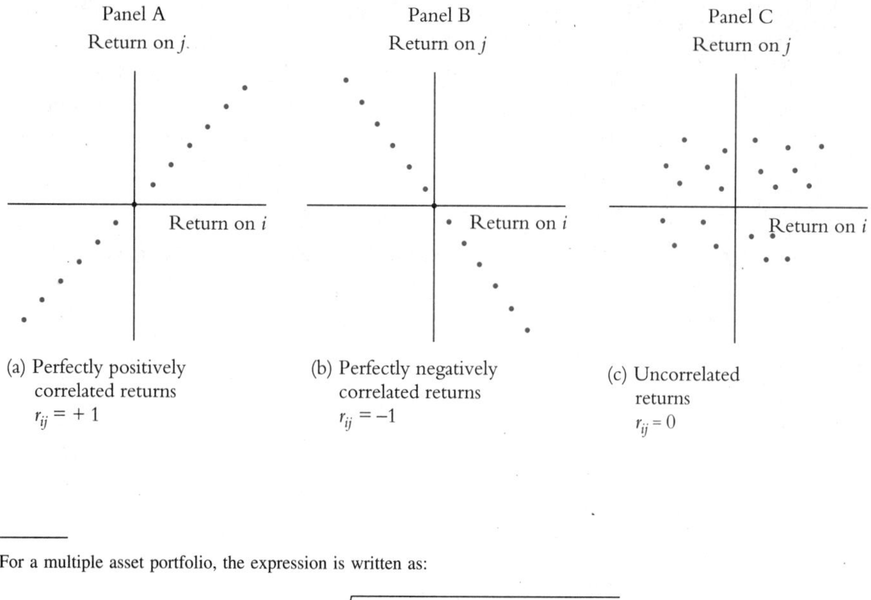

(a) Perfectly positively correlated returns $r_{ij} = +1$

(b) Perfectly negatively correlated returns $r_{ij} = -1$

(c) Uncorrelated returns $r_{ij} = 0$

---

[2] For a multiple asset portfolio, the expression is written as:

$$\sigma_P = \sqrt{\sum_{i=1}^{N} X_i^2\sigma_i^2 + 2\sum_{i=1}^{N-1}\sum_{j=1+1}^{N} X_iX_jr_{ij}\sigma_i\sigma_j}$$

N is the number of securities in the portfolio.

the correlation coefficient (r_{ij}) between our investment i and investment j is –0.70. This indicates the two investments show a high degree of negative correlation. Plugging this value into Formula 21–4, along with other previously determined values, the standard deviation (σ_p) for the two-asset portfolio can be computed[3]:

$$\sigma_p = \sqrt{X_i^2\sigma_i^2 + X_j^2\sigma_j^2 + 2X_iX_jr_{ij}\sigma_i\sigma_j} \qquad (21\text{–}4)$$

where:

$$X_i = 0.5,\ \sigma_i = 3.9$$
$$X_j = 0.5,\ \sigma_j = 5.1$$
$$r_{ij} = -0.70$$

$$\begin{aligned}\sigma_p &= \sqrt{(0.5)^2(3.9)^2 + (0.5)^2(5.1)^2 + 2(0.5)(0.5)(-0.7)(3.9)(5.1)}\\ &= \sqrt{(0.25)(15.4) + (0.25)(25.6) + 2(0.25)(-0.7)(19.9)}\\ &= \sqrt{3.85 + 6.4 + (0.5)(-13.93)}\\ &= \sqrt{3.85 + 6.4 - 6.97}\\ &= \sqrt{3.28} = 1.8\%\end{aligned}$$

The standard deviation of the portfolio of 1.8 percent is less than the standard deviation of either investment i (3.9 percent) or j (5.1 percent). Any time two investments have a correlation coefficient (r_{ij}) less than +1 (perfect positive correlation), some risk reduction will be possible by combining the assets in a portfolio. In the real world, most items are positively correlated; the extent that we can still get risk reduction from positively correlated items gives extra meaning to portfolio management. Note the impact of various assumed correlation coefficients for the two investments previously described in terms of individual standard deviations[4]:

Correlation Coefficient (r_{ij})	Portfolio Standard Deviation (σ_p)
+1.0	4.5
+0.5	3.9
0.0	3.2
–0.5	2.3
–0.7	1.8
–1.0	0.0

[3] Note that the squared values, such as $(3.9)^2 = 15.4$, are the reverse of earlier computations. Previously, we found the square root of 15.4 to be 3.9 (see computation under Formula 21–2). The use of rounding introduces slight discrepancies where we square numbers for which we previously found the square root.

[4] Each is assumed to represent 50 percent of the portfolio.

The conclusion to be drawn from our portfolio analysis discussion is that the most significant risk factor associated with an individual investment may not be its own standard deviation but how it affects the standard deviation of a portfolio through correlation. As we shall later observe in this chapter, there is not considered to be a risk premium for the total risk or standard deviation of an individual security, but only for that risk component that cannot be eliminated by various portfolio diversification techniques.

DEVELOPING AN EFFICIENT PORTFOLIO

We have seen how the combination of two investments has allowed us to maintain our return of 10 percent but reduce the portfolio standard deviation to 1.8 percent. We also saw in the preceding table that different coefficient correlations produce many different possibilities for portfolio standard deviations. A shrewd portfolio manager may wish to consider a large number of portfolios, each with a different expected value and standard deviation, based on the expected values and standard deviations of the individual securities and, more importantly, on the correlations between the individual securities. Though we have been discussing a two-asset portfolio case, our example may be expanded to cover 5-, 10-, or even 100-asset portfolios.[5] The major tenets of portfolio theory that we are currently examining were developed by Professor Harry Markowitz in the 1950s, and so we refer to them as Markowitz portfolio theory.

Assume we have identified the following risk-return possibilities for eight different portfolios (there may also be many more, but we will restrict ourselves to this set for now):

Portfolio	K_p	σ_p
A	10%	1.8%
B	10	2.1
C	12	3.0
D	13	4.2
E	13	5.0
F	14	5.0
G	14	5.8
H	15	7.2

In diagramming our various risk-return points, we show the values in Figure 21–3 on page 600.

[5] The incremental benefit from reduction of the portfolio standard deviation through adding securities appears to diminish fairly sharply with a portfolio of 10 securities and is quite small with a portfolio as large as 20. A portfolio of 12 to 14 securities is generally thought to be of sufficient size to enjoy the majority of desirable portfolio effects. See W. H. Wagner and S. C. Lau, "The Effect of Diversification on Risk," *Financial Analysts Journal,* November–December 1971, pp. 48–53.

FIGURE 21–3

Diagram of Risk-Return Trade-Offs

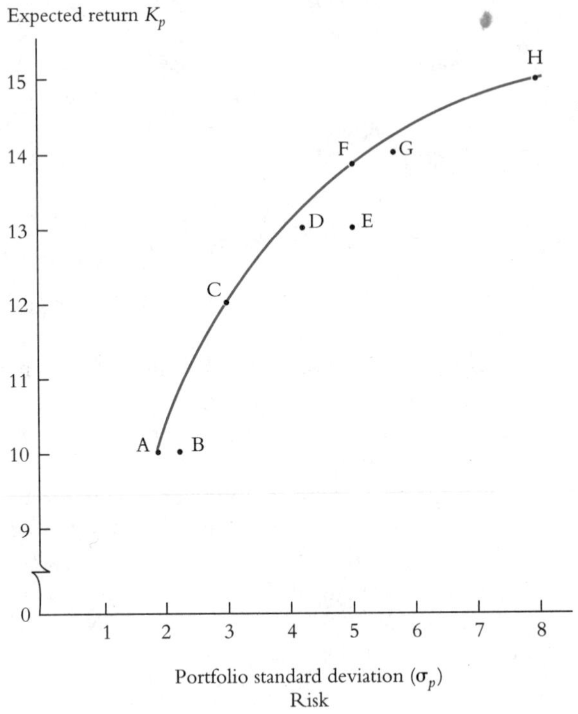

Though we have only diagrammed eight possibilities, we see an efficient set of portfolios would lie along the ACFH line in Figure 21–3. This line is efficient because the portfolios on this line dominate all other attainable portfolios. This line is called the **efficient frontier** because the portfolios on the efficient frontier provide the best risk-return trade-off. That is, along this efficient frontier we can receive a maximum return for a given level of risk or a minimum risk for a given level of return. Portfolios do not exist above the efficient frontier, and portfolios below this line do not offer acceptable alternatives to points along the line. As an example of *maximum return* for a given level of risk, consider point F. Along the efficient frontier, we are receiving a 14 percent return for a 5 percent risk level, whereas directly below point F, portfolio E provides a 13 percent return for the same 5 percent standard deviation.

To also demonstrate that we are getting *minimum risk* for a given return level, we can examine point A in which we receive a 10 percent return for a 1.8 percent risk level, whereas to the right of point A, we get the same 10 percent return from B, but a less desirable 2.1 percent risk level. One portfolio can consist of various proportions of two assets or two portfolios. For example, we can connect the points between A and C by generating portfolios that combine different percentages of portfolio A and portfolio C and so on between portfolio C and F and portfolio F and H. Though we have shown but

FIGURE 21–4 Expanded View of Efficient Frontier

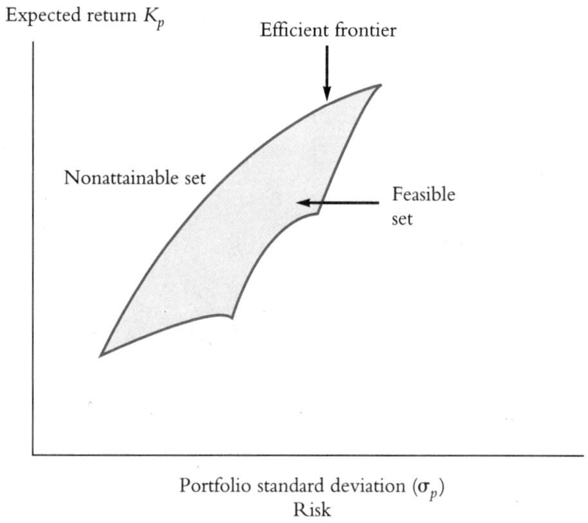

eight points (portfolios), a fully developed efficient frontier may be based on a virtually unlimited number of observations as is presented in Figure 21–4.

In Figure 21–4, we once again view the efficient frontier in relationship to the feasible set and note that certain risk-return possibilities are not attainable (and should be disregarded). At this point in the analysis, we can stipulate that the various points along the efficient frontier are all considered potentially optimal and a given investor must choose the most appropriate single point based on individual risk-return trade-off desires. We would say that a low-risk-oriented investor might prefer point A in Figure 21–3, whereas a more-risk-oriented investor would prefer point F or H. At each of these points, the investor is getting the best risk-return trade-off for his or her own particular risk-taking propensity.

Risk-Return Indifference Curves

To actually pair an investor with an appropriate point along the efficient frontier, we look at his or her indifference curve as illustrated in Figure 21–5 on page 602.

The **indifference curves** show the investor's trade-off between risk and return. The steeper the slope of the curve, the more risk-averse the investor is. For example, in the case of investor B (I_B in Figure 21–5), the indifference curve has a steeper slope than for Investor A (I_A). This means investor B will require more incremental return (more of a risk premium) for each additional unit of risk. Note that to take risks, investor B requires approximately twice as much incremental return as investor A between points X and Y. Investor A is still somewhat risk-averse and perhaps represents a typical investor in the capital markets.

FIGURE 21–5 Risk-Return Indifference Curves

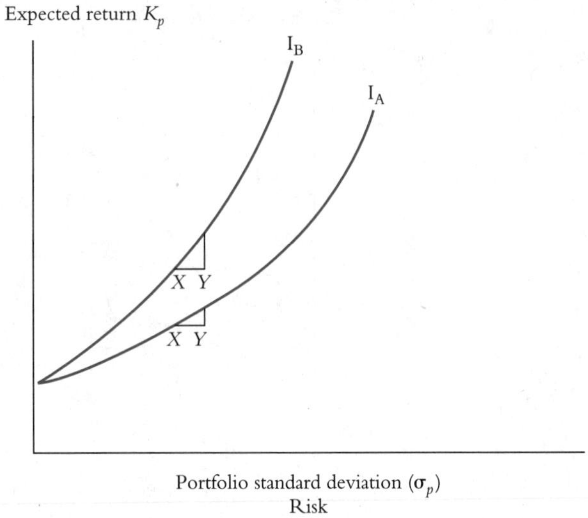

FIGURE 21–6 Indifference Curves for Investor A

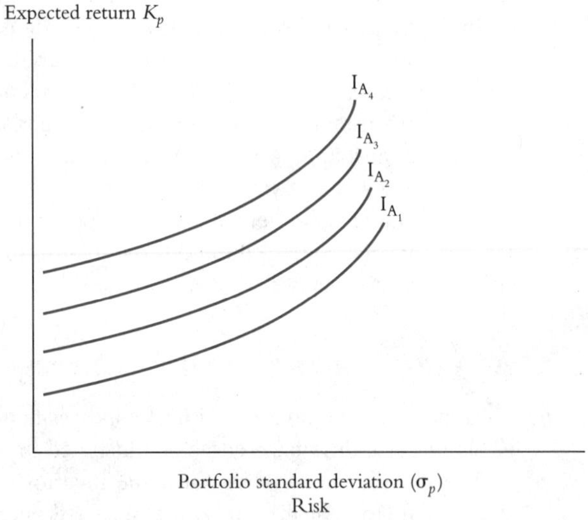

Once the shape of an investor's indifference curve is determined, a second objective can be established—to attain the highest curve possible. For example, investor A, initially shown in figure 21–5, would have a whole set of similarly shaped indifference curves as presented in Figure 21–6.

While he is indifferent to any point along a given curve (such as I_{A_4}), he is not indifferent to achieving the highest curve possible (I_{A_4} is clearly superior to I_{A_1}). I_{A_4} provides more return at all given risk levels. The only limitation to achieving the highest possible indifference curve is the feasible set of investments available.

Optimum Portfolio

The investor must theoretically match his own risk-return indifference curve with the best investments available in the market as represented by points on the efficient frontier. We see in Figure 21–7 that investor A will achieve the highest possible indifference curve at point C along the efficient frontier.

This is the point of tangency between his own indifference curve (I_{A_3}) and the efficient frontier. Both curves have the same slope or risk-return characteristics at this point. While a point along indifference curve (I_{A_4}) might provide a higher level of utility, it is not attainable. Also, any other point along the efficient frontier would cross a lower level indifference curve and be inferior to point C. For example, points B and D cross I_{A_2}, providing less return for a given level of risk that I_{A_3}. Investors must relate the shape of their *own* risk-return indifference curves to the efficient frontier to determine that point of tangency providing maximum benefits.

FIGURE 21–7 Combining the Efficient Frontier and Indifference Curves

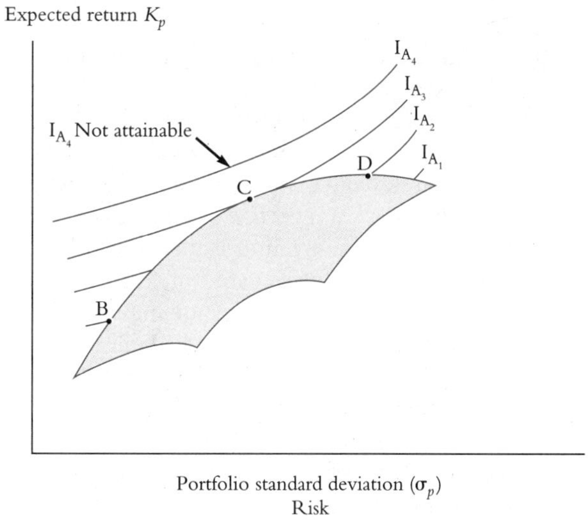

Students as Portfolio Managers—The Number of Programs Continues to Grow

It started at the University of Wisconsin more than two decades ago. Now students manage part of the university endowment in more than 30 colleges and universities. This is no simulation.

The largest such program is at Ohio State University, where the students are enrolled in courses that allow them to manage more than $8 million of the permanent endowment of the university. Other schools such as UCLA, Indiana University, the University of Southern California, Southern Methodist University, Notre Dame, Gannon College, Virginia Military Institute, DePaul University, and Texas Christian University have similar programs. Professor Edward C. Lawrence of the University of Missouri–St. Louis tracks all the programs across the country as to size, value, and source of funding.* Some schools operate with as little as a few thousand dollars, while the typical program size is $150,000 to $200,000.

The authors are most familiar with the student-managed fund at Texas Christian University, where they have both served as faculty advisors. The students manage $1.2 million in stocks and bonds and have power to make their own investment decisions. The faculty advisors do not even have veto power (don't ask if they sweat a lot!). The students receive six hours of academic credit for their work and do intensive work to analyze securities and balance the portfolio. The students also have their own committees operating in such areas as economics and accounting.

As would be true of other professional money managers, they provide annual reports, in which they compare their performance with their own goals as well as with the popular market averages.

*Edward C. Lawrence, "Financial Innovation: The Case of Student Investment Funds at United States Universities," *Financial Practice and Education,* Spring–Summer 1994, pp. 47–53.

CAPITAL ASSET PRICING MODEL

The development of the efficient frontier in the previous section gives insight into optimum portfolio mixes in an appropriate risk-return context. Nevertheless, the development of multiple portfolios is a rather difficult and tedious task. Professors Sharpe, Lintner, and others have allowed us to take the philosophy of efficient portfolios into a more generalized and meaningful context through the **capital asset pricing model**. Under this model, we examine the theoretical underpinnings through which assets are valued based on their risk characteristics.

The capital asset pricing model (CAPM) takes off where the efficient frontier concluded through the introduction of a new investment outlet, the risk-free asset (R_F). A risk-free asset has no risk of default and a standard deviation of 0 ($\sigma_{R_F} = 0$) and is the lowest assumed safe return that can be earned. A U.S. Treasury bill or Treasury bond is often considered representative of a risk-free asset. Under the capital asset pricing model, we introduce the notion of combining the risk-free asset and the efficient frontier with the development of the R_FMZ line as indicated in Figure 21–8.

The R_FMZ line opens up the possibility of a whole new set of superior investment opportunities. That is, by combining some portion of the risk-free asset as represented by (R_F) with M (a point along the efficient frontier), we create new investment opportunities that will allow us to reach higher indifference curves than would be possible simply along the efficient frontier. The only point along the efficient frontier that now has significance is point M, where the straight line from R_F is tangent to the old efficient frontier. Let us further examine the R_FMZ line.

FIGURE 21–8 Basic Diagram of the Capital Asset Pricing Model

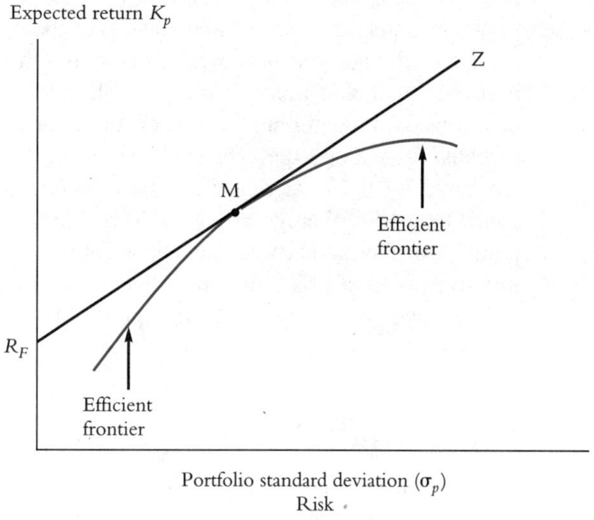

FIGURE 21–9 The CAPM and Indifference Curves

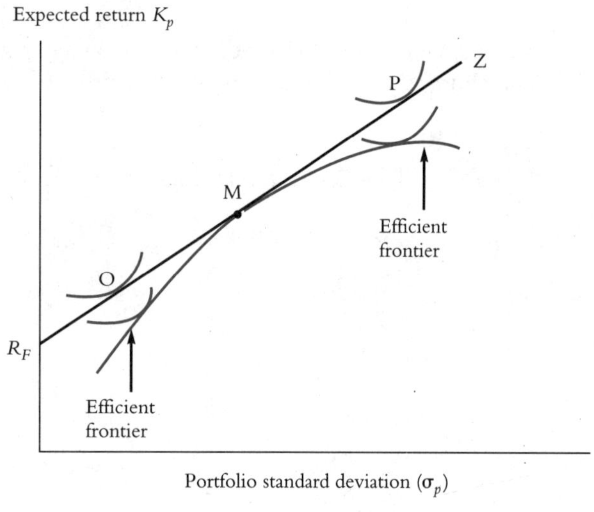

We can reach points along the R_FMZ line in a number of different ways. To be at point R_F, we would simply buy a risk-free asset. To be at a point between R_F and M, we would buy a combination of R_F and the M portfolio along the efficient frontier. To be at a point between M and Z, we buy M with our available funds and then borrow additional funds to further increase our purchase of the M portfolio (an example of this would be to be at point P in Figure 21–9). To the extent that M is higher than R_F and we can borrow at a rate

equal to R_F or slightly higher, we can get larger returns with a combination of buying M and borrowing additional funds to buy M. (Of course, this calls for greater risk as well.)

We also note that point M is considered the optimum "market basket" of investments available (though you may wish to combine this market basket with risk-free assets or borrowing). If you took all the possible investments that investors could acquire and determined the optimum basket of investments, you would come up with point M (because it is along the efficient frontier and tangent to the R_F line). Point M can be measured by the total return on the Standard & Poor's 500 Stock Average, the Dow Jones Industrial Average, the New York Stock Exchange Index, or similar measures. If point M or the market were not represented by the optimum risk-return portfolio for all investments at a point in time, then it is assumed there would be an instantaneous change, and the market measure (point M) would once again be in equilibrium (be optimal).

Capital Market Line

The previously discussed R_FMZ line is called the **capital market line (CML)** and is once again presented in Figure 21–10.

The formula for the capital market line in Figure 21–10 may be written as:

$$K_P = R_F + \left(\frac{K_M - R_F}{\sigma_M - 0}\right)\sigma_p$$

We indicate that the expected return on any portfolio (K_P) is equal to the risk-free rate of return (R_F) plus the slope of the line times a value along the horizontal axis (σ_P),

FIGURE 21–10 Illustration of the Capital Market Line

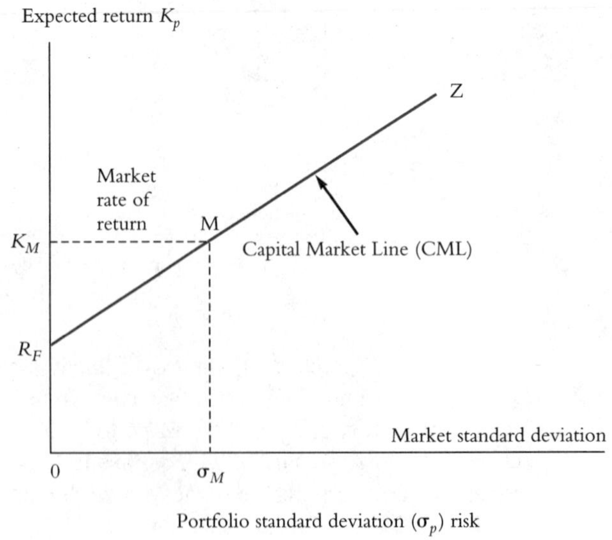

indicating the amount of risk undertaken. We can relate the formula for the capital market line to the basic equation for a straight line as follows:

$$\text{Straight line } Y = a + bX$$

$$\text{Capital market line } K_P = R_F + \left(\frac{K_M - R_F}{\sigma_M}\right)\sigma_P$$

In using the capital market line, we start with a minimum rate of return of R_F and then say any additional return is a reward for risk. The reward for risk or risk premium is equal to the market rate of return (K_M) minus the risk-free rate (R_F) divided by the market standard deviation (σ_M). If the market rate of return (K_M) is 12 percent and the risk-free rate of return (R_F) is 6 percent, with a market standard deviation (σ_M) of 20 percent, there is a risk premium of 0.3:

$$\frac{K_M - R_F}{\sigma_M} = \frac{12\% - 6\%}{20\%} = \frac{6\%}{20\%} = 0.3$$

Then, if the standard deviation of our portfolio (σ_P) is 22 percent, we can expect a return of 12.6 percent along the CML computed as follows:

$$K_P = R_F = \left(\frac{K_M - R_F}{\sigma_M}\right)\sigma_P \qquad (21\text{–}5)$$

$$K_P = 6\% + \left(\frac{12\% - 6\%}{20\%}\right)22\%$$

$$= 6\% + (0.3)\ 22\%$$

$$= 6\% + 6.6\% = 12.6\%$$

The essence of the capital market line is that the way to get larger returns is to take increasingly higher risks. Thus, the only way to climb up the K_P *return* line in Figure 21–10 is to extend yourself out on the σ_P *risk* line. Portfolio managers who claim highly superior returns may have taken larger than normal risks and thus may not really be superior performers on a risk-adjusted basis. We shall see in the following chapter that the best way to measure a portfolio manager is to evaluate his returns relative to the risks taken. Average to slightly above average returns based on low risk may be superior to high returns based on high risk. One does not easily exceed market-dictated constraints for risk and return.

RETURN ON AN INDIVIDUAL SECURITY

We have been examining return expectations for a portfolio; we now turn our attention to an individual security. Once again the return potential is closely tied to risk. However, when dealing with an individual security, the premium return for risk is not related to *all* the risk in the investment as measured by the standard deviation (σ). The reason for this is that the standard deviation includes two types of risk, but only one is accorded a premium return under the capital asset pricing model.

We now begin an analytical process that allows us to get at the two forms of risk in an individual security. The first form of risk is measured by the beta coefficient.

Beta Coefficient In analyzing the performance of an individual security, it is first important to measure its relationship to the market through the **beta coefficient**. Let us lay the groundwork for understanding beta. In the case of a potential investment, stock *i*, we can observe its relationship to the market by tracing its total return performance relative to market total return over the last five years.[6]

Year	Stock *i* Return (K)	Market Return (K_M)
1	4.8%	6.5%
2	14.5	11.8
3	19.1	14.9
4	3.7	1.1
5	15.6	12.0

We see that stock *i* moves somewhat with the market. Plotting the values in Figure 21–11, we observe a line that is upward sloping at slightly above a 45-degree angle.

FIGURE 21–11 Relationship of Individual Stock to the Market

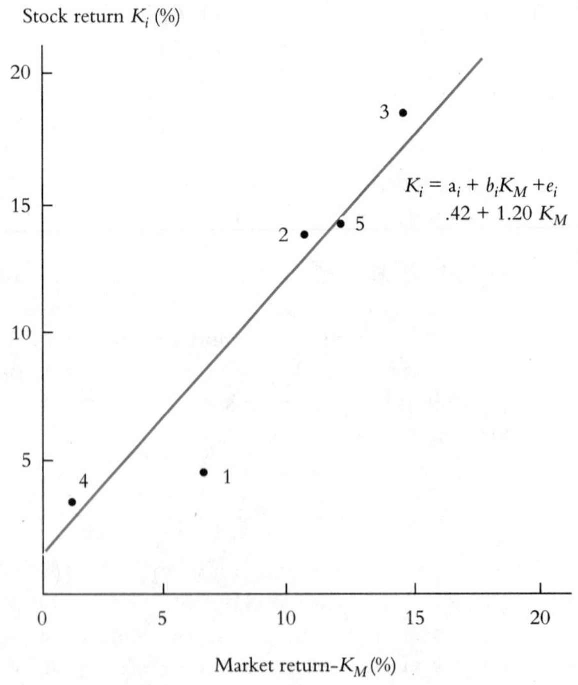

[6] Although monthly calculations are often used, we can satisfy the same basic learning objectives with annual data, and the analysis is easier to follow.

A straight line of best fit has been drawn through the various points representing the following formula:

$$K_i = a_i + b_i K_M + e_i \tag{21–6}$$

K_i represents the anticipated stock return based on Formula 21–6 where: a_i (alpha) is the point at which the line crosses the vertical axis; b_i (beta) is the slope of the line; K_M is the independent variable of market return; and e_i is the random error term. The $a_i + b_i K_M$ portion of the formula describes a straight line, and e_i represents deviations or random, nonrecurring movements away from the straight line. In the present example, the formula for the straight line is $K_i = 0.42 + 1.20\,K_M$ (indicating a beta or line slope of 1.2). These values can be approximated by drawing a line of best fit as indicated in Figure 21–11 or through the use of least squares regression analysis presented in Appendix 21B. Basically, the equation tells us how volatile our stock is relative to the market through the beta coefficient. In the present case, if the market moves up or down by a given percent, our stock is assumed to move 1.2 times that amount.

Since beta measures the correlation of a stock's total return to a market index, the beta of the market when regressed on itself will always be 1.0. With a beta of 1.2, our stock is considered to be 20 percent more volatile than the market and therefore riskier. A stock with average volatility would have a beta of 1.0, the same beta as the market. A stock having a beta of less than 1.0 would have less risk than the market.

Systematic and Unsystematic Risk

Previously, we mentioned the two major types of risk associated with a stock. One is the market movement or beta (b_i) risk. If the market moves up or down, a stock is assumed to change in value. This type of risk is referred to as **systematic risk** and was introduced in Chapter 1. The second type of risk is represented by the error term (e_i) and indicates changes in value not associated with market movement. It may represent the temporary influence of a competitor's new product, changes in raw material prices, or unusual economic and government influences on a given firm. These changes are peculiar to an individual security or industry at a given point and are not directly correlated with the market. This second type of risk is referred to as **unsystematic risk.**

Since unsystematic risk is associated with an individual company or industry, it may be diversified away in a large portfolio and is not a risk inherent in investing in common stocks. Thus, by picking stocks that are less than perfectly correlated, unsystematic risk may be eliminated. For example, the inherent risks of investing in cyclical semiconductor stocks may be diversified away by investing in countercyclical housing stocks. Researchers have indicated that all but 15 percent of unsystematic risk may be eliminated with a carefully selected portfolio of 10 stocks, and all but 11 percent, with the portfolio of 20 stocks.[7]

The systematic risk (beta) cannot be diversified away even in a large portfolio, and therefore, the market compensates an investor with a higher expected return when that investor buys securities with a high beta or a lower expected return than the market when

[7] Wagner and Lau, "The Effect of Diversification on Risk."

the investor buys securities with a beta less than the market. Using this method of risk adjustment, the capital asset pricing model creates a linear risk-return trade-off using the market as the reference point for risk and return.

Since unsystematic risk can be diversified away, systematic risk (b_i) is the only relevant risk under the capital asset pricing model. Thus, even though we can describe total risk as:

$$\text{Total risk} = \text{Systematic risk} + \text{Unsystematic risk}$$

in a diversified portfolio, unsystematic risk approaches 0.

Security Market Line

We actually express the trade-off between risk and return for an *individual stock* through the **security market line (SML)** in Figure 21–12. Whereas in Figure 21–11 on page 608, we graphed the relationship that allowed us to compute the beta (b_i) for a security, in Figure 21–12 we now take that beta and show what the anticipated or required return in the marketplace is for a stock with that characteristic. The security market line (SML) shows the risk-return trade-off for an individual stock in Figure 21–12 just as the capital market line (CML) accomplished that same objective for a portfolio in Figure 21–10.

Once again, we stress that the return is not plotted against the total risk (σ) for the individual stock but only that part of the risk that cannot be diversified away, commonly referred to as the systematic or beta risk. The actual formula for the security market line (SML) is:

$$K_i = R_F + b_i (K_M - R_F) \qquad (21\text{–}7)$$

The mathematical derivation of the formula is presented in Appendix 21C. As we did with the capital market line for portfolio returns, with the security market line we start out with a basic rate of return for a risk-free asset (R_F) and add a premium for risk. In this case, the premium is equal to the beta on the stock times the difference between the market rate

FIGURE 21–12 Illustration of the Security Market Line

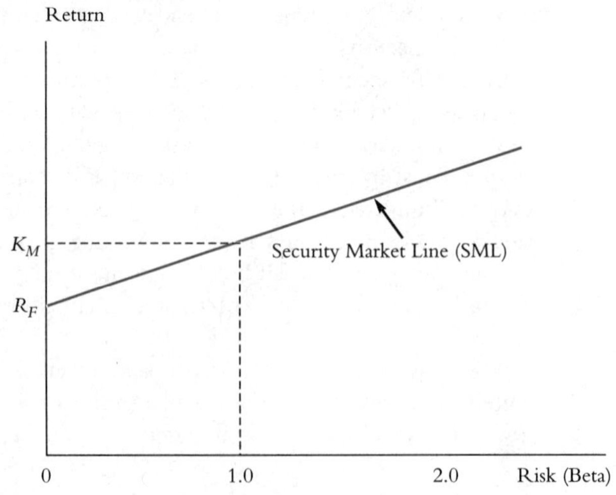

of return (K_M) and the risk-free rate of return (R_F). If $R_F = 6\%$, $K_M = 12\%$, and the stock has a beta (b_i) of 1, the anticipated rate of return, using Formula 21–7, would be the same as that in the market, or 12 percent.

$$K_i = 6\% + 1(12\% - 6\%) = 6\% + 6\% = 12\%$$

Since the stock has the same degree of risk as the market in general, this would appear to be logical. If the stock has a beta of 1.5, the added systematic risk would call for a return of 15 percent, whereas a beta of 0.5 would indicate the return should be 9 percent. The calculations are indicated below:

Beta = 1.5

$$K_i = 6\% + 1.5(12\% - 6\%) = 6\% + 1.5(6\%) = 6\% + 9\% = 15\%$$

Beta = 0.5

$$K_i = 6\% + 0.5(12\% - 6\%) = 6\% + 0.5(6\%) = 6\% + 3\% = 9\%$$

Since the beta factor is deemed to be important in analyzing potential risk and return, much emphasis is placed on knowing the beta for a given security. Merrill Lynch, Value Line, Standard and Poor's, and various brokerage houses and investment services publish information on beta for a large number of securities. A representative list is presented in the table below.

Corporation	Beta (September 1994)
Paine Webber	1.80
Compaq Computer	1.45
Colgate-Palmolive	1.20
Digital Equipment	1.15
Colgate-Palmolive Dupont	1.00
Shell Transport	.70
Piedmont Natural Gas	.60

ASSUMPTIONS OF THE CAPITAL ASSET PRICING MODEL

Having evaluated some of the implications of the CAPM, it is important that the student be aware of some of the assumptions that go into the model.

1. All investors can borrow or lend an unlimited amount of funds at a given risk-free rate.
2. All investors have the same one-period time horizon.
3. All investors wish to maximize their expected utility over this time horizon and evaluate investments on the basis of means and standard deviations of portfolio returns.
4. All investors have the same expectations—that is, all investors estimate identical probability distributions for rates of return.
5. All assets are perfectly divisible—it is possible to buy fractional shares of any asset or portfolio.

6. There are no taxes or transactions costs.
7. The market is efficient and in equilibrium or quickly adjusting to equilibrium.

Listing these assumptions indicates some of the necessary conditions to create the CAPM. While at first they may appear to be severely limiting, they are similar to those often used in the standard economic theory of the firm and in other basic financial models.

The primary usefulness in examining this model or similar risk-return trade-off models is to provide some reasonable basis for relating return opportunity with risk on the investment. Portfolio managers find risk-return models helpful in explaining their performance or the performance of their competitors to clients. A competitor's portfolio that has unusually high returns may have been developed primarily on the basis of high-risk assets. To the extent that this can be explained on the basis of capital market theory, the competitor's performance may look less like superior money management and more like a product of high risk taking. As we shall see in Chapter 22, many of the techniques for assessing portfolio performance on Wall Street are explicitly or implicitly related to the risk-return concepts discussed in this chapter.

Although empirical tests have somewhat supported the capital asset pricing model, a number of testing problems remain. To develop the SML in which stock returns (vertical axis) can be measured against beta (horizontal axis), an appropriate line must be drawn. Researchers have some disagreement about R_F. (Is it represented by short-term or long-term Treasury rates?) There is also debate about what is the approximate K_M, or market rate of return. Some suggest the market proxy variable will greatly influence the beta and that difficulties in dealing with this problem can bring the whole process under attack.[8]

When empirical data are compared with theoretical return expectations, there is some discrepancy in that the theoretical SML may have a slightly greater slope than the actual line fitted on the basis of real-world data as shown in Figure 21–13.[9]

There may also be a possible problem in that betas for individual securities are not necessarily stable over time (rather than remaining relatively constant at 1.3 or perhaps 0.7, they tend to approach 1 over time). Thus, a beta based on past risk may not always reflect current risk.[10] Because the beta for a portfolio may be more stable than an individual stock's beta, portfolio betas are also used as a systematic risk variable. A portfolio beta is simply the weighted average of the betas of the individual stocks. We can say:

$$b_P \text{ (portfolio beta)} = \sum_{i=1}^{n} x_i b_i \qquad (21\text{–}8)$$

and

$$K_P = R_F + b_P (K_M - R_F) \qquad (21\text{–}9)$$

---

[8] Richard Roll, "A Critique of the Asset Pricing Theory's Test," *Journal of Financial Economics*, March 1977, pp. 129–76. Also, "Ambiguity When Performance Is Measured by the Securities Market Line," *Journal of Finance*, September 1978, pp. 1051–69.

[9] Franco Modigliani and Gerald A. Pogue, "An Introduction to Risk and Returns," *Financial Analysts Journal*, March–April 1974, pp. 68–86, and May–June 1974, pp. 69–86.

[10] Robert A. Levy, "On the Short-Term Stationary of Beta Coefficients," *Financial Analysts Journal*, November–December 1971, pp. 55–62. Also, Marshall E. Blume, "Betas and Their Regression Tendencies," *Journal of Finance*, June 1975, pp. 785–95.

FIGURE 21–13 Test of the Security Market Line

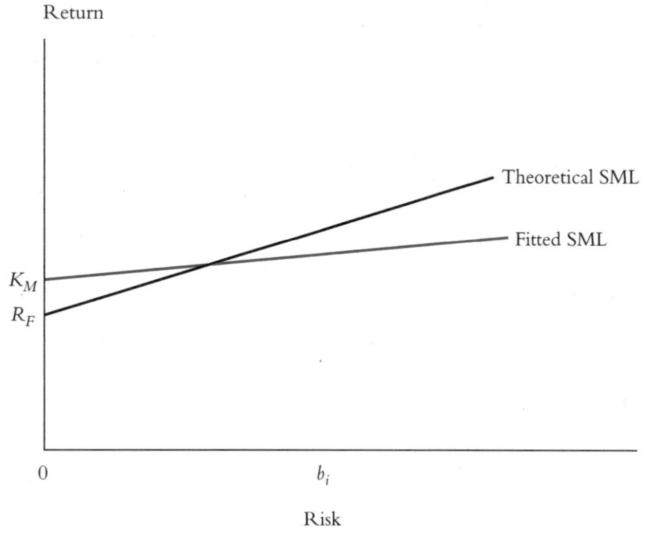

By examining portfolio betas rather than individual stock betas, we overcome part of the criticism leveled at the instability of betas in the capital asset pricing model. Many of the other criticisms have also evoked new research that may provide different approaches or possible solutions to past deficiencies in the model.

ARBITRAGE PRICING THEORY

Another theory for explaining stock prices and stock returns is arbitrage pricing theory (APT). This is a fairly sophisticated theory and will be of interest only to those who wish to learn more about asset pricing.

Arbitrage pricing theory assumes a linear return generating model that makes the return on an investment a function of more than one factor. The capital asset pricing model also uses a linear return generating model but assumes that returns are a function of a stock's sensitivity to the equity risk premium. APT acknowledges that a stock's return may be a function of many factors. The arbitrage pricing model is a more generalized model than the CAPM and less restrictive in its assumptions; it does not assume equilibrium markets or make assumptions about investor preferences. However, the concept of arbitrage behavior will drive markets to equilibrium as investors try to make risk-free profits.

Arbitrage behavior assumes one good should have the same price. If two different prices are found for gold in London and New York, an arbitrageur could sell short the high-priced gold and buy the low-priced gold. This behavior would drive the price of high-priced gold down and the price of low-priced gold up until the price of gold was the same. Theoretically, by selling short, the investor can use the proceeds from the short sale to buy long, and therefore, the transaction can be made without any investment. This makes the transaction a no-cost riskless transaction. Arbitrage relies on the behavior of market participants to take advantage of prices in disequilibrium, and through this arbitrage mechanism, prices will move into equilibrium.

The arbitrage pricing model describes the expected return on a stock as a function of several factors. While there is no universal agreement on what factors have the greatest impact on stock returns, Chen[11] and Roll and Ross[12] suggest there are a few major factors. These are changes in expectations about:

1. Interest-rate risk.
2. Business-cycle risk.
3. Inflation.
4. The risk of changing risk premiums.

The return-generating process using the APT model appears in Formula 21–10. We have listed four factors here, but there could be as few as one factor or many other factors. Three or four factors probably capture the most significant return sensitivities.

$$K_{i,t} = a_i + b_{i,1}F_{1,t} + b_{i,2}F_{2,t} + b_{i,3}F_{3,t} + b_{i,4}F_{4,t} + e_{i,t} \qquad (21\text{–}10)$$

where:

$K_{i,t}$ = Return on stock i at time t
a_i = Expected return on stock i
b_i, j = Sensitivity of stock i to factor j
$F_{j,t}$ = Value of factor j at time t
$e_{i,t}$ = Random term unique to stock i at time t

If a_i is the expected return on the stock, then the effect of the factors is expected to be zero (0). In other words, the market has already incorporated expectations about these factors into the stock's price. What will affect the actual return on stock i are any surprises in these factors that were not anticipated. For example, if factor 1 is changing real GDP and if real GDP goes up more than expected, stocks that are sensitive to changes in real GDP will go up, while those stocks that are not sensitive to the business cycle will be unaffected. Conversely, if inflation is factor 2 and if it increases more than expected, stocks that are subject to inflationary pressures will decline in price, while those that are not sensitive to changes in inflation will not be affected. The sensitivity to these various factors shows up in the b_i for each factor.

The random term e_i represents the unexpected portion of the return on security i, which is not explained by the factors. It captures unexpected events unique to firm i. For example, a new product announcement, a merger, or a takeover will affect firm i only. These unexpected events were not impounded into the stock's expected return, a_i.

The b_i's (factor sensitivities) reflect the sensitivity of the factor on the stock's return. Like the capital asset pricing model, the factor sensitivity for a portfolio is the sum of the weighted beta for each factor based on the percentage of market value that each stock contributes to the portfolio.

---

[11] Nai-fu Chen, "Some Empirical Tests of the Theory of Arbitrage Pricing," *Journal of Finance,* December 1983, pp. 1393–1414.

[12] Richard Roll and Stephen A. Ross, "An Empirical Investigation of the Arbitrage Pricing Theory," *Journal of Finance,* December 1980, pp. 1073–1103.

Let us take two stocks, x and y. Two factors affect the returns of both stocks, and the random variable e_i is eliminated because we assume that in a diversified portfolio, e_i approaches zero (0):

$$K_x = 12\% + 3F_{1,t} - 2F_{2,t}$$
$$K_y = 15\% + 1F_{1,t} - 6F_{2,t}$$

Each factor will have an impact on portfolio risk in proportion to the amount invested in each stock and the sensitivity of each factor on the stock's return. For example, if factor 1 represents the impact of changing real GDP (the business cycle risk), an unexpected increase in real GDP would increase the return on stock x by 3 percent. The same 1 percent unexpected change in GDP would increase the return on stock y by 1 percent. These effects show up in the factor sensitivities (b_i) of 3 for K_x and 1 for K_y.

If the second factor represents inflation, we can see that a 1 percent unexpected increase in inflation will cause a reduction in return of 2 percent for stock x and 6 percent for stock y. When we combine stocks x and y into a portfolio weighted 40 percent stock x and 60 percent stock y, we end up with portfolio risk dependent on the percentage of each stock in the portfolio and each stock's sensitivity to factors affecting risk. We multiply both sides of the return equations by the portfolio weights:

$$(0.4)\ K_x = (0.40) \times 12\% + (0.40) \times (3)F_{1,t} - (0.40) \times (2)F_{2,t}$$
$$(0.4)\ K_x = 4.8\% \qquad + 1.2F_{1,t} \qquad - 0.8F_{2,t}$$

Forty percent of stock x will contribute 4.8 percent expected return to the portfolio and will have a factor sensitivity of 1.2 to the business-cycle risk and a negative factor sensitivity of 0.8 to the inflation risk:

$$(0.6)\ K_y = (0.60) \times 15\% + (0.60) \times (1)F_{1,t} - (0.60) \times (6)F_{2,t}$$
$$(0.6)\ K_y = 9.0\% \qquad + 0.6F_{1,t} \qquad - 3.6F_{2,t}$$

Sixty percent of stock y will contribute 9.0 percent expected return to the portfolio and will have a factor sensitivity of 0.6 to the business-cycle risk and a negative factor sensitivity of 3.6 to the inflation risk. When we combine the two stocks into a portfolio, we end up with a portfolio having an expected return of 13.8 percent and having a sensitivity to factor 1 (business-cycle risk) of 1.8 and a negative sensitivity to factor 2 (inflation risk) of 4.4:

$$\text{Portfolio return } K_p = (4.8\% + 9\%) + (1.2 + 0.6) - (0.8 + 3.6)$$
$$K_p = 13.8\% \qquad + 1.8F_{1,t} \qquad - 4.4F_{2,t}$$

We have structured a portfolio that will be moderately sensitive to any unexpected events having to do with changes in real GDP and highly susceptible to unexpected changes in inflation.

It is important to understand that the sign in front of the factor sensitivity indicates whether the unexpected event is directly related to returns or inversely related to returns. For example, we assume unexpected increases in inflation reduce stock returns while unexpected decreases in inflation increase stock returns. Thus, we have a minus sign before the second factor.

Application to Portfolio Management

From the portfolio manager's point of view, the arbitrage pricing theory can help measure the sensitivity of a portfolio to various macro factors that could potentially affect the actual return on one stock or a portfolio. This model allows investment managers to structure portfolios that either are highly sensitive or insensitive to certain kinds of risk exposures. If a manager were concerned about a recession and this information were not yet factored into stock prices, he or she could create a portfolio that insulated the returns on the portfolio from unpleasant surprises. On the other hand, if the market had factored in expectations for a recession and the manager expected good business-cycle news, he or she could buy stocks sensitive to business-cycle news.

Let us look at one last arbitrage case that for simplicity assumes one factor affects two stocks:

$$K_{a,t} = 19\% + 3F$$
$$K_{b,t} = 13\% + 2F$$

Stock *a* has an expected return of 19 percent and a factor risk of 3, while stock *b* has an expected return of 13 percent and a factor risk of 2. Stock *b* has less risk than stock *a* because its factor sensitivity is 2 versus 3. To create a portfolio of equal risk to stock *b,* we can structure a portfolio consisting of two-thirds of stock *a* and one-third of a risk-free asset. If we can borrow at a risk-free rate of 6 percent, we can arbitrage our portfolio and increase our return. We would sell a portfolio consisting of only security *b* and buy a portfolio consisting of two-thirds of security *a* and one-third of the risk-free security. The portfolio we bought now has a factor sensitivity of 2 from the combined risk of stock *a* and the risk-free asset $[(2/3 \times 3F + (1/3 \times 0)]$. This risk of 2 for the risk factor F is the same risk as security *b*. This is because the risk-free security has no factor risk at all, and two-thirds of the factor risk in security *a* equals 2. What happens to our return? It goes up to 14.7 percent (two thirds of 19 percent from stock *a* plus one-third of 6 percent from the risk-free asset). Since we sold security *b* and bought security *a* and a risk-free security equal to the sales price of security *b,* we have increased the expected return from 13 percent to 14.7 percent without increasing our investment or risk. If opportunities like this one become available, arbitrageurs will follow the same strategy outlined and drive the price of security *b* down and the price of security *a* up until the two are in equilibrium with respect to their risk and return expectations.

Arbitrage pricing theory shows that market participants using arbitrage will create a unique equilibrium price of risk for each factor so that the expected return is a function of all the expected returns attributable to each factor.

SUMMARY

The investor is basically risk-averse and therefore will demand a premium for incremental risk. In an efficient market context, the ability to achieve high returns may be more directly related to absorption of additional risk than superior ability in selecting stocks (this remains a debatable point that proponents of fundamental and technical analysis would argue).

Risk for an individual stock is measured in terms of the standard deviation (σ_i) around a given expected value ($\overline{K}_i$).

The larger the standard deviation, the greater the risk. For a portfolio of stocks, the expected value (K_P) is the weighted average of the individual returns; but this is not true for the portfolio standard deviation (σ_P). The portfolio standard deviation is also influenced by the interaction between the stocks. To the extent the correlation coefficient (r_{ij}) is less than +1, there will be some reduction from the weighted average of the standard deviation of the individual stocks that we are combining. A negative correlation coefficient will provide substantial reduction in the portfolio standard deviation.

Under classic Markowitz portfolio theory, we look at a large array of possible portfolios in an attempt to construct an efficient frontier that represents the best possible risk-return trade-off at different levels of risk. Individuals then match their own risk-return indifference curves with the efficient frontier to determine where they should be along this optimal scale.

This was the prevailing theory until the capital asset pricing model (CAPM) was developed. The CAPM supersedes some of the findings of classic portfolio theory with the introduction of the risk-free asset as represented by (R_F) into the analysis. The assumption is that an individual can choose an investment combining the return on the risk-free asset with the market rate of return, and this will provide superior returns to the efficient frontier at all points except M, where they are equal. The investor may invest in any combination of R_F and M to achieve the risk-return positions described by the capital market line in Figure 21–10.

The capital market line describes the general trade-off between risk and return for portfolio managers in the economy. Any attempt to get higher portfolio returns must be matched by higher portfolio risks. Although the portfolio manager is investing in stocks and bonds, the general pattern set out for the risk-free asset and market combination is perceived to establish the limits for investment performance of any nature. Any increase in portfolio returns (K_P) must be associated with an increase in the portfolio standard deviation (σ_P).

The capital asset pricing model also calls for an evaluation of individual assets (rather than portfolios). The security market line in Figure 21–12 shows the same type of risk-return trade-off for individual securities as the capital market line did for portfolios. Investors in individual assets are only assumed to be rewarded for systematic, market-related risk, known as the beta (b_i) risk. All other risk is assumed to be susceptible to diversification.

A number of assumptions associated with the capital asset pricing model are subject to close review and challenge. Furthermore, there is some question about the appropriate measures for R_F and K_M as well as the stability of beta and the appropriate slope of the SML line. Nevertheless, the capital asset pricing model represents a generally useful device for portraying the relationship of risk and return in the capital markets over the long term.

Arbitrage pricing theory allows for several sources of systematic risk as opposed to one measure under the capital asset pricing model. It further assumes investors will appropriately hedge or arbitrage between securities and portfolios to establish expected returns. While arbitrage pricing theory offers some conceptual and empirical advantages over the capital asset pricing model, it is less widely used.

KEY WORDS AND CONCEPTS

expected value, 593
standard deviation, 594
correlation coefficient, 597
efficient frontier, 600
indifference curves, 601
capital asset pricing model, 604
capital market line (CML), 606
beta coefficient, 608
systematic risk, 609
unsystematic risk, 609
security market line (SML), 610
arbitrage pricing theory, 613

DISCUSSION QUESTIONS

1. Define risk.
2. What is an expected value?
3. What is the most commonly used measure of dispersion?
4. In a two-asset portfolio, is the portfolio standard deviation a weighted average of the two individual stocks' standard deviation? Explain.
5. What does the correlation coefficient (r_{ij}) measure? What are the two most extreme values it can take, and what do they indicate? In the real world, are more variables positively or negatively correlated?
6. What are the two characteristics of points along the efficient frontier? Do portfolios exist above the efficient frontier?
7. What does the steepness of the slope of the risk-return indifference curve indicate?
8. Describe the optimum portfolio for an investor in terms of indifference curves and the efficient frontier.
9. What new investment variable or outlet allowed market researchers to go from the Markowitz portfolio theory (including the efficient frontier) to the capital asset pricing model?
10. In examining the *capital market line* as part of the capital asset pricing model, to increase portfolio return (K_P) what other variable must you increase?
11. In terms of the capital asset pricing model:
    a. Indicate the two types of risks associated with an individual security.
    b. Which of these two is the beta risk?
    c. What risk is assumed not to be compensated for in the marketplace under the capital asset pricing model? Why?
12. What can be assumed in terms of volatility for a stock that has a beta of 1.2?
13. What does the security market line indicate? In general terms, how is it different from the capital market line?
14. In regard to the capital asset pricing model, comment on disagreements or debates related to R_F (the risk-free rate) and K_M (market rate of return).
15. Are betas of individual stocks necessarily stable (constant) over time?
16. Arbitrage pricing theory is more generalized than the capital asset pricing model because it assumes an investment's return is related to

more than just the one factor of risk. Suggest four factors that might influence return under arbitrage pricing theory as suggested by Chen, and Roll and Ross.

17. Under arbitrage pricing theory, how does an investor attempt to take advantage of economic events that are not yet fully recognized in the marketplace?

18. How does arbitraging tend to create equilibrium in the marketplace?

PROBLEMS

Expected value and standard deviation

1. An investment has the following range of outcomes and probabilities.

Outcomes (Percent)	Probability of Outcomes
6%	0.20
9	0.60
12	0.20

Calculate the expected value and the standard deviation (round to two places after the decimal point where necesary).

Portfolio expected value and standard deviation

2. Given another investment with an expected value of 12 percent and a standard deviation of 2.2 percent that is countercyclical to the investment in problem 1, what is the expected value of the portfolio and its standard deviation if both are combined into a portfolio with 40 percent invested in the first investment and 60 percent in the second? Assume the correlation coefficient (r_{ij}) is –0.40.

Portfolio standard deviation

3. What would be the portfolio standard deviation if the two investments in problem 2 had a correlation coefficient (r_{ij}) of +0.40?

Efficient frontier

4. Assume the following risk-return possibilities for 10 different portfolios. Plot the points in a manner similar to Figure 21–3 and indicate the approximate shape of the efficient frontier.

Portfolio	K_P	σ_P
1	9.0%	1.5%
2	9.0	2.0
3	10.0	3.0
4	10.0	4.0
5	12.0	4.0
6	11.5	5.0
7	13.5	5.5
8	13.0	6.0
9	15.0	7.0
10	14.5	7.8

Efficient frontier

5. Referring to problem 4, if a new portfolio, no. 11, has a K_P value of 13.8 percent and a standard deviation (σ_P) of 7.1 percent, will it qualify for the efficient frontier?

Capital market line

6. Using the formula for the capital market line (Formula 21–5), if the risk-free rate (R_F) is 8 percent, the market rate of return (M_K) is 12 percent, the market standard deviation (σ_M) is 10 percent, and the standard deviation of the portfolio (σ_P) is 12 percent, compute the anticipated return (K_P).

Capital market line

7. Recompute the answer to problem 6 based on a portfolio standard of 16 percent. In terms of capital market theory, explain why K_P has increased.

Security market line

8. Using the formula for the security market line (Formula 21–7), if the risk-free rate (R_F) is 7 percent, the beta (b_i) is 1.25, and the market rate of return (K_M) is 11.8 percent, compute the anticipated rate of return (K_i).

Beta consideration

9. If another security had a lower beta than indicated in problem 8, would K_i be lower or higher? What is the logic behind your answer in terms of risk?

Plotting best fit to data

10. Assume the following values for a stock's return and the market return.

Year	Stock *i* Return (K)	Market Return (K_M)
1	14.9	10.3
2	3.8	2.2
3	9.0	10.5
4	18.2	12.8
5	6.0	3.4

Plot the data and draw a line of best fit similar to that in Figure 21–11. No equation is necessary.

Least squares regression analysis

11. Using the formulas in Appendix 21B, compute a least squares regression equation for problem 10. (Round beta and alpha to two places after the decimal point.)

Rate of return

12. Use the beta (b_i) from problem 11, and plug it into the formula for the security market line (Formula 21–7). Assume the risk-free rate (R_F) is 7 percent and the market rate of return (K_M) is 12.6 percent. What is the value of the anticipated rate of return (K_i)?

Arbitrage pricing theory

13. Under arbitrage pricing theory, assume two stocks have the following equations:

$$K_x = 15\% + 2F_{1,t} - 3F_{2,t}$$

$$K_y = 11\% + 1F_{1,t} - 4F_{2,t}$$

The first factor relates to unexpected increases in real GDP, and the second factor relates to unexpected increases in interest rates.

If a portfolio consists of 60 percent of stock x and 40 percent of stock y, what will be the equation for portfolio return (K_P)?

Arbitrage pricing theory

14. Assume the following two stocks are available for purchase. (There is only one risk factor.)

$$K_a = 20\% + 4F$$

$$K_b = 12\% + 3F$$

We will sell stock *b* and replace three-fourths of its value with stock *a* and one-fourth of its value with a risk-free asset yielding 6 percent.

a. What is the new weighted average for the risk factor?

b. What is the new weighted average return?

c. Has the investor benefited from a risk-return perspective?

THE WALL STREET JOURNAL PROJECTS

Assume you are asked to find the average price and average beta for a portfolio composed of the following seven stocks. The weights represent the percent of the portfolio invested in each stock.

Corporation	Weights
Citicorp	10%
Colgate-Palmolive	15
Hewlett-Packard	18
Merrill Lynch & Co.	20
Philip Morris	5
Scott Paper	12
Texas Instruments	20
	100%

Each of the stocks is listed on the New York Stock Exchange, and its price can be found under "New York Stock Exchange Composite Transactions" in section C of *The Wall Street Journal.* The betas can be looked up in *The Value Line Investment Survey.*

1. To determine the average price for the portfolio, merely multiply each stock's price times its weight in the portfolio and sum.
2. To determine the average beta for the portfolio, follow the same general procedure. Does this appear to be a risky portfolio?

U.S. EQUITIES ONFLOPPY EXERCISES

Please use your U.S. Equities OnFloppy software and manual to complete the following exercises.

1. On page 611, the beta coefficients for Compaq Computer and Piedmont Natural Gas are given for September 1994 as 1.45 and 0.6, respectively. Put all companies with the same SIC code as Compaq Computer into one group and all those with the same SIC code as Piedmont Natural Gas into another group. Save the list of companies selected in each industry. Prepare a report that shows the beta for each industry. Prepare a report that shows the beta for each firm and the average beta for each industry. Comment on your findings.
2. On page 611, the beta coefficient as of September 1994 is shown for seven companies. Find a more recent beta for these seven companies using the most

recent data disk available for U.S. Equities OnFloppy. What do you observe about the stability of a stock's beta over time? What conclusions might be drawn from the observation?

3. a. Select the stocks that meet the screen specified in Chapter 10 problem 1*a* for U.S. Equities OnFloppy exercises. Construct two portfolios from the companies identified—one of the five highest beta stocks and one of the five lowest beta stocks.
   b. Determine the CAPM portfolio returns for these two portfolios using the current rate on one-year Treasury bills as the risk-free rate and 6 percent as the market-risk premium.
   c. Look up the stocks' prices exactly one year ago and compute the return over the past year. Compare the CAPM portfolio return to the actual return offered by these portfolios. Did the portfolios earn excess returns?

SELECTED REFERENCES

Portfolio Considerations

Blume, Marshall E., and Irwin Friend. "The Asset Structure of Individual Portfolios and Some Implications for Utility Functions." *Journal of Finance,* May 1975, pp. 585–603.

McEnally, Richard W. "Time Diversification: The Surest Route to Lower Risk?" *Journal of Portfolio Management,* Summer 1985, pp. 24–26.

Capital Asset Pricing Model

Fama, Eugene F. "Efficient Capital Markets: II." *Journal of Finance,* December 1991, pp. 1575–1617.

Friend, Iwrin; Randolph Westerfield; and Michael Granito. "New Evidence on the Capital Asset Pricing Model." *Journal of Finance,* June 1978, pp. 903–17.

Jensen, Michael C., ed. *Studies in the Theory of Capital Markets.* New York: Praeger Publishers, 1972.

Roll, Richard. "Ambiguity When Performance Is Measured by the Securities Market Line." *Journal of Finance,* September 1978, pp. 1051–70.

Sharpe, William F. "Factor Models, CAPMs, and the APT." *Journal of Portfolio Management,* Fall 1984, pp. 21–25.

________. "Capital Asset Prices: A Theory of Market Equilibrium under Conditions of Risk." *Journal of Finance,* September 1964, pp. 425–42.

Beta Measurement

Black, Fisher. "Return and Beta." *Journal of Portfolio Management,* Fall 1993, pp. 8–18.

Roll, Richard, and Steven A. Ross. "On the Cross-Sectional Relation between Expected Returns and Betas." *Journal of Finance,* March 1994, pp. 101–21.

Rosenberg, Barr. "Prediction of Common Stock Betas." *Journal of Portfolio Management,* Winter 1985, pp. 5–14.

Arbitrage Pricing Theory

Chen, Nai-fu. "Some Empirical Tests of the Theory of Arbitrage Pricing." *Journal of Finance,* December 1993, pp. 1393–1414.

Gehr, Adam. "Some Tests of the Arbitrage Pricing Theory." *Journal of the Midwest Finance Association,* Annual 1978 issue, pp. 91–105.

Roll, Richard. "A Critique of the Asset Pricing Theory's Test." *Journal of Financial Economics,* March 1977, pp. 129–76.

Roll, Richard, and Stephen A. Ross. "An Empirical Investigation of the Arbitrage Pricing Theory." *Journal of Finance,* December 1980, pp. 1073–1103.

Ross, Stephen A. "The Arbitrage Theory of Capital Asset Pricing," *Journal of Economic Theory,* December 1976, pp. 314–60.

APPENDIX 21A: The Correlation Coefficient

There are a number of formulas for the correlation coefficient. We shall use the statement:

$$r_{ij} = \frac{\text{cov}_{ij}}{\sigma_i \sigma_j} \qquad (21A\text{–}1)$$

Here, cov_{ij} (covariance) is an *absolute* measure of the extent to which two sets of variables move together over time. Once we have determined this value, we simply divide by $\sigma_i \sigma_j$ to get a relative measure of correlation (r_{ij}).

The formula for the covariance is:

$$\text{cov}_{ij} = \Sigma(K_i - \overline{K}_i)(K_j - \overline{K}_j)P \qquad (21A\text{–}2)$$

We take our K and P values from investment i and investment j in Chapter 21 to compute the following:

K_i	$\overline{K}_i$	$(K_i - \overline{K}_i)$	K_j	$\overline{K}_j$	$(K_j - \overline{K}_j)$	$(K_i - \overline{K}_i)(K_j - \overline{K}_j)$	P	$(K_i - \overline{K}_i)(K_j - \overline{K}_j)P$
5%	10%	−5%	20%	10%	+10%	−50%	0.20	−10.0%
7	10	−3	8	10	−2	+6	0.30	+1.8
13	10	+3	8	10	−2	−6	0.30	−1.8
15	10	+5	6	10	−4	−20	0.20	−4.0
								−14.0%

$$\text{cov}_{ij} = \Sigma(K_i - \overline{K}_i)(K_j - \overline{K}_j)P = -14.0\%$$

Using the values in the chapter for σ_i equal to 3.9 and σ_j equal to 5.1, we determine:

$$r_{ij} = \frac{\text{cov}_{ij}}{\sigma_i \sigma_j} = \frac{-14.0}{(3.9)(5.1)} = \frac{-14.0}{19.9} = -0.70$$

APPENDIX 21B: Least Squares Regression Analysis

We shall show how least squares regression analysis can be used to develop a linear equation to explain the relationship between the return on a stock and return in the market.

We will develop the terms in the expression:

$$K_i = a_i + b_i K_M + e_i$$

(e_i is the random error term and will not be quantified in our analysis.)
Using the data from the chapter,

Year	K_i	K_M
1	4.8%	6.5%
2	14.5	11.8
3	19.1	14.9
4	3.7	1.1
5	15.6	12.0

the normal or mathematical equation to solve for b_i is:

$$b_i = \frac{N\Sigma K_i K_M - \Sigma K_i \Sigma K_M}{N\Sigma K_M^2 - (\Sigma K_M)^2} \tag{21B–1}$$

For a_i, we use the following formula (which is dependent on a prior determination of b_i):

$$a_i = \frac{\Sigma K_i - b_i \Sigma K_M}{N} \tag{21B–2}$$

We compute four columns of data and plug the values into our formulas.

K_i	K_M	$K_i K_M$	K_M^2
4.8	6.5	31.20	42.25
14.5	11.8	171.10	139.24
19.1	14.9	284.59	222.01
3.7	1.1	4.07	1.21
15.6	12.0	187.20	144.00
$\Sigma K_i = 57.7$	$\Sigma K_M = 46.3$	$\Sigma K_i K_M = 678.16$	$\Sigma K_M^2 = 548.71$

Also N (number of observations) = 5.

$$\begin{aligned} b_i &= \frac{N\,\Sigma K_i K_M - \Sigma K_i \Sigma K_M}{N\,\Sigma K_M^2 - (\Sigma K_M)^2} \\ &= \frac{5(678.16) - 57.7(46.3)}{5(548.71) - (46.3)^2} \\ &= \frac{3390.80 - 2671.51}{2743.55 - 2143.69} = \frac{719.29}{599.86} = 1.20 \end{aligned}$$

Using our beta value, we now compute alpha:

$$a_i = \frac{\Sigma K_i - b_i \Sigma K_M}{N}$$

$$a_i = \frac{57.7 - 1.2(46.3)}{5}$$

$$a_i = \frac{57.7 - 55.6}{5} = \frac{2.1}{5} = 0.42$$

In summary:

$$K_i = a_i + b_i K_M$$

$$K_i = 0.42 + 1.20\,K_M$$

APPENDIX 21C: Derivation of the Security Market Line (SML)

First, we graph the SML based on covariance (Figure 21C–1).[13]

Along the vertical axis we show return, and along the horizontal axis, covariance of return with the market.[14] We can describe our equation for the SML in terms of the slope of the line as shown on page 626.

FIGURE 21C–1 Derivation of the SML

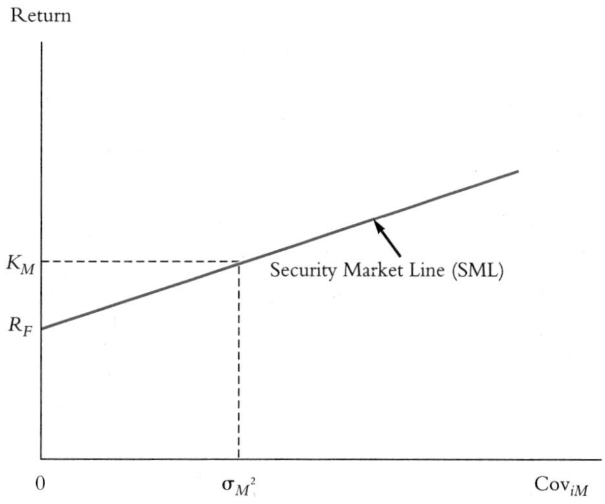

[13] The concept of covariance is described in Appendix 21A.

[14] Actually, σ_M^2 represents the covariance of the market with the market (a bit redundant). The cov_{MM} equals σ_M^2. The covariance of a variable with itself is equal to the variance.

$$K_i = R_F + \frac{(K_M - R_F)}{(\sigma_M^2 - 0)} \text{cov}_{iM} \tag{21C–1}$$

We then rearrange our terms:

$$K_i = R_F + \left(\frac{\text{cov}_{iM}}{\sigma_M^2}\right)(K_M - R_F) \tag{21C–2}$$

The systematic risk of an individual asset is measured by its covariance with the market (cov_{iM}). We can convert this to a relative measure by dividing through by the market variance (σ_M^2). The *relative* systematic movement of an individual asset with the market is referred to as the beta regression coefficient. Thus, we show in Formula 21C–3:

$$b_i = \frac{\text{cov}_{iM}}{\sigma_M^2} \tag{21C–3}$$

Substituting beta into Formula 21C–2, we show:

$$K_i = R_F + b_i(K_M - R_F) \tag{21C–4}$$

22

Measuring Risks and Returns of Portfolio Managers

In the bull market days of the mid-1980s, many portfolio managers turned in performances that were superior to the market averages. These high returns were often achieved by taking larger than normal risks through investing in small growth companies or concentrating in a limited number of high-return industries. These portfolio managers or their representatives proclaimed their superior ability in managing money and often extrapolated past returns into the future to indicate the potential returns to the investor. A typical statement might be: "The Rapid Growth Fund has earned 20 percent per year over the past 10 years. The investor who places funds with us has the possible opportunity to see the funds grow from a $100 investment today to $619.20 in 10 years at this historical growth rate of 20 percent." There was very little attempt to relate rate of return directly to risk exposure or to provide warnings about the likelihood of repeating past performance.

Thus, the bull market of the 1980s, like other bull markets, lulled investors into looking for the highest stock returns while paying little heed to the relative risk of individual stock portfolios. The crash of 1987 drove home risk-adjusted returns once more. If an investor had been invested in bonds rather than stock on October 19, 1987, he or she would have seen the value of bonds rise as the Federal Reserve pushed interest rates down by pumping liquidity into the market. Money market securities would have been another safe haven, but investors in common stock lost out during the crash on a worldwide basis.

In this chapter, we will examine actual studies of risk-return performance for professional money managers. We will evaluate the setting of objectives, the achievement of efficient diversification, and the measurement of return related to risk. In some of this discussion, we will relate back to the capital asset pricing model developed in Chapter 21.

Because mutual funds are professionally managed and publicly traded, a large amount of information is available to judge performance and evaluate risk-return objectives. For this reason, much of the research presented in this chapter relies on mutual fund data. However, there are many other important participants among professional money managers. These include pension funds, life insurance companies, property and casualty companies, bank trust departments, and endowment funds and foundations. These institutional investors are examined later in this chapter.

STATED OBJECTIVES AND RISK

A first question to be posed to a professional money manager is: Have you followed the basic objectives that were established? These objectives might call for maximum capital gains, a combination of growth plus income, or simply income (with many variations in between). The objectives should be set with an eye toward the capabilities of the money managers and the financial needs of the investors. The best way to measure adherence to these objectives is to evaluate the risk exposure the fund manager has accepted. Anyone who aspires to maximize capital gains must, by nature, absorb more risk. An income-oriented fund should have a minimum risk exposure.

A classic study by John McDonald published in the *Journal of Financial and Quantitative Analysis* indicates that mutual fund managers generally follow the objectives they initially set. As indicated in Figure 22–1, he measured the betas and standard deviations for 123 mutual funds and compared these with the funds' stated objectives. In panel (*a*), we see the fund's beta dimension along the horizontal axis and the fund's stated

FIGURE 22–1 Risk and Fund Objectives for 123 Mutual Funds, 1960–1969

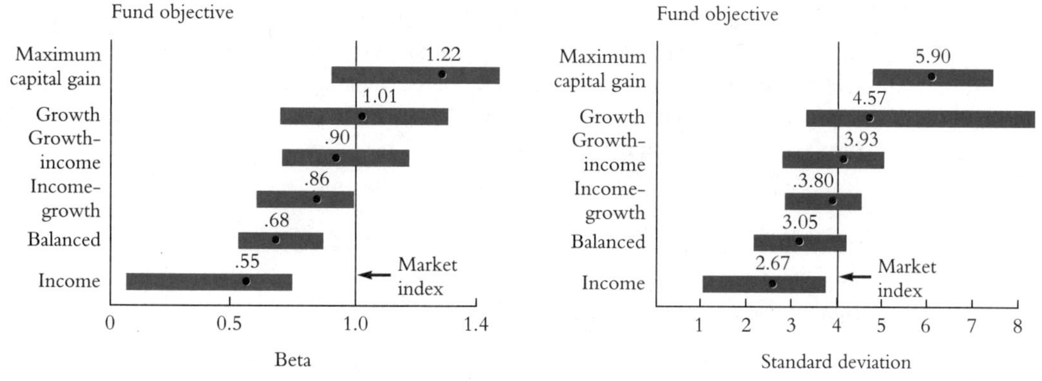

(a) Objective and systematic risk (beta)

(b) Objective and total variability

• Mean

Source: John G. McDonald, "Objectives and Performance of Mutual Funds, 1960–1969," *Journal of Financial and Quantitative Analysis*, June 1974, p. 316.

objective along the vertical axis. Inside the panel, we see the association between the two. For example, funds with an objective of maximum capital gains had an average beta of 1.22, those with a growth objective had an average beta of 1.01, and so on all the way down to an average beta of 0.55 for income-oriented funds. In panel (*b*) of Figure 22–1, a similar approach was used to compare the fund's objective with the portfolio standard deviation.

In both cases of using betas and portfolio standard deviations, we see that the risk absorption was carefully tailored to the fund's stated objectives. Funds with aggressive capital gains and growth objectives had high betas and portfolio standard deviations, while the opposite was true of balanced and income-oriented funds.

Adherence to objectives as measured by risk exposure is important in evaluating a fund manager because risk is one of the variables a money manager can directly control. While short-run return performance can be greatly influenced by unpredictable changes in the economy, the fund manager has almost total control in setting the risk level. He can be held accountable for doing what was specified or promised in regard to risk. Most lawsuits brought against money managers are not for inferior profit performance but for failure to adhere to stated risk objectives. Though it may be appropriate to shift the risk level in anticipation of changing market conditions (lower the beta at a perceived peak in the market), long-run adherence to risk objectives is advisable.

MEASUREMENT OF RETURN IN RELATION TO RISK

In examining the performance of fund managers, the return measure commonly used is excess returns. Though the term **excess returns** has many definitions, the one most commonly used is total return on a portfolio (capital appreciation plus dividends) minus the risk-free rate:

$$\text{Excess returns} = \text{Total portfolio return} - \text{Risk-free rate}$$

Thus, excess returns represent returns over and above what could be earned on a riskless asset. The rate on U.S. government Treasury bills is often used to represent the risk-free rate of return in the financial markets (though other definitions are possible). Thus, a fund that earns 12 percent when the Treasury bill rate is 6 percent has excess returns of 6 percent.

Once computed, excess returns are then compared with risk. We look at three different approaches to comparing excess returns to risk: the **Sharpe approach,** the **Treynor approach,** and the **Jensen approach.**

Sharpe Approach

In the Sharpe approach,[1] the excess returns on a portfolio are compared with the portfolio standard deviation:

$$\text{Sharpe measure} = \frac{\text{Total portfolio return} - \text{Risk-free rate}}{\text{Portfolio standard deviation}} \tag{22–1}$$

The portfolio manager is thus able to view excess returns per unit of risk. If a portfolio has a return of 10 percent, the risk-free rate is 6 percent, and the portfolio standard deviation is 18 percent, the Sharpe measure is 0.22:

$$\text{Sharpe measure} = \frac{10\% - 6\%}{18\%} = \frac{4\%}{18\%} = 0.22$$

This measure can be compared with other portfolios or with the market in general to assess performance. If the market return per unit of risk is greater than 0.22, then the portfolio manager has turned in an inferior performance. Assume there is a 9 percent total market return, a 6 percent risk-free rate, and a market standard deviation of 12 percent. Then the Sharpe measure for the overall market is:

$$\frac{9\% - 6\%}{12\%} = \frac{3\%}{12\%} = 0.25$$

The portfolio measure of 0.22 is less than the market measure of 0.25 and represents an inferior performance. Of course, a portfolio measure above 0.25 would have represented a superior performance.

Treynor Approach

The formula for the second approach for comparing excess returns with risk (developed by Treynor[2]) is:

$$\text{Treynor measure} = \frac{\text{Total portfolio return} - \text{Risk-free rate}}{\text{Portfolio beta}} \tag{22–2}$$

---

[1] William F. Sharpe, "Mutual Fund Performance," *Journal of Business,* January 1966, pp. 119–38.

[2] Jack L. Treynor, "How to Rate Management of Investment Funds," *Harvard Business Review,* January–February 1965, pp. 63–74.

The only difference between the Sharpe and Treynor approaches is in the denominator. While Sharpe uses the portfolio standard deviation—Formula 22–1, Treynor uses the portfolio beta—Formula 22–2. Thus, one can say that Sharpe uses total risk, while Treynor uses only the systematic risk, or beta. Implicit in the Treynor approach is the assumption that portfolio managers have diversified away unsystematic risk, and only systematic risk remains.

If a portfolio has a total return of 10 percent, the risk-free rate is 6 percent, and the portfolio beta is 0.9, the Treynor measure would be:

$$\frac{10\% - 6\%}{0.9} = \frac{4\%}{0.9} = \frac{0.04}{0.9} = 0.044$$

This measure can be compared with other portfolios or with the market in general to determine whether there is a superior performance in terms of return per unit of risk. Assume the total market return is 9 percent, the risk-free rate is 6 percent, and the market beta (by definition) is 1; then the Treynor measure as applied to the market is 0.03:

$$\frac{9\% - 6\%}{1.0} = \frac{3\%}{1.0} = \frac{0.03}{1.0} = 0.030$$

This would imply the portfolio has turned in a superior return to the market (0.044 versus 0.030). Not only is the portfolio return higher than the market return (10 percent versus 9 percent), but the beta is less (0.9 versus 1.0). Clearly, there is more return per unit of risk.

Jensen Approach

In the third approach, Jensen emphasizes using certain aspects of the capital asset pricing model to evaluate portfolio managers.[3] He compares their actual excess returns (total portfolio return − risk-free rate) with what should be required in the market, based on their portfolio beta.

The required rate of excess returns in the market for a given beta is shown in Figure 22–2 on page 632 as the **market line.** If the beta is 0, the investor should expect to earn no more than the risk-free rate of return since there is no systematic risk. If the portfolio manager earns only the risk-free rate of return, the excess returns will be 0. Thus, with a beta of 0, the expected excess returns on the market line are 0. With a portfolio beta of 1, the portfolio has a systematic risk equal to market, and the expected portfolio excess returns should be equal to market excess returns. If the market return (K_M) is 9 percent and the risk-free rate (R_F) is 6 percent, the market excess returns are 3 percent. A portfolio with a beta of 1 should expect to earn the market rate of excess returns ($K_M - R_F$), equal to 3 percent. Other excess returns expectations are shown for betas ranging from 0 to 1.5. For example, a portfolio with a beta of 1.5 should provide excess returns of 4.5.

---

[3] Michael C. Jensen, "The Performance of Mutual Funds in the Period 1945–1964," *Journal of Finance,* May 1968, pp. 389–416.

FIGURE 22–2 Risk-Adjusted Portfolio Returns

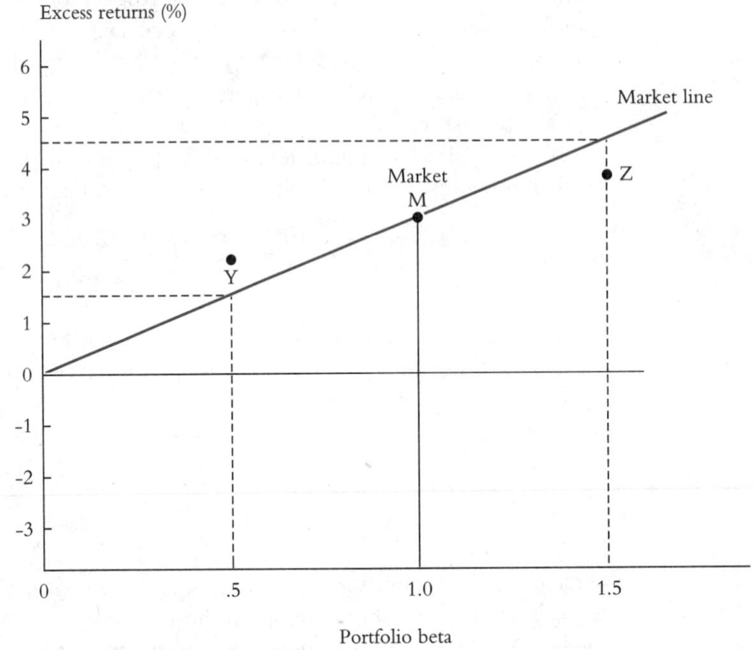

Adequacy of Performance

Using the Jensen approach, the adequacy of a portfolio manager's performance can be judged against the market line. Did he fall above or below the line? While it would appear that portfolio manager Y in Figure 22–2 had inferior returns in comparison with portfolio manager Z (approximately 2.1 percent versus 3.9 percent), this notion is quickly dispelled when one considers risk. Actually, portfolio manager Y performed above risk-return expectations as indicated by the market line, while portfolio manager Z was below his risk-adjusted expected level. The vertical difference from a fund's performance point to the market line can be viewed as a measure of performance. This value, termed **alpha** or **average differential return,** indicates the difference between the return on the fund and a point on the market line that corresponds to a beta equal to the fund. In the case of fund Z, the beta of 1.5 indicated an excess return of 4.5 percent along the market line, and the actual excess return was only 3.9 percent. We thus have a negative alpha of 0.6 percent (3.9% – 4.5%). Clearly, a positive alpha indicates a superior performance, while a negative alpha leads to the opposite conclusion.

Key questions for portfolio managers in general include the following: Can they consistently perform at positive alpha levels? Can they generate returns better than those available along the market line, which are theoretically available to anyone? The results of the classic study conducted by John McDonald on 123 mutual funds are presented in Figure 22–3.

The upward-sloping line is the market line, or anticipated level of performance based on risk. The small dots represent performance of the funds. About as many funds underperformed (negative alpha below the line) as overperformed (positive alpha above the line). Although a few high-beta funds had an unusually strong performance on a risk-adjusted basis, there is no consistent pattern of superior performance.

FIGURE 22–3 Empirical Study of Risk-Adjusted Portfolio Returns—Systematic Risk and Return

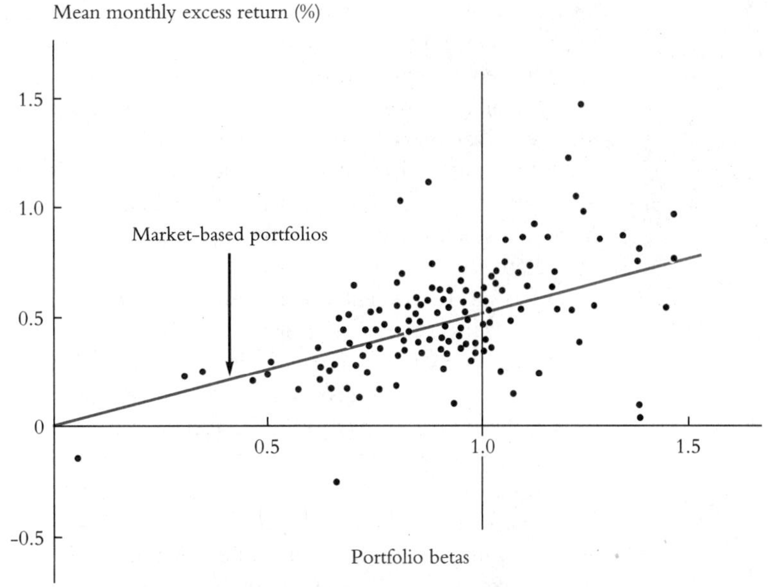

Source: John G. McDonald, "Objectives and Performance of Mutual Funds, 1960–1969," *Journal of Financial and Quantitative Analysis,* June 1974, p. 321.

Around this same time period (the 1960s), the studies by Sharpe and Jensen[4] actually showed that mutual funds underperformed common stock indexes. Since then, there has been a raging debate about the adequacy of performance of mutual funds. In an excellent 1993 article in the *Financial Analysts Journal,* Richard Ippolito analyzed 21 major studies relating to mutual fund performance over the last four decades.[5] In examining the Ippolito material, one is left with the impression that mutual fund managers are not inferior performers; however, one would be hard pressed to say that investing in mutual funds will provide returns that are higher than those reported in the popular common stock market indexes such as the Standard & Poor's 500 Index or New York Stock Exchange Index (after adjustment for the fund's risk).

What the Ippolito article suggests is that mutual funds are efficient gatherers of information and that, on average, they use the information well in their investment activities. However, there are costs associated with acquiring this information, and wise use of the information covers the cost of its acquisition. Thus, we are left with the conclusion that after all factors are considered and after four decades of debate, mutual funds are neither superior nor inferior to the overall market in terms of risk-adjusted returns. Studies of other types of money managers besides mutual funds, such as pension funds and endowment funds, have reached similar conclusions.[6]

---

[4] Sharpe, "Mutual Fund Performance"; Jensen, "The Performance of Mutual Funds in the Period 1945–1964."

[5] Richard A. Ippolito, "On Studies of Mutual Fund Performance, 1962–1991," *Financial Analysts Journal,* January–February 1993, pp. 42–50.

[6] Stephen A. Berkowitz, Louis D. Finney, and Dennis E. Logue, *The Investment Performance of Corporate Pension Plans,* New York: Quorum Books, 1988.

DIVERSIFICATION

An important service a money manager can provide is effective diversification of asset holdings. Once we at least partially accept the fact that superior performance on a risk-adjusted basis is a difficult achievement, we begin to look hard at other attributes money managers may possess. For example, we can ask: Are mutual fund managers effective diversifiers of their holdings?

As previously discussed in Chapter 21 and in this chapter, there are two measures of risk: systematic and unsystematic. Systematic risk is measured by the portfolio's (or individual stock's) beta. Under the capital asset pricing model, higher betas are rewarded with relatively high returns, and vice versa. As the market goes up 10 percent, our portfolio might go up 12 percent (beta of 1.2), and a similar phenomenon may occur on the downside. Unsystematic risk is random or nonmarket related and may be generally diversified away by the astute portfolio manager. Under the capital asset pricing model, there is no market reward for unsystematic risk since it can be eliminated through diversification.

The question for a portfolio manager then becomes: How effective have you been in diversifying away the nonrewarded, unsystematic risk? Put another way, to what extent can a fund's movements be described as market related rather than random in nature? If we plot a fund's excess returns over an extended period against market excess returns, we can determine the joint movement between the two as indicated in Figure 22–4. In panel (*a*) we plot the fund's basic points. In panel (*b*) we draw a regression line through these points. Of importance to the present discussion is the extent to which our line fits the data. If the points of observation fall very close to the line, the independent variable (excess market returns) is largely responsible for describing the dependent variable (excess returns for fund X).

The degree of association between the independent and dependent variables is measured by **R^2 (coefficient of determination).**[7] R^2 may take on a value anywhere between 0 and 1. A high degree of correlation between the independent and dependent variables will produce an R^2 of 0.7 or better. In panel (*b*) of Figure 22–4 it is assumed to be 0.90.

In Figure 22–5, the points do not fall consistently close to the regression line, and the R^2 value is assumed to be only 0.55. In this instance, we say the independent variable (excess market returns) was not the only major variable in explaining changes in the dependent variable (excess returns for fund Y).

The points in Figure 22–5 imply that the portfolio manager for fund Y may not have been particularly effective in his diversification efforts. Many other factors besides market returns appear to be affecting the portfolio returns of fund Y, and these could have been diversified away rather than allowed to influence returns. In this instance, we say there is a high degree of unsystematic, or nonmarket-related, risk. Since unsystematic risk is presumed to go unrewarded in the marketplace under the capital asset pricing model, there is evidence of inefficient portfolio diversification.

---

[7] R^2 also represents the correlation coefficient squared. Thus, we can square Formula 21A–1 in Chapter 21. Another statement is:

$$R^2 = 1 - \frac{\Sigma(y - y_c)^2/n}{\Sigma(y - \bar{y})^2/n}$$

where y_c represents points along the regression line, and y is the average value of the independent variable.

FIGURE 22–4 Relationship of Fund's Excess Returns to Market Excess Returns

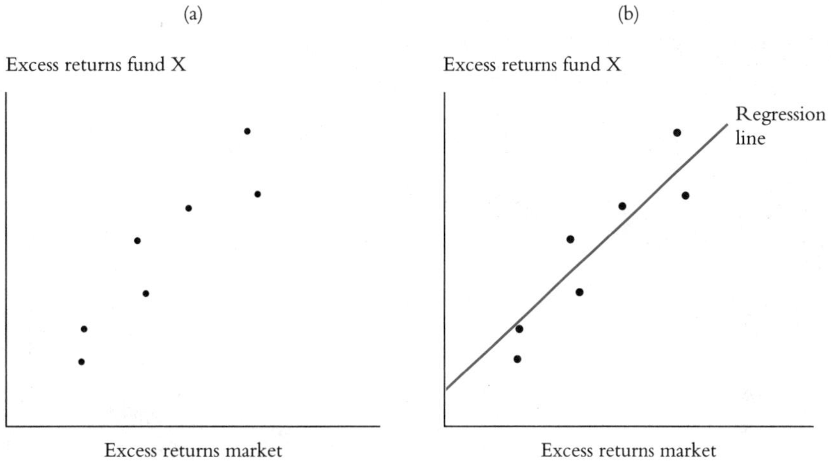

FIGURE 22–5 Example of Lower Correlation

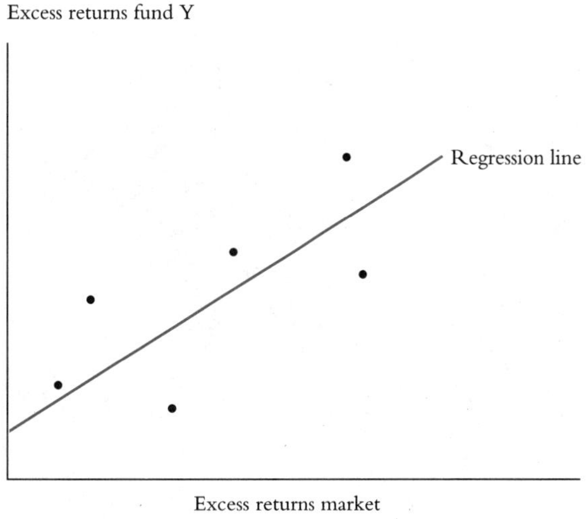

What does empirical data tell us about the effectiveness of portfolio managers in achieving diversification? How have they stacked up in terms of R^2 values for their portfolios? As indicated in Figure 22–6 on page 636, their record is generally good.

The Merrill Lynch study of 100 mutual funds in Figure 22–6 shows an average R^2 value of approximately 0.90 with very few funds falling below 0.70. The actual range is between 0.66 and 0.98. Studies by McDonald, Jensen, Gentry, and Williamson have led to similar conclusions (see Selected References for complete citations).

Although many mutual funds invest in 80 to 100 securities to achieve effective diversification, this is often more than is necessary. A high degree of diversification can be achieved with between 10 and 20 efficiently selected stocks, as is indicated in Table 22–1 on page 636.

FIGURE 22–6 Quarterly Returns Attributable to Market Fluctuations: 100 Mutual Funds, 1970–1974

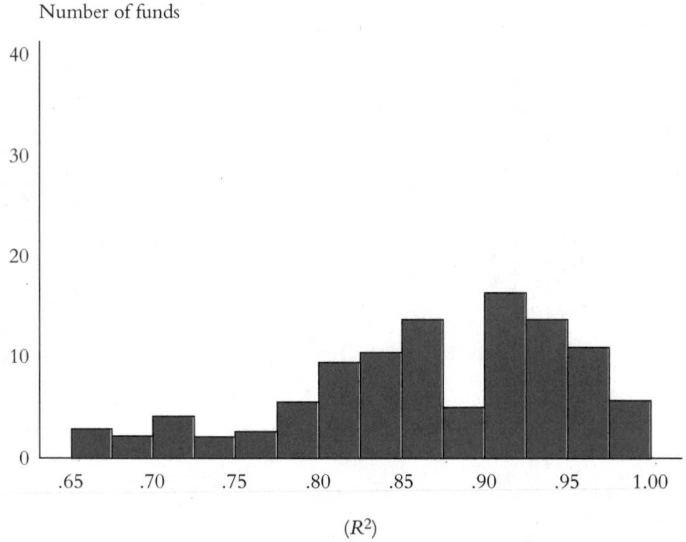

Source: Merrill Lynch, Pierce, Fenner & Smith. *Investment Performance Analysis, Comparative Survey,* 1974.

TABLE 22–1 Reduction in Portfolio Risk through Diversification

Number of Securities in Portfolio	Standard Deviation of Portfolio Returns, σ_p (Percent per Month)	Correlation with Return on Market Index*
1	7.0	0.54
2	5.0	0,63
3	4.8	0.75
4	4.6	0.77
5	4.6	0.79
10	4.2	0.85
15	4.0	0.88
20	3.9	0.89

* The market here refers to an unweighted index of all NYSE stocks.
Source: W. H. Wagner and C. S. Lau, "The Effect of Diversification on Risk," *Financial Analysts Journal,* November–December 1971, p. 53.

The Wagner and Lau study shows the number of securities in the portfolio, the portfolio standard deviation, and correlation with return on the market index (R^2).

OTHER ASSETS AS WELL AS STOCKS

This chapter has dealt primarily with the ability to measure risk and return as it relates to portfolios of common stock. Most professionally managed funds have portfolios that are also diversified across asset classes. Brinson, Hood, and Beebower (BHB) examined 91

large corporate pension plans from 1974 to 1983 and found that the average plan included investments in stocks, bonds, T-bills, and real estate.[8] The combined asset mix makes performance evaluation more complex than the Sharpe, Treynor, and Jensen measures discussed earlier in the chapter, which can be applied only to the stock portion of the portfolio.

BHB suggest that performance of portfolios diversified across asset classes be compared with a portfolio that consists of the pension plan's normal percentage distribution between asset classes. BHB use the Standard & Poor's 500 Index, the Shearson Lehman Government/Corporate Bond Index, and 30-day Treasury bills as the measurement indicator for each of these asset classes. For an investment manager to generate superior performance, he or she would have to outperform a passively managed portfolio maintaining the plan's mix of asset classes.

Ignoring real estate and focusing on stocks, bonds, and T-bills, BHB found that, in general, the actual mean average total return on managed portfolios over the period was 9.01 percent versus 10.11 percent for the benchmark portfolio. In other words, active management cost the pension plans 1.10 percent per year. Of course, over other time periods the managed portfolios could reflect superior results. Stressed throughout the BHB analysis is also the fact that determining the appropriate asset allocation mix (stocks versus bonds versus T-bills) is much more important than simply picking winning or losing stocks.

Asset managers lose their jobs not so much because they picked stock A over stock B, but because they had a poorly allocated portfolio under a given market condition. For example, Table 22–2 shows a typical portfolio composition for large pension fund managers. Equities of all types make up 55 percent of the portfolio. If in a bull market, one is only 40 percent invested in equities, he or she could be in real trouble even if individual stock selection was great.

TABLE 22–2 Typical Weighted Portfolio for Money Managers

Asset Class	Weight	
Equities		
Domestic large capitalization	30%	55%
Domestic small capitalization	15	
International	10	
Venture capital	5	
Fixed income:		
Domestic bonds	15	
International dollar bonds	4	
Nondollar bonds	6	
Real estate	15	
Cash equivalents	0	
	100%	

Source: Gary Brinson, Jeffrey J. Diermeier, and Gary C. Schlarbaum, "A Composite Portfolio Benchmark for Pension Plans," *Financial Analysts Journal,* March–April 1986, p. 15.

[8] Gary P. Brinson, Randolph Hood, and Gilbert L. Beebower, "Determinants of Portfolio Performance," *Financial Analysts Journal,* July–August 1986, pp. 39–44.

A SPECIFIC EXAMPLE—ASSET ALLOCATION

Suppose a portfolio manager is charged with the responsibility of overseeing the performance of a $100 million portfolio. At the end of each quarter, she must report her performance to the plan sponsor, which we shall assume is a pension fund committee for a large corporation.

After intensive analysis of the economy using many of the approaches presented in Chapter 5, she decides to allocate her funds in the manner shown in column 1 of Table 22–3. The second column represents her returns from each category during the course of the year. The third column shows the percentage invested (column 1) times the return (column 2) and, in effect, represents her weighted return for each category and her total return for the year.

On the right side of the table, we see a representative benchmark portfolio that is the standard for measuring her performance. In column 4, we see the asset allocation; in column 5, the return for each category; and in column 6, the weighted returns for the benchmark portfolio.

For ease of presentation, we shall assume the risk associated with her portfolio is the same as that for the benchmark portfolio. Later we will consider the implications of different risk exposure.

In observing Table 22–3, note the overall results in column 3 for the portfolio manager and those in column 6 for the benchmark portfolio. She outperformed the benchmark portfolio by 1.09 percent; that is, her total return was 11.84 percent, while the benchmark portfolio had a 10.75 percent return.

The question is, How was this superior result achieved? In this particular case, she held a larger equity position (70 percent) than the benchmark portfolio (55 percent),

TABLE 22–3 Comparison of Managed and Benchmark Portfolios

	Managed Portfolio			Benchmark Portfolio		
	(1) Asset Allocation	(2) Returns	(3) Weighted Returns	(4) Asset Allocation	(5) Returns	(6) Weighted Returns
Asset Class						
Equities:						
Domestic large capitalization	30%	9%	2.70%	30%	10%	3.00%
Domestic small capitalization	20	15	3.00	15	13	1.95
International	20	18	3.60	10	14	1.40
Total equities	70%		9.30%	55%		6.35%
Fixed income:						
Domestic bonds	11%	8%	0.88%	15%	9%	1.35%
Foreign bonds	8	10	0.80	10	12	1.20
Total fixed income	19%		1.68%	25%		2.55%
Real estate	7%	10%	0.70%	15%	11%	1.65%
Cash equivalents	4%	4%	0.16	5%	4%	0.20
Total portfolio	100%		11.84%	100%		10.75%

which turned out to be fortunate because the stock market was moving up throughout the year (all categories of equities had strong positive returns).

We can further break down the performance of equities based on the three major categories of stock. Actually, for domestic, large capitalization stocks (perhaps those with $5 billion or more in market value), she slightly underperformed the market (9 percent versus 10 percent). An appropriate market measure for the benchmark portfolio of large capitalization stocks would be the Standard & Poor's 500 Index.[9] Notice that her performance on small capitalization stocks was 2 percent higher than the market portfolio (15 percent versus 13 percent). An appropriate market measure for the benchmark portfolio of small capitalization stocks would be the NASDAQ Composite Index.

Finally, she achieved a high rate of return on international equities, exceeding the benchmark return by a full 4 percent (18 percent versus 14 percent). The appropriate benchmark portfolio measure might be the Dow Jones World Stock Index. We might even decide to break down our international equity investments and the benchmark comparisons by different areas of the world such as Mexico, Europe, Asia/Pacific, and so on. Further comparisons can be made among investments in established markets and emerging markets. The effect that the changing value of the dollar had on returns could also be considered.

In moving to fixed-income securities, our portfolio manager underperformed the benchmark portfolio, both domestically (8 percent versus 9 percent) and internationally (10 percent versus 12 percent). The same slight underperformance can be found in real estate (10 percent versus 11 percent). However, with only 19 percent of assets allocated to fixed income and 7 percent to real estate in the managed portfolio, this underperformance is not a problem.

In summary, our portfolio manager had a strong performance because of an equity position (70 percent) that was much higher than the benchmark portfolio (55 percent); that is, she benefited from superior asset allocation. She also gained from superior stock selection in the small capitalization and international equity areas; these factors more than overcame the slightly inferior performance in other categories.

Earlier in the chapter, we talked about risk considerations in measuring performance. Although we will not make a formal evaluation of risk in this case, certain factors are worthy of note. To the extent that the managed portfolio is riskier than the benchmark portfolio, the superior return would have to be partially discounted. Of course, if it is less risky than the market, the superior performance becomes even more meaningful.

While the higher equity component in the managed portfolio might imply greater risk, the large degree of international diversification could easily compensate for this factor. International securities may offset shocks in the U.S. market, and vice versa. Also, the managed portfolio appears to be more liquid than the benchmark portfolio, with real estate representing 7 percent of the holdings versus 15 percent for the benchmark portfolio. This is true in spite of a slightly lower cash position in the managed portfolio.

One last factor is worthy of note in discussing the performance of the portfolio manager. The results presented in Table 22–3 represent annual data. As mentioned earlier, the portfolio manager will not only need to present annual information for evaluation but normally meets quarterly with the investor as well. Because there is always

---

[9] We could also add another category of MidCap stocks, but we have omitted it to shorten the presentation.

strong pressure for performance, short-term swings in the market can test a portfolio manager's convictions. For example, when the stock market is going down, a portfolio manager with a large equity position (perhaps 70 percent or greater) may be under pressure to lighten up on stocks because of negative returns. However, down markets are normally the best time to buy, not to sell. This principle may be severely tested when a portfolio manager has to report a quarterly loss but, at the same time, suggests that unusually good buying opportunities now exist. While the stock market generally provides superior returns in comparison with other investments over the long term, such may not be the case over a short period of time. Well-informed portfolio managers, and those for whom they work, generally use a three- to five-year time horizon to determine whether performance is acceptable. However, in the world of money management, one or two bad quarters can sometimes mean the loss of an account.

THE MAKEUP OF INSTITUTIONAL INVESTORS

Having discussed measurement and portfolio management techniques for institutional investors, we will now take a more specific look at the participants. **Institutional investors** (as opposed to individual investors) represent organizations that are responsible for bringing together large pools of capital for reinvestment. Our coverage will center on investment companies (including mutual funds), pension funds, life insurance companies, bank trust departments, and endowments and foundations.

Investment Companies (Including Mutual Funds)

Investment companies take the proceeds of individual investors and reinvest them in other securities according to their specific objectives. Income and capital gains are generally distributed to stockholders and are subject to single taxation under Subchapter M of the Internal Revenue Code. Investment companies were discussed at some length in Chapter 19.

Other Institutional Investors

Other institutional investors (along with investment companies) and their extent of market participation are presented in Table 22–4. Total institutional holdings are over $5 trillion. We will briefly comment on pension funds, insurance companies, bank trust departments, and foundations and endowments.

Pension Funds Pension funds represent an important and growing sector of the institutional market and may be private or public. Private funds represent well over half of the pension fund market. The benefits that accrue under private pension funds may be insured or uninsured, with the latter arrangement occurring most frequently. Public pension funds are run for the benefit of federal, state, or local employees.

Insurance Companies Insurance companies may be categorized as either "life" or "property and casualty." Life insurance companies must earn a minimum rate of return

TABLE 22–4 Percentage of Institutional Market Held by Institutional Investors

	Percent
1. Private noninsured pension funds	26.2%
2. Open-end investment companies	15.5
3. Other investment companies	2.0
4. Life insurance companies	6.1
5. Property-liability insurance companies	4.9
6. Personal trust funds	27.8
7. Common trust funds	1.7
8. Mutual savings banks	1.1
9. State and local retirement funds	4.6
10. Foundations	7.4
11. Educational endowments	2.7
	100.0%

Source: Compiled from a review of annual reports from the Securities and Exchange Commission and the New York Stock Exchange.

assumed in calculating insurance premiums, and public policy emphasizes safety of assets. Part of life insurance company assets are in privately placed debt or mortgages, with the balance in bonds and stocks. Property and casualty insurance companies enjoy more lenient regulation of their activities and generally have a larger percentage of their assets in bonds and stocks.

Bank Trust Departments The emphasis in bank trust departments is on managing other people's funds for a fee. Banks may administer individual trusts or commingled (combined) funds in a common trust fund. Often a bank will establish more than one common trust fund to serve varying needs and objectives. The overall performance of bank trust departments has been mixed, with the usual number of leaders and laggards. Bank trust management is highly concentrated with a relatively small number of trust departments holding the majority of funds. Out of approximately 4,000 bank trust departments, the top 10 hold one-third of all assets, and the largest 60 hold two-thirds.

Foundations and Endowments Foundations represent nonprofit organizations set up to accomplish social, educational, or charitable purposes. They are often established through the donation of a large block of stock in which the donor was one of the corporate founders. Examples include the Ford, Carnegie, and Rockefeller foundations. Endowments, on the other hand, represent permanent capital funds that are donated to universities, churches, or civic organizations. The management of endowment funds is often quite difficult because of the pressure for current income to maintain operations (perhaps the university library) while at the same time there is a demand for capital appreciation. Measurement of performance for foundations and endowments is moving more to a total-return basis (annual income plus capital appreciation) rather than the traditional interest-earned or dividend-received basis.

Should Pension Funds Make Politically and Socially Desirable Investment Decisions?

Pension funds are responsible for managing the retirement funds for corporations, government entities, labor unions, universities, etc. They are charged by law to make financially correct (or at least prudent) decisions. The question is, Should they be making politically correct decisions also? The latter would imply investments in inner cities, minority-owned businesses, bridges and highways, and even in companies that do a good job of training workers for the future.*

Many pension funds worry that politically correct decisions may get them in trouble with the rules of the Employee Retirement Income Security Act (ERISA), which demands "prudent" investment of pension fund assets. To the extent that they do not attempt to maintain a high return consistent with controlling risk, they could be subject to government enforcement actions as well as lawsuits by people expecting to receive retirement funds.

But others would argue that financially correct and politically correct decisions can go hand in hand. For example, TIAA-CREF, the nation's largest pension fund with assets of well over $1 billion, sets aside a portion of its funds to invest in affordable housing for low- and middle-income city residents.

Some pension funds target their socially oriented investments through Multi-Employer Property Trust (MEPT), a real estate investment trust that places investments in the areas in which participating pension funds are located. More than 90 pension funds entrust part of their assets to MEPT. There is one added stipulation—any new project must be union built. Frank Russell Investment Management Company, a firm that measures investment performance, states that MEPT has earned more than a competitive return.

Of course, not all socially targeted investments turn out as well. Sometimes, state or local pension funds make the mistake of placing retirement funds in local businesses experiencing difficulty in hopes of keeping them open to spur the local economy and maintain jobs. Such was the case with the Kansas Public Retirement System, which invested $7.8 million in a Wichita steel mill only to see it close down two years later. This would appear to represent an example where prudent investment and social goals did not go hand in hand.

*Christian Del Valle, "The Politically Correct Pension Fund," *Business Week,* March 21, 1994, p. 108.

SUMMARY

The ability of portfolio managers to meet various goals and objectives is considered in this chapter. Many portfolio managers appear to demonstrate superior performances during market boom years. However, when this performance is adjusted for risk, any perceived superiority may quickly vanish.

Some concepts related to the capital asset pricing model may be used to evaluate the performance of money managers. Portfolio beta values are shown along the horizontal axis, while the market line indicates expected returns. Portfolio managers that are able to operate above the line (positive alphas) are thought to be superior managers, while the opposite would be true of those falling below the line. Research indicates that, on average, portfolio managers do not beat the popular averages or random portfolios on a risk-adjusted basis.

Nevertheless, mutual funds (or other managed portfolios) do have some desirable attributes. As indicated by a Merrill Lynch study (and others as well), mutual funds tend to be very efficient diversifiers. Their average correlation with the market (R^2) tends to be approximately 90 percent, indicating only 10 percent

unsystematic, or nonrewarded, risk. In general, mutual fund managers also do a good job of constructing portfolios that are consistent with their initially stated objectives (that is, maximum capital gains, growth, income, etc.).

In a specific evaluation of a professional money manager, one may wish to judge how assets were allocated between stocks, bonds, real estate, cash equivalents, etc., and whether this was effective over a given time period. Furthermore, the performance within each asset classification can be compared with a benchmark portfolio's return. All of this analysis enables one to determine the overall adequacy of performance and how it was produced.

The market of institutional investors is made up of investment companies (closed-end and mutual funds), pension funds, insurance companies, foundations, endowments, and other participants. Although the great weight of empirical research has dealt with mutual funds, the same basic conclusions about risk-adjusted returns can be applied to other institutional investors.

KEY WORDS AND CONCEPTS

excess returns, 629
Sharpe approach, 630
Treynor approach, 630
Jensen approach, 630
market line, 631
alpha (average differential return), 632
R^2 (coefficient of determination), 634
institutional investors, 640

DISCUSSION QUESTIONS

1. What is a risk-adjusted return?
2. In evaluating a mutual fund manager, what would be the first point to analyze?
3. How can adherence to portfolio objectives be measured?
4. How can risk exposure be measured?
5. How are excess returns defined?
6. What is the Sharpe approach to measuring portfolio risk? If a portfolio has a higher Sharpe measure than the market in general under the Sharpe approach, what is the implication?
7. How does the Treynor approach differ from the Sharpe approach? Which of the two measures assumes unsystematic risk will be diversified away?
8. Under the Jensen approach, how is the market line related to the beta?
9. Explain alpha as a measure of performance.
10. What conclusions can be drawn from the empirical studies of portfolio (fund) managers' performances? Are they superior?
11. If investment companies do not offer returns that are, on average, any better than the market in general, why would someone invest in them?
12. What does a high R^2 (correlation) between a fund's excess returns and the market's excess returns indicate

about the fund manager's ability to effectively diversify?

13. According to the Brinson, Hood, and Beebower (BHB) study, are asset allocation decisions (stocks versus bonds, etc.) more or less important than individual stock selection decisions?

14. What is meant by an institutional investor? Give some examples.

PROBLEMS

Sharpe approach to measuring performance

1. A firm that evaluates portfolios uses the Sharpe approach to measuring performance. How would it rank the following three portfolios? (Round to three places to the right of the decimal point.)

	Portfolio Return	Risk-Free Rate	Portfolio Standard Deviation
Grange Money Managers	10.0%	7%	14%
Harmon Group	10.2	7	18
Luckman Investment Company	14.0	7	22

Treynor approach to measuring performance

2. Assume a second firm that evaluates portfolios uses the Treynor approach to measuring performance. The firm is also evaluating the three portfolios in problem 1. The portfolio betas are as follows:

	Portfolio Beta
Grange Money Managers	1.18
Harmon Group	0.90
Luckman Investment Company	1.25

a. Using the Treynor approach, how would the second firm rank the three portfolios? (Round to three places to the right of the decimal point.)
b. Explain why any differences have taken place in the rankings between problem 1 and problem 2*a*.
c. If the Treynor approach is utilized and the market return is 10 percent (with a risk-free rate of 7 percent), which of the portfolios outperformed the market? The market beta is always 1.

Jensen approach to measuring performance

3. Assume the Jensen approach to portfolio valuation is being used.
a. Draw a market line similar to that in Figure 22–2. That is, show 0 excess returns at a 0 portfolio beta and 3 percent excess returns at a portfolio beta of 1.
b. Now graph the three portfolios. Which portfolio(s) over- or underperformed the market?

Asset allocation and returns

4. A portfolio manager has the following asset allocation and returns on his portfolio. Fill in the values in column 3. Use Table 22–3 as a guideline on how to proceed.

	(1) Portfolio Manager Asset Allocation	(2) Portfolio Manager Returns	(3) Portfolio Manager Weighted Returns
Asset Class			
Equities:			
Domestic large capitalization	25%	10%	
Domestic small capitalization	20	13	
International	5	20	
Total equities	50		
Fixed income:			
Domestic bonds	20%	7%	
Foreign bonds	7	8	
Total fixed income	27		
Real estate	3%	10%	
Cash equivalents	20%	5%	
Total portfolio	100%		

The benchmark portfolio with which he is being compared is shown below:

	(1) Benchmark Portfolio Asset Allocation	(2) Benchmark Portfolio Returns	(3) Benchmark Portfolio Weighted Returns
Asset Class			
Equities:			
Domestic large capitalization	30%	9%	2.70%
Domestic small capitalization	25	12	3.00
International	17	18	3.06
Total equities	72		8.76%
Fixed income:			
Domestic bonds	13%	6%	0.78%
Foreign bonds	6	7	0.42
Total fixed income	19		1.20%
Real estate	3%	9%	0.27%
Cash equivalents	6%	4%	0.24
Total portfolio	100%		10.47%

a. Explain why the portfolio manager under- or outperformed the benchmark portfolio.

b. If cash equivalents had been reduced by the portfolio manager to 5 percent and had been invested in international equities at his indicated rate of return, would the portfolio manager have under- or outperformed the benchmark portfolio?

THE WALL STREET JOURNAL PROJECT

1. Assume you are responsible for evaluating the market over the last 12 months. Using the asset allocation in column 1, fill in column 2 for market returns over the last 12 months and column 3 for weighted returns (column 1 times column 2). Use *The Wall Street Journal* as your source of information.

	(1) Asset Allocation	(2) Market Return Over the Last 12 Months (% Change)	(3) Weighted Returns
Asset Class			
Equities:			
Domestic large capitalization[a]	25%		
Domestic small capitalization[b]	15		
European stocks[c]	10		
Asia/Pacific stocks[c]	10		
Fixed income:			
U.S. Treasury securities (intermediate)[d]	15%		
U.S. corporate debt issues (high yield)[d]	5		
Mortgage backed securities (GNMA)[d]	8		
Convertible bonds (investment grade)[d]	12		______
Total weighted returns (Note: These returns only include price changes—not dividends or interest.)			______

[a] Use the S&P 500 Index found under the "Market Diary" on the first page of Section C of *The Wall Street Journal.*
[b] Use the NASDAQ Composite Index found under the "Markets Diary" on the first page of Section C of *The Wall Street Journal.*
[c] Use the "Dow Jones World Stock Index" found in Section C of *The Wall Street Journal.* It's shown in the index for Section C as "World Index."
[d] Use the "Bond Market Data Bank" found in Section C of *The Wall Street Journal.*

2. Generally speaking, did equities outperform fixed-income securities over the past 12 months? Comment.
3. Which one of the four classes of equities performed best? Which performed worst?
4. Which of the four classes of fixed-income securities performed best? Which performed worst?
5. With 20-20 hindsight, describe some of the changes you would have made in your asset allocation 12 months ago given what you now know.

U.S. EQUITIES ONFLOPPY EXERCISES

Please use your U.S. Equities OnFloppy software and manual to complete the following exercises.

1. a. Growth stocks are often thought to have more risk than income stocks. Select rapidly growing stocks by finding all the companies that have a compound annual rate of growth of earnings greater than 100 percent over the past five

years; that is, EA%C15 > 100. Also require earnings to be positive in each of the past three years; that is EA1, EA2, and EA3 > 0.

b. Prepare a report that shows EA%C15, the current dividend yield, DYL, and beta for each growth company selected above in part *a.*

c. Select income companies by finding all the companies that have a dividend yield greater than 7 percent; that is, DYL > 7. Again, also require earnings to be positive in each of the past three years.

d. Prepare a report as described in part *b* for each of the income companies.

e. Analyze the reports, and comment on your observations. In particular, compare the average beta for the growth portfolio with the income portfolio.

2. a. Sort the companies in the U.S. Equities OnFloppy by beta in ascending order. How many of the companies have NM (not meaningful) for their beta? Can you determine why their beta is specified as NM?

b. How many companies have a negative beta? What is the range of the negative betas?

c. Since there are relatively few negative beta companies, would you expect that the demand for these stocks by institutional portfolio managers would be strong or weak?

d. Compare the average level of institutional holdings for stocks with betas > −3.00 and < −1.1 versus those with betas > 1.00 and < 2.99. Comment on your findings.

SELECTED REFERENCES

Measuring Portfolio Performance

Berkowitz, Stephen A.; Louis D. Finney; and Dennis E. Logue. *The Investment Performance of Corporate Pension Plans.* New York: Quorum Books, 1988.

Brinson, Gary P.; Randolph Hood; and Gilbert L. Beebower. "Determinants of Portfolio Performance." *Financial Analysts Journal,* July–August 1986, pp. 39–44.

Coggin, T. Daniel; Frank J. Fabozzi; and Shafiqur Rahman. "The Investment Performance of U.S. Equity Pension Fund Managers: An Empirical Investigation." *Journal of Finance,* July 1993, pp. 1039–55.

French, Dan W., and Glenn V. Henderson, Jr. "How Well Does Performance Evaluation Perform?" *Journal of Portfolio Management,* Winter 1985, pp. 15–18.

Friend, Irwin; Marshall Blume; and Jean Crockett. *Mutual Funds and Other Institutional Investors.* New York: McGraw-Hill, 1970.

Ibbotson, Roger G.; Laurence B. Siegel; and Kathryn S. Love. "World Wealth: Market Values and Returns." *Journal of Portfolio Management,* Fall 1985, pp. 4–23.

Ippolito, Richard A. "On Studies of Mutual Fund Performance, 1962–1991." *Financial Analysts Journal,* January–February 1993, pp. 42–50.

Jensen, Michael C. "The Performance of Mutual Funds in the Period 1945–1964." *Journal of Finance,* May 1968, pp. 389–416.

______. "Risk, Capital Assets, and Evaluation of Portfolios." *Journal of Business,* April 1969, pp. 167–247.

McDonald, John G. "Objectives and Performance of Mutual Funds, 1960–1969." *Journal of Financial and Quantitative Analysis,* June 1974, pp. 311–33.

Sharpe, William F. "Mutual Fund Performance." *Journal of Business,* January 1966, pp. 119–38.

Treynor, Jack L. "How to Rate Management of Investment Funds." *Harvard Business Review,* January–February 1965, pp. 63–74.

Portfolio Strategy

Leibowitz, Martin L.; Stanley Kogelman; Lawrence N. Bader; and Ajay R. Dravid. "Interest Rate-Sensitive Asset Allocation." *Journal of Portfolio Management,* Spring 1994, pp. 8–15.

Lockwood, Larry J., and Scott C. Linn. "An Examination of Stock Market Volatility during Overnight and Intraday Periods, 1964–1989." *Journal of Finance,* June 1990, pp. 591–601.

McEnally, Richard W. "Latane's Bequest: The Best Portfolio Strategies." *Journal of Portfolio Management,* Winter 1986, pp. 21–30.

Wagner, W. H., and S. C. Lau. "The Effect of Diversification on Risk." *Financial Analysts Journal,* November–December 1971, pp. 48–53.

APPENDIXES

APPENDIX A Compound Sum of $1

Period	1%	2%	3%	4%	5%	6%	7%	8%	9%	10%	11%
1	1.010	1.020	1.030	1.040	1.050	1.060	1.070	1.080	1.090	1.100	1.110
2	1.020	1.040	1.061	1.082	1.103	1.124	1.145	1.166	1.188	1.210	1.232
3	1.030	1.061	1.093	1.125	1.158	1.191	1.225	1.260	1.295	1.331	1.368
4	1.041	1.082	1.126	1.170	1.216	1.262	1.311	1.360	1.412	1.464	1.518
5	1.051	1.104	1.159	1.217	1.276	1.338	1.403	1.469	1.539	1.611	1.685
6	1.062	1.126	1.194	1.265	1.340	1.419	1.501	1.587	1.677	1.772	1.870
7	1.072	1.149	1.230	1.316	1.407	1.504	1.606	1.714	1.828	1.949	2.076
8	1.083	1.172	1.267	1.369	1.477	1.594	1.718	1.851	1.993	2.144	2.305
9	1.094	1.195	1.305	1.423	1.551	1.689	1.838	1.999	2.172	2.358	2.558
10	1.105	1.219	1.344	1.480	1.629	1.791	1.967	2.159	2.367	2.594	2.839
11	1.116	1.243	1.384	1.539	1.710	1.898	2.105	2.332	2.580	2.853	3.152
12	1.127	1.268	1.426	1.601	1.796	2.012	2.252	2.518	2.813	3.138	3.498
13	1.138	1.294	1.469	1.665	1.886	2.133	2.410	2.720	3.066	3.452	3.883
14	1.149	1.319	1.513	1.732	1.980	2.261	2.579	2.937	3.342	3.797	4.310
15	1.161	1.346	1.558	1.801	2.079	2.397	2.759	3.172	3.642	4.177	4.785
16	1.173	1.373	1.605	1.873	2.183	2.540	2.952	3.426	3.970	4.595	5.311
17	1.184	1.400	1.653	1.948	2.292	2.693	3.159	3.700	4.328	5.054	5.895
18	1.196	1.428	1.702	2.206	2.407	2.854	3.380	3.996	4.717	5.560	6.544
19	1.208	1.457	1.754	2.107	2.527	3.026	3.617	4.316	5.142	6.116	7.263
20	1.220	1.486	1.806	2.191	2.653	3.207	3.870	4.661	5.604	6.727	8.062
25	1.282	1.641	2.094	2.666	3.386	4.292	5.427	6.848	8.623	10.835	13.585
30	1.348	1.811	2.427	3.243	4.322	5.743	7.612	10.063	13.268	17.449	22.892
40	1.489	2.208	3.262	4.801	7.040	10.286	14.974	21.725	31.409	45.259	65.001
50	1.645	2.692	4.384	7.107	11.467	18.420	29.457	46.902	74.358	117.39	184.57

APPENDIX A Compound Sum of $1 *(concluded)*

	Percent										
Period	12%	13%	14%	15%	16%	17%	18%	19%	20%	25%	30%
1	1.120	1.130	1.140	1.150	1.160	1.170	1.180	1.190	1.200	1.250	1.300
2	1.254	1.277	1.300	1.323	1.346	1.369	1.392	1.416	1.440	1.563	1.690
3	1.405	1.443	1.482	1.521	1.561	1.602	1.643	1.685	1.728	1.953	2.197
4	1.574	1.630	1.689	1.749	1.811	1.874	1.939	2.005	2.074	2.441	2.856
5	1.762	1.842	1.925	2.011	2.100	2.192	2.288	2.386	2.488	3.052	3.713
6	1.974	2.082	2.195	2.313	2.436	2.565	2.700	2.840	2.986	3.815	4.827
7	2.211	2.353	2.502	2.660	2.826	3.001	3.185	3.379	3.583	4.768	6.276
8	2.476	2.658	2.853	3.059	3.278	3.511	3.759	4.021	4.300	5.960	8.157
9	2.773	3.004	3.252	3.518	3.803	4.108	4.435	4.785	5.160	7.451	10.604
10	3.106	3.395	3.707	4.046	4.411	4.807	5.234	5.696	6.192	9.313	13.786
11	3.479	3.836	4.226	4.652	5.117	5.624	6.176	6.777	7.430	11.642	17.922
12	3.896	4.335	4.818	5.350	5.936	6.580	7.288	8.064	8.916	14.552	23.298
13	4.363	4.898	5.492	6.153	6.886	7.699	8.599	9.596	10.699	18.190	30.288
14	4.887	5.535	6.261	7.076	7.988	9.007	10.147	11.420	12.839	22.737	39.374
15	5.474	6.254	7.138	8.137	9.266	10.539	11.974	13.590	15.407	28.422	51.186
16	6.130	7.067	8.137	9.358	10.748	12.330	14.129	16.172	18.488	35.527	66.542
17	6.866	7.986	9.276	10.761	12.468	14.426	16.672	19.244	22.186	44.409	86.504
18	7.690	9.024	10.575	12.375	14.463	16.879	19.673	22.091	26.623	55.511	112.46
19	8.613	10.197	12.056	14.232	16.777	19.748	23.214	27.252	31.948	69.389	146.19
20	9.646	11.523	13.743	16.367	19.461	23.106	27.393	32.429	38.338	86.736	190.05
25	17.000	21.231	26.462	32.919	40.874	50.658	62.669	77.388	95.396	264.70	705.64
30	29.960	39.116	50.950	66.212	85.850	111.07	143.37	184.68	237.38	807.79	2,620.0
40	93.051	132.78	188.88	267.86	378.72	533.87	750.38	1,051.7	1,469.8	7,523.2	36,119.
50	289.00	450.74	700.23	1,083.7	1,670.7	2,566.2	3,927.4	5,988.9	9,100.4	70,065.	497,929.

APPENDIX B Compound Sum of an Annuity of $1 *(concluded)*

Period	12%	13%	14%	15%	16%	17%	18%	19%	20%	25%	30%
						Percent					
1	1.000	1.000	1.000	1.000	1.000	1.000	1.000	1.000	1.000	1.000	1 000
2	2.120	2.130	2.140	2.150	2.160	2.170	2.180	2.190	2.200	2.250	2.300
3	3.374	3.407	3.440	3.473	3.506	3.539	3.572	3.606	3.640	3.813	3.990
4	4.779	4.850	4.921	4.993	5.066	5.141	5.215	5.291	5.368	5.766	6.187
5	6.353	6.480	6.610	6.742	6.877	7.014	7.154	7.297	7.442	8.207	9.043
6	8.115	8.323	8.536	9.754	8.977	9.207	9.442	0.683	9.930	11.259	12.756
7	10.089	10.405	10.730	11.067	11.414	11.772	12.142	12.523	12.916	15.073	17.583
8	12.300	12.757	13.233	13.727	14.240	14.773	15.327	15.902	16.499	19.842	23.858
9	14.776	15.416	16.085	16.786	17.519	18.285	19.086	19.923	20.799	25.802	32.015
10	17.549	18.420	19.337	20.304	21.321	22.393	23.521	24.701	25.959	33.253	42.619
11	20.655	21.814	23.045	24.349	25.733	27.200	28.755	30.404	32.150	42.566	56.405
12	24.133	25.650	27.271	29.002	30.850	32.824	34.931	37.180	39.581	54.208	74.327
13	28.029	29.985	32.089	34.352	36.786	39.404	42.219	45.244	48.497	68.760	97.625
14	32.393	34.883	37.581	40.505	43.672	47.103	50.818	54.841	59.196	86.949	127.91
15	37.280	40.417	43.842	47.580	51.660	56.110	60.965	66.261	72.035	109.69	167.29
16	42.753	46.672	50.980	55.717	60.925	66.649	72.939	79.850	87.442	138.11	218.47
17	48.884	53.739	59.118	65.075	71.673	78.979	87.068	96.022	105.93	173.64	285.01
18	55.750	61.725	68.394	75.836	84.141	93.406	103.74	115.27	128.12	218.05	371.52
19	63.440	70.749	78.969	88.212	98.603	110.29	123.41	138.17	154.74	273.56	483.97
20	72.052	80.947	91.025	102.44	115.38	130.03	146.63	165.42	186.69	342.95	630.17
25	133.33	155.62	181.87	212.79	249.21	292.11	342.60	402.04	471.98	1,054.8	2,348.80
30	241.33	293.20	356.79	434.75	530.31	647.44	790.95	966.7	1,181.9	3,227.2	8,730.0
40	767.09	1,013.7	1,342.0	1,779.1	2,360.8	3,134.5	4,163.21	5,529.8	7,343.9	30,089.	120,393.
50	2,400.0	3,459.5	4,994.5	7,217.7	10,436.	15,090.	21,813.	31,515.	45,497.	280,256.	1,659,731.

APPENDIX B Compound Sum of an Annuity of $1

	Percent										
Period	1%	2%	3%	4%	5%	6%	7%	8%	9%	10%	11%
1	1.000	1.000	1.000	1.000	1.000	1.000	1.000	1.000	1.000	1.000	1 000
2	2.010	2.020	2.030	2.040	2.050	2.060	2.070	2.080	2.090	2.100	2.110
3	3.030	3.060	3.091	3.122	3.153	3.184	3.215	3.246	3.278	3.310	3.342
4	4.060	4.122	4.184	4.246	4.310	4.375	4.440	4.506	4.573	4.641	4.710
5	5.101	5.204	5.309	5.416	5.526	5.637	5.751	5.867	5.985	6.105	6.228
6	6.152	6.308	6.468	6.633	6.802	6.975	7.153	7.336	7.523	7.716	7.913
7	7.214	7.434	7.662	7.898	8.142	8.394	8.654	8.923	9.200	9.487	9.783
8	8.286	8.583	8.892	9.214	9.549	9.897	10.260	10.637	11.028	11.436	11.859
9	9.369	9.755	10.159	10.583	11.027	11.491	11.978	12.488	13.021	13.579	14.164
10	10.462	10.950	11.464	12.006	12.578	13.181	13.816	14.487	15.193	15.937	16.722
11	11.567	12.169	12.808	13.486	14.207	14.972	15.784	16.645	17.560	18.531	19.561
12	12.683	13.412	14.192	15.026	15.917	16.870	17.888	18.977	20.141	21.384	22.713
13	13.809	14.680	15.618	16.627	17.713	18.882	20.141	21.495	22.953	24.523	26.212
14	14.947	15.974	17.086	18.292	19.599	21.015	22.550	24.215	26.019	27.975	30.095
15	16.097	17.293	18.599	20.024	21.579	23.276	25.129	27.152	29.361	31.772	34.405
16	17.258	18.639	20.157	21.825	23.657	25.673	27.888	30.324	33.003	35.950	39.190
17	18.430	20.012	21.762	23.698	25.840	20.213	30.840	33.750	36.974	40.545	44.501
18	19.615	21.412	23.414	25.645	28.132	30.906	33.999	37.450	41.301	45.599	50.396
19	20.811	22.841	25.117	27.671	30.539	33.760	37.379	41.446	46.018	51.159	56.939
20	22.019	24.297	26.870	29.778	33.066	36.786	40.995	45.762	51.160	57.275	64.203
25	28.243	32.030	36.459	41.646	47.727	54.865	63.249	73.106	84.701	98.347	114.41
30	34.785	40.588	47.575	56.085	66.439	79.058	94.461	113.28	136.31	164.49	199.02
40	48.886	60.402	75.401	95.026	120.80	154.76	199.64	259.06	337.89	442.59	581.83
50	64.463	84.579	112.80	152.67	209.35	290.34	406.53	573.77	815.08	1,163.9	1,668.8

APPENDIX C Present Value of $1

Period	1%	2%	3%	4%	5%	6%	7%	8%	9%	10%	11%	12%
						Percent						
1	0.990	0.980	0.971	0.962	0.952	0.943	0.935	0.926	0.917	0.909	0.901	0.893
2	0.980	0.961	0.943	0.925	0.907	0.890	0.873	0.857	0.842	0.826	0.812	0.797
3	0.971	0.942	0.915	0.889	0.864	0.840	0.816	0.794	0.772	0.751	0.731	0.712
4	0.961	0.924	0.885	0.855	0.823	0.792	0.763	0.735	0.708	0.683	0.659	0.636
5	0.951	0.906	0.863	0.822	0.784	0.747	0.713	0.681	0.650	0.621	0.593	0.567
6	0.942	0.888	0.837	0.790	0.746	0.705	0.666	0.630	0.596	0.564	0.535	0.507
7	0.933	0.871	0.813	0.760	0.711	0.665	0.623	0.583	0.547	0.513	0.482	0.452
8	0.923	0.853	0.789	0.731	0.677	0.627	0.582	0.540	0.502	0.467	0.434	0.404
9	0.914	0.837	0.766	0.703	0.645	0.592	0.544	0.500	0.460	0.424	0.391	0.361
10	0.905	0.820	0.744	0.676	0.614	0.558	0.508	0.463	0.422	0.386	0.352	0.322
11	0.896	0.804	0.722	0.650	0.585	0.527	0.475	0.429	0.388	0.350	0.317	0.287
12	0.887	0.788	0.701	0.625	0.557	0.497	0.444	0.397	0.356	0.319	0.286	0.257
13	0.879	0.773	0.681	0.601	0.530	0.469	0.415	0.368	0.326	0.290	0.258	0.229
14	0.870	0.758	0.661	0.577	0.505	0.442	0.388	0.340	0.299	0.263	0.232	0.205
15	0.861	0.743	0.642	0.555	0.481	0.417	0.362	0.315	0.275	0.239	0.209	0.183
16	0.853	0.728	0.623	0.534	0.458	0.394	0.339	0.292	0.252	0.218	0.188	0.163
17	0.844	0.714	0.605	0.513	0.436	0.371	0.317	0.270	0.231	0.198	0.170	0.146
18	0.836	0.700	0.587	0.494	0.416	0.350	0.296	0.250	0.212	0.180	0.153	0.130
19	0.828	0.686	0.570	0.475	0.396	0.331	0.277	0.232	0.194	0.164	0.138	0.116
20	0.820	0.673	0.554	0.456	0.377	0.312	0.258	0.215	0.178	0.149	0.124	0.104
25	0.780	0.610	0.478	0.375	0.295	0.233	0.184	0.146	0.116	0.092	0.074	0.059
30	0.742	0.552	0.412	0.308	0.231	0.174	0.131	0.099	0.075	0.057	0.044	0.033
40	0.672	0.453	0.307	0.208	0.142	0.097	0.067	0.046	0.032	0.022	0.015	0.011
50	0.608	0.372	0.228	0.141	0.087	0.054	0.034	0.021	0.013	0.009	0.005	0.003

APPENDIX C Present Value of $1 *(concluded)*

Period	13%	14%	15%	16%	17%	18%	19%	20%	25%	30%	35%	40%	50%
1	0.885	0.877	0.870	0.862	0.855	0.847	0.840	0.833	0.800	0.769	0.741	0.714	0.667
2	0.783	0.769	0.756	0.743	0.731	0.718	0.706	0.694	0.640	0.592	0.549	0.510	0.444
3	0.693	0.675	0.658	0.641	0.624	0.609	0.593	0.579	0.512	0.455	0.406	0.364	0.296
4	0.613	0.592	0.572	0.552	0.534	0.515	0.499	0.482	0.410	0.350	0.301	0.260	0.198
5	0.543	0.519	0.497	0.476	0.456	0.437	0.419	0.402	0.320	0.269	0.223	0.186	0.132
6	0.480	0.456	0.432	0.410	0.390	0.370	0.352	0.335	0.262	0.207	0.165	0.133	0.088
7	0.425	0.400	0.376	0.354	0.333	0.314	0.296	0.279	0.210	0.159	0.122	0.095	0.059
8	0.376	0.351	0.327	0.305	0.285	0.266	0.249	0.233	0.168	0.123	0.091	0.068	0.039
9	0.333	0.300	0.284	0.263	0.243	0.225	0.209	0.194	0.134	0.094	0.067	0.048	0.026
10	0.295	0.270	0.247	0.227	0.208	0.191	0.176	0.162	0.107	0.073	0.050	0.035	0.017
11	0.261	0.237	0.215	0.195	0.178	0.162	0.148	0.135	0.086	0.056	0.037	0.025	0.012
12	0.231	0.208	0.187	0.168	0.152	0.137	0.124	0.112	0.069	0.043	0.027	0.018	0.008
13	0.204	0.182	0.163	0.145	0.130	0.116	0.104	0.093	0.055	0.033	0.020	0.013	0.005
14	0.181	0.160	0.141	0.125	0.111	0.099	0.088	0.078	0.044	0.025	0.015	0.009	0.003
15	0.160	0.140	0.123	0.108	0.095	0.084	0.074	0.065	0.035	0.020	0.011	0.006	0.002
16	0.141	0.123	0.107	0.093	0.081	0.071	0.062	0.054	0.028	0.015	0.008	0.005	0.002
17	0.125	0.108	0.093	0.080	0.069	0.060	0.052	0.045	0.023	0.012	0.006	0.003	0.001
18	0.111	0.095	0.081	0.069	0.059	0.051	0.044	0.038	0.018	0.009	0.005	0.002	0.001
19	0.098	0.083	0.070	0.060	0.051	0.043	0.037	0.031	0.014	0.007	0.003	0.002	0
20	0.087	0.073	0.061	0.051	0.043	0.037	0.031	0.026	0.012	0.005	0.002	0.001	0
25	0.047	0.038	0.030	0.024	0.020	0.016	0.013	0.010	0.004	0.001	0.001	0	0
30	0.026	0.020	0.015	0.012	0.009	0.007	0.005	0.004	0.001	0	0	0	0
40	0.008	0.005	0.004	0.003	0.002	0.001	0.001	0.001	0	0	0	0	0
50	0.002	0.001	0.001	0.001	0	0	0	0	0	0	0	0	0

APPENDIX D Present Value of an Annuity of $1

Period	1%	2%	3%	4%	5%	6%	7%	8%	9%	10%	11%	12%
1	0.990	0.980	0.971	0.962	0.952	0.943	0.935	0.926	0.917	0.909	0.901	0.893
2	1.970	1.942	1.913	1.886	1.859	1.833	1.808	1.783	1.759	1.736	1.713	1.690
3	2.941	2.884	2.829	2.775	2.723	2.673	2.624	2577	2.531	2.487	2.444	2.402
4	3.902	3.808	3.717	3.630	3.546	3.465	3.387	3.312	3.240	3.170	3.102	3.037
5	4.853	4.715	4.580	4.452	4.329	4.212	4.100	3.993	3.890	3.791	3.696	3.605
6	5.795	5.601	5.417	5.242	5.076	4.917	4.767	4.623	4.486	4.355	4.231	4.111
7	6.728	6.472	6.230	6.002	5.786	5.582	5.389	5.206	5.033	4.868	4.712	4.564
8	7.652	7.325	7.020	6.733	6.463	6.210	5.971	5.747	5.535	5.335	5.146	4.968
9	8.566	8.162	7.786	7.435	7.108	6.802	6.515	6.247	5.995	5.759	5.537	5.328
10	9.471	8.983	8.530	8.111	7.722	7.360	7.024	6.710	6.418	6.145	5.889	5.650
11	10.368	9.787	9.253	8.760	8.306	7.887	7.499	7.139	6.805	6.495	6.207	5.938
12	11.255	10.575	9.954	9.385	8.863	8.384	7.943	7.536	7.161	6.814	6.492	6.194
13	12.134	11.348	10.635	9.986	9.394	8.853	8.358	7.904	7.487	7.103	6.750	6.424
14	13.004	12.106	11.296	10.563	9.899	9.295	8.745	8.244	7.786	7.367	6.982	6.628
15	13.865	12.849	11.939	11.118	10.380	9.712	9.108	8.559	8.061	7.606	7.191	6.811
16	14.718	13.578	12.561	11.652	10.838	10.106	9.447	8.851	8.313	7.824	7.379	6.974
17	15.562	14.292	13.166	12.166	11.274	10.477	9.763	9.122	8.544	8.022	7.549	7.102
18	16.398	14.992	13.754	12.659	11.690	10.828	10.059	9.372	8.756	8.201	7.702	7.250
19	17.226	15.678	14.324	13.134	12.085	11.158	10.336	9.604	8.950	8.365	7.839	7.366
20	18.046	16.351	14.877	13.590	12.462	11.470	10.594	9.818	9.129	8.514	7.963	7.469
25	22.023	19.523	17.413	15.622	14.094	12.783	11.654	10.675	9.823	9.077	8.422	7.843
30	25.808	22.396	19.600	17.292	15.372	13.765	12.409	11.258	10.274	9.427	8.694	8.055
40	32.835	27.355	23.115	19.793	17.160	15.046	13.332	11.925	10.757	9.779	8.951	8.244
50	39.196	31.424	25.730	21.482	18.256	15.762	13.801	12.233	10.962	9.915	9.042	8.304

APPENDIX D Present Value of an Annuity of $1 (*concluded*)

Period	13%	14%	15%	16%	17%	18%	19%	20%	25%	30%	35%	40%	50%
1	0.885	0.877	0.870	0.862	0.855	0.847	0.840	0.833	0.800	0.769	0.741	0.714	0.667
2	1.668	1.647	1.626	1.605	1.585	1.566	1.547	1.528	1.440	1.361	1.289	1.224	1.111
3	2.361	2.322	2.283	2.246	2.210	2.174	2.140	2.106	1.952	1.816	1.696	1.589	1.407
4	2.974	2.914	2.855	2.798	2.743	2.690	2.639	2.589	2.362	2.166	1.997	1.849	1.605
5	3.517	3.433	3.352	3.274	3.199	3.127	3.058	2.991	2.689	2.436	2.220	2.035	1.737
6	3.998	3.889	3.784	3.685	3.589	3.498	3.410	3.326	2.951	2.643	2.385	2.168	1.824
7	4.423	4.288	4.160	4.039	3.922	3.812	3.706	3.605	3.161	2.802	2.508	2.263	1.883
8	4.799	4.639	4.487	4.344	4.207	4.078	3.954	3.837	3.329	2.925	2.598	2.331	1.922
9	5.132	4.946	4.772	4.607	4.451	4.303	4.163	4.031	3.463	3.019	2.665	2.379	1.948
10	5.426	5.216	5.019	4.833	4.659	4.494	4.339	4.192	3.571	3.092	2.715	2.414	1.965
11	5.687	5.453	5.234	5.029	4.836	4.656	4.486	4.327	3.656	3.147	2.752	2.438	1.977
12	5.918	5.660	5.421	5.197	4.988	4.793	4.611	4.439	3.725	3.190	2.779	2.456	1.985
13	6.122	5.842	5.583	5.342	5.118	4.910	4.715	4.533	3.780	3.223	2.799	2.469	1.990
14	6.302	6.002	5.724	5.468	5.229	5.008	4.802	4.611	3.824	3.249	2.814	2.478	1.993
15	6.462	6.142	5.847	5.575	5.324	5.092	4.876	4.675	3.859	3.268	2.825	2.484	1.995
16	6.604	6.265	5.954	5.668	5.405	5.162	4.938	4.730	3.887	3.283	2.834	2.489	1.997
17	6.729	6.373	6.047	5.749	5.475	5.222	4.988	4.775	3.910	3.295	2.840	2.492	1.998
18	6.840	6.467	6.128	5.818	5.534	5.273	5.033	4.812	3.928	3.304	2.844	2.494	1.999
19	6.938	6.550	6.198	5.877	5.584	5.316	5.070	4.843	3.942	3.311	2.848	2.496	1.999
20	7.025	6.623	6.259	5.929	5.628	5.353	5.101	4.870	3.954	3.316	2.850	2.497	1.999
25	7.330	6.873	6.464	6.097	5.766	5.467	5.195	4.948	3.985	3.329	2.856	2.499	2.000
30	7.496	7.003	6.566	6.177	5.829	5.517	5.235	4.979	3.995	3.332	2.857	2.500	2.000
40	7.634	7.105	6.642	6.233	5.871	5.548	5.258	4.997	3.999	3.333	2.857	2.500	2.000
50	7.675	7.133	6.661	6.246	5.880	5.554	5.262	4.999	4.000	3.333	2.857	2.500	2.000

APPENDIX E

TIME VALUE OF MONEY AND INVESTMENT APPLICATIONS

OVERVIEW

Many applications for the time value of money exist. Applications use either the compound sum (sometimes referred to as *future value*) or the present value. Additionally some cash flows are annuities. An **annuity** represents cash flows that are equally spaced in time and are constant dollar amounts. Car payments, mortgage payments, and bond interest payments are examples of annuities. Annuities can either be present value annuities or compound sum annuities. In the next section, we present the concept of compound sum and develop common applications related to investments.

COMPOUND SUM

Compound Sum: Single Amount

In determining the **compound sum,** we measure the future value of an amount that is allowed to grow at a given rate over a period of time. Assume an investor buys an asset worth \$1,000. This asset (gold, diamonds, art, real estate, etc.) is expected to increase in value by 10 percent per year, and the investor wants to know what it will be worth after the fourth year. At the end of the first year, the investor will have \$1,000 × (1 + .10), or \$1,100. By the end of year two, the \$1,100 will have grown by another 10 percent to \$1,210 (\$1,100 × 1.10). The four-year pattern is indicated below:

1st year: \$1,000 × 1.10 = \$1,100
2nd year: \$1,100 × 1.10 = \$1,210
3rd year: \$1,210 × 1.10 = \$1,331
4th year: \$1,331 × 1.10 = \$1,464

After the fourth year, the investor has accumulated \$1,464. Because compounding problems often cover a long time, a generalized formula is necessary to describe the compounding process. We shall let:

S = Compound sum
P = Principal or present value
i = Interest rate, growth rate, or rate of return
n = Number of periods compounded

The simple formula is:

$$S = P(1 + i)^n \qquad \text{(E–1)}$$

In the preceding example, the beginning amount, P, was equal to $1,000; the growth rate, i, equaled 10 percent; and the number of periods, n, equaled 4, so we get:

$$S = \$1{,}000\ (1.10)^4, \text{ or } \$1{,}000 \times 1.464 = \$1{,}464$$

The term $(1.10)^4$ is found to equal 1.464 by multiplying 1.10 four times itself. This mathematical calculation is called an exponential, where you take (1.10) to the fourth power. On your calculator, you would have an exponential key y^x where y represents (1.10) and x represents 4. For students with calculators, we have prepared Appendix F for both Hewlett-Packard and Texas Instruments calculators.

For those not proficient with calculators or who have calculators without financial functions, Table E–1 is a shortened version of the compound sum table found in Appendix A. The table tells us the amount $1 would grow to if it were invested for any number of periods at a given rate of return. Using this table for our previous example, we find an interest factor for the compound sum in the row where $n = 4$ and the column where $i = 10$ percent. The factor is 1.464, the same as previously calculated. We multiply this factor times any beginning amount to determine the compound sum.

When using compound sum tables to calculate the compound sum, we shorten our formula from $S = P(1 + i)^n$ to:

$$S = P \times S_{IF} \qquad \text{(E–2)}$$

where S_{IF} equals the interest factor for the compound sum found in Table E–1 or Appendix A. Using a new example, assume $5,000 is invested for 20 years at 6 percent. Using Table E–1, the interest factor for the compound sum would be 3.207, and the total value would be:

$$S = P \times S_{IF}\ (n = 20,\ i = 6\%)$$
$$S = \$5{,}000 \times 3.207$$
$$S = \$16{,}035$$

TABLE E–1 Compound Sum of $1 ($S_{IF}$)

Periods	1%	2%	3%	4%	6%	8%	10%
1	1.010	1.020	1.030	1.040	1.060	1.080	1.100
2	1.020	1.040	1.061	1.082	1.124	1.166	1.210
3	1.030	1.061	1.093	1.125	1.191	1.260	1.331
4	1.041	1.082	1.126	1.170	1.262	1.360	1.464
5	1.051	1.104	1.159	1.217	1.338	1.469	1.611
10	1.105	1.219	1.344	1.480	1.791	2.159	2.594
20	1.220	1.486	1.806	2.191	3.207	4.661	6.727
30	1.348	1.811	2.427	3.243	5.743	10.063	13.268

Example—Compound Sum, Single Amount

Problem: Mike Donegan receives a bonus from his employer of \$3,200. He will invest the money at a 12 percent rate of return for the next eight years. How much will he have after eight years?

Solution: Compound sum, single amount:

$$S = P \times S_{IF} \qquad (n = 8, i = 12\%) \qquad \text{Appendix A}$$
$$S = \$3{,}200 \times 2.476 = \$7{,}923.20$$

Compound Sum: Annuity

Our previous example was a one-time single investment. Let us examine a **compound sum of an annuity** where constant payments are made at equally spaced periods and grow to a future value. The normal assumption for a compound sum of an annuity is that the payments are made at the end of each period, so the last payment does not compound or earn a rate of return.

Figure E–1 demonstrates the timing and compounding process when \$1,000 per year is contributed to a fund for four consecutive years. The \$1,000 for each period is multiplied by the compound sum factors for the appropriate periods of compounding. The first \$1,000 comes in at the end of the first period and has three periods to compound; the second \$1,000 at the end of the second period, with two periods to compound; the third

FIGURE E–1 Compounding Process for Annuity

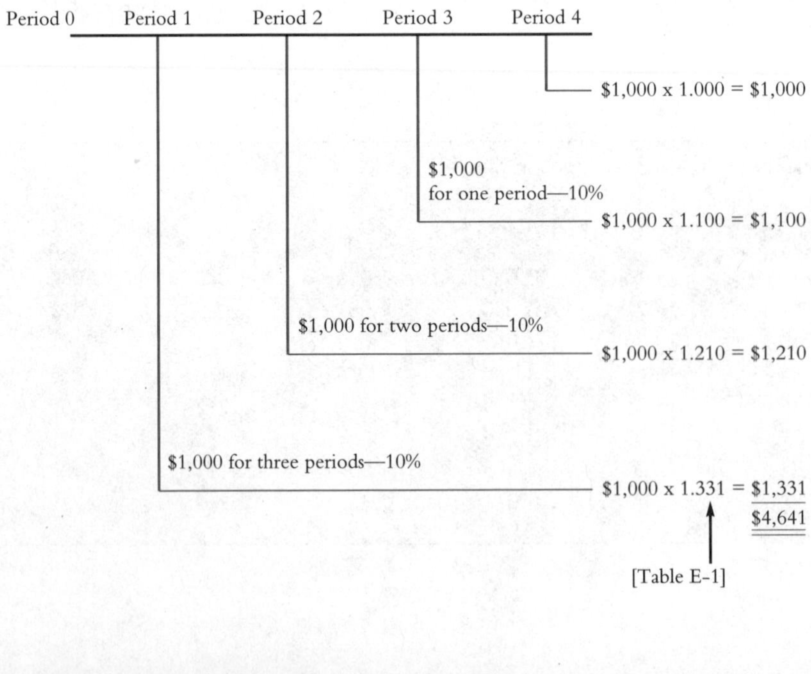

payment has one period to compound; and the last payment is multiplied by a factor of 1.00 showing no compounding at all.

Because compounding the individual values is tedious, compound sum of annuity tables can be used. These tables simply add up the interest factors from the compound sum tables for a single amount. Table E–2 is a shortened version of Appendix B, the compound sum of an annuity table showing the compound sum factors for a specified period and rate of return. Notice that all the way across the table, the factor in period one is 1.00. This reflects the fact that the last payment does not compound.

One example of the compound sum of an annuity applies to the individual retirement account (IRA) and Keogh retirement plans. The IRA allows workers to invest $2,000 per year in a tax-free account, and the Keogh allows a maximum of $30,000 per year to be invested in a retirement account for self-employed individuals. Assume Dr. Piotrowski shelters $30,000 per year from age 35 to 65. If she makes 30 payments of $30,000 and earns a rate of return of 8 percent, her Keogh account at retirement would be more than $3 million.

$$S = R \times SA_{IF}\ (n = 30,\ i = 8\%\ \text{return}) \qquad \text{(E–3)}$$
$$S = \$30{,}000 \times 113.280$$
$$S = \$3{,}398{,}400$$

While this seems like a lot of money in today's world, we need to measure what it will buy 30 years from now after inflation is considered. One way to examine this is to calculate what the $30,000 payments would have to be if they only kept up with inflation. Let's assume inflation of 3 percent over the next 30 years and recalculate the sum of the annuity:

$$S = R \times SA_{IF}\ (n = 30,\ i = 3\%\ \text{inflation})$$
$$S = \$30{,}000 \times 47.575$$
$$S = \$1{,}427{,}250$$

To maintain the purchasing power of each $30,000 contribution, Dr. Piotrowski needs to accumulate $1,427,250 at the estimated 3 percent rate of inflation. Since her rate of return of 8 percent is 5 percentage points higher than the inflation rate, she is adding additional purchasing power to her portfolio.

TABLE E–2 Compound Sum of an Annuity of $1 ($SA_{IF}$)

Periods	1%	2%	3%	4%	6%	8%	10%
1	1.000	1.000	1.000	1.000	1.000	1.000	1.000
2	2.010	2.020	2.030	2.040	2.060	2.080	2.100
3	3.030	3.060	3.091	3.122	3.184	3.246	3.310
4	4.060	4.122	4.184	4.246	4.375	4.506	4.641
5	5.101	5.204	5.309	5.416	5.637	5.867	6.105
10	10.462	10.950	11.464	12.006	13.181	14.487	15.937
20	22.019	24.297	26.870	29.778	36.786	45.762	57.275
30	34.785	40.588	47.575	56.085	79.058	113.280	164.490

Example—Compound Sum, Annuity

Problem: Sonny Outlook invests \$2,000 in an IRA at the end of each year for the next 40 years. With an anticipated rate of return of 11 percent, how much will the funds grow to after 40 years?

Solution: Compound sum, annuity:

$$S = R \times SA_{IF}\ (n = 40, i = 11\%) \qquad \text{Appendix B}$$
$$S = \$2{,}000 \times 581.83 = \$1{,}163{,}660$$

PRESENT VALUE CONCEPT

Present Value: Single Amount

The **present value** is the exact opposite of the compound sum. A future value is discounted to the present. For example, earlier we determined the compound sum of \$1,000 for four periods at 10 percent was \$1,464. We could reverse the process to state that \$1,464 received four years from today is worth only \$1,000 today if one can earn a 10 percent return on money during the four years. This \$1,000 value is called its present value. The relationship is depicted in Figure E–2.

The formula for present value is derived from the original formula for the compound sum. As the following two formulas demonstrate, the present value is simply the inverse of the compound sum.

$$S = P(1 + i)^n \text{ Compound sum}$$
$$P = S \times 1/(1 + i)^n \text{ Present value} \qquad \text{(E–4)}$$

The present value can be determined by solving for a mathematical solution to the above formula, or by using Table E–3, the Present Value of \$1. When we use Table E–3, the

FIGURE E–2 Relationship of Present Value and Compound Sum

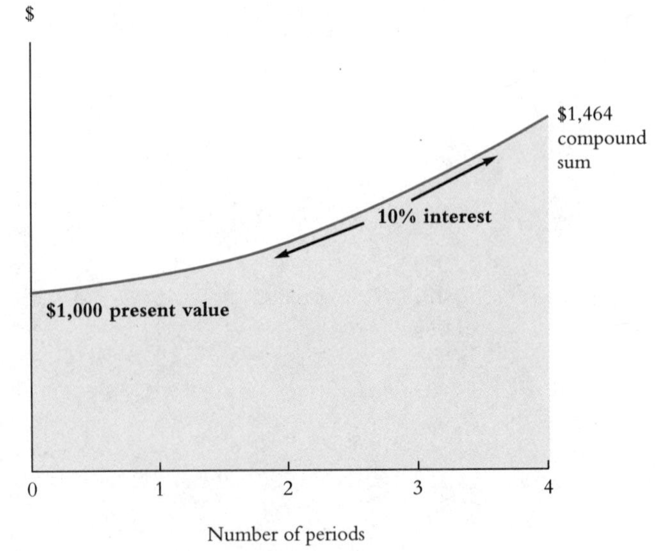

TABLE E–3 Present Value of \$1 (PV_{IF})

Periods	1%	2%	3%	4%	6%	8%	10%
1	0.990	0.980	0.971	0.962	0.943	0.926	0.909
2	0.980	0.961	0.943	0.925	0.890	0.857	0.826
3	0.971	0.942	0.915	0.889	0.840	0.794	0.751
4	0.961	0.924	0.888	0.855	0.792	0.735	0.683
5	0.951	0.906	0.863	0.822	0.747	0.681	0.621
10	0.905	0.820	0.744	0.676	0.558	0.463	0.386
20	0.820	0.673	0.554	0.456	0.312	0.215	0.149
30	0.742	0.552	0.412	0.308	0.174	0.099	0.057

present value interest factor $1/(1 + i)^n$ is found in the table and represented by PV_{IF}. We substitute it into the formula above:

$$P = S \times PV_{IF} \qquad \text{(E–5)}$$

Let's demonstrate that the present value of \$1,464, based on our assumptions, is worth \$1,000 today:

$$P = S \times PV_{IF}\ (n = 4,\ i = 10\%) \text{ Table E–3 or Appendix C}$$
$$P = \$1{,}464 \times 0.683$$
$$P = \$1{,}000$$

Present value becomes very important in determining the value of investments. Assume you think a certain piece of land will be worth \$500,000 10 years from now. If you can earn a 10 percent rate of return on investments of similar risk, what would you be willing to pay for this land?

$$P = S \times PV_{IF}\ (n = 10,\ i = 10\%)$$
$$P = \$500{,}000 \times 0.386$$
$$P = \$193{,}000$$

This land's present value to you today would be \$193,000. What would you have 10 years from today if you invested \$193,000 at a 10 percent return? For this answer, we go to the compound sum factor from Table E–1:

$$S = P \times S_{IF}\ (n = 10,\ i = 10\%)$$
$$S = \$193{,}000 \times 2.594$$
$$S = \$500{,}642$$

The compound sum would be \$500,642. The two answers do not equal \$500,000 because of the mathematical rounding used to construct tables with three decimal points. If we carry out the interest factors to four places, 0.386 becomes 0.3855 and 2.594 becomes 2.5937 and the two answers will be quite similar.

Near the end of the compound sum of an annuity section, we showed that Dr. Piotrowski could accumulate \$3,398,400 by the time she retired in 30 years. What would be the present value of this future sum if we brought it back to the present at the rate of inflation of 3 percent?

$$P = S \times PV_{IF} \; (n = 30, i = 3\%)$$
$$P = \$3{,}398{,}400 \times 0.412$$
$$P = \$1{,}400{,}141$$

The amount she will have accumulated will be worth $1,400,141 in today's dollars. If the rate of inflation averaged 6 percent over this time, the amount would fall to $591,322 ($3,398,400 × 0.174). Notice how sensitive the present value is to a 3 percentage point change in the inflation rate. Another concern is being able to forecast inflation correctly. These examples are simply meant to heighten your awareness that money has a time value and financial decisions require this to be considered.

EXAMPLE—PRESENT VALUE, SINGLE AMOUNT

PROBLEM: Barbara Samuels received a trust fund at birth that will be paid out to her at age 18. If the fund will accumulate to $400,000 by then and the discount rate is 9 percent, what is the present value of her future accumulation?

SOLUTION: Present value, single amount:

$$P = S \times PV_{IF} \; (n = 18, i = 9\%) \qquad \text{Appendix C}$$
$$P = \$400{,}000 \times 0.212 = \$84{,}800$$

Present Value: Annuity

To find the **present value of an annuity,** we are simply finding the present value of an equal cash flow for several periods instead of one single cash payment. The analysis is the same as taking the present value of several cash flows and adding them. Since we are dealing with an annuity (equal dollar amounts), we can save time by creating tables that add up the interest factors for the present value of single amounts and make present value annuity factors. We do this in Table E–4, a shortened version of Appendix D. Before using Table E–4, let us compute the present value of $1,000 to be received each year for five years. We could use the present value of five single amounts and Table E–3 on page 663.

TABLE E–4 Present Value of an Annuity of $1 ($PVA_{IF}$)

Periods	1%	2%	3%	4%	6%	8%	10%
1	0.990	0.980	0.971	0.962	0.943	0.926	0.909
2	1.970	1.942	1.913	1.886	1.833	1.783	1.736
3	2.941	2.884	2.829	2.775	2.673	2.577	2.487
4	3.902	3.808	3.717	3.630	3.465	3.312	3.170
5	4.853	4.713	4.580	4.452	4.212	3.993	3.791
8	7.652	7.325	7.020	6.773	6.210	5.747	5.335
10	9.471	8.983	8.530	8.111	7.360	6.710	6.145
20	18.046	16.351	14.877	13.590	11.470	9.818	8.514
30	25.808	22.396	19.600	17.292	13.765	11.258	9.427

Period	Receipt	IF @ 6%	
1	$1,000 ×	0.943 =	$ 943
2	$1,000 ×	0.890 =	$ 890
3	$1,000 ×	0.840 =	$ 840
4	$1,000 ×	0.792 =	$ 792
5	$1,000 ×	0.747 =	$ 747
		4.212	$4,212 Present value

Another way to get the same value is to use Table E–4. The present value annuity factor under 6 percent and 5 periods is equal to 4.212, or the same value we got from adding the individual present value factors for a single amount. We can simply calculate the answer as follows:

where:

$$A = \text{the present value of an annuity}$$
$$R = \text{the annuity amount}$$
$$PVA_{IF} = \text{the interest factor from Table E–4}$$

$$A = R \times PVA_{IF}\,(n = 5, i = 6\%) \qquad \text{(E–6)}$$
$$A = \$1{,}000 \times 4.212$$
$$A = \$4{,}212$$

Present value of annuities applies to many financial products such as mortgages, car payments, and retirement benefits. Some financial products such as bonds are a combination of an annuity and a single payment. Interest payments from bonds are annuities, and the principal repayment at maturity is a single payment. Both cash flows determine the present value of a bond.

Example—Present Value, Annuity

Problem: Ross "The Hoss" Sullivan has just renewed his contract with the Chicago Bears for an annual payment of $3 million per year for the next eight years. The newspapers report the deal is worth $24 million. If the discount rate is 14 percent, what is the true present value of the contract?

Solution: Present value, annuity:

$$A = R \times PVA_{IF}\,(n = 8, i = 14\%) \qquad \text{Appendix D}$$
$$A = \$3{,}000{,}000 \times 4.639 = \$13{,}917{,}000$$

Present Value: Uneven Cash Flow

Many investments are a series of uneven cash flows. For example, buying common stock generally implies an uneven cash flow from future dividends and the sale price. We hope to buy common stock in companies that are growing and have increasing dividends.

Assume you want to purchase Caravan Motors common stock on January 1, 1996. You expect to hold the stock for five years and then sell it at $60 in December 2000. You also expect to receive dividends of $1.60, $2.00, $2.00, $2.50, and $3.00 during those five years.

What would you be willing to pay for the common stock if your required return on a stock of this risk is 14 percent. Let's set up a present value analysis for an uneven cash flow using Appendix C, the present value of a single amount. Since this is not an annuity, each cash flow must be evaluated separately. For simplicity, we assume all cash flows come at the end of the year. Also, the cash flow in year 2000 combines the $3.00 dividend and expected $60 sale price.

Year	Cash Flow	PV_{IF} 14%	Present Value
1996	$ 1.60	0.877	$ 1.40
1997	2.00	0.769	1.54
1998	2.00	0.675	1.35
1999	2.50	0.592	1.48
2000	63.00	0.519	32.70
Present value of Caravan Motors under these assumptions:			$38.47

If you were satisfied that your assumptions were reasonably accurate, you would be willing to buy Caravan at any price equal to or less than $38.47. This price will provide you with a 14 percent return if all your forecasts come true.

EXAMPLE—PRESENT VALUE, UNEVEN CASH FLOW

PROBLEM: Joann Zinke buys stock in Collins Publishing Company. She will receive dividends of $2.00, $2.40, $2.88, and $3.12 for the next four years. She assumes she can sell the stock for $50 after the last dividend payment (at the end of four years). If the discount rate is 12 percent, what is the present value of the future cash flows? (Round all values to two places to the right of the decimal point.) The present value of future cash flows is assumed to equal the value of the stock.

SOLUTION: Present value, uneven cash flow:

Year	Cash Flow	PV_{IF} 12%	Present Value
1	$ 2.00	0.893	$ 1.79
2	2.40	0.797	1.91
3	2.88	0.712	2.05
4	53.12	0.636	33.78
			$39.53

The present value of the cash flows is $39.53.

Example—Present Value, Uneven Cash Flow

Problem: Sherman Lollar wins a malpractice suit against his accounting professor, and the judgment provides him with \$3,000 a year for the next 40 years, plus a single lump-sum payment of \$10,000 after 50 years. With a discount rate of 10 percent, what is the present value of his future benefits?

Solution: Present value, annuity plus a single amount:

Annuity

$$A = R \times PVA_{IF}\,(n = 40, i = 10\%) \qquad \text{Appendix D}$$

$$A = \$3{,}000 \times 9.779 = \$29{,}337$$

Single amount

$$P = S \times PV_{IF}\,(n = 50, i = 10\%) \qquad \text{Appendix C}$$

$$P = \$10{,}000 \times 0.009 = \$90$$

Total present value = \$29,337 + \$90 = \$29,427.

APPENDIX F

USING CALCULATORS FOR FINANCIAL ANALYSIS

This appendix is designed to help you use either an algebraic calculator (Texas Instruments BA-35 Student Business Analyst) or the Hewlett-Packard 12C Financial Calculator. We realize that most calculators come with comprehensive instructions, and this appendix is only meant to provide basic instructions for commonly used financial calculations.

There are always two things to do before starting your calculations as indicated in the first table: clear the calculator, and set the decimal point. If you do not want to lose data stored in memory, do not perform steps 2 and 3 in the first box below.

Each step is listed vertically as a number followed by a decimal point. After each step you will find either a number or a calculator function denoted by a box [ ]. Entering the number on your calculator is one step and entering the function is another. Notice that the HP 12C is color coded. When two boxes are found one after another, you may have an [f] or a [g] in the first box. An [f] is orange coded and refers to the orange functions above the keys. After typing the [f] function, you will automatically look for an orange-coded key to punch. For example, after [f] in the first Hewlett-Packard box (right-hand panel), you will punch in the orange-color-coded [REG]. If the [f] function is not followed by another box, you merely type in [f] and the value indicated.

	Texas Instruments BA-35	Hewlett–Packard 12C
First clear the calculator.	1. [ON/C] [ON/C]	1. [CLX] Clears Screen
	2. 0	2. [f]
	3. [STO] Clears Memory	3. [REG] Clears Memory
Set the decimal point. The TI BA-35 has two choices: 2 decimal points or variable decimal points. The screen will indicate Dec 2 or the decimal will be variable. The HP 12C allows you to choose the number of decimal points. If you are uncertain, just provide the indicated input exactly as shown on the right.	1. [2nd]	1. [f]
	2. [STO]	2. 4 (# of decimals)

The [g] is coded blue and refers to the functions on the bottom of the function keys. After the [g] function key, you will automatically look for blue-coded keys. This first occurs on page 673 of this appendix.

Familiarize yourself with the keyboard before you start. In the more complicated calculations, keystrokes will be combined into one step.

In the first four calculations on pages 669 and 670 we simply instruct you on how to get the interest factors for Appendixes A, B, C, and D. We have chosen to use examples as our method of instruction.

	Texas Instruments BA-35	**Hewlett–Packard 12C**
A. Appendix A	To Find Interest Factor	To Find Interest Factor
Compound Sum of $1		
	1. 1	1. 1
i = 9% or 0.09; n = 5 years		
	2. +	2. [enter]
$S_{IF} = (1 + i)^n$		
	3. 0.09 (interest rate)	3. 0.09 (interest rate)
Sum = Present Value × S_{IF}		
	4. [=]	4. [+]
$S = P \times S_{IF}$		
	5. [y^x]	5. 5 (# of periods)
Check the answer against the number in Appendix A. Numbers in the appendix are rounded. Try different rates and years.	6. 5 (# of periods)	6. [y^x] answer 1.5386
	7. = answer 1.538624	

	Texas Instruments BA-35	**Hewlett–Packard 12C**
B. Appendix B	To Find Interest Factor	To Find Interest Factor
Compound Sum of an Annuity of $1		
	Repeat steps 1 through 7 in part A of this section. Continue with step 8.	Repeat steps 1 through 6 in part A of this section. Continue with step 7.
i = 9% or 0.09; n = 5 years		
$SA_{IF} = \frac{(1+i)^n - 1}{i}$	8. [−]	7. 1
Sum = Receipt × SA_{IF}	9. 1	8. [−]
$S = R \times SA_{IF}$	10. [=]	9. 0.09
Check your answer with Appendix B. Repeat example using different numbers and check your results with the number in Appendix B. Numbers in appendix are rounded.	11. [÷]	10. [÷] answer 5.9847
	12. 0.09	
	13. [=] answer 5.9847106	

	Texas Instruments BA-35		Hewlett–Packard 12C	
C. Appendix C Present Value of $1	To Find Interest Factor		To Find Interest Factor	
$i = 9\%$ or 0.09; $n = 5$ years	Repeat steps 1 through 7 in part A of this section. Continue with step 8.		Repeat steps 1 through 6 in part A of this section. Continue with step 7.	
$PV_{IF} = 1/(1+i)^n$	8. [1/x]	answer 0.6499314	7. [1/x]	answer 0.6499
Present Value = Sum × PV_{IF}				
$P = S \times PV_{IF}$				
Check the answer against the number in Appendix C. Numbers in the appendix are rounded.				
D. Appendix D Present Value of an Annuity of $1	To Find Interest Factor		To Find Interest Factor	
$i = 9\%$ or 0.09; $n = 5$ years	Repeat steps 1 through 8 in parts A and C. Continue with step 9.		Repeat steps 1 through 7 in parts A and C. Continue with step 8.	
$PVA_{IF} = \dfrac{1-[1/(1+i)^n]}{i}$	9. [−]		8. 1	
Present Value = Annuity × PVA_{IF}	10. 1		9. [−]	
	11. [ ]		10. [CHS]	
$A = R \times PVA_{IF}$	12. [+/−]		11. 0.09	
Check your answer with Appendix D. Repeat example using different numbers and check your results with the number in Appendix D. Numbers in appendix are rounded.	13. [÷]		12. [÷]	answer 3.8897
	14. 0.09			
	15. [=]	answer 3.8896513		

On the following pages,you can determine bond valuation, yield to maturity, net present value of an annuity, net present value of an uneven cash flow, internal rate of return for an annuity, and internal rate of return for an uneven cash flow.

BOND VALUATION USING BOTH THE TI BA-35 AND THE HP 12C

Solve for V = Price of the bond, given:

C_t = \$80 annual coupon payments or 8 percent coupon (\$40 semiannually)

P_n = \$1,000 principal (par value)

n = 10 years to maturity (20 periods semiannually)

i = 9.0 percent rate in the market (4.5 percent semiannually)

You may choose to refer to Chapter 12 for a complete discussion of bond valuation.

	Texas Instruments BA–35	**Hewlett–Packard 12C**
Bond Valuation	Set Finance Mode [2nd] [FIN]	Clear Memory [f] [REG]
All steps begin with number 1. Numbers following each step are keystrokes followed by a box [ ]. Each box represents a keystroke and indicates which calculator function is performed.	Set decimal to 2 places	Set decimal to 3 places
	Decimal	[f] 3
	[2nd] [STO]	1. 9.0 (yield to maturity)
	1. 40 (semiannual coupon)	2. [i]
The Texas Instruments calculator requires that data be adjusted for semiannual compounding; otherwise it assumes annual compounding.	2. [PMT]	3. 8.0 (coupon in percent)
	3. 4.5 (yield to maturity) semiannual basis	4. [PMT]
The Hewlett-Packard 12C internally assumes that semiannual compounding is used and requires annual data to be entered. The HP 12C is more detailed in that it requires the actual day, month, and year. If you want an answer for a problem that requires a given number of years (e.g., 10 years), simply start on a date of your choice and end on the same date 10 years later, as in the example.	4. [%i]	5. 1.091995 (today's date month-day-year)*
	5. 1000 principal	6. [enter]
	6. [FV]	7. 1.092005 (maturity date month-day-year)*
	7. 20 (semiannual periods to maturity)	8. [f]
	8. [N]	9. [Price] Answer 93.496
	9. [CPT]	
	10. [PV] answer 934.96	Answer is given as % of par value and equals \$934.96.
	Answer is given in dollars, rather than % of par value.	If Error message occurs, clear memory and start over.
		*See instructions in the third paragraph of the first column.

YIELD TO MATURITY ON BOTH THE TI BA-35 AND HP 12C

Solve for Y = Yield to maturity, given:

V = \$895.50 price of bond

C_t = \$80 annual coupon payments or 8 percent coupon (\$40 semiannually)

P_n = \$1,000 principal (par value)

n = 10 years to maturity (20 periods semiannually)

You may choose to refer to Chapter 12 for a complete discussion of yield to maturity.

Yield to Maturity

All steps are numbered. All numbers following each step are keystrokes followed by a box [ ]. Each box represents a keystroke and indicates which calculator function is performed.

The Texas Instruments BA-35 does not internally compute a semiannual rate, so the data must be adjusted to reflect semiannual payments and periods. The answer received in step 10 is a semiannual rate, which must be multiplied by 2 to reflect an annual yield.

The Hewlett-Packard 12C internally assumes that semiannual payments are made and, therefore, the answer in step 9 is the annual yield to maturity based on semiannual coupons. If you want an answer on the HP for a given number of years (e.g., 10 years), simply start on a date of your choice and end on the same date 10 years later, as in the example.

Texas Instruments BA-35

Set Finance Mode [2nd] [FIN]

Set decimal to 2 places

Decimal

[2nd] [STO]

1. 20 (semiannual periods)
2. [N]
3. 1000 (par value)
4. [FV]
5. 40 (semiannual coupon)
6. [PMT]
7. 895.50 (bond price)
8. [PV]
9. [CPT]
10. [%i] answer 4.83%
11. [x]
12. 2
13. [=] answer 9.65% (annual rate)

Hewlett–Packard 12C

Clear Memory [f] [REG]

Set decimal [f] 2

1. 89.55 (bond price as a percent of par)
2. [PV]
3. 8.0 (annual coupon in %)
4. [PMT]
5. 1.091995 (today's date)*
6. [enter]
7. 1.092005 (maturity date)*
8. [f]
9. [YTM] answer 9.65%

In case you receive an Error message, you have probably made a keystroke error. Clear the memory

[f] [REG]

and start over.

*See instructions in the third paragraph of the first column.

NET PRESENT VALUE OF AN ANNUITY ON BOTH THE TI BA-35 AND THE HP 12C

Solve for A = Present value of annuity, given:

$$n = 10 \text{ years (number of years cash flow will continue)}$$
$$PMT = \$5{,}000 \text{ per year (amount of the annuity)}$$
$$i = 12 \text{ percent (cost of capital } K_a\text{)}$$
$$\text{Cost} = \$20{,}000$$

	Texas Instruments BA–35	Hewlett–Packard 12C
Net Present Value of an Annuity	Set Finance Mode [2nd] [FIN]	Set decimal to 2 places
All steps are numbered and some steps include several keystrokes. All numbers following each step are keystrokes followed by a box [ ]. Each box represents a keystroke and indicates which calculator function is performed on that number.	Set decimal to 2 places	[f] 2
	Decimal	[f] [REG] clears memory
	[2nd] [STO]	1. 20000 (cash outflow)
	1. 10 (years of cash flow)	2. [CHS] changes sign
	2. [N]	3. [g]
The calculation for the present value of an annuity on the TI BA-35 requires that the project cost be subtracted from the present value of the cash inflows.	3. 5000 (annual payments)	4. [CFo]
	4. [PMT]	5. 5000 (annual payments)
	5. 12 (cost of capital)	6. [g] [Cfj]
The HP 12C could solve the problem exactly with the same keystrokes as the TI. However, since the HP uses a similar method to solve uneven cash flows, we elected to use the method that requires more keystrokes but which includes a negative cash outflow for the cost of the capital budgeting project.	6. [%i]	7. 10 [g] [N_j] (years)
	7. [CPT]	8. 12 [i] (cost of capital)
	8. [PV]	9. [f] [NPV]
	9. [−]	answer $8,251.12
	10. 20,000	If an Error message appears, start over by clearing the memory with
To conserve space, several keystrokes have been put into one step.	11. [=] answer $8,251.12	[f] [REG]

NET PRESENT VALUE OF AN UNEVEN CASH FLOW ON BOTH THE TI BA-35 AND THE HP 12C

Solve for NPV = Net present value, given:

n = 5 years (number of years cash flow will continue)
PMT = \$5,000 (yr. 1); 6,000 (yr. 2); 7,000 (yr. 3); 8,000 (yr. 4); 9,000 (yr. 5)
i = 12 percent (cost of capital K_a)
Cost = \$25,000

Net Present Value of an Uneven Cash Flow

All steps are numbered and some steps include several keystrokes. All numbers following each step are keystrokes followed by a box [ ]. Each box represents a keystroke and indicates which calculator function is performed on that number.

Because we are dealing with uneven cash flows, each number must be entered. The TI BA-35 requires that you make use of the memory. In step 2, you enter the future cash inflow in year 1, and in step 3, you determine its present value, which is stored in memory. After the first 1-year calculation, following year present values are calculated in the same way and added to the stored value using the SUM key. Finally, the recall key RCL is used to recall the present value of the total cash inflows.

The HP 12C requires each cash flow to be entered in order. The CFo key represents the cash flow in time period 0. The CFj key automatically counts the year of the cash flow in the order entered and so no years need to be entered. Finally, the cost of capital of 12% is entered and the f key and NPV key are used to complete the problem.

Texas Instruments BA-35

Clear memory ON/C 0 STO

Set decimal to 2 places

Decimal

2nd STO

Set finance mode

2nd FIN

1. 12 %i
2. 5000 FV
3. 1 N CPT PV SUM
4. 6000 FV
5. 2 N CPT PV SUM
6. 7000 FV
7. 3 N CPT PV SUM
8. 8000 FV
9. 4 N CPT PV SUM
10. 9000 FV
11. 5 N CPT PV SUM
12. RCL (answer 24420.90)
13. −
14. 25000 (cash outflow)
15. = answer −\$579.10

Negative Net Present Value

Hewlett-Packard 12C

Set decimal to 2 places

f 2

f REG clears memory

1. 25000 (cash outflow)
2. CHS changes sign
3. g CFo
4. 5000 g CFj
5. 6000 g CFj
6. 7000 g CFj
7. 8000 g CFj
8. 9000 g CFj
9. 12 i
10. f NPV

answer −\$579.10
Negative Net Present Value

If you receive an Error message, you have probably made a keystroke error. Clear memory with

f REG

and start over with step 1.

INTERNAL RATE OF RETURN FOR AN ANNUITY ON BOTH THE TI BA-35 AND THE HP 12C

Solve for *IRR* = Internal rate of return, given:

n = 10 years (number of years cash flow will continue)
PMT = $10,000 per year (amount of the annuity)
Cost = $50,000 (this is the present value of the annuity)

	Texas Instruments BA-35	Hewlett-Packard 12C
Internal Rate of Return of an Annuity	Clear memory [ON/C] 0 [STO]	Set decimal to 2 places
	Set Finance Mode [2nd] [FIN]	[f] 2
All steps are numbered and some steps include several keystrokes. All numbers following each step are keystrokes followed by a box [ ]. Each box represents a keystroke and indicates which calculator function is performed on that number.	Decimal	[f] [REG] clears memory
	[2nd] [STO]	1. 5000 (cash outflow)
	1. 10 (years of cash flow)	2. [CHS] changes sign
	2. [N]	3. [g]
The calculation for the internal rate of return on an annuity using the TI BA-35 requires relatively few keystrokes.	3. 10000 (annual payments)	4. [CFo]
	4. [PMT]	5. 10000 (annual payments)
	5. 50000 (present value)	6. [g] [Cfj]
The HP 12C requires more keystrokes than the TI BA-35, because it needs to use the function keys [f] and [g] to enter data into the internal programs. The HP method requires that the cash outflow be expressed as a negative, while the TI BA-35 uses a positive number for the cash outflow.	6. [PV]	7. 10 [g] [Nj] (years)
	7. [CPT]	8. [f] [IRR]
	8. [%i]	answer is 15.10%
	answer is 15.10%	If an Error message appears, start over by clearing the memory with
To conserve space, several keystrokes have been put into one step.	At an internal rate of return of 15.10%, the present value of the $50,000 outflow is equal to the present value of $10,000 cash inflows over the next 10 years.	[f] [REG].

INTERNAL RATE OF RETURN WITH AN UNEVEN CASH FLOW ON BOTH THE TI BA-35 AND THE HP 12C

Solve for *IRR* = Internal rate of return (return which causes present value of outflows to equal present value of the inflows), given:

n = 5 years (number of years cash flow will continue)

PMT = \$5,000 (yr. 1); 6,000 (yr. 2); 7,000 (yr. 3); 8,000 (yr. 4); 9,000 (yr. 5)

Cost = \$25,000

Internal Rate of Return on Uneven Cash Flow

All steps are numbered and some steps include several keystrokes. All numbers following each step are keystrokes followed by a box [ ]. Each box represents a keystroke and indicates which calculator function is performed on that number.

Because we are dealing with uneven cash flows, the mathematics of solving this problem with the TI BA-35 is not possible. A more advanced algebraic calculator would be required.

However, for the student willing to use trial and error, the student can use the NPV method and try different discount rates until the NPV equals zero. Check Chapter 12 on methods for approximating the IRR. This will provide a start.

The HP 12C requires each cash flow to be entered in order. The [CFo] key represents the cash in time period 0. The [CFj] key automatically counts the year of the cash flow in the order entered and so no years need to be entered. To find the internal rate of return, use the [f] [IRR] keys and complete the problem.

Texas Instruments BA–35

Clear memory [ON/C] 0 [STO]

Set decimal to 2 places

Decimal

[2nd] [STO]

Set finance mode

[2nd] [FIN]

1. 12 [%i] (your IRR est.)
2. 5000 [FV]
3. 1 [N] [CPT] [PV] [STO]
4. 6000 [FV]
5. 2 [N] [CPT] [PV] [SUM]
6. 7000 [FV]
7. 3 [N] [CPT] [PV] [SUM]
8. 8000 [FV]
9. 4 [N] [CPT] [PV] [SUM]
10. 9000 [FV]
11. 5 [N] [CPT] [PV] [SUM]
12. [RCL] (answer 24,420.90)
13. [–]
14. 25000 (cash outflow)
15. [=] answer –\$579.10 Negative NPV.

Start over with a lower discount rate (try 11.15). Answer is 24999.75. With a cash outflow of \$25,000, the IRR would be 11.15%

Hewlett–Packard 12C

Set decimal to 2 places

[f] 2

[f] [REG] clears memory

1. 25000 (cash outflow)
2. [CHS] changes sign
3. [g] [CFo]
4. 5000 [g] [CFj]
5. 6000 [g] [CFj]
6. 7000 [g] [CFj]
7. 8000 [g] [CFj]
8. 9000 [g] [CFj]
9. [f] [IRR]

answer 11.15%

If you receive an Error message, you have probably made a keystroke error. Clear memory with

[f] [REG]

and start over with step 1.

Glossary

A

abnormal return Gains beyond what the market would normally provide after adjustment for risk.

adjustable rate mortgage A mortgage in which the interest rate is adjusted regularly to current market conditions. It is sometimes referred to as a variable rate mortgage.

advances Increases in the prices of various stocks as measured between two points in time. Significant advances in a large number of stocks indicate a particular degree of market strength. Also see *declines*.

after-acquired property clause The stipulation in a mortgage bond indenture requiring all real property subsequently obtained by the issuing firm to serve as additional bond security.

after-market performance The price experience of new issues in the market.

alpha The value representing the difference between the return on a portfolio and a return on the market line that corresponds to a beta equal to the portfolio. A portfolio manager who performs at positive alpha levels would generate returns better than those available along the market line.

American depository receipts (ADRs) These securities represent the ownership interest in a foreign company's common stock. The process is as follows: The shares of the foreign company are purchased and put in trust in a foreign branch of a New York bank. The bank, in turn, receives and can issue depository receipts to the American shareholders of the foreign firm. These ADRs (depository receipts) allow foreign shares to be traded in the United States much like any other security. Through ADRs, one can purchase the stock of Sony Corporation, Honda Motor Co., Ltd., and hundreds of other foreign corporations.

annuity Cash flows that are equally spaced in time and are constant dollar amounts.

anomalies Deviations from the basic proposition that the market is efficient.

anticipated realized yield The return received on a bond held for a period other than that ending on the call date or the maturity date. In computing the anticipated realized yield, the investor considers both coupon payments and expected capital gains.

arbitrage An arbitrage is instituted when a simultaneous trade (a buy and a sale) occurs in two different markets and a profit is locked in.

arbitrage pricing theory A theory for explaining stock prices and stock returns. While the capital asset pricing model bases return solely on one form of systematic risk (market risk), arbitrage pricing theory can utilize several sources of risk (GDP, unemployment, etc.). Under this theory, it is assumed the investor will not be allowed to earn a return greater than that dictated by the various sensitivity factors affecting returns. To the extent that he does, arbitrageurs will eliminate the extra returns by selling the security and buying other comparable securities—thus the term *arbitrage pricing theory.* Unlike the capital asset pricing model, there is no necessity to define K_M (the market rate of return).

asset-utilization ratios Ratios that indicate the number of times per year that assets are turned over. They show the activity in the various asset accounts.

automatic reinvestment plan A plan offered by a mutual fund in which the fund automatically reinvests all distributions to a shareholder account.

average differential return The alpha value that indicates the difference between the return on a portfolio or fund and a return on the market line that corresponds to a beta equal to the portfolio or fund.

B

balance sheet A financial statement that indicates, at a given point, what the firm owns and how these assets are financed in the form of liabilities and ownership interest.

balanced funds Mutual funds that combine investments in common stock, bonds, and preferred stock. Many balanced funds also invest in convertible securities as well. They try to provide income plus some capital appreciation.

banker's acceptance A short-term debt instrument usually issued in conjunction with a foreign trade

transaction. The acceptance is a draft that is drawn on a bank for approval for future payment and is subsequently presented to the payer.

***Barron's* Confidence Index** An indicator utilized by technical analysts who follow smart money rules. Movements in the index measure the expectations of bond investors whom some technical analysts see as astute enough to foresee economic trends before the stock market has time to react.

basis The difference between the futures price and the value of the underlying item. Thus, on a stock index futures contract, basis represents the difference between the stock index futures price and the value of the underlying index. The basis may be either positive or negative, with the former indicating optimism and the latter signifying pessimism.

basis point One basis point is equal to 0.01 percent. It is used as a unit to measure changes in interest rates.

best efforts The issuing firm, rather than the investment banker, assumes the risk for a distribution. The investment banker merely agrees to provide his best effort to sell the securities.

beta A measurement of the volatility of a security with the market in general. A greater beta coefficient than 1 indicates systematic risk greater than the market, while a beta of less than 1 indicates systematic risk less than the market.

beta-related hedge A stock index futures hedge in which the relative volatility of the portfolio to the market is considered in determining the number of contracts necessary to offset a given dollar level of exposure. If a portfolio has a beta greater than 1, then extra contracts may be necessary to compensate for high volatility.

beta stability The amount of consistency in beta values over time. Instability means prior beta values may not be reflective of future beta values.

Black-Scholes option pricing model A formal model used to determine the theoretical value of an option. Such factors as the riskless interest rate, the length of the option, and the volatility of the underlying security are considered. For a more complete discussion, see Appendix 15A.

blind pool A form of limited partnership for real estate investments in which funds are provided to the general partner to select properties for investment.

bond indenture A lengthy, complicated legal document that spells out the borrowing firm's responsibilities to the individual lenders in a bond issue.

bond price sensitivity The sensitivity of a change in bond prices to a change in interest rates. Bond price sensitivity is influenced by the duration of the bond in that the longer the duration of a bond, the greater the price sensitivity. A less sophisticated but acceptable approach is to tie price sensitivity to the maturity of the bond rather than the duration.

bond swaps The selling of a given bond position and immediately buying into another one with similar attributes in an attempt to improve overall portfolio return or performance.

bottom-up approach A method for choosing stocks that starts with picking *individual* companies and then looking at the industry and economy to see if there is any reason an investment in the company should not be made.

breadth of market indicators Overall market rules used by technical analysts in comparing broad market activity with trading activity in a few stocks. By comparing all advances and declines in NYSE-listed stocks, for example, with the Dow Jones Industrial Average, analysts attempt to judge when the market has changed directions.

bull spread An option strategy utilized when the expectation is that the stock price will rise. The opposite strategy is a bear spread.

business cycle Swings in economic activity encompassing expansionary and recessionary periods and, on average, occurring over four-year periods.

buying the spread A term indicating the cost from writing the call is more than the revenue of the short position. The opposite results in "selling the spread."

C

call option An option to buy 100 shares of common stock at a specified price for a given period.

call provision A mechanism for repaying funds advanced through a bond issue. A provision of the bond indenture allows the issuer to retire bonds before maturity by paying holders a premium above principal.

capital appreciation A growth in the value of a stock or other investments as opposed to income from dividends or interest.

capital asset pricing model A model by which assets are valued based on their risk characteristics. The required return for an asset is related to its beta.

capital gain or loss The difference between the cost of an asset and its sales price.

capital market line The graphic representation of the relationship of risks and returns with various portfolios

of assets. The line is part of the capital asset pricing model.

cash settlement Closing out a futures or options contract for cash rather than calling for actual delivery of the underlying item specified in the contract—for example, pork bellies and T-bills. The stock index futures markets and stock index options markets are *purely* cash-settlement markets. There is never even the implied potential for future delivery of the S&P 500 Stock Index or other indexes.

CBOE Chicago Board Options Exchange, the first and largest exchange for call options.

certificates of deposit Savings certificates that entitle the holder to the receipt of interest. These instruments are issued by commercial banks and savings and loans (or other thrift institutions).

certified financial planner (CFP) A financial planner who has been appropriately certified by the College for Financial Planning in Denver. He or she must demonstrate skills in risk management, tax planning, retirement and estate planning, and other similar areas.

chartered financial analyst (CFA) A security analyst or portfolio manager who has been appropriately certified through experience requirements and testing by the Association for Investment Management and Research (AIMR) in Charlottesville, Virginia.

charting Use by technical analysts of charts and graphs to plot past stock price movements that are used to predict future prices.

circuit breakers The temporary suspension of trading of futures contracts when the market is falling rapidly. For example, the Chicago Mercantile Exchange has a rule that prevents market participants from trading Standard & Poor's Stock Index Futures at lower prices for 30 minutes after the S&P 500 Index has fallen 12 points.

closed-end fund A closed-end investment fund has a fixed number of shares, and purchasers and sellers of shares must deal directly with each other rather than with the fund. Closed-end funds trade on an exchange or over-the-counter.

closing purchase transactions A transaction in which an investor who is a writer of an option intends to terminate the obligation.

closing sale transaction A transaction in which an investor who is the holder of an outstanding security intends to liquidate a position as a holder.

coincident indicators Economic indicators that change direction at roughly the same time as the general economy.

combined earnings and dividend model A model combining earnings per share and an earnings multiplier with a finite dividend model. Value is derived from both the present value of dividends and the present value of the future price of the stock based on the earnings multiplier (P/E).

commercial paper A short-term credit instrument issued by large business corporations to the public. Commercial paper usually comes in minimum denominations of $25,000 and represents an unsecured promissory note.

commission broker An individual who represents a stock brokerage firm on the floor of an exchange and who executes sales and purchases stocks for the firm's clients across the nation.

commodities Such tangible items as livestock, farm produce, and precious metals. Users and producers of commodities hedge against future price fluctuations by transferring risks to speculators through futures contracts.

commodity futures A contract to buy or sell a commodity in the future at a given price.

compound sum The future value of an amount that is allowed to grow at a given interest rate over a period of time.

compound sum of an annuity Constant payments are made at equally spaced time periods and grow to a future value.

constant-dollar method Adjusting for inflation in the financial statements by using the consumer price index.

constant-growth model A dividend valuation model that assumes a constant growth rate for dividends.

construction and development trust A type of REIT that makes short-term loans to developers during their construction period.

consumer price index An index used to measure the changes in the general price level.

contrary opinion rules Guidelines, based on such factors as the odd-lot or the short sales position, used by technical analysts who predict stock market activity on the assumption that such groups as small traders or short sellers are often wrong. Also see *smart money rules.*

conversion premium The amount, expressed as a dollar value or as a percentage, by which the price of the convertible security exceeds the current market value of the common stock into which it may be converted.

conversion price The face value of a convertible security divided by the conversion ratio gives the price of the underlying common stock at which the security is convertible. An investor would usually not convert the security into common stock unless the market price was greater than the conversion price.

conversion ratio The number of shares of common stock an investor receives when exchanging convertible bonds or shares of convertible preferred stock for shares of common stock.

conversion value The value of the underlying common stock represented by convertible bonds or convertible preferred stock. This dollar value is obtained by multiplying the conversion ratio by the per share market price of the common stock.

convertible security A corporate bond or a share of preferred stock that, at the option of the holder, can be converted into shares of common stock of the issuing corporation.

correlation coefficient The measurement of joint movement between two variables.

coupon rate The stated, fixed rate of interest paid on a bond.

covered options The process of writing (selling) options on stock that is already owned.

covered writer A writer of an option who owns the stock on which the option is written. If the stock is not owned, the writer is deemed naked.

creditor claims Claims represented by debt instruments offered by financial institutions, industrial corporations, or the government.

cross hedge A hedging position in which one form of security is used to hedge another form of security (often because differences in maturity dates or quality characteristics make a perfect hedge difficult to establish).

currency fluctuations Changes in the relative value of one currency to another. For example, the French franc may advance or decline in relation to the dollar. To the extent a foreign currency appreciates relative to the dollar, returns on foreign investments will increase in terms of dollars. The opposite would be true for declining foreign currencies.

currency futures Futures contracts for speculation or hedging in different nations' currencies.

current-cost method Adjusting for inflation in the financial statements by revaluing assets at their current cost.

current ratio Current assets divided by current liabilities.

current yield The annual dollar amount of interest paid on a bond divided by the price at which the bond is currently trading in the market.

cyclical indicators Factors that economists can observe to measure the progress of economic cycles. Leading indicators move in a particular direction in advance of the movement of general business conditions, while lagging indicators change direction after general conditions, and coincident indicators move in unison with the economy.

cyclical industry An industry, such as automobiles, whose financial health is closely tied to the condition of the general economy. Such industries tend to make the type of products whose purchase can be postponed until the economy improves.

D

database A form of organized, stored data. It is usually fed into the computer for additional analysis.

debenture An unsecured corporate bond.

debt-utilization ratios Ratios that indicate how the firm is financed between debt (lenders) and equity (owners) and the firm's ability for meeting cash payments due on fixed obligations, such as interest, lease payments, licensing fees, or sinking-fund charges.

declines Decreases in the prices of various stocks as measured between two points in time. Significant declines in a large number of stocks indicate a particular degree of market weakness. Also see *advances.*

deep discount bond A bond that has a coupon rate far below rates currently available on investments and that consequently can be traded only at a significant discount from par value. It may offer an opportunity for capital appreciation.

derivative products Securities that derive their existence from other items. Stock index futures and options are sometimes thought of as derivatives because they derive their existence from actual market indexes but have no intrinsic characteristics of their own.

diagonal spread A combination of a vertical and horizontal spread.

dilution The reduction in earnings per share that occurs when earnings remain unchanged yet the number of shares outstanding increases, as in the conversion of convertible bonds or preferred stock into common stock.

direct equity claim Representation of ownership interests through common stock or other instruments to purchase common stock, such as warrants and options.

discount rate The interest rate at which future cash flows are discounted to a present value.

dispersion The distribution of values or outcomes around an expected value.

diversification Lack of concentration in any one item. A portfolio composed of many different securities is diversified.

diversification benefits Risk reduction through a diversification of investments. Investments that are negatively correlated or that have low positive correlation provide the best diversification benefits. Such benefits may be particularly evident in an internationally diversified portfolio.

dividend payout ratio Annual dividends per share divided by annual earnings per share.

dividend valuation model Any one of a number of stock valuation models based on the premise that the value of stock lies in the present value of its future dividend stream.

dividend yield Annual dividends per share divided by market place.

dollar-cost averaging The investor buys a fixed dollar's worth of a given security at regular intervals regardless of the security's price or the current market outlook. This provides a certain degree of discipline and also means more shares will be purchased at low prices rather than high prices since the amount of the regular investment is fixed and only the number of shares purchased varies.

Dow Jones Equity Market Index An index that includes 700 stocks in 82 industry groups. Unlike the Dow Jones Industrial Average, it includes stocks from the New York Stock Exchange, the American Stock Exchange, and the NASDAQ National Market System and is much more broadly based.

Dow Jones Industrial Average An index of stock market activity based on the price movements of 30 large corporations. The average is price-weighted, which means each stock is effectively weighted by the magnitude of its price.

Dow Jones World Industry Groups A table in *The Wall Street Journal* that shows the leading and lagging industries for a given day around the world. Specific price change information on more than 100 industries is also provided.

Dow Jones World Stock Index An international stock index that covers 25 countries in three major sectors of the world. It shows this information individually and collectively.

Dow theory The theory, developed by Charles Dow in the late 1890s and still in use today, that the analysis of long-term (primary) stock market trends can yield accurate predictions for future price movements.

downside protection The protection that a convertible bond investor enjoys during a period of falling stock prices. While the underlying common stock and the convertible bond may both fall in value, the bond will fall only to a particular level because it has a fundamental, or pure, bond value based on its assured income stream.

downside risk The possibility that an asset, such as a security, may fall in value as a result of fundamental factors or external market forces. The limit of the downside risk for a convertible bond can be computed as the difference between the bond's market price and its pure bond value divided by the market price.

Du Pont analysis A system of analyzing return on assets through examining the profit margin and asset turnover. Also, the value of return on equity is analyzed through evaluating return on assets and the debt/total assets ratio.

duration The weighted average life of a bond. The weights are based on the present values of the individual cash flows relative to the present value of the total cash flows. Duration is a better measure than maturity when assessing the price sensitivity of bonds; that is, the impact of interest-rate changes on bond prices can be more directly correlated to duration than to maturity.

E

earnings per share The earnings available to holders of common stock divided by the number of common stock shares outstanding.

earnings valuation model Any one of a number of stock valuation models based on the premise that a stock's value is some appropriate multiple of earnings per share.

effective diversification The diversification of a portfolio to remove unsystematic risk.

efficient frontier A set of investment portfolios in which the investor receives maximum return for a given level of risk or a minimum risk for a given level of return.

efficient hedge A hedge in which one side of the transaction effectively covers the exposed side in terms of movement.

efficient market The capacity of the market to react to new information, to avoid rapid price fluctuations, and to engage in increased or reduced trading volume without realizing significant price changes. In an efficient market environment, securities are assumed to be correctly priced at any point in time.

efficient market hypothesis The concept that there are many participants in the securities markets who are profit maximizing and alert to information so that there is almost instant adjustment to new information. The weak form of this hypothesis suggests there is no relationship between past and future prices. The semistrong form maintains that all forms of public information are already reflected in the price of a security, so fundamental analysis cannot determine under- or overvaluation. The strong form suggests that all information, insider as well as public, is impounded in the value of a security.

efficient portfolio A portfolio that combines assets so as to minimize the risk for a given level of return.

electronic book The database system that covers all stocks listed on the New York Stock Exchange and keeps track of limit orders and market orders for the specialist.

emerging countries Foreign countries that have not fully developed their economic system and productive capacity. Examples might include Chile, Jordan, Korea, Thailand, and Zimbabwe. A number of these emerging countries may represent good risk-reduction potential for U.S. investors because the factors that influence their economic welfare may be quite different from critical factors in the United States. Investments in these countries, at times, may also provide high returns.

equal-weighted index Each stock, regardless of total market value or price, is weighted equally. It is as if there were $100 invested in every stock in the index. The Value Line Index is a prime example of an equal-weighted index.

equipment trust certificate A secured debt instrument used by firms in the transportation industry that provides for bond proceeds to purchase new equipment, which in turn is collateral for the bond issue.

equity participation The lender also participates in an ownership interest in the property.

equity risk premium An extra return that the stock market must provide over the rate on Treasury bills to compensate for market risk. It is defined as $(K_M - R_F)$ or the expected rate of return for common stocks in the market minus the risk-free rate.

equity trust A type of REIT that buys, operates, and sells real estate as an investment as opposed to mortgage trusts.

excess returns Returns in excess of the risk-free rate or in excess of a market measure such as the S&P 500 Stock Index.

exchange listing A firm lists its shares on an exchange (such as the American or New York Stock Exchange).

exchange privilege A feature offered by a mutual fund sponsor in which a shareholder is able to move money between various funds under the management of the sponsor at a very minimal processing charge and without a commission.

exercise price (warrant) The price at which the stock can be bought using the warrant.

expectations hypothesis The hypothesis that explains the term structure of interest rates, stating that a long-term interest rate is the average of expected short-term interest rates over the applicable time period. If, for example, long-term rates are higher than short-term rates, then according to the expectations hypothesis, investors must expect that short-term rates will be increasing in coming periods.

expected value The sum of possible outcomes times their probability of occurrence.

extraordinary gains and losses Gains or losses from the sale of corporate fixed assets, lawsuits, or similar events that would not be expected to occur often, if ever again.

F

Fed The Federal Reserve serves as the central banking authority for the United States. The Fed enacts monetary policy, and it plays a major role in regulating commercial banking operations and controlling the money supply.

federal deficit A situation in which the federal government spends more money than it receives through taxes and other revenue sources.

federal surplus A situation in which taxes and other government revenues provide more money than is needed to cover government expenditures.

FIFO A method of inventory valuation in which it is assumed that inventory purchased first is sold first (first-in, first-out).

financial asset A financial claim on an asset (rather than physical possession of a tangible asset) usually documented by a legal instrument, such as a stock certificate.

financial-service companies Firms that provide a broad range of financial services to diversify their consumer base. Services may include brokerage activities, insurance, banking, and so forth.

fiscal policy Government spending and taxing practices designed to promote or inhibit various economic activities.

floating-rate notes The coupon rate on the note or bond is fixed for only a short time and then varies with a stipulated short-term rate such as the rate on U.S. Treasury bills.

floor broker An independent stockbroker who is a member of a stock exchange and who executes trades, for a fee, for commission brokers experiencing excessive volumes of trading.

floor value A value that an income-producing security will not fall below because of the fundamental value attributable to its assured income stream.

flow-of-funds analysis Analysis of the pattern of financial payments between business, government, and households.

foreign currency effects To the extent a foreign currency appreciates relative to the dollar, returns on foreign investments will increase in terms of dollars. The opposite would be true for declining foreign currencies.

foreign political risks The risks associated with investing in firms operating in foreign countries. There is the danger of nationalization of foreign firms or the blockage of capital flows to investors. There also may be the danger of violent overthrow of the political party in power, with all the associated implications. Punitive legislation against foreign firms or investors is another political risk.

fourth market The direct trading between large institutional investors in blocks of listed stocks. The participants avoid paying brokerage commissions.

fully diluted earnings per share The value of earnings per share that would be realized if all outstanding securities convertible into common stock were converted.

fundamental analysis The valuation of stocks based on fundamental factors, such as company earnings, growth prospects, and so forth.

funded pension plan Current income is charged with pension liabilities in advance of the actual payment, and funds are set aside.

futures contract An agreement that provides for sale or purchase of a specific amount of a commodity at a designated time in the future at a given price.

futures contract on a stock market index A futures contract based on a market index, such as the Standard & Poor's 500 Stock Index or the NYSE Composite Index.

G

general obligation bonds A municipal bond backed by the full faith, credit, and "taxing power" of the issuing unit rather than the revenue from a given project.

GNMA (Ginnie Mae) pass-through certificate Fixed-income securities that represent an undivided interest in a pool of federally insured mortgages. GNMA, the Government National Mortgage Association, buys a pool of securities from various lenders at a discount and then issues securities to the public against these mortgages.

going public Selling privately held shares to new investors in the over-the-counter market for the first time.

government securities Bonds issued by federal, state, or local governmental units or government agencies. Whereas corporate securities' returns are paid through company earnings, government securities are repaid through taxes or the revenues from projects financed by the bonds.

graduated payment mortgage A type of mortgage in which payments start out on a relatively low basis and increase over the life of the loan.

greed index A contrary opinion index that measures how "greedy" investors are. Greed is thought to be synonymous with bullish sentiment, or optimism. Under the assumptions of the greed index, the more greedy or optimistic investors are, the more likely the market is to fall and vice versa.

gross domestic product (GDP) A measure of output from United States factories and related consumption in the United States. It does not include products made by U.S. companies in foreign markets.

growth company A company that exhibits rising returns on assets each year and sales that are growing at an increasing rate (growth phase of the life-cycle curve). Growth companies may not be as well known as growth stocks.

growth funds Mutual funds with the primary objective of capital appreciation.

growth stock The stock of a firm generally growing faster than the economy or market norm.

growth-with-income funds Mutual funds that combine a strategy of capital appreciation with income generation.

H

hedging A process for lessening or eliminating risk by taking a position in the market opposite to your original

position. For example, someone who owns wheat can sell a futures contract to protect against future price declines.

hidden assets Assets that are not readily apparent to investors in a traditional sense, but add substantial value to the firm.

horizontal spread Buying and writing two options with the same strike price but maturing in different months.

hybrid trust A form of REIT that engages in the activities of both equity trusts and mortgage trusts.

I

Ibbotson study A study examining comparative returns on stocks and fixed-income securities from the mid-1920s to the present.

immunization Immunizing or protecting a bond portfolio against the effects of changing interest rates on the ending value of the portfolio. The process is usually tied to a time horizon. In the process, if interest rates go up, there will be a decline in the value of the portfolio, but a higher reinvestment rate opportunity for inflows. Conversely, if interest rates go down, there will be capital appreciation for the portfolio, but a lower reinvestment rate opportunity. By tying all the investment decisions to a specified duration period, the portfolio manager can take advantage of these counter forces to ensure a necessary outcome.

income bond A corporate debt instrument on which interest is paid only if funds are available from current income.

income statement A financial statement that shows the profitability of a firm over a given period.

income-statement method A method of forecasting earnings per share based on a projected income statement.

index fund A fund investing in a portfolio of corporate stocks, the composition of which is determined by the Standard & Poor's 500 Index or some other index.

indifference curves These curves show the investor's trade-off between risk and return. The steeper the slope of the curve, the more risk-averse the investor is.

indirect equity claim An indirect claim on common stock such as that achieved by placing funds in investment companies.

individual retirement account (IRA) An IRA allows a qualifying taxpayer to deduct $2,000 from taxable income and invest the funds at a bank, savings and loan, brokerage house, mutual fund, or other financial institution. The funds are normally placed in interest-bearing instruments, or perhaps in other securities, such as common stock. The income on the funds is allowed to grow tax-free until withdrawn at retirement.

industry factors The unique attributes that must be considered in analyzing a given industry or group of industries. Examples include industry structure, supply/demand of labor and materials, and government regulation.

industry life cycles Cycles that are created because of economic growth, competition, availability of resources, and the resultant market saturation of the particular goods and services offered. The stages are development, growth, expansion, maturity, and decline.

inflation A general increase in the prices of goods and services.

inflation-adjusted accounting Restating financial statements to show the effect of inflation on the balance sheet and income statement. This is supplemental to the normal presentation based on historical data.

inflationary expectations A value representing future expectations about the rate of inflation. This value, combined with the real rate of return, provides the risk-free required return for the investor.

initial public offering (IPO) The process of bringing private companies to the public market for the first time.

insider trading Trading by those who had special access to unpublished information. If the information is used to illegally make a profit, there may be large fines and possible jail sentences.

institutional investor A type of investor (as opposed to individual investors) representing organizations responsible for bringing together large pools of capital for investment. Institutional investors include investment companies, pension funds, life insurance companies, bank trust departments, and endowments and foundations.

in the money A term that indicates when the market price of a stock is above the striking price of the call option. When the strike price is above the market price, the call option is out of the money.

interest-rate futures Futures contracts involving Treasury bills, Treasury bonds, Treasury notes, commercial paper, certificates of deposit, and GNMA certificates.

interest-rate swaps The trading of interest rate exposure between two or more parties so that each participant may be able to rebalance his portfolio with less risk. Fixed-rate exposure and variable-rate exposure are normally exchanged.

international tax problems Many foreign countries impose a 7.5 to 15 percent withholding tax against the dividends or interest paid to nonresident holders of equity or debt securities. However, it is often possible for tax-exempt U.S. investors to secure an exemption or rebate on part or all of the withholding tax. Also, taxable U.S. investors can normally claim a U.S. tax credit for taxes paid in foreign countries. The problem is more likely to be one of inconvenience and paper shuffling rather than loss of funds.

internationally oriented funds Mutual funds and closed-end investment companies that invest in worldwide securities. Some funds specialize in Asian holdings, others in South African, and so on.

intrinsic value Value of a warrant or option equal to market price minus the strike (exercise) price.

inverse pyramiding A process of leveraging to control commodities contracts in which the profits from one contract are used to purchase another contract on margin, and profits on this contract are applied to a third, and so on.

investment The commitment of current funds in anticipation of the receipt of an increased return of funds at some point.

investment banker One who is primarily involved in the distribution of securities from the issuing corporation to the public. An investment banker also advises corporate clients on their financial strategy and may help to arrange mergers and acquisitions.

investment banking The underwriting and distribution of a new security issue in the primary market. The investment banker advises the issuing concern on price and other terms and normally guarantees sale while overseeing distribution of the securities through the selling brokerage houses.

investment companies A type of financial institution that takes proceeds of individual investors and reinvests them in securities according to their specific objectives. A popular type of investment company is the mutual fund.

J

Jensen measure of portfolio performance Jensen compares excess returns (total portfolio returns minus the risk-free rate) to what should be required in the market based on the portfolio beta. For example, if the portfolio beta is 1, the portfolio has a systematic risk equal to the market, and the expected portfolio excess returns should be equal to market excess returns (the market rate of return minus the risk-free rate). The question then becomes: Did the portfolio manager do better or worse than expected? The portfolio manager's excess returns can be compared to the market line of expected excess returns for any beta level.

junk bonds High-risk, low-grade bonds rated below BBB. They often perform like common stock and may provide interesting investment opportunities.

K

K_e The term representing required rate of return based on the Capital Asset Pricing Model. It is the discount rate applied to future dividends and price.

key indicators Various market observations used by technical analysts to predict the direction of future market trends. Examples include the contrary opinion and smart money rules.

L

lagging indicators Economic indicators that usually change direction after business conditions have turned around.

leading indicators Economic indicators that change direction in advance of general business conditions.

least squares trendline A statistically developed linear trendline that minimizes the distance of the individual observations from the line.

leveraged buyouts The management of the company or some other investor group borrows the needed cash to repurchase all the shares of an existing company. The balance sheet of the company serves as the collateral base to make the borrowing possible. After the leveraged buyout, the company may be taken private for a time in which unprofitable assets are sold and debt reduced. The intent is then to bring the company to the public market once again (or resell it to another company) at a large profit over the initial purchase price.

LIFO A method of inventory valuation in which it is assumed inventory purchased last is sold first (last-in, first-out).

limit order A condition placed on a transaction executed through a stockbroker to assure that securities will be sold only if a specified minimum price is received or purchased only if the price to be paid is no more than a given maximum.

limited partnership A business arrangement in which there is the limited liability protection of a corporation

with the tax provisions of a regular partnership. All profits or losses are directly assigned to the partners for tax purposes. The general partner has unlimited liability.

Lipper Mutual Fund Investment Performance Averages Lipper publishes indexes for growth funds, growth-with-income funds, and balanced funds. Lipper also shows year-to-date and weekly performance for many other categories of funds.

liquidity The capacity of an investment to be retired for cash in a short period with a minimum capital loss.

liquidity preference theory A theory related to the term structure of interest rates. The theory states the term structure tends to be upward sloping more than any other pattern. This reflects a recognition of the fact that long maturity obligations are subject to greater price change movements than short maturity obligations when interest rates change. Because of increased risk of holding longer-term maturities, investors demand a higher return to hold such securities. Thus, they have a preference for short-term liquid obligations.

liquidity ratios Ratios that demonstrate the firm's ability to pay off short-term obligations as they come due.

long position A market transaction in which an investor purchases securities with the expectation of holding the securities for cash income or for resale at a higher price in the future. Also see *short position.*

long-term anticipation securities (LEAPS) Longer-term options with expiration dates of up to two years.

Lorie and Fisher study A University of Chicago study indicating comparative returns on financial assets over half a decade. It is similar to the Ibbotson and Sinquefield study in many respects.

M

margin account A trading account maintained with a brokerage firm on which the investor may borrow a percentage of the funds for the purchase of securities. The broker lends the funds at interest slightly above the prime rate.

margin maintenance requirement The amount of money that must be "deposited" to hold a margin position if losses reduce the initial margin that was put up.

margin requirements The amount of money that must be "deposited" to purchase a commodity contract or shares of stock on margin.

market A mechanism for facilitating the exchange of assets through buyer-seller communication. The communication, and not a central negotiating location, is the requisite condition for a market to exist, though some transactions (for example, trades at the various stock exchanges) do involve a direct meeting of buyers and sellers or their agents.

market capitalization The total market value of the firm. It is computed by multiplying shares outstanding times stock price.

market line On a graph, excess returns are shown on the vertical axis, the portfolio beta is shown on the horizontal axis, and the market line describes the relationship between the two.

market rate of interest The coupon rate of interest paid on bonds currently issued. Of course, a previously issued bond that is currently traded may be sold at a discount or a premium so that the buyer in effect receives the market rate even if the coupon rate on this older bond is substantially higher or lower than market rates. The market rate is also known as the yield to maturity.

market-segmentation theory A theory related to the term structure of interest rates that focuses on the demand side of the market. There are several large institutional participants in the bond market, each with its own maturity preferences. Banks tend to prefer short-term liquid securities to match the nature of their deposits, whereas life insurance companies prefer long-term bonds to match their long-run obligations. The behavior of these two institutions and of savings and loans often creates pressure on short-term or long-term rates but very little on the intermediate market of five- to seven-year maturities. This theory helps to focus on the accumulation or liquidation of securities by institutions during the different phases of the business cycle and the resultant impact on the yield curve.

maturity date The date at which outstanding principal must be repaid to bondholders.

merger price premium The difference between the offering price per share and the market price per share of the merger candidate (before the impact of the offer).

monetarist An economic analyst who believes monetary policy tools, and not fiscal policy, can best provide a stable environment of sustained economic growth.

monetary policy Direct control of interest rates or the money supply undertaken by the Federal Reserve to achieve economic objectives. Used in some cases to augment or offset the use of fiscal policy.

money market account Accounts offered by financial institutions to compete with money market funds. The minimum deposit is $500 to $1,000, with a maximum of three checks drawn per month.

money market fund A type of mutual fund that invests in short-term government securities, commercial paper, and repurchase agreements. Most offer check-writing privileges.

money supply The level of funds available at a given time for conducting transactions in our economy. The Federal Reserve can influence the money supply through its monetary policy tools. There are many different definitions of the money supply. For example, M1 is currency in circulation plus private checking deposits, including those in interest-bearing NOW accounts. M2 adds in savings accounts and money market mutual funds, and so on.

monopolies Dominance of an industry by one company. Monopolies are not common in the United States due to antitrust laws, but they do exist by government permission in the area of public utilities.

mortgage trust A form of REIT in which long-term loans are made to real estate investors.

multinational corporations Firms that have operations in a number of countries. Multinationals are frequently found in such industries as oil, mainframe computers, and banking.

municipal bonds Tax-exempt debt securities issued by state and local governments (including special political subdivisions).

mutual fund A pooling of funds by investors for reinvestment. The funds are administered by professional managers. Technically, only an open-end (see definition) investment fund is considered to be a mutual fund.

mutual fund cash position An overall market rule that asserts that by examining the level of uncommitted funds held by large institutional investors, analysts can measure the potential demand for stocks and thereby anticipate market movements.

N

naked options The process of writing (selling) options on a stock that is not currently owned. It is highly speculative.

NASDAQ indexes Index measures for components of the over-the-counter market. The OTC Indexes are value-weighted.

National Association of Securities Dealers Automated Quotations System (NASDAQ) A computerized system that provides up-to-the-minute price quotations on about 6,000 of the more actively traded OTC stocks.

net asset value The net asset value (NAV) represents the current value of an investment fund. It is computed by taking the total value of the securities, subtracting out the liabilities, and dividing by the shares outstanding.

net debtor-creditor hypothesis Since inflation makes each dollar worth less, it is often argued that a person or firm that is a net debtor gains from inflation because payments of interest and return of principal are made with continually less-valuable dollars. Conversely, a net creditor loses real capital because the loans are repaid in less valuable dollars.

net working capital Current assets minus current liabilities.

New York Stock Exchange Index A market value-weighted measure of stock market changes for all stocks listed on the NYSE.

no-load mutual fund A mutual fund on which no sales commission must be paid. The fund's shares are sold, not through brokers, but rather through the mail or other direct channels.

nominal GNP Gross national product expressed in current, noninflation-adjusted dollars.

nominal return A return that has not been adjusted for inflation.

nonconstant growth model Dividend valuation model that does not assume a constant growth rate for dividends.

O

odd-lot dealer A member of a stock exchange who maintains an inventory of a particular firm's stock in order to sell odd lots (trades of less than 100 shares) to customers of the exchange.

odd-lot theory The contrary opinion rule stating that small traders (who generally buy or sell odd lots) often misjudge market trends, selling just before upturns and buying before downturns. The theory has not been useful in predicting trends observed in recent years.

oligopolies Industries that have few competitors. Oligopolies are quite common in large, mature U.S. industries such as automobiles, steel, oil, airlines, and aluminum. The competition between companies in an oligopoly can be intense, and profitability can suffer as a

result of price wars and battles over market share. Increasingly, obligopolistic industries are facing international competition, which has altered their competitive strategies.

open-end fund An open-end investment fund stands ready at all times to sell or redeem shares from stockholders. There is no limit to the number of shares. Technically, a mutual fund is considered to be an open-end investment fund. Also see *closed-end fund.*

open-market operations The Federal Reserve's action of buying or selling government securities to expand or contract the amount of money in the economy.

opening purchase transaction A transaction in which an investor intends to become the holder of an option.

opening sale transaction A transaction in which an investor intends to be a writer of an option.

operating margin Operating income divided by sales.

option The right acquired for a consideration to buy or sell something at a fixed price within a specified period.

option premium The intrinsic value plus a speculative premium.

option price The specified price at which the holder of a warrant may buy the shares to which the warrant entitles purchase.

Options Clearing Corporation Issues all options listed on the exchanges that trade in options.

options on industry indexes An option index contract tailored to a given industry. Thus, one who wishes to speculate on a given industry's performance or hedge against holdings in that industry can use industry index options (subindexes).

options to purchase stock index futures An option to purchase a stock index futures contract at a specified price over a given time. This security combines the options concept with the futures concept.

organized exchanges Institutions, such as the New York Stock Exchange, the American Stock Exchange, or any of the smaller regional exchanges, that provide a central location for the buying and selling of securities.

OTC National Market system A segment of the OTC stock market made up of stocks that have a diversified geographical stockholder base and relatively large activity in their securities. Stocks in the National Market system receive enhanced market activity reporting through the NASDAQ system.

over-the-counter market Not a specific location but rather a communications network through which trades of bonds, nonlisted stocks, and other securities take place. Trading activity is overseen by the National Association of Securities Dealers (NASD).

overall market rules Guidelines, such as breadth of market indicators or mutual fund cash positions, used by technical analysts who predict stock market activity based on past activity.

P

par bonds Bonds that are selling at their par or maturity values rather than at premium or discounted prices. Par value on a corporate bond is generally $1,000.

par value (bond) The face value of a bond, generally $1,000 for corporate issues, with higher denominations for many government issues.

partial hedge A hedge position in which only part of the risk is eliminated or lessened.

peak The point in an economic cycle at which expansion ends and a recession begins.

perpetual bond A bond with no maturity date.

personal savings/personal disposable income The rate at which people are saving their disposable income. This has implications for the generation of funds to modernize plant and equipment and increase productivity.

portfolio The term applied to a collection of securities or investments.

portfolio effect The effect obtained when assets are combined into a portfolio. The interaction of the assets can provide risk reduction such that the portfolio standard deviation may be less than the standard deviation of any one asset in it.

portfolio insurance Protecting a large portfolio against a decline. A common strategy is to sell stock index futures contracts in anticipation of a decline.

portfolio manager One responsible for managing large pools of funds. Portfolio managers may be employed by insurance companies, mutual funds, bank trust departments, pension funds, and other institutional investors.

preferred stock A hybrid security that generally provides fixed returns. Preferred stockholders are paid returns after bondholder claims are satisfied but before any returns are paid to common stockholders. Though preferred stock returns are fixed in amount, they are classified as dividends (not interest) and are not tax deductible to the issuing firm.

present value The exact opposite of the compound sum. A future value is discounted to the present.

present value of an annuity The present value of an equal cash flow for several periods is determined.

price-earnings ratio The multiplier applied to earnings per share to determine current value. The P/E ratio is influenced by the earnings and sales growth of the firm, the risk or volatility of its performance, the debt-equity structure, and other factors.

price ratios Ratios that relate the internal performance of the firm to the external judgment of the marketplace in terms of value.

price-weighted average Each stock in the average is weighted by its price. The higher the price, the greater the relative weighting. The Dow Jones Industrial Average represents a price-weighted average.

primary earnings per share A firm's adjusted earnings after taxes divided by the number of shares of common stock outstanding plus common stock equivalents. Common stock equivalents include warrants and other options along with convertible securities that are paying low returns at the time of issue compared to other comparable securities.

primary market A market in which an investor purchases an asset (via an investment banker) from the issuer of that asset. The purchase of newly issued shares of corporate stock is an example of primary market activity. Subsequent transfers of the particular asset occur in the secondary market.

private placement The company sells its securities to private investors such as insurance companies, pension funds, and so on rather than through the public markets. Investment bankers may also aid in a private placement on a fee basis. Most private placements involve debt rather than common stock.

profitability ratios Ratios that allow the analyst to measure the ability of the firm to earn an adequate return on sales, total assets, and invested capital.

program trading Computer-based trigger points are established in which large volume trades are indicated. The technique is used by institutional investors.

prospectus A document that must accompany a new issue of securities. It contains the same information appearing in the registration statement, such as a list of directors and officers, financial reports certified by a CPA, the underwriters, the purpose and use for the funds, and other reasonable information that investors need to know.

public placement Public distribution of securities through the financial markets.

pure bond value The fundamental value of a bond that represents a floor price below which the bond's value should not fall. The pure bond value is computed as the present value of all future interest payments added to the present value of the bond principal.

pure competition Companies in pure competition do not have a differentiated product; they compete on price like farmers with corn, soybeans, and other commodities.

pure pickup yield swap A bond swap where a bond owner thinks he or she can increase the yield to maturity by selling a bond and buying a different bond of equal risk. This implies market disequilibrium.

put An option to sell 100 shares of common stock at a specified price for a given period.

put provision This provision enables a bond investor to have an option to sell a long-term bond back to the corporation at par value after a relatively short period (such as three to five years). This privilege can be particularly valuable if interest rates have gone up and bond prices have gone down.

Q

quick ratio Current assets minus inventory (i.e., cash, marketable securities, and accounts receivables) divided by current liabilities.

R

R^2—the coefficient of determination It measures the degree of association between the independent variable(s) and the dependent variable. It may take on a value anywhere between 0 and 1.

real asset A tangible piece of property that may be seen, felt, held, or collected, such as real estate, gold, diamonds, and so on.

real estate investment trust (REIT) An organization similar to a mutual fund where investors pool funds that are invested in real estate or used to make construction or mortgage loans.

real GDP Gross domestic product expressed in dollars that have been adjusted for inflation.

real rate of return The return that investors require for allowing others to use their money for a given period. This is the value that investors demand for passing up immediate consumption and allowing others to use their savings until the funds are returned. Because the term

real is employed, this means it is a value determined *before* inflation is added.

registered trader A member of a stock exchange who trades for his or her own account rather than for the client of a brokerage firm.

reinvestment assumption with bonds The assumed rate of reinvestment for inflows from a bond investment. It is normally assumed that inflows can be reinvested at the yield to maturity of the bond. This, however, may not be valid. Interest rates may go up or down as inflows from coupon payments come in and need to be reinvested. A more valid approach is to assign appropriate reinvestment rates to inflows and then determine how much the total investment will be worth at the end of a given period. This process is known as terminal wealth analysis.

reported income versus adjusted earnings Reported income is generally based on historical cost accounting, whereas adjusted earnings have been modified for inflation (on inventory and plant and equipment).

repurchase A purchase by a firm of its own shares in the marketplace.

required rate of return The total return required on an investment. For common stock, it is composed of the risk-free rate plus an equity risk premium. Once determined, it becomes the discount rate applied to future cash flows.

reserve requirements Percentages of bank deposit balances stipulated by the Federal Reserve as unavailable for lending. By increasing or reducing reserve requirements, the Fed can contract or expand the money supply.

resistance level The technical analyst's view that as long as a given long-term trend continues, prices of a particular stock or of the market as a whole will not rise above the upper end of the normal trading range (the resistance level) because at that point, investors sell in an attempt to get even or take a profit.

retention ratio The percent of earnings retained in the firm for investment purposes.

return on equity Net income divided by stockholder's equity.

revenue bond A municipal bond supported by the revenue from a specific project, such as a toll, road, bridge, or municipal coliseum.

risk Uncertainty concerning the outcome of an investment or other situation. It is often defined as variability of returns from an investment. The greater the range of possible outcomes, the greater the risk.

risk-adjusted return The amount of return after adjustment for the level of risk incurred to achieve the return.

risk-free rate The required rate of return before risk is explicitly considered. It is composed of the real rate of return plus a rate equivalent to inflationary expectations. It is referred to as R_F.

risk premium A premium assumed to be paid to an investor for the risk inherent in an investment. It is added to the risk-free rate to get the overall required return on an investment.

rotational investing An investment strategy that refers to the practice of moving in and out of various industries over the business cycle. As the business cycle moves from a trough to a peak, different industries benefit from the economic changes that accompany the business cycle.

Rule 80A Under this rule, all daily up or down movements in the Dow Jones Industrial Average of 50 points or more cause a "tick test" to go into effect. In down markets, sell orders can only be executed on an increase in price (a plus tick), and buy orders can only be executed on a decrease in price (a minus tick). The rule stays in effect all day unless the DJIA returns to within 25 points of the previous day's closing price. The rule specifically applies to stocks in the Standard & Poor's 500 Stock Index to protect again index arbitrage, that is, trading in stocks and stock index futures at the same time in order to profit from price differences between the two.

Russell 1000 Index The index includes the 1,000 largest firms out of the Russell 3000 Index. It is value-weighted.

Russell 2000 Index The index includes the 2,000 smallest firms out of the Russell 3000 Index. It is value-weighted.

Russell 3000 Index The index is composed of the 3,000 largest U.S. stocks as measured by market capitalization. It is value-weighted.

S

secondary market A market in which an investor purchases an asset from another investor rather than the issuing corporation. The activity of secondary markets sets prices and provides liquidity. Also see *primary market.*

sector funds Mutual funds that specialize in a given segment of the economy such as energy, medical technology, computer technology, and so forth. While they may offer the potential for high returns, they are

clearly less diversified and more risky than a typical mutual fund.

secured bond A bond that is collateralized by the pledging of assets.

Securities Act of 1933 Enacted by Congress to curtail abuses by securities issuers, the law requires full disclosure of pertinent investment information and provides for penalties to officers of firms that do not comply.

Securities Acts Amendments of 1975 Enacted to increase competition in the securities markets, this legislation prohibits fixed commissions on public offerings of securities and directs the Securities and Exchange Commission to develop a single, nationwide securities market.

Securities and Exchange Commission (SEC) The federal government agency created in 1934 to enforce securities laws. Issuers of securities must register detailed reports with the SEC, and the SEC polices such activities as insider trading, investor conspiracies, and the functionings of the securities exchanges.

Securities Exchange Act of 1934 Created the Securities and Exchange Commission to regulate the securities markets. The act further empowers the Board of Governors of the Federal Reserve System to control margin requirements.

Securities Investor Protection Corporation Created under the Securities Investor Protection Act of 1970, this agency oversees the liquidation of insolvent brokerage firms and provides insurance on investors' trading accounts.

security analyst One who studies various industries and companies and provides research reports and valuation studies.

security market line The graphic representation of risk (as measured by beta) and return for an individual security.

selling short against the box A short sale of securities with the objective of deferring the payment of taxes. This requires a short sale against shares already owned so that shares owned are delivered to cover the short position as the transaction is completed.

semistrong form of efficient market hypothesis The hypothesis states that all public information is already impounded into the value of a security, so fundamental analysis cannot determine under- or overvaluation.

serial payment A mechanism for repaying funds advanced through a bond issue. Regular payments systematically retire individual bonds with increasing maturities until, after many years, the entire series has been repaid.

settle price The term for the closing price on futures contracts.

shared appreciation mortgage A type of mortgage in which the lender participates in any increase in value associated with the property being mortgaged.

Sharpe measure of portfolio performance Total portfolio return minus the risk-free rate divided by the portfolio standard deviation. It allows the portfolio manager to view excess returns in relation to total risk. Comparisons between various portfolios can be made based on this relative risk measure.

shelf registration Large companies file one comprehensive registration statement that outlines the firm's plans for future long-term financing. Then, when market conditions seem appropriate, the firm can issue the securities through an investment banker without further SEC approval. Future issues are said to be sitting on the shelf, waiting for the most advantageous time to appear. An issue may sit on the shelf for up to two years.

short position (short sale) A market transaction in which an investor sells borrowed securities in anticipation of a price decline. The investor's expectation is that the securities can be repurchased (to replace the borrowed shares) at a lower price in the future. Also see *long position.*

short sales position theory The contrary opinion rule stating that large volumes of short sales can signal an impending market upturn because short sales must be covered and thereby create their own demand. Also, the average short seller is often thought to be wrong.

sinking-fund provision A mechanism for repaying funds advanced through a bond issue. The issuer makes periodic payments to the trustee, who retires part of the issue by purchasing the bonds in the open market.

small-firm effect A market theory that suggests small firms produce superior returns compared to larger firms on both an absolute and risk-adjusted basis.

smart money rules Guidelines, such as *Barron's* Confidence Index, used by technical analysts who predict stock market activity based on the assumption that sophisticated investors will correctly predict market trends and that their lead should be followed. Also see *contrary opinion rules.*

specialist or dealer hedge A specialist on an exchange or dealer in the over-the-counter market buys and sells stocks for his own inventory for temporary holding (as a part of his market-making function). At times, he may

assume a larger temporary holding than desired with all the risks associated with that exposure. Stock index futures or options can reduce the market, or systematic, risk, although they cannot reduce the specific risk associated with a security.

speculative premium The difference between an option or warrant's price and its intrinsic value. That an investor would pay something in excess of the intrinsic value indicates a speculative desire to hold the security in anticipation of future increases in the price of the underlying stock.

spot market The term applied to the cash price for immediate transfer of a commodity as opposed to the futures market where no physical transfer occurs immediately.

spreads A combination of options that consists of buying one option (going long) and writing an option (going short) on the same stock.

Standard & Poor's 100 Index An index composed of 100 blue-chip stocks on which the Chicago Board of Trade currently has individual option contracts.

Standard & Poor's 400 Industrial Index An index that measures price movements in the stocks of 400 large industrial corporations listed primarily on the New York Stock Exchange.

Standard & Poor's 500 Stock Index An index of 500 major U.S. corporations. There are 400 industrial firms, 20 transportation firms, 40 utilities, and 40 financial firms. This index is value-weighted.

Standard & Poor's International Oil Index A value-weighted index of oil firms. Options on the index have been traded on the Chicago Board Options Exchange.

Standard & Poor's MidCap Index An index composed of 400 middle-size firms that have total market values between $200 million and $5 billion.

standard deviation A measure of dispersion that considers the spread of outcomes around the expected value.

statement of cash flows Formally established by the Financial Accounting Standards Board in 1987, the purpose of the statement of cash flows is to emphasize the critical nature of cash flows to the operations of the firm. The statement translates accrual-based net income into actual cash dollars.

stock dividend A dividend paid by issuing more stock, which results in retained earnings being capitalized.

stock index futures A futures contract on a specific stock index, such as the Standard & Poor's 500 Stock Index or the NYSE Composite Index.

stock index options An option contract to purchase (call) or sell (put) a stock index. Popular contracts include the S&P 100 Index, the American Exchange Major Market Index, and others. The purchaser of a stock index option pays an initial premium and then closes out the option at a given price in the future.

stock pickers Investors who follow the bottom-up approach to selecting stocks. They pick an individual stock and then merely check it out against the industry and economy.

stock split The result of a firm dividing its shares into more shares with a corresponding decrease in par value.

stop order A mechanism for locking in gains or limiting losses on securities transactions. The investor is not assured of paying or receiving a particular price but rather agrees to accept the price prevailing when the broker is able to execute the order after prices have reached some predetermined figure.

straddle A combination of a put and call on the same stock with the same strike price and expiration date.

straight-line depreciation A method of depreciation in which the project cost is divided by the project life to calculate each year's depreciation amount.

strong form of the efficient market hypothesis A hypothesis that says all information, insider as well as public, is reflected in the price of a security.

Super Dot The computer system that allows New York Stock Exchange members to electronically transmit all market and limit orders directly to the specialist at the trading post or member trading booth.

support level Technical analyst's view that as long as a given long-term trend continues, prices of a particular stock or of the market as a whole will not fall below the lower end of a normal trading range (the support level) because at that point, low prices stimulate demand.

sustainable growth model A model that looks at how much growth a firm can generate by maintaining the same financial relationships as the year before. The interaction between return on equity and the retention of equity for reinvestment is considered.

syndicate A group of investment bankers that jointly shares the underwriting risk and distribution responsibilities in a large offering of new securities. Each participant is responsible for a predetermined sales volume. One or a few firms serve as the managing underwriters.

synergy A more-than-proportionate increase in performance from the combination of two or more parts.

systematic risk Risk inherent in an investment related to movements in the market that cannot be diversified away.

systematic withdrawal plan A plan offered by a mutual fund in which the investor receives regular monthly or quarterly payments from investment in the fund.

T

tax hedge An investor may have accumulated a large return on a diversified portfolio in a given year. To maintain the profitable position but defer the taxable gains until the next year, stock index futures or options contracts may be employed. For individual securities, individual stock options may be used when available.

tax swaps Selling of one bond position and buying into a similar one to take advantage of a tax situation. For example, one might sell a bond that has a short-term capital loss to take the deduction and replace it with a similar bond.

technical analysis An analysis of price and volume data as well as other related market indicators to determine past trends that are believed to be predictable into the future. Charts and graphs are often utilized.

term structure of interest rates This depicts the relationship between maturity and interest rates for up to 30 years.

terminal wealth table A table that indicates the ending or terminal wealth from a bond investment based on the reinvestment of the inflows at a specified rate (which may be different from the coupon rate). The initial investment can then be compared with the terminal wealth (compound interest plus principal) and an overall rate of return computed.

third market The trading between dealers and institutional investors, through the over-the-counter market, of NYSE-listed stocks. The third market accounts for an extremely small share of total trading activity.

Tokyo Nikkei 225 The most widely watched country index outside the U.S. It covers 225 large Japanese companies.

top-down approach A method for choosing stocks that goes from the macro-economic viewpoint to the individual company.

trading range The high and low spread of prices that a stock normally sells within.

Treasury bill A short-term U.S. government obligation. A Treasury bill is purchased at a discount and is readily marketable.

Treasury bond A long-term U.S. government bond.

Treasury note An intermediate-term (1 to 10 years) U.S. government bond.

Treasury stock Stock issued but not outstanding by virtue of being held (after it is repurchased) by the firm.

trend analysis Comparable analysis of performance over time.

Treynor measure of portfolio performance Total portfolio return minus the risk-free rate divided by the portfolio beta. Unlike the Sharpe measure, which uses the portfolio standard deviation in the denominator, the risk measure here is the beta, or systematic risk. It enables the portfolio manager to view excess return in relation to nondiversifiable risk. The assumption is that all other types of risk have been diversified away. Once computed, the Treynor measure allows for comparisons between different portfolios.

trough The point in an economic cycle at which recession ends and expansion begins.

U

underpricing In selling formerly privately held shares to new investors in the over-the-counter market, the price might not fully reflect the value of the issue. Underpricing is used to attempt to ensure the success of the initial distribution.

underwriter hedge A hedge, based on stock index futures or options contracts, used to offset the risk exposure associated with the underwriting of new securities by an investment banker. If the market goes down, presumably the loss on the stock being underwritten will be compensated for by the gain on the stock index futures or options contract as a result of being able to repurchase it at a lower price. This, of course, is not a perfect hedge. The stock could go down while the market is going up, and losses on both the stock and stock index contract would occur (writing options directly against the stock may be more efficient, but in many cases such options are not available).

unfriendly takeover A merger or acquisition in which the firm acquired does not wish to be acquired.

unfunded pension plan Payments to retirees are made out of current income and not out of prior funding.

unit investment trusts (UITs) These are formed by investment companies with the intention of acquiring a portfolio of fixed income to be passively managed over a fixed period. The trust is then terminated.

unseasoned issue An issue that has not been formerly traded in the public markets.

unsystematic risk Risk of an investment that is random in nature. It is not related to general market movements. It may represent the temporary influence of a competitor's new product, changes in raw material prices, or unusual economic or government influences on a firm. It may generally be diversified away.

V

valuation The process of attributing a value to a security based on expectations of the future performance of the issuing concern, the relevant industry, and the economy as a whole.

valuation model A representation of the components that provide the value of an investment, such as a dividend valuation model used to determine the value of common stock.

Value Line Index The index represents 1,700 companies from the New York and American Stock Exchanges and the over-the-counter market. Many individual investors use the Value Line Index because it more closely corresponds to the variety of stocks the average investor may have in his or her portfolio. It is an equal-weighted index, which means each of the 1,700 stocks, regardless of market price or total market value, is weighted equally.

value-weighted index Each company in the index is weighted by its own total market value as a percentage of the total market value for all firms in the index. Most major indexes such as the S&P 500, S&P 400, and the NYSE Index, are value-weighted. With value-weighted indexes, large firms tend to be weighted more heavily than smaller firms.

variability The possible different outcomes of an event. As an example, an investment with many different levels of return would have great variability.

variable rate mortgage A mortgage in which the interest rate is adjusted regularly.

variable-rate notes (See *floating-rate notes.*)

vertical spread Buying and writing two contracts at different striking prices with the same month of expiration.

vesting A legal term meaning pension benefits or rights cannot be taken away.

W

warrant A right or option to buy a stated number of shares of stock at a specified price over a given period. It is usually of longer duration than a call option.

warrant break-even The price movement in the underlying stock necessary for the warrant purchaser to break even, that is, recover the initial purchase price of the warrant.

weak form of efficient market hypothesis A hypothesis suggesting there is no relationship between past and future prices of securities.

weighted average life The weighted average time period over which the coupon payments and maturity payment on a bond are recovered.

white knight A firm that "rescues" another firm from an unfriendly takeover by a third firm.

Wiesenberger Financial Services An advisory service that provides important information on mutual funds.

Wilshire 5,000 Equity Index A stock market measure comprising 5,000 equity securities. It includes all New York Stock Exchange and American Stock Exchange issues and the most active over-the-counter issues. The index represents the *total dollar value* of all 5,000 stocks. By measuring total dollar value, it is, in effect, a value-weighted measure.

World Index A value-weighted index of the performance in 19 major countries as compiled by Capital International, S.A., of Geneva, Switzerland.

Y

yield curve A curve that shows interest rates at a specific point for all securities having equal risk but different maturity dates. Usually, government securities are used to construct such curves. The yield curve is also referred to as the term structure of interest rates.

yield spread The difference between the yields received on two different types of bonds, or bonds with different ratings. It is important to investment strategy because during periods of economic uncertainty, spreads increase because investors demand larger premiums on risky issues to compensate for the greater chance of default.

yield to call The interest yield that will be realized on a callable bond if it is held from a given purchase date until the date when it can be called by the issuer. The yield to call reflects the fact that lower overall returns may be realized if the issuer avoids some later payments by retiring the bonds early.

yield to maturity The internal rate of return or true yield on a bond. It is the interest rate (i) at which you can discount the future coupon payments (C_t) and maturity value (P_n) to arrive at the current value of a bond (v). It is synonymous with market rate of interest.

Ying, Lewellen, Schlarbaum, and Lease study A research study that indicates there may be an opportunity for abnormal returns on a risk-adjusted basis in the many weeks between announcement of listing and actual listing of a security.

Z

zero-coupon bonds Bonds designed to pay no interest, in which the return to the investor is in the form of capital appreciation over the life of the issue.

Index

C

N

Q

R

S

Y

Z